FOREWORD

Chronologies have a very special place in written history—they present a sequential record or chronicle of events, without attempting to interpret their significance. They serve as an important reference tool for historians, who provide the correlation and assign the meaning to the events that have taken place in any given period of history.

The Army Air Forces in World War II: Combat Chronology, 1941–1945 is no exception. It is precisely what its name indicates—a factual record of combat operations conducted by the United States Army Air Forces during World War II. No attempt has been made to interrelate the events—that task remains for those writing history. No attempt has been made to incorporate events of broader scope than combat operations of the AAF—for those the historian may consult other specialized chronologies. This volume does, however, fill in the fine, essential detail to the earlier seven-volume history of *The Army Air Forces in World War II*.

Washington, D.C.
1 December 1974

EARL G. PECK, Brig. Gen., USAF
Chief, Office of Air Force History

U.S. Army Air Forces in World War II

Combat Chronology

1941 – 1945

*Compiled
by*

Kit C. Carter
Robert Mueller

Center for Air Force History
Washington, DC 1991

Library of Congress Catalog Card No. 75-600031

Reprint of the 1973 edition, 1991

PREFACE

The chronology is concerned primarily with operations of the US Army Air Forces and its combat units between December 7, 1941 and September 15, 1945. It is designed as a companion reference to the seven-volume history of *The Army Air Forces in World War II*, edited by Wesley Frank Craven and James Lea Cate. The research was a cooperative endeavor carried out in the United States Air Force historical archives by the Research Branch of the Albert F. Simpson Historical Research Center.

Such an effort has demanded certain changes in established historical methodology, as well as some arbitrary rules for presentation of the results. After International and US events, entries are arranged geographically. They begin with events at Army Air Forces Headquarters in Washington then proceed eastward around the world, using the location of the headquarters of the numbered air forces as the basis for placement. For this reason, entries concerning the Ninth Air Force while operating in the Middle East follow Twelfth Air Force. When that headquarters moves to England in October 1943, the entries are shifted to follow Eighth Air Force. The entries end with those numbered air forces which remained in the Zone of the Interior, as well as units originally activated in the ZI, then designated for later movement overseas, such as Ninth and Tenth Air Forces. The ZI entries do not include Eighth and Twentieth Air Forces, which were established in the ZI with the original intent of placing them in those geographical locations with which they became historically identified. For these two units, original actions are shown either under AAF or in their intended geographic area of location.

All times and dates used are those of the area under discussion. The entry "1/2 Jun" indicates that an event occurred during the night between the two given dates, while "1-2 Jun" indicates an action over a period of time.

In dealing with people, again arbitrary decisions were implemented. For military men below the general officer or equivalent level, full grade and name were used. For general officers and those of equal grade in other US and foreign services, the complete rank (both that at the time first mentioned and the highest rank held prior to the end of the war) and name will be found in the index. Only an abbreviated rank (*e.g.*, Gen or Adm) and last name are used in the text. The exception is where two general officers had the same last name; in such cases, the first name is also included. Similarly for civilian leaders, only the last name is used; full name and title are given in the index.

Location of all towns, islands, etc., is also made in the index. In all cases, attempts were made to cite place names in use by the native population at the time of or immediately before the war. No names imposed by a conqueror are used. For example Pylos Bay, not Navarino Bay, is used. Further, as appropriate, native geographic terms are used: *Shima* for island in Japanese island groups, *See* for lake in Germany. However, two exceptions were made. In cases in which the place became infamous because of the actions of the conquering power, that name is preferred—for example Auschwitz would be used rather than the Polish name of Oswiecim. Also, in larger international cities, such as Roma, Köln and Wien, the anglicized name is used. Where a village or hamlet was difficult to locate or where there were several such places with the same name in a general area, the coordinates are given in the index. In some cases, with no extant navigational aids of the attacking force, the best possible guess was made based upon all available evidence. In other instances, such as the bridge at Hay-ti—attacked so often by Tenth Air Force—even a logical guess could not be made. In these cases, a question mark is placed in brackets after the index entry. Accent marks, such as umlauts, were omitted.

Abbreviations are found extensively throughout the text. These are all explained in the Glossary of Abbreviations. Similarly, a list of code names and descriptions for all operations is provided in a separate Glossary of Code Names.

In addition to the two compilers, many others played a major role in completing this volume. In addition to those in the Research Branch including reserve officers assigned as mobilization augmentees, particular recognition and thanks should go to Mr. Gurvis Lawson and other members of the Cartographic Information Division, Air University Library, who gave willingly and often of their talents and provided many valuable suggestions in identifying remote and almost uncharted villages, hamlets, and "populated" places.

Invaluable help in locating documents was provided by the members of the Circulation Section of the Center's Archives Branch. Dr. Maurer Maurer, head of the Research Branch when this chronology was begun, and now chief of the Center, accomplished the early editing and provided much of the direction and guidance necessary to carry the work to completion. The final manuscript was ably and patiently typed by Mrs. Myra Dean, Mrs. Jean Jocelyn and Mrs. Jane Hanlin of the Center. Final editing by Mr. Max Rosenberg, Deputy Chief Historian, in the Office of Air Force History, eliminated many of the more embarrassing errors which can creep into such a detailed work when the effort extends over a number of years. Mr. Lawrence Paszek of the same office maintained a close liaison with the Air Force's Publishing Division and the Government Printing Office, to insure timely resolution of problems so often encountered in the final printing phases. Special recognition must go to MSgt. Robert Jakob of the Research Branch at the Center, whose patient and detailed editorial assistance was invaluable in proofing the galleys and page-proofs for this work. Also providing much help in this effort was Airman LaVern Lowe.

Finally, it would be remiss not to mention the thorough and highly useful volume, *The U.S. Army in World War II: Chronology, 1941–1945*, prepared by the U.S. Army's Office of the Chief of Military History. This work was both an incentive and a guide and one can only hope this volume will serve as a complement thereto.

Maxwell AFB, Alabama
1 June 1973

JAMES N. EASTMAN, JR.
Chief, Research Branch
The Albert F. Simpson
    Historical Research Center

CONTENTS

1941

7 December

International: Japan attacks Hawaii and other US and British possessions in the Pacific without warning. Japan already is at war with China, and Great Britain is at war with the Axis powers, Germany and Italy, which control most of Western Europe. The RAF is conducting an aerial offensive against Germany, and the Luftwaffe is engaged in a campaign against Britain. Russians are fighting German forces that have invaded the USSR. British troops are battling Italians and Germans in Africa.

Hawaiian AF: First wave of Japanese carrier-based airplanes (almost 200) hits US naval base at Pearl Harbor and Hickam Field at 0755. Attacks follow quickly against Wheeler and Bellows Fields. A second wave of Japanese airplanes strikes other naval and military facilities. Hawaiian AF loses 163 men, with about 390 others wounded or missing; has 64 of its 231 assigned aircraft destroyed. Only 79 of the remaining aircraft are deemed usable, and much of the AF's ground facilities are destroyed. These losses are light in comparison with the Navy's: more than 2,000 killed or missing, and more than 900 wounded; 4 battleships sunk; 3 battleships, 3 cruisers, and 3 destroyers damaged; and over half of the Navy's 169 airplanes in the area destroyed. The Japanese lose 20 aircraft over Hawaii, including 4 claimed destroyed by 2d Lt George S Welch (47th Pur Sq) piloting a P–40, one of the few US ftrs to successfully attack airplanes during the day. About 20 other aircraft are lost by the Japanese during carrier landings. Altogether the Japanese pay a small price for the damage done to the Americans on Oahu. For the remainder of the day, following the attacks, AAF carries out fruitless searches for the carriers.

Air Force, Alaska Def Cmd: Upon learning of the Pearl Harbor attack, the Cmd's 6 B–18's and 12 P–36's take to the air to avoid being caught on their fields.

8 December

International: US, Great Britain, the Netherlands, Canada, Union of South Africa, New Zealand, Australia, Free France, and 8 Latin American republics declare war against Japan.

Far East AF: First word of Japanese attack on Pearl Harbor is received on Luzon in the Philippines by commercial radio between 0300–0330 local time. Within 30 minutes radar at Iba Field plots formation of airplanes 75 mi offshore, heading for Corregidor. AAF P–40's are sent out to intercept but make no contact. Shortly before 0930, after aircraft are detected over Lingayen Gulf heading toward Manila, B–17's at Clark Field

1

are ordered airborne to prevent being caught on the ground. Ftrs from Clark and Nichols Fields are sent to intercept the enemy but do not make contact. The airplanes swing E and bomb military installations at Baguio. Tarlac, Tuguegarao, and A/Fs at Cabantuan are also attacked. By 1130 the B–17's and ftrs sent into the air earlier have landed at Clark and Iba for refueling, and radar has disclosed another flight of aircraft 70 mi W of Lingayen Gulf, headed S. Ftrs from Iba make a fruitless search over S China Sea. Ftrs from Nichols are dispatched to patrol over Bataan and Manila. Around 1145 a formation is reported headed S over Lingayen Gulf. Ftrs are ordered from Del Carmen to cover Clark Field but fail to arrive before the Japanese hit Clark shortly after noon. HBs and many ftrs at Clark Field are caught on the ground, but a few P–40's manage to get airborne. 2d Lt Randall B Keator (20th Pur Sq) shoots down the first Japanese aircraft over the Philippines. The P-40's earlier sent on patrol of S China Sea return to Iba Field with fuel running low at the beginning of an attack on that A/F. They fail to prevent bombing but manage to prevent low-level strafing of the sort which proved so destructive at Clark. At the end of the day's action it is apparent that the Japanese have won a major victory. The effective striking power of Far East AF has been destroyed, the ftr strength has been seriously reduced, most B–17 maintenance facilities have been demolished, and about 80 men have been killed.

Air Force, Alaska Def Cmd: Start-ing today bmrs fly armed rcn each morning from Anchorage to Kodiak.

ZI: First and Fourth AFs are made responsible for air def on the E and W coasts, respectively. CG First AF orders I BC to begin over-water rcn with all available aircraft to locate and attack any hostile sur-face forces which might approach the E coast. Similar rcn is ordered off W coast. Aircraft of 1st Pur Gp from Selfridge Field begin to arrive at San Diego, being the first reinforcements of air strength on the W coast.

9 December

FEAF: Shortly after 0300 aircraft attack Nichols Field. This attack, added to the previous day's raids on Clark and Iba Fields, leaves FEAF strength reduced by half. Only 17 of 35 B–17's remain in commission; about 55 P–40's, 3 P–35's, and close to 30 other aircraft (B–10's, B–18's, and observation airplanes) have been lost in aerial combat or destroyed on the ground. During morning and afternoon, B–17's from Mindanao fly rcn missions and land on Clark and San Marcelino Fields. Several more B–17's are flown from Mindanao to these Luzon bases for resistance against possible invasion attempt.

ZI: Ftrs at Mitchel Field are dis-patched to intercept hostile airplane reported (falsely) to be approaching the E coast.

10 December

FEAF: B–17's, P–40's, and P–35's attack a convoy landing troops and equipment at Vigan and at Aparri in N Luzon. 1 transport at Vigan is destroyed. The strikes include the much publicized attack of Capt Colin

P Kelly Jr (14th Bomb Sq) on a warship off Aparri. Capt Kelly, who is killed when his B–17 is shot down by ftrs as he is returning to Clark Field, is later posthumously awarded the DSC for destroying a battleship. However, later information reveals that he attacked the heavy cruiser *Ashigara*, probably scoring near misses.

11 December

International: Germany and Italy declare war on US. Congress declares war on Germany and Italy.

Hawaiian AF: 6 B–18's fly sea-search mission from Hawaiian Islands. Similar missions by B–17's, B–18's, and A–20's are flown each day for the remainder of the year; several submarines are sighted and some are attacked but without positive evidence of hits.

ZI: Second and Fourth AFs are assigned to Western Def Cmd.

12 December

FEAF: More than 100 aircraft hit tgts at Clark Field, Batangas, and Olongapo. No hits are scored by the single B–17 that is sent against transports at Vigan.

13 December

FEAF: 1st Lt Boyd D Wagner (17 Pur Sq) shoots down 4 airplanes near Aparri while on rcn mission over N Luzon.

14 December

FEAF: B–17's are sent against beachhead at Legaspi. 1st Lt Hewitt T Wheless is later awarded DSC for bringing his bullet-riddled aircraft back from the mission to an emergency crashlanding at Cagayan.

16 December

FEAF: 1st Lt Boyd D Wagner (17th Pur Sq) leads dive-bombing raid on A/F at Vigan and shoots down his fifth aircraft, thereby becoming the first AAF "Ace" in World War II.

17 December

UK: Gen Chaney, Chief SPOBS, writes to AG, USA on "Construction Program of US Forces in UK," which indicates shortage of accomodations for proposed US forces in Scotland, N Ireland, and England.

FEAF: B–17's, evacuating Luzon, begin arriving at Batchelor Field. Capt Floyd J Pell arrives in Australia to begin arrangements for use of Australian facilities by FEAF.

18 December

Hawaiian AF: Gen Tinker succeeds Gen Martin as CG.

19 December

ZI: First AF is assigned to Eastern Theater of Operations (later Eastern Def Cmd).

22 December

International: Anglo-American conference (ARCADIA) opens at Washington to deal with war strategy. Churchill, Roosevelt, Harry Hopkins, Lord Beaverbrook, and American and British CoSs participate.

FEAF: 9 B–17's from Batchelor Field attack shipping in Davao Bay and land at Del Monte.

23 December

FEAF: 4 B–17's take off from Del Monte shortly after midnight during 22/23 Dec and bomb shipping in Lingayen Gulf. 12 P–40's and 6 P–35's strafe forces landing in San Miguel Bay. FEAF comes under control of newly-created USFIA. Gen Brereton, CG, receives orders establishing Hq FEAF at Darwin.

24 December

FEAF: 3 B–17's fly from Del Monte during 24/25 Dec, bomb A/F and shipping at Davao, and land at Batchelor Field. 2 airplanes leave Manila for Darwin with personnel of Hq FEAF. AAF units on Luzon, as well as ground forces, begin moving to Bataan Peninsula.

ZI: 95th Bomb Sq, at Pendleton Field, claims sub sunk off mouth of Columbia R, but this claim is not confirmed by committees of USN and British Admiralty which later assesses damage to enemy subs during World War II.

25 December

FEAF: Lt Col Charles H Caldwell sets up HQ FEAF on RAAF A/F at Darwin.

29 December

FEAF: Gen Brereton, CG, arrives at new HQ at Darwin. Col Harold H George remains at Manila in cmd of air elements left in the Philippines, the chief center of AAF activity in S Philippines being Del Monte, where air personnel are under cmd of Maj Ray T Ellsmore.

Air Force, Alaska Def Cmd: In response to repeated requests by this Cmd to the WD for additional aircraft to defend Alaska, the 77th Bomb Sq arrives at Elmendorf Field. The 11th Pur Sq arrives the next day.

1942

1 January

International: Declaration of United Nations is signed. Each signatory pledges not to make a separate peace and to employ its full resources against members of and adherents to Tripartite Pact with which it is at war.

2 January

Phil Is: Japanese occupy Manila and Cavite naval base.

Air Force, Alaska Def Cmd: The 77th Bomb Sq joins the 28th Comp Gp and the 11th Pur Sq joins the Prov IC, Alaska. Alaskan air strength is now 2 pur and 3 bomb sqs.

3 January

International: Roosevelt and Churchill announce creation of unified cmd in SW Pacific, with Gen Wavell as supreme cmdr of American, British, Dutch, and Australian (AB DA) forces in that area.

4 January

FEAF: Ftrs from Bataan attempt interception of bombing raid on Corregidor. The ftrs, failing to intercept until the enemy airplanes are over the tgt, have little effect on the raid. Several ftrs depart from Mindanao following the mission.

5 January

FEAF: B–17's from Malang stage through Samarinda during 4/5 Jan

and attack shipping in Davao Bay. USFIA, which controls FEAF, is redesignated USAFIA, and Gen Brett assumes cmd.

8 January

UK: Gen Chaney designated CG USAFBI; continues as Chief SPOBS.

9 January

FEAF: B–17's, flying out of Kendari, strike shipping in Davao Bay.

10 January

FEAF: Ftr units complete movement (begun 24 Dec 41) from various bases on Luzon to Bataan Peninsula.

11 January

FEAF: B–17's, out of Malang, attack landing forces on island of Tarakan.

13 January

International: American and British CoSs formally adopt agreement to begin movement of American air forces to UK as soon as possible in order to intensify attack on Germany.

14 January

International: ARCADIA conference ends. Major discussions include creation of CCS to direct US-British war effort, and employment of main military efforts against Germany while containing the Japanese offensive.

AAF: Col Claude E Duncan leaves Washington for Britain to prepare for arrival of Shadow Staff of BC.

FEAF: HQ moves from Darwin to Java.

15 January

FEAF: B–17's, flying out of Palembang, attack Sungei Patani A/F.

Air Force, Alaska Def Cmd: The Alaskan Air Force is activated at Elmendorf Field. Cmdr is Lt Col Everett S Davis.

16 January

Hawaiian AF: First significant deployment of aircraft from Hawaiian AF begins with movement of 6 B–17's, commanded by Lt Col Walter C Sweeney, to Palmyra for duty with TG 8.9.

17 January

FEAF: B–17's from Malang, staging through Kendari, hit Langoan A/F and ships in Menado Bay.

Hawaiian AF: Aircraft unsuccessfully attack submarines in Hawaiian area. B–17's of TG 8.9 proceed from Palmyra to Canton I.

18 January

US: First increment (1,400 men) of US forces to be sent to UK sails for N Ireland.

Hawaiian AF: Another unsuccessful attack on enemy submarines in Hawaiian area. B–17's of TG 8.9 conduct antisubmarine search from Canton I.

19 January

FEAF: B–17's, flying out of Malang, attack shipping at Jolo.

Hawaiian AF: B–17's of TG 8.9 fly antisubmarine mission from Canton I.

20 January

FEAF: Gen Brett, CG USAFIA, halts ferrying of aircraft from India to NEI. AAF has been sending HBs to Java by way of Africa and India, but the Japanese are able to inflict prohibitive losses on AAF aircraft on the last stops of the route by interception from newly acquired A/Fs near Java.

21 January

Hawaiian AF: B–17's of TG 8.9 fly from Canton I to Nandi.

22 January

FEAF: From this date through 3 Feb, B–17's launch at least 15 missions out of Malang against shipping moving through Makassar Strait. 4 missions abort due to bad weather, 6 end with negative results, and the remaining 5 suffer heavy losses but sink 4 ships.

23 January

Hawaiian AF: B–17's of TG 8.9 return from Nandi to Canton I.

ZI: Flying Trg Cmd is established and given jurisdiction over the Southeast Gulf Coast and West Coast Flying Trg Centers which had been established on 8 Jul 40.

24 January

US: Special Court of Inquiry on Pearl Harbor, headed by Supreme Court Justice Owen J Roberts, places main responsibility for the 7 Dec 41 disaster on Adm Kimmel and Gen Short, accusing them of neglecting to heed attack warning, failing to confer with each other, and taking only minimum precautions.

25 January

FEAF: The first AAF pur sq (17th Pur Sq), (Prov) under Maj Charles A Sprague, arrives in Java with 13 P-40's flown from Australia.

Hawaiian AF: B-17's of TG 8.9 fly from Canton I to Nandi.

26 January

AAF: Gen Arnold recommends to Army CoS that AAFIB be composed of a HQ and 3 cmds—bomber, interceptor, and base.

USAFBI: First increment of US troops arrives in N Ireland.

FEAF: Ftrs from Bataan bomb and strafe Nichols and Nielson Fields on Luzon during 26/27 Jan, inflicting considerable damage on aircraft and fuel storage.

27 January

Hawaiian AF: B-17's of TG 8.9 return to Canton I.

28 January

Eighth AF: Activated at Savannah AB, Col Asa N Duncan commanding. Originally designated as the air element of GYMNAST.

FEAF: B-17's from Malang and Palembang attack A/Fs at Kendari and Kuala Lumpur.

Hawaiian AF: B-17's of TG 8.9 fly unsuccessful antisubmarine mission from Canton I.

29 January

FEAF: B-17's, striking out of Palembang, hit Kuantan A/F scoring

numerous hits on runways and hangars.

Hawaiian AF: VII BC is activated. B-17's of TG 8.9 fly from Canton I to Palmyra.

30 January

Hawaiian AF: B-17's of TG 8.9 return to Hawaii, having completed a mission (began on 16 Jan 42) which afforded a pioneer look at the problem of air operations over vast Pacific areas, especially the problems of navigation and the servicing of aircraft.

31 January

AAF: Gen Eaker is designated CG, Bmr Cmd, USAFBI and ordered to proceed to UK.

1 February

Eighth AF: VIII BC is activated at Langley Field and VIII IC at Selfridge Field.

FEAF: P-40's from Bataan bomb and strafe landing barges off Quinauan Point during 1/2 Feb. These strikes, in conjunction with naval and field arty fire, cause considerable damage and casualties but fail to prevent the landings which take place S of the point, although the attempt to reinforce troops already on the point is thwarted.

2 February

Hawaiian AF: VII IC is activated in Hawaii, with Gen Davidson as cmdr. Gen Hale cmds VII BC.

3 February

FEAF: Bad weather from now until 18 Feb, along with effective interception by ftrs, thwarts attempts of HBs in Java to deliver damaging blows on shipping and A/Fs in NEI. B–17's strikes from Singosari against shipping at Balikpapan (8 Feb) and an A/F at Kendari (9 Feb) are repulsed by ftr attacks. B–17's on a shipping strike claim hits on a carrier near Sinjai.

5 February

AAF: Far East, Caribbean, Hawaiian, and Alaskan AFs are redesignated Fifth, Sixth, Seventh, and Eleventh AFs, respectively.

6 February

CCS: WD announces creation of US-British CCS in Washington.

9 February

Seventh AF: 12 B–17's are detached and released to CINCPAC for assignment to TF 11 for operations in S Pacific.

Fifth AF: Between this day and 18 Feb, HBs fly at least 14 missions, but they result in claims of only 3 hits on shipping.

12 February

AAF: Gen Arnold indicates that 16 HB gps, 3 pur gps, and 8 photorcn sqs will be sent to UK during 1942.

Tenth AF: Activated at Patterson Field.

Eighth AF: Gen Duncan, CG, requests that his force, inadequate for its intended mission under GYMNAST, be strengthened by several bomb and pur gps. This move, if carried out, would require diversion of units originally intended for other task forces.

14 February

Seventh AF: A B–17 flies photo rcn of Wake I.

15 February

SE Asia: Japanese forces on Malay Peninsula capture Singapore.

UK: Lt Col Townsend Griffiss, aide to Gen Chaney, is killed when the aircraft on which he is a passenger is mistakenly shot down by RAF Polish fliers. He is first US airman to die in line of duty in Europe since the US entered World War II. Eighth AF base at Bushy Park is later named Camp Griffiss in his honor.

17 February

Tenth AF: Col Harry A Halverson becomes CO.

Eleventh AF: Colonel Lionel H Dunlap arrives from ZI and becomes CO of the Eleventh.

19 February

Fifth AF: Operating out of Malang, Madioen, and Jogjakarta, A–24's, with P–40 escort, and B–17's attack vessels landing troops on Bali. The attacks, carried out during the afternoon of 19 Feb and throughout the morning of 20 Feb, cause considerable damage to vessels but fail to halt the landings. P–40's shoot down or turn back several bmrs sweeping W over Java. Japanese airplanes attack Darwin, bombing vessels loaded with troops destined for defense of Koepang on Timor I. 10 P–40's sent to Darwin to escort the convoy are almost entirely wiped out by the attack.

Seventh AF: VII AFBC is activated.

20 February

AAFIB: Gen Eaker arrives in UK with 6 staff officers.

21 February

Fifth AF: Gen Brett, Dep CG ABDACOM, informs WD of his decision to evacuate Fifth AF and other US troops from Java. Fifth AF bmrs at Java bases fly about 20 strikes, usually in 2- and 3-aircraft elements, against shipping in Java Sea and against tgts on Bali from this date through 1 Mar. 11 strikes are complete failures; the remainder, although causing some damage to vessels and A/F facilities, fail to deter the invasion of Java.

23 February

Eighth AF: HQ VIII BC established in UK; Gen Eaker assumes cmd.

Fifth AF: B–17's fly first mission against Rabaul. Operating out of Townsville, the force suffers mechanical trouble and runs into bad weather. Only 1 HB manages to bomb the tgt. Gen Brereton, CG, departs for India after issuing order terminating HQ Fifth AF. Until 3 Sep 42, units of Fifth AF will be initially under control of ABDACOM and then Allied AF (SWPA).

ZI: Japanese submarine I-17 fires 13 rounds of 5½-in shells from range of 2,500 yds at oil refinery N of Santa Barbara. Pur and bmr aircraft sent to the area are unable to destroy the sub.

24 February

Fifth AF: HB units begin evacuating Java.

ZI: Reports of unidentified aircraft approaching Los Angeles from the ocean during 24/25 Feb result in "Battle of Los Angeles" in which some 1,400 rounds of 3-in AA ammo is fired against various "targets." Later the Army will conclude that the "battle" had been touched off by 1 to 5 unidentified aircraft, but the Navy will maintain there was no reason for the firing.

25 February

AAF: AWPD recommends removal of GYMNAST from list of current projects. This proposal, if adopted, would leave Eighth AF uncommitted to any operation.

USAFBI: Gen Chaney instructs Gen Eaker and staff to VIII BC to proceed to HQ, RAF BC for study of bombing operations, and to make rcn of certain A/Fs and submit plans for reception and assignment of AAF units.

27 February

Fifth AF: Battle of Java Sea. Allied air and naval units try to stop convoy of some 80 ships approaching Java from NE. All available B–17's, A–24's, P–40's and LB–30's are put into the air but achieve only insignificant results. An Allied naval force, 5 cruisers and 11 destroyers, under Adm Doorman, Royal Netherlands Navy, meets the enemy near Surabaya and is decisively defeated, losing 5 ships. Most of Fifth AF ground echelon in Java is evacuated by sea. The *Sea Witch* delivers 27 crated P–40's to Tjilatjap, Java, but these will be destroyed to prevent their falling into Japanese hands. 32 P–40's aboard the USS *Langley*, which sailed from Australia for India on 23 Feb, are lost when the *Langley* is sunk by aircraft 100 mi S of Tjilatjap. The pilots are rescued by other vessels in the convoy, but the enemy sinks these ships with the exception of a destroyer, which delivers 2 of the pilots to Perth.

1 March

Fifth AF: Last HB mission flown from Java.

2 March

Fifth AF: 5 B–17's and 3 LB–30's (the last airplane taking off just before midnight) evacuate the last 260 men from Jogjakarta, the last A/F on Java in Allied hands. Ground forces are within 20 mi at this time. Bataan-based P–40's attack shipping in Subic Bay. The pilots claim considerable damage to the ships, but 4 of the few P–40's remaining on Bataan are lost.

3 March

US: CCS take under consideration recommendation to continue SUPERGYMNAST as an "academic study" only. Thus the proposed N African venture ceases to affect Eighth AF until it is revived later as TORCH.

Fifth AF: Japanese airplanes attack A/F and harbor at Broome, Australia at 1000, shortly after arrival of 8 HBs evacuating men from Java. The Japanese destroy 2 B–17's, 2 B–24's, 12 seaplanes, and 2 Hudsons, and kill at least 45 Dutch civilians and 20 US airmen.

4 March

Seventh AF: A lone Japanese aircraft attempts to attack Honolulu but drops its bombs short of the city. Overcast conditions prevent successful pursuit by Seventh AF airplanes.

5 March

Tenth AF: Gen Brereton who arrived in India from NEI on 25 Feb, formally takes cmd of Tenth AF, which at this time has 8 tac aircraft (B–17's).

ZI: Civil Air Patrol begins flying patrols off the E coast. XII IC (later redesignated XII FC) is activated at Drew Field.

8 March

Tenth AF: HQ Tenth AF begins moving from Patterson Field to India. Between this date and 13 Mar, the 8 B–17's in India transport 474 troops and 29 tons of supplies from India to Magwe and on the return flights evacuate 423 civilians.

Eleventh AF: Col William O Butler assumes cmd of the Eleventh with HQ at Ft Richardson.

9 March

AAF: Military reorganization, implementing Executive Order of 28 Feb, becomes effective. The Air Corps and the US Army Air Force Combat Cmd, which previously had made up the AAF under Gen Arnold as Chief, are discontinued, and the AAF is reorganized with Arnold as CG. Army Ground Forces under Gen McNair and Services of Supply (later Army Serv Forces) under Gen Sommervell are also organized. All are under control of Gen Marshall, CoS. In the Navy, Adm King, CinC US Fleet, assumes additional responsibilities as he succeeds Adm Stark as Chief of Naval Operations.

SE Asia: Japanese forces complete capture of Rangoon, dealing China a great blow by cutting off supplies from Burma Road.

12 March
Tenth AF: 10 P–40's arrive in Karachi by ship from Australia.

ZI: XII BC is activated at MacDill Field.

15 March
SOPAC: 67th Ftr Sq, the first AAF tac unit in the theater, arrives on New Caledonia.

Eleventh AF: XI FC is activated at Elmendorf Field; cmdr is Col Norman D Sillin. Its operational components are the 11th and the 18th Pur Sqs.

16 March
Fifth AF: 3 B–17's of 435th Rcn Sq, 19th Bomb Gp begin evacuating Gen MacArthur, his family, and his staff from Del Monte to Australia.

17 March
SWPA: Gen MacArthur arrives in Australia to assume cmd of United Nations forces in SWPA. He actually assumed cmd on 18 Apr.

20 March
AAF: "Plan for Initiation of US Army Bombardment Operations in the British Isles" further elaborates previous AAF plans outlining intention of launching strategic bombardment from UK against facilities supporting German national, economic, and industrial structure.

AAFIB: Report submitted by Gen Eaker in compliance with Gen Chaney's instructions of 25 Feb indicates completion of studies of RAF BC operations and of A/Fs, trg, tac doctrine, equipment, and methods of conducting air offensive in cooperation with RAF. Report also indicates much dependence upon British for the present but emphasizes the apparent compatibility of the tac doctrines of the US (daylight precision bombing) and RAF (night area bombing), and implies the principle of coordinating these attacks to complement each other.

25 March
Eighth AF: Maj Cecil P Lessig becomes first Eighth AF pilot to fly a mission over France in World War II. Flying a Spitfire with RAF 64 Sq, Lessig participates in a 36-aircraft ftr sweep that is recalled when 50 ftrs challenge them.

26 March
Fifth AF: 3 B–17's of 435th Rcn Sq, 19th Bomb Gp, evacuate Philippine Pres Quezon and his family to Australia.

28 March
ZI: Units of I BC engaged in anti-sub operations are placed under operational control of Cmdr, Eastern Sea Frontier.

31 March
AAF: Gen Spaatz suggests that the now "task-less Eighth" be made nucleus for AAFIB.

1 April
ZI: AC Proving Ground becomes Proving Ground Cmd, with main base at Eglin Field.

2 April
Tenth AF: Gen Brereton, CG, leads 3 HBs on raid on shipping in Andaman Is during 2/3 Apr. The HBs claim hits on a cruiser and a transport. 2 HBs are damaged by AA and ftrs, but all return to base. Earlier in the evening, a mission scheduled against Rangoon area is aborted when 1 HB crashes on takeoff and the other has mechanical trouble.

3 April
Tenth AF: 6 HBs from Asansol bomb warehouses and docks at Rangoon, starting 3 large fires. 1 B–17 fails to return.

6 April
Tenth AF: 10 DC–3's of Pan American Airways begin hauling 30,000 gals of fuel and 500 gals of lubricants from Calcutta to the airstrip at Asansol, completing the mission on the following day. This fuel, subsequently transferred via Dinjan to China, is for use by Lt Col James H Doolittle's Tokyo raiders, already at sea aboard the carrier *Hornet*.

7 April
US: WD officially states that Eighth AF will be established in UK as intermediate cmd between USA-FBI and the AF cmds. Gen Marshall notifies Gen Chaney of this decision.
Fifth AF: During 6/7 Apr the Japanese break the Philippine II Corps front on Bataan, thus necessitating immediate removal of all remaining ftrs to Mindanao, where for the next 3 days they will fly rcn, cover HBs (sent to Mindanao from Australia) operating against concentrations at Legaspi, Cebu, Iloilo, and Davao, and

carry out a strafing attack against aircraft at Davao. After the HBs return to Australia on 12 Apr, the ftrs will continue to fly rcn until Japanese forces envelop the troops on Mindanao on 1 May.

8 April
International: Harry Hopkins and Gen Marshall arrive in London for talks with British serv and supply chiefs concerning integration of US and British manpower and war production for action in Europe. Gen Marshall urges an offensive in the west to relieve pressure upon Russia, and promises a constant flow of US troops, including many air units, to UK.
Ninth AF: V A Spt Cmd (activated 1 Sep 41) is redesignated Ninth AF. HQ is at New Orleans AAB.

9 April
Eighth AF: HQ echelon is located at Bolling Field to prepare Eighth AF for move overseas.
Phil Is: Japanese capture Bataan after 3 months. US-Philippine forces surrender unconditionally. Japanese arty emplaced on Bataan opens fire on Corregidor in conjunction with air attacks.

12 April
AAF: Gen Arnold sends air plans for BOLERO to Gen Marshall in London. Plan calls for establishment of Eighth AF in UK.
Fifth AF: Australia-based B-25's, staging through Mindanao, hit harbor and shipping at Cebu while B-17's carry out single-bmr strikes from Mindanao against Cebu harbor and Nichols Field.

13 April

Fifth AF: Australia-based B–25's hit tgts in the Phil Is for second consecutive day. Staging through Valencia the B–25's take off just after midnight during 12/13 Apr and bomb Cebu shipping and installations at Davao. Later in the day the MBs again attack Davao, bombing the dock area.

SOPAC: Adm Ghormley is assigned as COMSOPAC. He is to cmd all Allied base and local def forces (land, sea, and air) in the South Pacific islands, with the exception of NZ land defenses.

14 April

International: British Government and CoSs accept Gen Marshall's BOLERO plan for Allied build-up in UK for attack on Germany.

15 April

Eighth AF: HQ of VIII BC established in Wycombe Abbey, in High Wycombe by Gen Eaker.

16 April

Tenth AF: HBs take off from Dum Dum A/F near Calcutta to bomb Rangoon. 6 B–17's, guided by flares, bomb the tgt. Numerous searchlights make it impossible to estimate the bombing results.

18 April

Doolittle Raid: 16 B–25's launched from carrier *Hornet* carry out first AAF attack on Japanese mainland. 15 of the B–25's bomb in Japan, the principal tgts being Tokyo, Kobe, Yokohoma, and Nagoya. Since the bmrs had to be launched earlier than scheduled they are unable to reach planned bases in China and have to be crashlanded or abandoned, 15 in China and the other in the USSR.

Fifth AF: Fifth AF units come under control of Allied AF (SWPA) which is created in Australia to control AAF, RAAF and Dutch elements.

20 April

Fifth AF: Gen Brett assumes cmd of Allied AF, which has units based in N and E Australia, with advanced facilities in the Port Moresby area.

22 April

Tenth AF: Aircraft begin to evacuate military and civilian personnel and supplies from Burma to India. By 15 Jun the Tenth has evacuated 4,499 passengers and 1,733,026 lbs of freight.

SOPAC: Joint US-NZ Naval Cmd ordered established under Adm Ghormley. It is to operate separately but in close liaison with Gen MacArthur and Adm Leary.

27 April

Eighth AF: ADVONs of HQ, Eighth AF and of bmr, ftr and base cmds, along with 15th Bomb Sq, 2d Air Depot Gp, and a weather dets totalling about 1,800 men, sail from Boston for UK.

Fifth AF: In Australia, US Army Air Services under Gen Lincoln takes over responsibility as an administrative, supply, maintenance, and engineering cmd under Allied AF.

28 April

Eighth AF: VIII GASC is activated at Bolling Field.

29 April

Tenth AF: Rangoon is again hit by a flight of HBs which pound dock area.

30 April

Burma: Japanese capture Lashio and begin move to drive Chinese back along Burma Road toward China and drive US and British forces back toward India.

Fifth AF: P–39's flying out of Port Moresby strafe airplanes and fuel dumps at Lae and Salamaua.

ZI: ATC is established.

1 May

Tenth AF: X ASC is activated under cmd of Gen Adler, who arrived in India on 26 Apr.

2 May

Eighth AF: Gen Spaatz is designated Eighth AF cmdr.

4 May

Fifth AF: B–26's bomb Vunakanau A/F at Rabaul. P–39's and B–17's hit A/F at Lae.

SOPAC: Battle of the Coral Sea begins with US carrier-based air attack on Tulagi.

5 May

Eighth AF: Gen Spaatz assumes cmd at Bolling Field.

Tenth AF: On a raid against Mingaladon A/F during 4/5 May, 4 B–17's bomb a hangar and parked aircraft. The crews claim 40 airplanes destroyed but searchlights make accurate observation impossible.

6 May

Phil Is: Corregidor surrenders. All US organized resistance to Japanese in Phil Is ends.

Tenth AF: Mingaladon A/F is hit for second consecutive night. 3 B–17's score direct hits on fuel dump at the field.

Fifth AF: B–17's unsuccessfully attack shipping in Bougainville area.

7 May

Fifth AF: Battle of the Coral Sea, which began on 4 May, approaches its climax as Allied naval forces intercept Japanese naval forces near Misima I. Navy divebmrs sink the carrier *Shoho*. Allied forces lose an oiler and a destroyer. Allied AF bmrs join the battle but their effect is limited. Several bmrs attack Allied vessels by mistake.

8 May

Fifth AF: Main action of Battle of the Coral Sea occurs as Allied and Japanese carrier forces clash. Allied bmrs join Navy airplanes in attacking enemy's main spt force which has swept around S of San Cristobal. The carrier *Shokaku* is severely damaged by aircraft from carriers *Lexington* and *Yorktown*. The *Lexington* is damaged so severely that it later is sunk by US naval fire. The *Yorktown* also suffers damage from aircraft. Both sides lose heavily in aircraft, US losses totalling 66 and the Japanese considerably more. The Allies turn back the sea assault against Port Moresby, a key base in New Guinea and of great importance to the security of Australia. The battle is the first major naval engagement in history in which the opposing warships do not exchange a shot. The Coral Sea battle marks the end of the period in which the Allied forces in SWPA are only on the defensive and paves the way for offensive operations. The rcn work of the AAF proves of greater importance than its bombardment operations, which have no real effects on the battle. Lack of Navy-AAF coordination is apparent from the Coral Sea action, and this eventually leads to better interservice communication.

9 May

Tenth AF: During 8/9 May, 6 B-docks at Rangoon.

Fifth AF: 8 B-26's and a single B-17 attack shipping and seaplanes at Deboyne I.

10 May

Fifth AF: B-25's bomb seaplane base at Deboyne I.

11 May

Eighth AF: The transport *Andes* 17's bomb Mingaladon and attack the docks in UK, carrying about 1,800 personnel for various Eighth AF units. This is first large shipment of AAF troops to UK.

Fifth AF: B-17's attack shipping at Kessa in N Solomons while B-26's hit seaplane base at Deboyne I.

12 May

Eighth AF: 39 officers and 348 enlisted men of HQ and the bmr, ftr, and serv cmds arrive at High Wycombe, UK, where VIII IC sets up HQ.

Tenth AF: HBs fly their first mission in direct def of air cargo line to China when 4 B-17's from Dum Dum A/F heavily damage runways and set fire to several parked aircraft at

Myitkyina. Myitkyina, which fell to the Japanese on 8 May, poses serious ftr threat to Allied base at Dinjan.

13 May

Eighth AF: Flying personnel of 15th Bomb Sq, the first US bomb unit sent to UK, arrive at Newport, UK, without aircraft.

Fifth AF: B-17's and B-26's hit shipping and A/F at Rabaul.

14 May

Eighth AF: Gen Eaker designated cmdr of Det HQ Eighth AF in addition to his duties as CG VIII BC. Gen Hunter assumes cmd of VIII IC.

Tenth AF: HBs pound Myitkyina for second time, scoring direct hits on runways and several buildings.

Fifth AF: B-17's, B-26's, and B-25's attack Rabaul and Lae.

15 May

AAF: Interceptor and pur organizations of AAF are redesignated "fighter."

16 May

Tenth AF: HQ completes its move from US to New Delhi. HBs again strike A/F at Myitkyina, pounding runways and buildings. Subsequent rcn indicates that the runways are unusable.

Fifth AF: B-25's, B-26's and B-17's hit A/F and storehouses at Lae and seaplane base at Deboyne I.

17 May

Eighth AF: Det, Eighth AF, with help of VIII BC staff, issues a directive defining its mission, which is the organization, trg and supplying of units of ADVONs of Eighth AF to prepare for immediate operations upon arrival of tac elements of the Eighth. 50 US intelligence officers arrive in UK for trg by RAF BC.

18 May

International: US and Panama sign agreement concerning use of Panama def areas by US forces.

Fifth AF: B–17's bomb shipping in Koepang Bay.

Seventh AF: Seventh AF is placed on alert in anticipation of a possible attack on Midway. For next 10 days the old B–18's on hand are used on search to supplement the B–17's. VII BC receives influx of B–17's during this period, and the 72d Bomb Sq is converted from B–18's to B–17's.

19 May

Eighth AF: Det, HQ Eighth AF, under Gen Eaker, assumes control of all AAF organizations in British Isles.

20 May

Fifth AF: B–17's attack A/F and AA guns at Koepang on Timor I.

SOPAC: Adm McCain, aboard USS *Tangier* at Noumea, assumes cmd as COMAIRSOPAC.

21 May

Fifth AF: B–26's bomb aircraft at Lae.

22 May

Fifth AF: B–17's pound A/F and shipping at Rabaul while B–26's hit A/F at Lae and attack shipping in the harbor.

23 May

Eighth AF: Agreement is reached

on plan to transfer repair depot at Burtonwood to US forces following period of joint control to begin at end of Jun. Burtonwood later becomes greatest AAF depot overseas.

Fifth AF: B–25's strike A/F and buildings at Lae.

24 May

Eighth AF: VIII AFBC, under overall logistical control of SOS, is given primary responsibility for all supply and maintenance peculiar to AAF, thus leaving much logistical autonomy to AAFIB.

Fifth AF: B–26's attack Lae A/F, but heavy AA and at least 15 intercepting Zeros prevent accurate bombing. Several of the MBs are shot down or badly damaged and forced to crashland.

ZI: Deployment of air units from eastern US is begun as a result of threat of a naval attack on the W coast. 12th Bomb Gp begins movement from La to Calif.

25 May

Tenth AF: 4 B–17's bomb Rangoon during 24/25 May.

Fifth AF: B–17's bomb Vunakanau A/F at Rabaul.

26 May

International: Gen Arnold, Adm Towers, and ACM Portal attend Anglo-American air conference in London. Topics of discussion include allocation of aircraft and establishment of US air forces in UK. Meeting begins at 10 Downing Street with Churchill.

ZI: Gulf TF, I BC is established and placed under operational control of Cmdr, Gulf Sea Frontier, for anti-sub operations in Gulf of Mexico.

27 May

Fifth AF: B–17's bomb base at Rabaul.

ZI: 54th Ftr Gp begins deployment from La to strengthen def of W coast.

28 May

Fifth AF: B–26's attack A/F at Lae.

Eleventh AF: A B–17 flies the first armed rcn mission from the secretly constructed A/F at Umnak over the Aleutian Chain, but finds no sign of the enemy. XI FC elements are now deployed at Umnak (P–40's, P–38's), Cold Bay (P–40's), Kodiak (P–39's), and Ft Richardson (P–38's, RCAF Kittyhawks).

ZI: 2 ftr sqs (58th and 59th) of 33d Ftr Gp begin deployment from E coast for def of W coast. Some HB units in W are redeployed for better def against Japanese Navy.

29 May

International: Molotov, who has been in London since 20 May for talks with Churchill, flies to Washington for conference with Roosevelt and US JCS. These talks, which end 2 Jun, deal mainly with the signing of a 20-yr Anglo-Soviet treaty for collaboration, shipments of materiel to USSR, and a second front in 1942.

Tenth AF: 4 HBs hit Myitkyina A/F in high-altitude strike. No activity is seen.

30 May

International: During conferences with ACM Portal, Gen Arnold pres-ents "Programme of Arrival of US Army Air Forces in the United Kingdom" providing for 66 combat gps, exclusive of obs sqs, by Mar 43.

Tenth AF: Myitkyina is again hit by HBs. Again no activity is observed and the attacks are discontinued.

Seventh AF: Seventh AF begins flying B–17's from Oahu to Midway in face of expected attack on that island.

31 May

Fifth AF: B–17's attack Lae and Salamaua.

Seventh AF: B–17's on DS at Midway begin search operations.

Eleventh AF: 54th Ftr Sq (P–38's) arrives at Elmendorf.

1 June

Tenth AF: 5 HBs attack Rangoon dock and harbor area, claiming 1 tanker sunk and another left listing.

Fifth AF: B–17's attack Lae, Salamaua, and Rabaul.

ZI: Fear of attack on W coast causes suspension of movement of aircraft and crews from US to UK.

2 June

Fifth AF: B–17's bomb dock and military camp area at Rabaul.

Seventh AF: 6 of 16 B–17's that have been on DS at Midway return to Oahu.

ZI: Aircraft and crews of 97th Bomb Gp, then in New England for movement to UK, are ordered to W coast as defensive measure against attack on US.

3 June

Tenth AF: A flight of 6 B–25's of

11th Bomb Sq earmarked for CATF, take off from Dinjan for China. They bomb Lashio en route to Kunming, but afterward 3 crash into an overcast-hidden mountain at 10,000 ft and another is abandoned when it runs out of fuel near Chan-i. The remaining 2 B–25's reach Kunming, 1 with its radio operator killed by a ftr.

Fifth AF: B–17's hit wharf, warehouse area, and military camp at Rabaul.

Seventh AF: Preliminary action begins in Battle of Midway. 9 B–17's, flying out of Midway, attack 5 large warships 570 mi off Midway, claiming 5 hits and several near misses. 7 other B–17's leave Oahu and fly to Midway.

Eleventh AF: Japanese carrier-based bmrs and ftrs bomb and strafe Ft Mears and Dutch Harbor in several waves inflicting little damage and killing 52 US personnel. P–40's from Cold Bay trying to intercept them arrive 10 min after the last attack wave departs. Other P–40's at Umnak are notified too late due to communication failure. 9 P–40's and 6 B–26's fly patrol but cannot find the fleet—180 mi S of Dutch Harbor—but 2 of the P–40's engage 4 carrier-based aircraft, shoot down one and damage another.

4 June

AAF: Schedule, with tables of composition and strength, indicating total of 3,649 airplanes, is set up for AAF in UK.

Tenth AF: 2 HBs bomb Rangoon, but are attacked by 10 ftrs. 1 HB is shot down and the other badly damaged. This raid ends 2 months of harassing strikes against Rangoon; soon all HBs are grounded by monsoon.

Seventh AF: Battle of Midway. 4 B–26's, in conjunction with Navy torpedo bmrs, attack carrier; 2 of the MBs are shot down. In further morning action 14 B–17's attack a TF approaching Midway at a distance of 145 mi; they claim several hits on carriers and 2 Zeros shot down. In late afternoon 2 B–17's attack carrier force at 31–40N 179–10W, claiming hits on a battleship and a carrier and 3 airplanes shot down. 4 other B–17's claim a hit on heavy cruiser 185 mi from Midway. 6 B–17's, en route to Midway from Hawaii, bomb ships 170 mi from Midway, claiming hits on a burning carrier, the *Hiryu*, hit earlier in the battle, and a destroyer, which is claimed sunk.

Eleventh AF: A carrier-borne force strikes again as 11 bmrs, 10 ftrs, and 8 torpedo bmrs attack Dutch Harbor in several waves. 2 P–40's intercept 4 bmrs just before noon over Umnak Pass and shoot down 3. During the afternoon P–40's intercept 9 ftrs. A dogfight claims one enemy aircraft and one P–40, the Eleventh's first combat casualty. AA fire claims another Japanese bmr. During the afternoon 2 B–17's and 5 B–26's attack the carrier force, and 3 more B–26's strike the cruiser *Takao*. No hits are scored. 1 B–24 and 1 B–25 fail to return.

5 June

Eighth AF: VIII AFBC, activated in US on 28 Jan 42, is redesignated VIII AFSC. Col Harold A McGinnis assumes cmd.

Fifth AF: B–17's hit wharves, warehouse, and coal jetty at Rabaul.

Seventh AF: Battle of Midway continues with Japanese fleet retiring westward. In the morning 8 B–17's hit force 130 mi from Midway, claiming hits on 2 large warships. During afternoon 6 B–17's claim hits on heavy cruiser 300 mi from Midway. The last strike by Seventh AF aircraft in the Battle of Midway is by 5 B–17's which bomb a heavy cruiser 425 mi from Midway. 1 B–17 is shot down and another lost due to fuel shortage. The battle ends with Midway's installations heavily damaged by bombs but still in US hands and with landing strips still intact. During the fighting (3–5 Jun) Seventh AF aircraft carried out 16 B–17 attacks (55 sorties) and 1 torpedo attack by 4 B–26's, claiming 22 hits on ships and 10 ftrs shot down. 2 B–17's and 2 B–26's were lost. One of the decisive battles of naval history, Midway will cost Japan the initiative and will be a turning point in the Pacific war.

Eleventh AF: 18 B–26's, 10 B–17's and 2 LB–30's search and attack sorties are flown against the carrier force, the B–26's splitting into 3 missions, the B–17's into 2. No contact is made. The B–17's using radar bomb tgts which look like ships, but later turn out to be the Pribilof Is. The 54th Ftr Sq begins moving into Umnak.

ZI: Aircraft and pilots of 1st Pur Sq, then at Dow Field for movement to UK, fly to Morris Field, en route to W coast for def against attack.

6 June

Seventh AF: B–17's maintain search out of Midway. 6 of the HBs mistakenly attack US submarine, which later reports no damage. More B–17's arrive on Midway from Oahu.

Eleventh AF: Various bmr search-attack missions are flown in an attempt to contact the fleet reported near Seguam I. No contact is made due to weather. 8 P–38's en route from Cold Bay to Umnak mistakenly attack a USSR freighter. Japanese begin to land on Kiska.

ZI: Aircraft and pilots of 1st Pur Gp at Morris Field return to Dow Field, following defeat of Japanese fleet in Battle of Midway.

7 June

Seventh AF: Gen Tinker, CG, is lost during 6/7 Jun while leading flight of LB–30's from Midway for predawn attack on Wake I.

Eleventh AF: Japanese troops invade Attu. More troops are put ashore on Kiska. An enemy airplane is sighted over Cold Bay but cannot be intercepted.

8 June

ETOUSA: ETO established by presidential directive. Gen Chaney is designated cmdr of all US forces of ETOUSA.

Eleventh AF: 1 LB–30 flies armed patrol over Kiska and Umnak and discovers Japanese naval units in Kiska Harbor.

9 June

Eighth AF: Second contingent of personnel for HQ Eighth AF and subordinate cmds, including main body of VIII AFSC, arrives in UK.

Fifth AF: B–17's, B–25's, and B–26's attack Lae and Salamaua.

Seventh AF: Gen Davidson, CG VII FC, also becomes CG Seventh

AF following loss of Gen Tinker (see 7 Jun 42).

Eleventh AF: Patrols are flown but encounter no aircraft.

10 June

Eighth AF: Main part of ground echelon, including ground echelons of 97th Bomb, 1st and 31st Ftr, 60th Transp, and 5th Air Depot Gps, and serv units arrive in UK aboard *Queen Elizabeth.*

Fifth AF: B–17's bomb aircraft and buildings at Rabaul.

Eleventh AF: Local patrol is flown at Umnak.

11 June

Eleventh AF: The Eleventh strikes at Kiska for the first time. 5 B–24's and 5 B–17's from Cold Bay load bombs at Umnak and hit Kiska harbor installations and shipping tgts. Low-altitude runs score near misses on 2 cruisers and a destroyer. AA downs a B–24. The other B–24's are pursued by 4 ftrs back to Umnak where US ftrs drive them off. Navy airplanes discover Japanese landing at Attu.

ZI: Aircraft and crews of 97th Bomb Gp, deployed temporarily to W coast, are ordered back to New England for movement to UK.

12 June

Eighth AF: Another contingent of personnel for HQ and subordinate cmds arrive in UK.

HALPRO: 13 B–24's of det under cmd of Col Harry A Halverson en route from US to China take off during 11/12 Jun from Fayid to bomb oilfields at Ploesti. Only 12 attack at dawn. 4 of the 13 land at base

in Iraq which was designated for recovery of the flight, 3 land at other Iraq fields, 2 land in Syria, and 4 are interned in Turkey. Though damage to tgt is negligible, the raid is significant because it is the first AAF combat mission in EAME Theater in World War II, and the first strike at a tgt which later will be famous.

Fifth AF: B–17's bomb building area and Vunakanau and Lakunai A/Fs at Rabaul.

Eleventh AF: 6 B–17's and 1 B–24 bomb shipping in Kiska Harbor. A cruiser is heavily damaged and one destroyer is seen burning.

13 June

Fifth AF: B–17's hit A/F at Rabaul.

Eleventh AF: An LB–30 flies weather mission and for the third straight day Kiska Harbor shipping is bombed by 5 B–17's and 3 B–24's. 2 HBs turn back. The others bomb partially cloud-obscured tgts. No effect observed.

14 June

AAF: Aircraft program for AAF in UK is revised downward from 3,649 to 3,266, and date of anticipated final strength is advanced 1 month to 1 Apr 43.

Eleventh AF: 4 B–17's and 3 B–24's bomb shipping in Kiska Harbor from an altitude of 700 ft, lowest altitude yet. 2 cruisers are hit and one scout seaplane is downed. 2 B–17's are heavily damaged but return to base. Japanese bomb Nazan Bay, Atka.

15 June

Eighth AF: Gen Spaatz, CG, arrives in UK. VIII BC takes significant step toward development of organization for control of combat operations by establishing 1st Bomb Wg, Prov, at Brampton Grange.

HALPRO: 7 B–24's, along with 2 RAF B–24's and RAF torpedo-carrying Beauforts, attack Italian fleet E of Malta. The B–24's bomb and damage a battleship and a cruiser, while the Beauforts sink a cruiser.

Eleventh AF: A bombing mission to Kiska by 3 B–17's and 2 B–24's is aborted due to weather.

16 June

Fifth AF: B–26's, B–25's, and B–17's pound Lae and Salamaua, hitting runways and buildings and starting several fires.

17 June

HALPRO: The det is ordered to vicinity of Cairo to report to Gen Russell L Maxwell, designated CG USAFIME.

Seventh AF: P–40's of 73d Ftr Sq aboard the *Saratoga* are flown off the carrier at Midway to replace Navy airplanes lost in the Battle of Midway. The P–40's begin dawn and dusk patrols which continue until the P–40's are relieved on 23 Jun 43.

Eleventh AF: A Kiska Harbor bombing mission is cancelled due to weather as is patrolling mission by HBs.

18 June

International: Churchill arrives in Washington for series of conferences (until 25 Jun) with Roosevelt. Subjects discussed include war production, shipping, help for China, diver-

sion of Germany from Eastern Front, and atomic research.

Eighth AF: HQ opens in London with Gen Spaatz commanding. Air Ministry publishes tentative list of 87 A/Fs to be made ready for Eighth AF.

Eleventh AF: 1 LB–30, 3 B–17's and 4 B–24's make a precision high-altitude attack on Kiska Harbor. A transport is left burning and sinking, another is mauled, and 2 scout planes are possibly shot down. 1 B–24 crashes at sea; part of its crew is saved.

19 June

USAFIME: Gen Maxwell, formerly head of US Military North African Mission, assumes cmd of USAFIME.

Fifth AF: B–17's pound shipping and Vunakanau A/F at Rabaul.

Eleventh AF: B–24's taking off to bomb Kiska abort due to fog. 1 of them and 2 of its crew are lost when forced to land in the water. A B–17 is dispatched to attack a reported submarine but makes no contact.

20 June

US: Gen Chaney, CG ETOUSA, is recalled from UK and will be replaced by Gen Eisenhower.

Eighth AF: Gen Marshall's letter of instruction to Gen Eisenhower reveals plan to integrate all US air units in UK into Eighth AF. Broad objective of AAF in ETO is to attain "air supremacy over Western Continental Europe" in preparation for future invasion of the Continent.

Fifth AF: B–17's bomb runway at Lae.

Seventh AF: Gen Hale becomes

CG Seventh AF, and Col Albert Hegenberger becomes temporary CO VII BC.

Eleventh AF: 1 LB–30, 1 B–17 and 7 B–24's take off on a search and bombing mission over Kiska. 3 aircraft abort mission due to weather, 3 bomb through overcast with unobserved results, and 3 others search in vain for B–24 lost on the preceding day.

21 June

International: Arnold-Portal-Towers agreement is signed. It deals with US air commitments and provides for strong air force for BOLERO.

HALPRO: 9 B–24's bomb Bengasi harbor after RAF Wellingtons light the tgt with flares and incendiaries.

Eleventh AF: WD authorizes XI AFSC—hitherto Prov Serv Cmd—which is activated at Elmendorf. It is charged with maintaining and supplying all of the Eleventh's bases. Weather cancels all missions except an armed weather sortie over Kiska. Ftrs fly local patrols.

22 June

Eleventh AF: A B–17 weather rcn aircraft flies over Kiska. Ftrs fly AB patrols. Bombing mission is cancelled due to weather.

23 June

Eighth AF: Gen Spaatz is informed that Operation ROUNDUP for invasion of European continent has been put off until Spring 43. This postponement is due to decision to mount Operation TORCH, which will necessitate diversion of large numbers of aircraft earlier slated for Eighth AF in UK.

Eleventh AF: Weather cancels bombing mission. A B–17 flies rcn mission over Kiska. A P–40 on defensive patrol crashes at Elmendorf.

24 June

ETOUSA: Gen Eisenhower arrives in UK.

HALPRO: B–24's bomb Bengasi harbor during 23/24 Jun.

Fifth AF: B–17's hit Vunakanau A/F. Bomb loads include several bundles of incendiaries which cause intense fires.

Eleventh AF: Weather cancels bombing. 1 B–17 flies weather rcn over Kiska. Ftrs patrol A/Fs.

25 June

US: Arnold-Portal-Towers agreement concerning air forces for BOLERO is approved by JCS.

Eighth AF: HQ is established at Bushy Park, a London suburb.

Fifth AF: B–25's bomb Salamaua.

Seventh AF: Gen Lynd becomes CG VII BC.

Eleventh AF: A field order bases the 404th Bomb Sq at Fairbanks, to operate out of Nome, to which 1 sq of the 54th Ftr Gp is also sent. Another sq of the 54th (P–39's) is sent to Ft Richardson. 2 B–17's, 4 B–24's and 1 LB–30 fly bombing and weather missions over Kiska, bombing N side of the harbor.

26 June

Eighth AF: Air echelons of 31st Ftr Gp are established at Atcham and High Ercall by this date. These are first combat personnel of VIII FC to reach UK.

HALPRO: B–24's fly a diversion

for RAF Albacore attack on 2 merchant vessels at Tobruk.

Tenth AF: Gen Naiden becomes CG Tenth AF, succeeding Gen Brereton who departs for ME with Gen Adler, CG X ASC, and several other key subordinates. Aircraft and crews of 9th Bomb Sq follow. This move leaves the Tenth AF almost a skeleton.

Seventh AF: 3 LB–30's bomb installations on Wake I. The raid takes place during 26/27 Jun and is staged through Midway.

Eleventh AF: 5 B–24's drop incendiaries and fire bombs on Kiska Harbor installations.

27 June

HALPRO: B–24's bomb harbor at Tobruk during 26/27 Jun in effort to disrupt movement of supplies.

Fifth AF: B–26's bomb Lae and Salamaua.

28 June

ETOUSA: Gen Eisenhower assumes cmd of ETOUSA, succeeding Gen Chaney.

USAMEAF: Gen Brereton arrives at Cairo, where USAFIME issues orders placing him in cmd of USAMEAF, which is activated immediately. USAMEAF is comprised of Halverson Det (HALPRO), Brereton's det (9th Bomb Sq and other personnel which Brereton brought from India), and Air Section of US Military North African Mission. Also activated is ASC, USAMEAF, under Gen Adler. B–24's of HALPRO bomb harbor and shipping at Tobruk.

Eleventh AF: A B–17 weather aircraft flies over Kiska. Solid weather front cancels bombing. On this and

the following day US adv rcn parties land on Adak from submarines.

29 June

N Africa: Rommel's *Afrika Korps* takes Matruh.

Eighth AF: Capt Charles C Kegelman (CO 15th Bomb Sq), flying on mission with 12 RAF Bostons against Hazebrouck M/Y, becomes first member of Eighth AF to drop bombs on enemy-occupied Europe. First pilot fatality of Eighth AF in ETO is suffered when 1st Lt Alfred W Giacomini of 31st Ftr Gp crashes a Spitfire while landing at Atcham.

Tenth AF: Col Robert C Oliver assumes cmd of X ASC.

Fifth AF: B–17's hit A/Fs at Rabaul and Lae during 28/29 Jun.

30 June

Eighth AF: Joint Anglo-American control of Burtonwood air depot begins with view toward subsequent exclusive control by AAF. VIII AFSC is designated US agent at Burtonwood.

USAMEAF: B–24's bomb Tobruk harbor during 29/30 Jun; first US combat casualties in ME are recorded as 1 B–24 is lost. Gen Brereton moves his det from Egypt to Palestine, as Rommel advances toward the Suez Canal.

Fifth AF: B–17's attack Dili, Koepang and Kendari; B–25's and B–26's hit Lae in New Guinea.

Eleventh AF: A B–17 flies weather rcn over Kiska.

1 July

AAF: BOLERO build-up is revised downward from 66 to 54 combat gps because of demands of other theaters. AAF Foreign Service Concentration Cmd is activated to handle movement of units and trooops to and from overseas theaters.

Eighth AF: The first B–17 (assigned to 97th Bomb Gp) of the BOLERO air movement via N Atlantic route lands at Prestwick.

Middle East: British forces check Axis adv at El Alamein.

USAMEAF: B–24's bomb harbor at Tobruk during 1/2 Jul.

Tenth AF: First combat mission of CATF takes place before the formal activation (4 Jul) of the unit. 4 B–25's from Hengyang, escorted by P–40's, bomb docks at Hankow. Bad weather handicaps the bombardiers, and the effects of the raid are inconsequential.

Fifth AF: B–26's bomb Salamaua. Other MB and HB strikes abort due to bad weather.

Eleventh AF: The XI Prov BC comprising the 28th Comp Gp and its assigned sqs is activated. Col William O Eareckson in cmd. A B–17 flies weather rcn over Kiska and lands early due to weather.

2 July

International: CCS approve of Arnold-Portal-Towers agreement.

USAMEAF: B–17's and B–24's bomb Tobruk harbor during 2/3 Jul.

Tenth AF: CATF B–25's and P–40's hit Hankow dock area for second consecutive day. This raid, more successful than the first, causes considerable damage. The Japanese retaliate during the night by attacking Hengyang but fail to hit the A/F.

Eleventh AF: 7 B–24's and 1 B–17 fly photo and bombing missions to Attu—which appears deserted—and

to Kiska and Agattu. Near misses are scored on a transport and a destroyer at Agattu.

3 July

USAMEAF: B–24's attack Tobruk harbor during daylight hrs and B–17's bomb supplies at Tobruk during 3/4 Jul.

Tenth AF: CATF airplanes bomb and strafe A/F at Nanchang, the probable base of the preceding night's raiders on Hengyang. Several parked aircraft are destroyed. During the night Japanese airplanes again strike at Hengyang and once more fail to hit A/F.

Fifth AF: B–17's attack barracks area at Koepang and A/F at Lae. 1 A–24 bombs Tulagi.

Eleventh AF: 7 B–24's and 2 B–17's bomb Kiska and Near Is, encountering neither ftr opposition nor AA. Results not observed.

4 July

Eighth AF: First AAF air operation over W Europe. 15th Bomb Sq, flying 6 American-built Bostons belonging to RAF, join RAF low-level attack on 4 A/Fs in the Netherlands. Aircraft flown by Capt Charles C Kegelman, sq CO, is severely damaged, but Kegelman succeeds in bringing it back to base at Swanton Morley. VIII AF Comp Cmd is activated in US. Second B–17 arrives in UK via N Atlantic ferry route.

USAMEAF: B–24's attack convoy in Mediterranean during 4/5 Jul, setting 1 tanker aflame.

Tenth AF: CATF is activated under cmd of Gen Chennault. This new cmd is successor to Chennault's AVG, which had attained 300 confirmed victories over Japanese airplanes at a cost of less than 50 aircraft and only 9 pilots. Only 5 pilots and a few ground personnel of AVG choose to join the AAF, although 20 other pilots agree to stay until replacements arrive in Kunming. Combat elements of CATF are 23d Ftr Gp, 16th Ftr Sq, and 11th Bomb Sq. Col Robert L Scott is to cmd the ftrs and Col Caleb V Haynes the bmrs. In air action in China, 5 B-25's, with ftr escort, heavily damage buildings, runways, and parked aircraft at Tien Ho A/F. P-40's over Kweilin intercept a formation of FBs, claiming 13 destroyed. The Japanese fail to bomb tgt.

Fifth AF: B-17's, B-26's, and B-25's bomb A/Fs at Lae and Salamaua.

ZI: ATC, which was established on 30 Apr 42, is redesignated I TCC and made responsible for trg and preparing units and personnel for TC (airborne) operations. Ferrying Cmd, which was established on 29 May 41, is redesignated ATC and made responsible for air transport and ferrying operations.

5 July

USAMEAF: B-24's bomb harbor and ships at Bengasi during 4/5 Jul.

Fifth AF: B-17's and B-26's attack Lae and Salamaua.

Eleventh AF: A B-17 flies a weather mission.

6 July

Eighth AF: RAF invites Eighth to share membership in important RAF operational committees dealing with tgts, operational research, interception, and bmr operations. VIII

AFSC sets up HQ at Bushy Park with Gen Frank as CG. 6 B-17's arrive in UK via N Atlantic ferry route.

Tenth AF: CATF B-25's bomb waterfront at Canton, marking their initial action against coastal facilities of Japanese-held Chinese ports.

Eleventh AF: 4 B-24's and 1 LB-30 fly bombing and weather missions to Kiska. Results are not observed.

Sixth AF: German sub, U-153, is damaged in attack by aircraft of 59th Bomb Sq off Panama, 12-50N 72-21W. The sub is sunk a week later by US destroyer *Landsdowne*.

7 July

SOPAC: Gen Millard F Harmon is designated COMGENSOPAC.

Eleventh AF: 1 B-17 and 7 B-24's fly weather, bombing and photo missions to Kiska, Attu, and Agattu. All bombs are returned to base due to weather. 1 seaplane is shot down.

ZI: An A-29 of 396th Bomb Sq sinks German sub, U-701, off NC 34-50N 74-55W. This is first sub sunk by AAF aircraft during World War II.

8 July

USAMEAF: B-24's bomb harbor and shipping at Bengasi during 8/9 Jul, while B-17's hit harbor at Tobruk.

Tenth AF: A single B-25 piloted by Col Caleb V Haynes, bombs Japanese HQ at Tengchung near Burma border. Bad weather, pilot fatigue, and maintenance halt major operations for several days.

Eleventh AF: 404th Bomb Sq arrives in the Alaskan Theater with

B-24's—originally destined for N Africa. 1 B-24 flies 2 photo missions over S shore of Kiska and over Little Kiska. Bombing mission cancelled due to weather.

9 July

Eighth AF: 7 P-38's arrive in UK via N Atlantic route, this being the first time single-seater AAF aircraft have flown this route.

USAMEAF: 6 B-24's dispatched against shipping are attacked by ftrs; 1 B-24 is lost and the others return to base without bombing tgts.

Eleventh AF: 5 B-24's fly photo, weather, and bombing missions to Kiska but return with the bombs due to weather.

10 July

AAF: AAF planners for BOLERO build-up estimate 137 AAF gps in UK by 31 Dec 43.

USAFMEAF: 57th Ftr Gp, en route from US, is assigned to USA-MEAF.

Seventh AF: Ground echelon of 11th Bomb Gp leaves Hawaii for S Pacific aboard USS *Argonne*.

Eleventh AF: 1 B-24 aborts a rcn mission to Kiska due to weather.

11 July

Eighth AF: First formal decoration ceremony held in Eighth AF takes place when Gen Spaatz pins DSC on Maj Charles C Kegelman for extraordinary gallantry and heroism during the raid of 4 Jul.

USAMEAF: B-24's attack harbor and shipping at Bengasi during 11/12 Jul.

Eleventh AF: 4 B-24's taking off

for weather, bombing and photo mission to Kiska are attacked by seaplane ftrs. No losses. A cruiser is bombed with unobserved results.

12 July

Eighth AF: 6 Bostons flown by US crews attack Abbeville/Drucat A/F.

Eleventh AF: 3 B-24's dispatched on weather, photo, and bombing missions to Kiska abort due to weather.

13 July

USAMEAF: During 13/14 Jul, B-17's bomb Tobruk harbor, and B-24's hit ships and harbor at Bengasi. Heavy AA fire accounts for loss of 1 B-24.

15 July

USAMEAF: B-24's strike harbor and ships at Bengasi during 15/16 Jul.

Tenth AF: India-China Ferrying Cmd is activated to replace Assam-Burma-China Cmd.

Eleventh AF: 3 B-24's on a bombing mission to Kiska turn back due to weather.

16 July

Tenth AF: 4 B-25's from Kweilin, with P-40 escort, bomb storage area at Hankow, starting a fire that is later reported to have burned 3 days. The MBs land at Hengyang during return flight to refuel, but are attacked by Japanese airplanes and have to take off immediately. Amidst the confusion a P-40 pilot mistakes a B-25 for a Japanese aircraft and shoots it down, the first bmr lost since

CATF began operations in China. The crew is saved.

Fifth AF: 1 B–17 bombs Salamaua.

Seventh AF: B–17's of 11th Bomb Gp begin leaving Hickam Field for S Pacific.

17 July

USAMEAF: Halverson Det is redesignated Hal Bomb Sq. B–24's bomb Bengasi harbor. B–17's hit Tobruk.

Fifth AF: B–17's bomb harbor at Rabaul.

Eleventh AF: 3 B–17's and 7 B–24's fly weather, bombing and photo missions. Shipping is bombed; North and South Heads of Kiska are photographed. Ftrs down 1 B–17.

18 July

International: Hopkins, Gen Marshall, Adm King, Churchill, and British COS begin conference in London on proposed invasion of N Africa (TORCH).

Tenth AF: 3 B–25's from Kweilin bomb Tien Ho A/F.

Eleventh AF: A B–17 flying weather and photo rcn over Kiska crashes on Umnak I.

19 July

USAMEAF: B–24's hit Bengasi while B–17's attack Tobruk in continuing effort to disrupt movement of supplies.

Tenth AF: In response to a Chinese request, 2 B–25's strike in spt of Chinese ground forces at Linchwan, a Japanese-held city under siege for some time. The Chinese CO later reports that the raid broke the

stalemate and the city was entered the next day.

Eleventh AF: Search missions are flown over Attu and Agattu.

20 July

USAMEAF: Hal Bomb Sq and 9th Bomb Sq (19 B–24's and 9 B–17's) are organized as 1st Prov Gp under Col Harry A Halverson's cmd at Lydda.

Tenth AF: 3 B–25's bomb docks and warehouses at Chinkiang on the Yangtze R. 4 escorting P–40's strafe junks on the river. This is last CATF bombing raid of Jul.

Eleventh AF: Gen Butler moves adv HQ to Umnak. 3 B–17's bomb Kiska (especially barracks) with incendiaries and demolition charges. 4 P–38's try to intercept 4 ftrs reported by Navy aircraft. No contact made.

21 July

US: Roosevelt calls Adm Leahy, Ambassador to France and former Chief of Naval Operations, to serve as CoS to CinC of US Army and Navy.

Eighth AF: Gen Eisenhower assigns to Eighth AF the mission of carrying out, in collaboration with RAF, the degree of air ops with the view of attaining air domination over W France by 1 Apr 43.

Fifth AF: B–26's attack convoy off Salamaua as invasion force heads for Buna, where it begins landings during 21/22 Jul. This move by the enemy forestalls Allied ops which were to have secured the same general area.

SOPAC: Initial sq of B–17's of 11th Bomb Gp arrives at Plaines des Gaiacs from Hawaii.

Eleventh AF: 4 B–24's fly search and bomb missions over Kiska but make no contact because of weather.

22 July

USAMEAF: B–24's bomb Suda Bay claiming hits on 2 vessels. B–17's hit Tobruk.

Fifth AF: P–40's and P–39's hit shipping and landing barges at Gona as Japanese forces continue to land in NE New Guinea with ultimate aim of pushing across the Owen Stanley Range to the Allied base at Port Moresby.

Eleventh AF: Of 8 B–24's and 2 B–17's dispatched to Kiska only 8 reach tgt and due to fog drop only 7 bombs with unobserved results. 1 B–24 missing on return flight.

23 July

USAMEAF: 98th Bomb Gp is assigned to USAMEAF.

Fifth AF: B–17's, B–26's, A–24's, and ftrs pound shipping, landing barges, storage dumps, AA positions, and troop concentrations at Buna and Gona as the enemy pushes inland along Kokoda trail. Ftrs also hit harbor at Salamaua.

SOPAC: 11th Bomb Gp B–17's in New Caledonia begin photo rcn of Guadalcanal-Tulagi-Gavutu area.

Seventh AF: 3 B–17's, staging through Canton I, carry out photo rcn of Makin.

24 July

US: JCS issue statement that HB and MB gps will be shifted from BOLERO assignments to Africa for TORCH. BOLERO resources are further depleted by decision to send 15 combat gps to Pacific theater.

USAMEAF: During 23/24 Jul, B–17's attack Tobruk harbor. B–24's hit harbor at Bengasi. A B–24 crashes on return to base, killing 1 crew member.

Fifth AF: B–26's, A–24's, and ftrs continue to pound AA positions and enemy troops at Gona as Japanese continue to push inland toward Kokoda.

25 July

USAMEAF: Reinforcements begin arriving from US as air echelon of 344th Sq of 98th Bomb Gp reaches Palestine.

Fifth AF: B–25's, and P–39's pound barges and concentrations at Gona and troops on the Gona and Kokoda trails. Japanese forces push to Oivi, within 6 mi of Kokoda.

SOPAC: Daily search missions over S Solomons are begun from New Caledonia.

26 July

Eighth AF: Lt Col Albert P Clark, Executive Officer of 31st Ftr Gp, is shot down while flying an RAF ftr on a sweep over France, thus becoming the first Eighth AF ftr pilot to be shot down in ETO. He survives and is taken prisoner by the Germans.

USAMEAF: During 25/26 Jul, B–17's and B–24's bomb harbor at Tobruk.

Fifth AF: A B–25 strike against Gasmata is repulsed by ftr interception. B–26's attack destroyer off Gona but fail to score hits. Australian troops flown into Kokoda fail to halt Japanese adv and Kokoda is evacuated.

27 July

Eighth AF: HQ VIII BC issues order establishing 1st Bomb Wg at Brampton Grange (replacing 1st Bomb Wg, Prov, established there on 15 Jun) and 2d Bomb Wg at Old Catton. 1st Wg is commanded by Col Claude E Duncan, 2d Wg by Col Newton Longfellow. US aircraft of 97th Bomb Gp and 1st Ftr Gp land at Prestwick, thus completing first series of flights in BOLERO, air movement across N Atlantic ferry route. 97th Bomb Gp becomes first US HB gp complete with air and ground echelons in UK. Gen Eaker and officers of RAF FC agree to use Spitfire IX's as high ftr cover for B–17's of VIII BC until VIII FC is ready for escort duty. This also will provide test of Spitfire IX's against FW 190's at high altitude.

Fifth AF: B–26's and A–24's hit Gona and tgts along Buna trail.

SOPAC: Gen Millard Harmon arrives at Noumea to assume cmd of USAFISPA with responsibility for trg all army (air and ground) personnel. Air units in the theater are under operational control of COMAIRSOPAC.

28 July

USSR: Soviet High Command admits Rostov's fall to the Germans.

USAMEAF: B–17's hit Tobruk during 27/28 Jul, while B–24's attack convoy in Mediterranean, claiming hits on 2 merchant ships.

Eighth AF: HQ VIII FC opens at Bushey Hall following move from temporary HQ at High Wycombe. Gen Hunter, designated CG VIII FC on 14 May in US, assumes cmd in England. Gen Candee, CG VIII

GASC, announces staff assignments and begins organization of his cmd in UK.

Fifth AF: 1 B–26 bombs installations at Gona. Gen Kenney, cmdr-designate of Allied AF, arrives in Australia.

Eleventh AF: Air coverage survey for Army ground operations to Adak and Tanaga Is is flown. Weather cancels bombing mission to Kiska.

29 July

Fifth AF: A–24's, with P–39 escort, and RAAF aircraft attack shipping off Gona, partially frustrating Japanese attempts to land more troops and supplies. Japanese recapture Kokoda, which they temporarily lost the previous day.

Eleventh AF: 4 B–24's and 5 B–17's bomb vessels and installations in Kiska Harbor area with unobserved results due to clouds.

30 July

USAMEAF: During 30/31 Jul, B–24's bomb convoy in Pylos Bay, claiming hits on 2 merchant ships. B–17's hit Tobruk harbor.

Tenth AF: The Japanese send about 120 airplanes against the base at Hengyang from which CATF is harassing the Yangtze Valley. The attacks last about 36 hrs. Fierce opposition by US P–40's prevents major damage to the base. 17 Japanese aircraft are shot down, 4 of them at night. 3 P–40's are lost.

Fifth AF: B–17's attack shipping in Solomon Sea E of Huon Gulf and S of New Britain.

SOPAC: B–17's of 11th Bomb Gp begin arriving at Espiritu Santo where they are to constitute a rcn and strike force over Guadalcanal-Tulagi-Gavutu area in preparation for amphibious assault by US Marines on Guadalcanal on 7 Aug.

Eleventh AF: 1 LB–30, 3 B–17's and 3 B–24's fly photo rcn and bombing missions to Tanaga and Kiska. Missions are unsuccessful due to weather.

31 July

UK: Units of Prov TCC are organized in UK.

USAMEAF: The complete air echelon of 57th Ftr Gp, commanded by Col Frank H Mears, has arrived in Palestine by this date; 12th Bomb Gp, commanded by Col Charles G Goodrich, is now arriving in Palestine. Thus USAMEAF has P–40's and B–25's to add to its B–24's and B–17's.

Fifth AF: B–17's hit Gona and a nearby transport which had been previously damaged, and bomb Kukum Beach and Lunga landing strip on N coast of Guadalcanal as US invasion forces leave Fiji Is for the Solomons.

SOPAC: Col LaVerne G Saunders leads 9 B–17's of his 11th Bomb Gp from Efate on strike against Guadalcanal, bombing landing strip and area about Lunga Pt. From this date until 7 Aug, the 11th Gp flies 56 strike and 22 search sorties in spt of the invasion of Guadalcanal.

Seventh AF: 1 B–17, from Midway, flies photo rcn of Wake. The HB is intercepted by 6 ftrs. In the ensuing fight US gunners claim 4 ftrs destroyed.

Eleventh AF: 1 B–24 and 1 LB–30 fly weather and photo rcn. Weather cancels combat mission to Kiska.

1 August

Eighth AF: Gen Eaker describes the mission of VIII BC as the destruction of carefully chosen strategic tgts in Europe.

USAMEAF: During 1/2 Aug, B–24's hit convoy in Mediterranean, scoring 3 direct hits on a large merchant ship which last aircraft reports sinking. 1 B–24 is lost in crash-landing at base.

Fifth AF: B–17's attack installations at Gona and shipping 75 mi E of Salamaua in Huon Gulf.

Eleventh AF: Weather and photo rcn is flown by 1 B–24 and 1 LB–30 over Korovin Bay and North Cape.

2 August

Fifth AF: 1 B–17 flies unsuccessful strike against cargo vessel 5 mi S of Salamaua while another bombs Gona.

3 August

Fifth AF: P–400's strafe Oivi and Kokoda.

Eleventh AF: 3 B–17's, 2 B–24's, and 1 LB–30 fly bombing and photo rcn mission to Tanaga and Kanaga and also bomb Kiska. 4 of the aircraft have mechanical trouble but all return.

4 August

USAMEAF: B–24's strike convoy in Mediterranean during 4/5 Aug, claiming hits on 2 merchant ships.

Tenth AF: P–40's sweep Japanese HQ at Linchwan and bomb HQ buildings and barracks and strafe transports.

Eleventh AF: 1 LB–30 flies a photo mission and 2 B–17's and 3 B–24's covered by 8 P–38's escort Navy tenders to Nazan Bay. 2 4-engine seaplane bmrs and a possible third are downed near Atka by 2 of the P–38's, in their first aerial combat in any theater. Weather cancels bombing mission to Kiska.

5 August

Eighth AF: VIII FC dispatches its first mission—11 aircraft of 31st Ftr Gp on a practice run over France.

USAMEAF: Gen Brereton, in his first strategic estimate of the Middle Eastern war, indicates that the 3 major objectives for the Allied AFs are to assist in the destruction of Rommel's *Afrika Korps* by spt to ground troops, secure sea and air comm on and over the Mediterranean, and carry out a sustained air offensive against Italy and against oil installations at Ploesti and in the Caucasus, if the latter should fall under Axis control.

Tenth AF: Japanese aircraft again attack US A/F at Kweilin. Notified well in adv by the Chinese warning net (previously set up under Gen Chennault while he was head of AVG), P–40's meet the Japanese over the tgt, shooting down 2, and another is downed by ground fire.

6 August

USAMEAF: B–24's hit harbor at Tobruk.

Tenth AF: B–25's bomb Tien Ho A/F, causing heavy damage to the runways and destroying several parked airplanes.

Fifth AF: B–25's and B–26's pound A/Fs at Lae and Salamaua.

Eleventh AF: 3 B–24's, 2 B–17's, and 10 P–38's provide air coverage for Navy tenders to Nazan Bay. Photo rcn is flown over Attu.

7 August

USAMEAF: Col Harry A Halverson relinquishes cmd of Hal Bomb Sq, to be succeeded by Lt Col George F McGuire.

Fifth AF: 13 B–17's of 19th Bomb Gp, led by Lt Col Richard H Carmichael, hit Vunakanau A/F in coordination with Marine landings on Guadalcanal. B–26's attack Lae, and a B–17 and a B–25 each attack a submarine in Gulf of Papua.

SOPAC: First Marine Div invades Guadalcanal.

Eleventh AF: 3 B–24's dispatched to bomb Kiska return with their bombs due to solid overcast. 4 more B–24's also depart for Kiska. 1 turns back with mechanical trouble, the others abort mission over tgt due to undercast. 1 B–24, 4 P–38's and an LB–30 fly 2 air coverage missions at Nazan Bay for Navy tenders.

8 August

Tenth AF: B–25's hit Canton area, bombing Tien Ho A/F and other tgts in the vicinity and claiming 2 interceptors shot down.

Fifth AF: P–400's dive-bomb Kokoda and Yodda. B–17's, B–25's and B–26's bomb runways and T/Os at Lae and Salamaua.

SOPAC: From this date through 23 Aug, B–17's fly search missions covering the lower Solomons in order to detect any attempt to make surprise attack on the forces consolidating the Guadalcanal beachhead.

Eleventh AF: 1 LB–30, 3 B–24's, and 8 P–38's on photo and bombing missions over Kiska cannot attack but Navy Catalinas also operating over and off Kiska hit freighters and transport, claiming 1 transport sinking, and score many hits on North Head and Main Camp.

9 August

Tenth AF: P–40's of the 23d Gp continue to spt Chinese ground forces by harassing the Japanese at Linchwan. 4 B–25's and 3 P–40's from Kweilin-Hengyang area, staging through Nanning, bomb docks and warehouses at Haiphong, causing considerable damage and claiming a freighter sunk in the harbor; this is first CATF raid over Indochina.

Fifth AF: B–17's bomb shipping and A/Fs at Rabaul and Gasmata while B–26's hit harbor area at Salamaua.

Eleventh AF: 6 bmrs fly armed rcn over Kiska and Attu and hit Kiska.

10 August

Tenth AF: B–25's bomb Hankow. Afterwards the P–40 escorts, led by Col Robert L Scott, strike ammo dumps and military warehouses at Sienning, causing heavy destruction of material which the Japanese have accumulated to use against Hengyang and other US bases in C China.

Eleventh AF: 5 B–17's and 3 B–24's bomb Kiska tgts. Ftrs and AA down 1 B–24. Only its pilot is saved.

11 August

Eighth AF: Referring to TORCH, Gen Spaatz informs Gen Arnold that, in his opinion, UK remains the only base from which air supremacy over Germany can be established.

Tenth AF: P–40's hit A/Fs at Yoyang and Nanchang from which the enemy has been attacking Hengyang.

Eleventh AF: 1 B–24 flies photo

rcn over W Semichi Is and N Attu coast.

12 August

International: Churchill and British COS, along with Harriman of US, arrive in Moscow for conference with Stalin. Stalin is told about plan for TORCH. Talks, which end on 15 Aug, also include discussion of Second Front in Europe.

Eighth AF: 31st Ftr Gp at Westhampnett is declared fully operational and ready for combat operations under RAF control until it gains enough experience to be able to fight as a group. This is first US ftr unit in UK to reach this operational status.

Fifth AF: B–17's bomb shipping at Rabaul, scoring damaging hits on 3 vessels.

Eleventh AF: 1 B–24 flies photo rcn over Amlia and Atka.

13 August

Fifth AF: Convoy, headed toward Basabua near Gona, with 3,000 construction troops, is attacked first by B–17's 76 mi NE of Gona, followed by B–26's 20–25 mi N of Gona, and another B–17 attack as the convoy approaches landing position. Japanese ground forces attack at Deniki, driving Allied forces back about 5 mi and firmly securing Buna-Kokoda trail.

Eleventh AF: 1 B–24 flies photo rcn over Kiska.

14 August

Iceland: 2d Lt Joseph D Shaffer (33d Ftr Sq) and 2d Lt Elza E Shahan (27th Ftr Sq) jointly shoot down FW 200 off coast of Iceland.

This is first aerial victory of AAF in ETO.

USAMEAF: B–24's bomb Tobruk harbor during 14/15 Aug.

Fifth AF: B–17's attack shipping off Gona.

Eleventh AF: A B–24 trying to fly photo rcn over Tanaga and Adak aborts over Kiska due to weather.

ZI: AAF Foreign Serv Concentration Cmd is redesignated I Concentration Cmd.

16 August

USAMEAF: Personnel strength is greatly increased and supply and maintenance prospects are much improved by arrival of ground echelons of 57th Ftr, 12th and 98th Bomb, and 323d Serv Gps.

Eleventh AF: A B–24 aborts photo rcn flight over Adak because of mechanical failure.

17 August

Eighth AF: 12 B–17's of 97th Bomb Gp, escorted by Spitfires, launch first AAF HB attack from UK against W Europe. Tgt is Rouen-Sotteville M/Y. Sgt Kent R West shoots down German ftr, thus becoming the first Eighth AF gunner to receive credit for a combat kill. VIII GASC opens its HQ at Membury.

USAMEAF: HQ USAMEAF announces designation of Gen Strickland as CG IX FC. B–25's of 81st Bomb Sq hit stores, depot and tank repair shops at Matruh. This marks debut of the MBs of the 12th Bomb Gp in ME.

Fifth AF: A single B–17 bombs Kavieng.

Eleventh AF: 1 B–24 flies photo rcn over Buldir, Kiska and Amchitka Is despite heavy rain.

18 August

Middle East: Gen Alexander assumes cmd of British imperial forces in ME.

Tenth AF: Gen Bissell becomes CG Tenth AF, relieving Gen Naiden who now devotes full time to cmd of India-China Ferry Cmd.

Fifth AF: For second consecutive day a single B–17 attacks Kavieng; bombs fall in A/F dispersal area.

Eleventh AF: A B–24 takes obliques of Amchitka and Tanaga. Heavy fog over Kiska and Attu precludes armed rcn.

19 August

Eighth AF: 22 B–17's drop 34 tons of bombs on Abbeville/Drucat A/F causing extensive damage. This mission is flown to occupy enemy ftrs and prevent them from opposing an invasion by over 5,000 Allied troops, mostly Canadians, who raid Dieppe. 2d Lt Samuel F Junkin Jr of 309th Ftr Sq, 31st Ftr Gp, flying a Spitfire in spt of the amphibious raid on Dieppe, shoots down a German ftr, this being the first aerial victory won by an Eighth AF ftr pilot flying from the UK.

Fifth AF: B–17's bomb shipping at Faisi on Shortland I.

Eleventh AF: Mechanical failure prevents a B–24 from flying rcn over Tanaga.

20 August

Eighth AF: Principle of coordinated day and night bombing receives its first formal definition in "Joint British/American Directive on Day Bomber Operatons involving Fighter

Cooperation." Emphasis is placed on achieving continuity in bombing offensive from UK. 11 HBs attack Longeau M/Y at Amiens, a vital point in the traffic flow between France and Germany.

Eleventh AF: 1 B–24 flies photo rcn over Kiska. Patrol is flown over Shumagin I.

ZI: Twelfth AF is activated at Bolling Field.

21 August

Eighth AF: At Gen Arnold's request, Gen Eisenhower gives Gen Spaatz additional duties as Air Officer for ETOUSA and head of the air section of its staff, thus assuring active participation by Eighth AF in theater planning. 12 airplanes are dispatched to bomb shipyards at Rotterdam, but mission is aborted due to attack by 25 Me 109's and FW 190's. Lack of proper coordination with Spitfire escort is major factor in failure of mission.

USAMEAF: B–24's from 2 sqs hit convoy SW of Crete, claiming 2 ships probably sunk. Ftrs attack straggling B–24 and force it to crashland at sea.

Eleventh AF: 1 B–24 trying to fly rcn over Kiska aborts due to weather.

22 August

USAMEAF: B–25's hit tank and motor repair shop and storage dumps at Matruh. A B–25 is mistakenly shot down by an RAF Beaufighter.

Fifth AF: B–17's bomb A/Fs at Lae and Rabaul.

SOPAC: First AAF airplanes, 5 P–400's of 67th Ftr Sq, arrive at Henderson Field, Guadalcanal, joining Marine aircraft which arrived earlier. These P–400's, which operate under control of Marine Aircraft Wing One, prove no match for Japanese Zeros or bmrs at high altitudes.

Eleventh AF: Photo rcn mission over Kiska is aborted due to overcast.

Sixth AF: German sub, U–654, is sunk off Panama, 12–00N 79–56W, by aircraft of 45th Bomb Sq.

ZI: XII AFSC is activated at Mac-Dill Field, under Maj John L Cheesebrough.

23 August

Fifth AF: A lone B–17 bombs Buka I.

Eleventh AF: Fog cancels photo mission.

24 August

Eighth AF: 12 HBs hit the shipyard of Ateliers et Chantiers Maritime de la Seine at Le Trait. Gen Spaatz reports RAF attitude towards US daylight precision bombing seems to be changing from one of skepticism to one of tentative approval.

USAMEAF: B–24's attack Tobruk harbor.

Fifth AF: B–17's hit town of Gasmata and A/Fs at Rabaul. Japanese amphibious forces leave Buna in barges and New Ireland in transports, heading for Milne Bay. Barges are detected by Australian coastwatcher during the afternoon.

SOPAC: In the Battle of the Eastern Solomons, 7 B–17's and USN dive and torpedobmrs from the *Enterprise* and *Saratoga* attack a TF covering a transport formation heading for Guadalcanal; Navy airplanes sink the carrier *Ryujo*. During the night 4 warships shell the airstrip on Guadalcanal.

Eleventh AF: 404th Bomb Sq begins to operate from Umnak. Photo rcn sortie is cancelled due to overcast.

ZI: XII FC is assigned to Twelfth AF.

25 August

Eighth AF: Units of Prov TCC, organized in UK on 31 Jul pending arrival of VIII TCC, are transferred to VIII GASC after plans to organize VIII TCC have been abandoned.

USAMEAF: B–25's bomb shipping and landing grounds. B–24's attack Corinth Canal.

Fifth AF: Amphibious forces bound for Milne Bay from Buna are stranded on Goodenough I when P–40's from Milne Bay destroy all of their beached barges. P–40's also attack a convoy proceeding from New Ireland toward Milne Bay but are hampered by bad weather and fail to halt landings at 3 points E of Rabi during 25/26 Aug. P–400's hit A/F and AA positions at Buna.

SOPAC: The invasion force sailing toward Guadalcanal (see 24 Aug) is hit hard by Marine dive bmrs 125 mi from the island at 0835. B–17's from Espiritu Santo sink the destroyer *Mutsuki* as it is attempting to sink the damaged transport *Kinyru Maru*. By noon the force is heading N in retreat. The enemy has lost about 90 aircraft in the battle.

Eleventh AF: Photo rcn airplane flies over Kiska, Attu, and Adak, then turns back because of mechanical failure.

26 August

USSR: Russians make 7 counterattacks NW of Stalingrad.

Tenth AF: B–25's, which have moved temporarily from C China to Yunnani, bomb Lashio, an important rail center, highway junction, and air base. Covering P–40's strafe numerous T/Os and shoot down at least 2 ftrs.

Fifth AF: P–40's, B–25's, B–26's, and B–17's, plus RAAF Hudsons, pound forces in Milne Bay. A large transport is damaged and most of the supplies on the beachheads E of Rabi are destroyed. P–400's strafe A/F at Buna.

Eleventh AF: Photo mission aborted over Atka due to weather.

27 August

Eighth AF: 7 HBs attack Wilton shipyards on outskirts of Rotterdam. These yards, the most modern in the Netherlands, are fully employed by the Germans for servicing vessels. 92d Bomb Gp completes nonstop flight of the last of its 4 sqs from Newfoundland to UK without a loss. A CCRC, the first in Eighth AF, is established at Bovingdon.

USAMEAF: B–24's bomb a convoy, hitting 1 merchant ship which is reported sinking.

Fifth AF: B–26's and P–400's bomb A/F at Buna while P–40's strafe beachhead and fuel dumps at Milne Bay.

Eleventh AF: 4 B–17's, 6 B–24's, and 2 P–38's fly weather, rcn and patrol missions over Kiska and Atka. Enemy begins to transfer Attu garrison to Kiska, which is completed on 16 Sep 42.

28 August

Eighth AF: 11 B–17's bomb airplane factory of Avions Potez at

Meaulte, an important repair depot for German ftrs.

USAMEAF: 2 B–24 sqs bomb docks, shipping, and jetties in Tobruk harbor.

Tenth AF: 8 B–25's hit barracks and ammo dumps at Hoang Su Phi and a fuel dump at Phu Lo. This is the largest force of MBs used by CATF to date, and the first MB mission flown without escort.

Fifth AF: B–26's pound forces at Milne Bay.

Eleventh AF: Of 3 B–17's bombing Kiska, 1 fails to return. All available B–24's and 2 flts of P–38's fly naval cover at Nazan Bay. An attack mission to Attu is cancelled due to weather.

ZI: Lt Col Harold L Neely takes cmd of Twelfth AF.

29 August

Eighth AF: 12 B–17's attack Courtrai/Wevelghem A/F, an FW 190 base.

USAMEAF: B–24's fail to locate shipping near Crete and return without bombing. B–25's bomb landing ground during 29/30 Aug.

Tenth AF: B–25's pound Lashio, scoring numerous hits on the airport and starting 3 large fires in warehouse area SE of the city.

Fifth AF: B–26's and P–400's hit A/F at Buna; B–17's pound A/F at Rabaul, and P–40's hit facilities in Milne Bay area as enemy ground forces continue drive over the Owen Stanley Range toward Port Moresby.

Eleventh AF: A Navy Catalina reports force of 3 cruisers and 4 destroyers NW of Umnak. Thereupon all aircraft of the Eleventh go on at-

tack alert. Surface force then identifies itself as friendly.

30 August

USAMEAF: B–24's bomb docks and jetties in Tobruk Harbor.

Tenth AF: Myitkyina, northern-most Japanese supply depot and A/F in Burma, from which ftrs could hit Dinjan (terminus of Assam-Burma Ferry), is bombed for first time by 8 China-based B–25's.

Fifth AF: B–17's attack shipping in Saint George Channel.

Eleventh AF: US troops occupy Kuluk Bay, amidst a terrific storm and start building a runway. 5 B–24's photograph Kiska but do not bomb due to overcast, and then fly patrol and photo rcn over Amchitka and Tanaga. P–38's fly patrol between Great Sitkin and Little Tanaga.

31 August

Twelfth AF: XII BC is assigned to Twelfth AF with HQ at High Wycombe.

USAMEAF: B–25's attack aircraft on a landing ground, and B–24's raid harbor at Tobruk. P–40's of 66th Ftr Sq, 57th Gp, escort RAF bmrs during raid on Maryut. B–25's, in conjunction with RAF Bostons, attack troop concentrations and military vehicles as battle of Alam-el-Halfa begins along the El Alamein line.

Tenth AF: MBs from China bomb Myitkyina for second consecutive day.

Fifth AF: B–26's and A–20's bomb A/F at Lae; B–17's bomb ammunition dump at Buna; P–400's strafe positions at Wairopi; and P–40's bomb landing barges and strafe gun positions in Milne Bay area where Australian ground forces now take the offensive.

Eleventh AF: Of 2 B–24's flying weather, rcn and patrol missions over Tanaga, 1 returns due to weather.

1 September

USAMEAF: B–24's attack harbor at Candia, Crete, scoring several direct hits on 1 vessel and hitting 2 others. 2 sqs of 57th Ftr Gp fly escort missions and sweeps with RAF. B–25's, in conjunction with RAF LBs, hit trucks and tanks in battle area of Alam-el-Halfa.

Fifth AF: P–40's hit Japanese HQ at Wagga Wagga on Milne Bay while P–400's strafe Kokoda and Kokoda Pass in the Owen Stanley Range. Australian ground forces continue slow retreat over the range but make progress in Milne Bay offensive.

Eleventh AF: US forces complete occupation of Adak.

2 September

Twelfth AF: Col Claude E Duncan becomes CO XII BC.

USAMEAF: B–24's hit docks and jetties at Tobruk harbor. B–25's bomb aircraft and landing ground and, with RAF, attack troops and vehicles in battle area around Alamel-Halfa ridge. P–40's fly escort and sweep missions over battle area in conjunction with RAF.

Tenth AF: P–40's hit barges and junks carrying rice in the Poyang Lake region, strafe HQ and runways at Nanchang A/F, attack railroad stations and warehouses at Hua Yuan, and sink a launch, damage 4 junks, and wreck a train on Wuchang Peninsula.

Fifth AF: P–400's bomb and strafe

forces in Kokoda and Alola areas as Japanese continue to push toward Port Moresby.

SOPAC: The mission of the 67th Ftr Sq P–400's on Guadalcanal is shifted from air def to close spt for Marine ground forces and attacks on shipping, tasks for which they are better suited.

Eleventh AF: 6 bmrs and 12 P–38's fly cover and photo rcn over Nazan and Kuluk Bays, and Amchitka and Semisopochnoi Is.

3 September

USAMEAF: B–24's attack convoy at sea. B–25's hit troop concentrations, vehicles, and A/F installations in battle area of Alam-el-Halfa and behind enemy lines. P–40's, mostly operating with RAF, escort bmrs and engage ftrs in combat, claiming at least 1 shot down.

Tenth AF: 1 B–25 dumps bombs and pamphlets on Hanoi in first US raid against that city. Munitions, supplies, and several parked aircraft are destroyed or damaged. 9 interceptors pursue the MB for about 30 mi but fail to make contact. For the next 3 weeks, bad weather and inaccurate Chinese weather forecasts severely limit bmr operations.

Fifth AF: Gen Kenney assumes cmd of Fifth AF in Brisbane, where the Fifth's HQ is remanned. Gen Kenney retains cmd of Allied AF. P–400's bomb and strafe Kokoda Pass area, hitting A/F at Kokoda and in the vicinity of Alola, Isurava, and Missima. B–25's and A–20's pound Mubo-Busama-Salamaua area. A B–17 strafes seaplanes at Faisi I.

Eleventh AF: The 21st Bomb Gp arrives at Umnak. Of 6 bmrs and 5

P–38's off to bomb Kiska and flying air cover over Kuluk Bay, 5 bmrs and 3 ftrs abort due to weather. The others strafe seaplanes and boats in Kiska Harbor and nearby installations. Between 1 and 4 seaplanes are claimed destroyed on the water. This is the longest over-water attack flight thus far in World War II. The 2 ftrs which reach the tgt area return from the 1,260 mi round trip with only 40 gals of fuel.

4 September

USAMEAF: B–24's, in conjunction with RAF and RN, attack convoy at sea. 2 merchant ships are reported sunk and 1 left burning. B–25's and RAF Bostons, repelling counterattacks during Alam-el-Halfa battle, hit troop concentrations and vehicles, while P–40's, operating with RAF, escort bmrs and engage in combat over battle area, claiming 1 ftr destroyed.

Fifth AF: P–40's bomb and strafe forces in Milne Bay area at Goroni, Wagga Wagga, Ahioma, and N of Lilihoa. Australian ground forces pushing E along Milne Bay reach Goroni; Japanese begin evacuation of the area.

Eleventh AF: 2 bmrs and 1 P–38 bomb and patrol Nazan and Kuluk Bays, but bombing of Kiska is cancelled due to weather.

5 September

Eighth AF: Because of Gen Spaatz's convincing protests, Gen Eisenhower changes his mind concerning his recent orders to suspend Eighth AF operations from UK in order to devote total air effort to spt of Twelfth AF and the forth-coming African campaign. Gen Eisenhower informs Gen Marshall that he considers air operations in UK and in Africa mutually complementary. 31 B–17's bomb the locomotive depot at Rouen-Sotteville M/Y. This is largest force of Eighth AF HBs to attack to date. Almost 1/5 of the HE bombs burst within the M/Y.

USAMEAF: B–24's strike shipping and dock area in Candia Bay. P–40's escort RAF bmrs over battle area SE of Alam-el-Halfa ridge near Rayil Dayr Ar Depression as enemy offensive falters and is pushed back.

Fifth AF: Gen Walker becomes CG V BC. P–400's strafe Kokoda, Kaile, Isurava, Alola, Buna, Sanananda, and Buna-Kokoda trail. A/F at Buna is strafed and bombed by P–400's and A–20's. As Japanese withdraw from Milne Bay area, Australian ground forces capture Wagga Wagga supply dump.

Eleventh AF: 3 B–24's abort bombing of Kiska due to overcast.

6 September

USSR: Germans announce capture of Novorossisk, key Soviet port on Black Sea since fall of Sevastopol.

Eighth AF: 30 B–17's strike Avions Potez aircraft plant at Meaulte, while a smaller force bombs 2 A/Fs near Saint-Omer. 12 DB–7's attack Abbeville/Drucat A/F. 2 B–17's are shot down over Meaulte by ftrs, marking VIII BC's first loss of aircraft in combat.

USAMEAF: P–40's fly offensive sweep over battle area near Rayil Dayr Ar Depression, claiming 3 Ju 87's shot down. P–40's also escort RAF bmrs and fly 2 interceptor missions.

Fifth AF: P–400's, A–20's, and B–17's strafe and bomb positions, troops, and shipping at Myola, Mubo, Kokoda, Myola Lake, Eora Creek, and Milne Bay. Australian ground forces continue to clear enemy from Milne Bay area while Australian troops in the Owen Stanley Range fall back to vicinity of Efogi Spur beyond Gap Mountain, where defensive positions are already established.

Eleventh AF: A B–24 flying patrol and armed rcn over Tanaga sinks a mine layer and strafes a tender as well as nearby tents and buildings.

7 September

EIGHTH AF: 7 B–17's of 29 dispatched, ineffectively raid the Wilton shipyards at Rotterdam in bad weather. 2 HBs seek T/Os in vicinity of Utrecht. Heavy ftr opposition is successfully repulsed with bmr crews claiming 12 destroyed.

USAMEAF: B–24's bomb convoys at sea, hit other shipping, and attack Maleme A/F and Suda Bay.

Fifth AF: A–20's and P–400's strafe and bomb positions at Myola Lake and Efogi in Owen Stanley Range. P–40's and RAAF Hudsons, Beauforts, and Beaufighters attack cruiser and destroyer 17 mi ENE of Cape Karitahua. Organized Japanese resistance in Milne Bay sector ends.

Eleventh AF: 3 B–24's patrol and bomb Kiska Harbor and camp area and also patrol Tanaga. They are attacked by 3 sea ftrs of which at least 1 is downed.

8 September

Eighth AF: "Joint British American Directive on Day Bomber Op-erations Involving Fighter Cooperation" is issued. Worked out between Gen Spaatz and the RAF, it consigns night bombing to the RAF and day bombing to the Eighth AF. Purpose is to achieve continuity in the bombing offensive and secure RAF ftr spt for US bmrs. Gen Spatz orders all tac operations to give way to activity in spt of TORCH. Processing of units of newly created Twelfth AF destined for N Africa takes priority over combat operations for the present.

USAMEAF: B–24's attack shipping and harbor at Suda Bay.

Fifth AF: P–400's bomb and strafe Efogi area where Australian forces are hard pressed by the Japanese. B–17's and RAAF Hudsons attack cruisers and a destroyer N of the D'Entrecasteaux Is.

Eleventh AF: 1 B–24 and 1 B–26 fly photo rcn over Agattu, Attu, and Kiska.

9 September

US: Japanese airplane, launched from sub off coast, drops incendiary bomb on mountain slope near Brookings, causing small forest fire. This comprises total bombing of continental US by enemy aircraft during World War II.

AAF: Gen Arnold submits to the CoS a plan (AWPD–42) estimating size of air force necessary to attain air ascendancy over the enemy and outlining suggestions for use of these forces in the several theaters. This plan, which by 17 Nov has been approved by WD and the President, includes buildup of depleted Eighth AF in UK and contains the seeds of the CBO.

USAMEAF: B–24's attack Tobruk harbor and shipping.

Fifth AF: P–40's strafe Galaiwa Bay area on Goodenough I. A–20's, in spt of encircled Australian ground forces, strafe and bomb troops in Efogi Spur area.

Eleventh AF: 1 B–26 patrols Tanaga and Adak.

10 September

Eleventh AF: Weather, photo rcn, and patrol missions are flown during morning over Tanaga, Nazan Bay, Adak, and Amchitka. Poor weather is encountered at Kiska, Attu, and Agattu.

11 September

USAMEAF: P–40's fly uneventful sweep with RAF during lull after Battle of Alam-el-Halfa.

Fifth AF: A–20's and B–26's hit Efogi and Menari in the Owen Stanley Range and A/F at Buna. B–17's, along with RAAF Hudsons, attack 2 destroyers 20 mi E of Normanby I. A B–17 scores a direct hit on stern of the destroyer *Yayoi*, which later sinks.

SOPAC: Island combat control gps are authorized for New Caledonia and Fiji. These units, under immediate control of COMGENSOP AC, are to take over local operational direction of ftr aircraft and all other units in the island combat team.

Eleventh AF: 343d Ftr Gp, constituted on 3 Sep, is activated on this day and immediately begins to operate. It is composed of the 11th, 18th, 54th, and, as of 10 Oct, 344th Ftr Sqs. A weather, photo, and patrol aircraft draws AA fire over Chicha-

gof Harbor and also covers Tanaga, Amchitka, and Semichi.

12 September

Eighth AF: HQ VIII AF Comp Cmd arrives in N Ireland and is temporarily stationed at Long Kesh. HQ 3d Bomb Wg arrives in UK and is established at Elveden Hall. HQ 4th Bomb Wg is established at High Wycombe but soon loses its personnel to XII BC and is not manned again until Jan 43. 4th Ftr Gp is activated in UK to be manned by US pilots who formerly flew with RAF Eagle Sqs.

Twelfth AF: HQ of Twelfth AF, XII FC and XII AFSC arrive in UK.

USAMEAF: P–40's fly 3 uneventful scramble missions along frontlines.

Fifth AF: P–400's, B–26's, A–20's, and B–17's bomb A/F and strafe barges at Buna. P–40's strafe Gadaibai on Goodenough I. A B–17 strafes vessel in Bismarck Sea S of Kavieng.

Eleventh AF: A weather and patrol rcn aircraft finds overcast at Kiska but takes photos over Tanaga, Kanaga, and Attu. The runway at Adak is completed.

13 September

USAMEAF: During 13/14 Sep, B–24's attack Tobruk and shipping in Bengasi harbor while B–25's hit landing grounds SE of Matruh.

Fifth AF: B–26's pound A/F at Lae. B–17's unsuccessfully attack cruiser SE of Rabaul. P–40's strafe buildings on Goodenough I.

Eleventh AF: 14 B–24's of the 21st and 404th Bomb Sqs move up to Adak. 1 LB–30 and 2 P–38's fly photo rcn, antisub coverage and strafing mission over Kiska lakes and harbor. A tender in harbor is slightly damaged, 1 float ftr is downed. A P–38 is hit by AA fire and ftrs damage the LB–30.

14 September

Twelfth AF: HQ of Twelfth AF, XII FC, XII AFSC, and XII BC are attached to corresponding units of Eighth AF in UK. The Eighth subsequently handles the buildup of the Twelfth by assigning a large number of its own units to the new AF (appropriately dubbed JUNIOR) and supervises its trg. The first increment of tac and serv units includes 2 HB gps, 3 MB gps, 1 LB gp, 4 ftr gps, 3 TC gps, and several engineer, signal, and serv units of varying sizes.

USAMEAF: B–24's attack shipping at Suda Bay, setting 1 vessel afire, while other HBs hit Tobruk. P–40's fly sweep with RAF over frontlines.

Fifth AF: A single A–20 bombs ground forces and installations at Myola.

Eleventh AF: In the first combined heavy mission over Kiska 13 B–24's, 1 B–17, 14 P–38's, and 14 P–39's fly low-altitude and photo runs. The P–39's shell 3 subs in the harbor. The other aircraft bomb and strafe many installations including AA guns and the submarine base. A single aircraft also strafes Segula. Enemy losses are 5 float planes shot down and 1 flying boat destroyed on the water; 2 mine sweepers sunk and another vessel slightly damaged; while a large cargo vessel and several small barges and vessels sustain hits. 2 P–38's are lost, colliding head-on while after a ftr.

15 September

USAMEAF: 57th Gp is first ftr gp to arrive in Egypt from Palestine. A lone B–24 drops 1 bomb on tanker in Suda Bay. B–24's bomb behind enemy lines while P–40's, along with RAF, fly escort and carry out scramble missions over area W of El Alamein.

Fifth AF: MBs hit Buna and Sanananda and attack camps at Efogi and Myola. B–17's bomb harbor and A/F at Rabaul. First US inf troops, elements of 32d Div, arrive at Port Moresby.

Eleventh AF: 1 B–17 and 1 B–24 fly armed rcn over Kiska, and at Amchitka blast buildings in Constantine Harbor area. Ftrs strafe Kiska Camp area and down 4 intercepting aircraft.

16 September

Eighth AF: VIII AFSC selects Honington and Watton as sites for BC adv depots. Site for FC awaits final settlement of question of location and mission of FC.

USAMEAF: Gen Brereton is officially assigned to the ME as a result of pressure from Gen Bissell, new CG Tenth AF, for clarification of status of Brereton and other key staff officers and combat crews who had gone from India to ME in Jun and Jul 42.

Fifth AF: B–17's bomb wharf and A/F at Rabaul and A/F at Gasmata. A lone B–17 attacks landing barges in Sanananda area while a single A–20 bombs and strafes positions at Nauro and Menari in Efogi area. Japanese ground offensive toward Port Moresby comes to a halt at Ioribaiwa. Australians are entrenched on

Imita Range where they are preparing a counteroffensive.

Eleventh AF: Enemy completes transfer of Attu garrison to Kiska, begun on 27 Aug. 1 B–17 and 1 B–24 fly photo and rcn runs over Adak.

17 September

USAMEAF: During 16/17 Sep, B–24's bomb Bengasi harbor. During the day, tgts for B–24's are in Greece: shipping in Pylos Bay and shipping and piers near Sphakia, and in Khalones and Pylos I. P–40's make offensive sweep with RAF over front lines.

Fifth AF: B–17's, carrying out single-bmr attacks, bomb A/Fs at Rabaul and Lae, and hit a beached cargo vessel at Salamaua. P–400's, P–40's, and P–39's strafe and bomb landing barges at Buna and Sanananda Pt. Japanese ground forces, halted within sight of Port Moresby, are unable to attack without reinforcements and supplies, neither of which is available.

Twelfth AF: XII GASC is activated at Birmingham, Ala. The only Twelfth AF cmd to be completely organized in US, it eventually will proceed directly to N Africa as part of WTF.

18 September

Eighth AF: VIII GASC is redesignated VIII A Spt Cmd.

Twelfth AF: 12 British units—signal, observer, radar, and air warning—are attached to XII FC in UK. Col Rosenham R Beam becomes CO XII GASC.

Fifth AF: 1 B–17 bombs Salamaua while a B–25 strafes pack trains on Kokoda trail in Andemba-Wairopi-Kokoda area.

19 September

USAMEAF: B–24's bomb Pylos Bay area, Pylos I and Khalones during 19/20 Sep.

Tenth AF: B–25's strike Lungling. The raid is ineffective due to bad weather but results in discovery of much Japanese activity which further rcn reveals as part of heavy movement of enemy and supplies along Burma Road toward Salween front.

Fifth AF: A–20's and B–26's strafe and bomb A/F at Lae. B–17's attack cargo vessels near Umboi (Rooke) I. Whaling vessel is strafed by ftrs off Goodenough I.

20 September

Fifth AF: In Owen Stanley Range, A–20's bomb and strafe troops and installations at Sangara, Arehe, and along the Popondetta-Andemba road, and P–40's strafe A/F at Kokoda, bridges on trail near Wairopi, and troops at Myola, Efogi, and Kagi.

SOPAC: Adm Fitch becomes COMAIRSOPAC.

21 September

Fifth AF: P–40's bomb and strafe bridges and T/Os along Buna-Kokoda trail.

Eleventh AF: The 21st Bomb Sq begins to operate from Adak. Bmrs fly rcn over Kiska and bomb and fire Constantine Harbor installations at Amchitka.

22 September

Twelfth AF: Gen Cannon takes cmd of XII GASC.

USAMEAF: B–24's bomb shipping in Bengasi harbor. Direct hits are made on 1 large vessel while a smaller vessel and other tgts receive lesser hits.

Fifth AF: A–20's bomb and strafe occupied areas at Menari, Efogi, Nauro, Yodda, and Kokoda. P–40's strafe AA positions, huts, and barges at Buna and Salamaua and bomb and strafe Wairopi bridge, strafe buildings at Yodda, A/F at Buna, and AA positions and other tgts along Buna-Kokoda trail. 1 B–25 bombs N end of Buna A/F and coastal end of Sanananda track. B–17's bomb A/F and shipping at Rabaul.

Eleventh AF: 9 B–24's, 2 B–17's, and 1 LB–30, accompanied by 15 P–39's and 20 P–40's, abort Kiska bombing mission due to weather. Photo rcn suggests that Chichagof Harbor is abandoned.

23 September

Twelfth AF: Gen Doolittle assumes cmd of Twelfth AF in Great Britain.

Fifth AF: P–40's, P–39's, P–400's, and B–17's hit tanks, buildings, and A/F at Buna, Wairopi bridge and T/Os on Buna-Kokoda trail, and Taupota Mission near Goodenough Bay.

SOPAC: 72d Bomb Sq (B–17's) of 5th Bomb Gp joins 11th Bomb Gp on Espiritu Santo.

Seventh AF: Movement of 72d Bomb Sq to SOPAC, plus subsequent movement of other sqs of 5th Bomb Gp to SOPAC, makes it difficult for some time to maintain the minimum force of 35 HBs considered necessary for def of the Hawaiian Is. This situation is relieved by 90th Bomb Gp, which stops in Hawaii while en route to SWPA, and by 307th Bomb Gp, which is assigned to Seventh AF for a time.

Eleventh AF: Weather causes mission abort to Kiska. Photo rcn over Attu confirms abandonment by enemy. A Navy PBY escorted by 2 P–38's lands off Amchitka with a scouting party which determines that the island is unsuited as an A/F. The P–38's also bomb a radio shack and sink a submarine at Amchitka.

24 September

Twelfth AF: XII GASC is redesignated XII A Spt Cmd.

Fifth AF: B–17's bomb shipping at Rabaul. P–40's and A–20's hit Mubo while B–17's bomb wrecked vessel at Gona. P–40's hit A/F at Kokoda and tgts along Kokoda-Wairopi trail, including bridge at Wairopi.

Eleventh AF: 3 B–24's bomb Main Camp, storage dumps, and dock areas, starting several fires.

25 September

USAMEAF: B–24's fail to locate shipping convoy S of Crete and return without bombing. Other B–24's bomb Bengasi.

Tenth AF: 4 B–25's, with escort of 10 P–40's, attack Hanoi. The strike force is intercepted by 10 ftrs but the MBs place several bombs on the runway at Gia Lam A/F. The P–40's claim at least 9 ftrs shot down. CATF bmrs fly 11 missions during remainder of Sep and early Oct to spt Chinese ground forces attempting to hold the Japanese on W bank of the Salween.

Fifth AF: P–40's again bomb bridge at Wairopi, scoring direct hit on NE end, which is demolished. Australian ground forces open counteroffensive, attacking strongly toward Ioribaiwa to drive enemy back along Port Moresby-Kokoda trail.

Eleventh AF: 9 B–24's, 1 B–17, and 1 B–24 photo airplane, escorted by 11 P–39's and 17 P–40's, fly first of 2 missions to Kiska. RCAF Kittyhawks participate in this first combined Canadian-American mission of the Eleventh. Later 2 B–24's and a B–17, escorted by 15 P–39's, pound Little Kiska and Kiska. Radar installations at Little Kiska are destroyed and explosions and fires are caused in the Main Camp area. Other tgts include shipping, stores, and tents. The P–39's also strafe 2 subs. 2 float planes are downed. 5 to 8 biplanes are probably destroyed on the water. 1 large transport vessel is hit and lists badly. 150 personnel are believed killed.

26 September

Eighth AF: Approximately 75 HBs are dispatched to attack Cherbourg/Maupertus and Morlaix/Poryeau A/Fs and to execute diversionary sweeps. All bmrs return without bombing their tgts due to adverse weather.

USAMEAF: B–24's of 3 sqs sent on shipping strikes fail to locate tgts.

Tenth AF: 4 B–25's devastate village of Luchiangpa in SW China.

Fifth AF: A–20's bomb and strafe forces N of Ioribaiwa and along Efogi-Menari trail in spt of Australian counteroffensive in Papua. A B–17, along with RAAF airplanes, bombs A/F at Buna. B–17's strike shipping and A/F at Rabaul.

Eleventh AF: 1 destroyer and 1 freighter are bombed at 53–30N 174–20E. 2 near misses are scored on the freighter.

27 September

Twelfth AF: Following a series of cmd changes between 16 and 27 Sep, Col Thomas W Blackburn becomes CO XII FC. WD assigns to XII A Spt Cmd the units which are to constitute its force for the invasion of N Africa: a ftr wg (2 gps), a bomb wg (1 LB gp and 1 obs gp), and 10 signal, serv, and engineer units of various sizes.

USAMEAF: B–24's are dispatched to attack an 8,000-ton vessel at Bengasi. No bombs hit tgt but several straddle a jetty in the harbor.

Tenth AF: 4 B–25's over SW China blast Mengshih, claiming about 30 trucks and 400 troops destroyed. The MBs also bomb Tengchung, leaving it aflame. 3 flights of P–40's strafe T/Os along Burma Road, claiming 15 trucks destroyed and 5 barracks groups damaged.

Fifth AF: A–20's continue to pound forces N of Ioribaiwa in area between Kagi and Efogi and in Myola and Menari areas. Japanese abandon Ioribaiwa Ridge and are in full retreat under heavy pressure from Australian ground forces.

Eleventh AF: Shore and harbor areas of Kiska are bombed: 8 B–24's and 1 B–17, escorted by 1 P–38, 13 P–39's and 4 P–40's take off first, and are followed by 6 unescorted B–24's. Weather turns back 13 of the ftrs. An LB–30 flies photo-weather rcn over Attu, Buldir, the Semichis, Agattu, and Amchitka.

28 September

Fifth AF: P–40's and P–400's bomb and strafe Wairopi bridge, village of Kagi, Myola Lake area, and T/Os along Buna-Kokoda trail. 1 B–17 bombs A/F at Lae. Main body of 126th Inf, US 32d Div, arrives at Port Moresby and is assigned to New Guinea Force to join Australian adv on Wairopi.

Eleventh AF: 2 bombing missions are flown to Kiska and Attu by 7 B–24's, 1 B–17, and 1 LB–30, escorted by 17 ftrs. Installations on Kiska and a freighter nearby are bombed. 1 of the B–24's and the LB–30 bomb village and Chichagof Harbor on Attu and on returning silence AA guns on a freighter. 5 floatplanes are shot down, and 1 submarine is sunk. 1 P–39 is shot down.

29 September

Eighth AF: US pilots who had been members of 3 RAF Eagle Sqs are taken over by VIII FC and organized into 4th Ftr Gp.

USAMEAF: B–24's hit harbor installations at Suda Bay. P–40's fly offensive sweep over battle area, and carry out interception mission against *Stukas* over frontline near El Alamein.

Fifth AF: B–17's bomb AA positions at Buna and A/F at Salamaua. A single A–20 bombs Menari area.

Eleventh AF: Morning armed rcn mission is flown by an LB–30 over Semichis and Attu. It strafes a ship at Attu. 3 B–24's bomb and strafe sea transport, scoring no hits.

30 September

Twelfth AF: Gen Dunton assumes cmd of XII AFSC.

Fifth AF: B–17's, A–20's, and P–40's pound occupied areas at Menari, Myola Lake, Kagi, and Efogi and bridge at Wairopi.

Eleventh AF: Of 9 B–24's off to bomb Kiska and Attu, 2 turn back. The others blast Attu Camp area, and at Kiska Harbor score at least 1 direct hit and near misses on a ship. 8 ftrs intercept over Kiska and Little Kiska but inflict no losses.

1 October

USAMEAF: B–24's bomb shipping in Pylos Bay, claiming 2 direct hits and several near misses on a large vessel. Other B–24's dispatched to bomb convoy at sea fail to find tgt.

Fifth AF: B–17's and P–400's pound forces and comm in Owen Stanley Range, hitting Menari, Kagi, Myola Lake, Kokoda area, Wairopi bridge, and Buna-Wairopi trail.

Eleventh AF: A Japanese rcn airplane over Adak establishes US occupation on the island. 7 B–24's on a search-attack and photo rcn mission over Kiska hit hangars and ramps, starting several fires. 4 ftrs appear and are engaged. 1 probable victory is claimed. 2 other B–24's take off, after Navy Catalinas contact transport, but cannot locate it.

2 October

Eighth AF: Avions Potez aircraft factory at Meaulte is bombed by 30 B–17's. A small group attacks Saint-Omer/Longuenesse A/F. Some 400 ftr escorts provide cover which is frequently penetrated by German ftrs. The B–17's show remarkable defensive strength.

Fifth AF: In Owen Stanley Range,

A–20's bomb and strafe Japanese campsites around Myola and hit several trails in the area, while P–400's strafe bridges at Sirorata and Wairopi and village NE of Wairopi. B–17's bomb shipping and A/F at Rabaul.

Sixth AF: German sub, U–512, is sunk off French Guiana, 06–50N, 52–25W, by aircraft of 99th Bomb Sq.

Eleventh AF: 11 B–24's and 6 P–39's bomb 2 cargo ships at Kiska Harbor (no hits observed) drop demolition charges throughout Main Camp area, and hit hangar S of seaplane ramp. 4 floatplanes and 1 biplane are shot down. Enemy aircraft bomb Adak A/F without inflicting damage.

3 October

USAMEAF: B–24's attack shipping in Pylos Bay during 3/4 Oct. The HBs claim 2 ftrs shot down.

Tenth AF: IATF is activated at Dinjan to spt Chinese resistance along Salween R by hitting supply lines in C and S Burma. The new task force, cmd by Col Caleb V Haynes, includes all AAF combat units in India—the 7th and 341st Bomb and 51st Ftr Gps.

Fifth AF: A–20's bomb and strafe Efogi and Myola Lake, P–40's strafe Efogi-Buna trail, B–25's hit bridge at Wairopi, and a lone B–17 bombs camp on Kumusi R.

Eleventh AF: 6 B–24's, 4 P–38's, and 8 P–39's bomb and strafe 7 vessels in and around Kiska Harbor hitting a beached cargo vessel and the camp. The ftrs down 6 float ftrs attempting interception. Enemy bombs Adak A/F but inflicts no damage.

4 October

Fifth AF: P–40's strafe forces and occupied areas at Myola Lake, Kokoda, Wairopi, Yodda, and Buna. US rcn party from 126th Inf, 32d Div reaches Jauri, completing rcn of Kapa Kapa-Jauri trail, which is found to be difficult but practicable for use as a route in contemplated offensive against Buna-Gona area.

Eleventh AF: 3 B–24's abort weather, bombing and photo missions over Kiska due to weather and instead attack a cargo vessel. Ship's rudder is probably damaged. 1 B–24 is damaged.

5 October

Fifth AF: B–25's attack convoy off Buna; A–20's hit AA positions at Sanananda Pt and bomb village of Sanananda; B–17's bomb A/Fs at Buna and also hit Rabaul A/Fs.

Eleventh AF: 6 B–24's, 3 P–38's and 3 P–39's abort a bombing, weather, and photo mission over Kiska due to weather.

6 October

USAMEAF: B–24's hit Bengasi harbor, scoring large number of near misses but no direct hits. 1 HB bombs Bardia during return flight. AA is heavy and accurate and ftrs attack 6 HBs over tgt. 2 B–24's are lost.

Fifth AF: Fifth AF aircraft complete movement of reinforced Australian 18th Brig to Wanigela on peninsula between Dyke Acland and Collingwood Bays on E coast of Papua. This is part of move aimed at capture of Buna-Gona area.

Eleventh AF: 8 B–24's, 1 B–17, 10 P–39's, and 8 P–38's fly bombing and weather missions over Kiska. A large transport is bombed in the harbor which is left sinking. Hits are scored on a corvette and on a large freighter at Gertrude Cove and on a hangar in Main Camp. The radio station is damaged. A float ftr is strafed and set afire, and 6 Zeros are hit on the water.

7 October

USAMEAF: B–24's score 7 direct hits on a tanker and 8 on fuel installations at Suda Bay. 66 P–40's escort bmrs over battle area W of El Alamein.

Eleventh AF: 3 B–24's taking off to bomb Kiska and patrol Near Is abort mission due to mechanical failure and instead fly rcn over Agattu, Attu, and Semichi Is with negative results.

8 October

USSR: German High Cmd abandons attempt to storm Stalingrad; announces plans to take city by arty siege.

Eighth AF: In letter to Gen Stratemeyer, Gen Eaker indicates plans for developing highly-skilled intruder force capable of using bad weather as a cloak for small blind-bombing operations. These missions are also to serve purpose of keeping the enemy from resting during periods of bad weather when big strategic missions cannot be flown.

USAMEAF: B–24's of 343d and 344th Sqs, 98th Bomb Gp, fail to reach tgt at Bengasi because of bad weather. Hal Bomb Sq manages to attack shipping at Bengasi.

Fifth AF: B–25's bomb Buna area while A–20's pound Buna-Kokoda

trail. Japanese withdrawal NE across Owen Stanley Range slows as they prepare to make a stand at Templeton's Crossing N of Myola.

Eleventh AF: 9 B–24's, 3 B–17's, and 12 P–38's blast Kiska Harbor installations (starting fires in Main Camp), and strafe AA positions, hangars, a corvette (silencing her guns), and a freighter.

9 October

Eighth AF: B–24's join air assault in first US mission in which more than 100 bmrs are dispatched from UK. The principal tgts are the steel and engineering works of the Compagnie de Fives at Lille and the locomotive and freight car works of Ateliers d'Hellemmes at Lille, which are attacked by 69 B–17's and B–24's. Other tgts attacked (by 10 HBs) are Courtrai/Wevelghem and Saint-Omer A/Fs and the city of Roubaix.

USAMEAF: B–24's strike shipping and harbor facilities at Bengasi. P–40's fly escort and strafe a landing ground W of El Daba and emplacements in battle area W of El Alamein.

Fifth AF: 14 B–25's hit A/F at Lae. 30 B–17's pound numerous tgts at Rabaul.

Eleventh AF: 7 B–17's and 10 B–24's escorted by 6 P–38's and 4 P–39's bomb Kiska Harbor, installations and shipping 6 times. Tgts include shipping in Gertrude Cove, small cargo vessels in Kiska Harbor, installations at North Head, hangar, Main Camp area (hit several times), and various shore facilities.

10 October

USAMEAF: B–24's bomb shipping and dock area at Bengasi, while B–25's hit landing grounds.

Fifth AF: B–17's pound Rabaul and nearby Lakunai A/F. A–20's hit tgts along Buna-Kokoda trail and, with P–400's, strike villages in area of Asisi and Sanananda.

Eleventh AF: 10 B–24's, 7 B–17's, and 4 P–38's fly 4 missions to Kiska. Third mission (3 B–17's) does not make contact. The others bomb and strafe Main Camp area, hit shipping in Trout Lagoon and off South Head, where gun positions and installations are also blasted. Fires are started in the Main Camp and hangar areas.

11 October

USAMEAF: B–24's attack convoy in the Mediterranean, hitting 1 vessel and claiming 1 ftr shot down.

SOPAC: B–17's sight TF of cruisers and destroyers bearing down on Guadalcanal in the afternoon. During 11/12 Oct, in the Battle of Cape Esperance, Adm Scott's cruisers drive away the vessels. Search has been and continues to be the most useful service of the B–17's in SOPAC.

Eleventh AF: Kiska is hit by 3 bombing and strafing missions flown by 10 B–24's and 3 B–17's. The B–17's make no contact. The B–24's blast harbor tgts and Main Camp.

12 October

Eighth AF: VIII FC is made responsible for preparation and movement of air echelons of Twelfth AF from UK to N Africa.

USAMEAF: BC USAMEAF is organized at Cairo with Col Patrick W Timberlake as CO. This step comes about as part of a move to preserve Arnold-Portal-Towers agreement that

US combat units in theaters of British strategic responsibility are to be organized in homogeneous "American formations" and under "strategic control only" of a British CinC. B–17's hit shipping at Tobruk harbor.

Fifth AF: A–20's hit village of Isivita and tgts on trail near Wairopi. B–25's bomb Buna, Wairopi bridge, and tgts along Buna-Kokoda trail.

SOPAC: 5 B–17's bomb installations at Buka.

Eleventh AF: 2 B–24's abort bombing of Kiska due to overcast and instead fly shipping search W of Attu.

13 October

USAMEAF: P–40's fly ftr sweep, patrol, and interception missions W of El Alamein. Ftrs claim 2 Me 109's destroyed and 1 damaged.

Fifth AF: B–17's again pound Rabaul, concentrating on Vunakanau and Lakunai A/Fs. A B–17 bombs Buna.

SOPAC: 6 B–17's bomb Buka and Tonolai. Japanese aircraft from Rabaul pound Henderson Field during the day and hit troops of the Americal Div disembarking at Lunga Pt. Arty also begins shelling the airstrip. During 13/14 Oct the battleships *Kongo* and *Haruna* hit Henderson with a terrific bombardment. The field is damaged severely and many airplanes are destroyed or damaged.

Eleventh AF: A search mission is not completed due to weather.

14 October

USAMEAF: B–17's hit shipping at Tobruk, scoring 2 direct hits on a large vessel and demolishing a smaller ship moored alongside. P–40's fly patrols, rcn and interception missions between El Alamein and Burg el Arab.

Fifth AF: B–25's attack Lae, a bridge 40 mi N of Port Moresby, and area of Wairopi bridge. On Kokoda trail Japanese offer fierce resistance to Australians pushing NE in vicinity of Templeton's Crossing. Fifth AF airplanes begin flying a force of Australians and Americans to Wanigela.

SOPAC: B–17's which have been temporarily operating out of Henderson Field are evacuated. Field is again pounded by arty and naval bombardment, and by afternoon is out of operation. Aviation fuel supply is low.

Eleventh AF: 9 B–24's, 6 B–26's, 1 B–17 and 12 P–38's bomb and strafe Kiska installations and shipping. Fire bombs are dropped on hangars and Main Camp area where a large fire is started. 2 torpedo attacks on shipping in Gertrude Cove score no hits. The P–38's destroy 3 floatplanes on water. 1 P–38 is shot down.

15 October

Fifth AF: A–20's and P–40's pound forces S of Templeton's Crossing and at Popondetta. B–25's bomb Salamaua and hit tgts in Owen Stanley Range and in area around bridge at Wairopi. A single B–17 attacks shipping near Treasury Is.

SOPAC: Aviation fuel arrives at Henderson Field from Espiritu Santo by aircraft and ship.

Eleventh AF: 3 B–26's bomb and 1 B–24 flies photo rcn over Kiska and Attu. The B–26's hit a large cargo

ship in Gertrude Cove, starting fire, and hit buildings on Attu. AA claims 1 B–26.

ZI: AAF Antisub Cmd is activated to take over antisub operations of I BC, which is inactivated.

16 October

USAMEAF: B–24's bomb shipping in Bengasi harbor. B–17's and B–24's dispatched to attack Tobruk and Bengasi are forced by bad weather to abort.

Fifth AF: A–20's and B–25's hit village of Pawaia, trails in Kokoda area, Buna-Kokoda trail, and villages at mouth and along Mambare R; B–25's also bomb Mubo-Salamaua trail. B–17's bomb A/F at Rabaul and attack tgts in the Solomons, including A/F at Buin, and shipping off Moila Pt and Shortland Is.

SOPAC: Seabees on Guadalcanal patch up Henderson Field runways enough for use by ftrs. Marine ftrs and AAF P–400's and P–39's begin pounding invasion force landing at Kokumbona-Doma Reef area just 8 mi away. However, the enemy continues to bombard Henderson by air strike and arty and to land troops.

Eleventh AF: 1 B–17, 6 B–26's, and 4 P–38's bomb Kiska and low-level bomb and sink 2 destroyers just N of there. Duds hit large freighter beached off Trout Lagoon. 1 B–26 is shot down.

17 October

Eleventh AF: 5 B–24's bomb Kiska Main Camp area and beached vessel in Trout Lagoon. Results unobserved due to clouds. 1 B–24 flying weather rcn finds no trace of 2 destroyers, confirming their sinking on 16 Oct.

18 October

Fifth AF: B–25's hit Wairopi bridge in Owen Stanley Range, village of Mubo, and dock and occupied area on Pilelo I. B–17's attack shipping and aircraft in Faisi area, schooners and buildings at Lorengau on Manus, Kahili A/F, and shipping off Kahili, Pupukuna Pt, and Buin. Fifth AF completes air movement of most of 128th Inf, 32d Div, to Wanigela.

SOPAC: Adm Halsey succeeds Adm Ghormley as COMSOPAC.

Eleventh AF: 4 B–24's bomb Main Camp, score near misses on beached vessel in Trout Lagoon, and hit gasoline storage area. Weather aircraft flies rcn over Attu, Segula, Little Sitkin, and Gareloi.

19 October

Eighth AF: HQ VIII A Spt Cmd moves from Membury to Sunninghill Park, Berkshire.

USAMEAF: Air offensive preliminary to the British Eighth Army ground attack W of El Alamein begins as B–25's hit landing ground and B–24's score direct hit on vessel at Tobruk.

Eleventh AF: A B–17 flies weather rcn and bomb runs over Attu, Semichis, Kiska, and Amchitka. 6 B–24's dispatched to bomb Kiska abort mission due to weather.

20 October

Eighth AF: Gen Eisenhower issues directive reflecting immediate urgency of TORCH as the currently important item of Allied strategy and requiring Eighth AF, as a matter of first priority, to protect movement of men and supplies from UK to N Africa by attacking German submarine bases on W coast of France, with shipping docks on the French W coast as secondary tgts for these missions and with German aircraft factories and depots in France as second priority.

USAMEAF: Air action is intensified with aim of attaining strong air superiority preceding Gen Montgomery's El Alamein offensive. B–17's and B–24's sent to attack shipping at Tobruk fail to locate tgt due to bad weather and poor visibility. 3 of the B–17's bomb coastal road near Bardia during return trip. B–25's, in conjunction with RAF, attack landing grounds.

SOPAC: Adm Halsey sends 147th Inf to Guadalcanal and also institutes construction of another bmr strip to be located at Koli Pt, 12 mi SE of Henderson Field.

Eleventh AF: 6 B–24's take off for Kiska but return due to weather. Rcn is flown to 70 mi E of Attu. A negative search is made for a missing C–53.

21 October

Eighth AF: VIII BC flies its first mission against submarine bases. 15 B–17's hit U-boat pens at Lorient-Keroman. 8 HBs strike at Cherbourg/Maupertus A/F. The strike against the sub pens is flown at 17,-500-ft level, 5,000 to 10,000 ft lower than usual. 36 FW 190's intercept; 3 US bmrs are shot down.

USAMEAF: B–24's dispatched against shipping at Bengasi fail to locate tgt because of bad weather. During return flight, several HBs bomb tent areas along coast and also hit landing grounds. B–25's, co-operating with RAF, bomb landing ground and tent area.

Tenth AF: B–24's of IATF stage through Chengtu to bomb Lin-hsi coal mines. The plan is to blast nearby power stations and pumping facilities and flood the mines. The attack fails to flood the mines but inflicts considerable damage to the tgt area. This marks the first use of HBs in China and the first AAF strike N of the Yangtze and Yellow Rivers.

Fifth AF: B–25's hit Luscan Harbor on S coast of New Britain.

Eleventh AF: Weather rcn aircraft returns twice due to fog.

22 October

Twelfth AF: First echelon of HQ begins move from UK to N Africa.

USAMEAF: Adv US Air HQ, previously attached to RAF Advanced Air HQ, Western Desert, to gain field experience, becomes HQ of DATF, located at Burg el Arab, with Gen Brereton as CG and Gen Adler attached with adv HQ of ASC. CoS of DATF is Gen Strickland. B–25's bomb dispersed aircraft. P–40's escort bmrs, attack tent areas and motor transport along coastal road near El Hammam, fly rcn and ftr sweeps W of El Daba, and bomb arty positions. P–40's claim 2 ftrs destroyed. B–17's sent to hit Candia abort because of weather.

SOPAC: Henderson Field is out of operation again as result of enemy action.

Eleventh AF: Weather rcn aircraft reports submarine at 52–08N 177–21 W. Navy airplane later makes contact and drops depth bomb. Result unknown.

23 October

USAMEAF: B–17's and B–24's sent to attack Candia and Bengasi turn back short of tgt due to bad weather. El Alamein offensive by British Eighth Army begins at 2140 with arty barrage by more than 1,000 guns aimed at enemy batteries. At 2200 barrage switches to enemy forward positions as British troops move forward. Heavy fighting continues during 23/24 Oct.

Fifth AF: A–20's bomb and strafe Deniki and Deniki-Kokoda trail. B–17's thoroughly pound shipping at Rabaul.

SOPAC: Henderson Field is again made operational by Seabees, and Marine and AAF ftrs begin to inflict heavy losses on naval aircraft. Japanese ground forces assault def lines around the A/Fs but are thrown back.

Eleventh AF: Armed rcn by 7 bmrs, escorted by 6 P–38's, is flown over Kiska installations, chiefly the submarine base and Main Camp. Visibility is excellent and direct hits are scored, including 1 on submarine base.

24 October

USAMEAF: B–25's spt British Eighth Army Offensive W of El Alamein between Mediterranean Sea and Qattara Depression as 30 Corps, with 4 divs in assault, secures 2 corridors through enemy minefields on British N flank, while 13 Corps on S flank breaks through minefields N of Himeimat and establishes small bridgehead. The MBs hit troop concentrations, tent areas, gun emplacements, and vehicles. P–40's, working with RAF and SAAF, escort MBs and LBs and hit motor transports and tanks.

Fifth AF: B–25's hit Lae A/F. Organized Japanese resistance on Goodenough I ceases.

SOPAC: Marine and AAF ftrs at Henderson Field continue to inflict damaging losses upon Japanese naval air force. Japanese ground forces, attacking aggressively, are again repulsed by defenses around Henderson area.

Eleventh AF: 3 B–17's hit Kiska submarine base. Results not observed. Weather rcn flight is made over Attu.

25 October

USAMEAF: Battle of El Alamein continues as Gen Montgomery decides to make main effort on N flank of 30 Corps. Australian 9th Div drives N toward coastal road to Rahman. B–25's disperse motor transport and other tgts in spt of ground forces. P–40's on escort attack vehicles and other tgts. Ftrs claim several airplanes destroyed in combat. HBs sent to bomb Bengasi harbor and a convoy at sea fail to reach tgts as bad weather prevails.

Tenth AF: Japanese aircraft attack A/Fs connected with the India-China air transport route, heavily bombing Dinjan and Chabua fields and scoring hits also at Mohanbari and Sookerating. 10 US airplanes are destroyed and 17 badly damaged; 9 Japanese aircraft are downed. 12 B–25's and 7 P–40's of CATF, led by Col Merian C Cooper, hit Kowloon Docks at Hong Kong. 21 airplanes intercept. 1 B–25 and 1 P–40 are shot down. This marks the first loss of a CATF B–25 in combat. The Japa-

nese interceptors are virtually annihilated. During 25/26 Oct 6 B–25's, on first CATF night strike, continue pounding Hong Kong, bombing North Pt power plant which provides electricity for the shipyards. 3 other B–25's bomb the secondary tgt, Canton warehouse area, causing several large explosions and fires.

Fifth AF: B–17's bomb shipping at Rabaul. A–20's bomb and strafe Isurava-Kokoda trail, W bank of Kumusi R, and area N of Asisi as Australian ground forces push toward Kokoda in the Owen Stanley Range.

SOPAC: Japanese ground assaults on def lines around Henderson Field are again thrown back. Marine and AAF ftrs continue to inflict telling losses on Japanese Navy aircraft. During the afternoon, a B–17 on sea-search mission sights powerful TF NW of Santa Cruz Is, heading for Guadalcanal.

Eleventh AF: Alert only as weather permits.

26 October

USAMEAF: Momentum of British drive decreases in El Alamein battle. 30 Corps takes Kidney Ridge, and Gen Montgomery decides to regroup for a break-out assault. Allied aircraft continue strong spt to ground forces and disperse enemy concentrations preparing for attack. B–25's hit transport, troop concentrations, and tanks. P–40's fly sweeps over El Daba area and attack motor transport and other tgts. Enemy air action increases and considerable aerial combat ensues. US ftrs claim 4 airplanes shot down. More than 30 B–17's and B–24's attack shipping off coast of Libya.

Tenth AF: Japanese again hit

A/Fs in Assam connected with India-China transport route, concentrating on Sookerating. A freight depot, containing food and medical supplies for China, is destroyed but no US airplanes are lost. Due to lack of warning, no ftrs intercept the attacking force. CATF MBs move to W China to carry out neutralization of Lashio, where the Japanese have aircraft they are using against the Dinjan area. P-40's continue to hit Hong Kong-Canton area, using dive-bombing tactics for first time in the area.

Fifth AF: B-25's hit Salamaua and A/F at Lae. A-20's, escorted by P-40's, bomb and strafe trails in Missima-Kaile-Deniki area.

SOPAC: Carrier aircraft from the *Hornet* and *Enterprise* fight fierce air action with TF in Battle of Santa Cruz Is. B-17's also attack the TF but report no hits. With 3 of his carriers hit and almost 100 airplanes lost, VAD Nagumo retires toward Truk. *Hornet* is severely damaged and is sunk the following day by Japanese aircraft and destroyer with bombs and torpedos.

27 October

Eighth AF: Last 2 sqs of 14th Ftr Gp leave UK for Twelfth AF in N Africa. This completes transfer of VIII FC's fighting units to XII FC and leaves VIII FC with only 1 ftr gp (4th) operational.

USAMEAF: B-25's, with ftr escorts, bomb Matruh and attack motor transports, tanks, and other ground tgts. Enemy reinforcements brought up from the S, counterattack Kidney Ridge and are repulsed. Bri-

tish Eighth Army continues regrouping for assault.

Tenth AF: B-25's of CATF bomb A/F at Lashio.

Fifth AF: A-20's hit trails in SE Papua around Alola, Isurava, and Abuari. P-39's escort RAAF Hudsons in strike against small craft at Ferguson I in D'Entrecasteaux group.

Eleventh AF: 6 B-24's flying attack on Kiska submarine base turn back due to weather. Weather airplane flies rcn over Gareloi, Segula, Kiska, and Attu.

28 October

USAMEAF: B-17's, dispatched to attack convoy at sea, fail to locate tgt but attack cruisers in Pylos Bay. B-25's attack tanks, motor transports, and landing grounds. P-40's fly MB and LB escort, bomb and strafe landing grounds and other tgts, and engage aircraft in combat, mostly in area between El Alamein and El Daba. Ftrs claim 3 Me 109's destroyed. Attacks by US and RAF aircraft cause enemy to abandon plan for counterattack on Kidney Ridge.

Fifth AF: B-17's pound shipping in harbor at Rabaul, while B-25's bomb Gasmata A/F.

Eleventh AF: 6 B-24's turn back from an attempted attack on Kiska sub base because of adverse weather. A B-17 bombs Attu with unobserved results and flies weather rcn over Kiska, Amchitka, and Tanaga.

29 October

US: A 1943 production objective of 107,000 airplanes is given top priority by Roosevelt in his instructions to Donald M Nelson, Chairman of War Production Board.

USAMEAF: B–24's and B–17's strike Maleme A/F. B–25's bomb landing grounds, motor transports, and tanks. P–40's fly escort, then bomb and strafe road E of El Daba, and attack troop concentration and vehicles. In view of strong German reinforcements on his N flank near coast, Gen Montgomery alters breakout plan. Instead of pushing W along coast, he decides to shift point of adv S in order to attack against Italian troops.

Fifth AF: A–20's hit Isurava-Deniki and Abuari-Kaile trails. B–17's attack shipping in Bougainville Strait between Buin and Faisi.

Eleventh AF: Japanese reoccupy Attu. Special rcn flown with Gen Buckner, covers Tanaga, Amchitka and Kiska.

30 October

USAMEAF: B–24's bomb Maleme A/F. 1 HB bombs main jetty in Suda Bay. B–25's attack landing grounds at Fuka-Bagush and El Daba. P–40's fly escort. British Eighth Army sends 9th Australian Div N to the sea and then E, trapping large force in pocket, as Allied aircraft provide excellent spt. Enemy tanks breaking through from W, however, enable most of the surrounded force to escape.

Fifth AF: B–17's bomb harbor and shipping at Buin.

Eleventh AF: 1 B–24 twice flies rcn over Kiska and Agattu. No bombing mission as all bmrs are on alert for possible navy tgts.

31 October

Eighth AF: Gen Spaatz informs Gen Arnold that operations against sub pens may prove too costly for results obtained. Believing the pens impervious to normal high-altitude bombing, Spaatz plans to operate as low as 4,000 ft and accept higher casualty rates.

USAMEAF: B–25's hit landing ground. The MBs claim 1 ftr shot down while P–40's flying escort claim 3. B–24's sent to bomb Maleme dispersal area fail to locate tgt because of overcast. 376th Bomb Gp is activated at Lydda, replacing the 1st Prov Gp. CO is Col George F McGuire, who had commanded 1st Prov Gp. The 376th is intended to become part of an Anglo-American air force to be sent to the Caucasus to aid the USSR, but the plan falls through and the 376th remains in the ME.

Fifth AF: A–20's bomb and strafe Nauro and area to N. B–25's strafe supply trucks SE of Gona. B–17's bomb shipping at Rabaul and in Buin-Faisi-Tonolai area.

Eleventh AF: Weather and rcn flight over Attu and Kiska. Over Kiska, weather airplane draws AA fire from Little Kiska. No other missions as all combat aircraft are alerted for possible navy tgt.

1 November

USAMEAF: B–24's strike A/F and dispersal areas at Maleme. P–40's escort bmrs and hit ground tgts in battle area. An air depot, 2 serv gps, and 1 MP co are assigned to USAMEAF.

Fifth AF: B–25's bomb A/F and dump area at Lae. B–17's strike shipping in Buin-Faisi-Tonolai area.

Kahili A/F on Bougainville is also attacked.

2 November

Eighth AF: CG VIII A Spt Cmd states that the effort expended and personnel lost in organizing Twelfth AF and preparing for its move from UK to N Africa has severely retarded organization of his HQ and staff.

USAMEAF: British Eighth Army opens assault (SUPERCHARGE) W of Tell el-Eisa, with 2d NZ Div in lead. B–25's bomb track extending S from Rahman as British 9th Armd Brig establishes bridgeheads across the track. Other B–25's attack tanks and other tgs in spt of the assault. P–40's fly escort and strafing missions in battle area. B–17's bomb shipping and jetties in Tobruk harbor.

Fifth AF: B–26's bomb Dili. B–17's attack shipping NE of Buna while B–25's strike at convoy S of New Britain. In Owen Stanley Range, Australian ground forces seize Kokoda with its A/F after long days of fighting. This will greatly facilitate supply and reinforcement of troops in this area as they push over the mountains toward Buna-Gona area.

3 November

USAMEAF: B–25's bomb tanks, motor transports, landing ground, ammo dumps, mainly in Rahman Track area and on road between Fuka and El Daba, and also hit town of Fuka and Ghazal station. P–40's fly several escort and FB missions, attacking ground tgs in spt of British Eighth Army. Allied aircraft fly more than 400 sorties against troops retreating along coastal road. During

3/4 Nov, British and Indian troops outflank and break enemy tank screen in sector S of Tell el Aqqaqir.

Fifth AF: B–26's bomb Dili. B–17's bomb A/F and wharf at Lae, and attack ship S of Gasmata.

4 November

USAMEAF: 9 B–24's bomb Bengasi harbor, hitting 3 ships and claiming 1 enemy ftr shot down. B–25's and P–40's attack motor transports and troops retreating W from El Alamein battleline with British in pursuit. 10 Corps armor clashes with rearguard S of Ghazal. Gen Andrews replaces Gen Maxwell as CG USAFIME.

Fifth AF: B–17's and B–25's bomb town and harbor of Salamaua; A–20's hit troop concentrations at Oivi, where Australian attack meets firm resistance; and B–26's bomb Aileu. Transports fly most of the remainder of 128th Inf, 32d Div, to Wanigela.

Eleventh AF: Bad weather at Umnak and Dutch Harbor and flooded field at Adak preclude missions. New Adak runway permits an air alert.

5 November

USAMEAF: Gen Montgomery announces victory of British Eighth Army in Egypt. 10 Corps, pushing rapidly W, overcomes rearguard action near Fuka. As FM Rommel retreats W from El Alamein, P–40's bomb tgs on Fuka road and patrol Sidi Hanaish area. B–25's also bomb motor transports.

Tenth AF: IATF HBs carry out raid on Rangoon.

Fifth AF: B–25's unsuccessfully attack schooner near Arawe.

Eleventh AF: Weather rcn is flown over Kiska and Little Kiska.

6 November

USAMEAF: B–24's hit harbors of Tobruk and Bengasi, scoring hits on 2 vessels. Heavy rains delay British pursuit of retreating enemy in Matruh area.

Fifth AF: A single B–25 attacks destroyer off S tip of New Ireland. No hits are scored. Gen MacArthur arrives in Port Moresby, where AD VON of GHQ opens to direct operations.

Eleventh AF: Weather airplane is forced back near Kiska.

7 November

Eighth AF: 34 HBs attack U-boat pens at Brest.

Twelfth AF: Air movement of Twelfth AF from UK to N Africa begins. Other elements of Twelfth moving from UK and US are aboard Allied ships approaching Algerian and Moroccan coasts.

USAMEAF: 376th Bomb Gp begins move from Palestine to Egypt.

Fifth AF: A–20's bomb and strafe forces at Kakandeta in Owen Stanley Range. B–25's attack shipping at Maklo I and seaplanes at Lasonga I.

Eleventh AF: 6 B–24's and 2 B–26's attack submarine base in Kiska Harbor, slightly damaging float ftrs and a seaplane beached by storm. A B–17 flies rcn over A/F W of Holtz Bay, and bombs submarine base and a previously-damaged freighter in Gertrude Cove.

8 November

Eighth AF: 41 HBs bomb the Abbeville/Drucat A/F and the Atelier d'Hellemmes locomotive works at Lille.

Twelfth AF: Invasion of N Africa (TORCH) begins. C–47's of 60th TC Gp attempting to land troops at La Senia A/F find the French unexpectedly hostile and have several aircraft shot down by ftrs and AA; several other C–47's are damaged when trying to land on a dry lakebed of Sebkra d'Oran. Spitfires of 31st Ftr Gp, flying from Gibraltar into Tafaraoui A/F during afternoon of D-Day, claim 3 hostile French ftrs destroyed.

Fifth AF: A–20's hit forces in Oivi area in Owen Stanley Range as Australian ground forces push over mts toward Gona-Buna area. Fifth AF transports fly final elements of 128th Inf, 32d Div, from Port Moresby to Wanigela. B–25's bomb radio station and A/F at Gasmata.

Eleventh AF: Intermittent air alert. Weather airplane returns due to icing.

9 November

Eighth AF: Gen Spaatz, in memo to Gen Eisenhower, agrees that any increase in air commitments to N Africa must necessarily be made at expense of US forces in UK as US forces in other theaters are considered irreducible. VIII BC attacks U-boat base at Saint-Nazaire from reduced altitude. 12 B–24's at 17,500 to 18,300 ft suffer little AA damage, but 31 B–17's at 7,500 to 10,000 ft lose 3 of their number and have 22 damaged by AA fire. This ends experiment with low-level attacks of HBs against submarine bases.

Twelfth AF: Spitfires of 31st Ftr Gp attack and halt an armored column moving N toward Tafaraoui, and also attack arty and AA batteries SE of Tafaraoui and along coastal road. At 1605, Gen Doolittle arrives in Algeria from Gibraltar by B–17, escorted by 12 Spitfires from 52d Ftr Gp.

Tenth AF: IATF HBs raid Rangoon.

Fifth AF: A–20's hit troops at Oivi in spt of Australian offensive in Owen Stanley Range. B–26's bomb Buna while B–25's score hit on merchant vessel off S tip of New Ireland and attack schooner off Salamaua. Airlift of elements of 126th Inf, US 32d Div, from Port Moresby to forward areas begins. First elements are flown to Abel's Field and moved overland to Pongani.

Eleventh AF: 2 B–26's and 4 P–38's bomb a cargo ship in Gertrude Cove. No hits. 2 P–38's then strafe Kiska Harbor area. 1 B–17 and 4 P–38's attack Holtz Bay and Attu A/F, destroying 8 float Zeros. 1 B–17 flies weather rcn over Attu, Kiska, and Segula.

10 November

Twelfth AF: US Spitfires escort convoy, fly rcn, and attack tanks and other vehicles in Oran area. 72 P–40's of 33d Ftr Gp, catapulted from US carrier *Chenango*, land in Port Lyautey area. French Adm Darlan broadcasts orders for French forces in N Africa to cease resistance against Allies.

USAMEAF: B–24's hit Bengasi harbor. B–17's hit Candia harbor.

Fifth AF: B–26's bomb AA positions and supply dumps along Sanananda-Soputa trail. A–20's hit positions at Soputa as Australian ground

forces push Japanese from Oivi toward mouth of the Kumusi.

Eleventh AF: Rcn is flown over Attu, Semichi, Segula, Alaid, and Kiska islands. 5 B–24's and 1 B–17 bomb Kiska, but they cannot bomb Kiska submarine base and return with some bombs. 2 P–38's and 1 OA–10 fly local air coverage.

11 November

Europe: German troops enter part of France previously unoccupied by Axis forces.

Twelfth AF: Ftrs fly rcn over Oran-Tafaraoui area and escort C–47's carrying paratroops from Gibraltar to Algiers. All French resistance against Allies in NW Africa ceases in the early morning.

USAMEAF: B–24's hit shipping N of Bengasi, claiming 4 direct hits and several near misses on 1 vessel. P–40's fly sweep over Gambut area, claiming 3 *Stukas* destroyed. British Eighth Army drives last of enemy from Egypt and crosses into Libya, taking Bardia without opposition.

Tenth AF: 9 P–40's hit Shinghbwiyang, causing heavy damage.

Fifth AF: A–20's bomb and strafe tgts in Wairopi area. B–17's attack shipping off S coast of Bougainville. HQ, 126th Inf, US 32d Div, is flown from Port Moresby to Pongani. Col Paul B Wurtsmith becomes CO V FC.

SOPAC: Search aircraft from Guadalcanal report at least 61 Japanese ships in Buin-Tonolai area. Other ships are massed at Rabaul.

Eleventh AF: 3 B–26's, 3 B–17's, and 3 B–24's are over Kiska. The B–26's make unsuccessful runs on ship in Gertrude Cove. The B–17's and B–24's find submarine base closed by weather. Weather aircraft flies over Attu and Amchitka.

12 November

Twelfth AF: Ftrs fly patrols over wide area around Oran and escort C–47's which drop US paratroops at Duzerville A/F SE of Bone. Duzerville A/F is bombed by Axis aircraft during 12/13 Nov.

Ninth AF: USAMEAF is dissolved and replaced by Ninth AF, commanded by Gen Brereton. Major components are: IX BC (Gen Timberlake), IX FC (Col John C Kilborn), and IX ASC (Gen Adler). 79th Ftr Gp begins arriving in Egypt from US.

Fifth AF: B–17's bomb shipping at Tonolai harbor. 3d Bn of 126th Inf, US 32d Div, is airlifted from Port Moresby to Pongani. The troops immediately start overland toward Natunga. 2d Bn, flown in earlier, reaches Bofu.

SOPAC: 11 transports carrying 13,500 troops and supported by a force of cruisers and 2 battleships (*Kirishima* and *Hiei*) leave Shortland Is area and head for Guadalcanal. During the afternoon the rcn value and defensive capability of the B–17 are ably demonstrated when a single HB sights a carrier 350 mi off Guadalcanal and maintains contact for 2 hrs before returning to base with claims of 6 Zeros shot down. Naval Battle of Guadalcanal (12–15 Nov) opens as Japanese aircraft attack transports unloading troops in Lunga Roads. First 12 P–38's of 339th Ftr Sq, as well as Marine and Navy airplanes, are moved from Tontouta and Espiritu Santo to Henderson Field to bolster defenses of Guadalcanal.

Eleventh AF: Bmrs are on alert at Umnak and Adak to attack any reported naval tgts. Intermittent ftr patrols fly over Adak.

ZI: AAF School of Applied Tactics is established at Orlando AAB.

13 November

Eighth AF: HQ VIII AF Comp Cmd moves from temporary station at Long Kesh to Kirkassock House, N Ireland.

Ninth AF: 98th Bomb Gp arrives in Egypt from Palestine. Tobruk falls to 10 Corps, British Eighth Army.

Twelfth AF: C–47's, with P–38 escort, fly AA guns and aviation gasoline to Duzerville A/F. US Spitfires patrol Oran-Tafaraoui area.

Fifth AF: B–17's bomb shipping off Tonolai-Komaleai Pt and A/F at Kahili. A B–17 strafes a schooner in Lorengau harbor on Manus I.

SOPAC: Air strength at Guadalcanal is raised by arrival of 3 B–26's of 69th and 70th Bomb Sqs from New Hebrides as naval battle of Guadalcanal continues. Japanese cruisers and destroyers bombard Henderson Field during 13/14 Nov, and destroy one of the new P–38's.

Eleventh AF: Rcn over Attu and Agattu reveals 5 landing barges in Chichagof harbor.

14 November

Eighth AF: 24 HBs strike U-boat works at Saint-Nazaire.

Twelfth AF: US Spitfires fly routine patrols in Oran-Tafaraoui area and escort C–53's carrying paratroops from Gibraltar to Algiers.

Ninth AF: 79th Ftr Gp and HQ 19th Bomb Wg, now arriving from US, are assigned to Ninth AF. 6 B–17's are dispatched to attack harbor at Bengasi, but only 1 locates tgt and drops its bombs.

Fifth AF: 1 B–25 bombs and strafes track N of Soputa. Fifth AF airplanes drop bridging equipment at Wairopi on Kokoda trail where the Australian 25th Brig is crossing on improvised bridge. US and Australian forces are consolidating at Natunga and in Oro Bay-Embogu-Embi areas. 2 B–17's attack transport in the Solomons.

SOPAC: Airplanes from the US carrier *Enterprise* are joined by land-based Marine and AAF aircraft in driving off the force that bombarded Henderson Field the previous night. In view of the pressing need for aircraft in SOPAC, Adm Nimitz (CINCPOA) is given more freedom to deploy his air weapons. He receives authority to distribute as he sees fit all available air units assigned to S and C Pacific provided he move units rather than individual airplanes and crews.

Eleventh AF: 1 B–24 flies armed rcn over Kiska and Attu and bombs Holtz Bay and Chichagof with negative results. Bmrs at Adak and Umnak are alerted for shipping tgts.

15 November

Twelfth AF: C–47's fly airborne operation from Algiers to Youks-les-Bains. Escort is provided at intervals by RAF Spitfires and Hurricanes. British First Army ground forces reach Tunisia at Taberka. 15th Bomb Sq flying DB–7's from UK, arrives at Oran.

Ninth AF: B–24's from 2 gps are sent to bomb Tripoli, but unfavorable weather prevents them from reaching tgt. 1 gp bombs a motor convoy,

as well as A/F and crowded roads in Bengasi area. P–40's fly sweeps and FB missions against retreating enemy W of Martuba. Martuba A/Fs are captured by British 10 Corps and soon occupied by 57th Ftr Gp.

Fifth AF: A–20's strafe tgts near Gona while B–25's and B–26's pound AA positions at Buna and Soputa as US-Australian ground forces prepare to move against Buna-Gona beachhead. B–17's hit shipping at Rabaul.

SOPAC: Adm Lee's force of 2 battleships and 3 destroyers meets and turns back a larger Japanese force, sinking the battleship *Kirishima* and a destroyer while losing a destroyer. This ends the Naval Battle of Guadalcanal (12–15 Nov) which involved sqs of the 11th Bomb Gp, as well as the 69th, 70th, and 72d Bomb Sqs, and the 39th and 339th Ftr Sqs.

16 November

Twelfth AF: As British First Army continues into Tunisia, Twelfth AF C–47's drop British paratroops at Souk el Arba. 6 B–17's, of the 97th Bomb Gp based at Algiers, raid Sidi Ahmed A/F at Bizerte. Thus the 97th which flew first US HB mission from the UK (on 17 Aug), becomes the first Twelfth AF bomb gp to fly a combat mission in Africa.

Ninth AF: P–40's patrol over Germiston area.

Fifth AF: B–26's, B–25's, and A–20's pound areas around Buna, Gona, Soputa, Sanananda, and Giruwa, hitting AA positions, buildings, barges, and troop concentrations as US 32d and Australian 7th Divs move forward against Buna-Gona beachhead.

Eleventh AF: Weather rcn flight is flown over Kiska and Attu. Demo-

lition charges are dropped on Holtz
Bay, AA guns, and on Attu village.
Results not observed.

17 November

Eighth AF: 35 HBs pound U-boat
pens at Saint-Nazaire with 102 tons
of bombs.

Twelfth AF: Air action is limited
to routine patrols in Tafaraoui area.

Ninth AF: P–40's patrol over Tobruk and Derna road.

Fifth AF: B–26's hit Gona Mission
as US 32d and Australian 7th Divs
continue to move toward Buna-Gona
beachhead. B–25's bomb A/Fs at Lae
and Gasmata. A lone B–24 bombs
wharf area at Rabaul.

Eleventh AF: Weather rcn aircraft is forced back by weather W
of Kiska. Bmrs are on alert to attack
surface vessels.

18 November

Eighth AF: VIII BC conducts
missions against 3 U-boat bases. 19
HBs attack at La Pallice, 13 at Lorient-Keroman, and 19 at Saint-Nazaire.

Twelfth AF: P–38's of 14th Ftr
Gp arrive from UK for HB escort
duty. Several are damaged in enemy
air raid on Maison Blanche A/F.

Ninth AF: B–17's bomb M/Y and
docks at Bengasi.

Fifth AF: B–25's bomb A/Fs at
Lae and Salamaua. B–17's attack
warships 50 mi SW of Gasmata, 17
mi N of Buna, and between Gona
and Cape Ward Hunt. B–26's bomb
and strafe area between Cape Endaiadere and Buna.

Eleventh AF: Armed rcn is flown
over Kiska and Attu. No bombs are
dropped.

19 November

Eighth AF: Submarine yards at
Vegesack, Bremen, and Kiel are added
to day bombardment program as top
priority objectives.

Twelfth AF: B–17's, escorted by
P–38's, bomb El Aouina A/F.

Eleventh AF: Rcn aircraft over
Attu and Agattu sights 2 unidentified float monoplanes E of Buldir I.

20 November

Twelfth AF: During 20/21 Nov,
enemy airplanes bomb harbor and
Maison Blanche A/F at Algiers, destroying several aircraft at the field.

Ninth AF: P–40's patrol over battle area near Bengasi, as that city
falls to British 10 Corps.

Tenth AF: 8 HBs bomb M/Y at
Mandalay as IATF B–24's, commanded by Col Conrad F Necrason,
intensify their campaign against
Burma and Thailand.

Eleventh AF: Rcn aircraft over
Kiska draws heavy AA from
Gertrude Cove.

21 November

Twelfth AF: P–38's of 1st Gp arrive at Nouvion to replace 14th Gp
in escorting B–17's. B–17's hit El
Aouina A/F. During 21/22 Nov enemy airplanes again hit Algiers, damaging several aircraft and destroying
a B–17.

Ninth AF: B–24's flying out of
Gambut bomb Tripoli harbor, scoring direct hit on warehouse. RAF
HBs follow US raids with staggered
attacks during 21/22 Nov. P–40's patrol battle area S of Bengasi.

Fifth AF: A–20's and B–25's
pound A/F, AA positions, and bridge
at Buna and hit village of Sanananda

in spt of Allied ground forces. Australian-US force is advancing from Soputa toward Sanananda. US forces driving on Buna are halted by strong bunker positions at The Triangle where trails to Buna mission and Buna village meet.

Eleventh AF: Rcn is flown over Kiska, Attu, and Agattu islands.

22 November

USSR: Soviet Army opens offensive at Stalingrad.

Eighth AF: 11 HBs attack Lorient-Keroma 17 U-boat base.

Twelfth AF: US HBs based at Algiers move back to Tafaraoui because of enemy bombing raids on Maison Blanche A/F. P–38's of 14th Gp move into Youks-les-Bains A/F.

Ninth AF: P–40's patrol over Derna area.

Tenth AF: 6 HBs inflict heavy damage on railroad center at Mandalay.

Fifth AF: A–20's pound trails around Sanananda while B–26's hit Buna area. B–17's and B–25's hit A/F at Lae and barges between Lae and Salamaua, and attack warships 68 mi SW of Arawe and elsewhere in the Solomon Sea.

SOPAC: The critical lack of aircraft repair and maintenance facilities is alleviated somewhat by the arrival of the 13th Air Depot and the 6th and 29th Serv Gps. The units are based on New Caledonia and Espiritu Santo.

Eleventh AF: 1 B–24 flies rcn over Kiska, Attu, and Agattu. Bmrs and ftrs are alerted for 23 Nov mission to find and destroy a reported 5-vessel convoy.

23 November

Eighth AF: 36 HBs hit Saint-Nazaire submarine base for the fifth time in 2 weeks. Cumulative effect of operation on the base is large though the sub shelter shows little permanent damage. HB crews report change in ftr tactics from rear to head-on attack as they learn that the B–17 and B–24 are weak in forward firepower. Sir Pound, First Lord of the Admiralty, writes to Gen Eaker praising the effects of US bmr attacks on disorganizing the servicing schedule of the German U-boat bases on the French W coast.

Twelfth AF: Main HQ Twelfth AF is moved from Gibraltar to Algiers. B–17's, with P–38 escort, sent to bomb A/F at Elmas abort due to bad weather.

Tenth AF: 9 B–25's and 7 P–40's of CATF feint at Hong Kong, then fly to Gulf of Tonkin and sink a freighter and damage 2 others near Haiphong. 6 B–25's and 17 P–40's pound Tien Ho A/F claiming more than 40 aircraft destroyed on the field. These strikes follow 3 weeks of missions in spt of Chinese forces along the Siang-Chiang R.

Fifth AF: A–20's and B–26's pound Sanananda Pt E as Australian forces begin assault on Gona and US forces approach Sanananda.

Eleventh AF: Rcn is flown over Kiska, Attu, Agattu, and Amchitka.

24 November

Twelfth AF: B–17's, with P–38 escort, are dispatched against Bizerte harbor but must abort because of bad weather. Ftrs patrol Oran-Nouvion-Tafaraoui area, fly sea patrol off Oran, and destroy several aircraft and attack ground tgts in vicinity of Gabes.

Ninth AF: P–40's patrol over Bengasi and Derna areas.

Fifth AF: A–20's, B–25's, B–26's, B–17's, P–40's, P–39's, and P–400's hit Sanananda Pt, Buna area, Sanananda-Soputa trail S of Sanananda, and area between Cape Killerton and Sanananda Pt as Allied forces launch ground assault on The Triangle. The attack is repelled by fierce resistance. B–17's also bomb 2 destroyers and a light cruiser off New Guinea between Lae and Finschhafen.

SOPAC: Search airplanes over Buin area report large number of destroyers and cargo vessels in the harbor. By this date elements of Americal Div have pushed along N coast of Guadalcanal to a position S of Pt Cruz where they wait until a general offensive can be prepared following the arrival of reinforcements. Throughout these operations P–39's have continually hit ground positions and troops all along the coast, flying as many as 11 strikes on some days.

Eleventh AF: 1 B–24 flies rcn over Kiska. Weather precludes westward continuation of rcn. A scheduled mission of 8 B–24's and 4 B–26's to Kiska is called off due to icing conditions.

25 November

Twelfth AF: Spitfires and P–38's fly widespread rcn missions over coastal Algeria.

Ninth AF: Air echelon of 316th TC Gp (except for 1 sq which arrives 10 days later) arrives in Egypt, and begins operations almost immediately. This does much to relieve the transport situation in the Western Desert. P–40's escort minesweepers in vicinity of Bengasi harbor. RAF raids Tripoli harbor during 25/26 Nov.

Tenth AF: B–25's and P–40's cripple 3 freighters on Pearl R near Canton.

Fifth AF: P–38's hit A/F at Lae. A lone B–25 scores hit on cruiser off Tami I.

Eleventh AF: Rcn is flown over Kiska, Attu and the Semichis.

26 November

Ninth AF: B–24's fly 3 missions against Tripoli, scoring direct hits on 2 vessels. 1 HB bombs ship at Homs harbor. P–40's patrol over Bengasi and Derna area.

Fifth AF: US and Australian ground forces carry out limited attacks on Buna front, making little progress. In an effort to break Japanese air superiority over Buna, Fifth AF P–40's, A–20's, and B–25's pound A/Fs and AA positions in the area. B–26's strike Salamaua area.

Eleventh AF: A B–24 reconnoitering Holtz Bay harbor spots shipping tgts which are subsequently hit by 4 B–26's escorted by 4 P–38's. 1 large vessel is claimed afire and sinking. Rcn is flown over Rat I, Kiska shipping, Agattu, Semichi and N coast of Attu. 2 P–38's and 1 B–26 sustain minor damage.

27 November

France: Adm de Laborde orders French fleet at Toulon scuttled to prevent it from falling into German hands.

Ninth AF: B–17's bomb Portolago Bay, hitting 2 vessels.

Tenth AF: 10 B–25's and more

than 20 P–40's, the largest CATF effort in China to date, hit shipping and harbor installations at Hong Kong, firing warehouses and claiming 2 freighters and numerous barges sunk. A large force of ftrs intercept during the return trip but are driven off by the escort. The P–40's and B–25's claim several airplanes shot down.

Fifth: B–26's pound Buna area, hitting buildings, A/F, and other tgts, as Allied ground forces prepare to renew attacks in the Buna-Gona area.

Eleventh AF: Photo rcn covers Kiska, Amchitka and Attu. Ship attacked in Holtz Bay on previous day is observed lower in water and still burning.

28 November

Twelfth AF: 35 B–17's of the 97th Gp and newly-arrived 301st Gp bomb Bizerte A/F and dock area. Because of mud, no P–38 escort is provided. 2 HBs are lost to ftr attacks. B–26's of newly-arrived 319th Gp bomb oil tanks, warehouses, and rail yards at Sfax, marking debut of Twelfth AF MBs in NW Africa.

Fifth AF: B–26's bomb A/Fs at Lae and Buna. Elements of 126th Inf, US 32d Div arrive on Sanananda front from Wairopi.

Eleventh AF: A B–24 photographs beached freighter at Holtz Bay drawing no AA fire during 10 runs over Bay, and flies rcn over Kiska.

29 November

Twelfth AF: British First Army, after taking Tebourba on 27 Nov, is stalled at Djedeida. In an effort to rejuvenate the drive on Tunis,

elements of British 1st Parachute Brig are dropped at Depienne by Twelfth AF C–47's, but the objective of capturing Oudna A/F and threatening Tunis (10 mi to the N) fails because of overwhelming def of the A/F. Over 300 casualties are suffered by the paratroops. P–38's and DB–7's attack Gabes A/F while other US ftrs operate with RAF out of Bone, furnishing air cover for ground units in battle area.

Ninth AF: B–24's bomb Tripoli harbor at dusk, hitting docks, warehouses, 2 vessels, and silencing an AA battery.

Tenth AF: B–25's bomb Hongay and Campho on Indochina coast.

Fifth AF: B–17's, P–40's, and A–20's pound Gona area while B–25's and a single A–20 bomb A/F at Lae. B–17's intercept force of 4 troop-carrying destroyers proceeding through Vitiaz Strait without air cover. The HBs damage 2 vessels and cause the others to turn back, thus preventing reinforcement of Gona with fresh troops from Rabaul.

Eleventh AF: A B–24 over Holtz Bay reports vessel bombed and damaged on 26 Nov as still sinking. 1 B–26 flies uneventful rcn over S shore of Kiska.

30 November

Eighth AF: In a meeting at the Air Ministry a joint decision is made on allocation of responsibility, with RAF to provide aerial def of sectors in which US A/Fs are located while VIII FC operates principally as escort for bmr strikes against Continent.

Twelfth AF: B–17's bomb N quay at Bizerte; B–26's hit A/F and railroad at Gabes; DB–7's attack bridge and railway station at Djedeida. P–38's escort all 3 missions. Other P–38's strafe Gabes A/F, fly rcn, and shoot down an Me 109 in aerial battle near Tunis. Elements of British First Army remain hard pressed at Djedeida.

Tenth AF: IATF HBs attack shipping at Port Blair in the Andaman Is, claiming damage to one vessel by near misses. This strike begins a series of raids on this water approach to Burma.

Fifth AF: B–25's and B–26's pound A/F, AA positions, and defenses in Buna area. 3 attempts by Allied ground forces to take Buna fail. US forces establish a block behind enemy forces on Soputa-Sanananda trail but frontal and flanking assaults make little headway.

SOPAC: Battle of Tassafaronga. USN turns back Japanese effort to land troops in Tassafaronga area of Guadalcanal during 30 Nov/1 Dec.

Eleventh AF: Fog prevents rcn over Kiska, while a B–24 on rcn is turned back at Buldir.

1 December

Eighth AF: Gen Eaker replaces Gen Spaatz as CG. Spaatz flies to Algeria to serve as air adviser to Gen Eisenhower, Theater Cmdr.

Twelfth AF: DB–7's and later B–17's bomb El Aouina A/F, with P–38's escorting both forces. P–38's on sweep over Djedeida area attack tanks NW of town. Enemy counterattack is launched toward Tebourba, inflicting heavy tank losses on BLADE Force, which, along with

part of US 1st Armd Div, was prepared to attack Tunis on 2 Dec.

Fifth AF: B–26's, A–20's, P–400's, and B–25's pound Buna area, but ground forces fail in another attempt to capture the village. Australian 21st Brig, however, turns back from Giruwa 3 large loads of reinforcements destined for Gona, then attacks and takes Gona, forcing enemy back to Gona Mission for final stand.

Eleventh AF: B–24 flies rcn over Semichis and Attu. Other flights prevented by weather.

2 December

Eighth AF: Gen Longfellow replaces Gen Eaker as CG VIII BC.

Twelfth AF: B–26's bomb El Aouina A/F following DB–7 raid on same tgt; B–17's hit Sidi Ahmed A/F and Bizerte harbor; and B–25's attack AA guns near Gabes A/F. P–38's provide escort and fly rcn missions and sweeps, claiming 8 aircraft and 1 tank destroyed. British First Army withstands another counterattack on Tebourba.

Fifth AF: B–17's, B–25's, A–20's, and P–400's attack 4 destroyers off Buna and Gona, and A/F and positions in Buna area and between Watutu Pt and Cape Killerton. As the result of the strike against shipping, the destroyers, originally bound for Gona with 800 reinforcements, land the troops near mouth of the Kumusi R 12 mi to the N. After bombardment of Gona, Allied ground forces attack in strength but are again halted short of the village.

Eleventh AF: A B–24 finds Semichi negative in detailed rcn, and Attu unchanged. B–26 rcn finds Kiska closed by fog.

3 December

Twelfth AF: B–17's hit docks and shipping at Bizerte harbor. 2 of the escorting P–38's are shot down by Me 109's. DB–7's, with P–38's as escort, bomb El Aouina A/F. Spitfires and P–38's fly patrols and photo rcn over wide areas of NW Africa, and carry out ftr sweeps during which several ground tgts, including Gabes A/F, are attacked. British First Army withdraws from Tebourba as German forces, through continuous attacks, occupy the city during 3/4 Dec.

Fifth AF: A–20's, P–400's, and B–25's bomb and strafe Sanananda Pt and Buna areas and attack small torpedo boat in Dyke Acland Bay. A lone B–17 attacks sub 75 mi SE of Rabaul. During 3/4 Dec, B–17's bomb A/Fs at Lae and Salamaua. US roadblock on Soputa-Sanananda trail remains precarious as Japanese maintain attacks from all sides and hold off reinforcements.

Eleventh AF: 2 bmrs and several ftrs fly rcn over Semichis, Kiska and Attu. Constant air alert in Adak.

4 December

Twelfth AF: B–17's bomb shipping and docks at Bizerte. B–26's, with ftr escort, attack the same tgt a half hour later. P–38's, F–4's, and a B–17 fly rcn, while P–38's attack vehicles and troop concentrations, mainly in Gabes and Sfax areas.

Ninth AF: B–24's, in first attack by US bmrs on Italy, hit Italian fleet and docks at Naples. Hits are scored on numerous harbor installations, a railroad yard, and 3 or 4 ships, including a battleship.

Eleventh AF: 7 B–24's and 9 B–26's escorted by 16 P–38's take off upon a PBY rpt of surface force SE of Amchitka. At interception point, area is searched without result. PBY pilot later reports he saw "clouds." Rcn is flown over Attu, Agattu, Semichi, Kiska, and Amchitka.

5 December

Twelfth AF: Gen Spaatz is announced as Acting Dep CinC for Air, Allied Force in NW Africa. B–17's bomb docks and shipping at Tunis. B–25's hit Sidi Ahmed A/F; DB–7's follow shortly with raid on same tgt while another small force of the LBs hit Faid. Each raid is escorted by P–38's. P–38's fly rcn over wide areas of Tunisia, a B–17 photographs Sousse-Sfax-Gabes region, a Mosquito covers A/Fs and harbors in W Sicily, and an F–4 flies photo rcn over S Sardinia.

Fifth AF: A–20's and B–25's pound Buna area. Allied ground forces again fails to take the village, but some elements push to within 50 yards of Buna, some break through to the sea, and others invest W bank of Entrance Creek. Buna is thus completely isolated. B–24's bomb Kavieng A/F.

SOPAC: Gen Marshall informs CO MGENSOPAC that AAF units in SOPAC are designated Thirteenth AF. This is first official step toward creation of the new AF.

Seventh AF: 5th and 11th Bomb Gps are formally transferred to SO PAC, along with 12th and 44th Ftr Sqs and an ordnance and a chemical co.

Eleventh AF: Negative rcn covers Attu, Agattu, the Semichis, Amchitka and Kiska.

ZI: I Concentration Cmd is disbanded, its functions being taken over by the 4 domestic AFs and ATC.

6 December

Eighth AF: 36 HBs attack Atelier d'Hellemmes locomotive works at Lille while a smaller group of aircraft bomb Abbeville/Drucat A/F.

Twelfth AF: DB–7's, with ftr escort, bomb bridge over Medjerda R at El Bathan. P–38's and F–4's fly patrols and rcn missions over parts of Algeria and Tunisia. In ground fighting, German attack penetrates positions of US 1st Armd Div (with British First Army) on El Guettar Mountains.

Ninth AF: B–24's sent to attack shipping at Tobruk fail to locate tgt due to bad weather, but a few aircraft manage to bomb Misurata and 2 enemy A/Fs. P–40's fly top cover for RAF airplanes attacking Marble Arch.

Fifth AF: B–17's bomb Lakunai A/F and town of Rabaul. B–25's bomb A/F at Lae.

SOPAC: P–39's, strafing Munda, discover trucks, steam rollers, and other construction equipment, and evidence of 2 airstrips under construction. B–17's will bomb Munda 21 times in Dec and continue to hit it in Jan 43, as the Japanese continue to work at building the strips despite the constant air strikes.

Eleventh AF: Rcn is flown over Attu, Agattu, Amchitka, Kiska and the Semichis.

7 December

Twelfth AF: B–17's, escorted by P–38's, attack docks and shipping at Bizerte. Escorted DB–7's attack tanks in Tebourba-El Bathan area where elements of British First

Army continue to be hard pressed. Other DB–7's sent to bomb at La Hencha and Sousse abort because of bad weather. P–38's and P–40's fly numerous rcn missions over Sousse-Sfax-Gabes area and patrols over Oran. B–17's and F–4's fly photo rcn over Sousse-Sfax-Gabes and Tunis-Bizerte areas. 3 sqs of B–24's of 93d Bomb Gp arrive in Africa from Eighth AF in UK. Ground fighting subsides as enemy attacks in Tebourba area decrease in intensity.

Fifth AF: B–25's pound area around Buna as ground forces attack the village and clear trench at S edge. B–17's attack wrecked vessel off Gona and a tanker off Gasmata. B–25's hit A/F at Lae.

Eleventh AF: Rcn mission over Semichis and Attu is flown. Rcn of Kiska is aborted due to weather.

8 December

Eighth AF: VIII BC study of air attacks on sub pens indicates that available US bombs are incapable of penetrating roofs of the pens from any bombing level low enough to maintain accuracy.

Twelfth AF: Ftrs of 31st and 52d Gps patrol in Oran-La Senia-Tafaraoui area. Weather prevents operations of all bmr and ftr units in E Algeria. British First Army obtains permission to withdraw from areas W of Tebourba and E of Medjez el Bab to more favorable positions slightly to the W from which to prepare for move on Tunis.

Ninth AF: P–40's fly FB missions in battle area E of El Agheila.

Fifth AF: A–20's and B–25's pound AA positions at Buna and area around Buna Mission and Cape Endaiadere as ground forces attack bunker positions on S edge of Buna. P–38's hit wrecked vessel off Gona. B–24's bomb Gasmata A/F. 6 destroyers carrying troops to reinforce Buna-Gona beachhead are bombed by B–17's and a lone B–24 and turn back to Rabaul.

Eleventh AF: Attempted bombing mission of Attu and Kiska by 6 B–24's and 6 B–26's, escorted by 8 P–38's, is forced back by weather. Uneventful rcn is flown by a B–24 and a B–26 over Attu, Agattu, Amchitka, Kiska, and the Semichis.

9 December

Eighth AF: Special report on first 1,100 bmrs dispatched by VIII BC, 17 Aug to 23 Nov justifies high-level daylight precision bombing.

Twelfth AF: Heavy rains stop most air operations in E Algeria and Tunisia. A few P–38's fly rcn S of Gafsa, and P–40's fly intercept mission over Youks-les-Bains, damaging 1 airplane.

Ninth AF: P–40's fly ftr sweep over El Agheila region.

Fifth AF: B–26's pound Buna area as ground forces prepare for final assault on the village. P–40's hit area along Sanananda-Soputa trail. In nearby Gona, following air and arty bombardment, Australian forces overcome resistance, taking the village in hand-to-hand combat.

SOPAC: Cmd at Guadalcanal passes from Gen Vandegrift, CG First Marine Div, to Gen Patch, CG Americal Div. The battle-weary First Marine Div gradually withdraws from Guadalcanal during Dec.

Eleventh AF: The daily weather aircraft cannot return to base due to a sudden snow squall and crashlands at Atka I. Attempted bombing mission to Kiska Harbor by 3 B–26's and 6 P–38's is forced back by weather.

10 December

Twelfth AF: Due to heavy rains and waterlogging of A/Fs, aerial activity in Algeria-Tunisia area practically ceases. Allied troops repulse another armd and inf attack on Medjez el Bab. During 10/11 Dec, elements of British 78th Div and US 1st Armd Div begin withdrawal to Bedja area to refit. 1st Armd Div sustains heavy loss of equipment as it withdraws.

Eleventh AF: The weather aircraft which crashlanded at Atka on the previous day is sighted on the W end of the island, its fuselage broken off aft of the wings. Crew, later brought back, is unharmed except for light injuries of Gen Lynd, visiting IG. Uneventful rcn covers Attu, Kiska and the Semichis. 4 B–26's and 6 P–38's abort a bomb run to Kiska due to weather.

11 December

Twelfth AF: Twelfth AF creates 5 area cmds covering NW Africa from W coast of Morocco to E coast of Tunisia. From W to E these are: Moroccan Comp Wg (Col Rosenham R Beam); W Algerian Comp Wg (Col Lawrence P Hickey); C Algerian Comp Wg (Col Paul L Williams); XII BC (Col Charles T Phillips); and XII FC (Gen Blackburn). Gen Cannon becomes overall cmdr of the 2 wgs in Algeria. B–25's with ftr escort, attack rail bridge at La Hencha. P–38's fly sea patrol off N coast and

over Gulf of Tunis and rcn over Sousse region. Spitfires sweep over Medjez
el Bab, and Bone.

Ninth AF: B–24's bomb harbor
and surrounding areas at Naples
with good results. P–40's fly several
FB missions and sweeps over battle
area in preparation for ground assault on El Agheila which Gen Montgomery schedules for 14 Dec.

Tenth AF: HBs of IATF attack
shipping at Port Blair, with negative
results.

Fifth AF: B–26's bomb A/F and
T/O in Buna area. B–25's and B–26's
hit A/F at Lae.

Eleventh AF: Uneventful rcn covers Attu, Agattu, Amchitka, Kiska,
and the Semichis. 3 B–26's and 4 P–
38's rebomb and strafe previously
bombed cargo vessel in Kiska Harbor,
scoring 2 more direct hits. The P–
38's also strafe and bomb Kiska Harbor submarine base and seaplane
hangars, camp area, and nearby gun
emplacements.

12 December

Eighth AF: 17 HBs bomb Rouen-
Sotteville M/Y. Bad weather prevents
large attack planned for air installations at Romilly-sur-Seine.

Twelfth AF: B–17's, with P–38 escort, bomb rail facilities and harbor
area at Tunis. B–26's on mission to
bomb at Sousse or La Hencha abort
due to very bad weather. P–38's and
P–40's fly widespread rcn operations.

Ninth AF: P–40's fly sweeps and
attack ground forces in El Agheila
and Brega area. RAF Liberators, under IX BC operational control, attack
dock area at Naples.

Fifth AF: A–20's strafe barges off

Sanananda Pt while B–17's bomb
A/Fs at Lae and Salamaua.

SOPAC: US HBs begin series of
daily attacks on Japanese A/Fs near-
ing completion at Munda.

Eleventh AF: Attempted photo rcn
over Kiska by a B–24 and 2 P–38's returns without result due to weather.
Another rcn B–24 is turned back by a
weather front W of Buldir I.

13 December

Twelfth AF: 15 B–17's of 97th Gp
hit harbor and docks at Tunis. 10
B–17's of 301st Gp bomb harbor and
docks at Bizerte and are shortly followed by 19 B–24's of Eighth AF's
93d Gp attacking same tgt. B–25's
hit harbor area at Sousse while B–
26's blast bridge N of Sfax. P–38's
escort both MB raids. P–38's, P–40's,
and Spitfires fly rcn and patrols over
much of NW Africa. P–38's attack
several tgts including vehicles N of
Gabes and a schooner off Cape
Dimasse. C–47's fly 17 transport missions between various points in NW
Africa.

Ninth AF: Aircraft of WDAF, including more than 100 US P–40's, fly
strafing and bombing missions
against ground forces which begin
withdrawing from El Agheila during
early morning. British 51st Inf Div
penetrates E defenses of the town.

Fifth AF: Convoy of 5 destroyers
is detected off Madang, as it attempts
to bring in reinforcements for beachhead in Buna area. B–17's and B–24's
attack as it moves S but fail to deter
its progress. A–20's bomb and strafe
Cape Killerton area while B–17's
bomb Salamaua area. B–26's hit A/F
at Gasmata.

Eleventh AF: Largely negative

rcn is flown over Attu, Agattu, Kiska, Amchitka, and the Semichis by 2 B–24's and 2 P–38's.

14 December

Eighth AF: IG report states that drain of stocks from Eighth AF for purpose of equipping Twelfth AF is hindering greatly the trg and combat program of Eighth AF gps.

Twelfth AF: B–24's bomb harbor and shipping at Bizerte while B–17's hit similar tgts at Tunis. DB–7's make 2 attacks on M/Y at Sfax. P–38's and P–40's fly escort. P–38's attack vessels off N Tunisian coast, road between Tunis and Bizerte, train near Kerker, trucks near Chaaba, and El Djem, and train near La Hencha. P–40's fly sweeps; F–4's carry out photo rcn over areas of Tunisia; C–47's fly 19 transport missions between various points in NW Africa.

Ninth AF: P–40's continue to pound retreating forces E of El Agheila. As British 7th Armd and 51st Inf Divs push W, 2d NZ Div pushes SW and rounds enemy's right flank, then heads NW towards coast to cut off retreat.

Fifth AF: Troop-carrying destroyers, attacked by Fifth AF aircraft on 13 Dec, reach mouth of Mambare R and unload without being detected. However, Fifth AF MBs, LBs and ftrs, along with RAAF airplanes, subsequently deliver damaging blows against these troops and their supplies and also hit forces along Kumusi R, in Cape Endaiadere area, and along the Mambare R. The destroyers are attacked off Cape Ward Hunt by MBs and HBs. A/Fs at Lae and Gasmata are also bombed.

15 December

Twelfth AF: B–26's attack El Aouina A/F while B–17's bomb harbor area. Other B–17's hit harbor at Bizerte. F–4's fly several photo rcn missions over coastal Tunisia covering area from Bizerte to Gabes, ftrs fly routine patrols, and C–47's carry out numerous courier and transport missions in NW Africa.

Ninth AF: B–24's, opening Ninth AF offensive against Tunisian ports, hit railroad yard, repair shop, and roundhouse at Sfax. RAF B–24's, operationally controlled by IX BC, hit Naples harbor during 15/16 Dec. B–25's and P–40's strike at retreating troops and vehicles between El Agheila and Merduma, as 2d NZ Div drives to coast in Merduma area to obstruct the retreating forces.

Fifth AF: A–20's hit forces along Mambare R while a B–24 bombs wrecked ship at Gona.

16 December

Twelfth AF: DB–7's bomb rail junction E of Mateur and hit town area of Massicault and nearby vehicle dispersal area. P–38's attack ships off N coast of Tunisia scoring hit on 1 vessel. Other P–38's fly rcn missions, exchanging ineffective fire with enemy airplanes. C–47's continue transport and courier missions in NW Africa. Col Carlyle H Ridenour takes over as CO XII BC.

Ninth AF: P–40's fly FB missions and sweeps over battle area as enemy, breaking into small dets, manages to withdraw from El Agheila positions after hard fighting and heavy losses. B–25's hit concentrations and transport tgts.

Fifth AF: A–20's and B–26's bomb

forces in Buna area and at mouth of Kumusi R, and strafe barge and lagoon shoreline S of the Kumusi's mouth. B–24's attack wreck off Gona, cargo vessel in Bismarck Sea, and a destroyer, 2 cargo ships, and 2 tankers in Solomon Sea, SE of Cape Orford.

17 December

N Africa: Adm Darlan announces French Fleet units at Alexandria, Dakar, and N African ports are joining Allied forces.

Twelfth AF: 36 B–17's hit harbors and docks at Tunis and Bizerte, claiming damage to both tgts and destruction of 1 vessel and 3 aircraft at Tunis. DB–7's and A–20's hit military installations N and W of Gabes A/F and landing ground near Sidi Tabet. B–25's and B–26's on shipping raid in Gulf of Tunis fail to sight vessels. P–38's and Spitfires escort all the bomb missions. P–38's on sea mission off N Tunisia engage German aircraft in combat, claiming 1 destroyed. Other P–38's and F–4's fly rcn over Tunisia.

Tenth AF: CATF planes pound Lashio.

Fifth AF: B–26's bomb Buna mission while US ground forces make fruitless attacks on The Triangle now dubbed "Bloody Triangle."

SOPAC: US 132d Inf opens preliminaries for offensive on Guadalcanal with attack on positions in Mount Austen area which overlooks Henderson Field. The enemy offers bitter resistance. AAF aircraft, especially P–39's, and Marine SBD's, provide spt and continue to do so as the offensive progresses, cutting off Japanese forces from coastal supply points, hitting reinforcements moving through the jungle, and destroying ammo dumps.

Eleventh AF: A rcn sortie is flown over Attu, Agattu, Kiska, Amchitka, and the Semichis. 2 attacks by 5 B–24's, 2 B–25's, and 4 B–26's—the second attack escorted by 8 P–38's—take off for Kiska. Only the first mission, 4 B–24's, gets through and hits submarine base area, marine railway, buildings, and communication facilities. Second mission aborts due to weather. P–38's and B–24's also fly offshore patrol between Vega Pt and Little Kiska.

18 December

Twelfth AF: B–17's, with P–38 escort, hit Bizerte harbor and shipping offshore. Direct hit scored on 1 vessel. Attacks by ftrs result in loss of 1 HB and 4 ftrs. 3 enemy ftrs are destroyed and others damaged. B–26's and P–38 escorts attack M/Y at Sousse, hitting station, roundhouse, and other buildings, tracks, and a train. Heavy AA accounts for 2 MBs. DB–7's, with ftr escort, hit landing ground and dispersal area near Mateur and attack railroad yards in the town. P–38's and P–40's fly rcn missions and sweeps over Tunisia and attack ground tgts, including a train N of Sfax and trucks near Sainte-Marie-du-Zit. C–47's continue transport missions in NW Africa.

Ninth AF: 93d Bomb Gp, Eighth AF, is attached to IX BC for operations. P–40's fly rcn and patrol as British Eighth Army's lead div, 2d NZ, clashes with enemy rear guards at Nofilia. B–17's hit shipping and harbor installations at Sousse. RAF B–24's, under IX BC, follow with raid on same tgt during 18/19 Dec.

Fifth AF: A–20's hit positions at Kurenada in Cape Endaiadere area where Allied ground forces launch concerted assault. B–17's attack convoy in Astrolabe Bay off Madang, while B–24's bomb Alexishafen area. B–24's bomb A/F at Lae and attack the convoy off Madang and a transport NW of Lorengau.

Eleventh AF: A B–24 flies rcn over Kiska, Attu, Agattu, and Semichis.

19 December

Twelfth AF: Rain curtails operations. A–20's and DB–7's, with ftr escort, hit M/Y at Sfax. Ftrs fly routine patrol in Oran area.

Fifth AF: A–20's and B–25's hit Buna Mission area in which Australian forces again attacking The Triangle are halted by fierce crossfire. B–24's and B–17's attack warships, transports, and cargo vessels off Madang in Astrolabe Bay and NNW of Finschhafen off coast of Huon Peninsula. B–25's bomb A/F at Lae.

Eleventh AF: 2 B–24's fly rcn and patrol over Amchitka and Kiska. 4 escorting P–38's turn back due to weather and mechanical difficulties.

20 December

Eighth AF: 72 HBs attack air depot at Romilly-sur-Seine in effective raid. 6 bmrs are lost to ftrs.

Twelfth AF: Operations are severely curtailed as result of heavy rains. C–47's maintain transport and courier service. Ftrs fly rcn and scramble missions.

Ninth AF: B–24's sent to attack Sousse harbor, abort because of

weather; 3 bomb wrecked vessel N of Sfax.

Tenth AF: CATF bmrs hit Lashio. Japanese airplanes bomb Calcutta and vicinity, hitting docks, shipping, and A/Fs in the area.

Fifth AF: A–20's and B–25's pound Giropa Pt and area around Buna Mission near which are located strong bunker positions. After preparatory bombardment Australian forces again assault the positions, attacking twice under cover of smoke, but are beaten back. A decision is made to bypass The Triangle.

Eleventh AF: 4 B–26's, 5 B–24's, 4 B–25's, and 9 P–38's make a coordinated bombing, strafing, and incendiary attack on Kiska Harbor installations and vicinity, especially on the submarine base and near the marine railway and gun emplacements. A direct hit is scored on a probable ammo dump. P–38's also strafe previously damaged cargo ship off Trout Lagoon. 1 B–24 and 2 P–38's fly photo and rcn patrol over Attu, Agattu, Semichis, and Amchitka.

21 December

Twelfth AF: Weather prevents B–17's from bombing Sfax or secondary tgt, Gabes. P–38's on scramble over Youks-les-Bains down 2 Ju 88's. P–40's destroy a tank and several cars and trucks with trailers in Kairouan area. F–4's fly 3 photo rcn missions over area between Bizerte and Gabes while C–47's continue transport and courier missions.

Ninth AF: B–24's of 93d Bomb Gp abort mission against Sousse harbor due to weather. 6 RAF Liberators, under IX BC control, attack the harbor; results are not observed. Light forces of British Eighth Army overtake enemy rearguard at Sirte and are halted temporarily.

Fifth AF: B–17's attack vessels in Finschhafen harbor while B–24's carry out single-bmr strikes on cargo ship N of Finschhafen and barges at mouth of the Mambare R and off Cape Ward Hunt.

Eleventh AF: 1 B–24 flies uneventful rcn over Amchitka, Kiska, Semichis, and Attu. A B–24 and 2 P–38's abort photo mission due to weather.

22 December

Twelfth AF: Solid overcast prevents B–17's from bombing Bizerte or alternate tgts of Sousse and Sfax. P–40's shoot up train in Kairouan and destroy trucks on Sfax-Faid road. F–4's continue rcn between Bizerte and Gabes-Medenine area. C–47's continue courier missions. British 5 Corps of First Army renews drive on Tunis. 2d Coldstream Gds attack Djebel el Ahmera (Longstop Hill) NE of Medjez el Bab.

Ninth AF: B–24's of 93d Gp and RAF Liberators are dispatched against harbor at Sousse. Only 2 HBs reach tgt. Others are forced to return because of weather, but a few manage to bomb Monastir and railroads at Mahdia.

Tenth AF: CATF aircraft bomb Lashio.

Fifth AF: B–25's pound Maimba mission and village near Buna when ground forces continue to resist stubbornly. B–17's hit ship in harbor at Arawe while a single B–24 attacks a transport off Gasmata.

Seventh AF: 26 B–24's staging through Midway from Hawaii bomb Wake I during 22/23 Dec.

Eleventh AF: All missions including a B–24 weather run cancelled due to weather.

23 December

AAF: Committee of Operations Analysts, in process of formulating a basis for tgt selection, presents an interim report stating principle of concentration of bombardment against a few essential industries or services.

Twelfth AF: Total cloud cover causes B–17's, escorted by P–38's, to abort bombing mission against Tunis and Bizerte A/Fs. Spitfires fly routine patrol over Oran-Tafaraoui area. C–47's fly courier missions. Elements of US 1st Div, after relieving 2d Coldstream Gds on Djebel el Ahmera, are forced to withdraw by German counterattack.

Ninth AF: 324th Ftr Gp arrives in Egypt to join Ninth AF.

Fifth AF: A–20's strafe troops near Gona and at Woiba Is. B–25's bomb Cape Gloucester A/F, and attack ship at Pilelo I. B–24's carry out single-bmr attacks on transport WSW of Cape Orford, a vessel NW of Lorengau, a cargo ship at Arawe, and the Cape Gloucester A/F.

24 December

Eighth AF: First P–47's arrive in ETO. However, because of VHF radios and engine difficulties, the P–47's are not sent into combat until Apr 43.

N Africa: Adm Darlan is assassinated in Algiers. Gen Giraud becomes acting French ruler of African colonies.

Twelfth AF: Weather restricts operations to routine C–47 courier flights, Spitfire patrols in Oran-Tafaraoui area, and an attack by 4 P–40's on bridge N of Gabes. During conference with Gen Eisenhower, Gen Sir Anderson, CG British First Army, decides to cease attack on Tunis until after rainy season. British forces retake positions on Djebel el Ahmera.

Ninth AF: B–24's sent to bomb Tunis abort because of weather. B–24's attack harbor at Naples during 23/24 Dec; 1 bombs Taranto.

Fifth AF: A–20's strafe troops near Kel Kel and along N Amboga R and trail. B–17's and B–24's hit shipping and A/F at Gasmata. Other B–24's, operating singly, bomb Lae, a schooner in Vitiaz Strait, and the harbor at Arawe.

SOPAC: P–39's and USMC F4F's and SBD's carry out their most devastating raid on Munda, claiming 24 ftrs destroyed on the ground and in the air. None of the attacking ftrs are lost.

Eleventh AF: The rcn aircraft over Kiska finds shipping there unchanged. Weather cancels other missions.

25 December

Twelfth AF: P–40's bomb troop concentration at Sfax. P–38's sent to bomb convoy off N Tunisia fail to sight ships. Germans retake Djebel el Ahmera.

Fifth AF: A B–17 attacks sub in Wide Bay off New Britain; 1 B–24 attacks runways at Cape Gloucester and another bombs Lae.

Eleventh AF: A B–24 takes photos of Kiska and Attu and unsuccessfully bombs 5 barges between Gertrude Cove and Kiska Harbor. The B–24 then sights 8 float Zeros. 3 unsuccessfully attempt to attack the HB.

26 December

Twelfth AF: B–17's, with ftr escort, hit harbor and shipping at Bizerte; heavy AA and ftr attacks account for 2 HBs and 2 P–38's; P–38's claim 2 FW 190's destroyed. Other B–17's, with P–40 escort, bomb harbor and shipping at Sfax; HBs claim 3 vessels sunk. P–38's on rcn attack locomotives and motor vehicles S of Tunis and W of Sousse. P–40's strafe barges off Sousse, destroying 1 of them, and strafe ground tgts during rcn over Kairouan-Sousse-Kasserine area. Spitfires patrol Oran area. C–47's continue transport runs. During 26/27 Dec transports drop det of US paratroops at bridge N of El Djem.

Ninth AF: B–24's are dispatched against Tunis harbor during 26/27 Dec; 3 hit primary tgt while 2 others bomb Sousse and Sfax.

Tenth AF: 12 IATF B–24's bomb railroad station, dock area, arsenal, and power plant at Bangkok. CATF B–25's hit Lashio.

Fifth AF: HBs carry out single-bmr attacks against Cape Gloucester, Finschhafen, and Madang, and attack shipping off New Britain. Japanese aircraft from Rabaul attack Doboduru but are driven off by Fifth AF ftrs.

SOPAC: Gen Mulcahy, USMC, arrives on Guadalcanal with Second Marine Aircraft Wg and assumes operational control of all aircraft on the island, including those of the AAF.

Eleventh AF: 6 B–24's and 9 P–38's attack Holtz Bay but do not find the 8 float Zeros seen there the previous day. The P–38's strafe Attu installations at minimum altitude. The B–24's bomb Sarana Bay. AA fire downs one P–38 and damages another. Later 6 B–25's and 4 P–38's over Kiska and Gertrude Cove abort due to low ceiling. An OA–10 flies rcn over NE Kiska.

27 December

Twelfth AF: B–17's, escorted by P–38's, bomb shipping and dock facilities at Sousse, damaging docks and warehouses and claiming direct hits on 4 vessels. P–38's and P–40's fly several rcn missions over Tunisia while Spitfires patrol Oran and Bone areas. C–47 transport flights continue. British First Army repels attack in Medjez el Bab area.

Fifth AF: B–17's pound shipping at Rabaul while B–26's hit tgts in Gona area. A single B–24 hits runway at Finschhafen.

Eleventh AF: 2 B–24's flying rcn over Kiska and Amchitka abort in bad weather.

28 December

Twelfth AF: B–17's bomb dock and harbor installations at Sousse. P–38's provide escort. P–38's and P–40's on patrol and rcn missions claim 4 airplanes downed in combat and several vehicles destroyed at various points in Tunisia. C–47's, some escorted by Spitfires, continue courier and ferry missions. F–4's fly rcn over Tunis, Sousse and Sfax areas, and Spitfires patrol Oran and Bone areas.

Ninth AF: During 27/28 Dec and during day, B–24's, including RAF Liberators under IX BC control, bomb harbor at Sousse, hitting vessels and dock installations. British Army patrols reach point E of Buerat, overlooking Wadi el Chebir, without opposition.

Tenth AF: CATF B–25's, with ftr spt, hit Magwe.

Fifth AF: B–24's bomb Rabaul, Gasmata and Lae.

Eleventh AF: Icing conditions and low visibility prevent all flying.

29 December

Twelfth AF: B–17's attack Sousse docks and harbor; P–38's provide escort. DB–7's and A–20's hit bridges at La Hencha; escorting P–40's strafe flatcars and locomotive at Sainte-Juliette. P–38's attack tank depot SE of Pont-du-Fahs; DB–7's and A–20's follow with attack on same tgt. P–38's and P–40's fly rcn missions and patrols over wide areas of Algeria and Tunisia. C–47's continue transport missions throughout NW Africa.

Ninth AF: B–24's sent to bomb Tunis harbor during 29/30 Dec find tgt obscured by clouds and attack Sousse instead.

Tenth AF: 12 B–24's attack shipping in Rangoon vicinity.

Fifth AF: A–20's strafe forces and occupied areas at Lokanu and along W bank of Amboga R. B–24's carry out single-bmr attacks on A/Fs at Lae and Gasmata.

Eleventh AF: B–24 flies negative rcn over Rat I and Amchitka. Scheduled Kiska attack and Amchitka rcn missions are cancelled by bad weather.

30 December

Eighth AF: 40 HBs hit submarine base at Lorient, which now shows cumulative effect of repeated bombardment.

Twelfth AF: B–17's, with P–38 escort, attack docks and M/Y at Sfax. B–25's escorted by P–38's, follow with attack on same M/Y. DB–7's hit troop concentration near Gabes, this attack being followed by A–20 raid on the A/F. During afternoon more DB–7's hit Gabes, concentrating on the A/F. P–40's and P–38's furnish escort for the raids on Gabes. A–20's hit fuel dump at El Aouinet; on return flight, escorting P–40's strafe near El Guettar. P–38's fly 2 rcn missions to Tripoli, 1 flight destroying several trucks on return trip. P–40's and F–4's fly uneventful rcn missions.

Fifth AF: B–17's bomb shipping at Rabaul. A–20's strafe forces in Duvira Creek area while B–24's carry out single-bmr attacks on A/F at Lae, Madang Village, and troops and vehicles at Wewak. A B–17 strafes a schooner in Jacquinot Bay.

Eleventh AF: B–25's and 14 P–38's approach Kiska Harbor at minimum altitude for a bombing and strafing attack. 2 ships and 3 submarines, newly arrived, are covered by Zeros. 4 of them engage the approaching P–38's in a dogfight. 2 P–38's are shot down and 4 Zeros are scored as probables. The B–25's meanwhile attack the ships with unobserved results. One B–25 is shot down off Little Kiska. A PBY picks up survivors, but fails to return. Kiska Harbor is then attacked once more by 5 B–24's, 4 B–25's, and 4 B–26's. They claim

hits on both vessels observing explosions on the smaller ship. A B–24 photographs Amchitka. Weather rcn of Near Is is cancelled due to weather. Aerial rcn observes for first time Japanese use of smoke screen at Kiska Harbor.

31 December

Ninth AF: B–24's, including RAF Liberators, bomb shipping and dock area at Sfax with good results.

Twelfth AF: LBs, with ftr escort, make 2 attacks on Sousse, bombing railroad yards and docks. Escorted B–17's hit harbor at Sfax while B–26's, with ftr protection, hit A/F area at Gabes and shipping and rail bridges in Bizerte-Tunis area. P–38's and P–40's, flying rcn, destroy several vehicles. Other ftrs fly routine patrols and escort C–47's on transport missions.

Tenth AF: P–40's on armed rcn hit railroad T/Os from Naba to Pinbaw.

Fifth AF: A–20's strafe forces in Sanananda and Giruwa area and along Amboga R. B–26's pound forces on N shore of Markham R near its mouth, while A–20's strafe parked aircraft at Lae. B–24's operating singly, bomb A/F at Gasmata and attack shipping in Wide Bay and Saint George Channel.

SOPAC: B–26's of 69th Bomb Sq arrive on Guadalcanal.

Eleventh AF: 6 B–24's, covered by 9 P–38's, attack Kiska Harbor, hitting 2 cargo vessels. 1 of 6 intercepting ftrs is probably shot down. 1 B–25 searching for a Navy aircraft missing since the previous day also flies rcn over Semisopochnoi, Segula, Little Sitkin, Gareloi, and Amchitka.

1943

1 January

Twelfth AF: Gen Cannon becomes CG, XII BC. Col Peter S Rask takes cmd of XII A Spt Cmd. B–17's hit harbor at Tunis, while B–26's hit M/Y. B–25's on mission against shipping near La Goulette abort due to weather. Ftrs escort bmr missions and C–47 transport runs and carry out routine patrols.

Ninth AF: B–24's strike harbor at Tunis, hitting turning basin, area just SW of it, and nearby rail junction. A few of the aircraft bomb SW and SE coast of Sicily.

Tenth AF: 6 B–25's attack railroad bridge near Myitnge, claiming several hits on the tgt. The nearby A/F is also bombed.

Fifth AF: B–24's and B–17's bomb A/Fs at Rabaul, Gasmata, and Lae, and attack shipping at Rabaul.

2 January

Eighth AF: 4 radar-equipped B–24's fly "moling," or intruder, mission aimed at harassing enemy in weather unsuitable for large missions by alerting air-raid crews in area north of the Ruhr. This mission and 2 subsequent missions in Jan are foiled by clear weather over tgt area.

Twelfth AF: B–17's bomb harbor and shipping at La Goulette. Escorting P–38's and Me 109's engage in air battle, each side losing 2 airplanes. A–20's and DB–7's, with ftr escorts, consecutively raid Sousse

harbor. In afternoon, DB–7's again hit the harbor. B–26's, with ftr protection, hit bridge N of El Djem. Ftrs fly escort, patrol, and rcn missions, attacking enemy vehicles and aircraft. Several trucks and ftrs are claimed destroyed.

Ninth AF: B–25's bomb A/F at Heraklion. B–24's hit A/F at Kastelli/Pediada.

Tenth AF: CATF ftrs continue to hit transportation tgts, strafing truck convoy on Burma Road. The strikes begin near Loiwing and cover 30 mi of highway. At least 5 trucks are destroyed and others damaged. 6 B–25's bomb Monywa A/F.

Fifth AF: A–20's, B–25's, B–26's, and B–24's, hit A/F and T/Os at Lae and Gasmata. Buna Mission is finally overrun by Australian and US forces.

Eleventh AF: 3 B–25's, 3 B–26's, and 8 P–38's heading for Kiska are forced back by bad weather. The weather aircraft cannot see into Kiska Harbor or Gertrude Cove. 2 B–24's fly photo rcn over Amchitka and encounter poor weather. An OA–10 unsuccessfully searches islands E of Segula for missing OA–10.

3 January

Eighth AF: 68 HBs of VIII BC strike Saint-Nazaire U-boat base in first attack on that installation since 23 Nov 42, and the heaviest attack to date against submarine bases. Formation (instead of individual) precision bombing is used for the first time by VIII BC, and considerable damage is done to dock area. There is heavy ftr opposition, and German flak is thrown up in an effective predirected barrage rather than in the usual attempt to track the bmrs. 7 aircraft are lost and 47 damaged; 70 men are missing and 5 killed.

Twelfth AF: All XII FC units in Tunisia (ftrs and LBs) attack tanks which, with inf and arty spt, have overrun French troops at Fondouk el Aouareb. The ftrs and LBs attack the tanks as they move W from Fondouk. Several tanks are reported destroyed or aflame and numerous other tanks and vehicles damaged. Spitfires based in Algeria escort C–47's on transport missions.

Ninth AF: RAF Baltimores, operating under IX BC, bomb Suda Bay and Timbakion A/F. A few of the aircraft bomb Kapistri.

Fifth AF: P–40's strafe troops in waters off Buna as US-Australian ground forces are mopping up in nearby Buna Mission area. B–26's, along with a single B–24, bomb A/F at Lae while a B–24 bombs Madang and an A–20 hits Salamaua. A lone B–24 strafes A/F at Gasmata.

Eleventh AF: All but 2 searches are cancelled because of weather.

4 January

Twelfth AF: B–17's sent, in 2 forces, to bomb Bizerte are forced to abort by heavy clouds over tgt. B–25's hit railroad yards at Kairouan while A–20's attack Cherichera. Ftrs provide escort for the bmrs and for C–47 transport runs, and fly rcn and patrol missions.

Ninth AF: Col Robert Kauch replaces Gen Adler as CO IX ASC.

Tenth AF: HBs from Gaya and Pandaveswar pound M/Y at Mandalay, halting northbound flow of supplies. Tracks and cars in S half of the M/Y are heavily bombed, causing fires visible for 70 mi. HBs also damage 15,000-ton transport at mouth of Rangoon R. 1 B–25 and 9 P–40's hit rail tgts at Naba.

Fifth AF: B–26's pound Sanananda Pt area as preparations for allied offensive in that sector get underway. A–20's and B–25's hit A/F, AA positions and buildings at Lae. B–24's, on single-plane flights, bomb A/F at Lae and attack schooners off Gasmata and Cape Kwoi.

Eleventh AF: 6 B–24's, 3 B–25's, 3 B–26's, and 10 P–40's en route to Kiska, are forced back near Segula by snow squalls and low ceiling. The weather aircraft flies unsuccessful rcn over Kiska. Photo rcn is flown over Amchitka. An OA–10 investigates flares reported near Kagalaska Strait.

5 January

AAF: Gen Spaatz is designated Air CinC, Allied AF, in N Africa and, as such, Chief Air Adviser to Gen Eisenhower, the CinC Allied Forces.

Twelfth AF: Allied AF is activated. It includes Twelfth AF, EAC (RAF) and such French air units as might be assigned or attached to it. The cmd serves under direction of CinC, Allied Forces. System of area cmds in NW Africa is reorganized. HQ announces that the Moroccan, W Algerian, and C Algerian Comp Wgs are to be replaced by 2d, 1st, and 3d

Air Def Wgs, respectively, upon arrival of these units in the theater.
B–17's, with large P–38 escort, attack Sfax power station. Ftr-escorted
B–26's hit Kairouan A/F. Other ftrs
fly patrols, rcn, and C–47 escort.

Ninth AF: B–24's of 93d Gp bomb
Sousse harbor (clouds obscure primary tgt at Tunis). RAF Liberators
of 160 Sq during 5/6 Jan, hit harbors
at Tunis and Sousse. Severe 2-day
storm (4–5 Jan) sharply decreases
capacity of Bengasi port and forces
British Eighth Army to make greater
use of more distant port of Tobruk.

Fifth AF: B–26's again pound
Sanananda Point area as Australian
inf and armd elements reach Soputa
and US forces of 128th Inf start NW
along coast toward Tarakena as preliminary moves to all-out assault on
Sanananda get under way. B–17's,
A–20's, B–25's, and B–24's hit A/F at
Lae, and harbor, shipping, and A/F
at Rabaul.

Eleventh AF: 3 B–25's sink a
6,500-ton cargo vessel previously
sighted by a PBY off Holtz Bay,
where a weather and armed rcn B–24
with direct bomb hits sinks another
freighter shortly afterwards. A B–24
flies photo rcn over Amchitka, concentrating on Constantine Harbor. A
Kiska attack mission of 6 HBs, 6
MBs, and 12 ftrs is cancelled due to
weather.

6 January

Twelfth AF: A–20's, in 2 forces,
hit military camp S of Kairouan. B–
25's hit Kairouan railroad yards.
Ftrs escort bmrs, carry out patrols
and rcn flights, and accompany C–
47's on transport operations.

Fifth AF: B–26's pound forces in

Sanananda Pt area; A–20's hit Lae
A/F; B–17's, B–24's, B–26's, and P–
38's attack convoy heading SW off
coast of New Britain bound for Lae;
a single B–24 bombs Gasmata A/F.

Eleventh AF: Rcn is flown over
Amchitka, the Semichis, Agattu, and
Attu. Flotsam sighted outside of
Holtz Bay confirms that freighter
bombed on previous day sank. 6 B–
24's, 6 B–25's, and 12 P–38's take
off to attack Kiska. The P–38's and
1 B–24 turn back due to weather.
The B–25's find the tgt obscured and
5 Zeros waiting to intercept them,
whereupon they turn back without
attacking. The 5 remaining B–24's
circle Kiska without contacting enemy airplanes. One of the B–24's, ex-
ploiting a break in cloud cover, bombs
Kiska submarine base area which the
others then bomb also through the
clouds.

7 January

Twelfth AF: Allied AF GO makes
Twelfth AF responsible for air spt
of US land forces in N Africa, and
EAC responsible for spt of British First Army. However, units are
to be placed under operational control
of the other as the situation might
dictate. B–26's bomb A/F and barracks at Gabes while A–20's attack
troop concentrations at Kairouan.
Ftrs escort both raids. Ftrs carry out
several rcn missions and escort transports of 51st TC Wg on routine missions.

Ninth AF: B–24's hit shipping in
harbor at Palermo. Several other
HBs abort because of bad weather.
1 B–24 on special mission bombs
Maiouli Quay at Piraeus.

Tenth AF: P–40's blast fuel storage at Mangshih. CATF aircraft begin a series of raids, lasting through 10 Jan, during which they destroy trucks along Burma Road, barges on the Irrawaddy R, and stores in the Bhamo area.

Fifth AF: Japanese convoy bound for Lae from New Britain is again attacked by HBs, MBs, LBs, and ftrs (along with RAAF planes) in Solomon Sea off Finschhafen and during its progress off S coast of Huon Peninsula through Huon Gulf to Lae. Despite the heavy air resistance the convoy reaches its destination. Ftrs also hit A/F at Lae.

Eleventh AF: 6 B–25's and 12 P–38's dispatched to Kiska turn back due to cloud cover. 6 B–24's circle over Kiska for 2 hrs until 4 can bomb the submarine base. AA fire damages 3 of the attackers. Negative rcn is flown over Amchitka, Kiska, Agattu, and Attu. Photos taken reveal use of smoke pots by the defenders and also suggest construction of a ftr strip along the ridge S of Salmon Lagoon.

8 January

Twelfth AF: B–17's hit docks at Ferryville and naval base at Bizerte. B–25's hit bridges and rail junctions at Graiba and at Kalaa Srira while B–26's hit Kairouan A/F. The HBs and MBs are escorted by P–38's. A–20's, escorted by P–40's, bomb tank concentration near Gabes. Other ftrs fly numerous patrols and rcn missions.

Ninth AF: B–24's hit Tunis after weather and engine trouble prevent planned attack on Bizerte. RAF Liberators, under IX BC operational control, attack rail junction near Tripoli.

Tenth AF: 6 P–40's bomb and strafe Watugyi and Nsopzup and strafe other tgts. 6 B–25's bomb storage area at Bhamo.

Fifth AF: HBs, MBs, and LBs, with ftr cover, join RAAF airplanes in continued pounding of convoy as it unloads about 4,000 reinforcements at Lae. Enemy ftr cover and allied aircraft continue fierce air combat.

Eleventh AF: A B–24 flies photo rcn over Amchitka. Another B–24 aborts a weather run over Kiska because of instrument trouble.

9 January

Twelfth AF: B–26's, with ftr escort, hit A/F 10 mi S of Tripoli while B–25's attack shipping off N Tunisian coast. Ftrs fly rcn and patrol, and escort C–47's.

Ninth AF: 20 P–40's fly cover mission for RAF.

Tenth AF: 5 B–25's, with escort of 9 P–40's, bomb Bhamo. Other ftrs strafe T/Os in Wanling, Bhamo, and Loiwing areas.

Fifth AF: US HBs, MBs, LBs, and ftrs, along with RAAF planes, continue to pound convoy as it leaves Lae. A/Fs, supply dumps, and troop concentrations at Lae and at Salamaua are also hit. 4 days of attacks on the convoy result in 2 transports sunk, several vessels damaged, and about 80 airplanes destroyed.

Eleventh AF: 50-plus knot winds at Adak prevent missions.

10 January

Twelfth AF: Gen Craig takes cmd of XII A Spt Cmd. B–26's, with P–38 escort, attack M/Y and oil tanks at Gabes. B–26's, sent against Sousse abort because of bad weather. A–20's, with P–40 cover, hit military camp at Kebili. Ftrs escort C–47 missions and fly rcn and patrols. 1 P–40, on special mission, bombs German HQ at Kairouan.

Ninth AF: B–24's forced by overcast to divert from primary tgt of Bizerte, strike La Goulette, the seaport of the city of Tunis. P–40's fly rcn missions.

Tenth AF: MBs and HBs jointly attack Myitnge bridge, knocking out a span and causing considerable damage to the entire tgt.

Fifth AF: Allied aircraft operating over Solomon Sea S of New Britain continue to attack vessels of convoy which departed Lae on 9 Jan after unloading reinforcements and supplies. Supply dumps and AA positions in Lae area are also bombed.

SOPAC: P–39's and SBD's spt ground forces in Guadalcanal battle area. Strongpoint and ammo dump are destroyed.

11 January

Twelfth AF: B–17's bomb fort and town of Gadames and attack rail bridge and highway bridge across the Oued el Akarit, NNW of Gabes. Escorting P–38's engage in 25-min combat with attacking ftrs, shooting down 1 and severely damaging another. 2 P–38's are lost. B–25's bomb shipping at NE Tunisian coast. Escorting P–38's claim 3 aircraft shot down. Other ftrs fly patrol and rcn, and escort C–47 transport missions.

Ninth AF: During 10/11 Jan, RAF Liberators, under IX BC control, bomb road junction at Tripoli. During daylight, US B–24's hit harbor at Naples. P–40's fly rcn and escort missions.

Tenth AF: Ftrs attack Bhamo, destroying barges, tugs, warehouses, and other port facilities. The ftrs also strafe fuel drums along road between Chefang and Mangshih and hit a truckful of soldiers near Ho-lu.

SOPAC: B–26's and P–39's hit Munda area.

12 January

Twelfth AF: B–17's bomb Castel Benito A/F S of Tripoli, claiming destruction of at least 20 parked airplanes. HBs claim destruction of 14 attacking aircraft in aerial combat. B–25's sent to hit shipping in Straits of Sicily and in Gulf of Gabes fail to find tgts and return with bombs. B–26's hit bridges at La Hencha and Chaaba, completely destroying 1 bridge. Ftrs fly patrols, rcn, and C–47 escort, and strafe moored seaplanes and destroy numerous trucks during sweep over Ben Gardane area.

Ninth AF: P–40's carry out 3 scramble interceptor missions, claiming 2 ftrs shot down. RAF Liberators, under IX BC, hit Tripoli.

Fifth AF: B–24's, in single-plane actions, bomb Finschhafen and Madang areas.

SOPAC: B–26's, P–38's, P–39's, and P–40's attack Munda. Other P–39's hit forces on Guadalcanal.

Eleventh AF: 2 B–24's cover a small US Army and Navy force landing unopposed at Amchitka. 2 B–25's and 4 P–38 escorts also on this cover mission turn back due to weather. Weather rcn is flown over Attu, Agattu, Semichis and, lastly, over Kiska Harbor, where 4 ships are observed.

13 January

Eighth AF: 64 HBs drop approximately 125 tons of bombs on the steel works, locomotive works, and M/Y at Lille. Locomotive construction and repair work are seriously impaired.

Twelfth AF: B–25's, with P–38 escort, bomb partially sunken freighter between Tunisia and Sicily. Ftrs fly uneventful rcn and patrol.

Ninth AF: Weather prevents B–24's from attacking Tripoli and also causes B–25's sent to bomb Bir Dufan to abort. P–40's fly cover for RAF Baltimores.

Fifth AF: A–20's bomb and strafe Sanananda Pt area and forces along Sanananda track. HBs and MBs hit dock facilities at Lae and A/Fs at Lae and Salamaua.

Thirteenth AF: Thirteenth AF, XIII BC, and XIII FC are activated in S Pacific. Thirteenth AF HQ is established on Espiritu Santo, FC HQ on New Caledonia, and BC HQ on Espiritu Santo. Cmdrs are: Gen Twining, Thirteenth AF; Col Harlan T McCormick, BC; Col Dean C Strother, FC. P–39's strafe forces on the beach at Kokumbona and hit Visale in spt of ground offensive. Also MBs and ftrs hit A/F and adjacent areas at Munda, and pound Rekata Bay area.

Eleventh AF: 3 bmrs and 4 ftrs are in the air. Weather rcn airplane returns W of Kiska due to high winds. Constantine Harbor is patrolled until weather forces aircraft to return. Attack on Kiska is cancelled.

14 January

International: Casablanca Conference opens. Churchill, Roosevelt, and CCS discuss offensive in the Mediterranean and pledge to accept only unconditional surrender.

Eighth AF: One sq of 4th Ftr Gp becomes the first in Eighth AF to be completely equipped with P–47's.

Twelfth AF: B–17's, with ftr escort, attack docks and shipping at Sousse and Sfax. B–25's, with P–38's, fly anti-shipping sweep in Straits of Sicily; no ships are sighted but vehicles and troop concentrations are strafed by ftrs on return trip. B–26's, with ftr escort, attack rail junction at Kalaa Srira and junction and warehouse at Mahares. Ftrs fly rcn, patrols, and C–47 escort.

Ninth AF: B–25's strike motor transport near Gheiada, with P–40's providing cover. B–24's fail, because of weather, to locate Sousse harbor (primary tgt), but several bomb in tgt area and along road near Teboulba. RAF Liberators, under IX BC, hit Tripoli, Tagiura, and supply dump at Misurata.

Fifth AF: A–20's strafe Labu area and small boats in Sachsen Bay. B–25's bomb fuel dump and other supplies along beach in vicinity of Voco Point near Lae. B–24's carry out single-plane attacks on Madang and Finschhafen, and also bomb Gasmata.

Thirteenth AF: P–39's, dropping improvised gasoline bombs in Guadalcanal battle area around Mount Austen and Kokumbona pound forces and supplies throughout the day. Others hit barges and launches at Kaimana Bay and Aruligo Point.

15 January

Twelfth AF: B–26's attack railroad and highway bridge across Oued el Akarit, NNW of Gabes. Escorting

P-38's fight long battle with ftrs. 2 MBs and 2 P-38's are shot down. B-25's and B-26's fly 3 counter-shipping missions N and NE off Tunisia, claiming 1 vessel left in flames. Escorting ftrs strafe trucks and claim 10 aircraft shot down. Ftrs fly several rcn and patrol operations, intercept enemy airplanes attacking A/Fs in Labasse area, and escort transport aircraft.

Ninth AF: B-24's bomb harbor at Tripoli, scoring hits on vessels and on shore areas near the harbor. P-40's fly sweep and FB operations as British Eighth Army begins assault on Buerat line and drive on Tripoli. RAF Liberators, under IX BC, hit road junction at Tripoli.

Tenth AF: 6 B-24's hit shipping in Rangoon area, claiming 1 vessel sunk and another damaged. 6 P-40's bomb barges at Bhamo; 6 others bomb Nsopzup; 3 more hit footbridges and T/Os at Taihpa Ga, Yupbang Ga, and other points in N Burma.

Fifth AF: A-20's strafe Sanananda Pt area as US troops envelop pockets along Soputa-Sanananda road. B-25's bomb supply dumps at Lae while B-24's hit A/F at Gasmata. B-24's carry out single-plane attacks on bridge construction at Wewak and runway at Cape Gloucester.

Thirteenth AF: B-17's, P-40's, P-39's, and P-38's attack shipping in C Solomons; 1 HB bombs Ballale I. Other P-39's hit forces in Guadalcanal battle area and attack vessel off Kolombangara.

Eleventh AF: A total of 8 P-38's, 3 B-25's and a B-24 patrol Constantine Harbor, fly rcn over Kiska, where 1 ship is sighted, and fly negative armed rcn runs over Attu, the Semichis, and Buldir.

16 January

RAF: RAF HBs attack Berlin during 16/17 Jan for first time since 7 Nov 41. Tgt indicator bombs are used for the first time.

Twelfth AF: B-26's on shipping strike in Straits of Sicily fail to find ships. A-20's on armed rcn return to base with bombs when no tgts are sighted. Ftrs and F-4's fly rcn and patrols. Spitfires escort C-47's on ferry runs.

Ninth AF: B-24's hit Tripoli harbor and town area. RAF Liberators of 178 Bomb Sq bomb road junction and Benito Gate at Tripoli. P-40's fly patrol, scramble, and FB missions as British Eighth Army, having passed through enemy's main defenses at Buerat, pushes toward Tripoli.

Tenth AF: P-40's intercept aircraft that attempt strike on Yunnani and claim 7 Zeros shot down in the air battle. Anticipating that the Japanese planes will land at Lashio A/F, Chennault sends 6 MBs and 11 ftrs to that field in hopes of catching the enemy on the ground. Finding no aircraft there, the MBs and ftrs attack town of Lashio. This is last raid by CATF before fuel shortage grounds the ftrs for the remainder of the month and the MBs for 33 days. IATF B-25's hit Mandalay-Lashio and Sagaing-Ye-u branch railroad lines with 3 strikes on 16 and 17 Jan, knocking out 2 important rail hubs. 10 B-25's bomb railroad yards at Maymyo.

Fifth AF: A-20's pound Soputa-Sanananda trail, Kurenada area, and area S of Kumusi R, after which US and Australian ground forces open assault on Sanananda which falls the next day. B–25's again bomb supplies at Lae. B–24's carry out single-plane attacks on A/Fs at Gasmata and town of Finschhafen, and cruiser ESE of Cape Orford.

Thirteenth AF: B–26's from Espiritu Santo join P–39's and P–38's in Guadalcanal campaign, pounding the Japanese at Tassafaronga. Munda area is also bombed. B–17's bomb Buin-Faisi area, concentrating on Kahili A/F on Bougainville and Ballale A/F on Shortland I.

Eleventh AF: 6 B–24's off to hit Kiska return due to weather. A B–24 flies negative rcn over Buldir, the Semichis, Attu, and Agattu.

17 January

Twelfth AF: B–25's, with P–38 cover, attack rail junction at Graiba. Other B–25's on shipping strike fail to locate vessels and return with bombs. Ftrs fly routine rcn and patrols and escort C–47 missions.

Ninth AF: B–24's bomb Tripoli harbor. P–40's fly rcn, patrol, top cover, and FB missions as British ground forces pursue enemy toward Tripoli, reaching positions 10 mi E of Misurata on coast with Beni Ulid on the S flank. During 17/18 Jan, RAF Liberators hit Castel Benito A/F and road junction W of Homs.

Tenth AF: 6 B–25's bomb railroad T/Os N of Monywa. 3 others bomb rail junction at Maymyo.

Fifth AF: A–20's strafe Mambare Delta and hit positions between Bakumbari and Salamaua. B–17's bomb landing grounds and shipping in Rabaul. B–25's again pound supply

stores at Lae. B–24's, operating individually, attack Finschhafen and Madang wharf areas, Malahang A/F, A/F at Gasmata, and a vessel SE of Rambutyo Is.

Thirteenth AF: P–39's pound mortar positions near Allied lines on Guadalcanal. Ground supply lines to Mount Austen battle area reopen after 3 days of being closed because their extension outran the capacity of the native carriers. During the 3 days, B–17's from Henderson Field airlift rations, water, and ammo to the troops, using what improvised cargo parachutes are available and in many cases wrapping the supplies in burlap or canvas and pushing them out.

18 January

Twelfth AF: B–17's, with ftr escort, bomb Castel Benito A/F. B–26's attack 2 vessels in Gulf of Hammamet. Ftrs fly rcn and patrols and escort C–47 runs.

Ninth AF: B–24's strike Tripoli harbor. P–40's fly top cover and FB mission. Gen Montgomery orders accelerated day and night pursuit toward Tripoli as contact with Rommel's forces is temporarily lost due to terrain and obstacles.

USSR: Siege of Leningrad is raised after 17 months of bombardment.

Tenth AF: 8 P–40's and a B–25 strike Kamaing.

Fifth AF: B–25's bomb motor pool and supply dumps at Lae. B–24's, operating individually, bomb Madang and Malahang A/Fs and attack cargo ship SE of Rambutyo I.

Thirteenth AF: B–17's, P–38's, and P–40's attack shipping at Shortland I, bomb Ballale I, and attack schooner S of Santa Isabel. Hits are scored on 2 vessels.

Eleventh AF: A B–24 on rcn reports 2 vessels in Kiska Harbor. Thereupon 4 B–24's, 4 B–26's, 1 B–25, and 6 P–38's fly out of Adak. Mechanical trouble forces 2 B–26's to return. Bomb run is negative. Meanwhile bad weather closes in on Kiska and Adak. 6 aircraft are lost. 1 B–24 lands in a 20 mph downwind and crashes into 2 P–38's while 3 other B–24's are missing on return flight.

19 January

Twelfth AF: B–17's hit industrial area just S of Tunis and M/Y at Jabal al Jallud. P–38's provide cover for HBs. B–25's hit Medenine and nearby motor park. Ftrs continue routine rcn, patrol, and C–47 escort missions.

Ninth AF: B–24's hit harbors at Tripoli and Sousse. B–25's hit Castel Benito A/F and motor transport on road. Ground forces regain contact with enemy. Coastal force reaches Homs while S column presses toward Tarhunah.

Tenth AF: B–24's from Pandaveswar fly missions over Burma and Thailand. 1 flight bombs Thazi, a railroad junction S of Mandalay. The other flight carries out photo rcn of Kanchanaburi and bombs docks at Bassein during return trip. This rcn flight, the largest mission in the theater to date, reveals construction of a new railline from Thailand to Burma. 14 P–40's and a B–25 pound Kamaing.

Fifth AF: A–20's strafe troops in Kurenada area. B–25's hit barracks area and supply dumps at Toeal and pound supply dumps at Lae. HBs carry out individual attacks on various tgts at Lae, Madang, Cape Hollman, Cape Saint George, Finschhafen, and Gasmata.

Thirteenth AF: B–17's, escorted by P–38's and P–40's, bomb runway and revetments at Munda.

Eleventh AF: The crew of one of the 3 B–24's missing from previous day's mission, which had crash-landed at Great Sitkin I, is picked up by a Navy tender. Weather precludes missions and searches.

20 January

Twelfth AF: B–17's hit Cap Mangin near Gabes when cloud cover prevents bombing of primary tgt, Tripoli. B–25's hit shipping in Straits of Sicily. Ftrs continue rcn and patrols, and C–47's continue transport flights with ftr escort.

Ninth AF: B–24's hit harbor at Tripoli. P–40's fly top cover and FB operations as enemy resistance to British adv stiffens in Homs-Tarhunah area.

Fifth AF: B–25's bomb supply dumps at Lae. B–24's, operating singly, attack Cape Gloucester, Gasmata, Madang, and Finschhafen. B–25's attack tgts in Aroe Is.

Thirteenth AF: B–26's claim hit on destroyer off S Bougainville.

Seventh AF: Col Truman H Landon becomes CO VII BC.

Eleventh AF: Weather aircraft aborts shortly after takeoff. A B–24 and a Navy PBY search without results for the 2 missing B–24's.

21 January

CCS: "Casablanca Directive" is issued. It broadly outlines the operations of the BCs of the US and Britain located in UK as having primary object of destruction of German military, economic, and industrial systems and undermining of morale of German people. Primary tgts listed in order of priority are submarine construction yards, aircraft industry, transportation, oil plants, and other war industries. It largely relieves VIII BC of supporting N African operations.

Eighth AF: Gen Eaker completes paper called "The Case For Day Bombing" which he presents to Gen Arnold at Casablanca Conference. Eaker then discusses these ideas on the merits of daylight bombing with Churchill in attempt to convince him of its effectiveness. Churchill later concurs. This paper leads to development of CBO program.

Twelfth AF: B–25's bomb highway and railroad bridge just N of Pont-du-Fahs. B–26's hit 2 freighters NE of Cap Bon, sinking 1 and damaging the other. Ftrs fly bmr and C–47 escort and fly sweeps and rcn, attacking and destroying large number of trucks on Gabes-Ben Gardane road. A–20's and ftr escort bomb and strafe tank and truck concentration near Ousseltia in spt of elements of US 1st Armd Div which begins Allied assault in effort to push enemy back in Ousseltia Valley into which new enemy offensive under new Axis CG, Col Gen von Arnim, has advanced in 4-day push.

Ninth AF: B–24's bomb Tripoli harbor. B–25's attack tgts along Surman-Az Zawiyah road. P–40's fly FB missions against ground tgts as British Eighth Army overcomes resistance in area. Enemy strengthens Tarhunah area at expense of Homs front, causing Gen Montgomery to decide to make main effort along coast.

Fifth AF: B–17's bomb A/F and shipping in Rabaul. In NE New Guinea B–25's hit supply dumps and A/F. A single B–24 attacks cruiser at Amboina harbor.

Thirteenth AF: HQ moves from New Caledonia to Espiritu Santo. B–17's, B–26's, and P–39's pound bivouac and other tgts in Munda. B–17's also attack shipping E of Kieta.

Eleventh AF: Weather rcn airplane flies. An attack run over Kiska and patrol over Amchitka are called off due to weather. Air searches for 2 B–24's missing since 18 Jan continues.

22 January

Twelfth AF: Another step is taken toward amalgamation of US and RAF air strength in Allied AF. Air spt for US and British land forces in N Africa is coordinated by formation of a new combined HQ, Allied A Spt Cmd, subordinate to Allied AF and under cmd of Gen Kuter. The cmd consists of XII A Spt Cmd, 242 Gp (RAF), a photo rcn unit, and other units that might be assigned to it. B–17's, operating in 2 forces, bomb El Aouina A/F in the morning. B–26's hit the A/F shortly after noon and B–25's attack later in the afternoon. Other B–26's, on shipping strike, severely damage a freighter in Straits of Sicily. Ftrs fly escort for bmrs and for C–47's and carry out numerous rcn and patrol missions. P–39's and P–40's spt allied ground assault in Ousseltia Valley which has been halted by strong opposition. The ftrs silence several machinegun positions.

Ninth AF: B–25's bomb road junction near Tripoli. P–40's fly cover and FB missions as British Eighth Army's 22d Armd Brig passes through 51st Inf Div at Homs and drives beyond Castelverde. Forces to S adv to within 17 mi of Tripoli.

Tenth AF: 9 P–40's bomb and strafe Nsopzup and hit T/O S of town.

Fifth AF: B–25's bomb Lae terrace area. B–24's bomb Simpson Harbor and shipping and searchlights at Rabaul, and attack vessel off Amboina. A–20's strafe small boats in Baden Bay and at Woiba I. On this date Papua Campaign ends with collapse of organized resistance on Sanananda front. A decisive victory has been won by the Allied forces, the first of the war against the Japanese on land.

Thirteenth AF: XIII FC moves from New Caledonia to Espiritu Santo.

Eleventh AF: Weather rcn aircraft finds Kiska closed in and flies negative search mission for 2 missing B–24's. For first time weather airplane draws AA fire through overcast at Kiska, suggesting that the Japanese have fire-control radar.

23 January

Eighth AF: 19 HBs bomb port facilities and U-boat base at Brest while 35 attack the sub pens and supply shed at Lorient-Keroman. At Lorient, enemy ftrs use new tactics of coordinated attacks in groups of 6 aircraft. 5 bmrs are shot down.

Twelfth AF: B–17's, in 2 forces, hit Bizerte naval base and shipping in the immediate area. Much damage is done to base facilities and 1 motor vessel is sunk. 75 to 100 ftrs attack formations, and HBs and escorting P–38's claim 20 destroyed. B–26's hit shipping off NE Tunisia, attacking several vessels and claiming 1 destroyed. Escorting ftrs hit trucks and tanks near Enfidaville during return flight. A–20's, and escorting P–40's, attack heavy gun battery, machinegun nests, and 2 inf cos while supporting ground forces in battle area S of Ousseltia. Ftrs of XII A Spt Cmd destroy over 20 vehicles on Gabes-Ben Gardane highway.

Ninth AF: During 23/24 Jan, B–24's bomb Palermo harbor. P–40's fly cover and FB missions during the day as Tripoli falls to Gen Montgomery's Eighth Army.

Fifth AF: B–17's attack A/Fs at Rabaul and shipping off Cape Gazelle. B–25's pound supply dumps in terrace area of Lae. B–24's, operating individually, hit Madang and Finschhafen, and attack transports N of Rabaul and at Simpson Harbor.

Thirteenth AF: US ground forces, aided by P–39's and USMC FBs, have by this date pushed up Guadalcanal coast and taken Kokumbona and Poha R Valley. The enemy has now lost control of good landing beach W of the A/Fs. Captured with the beach are the arty pieces that have menaced Henderson Field and ground forces in Mount Austen area. The enemy's supply routes, comm systems, and ammo dumps are also lost.

Seventh AF: 24 P–40's of 78th Ftr Sq fly from Barking Sands, Kauai, in the Hawaiian Is to Midway (where they carry out patrols until 23 Apr 43). This flight of about 1,100 nautical mi is the longest over-water massed flight of single-engine planes made as of this date. The 78th replaces the P–40's of the 73d Ftr Sq on Midway.

Eleventh AF: Weather rcn over Kiska and search mission for missing B–24's reveal nothing. Enemy airplanes appear over Amchitka twice but inflict no damage. During 18–23 Jan, a period of continuous storm and sudden changes to extreme foul weather, non-combat losses were exceptionally high as 13 aircraft were lost. No losses resulted from enemy action.

24 January

Twelfth AF: Col Paul L Williams assumes cmd of XII A Spt Cmd. B–25's and B–26's, operating in 2 forces, attack Medenine A/F. B–17's hit shipping in Sousse harbor. Ftrs escort bmrs and attack vehicles and troop concentrations along battleline in Tunisia.

Ninth AF: B–25's strike Medenine A/F. P–40's fly cover and FB missions as Axis forces retreat W from Tripoli.

Tenth AF: 492d Bomb Sq, not previously tried in battle, borrows 4 B–24's and 1 crew from 436th Sq and mounts a 9-plane strike against docks at Rangoon. Hits are scored on the wharves, storage areas, and a 6,000-ton vessel in the harbor. P–40's bomb and strafe ammo stores at Shaduzup.

Fifth AF: B–17's bomb A/F, harbor, and shipping at Rabaul. B–25's hit supply dumps in terrace area of Lae. Single B–24's attack runways at Cape Gloucester and Gasmata, and bomb Dili.

Eleventh AF: 6 HBs and 6 MBs attempt attack on Kiska. MBs abort over Semisopochnoi. HBs circle Kiska until weather closes in. 2 aircraft bomb Amchitka harbor area before US interceptors, 6 P–38's and 1 B–24, arrive. 2 P–38's return due to mechanical troubles. The others fly negative search over Kiska.

25 January

Twelfth AF: Bad weather cancels HB and MB missions. Ftrs fly rcn, patrol, and C–47 escort.

Ninth AF: P–40's carry out FB operations. 7th Armd Div, in pursuit of enemy, reaches Az Zawiyah.

Tenth AF: 5 B–25's from Argatala bomb bridge (which the enemy is striving to rebuild) at Myitnge. The S approach to the bridge is destroyed and repair work on the bridge suspended. 3 B–25's add to destruction at Mandalay M/Y, tearing up tracks, wrecking about 75 railroad cars, and setting the freight house aflame. 3 other B–25's inflict similar damage on M/Y at Naba. 6 B–24's pound Rangoon dock area.

Fifth AF: A–20's strafe areas in NE Papua where there appears to be some enemy movement. B–25's blast supply dumps and AA and machinegun positions around Lae. Single B–24's attack runways at Gasmata and Cape Gloucester, and runway and beached ship at Finschhafen.

SOPAC: Final phase of Guadalcanal offensive begins with orders of Gen Patch to begin pursuit of enemy along NW coast toward Cape Esperance. Enemy retreat is to be cut off by landing of a US bn just SW of the cape.

Thirteenth AF: B–26's and P–38's

hit A/F at Munda and bomb the wharf at Repirepi, demolishing it. Other P-38's bomb installations in Rekata Bay area, Santa Isabel I.

Seventh AF: 6 B-24's, staging through Midway from Oahu, carry out photo rcn mission over Wake and drop 60 bombs. They claim 1 ftr shot down.

Eleventh AF: P-38's are dispatched too late to engage 2 floatplanes bombing Amchitka. Rcn is flown over Kiska, Buldir, Semichis, Attu, and Agattu. 1 B-24 and 4 P-38's fly 2 patrol missions over Amchitka. An attack mission to Kiska is turned back by weather. B-25's unsuccessfully search for missing aircraft.

26 January

Twelfth AF: B-26's on shipping strike abort because of weather which limits air activity. Ftrs fly rcn and local patrol missions.

Ninth AF: Headwinds prevent B-24's from reaching Naples (primary tgt) before dark, so they divert to Messina, bombing town and area around train ferry terminal. P-40's fly FB operation, refueling at Castel Benito.

Tenth AF: 7 B-24's bomb shipping and dock area at Rangoon. 12 B-25's bomb Mandalay M/Ys. 15 P-40's and 3 B-25's hit town area and bridge at Shaduzup, railroad SW of Meza, and Naba M/Y.

Fifth AF: B-17's bomb shipping and Rapopo airstrip in Rabaul area. A-20's and B-25's pound Lae area, concentrating on supply storage dumps. B-24's carry out individual attacks on runways at Cape Glou-

cester and Gasmata and hit Finschhafen.

Thirteenth AF: B-17's bomb A/F on Ballale I. P-39's, along with Navy aircraft, bomb AA positions and revetment area at Munda.

Seventh AF: 3 B-24's, taking off from Funafuti in the Ellice Is, fly photo rcn mission over Tarawa, Maiana, Abemama, Beru, and Tomama in the Gilberts. The HBs attack merchant vessel in lagoon at Tarawa. P-40's of 73d Ftr Sq fly from Midway to Kaneoke NAS in the Hawaiian Is, a distance of about 1,400 mi, thus breaking the record set by the 78th Sq on 23 Jan.

Eleventh AF: All missions cancelled due to weather. 2 enemy airplanes strafe Constantine Harbor.

27 January

Eighth AF: 53 HBs make first Eighth AF attack on Germany, bombing naval base, U-boat construction works, power plant, and docks at Wilhelmshaven. 2 other HBs bomb submarine base at Emden.

Twelfth AF: B-25's hit shipping off N coast of Algeria, attacking 2 destroyers and leaving 1 on fire. B-26's on shipping strike fail to attack sighted vessels because of weather. A-20's attack town of Al Mazzunah. Ftrs escort bmrs and fly rcn and local patrols.

Ninth AF: During 26/27 Jan, B-24's bomb Naples and Messina. In afternoon, other B-24's hit Palermo, after weather causes diversion from primary tgt at Naples. British Eighth Army's 7th Armd Div meets stiffening resistance near Zuwarah.

Fifth AF: A-20's hit huts and AA positions at Garrison Hill while B-

25's pound supply storage and runway at Malahang. Individual B–24's bomb Finschhafen town, runway on tip of Huon Peninsula, and Gasmata A/F.

Thirteenth AF: Gen Twining and a crew of 14 are down at sea between Guadalcanal and Espiritu Santo. The entire group is rescued 6 days later. Gen Twining's rubber raft had no radio, an item which COMGEN SOPAC, Gen Millard Harmon, had been requesting for some time. This incident results in the rapid appearance of dinghy radio sets in the area. 6 B–26's and 8 P–39's attack A/F at Munda.

Eleventh AF: Negative weather rcn sortie over Kiska. 4 P–38's fly protective patrol over Amchitka. Upon their departure, 3 Japanese aircraft appear and unsuccessfully bomb shipping but cause 3 casualties.

28 January

Twelfth AF: 60 HBs and MBs in 3 waves (B–17's, B–25's, and B–26's) attack harbor, shipping, and M/Ys at Sfax. All missions are escorted by P–38's. P–40's of XII A Spt Cmd attack inf and arty while supporting French and US ground forces in Ousseltia Valley where Allies gain control of W exit and half of Kairouan Pass.

Fifth AF: A–20's bomb area from Garrison Hill to Komiatum Track and B–17's hit Wewak area. B–24's carry out individual attacks at Salamaua, on cargo vessel in Open Bay and nearby village in New Britain, and on transport off Amboina.

Thirteenth AF: 5 B–26's and 12 P–39's attack A/F at Vila on Kolombangara. P–38's and P–40's, along

with Navy aircraft, hit shipping between Choiseul and Kolombangara, claiming hits on a tanker and a smaller vessel.

Seventh AF: 1 B–24 flies photo rcn over Nauru and Ocean I.

Eleventh AF: Weather airplane encounters poor visibility over Kiska. 2 patrols fly over Amchitka. The second runs into poor weather and aborts. Attack on Kiska is cancelled due to weather.

29 January

Twelfth AF: 3 consecutive waves of B–17's attack docks and shipping at Bizerte. B–26's hit El Aouina A/F while others on shipping strike between Tunisia and Sicily severely damage a cargo liner. Ftrs escort bmrs and C–47's and carry out rcn.

Fifth AF: B–25's pound area around Mubo, concentrating on positions on Garrison and Mat Mat Hill. Single B–24's bomb runways at Cape Gloucester and Gasmata.

Thirteenth AF: B–26's and P–39's hit bivouac area at Vila, Kolombangara and A/F at Munda Pt. B–17's bomb Kahili A/F.

Eleventh AF: Weather rcn over Kiska and patrol over Rat I, flown by 1 B–24, 2 B–25's, and 4 P–38's, are recalled early due to weather. All other missions cancelled.

30 January

Twelfth AF: Over 50 B–17's bomb docks and shipping at Ferryville. B–25's hit railroad installations and warehouses at El Aouinet while B–26's bomb railroad S of Reyville. Ftrs and A–20's carry out numerous strafing and bombing operations against tanks, motor transport, and troop concentrations along battleline in Tunisia between El Guettar and Faid.

Ninth AF: B–24's bomb train ferry terminal at Messina. Direct hits are scored on a ship and AA battery near terminal.

Fifth AF: B–17's bomb shipping and wharf facilities at Rabaul. A–20's strafe and bomb Lae and area around Mubo in vicinity of Garrison Hill and along Komiatum Track. B–24's, operating individually, bomb runway at Gasmata and attack transport vessel in Open Bay.

Thirteenth AF: AA positions and A/F area at Munda Pt are pounded by B–17's, B–26's, P–40's and P–39's.

Eleventh AF: 2 patrols, each composed of 1 B–25 and 4 P–38's, fly over Amchitka and are recalled early due to weather. 1 B–17, upon an alleged submarine sighting, drops 4 depth charges and 1 bomb whereupon a whale breaks water. Weather cancels other missions.

31 January

USAFIME: Gen Brereton, CG Ninth AF, assumes cmd of US AFIME.

Twelfth AF: B–17's hit harbor and shipping at Bizerte. B–26's bomb Gabes A/F. Ftrs escort bmrs and attack ground tgts and furnish cover for ground forces along battleline in Tunisia, mainly between Gafsa and Faid.

Ninth AF: IX FC begins functioning at its HQ station at Kabrit, Egypt, Gen Strickland is CG. B–24's hit railroad ferry installations at Messina harbor. British 7th Armd Div finishes clearing Zuwarah.

Fifth AF: A–20's continue to

pound positions between Mubo and Komiatum. B–17's pound A/Fs, shipping, and town area at Rabaul. A single B–24 bombs runway at Cape Gloucester, while a lone B–17 bombs runway at Wewak. Other B–24's unsuccessfully attack isolated vessels over widespread areas in Banda Sea and Solomon Sea.

Thirteenth AF: P–39's join Navy aircraft in attacks on shipping in Vella Gulf. Hits are claimed on a destroyer. B–17's bomb ammo dump and A/F at Vila. P–39's, P–38's, P–40's, and other Allied ftrs carry out sweeps over Vila and over Munda.

Eleventh AF: Weather and photo rcn aircraft flies twice over Kiska. During first mission near Attu the airplane is jumped by 6 ftrs which it eludes. 4 B–17's, 2 B–24's, 6 B–25's, 4 P–38's, and 4 P–40's then attempt attack on Kiska. P–40's turn back with mechanical troubles. The other aircraft find Kiska closed in and abort mission. 2 patrol missions, each by 1 B–25 and 4 P–38's, fly over Amchitka. 2 enemy floatplanes bomb Constantine Harbor without results.

1 February

Twelfth AF: B–17's bomb harbor and shipping at Tunis and shipping in La Goulette harbor. Ftrs escort bmrs and cover ground forces in Sened-Maknassy area. A–20's and P–40's bomb tank and vehicle concentration near Sidi Khalif.

Ninth AF: HQ 9th Ftr Wg arrives in Egypt.

Tenth AF: 7 B–24's from Pandaveswar bomb Arakan tea sheds on Rangoon R near Rangoon harbor.

Fifth AF: B–17's bomb runway and aircraft dispersal areas at

Rabaul. A lone B–24 bombs runway at Finschhafen, then flies E to New Britain where it bombs runway at Cape Gloucester and unsuccessfully attacks ship in Open Bay.

Thirteenth AF: P–38's, P–40's, and P–39's, along with Navy and Marine airplanes, attack 4 destroyers N of Vangunu I. Hits on 2 of the ships cause fires. B–17's attack shipping in Shortland-Bougainville area, claiming 3 direct hits on cargo vessels.

Eleventh AF: All missions cancelled due to weather. Enemy aircraft bomb and strafe Amchitka harbor and shipping without inflicting damage.

2 February

Twelfth AF: B–25's and B–26's, in coordinated attacks, bomb El Maou A/F at Sfax. A–20's, with P–40's and P–39's escorting, bomb munitions dump in battle area. Other ftrs fly cover missions for ground forces along battleline and carry out rcn operations.

Tenth AF: P–40's strafe aircraft, AA positions, and T/Os at Kentung.

Fifth AF: B–17's bomb A/F at Rabaul. B–24's attack shipping between Lolobau Is and New Britain and N of Open Bay, bomb Gasmata runway, and hit Timika. A–20's continue to bomb and strafe positions on high points between Mubo and Komiatum.

Thirteenth AF: B–17's, along with escorting P–40's and P–38's, attack shipping off Shortland I. Of 20 Japanese aircraft which intercept, 9 are claimed destroyed. Other B–26's, P–38's, and P–39's attack Munda A/F.

3 February

Twelfth AF: B–26's attack Gabes and vessels between Tunisia and Sicily. B–25's hit bridges over river N of Maknassy, damaging railroad bridge. A–20's hit tanks and vehicles further N, and attack a large howitzer and numerous trucks E of Ousseltia.

Ninth AF: B–24's hit harbors at Palermo and Messina; 1 bombs Plati.

Fifth AF: A–20's continue to strike along Mubo-Komiatum Track. B–17's and B–24's attack Gasmata runway, Simpson Harbor, Cape Gazelle area, and A/F at Cape Gloucester. B–25's bomb Dobo on Wamar I.

Thirteenth AF: P–39's, P–38's, and P–40's, along with Navy and Marine planes, attack Munda A/F.

4 February

JCS: Gen Andrews assumes cmd of ETOUSA. NATOUSA is established with Gen Eisenhower as cmdr.

Eighth AF: 32 HBs attack M/Y, port area and industries in Emden, and a few strike at industries in Osnabruck. Bmrs are opposed for first time by twin-engine ftrs (Me 110's and Ju 88's).

Twelfth AF: B–17's hit Gabes A/F and a landing ground W of the town. Weather prevents completion of a MB mission against landing ground further SW. Ftrs escort bmrs and C–47's and fly rcn over battle area.

Tenth AF: 6 B–25's and 7 B–24's bomb Myitnge bridge S of Mandalay, damaging S approach. 3 other B–25's bomb Myitnge railroad shops.

Fifth AF: A–20's and B–25's bomb Lae A/F and harbor and nearby AA positions, and hit forces in Mubo,

Komiatum, Zaka, and Wau areas. Japanese forces begin retreating in disorder from Wau area toward Mubo. HBs hit A/Fs at Rabaul, Gasmata, and Cape Gloucester, score hits on vessel off Arawe, and attack small boats at Lorengau, sinking 1 boat.

Thirteenth AF: A single B-17 joins Navy aircraft in pounding Kahili A/F. Other Navy airplanes hit Munda A/F.

Eleventh AF: The weather rcn plane over Kiska, jumped by 3 ftrs, shoots 1 down. It is followed by 3 B-17's, 3 B-24's, 3 B-25's, 4 P-38's, and 8 P-40's. The B-24's blast North Head submarine base, and score near misses on cargo ship. The B-25's hit vicinity of Main Camp area. 3 of 5 floatplanes which intercept are shot down. The P-40's strafe Kiska ground installation and sight a ftr strip SW of Salmon Lagoon. 2 Amchitka ftr patrols are flown. The first also strafes gun emplacements on Vega Pt. 5 enemy bmrs strike Amchitka.

5 February

Twelfth AF: Bad weather cancels HB and MB missions. Ftrs fly rcn missions (strafing trucks near Jabal Ash Shamsi), local patrols, and escort for C-47's.

Tenth AF: 6 B-24's bomb railroad station area at Rangoon. P-40's bomb railway cut W of Meza, and having blocked the line, strafe a halted train. 6 B-25's attack Myitnge bridge but fail to knock out the tgt. P-40's hit T/Os in Kentung area.

Fifth AF: B-17's bomb Rabaul A/Fs while B-24's blast docks and shipping at Amboina. B-25's hit Dobo. A-20's continue to bomb and strafe forces around Zaka, Sappa,

Mubo, and Gona. HBs carry out individual attacks on shipping off Papua and New Britain and hit town of Rabaul and A/F at Gasmata.

6 February

Twelfth AF: XII BC cancels missions because of weather. P-40's and P-39's fly rcn and strafing mission between Sidi bou Zid and Sfax. Spitfires escort transport and evacuation missions.

Tenth AF: 16 ftrs follow Mali R to Hpunkizup where they destroy about 20 trucks loaded with bridge repair equipment and completely decimate the village. HBs attack bridge at Myitnge but fail to seriously damage the tgt.

Fifth AF: A-20's bomb and strafe forces along track from Mubo to Komiatum to Salamaua and hit the enemy in the Mambare R delta. B-25's hit A/F at Lae. A single B-24 hits cargo vessels off Finschhafen and Powell Pt, claiming 1 vessel destroyed, and attacks troop barges in Riebeck Bay, causing several casualties. Japanese aircraft attack Wau A/F; Allied ftrs (P-40's, P-39's, P-400's, and P-39's) effectively intercept the attacks during the late morning and midday hours, claiming 24 of the enemy shot down in air combat. No allied aircraft are shot down.

Eleventh AF: Weather rcn is flown over Kiska and Attu.

7 February

Twelfth AF: Over 50 B-17's and B-26's bomb Elmas A/F and seaplane base at Cagliari. P-38's provide escort. Ftrs and A-20's fly rcn over large areas of E Tunisia. Ftrs strafe gun batteries in Gafsa-Maknassy area.

Ninth AF: B–24's hit harbor at Naples, scoring direct hit on 1 vessel and hits on others.

Fifth AF: A single B–24 bombs Dobo and Babo, while another bombs Timika and Kaukenau.

Eleventh AF: 1 B–17 flies weather rcn over Kiska.

8 February

Twelfth AF: B–17's bomb docks and shipping at Sousse. B–26's and B–25's bomb Gabes A/F, also hitting nearby M/Y. 2 forces of A–20's attack vehicle and troop concentration E of Faid. Ftrs escort bmr missions, strafe Sened-Maknassy area and landing ground at Kebili, and fly routine rcn and patrols.

Ninth AF: B–24's attack ferry installations at Messina.

Tenth AF: 18 B–24's pound Rangoon M/Y, wrecking locomotive shops and destroying railroad station. 3 other HBs bomb runway at Mingaladon.

Fifth AF: A–20's pound Japanese forces in Mubo area. B–25's bomb Dobo town area. A single B–24 bombs Gasmata A/F.

Thirteenth AF: P–38's and Navy aircraft bomb Munda A/F.

Eleventh AF: Weather rcn is flown over Kiska, Agattu, and Attu. 5 B–24's and 5 B–25's bomb Kiska Camp area and hit water tank and bldgs. 2 B–25's bomb North Head through overcast. 4 P–38's and 1 B–25 patrol over Amchitka.

9 February

Twelfth AF: B–17's bomb Kairouan A/F. Ftrs strafe AA and machineguns and trucks in Faid Pass, buildings near Mezzouna, trucks in Station de Sened area, and fly escort and rcn missions.

Ninth AF: B–25's bomb A/Fs on Crete.

Fifth AF: B–24's bomb Kendari A/F. A–20's hit Malahang area.

Thirteenth AF: B–26's, P–38's, and P–39's pound A/F at Vila. Other P–38's join Navy aircraft in attacking Munda A/F. Organized Japanese resistance ends on Guadalcanal.

10 February

Atlantic: German sub, U–519, is sunk NW of Spain, 47–05N 18–34 W, by aircraft of 2d Antisub Sq.

Twelfth AF: B–25's attack shipping between Tunisia and Sicily, claiming 1 vessel sunk and another badly damaged. Weather cancels other bmr missions. P–39's and Spitfires of XII A Spt Cmd strafe gun batteries, machinegun nests, vehicles, and troops in Maknassy-Station de Sened-Bou Hamran area.

Ninth AF: B–24's sent to attack Palermo are forced to abort because of bad weather. They jettison bombs or return with them to base. 1 aircraft scores direct hits on Italian highway. Rainfall delays British Eighth Army assault on Mareth Line positions at Ben Gardane.

Tenth AF: 8 B–25's bomb rolling stock at Maymyo.

Thirteenth AF: P–38's and Navy aircraft attack Munda A/F.

Eleventh AF: The weather rcn aircraft aborts due to radio failure. 4 B–24's, 2 B–17's, 8 B–25's, and 8 P–38's attack Kiska. Hits are observed on landing strip and near hangar and buildings. 2 patrol missions, each by

4 P–38's and 1 B–25, are flown over Amchitka.

11 February

Twelfth AF: Bad weather cancels HB and MB missions. A–20's hit Station de Sened. Ftrs escort LBs and transports, and fly rcn and patrols.

Ninth AF: RAF Liberators, under IX BC, are sent against Heraklion A/F during 10/11 Feb. Severe weather causes them to abort near S coast of Crete.

Fifth AF: During predawn hours a B–17 carries out harassing strike over Rabaul.

Thirteenth AF: B–26's, P–38's, anl P–39's bomb A/Fs at Munda and Vila.

12 February

Twelfth AF: HB and MB missions are cancelled because of weather. A–20's attack gun installations W of Station de Sened. Ftrs escort A–20's and C–47's, and fly routine patrols.

Tenth AF: 7 B–24's pound Myitnge bridge area but fail to damage bridge itself. This strike marks first use of 2,000-lb blockbusters in the CBI. 12 other B–24's bomb Mahlwagon M/Y and railway station at Rangoon. 12 P–40's hit barracks near Lonkin.

Fifth AF: B–24's, operating individually, attack sawmill at Ubili, runway at Cape Gloucester, and harbor and A/F at Rabaul, and score possible hit on 6,000-ton vessel in Solomon Sea between New Britain and Bougainville.

Thirteenth AF: P–38's, along with Navy aircraft, attack Munda area, hitting AA at Rapa and setting fires at Kokengolo. B–26's and P–39's fol-

low with strike on the Munda A/F.

Eleventh AF: Weather rcn and attack missions on Kiska and a ftr patrol over Amchitka are broken off due to weather.

13 February

Twelfth AF: B–26's bomb El Aouina A/F. Ftrs escort MBs, strafe tanks near Station de Sened, and destroy several trucks and staff cars in the Faid area.

Ninth AF: B–24's bomb Naples area and Crotone A/F and city area under storm conditions. During late afternoon and early evening RAF Liberators hit Heraklion A/F. 1 HB hits Kastelli/Pediada A/F on return trip.

Tenth AF: 7 HBs from Gaya bomb Rangoon M/Y, scoring over 30 direct hits on the tgt. P–40's hit HQ at Lonkin, burning 12 barracks. 9 B–25's hit rolling stock in M/Y at Paukkan and along rail line from Shwebo to Sagaing.

Fifth AF: A–20's pound forces in and around Mubo while B–25's hit Lae area. A single B–24 bombs sawmill area at Ubili and a B–17 hits T/Os in Rabaul area.

Thirteenth AF: 6 B–24's, with light ftr cover from Guadalcanal, bomb Buin and shipping in nearby Shortland Is area. Ftr opposition is aggressive; 3 HBs, plus 3 ftrs, are shot down. This is the baptism of fire in the Solomons for the B–24's of 424th Bomb Sq, 307th Bomb Gp.

Eleventh AF: Weather rcn is flown over Kiska, Attu, Agattu, the Semichis, and Buldir I. 5 HBs, 6 MBs, and 10 P–38's bomb and strafe Kiska tgts including Camp area, landing strip, and shipping. Of 5 float-type ftrs which attack, P–38's shoot down 3. 4 P–38's and 1 B–25 fly patrol mission over Amchitka and Little Kiska. A B–25 shoots down a float-plane.

14 February

Twelfth AF: B–25's on shipping strike return with bombs when no vessels are sighted. Other MB and HB operations are cancelled by bad weather. Ftrs strafe vehicles and gun emplacements in El Guettar-Sened-Maknassy areas, and hit tanks and trucks near Sidi Saad. A–20's bomb tanks in Faid Pass, trucks near Maknassy and SW of Faid, town of Maknassy, and railroad yards at Station de Sened. Enemy ground forces (armd and inf) begin drive, supported by arty and dive bmrs, against Allied forces E of Sidi bou Zid.

USSR: Soviet Army takes Rostov, key comm center for German forces.

Tenth AF: MBs unsuccessfully attack bridge at Myitnge. 14 FBs hit town area of Maingkwan and barracks to the SW.

Fifth AF: B–17's and B–24's administer a thorough pounding to the Rabaul area, and also bomb Kokopo area, Watom I, vessels off Kokopo and off Cape Nelson. Individual B–24's attack Madang area and hit saw-mill at Ubili. B–25's bomb A/F at Lae.

Thirteenth AF: 9 B–24's, with light ftr protection, again attack Buin. Japanese ftrs again put up rugged opposition and shoot down 2 B–24's. As a result of the loss of 5 HBs in 15 sorties in 2 days, all daylight bombing missions in N Solomons are halted till adequate ftr protection can

be furnished. P–39's and Navy aircraft bomb and strafe Munda A/F and hit AA position and other tgts at Munda Pt. P–38's and Navy aircraft report hits on small vessel near Kahili and claim 11 shot down. 8 more Allied airplanes are lost.

Eleventh AF: Weather rcn airplane turns back due to weather, as does morning patrol of 1 B–25 and 4 P–38's flying over Amchitka. Other missions from Adak are also called off. 7 enemy float-type planes bomb and strafe Constantine Harbor area without effect.

15 February

Eighth AF: 21 HBs strike shipping at Dunkirk.

Twelfth AF: B–17's hit harbor and shipping at Palermo, while B–25's and B–26's attack Kairouan A/F. Ftrs spt Allied ground forces being pushed back from Faid-Sidi bou Zid area to position at Sbeitla, Kasserine, and Feriana. Enemy troops, vehicles, gun positions, and tanks are repeatedly attacked. Ftrs hit similar tgts in Gafsa-Bou Hamran area.

Ninth AF: DATF is established with Gen Strickland as CG. Whereas Desert Air Task Force HQ, organized 22 Oct 42, controlled USAMEAF tac operations in the Western Desert, this new organization, with HQ at Tripoli, supervises, operationally and administratively, all of Ninth AF W of, and including, Marble Arch. In addition the CG is cmdr of all US troops in the area. Col Hugo P Rush succeeds Gen Timberlake as CO of IX BC, which begins functioning from its new station at Bengasi. B–24's attack harbor at Naples, scoring direct hits on 2 vessels. British Army ground forces resume operations toward Mareth Line as weather improves.

Tenth AF: For second consecutive day HB strikes against bridge at Myitnge cause little damage.

Fifth AF: B–17's again bomb town of Rabaul and hit area nearby W of Simpson Harbor. A single HB attacks Rapopo A/F. B–24's pound shipping and town area at Amboina. B–25's attack town and A/F of Dili and pound supply dumps at Malahang. B–24's operating singly bomb runway at Finschhafen, and claim direct hit on vessel in Stettin Bay.

Thirteenth AF: B–26's, P–39's, and P–40's attack Vila A/F. B–24's, hindered by effective AA fire, bomb A/Fs at Kahili and on Ballale I. 2 B–24's are lost.

Eleventh AF: Weather rcn B–24 is soon called off due to weather. All other missions cancelled. 6 float-type enemy aircraft bomb and strafe Amchitka, hitting runway and inflicting casualties.

16 February

Eighth AF: 65 HBs hit locks and U-boat base at Saint-Nazaire. Unsuccessful air-to-air bombing attempt is made by German ftrs. 8 aircraft are lost during mission.

Twelfth AF: B–25's on shipping strike abort due to weather. Other XII BC operations are cancelled. A–20's, in spt of hard-pressed Allied ground forces, bomb gun positions W of Sidi bou Zid. Ftrs fly repeated strafing missions against troops and vehicles in Gafsa area.

Ninth AF: During 16/17 Feb, RAF Liberators, under IX BC, bomb Heraklion A/F. British Eighth Army's 7th Armd Div drives into

Ben Gardane, outpost of Mareth Line.

USSR: Soviet Army takes Kharkov, stronghold of German line in S Russia since Oct 41.

Tenth AF: 18 P–40's hit T/Os in Nsopzup and Hpunkizup areas.

Fifth AF: B–25's bomb Malahang A/F and strafe T/Os on Salamaua peninsula. B–17's bomb warehouse at Ubili.

SOPAC: Adm Mason becomes CO MAIRSOLS with cmd of all aircraft in the Solomons.

Eleventh AF: Weather rcn airplane flies over Kiska, Attu, Agattu, the Semichis, and Buldir. 5 HBs, 6 MBs, 6 P–38's, and 1 MB photo airplane take off for Kiska but do not attack due to weather. 1 P–40, accompanying several P–38's on Amchitka ftr patrol, lands on Amchitka strip. An afternoon patrol of 7 P–40's and 1 transport aircraft also land at the strip which is now safe for limited operations.

17 February

Twelfth AF: Twelfth AF and other organizations of Allied AF are transferred to NAAF which supplants Allied AF. NAAF, in turn, becomes part of MAC, a new air cmd which comes into existence on this date with ACM Tedder as cmdr. MAC also includes Middle East Air Cmd (later RAF, Middle East) and Malta Air Cmd (later RAF, Malta). NAAF CG is Gen Spaatz. Over 40 B–17's bomb Elmas A/F. B–25's and B–26's hit Sardinian A/Fs of Villacidro and Decimomannu. Ftrs escort bmrs and spt ground forces in Sbeitla-Kasserine-Feriana area. The ftrs, along with A–20's, attack and destroy numerous tanks, trucks, and other vehicles moving against hard-pressed British First Army forces.

Fifth AF: B–24's operating individually, strike Gasmata A/F and Pondo Harbor, Babo, and sawmill at Ubili.

Thirteenth AF: P–39's join Navy ftrs and dive bmrs in strike against Munda A/F. Single B–24's bomb Nusave I, and A/Fs on Ballale I and at Kahili.

Eleventh AF: Weather cancels all missions and also laying of mat at Amchitka airstrip.

18 February

NAAF: HQ NAAF is set up (under Gen Spaatz) and 6 principal subordinate cmds are specified: NAT AF, NASAF, NACAF, NATC, NAASC, and NW African Photo Rcn Wg.

Twelfth AF: Weather cancels bmr missions. Ftrs provide direct spt for British First Army in Sbeitla-Kasserine-Feriana areas.

Fifth AF: B–25's bomb Barar area and unsuccessfully attack shipping off Dili. Individual B–24's bomb Finschhafen landing ground and Madang area, and unsuccessfully attack shipping off Cape Gloucester and Cape Orford.

Thirteenth AF: B–24's pound A/F at Munda. B–17's attack Kahili area and shipping nearby.

Eleventh AF: Weather rcn B–24 determines 3 ships at Attu to be friendly. P–40's on local patrol over Amchitka encounter and shoot down 2 ftrs.

19 February

Twelfth AF: Weather prevents bmr operations. Ftrs and LBs of XII A Spt Cmd are grounded and unable to spt ground forces as enemy opens attack on Kasserine with inf and tanks supported by arty.

Ninth AF: B–25's bomb Gabes W area through heavy clouds.

Tenth AF: Ftrs dive-bomb a Japanese HQ at Hpunkizup and afterwards strafe rail defile S of Meza, burying about 100 ft of track. 5 B–25's bomb rail terminal at Sagaing.

Fifth AF: B–17's bomb shipping and seaplane base between Buin and Faisi and at Ballale I, and hit Kahili A/F. A–20's bomb and strafe forces in Butibum and Angari areas. B–24's carry out single-plane attacks against shipping at Salamaua, off Cape Gloucester, and at Gasmata.

Eleventh AF: Weather cancels all missions except limited weather rcn.

20 February

Twelfth AF: Weather again severely limits operations. A handful of P–39's strafe trucks and half-tracks in Kasserine area as enemy breaks through Kasserine Pass and thrusts N and W toward Thala and Tebessa.

Ninth AF: During 19/20 Feb, RAF Liberators bomb Heraklion and Kastelli/Pediada A/F. B–24's bomb Crotone, Naples, Amantea, Palmi, Nicotera, and Rosarno.

Tenth AF: 17 P–40's bomb factory, oil tanks, and railroad tracks at Sahmaw. 13 B–24's attack Gokteik Viaduct but fail to damage the structure.

Fifth AF: B–17's bomb landing

strips at Kahili and at Ballale I, and Gasmata A/F.

Thirteenth AF: B–17's and Navy PBY's bomb Ballale I and Kahili. B–24's pound Vila. During 19/20 Feb and day strikes, P–39's and Navy airplanes attack Munda area, hitting A/F and nearby Lambeti and Munda Pt.

Seventh AF: 3 B–24's, from Canton I, photograph Makin, Abaiang, and Tarawa, and attack shipping at Tarawa.

Eleventh AF: Rcn over Kiska finds weather favorable. Therefore 5 B–24's, 7 B–25's and 8 P–38's take off. The ftrs blast Main Camp area. The bmrs bomb North Head, Camp area, and runway.

21 February

NAAF: WDAF passes under operational control of NATAF; AAF gps of WDAF remain under administrative control of Ninth AF. B–25's hit Gafsa railroad yards. Weather foils 3 attempts by P–39's and Spitfires to furnish spt to ground forces battling enemy drive N and W of Kasserine Pass. Only 2 P–39's are able to reach the enemy and strafe tanks and trucks.

Ninth AF: 93d Bomb Gp is relieved from duty with Ninth AF in the ME for return to duty with Eighth AF in UK.

Fifth AF: B–24's bomb harbor and shipping at Amboina. A–20's bomb and strafe several occupied villages and tracks throughout Mubo-Komiatum-Salamaua region.

Thirteenth AF: Thirteenth AF ftrs and others (USN, USMC, and RN ZAF) from Guadalcanal provide air spt as 43d Div lands in Russell Is to

begin the long push up the Solomons toward Rabaul. SWPA forces had aided by bombing A/Fs in Buin, Kahili, and Ballale areas preceding the invasion (see Fifth AF, 19 and 20 Feb).

Eleventh AF: Weather prevents all flying from Adak. Amchitka-based ftrs patrol Kiska.

22 February

NAAF: A–20's and ftrs, flying close spt to ground forces, aid in repulsing FM Rommel's drive toward Thala and Tebessa. At 1915 the enemy begins general withdrawal toward Kasserine. B–17's bomb Kasserine Pass while B–25's hit nearby bridge. Escorting P–38's strafe retreating troops. Other B–25's hit Gafsa railway yards.

Tenth AF: During 22/23 Feb, 10 B–24's mine Gulf of Martaban between Pagoda Pt and mouth of Rangoon R. 24 US and RAF Liberators fly diversionary strike against city of Rangoon and Mingaladon A/F.

Fifth AF: B–25's pound Lae area while to the S A–20's hit forces at Buibuining, Waipali, Guadagasal, and along trails in the surrounding areas. A single B–17 bombs Lae, and a B–24 hits Lorengau A/F.

Thirteenth AF: P–38's, P–39's, and Navy aircraft hit Rekata Bay area and barges in Sambi Bay.

Eleventh AF: 16 bmrs and 8 ftrs abort Kiska attack mission due to weather.

23 February

NAAF: B–25's attack shipping N of Cap Bon, claiming 1 vessel sunk. B–17's bomb Kairouan A/F and hit troops retreating through Kasserine Pass. B–25's and B–26's hit Kasserine

Pass and bridge nearby. A–20's and ftrs also attack retreating columns in Kasserine area.

Ninth AF: B–24's attack Messina ferry slip, scoring several direct hits and leaving tgt area burning. During the late evening B–25's hit Arram in the Mareth Line.

Tenth AF: 46 Japanese bmrs and ftrs are intercepted over Chabua A/F by P–40's. In running battle the P–40's claim at least 14 planes shot down. 8 P–40's knock out railroad bridge W of Myitkyina. Several HBs attack bridge at Myitnge; the strike fails to damage the structure itself but batters the S approach.

Fifth AF: A–20's continue to pound occupied villages and trails in Buibuining-Waipali and Guadagasal-Mubo areas. B–25's bomb and strafe Angari and Yangla. B–17's bomb town and harbor area of Rabaul.

Eleventh AF: Over Kiska 17 bmrs and 8 ftrs bomb Main Camp area while an F–5A flies a photo mission.

24 February

Eighth AF: Gen Eaker, CG, is advised by WD of CCS decision to employ his ftr units primarily in an offensive role in spt of bmrs.

NAAF: B–17's bomb Kairouan A/F. B–25's sink several barges NE of Cap Bon. B–26's and B–17's bomb enemy columns in Kasserine Pass and hit town of Kasserine, while B–25's attack highway traffic near Sbeitla. A–20's and ftrs hit motor transport in wide area around Kasserine and Sbeitla.

Tenth AF: P–40's knock out S span of railroad bridge NE of Pinbaw.

Fifth AF: A–20's continue to at-

tack forces at Guadagasal Saddle, Waipali, trails from Waipali to Guadagasal Saddle and Mubo, and in area of Waria R mouth. B–25's pound Lae, Angari, Yangla, Malahang landing strip, and smaller villages in the area. B–17's again hit shipping at Rabaul. B–24's continue single-plane harassing strikes on shipping and A/Fs in coastal areas of Portuguese and NE New Guinea and in Solomon Sea off Cape Saint George.

Thirteenth AF: B–24's bomb Kahili and Faisi.

Eleventh AF: All except one mission of 4 P–40's, to Kiska, are called off. The P–40's make no contacts, however.

25 February

RAF: RAF starts round-the-clock operations against the enemy from UK.

NAAF: B–17's bomb El Aouina A/F. Ftrs and A–20's hit troops and military traffic in Thala-Kasserine-Sbeitla areas and along Gafsa-Feriana road. Other ftrs carry out widespread rcn and patrol missions. British First Army and US troops of II Corps occupy Kasserine Pass.

Ninth AF: During 24/25 Feb, B–24's bomb Naples harbor and Crotone. B–25's attack motor transport on Arram road.

Tenth AF: Ftrs from Dinjan dive-bomb bridge 10 mi W of Myitkyina. A single span is knocked out and another damaged. HBs again fail to damage Myitnge bridge. More than 40 Japanese airplanes attack Dinjan A/F; 32 intercepting P–40's claim at least 9 aircraft shot down.

Fifth AF: A–20's again bomb and strafe forces at Guadagasal Saddle and vicinity. HBs continue to attack shipping, A/F, and town area at Rabaul. Gasmata A/F is also bombed.

Thirteenth AF: P–38's, P–40's, and F4U's sweep Kahili area.

Eleventh AF: 4 P–40's sweep Kiska. 6 B–24's and 5 B–25's bomb Main Camp and North Head areas.

26 February

Eighth AF: 65 HBs bomb U-boat yards and naval base at Wilhelmshaven. Docks and surrounding areas are also hit. This mission is originally intended for Bremen but strikes Wilhelmshaven because primary tgt is obscured by clouds. Germans attempt air-to-air bombing by ftr aircraft and use of parachute-bombs fired by arty.

Twelfth AF: Gen Doolittle assumes cmd of XII BC.

NAAF: B–17's, with P–38 escort, attack docks and shipping at Bizerte after Wellingtons hit same tgt the previous night. Ftrs hit trucks in Pichon-Ousseltia area and fly numerous rcn missions. Von Arnim's 5th Panzer Army opens offensive on broad front toward Bedja and Medjez el Bab.

Ninth AF: Gen Montgomery sets 20 Mar as D-Day for attack on Mareth Line. P–40's carry out FB missions as ground forces maintain pressure on enemy along coast and on Gabes road. B–25's attack roads and motor transport in Arram area during 26/27 Feb.

Tenth AF: Dinjan-based P–40's hit bridge NE of Pinbaw, destroying a span and damaging other parts of the bridge.

Fifth AF: A–20's hit Buibuining-Waipali area while a single B–17

bombs A/Fs at Lae and Salamaua. B–17's and B–24's bomb A/F at Gasmata, other B–17's attack shipping and A/F at Wewak and a single B–17 attacks shipping in Hixon and Open Bays.

Thirteenth AF: P–38's and Navy aircraft hit Vila during 25/26 Feb.

27 February

Eighth AF: 60 HBs strike U-boat pens, port, and naval facilities at Brest.

NAAF: B–17's bomb Cagliari area and ships N of Capo d'Orlando. Wellingtons hit Bizerte. Ftrs fly sweeps and rcn, attacking ground forces at points along battleline, including Medjez el Bab area where enemy adv is being halted.

Ninth AF: P–40's fly top cover, strafing, and FB missions against positions along Mareth Line.

Tenth AF: 24 P–40's bomb and strafe Waingmaw. Direct hits are scored on warehouse and fuel and ammo dump.

Fifth AF: B–25's hit Japanese-occupied villages in Labu area. B–17's, operating individually, strafe schooner off Matiu Pt and bomb Finschhafen A/F.

Thirteenth AF: P–40's and P–38's join Navy airplanes in attack on small vessels off Vella Lavella I. Hits are claimed on 2 vessels.

Eleventh AF: 6 B–24's, 6 B–25's, and 4 P–38's bomb and strafe Main Camp area. On return trip, weather airplane flies rcn and makes bombing and strafing run on Attu and nearby barges with negative results.

28 February

NAAF: Ftrs and FBs hit troops,

tanks, and motor transport along Tunisian battleline SW of Mateur, at Sidi Nsir near Pont-du-Fahs, NE of Bedja, and in Goubellat area.

Tenth AF: P–40's from Dinjan knock out bridge near Kazu and bomb and strafe Nsopzup. 6 B–25's from Kunming, with ftr escort, bomb storage area at Mangshih. 8 B–25's from Ondal hit Thazi railroad junction.

Fifth AF: A lone B–17 bombs Lae A/F.

Thirteenth AF: P–38's and Navy aircraft attack Vila A/F. B–24's bomb Kahili A/F and hit Ballale I.

Eleventh AF: Rcn is flown over Kiska, Buldir, Semichis, Attu, and Agattu, with negative results. 6 B–24's and 6 B–25's bomb Main Camp area.

1 March

NAAF: Gen Cannon takes cmd of NATC. B–17's bomb docks and shipping, also hit railroad yards and town area, at Cagliari. B–25's and B–26's of NASAF attack bridges and AA gun positions in La Hencha area. Other B–26's attack freighter NE of Bizerte. Ftrs escort bmrs and hit ground forces in battle areas around Sidi Nsir and Bedja. B–25's of NA TAF bomb Mateur area.

Twelfth AF: Gen Spaatz assumes cmd of Twelfth AF in Algeria. Col Lawrence P Hickey becomes acting cmdr of XII FC until arrival of Gen Quesada.

Ninth AF: B–24's raid harbor at Naples; 1 bombs Soverato while 2 others hit Staletti and Catanzaro as T/Os. AA fire is accurate and several HBs are hit over Naples and Palmi.

Tenth AF: 46 P–40's hit T/Os in

Nsopzup area and throughout Hukawng Valley.

Fifth AF: A–20's bomb and strafe forces at Guadagasal and along trails throughout Mubo, Komiatum, and Salamaua area. B–17's bomb runway at Gasmata. B–24's carry out single-plane attacks on shipping off Soemba and Soembawa, and in Solomon Sea.

Eleventh AF: P–40's jettison their bombs when bad weather prevents a sweep over Kiska.

2 March

NAAF: NASAF B–17's bomb shipping and harbor area at Palermo. B–26's attack bridges and flak positions at La Hencha. NATAF ftrs hit troops, tanks, and motor transport S of Mateur and NE of Bedja as enemy renews attack along Mateur-Taberka road near Jefna.

Tenth AF: More than 20 B–24's pound tgts in Burma. 7 splinter part of Ahlone docks and destroy a nearby warehouse, 6 hit Mahlwagon roundhouse, and 9 attack bridge at Pazundaung, tearing up its S approach. 6 B–25's, with P–40 escort, hit camp and storage area at Lamaing while 24 B–25's, also with ftr escort, pound Myitkyina.

Fifth AF: Battle of the Bismarck Sea begins. B–17's and B–24's attack convoy of 8 transports and 8 destroyers as it proceeds from Rabaul towards Huon Gulf. The HBs first hit the convoy N of New Britain. The last air strike of the day takes place WNW of Umboi I between New Guinea and New Britain. By the end of the day, half of the transports are sunk or sinking.

Thirteenth AF: P–40's, P–38's,

and a single PB4Y fly photo rcn over Munda A/F.

3 March

NAAF: B–17's bomb docks and shipping at Tunis and shipping and power plant at La Goulette harbor. Ftrs and MBs of NATAF hit ground forces in areas around Bedja, Bou Arada, and Mateur. Fighting around Bedja subsides but enemy forces take Sedjenane.

Ninth AF: B–24's dispatched against Naples fail to reach primary tgt. Several bomb secondary tgt, Messina, while 3 bomb bridges at Bianco and Siderno Marina. P–40's fly FB missions along Mareth Line as probing attack against British 51st Div positions near Mareth is driven back. German *Afrika Korps* issues plan for counterattack from Mareth Line.

Tenth AF: 13 B–24's bomb Mahlwagon M/Y and dock area at Rangoon. 9 others attack Pazundaung railroad bridge but fail to knock it out. 6 B–25's bomb railroad sheds at Maymyo.

Fifth AF: Battle of Bismarck Sea continues as HBs are joined by MBs, LBs, and ftr aircraft (US and Australian) in pounding convoy as it moves into Huon Gulf. PT boats of US Seventh Fleet also close with the enemy. By the end of the day all 8 transports have been sunk and Allied aircraft have destroyed 4 of the 8 destroyers and a large number of ftr aircraft covering the convoy.

Eleventh AF: 4 P–40's sweep Kiska dropping demolition and fragmentation bombs. Adm Kinkaid, CO Alaska Def Cmd tables Kiska invasion

plan and substitutes an Attu invasion plan.

4 March

Eighth AF: 42 HBs fly missions over Germany and the Netherlands, 28 hitting the shipyards at Rotterdam and 16 attacking Hamm M/Y. This is first Eighth AF attack on a Ruhr industrial tgt.

NAAF: B–25's and B–26's fly unsuccessful missions against shipping between Tunisia and Sicily. B–17's attack convoy NW of Bizerte, claiming 4 vessels sunk.

Ninth AF: P–40's fly top cover mission as British Eighth Army completes concentration of troops and weapons in forward areas and awaits attack which seems imminent in view of troop movement in mts W of Medenine.

Tenth AF: 3 B–25's bomb railroad facilities at Ywataung.

Fifth AF: Allied aircraft continue to bombard remnants of Japanese convoy in Huon Gulf, thus ending Battle of Bismarck Sea, a decisive Allied victory. Fifth AF and RAAF aircraft sink 12 vessels in 3 days. This is last enemy attempt to use large vessels to reinforce positions on Huon Gulf. After World War II Gen MacArthur calls this the decisive aerial engagement in his theater. A–20's hit Lae A/F and vicinity, B–17's attack Ubili and power launches off Lae and Cape Gloucester, and several B–25's and single B–17's and B–24's hit harbor and A/F at Lae and barges off Finschhafen.

Thirteenth AF: B–24's hit A/F on Ballale I and bomb Kahili.

Eleventh AF: 4 P–40's fly over

Kiska but drop no bombs due to weather.

5 March

NAAF: NASAF B–17's hit convoys NW of Bizerte while B–26's attack motor vessels between Tunisia and Sicily. NATAF ftrs and MBs hit Djedeida, Sidi Nsir area, and ground forces in Bedja-Mateur areas.

Ninth AF: RAF Liberators, under IX BC, bomb harbor at Naples during 4/5 Mar.

Fifth AF: A–20's pound Lae A/F while HBs, operating individually, hit Lae, Alexishafen, Gasmata, and Saumlakki.

Eleventh AF: 1 B–24 flies negative weather rcn over Kiska, Semichis, Attu, Agattu, and Buldir.

6 March

Eighth AF: 63 HBs strike power plant, bridge, and port area at Lorient. 15 B–24's make diversionary attack on bridge and U-boat facilities at Brest.

NAAF: Weather cancels NASAF bmr missions. Ftrs fly rcn along battle line in Tunisia.

Ninth AF: 35 planes strafe and bomb installations in the Mareth Line as Rommel's expected attack in Tunisia takes place and is defeated. 4 thrusts toward Medenine are repulsed by British, and enemy retreats after nightfall, having lost about 50 tanks.

Tenth AF: 4 B–24's over Burma bomb shipping near Pagoda Pt, scoring near misses. On return flight, they strafe lighthouse on Alguada Reef, a lightship off China Park, and a radio station at Diamond I. 3 B–24's intending to bomb Pazundaung bridge fail to reach tgt. 1

manages to bomb A/F at Pagoda Pt. The others return to base without bombing. 6 B–24's unsuccessfully attack Myitnge bridge.

Fifth AF: A–20's hit Guadagasal area. Single B–24's attack shipping off Manus and off Talasea, and hit A/F at Gasmata.

Thirteenth AF: B–24's bomb Kahili and Ballale I A/Fs.

Eleventh AF: 1 B–24 flies uneventful rcn over Kiska, Attu, Agattu, Buldir, and the Semichis.

7 March

NAAF: B–25's hit shipping between Tunisia and Sicily while B–17's bomb convoy in Gulf of Tunis and shipping and M/Y at Sousse.

Tenth AF: 12 B–25's attack Gokteik Viaduct, causing only minor damage.

Fifth AF: A–20's attack Guadagasal area and barges offshore. B–25's bomb Toeal. Single B–24's attack ship NW of Madang and bomb Salamaua, Gasmata, and Cape Gloucester.

Thirteenth AF: Single B–24's hit A/Fs at Vila and Kahili. 3 HBs bomb Munda A/F.

Eleventh AF: 343d Ftr Gp moves to Adak, and the first flight of MBs is brought up to Amchitka. This enables stepped-up raids on Kiska. 8 B–24's and 4 P–38's bomb and strafe Chichagof Harbor area and Holtz Bay installations. A ftr sweep, 6 B–24's, and 10 B–25's hit North Head and Main Camp area.

8 March

AAF: Committee of Operations Analysts, composed of military and civilian members, submits to Gen Arnold a report attempting to set forth industrial objectives, the destruction of which would weaken Germany most decisively in the shortest time. This report, which lists German aircraft industry as first priority, is basis for much of CBO plan.

Eighth AF: 54 HBs hit Rennes M/Y while 13 strike M/Y at Rouen. Bomb run over Rouen is considerably disrupted by well-executed attack of ftrs which down 2 bmrs including lead aircraft. This action is preceded by an earlier wave of German ftrs which occupy the ftr escort while the second wave attacks the bmrs.

NAAF: NASAF B-17's and B-25's attack shipping between Tunisia and Sicily, claiming destruction or heavy damage of several motor vessels. Other B-17's hit shipping and M/Y at Sousse. P-38's escort the bomb missions. Ftrs of NATAF fly several rcn and patrol missions along Tunisian First Army (British) battle-front while WDAF P-40's and Spitfires hit rear of columns attacking Medenine from the W.

Tenth AF: 12 B-25's strike at Myitnge bridge and AA positions. Results are poor. 4 B-24's bomb Bassein docks. P-40's hit military tgs near Pebu and Wan-hat.

Fifth AF: HBs, operating individually, hit occupied areas in SE coastal region of NW New Guinea and also strike at Saumlakki and Babo.

Thirteenth AF: A/Fs at Munda and Vila are again hit by light B-24 raids.

9 March

NAAF: Bad weather cancels NASAF operations and restricts other cmds to rcn, patrol, and transport missions.

Tenth AF: P-40's hit town area and bridge at Mogaung. Many fires are started and the bridge is severely damaged.

Thirteenth AF: 3 B-24's bomb A/Fs at Munda, Kahili, and Ballale I.

Eleventh AF: 6 B-24's, 10 B-25's, 12 P-38's and 4 P-40's attack Kiska. The P-40's and 6 of the MBs return to base due to bad weather; the other bmrs bomb Main Camp area, North Head and submarine base.

10 March

Eighth AF: A few P-47's take part for first time in ftr sweep from UK. Aircraft-to-aircraft communication proves impossible because of VHF radio malfunctions.

NAAF: B-17's bomb El Aouina A/F and La Marsa landing ground, destroying several parked airplanes, and hit town of Gafsa. Ftrs escort the B-17's and carry out numerous rcn missions.

Ninth AF: Flight echelon of 340th Bomb Gp (M) begins arriving in Egypt.

Tenth AF: HBs strike Rangoon area at 2 points. 5 B-24's hit Pazundaung bridge. 4 others pound runways, buildings, and revetments at Mingaladon A/F. After the attack, several ftrs attack the flight. The HBs claim 3 shot down. CATF is absorbed by Fourteenth AF.

Fourteenth AF: Fourteenth AF is activated at Kunming with Gen Chennault as CG. P-40's from Kunming fly armed rcn into Burma, crossing the Salween and covering areas SW of Lashio.

Fifth AF: B–17's bomb A/F and shipping at Wewak. Single HBs attack shipping off New Guinea.

Eleventh AF: Rcn airplane is attacked by 5 aircraft. Kiska attack mission is flown by 10 B–25's, 6 B–24's, 12 P–38's (4 of them flying top cover), and 1 F–5A. 8 of the P–38's strafe ground installations. The B–25's bomb radar site and pound North Head, silencing AA fire. The B–24's hit Main Camp area. 4 Amchitka-based P–40's bomb submarine base.

11 March

NAAF: B–26's attack convoy between Tunisia and Sicily. B–25's in the area carry out no attacks on vessels. Ftrs escort MBs and attack guns, vehicles, and tanks in Sedjenane, Jefna, and Bedja areas.

Tenth AF: 7 B–25's bomb Myitnge bridge, causing little damage.

Fifth AF: A–20's bomb and strafe Vickers Ridge and Guadagasal area. B–24's bomb A/F at Rabaul. Single HBs attack Finschhafen, Cape Gloucester, and shipping off Powell Pt.

12 March

Eighth AF: 63 HBs strike Rouen-Sotteville M/Y. Good ftr escort is major factor in this no-loss mission.

NAAF: B–17's bomb docks and M/Ys at Sousse. B–26's pound supply dumps and score near misses on bridges at Enfidaville, while B–25's bomb shipping between Tunisia and Sicily. Ftrs escort the bmrs and carry out attacks on ground tgts, destroying several vehicles in Pichon area and S of Pont-du-Fahs. Wellingtons bomb Tunis docks during 12/13 Mar.

Tenth AF: 6 B–24's attack Pazun-

daung bridge, causing negligible damage.

Fifth AF: A–20's attack Guadagasal Gap area and Salamaua A/F. B–24's and B–25's attack shipping at Amboina and bomb Fuiloro. B–17's bomb Rabaul A/F while individual B–24's hit wreck off Talasea and bomb Cape Gloucester.

Thirteenth AF: A/Fs at Munda, Ballale I, and Kahili are again hit by light B–24 raids. P–38's destroy small vessel off NE coast of Rendova I.

Seventh AF: VII AFBC is redesignated VII AFSC.

Eleventh AF: 12 Amchitka-based P–40's scout Kiska.

13 March

Eighth AF: 74 HBs hit area around Amiens and Abbeville. Largest effort is aimed at Longeau railroad facilities and M/Y at Amiens. No aircraft are lost as ftr protection is excellent.

NAAF: B–25's are sent against shipping NE of Bizerte but fail to locate tgt. Ftrs hit positions and movement in Mareth Line area, and fly patrols and rcn.

Ninth AF: Gen Brereton, CG, directs that HQ, DATF be redesignated Adv HQ, Ninth AF, and that the AAF tac units with the HQ be designated DATF. B–24's bomb Naples harbor through heavy clouds. P–40's fly top cover and ftr sweep, and engage about 25 ftrs in combat, claiming 3 destroyed but also losing 3.

Tenth AF: 4 B–24's attack and slightly damage Pazundaung bridge.

Fifth AF: B–17's bomb A/F and shipping at Wewak. A B–17 bombs Gasmata A/F and warehouses on

Wide Bay, while a B–24 attacks shipping off Netherlands New Guinea.

Thirteenth AF: Vila and Munda A/Fs are again attacked by B–24's in light raids. Also bombed is Faisi I.

Eleventh AF: A B–24 on rcn returns early because of adverse weather. 12 P–40's strike Kiska beach, camp and runway. Hits are observed on these tgts and among 14 parked airplanes. 8 P–38's with 8 P–40's flying top cover again take off for Kiska. Only 3 of the P–38's reach the tgt and strafe aircraft on beach. Another sights a submarine SW of Rat I.

14 March

NAAF: Weather cancels all missions except NATAF ftr rcn in Enfidaville-Sfax area and between Tunisia and Sicily.

Ninth AF: During 13/14 Mar, RAF Liberators under IX BC control hit harbor at Naples. During the day, ftrs fly cover and sweep over battle area.

Tenth AF: 4 B–24's bomb Moulmein docks. 8 B–25's hit the oft-bombed Gokteik Viaduct but the structure remains serviceable.

Fifth AF: B–17's and B–24's bomb Wewak, Tring, and Madang. Single B–17's bomb Gasmata, and strafe vessel off Talasea, AA position at Cape Gloucester, and Finschhafen A/F. A lone B–24 bombs Dili.

15 March

NAAF: NASAF B–26's, with ftr escort, attack landing ground at Mezzouna. B–25's follow with attack on same tgt. B–17's, with ftr escort, hit shipping off N Tunisia. Ftrs of NA

TAF fly tac rcn over battle area as British 18 Army Gp's II Corps (US) prepares to attack E from Gafsa area. Gen Dunton is designated CG of NW African Air Service Cmd (NA ASC), to which are assigned HQ and HQ Sq, XII AFSC; all serv gps, depot gps, arms and serv units of XII AF SC, all maintenance, aircraft repair, aircraft assembly, embarkation, and mobile parachute servicing units, and base depots formerly assigned to EAC (RAF) and numerous RAF personnel.

Ninth AF: B–25's, escorted by P–40's of 79th Gp (the gp's first operation in the theater) bomb Zarat. Ftrs also fly strafing and bombing raids against ground tgts.

Tenth AF: 8 B–25's bomb Gokteik Viaduct and 8 others attack Myitnge. Neither tgt suffers effective damage. 8 FBs damage bridge at Kadrangyang.

Fifth AF: B–25's and B–24's, along with RAAF airplanes, bomb shipping at Dobo and Wokam. B–17's, on single-plane flights bomb Gasmata and Cape Gloucester.

Thirteenth AF: Single B–17's hit Munda and Vila A/Fs. P–38's strafe A/F at Viru.

Eleventh AF: 6 B–25's, with 4 P–38's flying top cover, bomb North Head, hitting Main Camp and gun emplacements. 6 B–24's with 4 P–38's for top cover then bomb Main Camp. Revetments and hangar area are strafed by the P–38's one of which is lost to AA. Next, 5 B–24's and 16 P–38's bomb and strafe Main Camp area and North Head. 4 P–40's then unsuccessfully search for 3 enemy ftrs which had earlier attacked weather airplane. Main Camp is hit two more times, by 3 B–25's and by 8 P–38's.

16 March

NAAF: B–17's attack shipping between Tunisia and Sicily, leaving 2 small vessels aflame. Weather prevents completion of other bmr operations. Ftrs fly rcn and patrols but bad weather hides enemy ground activity.

Ninth AF: 1st Prov Trg Unit is established to train repl crews for MB and ftr gps. Personnel is drawn from HQ Sqs of IX FC, 9th Ftr Wg, and 8th Ftr Wg. P–40's fly FB operations against enemy positions as British ground forces prepare to conduct limited attacks as a preliminary to main assault against Mareth Line.

Tenth AF: 6 B–24's damage approaches to Pazundaung bridge. 8 B–25's attack Myitnge bridge, scoring at least 2 hits, but the structure remains intact. P–40's hit positions N of Sumprabum.

Fourteenth AF: P–40's strafe Mong Yaw storage area and docks, warehouse area, and rail-river terminal (for phosphate mines) at Lao Kay.

Fifth AF: B–25's bomb Lae. B–17's bomb Rapopo airstrip and attack Ubili, sub off Cape Turner, town of Marienberg, and Cape Gloucester area. B–24's unsuccessfully attack cargo ships between Bitsjaroe Bay and Fak Fak.

Thirteenth AF: B–17's and B–24's on harassing raids bomb Kahili, Vila, and Ballale A/Fs.

Eleventh AF: 16 B–25's, 13 B–24's, 8 P–40's and 32 P–38's (cover/escort) sorties are flown to Kiska in one weather rcn and 2 attack missions from Adak, and in 3 more missions from Amchitka. Tgts hit are North Head, Main Camp area, radar sites and submarine base. On last Amchitka mission 1 enemy floatplane is shot down with 2 more probables. 4 HBs are hit and 1 B–25 does not return.

17 March

NAAF: Weather cancels NASAF bmr operations. Tac ftrs and LBs fly numerous armed rcn missions and sweeps over Sedjenane, Cap Serrat, and Sidi Nsir area and attack ground forces E of Gafsa in preparation for allied assault. NACAF aircraft continue coastal and sea patrols. US II Corps opens offensive to the E from Gafsa area after air and arty preparation.

Ninth AF: P–40's fly scramble and FB operations as British ground forces continue local operations in preparation for assault on Mareth Line.

Tenth AF: 8 B–25's again attack bridge at Myitnge, damaging N approach. 14 P–40's hit bridges at Kadrangyang and NE of Myitkyina and motor pool at Hpunkizup. The motor pool suffers considerable damage.

Fifth AF: B–25's bomb Langgoer.

Thirteenth AF: B–17's continue harassing raids against Vila, Kahili, and Ballale.

Eleventh AF: 8 P–38's patrol Kiska without making contacts.

18 March

Eighth AF: 97 HBs strike submarine yards at Vegesack. 7 U-boat hulls appear severely damaged. This mission marks first successful combat use of automatic flight control linked with bombsights.

NAAF: Weather cancels operations of NASAF bmrs. NATAF ftrs fly sweeps and rcn over Sidi Nsir-Sedjenane-Medjez el Bab areas and attack railway station, other buildings, railroad sidings, and motor transport at Temara.

Ninth AF: B–24's, escorted by P–40's, bomb harbor at Naples.

Tenth AF: 16 P–40's bomb and strafe stronghold of Seniku, claiming high enemy casualty rate. 7 others attack Nalong. 16 B–24's bomb Pazundaung bridge, causing considerable damage to the structure. 8 B–25's damage the Myitnge bridge; 8 other B–25's hit AA positions in the Myitnge general area.

Fifth AF: B–24's pound town of Madang. Single B–17's strafe launch at Talasea and barges NE of Cape Gloucester, while a lone B–24 bombs Timoeka and Langgoer.

Eleventh AF: Taking off from Adak, 6 B–24's bomb Main Camp area, 6 B–25's bomb North Head, and 12 P–38's fly top cover and strafing attacks. 12 Amchitka-based P–38's then blast Kiska runway and Main Camp area, starting fires. At Amchitka, the 54th Ftr Sq is reinforced by several F–5A's.

19 March

NAAF: NAAF TCC (Prov), consisting of 51st TC Wg and its subordinate units which are transferred from XII AFSC, is activated. Col Ray A Dunn is acting CO. Landing grounds are non-operational due to continued bad weather. NASAF and NATAF cancel missions. NACAF airplanes fly routine patrols.

Ninth AF: Col Uzal G Ent assumes cmd of IX BC, replacing Col Hugo P Rush.

Tenth AF: 8 B–25's pound bridge at Myitnge, rendering it unserviceable. A single P–40 uses a 1,000-lb bomb against bridge near Mogaung in a test to see if the ftr can carry such "blockbusters" and deliver them effectively. Despite negligible damage suffered by the tgt, both the carrying and releasing of the bomb are considered successful. 12 B–25's, with P–40 escort, bomb rail and river terminal at Lao Kay and afterwards strafe the area, causing widespread destruction.

Fourteenth AF: 12 B–25's, with escort of 6 P–40's, bomb power plant and railroad yards at Lao Kay. The P–40's strafe the tgt area and a barracks a few miles down the Red R.

Fifth AF: A–20's pound forces in Mubo area while B–25's bomb submarine and barges in Lae harbor. B–24's hit Amboina. Single B–17's strike Arawe, Gasmata, Cape Gloucester, barges off Cape Gauffre and cargo boat at Lorengau.

Thirteenth AF: B–17's and B–24's on armed rcn bomb Kahili and Ballale A/Fs.

Eleventh AF: XI BC, constituted on 4 Mar, is activated at Adak. All missions cancelled due to weather except local ftr patrols.

20 March

NAAF: NATBF is formed under NATAF with a small combined HQ which has under it 47th Bomb Gp, 326 Wg (RAF), and air echelons of 2 sqs of 12 Bomb Gp which are attached for operational control. B–26's and B–25's launch consecutive attacks against landing ground at Djebel Tebaga. Other B–25's bomb shipping between Tunisia and Sicily. Ftrs fly escort and carry out numerous rcn missions as Eighth Army opens assault on Mareth Line.

Ninth AF: B–25's bomb Mareth area. AA is intense and all MBs suffer hits. P–40's escort bmrs and carry out FB and top cover operations as British ground troops open assault on positions with inf and arty. 30 Corps gains bridgehead across Oued Zigzaou.

Tenth AF: 7 B–25's again attack Myitnge bridge, inflicting little additional damage to the structure.

Fifth AF: B–25's bomb Langgoer and Kaimana. Landing strip at Finschhafen and harbor area at Salamaua are bombed by single B–24's.

Thirteenth AF: During 19/20 Mar 42 Navy and Marine aircraft lay mines off Bougainville coast in Buin-Tonolai area while 18 B–17's and B–24's pound Kahili A/F in diversionary strike. This mission inaugurates mine-laying operations by aircraft in SOPAC.

21 March

NAAF: During 20/21 Mar, Wellingtons bomb docks at Ferryville. On morning of 21 Mar, B–17's, with P–38 escort, attack landing grounds at Djebel Tebaga. NATAF ftrs, LBs, and MBs hit Djebel Tebaga, and Mezzouna. US 1st Armd Div elements push toward Maknassy, placing it under arty fire in preparation for assault on the town.

Ninth AF: During 20/21 Mar, B–24's attack harbor and surrounding area at Naples, hitting a vessel, city area, and vicinity of railroad yards.

During day B–25's bomb tgts, including a highway, in Gabes area. They are escorted by almost 100 P–40's.

Tenth AF: 15 B–24's pound Gokteik Viaduct, causing considerable damage to the structure. 6 other B–24's, unable to bomb the viaduct due to haze and clouds, attack the previously damaged bridge at Myitnge. P–40's again dive-bomb tgts in Mogaung area, using 1,000-lb. bombs for second time. 3 of the ftrs bomb town area, causing heavy destruction over 2 blocks. 3 others attack bridge S of town, claiming damaging hits in the area. Others attack T/Os in N Indochina.

Fourteenth AF: P–40's strafe Lao Kay phosphate mine area and T/Os in the vicinity.

Fifth AF: 1 B–24 claims direct hit on cargo vessel ESE of Cape Gloucester. Other isolated attacks on shipping are unsuccessful.

Thirteenth AF: During 20/21 Mar 40 Navy and Marine airplanes lay mines in Buin-Tonolai area while 19 B–17's and B–24's bomb Kahili A/F in diversionary attack.

Eleventh AF: 13 B–24's, 9 B–25's, 50 P–38's, 16 P–40's, and 2 F–5A's fly 8 bombing and strafing missions to Kiska. Some of the missions abort due to weather. The others hit Main Camp area, while 2 P–40's make no contact when trying to intercept reported enemy aircraft.

22 March

Atlantic: German sub, U–524, is sunk N of Canary Is, 30–15N 18–13W, by aircraft of 1st Antisub Sq.

Eighth AF: 84 HBs attack Wilhelmshaven U-boat yards.

NAAF: NASAF Wellingtons hit

landing ground near Sfax during 21/ 22 Mar. On 22 Mar, B–26's on sea sweep attack vessels near Zembra I while B–17's bomb shipping in harbor at Palermo. NATAF ftrs fly numerous rcn and patrol missions while A–20's bomb Mezzouna and FBs hit motor transport and tanks in N Tunisian battle area.

Ninth AF: Col John D Corkille succeeds Gen Kauch in cmd of IX ASC. During 21/22 Mar, RAF Liberators, under IX BC, bomb Naples. During the day, B–25's hit Gabes area, bombing road junction, motor transport, and troop concentration. P–40's fly 5 escort missions during the day. British ground forces, after expanding Oued Zigzaou bridgehead during 21/22 Mar, are severely handicapped by heavy rain. Enemy counterattack forces 50th Div to give ground.

Tenth AF: 17 B–25's, operating in 2 forces, bomb Gokteik Viaduct. Several damaging hits are scored on the base and structure. 7 B–25's pound Thazi rail junction. Considerable damage is caused to warehouses, yards, sidings, tracks, and rolling stock.

Fourteenth AF: P–40's again strafe phosphate mine area at Lao Kay.

Fifth AF: HBs pound Gasmata A/F and, in single-plane strikes, attack Finschhafen, Lae, Madang, and harbor at Lorengau.

Thirteenth AF: P–38's strafe Rekata Bay area.

Eleventh AF: 6 B–25's, 12 B–24's, and 22 P–38's attempt 3 missions to Kiska. Only 8 of the P–40's get through but fly uneventful patrol.

23 March

NAAF: During 22/23 Mar Wellingtons hit El Maou A/F near Sfax. During the day, B–17's bomb shipping in Bizerte harbor. Ftrs fly rcn and patrol, bomb and strafe trucks, tanks, and troops near Bir Zallujah hit tanks and trucks E of Mezzouna and Maknassy, and E of El Guettar, where enemy ground forces are making thrusts toward the town.

Ninth AF: B–24's bomb Messina, concentrating on ferry slip. B–25's hit Mareth area. P–40's fly FB operations and bmr escort over battle area as British 50th Div withdraws Oued Zigzaou bridgehead under cover of arty fire.

Tenth AF: 9 B–25's bomb barracks, warehouse, railroad tracks, and A/F at Meiktila.

Fourteenth AF: P–40's strafe operations building at Dong Cuong and hit troop trucks between Tuyen Quang and Ha Giang.

Fifth AF: B–17's thoroughly pound A/Fs in the Rabaul area and strafe vessel off Cape Gazelle. A–20's bomb and strafe forces in Mubo area and at mouth of Bitoi R. B–25's strafe T/Os in Salamaua, Labu Lagoon and Nadzab areas, and at mouth of Markham R. Single B–24's attack Lorengau harbor and A/Fs at Gasmata and Salamaua.

Eleventh AF: Weather grounds all missions except weather rcn and an unsuccessful intercept attempt of an enemy rcn airplane by 2 P–40's.

24 March

NAAF: NASAF B–17's hit shipping and dock area at Ferryville. B–26's bomb La Smala des Souassi landing ground and B–25's hit Djebel

Tebaga N landing ground. NATAF
A–20's and B–25's hit troop concentrations near El Guettar (where US
1st Div is under attack) and landing
ground at Djebel Tebaga. Ftrs escort
bmrs and strafe ground forces along
battleline.

Ninth AF: B–24's attack ferry installations at Messina. Direct hits are
scored in tgt area and adjacent railroad yards and naval oil and storage
tanks are set afire. B–25's hit Zarat.
P–40's fly escort, armed rcn, and
strafing mission. Just before midnight RAF Liberators, under IX BC
control, blast docks at Messina. British Eighth Army prepares to assault
W flank of Mareth Line.

Tenth AF: 23 B–24's and 2 B–17's
attack bridge at Myitnge but fail to
score damaging hits. 8 B–25's bomb
engine sheds at Maymyo.

Fifth AF: B–25's hit Langgoer and
Faan. B–25's and B–17's, operating
individually, attack shipping in NEI
and A/Fs and T/Os at Gasmata and
Mubo.

Thirteenth AF: B–17's and Navy
dive-bmrs hit A/F at Kahili.

Eleventh AF: 10 B–24's, 3 B–25's,
and 12 P–38's fly 5 attack missions
to Kiska. North Head runway and
Main Camp area are bombed.

25 March

NAAF: NASAF B–17's bomb
docks and shipping at Sousse. B–25's
hit Djebel Tebaga landing ground.
NATAF ftrs fly numerous patrols,
sweeps, and rcn flights over battle
areas. NATBF bmrs hit Djebel Tebaga A/F and motor transport W of
Sfax and Sousse (during 24/25 Mar).
XII A Spt Cmd MBs and ftrs hit
Djebel Tebaga A/F, vehicles near

Gabes, Mezzouna, Maknassy, and at
several other points in battle areas.

Ninth AF: B–25's, in early daylight hours, bomb installations in
Mareth area. P–40's attack motor
transport, tanks, and comm tgts in
battle area. During 25/26 Mar HBs,
MBs, and LBs blast forces gathering
in El Hamma area.

Tenth AF: 8 B–25's bomb engine
sheds at Maymyo for second consecutive day. Considerable damage is
done although main shed is not hit.

Fifth AF: B–24's pound Rabaul
and shipping, wharf, and town area
at Amboina. Single B–17's hit Lae,
Gasmata, and Ubili.

Eleventh AF: Weather airplane
take photos of Holtz Bay and Chichagof Harbor. 14 B–24's, 3 B–25's,
12 P–38's, and 2 P–40's fly 4 missions to Kiska. The tgts include beach,
runway, hangar area, North Head,
the Main Camp and submarine base.

26 March

NAAF: B–25's bomb Grombalia
area. Other B–25's and B–17's of NA
SAF fail to complete missions because of weather. P–39's destroy several trucks in Maknassy-Mezzouna
area. NATAF ftrs, LBs, and MBs
bomb fuel dump at Oudref, roads and
railway near Cekhira, docks at Sfax,
and A/F at Djebel Tebaga. Ftrs strafe
vehicles during armed rcn between
Faid and Gabes.

Ninth AF: B–25's attack Mareth
area, dropping over 57,000 lbs of
bombs during 2 strikes. P–40's fly
FB and strafing missions, destroying
or damaging over 50 military transport vehicles, tanks, and gun emplacements. Intense ground fire downs
several US ftrs. Following aerial bom-

bardment, allied ground forces renew assault on Mareth Line.

Tenth AF: 6 B–24's mine Rangoon R during 26/27 Mar. 6 others fly diversion raid on city of Rangoon, scoring hits on Mingaladon A/F, between central railroad station and Pazundaung Creek, and in Syriam area.

Fifth AF: B–17's attack shipping, harbor and town area at Wewak. A–20's pound forces and T/Os in Mubo, Malahang, and Salamaua area. A single B–17 bombs Finschhafen and unsuccessfully attacks ship E of Talasea.

Thirteenth AF: B–24's bomb A/F on Nauru I.

Eleventh AF: A rcn aircraft covers Attu, Agattu, Semichi and Alaid where cabin is strafed. Upon report of Navy contacts with enemy surface force (Battle of Komandorskies), 13 B–24's, 11 B–25's and 8 P–38's are ordered to hit the enemy, reported 150 mi W of Cape Wrangell (Attu). Because of mechanical failures and weather, airplanes cannot take off until 6 hrs after surface force is sighted. Thus, Japanese ships have fled when aircraft arrive at interception point. Some of the returning B–25's bomb radar site, hangar, and Main Camp area on Kiska.

27 March

NAAF: NATAF ftrs attack machinegun installations NE of Maknassy and train at Mezzouna, and hit Djebel Naimia. NACAF ftrs on patrol claim several aircraft shot down. Weather prevents completion of antishipping sweep by NASAF B–25's.

Tenth AF: 5 B–24's mine Rangoon R for second consecutive night.

Fifth AF: B–25's hit Lae and Salamaua. B–24's bomb Saumlakki and attack harbor and shipping at Bogia.

Thirteenth AF: P–39's join Navy aircraft in attack on Vila A/F.

Eleventh AF: 7 B–24's from Adak and 6 Amchitka-based B–25's attempt unsuccessfully to attack naval tgts. From Amchitka, 1 B–25 and 6 P–38's (of which 1 turns back with mechanical trouble) provide cover for US surface force until 1300. 6 P–38's and 1 B–17 depart Adak for a second cover mission, but do not find surface force.

28 March

Eighth AF: 70 HBs hit Rouen-Sotteville M/Y.

NAAF: Weather again prevents completion of NASAF B–25 shipping strike. NATAF ftrs attack trucks S of Maknassy and near Gabes, hit gun positions and tanks near Mezzouna, where fierce ground fighting is taking place, and fly patrols and rcn throughout battle areas of Tunisia. Bmrs hit roads, railroads, and military transport in Sousse and Sfax areas during 28/29 Mar.

Ninth AF: P–40's launch FB attack against El Hamma, which enemy has held as escape corridor through which troops have been withdrawing during 27/28 Mar.

Fifth AF: MBs and HBs on individual missions attack Langgoer, Dobo, Gasmata, and barges and small boat off Finschhafen and Kerema.

Thirteenth AF: Last remaining personnel of the battle-weary 11th Bomb Gp (B–17's) leave SOPAC to return to Hawaii. P–38's and Corsairs hit seaplane bases at Poporang and Shortland, claiming 8 aircraft destroyed, and attack destroyer E of Shortland I, leaving it listing.

29 March

NAAF: Weather cancels all NA SAF operations. NATAF ftrs bomb and strafe truck column S of Djebel Chemsi, troop concentration near Mezzouna, and vehicles at other points along Tunisian battlefront.

Ninth AF: B–25's attack Sfax and El Maou area, scoring hits on several parked aircraft. P–40's fly escort and FB missions as British ground forces pursue enemy N through Gabes. British Eighth Army completes occupation of Mareth Line.

Tenth AF: 4 B–24's bomb shipping and dock area at Tavoy. 9 B–25's bomb Maymyo railroad yards, 7 P–40's blast possible Japanese HQ N of Maingkwan. 8 others pound positions WNW of Sumprabum.

Fourteenth AF: P–40's strafe trucks at Bhamo and fuel drums at Chefang.

Fifth AF: A lone B–17 bombs Gasmata A/F while another attacks Mur-Weber Pt area.

Thirteenth AF: B–17's and B–24's pound Buin and Kahili. P–38's strafe seaplane base at Faisi.

Eleventh AF: 7 MBs and HBs, with ftr escort, bomb and strafe Kiska runway and nearby Main Camp area. Heavy AA fire damages 5 bmrs and 2 P–38's.

30 March

NAAF: Weather halts all NASAF missions except ftr rcn. NATAF ftrs bomb area NE of Oued Zarga, attack tanks, trucks, and troops SE of Slourhia, at Djebel ben Kheir, at Djebel Chemsi, near El Ayacha and El

Avoua, along El Guettar-Mahares road, and in El Agahea area. A–20's bomb La Fauconnerie A/F, hit troops at Djebel Chemsi, and bomb tanks and troops at Djebel Berda which is being assulted by US 9th Div.

Ninth AF: 3 B–24's sent to bomb Messina ferry slip are unable to rendezvous because of bad weather. 1 HB bombs Crotone chemical factory, hitting center of factory area, warehouses, and rail facilities. RAF Liberators sent against same tgt return without bombing. B–25's hit landing ground at Sfax, scoring direct hits on 4 aircraft. P–40's fly escort missions. British ground forces make contact with enemy's new line along Oued el Akarit.

Tenth AF: 5 B–25's bomb Maymyo railroad yards, scoring hits on machine shops, sheds, and tracks. 16 P–40's hit T/Os at Npyentawng, Wuja, and Mohnyin.

Fourteenth AF: P–40's strafe 8 locomotives SW of Lashio, exploding 3 of them.

Fifth AF: A–20's, B–25's, B–24's, and B–17's pound shipping, harbor, and town area at Finschhafen. Other B–24's hit Gasmata. Single aircraft attack several tgts, mostly shipping and coastal areas, in NEI, NE New Guinea, and New Britain.

Thirteenth AF: HBs continue snooper strikes on Vila and Kahili A/Fs.

Eleventh AF: 6 missions are dispatched against Kiska and Attu. From Adak, 6 B–24's, 6 B–25's, and 4 P–38's are over Kiska at noon but cannot bomb due to weather. 4 B–24's, 4 P–38's, and 2 F–5A's then bomb runway at Attu. Next, 5 B–24's and 4 P–38's bomb Main Camp; intense AA fire downs 1 B–24. From Amchitka, 4 P–38's bomb Little Kiska. Next, 4 P–38's bomb Kiska through overcast, followed by 6 B–25's bombing and strafing radar, radio installations, Main Camp, runway, and personnel.

31 March

Eighth AF: Rotterdam shipyards and dock area are hit by 33 HBs, while others attack ship docks at Schiedam and city area of Bocholt.

NAAF: During 30/31 Mar, Wellingtons bomb Decimomannu A/F. During the day, B–17's hit Villacidro, Monserrato and Decimomannu A/Fs and Cagliari harbor. B–25's hit shipping off NE Tunisia. The B–17 and B–25 missions are escorted by P–38's. NATAF ftrs, LBs, and MBs attack La Fauconnerie A/F, hit concentrations on El Guettar-Gabes road (enemy positions through which US II Corps is trying to break), bomb transport in Djebel Tabouna area, attack roads in Mezzouna-Mahares-Sfax-Sousse areas, hit trucks, half-tracks, and tanks S of Djebel Berda and in Djebel Berrani area, bomb Djebel Chemsi Pass, strafe trucks on Djebel Hadifa-Sidi Rouda road and in Ofel-El Guettar area. WDAF hits El Maou landing ground.

Ninth AF: B–25's bomb Sfax A/F. Bombs explode among 6 parked airplanes. P–40's escort bmrs and fly FB operations, during which motor transport along highway N of Gabes is hit.

Tenth AF: 9 B–25's bomb M/Y at Pyinmana, blasting railroad tracks and warehouses.

Fifth AF: A–20's hit Salamaua, while B–24's bomb Babo. Individual B–24's attack Lae A/F, Finschhafen, and Samoa Pt and Timper R bridges.

Thirteenth AF: P–40's and P–38's hit Suavanau Pt area on Rekata Bay.

Eleventh AF: Rcn airplane finds impenetrable weather and returns to base. 2 P–38's make uneventful sweep.

1 April

NAAF: During 31 Mar/1 Apr, Wellingtons bomb Bizerte docks and Karouba Bay seaplane base. During day, A–20's bomb La Fauconnerie and El Djem A/Fs. Ftrs, carrying out rcn missions over wide areas of Tunisia, attack motor transport, tanks, and guns in Sidi Mansour-Djebel Tebaga area. British MBs, LBs, and ftrs hit gun positions N of Oued el Akarit and hit Sfax-El Maou A/F.

Ninth AF: P–40's escort bmr missions. MBs and LBs hit parked airplanes and AA batteries at El Maou A/F at Sfax.

Tenth AF: 16 B–25's bomb Maymyo railroad sheds. 8 others hit railroad yards at Ywataung. 12 P–40's intercept 9 Zeros near Lingling, claiming 7 shot down. 1 P–40 is lost.

Fourteenth AF: Japanese force of 9 ftrs is intercepted in Lingling area by P–40's. 7 ftrs are shot down. 1 P–40 is lost.

Fifth AF: B–17's attack convoy off Kavieng, A/Fs at Gasmata and Cape Gloucester, and town of Madang. Flights of from 1 to 3 MBs or HBs hit several other tgts, mostly isolated shipping and coastline tgts, in NEI and in Solomon Sea.

Thirteenth AF: 42 ftrs (P–38's and Navy and Marine aircraft) are sent over the Russells to intercept Japanese aircraft trying to hit US stockpiles on Guadalcanal, naval base at Tulagi, and the incomplete airstrips in the Russells. The air battle lasts for nearly 3 hours. 6 US ftrs are lost, against claims of 20 Japanese airplanes.

Eleventh AF: A joint directive by CINCPAC and CG Western Def Cmd orders preparations for LANDGRAB (invasion of Attu). 16 B–24's, 5 B–25's, and 12 P–38's sorties are flown against Kiska from Adak and Amchitka. Tgts include ship in Gertrude Cove, North Head area, Main Camp and beach. AA fire damages 2 bmrs. Rcn covers Kiska, Attu, Buldir, and Semichis.

2 April

NAAF: B–25's and A–20's bomb A/F at La Fauconnerie.

Ninth AF: During 1/2 Apr, RAF Liberators, under IX BC, bomb ferry terminal at Messina and A/F at Crotone. During the day, 2 B–24's on special mission bomb ferry terminals at Messina and Villa San Giovanni. 24 B–24's sent to attack Palermo abort because of heavy clouds over tgt. 27 B–24's sent against Naples find the tgt totally obscured by clouds; 9 bomb the area through overcast and 3 bomb Augusta and Crotone. P–40's fly 9 armed rcn and 6 FB and escort missions.

Tenth AF: 8 B–25's hit Thazi railroad junction.

Fifth AF: A–20's hit Kitchen Creek area and Labiabi-Duali area. Single B–24's attack Salamaua, Finschhafen, bridge at Rempi, and A/Fs at Gasmata and Cape Gloucester.

Thirteenth AF: P–38's and P–40's

attack and set fire to a small cargo vessel in Kokolope Bay.

Eleventh AF: 18 B–24's bomb Kiska tgts including North Head. 6 B–25's, 16 P–38's, and 24 P–40's in 6 missions from Amchitka to Kiska, bomb Main Camp and submarine base areas. 4 B–24's bomb runway at Attu. All aircraft, including 2 B–25's colliding in the air, return safely.

3 April

NAAF: Weather cancels NASAF bmr operations. NATAF ftrs strafe tanks and trucks at Kebira and Jabal Nasir Allah, and claim 14 aircraft downed in aerial combat over Djebel Berda. B–25's bomb A/F at Sainte-Marie du Zit. WDAF LBs hit motor transport and gun positions N of Oued el Akarit.

Ninth AF: B–25's bomb Sfax-El Maou area during 2/3 Apr. P–40's fly FB missions N of Gabes.

Tenth AF: 17 B–25's, operating in 2 forces, bomb Myitnge bridge, scoring hits on both approaches.

Fifth AF: A–20's hit Kitchen Creek. B–17's pound shipping and A/F at Kavieng. Single B–24's bomb Kavieng and hit Korindindi.

4 April

Eighth AF: 85 HBs hit industrial installations in Paris area, including Renault armament works and motor works, which are severely damaged. Fierce ftr opposition accounts for 4 US bmrs.

NAAF: B–25's bomb small shipping at Carloforte and landing ground at El Djem. B–17's hit Capodichino A/F and M/Y at Naples. P–38's dive-bomb beached freighter off Cape Zebib. Other P–38's escort the bombing raids. NATAF A–20's hit La Fauconnerie A/F while B–25's hit El Djem and Sainte-Marie du Zit A/Fs. Ftrs accompany LBs and MBs on attacks, and carry out numerous patrols, rcn flights, and ftr sweeps over battle areas of Tunisia.

Ninth AF: B–24's attack Naples, concentrating on dock area. RAF Liberators, under IX BC, bomb Palermo.

Tenth AF: 8 B–25's hit Maymyo engine sheds. 9 others bomb Pyawbwe railroad yards. 7 B–24's heavily damage Thilawa oil refinery.

Fifth AF: B–25's and A–20's pound areas along Huon Gulf, around Kitchen Creek and Heaths and Lane Plantations. B–17's bomb town area, and A/F at Kavieng. Single B–17's bomb Salamaua and Cape Gloucester.

SOPAC: Adm Mitscher assumes position of COMAIRSOLS.

5 April

Eighth AF: 82 HBs bomb industrial tgts in Antwerp area. Main force is directed at Erla aircraft factory and Erla engine works. Strong ftr opposition claims 4 bmrs.

NAAF: During 4/5 Apr, NASAF Wellingtons bomb Trapani docks and shipping. During day, B–17's bomb A/Fs at Sidi Ahmed, Tunis, Boccadifalco, and Milo. B–25's hit A/F at Bo Rizzo and attack convoy off Cap Bon. P–38's fly several ftr sweeps over Straits of Sicily. 1 force of ftrs claims 16 airplanes destroyed. NATAF A–20's hit A/F at El Djem and La Fauconnerie. Ftrs attack E-boats off Pont-du-Fahs and vehicles S of Bou Hamran, and fly sweeps, rcn, and patrol over battle area in Tunisia. WDAF and NACAF airplanes hit

motor transport W of Cekhira, bomb Djebel Zitouna A/F, and strike shipping in Straits of Sicily. During the day NAAF aircraft claim destruction of nearly 50 aircraft in aerial combat. Today starts Operation FLAX (5–22 Apr) which is designed to destroy, in air and on ground, enemy air transports and escorts employed in ferrying personnel and supplies to Tunisia.

Tenth AF: 17 B–25's bomb railroad tgts at Mandalay; 2 others hit Ngamya. 3 B–24's bomb Prome railroad yards; 5 hit Mahlwagon yards and roundhouse. 12 P–40's and a B–25 spt ground forces in N Burma.

Fourteenth AF: P–40's on armed rcn strafe 15 horse-drawn wagons at Wanling.

Fifth AF: Single B–17's attack occupied areas at several points along Huon Gulf coast, hit Finschhafen on Huon Peninsula, bomb Madang and other points on N coast of New Guinea and hit Cape Gloucester.

Eleventh AF: Rcn covers all islands W of Kiska with negative results. 16 B–24's and 6 B–25's bomb Attu runway and Kiska's Main Camp and runway. 4 P–38's fly top cover. Later, 3 B–25's, 16 P–40's, and 16 P–38's bomb Kiska again.

6 April

NAAF: During 5/6 Apr, Wellingtons bomb dock and shipping at Tunis. During day, B–25's and P–38's attack shipping in Straits of Sicily. 2 forces of B–17's bomb convoy further W, near Zembra I, and hit convoy off Bizerte. Other B–17's bomb docks and ships at Trapani. B–25's and A–20's attack landing grounds and A/Fs at Enfidaville, La Fauconnerie, and El Djem. La Fauconnerie bears brunt of attacks and is well covered. Ftrs escort the bombing raids, fly rcn missions, and attack scattered enemy movement.

Ninth AF: B–25's fly 2 missions against concentrations in Oued el Akarit region, scoring hits on buildings, tanks, and numerous vehicles. B–24's hit ferry and slips at Messina harbor. RAF HBs, under IX BC control, bomb Naples area and rail facilities in Messina. P–40's fly escort, ftr sweep, and strafing operations, attacking guns, vehicles, and personnel as British Eighth Army begins assault on Oued el Akarit from which enemy begins withdrawing during the night.

Tenth AF: 6 B–24's attack Pazundaung bridge, damaging S approach.

Fifth AF: B–25's bomb town area and AA positions at Salamaua. Single B–17's bomb Gasmata and Finschhafen while another strafes Cape Gloucester.

Thirteenth AF: Col James M Fitzmaurice becomes CO XIII BC.

7 April

NAAF: NASAF Wellingtons attack Tunis and Jabal al Jallud M/Y. Weather cancels all other NASAF missions except for 2 rcn sorties. All available airplanes of XII A Spt Cmd and WDAF hit ground forces which are retreating in all sectors. Ftrs fly sweeps over Medjez el Bab (claiming 3 ftrs downed), scramble mission NW of Oued Zarga (5 ftrs are claimed destroyed), and over 100 other sorties (no encounters). Highway and motor transport are bombed between Sfax and Sousse. LBs, MBs, and FBs attack concentrations N of Oued el Akarit line. US II Corps makes contact with British Eighth Army on Gabes-Gafsa road.

Ninth AF: B–24's attack Palermo harbor. B–25's bomb retreating columns which are being pursued N of Oued el Akarit by British Eighth Army's 30 and 10 Corps. Ftrs carry out bombing and strafing operations in battle area.

Tenth AF: 2 MBs temporarily knock out bridge on Ye-u railroad branch, crossing the Mu R between Ywataung and Monywa. 18 B–25's, in 2 forces, bomb Ywataung M/Y. P–40's spt ground forces N of Shingbwiyang. 6 B–24's bomb Japanese HQ at Toungoo.

Fifth AF: B–25's hit areas along NE coast of New Guinea from Mur to Singor. B–24's bomb landing ground at Babo and town area of Fak Fak. Single HBs attack shipping and coastal tgts at Lae, Salamaua, Finschhafen, Wewak, Cape Gloucester, and off Lorengau and Kavieng.

Thirteenth AF: A large force of Japanese dive bmrs and ftrs is reported by coast watchers to be moving down the "Slot." In its path are a convoy off E coast of Guadalcanal, shipping at Koli Pt, and a TF at Tulagi. Every operable ftr (76) on Guadalcanal is sent up, and the bmrs are moved to SW tip of the island for safety. The air battle takes place off the Russells, near Tulagi, and over the convoy. AAF P–38's and P–39's and Marine and Navy Corsairs and Wildcats claim 39 aircraft shot down, 13 by AAF ftrs. Allied losses total 7 ftrs.

Eleventh AF: The rcn airplane aborts shortly after takeoff due to weather.

8 April

Eighth AF: 56th and 78th Ftr Gps become operational. Added to 4th Gp (already operational), this enables VIII FC to increase activity and paves way for its coming role of escorting bmrs on deep penetrations into enemy territory.

NAAF: Weather prevents all NA SAF operations except minimum weather rcn. NATAF P–40's and Spitfires fly sweeps and armed rcn over Faid Pass-Fondouk el Aouareb-Kairouan-Ousseltia area as British IX Corps attacks Fondouk. Other ftrs fly widespread rcn and sweeps, attacking motor transport S of Zaghouan. WDAF ftrs hit retreating columns in Cekhira-Sfax area.

Ninth AF: P–40's fly 29 bmr escort, armed rcn, and FB missions against retreating columns along coast N of Gabes.

Tenth AF: 9 B–25's bomb Meiktila A/F. 6 B–24's attack A/F at Heho. Ft Bayard A/F is strafed by 9 P–40's. Enemy stores at Ningam are hit by 4 P–40's and a B–25.

Fifth AF: B–17's and B–24's carry out small harassing strikes, bombing Ulamoa, Finschhafen, and A/F at Kavieng.

Eleventh AF: Weather airplane scouts Kiska and islands W of it with negative results.

9 April

NAAF: Ftrs continue rcn of N half of Tunisia and Straits of Sicily and hit enemy movement and defs over wide areas between Sfax and Enfidaville.

Ninth AF: 340th Bomb Gp is assigned to Ninth AF. P–40's in FB role attack Sfax, as British Eighth Army, in pursuit of retreating enemy, reaches position a few mi to the SW on the coast.

Fifth AF: B–25's bomb and strafe A/F and town and dock areas at Madang. A–20's hit Kitchen Creek-Mubo area. Single B–17's attack barges at Bogia, Alexishafen, and Finschhafen, and hit town of Wewak. Vehicles at Lorengau on Manus are strafed.

Eleventh AF: A B–24 flies rcn over Kiska, Attu, and the Semichis. P–40's fly rcn over Kiska.

10 April

NAAF: During 9/10 Apr, Wellingtons bomb troops and transport on roads in area surrounding Enfidaville. The following day, B–17's hit ships at La Maddalena while B–26's follow up the Wellingtons with raid on roads and military concentrations near Enfidaville. FBs also hit ground tgts in Enfidaville areas. Ftrs escort bmrs, carry out rcn, and fly sweeps over battle area from Medjez el Bab to Sousse.

Ninth AF: HQ IX FC is transferred to Tripoli. Personnel are to be moved from Egypt, over a period of several weeks. B–24's bomb harbor at Naples. RAF Liberators, under IX BC control, hit Palermo. Allied ground forces take Sfax and continue N to La Hencha.

Fifth AF: B–17's and B–24's pound town and dock area of Wewak. Some of the B–17's also bomb Cape Boram and Kairiru I, while some of the B–24's hit Alexishafen and shipping off Wewak. B–25's pound harbors at Bobia and Uligan. A lone B–17 strafes barges SE of Bogia and trucks at Cape Croisilles while another bombs A/F at Arawe.

Thirteenth AF: B–24's continue to fly harassing strikes as 3 of the HBs hit Kahili A/F.

Eleventh AF: Weather rcn B–24 observes 4 unidentified aircraft near Segula. 3 B–25's, 17 P–40's, and 6 P–38's fly 5 attack missions to Kiska, and negative searches for unidentified airplanes at Segula. Last mission finds Kiska closed in and returns with bombs.

11 April

NAAF: During 10/11 Apr, Wellingtons bomb A/Fs at Decimomannu and Monserrato. During day, P–38's carry out ftr sweeps and rcn flights, claiming numerous aircraft shot down, including 21 transports destroyed between Cap Bon and Marsala. B–26's bomb Oudna A/F, B–25's hit Sainte-Marie du Zit A/F, and B–17's strike harbors of Tunis, Marsala, and Trapani. FBs and LBs blast trucks S of Enfidaville road, trucks E of Kairouan, Sousse docks, and numerous other tgts in the NE quarter of Tunisia.

Ninth AF: Col Wycliffe E Steele assumes cmd of IX ASC, succeeding Col John D Corkille. B–24's attack Naples harbor. AA is intense and ftrs attack B–24's from all sides, knocking 1 down. The B–24's claim destruction of 3 ftrs. B–25's attack motor transport and concentrations N of Sfax as Allied ground troops push toward Sousse.

Fifth AF: B–17's bomb Lae and Finschhafen. Single B–24's bomb Finschhafen 3 times and hit Madang once. B–25's hit Vila Salazar and another village on Timor. Enemy airplanes attack Oro Bay and destroy 2 merchant vessels.

Thirteenth AF: P–38's and Navy ftrs strafe gun positions in Rekata Bay area. B–17's bomb A/Fs at Kahili and on Ballale I.

Eleventh AF: 4 B–25's, 22 P–40's, and 8 P–38's hit Kiska 5 times. Last mission aborts due to weather. The other 4 bomb various tgts starting large fires. Some ftrs strafe Little Kiska.

12 April

Eighth AF: Board of 5 officers of Eighth AF and one of RAF complete formulation of plan for CBO from UK in accordance with mission prescribed by CCS in Casablanca Directive.

NAAF: B–17's bomb harbors at Bizerte, and Trapani, and hit shipping in Straits of Sicily. B–25's and A–20's bomb A/Fs at Oudna and Sainte-Marie du Zit. Aircraft of tac units hit enemy movements and fly sweep and rcn throughout NE Tunisia following attack during 11/12 Apr by British aircraft, mainly in Enfidaville, Zaghouan, and Bou Ficha areas.

Ninth AF: B–24's of 376th Gp, sent to attack Naples harbor, are prevented by bad weather from bombing primary. About half return without bombing while the others hit Cosenza and Crotone. Other HBs of same group, in subsequent mission, bomb Naples and secondary tgt of Pizzo. RAF Liberators, under IX BC, are dispatched against Palermo. The primary is attacked, in spite of total cloud cover, but most of bomb tonnage is dropped in Messina harbor. In ground action, British 10 Corps captures Sousse and heads N.

Tenth AF: 9 B–25's hit A/F at

Magwe. P–40's bomb and strafe ammo and supply dump at Walawbum.

Fourteenth AF: P–40's strafe more than 20 vehicles 25 mi E of Loiwing.

Fifth AF: B–24's and B–17's pound A/Fs at Rabaul and Gasmata, shipping in Saint George Channel, T/Os in Ubili and Talasea areas, shipping in Hansa Bay, A/Fs at Lae and Nubia, and Bogia harbor. B–24's, operating individually, attack several tgts, scoring hits on Madang dock area and at Toeal. Japanese planes attack Port Moresby in strength but do little damage.

Thirteenth AF: Single B–24's continue snooper strikes, hitting Kahili A/F twice during the evening.

Eleventh AF: 3 B–25's, 24 P–40's, and 13 P–38's fly 7 missions to Kiska. The ftrs also strafe Little Kiska. AA fire damages 1 P–40 and 1 P–38. The P–38 force-lands safely.

13 April

NAAF: B–17's pound A/Fs at Castelvetrano and Milo, B–25's hit Oudna A/F, and P–38's bomb cruiser at La Maddalena and other shipping at Porto Torres. Ftrs maintain sweeps and armed rcn over NE Tunisia and Straits of Sicily. During 12/13 Mar, British airplanes bomb Megrine landing ground.

Ninth AF: B–24's are dispatched against harbor at Catania. Total cloud cover prevents visual contact with tgt. 1 drops bomb in tgt area, but others jettison load or return to base without bombing. P–40's fly convoy escort. British Eighth Army's 10 Corps, continuing N reaches antitank ditch guarding new enemy positions at Enfidaville and unsuccess-

fully attempts, on limited scale, to force retreat before the line can be strengthened.

Tenth AF: 9 B–25's bomb Myitnge bridge without inflicting further damage to the structure. 9 others hit Monywa A/F. 6 P–40's knock out bridge at Shaduzup.

Fifth AF: A–20's bomb and strafe Labiabi area while a single B–17 bombs runway at Finschhafen.

Thirteenth AF: P–38's and Navy aircraft bomb A/F at Munda and strafe barge at Bambatana.

Eleventh AF: 15 B–24's, 15 B–25's, 28 P–38's and 20 P–40's fly 11 attacks to Kiska. 43 tons of bombs are dropped on Main Camp, North Head, and runway. Ftrs attack Main Camp causing large fires, and also strafe aircraft on the beach. Heavy AA fire damages 2 P–38's, 1 of which later crashes into the sea, and 1 B–25.

14 April

NAAF: During 13/14 Apr, NA TAF Hurricanes and Bisleys bomb La Sebala A/F and attack transport on Tunis-Pont-du-Fahs road, and WDAF LBs and MBs hit A/Fs at Sainte-Marie du Zit and Korba during 13/14 Apr. During the day, B–17's bomb Elmas, Monserrato, and El Aouina A/Fs. P–38's escort HBs and fly bombing and strafing mission against beached vessel SE of Cape Zebib. A–20's bomb Bordj Toum. FBs hit motor convoy near Grich el Oued and trucks NE of Dechret Ben Saidane and battery E of Djedeida. Ftrs fly rcn and sweeps throughout Tunisian battle area. NACAF planes maintain sea rcn and patrols.

Ninth AF: P–40's fly convoy escort, and carry out ftr sweeps over battle area as British Eighth Army's 10 Corps continues to make quick jabs at positions at Enfidaville. These attempts to force enemy retreat are unsuccessful.

Tenth AF: P–40's, dropping 1,000-lb bombs, hit A/Fs at Myitkyina and Manywet, rendering runways at both unusable.

Fourteenth AF: P–40's strafe pack horses S of Tengchung, barracks and warehouses in Lungling, and cattle and trucks N of Lungling.

Fifth AF: HBs and MBs carry out widespread but unsuccessful attacks on individual enemy vessels. Japanese aircraft carry out heavy attack on Milne Bay area, severely damaging 1 vessel, beaching 1 vessel, and hitting 2 others, but doing very little damage to AAF facilities in the area. AA defenses and the 40-plus P–40's and P–38's that intercept the enemy strike claim 14 airplanes shot down.

Thirteenth AF: XIII AFSC is activated.

Eleventh AF: 30 P–40's, 17 P–38's, 9 B–24's and 6 B–25's fly 10 missions to Kiska, bombing and strafing runway, North Head area, installations, parked seaplanes, and facilities on Little Kiska.

ZI: Weather Wg is activated to assume responsibility from HQ AAF for supervision of AAFWS (established in 1937 and designated AAFWS in 1942).

15 April

NAAF: NASAF Wellingtons bomb Decimomannu, Villacidro, and Elmas A/Fs during 14/15 Apr. NATAF ftrs attack tanks and trucks at Oum El Djema and concentration near Sidi Ahmed, while others fly rcn and

patrols during the day. NACAF B–26's on armed rcn of Naples area attack vessel S of Ustica I.

Ninth AF: B–24's attack Catania and Palermo. B–25's hit A/F and area near fuel dump at Sainte-Marie du Zit. P–40's fly rcn and sea patrol. RAF Liberators, under IX BC, hit Naples and Messina.

Tenth AF: 10 B–25's bomb Mandalay M/Y; 9 more bomb M/Y at Ywataung. 8 B–24's hit Thilawa oil refinery while 7 others hit Prome.

Fifth AF: B–17's bomb A/Fs at Rabaul, Gasmata, and Lae.

Eleventh AF: Rcn over Kiska, Attu, Semichis, and Agattu spots no new enemy activities. 2 bmr missions from Adak and 11 ftr missions from Amchitka, composed of 23 B–24's, 20 B–25's, 25 P–38's, and 44 P–40's, hit Kiska. 1 F–5A takes photos. 85 tons of bombs are dropped. Fires result on North Head and Little Kiska. 1 B–24 shot down in flames, 4 bmrs receive battle damage.

16 April

Eighth AF: 2 groups of HBs, totaling 77, hit bridges, ports, and naval facilities at Lorient and Brest. Ftr opposition strong.

NAAF: NATAF ftrs strafe trucks during 15/16 Apr and during following day. A–20's and FBs bomb Djqobel el Raar and concentrations located in various wadis in battle area. NACAF maintains sea rcn and patrols. NASAF B–17's bomb dock area at Palermo. B–25's and B–26's hit Oudna landing ground while P–38's bomb vessels near Cape Zebib and at Cape el Ahmar.

Ninth AF: B–24's attack tanker in Catania harbor, scoring several hits on tgt and in surrounding area. Ftrs fly sea patrol. British Eighth Army abandons attempts to force retreat from Enfidaville by quick jabs and prepares to launch full-scale assault during 19/20 Apr.

Tenth AF: P–40's, bombing railroad bridge near Mogaung, score a direct hit on the tgt and blow up both approaches, leaving the bridge temporarily unserviceable. Later in the day the bridge near Pinbaw is demolished by direct hits. 8 B–24's hit Rangoon M/Y. 9 B–25's bomb Thazi rail junction, while 9 more, weathered out of Maymyo, hit rail tgts in Mandalay.

Fourteenth AF: P–40's strafe group of buildings E of Tengchung.

Fifth AF: B–24's bomb Kaimana, Wewak, Madang, and Lae. B–17's pound shipping at Wewak, leaving 3 vessels sunk or in sinking condition. B–25's bomb Vila Salazar.

Thirteenth AF: B–17's bomb Kahili A/F.

Eleventh AF: Kiska is bombed and strafed 13 times. A total of 13 B–24's, 12 B–25's, 32 P–40's, 29 P–38's, and 2 F–5A's cover tgts which include installations in the Holtz Bay area and gun positions on North Head.

17 April

Eighth AF: 106 HBs attack Focke-Wulf factory at Bremen in the Eighth's largest mission to date. A mass of ftrs attacks during bomb run, shooting down 15 bmrs while flak claims another. CG, VIII FC, expresses need for 20 ftr gps to neutralize growing German ftr opposition to CBO.

NAAF: During 16/17 Apr, NASAF Wellingtons bomb N quay in Bizerte harbor. Shortly after noon B–17's bomb shipping and docks at Ferryville and Palermo. B–25's hit town area and M/Y at Mateur. Ftrs provide escort. NATAF Bisleys bomb La Sebala A/F and A–20's hit Ksar Tyr and concentrations NE of Grich el Oued. Ftrs fly escort and rcn missions. NACAF airplanes fly sea patrol and rcn and attack shipping in Strait of Sicily.

Ninth AF: B–24's (including RAF 178 Sq, under IX BC control) bomb Catania. P–40's fly sweeps, sea patrol, and FB missions.

Tenth AF: 7 MBs bomb Myitnge bridge, scoring 4 damaging hits. 10 others hit Myitnge railway works. 16 P–40's damage bridge at Kamaing, attack town of Nanyaseik, and score hits on N approach to bridge at Namti. 6 B–24's damage S approach to Pazundaung railroad bridge.

Fifth AF: B–24's bomb Amboina. A single B–24 scores hits on NW shore of Hollandia Bay.

Thirteenth AF: B–17's during 16/17 Apr again fly strike against Kahili A/F.

Eleventh AF: 7 B–24's bomb and score 8 direct hits on runway and gun emplacements at Attu. 1 B–24 and 2 F–5A's abort due to weather. 4 B–25's, 31 P–38's, and 14 P–40's hit Kiska 9 times, bombing installations and strafing gun emplacements and 3 parked airplanes.

18 April

NAAF: During 17/18 Apr, Wellingtons bomb Tunis docks and M/Y. During day, over 75 B–17's attack Boccadifalco A/F and Palermo M/Y while B–25's hit Alghero-Fertilia

A/F and shipping at Porto Torres. P-38's escort •the B-17's and B-25's. NATAF Bisleys hit La Marsa landing ground while ftrs fly rcn and scramble missions. NACAF ftrs fly rcn and patrols, attacking vessels, troop columns, and trucks in Tunisian coastal area, and Beaufighters attack Decimomannu A/F.

Ninth AF: 57th Ftr Gp is credited with 77 German transport planes over Cap Bon area. B-24's attack Catania. P-40's fly sweeps, armed rcn, escort, and FB missions. B-25's hit landing grounds.

Fourteenth AF: P-40's strafe enemy-held supply village SE of Tengchung.

Fifth AF: B-25's bomb A/F at Penfoei. Single B-24's hit Finschhafen and Saidor area.

Thirteenth AF: Maj John W Mitchell leads flight of 16 P-38's (2 others abort) on a low-level, circuitous, over-water trip from Guadalcanal to a spot up the Bougainville coast from Kahili to intercept flight of Adm Yamamoto, head of Imperial Japanese Navy, who, according to US intelligence, is on an inspection trip in the S Pacific and is due in Ballale at 0945. Adm Yamamoto's well-known punctuality is calculated to allow the interception to take place at 0935 at a point 35 mi from Kahili. 2 hrs and 15 mins after takeoff at 0725, as the P-38's streak toward Bougainville at almost sea level, the flight of 2 bmrs and 6 Zeros appears just ahead. The 4-aircraft attack section under Capt Thomas G Lanphier Jr bores in. The Zeros spot the attacking P-38's at about 1 mi and try in vain to cut off the attack as the bmrs attempt to escape. In the air

battle, Capt Lanphier and 1st Lt Rex T Barber shoot down the bmr carrying Yamamoto.

Eleventh AF: 22 P-38's (some flown by RCAF pilots), and 37 P-40's hit Kiska 9 times. Submarine base and gun emplacements on North Head are bombed and gun emplacements near submarine base are silenced.

19 April

NAAF: During 18/19 Apr, NATAF Bisleys bomb La Marsa landing ground and roads nearby, and attack activity on beach at Reyville. During day, NASAF B-17's bomb shipping at Tunis. B-25's and A-20's raid La Sebala A/F. FBs attack tanks in battle area. NACAF maintains sea rcn and patrols as far as Sardinia and sea approaches to Naples. NAAF aircraft claim over 100 aircraft destroyed during the day.

Ninth AF: B-25's hit landing grounds and defensive positions, and P-40's escort bmrs and fly ftr sweeps as British Eighth Army opens assault on Enfidaville positions.

Tenth AF: P-40's hit bridges in Burma, seriously damaging Namti railroad bridge between Mogaung and Myitkyina. 9 B-24's bomb Rangoon's main railroad station.

Fifth AF: Col Roger M Ramey succeeds Gen Howard K Ramey as CO V BC. Single MBs or HBs bomb A/Fs at Hollandia, Lae, Cape Gloucester, and Gasmata.

Eleventh AF: 9 missions involving 14 B-24's, 12 B-25's, 32 P-40's, and 23 P-38's are flown to Kiska. First mission is weathered out of primary tgt, Attu, and directed to Kiska. Bombing and strafing concentrates on 4 grounded ships and submarine base area where fires are started. One ship, believed to serve as power station, is set afire.

20 April

NAAF: NASAF B–17's and B–25's bomb landing grounds of Mabtouha, La Marsa, La Sebala, Sidi Ahmed, Creteville, and near Protville. NATAF ftrs fly escort, carry out rcn, and attack various Tunisian A/Fs. NACAF continues sea patrols and rcn as far-reaching as the approaches to Naples.

Ninth AF: P–40's fly sweeps, rcn, and FB missions as British ground forces take Enfidaville and push N. Forces on left are checked by stubborn enemy resistance at Djebel Garci.

Tenth AF: 8 B–25's bomb engine sheds at Thazai.

Fifth AF: B–17's bomb Wewak, Nubia, and Boram A/Fs and shipping off Wewak. B–24's bomb Kaimana and T/Os on Kendari I.

Seventh AF: 22 B–24's, from Funafuti, carry out photo-bombing mission over Nauru. Several direct hits on runways and dispersal areas are claimed.

Eleventh AF: 10 bombing and strafing missions by 15 B–24's, 16 B–25's, 10 P–38's, and 32 P–40's hit shipping in harbor at Kiska and gun positions in North Head. Other tgts include buildings in Main Camp area and runway.

21 April

NAAF: Weather prevents completion of any missions by NASAF. NATAF ftrs and LBs hit landing grounds and military traffic on roads,

fly sweeps and armed rcn, and attack ground forces and aircraft in Medjez el Bab-Goubellat area where an enemy counterattack by armd and inf columns during 20/21 Apr ends in costly failure.

Ninth AF: RAF Liberators, under IX BC control, bomb Naples. P–40's bomb and strafe barges along coast. British Eighth Army meets such fierce opposition at Takrouna that Gen Montgomery decides to confine offensive to coastal region.

Tenth AF: 8 B–25's bomb railroad yards at Maymyo, and 9 more bomb area around Myitnge bridge. 16 B–24's are dispatched to bomb Bangsue Arsenal and other tgts in Bangkok, but only 4 reach tgt area and loose bombs over the city.

Fifth AF: B–25's bomb Kaimana and Laga. Single B–17's attack coastal villages in NE New Guinea and hit Ubili and Gasmata.

Eleventh AF: Cmdr NORPACFOR places all Army and Navy Air Forces (TG 16.1) under Gen Butler. The Army Air Striking Unit (Eleventh AF) is designated Task Unit 16.1.1 and the Naval Air Search Unit (Patrol Wing Four) is designated Task Unit 16.1.2. 2 P–38's take off for Kiska but abort mission.

22 April

NAAF: NASAF B–25's bomb 2 landing grounds near Protville while B–26's hit harbor at Carloforte. NATAF ftrs and LBs fly sweeps, rcn, and patrols and attack positions at Djebel el Ahmera, (Longstop Ridge) Sidi Nsir, Djebel el Ajred (Bald Hill), and other points as British First Army's 5 Corps launches start of final phase of assault on Tunis and

Bizerte, attacking on front N and S of Medjez el Bab.

Ninth AF: P–40's fly ftr sweeps over battle area along Gulf of Hammamet.

Fifth AF: A–20's and B–25's pound Lababia-Duali area on Nassau Bay. Single B–17's bomb Dobo and Nubia area, and strafe Ubili.

Seventh AF: A/F on Funafuti is bombed twice during 21/22 Apr by Japanese. 2 B–24's are destroyed and 5 others damaged.

23 April

International: CCS issues directive making British Gen Morgan CoS to Supreme Allied Commander (Designate). This title, COSSAC, describes both the office and the man who heads it. COSSAC is the seed of Supreme Headquarters, Allied Expeditionary Force. It is charged with continuance of planning for eventual invasion of Western Europe.

NAAF: NASAF B–25's and B–26's bomb Arbatax harbor, vehicles, and railroad at Mateur, and Mateur- Bedja road. B–17's attack vessels N of Sicily. NATAF ftrs, LBs, and MBs carry out large number of missions against positions in NE Tunisia and particularly along battleline area from near Pont-du-Fahs N to the Mediterranean as US II Corps begins drive on Bizerte in Jefna-Sidi Meftah area.

Ninth AF: B–25's attack a landing ground, troops, and arty N of Enfidaville. P–40's fly escort, sweeps, and FB missions in battle area.

Tenth AF: 9 B–25's bomb Mandalay warehouse area. 5 P–40's damage approaches to bridge at Shaduzup.

Fourteenth AF: P–40's strafe 15-truck convoy SW of Lungling.

Fifth AF: Single B–24's bomb A/F and town area at Finschhafen and score direct hit on cargo vessel SE of Kavieng.

Seventh AF: 12 B–24's from Funafuti attack Tarawa Atoll, bombing gas storage and barracks areas.

24 April

NAAF: NASAF Wellingtons bomb N quay at Bizerte harbor during 23/24 Apr. Bad weather the following morning cancels NASAF operations. NATAF ftrs, although hampered by bad weather, attack guns, troops, and trucks in battle area from Pont-du-Fahs N to the sea. Fierce ground fighting continues in Jefna area.

Ninth AF: RAF Liberators, under IX BC, bomb Naples. P–40's escort bmrs, fly sweeps, and carry out FB operations against troops in battle area N of Enfidaville.

Fourteenth AF: 9 B–25's, escorted by 11 P–40's, bomb Namtu mines and railroad yards. 7 of the P–40's strafe mine and smelter area. 13 P–40's intercept 25 ftrs near Lingling and shoot down 5.

Fifth AF: B–24's bomb Kendari A/F. B–25's pound Dili A/F. A–20's bomb and strafe positions in Mubo area. Single B–24's attack Lae, Gumbi, Biliau, and Singor, and bomb runway at Cape Gloucester.

Eleventh AF: 2 P–38's bomb Kiska and strafe personnel near Mutton Cove. Weather cancels other missions.

25 April

NAAF: Weather prevents NASAF bombing missions. NATAF ftrs attack positions and vehicles in battle area. LBs and MBs bomb S landing ground at Soliman, positions NW of Enfidaville, and several other points in battle area as Allied ground forces continue adv on Bizerte and Tunis.

Ninth AF: B–25's attack landing grounds, concentrations, and vehicles N and NW of Enfidaville. P–40's escort bmrs and fly ftr sweeps over battle area.

Tenth AF: 11 B–25's attack Ywataung railroad yards and vicinity.

Fifth AF: B–17's bomb Wewak A/F and towns of Madang and Saidor. A–20's bomb and strafe positions at Green's Hill. Single B–24's hit A/Fs at Madang and Finschhafen.

Thirteenth AF: 3 B–24's fly harassing strike during 25/26 Apr against Kahili A/F. 12 others bomb same tgt later during the night.

Eleventh AF: 15 B–24's, 12 B–25's, 32 P–40's, 23 P–38's, and 1 F–5A fly 12 missions to Kiska and Attu. Tgts include Holtz Bay, North Head, South Head, beach areas, runway, shipping, and submarine base.

26 April

NAAF: During 25/26 Apr, NAS AF Wellingtons bomb Decimomannu, Elmas, and Villacidro A/Fs. On following afternoon, B–17's strike A/F at Grosseto. B–25's bomb railroads at Mateur and town of Tebourba, while B–26's and P–38's hit shipping near Marettimo and Porto Ponte Romano. NATAF ftrs, LBs, and MBs hit area NW of Enfidaville, bomb Soliman S landing ground, hit vessels off Cap Bon, and attack Ksar Tyr, roads in Pont-du-Fahs-Zaghouan-Cheylus area, Massicault area, and numerous positions along battleline in NE Tunisia.

Ninth AF: B–24's bomb A/F, hangars, and dispersal area at Bari. B–25's hit landing ground at Soliman S. RAF Liberators, under IX BC control, hit Bari and Barletta, P–40's, escorting bmrs, claim 4 Me 109's destroyed.

Tenth AF: 7 B–24's bomb warehouses WSW of C railroad station at Rangoon. 7 others blast Thilawa oil refinery, causing heavy damage. 10 B–25's pound Heho A/F and 16 attack Kanaung A/F.

Fourteenth AF: A Japanese force of 12 bmrs and 15 ftrs hit Yunnani A/F with surprise raid. 5 P–40's and 1 C–47 are destroyed. 15 other P–40's are damaged. 5 US personnel and several Chinese laborers are killed.

Fifth AF: B–24's bomb Lae and Finschhafen. A single B–17 carries out harassing attacks on Arawe, Ubili, and Gasmata.

Eleventh AF: 11 B–24's, 15 B–25's, 36 P–40's, 21 P–38's and 1 F–5A fly 15 missions to Kiska. 24 of the P–40 sorties are flown by RCAF pilots. 5 B–25's abort mission due to weather. Bombs are dropped on North Head runway and nearby area, radar, gun installations, Main Camp and on Little Kiska.

ZI: Comm Wg is activated to assume responsibilities from HQ AAF for supervision of AACS (established in 1938).

27 April

Twelfth AF: Gen Quesada is named CG XII FC but had actually assumed office in mid-Mar.

NAAF: NASAF B–25's hit shipping W of Zembra I off Cap Bon. B–17's, with P–38 escort, bomb Villacidro A/F. NATAF planes (ftrs, LBs, and MBs) hit numerous tac tgts in NE Tunisia, including Sidi Ahmed A/F and troops, tanks, trucks, and gun positions at Massicault, on Pont-du-Fahs road, Ksar Tyr, Bir Meherga, and other points along battleline.

Ninth AF: P–40's bomb and strafe concentrations N and NW of Enfidaville.

Tenth AF: 19 B–25's bomb engine sheds at Thazi. P–40's hit positions S of Sarenghkyet.

Fifth AF: A–20's bomb and strafe forces in Green's Hill-Mubo area. B–25's bomb village near Beru. HBs, operating individually, attack vessels NNW of Dobo, Nabire, Cape Gloucester, Cape Goltz, Gasmata, New Britain, and small vessels and T/Os in Marienberg, Wewak, and Finschhafen areas.

Thirteenth AF: B–24's pound Vila and A/F on Ballale I. B–17's hit Kahili A/F.

Eleventh AF: 1 B–25 unsuccessfully investigates reported submarine 4 mi W of Bay Is. 4 P–38's bomb Main Camp, then scout Buldir.

28 April

NAAF: NASAF B–25's and P–38's attack 2 vessels off NE Tunisia in Straits of Sicily. Other B–25's hit Tunis shipping while B–26's bomb landing grounds at Mabouban and Mabtouha. NATAF aircraft bomb concentrations near Saint-Cyprien and Ksar Tyr, shipping off Tunis, and numerous positions and vehicles along Tunisian battleline and surrounding areas as US 9th Div continues W astride the Sedjenane R and 1st and 34th Divs continue to face fierce opposition S of Jefna in Sidi Meftah area.

Ninth AF: B–24's attack harbor at Naples and ferry slip at Messina. Gunners claim 5 ftrs destroyed. P–40's escort bmrs and attack troops in battle area N of Enfidaville.

Tenth AF: 9 P–40's intercept 21 MBs and 21 ftrs about 100 mi SW of Kunming. The P–40's claim 11 airplanes shot down. 9 B–25's pound docks at Monywa. 10 others attack river traffic in Katha vicinity.

Fourteenth AF: About 20 Japanese MBs and a like number of ftrs attack A/Fs at Kunming. High winds prevent bombing accuracy and little damage is done to the A/F. Several Chinese villagers near the field are killed. Gen Glenn, recently arrived to become Gen Chennault's CoS, is wounded. Defending P–40's shoot down 10 aircraft.

Fifth AF: B–25's attack 2 vessels NNW of Dobo. Single B–17's hit buildings N of Finschhafen A/F, Wilwilan village, and T/Os along coast of NE New Guinea from Nankina R to Mur.

Thirteenth AF: 3 B–24's continue snooper missions over Bougainville, bombing A/F at Kahili.

29 April

NAAF: During 28/29 Apr, NASAF Wellingtons bomb El Aouina A/F. On following morning, P–38's hit shipping S of Marettimo I. In afternoon B–26's bomb landing ground near Protville and P–40's hit vessels along NE Tunisian coast. NATAF ftrs, LBs, and MBs attack shipping in Gulf of Tunis, positions at Mateur and Derourhi, concentrations SW of Saint-Cyprien and NE of Ksar Tyr, and landing craft near Tunis.

Ninth AF: B–25's attack ground

installations in battle area. P–40's escort bmrs and fly bombing and strafing operations against vessels as far N as Zembra I.

Tenth AF: 9 B–25's attack shipping at Rangoon. 18 others bomb Myitnge engine sheds and the oft-attacked Myitnge bridge. 6 P–40's bomb and strafe Tahona.

Fifth AF: B–25's bomb Koepang. B–24's hit Halong while individual HBs attack Finschhafen, Madang, Gumbi, and in Singor area.

Thirteenth AF: Single B–24's bomb Numa Numa and Vila. 2 B–17's hit Kahili. P–38's, along with Navy and Marine airplanes, pound Gatere and Pelipelpi Bay. 6 B–24's hit Kieta while P–39's join Navy aircraft in pounding bivouac area at Vila A/F.

30 April

NAAF: NASAF B–26's and P–38's hit shipping off Tunis while B–25's strike shipping near Cap Bon and Tunis-Medjez el Bab highway. NATAF ftrs, LBs, and MBs, hit positions near Mateur, Bir Meherga, and Ksar Tyr, concentrations near Furna, shipping in Gulf of Tunis and near Cap Bon, and attack isolated vehicles and troops along battleline as US II Corps makes substantial gains in Jefna area.

Ninth AF: B–24's attack Messina ferry; bombs hit tgt area and nearby M/Y and city area. P–40's fly FB missions against shipping with excellent results, claiming 1 destroyer and 3 other vessels sunk, and 2 destroyers and 2 boats damaged. Ftrs claim 5 Me 109's shot down. 3 P–40's are lost.

Tenth AF: 16 B–25's pound Gokteik Viaduct, damaging the N end. 4 others bomb Maymyo railroad yards. 5 B–24's bomb Sule Pagoda wharves at Rangoon. 4 P–40's and a B–25 hit Mohnyin, while 6 P–40's attack camp S of Weshi.

Fifth AF: Single B–24's bomb Lae and A/Fs at Cape Gloucester and Gasmata.

Thirteenth AF: 5 B–17's bomb bivouac area and revetments at Kahili A/F.

Eleventh AF: 4 B–25's, 17 P–38's, and 7 P–40's fly 4 missions to Kiska. Only the P–38's get through and blast Gertrude Cove, Main Camp, the submarine base and a ship.

1 May

Eighth AF: 56 HBs in 2 waves strike Saint-Nazaire U-boat base and shipyard.

NAAF: NASAF B–26's and P–38's fly uneventful shipping sweeps. NA TAF ftrs and LBs hit shipping in Gulf of Tunis and jetties at Sidi Daoud and Kelibia, and attack position in NE Tunisian battle area as Allied ground forces regroup for final Tunisian offensive.

Ninth AF: B–24's bomb harbor at Reggio di Calabria. P–40's bomb and strafe shipping and shore installations on NE Tunisian coastline.

Fourteenth AF: Forward echelon of Fourteenth AF, under Col Clinton D Vincent and Lt Col David L ("Tex") Hill, moves into E China along the Hengyang-Kweilin line. This brings US aircraft within range of all major Japanese-held bases from N China to Indochina and Thailand, and makes shipping in China Sea more vulnerable to US air strikes.

Fifth AF: B–24's bomb landing

strip at Nabire and hit vessel in Man-okwari harbor.

Eleventh AF: 16 attack missions on Kiska and Attu are flown by 16 B–24's, 15 B–25's, 35 P–38's, 38 P–40's, and 4 F–5A's. Kiska tgts include Main Camp, hangar, submarine base (where fire is started), runway, radar, ship, North Head, AA guns and Gertrude Cove. Attu tgts include E Attu, Holtz Bay and Chichagof Harbor installations.

ZI: I BC (inactivated on 15 Oct 42) is activated and assigned to Second AF as a trg organization for bomb units.

2 May

NAAF: Bad weather restricts NASAF to rcn missions. NATAF ftrs hit tank and troop concentrations near Massicault and Tebourba and fly battle area rcn as US II Corps occupies Kef en Nsour while enemy withdraws toward Bizerte.

Ninth AF: P–40's attack shipping off Tunisian coast.

Fourteenth AF: 17 P–40's intercept 30–40 ftrs near Lingling and in a running battle to just N of Changsha claim at least 7 Zeroes downed. 1 P–40 is shot down.

Fifth AF: B–25's bomb Penfoei. Others unsuccessfully attack vessel off Toeal. A single B–17 bombs dock area at Finschhafen.

Thirteenth AF: B–17's on harassing strikes hit Rekata Bay area and Munda A/F. P–38's and P–39's join Navy aircraft in pounding runway area at Munda.

Eleventh AF: 6 B–25's, 8 P–40's, and 8 P–38's fly bombing, photo and attack missions to Kiska. Tgts include North Head, South Head and build-ings and AA gun batteries on Gertrude Cove.

3 May

Iceland: Gen Andrews, CG ET OUSA, is killed in aircraft crash while landing.

NAAF: NASAF B–25's bomb landing ground near Protville and B–17's hit shipping at Bizerte. NATAF ftrs fly numerous rcn missions over battle area as Mateur falls to US 1st Armd Div. Other ftrs escort NASAF bmrs. FBs bomb Massicault area.

Ninth AF: P–40's fly FB missions against bridge, buildings, and docks in NE Tunisia.

Fifth AF: B–25's strafe A/F at Gasmata. A B–17 strafes launches N of Lolobau I, claiming 1 boat sunk.

Thirteenth AF: P–40's and P–38's join Navy dive bmrs and ftrs in attacks on buildings and AA positions in Rekata Bay area.

Eleventh AF: 7 B–24's, 11 B–25's, 20 P–38's, 27 P–40's and 2 F–5A's participate in a weather rcn mission to Attu and in 9 attack missions to Kiska. Kiska tgts include Main Camp, North Head, radar, and runway.

4 May

Eighth AF: 65 HBs strike former Ford and General Motors plants at Antwerp. With this mission, P–47's begin providing ftr escort up to 175 mi. More than 30 B–17's and B–24's fly successful diversionary feint toward French coast, arousing more than 100 German ftrs (about half of total number in the region) and keeping many of them airborne long enough to prevent their attacking main effort.

NAAF: Weather restricts NASAF

operations to rcn and uneventful shipping sweep, NATAF ftrs attack gun positions and vehicles near Zaghouan and Massicault and at other points in surrounding areas. LBs and MBs hit Zaghouan in spt of French adv.

Ninth AF: B-24's attack shipping at Reggio di Calabria and Taranto. B-25's hit Zaghouan, including landing ground and road running to Bou Ficha. P-40's fly sea patrol and escort, as well as FB missions in Zaghouan area.

Fourteenth AF: 18 B-24's bomb dock installations, coal yards, and oil storage area at Samah on Hainan I. 9 B-25's pound docks at Haiphong. 19 P-40's escort HBs and MBs to Hanoi and then proceed with MBs to Haiphong and strafe the tgt area following the bombing strike.

Fifth AF: B-24's bomb Babo and town area, harbor, and shipping at Wewak. Single B-24's hit barges off N coast of New Britain.

Thirteenth AF: B-17's fly snooper strikes during 3/4 May against Vila A/F and Rekata Bay area. P-40's join Navy aircraft in strike on Vanga-vanga.

Eleventh AF: 36th Bomb Sq begins to operate from Amchitka. 5 B-24's, 6 B-25's, 8 P-38's, 2 P-40's and 2 F-5A's take off on 2 Kiska and 1 Attu missions. Missions to Kiska abort due to weather. At Attu tgts include Chichagof Harbor, AA positions at Holtz Bay, and a floatplane.

5 May

NAAF: NASAF B-17's bomb vessel off Capo San Vito, hit Tunis harbor, and attack ships and docks at La Goulette. B-25's and B-26's bomb shipping off Marettimo I and E of Cape Zebib, and hit landing ground at Galaat el Andeless and near Protville. NATAF ftrs and bmrs fly 6 missions against strongholds on NE and E slopes of Djebel Bou Aoukaz as British 5 Corps' 1st Div attacks and gains the position. Ftrs hit shipping in Gulf of Tunis and attack landing grounds and concentrations near Protville. Wellingtons bomb roads at Bir Meherga.

Ninth AF: P-40's strafe and bomb bridge, vessels, docks, warehouses, and other buildings at Nabeul harbor.

Fifth AF: B-25's pound Toeal. A lone B-24 bombs A/Fs at Cape Gloucester and Gasmata.

Thirteenth AF: P-38's and Navy F4U's administer thorough strafing to Nyanga.

Eleventh AF: Weather rcn airplane over Attu observes floatplane burning on water. 14 B-24's, 17 B-25's, 16 P-38's, 32 P-40's, and 5 F-5A's fly 4 attack missions to Attu and 6 (partly with RCAF pilots) to Kiska. Bombs are dropped on Attu installations and ftrs strafe and set afire 1 seaplane and silence AA guns. Tgts include Main Camp, radar site, North and South Head, runway, and Gertrude Cove installations.

6 May

NAAF: 18 Army Gp opens final assault on Tunis and Bizerte before dawn. Assault is supported by massed arty fire and the most intensive air bombardment yet employed in N Africa. NATAF airplanes bomb El Aouina, La Sebala, and Ariana A/Fs during 5/6 May. On 6th, ftrs, LBs, and MBs fly over 1,400 sorties, attacking Protville and La Sebala A/Fs, trucks on Massicault-Tunis road,

Bordj Frendj, Djebel Achour, traffic SW of Tunis, troops N of Massicault, Djedeida-Saint-Cyprien road, road S of Djedeida, and numerous other points of strength in extreme NE Tunisia. NASAF B–17's bomb Marsala and Trapani. B–25's and B–26's bomb convoy SW of Marettimo I, 2 beached vessels at Cape Zebib, port of Favignana, vessels W of Marettimo, and ships, lighthouse, and parked aircraft near Capes Fortass, Zebib, Cap Serrat and at Protville. Ftrs escort bombing missions.

Ninth AF: B–24's bomb Reggio di Calabria harbor, hitting several vessels and shore installations. B–25's attack Furna and Massicault and surrounding areas. P–40's hit shipping in Gulf of Tunis and vehicles and buildings along coast.

Fifth AF: A–20's hit forces in Green's Hill area. Single B–24's hit Madang and Finschhafen. B–25's pound Dili while B–24's hit Manokwari and Toeal.

Thirteenth AF: P–40's and Navy dive bmrs and ftrs hit Munda A/F. During the evening B–24's carry out harassing strikes on Kahili A/F and on Fauro and Ballale Is.

Eleventh AF: MBs, HBs, and P–38's drop over 52 tons of bombs on Attu tgts incl Holtz Bay, Sarana Bay, and Chichagof Harbor area and nearby gun positions. Kiska is also hit. Tgts include radar, gun positions and Gertrude Cove and Main Camp areas. Returning P–38's also bomb and strafe hut on Rat I. P–40's blast Kiska and Little Kiska.

7 May

ETO: Gen Devers is appointed cmdr of ETO.

NAAF: During 6/7 May, NASAF Wellingtons bomb docks and shipping at Trapani as diversion for minelaying mission off Malta. Next morning, P–40's attack motor vessels, quay and dock area at Tunis harbor. NATAF ftrs, LBs, and MBs hit El Aouina A/F and traffic on roads around Tunis, especially Tunis-Bizerte road, as Allied forces of Gen Alexander's 18 Army Gp overrun both Tunis and Bizerte, splitting the enemy's forces.

Ninth AF: B–25's hit town of Kelibia. P–40's bomb and strafe shipping in Gulf of Tunis, severely damaging 3 boats.

Fifth AF: B–17's and B–24's bomb A/F, supply dumps, and other tgts at Madang while A–20's hit forces in Green's Hill area. B–25's pound Penfoei.

Eleventh AF: An attempted mission to Kiska by 6 P–40's aborts due to weather.

8 May

NAAF: NASAF B–26's and P–40's attack small vessels off NE Tunisia. Weather prevents success of other shipping sweeps, but P–38's bomb Pantelleria A/F and B–25's hit road junction and railroad at Korba and highway N of Beni Khalled. P–40's bomb docks near Thonara. NATAF ftrs and LBs bomb landing ground on Pantelleria, shipping between Tunisia and Sicily, convoys and road network near Soliman and Hammamet, tanks near Protville, troops, emplacements, trucks, landing grounds, and vessels on and near Cap Bon and in area S of Tunis. On ground, *Corps Franc D'Afrique* makes official entry into Bizerte as British 7th Armd Div pushes N from Tunis toward US II Corps zone. The British 6th Armd and Indian 4th Inf Divs, pushing SE toward Hammamet, are stopped at Hammam Lif as enemy strives to keep line of retreat to Cap Bon peninsula open. 5 Corp 1st Div and 4th Indian Div push E with French 19th Corps which meets firm resistance near Zaghouan.

Ninth AF: B–25's hit landing ground on Pantelleria. P–40's strafe and bomb shipping in Cap Bon area and shipping and shore installations on Gulf of Tunis. Ftrs claim 5 Me 109's destroyed.

Fourteenth AF: 16 B–24's and 11 B–25's bomb Tien Ho A/F, shop and factory area, and White Cloud A/F at Canton. The 24 escorting P–40's strafe tgt areas following the bombing strikes. Considerable damage is done, including the destruction of about 20 enemy aircraft.

Fifth AF: B–25's claim destruction of 2 cargo vessels at Madang. B–17's bomb A/F at Rabaul, and single B–17's attack barges and small boats off N coast of New Britain.

Thirteenth AF: P–40's join Navy aircraft in attack on destroyers in Blackett Strait. Other P–40's and P–38's hit AA positions at Vila.

9 May

NAAF: During 8/9 May, NASAF Wellingtons bomb Villacidro, Elmas, and Decimomannu A/Fs, and NA TAF Bisleys, bomb troops and vehicle concentrations in Hammamet-Nabeul-Menzel Bou Zelfa-Soliman-Tazorhrane areas. During day, B–17's, with P–38 escort, bomb Palermo; B–26's follow immediately with attack on same tgt. Ftrs fly

sweeps over battle area, provide cover for destroyers, strafe barges, bomb buildings in battle area, strafe trucks between Hammamet and Soliman and bomb landing ground near Menzel Temime. LBs and MBs also bomb shipping, hit concentrations in battle area and in town of Soliman, and bomb A/F on Pantelleria. US II Corps receives unconditional surrender of enemy troops in its zone.

Ninth AF: B–24's attack harbor facilities at Messina, scoring hits on ferry terminal, round house, 2 ferries, and a ship. B–25's hit landing ground on Pantelleria. Over 300 P–40's fly escort and rcn missions, and strafing and bombing raids on landing ground, vessels, vehicles, bridges, and gun positions in areas of Zembra Is, Cap Bon, and Pantelleria.

Fifth AF: B–24's and B–17's bomb Manokwari, Nabire, Kaimana, and Madang A/F, and Wewak-But area. B–25's hit A/F at Gasmata.

10 May

NAAF: During 9/10 May, NA SAF Wellingtons bomb Palermo and surrounding area. B–17's follow up, shortly past noon, with raids on A/Fs at Milo and Bo Rizzo. NATAF ftrs, LBs, and MBs attack Pantelleria harbor, Korba bridge, Menzel Temime landing ground, Kelibia areas, and town of Menzel Bou Zelfa. Numerous motor transport and troop concentrations on Cap Bon peninsula are bombed and strafed as British 6th Armd Div drives to Hammamet, cutting off the peninsula.

Ninth AF: B–25's bomb Pantelleria landing ground. P–40's bomb Pantelleria and Cap Bon peninsula. Ftrs claim 4 airplanes destroyed.

Tenth AF: 6 P–40's bomb and strafe Kwitu, leaving several areas burning fiercely.

Fourteenth AF: 8 P–40's fly offensive sweep against comm in Nam Dinh and Hanoi areas. 4 locomotives and 3 riverboats are destroyed, a train carrying troops and supplies is heavily damaged, and several trucks of troops are destroyed.

Fifth AF: A–20's bomb and strafe Labu area while B–25's pound Cape Gloucester A/F. B–17's and B–24's, operating individually, attack coastline tgts in NE New Guinea, New Britain, and on Jamdena I.

Thirteenth AF: P–38's join Navy and Marine aircraft in strike against gun emplacements, runway, and revetments at Munda A/F.

11 May

NAAF: NASAF B–17's, B–26's, and B–25's bomb Marsala, hitting warehouse, docks, railroad yards, seaplane base, and city area. P–40's bomb and strafe harbor at San Michele. NATAF ftrs and LBs attack vehicles, gun positions and troop concentrations in Zaghouan-Sainte-Marie du Zit area and on Cap Bon as British 4th Div completes uneventful sweep around Cap Bon peninsula, revealing no important forces there. Resistance in Zaghouan sector weakens.

Ninth AF: B–24's strike Catania harbor, severely damaging harbor area and several ships. B–25's strike battle area in NE Tunisia. P–40's fly escort and armed rcn, and carry out bombing and strafing missions in Cap Bon area against motor transport, concentrations, roads, docks, and AA batteries.

Tenth AF: 6 B–24's pound Syriam, causing large fires in the town area.

Fifth AF: B–17's and B–24's hit A/F and general area at Rabaul. B–25's bomb Penfoei and Dili.

Thirteenth AF: B–17's fly harassing strikes during 10/11 May against Kahili A/F and against Shortland I.

Eleventh AF: The following missions spt US forces landing on Attu: 1 air-ground liaison sortie by 1 B–24; and B–24 supply sortie dropping supplies to ground forces, and 5 attack missions, flown by 11 B–24's and 12 B–25's. First attack mission cannot find tgt and instrument-bombs tgts which include runway, radar, submarine base, and camp area. Because of poor visibility next 2 missions hit Kiska, where runway and Main Camp are attacked. 2 B–24's then bomb Chichagof Harbor area through fog while another drops leaflets on Attu.

12 May

International: Churchill, Roosevelt, and CCS in Washington discuss strategy in light of events in USSR, Tunisia and Aleutians. Other topics are: setting date for invasion of W Europe, war plans for ETO and MTO, knocking Italy out of the war, and C Pacific offensive against Japan.

NAAF: NASAF Wellingtons bomb docks at Marsala during 11/12 May. Some bombs fall on Mazara del Vallo and Trapani. During day, NATAF ftrs, LBs, and MBs fly sweeps and tac rcn over battle area and hit positions S of Bou Ficha which form last link between enemy forces and the sea. By night enemy resistance in S is almost ended. Enemy troops, including Gen von Arnim, CinC, Army Gp Africa, are surrendering en masse.

Twelfth AF: Gen Cannon takes cmd of XII A Spt Cmd.

Ninth AF: B–25's bomb tgts in battle area in NE Tunisia.

Fifth AF: B–25's bomb A/F and surrounding area at Finschhafen. B–24's hit Saumlakki, and single HBs hit Salamaua and Gasmata.

Thirteenth AF: During 11/12 May, B–17's fly snooper strikes against Kahili A/F. During early morning hrs, P–40's and Navy aircraft hit AA positions, runway, and revetments there.

Eleventh AF: A P–39 rcn sortie over Kiska and Rat Is encounters poor weather and turns back. At Attu, air-ground liaison B–24 watches US forces land on beach "Red" while another B–24 drops supplies. 7 attack missions flown by 10 B–24's, 12 B–25's, and 24 P–38's bomb and strafe assigned Attu tgts. 4 barges are set afire in W arm of Holtz Bay.

13 May

Eighth AF: 119 HBs attack Meaulte industrial areas and Saint-Omer/Longuenesse A/F. The major effort is directed at Avions Potez aircraft factory at Meaulte. Four additional B–17 gps (94th, 95th, 96th, and 351st) become available for combat operations on 13–14 May.

NAAF: NASAF Wellingtons bomb area of railroad station, M/Y and docks in Naples during 12/13 May. The following day, B–17's, B–25's and B–26's from 7 bomb gps, escorted by ftrs from 4 ftrs gps, bomb Cagliari, hitting shipping, dock area, M/Y, oil dump, chemical plant, and

city area. Tunisian campaign ends with surrender of Marshal Messe, cmdr of Axis forces in Africa.

Ninth AF: B–25's bomb Augusta. RAF Liberators, under IX BC, attack Messina ferry terminal.

Fifth AF: B–17's bomb A/Fs at Rabaul, Wewak, and Boram. B–25's blast A/F, town area, and T/Os at Gasmata while A–20's hit Cape Gloucester A/F and area. Single B–24's and B–17's attack various shoreline and offshore tgts, including landing strips, buildings, gun positions, barges, and vessels, on NE New Guinea coast, New Britain, and in Admiralty Is.

Thirteenth AF: During 12/13 May 2 B–24's on snooper missions bomb Kahili and Ballale A/Fs. They are followed shortly by 6 B–17's which pound the same tgts. During day, 34 P–38's, P–39's, and P–40's, along with 62 Navy and Marine ftrs and 6 RNZAF P–40's, intercept 20-plus airplanes over Russell Is-Tulagi area. Allied pilots claim 16 aircraft shot down (1 by AAF ftrs). During early evening, 5 B–17's again hit Kahili and Ballale A/Fs.

Eleventh AF: Bad weather keeps air-ground liaison B–24 from observing or hearing friendly ground forces on Attu and returns to base. Air-ground spt mission of 6 B–24's is diverted from Attu to Kiska. 2 of the bmrs don't get the message, proceed to Attu, and bomb Chichagof Harbor and Holtz Bay. The other 4 bomb Main Camp area. 8 P–40's dispatched to Kiska in 2 waves cannot see tgt and instead bomb Little Kiska installations.

14 May

Eighth AF: Maximum force is put in air as part of combined offensive against *Wehrmacht*. 198 HBs of VIII BC plus a small group of MBs launch simultaneous attacks on 4 tgts. The principal attack is against submarine yards and naval installations at Kiel with other objectives being Courtrai A/F, former Ford and General Motors plants at Antwerp, and the Velsen power station at Ijmuiden. This is first time more than 200 US bmrs are dispatched. The attack at Ijmuiden is made at low level by 11 B-26's of 322d Bomb Gp, first US MB gp to become operational in UK. No MBs are lost during attack though 1 MB crashes while landing on return to base.

NAAF: During 13/14 May, Wellingtons hit Cagliari. During day, P-38's bomb tunnel, barracks, A/F, industry, power station, and town areas at Sassari, Alghero, Porto Torres, and Abbasanta. B-25's and P-38 escorts bomb dock and town area of Olbia, claiming destruction of 3 vessels. B-26's hit Porto Ponte Romano while B-17's bomb Civitavecchia.

Ninth AF: P-40's fly sea patrol and escort for bmrs.

Fifth AF: B-25's administer thorough pounding to A/F and surrounding area at Gasmata while B-24's and B-17's pound Rabaul A/F. Other B-25's bomb Penfoei A/F and Dili area. Single HBs hit various tgts in NE New Guinea, New Britain and NEI.

Thirteenth AF: Single B-24's fly early evening snooper strikes against A/Fs at Kahili, Ballale, and Munda. During 14/15 May, B-17's on snooper mission bomb Kahili.

Eleventh AF: Poor weather curtails bombings. Air-ground liaison B-24 flies rcn and photo rcn over Attu throughout the day. 1 B-24 carrying supplies for ground forces hits mountain side 10 mi W of dropping zone. 6 B-24's and 5 B-24's fly ground spt bombing misions over Attu. 2 P-40's bomb Kiska through overcast.

15 May

Eighth AF: 135 bmrs attack various tgts as well as A/F and naval installations on Helgoland; U-boat yard, M/Y and A/F at Emden; naval base and submarine construction works at Wilhelmshaven; and air facilities at Caen and Poix.

NAAF: NASAF Wellingtons bomb Palermo during 14/15 May. NACAF maintains sea patrol and rcn over large area of Mediterranean from W coast of Italy over Sicily, Corsica, Sardinia, and as far N as Marseille.

Ninth AF: P-40's fly sea patrol.

Fourteenth AF: 25-35 Japanese bmrs and 30-40 ftrs attack Kunming. Nearly all of the bombs fall in the W and SW of the A/F, causing little damage. 28 P-40's intercept, claiming 13 ftrs and 2 bmrs shot down.

Fifth AF: B-25's pound A/Fs at Lae and Gasmata. A-20's strafe airplanes and buildings at Lae. B-24's bomb A/F at Rabaul and hit Nabire. Single HBs hit Gasmata, Cape Gloucester, and barges SW of Ubili.

Seventh AF: 7 B-24's from Midway bomb Wake. 4 others abort and 7 others fail to find tgt. 22 ftrs intercept the formation. The B-24's claim 4 shot down. 1 HB is lost.

Eleventh AF: Weather again curtails operations. Air-ground liaison B-24 observes and directs air operations at Attu throughout the day as visibility permits and directs supply drop for ground forces by another B-24 in 2 air-ground spt missions. 6 B-24's bomb Holtz Bay and Chichagof Harbor; 6 P-38's strafe AA installations in Holtz Bay area.

16 May

NAAF: NASAF Wellingtons bomb Trapani during 15/16 May. NATAF and NACAF planes fly sea patrol, rcn, and convoy escort.

Ninth AF: P-40's escort shipping off Mediterranean coast.

RAF: Lancasters breach Mohne and Edersee dams, flooding large portions of Ruhr Valley.

Fifth AF: B-24's bomb Kendari A/F area. Single HBs attack coastal or offshore tgts in NE New Guinea, New Britain, and New Ireland.

Eleventh AF: Air-ground liaison B-24 bombs Chichagof Harbor with unobserved results. Another B-24 drops supplies to ground forces on Attu. 8 B-24's, 12 B-25's, and 12 P-38's fly ground spt missions to Attu. Because of weather, only the P-38's get through and strafe AA guns, installations and barges, scoring several hits. The bmrs are directed to bomb Kiska. 2 P-40's fly rcn mission over Kiska.

17 May

Eighth AF: 118 HBs hit port area and U-boat base at Lorient while a smaller force strikes the docks and sub pens at Bordeaux. 10 of 11 B-26's of 322d Bomb Gp are lost when sent on low-level mission to bomb power stations at Haarlem and Ijmuiden. This mission prompts Eighth AF to abandon low-level MB attacks.

NAAF: NASAF Wellingtons bomb Lido di Roma seaplane base and drop leaflets over Rome.

Fifth AF: B-25's bomb Gasmata, Dili, Penfoei, and Barique. Single HBs hit Lae, Finschhafen, Gasmata, and Cape Gloucester.

Thirteenth AF: P-39's and Navy airplanes bomb and strafe bivouac and AA positions in Rekata Bay area.

Eleventh AF: Two attempted ground spt missions to Attu by 1 B-24, 5 B-25's, and 6 P-38's are recalled due to weather.

18 May

Eighth AF: CBO plan for round-the-clock bombing of the enemy from UK by RAF and Eighth AF is approved by CCS. Eighth AF now has authorization to proceed with daylight strategic bombing within the type of combined offensive it has long wished to initiate. CBO plan lists the destruction of German ftrs as the immediate priority objective. Primary objectives in order are German submarine yards and bases, the German aircraft industry, ball bearings, and oil (the last being contingent upon attacks from the Mediterranean against Ploesti). Secondary objectives in order of priority are synthetic rubber and tires, and military motor transport vehicles.

NAAF: Gen Williams takes cmd of NAAF TCC (Prov). During 17/18 May, Wellingtons bomb Alghero-Sassari area. During day NAAF begins strong air offensive against Pantelleria in conjunction with naval blockade. Over 80 B-25's and B-26's, escorted by P-38's, blast the island, hitting Porto di Pantelleria and Marghana A/F. B-17's, with ftr escort, bomb Trapani.

Fifth AF: HBs, operating individually, hit Gasmata and Rabaul A/Fs twice and Cape Gloucester, Arawe, and Lorengau once.

Eleventh AF: 6 B-24's, weathered out of Attu, bomb Gertrude Cove area leaving large fires. 4 P-40's reconnoiter Kiska and strafe barges. 1 B-25 flies photo rcn over Kiska.

19 May

Eighth AF: 102 HBs hit U-boat yards at Kiel. A smaller force bombs naval yards at Flensburg.

NAAF: B-25's hit Milis and Villacidro A/Fs while B-26's bomb Monserrato and Elmas A/Fs, outskirts of Quarto Sant'Elena, and Cagliari harbor. B-17's bomb Milo A/F at Trapani.

Ninth AF: After 2 days of sand storms, Ninth AF aircraft are again airborne. P-40's fly escort for ships in area E of Kelibia off Cap Bon peninsula.

Fifth AF: B-24's hit Penfoei and A/F at Gasmata. B-25's attack Salamaua area and T/Os off NE coast of Huon Peninsula. Single HBs hit Gasmata twice during the day.

Eleventh AF: 6 B-24's and 11 B-25's fly 3 air-ground spt missions to Attu, bombing Sarana Valley. 4 P-40's fly 2 rcn missions to Kiska.

20 May

Ninth AF: P-40's escort ships and fly sea patrol off Cap Bon and Kelibia area.

NAAF: During 19/20 May, NA SAF Wellingtons bomb Villacidro and Decimomannu A/Fs. During day, P-38's bomb docks on Gulf of Aranci,

railroad bridge NE of Perfugas, Milis A/F, Macomer rail junction, and T/Os at Sassari, Bonnanaro, Chilivani, and Bonorva. Other P-38's and P-40's strafe and bomb Pantelleria. B-25's bomb Villacidro, Alghero, and Decimomannu A/Fs while B-17's strike Grosseto A/F.

Fifth AF: A/F and surrounding area at Gasmata are hit by A-20's during 20/21 May and by B-17's during day. B-17's and B-24's bomb Vunakanau A/F. B-25's sink several barges offshore between Madang and Cape Cretin.

Thirteenth AF: During 20/21 May, HBs on snooper missions bomb Kahili area and Ballale I.

Eleventh AF: All air-ground spt missions to Attu are cancelled due to weather. 20 P-40's bomb Main Camp and submarine area at Kiska, and strafe barges in the harbor. The remaining Japanese on Attu are concentrated in the Chichagof Harbor area.

21 May

Eighth AF: 123 bmrs of VIII BC hit German U-boat yards. Main effort is directed at Wilhelmshaven while smaller number of planes strike at Emden. At Wilhelmshaven German ftrs are reported firing rockets.

NAAF: During 20/21 May, Wellingtons hit Villacidro and Decimomannu A/Fs and T/Os on Sardinia. During day, B-25's and B-26's bomb the same A/Fs. P-40's attack gun positions and T/Os on Pantelleria, and B-17's hit hangars, repair shops, dispersal points, and a gun battery at Castelvetrano.

Ninth AF: During 20/21 May, RAF Liberators, under IX BC, bomb

Messina and Reggio di Calabria. During day, B–24's hit Villa San Giovanni and Reggio di Calabria; gunners claim 4 ftrs destroyed. P–40's fly sea patrol off NE Tunisian coast.

Fifth AF: B–17's bomb A/Fs in Rabaul area while B–24's hit A/F at Gasmata. Nabire A/F is hit by B–24's while B–25's blast AA positions, supply dumps, and town area at Saumlakki.

Eleventh AF: Of 10 B–24's, 12 B–25's, and 24 P–38's dispatched to Attu only 3 missions, totalling 6 P–38's and 1 B–24, are able to bomb and strafe troops and installations. 4 other missions, after vainly waiting for a break in the overcast over Attu, bomb Kiska submarine base through overcast.

22 May

NAAF: As diversion for convoy passing off Sicily during 21/22 May, NASAF Wellingtons fly intrusion mission over Sicily, dropping bombs on Castelvetrano, Sciacca, Milo, and Bo Rizzo A/Fs. NATAF ftrs fly convoy escort.

Ninth AF: P–40's fly sea patrol off NE Tunisia.

Fifth AF: B–24's bomb town of Kaimana and strafe power launches at Koer I.

Eleventh AF: Bad weather forces cancellation of all missions. 15 enemy bmrs make a torpedo attack on cruiser *Charleston* and destroyer *Phelps* patrolling Attu. The ships suffer only negligible damage.

23 May

NAAF: Col John W Monahan takes cmd of NATC. NASAF B–25's and B–26's bomb docks and A/F of Pantelleria and P–40's attack gun positions on the island. P–38's attack zinc works at Iglesias and Carloforte harbor.

Ninth AF: P–40's fly convoy escort off Tunisia.

Fifth AF: B–24's and B–17's hit harbor and A/F at Kavieng, A/F at Gasmata, and village of Ubili.

Thirteenth AF: 5 B–24's bomb A/Fs at Kahili and Ballale I during 23/24 May. 10 B–17's, attempting follow-up strike, abort because of bad weather. While other aircraft are successfully laying mines in N Solomons in Buin area, 19 B–17's and B–24's, in diversionary raid, bomb Buin-Kahili-Tonolai shoreline area.

Seventh AF: A flight of P–40's on patrol from Kauai bomb submarine from 1,500 ft, after which oil slick and debris are seen.

Eleventh AF: 6 B–24's and 12 B–25's fly 3 air-ground spt missions to Attu. Due to bad weather they are routed to Kiska. Weather there is also poor and only 1 B–25 bombs Main Camp area. Next, 3 B–24's and 18 P–38's fly 3 air cover missions to Attu. The last of these missions is notified by a PBY that 16 bmrs are W of Attu. 5 of the P–38's then intercept the bmrs over Attu, which jettison their bombs and close formation. The P–38's score 5 kills and 7 probables. 2 P–38's are lost.

24 May

NAAF: During 23/24 May, NASAF Wellingtons bomb harbor and A/F at Pantelleria. During day, NASAF and NATAF ftrs follow with more attacks on the A/F. P–40's, P–38's, B–25's, B–26's, and B–17's, bomb tgts on Sardinia, including Carloforte harbor, factories, hangars, and oil dump at Alghero and seaplane base at Porto Conte, railroad bridge at Arbatax, area near Macomer, town of Iglesias, harbor at La Maddalena I, harbor, warehouses, and dump at Terranova, and A/F at Olbia.

Twelfth AF: Col Lawrence P Hickey assumes cmd of XII A Spt Cmd.

Ninth AF: B–24's hit Villa San Giovanni ferry slip and railroad yards, and ferry terminal and nearby tanker at Reggio di Calabria.

Fifth AF: B–24's pound Lakunai A/F at Rabaul while B–25's hit runway at Gasmata. Other B–25's bomb Penfoei.

Eleventh AF: 2 of 3 air-ground spt missions to Attu, together 6 B–24's, 11 B–25's, and 1 F–5A, bomb Attu. Third mission is cancelled, except for 2 B–25's which do not hear cancelling order. 3 B–24's and 14 P–38's fly 3 more air cover missions over Attu but make no contacts.

25 May

NAAF: During 24/25 May, Wellingtons bomb docks and M/Y at Olbia. NASAF ftrs, MBs, and HBs bomb Portoscuso, Terranova, tunnel near Macomer, Porto Empedocle, Boccadifalco A/F, Licata harbor, Milo A/F, Messina, and Pantelleria. NATAF P–40's and B–25's hit A/F, shipping, and military concentrations at Pantelleria.

Ninth AF: B–24's attack Messina ferry docks and railroad yards.

Fifth AF: Single HBs bomb coastal A/Fs and villages, hitting Madang, Kakakog, Simbang, and Cape Gloucester, and attacking barges off Gavuvu.

Eleventh AF: 12 B–25's and 15 B–24's fly air-ground spt and 4 B–24's and 20 P–38's fly air cover all over Attu. 18 P–40's fly 1 rcn and 2 attack missions to Kiska and Little Kiska.

26 May

NAAF: NASAF MBs and HBs hit A/Fs at Ponte Olivo, Biscari, and Comiso. P–40's attack gun emplacements, trucks, and troops on SE coast of Pantelleria. P–38's hit Porto Ponte Romano shipping, Tirso power dam, Golfo Aranci harbor, and Villacidro A/F. NATAF P–40's bomb Pantelleria.

Fifth AF: 3 B–24's and B–25's bomb Madang town area and A/F.

Seventh AF: 3 B–24's from Canton I fly rcn-bombing mission over Abemama. Bombs are dropped on barracks area.

Eleventh AF: 8 B–24's and 11 B–25's, flying air-ground spt, bomb enemy positions. 2 B–24's and 12 P–38's fly air cover sorties and also patrol and strafe Attu. Kiska is covered by 3 F–5A's photo sorties and 3 attack missions, flown by 9 B–25's and 16 P–40's. Tgts include gun emplacements on North Head and E end of runway.

27 May

Eighth AF: 11 bmrs raid docks and submarine pens at Saint-Nazaire.

NAAF: P–40's bomb harbor defenses on Pantelleria. B–25's and B–26's hit Villacidro and Decimomannu A/Fs. NATAF P–40's attack tgts on S coast of Pantelleria.

Fifth AF: B–24's and B–25's pound Lae town area and A/F. Other B–25's hit enemy forces at Labu and

Jacobsens Plantation. Finschhafen, Saidor, Kakakog, and Langgoer are hit by single-plane strikes.

Eleventh AF: Attu is covered by 1 B-25 flying ground spt, bombing and strafing troops and dropping photos taken on previous day to friendly forces, and by 1 B-24 and 6 P-38's flying air cover. 6 P-40's fly attack and rcn missions to Kiska, concentrating on Little Kiska and on the Main Camp area.

28 May

NAAF: During 27/28 May, NA SAF Wellingtons bomb Villacidro, Decimomannu, and Elmas A/Fs. During day, P-40's hit Pantelleria, B-17's bomb oil refinery, M/Y, harbor, and shipbuilding yards at Leghorn, while MBs attack A/Fs of Sciacca, Castelvetrano, Milo, and Bo Rizzo. NATAF A-20's bomb Pantelleria.

Ninth AF: During 27/28 May, RAF Liberators, under IX BC, bomb Augusta. During day, B-24's of 2 gps hit Foggia A/F and surrounding area.

Fourteenth AF: 16 P-40's, operating in 2 forces, dive-bomb railroad yards at Yoyang. Tracks, warehouses, and the roundhouse are damaged.

Fifth AF: B-17's and B-24's attack Wewak, Dagua, and Boram A/Fs and bomb Wewak-Dagua coast road.

Thirteenth AF: P-38's and P-40's, along with naval aircraft, attempt strike on Kolombangara area and Munda but are hampered by bad weather. Some of the dive bmrs (TBF's) manage to bomb runway and revetment area at Munda.

Seventh AF: 3 B-24's from Canton I fly rcn-bombing mission over Abemama I, dropping 6 500-lb bombs.

29 May

Eighth AF: 147 HBs hit submarine pens and locks at Saint-Nazaire. Smaller strikes are made at Rennes naval depot and U-boat yards at La Pallice. 7 YB-40's, heavily armored B-17's with increased firepower for escorting bmrs, fly their first mission (to Saint-Nazaire). YB-40's show inability to keep up with B-17's and need for modification of waist and tail gun feeds and ammunition supplies.

NAAF: During 28/29 May, NA SAF Wellingtons bomb town areas, docks, and A/F at Castelevtrano, Bo Rizzo, Trapani, and Marsala. During day, NASAF P-38's bomb Porto Ponte Romano. P-40's, P-38's, and B-26's of NASAF and NATAF attack gun positions, radar station, and town area on Pantelleria.

Fourteenth AF: 9 B-24's bomb Ichang. 4 P-40's hit T/Os in Tengchung and Lungling areas.

Fifth AF: B-17's bomb Madang and Alexishafen. HBs and MBs, operating individually or in flights of 2 bmrs, attack town, A/Fs, shipping, docks, and other tgts at various places, including Dili, Penfoei, Damar I, Soemba, Soembawa, Babo, Nabire, Saidor, Finschhafen, Manam I, and Cape Gloucester.

Eleventh AF: No missions flown. All of Attu is secure after 19 days of fighting. US ground forces land on Shemya.

30 May

NAAF: During 29/30 May, NA SAF Wellingtons bomb Pantelleria. The following morning MBs and ftrs also hit the island. P-38's bomb Chilivani railway station and M/Y, hit port and railroad at Aranci, and strafe T/Os in Sardinia. B–17's bomb Pomigliano aircraft factory and landing ground and Capodichino A/F and M/Y. NATAF ftrs hit Pantelleria.

Ninth AF: B–24's hit Foggia, A/F, damaging buildings and hangars, and destroying several aircraft. B–25's attack concentrations on NE slope of Pantelleria.

Fourteenth AF: 7 B–24's bomb arty positions S of Ichang. 4 P–40's bomb and strafe Tengchung and T/Os along Burma Road and at Lamaing; 8 others on offensive sweep strafe several T/Os in Ichang area; 11 others hit riverboats at Shasi and trains NE of Yoyang.

Fifth AF: B–17's bomb Wewak, Boram, and Madang. B–24's hit Kendari area.

Eleventh AF: 8 P–40's fly 4 rcn missions to Kiska. 3 air-ground spt missions to Attu by 7 B–24's and 12 B–25's drop no bombs there and instead bomb Kiska installations. 2 B–24's and 12 P–38's fly air cover missions over Attu and patrol area. 3 F–5A's fly photo rcn and 8 P–40's attack and strafe tents and troops and blast runway at Kiska.

31 May

NAAF: NASAF B–17's bomb A/F and M/Y at Foggia. MBs and ftrs hit defended positions on Pantelleria. P–38's bomb Cagliari, factory at Guspini, and power station at Santa Caterina. NATAF P–40's hit Pantelleria.

Ninth AF: RAF HBs, including Liberators of 178 Bomb Sq under IX BC control, bomb oil stores, harbor, and seaplane base at Augusta.

Fourteenth AF: 9 B–24's, escorted by US and Chinese P–40's, bomb Ichang A/F. The HBs and ftrs shoot down 5 ftrs of an intercepting group of about 20. 1 Chinese P–40 is lost. 6 P–40's on armed rcn over Siaokan area blast a train and strafe troop concentration.

Fifth AF: B–24's pound Lae A/F and town area.

Thirteenth AF: 3 B–24's on armed rcn over S Bougainville bomb Numa Numa area and Tinputs. Small coastal vessel at Tinputs is set afire.

Eleventh AF: 5 F–5A's fly separate photo missions. 6 B–24's, 10 B–25's, 37 P–40's and 8 P–38's fly attack missions to Kiska. Their tgts include Gertrude Cove, AA installation, trenches, North Head runway, and a vessel.

1 June

NAAF: An attack by Wellingtons against Pantelleria during 30 May/1 Jun is followed by NASAF P–38's and B–17's while NATAF P–40's attack gun positions on the island during the day. NASAF P–40's strafe seaplane base on Stagnone I. P–38's bomb railroad near Balestrate. P–38's, B–26's, and B–25's, bomb Porto Torres harbor, Porto Ponte Romano, and Olbia harbor.

Fourteenth AF: 20 P–40's dive-bomb warehouses and railroad yards at Changanyi.

Fifth AF: B–25's hit Bogadjim and vicinity. B–24's bomb Lae A/F and nearby area.

Eleventh AF: 2 P–40's, 1 B–24, and 1 F–5A fly weather rcn and photo runs and 8 B–25's, 18 P–38's, and 20 P–40's, fly 7 attack missions to Kiska. Tgts include parked aircraft and installations, runway, gun positions, radar, and tents on South Head, North Head, Gertrude Cove and Main Camp.

2 June

NAAF: During 1/2 Jun, Wellingtons of NASAF hit Pantelleria and drop pamphlets on Naples. Ftrs and MBs hit the island during following morning and afternoon. P–38's attack Milo A/F while P–40's strafe T/Os in Sardinia.

Fourteenth AF: 5 B–25's, escorted by 10 P–40's, bomb Pailochi A/F. 18 P–40's strafe troop barges and launches at Itu and 6 long columns of troops E of Changyang.

Fifth AF: B–17's and B–24's bomb A/Fs at Wewak, Boram, Dagua, and But. Isolated shipping strikes result in little damage to vessels and barges.

Thirteenth AF: 2 B–24's on armed rcn attack gun positions, cargo boats, and shipping at Numa Numa and Tinputs.

3 June

NAAF: Ftrs, LBs, and MBs of NASAF and NATAF attack defended positions on Pantelleria following a raid on town area and docks by Wellingtons during 2/3 Jun.

Ninth AF: Col Charles D McAllister assumes cmd of IX FC, succeeding Gen Strickland. At the same time McAllister assumes cmd of DATF.

Fifth AF: B–24's bomb supply dump area at Dobo. Other tgts attacked in NEI suffer little damage.

Thirteenth AF: During 3/4 Jun, B–17's bomb Kahili A/F and Moliko R area. B–24's attack small vessels at Tinputs and Teop, sinking 1 and firing the other.

Eleventh AF: Weathered out from

Kiska are 3 weather missions flown by 2 B–24's and 2 P–40's, as well as 2 attack missions by 2 HBs and 6 ftrs.

4 June

NAAF: During 3/4 Jun, NASAF Wellingtons bomb Syracuse, Catanzaro, and Pantelleria, which is also hit on the following day by ftrs, LBs, MBs, and HBs, of NASAF and NATAF.

Ninth AF: B–24's attack Grottaglie A/F, leaving hangars and other building in flames. Gunners claim 3 ftrs shot down.

Fifth AF: B–17's and B–24's bomb A/Fs at Boram, Wewak, and Dagua. B–25's hit Koepang and Lautem.

Eleventh AF: 404th Bomb Sq begins to operate from Amchitka. 6 B–24's following a Navy Ventura make a radar-bombing run over North Head. 14 P–40's and P–38's bomb North Head, Main Camp and Little Kiska. 4 P–38's and 1 B–24 flying air cover over Attu make no enemy contact.

5 June

NAAF: During 4/5 Jun, Wellingtons hit docks and town area of Pantelleria. The following day, B–25's and P–38's extend the attack on the island, hitting mainly gun positions. B–17's hit harbor and shipping at La Spezia. B–26's bomb Porto Ponte Romano while P–38's hit A/Fs of Monserrato and Capoterra.

Ninth AF: During early morning, RAF HBs, under IX BC control, attack Catania harbor.

Fourteenth AF: P–40's strafe troop columns near Peiyang and hit barge and boat NW of Yoyang.

Eleventh AF: 7 B–24's, 6 B–25's, and 6 P–40's fly weather rcn and radar-bombing missions over Kiska, being handicapped by poor weather and mechanical trouble.

6 June

NAAF: NASAF Wellingtons hit town and docks of Pantelleria during 5/6 Jun. The following afternoon, Spitfires, P–40's, P–38's, B–26's, A–20's, DB–7's, A–36's, and B–25's of NASAF and NATAF continue pounding the island. Allied air bombardment increases and is concentrated on coastal batteries and other gun emplacements as second phase of air offensive against Pantelleria starts.

Ninth AF: B–24's strike harbor areas of Villa San Giovanni and Reggio di Calabria, and ferry slips and railroad yards at Messina. Gunners claim 8 ftrs destroyed. B–25's of 2 gps hit Pantelleria.

Fourteenth AF: 5 P–40's strafe trucks, barracks, and personnel at Tangyang; at least 15 trucks are burned and considerable damage is done to the barracks area. 11 P–40's hit approaches to bridge at Puchi. 2 locomotives in the area are destroyed. 10 other P–40's attack Shasi A/F and hit river shipping in the general area. 7 B–25's bomb A/F at Pailochi.

Fifth AF: B–24's hit town of Koepang and A/F at Penfoei.

Thirteenth AF: P–38's, P–40's, and Navy and Marine ftrs and dive bmrs attack shipping off Buin, scoring damaging hits on a destroyer and 2 smaller vessels. 15 Japanese airplanes are claimed shot down. Other P–38's and P–40's strafe Luti Bay area of Choiseul I.

7 June

Eighth AF: Eighth AF continues to be hit by requirements for N Africa as 389th Bomb Gp, originally scheduled for UK, is diverted by WD to Mediterranean.

NAAF: Following night raid by Wellingtons on Pantelleria, HBs, MBs, LBs, and ftrs of NASAF and NATAF pound the island throughout the afternoon.

Ninth AF: B–25's bomb gun emplacements at Pantelleria A/Fs.

Fifth AF: B–17's and B–24's attack Wewak, Lae, Madang, and Kesup, hitting town areas and A/Fs, and strafe sampans on Sepik R.

Thirteenth AF: P–38's and P–40's, along with RNZAF P–40's and Navy and Marine ftrs, intercept large force of ftr-escorted dive bmrs on mission against Allied shipping off Guadalcanal. Ftrs from the newly-opened Russell Is bases initiate the interception. A running fight develops and extends down to Guadalcanal. More than 20 Japanese aircraft are downed. 9 Allied ftrs are lost but all the pilots are recovered.

8 June

NAAF: NASAF Wellingtons pound town and docks on Pantelleria during 7/8 Jun. Air offensive against the island increase during the following day as ftrs, LBs, MBs, and HBs of NASAF anl NATAF continue to bomb throughout the day. Naval forces bombard harbor and shore batteries. Surrender requests, dropped by airplane, bring no response. P–38's attack barracks N of Segariu and A/F at Villacidro.

Ninth AF: RAF HBs bomb Messina ferry terminal. B–25's of 2 gps hit Pantellería, directing major effort at gun emplacements.

Fourteenth AF: 7 B–24's and 6 B–25's, with P–40 escorts, are dispatched to bomb shipping and dock installations at Haiphong. Bad weather prevents striking the primary tgts; alternates, including Hongay shipping, rail yard, and power facilities, Gia Lam A/F and warehouses E of Hanoi are bombed. P–40's bomb and strafe Japanese HQ at Tatung, barracks E of Lamaing on the Salween R, and a camp N of Lungling.

Fifth AF: B–25's bomb Koepang and hit area SE of Dili. B–24's unsuccessfully attack shipping at Waingapoe and off Wewak.

Thirteenth AF: B–24's on armed rcn bomb Kahili A/F and Ballale I.

Eleventh AF: A C–47 is the first AAF airplane to land at Attu, landing ftr crews at Alexai Pt. All other flying cancelled due to weather.

9 June

NAAF: Ftrs, MBs, and HBs of NASAF continue pounding of Pantelleria in predawn hours and during the afternoon.

Ninth AF: B–24's bomb landing ground at Gerbini and A/F at Catania. B–25's hit Pantelleria. Ftrs escort bmrs and fly patrols and ftr sweeps.

Fourteenth AF: 6 P–40's damage railroad bridge at Puchi and strafe nearby railroad yards.

Fifth AF: 2 B–24's bomb town area of Manokwari and A/F at Nabire. A lone B–17 bombs Unea I.

Thirteenth AF: B–24's on rcn attack small vessel WNW of Cape Henpan. B–17's, P–40's, and P–38's pound A/F at Munda and Vila.

10 June

Eighth AF: CCS issues directive through C/AS, RAF, marking official beginning of CBO of USAAF and RAF against sources of German war power. RAF is to bomb strategic city areas at night, and American force to hit precise tgts by daylight. CCS sanctions Combined Operational Planning Committee as the agency for coordinating the efforts of the CBO forces.

NAAF: Following attacks during 9/10 Jun by FBs, NASAF and NATAF aircraft (ftrs, LBs, MBs, and HBs) maintain all-day attack on Pantelleria. Over 1,000 sorties are flown.

Ninth AF: B–25's, escorted by ftrs, bomb Pantelleria. The escorting ftrs dive-bomb tgts on the island. Later, RAF HBs attack Reggio di Calabria A/F.

Fourteenth AF: 9 P–40's on armed rcn strafe 10 barges and a gunboat at Chienli; 1 barge is set aflame. 10 P–40's intercept about 25 airplanes over Hengyang; 1 enemy bmr is shot down.

Fifth AF: More than 20 B–17's and B–24's pound A/Fs in the Rabaul area. A single B–24 bombs town of Sorong and shipping at Kokas.

Thirteenth AF: P–38's and Navy ftrs claim 4 aircraft downed off N tip of Malaita I. B–17's and B–24's pound A/F at Kahili twice during the day.

Eleventh AF: 7 B–24's, 8 B–25's, 12 P–40's, and 2 F–5A's fly weather rcn, attack, and photo missions to Kiska and Little Kiska. Tgts include gun batteries, runway, North Head and Main Camp.

11 June

Eighth AF: 168 aircraft of VIII BC hit Wilhelmshaven U-boat yards. Smaller raid is made on port area of Cuxhaven. The raid on Wilhelmshaven demonstrates difficulty of operating beyond range of ftr escort as enemy ftr attacks prevent accurate bombing of the tgt.

NAAF: Attack during 10/11 Jun on Pantelleria by Wellingtons is followed by morning and afternoon attacks by ftrs and bmrs of NAAF, in conjunction with naval bombardment of the island.

Ninth AF: B–25's attack islands of Pantelleria and Lampedusa. Ftrs escort the MBs to Pantelleria and fly cover during bomb runs. After British 1st Div is landed unopposed, Pantelleria surrenders unconditionally.

Fourteenth AF: 8 P–40's hit camp on the Salween R, trucks at Mangshih, and warehouses at Tungling.

Fifth AF: B–24's again bomb A/F in Rabaul and hit T/Os at Gasmata and along shore of Keravia Bay. B–25's pound areas along Huon Gulf coast, hitting Kela Pt, Salamaua, and bridge at Nuk Nuk. Koepang is thoroughly blasted by B–24's while Penfoei and Dili A/Fs are hit by light B–25 attacks. P–40's strafe sub off Cape Nelson.

Eleventh AF: 7 B–24's, 8 B–25's, 10 P–40's, 4 P–38's, and 2 F–5A's fly weather, photo, rcn, and attack missions to Kiska. Main tgts are Gertrude Cove and Main Camp, South Head, North Head, runway, and offshore barges. Ftr bombing and strafing, and subsequent bmr runs over emplacements, are effectively coordinated.

12 June

NAAF: NASAF and NATAF ftrs, LBs, MBs, and HBs hit Lampedusa I. B–17's and B–26's bomb Castelvetrano, Boccadifalco, and Milo A/Fs.

Ninth AF: B–25's, escorted by P–40's, attack Lampedusa I. The island surrenders unconditionally, and Coldstream Gds go ashore and take charge.

Fifth AF: B–24's hit runways at Nabire and Kaimana. A lone B–25 bombs and strafes barges S of Langemak Bay.

Thirteenth AF: AAF ftrs, along with RNZAF, USN, and USMC ftrs, claim over 30 aircraft shot down during interception of enemy strike on Guadalcanal. 6 Allied ftrs are lost.

13 June

Eighth AF: 102 HBs hit Bremen U-boat yards while a smaller force strikes at Kiel sub yards. Heaviest ftr attack to date against Eighth accounts for 26 HBs, mostly of force attacking Kiel.

NAAF: NATAF and NACAF carry out land and sea patrols and rcn flights. NW African Photo Rcn Wg covers areas of Sardinia, Sicily, and Italian mainland.

Twelfth AF: Gen House becomes CG XII A Spt Cmd.

Ninth AF: US and RAF HBs attack Catania and Gerbini A/Fs, causing severe damage to aircraft, runways, hangars, and other installations. HBs claim 5 ftrs. 2 B–24's are down at sea.

Tenth AF: 9 B–25's attack Meza railway bridge on Mandalay-Myitkyina line, causing minor damage.

Fourteenth AF: 11 B–25's supported by 14 P–40's, bomb hangars and depot area at Nanchang A/F.

Fifth AF: B–17's and B–24's bomb A/Fs in Rabaul area and at Gasmata. B–25's hit Dili and Koepang and bomb and strafe barges off Huon Peninsula, at Jabob I, off Cape Gerhards, and S of Cape Cretin. Single B–24's bomb Malahang A/F and attack freighter in Humboldt Bay.

Thirteenth AF: B–24's and B–17's again bomb Kahili A/F.

14 June

NAAF: During 13/14 Jun NASAF Wellingtons bomb Messina. Other NASAF and NATAF airplanes continue patrols and rcn. NW African Photo Rcn Wg maintains flights over Sardinia and Sicily.

Fourteenth AF: 8 P–40's intercept about 8 bmrs and 20 ftrs 25 mi SW of Nanchang. The P–40's claim 7 ftrs shot down.

Fifth AF: A single B–24 bombs Lakunai A/F at Rabaul.

Thirteenth AF: 18 B–25's, escorted by F4U's, hit Vila A/F. 11 B–17's and B–24's bomb Kahili A/F and hit nearby Shortland I.

Seventh AF: 1 B–24 from Funafuti bombs runways at Tarawa.

15 June

Eighth AF: Additional modifications of YB–40 escort bmrs are completed in UK. It is now hoped that these B–17's converted to heavily armored aircraft with great firepower will solve the problem of long-range escort for bmrs.

NAAF: During 14/15 Jun, NASAF Wellingtons bomb Milo, Sciacca, Castelvetrano, and Boccadifalco A/Fs. B–17's, B–25's, B–26's, and P–

38's follow during morning hours with raids on same tgts and hit Bo Rizzo A/F and radio stations near Marsala. Widespread photo rcn of mainland Italy, Sicily, and Sardinia continues.

Twelfth AF: Col Harold A Barton takes cmd of XII AFSC.

Tenth AF: MBs score 2 direct hits on bridge at Myitnge.

Fourteenth AF: 10 B–25's, escorted by 12 P–40's, spt Chinese ground forces by bombing positions at Owchihkow.

Fifth AF: B–24's bomb A/Fs at Rabaul in predawn strikes and hit Kendari A/F in the evening. A single B–25 attacks power boat in Hanisch Harbor and strafes beach near Finschhafen.

Thirteenth AF: B–24's bomb Ballale I A/F.

16 June

NAAF: NW African Photo Rcn Wg continues coverage of areas of mainland Italy, Sicily, and Sardinia.

Fifth AF: B–25's bomb Koepang and Oeikoesi and, along with A–20's, hit barges and shore tgts at several points along coasts of NE New Guinea and New Britain.

Thirteenth AF: Gen Jamison becomes CG XIII BC. Search aircraft report nearly 250 Japanese airplanes at Rabaul and other A/Fs jammed with aircraft. In air action in the Solomons, about 120 Japanese aircraft converging on Allied vessels off Tulagi and Guadalcanal are met by more than 100 Allied ftrs (Thirteenth AF, RNZAF, USN, and US MC). The skies over Savo I, Tulagi, Cape Esperance, and Koli Pt are filled with dogfights and flak from ship and ground guns. The battle results in the largest single-day Allied aerial victory of the Solomons campaign. 79 airplanes are claimed shot down by Allied ftrs, and AA claims 17 more. 6 Allied ftrs are lost. The Japanese succeed in damaging 3 ships (2 of which have to be beached) and cause considerable destruction on Guadalcanal.

17 June

NAAF: During 16/17 Jun, Wellingtons bomb docks and M/Y at Naples.

Ninth AF: B–24's attack A/Fs at Biscari and Comiso.

Fourteenth AF: P–40's strafe warehouse and train S of Chiuchiang and a train N of Nanchang. Road traffic E of Hanoi is also attacked.

Fifth AF: B–25's administer thorough pounding to Madang and Salamaua areas. B–24's bomb Sorong and Boela. A single B–24 bombs Cape Gloucester A/F and during 17/18 Jun a B–25 attacks power launches nearby, sinking 1 and badly damaging 2 more.

Seventh AF: During 17/18 Jun, 4 B–24's take off from Funafuti at 2-hr intervals to bomb Tarawa. 1 aborts and another fails to find tgt. The 2 HBs bombing the tgt hit runways, silence an AA battery, and blow up an ammo dump. The raid is a diversion in spt of the first night photo-rcn mission by VII BC, during which 3 B–24's photograph Mille Atoll and nearby waters in the Marshalls.

18 June

NAAF: B–17's strike Messina ferry slip and railroad yards while P–38's bomb Milo A/F. B–26's and B–25's, with P–38 escort, hit docks and shipping at Olbia and shipping at Golfo Aranci. NATAF and NACAF airplanes maintain patrol and rcn flights. NAAF aircraft claim over 40 aircraft destroyed.

Fifth AF: B–25's bomb and strafe power launches off Cape Gloucester and Finschhafen, sinking 1 and damaging 2 near the Cape. A single B–17 bombs Unea I while an A–20 on armed rcn during 18/19 Jun bombs and strafes Salamaua and nearby coastal areas.

Thirteenth AF: B–24's bomb Kahili A/F while B–25's hit Ballale I and strafe barges in Wilson Strait.

19 June

NAAF: During 18/19 Jun, NASAF Wellingtons bomb Syracuse. NATAF, NACAF, and NW African Photo Rcn Wg airplanes maintain patrols and rcn over areas of N Africa, the Mediterranean, Sicily, Sardinia, and mainland Italy.

Ninth AF: B–24's attack ferry and railroad yards at Villa San Giovanni, ferries in Straits of Messina, and harbor of Reggio di Calabria.

Fifth AF: B–17's and B–24's thoroughly pound Vunakanau A/F. A–20's hit barges in Hanisch Harbor and trail near village of Tamigudu. Single B–24's bomb Finschhafen area and Rapopo airstrip.

Thirteenth AF: During 18/19 Jun, B–24's bomb Nauru.

Seventh AF: During 18/19 Jun, 2 B–24's fly photo rcn of Jaluit from Funafuti.

20 June

NAAF: NASAF Wellingtons bomb Messina during 19/20 Jun. The following morning B–26's bomb Milo,

Castelvetrano and Bo Rizzo A/Fs. NATAF and NACAF maintain patrols, rcn, and convoy escort while NW African Photo Rcn Wg continues coverage of areas in Sicily and mainland Italy.

Fifth AF: B–24's bomb airstrip at Rapopo, and A/Fs at Keravat and Rabaul, and also hit Rabaul town area. A–20's pound Lae A/F. 2 B–25's and an A–20 hit Finschhafen and barges and shoreline tgts along coast of New Britain.

Thirteenth AF: P–40's join Marine and Navy airplanes in strike against Vila A/F. Hits are scored on runway and dump area. B–24's blast A/F and other tgts at Kahili and also bomb Kieta.

Seventh AF: During 19/20 Jun, 3 B–24's from Funafuti fly photo rcn of Jaluit.

21 June

NAAF: Wellingtons bomb Naples during 20/21 Jun. The following day, B–17's hit Naples railroad yards, Salerno M/Y and trestle, Battipaglia M/Y, and Cancello Arnone air depot. Ftrs fly patrol, rcn, and convoy escort.

Ninth AF: B–24's attack ferry terminal and surrounding areas at Villa San Giovanni, and harbor area and railroad yards at Reggio di Calabria. RAF HBs follow up with raids on same tgts.

Fourteenth AF: 7 B–25's, with escort of 8 P–40's, bomb village of Shihshow. 8 other B–25's, supported by 9 P–40's, are dispatched to attack Japanese-held village of Hwajung but mistakenly bomb friendly village of Nanhsien, killing over 50 Chinese.

Fifth AF: In predawn strike B–25's bomb Koepang. A–20's bomb and strafe A/Fs at Lae and Malahang while B–25's blast A/F and general area at Salamaua. A single B–24 bombs MacDonald's Junction and strafes T/Os along coast S of Buka.

Seventh AF: 1 HB carries out armed photo rcn over Nonouti, Beru, and Nukunau Is.

Eleventh AF: A ftr strip is completed at Shemya. All missions are cancelled due to weather for tenth straight day.

22 June

Eighth AF: In first large-scale daylight raid on Ruhr, 182 HBs hit chemical works and synthetic rubber plant at Huls in main attack. This plant, representing a large percentage of the country's producing capacity, is severely damaged. 11 YB–40's accompany the Huls raid; 1 is lost. Other HBs bomb former Ford and General Motors plants at Antwerp.

NAAF: NASAF Wellingtons bomb Salerno during 21/22 Jun. NACAF Beaufighters sink small vessel off E Sardinia.

Ninth AF: P–40's patrol over Pantelleria; no encounters with enemy.

Tenth AF: HBs join MBs in pounding Ywataung M/Y. Monywa is also thoroughly bombed.

Fifth AF: B–24's bomb Taberfane area.

Seventh AF: 3 B–24's from Canton I fly photo rcn of Beru, Nukunau, Tabiteuea, Onotoa, Tarawa, and Arorae. 1 of the HBs strafes Arorae.

Eleventh AF: A P–40 sights a submarine 5 mi E of Zeto Pt. A B–24 then searches the area but makes no contact.

23 June

NAAF: NASAF Wellingtons bomb town of Olbia and lay mines in the harbor during 22/23 Jun. Photo rcn airplanes continue missions, flying over areas of mainland Italy, Sicily, Sardinia, Corsica, and S coast of France.

Ninth AF: RAF B–24's, under IX BC, hit Comiso A/F. Ftrs patrol over Pantelleria without incident.

Fifth AF: 17 B–24's bomb shipping, dock area, factory and residential areas of Makassar. 2 light cruisers are damaged and many buildings along Juliana Quay and in town area are damaged or demolished. A single B–24 or armed rcn bombs Lae A/F.

Thirteenth AF: B–25's and Navy ftrs and dive bmrs hit Buki village.

24 June

NAAF: During 23/24 Jun, Wellingtons strike Catania M/Y and industrial area. The following day, B–26's and B–25's bomb Chilivani rail junction, Alghero-Fertilia and Venafiorita A/Fs, and Golfo Aranci shipping and shore installations and other tgts in Sardinia. P–40's sweep S Sardinia, strafing and destroying trucks near La Maddalena, 2 small vessels in Gulf of Cagliari and off Capo Spartivento, and aircraft at Capoterra landing ground.

Ninth AF: B–24's strike Sedhes A/F near Salonika.

Tenth AF: B–25's attack road bridge at Shweli. Damage to tgt is slight.

Fifth AF: B–25's strafe and considerably damage Salamaua A/F and bomb villages in the area, demolishing 2 villages.

Seventh AF: 3 HBs from Funafuti fly visual rcn of Nonouti, Tabiteuea, Onotoa, Tamana I, Arorae, and Abemama. 2 other HBs fly sea-search mission from Canton I.

Eleventh AF: 16 bmrs fly 2 weather, an armed rcn, and 2 attack missions hitting barges near Vega Pt, Main Camp area, and North Head.

25 June

Eighth AF: 167 HBs make scattered attacks on T/Os in NW Germany when primary tgts at Bremen and Hamburg are obscured by clouds. Of 7 YB–40 escort bmrs dispatched only 4 are able to accompany formations to tgt area.

NAAF: NASAF Wellingtons bomb docks and M/Y at Olbia during 24/25 Jun. On following day B–17's drop over 300 tons of bombs on Messina bombing M/Y, W and N part of town, warehouse area and part of commercial quay.

Fifth AF: B–25's bomb and strafe several occupied villages in Sepu area.

Thirteenth AF: During 24/25 Jun B–24's attack Kahili area and hit A/F on Buka I. During the following day B–25's, escorted by P–40's, hit runway at Vila A/F.

Eleventh AF: 2 photo and weather rcn missions by 2 B–24's and 6 attack missions by 25 B–25's, 12 B–24's, and 2 P–38's hit Kiska. Tgts include gun revetments at Gertrude Cove and AA batteries.

26 June

Eighth AF: 93d Bomb Gp leaves UK for N African duty as demands for planned heavy bombardment in that area (invasion of Sicily and raid on Ploesti) make further inroads on strength of the Eighth. AM Leigh-Mallory is given responsibility for drafting air plans for invasion of Continent. His dep is Gen Hansell. 39 HBs hit Triqueville A/F. Smaller group strikes aircraft industry at Villacoublay. 5 YB–40 escort bmrs take off to accompany HBs but none are able to complete the attack.

NAAF: Wellingtons bomb Bari oil refinery during 25/26 Jun. 33d Ftr Gp (P–40) becomes first gp established on Pantelleria.

Ninth AF: During 25/26 Jun RAF HBs, under IX BC control, bomb Messina.

Fifth AF: During predawn and early morning hrs B–24's and B–17's bomb A/F and harbor at Rabaul and town of Lae. During midday B–25's hit Lae A/F and town of Salamaua. In early evening B–25's bomb Penfoei.

Thirteenth AF: During 25/26 Jun, B–24's pound Ballale I A/F and bomb Poporang-Buin-Faisi area. P–38's strafe Rekata Bay area.

Eleventh AF: 16 bmrs and 28 ftrs fly 7 attack, weather rcn and photo missions to Kiska and Little Kiska, starting fires. Intense machinegun fire damages 4 P–38's.

27 June

Eighth AF: 44th Bomb Gp leaves for duty in N Africa as Eighth continues to send combat units to the Mediterranean campaign.

NAAF: During 26/27 Jun, Wellingtons bomb Naples M/Y and port area.

Ninth AF: Beginning this date, 201st Bomb Wg (Prov)—93d, 44th, and 389th Bomb Gps—of Eighth AF

is attached to Ninth AF for operations. B–24's hit A/Fs at Kalamaki and Eleusis, damaging buildings, runways, and parked airplanes. HBs claim 7 ftrs shot down.

Fifth AF: B–25's bomb and strafe occupied areas at Dumpu, Kaigulin, and Kaiapit while A–20's strafe barges and shore installations at Labu Lagoon. B–24's hit Taka, Saumlakki, Boeroe I, and Malo I.

Thirteenth AF: B–24's bomb Kahili A/F and hit Ballale I. A single HB on armed rcn bombs Munda A/F.

Eleventh AF: 8 B–24's make a radar run over Kiska but return with their bombs due to weather. Later, 5 B–24's and 7 B–25's bomb Kiska Main Camp area and vicinity N of Salmon Lagoon. 14 B–25's bomb Gertrude Cove, camp areas, and North Head, while 7 others abort due to weather. 2 P–40's fly rcn over Segula I but overcast prevents observations.

28 June

Eighth AF: 158 HBs bomb locks and submarine pens at Saint-Nazaire. Beaumont-le-Roger is hit by smaller attack.

NAAF: During 27/28 Jun NASAF Wellingtons bomb Messina M/Ys and Villa San Giovanni. The following day, B–17's hit Leghorn, B–25's hit A/Fs near Olbia and Alghero, B–26's attack Milis landing ground, and ftrs hit Decimomannu A/F.

Seventh AF: Bombing mission against Nauru from Funafuti is hampered by engine trouble and bad weather. 1 B–24 had crashed at Palmyra the previous day while en route from Hawaiian Is to staging base at Funafuti. Of the 18 arriving at the forward base, 2 are released from duty because of engine trouble, 2 crash on takeoff, and 8 are grounded after second crash. 6 HBs are airborne for the mission, 2 abort, 2 fail to find Nauru because of heavy front, and 2 drop bombs on the island, with unobserved results.

Eleventh AF: 6 B–25's bomb Gertrude Cove, Little Kiska and southern Main Camp area through holes in overcast. Mission is partly ineffective because of faulty bomb-release mechanisms.

29 June

Eighth AF: 76 HBs attack aero-engine works at Le Mans. Heavy cloud over tgt prevents attack by most of the 232 planes dispatched. No planes are lost. Both of the 2 YB–40's dispatched as escorts are forced to abort. The lack of success of the YB–40's in this and previous missions in Jun 43 convinces Gen Eaker, CG, that if the escort bmr is to succeed it must be able to carry bombs and must be endowed with the same flight performance as the B–17.

NAAF: Wellingtons during 28/29 Jun raid ferry slips and M/Y at Messina. Photo rcn airplanes cover areas in N and S Italy, E Sicily, Sardinia, Corsica, and S France.

Ninth AF: RAF HBs hit Reggio di Calabria A/F. P–40's patrol sea off Cap Bon area; no incidents.

Fifth AF: B–25's bomb and strafe strong points along Bitoi R and A–20's pound supply dump on S side of Nassau Bay in preparation for allied amphibious landings which are to begin during 29/30 Jun. A lone B–24 bombs building area W of Parsee Pt near Salamaua. Other B–24's bomb Nabire.

30 June

Eighth AF: VIII FC becomes independent of RAF operational control. All ftr gps are placed under control of 65th Ftr Wg.

NAAF: During 29/30 Jun over 60 Wellingtons hit area NW of Cape San Marco and M/Y and surrounding area at Messina. The following day, B–17's bomb Palermo and Boccadifalco A/F, B–25's hit Sciacca A/F, and B–26's strike Bo Rizzo A/F. NACAF airplanes sink 2 schooners off S and E Sardinia and damage vessel off W coast of Italy.

Ninth AF: P–40's fly escort for a sea rescue airplane 35 mi N of Cap Bon.

Fifth AF: Allied amphibious forces begin landings, unopposed, at Nassau Bay during 29/30 Jun. Forces push N and S toward Bitoi R and Tabali Creek, respectively. Troops make contact with enemy forces in Cape Dinga area S of Nassau Bay. Australians open assault on Bobdubi Ridge and maintain pressure on enemy in Mubo area. B–25's pound Bobdubi Ridge in spt of the assault and hit forces at Logui and Salamaua. B–25's also bomb A/F at Cape Chater. B–24's and B–17's bomb Rabaul A/F. 1 HB scores hit on cargo vessel off Cape Gloucester.

Thirteenth AF: Invasion of New Georgia begins with amphibious landings by Army and Marine forces on nearby Rendova I. Subsidiary landings take place at other points in the New Georgia area. Thirteenth AF and other allied ftrs cover the landings. At 1100 30-plus Zeros attack the beachhead; Allied ftrs intercept, claiming 16 shot down. At 1500 a large force of ftrs, dive bmrs, and torpedo-carrying bmrs attack the vessels of the TF which is handling the landings. F4U's, F4F's and AA down all the torpedo-carrying bmrs as they attack vessels. However, a torpedo strikes the flagship *McCawley* amidship, severely damaging the vessel (later mistakenly sunk by US PT boats). Early in the evening about 30 more Japanese aircraft return to the assault area. Allied ftrs claim 18 of these shot down. B–25's and Navy dive bmrs bomb Munda A/F. B–24 strike on Kahili aborts because of bad weather.

1 July

AAF: Memo by Gen Giles for Gen Arnold stresses great need for more ftr escort for strategic bombing missions. The present ratio of less than 1 ftr gp to 4 HB gps is held to be completely insufficient and a minimum ratio of 1 to 2 is suggested.

Eighth AF: Gen Frederick L Anderson Jr replaces Gen Longfellow as CG VIII BC.

NAAF: During 30 Jun/1 Jul Wellingtons bomb Cagliari barracks and railway station. NACAF flies patrol, rcn, and convoy protection.

Ninth AF: P–40's, along with Twelfth AF ftrs, fly armed rcn of S Sicily and convoy patrol in Cap Bon area and off Kebili. RAF Halifaxes hit Catania railway yards.

Fifth AF: A–20's bomb and strafe forces in Duali area as nearby Allied troops consolidate positions along S arm of Bitoi R. Other A–20's strafe Lae area. B–25's hit Kela Pt and Logui. B–17's and B–24's bomb A/Fs at Rabaul.

2 July

NAAF: NASAF Wellingtons hit Palermo and Cagliari during 1/2 Jul. NATAF B–25's hit Castelvetrano during the day. NACAF aircraft attack 2 vessels off W coast of Italy and fly patrols, rcn, and convoy protection.

Ninth AF: 44th, 93d, and 389th Bomb Gps, on loan from Eighth AF, begin operations (2 Jul–21Aug) with Ninth AF. B–24's bomb A/Fs at Lecce, Grottaglie, and San Pancrazio Salentino. B–25's hit A/F and surrounding area at Sciacca. P–40's, escorting bmrs to Sciacca, shoot down ftr and damage 1. 2 P–40's are lost.

Fifth AF: B–25's pound defenses in Kela Pt area and trail near Logui. A lone B–24 bombs Salamaua area. Allied invasion force (MacKechnie Force) holds firm beachhead on Nassau Bay and makes contact with Australian forces to the N. B–17's and B–24's again attack A/Fs in Rabaul.

Thirteenth AF: B–25's and Navy F4U's bomb and strafe small vessel in Baeroko anchorage.

Eleventh AF: 3 bmrs and 4 P–38's fly 4 rcn missions over Kiska and Segula. 17 B–24's and 16 B–25's then attack Kiska in 5 missions, 2 of them radar-guided. Fires are started at several of the tgts, which include Gertrude Cove, the harbor, and buildings in Main Camp area. Intense AA fire damages 3 aircraft. 2 B–25's on a submarine attack hit Kiska seaplane ramp after making no contact with tgt. 2 P–40's cover troops which make unopposed landing on Rat I.

3 July

Eighth AF: Gen Devers, CG ET OUSA, in report to Gen Arnold, praises proficiency of VIII BC bombardiers but stresses dire need for high-altitude gunnery trg.

NAAF: During 2/3 Jul, NASAF Wellingtons attack Olbia and Trapani. The following day, B–17's and B–25's hit Chilivani, Monserrato, and Alghero A/Fs. Ftrs hit radar station at Pula and Alghero, while B–26's bomb Milis and Capotera A/Fs. NATAF LBs hit area around Marsala and A/Fs at Sciacca and Trapani.

Ninth AF: B–25's hit A/F at Comiso. P–40's fly escort over Sicily and over Pantelleria, claiming destruction of 1 ftr.

Tenth AF: B–25's hit the oft-bombed bridge at Myitnge, knocking the S end span into the river.

Fifth AF: B–24's bomb A/Fs in Rabaul area and hit Kendari A/F. Koepang is attacked by 2 B–25's. A lone B–17 bombs landing strip at Cape Gloucester.

Thirteenth AF: B–25's bomb A/F and AA positions at Munda.

Eleventh AF: 6 B–24's bomb Main Camp and take photos of Segula.

4 July

Eighth AF: 237 HBs strike in very effective attacks on aircraft factories at Le Mans and Nantes and also hit submarine yards at La Pallice. Bombing is extremely accurate.

NAAF: During 3/4 Jul, Wellingtons hit Trapani and Lido di Roma. Leaflets are dropped in Rome area. B–17's and B–26's hit Catania and Gerbini A/Fs. B–25's bomb 2 satellite A/Fs near Gerbini. NATAF LBs and MBs hit A/F at Comiso, Trapani, Sciacca, and Castelvetrano.

Ninth AF: RAF Halifax aircraft bomb Catania, railroad yards during

3/4 Jul. B–25's hit Comiso A/F. P–40's escort bmrs and convoy and fly sea-search for missing pilot. Ftrs claim 3 Me 109's shot down. 4 P–40's are lost.

Tenth AF: HBs attack Shweli road bridge but fail to cause appreciable damage.

Thirteenth AF: B–17's pound Bairoko.

5 July

NAAF: NASAF Wellingtons bomb Villacidro A/F and Catania during 4/5 Jul. NASAF ftrs, MBs, and HBs hit main and satellite A/Fs at Gerbini and radar stations at Marsala and Licata. NATAF LBs and MBs hit Sciacca and A/Fs at Trapani, Comiso and Biscari. NACAF airplanes maintain sea patrol, rcn, and convoy escort.

Ninth AF: B–24's attack harbor, harbor installations, railway yards, and oil storage at Messina. B–25's hit Sciacca and Biscari A/Fs. P–40's fly uneventful sea patrol. RAF HBs strike railroad yards at Catania.

USSR: German Army begins its ill-fated offensive toward Kursk.

Fifth AF: B–25's bomb and strafe A/F at Salamaua, Komiatum Track, and HQ areas at Kela and Salamaua.

Thirteenth AF: 9 B–24's over Buin fail to find shipping and bomb Munda and Ballale I instead.

6 July

NAAF: NASAF Wellingtons hit Gerbini A/F and 2 satellites during 5/6 Jul. During predawn hours and throughout the day, LBs and MBs of NATAF bomb A/Fs at Biscari, Sciacca, Trapani, and Comiso. NASAF B–17's again hit Gerbini A/F and 3

satellite fields. B–25's bomb Biscari A/F. NACAF maintains sea patrol and convoy protection.

Ninth AF: B–24's strike satellite A/Fs at Gerbini. B–25's hit A/F at Biscari and Gerbini. P–40's escort bmrs, patrol, and carry out dive-bombing operations in Sicily.

Fourteenth AF: 5 B–25's and 8 P–40's hit runway and revetment area at Pailochi A/F.

Fifth AF: B–25's attack Penfoei A/F and hit Labu Lagoon area.

Thirteenth AF: B–17's and B–24's pound A/Fs at Kahili, on Ballale and on Buka Is. B–25's hit beached destroyer at Bamberi.

Eleventh AF: 2 B–24's and 2 P–40's on 3 weather rcn missions report Kiska overcast, and take photos of Segula. 6 B–24's bomb Main Camp. 8 B–25's abort a radar run over Kiska when 1 has engine trouble and the others fail to locate Ventura Pathfinder. They sight a submarine which crash-dives immediately.

7 July

Atlantic: German sub, U–951, is sunk in E Atlantic, 37–40N 15–30W, by aircraft of 1st Antisub Sq.

NAAF: NASAF Wellingtons bomb Palermo and A/Fs at Villacidro, Milis, and Pabillonis during 6/7 Jul. During the day, B–17's, B–25's, and B–26's bomb Gerbini satellite fields and Bo Rizzo A/F, as P–40's fly diversionary sweep over W part of Sicily. NATAF LBs hit Sciacca during 6/7 Jul, and the following day bomb A/Fs at Trapani, Biscari, Comiso, Bo Rizzo, and Mazara del Vallo, and hit Sciacca, Marsala radar station, Caltanissetta, and Porto Empedocle.

Ninth AF: B–24's hit A/Fs at Gerbini and rail line N of Brucoli. B–25's bomb A/F and surrounding areas at Biscari and Comiso. P–40's bomb and strafe A/F at Lucca.

Fourteenth AF: 7 B–25's and 22 P–40's attack shipping at Canton. At least 2 interceptors are shot down.

Fifth AF: B–24's and B–25's, along with RAAF airplanes, operate in direct spt of Allied ground operations in Mubo area, dropping over 100 tons of bombs on numerous tgts as MacKechnie Force begins assault on Bitoi Ridge and Australian forces (2/6 Bn) capture Observation Hill, an important terrain feature W of Mubo.

Thirteenth AF: B–25's and P–38's attack Vila A/F. B–24's bomb Kahili A/F.

ZI: AAF Trg Cmd is established to take over functions formerly assigned to the Technical Trg and Flying Trg Cmds.

8 July

Atlantic: German sub, U–232, is sunk off Portugal, 40–37N 13–41W, by aircraft of 2d Antisub Sq.

NAAF: NASAF Wellingtons bomb A/Fs at Comiso and Catania during 7/8 Jul. During the day, B–17's, B–25's, and B–26's make several strikes against Gerbini and its satellite fields. P–38's strafe radar installations in E part of Sicily. NATAF LBs hit Sciacca A/F while MBs hit A/Fs at Biscari and Comiso. A–36's attack trucks, train, railroads, highways, sulphur plant, and a M/Y at several points in Sicily.

Ninth AF: B–24's attack Catania railway station, telegraph and telephone buildings, and industrial area. B–25's hit Biscari and Comiso A/Fs and nearby areas. P–40's attack Biscari A/F, escort bmrs over Sicily, and carry out sea patrol.

Fourteenth AF: 22 B–24's, escorted by 13 P–40's, attack shipping, docks, and cement works at Haiphong.

Fifth AF: B–25's continue to pound enemy positions around Mubo and along coast of NE New Guinea, hitting Kela Pt and village, Malolo, Buigap Creek, and trails from Salamaua A/F and Kennedy's Crossing to Logui.

Eleventh AF: 9 B–25's fly a special mission to Attu.

9 July

NAAF: During 8/9 Jul, NASAF Wellingtons bomb Catania, Gerbini, and Comiso A/Fs, and throughout the following day B–17's, B–25's, B–26's, and ftrs attack other tgts in Sicily, including Sciacca and Biscari A/Fs, Gerbini satellite field, and Cape Passero I radar stations. NATAF planes hit Sciacca and Milo A/Fs during 8/9 Jul, and on 9 Jul hit Milo and Biscari A/Fs, Sciacca, Porto Empedocle, HQ at Taormina, junction NE of Gela, Canicatti area, and T/Os.

Ninth AF: B–24's bomb A/Fs at Maleme, Comiso, and Taormina. B–25's hit Sciacca landing ground and Biscari A/F and dispersal areas. P–40's escort bmrs over Castelvetrano and Milo A/Fs. This pre-invasion air bombardment of Sicily provides air superiority over the enemy. British and US airborne contingents are dropped on the island during 9/10 Jul to help facilitate amphibious assault of seaborne troops which are to land on morning of 10 Jul. This is first major airborne operation to be undertaken by Allies in World War II, and subsequently becomes subject of intensive study.

Tenth AF: B–25's bomb railroad bridge on the Mu R between Ywataung and Monywa, scoring 2 direct hits and leaving the bridge temporarily unusuable.

Fifth AF: B–25's hit forces in vicinity of Old Bobdubi, Malolo, and Busama. B–25's hit landing fields on Timor, Dili, and Cape Chater.

Thirteenth AF: During 8/9 Jul, B–24's bomb Kahili A/F, Buin, and Poporang. B–25's and several ftrs sent against forces near Vella Lavella I fail to locate tgt and strafe Buki and Ganongga and a destroyer beached on SE Kolombangara.

10 July

Eighth AF: 70 HBs strike Caen/Carpiquet and Abbeville/Drucat A/Fs.

NAAF: During 9/10 Jul NASAF Wellingtons bomb Catania, Syracuse, Syracuse Isthmus, seaplane base and railroad station at Syracuse, and Caltagirone; NAAF TTC flies airborne operations to drop British and US paratroops on Sicily. US Seventh and British Eighth Armies make amphibious landings on S and SE coast of Sicily. NATAF A–36's hit railroads, road junctions, trains, and vehicles while P–40's fly cover for amphibious landings. NATAF LBs and MBs hit A/Fs at Sciacca, Canicatti, Ponte Olivo, and Trapani, and towns and surrounding areas of Caltagirone and Palazzolo. Throughout the day NASAF B–17's and B–25's bomb Milo and Sciacca A/Fs, Gerbini satellite fields, and towns of Palazzolo and Caltanissetta. P–38's on sweep strafe radar installation.

Ninth AF: B-24's attack M/Y at Catania and A/F at Vibo Valentia. B-25's hit Palazzolo, Sciacca, Catania and Agrigento, Floridia, Giarratana, Biscari, Syracuse, and Piazza Armerina. Ftrs cover assault beach areas in Sicily.

Fourteenth AF: 9 B-24's bomb dock area at Haiphong.

Fifth AF: B-25's pound Salamaua, Logui, and SE bank of Francisco R as Allied ground forces effect junction at Buigap Creek cutting comm between Salamaua and Mubo. A single B-24 bombs village of Kela. B-24's bomb Boela and Babo.

Thirteenth AF: B-24's pound Kahili A/F. Seabees report 3,300-ft airstrip at Segi Pt available for limited operations. This provides an emergency landing field only 40 mi from Japanese facilities at Munda.

Eleventh AF: The Eleventh attacks the Japanese Home Islands for the first time as 8 B-25's raid Paramushiru, scoring hits on the S part of Shimushu I, Paramushiru Strait, and northern Paramushiru, in dead reckoning runs when solid cloud cover prevents maximum altitude attack. No AA fire encountered, no enemy aircraft sighted. The B-25's stage through Attu on returning to Adak. 6 B-24's, originally slated to accompany the B-25's to Paramushiru, and 5 other B-25's are on short notice dispatched to attack a convoy off Attu. They claim 2 medium freighters sunk in deck-level strikes.

11 July

NAAF: NASAF planes hit Milo and Sciacca A/Fs during 10/11 Jul and numerous tac tgts during the day, including town areas, vehicle convoys, bridges, trains and roads. NASAF B-17's bomb Catania M/Y while B-26's hit Milo A/F and Gerbini satellite A/Fs. B-25's and P-38's hit Sciacca A/F and town of Caltanissetta. Throughout the day NASAF ftrs attack truck convoys on Sicilian highways, and hit gun positions and T/Os.

Ninth AF: B-24's hit A/Fs at Vibo Valentia and Reggio di Calabria. B-25's hit A/Fs at Trapani, Milo and Bo Rizzo, and areas between Sciacca and Enna. P-40's escort bmrs and provide beach cover as invasion forces push inland in Sicily. US Seventh Army's II Corps is hit by counterattack, mainly in Gela region. Attack is repelled, but airdrop of contingent of 82d Airborne Div troops results in heavy casualties.

Tenth AF: A few HBs hit port of Haiphong.

Fourteenth AF: 3 B-24's bomb Haiphong harbor area, 3 bomb shipping in Campha Port area, and 8 pound positions and barracks area at Kunlong. P-40's strafe traffic between Lao Kay and Cha Pa and hit oil storage area SW of Lao Kay.

Fifth AF: A-20's and B-25's blast positions in battle zone from Nassau Bay inland to Mubo area, hitting trail between Logui and Kennedy's Crossing, Bobdubi and Bobdubi Ridge areas, Salamaua, Kela Pt, and villages scattered through the area. Other B-25's bomb Penfoei. B-17's and B-24's pound A/Fs in Rabaul area.

Thirteenth AF: B-24's and B-17's attack Kahili A/F, hitting revetments E and W of the strip.

Seventh AF: 3 B-24's from Funafuti fly photo rcn mission to Little Makin; 2 of the HBs bomb the island.

Eleventh AF: 5 B–24's take off to attack Paramushiru and fly shipping search but are turned back by bad weather. A shipping search by 5 B–25's finds nothing. 6 B–25's and 6 B–24's in 3 missions (one by radar) attack North Head and Main Camp on Kiska with unobserved results. 4 P–40's fly rcn over Kiska sighting new excavations near Sredni Pt, strafe tent near Haycock Rock, and also fly over Segula I.

12 July

Atlantic: 1st Antisub Sq sinks U–506 near Portugal, 42–30N 16–30W.

NAAF: During 11/12 Jul, NASAF Wellingtons pound Trapani, Marsala, and Mazara del Vallo, and Montecorvino-Rovella A/F, and NAAF TCC drops paratroops in front of forward lines in battle area during 11/12 Jul. More than 20 C–47's fail to return from mission. During following day, B–17's hit Messina railroad bridges. MBs and LBs hit Gerbini satellite field, Agrigento, Canicatti, and Milo A/F. Ftrs hit trucks, trains, troops, tanks, and other T/Os during sweeps over Sicily. NATAF ftrs and LBs hit Milo A/F, Sicilian beaches, Termini harbor and town, Ninfa rail junction, several trains, numerous vehicles, and comm tgts throughout Sicily. NACAF aircraft fly convoy escort and carry out shipping strikes in Tyrrhenian Sea and W of Corsica and Sardinia.

Ninth AF: B–24's attack harbor, ferry slip, and M/Y at Reggio di Calabria, and ferry slip and railroad yards at Villa San Giovanni. B–25's hit Bo Rizzo A/F while P–40's patrol over Licata area. With bridgeheads firmly established in Sicily by end of day, British and US troops make contact at Ragusa. RAF HBs bomb Reggio di Calabria A/F.

Fourteenth AF: 7 B–24's attack docks and shipping at Campha Port, shipping at Ha Long Bay, and railroad yards, power plant, and warehouses at Hongay. The HBs claim critical damage to 2 freighters. P–40's strafe trucks S of Ha Giang.

Fifth AF: 13 B–24's bomb A/Fs and town area in Rabaul and vicinity. 2 B–25's hit Lingat A/F and Selaroe I villages. A lone B–17 bombs Garove I.

Thirteenth AF: 10 B–25's attack Vila A/F, which is hit later in the day by B–24's on armed rcn. 17 B–24's pound A/F on Ballale I. Several ftrs join Navy dive bmrs in strikes on AA and bivouacs in Munda area.

13 July

NAAF: During 12/13 Jul, NASAF Wellingtons hit Caltanissetta, Gerbini A/F, and Enna. During day, B–17's, B–25's, B–26's, and ftrs attack Enna, Milo A/F, Carcitella landing ground, Randazzo, and T/Os in Sicily. NATAF aircraft hit truck convoys, trains, railway stations, troops, and numerous T/Os over wide areas in Sicily. NACAF continues sea patrols, rcn, and convoy protection and attacks ship convoy NE of Palermo. British effort to break out onto Catania Plain by establishing bridgehead over Simeto R near Lentini is firmly opposed.

Ninth AF: B–24's strike A/Fs at Crotone and Vibo Valentia. B–25's attack Leonforte road and harbor on Termini. P–40's patrol Licata area.

Tenth AF: 16 B–25's lay mines in Irrawaddy R.

Fifth AF: B–17's and B–24's, operating individually, bomb A/F, town area, harbor, and other tgts in Lae area. B–25's blast positions in Salamaua area, along road between Kela and MacDonald's Junction, and hit AA guns at Salamaua and MacDonald's Junction. Ground forces clear Mubo area and Lababia Ridge of enemy.

14 July

Eighth AF: 101 HBs attack aircraft works at Villacoublay. Le Bourget and Amiens A/Fs are also hit by sizeable forces.

NAAF: During 13/14 Jul NASAF Wellingtons bomb Palermo and Messina, and C–47's drop paratroops in adv of Allied troops to secure bridge at Primosole. NATAF aircraft hit ammo dumps, trains, rail junctions, bridges, vehicle convoys, and other T/Os in Sicilian countryside, and bomb several town areas including Enna and Palermo during several raids throughout 13/14 Jul and the following day. During day, B–17's, B–26's, B–25's, and ftrs hit Naples, Messina, Enna, Marsala, and Randazzo, and numerous T/Os throughout Sicily. NACAF continues sea patrols, rcn, and convoy protection. British forces attempting to establish bridgehead at Primosole bridge on Simeto R near Lentini continue to face strong opposition.

Ninth AF: B–24's and RAF HBs hit railroad, M/Y, harbor, and oil storage at Messina. B–25's hit Enna and Palermo areas. P–40's patrol Licata and attack Lentini area.

Fifth AF: A–20's bomb and strafe Orodubi area. A single B–17 hits Lae. B–24's bomb Koepang.

Thirteenth AF: B–25's and P–40's strike small craft in Hunda Cove and Beagle Channel off New Georgia. 2 barges and a small vessel are claimed destroyed. B–24's and B–17's pound A/Fs at Ballale and Buka Is and at Kahili.

15 July

NAAF: During 14/15 Jul, Wellingtons of NASAF hit A/Fs and docks at Naples while NATAF LBs and MBs bomb Palermo and fly armed rcn, attacking roads and convoys, over extensive areas of Sicily. During the day, NASAF MBs bomb Vibo Valentia, while HBs hit Villa San Giovanni. NASAF ftrs fly numerous strafing and bombing missions against trains, road junctions, radar installations, truck convoys, railway stations, and T/Os throughout Sicily. NACAF airplanes fly sea patrols, rcn, convoy escort, and hit shipping off W. coast of Corsica and E coast of Sardinia.

Ninth AF: B–24's strike main A/F and 2 satellite fields at Foggia. B–25's bomb Palermo, Cape Gallo, Salina I, and Cape Zafferano. P–40's patrol over Licata area.

Fifth AF: A–20's hit positions along Orodubi-Komiatum Track.

Thirteenth AF: B–25's, P–40's, and P–38's strafe 2 barges NE of Ganongga, leaving them sinking. A large enemy force, estimated at 27 bmrs and 40–50 Zeros, is intercepted over Vella Lavella by AAF and other Allied ftrs, which claim 15 bmrs and 30 Zeros destroyed, against 3 losses.

Eleventh AF: 1 B–24 and 2 P–39's fly rcn over Kiska and Segula I. 9 B–24's and 14 B–25's bomb Kiska tgts including AA batteries at North Head, Jeff Cove and Gertrude Cove. Fires are started. 1 bmr turns back with 3 engines and jettisons bombs, another crashes on return. AA fire damages a B–25.

16 July

Eighth AF: 14 B–26's attack M/Y at Abbeville. With this mission, VIII A Spt Cmd begins combat operations, having acquired the 322d, 323d, 386th, and 387th Bomb Gps.

NAAF: During 15/16 Jul, NASAF Wellingtons bomb dock, M/Ys, and A/Fs at Vibo Valentia, Crotone, Reggio di Calabria, and Villa San Giovanni, while NATAF LBs and MBs carry out numerous missions against Randazzo and roads in Sicily. During day NATAF ftrs, LBs, and MBs bomb Valguarnera and T/Os in NC Sicily. British troops establish bridgehead across the Simeto.

Ninth AF: B–24's attack Bari A/F. Enemy ftrs attack persistently, and 3 B–24's are shot down. HBs claim 11 ftrs destroyed in combat. B–25's bomb Randazzo and Valguarnera. RAF HBs hit Reggio di Calabria A/F.

Fifth AF: A single B–24 bombs forces at MacDonald's Junction. RAAF airplanes hit positions to the SW.

Thirteenth AF: More than 30 B–24's and B–17's pound Kahili A/F. In Buin-Faisi area, 7 B–24's join 70-plus Navy dive bmrs and more than 100 AAF, RNZAF, Navy, and Marine ftrs in attack on shipping. Allied airplanes claim more than 40 aircraft destroyed or damaged. 7 vessels, including a destroyer, are sunk.

17 July

Eighth AF: 21 HBs hit aircraft factory at Amsterdam in main attack. Other planes bomb industrial tgts in NW Germany.

NAAF: During 16/17 Jul and following day NATAF ftrs, LBs, and MBs, hit Catania, Paterno, Riposto railroad station, and T/Os (vehicles, tanks, trains, guns) throughout Sicily. During day, over 200 B–25's, B–26's, and B–17's bomb Naples, concentrating on M/Y. US 45th and 1st Inf Divs cross Salso R S and E of Caltanissetta. British 30 Corps expands Simeto R bridgehead and drives toward Catania in coastal sector while 51st Div crosses Simeto and reaches to within 10 mi of Paterno.

Ninth AF: About 80 B–24's bomb Naples M/Y in face of fierce ftr opposition. 1 B–24 is shot down and several are damaged. The HBs claim 23 ftrs destroyed in combat. B–25's hit Catania and rail yards and roads at Paterno. P–40's fly escort to Gela and Comiso. RAF HBs hit Reggio di Calabria.

Fifth AF: During 17/18 Jul, B–25's bomb Lautem while B–24's bomb Adaoet I. During day, B–25's pound A/F, Army HQ and defensive positions, and general area in and around Salamaua as Allied forces from Nassau Bay-Mubo area begin drive on Salamaua. The drive is a secondary effort designed to divert enemy attention from subsequent Allied campaign to secure Markham R Valley and Huon Peninsula and thus gain control of Vitiaz and Dampier Straits.

Thirteenth AF: 7 B–24's and more than 70 Navy and Marine airplanes, escorted by more than 100 Thirteenth AF and Allied ftrs, attack shipping off Buin. The HBs claim hits on 2 cargo vessels, and the dive bmrs claim serious damage of 3 destroyers, a patrol ship, an oiler, a merchant ship, and the 2 cargo vessels. In the air battle, Allied aircraft claim more than 40 Zeros and at least 4 float planes shot down. 5 Allied airplanes are lost.

18 July

NAAF: During 17/18 Jul NASAF Wellingtons bomb A/Fs at Montecorvino and Pomigliano, while NATAF LBs bomb Catania and carry out rcn of extensive areas of Sicily. During the day, NATAF A–36's hit Santa Caterina, Adrano, Lercara, and Termini Imerese. US Seventh Army makes rapid progress against light opposition. British Eighth Army continues adv, but 13 Corps continues to meet strong resistance near Catania.

Ninth AF: B–25's bomb Randazzo and Catania.

Fourteenth AF: 7 B–24's bomb shipping at Haiphong and Hongay.

Fifth AF: During 18/19 Jul, B–24's bomb harbor area at Makassar. Several B–25's, a B–24, and an A–20 bomb and strafe Lokanu, Boisi, Tambu Peninsula, Dot Is, Salamaua, and Komiatum as US forces secure S headland of Tambu Bay for a supply base. Other B–25's attack barges and shipping off New Britain, sinking small cargo vessel off Cape Kwoi.

Thirteenth AF: 21 B–24's, more than 20 P–40's and P–38's, and 140-plus Navy and Marine dive bmrs and ftrs thoroughly blast the Kahili area. 15 of the HBs concentrate on the A/F. Many AA positions are attacked, as are revetments and runways. Hits are claimed on 2 destroyers, and a

light craft is sunk. The allied airplanes claim 21 ftrs shot down. 9 US Navy aircraft are lost. A B–25 off New Georgia strafes a motor launch.

Seventh AF: 6 B–24's, flying out of Funafuti, bomb Betio I, Tarawa Atoll. Japanese bmrs raiding Canton I are forced to jettison bombs at sea because of intense AA and ftr def.

Eleventh AF: 2 B–24's and 6 B–25's bomb Gertrude Cove and Main Camp at Kiska. 6 B–24's bomb shipping tgts between Paramushiru and Shimushu and completed runway at Murakami Bay on Paramushiru, which is also photographed. They observe fires among buildings S and E of this runway. Some of observed aircraft take to the air and vainly pursue the attackers.

19 July

NAAF: During 18/19 Jul, Wellingtons drop over 800,000 leaflets on Rome. NATAF LBs attack Catania. During the following day, about 150 NASAF B–17's bomb Rome railroad yards; B–25's and B–26's hit nearby Ciampino A/F. P–40's bomb rail facilities in Alcamo area. NATAF A–36's attack trains and motor transport in W Sicily. US Seventh Army continues to push N and NW while British Eighth Army's 13 Corps still faces firm resistance near Catania.

Ninth AF: Over 100 B–24's attack Littoria M/Ys and nearby A/F. On return flight railroads at Orlando and Anzio are bombed. B–25's hit Catania and Randazzo. P–40's escort DC–3's.

Tenth AF: B–25's damage approaches to Shweli road bridge.

Fourteenth AF: 4 B–24's attack cement works at Haiphong.

Fifth AF: A B-25 bombs bridge over mouth of Francisco R. A B-17 hits Finschhafen A/F. RAAF Bostons attack gun position at Komiatum and military camp at Erskine Creek.

Thirteenth AF: B-17's bomb Kahili A/F. B-17's and B-25's hit Ballale I A/F. B-25's in spt of ground forces hit positions at Bairoko battle area where enemy resistance is fierce.

20 July

Bay of Biscay: 19th Antisub Sq sinks U-588, 45-10N 09-42W.

NAAF: During 19/20 Jul, NASAF Wellingtons bomb Aquino and Capodichino A/Fs while NATAF MBs and LBs attack vehicles, roads, and town areas around and in Randazzo, Santo Stefano di Camastra, Orlando, and Nicosia in Sicily. During day, NASAF FBs attack T/Os in W Sicily while NASAF MBs strike Montecorvino A/F. US Seventh Army and British Eighth Army continue to push NW and N. 82d Airborne Div (US) takes Sciacca and Menfi. 3d Inf Div (US) clears Santo Stefano Quisquina and heights N of Mussomeli. 2d Armd Div, with British units, takes Enna and drives on to Villapriolo. Canadian 1st Inf Div pushes to Leonforte area. British 51st Div attacks German A/F near Sferro. 13 Corps is halted by strong opposition on Catania Plain.

Ninth AF: B-25's attack Randazzo and Taormina. RAF HBs hit Vibo Valentia A/F.

Tenth AF: HBs attack Mandalay.

Fourteenth AF: 4 P-40's bomb warehouse area at Tengchung. 6 others strafe river traffic and railroad T/Os at Sinti, Changanyi, Tingszekiao, Kaiyu, and near Puchi.

Fifth AF: As US ground forces begin struggle for heights commanding Tambu Bay and Dot Inlet, A-20's and B-25's pound Madang A/F and area, Komiatum, Logui, areas along Gum R and S of Gogol R, Gori R bridge area, and Bogadjim. B-25's bomb Lautem, Dili, and Cape Chater A/F. A single B-24 bombs Arawe.

Thirteenth AF: 18 B-24's bomb A/Fs at Kahili and on Ballale I. Ftrs strafe barges in Pakoi Bay.

21 July

NAAF: During 20/21 Jul, Wellingtons of NASAF hit Crotone A/F and Naples M/Y; NATAF LBs hit motor transport convoys in Randazzo area. During day, NASAF B-17's bomb A/F at Grosseto. Rangers seize Castelvetrano and airport. 82d Airborne Div takes San Margherita and 3d Inf Div takes Corleone. 45th Inf Div, pushing NW, takes Valledolmo. 1st Inf Div clears Alimena. In British 30 Corps area, Canadian 1st Inf Div takes Leonforte.

Ninth AF: About 20 B-25's bomb Randazzo. P-40's escort C-47's to Licata and return.

Fifth AF: More than 50 B-25's again thoroughly pound Madang area. Other B-25's hit junction of Gori and Ioworo Rivers and village of Bogadjim. B-26's bomb barges and jetties W of Voco Pt. Single B-24's bomb Finschhafen A/F and town of Rabaul.

Thirteenth AF: In a series of sorties in spt of ground forces, 22 B-25's, more than 50 AAF and Navy ftrs, and more than 170 Navy dive bmrs blast positions in Bairoko area. 135 tons of bombs are dropped.

Eleventh AF: 9 B-24's bomb Kiska

tgts, including runway, North Head, and Main Camp area where fires are observed. Poor weather cancels other scheduled missions

22 July

Eighth AF: Results of first phase of CBO are good according to a report of Joint Intelligence Committee (British). The report maintains CBO has caused Germany to adopt a defensive air strategy resulting in more than half its ftr strength being employed on Western Front at expense of Eastern and Mediterranean Fronts as well as causing considerable damage to transportation, synthetic rubber industry, and the fuel, iron, and coal industries of the Ruhr.

NAAF: During 21/22 Jul, NASAF Wellingtons bomb Capodichino A/F and Salerno M/Y. NATAF LBs hit Randazzo, railroad at Falcone, and road W of Marina. During day, over 100 B–17's bomb Battipaglia M/Y and Foggia. B–26's hit Salerno bridge and M/Y. Ftrs fly sweep over Maddalena I, strafing factories, trucks, and small vessels. NATAF LBs bomb Adrano, Paterno, Troina, and Misterbianco. US Seventh Army troops take Palermo. 1st Inf Div continues N, taking Bompietro.

Ninth AF: P–40's escort C–47's to Ponte Olivo.

Fifth AF: More than 50 B–24's, B–25's, and B–26's blast troops, AA guns, defensive positions, and T/Os in battle zones at Komiatum, on Komiatum Ridge, at Kela Mt, at Salamaua, and along trails near Komiatum and Salamaua. B–24's bomb oil refinery, docks, and railroad yards at Soerabaja. B–25's hit T/Os on Selaroe.

Thirteenth AF: More than 20 B–17's and B–24's, 40-plus Navy dive bmrs, and more than 100 Allied ftr aircraft attack shipping in area off Buin. A sea-plane carrier is sunk, and damaging hits are claimed on several other vessels.

Eleventh AF: 26 B–25's, 17 B–24's, 13 P–40's, and 20 P–38's hit North Head, Main Camp, and the submarine base at Kiska, as well as coastal defenses and AA guns at both Kiska and Little Kiska, starting numerous fires. Intense and heavy AA fire downs one B–25 (crew saved) and damages 18 aircraft of which another B–25 crashes at base. 1 B–25 photographs S and W Kiska shores. 1 B–24 flies radar rcn over Kiska.

23 July

NAAF: NASAF B–17's, B–25's, and B–26's bomb Leverano, Crotone, and Aquino A/F. NATAF MBs and ftrs bomb and strafe Misterbianco, transport in Nicosia-Troina-Randazzo areas, and bridges and landing craft in coastal area around Santo Stefano di Camastra and Orlando. US Seventh Army mops up in W Sicily. British Eighth Army's 30 Corps meets firm opposition as it moves E from Leonforte.

Ninth AF: P–40's escort C–47's to Licata. RAF HBs hit Reggio di Calabria A/F.

Fifth AF: B–25's, B–26's, B–24's, and B–17's again pound tgts in coastal NE New Guinea, hitting Malolo, Asini, Busama, Voco Pt, and Salamaua, blasting barges from Hanisch Harbor to Wald Bay and Cape Busching, and thoroughly bombing Bogadjim.

Thirteenth AF: B–25's and P–40's,

along with Navy dive bmrs, pound Rekata Bay area.

24 July

Eighth AF: 167 HBs execute very successful attack on nitrate works at Heroya. This is Eighth's first mission to Norway and its longest (1,900 mi round trip) to date. Work at the plant is disrupted for 3½ months, and unfinished aluminum and magnesium plants are damaged and subsequently abandoned by the Germans. Naval installations at Trondheim also are hit. Crews successfully experiment with new assembly procedure for occasions when bad weather conditions prevent ascent in formation. Aircraft take off individually on instruments, proceed to designated splasher beacon for group formation, and then along line of 3 splasher beacons for force assembly. The method works well and makes possible many future missions which might otherwise have been abandoned.

NAAF: NASAF B–17's and B–25's bomb Bologna railroad yards. B–26's hit Paola railroad yards. NATAF FBs hit barges, warships, and docks in Messina-Milazzo area and transport NE of Mount Etna. US Seventh Army continues to mop up W part of Sicily. Further E, 45th Inf Div takes Cefalu and Castelbuono while 1st Inf Div seizes Gangi and heads toward Nicosia.

Ninth AF: P–40's fly armed rcn and FB missions over Adrano and Milazzo areas. Attacks are concentrated against motor transport tgts.

Fifth AF: B–25's bomb Lautem, Fuiloro, Koepang, Tenau, and A/F and surrounding areas at Lae, and attack barges in Wapelik and Cape Busching areas and villages on Itni R.

Thirteenth AF: 48 ftrs join Navy and Marine dive bmrs in spt of ground forces in Bairoko area. Later in the day gun positions at Bibolo Hill near Munda are hit, along with other tgts.

Seventh AF: 8 B–24's from Midway attack Wake, bombing oil storage, barracks, and a gun emplacement. 20–30 Zeros attack the formation. 9 ftrs are claimed destroyed. 1 HB is lost in collision with falling Japanese ftr.

Eleventh AF: 62 P–40's fly 9 missions to Kiska (2 of them with RCAF pilots) bombing runway and scoring many hits. An AA battery takes a direct hit and explodes. AA guns are strafed on North Head and Little Kiska. Intense AA fire downs 1 P–40.

25 July

Eighth AF: 218 HBs bomb tgts in Germany, with shipyard at Hamburg and U-boat base at Kiel as major tgts. 19 HBs are lost, mostly to effective formation attacks by German ftrs. This raid on Hamburg is part of 6 CBO missions against that port city and follows a raid of the previous night during which nearly 750 RAF HBs did tremendous damage to the tgt. Bergen, one of the scheduled tgts, is completely obscured by clouds and no bombing attempt is made there because of the policy of no indiscriminate bombing over enemy-occupied countries. 13 B–26's hit coke ovens at Ghent.

NAAF: NATAF, MBs, LBs, and ftrs during night and day raids, attack shipping and docks at Milazzo and in Santo Stefano di Camastra-Orlando area, and hit roads and motor transport, bridges and armor concentration in Orlando-Adrano-Troina-Nicosia areas. US Seventh Army makes slow progress along N coastal road, while British Eighth Army's 30 Corps takes part in hard fighting in Agira area.

Ninth AF: B–25's bomb docks and shipping at Milazzo. Almost 100 P–40's strafe and bomb Milazzo, Taormina, and Catania harbor. Other P–40's escort C–47's.

Italy: King Victor Emmanuel III announces fall of Mussolini government. Marshall Badoglio becomes premier and takes cmd of Italian army.

Fourteenth AF: 9 B–25's, escorted by 17 P–40's and P–38's, bomb Hankow A/F.

Fifth AF: Single B–24's attack large transport vessel WNW of Buka Passage and bomb Lingat, Adaoet, and area near Finschhafen.

Thirteenth AF: Gen Twining becomes COMAIRSOLS. FC and BC, Solomons, are taken over by Gen Strother and Col William A Matheny, respectively; Strother retains his position as CG XIII FC. The Japanese try to hit US forces on Rendova I but Allied ftrs shoot down several Zeros (8 claimed) and force the enemy bmrs to drop their bombs indiscriminately. Final push on Japanese base at Munda opens with bombardment by 7 destroyers and the heaviest air attack in SOPAC to date. 170-plus B–24's, B–25's, B–17's, TBF's, and SBD's, covered by more than 70 ftrs, pound the tgt thoroughly, dropping more than 145 tons of bombs in little more than a

half hr. Later in the afternoon 10 more B–24's, with ftr cover, bomb Bibolo Hill, and SBD's and TBF's dive-bomb gun positions. Later in the day, gun positions NE of Kindu Village are hit. 43d and 37th Divs open ground assault against firmly entrenched enemy.

Eleventh AF: 343d Ftr Gp moves from Adak to Amchitka. 40 P–40's fly 7 attack missions (2 by RCAF pilots) bombing and strafing North Head AA batteries, runway, Main Camp, and Little Kiska.

26 July

Eighth AF: 92 HBs bomb rubber factories at Hannover as main objective. 54 attack shipbuilding yards at Hamburg. Results are good but costly. 24 aircraft are lost, mostly to enemy ftrs. 15 B–26's bomb Saint-Omer/Longuenesse A/F.

NAAF: During 25/26 Jul, NATAF MBs attack Milazzo, Adrano, and Paterno. Throughout day LBs hit Regalbuto at intervals, and FBs harrass shipping, rail, and road movements. NASAF B–26's bomb Marina di Paola M/Y.

Ninth AF: B–25's bomb Milazzo, Paterno, and Adrano. P–40's strafe and bomb Catania and shipping at Riposto harbor.

Fourteenth AF: 5 B–25's, escorted by 12 ftrs, bomb Hankow A/F. An estimated 30–50 ftrs intercept the force. The MBs and ftrs claim 14 airplanes shot down and 17 probably destroyed. 1 P–40 is lost.

Fifth AF: More than 40 B–24's and B–17's bomb Salamaua, Malolo Mission, Komiatum, Komiatum Ridge, and Lae A/F.

Thirteenth AF: B–24's, P–38's, P–40's, and Navy aircraft hit bivouac area and runway at Kahili. B–25's, P–40's, and USN ftrs over S Kolombangara hit E shore of Webster Cove and bivouac area and buildings on Simbo I.

Seventh AF: Last mission against Wake from Midway is flown. 8 B–24's bomb tgts including oil storage area. 20-plus ftrs (including an aircraft identified as a possible FW 190) intercept the formation. HBs claim 11 of the ftrs shot down.

Eleventh AF: 3 bmrs and 5 ftrs fly 5 armed rcn missions to Kiska. 32 B–24's, 38 P–40's, and 24 P–38's fly 13 attack raids, bombing and scoring hits on numerous Kiska and Little Kiska tgts, including North Head, Main Camp, runway, Gertrude Cove, AA batteries, and on suspected submarine in Kiska harbor. A submarine is sighted near Rat I. AA fire claims 1 P–40 (pilot rescued), and damages 3 others. 1 B–25 and 15 P–38's fly 2 air cover missions to Kiska for the Navy. Over 104 tons of bombs are dropped on Kiska this day, highest one-day bomb load so far dropped by the Eleventh.

27 July

Eighth AF: 17 B–26's raid A/F at Triqueville.

NAAF: NASAF B–17's hit A/F at Capua and railroad at Lioni. B–25's and B–26's bomb Scalea landing ground. NATAF ftrs and LBs continue bombing and strafing of ports, shipping, bridges, landing grounds, and motor transport in Sicily as US Seventh Army reaches Tusa and San Mauro and pushes toward Nicosia.

Ninth AF: P–40's attack tac tgts in battle area in NE Sicily, and others hit shipping at Catania.

Fourteenth AF: 10 B–24's attack shipping in Samah Bay area, claiming severe damage to 2 vessels. 25–30 ftrs intercept the HBs. 13 ftrs are claimed shot down. No B–24's are lost. 6 B–25's, supported by 14 ftrs, attack T/Os on Stonecutter's I in Hong Kong area after failing to locate a reported freighter in the area.

Fifth AF: 35 B–25's and 18 B–24's pound Salamaua area in one of the largest single-strike attacks of SWPA. A/F and supply storage at Salamaua, town of Kela and nearby hilltop positions, and defensive positions between road and beach at Logui are hit. 5 other B–25's hit barges between Pommern Bay and Finschhafen, and 6 B–26's bomb barge concentration and supply area at Voco Pt. A lone B–24 on armed rcn bombs T/Os on Mundua and Unea Is.

Thirteenth AF: Gen Owens becomes CG, Thirteenth AF. B–17's bomb A/Fs at Kahili and Ballale I. 8 P–38's and 70-plus Navy and Marine aircraft again attack Munda area, hitting positions on Bibolo Hill and tgts at Gurasai, Munda Pt, and Munda A/F.

Eleventh AF: 12 bmrs and 20 ftrs take off on 5 attack missions to Kiska. Several of the ftrs jettison bombs. The other aircraft hit Main Camp, North Head and Little Kiska.

28 July

Bay of Biscay: German sub, U–404, is sunk by aircraft of 4th Antisub Sq and RAF 224 Sq, at 45–53N 09–23W.

Eighth AF: Over 300 HBs are dispatched in 2 forces to bomb German tgts. Bad weather prevents majority from completing mission, but 49 bomb aircraft works at Kassel and 28 attack major FW 190 factory at Oschersleben, marking deepest US bmr penetration into Germany to date. Raid achieves good results. However, 22 HBs are lost as ftrs score first effective results with rockets. 105 P–47's, equipped with jettisonable belly tanks for first time on mission, escort the B–17's into Germany; other P–47's, going more than 30 mi deeper into Germany than they have penetrated before, meet the returning bmrs. They surprise about 60 German ftrs and destroy 9 of them; one P–47 is lost. 17 B–26's hit Zeebrugge coke ovens. MB mission to bomb Triqueville A/F aborts because of failure to meet ftr escort in bad weather.

NAAF: NASAF ftrs sweep over S Sardinia. NATAF LBs hit Regalbuto, Milazzo, and Centuripe. A–36's and P–40's hit heavy traffic on Troina-Randazzo road, bridges and roads N and W of Cesaro, landing ground at Falcone, and buildings near Randazzo. US Seventh Army takes Nicosia and pushes toward Santo Stefano di Camastra. British Eighth Army takes Agira. Allied cargo vessels begin arriving at Palermo, and Gen Alexander, 15 Army Gp CG, moves his HQ to Sicily.

Ninth AF: Almost 100 P–40's hit shipping at Catania and Santa Teresa, fly patrol over Straits of Messina and bomb encampments.

Fourteenth AF: 6 B–25's, with escort of 9 P–40's, bomb Taikoo Docks at Hong Kong.

Fifth AF: B–25's attack barges and fuel dump between Cape Raoult and Rein Bay, and hit A/F at Cape Gloucester and 2 destroyers offshore.

Single B–24's bomb Unea I and unsuccessfully attack shipping in Saint George Channel. B–24's bomb Manokwari, Larat, and Boela. B–25's hit town of Lautem and A/F at Cape Chater.

Thirteenth AF: B–25's and Navy aircraft hit gun positions and other tgts at Webster Cove.

29 July

Eighth AF: 91 HBs bomb U-boat yards at Kiel, and 81 attack Heinkel aircraft factory at Warnemunde. MBs hit Saint-Omer/Ft Rouge A/F. Mission to Schiphol A/F aborts due to navigational error.

NAAF: NASAF B–26's hit Aquino A/F. B–17's bomb Viterbo A/F. NATAF ftrs and LBs hit Regalbuto, Milazzo, shipping off Messina, and gun positions and motor transport in NE Sicily. US Seventh Army almost completes mopup of W Sicily, approaches Santo Stefano Quisquina, advances on Mistretta, and takes 3 islands off Trapani. British Eighth Army opens assault during 29/30 Jul along axis of Catenanuova-Adrano.

Ninth AF: Over 200 P–40's, to date the largest number of ftrs operating in 1 day during Sicilian campaign, attack Messina Riposto, shipping at Catania, Santa Teresa di Riva, Taormina, Milazzo, and in Straits of Messina.

Tenth AF: 2 flights of B–25's blast the previously bombed Mu R bridge between Ywataung and Monywa. The bridge is hit heavily with 1 span left submerged in the river.

Fourteenth AF: 18 B–24's, with ftr escort, bomb shipping and dockyard installations at Hong Kong. Kowloon and Taikoo Docks and the old Royal Navy yards are hit. 4 P–40's attack Japanese force of 23 bmrs and 30 ftrs attacking Hengyang. 1 Japanese ftr is downed.

Fifth AF: B–17's, B–24's, and B–25's bomb Kela Pt and village, and Salamaua town and peninsula area. B–25's, B–26's, and a B–24 attack Army HQ, barges, and villages in Natamo vicinity, shipping off Cape Gloucester, and barges off Cape Dampier, in Borgen Bay, and along coast from Ring Ring Plantation to Roebuck Pt. P–40's strafe T/Os.

Eleventh AF: 1 B–17 scouts Kiska and bombs Main Camp area.

30 July

Eighth AF: 134 HBs bomb aircraft works and M/Y at Kassel. P–47's with auxiliary tanks surprise attacking German ftrs over Bocholt as enemy is not yet accustomed to ftr escort penetration beyond coastal fringe. Small number of MBs hit A/F at Woensdrecht. Bad weather causes multiple aborts on this mission and abandonment of attack on Courtrai A/F.

NAAF: NASAF B–17's bomb Grottaglie A/F. B–25's hit A/F at Pratica di Mare. NATAF A–20's bomb Milazzo and hit gun positions N and E of Centuripe. Ftrs hit shipping off Milazzo. Enemy evacuates Santo Stefano Quisquina, with rear guard action. British take Catenanuova and push on to NE.

Ninth AF: Over 100 P–40's attack shipping at Milazzo, Messina, and Riposto, and hit tgts in battle area.

Fourteenth AF: 15 P–40's over Hengyang area make contact with 39 Japanese ftrs and 24 bmrs. In the ensuing battle, 3 bmrs and 2 ftrs are downed; 2 P–40's are lost.

Fifth AF: B–24's bomb Salamaua and Kela. B–25's hit barges off Huon Peninsula and villages in Finschhafen area. A–20's destroy several barges at Hanisch Harbor and Langemak Bay. Single B–24's bomb Cape Gloucester and Unea I.

Thirteenth AF: 9 B–24's, with escort of 16 P–38's and P–40's and 40-plus Navy F4U's, pound Ballale I A/F.

31 July

Eighth AF: MBs under heavy ftr escort carry out raids on A/Fs at Merville, Abbeville, Poix, Saint-Omer, and Triqueville. Lille and Amiens are bombed by RAF bmrs, also ftr-escorted, in conjunction with US raids.

NAAF: NASAF B–26's bomb Adrano. NATAF ftrs, LBs, and MBs hit Paterno, Santa Maria di Licondia, and Centuripe, general area around Paterno, and vessels in Milazzo-Orlando area. US ground forces in Sicily prepare to attack E along coast, and further inland press toward Troina. British, to the S, are fiercely opposed W of Regalbuto.

Ninth AF: P–40's fly escort missions and hit shipping in Milazzo area.

Tenth AF: 9 B–24's mine Rangoon R during 31 Jul/1 Aug.

Fifth AF: B–25's hit Finschhafen area and barges at Hanisch Harbor and Mange. B–25's and A–20's blast several barges in Cape Gloucester area. B–24's bomb Waingapoe.

Thirteenth AF: 17 P–40's and P–39's join 90-plus Navy and Marine aircraft in pounding guns and defensive positions on Bibolo Hill as

Allied ground forces close in on Munda A/F. B–17's, B–25's, P–40's, and Navy aircraft attack Vila A/F.

1 August

NAAF: During 31 Jul/1 Aug NA SAF Wellingtons drop leaflets on Rome and Naples, and bomb Randazzo and Adrano. During following day, B–17's bomb Capodichino A/F, and B–25's hit Milazzo. NATAF LBs and MBs hit Paterno, Randazzo, Adrano, Bronte, Santa Maria di Licondia, and motor transport in Orlando area. NACAF Beaufighters score hits on shipping between Sardinia and Italy. US ground forces adv E along coast of Sicily, approach Troina further inland, and begin movement to flank defenses. British, to S, penetrate into Regalbuto.

Ninth AF: 177 B–24's, of IX BC (including HBs on loan from Eighth AF) are dispatched to bomb oil refineries at Ploesti and nearby Campina. The operation (TIDALWAVE) is costly, 54 planes and 532 airmen being lost, but damage to the tgts is severe. More than 230 P–40's, largest Ninth AF total to date, attack Adrano, area near Randazzo, Messina, Milazzo, Taormina, and shipping in Straits of Messina.

Tenth AF: 8 B–25's hit E approach of the road bridge at Shweli, damaging cable anchorages and pylons but leaving bridge usable.

Fifth AF: A lone B–24 bombs A/F at Lae.

Thirteenth AF: P–40's and Navy aircraft again hit Munda, bombing AA positions, ammo dumps, and other tgts. 21 B–24's, 16 P–38's, and P–40's, and 30-plus Navy airplanes

pound Kahili A/F; other P–40's and 80-plus Navy aircraft hit shipping in nearby waters.

Eleventh AF: 7 B–24's bomb Kiska Main Camp area through overcast.

2 August

Atlantic: 4th Antisub Sq sinks U–706 in E Atlantic, 46–15N 10–25W.

Eighth AF: MBs attack Merville and Saint-Omer/Ft Rouge A/Fs.

NAAF: NATAF ftrs, LBs, and MBs hit trucks, dump and road junction in NE Sicily, docks and shipping at Milazzo, Messina and in Reggio di Calabria area, and T/Os (mainly motor transport) from Barcellona S to Adrano. In Sicily, US ground forces push slowly W while British troops gain control of Regalbuto and fight indecisively in streets of Centuripe.

Ninth AF: P–40's attack shipping in Straits of Messina and off Milazzo.

Fifth AF: B–17's bomb supply dumps on shores of Hansa Bay and T/Os along Francisco R. A–20's hit Buiambun and B–25's pound barges from Lae to Bogadjim, from Lae to Kepler Pt, and from Bubui R to Lepsius Pt. B–24's bomb Lae harbor, Salamaua, and W shore of Voco Pt.

Thirteenth AF: B–25's, B–17's, P–40's, and Navy ftrs pound shores of Bairoko harbor. B–24's, B–25's, P–40's and Navy F4U's hit supply area on W side of Webster Cove.

Eleventh AF: 8 B–24's, 9 B–25's, and 8 P–38's hit Kiska in 2 waves bombing and strafing North Head, and coast guns on Little Kiska, scoring several hits. 1 or 2 enemy aircraft over Attu cannot be intercepted due to weather.

3 August

Eighth AF: Gen Kepner becomes CG, VIII FC.

NAAF: NATAF LBs hit tac tgts in battle area in Sicily. Ftrs, LBs, and MBs hit shipping in Straits of Messina and at Milazzo and attack Adrano and Biancavilla and gun emplacements and bridges in the area. US forces continue E along N coast toward Furiano R. At Troina, further inland, enemy continues firm resistance.

Ninth AF: B-25's bomb Adrano and its highway approaches. Over 300 P-40's, largest Ninth AF total to date, attack harbors and shipping at Milazzo and Messina, and give direct spt to British ground forces in Catania-Bronte area.

Fifth AF: B-25's, B-17's, and B-24's bomb barges, small craft, villages, grounded planes, trails, and military camps at numerous points, including areas in or around Bogadjim, Salamaua, Manokwari, and Larat and along Bubui, Masaweng, Mindjim, and Kofebi Rivers and Bogadjim Road. Also bombed are W coast of Borgen Bay and island in Marien Harbor.

Eleventh AF: 6 attack missions—2 of which abort—are flown to Kiska by B-24's, B-25's, P-38's, and P-40's. Numerous tgts hit and strafed include installations at North Head and South Head.

4 August

Eighth AF: 33 B-26's hit shipyards at Le Trait.

NAAF: NASAF B-17's bomb Naples submarine base. B-26's and B-25's hit railroad bridge at Catanzaro and railroad at Paola. NATAF MBs,

LBs, and ftrs attack comm tgts, gun positions, and storage areas in Milazzo-Adrano-Biancavilla and Bronte-Riposto-Fiumefreddo areas. A number of NATAF aircraft hit rail sidings on toe of Italy and attack shipping off Messina. In Sicily, British cross Salso R with 2 divs, while other forces prepare to drive on Catania and others continue toward Misterbianco.

Ninth AF: P-40's attack shipping at Messina and spt ground forces at N end of Mount Etna. US troops are halted by fierce opposition at Furiano R and at Troina.

Fifth AF: B-25's bomb and strafe Itni R area and hit several villages on Selaroe I. Single B-24's bomb dump area on Francisco R and Cape Gloucester A/F.

Thirteenth AF: B-25's, and Navy dive bmrs, bomb Gurasai-Kindu area. Some of the MBs also strafe areas emitting intense small arms fire, silencing it. P-38's and P-40's claim 11 ftrs downed in series of running battles over C Solomons.

Eleventh AF: Between 0855 and 1846, 153 tons of bombs are dropped on Kiska, a new one-day record. 6 armed weather, photo and rcn missions, flown by 3 B-24's, 2 P-40's, and 2 F-5A's bomb through clouds, take photos and observe fires in Main Camp and on Little Kiska. Later 48 B-25's, 22 B-24's, 16 A-24's, 8 P-40's, and 40 P-38's fly 17 bombing and strafing attacks to Kiska. Tgts hit include buildings near radio station, and gun battery area on North Head. Little Kiska and Segula I are also strafed.

5 August

NAAF: NATAF ftrs, LBs, and MBs attack troops, roads, and gun positions at Adrano and Troina and surrounding areas in spt of Allied ground forces, hit motor transport behind enemy lines in Sicily and on toe of Italy, and sink or damage over 20 small vessels and barges at Milazzo and in Straits of Messina. NASAF B-17's, operating in 2 forces, hit Messina docks and railroad yards. B-25's bomb Guspini switching station, and P-40's, after escorting the B-25's, attack and probably sink U-boat off SW Sardinia. US forces open assault on San Fratello ridge, and further inland gain positions overlooking Troina. Enemy withdraws from town during night. British 13 Corps overruns Paterno, Misterbianco, and Catania, British 30 Corps continues toward Adrano.

Ninth AF: B-25's bomb town, roads, and road junctions of Francavilla. P-40's attack Messina harbor and shipping in the Straits of Messina.

Fifth AF: More than 30 B-25's pound barges near Madang and at Alexishafen, and hit Nuru R bridge and towns of Bogadjim and Saidor. A single B-24 bombs Finschhafen while another hits Vitu Is. Lt Col Malcolm A Moore takes cmd of newly formed Second Air TF based at recently constructed adv A/F at Tsili Tsili. Strikes from here will facilitate operations against Lae.

Thirteenth AF: B-24's bomb shore of Rekata Bay W of Brokeiello Pt area. B-25's and Navy ftrs strafe barges on NE coast of Gizo I. Munda A/F, principal objective of C Solomons campaign, is taken by XIV

Corps forces after 12 continuous days of fierce fighting in jungle area.

6 August

Caribbean: 10th Bomb Sq and USN land-based aircraft sink U-615 at 12-38N 64-15W.

NAAF: NASAF B-17's bomb coastal roads near Messina. B-26's and B-25's hit road junction SW of Badiazza and railroad bridges N of Gesso. NATAF LBs and MBs hit roads, junctions, and buildings in Troina, Adrano, Bagnara, Biancavilla, Tortorici, Bronte, Piraino, and Randazzo areas. FBs hit shipping from Vibo Valentia, S to Straits of Messina. US troops are unable to cross Furiano R as fierce resistance continues. At Troina troops push through town and 1 mi to E before opposition halts them. British take Biancavilla, and Adrano falls as enemy pulls out during 6/7 Aug.

Ninth AF: 60-plus B-25's hit Bronte, Catania, and Randazzo and the area N of Adrano-Biancavilla road. Over 20 others bomb road intersections in Adrano and Bronte. Over 100 P-40's attack shipping and shore tgts in Messina area while 30 others attack shipping on W coast of Sicily.

Fifth AF: B-24's, during 6/7 Aug bomb Laha A/F.

Thirteeenth AF: 20 P-39's and P-40's hit Tanagaba Harbor area. 24 B-17's and B-24's, 24 B-25's, and 50-plus Navy and Marine ftrs and dive bmrs pound Rekata Bay area, hitting bivouac and supply areas.

7 August

NAAF: Throughout the day NA TBF MBs and LBs pound Randazzo, the enemy's key withdrawal point. Maletto is also bombed. P–40's and A–36's strafe and bomb small craft between Sicily and mainland Italy, motor transport near Randazzo, warehouse N of Messina, dumps on toe of Italy, and vehicles and comm tgts in Sant' Agata di Militello, Bronte, Cesaro, Tortorici, Castiglione di Sicilia and Riposto areas. NASAF B–25's in 2 forces hit Crotone landing ground while B–26's bomb Marina di Catanzaro railroad bridge and highway bridge over Angitola R. US forces improve positions on N coast in San Fratello region against heavy resistance. During 7/8 Aug, small amphibious force lands on coast 2 mi E of Sant' Agata di Militello, greatly aiding progress along coast. Other forces begin drive on Randazzo.

Ninth AF: 150 B–25's attack Randazzo. Over 140 P–40's attack shipping at Messina and in the Straits, and shipping and shore-supply stores along NE coast of Sicily.

Fifth AF: B–24's thoroughly pound Salamaua area and also hit Kela village. B–25's hit Cape Chater A/F and Lautem.

Thirteenth AF: 16 HBs and 40-plus MBs, plus nearly 30 Navy airplanes, pound harbor and shore areas of Bairoko.

ZI: AAF Redistribution Center is established to receive, rehabilitate, and reassign personnel returning from overseas.

8 August

NAAF: NASAF B–26's hit highway and rail bridges at Angitola, while P–38's strafe trains and other T/Os SW of the town. NATAF LBs and MBs pound Randazzo. Ftrs hit road tgts N of Etna, shipping in Straits of Messina and cover ground forces at Sant' Agata di Militello.

Ninth AF: Over 90 B–25's bomb Randazzo area. More than 130 P–40's hit shipping at Messina and provide ground spt in NE Sicily as US and British forces push E and N, capturing Sant' Agata di Militello, Monte Camolato, and Bronte.

Fifth AF: B–24's attack Larat, shipping at Semboh, and barges at Kokas.

Thirteenth AF: 23 B–25's, with P–38's, P–39's, and Navy F4U's as cover, bomb Vila and Buki harbor.

9 August

NAAF: NASAF B–17's bomb crossroads N of Messina, B–25's hit Catanzaro and Soverato R bridges, B–26's attack Angitola R bridges, P–40's sweep over S Sardinia, and P–38's hit lighthouse and other T/Os in S Italy. NATAF bmrs hit Gesso road junction. Ftrs concentrate on highways and junctions and also hit rail sidings and gun positions in areas around Linguaglossa, Floresta, Falcone, Patti, Orlando, Novara di Sicilia, and Milazzo. US troops reach Torrenuovo, and, to the S, drive enemy back to Simeto R between Cesaro and Randazzo.

Ninth AF: B–25's hit Divieto and nearby tunnel W of Spadafora San Martino, and attack special points in battle area of NE Sicily. P–40's hit shipping at Messina, Milazzo, and Palmi.

Fifth AF: B–17's, B–24's, and B–25's bomb Salamaua, Lae, Nuk Nuk, Samoa harbor at mouth of Francisco R, barge near Reiss Pt, and bridges on Bogadjim-Ramu road. Barges and machinegun positions along Borgen Bay, installations at Unea I, and T/Os at Alilit are bombed. Amboina is thoroughly pounded.

Thirteenth AF: 10 B–25's, with ftr cover, bomb Vila. Shortly thereafter 22 B–24's strike the same tgt.

Eleventh AF: 1 B–24 flies photo rcn over various Kiska sites.

10 August

NAAF: Gen Dunn takes cmd of NAAF TCC (Prov). NASAF P–38's bomb and strafe comm tgts on toe of Italy. Bridges at Angitola and N of Locri are attacked. NATAF planes fly anti-shipping sweeps over coastal areas of NE Sicily and Straits of Messina, carry out armed rcn over battle areas and toe of Italy, and bomb Randazzo. US Seventh Army forces pursue enemy to point W of Naso near N coast of Sicily. During 10/11 Aug, 3d Inf Div makes amphibious landing on coast, outflanking enemy E of Capo d'Orlando. 9th Inf Div reaches point N of Bronte.

Ninth AF: B–25's attack Randazzo while P–40's bomb and strafe shipping on SW coast of Italy and in Straits of Messina.

Fifth AF: Over 20 B–24's pound A/Fs in Salamaua area. 12 B–25's hit barges in Lae area and AA positions W of Borgen Bay. 6 A–20's bomb and strafe barges in Labu Lagoon and in Gasmata area.

Thirteenth AF: Col William A Matheny becomes acting CG, XIII BC, a position he is officially assigned to on 30 Sep. P–40's and P–39's turn back about 40 ftrs attacking US bulldozers working on Munda A/F.

Eleventh AF: P–38's, P–40's, A–24's, B–24's and B–25's bomb and strafe various Kiska tgts. Direct hits are scored on revetments W of Wheat Grove and on gun emplacements, as well as on buildings on Little Kiska.

11 August

International: Quebec Conference begins. Roosevelt and Churchill discuss entire spectrum of world operations and decide on future action of Anglo-US armed forces.

NAAF: NASAF again hits comm tgts on toe of Italy. B–17's hit Terni M/Y, B–25's bomb Angitola R bridges, and B–26's and P–38's attack bridge at Catanzaro. NATAF FBs spt US Seventh Army's landing E of Orlando by attacking troop concentrations, gun positions, and comm lines leading to the area. US Seventh Army forces take Naso and press closer to Randazzo. MBs spt British Eighth Army by raiding Fiumefreddo and Randazzo area.

Ninth AF: Over 90 B–25's bomb bridge, roads, railway, and city area in and about Randazzo. About 170 P–40's hit Randazzo, shipping at Milazzo and Messina, road and train near Messina, and troop movements and evacuations in NE Sicily.

Fifth AF: A B–24 on armed rcn sinks enemy freighter NW of Kavieng. Second Air TF completes movement to Tsili Tsili A/F.

Thirteenth AF: 5 B–24's hit supply area on E side of Suavanau Pt and at Papatura Fa I.

Eleventh AF: B–24's, B–25's, A–24's, and P–38's pound Kiska tgts in 11 attack missions. Later, 10 rcn, strafing and photo missions to Kiska are flown by 3 P–38's, 26 P–40's, 4 F–5A's and 1 B–24. 9 B–24's from Attu drop bombs and incendiaries on

Paramushiru I tgts, including Kashiwabara A/F and Shimushu I where
Kataoka naval base and staging area
are hit. 40 enemy aircraft challenge
the attackers, which score 4 confirmed kills, 1 probable, and 4 possi-
bles.

12 August

Eighth AF: 243 HBs attack tgts
in the Ruhr, concentrating on manufacturing installations at Bonn and
synthetic oil industries at Gelsenkirchen. 25 airplanes are lost on mission.

NAAF: NASAF B–25's attack
landing grounds at Crotone, and B–
26's hit Grazzanise A/F. MBs claim
9 ftrs shot down. NATAF P–40's and
A–36's hit shipping along NE coast
of Sicily and in Straits of Messina, attack gun positions and vehicles at
Capo Calava and E of Randazzo, and
hit bridge at Taormina and roads in
Maletto-Fiumefreddo areas. NATAF
bmrs attack Patti, Falcone, Barcellona, and Nunziata. US Seventh
Army continues to pursue enemy E
along N coast. Further inland US
forces gain favorable position from
which to assault Randazzo, but enemy
withdraws during 12/13 Aug, preclud-
ing attack. British Eighth Army
seizes Maletto and Riposto.

Ninth AF: 79 B–25's attack Falcone, Patti, Novara di Sicilia, and
Barcellona. P–40's bomb and strafe
shipping at Messina.

Fifth AF: B–25's hit Bogadjim-
Yaula road. A–20's bomb and strafe
Gasmata and nearby barges. A B–24
hits Cape Gloucester A/F.

Thirteenth AF: 20-plus B–24's,
with P–40 and F4U cover, bomb
Kahili A/F, causing considerable

damage in dispersal and runway
areas. The Allied airplanes claim 11
Zeros shot down. 1 P–40 and 1 F4U
are lost.

Eleventh AF: From Adak B–24's
and B–25's fly 26 bombing, strafing,
and radar and photo rcn sorties over
Kiska tgts. From Amchitka P–40's,
P–38's, B–24's, B–25's, and A–24's fly
70 bombing sorties over the island
and are joined by B–24's, P–40's, and
F–5A's flying 6 rcn and photo sorties.
Tgts include runway, harbor and
shipping installations, army barracks,
and Rose Hill area.

13 August

NAAF: NASAF B–17's bomb Lor-
enzi M/Y, and B–25's and B–26's hit
Littoria M/Y. Other B–25's hit vessel off Pizzo. P–40's fly sweep over
S Sardinia, strafing small boats, power station, and railroad junction
NATAF LBs and MBs bomb Piedimonte, Falcone, and bridges N of
Scaletta. A–36's and ftrs hit tgts in
NE Sicily, Straits of Messina and on
toe of Italy, including Gioia Tauro,
Barcellona, road junction E of Randazzo, M/Y and trucks at Spadafora,
trucks between Taormina and Bar-
acca, and barges, ferries, and small
vessels in the Strait of Messina. US
Seventh Army enters Randazzo without opposition. Coastal forces continue
E toward Patti.

Ninth AF: 61 B–24's hit aircraft
factory at Wiener-Neustadt in first
Ninth AF raid on Austria. Over 80
B–25's hit Piedimonte, Falcone, and
shipping at Messina. More than 200
P–40's attack shipping and bridges
along SW Italian coast, hit shipping
in Straits of Messina, and fly armed
rcn and FB operations in NE Sicily.

Fourteenth AF: 4 P–40's bomb and strafe enemy installations at Lungling.

Fifth AF: 59 B–24's, B–17's, and B–26's drop 175 tons of bombs in Salamaua area in the heaviest single-day strike by Fifth AF to date. 9 other B–24's bomb oil center at Balikpapan during late night raid; the round trip covers 1,200 mi.

Thirteenth AF: 4 P–40's become the first Allied aircraft to land on the reconstructed Munda A/F; after refueling, they are sent on a sweep of the Kolombangara coast. 9 B–17's, with ftr cover, bomb Kape Harbor depot; 2 others on armed rcn bomb Vila. 12 B–25's bomb supply areas in Rekata Bay area. 2 B–24's on armed rcn hit Suavanau Pt, 8 bomb Ballale I A/F, and 13 bomb Kahili A/F.

Eleventh AF: 7 B–25's from Adak bomb tgts at Main Camp and North Head at Kiska and Little Kiska. A B–24 flies a special rcn mission. From Amchitka B–24's, B–25's, A–24's, and P–38's fly 8 more bombing missions against Kiska pounding Camp area, gun emplacements, buildings, shipping, and airstrip revetments.

14 August

NAAF: NASAF P–38's sweep toe of Italy but find little enemy movement. NATAF ftrs, MBs, and LBs, hit refueling depot at Nicola, near Gesso, road junction N of Palmi, shipping in straits and along W coast of Italy N to Gioia, and numerous T/Os in NE Sicily and S Italy as enemy continues orderly evacuation from Sicily to mainland Italy across Straits of Messina. US troops speed E along coast to Barcellona area and

also continue pursuit of enemy E of Randazzo.

Ninth AF: 61 B–24's, on loan from Eighth AF bomb Me 109 factory at Wiener-Neustadt. B–25's attack road junctions and vehicle concentrations along NE coast of Sicily and bomb crossroads N of Palmi. P–40's hit shipping in Milazzo and Messina area and along Italian coast in Palmi area.

Fifth AF: More than 50 B–24's, B–17's, and B–25's pound Salamaua area battle zone. With close air and arty spt, US forces push to crest of Roosevelt Ridge. Enemy retains several ridges along Dot Inlet. A–20's strafe barges near Finschhafen. B–25's hit barges at Talasea and Rein Bay, and B–25's bomb Koepang.

Thirteenth AF: 9 B–17's bomb Rekata Bay area.

Eleventh AF: 2 B–24's fly special radar ferret and rcn missions. 1 B–25, 8 B–24's, and 10 P–38's then fly 2 attack missions to Kiska, bombing with unobserved results.

15 August

Eighth AF: Over 300 HBs are dispatched to bomb GAF A/Fs in France and the Netherlands. The majority concentrates on Vlissingen A/F and on A/Fs at Lille and Merville. MBs attack Saint-Omer/Ft Rouge A/F and the M/Y at Abbeville.

NAAF: NASAF B–25's and B–26's bomb Sibari railroad junction and M/Y, and P–38's hit trains, troops, radar, and Staletti railroad tracks and tunnel. P–40's attack bivouac area near Monserrato. During 15/16 Aug, US Seventh Army troops land on Sicilian N coast NW of Barcellona to block enemy withdrawal. 3d Inf Div heads along N coast to Spadafora. British Eighth Army troops complete drive around Mount Etna as Randazzo-Linguaglossa road is closed. Linguaglossa and Taormina are taken.

Ninth AF: B–25's hit shipping along beaches of Sant' Agata di Militello. Over 180 P–40's attack shipping at Messina and in the Straits of Mesina. Enemy forces withdrawing to mainland Italy are pounded severely by constant air attacks.

Fifth AF: HBs again hit Salamaua area. 12 Japanese bmrs, escorted by more than 20 ftrs, attack Tsili Tsili A/F for first time. Intercepting P–39's claim 14 airplanes downed. 3 P–39's are lost.

Thirteenth AF: COMAIR, New Georgia cmd post, recently opened at Munda Pt by Gen Mulcahy, USMC, conducts its first full day of operations. Ftrs are sent to cover amphibious landings at Vella Lavella I where elements of 25th Inf Div, and supporting units, go ashore in Barakoma area and establish beachhead. Allied airplanes knock down about 25 Japanese aircraft (7 by AAF ftrs) attacking the landings. Corsairs also claim 10 Japanese shot down over Kahili. B–25's bomb Papatura Fa and Ighiti Is in Rekata Bay area.

Eleventh AF: US and Canadian troops invade Kiska and discover that the Japanese, under the cover of fog, evacuated their garrison. A P–38 bombs and strafes Sniper Hill.

16 August

Eighth AF: 169 HBs, escorted all the way to the tgt by P–47's using drop tanks, hit Le Bourget air depot in the Paris area. Smaller strikes are made at Poix and Abbeville/Drucat A/Fs. MBs hit locomotive works at Denain, and A/Fs at Beaumont-le-Roger, and Bernay/Saint Martin.

NAAF: NASAF MBs hit Staletti and temporary bridge at Angitola. NATAF LBs and MBs hit shipping in Straits of Messina and from N of Messina to Capo Peloro. A–36's and P–40's concentrate on comm tgts on toe of Italy, hitting trains, trucks, railroad yards, and sidings at Nicastro, Lamezia, Amantea, and Sambiase. Also bombed are barges, ferries, and small vessels off Messina and in Golfo di Sant' Eufemia.

Ninth AF: 86 B–24's bomb city area and A/Fs at Foggia. Over 50 B–25's hit landing craft concentrations near Ganzirri and Messina, and 100-plus P–40's hit shipping at Messina and in Straits of Messina, as enemy continues withdrawal of rear guard troop to mainland Italy. Before midnight, US patrols enter Messina, which is under fire from Italian coast.

Tenth AF: Bmrs hit and claim 2 small vessels sunk about 130 mi S of Rangoon.

Fourteenth AF: 4 P–40's bomb town of Tengchung.

Fifth AF: Oil tanks at Balikpapan are hit by 2 B–24's. 5 B–25's bomb Larat. 15 P–38's and 32 P–47's intercept 25 ftrs preparing to attack transport vessels near Tsili Tsili. The strike is completely thwarted and 12 ftrs shot down. This marks first combat use of the P–47 in SWPA.

Thirteenth AF: 9 B–24's bomb Papatura Fa I. 12 B–25's, 5 B–17's, and 30-plus Navy planes attack Vila A/F.

Eleventh AF: A B–24 rcn flight reconnoiters North Head, Main Camp, and northern Kiska, and observes friendly forces' unopposed adv into Main Camp.

17 August

Eighth AF: On first anniversary of US HB operations from UK, 315 B–17's launch two-pronged attack into Germany, marking deepest penetration of German territory to date. The critical tgts are the Messerschmitt complex at Regensburg and the antifriction-bearing factories at Schweinfurt. The bmrs unload a 724-ton bomb load, causing extensive damage. Every important building in the complex at Regensburg is damaged, and there are 80 HE hits on the 2 main bearing plants at Schweinfurt. 60 US aircraft are lost in fierce air battle that extends to the tgts and continues after the bombing. 4th Bomb Wg, after bombing Regensburg, continues to bases in N Africa. During 17/18 Aug RAF begins CROSSBOW, massive attacks on German V-weapon sites. About 570 aircraft drop 2,000 tons of bombs on Peenemunde.

NAAF: Sicily campaign ends with official entry of US Seventh Army's 3d Div into Messina at 1000. British force from Ali arrives shortly thereafter. Fall of Sicily paves way for stepped-up air offensive against Italy. About 180 NASAF B–17's attack Istres-Le-Tube and Salon-de-Provence A/Fs. Around 100 MBs attack comm tgts on N part of Italian toe, hitting Battipaglia and Castrovillari with damaging effect; escorting P–38's strafe vehicles in the area. NATAF ftrs and LBs pound shipping in Straits of Messina and Gulf of Gioia, hit rail center at Lamezia, and harass enemy movement on the Italian toe.

Ninth AF: More than 200 P–40's hit shipping at Messina, at Palmi, and in Gulf of Gioia.

Fourteenth AF: 23 B–24's, operating in 3 waves, bomb barracks at Cau Lo. 4 P–40's bomb town of Mangshih.

Fifth AF: More than 50 B–24's and B–17's make predawn attack on Wewak and satellite A/Fs at Boram, Dogaw, and But, and also hit Tadji and Madang. During midmorning, 30-plus B–25's, with over 80 P–38's covering, carry out the day's second bombing and strafing strike on Boram, Wewak, and Dagaw. This begins campaign to neutralize Japanese A/Fs in preparation for offensive against Lae. A–20's again hit enemy forces in Salamaua area. B–24's bomb oil facilities at Balikpapan.

Eleventh AF: 1 B–24 flies over Kiska watching friendly forces land on shore of E Kiska Lake.

18 August

Eighth AF: MBs hit A/Fs at Woensdrecht and Ypres-Vlamertinge. Primary tgt of Lille/Vendeville A/F is not bombed because of mechanical trouble with comm equipment and bombsight in lead plane.

NAAF: NASAF ftrs and MBs hit barracks and railroad at Gonnesa, sink small vessel in Golfo di Sant' Eufemia, and bomb and strafe railway station, bridge, and tracks at Soverato, bridges and road junction at Angitola, and highway and road junction at Staletti. NATAF airplanes hit gun positions and road and rail transport in S Italy.

Ninth AF: P–40's attack motor transport between Scilla and

Bagnara, and bomb shipping off Scilla.

Fifth AF: More than 70 B–24's, B–25's, and B–17's, with cover of almost 100 ftrs, blast A/Fs at Wewak, Boram, Dagua, and But. The mid-morning attacks cause heavy destruction of Japanese airplanes on the ground, and US ftrs and bmrs claim over 30 enemy aircraft shot down.

19 August

Eighth AF: 93 HBs hit A/Fs at Flushing and Gilze-Rijen. Smaller numbers strike at Amiens and Poix. MBs attack Amiens/Glisy and Poix A/Fs.

NAAF: Over 150 NASAF B–17's bomb Foggia M/Y, while almost 100 MBs hit M/Ys at Sapri and Salerno. The HBs, MBs, and escorting P–38's claim 34 enemy planes shot down, against 8 losses. NATAF A–36's attack Catanzaro M/Y. P–40's on sweeps over Italian toe attack train near Melito di Porto Salvo and strafe small number of trucks.

Ninth AF: About 70 B–24's bomb M/Y at Foggia. P–40's fly coastal rcn over toe of Italy and bomb roads and buildings.

Tenth AF: Gen Davidson becomes CG Tenth AF.

Fifth AF: B–24's attack Manok-wari, sink small craft near Babo, and bomb Larat and Saumlakki. B–25's hit Koepang, Fuiloro, and Lautem.

Thirteenth AF: B–25's, operating in pairs and with ftr escort, hit barges at Timbala Bay and Kakasa, radio station on Gill I, and beached vessel in Paraso Bay. From this date through 26 Aug, Japanese airplanes attack Allied forces in Barakoma area of Vella Lavella, losing a considerable

number of aircraft (claims total about 50) to Allied ftrs and ground fire without doing any great damage to the Allies.

20 August

Eighth AF: B–26's and A–20's carry out light raids on Dornier airframe factory at Flushing and M/Y at Abbeville.

NAAF: NASAF B–26's hit Capua and Aversa M/Y, while B–25's bomb Benevento M/Y, and P–40's attack A/F at Monserrato. NATAF ftrs hit road and railway at Gioia and trucks near Locri during missions along E and W coast of Italian toe.

Ninth AF: P–40's strafe and bomb shipping off Italian toe and comm tgts on land. Hits are scored on bridges, railway yards, and railway cars.

CBI: AAF, India-Burma Sector, China-Burma-India Theater is activated at New Delhi. Gen Stratemeyer assumes cmd. Components include Tenth AF, CBI ASC (Prov), CBI Trg Unit (Prov), and several lesser units.

Tenth AF: X AFSC personnel and organizations are absorbed by CBI ASC (Prov) which is activated on this date at New Delhi. Gen Oliver, CG X AFSC, becomes CG CBI ASC.

Fourteenth AF: 6 B–25's, with ftr escort, bomb Tien Ho A/F at Canton; the MBs and ftrs claim 5 interceptors shot down. 15 P–40's intercept 21 ftrs over Kweilin; 2 P–40's and 2 Zeros are shot down.

Fifth AF: 24 B–24's, escorted by 46 P–38's, hit Boram A/F in late morning; P–38's claim 19 ftrs shot down. A–20's bomb Lae and hit Sala-maua area where enemy forces have abandoned positions on Mount Tambu and Komiatum Ridge and are manning last-ditch defensive position at Salamaua. B–25's strafe barges near Cape Gloucester.

Thirteenth AF: HQ XIII BC moves from Espiritu Santo to Guadalcanal.

21 August

NAAF: NASAF B–26's and B–17's bomb M/Ys at Villa Literno and Aversa. P–38 escort also attacks Aversa. NASAF aircraft claim over 20 enemy ftrs shot down. NATAF FBs hit traffic on Bovalino-Bagnara road.

Ninth AF: B–24's attack railroad station, M/Y, and air depot at Cancello Arnone.

Fourteenth AF: 14 B–24's, 7 B–25's, and 11 P–40's attack docks and A/F at Hankow. A large force of ftrs, estimated at more than 50, attacks the HB formation, shooting down 2 of the B–24's. Gunners on HBs claim more than 40 ftrs shot down. In Hengyang area, 19 P–40's battle 33 airplanes, shooting down 5 Zeros. S of Changsha, 9 P–38's clash with 12 Zeros, shooting down 3.

Fifth AF: B–25's pound But and Dagua A/Fs. B–17's bomb Bogadjim area. Single B–24's hit Salamaua area and T/O at Malahang. B–24's carry out damaging strike against Pombelaa.

Thirteenth AF: B–25's and ftrs strafe barges in Doveli Cove and Marquana and Paraso Bays.

Eleventh AF: During the Aleutian Campaign—3 Jun 42–21 Aug 43—Eleventh AF destroyed 69 aircraft, sank 21 and damaged 29 ships, and lost 29 of its own aircraft.

22 August

Eighth AF: 35 B–26's hit Beaumont-le-Roger A/F.

NAAF: NASAF B–26's, with escort of NATAF A–36's, bomb M/Y at Salerno. MBs and escort claim 26 enemy ftrs destroyed. NATAF ftrs on armed rcn hit motor transport S of Locri-Gioia Tauro area and NE of Bagnara.

Ninth AF: All ftr and MB gps of Ninth AF are transferred to Twelfth AF.

Fourteenth AF: 4 P–40's bomb Japanese HQ and supply dump at Tengchung, and strafe trucks and troops in the area; 2 others strafe road traffic between Tengchung and Lungling.

Fifth AF: B–25's strike Dili. As result of air offensive against Wewak and satellite A/Fs, Japanese airpower on New Guinea is sufficiently neutralized for 4 Allied destroyers to proceed along coast from Milne Bay to Finschhafen. After bombarding Finschhafen during 22/23 Aug, the warships return to Milne Bay.

Thirteenth AF: B–25's and naval dive bmrs, escorted by ftr aircraft, bomb barge centers on W Vella Lavella I.

23 August

Ninth AF: B–24's hit M/Y at Bari.

NAAF: NASAF B–26's bomb Battipaglia M/Y. FBs hit factory and barracks near Cagliari. NATAF P–40's and A–36's escort NASAF B–26's, and Spitfires fly uneventful tac rcn over NE Sicily and toe of Italy.

Tenth AF: B–25's fly low-level strike against Myitnge bridge, knocking out a center span and badly damaging 2 others.

Fifth AF: B–24's bomb town and A/F of Kendari. B–25's hit tgts in Aroe Is. B–26's pound Kela. B–25's hit Marawasa, Finschhafen, and Lillum Saun.

Thirteenth AF: B–24's and P–39's strafe T/Os on Wagina I.

24 August

Eighth AF: 86 HBs hit aircraft works in main strike at Villacoublay. Other planes bomb A/Fs at Conches and Evreux. 84 B–17's, which had flown to N Africa after attacking Regensburg on 17 Aug, bomb Bordeaux on return flight to UK.

NAAF: NATAF FBs hit railroad tunnel and cruiser offshore at Sapri, tracks and buildings at Castrovillari, and town area at Sibari. DAF (British) airplanes strafe motor transport N of Reggio di Calabria and provide withdrawal cover for the NATAF FBs.

Fourteenth AF: 7 B–24's and 6 B–25's, escorted by 22 P–40's and P–38's, bomb A/Fs at Hankow and Wuchang. 4 B–24's are lost. The HBs, MBs, and ftrs claim 24 enemy interceptors shot down.

Fifth AF: B–24's thoroughly pound Wewak and bomb Salamaua. B–25's bomb Larat and barges E of Wotap.

Thirteenth AF: 25 B–24's, with ftr escort, bomb Papatura Fa I and attack E shore of Ringa Cove. P–39's strafe barges at Kakasa.

ZI: AAF Antisub Cmd is redesignated I BC after AAF and USN reached agreement under which the AAF withdrew from antisub operations; subsequently, I BC, Second AF, is redesignated XX BC.

25 August

Eighth AF: US HBs are assigned role of bombing important GAF targets in Operation STARKEY, designed to contain enemy forces in west to prevent their transfer to Eastern Front, and to serve as dress rehearsal in Pas de Calais area for invasion of W Europe. Allies hope to provoke Luftwaffe into prolonged air battle. MBs hit A/Fs of Triqueville, Bernay/Saint Martin, and Beaumont-le-Roger and the power station at Le Grand-Quevilly.

NAAF: Around 135 B–17's and 140 P–38's attack satellite A/Fs at Foggia. NATAF FBs hit trucks S of Sinopoli.

Ninth AF: B–24's bomb M/Y at Foggia.

Fourteenth AF: 8 B–25's, with ftr escort, bomb Kowloon Docks at Hong Kong.

SE Asia: Adm Mountbatten is appointed Supreme Allied Cmdr, SE Asia.

Fifth AF: Almost 100 B–24's, B–25's, and B–17's carry out an hourlong strike against Hansa Bay area, Nubia, and Awar, and nearby shipping. Small flights of B–24's attack Finschhafen and hit transport off New Hanover. A–20's hit Gasmata. B–25's bomb tgts on Timor.

Thirteenth AF: 13 B–25's, along with 40-plus dive bmrs and an escort of ftr aircraft, pound barge centers at Webster and Ringa Coves. 6 B–24's, along with 24 ftrs, hit Kahili A/F. Other P–40's strafe large motor vessels and a barge in NW part of the Slot.

26 August

Eighth AF: 36 MBs raid Caen/Carpiquet A/F.

NAAF: DAF is assigned to NA TAF, along with American units of Ninth AF which have been an operational part of DAF and NATBF. Over 80 NASAF B–17's, with P–38 escort, bomb Capua A/F. More than 100 ftr-escorted MBs hit Grazzanise A/F and satellite field. P–40's bomb Carloforte and strafe S part of Sardinia. NATAF MBs and LBs bomb tgts on toe of Italy, including railroad junction at Locri and gun positions at Reggio di Calabria and Villa San Giovanni.

Ninth AF: 316th TC Gp, less 1 sq, is transferred to Twelfth AF.

Fourteenth AF: 15 B–24's, with escort of 17 ftrs, bomb Kowloon Docks at Hong Kong. 5 Japanese interceptors are shot down. 5 B–25's, supported by 11 P–40's, bomb Tien Ho A/F at Canton; in a battle with enemy interceptors 1 P–40 is lost; the MBs and P–40's claim 5 Zeros downed.

Thirteenth AF: 11 B–25's and 50-plus Navy dive bmrs, escorted by ftrs, pound AA positions and barges at Ringa and Webster Coves and at Nusatuva I. P–40's strafe 2 large motor boats and a 100-ft steam vessel off Ganongga. 7 B–24's bomb Papatura Ite and supply areas on Papatura Fa. 15 B–24's, with ftr escort, bomb Kahili A/F. P–39's strafe buildings on Gizo I and at Kolulavabae Inlet.

Eleventh AF: The Eleventh's striking power shrinks rapidly as the 36th, 73d, 21st, and 406th Bomb Sqs are ordered to prepare for departure to CONUS.

27 August

Eighth AF: Over 180 HBs attack German rocket-launching site construction at Watten. This is the first of the Eighth's missions against V-weapon sites (later designated NO-BALL tgts). 36 B–26's hit Poix A/F. Mission to bomb Rouen power station is aborted because of bad weather and extremely heavy enemy ftr opposition.

NAAF: NASAF B–17's bomb Sulmona M/Y, and MBs hit Benevento and Caserta M/Ys. Nearly 150 P–38's escort the bmrs. NATAF MBs, LBs, and ftrs attack tgts in S Italy, including Catanzaro rail and road junction, guns near Reggio di Calabria, Sibari rail junctions, Cetraro M/Y, barracks at Tarsia, train and repair shops at Paola, and barge at Diamante.

Fourteenth AF: 5 P–40's strafe large truck convoy between Sintsiang and Yoyang, destroying 5 trucks and damaging 15 others; 1 P–40 is downed by ground fire. 6 other P–40's hit comm lines between Yoyang and Hankow; tgts include 2 small steamboats, a gunboat, several railroad cars, and a water tower.

Fifth AF: B–26's attack bridges in Bogadjim area. A–20's bomb and strafe barges and troops along Bubui R in Lae area. B–25's bomb Dili and Cape Chater airstrip.

Thirteenth AF: 10 SB–24's (Snoopers) equipped with radar devices that permit blind bombing, begin operations from Camey Field, Guadalcanal. 12 B–25's, 8 P–40's, and 8 Navy F4U's strafe barges and shoreline tgts at Kakasa. P–39's strafe barges and shore tgts at Ringa Cove.

28 August

NAAF: NASAF B–17's bomb M/Y at Terni. B–26's hit Aversa M/Y and Sparanise. B–25's hit Cancello Arnone M/Y. P–40's fly intruder mission over Sardinia, bombing and strafing industry and town area. NA TAF LBs and MBs attack railroad facilities at Lamezia and Catanzaro. FBs hit road and rail junctions, and M/Ys at Castrovillari, Cosenza, and Catanzaro.

Fifth AF: 26 B–25's bomb and strafe dumps and shipping in Hansa Bay area, sinking a small freighter, a power launch, and 8 barges and luggers. 20 B–17's and A–20's bomb jetties at Lae and Voco Pt and hit barges in Samoa Harbor between Lae and Salamaua.

Thirteenth AF: B–25's, P–40's, and Navy F4U's bomb and strafe barges, buildings, and personnel in Sigolehe I-Barora Ite I area.

29 August

Eighth AF: Gen Kepner succeeds Gen Hunter as CG VIII FC.

NAAF: NASAF B–17's hit Orte M/Y, and B–26's bomb Torre Annunziata. NATAF ftrs escort the NA SAF bmrs, hit rail junction at Bagnara, bridge and town of Angitola, gun positions in Villa San Giovanni-Reggio di Calabria areas, and M/Y at Lamezia.

Fourteenth AF: 9 B–25's, with ftr escort, bomb A/F at Chingmen.

Fifth AF: 35 B–24's, escorted by 44 P–38's, strike A/Fs at Wewak and Boram. 48 B–25's and 2 B–17's bomb and strafe Alexishafen and Bogadjim areas. A–20's hit dumps in Gasmata area. B–24's bomb Babo and Adodo.

30 August

Eighth AF: 482d Bomb Gp, a Pathfinder gp fitted with British Oboe and H2S and US H2X blind-bombing equipment, becomes operational. 31 B–26's raid ammunition dump at Foret d'Eperlecques near Saint-Omer.

NAAF: B–17's of NASAF bomb Viterbo A/F. B–25's hit Civitavecchia M/Y. B–26's bomb Aversa M/Y. P–40's strafe radar station at Pula. NATAF MBs and LBs attack M/Ys at Marina di Catanzaro and Paola, and gun emplacements and bivouac S of Reggio di Calabria. A–36's bomb M/Ys at Sapri and Lamezia and hit town of Pellaro.

Fourteenth AF: 13 B–25's, some with P–40 spt, attack Owchihkow and Shihshow, blasting fuel stores and several buildings; the P–40's strafe gun positions outside Shihshow. 10 P–38's and P–40's on armed rcn from Sinti to Yoyang to Sienning, strafe and bomb several T/Os; 3 locomotives are exploded and another damaged, a water tank is knocked down, and several railroad stations are heavily damaged. 4 other P–40's attack convoy E of Hong Kong; 1 freighter is hit amidships, causing heavy damage; 2 other vessels are also effectively damaged.

Fifth AF: B–24's pound Dagua, But, and Tadji. A–20's hit barges on Bubui R. B–26's bomb Cape Gloucester A/F while B–25's sweep along NW coast, bombing and strafing barges and enemy-occupied villages.

Thirteenth AF: 24 B–24's, along with 20 P–40's and P–39's and 20-plus Navy F4U's, pound Kahili A/F. Allied airplanes claim more than 30 Japanese shot down. 6 US aircraft are lost.

31 August

Eighth AF: 106 HBs hit Amiens/Glisy A/F and nearby tgts; A/F is severely damaged. 36 B–26's bomb Lille/Vendeville A/F, and 34 others strike power station at Mazingarbe.

NAAF: About 150 NASAF B–17's blast Pisa M/Y, doing large amount of damage. NATAF MBs and LBs bomb Cosenza M/Y and road-railway junction in Catanzaro during morning, and in afternoon bomb area around Cosenza when clouds prevent hitting specific tgts. FBs hit Sapri railroads and seaplane base. During night LBs hit bivouac areas SE of Reggio di Calabria.

Ninth AF: B–24's bomb Pescara M/Y. HBs claim 9 enemy ftrs destroyed.

Fourteenth AF: 7 B–24's bomb Gia Lam A/F. 22 P–40's and 2 P–38's bomb dike near Co Bi barracks. 6 B–25's hit Ichang A/F while 3 others attack oil storage area to the E. P–40's also hit the oil stores. 3 P–40's claim heavy damage to freighter off Stonecutter's I near Hong Kong. 4 P–38's dive-bomb Yoyang railroad yards and Sinti warehouses. A P–38 is shot down by ground fire.

Fifth AF: Bmrs fly scattered strikes against shipping and shore tgts in Saint George Channel, and NEI.

Thirteenth AF: P–40's, in running battle over Vella Lavella, claim 5 Japanese airplanes shot down. Other P–40's strafe barges in Timbala Bay. 22 B–25's and 50 Navy airplanes bomb gun positions and radio station at Vila.

1 September

Twelfth AF: All administrative functions of the AAF elements of NAAF are transferred to the appropriate Twelfth AF organizations: HQ NAAF to HQ Twelfth AF, NASAF to XII BC, NATAF to XII A Spt Cmd, NACAF to XII FC, NAASC to XII AFSC, NAAF TCC to XII TCC (Prov), NW African Photo Rcn Wg to Photo Rcn Wg (Prov), and NATC to XII Trg Cmd (Prov). Operational control remains with NAAF. P–40's bomb zinc plant at Iglesias and strafe factory N of Gonnesa. MBs and LBs hit Bova Marina, areas near Salina and Sant' Eufemia d'Aspromonte town area and bridge at Oliveto, and radar station and lighthouse at Capo Spartivento.

Fourteenth AF: 7 B–25's, supported by 8 P–40's, attack Japanese destroyer at Shihhweiyao; no hits are scored on the ship but considerable damage is done to surrounding dock area. 6 P–40's sink small tanker down river from Ichang, damage 2 large boats between Ocheng and Shihhweiyao, and strafe cav troops at Ocheng. 3 other P–40's heavily damage small ship at Swatow harbor and strafe nearby A/F. 3 P–38's and a P–40 dive-bomb and strafe barracks at Yangsin, demolishing 3 buildings. 2 nearby locomotives are also destroyed. The FBs then heavily damage small steamer at Wuchang, sink 1 tug and damage another at Kutang, and blast a train and AA position S of Puchi.

Fifth AF: More than 70 B–24's and B–25's hit Alexishafen-Madang area, dropping 201 tons of bombs (heaviest by Fifth AF to date). Other B–25's hit Iboki Plantation, barges on Bubui R, Rein Bay area and several villages in New Britain. B–17's bomb Labu I. B–26's attack Cape

Gloucester area. B–24's and B–25's strike tgts in Lesser Sunda Is.

Seventh AF: From this date through 14 Sep, 6 B–24's conduct daily sea-search operations out of Canton I.

Eleventh AF: 2 P–40's attempting to intercept aircraft reported near Attu abort because of weather.

2 September

Eighth AF: 5 forces totaling 319 B–17's are dispatched to attack GAF A/Fs in France. Because of unfavorable cloud conditions only part of one force is able to attack a tgt. 16 B–17's hit Denain/Prouvy A/F and 18 bomb Mardyck A/F. Over 100 MBs attack Foret D'Hesdin and power station at Mazingarbe.

Twelfth AF: Almost 200 B–17's and B–25's of XII BC bomb M/Ys at Bologna, Trento, Bolzano, and Cancello Arnone. Bmrs and ftrs escorting the B–25's claim 28 enemy airplanes shot down. Tac aircraft (including RAF and Ninth AF airplanes) hit gun positions and other tgts on Italian toe, bomb rail comm at Bova Marina, Locri, Marina di Monasterace, Siderno Marina, Lamezia, and Catanzaro, and attack barges in Golfo di Sant' Eufemia and ammo dump at Sapri.

Fourteenth AF: 10 B–25's and 5 P–40's bomb Kowloon area and attack shipping off Stonecutter's I and in Lai Chi Kok area.

Fifth AF: B–25's, with P–38 escort, attack shipping at Wewak harbor, claiming 1 vessel sunk and 2 left aflame. 10 enemy interceptors are claimed destroyed. Barrage balloons offer some protection to the enemy ships. This is first AAF observation of Japanese use of such balloons in SWPA.

Thirteenth AF: 24 B–25's and 60-plus Navy aircraft pound Vila, hitting AA and arty positions and area E of Ringa Cove. 18 B–24's, 20-plus P–40's and P–39's, and more than 60 Navy planes attack Kahili. Shore installations, the A/F, and bridges N of the strip are hit.

3 September

Eighth AF: 140 HBs severely damage German A/F at Romilly-sur-Seine. Lesser air strikes take place at Meulan-Les Mureaux and at industrial areas around Paris. Almost 100 MBs hit A/F of Lille/Nord, Beauvais/Tille, and Beaumont-le-Roger.

Twelfth AF: P–40's on sweep over Sardinia hit Pula and Capo Carbonara radar installations. A–20's, A–36's, ftrs (and RAF LBs) hit gun positions throughout toe of Italy, attack A/Fs at Crotone and Camigliatello, and hit railway yards at Marina di Catanzaro and Punta di Staletti, troop concentration near Santo Stefano d'Aspromonte and road junctions and bridges at Cosenza. British Eighth Army lands on toe of Italy between Reggio di Calabria and Villa San Giovanni (Operation BAYTOWN). Italian government signs surrender terms.

Ninth AF: B–24's bomb M/Y at Sulmona. Fierce attacks by enemy ftrs account for 6 losses. HBs claim 11 enemy ftrs destroyed.

Fourteenth AF: 11 P–40's and 2 P–38's blast barracks area at Pho Lu.

Fifth AF: HBs and MBs blast gun emplacements and terrace defenses in Lae area. Other HBs hit Cape Gloucester area. Light raids are flown against tgts on Ceram and Timor.

Thirteenth AF: 20-plus B–24's, 14 P–40's, and 30-plus Navy airplanes attack Kahili A/F. Vila A/F is bombed by 5 B–24's and 10 Navy aircraft. P–40's strafe Webster Cove wharf.

4 September

Eighth AF: Over 100 MBs launch four-pronged attack on M/Ys at Hazebrouck, Lille, Saint-Pol/Siracourt, and Courtrai.

Twelfth AF: Bad weather prevents XII BC B–17's from locating their tgts (A/Fs in Italy). P–38's sent to hit landing grounds at Grazzanise also fail to find tgts, but attack T/Os in the general area. US FBs and RAF LBs hit motor transport scattered along Italian toe, and bomb gun positions NE of Reggio di Calabria and roads and railroad junction in Cosenza-Catanzaro-Nicastro area and at Colosimi.

Fourteenth AF: 10 B–25's and 11 P–40's pound Tien Ho A/F at Canton. 3 of 15 intercepting Zeros are shot down.

Fifth AF: Allied offensive against Lae begins as forces land at Hopoi and mouth of Buso R. B–24's spt landings by pounding Lae A/F, B–25's hit Hopoi area and bomb A/F at Cape Gloucester, and A–20's and RAAF planes hit Gasmata A/F. Supporting P–38's intercept more than 100 enemy ftrs and bmrs, which are airborne despite the attacks on A/Fs, and claim 20 shot down.

Thirteenth AF: 23 B–25's hit Dulo Cove area. 9 B–24's, 15 AAF ftrs, and 20-plus Navy ftrs hit Ballale I A/F.

5 September

Eighth AF: Over 60 MBs raid 2 M/Ys at Ghent. Bad weather causes recall of a mission intended to bomb Courtrai M/Y.

Twelfth AF: Over 130 XII BC B–17's bomb Viterbo A/F and town of Civitavecchia. Over 200 B–25's and B–26's hit landing grounds at Grazzanise. Other MBs and ftrs hit Pula radar station and town of Pabillonis. Weather hampers operations of the ftrs, MBs, and LBs of NATAF (Twelfth AF and RAF aircraft) and only a few tgts (guns, roads, railroads, and troops) are attacked during missions over toe of Italy.

Ninth AF: Gen Strahm, CoS, assumes temporary cmd during absence of Gen Brereton. Col John C Kilborn assumes cmd of IX BC upon departure of Gen Ent from the theater.

Fourteenth AF: 15 FBs pound M/Y SE of Lao Kay; 16 others hit barracks in the city.

Fifth AF: 82 C–47's drop paratroops at Nadzab A/F (first such landings in SWPA) following bombardment of drop zone by 52 MBs and pounding of Lae A/F by 24 HBs. Smoke screen is laid over landing area by A–20's. Nadzab A/F is quickly put into operational condition and will subsequently become a major Allied airbase.

6 September

Eighth AF: Eighth sets new record in number of HBs dispatched. 69 of the 407 dispatched are to fly diversionary sweep over N Sea and the rest are to bomb aircraft and bearing factories in and around Stuttgart. Bad weather frustrates original tgt plans but 262 HBs bomb T/Os in

Germany and France. Strong ftr opposition is encountered and 45 HBs
are lost. Over 120 MBs strike M/Ys
at Rouen, Serqueux, and Amiens. 2
gps of MBs sent to bomb at Ghent
are recalled when bad weather prevents ftr escort from taking off.

Twelfth AF: XII BC B–17's hit
Capodichino A/F, Villa Literno M/Y,
Gaeta harbor, and Minturno railroad
facilities. Weather prevents B–17 attack on Pomigliano A/F. B–25's and
B–26's hit Capua A/F and landing
grounds at Grazzanise. P–40's hit
landing ground at Pabillonis. US and
RAF planes of NATAF operate on
reduced scale, flying patrols and hitting railroads and T/Os on Italian
toe.

Fourteenth AF: 6 FBs attack
wharves, vessels, and destroy small
factory building in Yoyang-
Shihhweiyao area. 5 others hit trucks,
trains, gun emplacements, and railway facilities in areas around Sintsiang and Puchi.

Fifth AF: HBs pound Lae A/F and
surrounding area, and MBs bomb and
strafe enemy defenses in Malahang
and vicinity, as Allied ground forces
push toward Lae. US ftrs claim 8
enemy aircraft downed over Lae. B–
25's fly sweep against barges along
coast of New Britain and bomb tgts
on Timor.

Thirteenth AF: B–25's and P–39's
hit enemy positions at Kakasa. B–24's
blast gun positions at Vila. P–39's
join Navy aircraft in strike on suspected radar site at Morgusaia I. 5
Zeros are claimed shot down. 2 P–39's
are lost.

7 September

Eighth AF: Over 100 HBs strike

industrial area and A/F at Brussels
while smaller number of HBs bomb
tgts (including NOBALL site) at
Watten, and shipping off Texel I.
M/Y at Saint-Pol/Siracourt is hit by
over 80 MBs. Ftr escort is excellent.
No aircraft are lost.

Ninth AF: HQ AAF decides to
transfer Gen Brereton, CG, and his
HQ staff from Africa to UK to re-
form Ninth AF in ETO by absorbing
VIII A Spt Cmd.

Twelfth AF: XII BC B–17's bomb
2 satellite A/Fs at Foggia. B–25's and
B–26's hit road and rail bridges at
Sapri and Trebisacce and roads at
Lauria. P–40's hit landing ground at
Pabillonis and barges off Portoscuso.
US A–20's of NATBF spt British
landing on 7/8 Sep near Pizzo in
an unsuccessful attempt to cut off
enemy retreat up W coast of Italian
toe. MBs and LBs, in afternoon raids,
bomb Crotone A/F and roadblock
and gun batteries N of Catanzaro.

Tenth AF: B–25's attack Gokteik
Viaduct, causing minor damage.

Fifth AF: B–24's and B–26's bomb
Lae area. B–25's bomb and strafe
nearby tgts on road to Markham. P–
38's successfully turn back enemy
bombing attack on Morobe. C–47's
begin flying Australian 7th Div to
Nadzab. A–20's hit Gasmata area.

Thirteenth AF: 2 B–25's bomb
barge depot and supply area E of
Ringa Cove.

8 September

Eighth AF: 44th and 93d Bomb
Gps resume operations in UK after
DS in Africa; 389th, previously diverted to Africa, becomes operational
in UK. Over 200 MBs attack coastal
defenses in Boulogne-sur-Mer area

and Lille/Nord and Lille/Vendeville A/Fs.

Ninth AF: B–24's bomb landing ground at Foggia, as convoys approach Salerno to begin US invasion of Italy (Operation AVALANCHE).

Twelfth AF: About 130 XII BC B–17's bomb Frascati. More than 160 MBs hit highway at Lauria and bridges at Trebisacce and Sapri. Ftrs hit Pabillonis, cover Allied forces near Pizzo, and bomb and strafe roads and vehicles in Lamezia-Vibo Valentia-Pizzo-Catanzaro areas. Bmrs hit roads and junctions in Naples area during 8/9 Sep.

Tenth AF: 6 B–24's mine Rangoon R during 7/8 Sep. B–25's hit Gokteik Viaduct for second consecutive day, scoring 5 hits at the base of the structure, which remains usable.

Fifth AF: B–17's, B–24's, B–25's and B–26's pound Lae area, and A–20's hit Salamaua. Japanese at Salamaua are ordered to prepare to fall back to Lae in face of approaching Australian 5th Div. Elements of Australian 9th Div, moving W on Lae, reach flooded Busu R where Japanese hold W bank. Other HBs and MBs carry out light raids on tgts in W part of Netherlands New Guinea and in islands of NEI.

Thirteenth AF: 12 B–25's hit Vila A/F area.

Seventh AF: B–24's operating from Canton I fire on flying boat, scoring hits but causing no visible damage.

9 September

Eighth AF: On D-day for Operation STARKEY (rehearsal for the invasion of France), Eighth AF dispatches a record number of 330 HBs, which attack Paris and Beaumont-sur-Oise, Beauvais/Tille, Lille/Nord, Lille/Vendeville, Saint-Omer/Longuenesse, Saint-Omer/Ft Rouge, Abbeville/Drucat, and Vitry-en-Artois A/Fs, as well as industrial area around Paris. More than 200 MBs attack coastal installations around Boulogne-sur-Mer. STARKEY is a disappointment as Germans refuse to commit ftr defenses on large scale, thus preventing possible destruction of many of their aircraft, which Allied air forces hoped to accomplish.

Twelfth AF: Gen Williams assumes cmd of XII TCC (Prov). Over 100 XII BC B–17's bomb bridges at Capua and Cancello Arnone, and over 240 B–25's and B–26's hit railroad bridges at Potenza and landing ground at Scanzano. P–40's fly uneventful sweep over Sardinia. XII A Spt Cmd ftrs maintain patrols over Salerno, and other NATAF planes bomb and strafe motor transport, roads, and other tgts in Catanzaro-Auletta-Rogliano area and NNW of Salerno, as Gen Clark's Fifth Army invades Italy, landing near Salerno (Operation AVALANCHE) and British forces make airborne landing on heel of Italy, taking Taranto (Operation SLAPSTICK).

Ninth AF: B–24's hit satellite A/F at Foggia.

Tenth AF: B–24's again mine Rangoon R, during 8/9 Sep.

Fourteenth AF: 8 B–25's and 11 P–40's hit White Cloud A/F. 4 P–38's bomb Whampoa docks. 8 P–40's and P–38's hit Yangtze R shipping near Chiuchiang, Kichun, Wusueh, Ocheng, and Changanyi, and strafe T/Os in the general area.

Fifth AF: B–25's bomb and strafe

coastal area from Alexishafen to Finschhafen and hit points on New Britain coast. HBs attack Garove I. Selaroe I is hit by light MB strike.

Thirteenth AF: 12 B–25's and 50-plus naval dive bmrs pound Vila A/F and barges at Disappointment Cove. 18 B–24's, with ftr escort, bomb Kahili A/F. 2 nearby coastal guns are also hit.

Eleventh AF: At Umnak, the RC AF 14th Ftr Sq prepares to depart for Canada.

10 September

Twelfth AF: XII BC MBs hit railroad and road junctions and road net in Castelnuovo-Pescopagano-Cassino-Capua-Formia areas. HBs attack Ariano intersection and highway bridge (and bridges and roads in the area), bridges near Botena and over the Tiber SW of Rome, and roads, buildings, and railroad facilities at Isernia. XII A Spt Cmd and RAF airplanes of NATAF blast heavy road movement N from Lauria and cover beachheads in Salerno area as British Eighth Army increases pressure on its front in effort to prevent Germans from concentrating against US Fifth Army's Salerno beachhead. German troops occupy Rome. During 10/11 Sep B–25's of 12th Bomb Gp hit comm centers at Corleto, Perticara, Auletta, and Sapri.

Ninth AF: B–24's bomb a satellite A/F at Foggia.

Tenth AF: B–25's again bomb Gokteik Viaduct. The approaches are battered but the viaduct remains usable.

Fourteenth AF: 10 B–25's and 7 P–40's hit cotton warehouse N of Wuchang and docks at Hankow; 9

of 20 intercepting Zeros are claimed destroyed. 6 P–38's bomb docks at Whampoa.

Fifth AF: B–25's attack barges along New Britain coast. Australian 7th Div, having been flown to Nadzab in C–47's, begins push E toward Lae.

Eleventh AF: 9 B–24's fly from Adak to Attu in preparation for Paramushiru mission on the next day.

ZI: First and Fourth AFs are relieved from their assignments to Eastern and Western Def Cmds and hereafter serve primarily as trg organizations.

11 September

Eighth AF: 32 B–26's attack Beaumont-le-Roger A/F. 19 others bomb Le Trait shipyards when primary tgt, Rouen power station, is obscured by clouds.

Twelfth AF: XII BC B–17's bomb Benevento M/Y and bridge and highway junction nearby. B–25's and B–26's hit highways and junctions at Castelnuovo, Ariano, Mignano, and Isernia. P–40's fly uneventful sweep over S Sardinia. US and RAF airplanes of NATAF continue to provide beachhead cover in Salerno area, hit road comm throughout the day, and attack road and rail bridges, junctions, A/F, and town areas at Sapri, Corleto, Perticara, Auletta, and Gioia del Colle.

Fourteenth AF: 10 B–25's and 11 P–40's attack Hankow docks and Wuchang cotton mills. 3 P–38's bomb ammo and fuel depots at Tayeh and strafe warehouses and barracks at Yangsin.

Fifth AF: B–24's bomb Makassar. Australian forces cross Francisco R to Salamaua A/F as Japanese forces begin to evacuate Salamaua and withdraw toward Lae.

Thirteenth AF: 18 B–25's pound area W of Vila A/F and W of Disappointment Cove. The A/F is hit again in the evening by 3 B–24's. 25 B–24's, with ftr escort, bomb Kahili A/F. HBs and ftrs claim 7 aircraft shot down. P–40's and P–39's spt Navy dive bmrs in striking gun positions at Hamberi.

Eleventh AF: 12 B–25's and 8 B–24's attack Paramushiru for the third and last time this year. 6 HBs bomb Kashiwabara staging area. Shipping is bombed and strafed in Kashiwabara harbor and Paramushiru Straits. 1 freighter and 1 large transport is sunk while 1 transport and 2 cargo ships are damaged. 2 other cargo vessels sustain possible hits. Tgts hit on land include 2 bldgs and a AA battery on Shimushu. Of 40 ftrs giving battle, 13 are shot down and 3 more are probables. 2 HBs force-land in USSR, one with mechanical defect, the other after being hit. 1 B–24 is downed by AA fire. Losses are 7 B–25's and 2 B–24's in this most disastrous day for the Eleventh. It will be another 5 months before it is able to strike at the Kurils again.

12 September

Twelfth AF: XII BC B–17's bomb Mignano road defiles, Benevento road bridge, and Frosinone A/F. MBs hit Ariano (and trucks and road nearby), Isernia, and Castelnuovo and Formia road junctions. US and RAF aircraft of NATAF attack motor transport movement, roads, and bridges in Potenza-Auletta areas, maintain cover over Fifth Army in Salerno invasion area (where the enemy launches a fierce effort to reduce the beachhead), and during 12/13 Sep fly intruder missions over 6 A/Fs between Rome and Pizzo, finding little activity. British Eighth Army forces on toe of Italy capture Crotone and push N, and on Taranto front occupy territory up to N of Castelaneta.

Ninth AF: B–24's hit Kalathos and Maritsa A/Fs.

Fourteenth AF: 8 P–38's bomb shipping in Hong Kong area, 4 hit Yangtze R traffic at Chiuchiang, and 4 P–40's strafe barracks and destroy locomotive W of Shihhweiyao.

Fifth AF: B–17's and B–24's pound Lae as Japanese begin withdrawal in face of Australian 9th and 7th Divs moving in from E and W. Australian 5th Div occupies Salamaua and surrounding area. First Allied airplane lands at Salamaua A/F. B–25's strafe between Saidor and Langemak Bay. B–25's hit barges near Cape Gloucester, and A–20's bomb radio station at Gasmata.

Eleventh AF: XI FC moves up to Adak.

13 September

Eighth AF: 1st, 2d, and 3d Bomb Divs are activated in UK. They are formed from complements of VIII BC's 4 bomb wgs. Each bomb div is organized into combat bomb wgs. COs of the Bomb Divs are Gen Williams (1st), Gen Hodges (2d), and Col Curtis E LeMay (3d).

Twelfth AF: B–17's of XII BC bomb roads in Torre del Greco area, highway at Sala Consilina, and road junction, railway and bridge at Atena Lucana. B–25's attack viaduct, rail and road junctions, and rail lines in Pompeii-Castellammare di Stabia-

Torre Annuziata areas. XII A Spt Cmd A–36's destroy 25 to 30 vehicles near Potenza, and ftrs maintain convoy patrol. US and RAF LBs and MBs of NATBF hit town areas, road junctions, and vehicles in Auletta-Pompeii-Sala Consilina-San Severino Rota areas. Over 80 troop transports drop contingents of 82d Airborne Div S of Sele R to strengthen bridgehead in face of enemy counterattacks which threaten US Fifth Army beachhead in Salerno area.

Ninth AF: RAF HBs, under IX BC, hit Potenza. Col Frederick M Byerly replaces Col Charles D Mc-Allister as cmdr of IX FC.

Fifth AF: B–24's escorted by P–38's, bomb A/Fs and ammo dumps in Wewak area. B–25's hit Lae.

Eleventh AF: Gen Johnson succeeds Gen Butler as CG of the Eleventh.

14 September

Eighth AF: Over 100 MBs of 3 gps sent to attack Woensdrecht and Lille/Nord A/Fs are forced to abort mission because of bad weather.

Twelfth AF: Elements of British Eighth Army enter Bari. At Salerno, US Fifth Army, throwing reserves and serv troops into line, and receiving much naval and air spt, holds off enemy onslaughts against beachhead. XII BC B–17's, B–25's, and B–26's attack highways, road junctions and defiles, bridges, town areas, railroads, M/Y, barracks, and numerous T/Os, including several gun positions, in or near Avellino, Pompeii, Torre Annunziata, Auletta, Baronissi, San Severino Rota, Battipaglia, and Eboli. US and RAF FBs, LBs, and MBs of NATAF fly well over

500 sorties, mainly against roads, bridges, and towns in battle areas, in or around Battipaglia, Eboli, Potenza, Torre Annunziata, Benevento, Auletta, and Avellino. Troop transports drop more contingents of 82d Airborne Div S of Sele R to strengthen beachhead, and also behind enemy lines near Avellino to disrupt enemy comm.

Ninth AF: B–24's hit M/Y at Pescara. RAF HBs, under IX BC, hit Potenza.

Fourteenth AF: 15 B–24's are dispatched against Haiphong. First flight aborts due to bad weather but second flight reaches tgt area and bombs docks and shipping. 4 P–38's severely damage 2 vessels at Chiuchiang.

Fifth AF: B–25's attack Lae and barges in Hansa Bay. B–24's bomb Kendari.

Thirteenth AF: Allied A/Fs and other facilities on Guadalcanal, at Barakoma, and at Munda are attacked by Japanese airplanes throughout the day. B–24's, with AAF and Navy ftr escorts, bomb Kahili A/F 3 times during the day. More than 30 of the HBs unload on dispersal and revetment areas and on runways, causing considerable damage. 8 Japanese interceptors are claimed shot down. 3 B–25's bomb Vila A/F. 2 B–24's and 6 B–34's attack Vila area. P–39's join Navy ftrs and dive bmrs in attack on Ballale I A/F.

Eleventh AF: The 36th Bomb Sq (H) departs for the ZI.

15 September

Eighth AF: Almost 140 HBs attack aircraft engine works, Renault motor works, and ball bearing plant at Paris. Comparable numbers of aircraft bomb A/Fs at Chartres and Romilly-sur-Seine. About 70 B–26's hit Merville A/F. Mission to Lille is abandoned due to bad weather. Small number of HBs fly night mission with RAF against Montlucon Dunlop tire factory.

Twelfth AF: B–17's of XII BC bomb highways and railroad at Torre del Greco while B–25's and B–26's hit highways and road junctions at or near Torre Annunziata, Battipaglia, Eboli, Serre, Auletta, and Polla. XII A Spt Cmd and other NATAF elements attack buildings, railroads, highways and motor transport in spt of US Fifth Army as German counterattacks astride Sele R subside. British Eighth Army forces reach Sapri, threatening the enemy with entrapment between US and British forces.

Ninth AF: B–24's hit M/Y at Potenza and attack railroads and warehouses in areas around Potenza, Altamura, Gravina di Puglia, and Matera.

Fourteenth AF: 5 B–24's attack Haiphong cement plant. More than 50 Japanese ftrs attack the HBs, shooting down 4 of them. The 1 returning B–24 claims 10 ftrs downed. 6 B–25's and 14 P–40's attack Wuchang cotton mill area.

Fifth AF: B–24's, with P–38 escort, bomb A/Fs in Wewak area, destroying 10 enemy aircraft on the ground. 14 more are claimed destroyed in air combat. B–17's bomb Lae area. B–25's sink about 15 barges between Alexishafen and Finschhafen, blast ammo and supply dump near Bogadjim, and attack AA positions at Bostrem Bay.

Thirteenth AF: B–25's bomb Vila, Kahili, and Kara A/Fs. B–24's, with ftr escort, later pound Kahili runway area; others hit Parapatu Pt. During the night, B–25's hit Kahili A/F twice and HBs bomb A/Fs on Buka and Ballale. Ballale I A/F is also hit by Navy dive bmrs, supported by AAF, Navy and Marine ftrs. Bivouac area, revetments, supply dumps and gun positions are hit. Runway appears badly damaged by the strikes.

16 September

Eighth AF: More than 130 HBs attack port area and Chateau-Bougon A/F, more than 70 hit La Pallice harbor installations and Laleu A/F near La Rochelle, and 21 strike at Cognac/Chateaubernard A/F. Nearly 70 MBs attack Beaumont-le-Roger and Triqueville A/Fs. 5 B–17's fly night mission with 340 RAF HBs against Modane M/Y. This mission is flown from UK at the request of Gen Eisenhower. 3 B–24 gps in UK (44th, 93d, and 389th) are sent on loan to N Africa for second time at Gen Eisenhower's request for spt of the crucial campaign in this theater.

Twelfth AF: B–17's of XII BC hit bridges, rail line, M/Y, trains, and railroad-highway intersection in Benevento area, and roads and railway facilities in Caserta area. MBs hit roads, railroads, junctions, and bridges at Isernia, Formia, Mignano, and Capua. XII A Spt Cmd FBs maintain continuous sweeps over Salerno beachhead and surrounding battle zone while other US and RAF elements of NATAF (ftrs, LBs, and MBs) blast enemy aircraft, motor transport, troop concentrations and comm tgts in Contursi and Eboli areas. US and British make patrol contact near Vallo della Lucania. US Fifth Army ties in with Taranto invasion force to form Allied line across S Italy.

Ninth AF: B–24's hit road junctions and a supply dump at Potenza, following RAF raid of previous night.

USSR: Red Army takes Novorossisk.

Fourteenth AF: 8 B–25's and 12 P–40's hit warehouses, barracks, ammo dumps, and HQ at Liujenpa.

Fifth AF: B–17's, B–26's, B–25's, and A–20's pound enemy positions at Lae, after which the A/F and town (evacuated by Japanese) are occupied by Australian forces. B–24's carry out light strike on Sorong.

Thirteenth AF: P–40's join Navy ftrs in covering Navy dive bmr strike on Ballale I A/F.

17 September

Twelfth AF: XII BC B–17's and B–26's bomb A/Fs at Ciampino and Pratica di Mare. B–25's attack small craft and barges off mouth of Tiber R. P–38's fly 27 dive-bombing missions against roads, junctions, railways, bridges, and T/Os in battle area and towns of Vallo della Lucania, Acerno, Nocera, Avellino, Gragnano, Serre, Lioni, Fisciano, Monteforte Irpino, Cava de' Tirreni and Auletta. XII A Spt Cmd, NATBF, and other elements of NATAF fly sweeps over battle area, patrol beaches, escort naval vessels, and bomb rail and road junctions, motor transport, M/Y, town areas, and various T/Os in Pompeii, Torre Annunziata, Salerno, Campagna, Sarno, Solofra, Montella,

and Acerno areas. US Fifth Army forces advancing on Altavilla are pinned down. However enemy retires to the N, completing withdrawal from battleline during night. British Eighth Army begins general adv N toward Potenza and Auletta.

Ninth AF: B–24's attack M/Y, road junction, and rail junction at Pescara on E coast of Italy. RAF HBs again hit Potenza.

Fifth AF: B–25's carry out coastal sweep against barges and villages from Reiss Pt to Langemak Bay.

18 September

Eighth AF: 36 MBs attack Beauvais/Tille A/F. Attacks of MBs on Rouen power station and Beaumont-le-Roger A/F are aborted because of failure to rendezvous with ftr escort and bad weather, respectively.

Twelfth AF: B–17's of XII BC hit Viterbo A/F and Salerno-Avellino road, while B–25's and B–26's bomb A/F at Ciampino and Pratica di Mare. B–25's fire 75mm shells at small vessels and lighthouse near Capraia and between Pianosa and Corsica. P–38's on DS with NATAF strafe 4 satellite A/Fs at Foggia and bomb roads, railroads, bridges, and towns in battle area. Seventh Army forces take Altavilla, Persano, and Battipaglia without opposition.

Ninth AF: B–24's hit Pescara M/Y.

Fourteenth AF: 4 B–25's and 7 P–40's attack rail yards and blast furnaces at Shihhweiyao.

Fifth AF: A–20's hit Tami Is in Lae area. B–26's and RAAF airplanes bomb and strafe Finschhafen.

Thirteenth AF: B–24's bomb A/F and attack phosphate plant and radio station on Nauru.

Seventh AF: 24 B–24's, flying out of Funafuti and Canton I, bomb Betio, Maiana, and Abemama Is in the Gilbert chain during 18/19 Sep. This action is part of a coordinated Army-Navy attack on Tarawa, aimed at preventing Japanese attacks on US installations at Baker I and in the Ellice Is.

19 September

Eighth AF: MBs hit Lille/Nord A/F. Other MB attacks on Lille and Merville are recalled due to bad weather.

Twelfth AF: FBs of XII A Spt Cmd and planes of other NATAF elements (US and RAF) concentrate on attacking roads and vehicles in Benevento-Montesarchio-Contursi-Potenza-Avellino areas, and hit railway station at Castelnuovo. Fifth Army gains firm control of Salerno plain, while British Eighth Army troops take Potenza and Auletta.

Tenth AF: HBs hit Monywa.

Fifth AF: B–25's and B–26's pound Finschhafen in preparation for Allied landings on 22 Sep. B–17's and B–24's bomb A/F and surrounding area at Cape Gloucester. B–24's and B–25's fly small strikes against Amboina, Selaroe, and Penfoei.

Thirteenth AF: B–25's and Navy dive bmrs, covered by ftrs, bomb Vila A/F and a causeway, enemy positions, and ammo dump at Disappointment Cove. Other B–25's bomb and strafe barge centers at Ringa and Webster Coves.

Seventh AF: 20 B–24's, out of Funafuti and Canton I, bomb Tarawa and Abemama and obtain photo coverage of Betio. 1 B–24 is lost to interceptors.

Eleventh AF: The 21st Bomb Sq (H) departs for the ZI.

20 September

Twelfth AF: XII BC B–17's and B–26's bomb Castelnuovo road junction, town of Formia, Torre Annunziata area roads, and roads and railroad SW of Sarno. XII A Spt Cmd A–36's attack and disperse enemy tank and troop concentrations forming near Nocera for a counterattack. Other US and RAF aircraft of NA TAF hit enemy movement in Avellino-Naples-Potenza-Benevento-Calabritto-Pomigliano-Pescopagano areas. US Seventh Army starts into mts N of Salerno.

Ninth AF: 98th and 376th Bomb Gps, along with 43d Serv Gp and several MP and engineer units, are to be transferred to Twelfth AF, effective on their arrival in Tunis. IX BC makes its last raid on Italy. B–24's of 98th and 376th Bomb Gps are dispatched against Castelfranco Veneto M/Y. Clouds obscure tgt, but 98th Gp drops bombs on estimated time of arrival. 376th bombs M/Y and A/F at Pescara during return trip.

Tenth AF: B–24's bomb Sagaing and Naba.

Fourteenth AF: 27 Japanese bmrs and 20 ftrs attack A/F at Kunming. 24 P–40's and 3 P–38's intercept, claiming 17 airplanes shot down. 1 US ftr is lost. Damage to the A/F is negligible.

Fifth AF: B–25's and B–17's hit roads from Kaiapit to Madang, destroying 3 key bridges. P–39's strafe and dive-bomb Bogadjim-Yaula area. B–24's bomb Wewak and Boram A/Fs. B–25's hit Penfoei.

Thirteenth AF: 1st Lt Henry Meigs II (6th Night Ftr Sq), flying a P–38 against Japanese night attackers over Bougainville, shoots down 2 aircraft within 60 seconds.

21 September

Eighth AF: Over 40 B–26's bomb Beauvais/Tille A/F. Bad weather causes more than 20 MBs to abort.

Twelfth AF: XII BC B–17's hit bridge and town area at Benevento. B–25's and B–26's hit landing craft and ferry near Elba and bridges at Cancello Arnone and Capua. B–24's on DS from Eighth AF bomb Leghorn and Bastia. MBs and FBs of NATBF and XII A Spt Cmd hit town areas, troop concentrations, trucks and tanks, and T/Os in Solofra-Avellino-Benevento areas.

Ninth AF: HQ IX FC at Tripoli closes.

Fifth AF: A–20's, B–26's, and RAAF aircraft hit Tami Is and pound Finschhafen in preparation for Allied amphibious assault on following day. B–25's bomb and strafe Bogadjim area. B–24's hit Cape Gloucester and a freighter near Talasea. A–20's, and RAF aircraft bomb Gasmata. B–25's attack Langgoer.

Fourteenth AF: 8 B–25's and 8 P–40's attack railroad yards and warehouses at Chiuchiang, causing considerable destruction.

Thirteenth AF: 20-plus B–24's bomb runway and revetment area at Buka I A/F. About 20 Japanese ftrs intercept. 2 Zeros are shot down.

22 September

Eighth AF: 70 B–26's bomb Evreux/Fauville A/F. MB mission to attack Beauvais/Tille A/F aborts due to bad weather. 4 gps of P–47's sweep over NE France and Belgium and 3 gps sweep over N Belgium and Dutch Is. A few B–17's fly night attack on Hannover with RAF.

Twelfth AF: XII BC B–25's and B–26's bomb roads, railroad, and bridges at or near San Martino Sannita, Grottaminarda, Amorosi, and Mignano. B–25's on DS to NATAF attack small vessels near Elba with 75mm cannon. NATBF and XII A Spt Cmd airplanes hit troop concentrations and gun positions near Serino and Santa Lucia di Serino, road block at Nocera, town and roads at Fisciano, town of Pagani, tanks and trucks between Acerno and Montella and in Foggia area, vessels and docks at Manfredonia, town of Camarella, and landing ground at Capua.

Ninth AF: Ninth AF flies its final mission from Africa. B–24's bomb Maritsa and Eleusis A/Fs. The bomb gps of IX BC subsequently are transferred to Twelfth AF.

Tenth AF: MBs attack Ye-u branch line railroad bridge over Mu R between Ywataung and Monywa. Negligible damage is done to the tgt.

Fifth AF: After preparatory naval bombardment, elements of Australian 9th Div land at mouth of Song R N of Finschhafen and push to S. B–25's pound defenses in Finschhafen area. Almost 90 Fifth AF ftrs battle aircraft attacking the convoy. 38 enemy aircraft are claimed shot down. A–20's and B–25's hit Lae area. B–24's and B–25's bomb Gasmata A/F. B–24 hit Amboina.

23 September

Eighth AF: More than 150 HBs hit port area at Nantes and Vannes/Meucon and Kerlin/Bastard A/Fs. 80 HBs strike Rennes/Saint-Jacques A/F and port area and ships at Nantes. MBs attack Conches/Evreux and Beauvais/Tille A/Fs. Mannheim is attacked by RAF, along with a few Eighth AF B–17's, in a night raid.

Twelfth AF: XII BC B–26's bomb bridges at Cancello Arnone and 3 mi NE of Capua. Planes of NATBF and XII A Spt Cmd attack motor transport, roads, railroads, town areas, gun positions, and T/Os in areas of San Severino Rota, Avellino, Sarno, Torre Annunziata, Aversa, Nocera, Resina, Serino, Pompeii, and Camarella.

Fifth AF: B–25's bomb and strafe villages in upper Markham R Valley. P–40's bomb Gasmata.

Thirteenth AF: 23 B–24's, 16 P–38's, and 60-plus Navy dive bmrs, covered by AAF, Marine, Navy, and RNZAF ftrs, attack Kahili. Allied aircraft claim at least 9 ftrs shot down. 21 B–24's bomb area from Stanmore Plantation to mouth of Vila R. P–39's strafe 2 barges, at Sasamunga and Malanono, leaving both aflame.

Eleventh AF: Adm Kinkaid issues Op Plan 9–43 which reorganizes Alaskan Army and Navy air strength. CG Eleventh AF becomes Cmdr of TF 90, composed of TG 90.1, designated the Air Striking Unit (comprising 16 MBs, 12 HBs, 100 ftrs) and of TG 90.2, designated the Air Search Gp, a Navy air arm. For operations the Eleventh is now under the jurisdiction of COMNORPAC Forces. There is no administrative change.

24 September

Eighth AF: 71 MBs hit Evreaux/Fauville A/F in main attack. Other aircraft attack tgts at Beauvais.

Twelfth AF: B–25's and B–26's of XII BC hit roads, railways, bridges, and junctions at Grottaminarda, Maddaloni, Benevento, Avellino, Capua, Cancello Arnone, Amorosi, Ponte, and Mignano, and attack destroyer between Corsica and Elba. B–24's on DS from Eighth AF bomb M/Y at Pisa. US and RAF planes of NATBF, XII A Spt Cmd, and other elements of NATAF attack vehicles, roads, troop concentrations, and gun positions around Santa Lucia di Serino, Serino, Caserta, Benevento, Camarella, Baronissi, Nocera, Montemarano, and San Severo.

Fifth AF: B–24's fly small strike against Sorong and Manokwari.

25 September

Eighth AF: 72 B–26's attack Saint-Omer/Longuenesse A/F.

Twelfth AF: About 90 B–17's of XII BC hit Bologna M/Y; 14 others hit Bolzano railroad bridge. B–25's and B–26's bomb A/Fs at Pisa, Lucca, and Bastia/Borgo, highway at Mignano, road junction at Maddaloni, and railroad and road bridges at Cancello Arnone, Caiazzo, and Ponte. US and RAF aircraft of NATBF, XII A Spt Cmd, and DAF hit Serino (causing roadblock), troop concentrations at Sarno, gun positions, troops, and vehicles near Nocera, Aquino A/F, storage dump N of Foggia, and a dredger at Termoli.

USSR: Soviet Army captures Smolensk.

Fifth AF: Nearly 40 B–17's, B–

24's, and B–25's bomb installations and supply lines from Bogadjim to villages on Ramu and Markham Rivers. A–20's and RAAF airplanes pound positions near Finschhafen as Australian 9th Div, having crossed Buni R previous day, pushes S toward the town. B–25's bomb and strafe AA positions at Rein Bay.

Thirteenth AF: B–25's join Navy TBF's and SBD's in pounding gun positions in areas around Vila A/F and Disappointment Cove.

26 September

Eighth AF: 40 HBs hit Reims/Champagne air depot. Bad weather prevents bombing by more than 160 other HBs dispatched to tgts in N France.

Twelfth AF: Ftrs, LBs, and MBs of XII A Spt Cmd, NATBF, and DAF patrol battle zone, escort convoys, carry out bombing and strafing sweeps against motor transport in Benevento-Melfi area and N of Foggia, bomb Pomigliano landing ground, and hit town of Sarno and military concentrations to the N. Bad weather prevents XII BC HB missions.

Fifth AF: B–24's bomb But and Dagua A/Fs. P–38's claim 9 enemy ftrs shot down in But-Dagua-Wewak areas. Other B–24's hit Nubia and Potsdam Plantations.

Thirteeenth AF: 21 B–24's, covered by 14 P–38's, bomb bivouac near Kahili. 30 P–40's and P–39's and 15 Navy F4U's spt more than 50 Navy dive bmrs in strike on Kahili A/F hangar area and gun positions at Kangu Hill and Jakohina.

27 September

Eighth AF: HBs equipped with

H2S fly first large daylight mission in ETO against cloud-covered tgt. Two of these pathfinder aircraft lead main attack of 244 other B–17's on port area at Emden. P–47's with belly tanks escort bmrs entire way to tgt in Germany for first time. More than 130 B–26's attack A/Fs at Conches and Beauvais/Tille. A few B–17's fly with RAF on night raid against Hannover.

Twelfth AF: Weather almost halts Twelfth AF operations. XII A Spt Cmd ftrs strafe Viterbo A/F and Bracciano seaplane base, bomb road junction at San Severo, and strafe locomotive and train station. Other NATAF airplanes hit trucks in Benevento area.

Fifth AF: 117 B–24's and B–25's, escorted by 129 P–38's and P–40's, attack A/Fs and shipping in Wewak area. About 40 aircraft are destroyed on the ground and 8 are claimed shot down in combat. The bmrs claim 10 ships (totalling about 28,000 tons), 11 luggers, and a launch sunk. Finschhafen is bombed twice during the day.

Thirteenth AF: 27 B–24's, 20-plus P–40's and P–39's, and several Navy ftrs pound Kahili area. P–39's over Choiseul strafe (and explode) 3 barges off Wogai Pt, and strafe 2 others off Bambatana, leaving 1 ablaze.

28 September

Twelfth AF: Weather prevents completion of XII BC B–17 missions against Bologna M/Y and Bolzano railroad bridge, except for 1 HB which bombs Bolzano. Tac aircraft operations are also severely curtailed by weather. FBs bomb and strafe motor transport in Benevento-Caserta area. US Fifth Army is ready for assault on Naples and Avellino. Castellamare di Stabia, Nocera, and Sala Consilina are taken.

Fifth AF: The Wewak area is again hit, the 40 attacking B–24's being escorted by 29 P–38's which claim 8 ftrs shot down. A–20's and RAAF Vengeances attack Finschhafen and Lae area. B–24's and P–39's hit road near Bogadjim.

Thirteenth AF: 5 SB–24 snoopers attack convoy in N Solomons waters and claim several damaging hits. The convoy reverses its course.

29 September

Twelfth AF: XII BC B–25's and B–26's bomb bridges at or near Piana, Castelvenere, Amorosi, and Cancello Arnone. P–38's bomb Ausonia defile and bridge near San Apollinare. US and RAF tac aircraft hit town of San Giorgio del Sannio and roads in the area S of Benevento. US Fifth Army opens attack on Avellino during 29/30 Sep. Gen Eisenhower and Marshal Badoglio sign Italian surrender document on HMS *Nelson* off Malta.

USSR: Soviet Army takes Kremenchug.

Fourteenth AF: 9 B–24's bomb Myitkyina and Sadon during routine ferry trips over the Hump.

Fifth AF: B–24's on armed rcn attack scattered shipping in NEI and Solomon and Bismarck Seas.

Thirteenth AF: P–40's, P–38's, and P–39's join Navy ftrs in supporting a strike by Navy dive bmrs on barge depot at Kakasa. Other P–40's strafe and set afire a barge off Sambi Pt.

30 September

Twelfth AF: XII BC P–38's, B–25's, and B–26's bomb road and rail and road bridges at Ausonia, Piana, Castelvenere, Amorosi, and Capua, and carry out sweeps from Bastia to Elba I. 7 B–25's hit Benevento and surrounding rail and road comm. XII A Spt Cmd FBs carry out strafing and bombing missions N and NE of Naples as Avellino falls to US 3d Div.

Fourteenth AF: 2 B–25's and 4 P–40's claim heavy damage to gunboat at Ft Bayard.

Fifth AF: B–24's and B–25's fly light raids against Boela, Sorong, and Manatuto.

Thirteenth AF: 16 B–24's, covered by 20-plus P–38's and P–40's and a few Navy F4U's, pound Kahili A/F area, hitting supply and bivouac area NE of the strip. 6 B–25's bomb Kakasa.

1 October

Eighth AF: Report by intelligence section of Eighth AF shows that despite recent efforts of Allies to destroy the German aircraft industry, ftr production has expanded greatly and enemy ftr strength on the Western Front has increased.

Twelfth AF: XII BC B–26's hit comm tgts in Capua, Grazzanise, Arce, and Mignano areas. B–24's, including HBs on DS from Eighth AF, bomb Wiener-Neustadt. B–17's, sent against airplane factory at Augsburg, fail to locate tgt, and bomb several alternate tgts and T/Os in Austria, Italy, and off Corsica and Elba. NA TBF and XII A Spt Cmd MBs, LBs, and FBs hit Benevento town area and M/Y, bridge at Capua, and motor transport, trains, and railroads mainly in Isernia area and N to Avezzano. British King's Dragoon Gds (with US Fifth Army) occupy Naples. British Eighth Army troops occupy Foggia A/Fs.

Tenth AF: Tenth AF ftr situation has improved with arrival of the 80th Ftr Gp (P–40's) and 311th FB Gp (A–36's and P–51's), and the activation of an additional sq for the 80th Gp. The new sq, 459th, flies P–38's, the first to be used in India.

Fourteenth AF: 21 B–24's, supported by 21 ftrs, bomb power plant, warehouse and dock area at Haiphong. 40–65 ftrs intercept, shooting down 2 US aircraft. 30 ftrs are claimed destroyed by Fourteenth in the air battle.

Fifth AF: A–20's and RAAF aircraft bomb and strafe Finschhafen area as Australian 9th Div pours more troops into the assault on the town. B–25's strafe power boat near Gasmata.

Thirteenth AF: 24 B–24's bomb supply and bivouac area N of Vila A/F. B–25's and P–38's join Navy dive bmrs in strike on barge depot at Kakasa.

2 October

Eighth AF: About 340 HBs led by 2 Pathfinders attack industrial areas of Emden. 6 of 72 B–26's dispatched bomb Saint-Omer/Longuenesse A/F; unable to identify tgt because of cloud formations above it, remainder of aircraft refrain from bombing.

Twelfth AF: Gen Saville becomes CG, XII FC. Weather curtails operations. FBs of XII A Spt Cmd attack motor transport, roads, and bridges during armed rcn missions from Vol-

turno Valley N to Isernia and W to Benevento.

Fourteenth AF: 5 P–40's dive-bomb and strafe Yangtze R shipping in Chiuchiang area. Strafing damages several small craft.

Fifth AF: B–25's strafe villages in Talasea area and barges off Gasmata. B–26's bomb Hoskins A/F. A B–24 bombs Cape Gloucester A/F. Other B–24's bomb Amboina. Australian forces take town and harbor of Finschhafen and prepare to take nearby commanding positions still held by the Japanese.

Thirteenth AF: 6 B–25's join Navy dive bmrs in attacking Hamberi Cove barge hideout near Vila.

3 October

Eighth AF: Almost 200 B–26's bomb A/Fs of Woensdrecht, Haamstede, Schiphol, and Beauvais/Tille. No aircraft are lost.

Twelfth AF: XII BC B–26's, B–25's, and P–38's bomb railroad, highway, and pontoon bridges, overpass, and road junction at Capua, Castel Volturno, Piana, Arce, Mignano, and Isernia. P–38's also hit shipping between Corsica and Italy. XII BC FBs hit motor transport in battle area as US Fifth Army troops take Benevento.

Fourteenth AF: 7 P–40's damage a 250-ft vessel on the Yangtze R near Chiuchiang. 4 P–38's bomb Chiuchiang docks. 6 B–24's damage a 100-ft coastal freighter off Tonkon Pt.

Fifth AF: B–25's continue to hit barges along W coast of New Britain.

Thirteenth AF: P–39's strafe several barges W of Choiseul.

4 October

Eighth AF: 282 HBs attack industrial areas of Frankfurt/Main, Wiesbaden, and Saarlautern, M/Ys at Sarreguemines and Saarbrucken, and Saint Dizier/Robinson A/F. The raid on Frankfurt is followed by a night raid on that city by more than 350 RAF HBs.

Twelfth AF: Over 100 XII BC B–17's bomb Pisa M/Y and Bolzano bridges. B–25's and B–26's attack A/F at Argos, road defiles at Terracina and Isernia, highway overpass at Mignano, and shipping at Bastia. Allies now have complete control of Corsica. NATBF aircraft hit road and rail junctions on main road N from Capua. XII A Spt Cmd FBs hit trains, roads, railroads, and vehicles near Isernia, Avezzano, Pescara, and Isolella.

Ninth AF: Lt Col Ray J Stecker becomes cmdr of IX FC.

Fourteenth AF: 17 Japanese bmrs and 25 Zeros attack Kweilin A/F. The bombs, dropped from 20,000 ft, fail to hit tgt. Fourteenth AF ftrs fail to make effective contact with the force.

Fifth AF: B–25's bomb and strafe barges, small craft, and villages in Vitu Is.

Thirteenth AF: 23 B–24's, covered by 16 P–38's and several Navy F4U's, bomb Kahili A/F. 20–30 ftrs intercept, and a running battle occurs between Bougainville and Vella Lavella. US ftrs and bmrs claim 9 ftrs downed. No American losses are suffered. 4 P–39's and 4 Corsairs sink 16 barges in strike along W coast of Choiseul I. The P–39's are especially effective because of their nose cannon.

5 October

Twelfth AF: Gen Doolittle assumes cmd of Twelfth AF during absence of Gen Spaatz. XII BC B–17's hit Bologna M/Y. B–25's and B–26's bomb Formia road, road loop N of Mignano, and Isernia chokepoint. NATBF, XII A Spt Cmd, and DAF aircraft bomb numerous tgts in and N of battle area, including heavy traffic in Isernia area, petrol dumps at Alfedena, trains at Termoli, and towns of Venafro and Isolella.

Fourteenth AF: A few B–25's and P–40's attack foundry at Shihhweiyao. Damaging hits are scored on barracks, on AA position, blast furnaces, hoppers, and a steam plant. 10 ftrs intercept a force of about 50 Zeros W of Kweilin, shoot down 1 enemy ftr. The enemy force turns back.

Fifth AF: B–25's carry out coastal sweep W to Madang, bombing and strafing villages and barges. B–17's hit Bogadjim Road and jetties at Erima. B–24's bomb Babo area.

6 October

Twelfth AF: XII BC B–17's bomb Mestre M/Y while B–26's hit highway chokepoint at Isernia, highway at Mignano, and road junction at Formia. P–38's strafe Araxos A/F. NATBF planes on road-blocking missions hit tgts at Teano, at Alfedena, between Cassino and Capua, and near Sessa Aurunca. XII A Spt Cmd P–40's and A–36's attack roads and vehicles N of US Fifth Army battle zone and patrol Naples area. Fifth Army reaches S bank of Volturno R. Capua falls to British units.

Fourteenth AF: 7 P–40's from Suichwan intercept an attacking force of 27 bmrs and 21 Zeros. 1 bmr and

1 ftr are shot down, and the attackers retire in the direction of Canton without dropping their bombs.

Fifth AF: B–25's sweep along coastal areas of New Britain and through islands to the N and W, bombing and strafing T/Os.

Thirteenth AF: 8 P–39's and 8 Navy F4U's strafe barges off W coast of Choiseul. 24 B–25's and 14 P–38's carry out low-level strike against Kahili A/F, damaging or destroying several parked aircraft.

7 October

Eighth AF: First of a series of Eighth AF night missions to drop propaganda leaflets is flown over Europe.

Twelfth AF: Bad weather cancels many operations. NATBF MBs and LBs strike roads, railway, junction, and town areas in Capua and Guglionesi regions. DAF FBs hit trucks in Termoli-Vasto areas.

Fourteenth AF: 4 B–25's attack 2,500-ton freighter 100 mi S of Amoy, scoring 3 direct hits. Vessel is left burning and listing. 9 B–24's and 22 ftrs hit cement plant at Haiphong, causing heavy damage to the kiln building.

Fifth AF: A B–24 on patrol bombs Umboi I, scoring damaging hits on several buildings.

8 October

Eighth AF: More than 350 HBs attack city and industrial areas of Bremen and U-boat yards at Vegesack. Nearly 30 US aircraft are lost in the main attack on Bremen. On this mission the Eighth uses, for first time, airborne transmitters (Carpet equipment) to jam German radar.

Over 140 MBs are recalled from missions to bomb A/Fs of Chievres and Lille/Vendeville due to thick haze and generally unsuitable weather.

Twelfth AF: XII BC B–24's bomb Tatoi and Eleusis A/Fs at Athens, A/Fs at Kastelli and Heraklion, and Maritsa A/F on Rhodes. B–25's also hit Eleusis A/F. P–38's fly convoy cover, patrols, and sweeps over the Aegean Sea. Weather prevents XII A Spt Cmd from operating. NATBF and DAF hit bridge at Minturno and road junction and military concentration at Termoli.

Fourteenth AF: 9 B–24's, supported by 20 P–40's, bomb Gia Lam A/F. While on ferry mission over the Hump, 3 B–24's bomb Tengchung, scoring hits on warehouses, barracks, and HQ area.

Fifth AF: A single B–24 on armed rcn bombs Cape Gloucester A/F.

Thirteenth AF: B–25's and P–40's sink barge off W coast of Choiseul I.

9 October

Eighth AF: 68 B–26's bomb Woensdrecht A/F. 352 HBs strike industrial areas at Anklam and Marienburg, U-boat yards at Danzig, and port area at Gdynia. 28 HBs are lost.

Twelfth AF: XII BC B–17's bomb A/Fs at Larissa, Athens, Salonika, and Argos. B–24's hit Kastelli/Pediada A/F. P–38's fly sweep between island of Corfu and Dubrovnik, and escort shipping in Karpathos Straits. XII A Spt Cmd does not operate, but NATBF and DAF hit traffic in Termoli and Montenero area, guns N of Capua, HQ at Palata, and roads and railroads N of Naples.

Fourteenth AF: 4 B–25's on shipping sweep off SE China coast in

Amoy-Quemoy area sink a 150-ft tanker and damage a patrol vessel, and a freighter. 1 MB crashes into a hill and explodes. 10 P–40's bomb fuel storage and barracks at Mangshih. 1 P–40 is downed by ground fire.

Fifth AF: A–20's and RAAF airplanes bomb and strafe defensive positions in Sattelberg and Finschhafen areas. B–24's bomb Makassar.

Thirteenth AF: B–25's and P–40's hit barges and concentrations on W Choiseul. P–39's and Navy F4U's strafe buildings, radar station, and gun positions at Poporang I.

Eleventh AF: 12 Kuril-based enemy bmrs attack Attu.

10 October

Eighth AF: 236 HBs attack railroads and waterways in and around Munster.

Twelfth AF: B–17's bomb 2 A/Fs at Athens. B–24's hit Maritsa, Calato, and Heraklion A/Fs. P–38's escort shipping off Rhodes I, hit Antimachia A/F in Dodecanese Is, and attack vessels in Corfu harbor, in Kotor harbor, and off Tivat, and hit T/Os in Aegean and along its E coastline. NATBF and DAF concentrate on gun positions on both US Fifth and British Eighth Army battlefronts. Vehicles, railroads, and town areas also are hit. Attacks take place NE of Capua, at Guglionesi, at Cassino and Mondragone, between Rome and Terracina, and around Termoli-Isernia-Pescara areas.

Tenth AF: 7 B–24's pound Meza railway bridge, destroying the 3 spans on the E end and dropping the end of a central span into the river.

Fourteenth AF: 20 B–24's and 18 P–40's pound docks at Haiphong. 8 P–40's bomb match factory and ammo dump at Tengchung; 8 others hit supply dump and T/Os in Lungling area.

Fifth AF: A–20's, along with RAAF airplanes, again pound Sattelberg area. B–25's hit Saumlakki 10/11 Oct.

Thirteenth AF: 24 B–24's, 50-plus P–38's, P–40's, and P–39's, and 50-plus Navy ftrs and dive bmrs pound Kahili A/F and surrounding areas, hitting runways, fuel dump, supply area, buildings, and Malabita Hill gun positions. US airplanes claim 15 interceptors shot down.

11 October

Twelfth AF: XII BC B–25's bomb Garitsa A/F and P–38's hit vessel in Corfu harbor. XII A Spt Cmd and NATBF operations are cancelled or aborted due to weather, but DAF ftrs hit trains, trucks, and gun positions near Montesilvano and Vasto.

Fourteenth AF: 8 B–24's bomb town areas of Tengchung, Sadon, and Myitkyina.

Fifth AF: B–24's attack towns of Manokwari, Bira, and Fak Fak and score hits on small vessel at Fak Fak. B–25's bomb Cape Chater A/F and Lautem during 11/12 Oct.

Thirteenth AF: 22 B–24's join 30-plus Navy dive bmrs in pounding Kahili A/F and nearby area. Hits are scored on the airstrip, fuel dumps, supply areas, gun positions, bridges between Kangu and Jakohina, barges at mouth of Uguima R, and several other tgts. The HBs and the Navy and AAF ftrs covering the attack claim 12 airplanes downed.

12 October

Twelfth AF: XII BC operations are canceled by weather. XII A Spt Cmd and other NATAF elements (NATBF and DAF) operate on reduced scale, hitting road junctions at Vasto and Fossacesia, Aquino A/F, motor transport on Itri-Pico road and on road N of Rome in Bolsena and Capranica areas, roads near Tarquinia, rail facilities at Cisterna di Latina, trains between Pescara and Benedello, and guns and troops near Cercemaggiore.

Fourteenth AF: 5 B–24's bomb warehouse area and railroad yards at Myitkyina.

Fifth AF: Allied AF begins major air offensive against Rabaul with aim of isolating and neutralizing Bismarck Archipelago. Almost 350 B–24's, B–25's, P–38's, and RAAF airplanes pound the town, habor, and A/Fs in the area. More than 50 aircraft are destroyed, 3 ships are sunk and several damaged, and several small harbor craft are sunk. B–25's fly small strikes against tgts on Timor and other areas of NEI.

Thirteenth AF: 2 B–25's skip-bomb 2 small vessels in Matchin Bay.

13 October

International: Italy declares war against Germany.

Twelfth AF: XII BC B–25's and B–26's bomb town of Alife, road junction at Sessa Aurunca, and A/F at Tirana. XII A Spt Cmd, supplemented by DAF ftrs, supports US Fifth Army, which begins assault crossing of Volturno R on 40-mi front during 12/13 Oct. Ftrs and FBs hit troop and tank concentrations, trains, trucks, and comm lines in forward areas, especially around Ortona, Giulianova, and Campobasso. NATBF LBs join in the attacks, hitting road junctions in Vairano, Carinola, Dragoni, Vasto, Terracina, and Minturno areas.

Tenth AF: Japanese ftrs appear in strength over Sumprabum to attack over-the-Hump flights. The enemy evades US patrols and shoots down 3 transports. FB offensive against A/Fs in Burma from which ftrs might operate against Hump transports opens with attack by P–40's on Myitkyina.

Fourteenth AF: 3 B–25's on sea sweep off SE China hit shipping in Amoy harbor, claiming 1 freighter sunk and another damaged.

Fifth AF: More than 100 B–24's and B–25's are sent against Rabaul. Bad weather forces the bmrs to turn back, but 40-plus B–24's hit tgts on New Britain including Hoskins, Lindenhafen, Gasmata, and Cape Gloucester.

Eleventh AF: 11 P–40's unsuccessfully intercept 8 MBs attacking Massacre Bay and the nearby A/F.

14 October

Eighth AF: Almost 230 HBs attack city area and ball bearing plants at Schweinfurt. The attack which causes great damage and interference with production, results in German reorganization of bearing industry. Fierce opposition of great numbers of ftrs, many of them firing rockets, accounts for 60 US aircraft shot down. As a result of these heavy losses, daylight bombing against strategic tgts deep in Germany are discontinued for a short period.

Twelfth AF: XII BC B–25's hit

Argos A/F. B–17's bomb Terni M/Y. Other B–17's and B–24's attack bridge at Giulianova, town area of Piano-Vomano and railroad and highway bridges N of Pescara and along E coast of Italy. Weather hinders tac aircraft operations, but XII A Spt Cmd and DAF hit trains and vehicles and fly patrols from N of Volturno R to Formia and N of Pescara.

Fourteenth AF: 4 B–25's attack shipping in Amoy area, damaging 2 freighters, and also bomb Amoy A/F.

Fifth AF: More than 60 MBs pound Cape Gloucester and Alexishafen. 3 others fly harassing strikes against Dili and Lautem.

Thirteenth AF: A single B–24 on armed rcn bombs 4 barges W of Taiof I, leaving 1 sinking.

15 October

USAAFUK: HQ USAAFUK is activated to exercise supervision over and provide coordination between Eighth and Ninth AFs in UK. Gen Eaker is appointed CG in addition to his duties as CG Eighth AF.

Eighth AF: A much needed P–38 gp (55th Ftr) becomes operational in UK.

Twelfth AF: B–25's of XII BC hit A/Fs at Salonika and Megalo Mikra. XII A Spt Cmd and other elements of NATAF hit roads, railroads, bridges, junctions, railway facilities, town areas, and motor transport at or near Piedimonte, Vairano, Termoli, Petacciato, Sparanise, and Civitanova, and hit gun positions and comm in general battle area N of Volturno R.

Fifth AF: More than 50 P–38's and P–40's intercept around 100 aircraft attacking Allied shipping in Oro Bay. The US ftrs claim more than 40 shot down. 4 other P–40's, encountering 20-plus airplanes E of Finschhafen, claim 5 destroyed. More than 70 MBs hit positions and villages from Sio to Saidor. 6 B–24's bomb Boela.

Thirteenth AF: 21 B–24's, 12 P–38's, and 17 Navy F4U's pound Kahili A/F supply and personnel area. 6 Zeros are claimed shot down. During the late evening B–25's bomb A/F at Buka I.

16 October

US: JCS sends to Gen Eisenhower a proposed directive, submitted by Gen Arnold on 9 Oct, for establishment of a new AF (Fifteenth) in Italy to be used when needed as part of CBO against strategic tgts in Germany.

Ninth AF: Ninth AF is established in UK as tac AF with Gen Brereton as CG. 3d Bomb Wg is transferred from VIII A Spt Cmd to IX BC commanded by Gen Frederick L Anderson. IX FC is re-formed in UK. IX TCC (constituted on 11 Oct 43) is activated in UK with Gen Giles as CG. IX ASC is re-formed in UK under Gen Miller.

Twelfth AF: XII BC B–25's bomb M/Y and rail lines, railroad tunnel, highway underpass, warehouses, industrial buildings, and gas works in or near Bologna. P–38's bomb a vessel in Leukas Channel off W coast of Greece. XII A Spt Cmd and other NATAF elements provide close spt to US Fifth and British Eighth Armies. Ftrs, LBs, and MBs hit comm centers of Venafro, Vairano, Sparanise, Latina, Alife, and town of

Pietravairano; roads, railroads, and junctions in areas SE of Rome to bomb line, between Vasto and Pescara, and at Mondragone; gun positions, trucks, and military concentrations near Vinchiaturo, Boiano, and Termoli; landing ground of Cisterna di Latina; and several other tgts in area between Rome and Ancona.

Tenth AF: Ftr patrols are increased from 4 to 8 aircraft with little effect on enemy marauders over the Hump. 3 A–36's fail to return from mission over Sumprabum.

Fifth AF: More than 60 B–25's attack Alexishafen area, hit coastal tgts between Reiss Pt and Sio, and bomb A/F at Wewak. A–20's bomb and strafe Gasmata. A lone B–24 destroys a patrol craft between Hoskins and Rabaul.

Thirteenth AF: 8 B–24's bomb Kara A/F. 6 B–25's hit Ballale I A/F.

17 October

Twelfth AF: Weather prevents operations by XII BC. US and RAF units of NATAF operate at reduced pace. LBs and MBs hit towns of Teano and Alife and motor transport at Benedello, Penna, and Pedaso. FBs bomb and strafe troops, trucks, guns, train stations, and bridge near Vinchiaturo, Benedello, Teramo, and Sparanise. Other ftrs strafe locomotives S of Ancona.

Tenth AF: HBs and MBs bomb Naba.

Fourteenth AF: 7 B–24's bomb Htawgaw.

Fifth AF: 18 A–20's and B–25's bomb and strafe Sattelberg and 7 B–25's hit Wewak and Boram A/F with low-level attack during which 15 aircraft are destroyed on the ground and 4 claimed shot down. 4 P–39's intercept 18 airplanes attacking Finschhafen, claiming 6 shot down. 40-plus ftrs intercept large group of enemy aircraft attempting to attack Oro Bay; US ftrs claim 24 shot down. 6 B–24's bomb Ternate, a 2,200-mi round trip.

18 October

Ninth AF: 228 MBs dispatched to bomb 4 A/Fs in France are recalled before attacking because of unfavorable weather. Gen Quesada becomes CG IX FC.

Twelfth AF: XII BC B–25's bomb M/Y at Skoplje. P–38's follow with strafing mission, damaging or destroying several locomotives and vehicles. XII A Spt Cmd A–36's hit Venafro railroad yards, and other FBs hit gun positions, troops, and railway stations in or near Boiano, Petacciato, and Vairano. Ftrs strafe A/Fs around Rome and also hit Viterbo, Grosseto, and seaplane base at Bracciano, and attack trains on Rome-Orte and Rome-Naples lines. NATBF LBs bomb road and railway near Cassino, town of Carpinone, road junction at Castiglione della Valle, and roads, bridges, and motor transport near Minturno and Chieti.

Fifth AF: Nearly 80 HBs and ftrs sent against Rabaul are forced to abort by bad weather. However, more than 50 B–25's slip beneath low clouds and pound town, A/Fs, and shipping from treetop and mast-height level. The MBs sink 2 vessels and claim more than 70 planes destroyed on the ground and in the air. 13 of the HBs bomb Cape Hoskins; 7 others bomb Cape Gloucester and hit Sio. B–25's bomb and strafe Bogadjim road.

Thirteenth AF: 28 B–24's and 40-plus Navy dive bmrs, with cover of more than 50 ftrs, hit Ballale I A/F. 14 P–39's join 20-plus Navy aircraft in strike on Kakasa village and tent area on Choiseul.

Eleventh AF: The 406th Bomb Sq departs for the ZI.

19 October

International: Tripartite conference opens in Moscow. Hull, Eden, and Molotov discuss measures to shorten the war and promote postwar cooperation.

Twelfth AF: During low-level raid, XII BC B–24's bomb bridges at Porto Civitanova, S of Porto Sant' Elpidio, N of Pedaso, and N of Cupra Marittima. Ftrs, FBs, and LBs of XII A Spt Cmd, NATBF, and DAF attack town of Boiano, gun positions and troop concentrations on the outskirts of town, and ammo dump and railroad tunnel nearby, Viterbo and Tarquinia landing fields, towns of Cassino and Anzio, railroad N of Pesaro and near Pineto, trains near Barisciano, troops near Minturno, and vehicles at several points.

Fifth AF: A–20's and RAAF airplanes hit Sattelberg and surrounding areas and bomb Gasmata. B–25's and RAAF Hudsons bomb Fuiloro. Enemy air raid on Finschhafen causes no effective damage.

Thirteenth AF: Kara and Kahili A/F are hit by B–24's, B–34's, P–38's, P–40's, and Navy ftrs and dive bmrs.

20 October

Eighth AF: 114 HBs bomb industrial areas of Duren. Failure of blind-bombing equipment (Oboe) is major cause of aborts by nearly 100 other HBs.

Twelfth AF: XII BC B–17's, B–26's, B–25's and P–38's bomb Rome-Casale landing ground, Marcigliana and Cerveteri A/Fs, railroad bridges at Montalto di Castro, Grosseto, and 13 mi SE of Orvieto, and M/Y at Nish, obstructing Belgrade-Sofia line. XII A Spt Cmd, NATBF, and other aircraft of NATAF devote most of their efforts to bombing gun positions, trucks, and rail and road comm S of Vasto, at Mignano, N of Cassino, in Cassino and Chieti, at Castropignano, Carpinone, Arce, Tratella, and at various other points along highways and railroads. FBs also hit shipping along Dalmatian coast, claiming 2 vessels sunk.

Tenth AF: Bridge at Meza, being repaired after being damaged severely on 10 Oct, is attacked and damaged by B–25's.

Fifth AF: B–25's bomb and strafe Bogadjim area. A–20's hit Gasmata. B–24's hit 2 freighters near Manokwari and bomb Manokwari area. Attack on Finschhafen by 30 enemy aircraft causes minor damage.

Thirteenth AF: Kakasa is attacked 3 times by B–34's, P–40's, and Navy ftrs and dive bmrs. 24 P–40's and nearly 50 Navy F4U's sweep Kahili. One force of F4U's encounters ftrs, claiming 3 destroyed.

21 October

Ninth AF: Bad weather causes 72 MBs sent to bomb Evreux/Fauville A/F to abort mission.

Twelfth AF: Col Arthur Thomas takes cmd of XII AFSC. XII BC B–17's hit railroad viaduct at Terni and rail and road bridges in Albania. B–24's hit Orvieto railroad bridge. B–26's and B–25's bomb bridges at Montalto di Castro and NW of Acquapendente and railroad at Orbetello. P–38's bomb radar station at Pellegrino and M/Y at Skoplje. RAF and US NATAF LBs and MBs concentrate on Cassino, hitting town, bivouac area nearby, and railroad to the S. Vessels along Dalmatian coast are also attacked. XII A Spt Cmd ftrs and FBs patrol Naples area and attack numerous roads, railroads, bridges, junctions, trucks, gun emplacements, and other tgts in battle area.

Fourteenth AF: 6 B–24's bomb Nawlang; barracks area is blasted by at least 3 direct hits. 6 P–40's pound barracks area at Kunlong.

Fifth AF: More than 50 B–24's bomb positions at Sattelberg. 19 B–25's follow with low-level strike. Other B–25's carry out sweep along Bogadjim road. P–40's bomb Gasmata area and attack 2 light cruisers off New Ireland, damaging 1 of them.

Thirteenth AF: 12 B–25's, with escort of 36 ftrs, attack Kara A/F. Runway and several buildings suffer direct hits.

22 October

CCS: CCS approve plan, submitted by Gen Arnold and JCS, to create a new AF (Fifteenth) in Italy from part of the Twelfth AF to be used in strategic bombing against Germany as well as in spt of ground operations.

Ninth AF: About 60 B–26's bomb Evreux/Fauville A/F. Over 140 others abort missions against other A/Fs because of bad weather.

Twelfth AF: XII AF Engineer

Cmd (Prov) is activated. XII BC B–26's bomb railroad bridges N and SE of Orvieto. B–25's hit railroad bridge S of Grosseto and Eleusis A/F. XII A Spt Cmd, along with other elements of NATAF, hit town areas, highways, vehicles, gun positions, railroad comm, strongpoints, and T/Os at or near San Salvo, Teano, Venafro, Cantalupo hel Sannio, Isernia, Cassino, Montenero, and Boiano. Aquino A/F is also bombed.

Tenth AF: MB strike against railroad bridge on Ye-u branch line over Mu R between Ywataung and Monywa fails to damage the structure. This raid marks the final assault of the year on this bridge.

Fifth AF: 20-plus B–25's carry out low-level attack on Wewak area, sinking 2 small freighters, and strafing barges and airplanes. Madang is strafed by 4 P–39's and 2 RAAF Boomerangs. More than 50 P–40's hit Gasmata. 11 B–24's bomb Pombelaa nickel mines.

Thirteenth AF: Kahili A/F and surrounding areas are pounded by 22 B–24's, 30-plus P–39's and P–40's and about 160 Navy ftrs and dive bmrs. 18 B–24's and Navy airplanes hit tgts in Choiseul I area. Other Navy aircraft hit Kara A/F. A single B–24 claims hits on a carrier NW of Buka.

23 October

Twelfth AF: XII BC B–26's bomb railroad and road bridges at Marsicano and Montalto di Castro. P–38's hit A/F at Tirana. B–25's hit bridge in Albania. XII A Spt Cmd, DAF, and NATBF attack troop concentrations in Spinete area, and town areas, vehicles, trains, railroads, highways, bridges, and gun positions at or near Gaeta, Pescara, Vasto, Isolella, Sulmona, Isernia, Vairano, and Ancona.

Tenth AF: MBs bomb Meza railroad bridge, which is still being repaired following damaging raid of 10 Oct. Damage is done to approaches.

Fourteenth AF: 6 B–24's bomb Htawgaw.

Fifth AF: 40-plus B–24's escorted by P–38's, bomb Rapopo airstrip, destroying about 20 airplanes on the ground. 20 enemy interceptors are claimed shot down. 9 B–25's hit Bogadjim area.

Thirteenth AF: 11 B–24's and 16 P–38's hit Kahili A/F. 36 P–40's and P–39's join 60-plus Navy dive bmrs and ftrs in strike on Kara A/F. Both Kahili and Kara are attacked again later in the day, the former by 6 B–24's and 16 Navy ftrs and the latter by 35 AAF ftrs and 42 Navy dive bmrs. 6 B–24's bomb Kakasa.

Seventh AF: Ftrs shoot down a Japanese flying boat 70 mi S of Baker I.

24 October

Ninth AF: 200 B–26's bomb A/Fs at Montdidier, Beauvais/Nivillers, and Saint-Andre-de-L'Eure.

Twelfth AF: XII BC B–24's of 98th Bomb Gp hit Wiener-Neustadt. 376th Gp fails to complete mission because of clouds. MBs hit Tirana A/F, railroad bridge N of Orvieto, and viaduct at Terni. XII A Spt Cmd, NATBF, and DAF attack comm and shipping tgts, hitting vessels, vehicles, trains, roads, bridges, and town areas in and around Formia, Sora, Chieti, Minturno, Sessa Aurunca, Popoli, Terracina, between Ancona-Pedaso, Frosolone (just be-

fore it is taken by allied ground forces), and along Dalmatian coast.

Fourteenth AF: 14 B–24's and 13 P–40's pound Co Bi barracks area. 8 B–24's bomb Htawgaw while on ferry flight over the Hump.

Fifth AF: At least 45 bmrs are destroyed on the ground at Vunakanau, Rapopo, and Tobera airstrips during attacks by 50-plus B–25's. The MBs and the more than 50 escorting P–38's claim over 40 airplanes shot down. A–20's hit enemy positions in Lae area. B–24's carry out light attack on Manokwari.

Thirteenth AF: 36 B–25's, along with 24 RNZAF P–40's and 4 Navy F4U's, in 1 force, and 20 AAF ftr and 70-plus Navy ftrs and dive bmrs in another force, pound Kahili A/F.

25 October

Twelfth AF: XII BC P–39's strafe and bomb landing ground at Podgorica. XII A Spt Cmd, NATBF and DAF concentrate on blocking roads and destroying bridges. Town areas, vehicles, radio stations, trains, and vessels are also attacked. Tgts attacked are in or near Frosinone, Formia, Gaeta, Cetraro, along Sangro R, Kuna, along Dalmatian coast, W of Lagosta I and S of Rome. Tarquinia A/F is also bombed.

Fourteenth AF: 6 P–40's strafe shipping at Haiphong, claiming 3 small boats sunk and damaging 6 larger boats. 2 B–25's and 4 P–40's attack shipping in Gulf of Tonkin, claiming a 150-ft tanker sunk and 200-ft freighter damaged.

Fifth AF: More than 60 B–24's bomb Rabaul area, destroying more than 20 airplanes on the ground. Of the 60–70 ftrs which intercept, the

HBs claim over 30 shot down. A–20's hit positions near Lae. B–24's carry out light strike against Manokwari.

26 October

Twelfth AF: B–25's and P–38's of XII BC attack A/Fs of Salonika/Sedhes and Megalo Mikra. XII A Spt Cmd and DAF ftrs and FBs attack gun emplacements and road junctions in battle area along E coast and in center of Italy, destroying also many vehicles and parked aircraft in Ancona area, where railroad facilities are also hit. Schooner at Porto Civitanova is left smoking. MBs of NATBF bomb Terracina and an ammo dump.

Fourteenth AF: 13 B–24's and 15 P–40's pound railroad yards at Haiphong. 2 B–25's attack several vessels at Kiungshan, claiming 4 sunk or badly damaged. Later 6 more B–25's hit shipping nearby, claiming 1 freighter sunk. A/F at Kiungshan is strafed by 1 of the MBs.

Fifth AF: B–24's fly small raid against Pombelaa. Ftrs shoot down 2 HBs. US gunners claim 11 aircraft downed. B–25's hit tgts in Tanimbar Is.

Thirteenth AF: Kahili A/F is hit twice during the day by B–24's, B–25's, P–38's, P–40's, P–39's, and Navy ftrs and dive bmrs. Buka I A/F is strafed by P–38's and then bombed and strafed by B–25's and P–38's. P–39's and P–40's join Navy ftrs and dive bmrs in strike on Kara A/F.

27 October

Twelfth AF: More than 150 B–17's and B–24's bomb Wiener-Neustadt and railroad tracks and installations and bridges at Friedberg and Ebenfurth. Weather severely curtails NA

TBF missions and XII A Spt Cmd operation in spt of ground forces. FBs attack Gaeta and bomb small vessels on Dalmatian coast at Opuzen.

Fourteenth AF: 6 B–24's bomb city of Tungling, claim 8 intercepting Zeros shot down.

Fifth AF: P–40's and P–39's intercept escorted bmr force dropping supplies over Sattelberg area. The US ftrs claim 12 airplanes downed. A–20's hit harbor and supply dump area at Gasmata.

Thirteenth AF: B–24's pound Kahili and Kara A/Fs. P–40's over Kahili claim 3 Zeros shot down. P–38's, P–40's, and P–39's, plus some RN ZAF P–40's and P–39's, cover landing by NZ troops on Stirling and Mono Is. The ftrs claim destruction of 12 Japanese dive bmrs attacking the landing force and afterwards claim 3 ftrs shot down.

28 October

Twelfth AF: Weather prevents most Twelfth AF operations planned for the day. No missions are flown by XII BC. XII A Spt Cmd A–36's hit several highways and bridges in adv of battleline and attack gun positions in Vairano area and transportation tgts in Rome area.

Fourteenth AF: 7 B–24's bomb Mangshih. 6 P–40's strafe warehouse and revetments at Yoyang A/F. 3 B–25's and 7 P–38's hit barracks at Ft Bayard. 2 B–25's on shipping sweep over S China Sea damage 2 freighters near Saint John I and sink a junk W of Kwangchow Wan.

Fifth AF: P–40's hit Gasmata area. P–47's attack barges at Talasea and strafe surrounding area. P–47's also strafe area from Sio to Fortification Pt.

Thirteenth AF: P–40's and P–39's join Navy ftrs and dive bmrs in attacks on Kara and Ballale I A/Fs. Almost 200 aircraft are involved in the 2 strikes. Kara A/F is also pounded by 19 B–24's.

ZI: AAF School of Applied Tactics is redesignated AAF Tac Center.

29 October

Twelfth AF: More than 100 XII BC B–17's, escorted by P–38's, bomb Genoa M/Y and also hit Sampierdarena M/Y, San Giorgio instrument factory, and ordnance, electric, and fitting plants and bridges at Genoa-Ansaldo. XII A Spt Cmd, NATBF, and DAF are forced by bad weather to abandon several missions in spt of ground forces. Troops and gun positions are attacked on 2 occasions and several bridges are hit. Giulianova harbor and shipping are successfully attacked.

Fourteenth AF: 14 B–24's and 16 P–40's pound smelter area at Quang Yen. 2 B–25's bomb administration building and runway at Ft Bayard A/F. 9 P–40's on offensive rcn in Chiuchiang area strafe 200-ft steamer and attack a train, destroying the locomotive.

Fifth AF: 37 B–24's, escorted by 53 P–38's, pound Rabaul area, claiming 45 airplanes destroyed on the ground and in the air. 17 B–25's hit Madang area. P–47's attack shipping in Hansa Bay and strafe Cape Gloucester area. B–25's sink vessel off Tanimbar Is while B–24's bomb Selaroe airstrip and attack Waroe Bay area.

Thirteenth AF: B–25's and B–24's, along with 40-plus Navy aircraft, bomb A/Fs at Buka and Bonis.

30 October

Ninth AF: 5 A–20's bomb Cherbourg/Maupertus A/F.

Twelfth AF: XII BC B–24's bomb Genoa M/Y and nearby Sampierdarena and Genoa-Ansaldo steel works. B–17's bomb Savona and Varazze, Porto Maurizio, and Imperia M/Y. Weather reduces efforts of NATAF elements. NATBF B–25's bomb Frosinone. FBs, mainly of XII A Spt Cmd, hit bridges, junctions, shipping, M/Y, gun positions, and vehicles at several locations, including Giulianova, Ancona, Ortona, Sessa Aurunca, Mignano, and Cassino.

Fourteenth AF: 7 B–25's and 12 P–40's pound motor pool and barracks at Shayang. 9 P–38's hit Chiuchiang dock area. 2 interceptors are shot down.

Fifth AF: B–25's strafe barges in Rein Bay.

Thirteenth AF: Kara A/F is bombed by 16 B–24's and shortly afterwards is hit by 90-plus Navy dive bmrs escorted by Navy and AAF ftrs. Airstrip and other tgts at Kieta are attacked by 6 B–25's, 12 P–39's and Navy aircraft. Tonolai harbor area is hit by 8 P–40's and 17 Navy planes.

31 October

Twelfth AF: XII BC B–17's bomb Antheor viaduct. B–26's hit Anzio. B–25's attack docks and shipping at Civitavecchia. P–38's strafe and bomb Tirana A/F. Weather cancels all NATAF attacks except for 11 P–40's which bomb and strafe tanker off Split, leaving it burning. XII A Spt Cmd ftrs fly uneventful naval escort.

Tenth AF: In an attempt to knock out Japanese base from which ftrs are attacking ferrying operations, P–40's carrying 1000-lb bombs fly 4 strikes against Myitkyina. Following the bomb runs, the ftrs strafe AA positions. The attacks cause considerable damage to the base. MBs attack Meza railroad bridge, scoring hits on approaches but missing the structure. The bridge remains unusable due to damage caused by the 10 Oct strike.

Fifth AF: P–40's sink barge off New Britain coast.

Thirteenth AF: 20-plus B–25's, with ftr spt, bomb Kara A/F.

1 November

Eighth AF: Progress report, assessing results of CBO, estimates that 19 important German towns and cities have been virtually destroyed, 19 severely damaged, and 9 more effectively damaged. Joint report of Ministry of Economic Warfare and Air Ministry Intelligence Branch claims that 10 percent of total war potential of Germany has been destroyed.

Ninth AF: Ninth AF comes under operational control of AEAF which is activated on this date to provide the tac air force for the invasion of W Europe (OVERLORD).

Twelfth AF: With activation of Fifteenth AF on this date, the units of XII BC transfer to the new AF. NATBF aircraft bomb shipping in harbors of Ancona and Split, hit tunnel mouth near Antrodoco, and attack scattered gun positions and motor transport on both US Fifth and British Eighth Army fronts. XII A Spt Cmd hits numerous bridges and junctions and town of Pontecorvo. DAF hits inland roads and vehicles in adv of battleline, shipping at Split, and town of Carpinone.

Fifteenth AF: Fifteenth AF is activated, with HQ at Tunis and Gen Doolittle as CG. The Fifteenth AF includes 6 HB gps, 5 MB gps, and 4 ftr gps. B–17's bomb town and harbor of La Spezia and railroad bridge at Vezzano. B–25's hit M/Ys at Rimini and Ancona. Ftrs fly escort.

Fourteenth AF: 6 B–25's and 9 P–40's bomb Yoyang railroad yards.

Fifth AF: 11 B–24's bomb Maniang I and nearby Pombelaa. A lone B–24 scores hit on ship off Kavieng.

Thirteenth AF: US Marines land on Bougainville. This operation is aimed at eliminating the last Japanese strongholds SE of Rabaul. Allied ftrs covering the operations shoot down more than 20 Japanese aircraft. Naval gunfire accounts for several more. 21 B–24's bomb Kahili A/F. Kara A/F is attacked by 19 B–24's, 30-plus P–40's and P–39's, and more than 70 Navy ftrs and dive bmrs. P–38's on sweep over waters NW of the Solomons claim 7 Zeros shot down. B–25's strafe barges and wharf area at Faisi. During 1/2 Nov 2 SB–24's attack convoy W of Cape Saint George.

2 November

Twelfth AF: NATBF LBs and MBs hit gun positions and ammo dump on Eighth Army front, railroad facilities at Aquila, and coast road at Terracina. At night LBs hit Zara and Penna Pt. XII A Spt Cmd and DAF ftrs and FBs attack gun positions and ammo dumps along British Eighth Army front, hit gun positions S of Isernia, bomb Fondi, and attack several bridges and junctions in adv of US Fifth Army front. Numerous trucks and a train also are strafed.

Fifteenth AF: B–17's and B–24's bomb aircraft factory and surrounding industrial complex at Wiener-Neustadt. The HBs claim over 50 attacking ftrs destroyed. B–25's bomb Ancona M/Y. B–26's bomb Civitavecchia harbor and miss railroad bridge near Amelia. P–38's escort the HBs and the B–26's.

Fourteenth AF: 5 B–25's and 12 P–40's pound docks and warehouses at Shasi.

Fifth AF: In direct spt of Allied landings on Bougainville, 75 B–25's, with escort of 70 P–38's, attack Rabaul A/Fs and harbor. 3 destroyers and 8 merchant vessels are sunk or left sinking. The MBs and ftrs claim 12 aircraft destroyed on the ground and 68 shot down. AA and air opposition is the strongest thus far encountered by the Fifth AF. 21 US airplanes are lost. P–39's pound road in Bogadjim area. A–20's bomb and strafe comm routes near Fortification Pt.

Thirteenth AF: 20 B–24's bomb Kahili A/F.

3 November

Eighth AF: 539 B–17's and B–24's, including 11 Pathfinders, 9 using new H2X blind-bombing device (first time on a US mission) and 2 using H2S, attack port of Wilhelmshaven. This is first Eighth AF blind-bombing mission in which aiming point is completely destroyed and is also

the Eighth's first 500-plane mission. P–38's escort the HBs almost the entire trip and see their first real ETO combat, claiming 3 aircraft shot down.

Ninth AF: 71 B–26's bomb A/F at Saint-Andre-de-L'Eure, 71 attack Triqueville A/F, and 65 bomb Schiphol A/F.

Twelfth AF: B–25's, escorted by P–38's, attack Araxos A/F. NATBF hits dump at Cupello, railway station at Cesano, road junction at Alfedena, town areas of Ceprano and Palmoli, and numerous vehicles. XII A Spt Cmd and DAF ftrs and FBs attack gun positions at Cupello, landing grounds near Pescara and Ancona, A/F at Cisterna di Latina, Ceccano railroad yards, town of Pozzilli, roads in Venafro-Cassino area, and several bridges and junctions. Many of the day's missions are flown in direct spt of British Eighth Army's adv.

Fifteenth AF: The 2 B–25 gps of the Fifteenth AF are transferred to the Twelfth. P–38's escort B–25's on raid against Araxos A/F. The tgt is well covered and several parked airplanes are destroyed.

Fourteenth AF: 21 B–24's, supported by 30 ftrs, pound Kowloon Docks. 4 ftrs are claimed shot down. 9 B–25's and 12 P–40's pound various tgts in Shihshow-Hwajung-Owchihkow area. 8 P–40's bomb runways and installations at Lashio.

Fifth AF: B–25's hit barges between Alexishafen and Bogadjim. B–24's fly light strikes against shipping (sinking 1 vessel) between Talasea and Cape Gloucester, and bomb Boela.

Thirteenth AF: 19 B–24's attack

convoy about 150 mi SE of Mussau I. HBs claim hits on 3 vessels.

4 November

Ninth AF: Ninth AF HQ issues letter ordering small det of HQ (IX AF Eng Section) to assume functions of a cmd under Col Karl B Schilling, thus beginning the creation of IX Engineer Cmd.

Twelfth AF: Gen Davison takes cmd of XII AF Engineer Cmd (Prov), following the cmd's assignment to Twelfth AF on 1 Nov. XII A Spt Cmd and RAF ftrs and FBs hit trucks and trains in Sora-Avezzano area, small vessels off Solta and Pescara, and A/Fs of Furbara and Tarquinia.

Fifteenth AF: B-17's bomb railroads between Montalto di Castro and Orbetello, between Orbetello and Talamone, and between San Vincenzo and Cecina. Bomb-carrying P-38's, escorted by others, hit tunnel N of Terni and strafe Montalto di Castro.

Fourteenth AF: Chinese-American Comp Wg enters combat on this date. Its B-25's hit Amoy and Swatow, successfully bombing and strafing ground troops, supply facilities, and shipping. The MBs claim 4 cargo ships badly damaged and possibly sunk.

Fifth AF: P-40's bomb Palmalmal Plantation. B-24's on armed rcn claim 1 vessel sunk N of New Britain.

Thirteenth AF: 23 B-24's strike Buka A/F.

5 November

Atlantic: 1st Comp Sq and USN land-based aircraft sink U-848 in S Atlantic, 10-09S 18-00W.

Eighth AF: 436 HBs, including 9

Pathfinder aircraft, attack M/Y and oil plants at Gelsenkirchen and M/Y at Munster.

Ninth AF: Eighth AF training officer arrives to assist Ninth FC HQ in setting up comprehensive training system for ftr pilots. Trg is based on the Eighth AF system. Eighth AF and RAF cooperate with the Ninth in instituting this program. Over 150 MBs bomb construction works at Mimoyecques. Poor visibility causes one gp to bomb area SW of primary tgts, and bad weather causes numerous aborts.

Twelfth AF: XII A Spt Cmd B-25's hit Berat-Kucove A/F in Albania. NATBF bombs roads E of Atina and N of Rome, and hits vehicles moving S from Pescara. XII A Spt Cmd and DAF ftrs and FBs attack motor transport N of Vasto, bridges and roads W of Isernia, Cassino, and Atena Lucana, town of Castrocielo, and vessels off Split.

Fifteenth AF: 3 B-24's on low-level raid bomb Falconara-Marittima railroad bridge and highway bridge. P-38's escort a XII A Spt Cmd raid on Berat-Kucove A/F.

Fifth AF: 90-plus HBs and ftrs attack wharf areas of Rabaul while Japanese airplanes from surrounding A/Fs search for carrier force that hit Rabaul earlier in the day. B-26's and P-39's hit Bogadjim Road, B-25's pound positions NW of Dumpu, and P-39's bomb and strafe Madang area. P-47's over Wewak encounter force of ftrs and claim about 20 shot down.

Thirteenth AF: 6 B-25's hit bivouac area at Kieta and sink at least 6 barges between Kieta and Banin Harbor. Allied ftrs from Munda area cover carrier strike which causes considerable damage to shipping in harbor at Rabaul.

6 November

Ninth AF: IX FC personnel debark in UK, after traveling by ship from Suez.

Twelfth AF: XII A Spt Cmd FBs strike gun positions, bridges, and roads around Mignano, vehicles N of Cassino, and train N of Aquino A/F. Other NATAF ftrs attack numerous road and rail transport tgts throughout Italy N of battleline and in Yugoslavia.

Fifteenth AF: 4 B–17's attack Fiora R bridge, 3 attack bridge N of Orbetello, and 11 P–38's attack bridge S of Orvieto. P–38's escorted by others, hit approaches to bridge near Monte Molino, and the escorting ftrs afterwards strafe Tarquinia A/F, a train N of Civitavecchia, and vehicles between Montefiascone and Vetralla.

USSR: Soviet Army retakes Kiev.

Tenth AF: 2 B–24's lay mines in Rangoon R during 6/7 Nov.

Fifth AF: P–40's hit Gasmata area. Enemy airplanes attack Nadzab, Dumpu, and Finschhafen but cause no major damage.

Thirteenth AF: 9 B–25's with Navy ftr spt hit Buka A/F and harbor. 1 other bombs Kieta and attacks Tinputs Harbor. 7 barges and small vessels are claimed sunk. 24 B–25's with ftr spt follow Navy dive bmrs and ftrs in attack on Kara A/F. 17 B–24's bomb Bonis A/F.

Seventh AF: Advanced HQ, Seventh AF, is set up on Funafuti to provide a HQ closer to tgts in the Gilbert and Marshall Is. VII AFSC and VII BC also establish forward echelons at Funafuti. Landing fields are being built at Baker, Nukufetau, and Nanumea to be used, along with existing fields at Canton I and Funafuti, as operational bases for attacks on Tarawa, Makin, Mille, Maloelap, Jaluit, and Nauru. These operations will mark the assumption of the offensive by Seventh AF and will play a conspicuous role in the invasion and occupation of the Gilbert and Marshall Is.

7 November

Eighth AF: 112 B–17's attack industrial areas of Wesel and Duren.

Ninth AF: Over 200 MBs dispatched to attack A/Fs at Montdidier and Meulan-Les Mureaux are forced to abort mission because of bad weather.

Twelfth AF: NATBF bmrs hit gun position along British Eighth and US Fifth Army fronts, shipping at Ancona harbor, and town of Ulcinj. Durazzo is bombed at night. XII A Spt Cmd and other ftrs of NATAF hit harbor and shipping at Split and train near Metkovic, and attack bridges, road junctions, town area, and trucks in Mignano-Cassino and Pontecorvo areas.

Fifteenth AF: Bad weather cancels HB operations.

Fourteenth AF: 2 B–25's pound Amoy harbor, claiming several boats sunk. 6 P–40's attack bridge at Hsiangyangchiao, causing only minor damage.

Fifth AF: 25 B–24's, with escort of more than 60 P–38's, bomb Rapopo airstrip. A large force of enemy ftrs intercepts the formations and in the ensuing battle 5 P–38's are lost. US airplanes claim more than 20 ftrs shot down and several more destroyed on the ground. 9 B–25's bomb Wewak and more than 40 others turn back when ftr escort is intercepted by airplanes over Nadzab. Enemy aircraft attack Nadzab and Bena Bena. 16 US aircraft are destroyed or damaged by the raids, but 14 airplanes are shot down by US ftrs.

Thirteenth AF: 8 B–25's bomb barge concentration and beach tgts in Atsinima Bay. 21 B–24's pound Buka A/F.

8 November

Ninth AF: IX FC is assigned its first tac ftr unit, the 354th Ftr Gp (P–51).

Twelfth AF: Weather cancels all XII A Spt Cmd missions except ftr patrols. NATBF bmrs and DAF ftrs fly only 6 missions, hitting gun positions along battleline, vehicles W of Sangro R, and trains at Civitanova and Pescara.

Fifteenth AF: 81 B–17's bomb Turin ball bearing works, M/Y, and nearby motor and aircraft engine works. P–38's provide escort as far N as Imperia.

Tenth AF: 5 B–24's lay mines in Rangoon R during 8/9 Nov.

Fourteenth AF: 2 B–25's bomb Kiungshan A/F, scoring direct hits on 2 hangars. 6 P–40's attack Hsiangyangchiao bridge, causing little damage.

Fifth AF: B–24's on armed rcn bomb Garove I and hit Kaimana.

Thirteenth AF: 22 B–24's bomb Bonis A/F. 6 B–25's hit T/Os at mouth of Laruma R and NW of Torokina I while 6 others bomb Kieta.

9 November

Twelfth AF: NATBF bombs Formia and Itri as diversion to naval bombardment of Formia and Gaeta. XII A Spt Cmd FBs attack roads and bridges in Mignano-Ceprano area while other NATAF FBs hit shipping in Split harbor. Ftrs strafe road and rail tgts in Rome-La Spezia area and vessels, radio stations, and gun emplacements off coast of Albania.

Fifteenth AF: B–24's attack Villarperosa ball-bearing works at Turin, and B–17's hit Genoa-Ansaldo steel works. P–38's provide escort.

Fifth AF: 40-plus B–25's and A–20's, escorted by P–38's and P–47's, pound A/F at Alexishafen, destroying at least 12 enemy airplanes. US ftrs claim destruction of 10–15 interceptors in combat. Other ftrs claim over 20 aircraft shot down over Sek Harbor, Markham R Valley, and Lae. B–25's bomb fuel dump and shipping in Rein Bay area, and P–40's bomb Gasmata dumps. B–24's on patrol claim sinking of a destroyer near Kavieng.

Thirteenth AF: B–25's bomb Kieta and hit Buka A/F. 20-plus B–24's pound Kara and Kahili A/Fs. P–39's join Navy aircraft in strikes on Kara and on Ballale I A/Fs.

10 November

Ninth AF: Around 60 B–26's bomb Chievres A/F. Bad weather causes force sent to bomb Lille/Vendeville A/F to abandon mission, though a few MBs manage to bomb other tgts in the area. A force of 72 B–26's dispatched to attack Montdidier A/F suffers numerous aborts due to weather. 6 MBs manage to bomb A/F believed to be secondary tgt of Amiens/Glisy.

Twelfth AF: NATBF bmrs hit shipping at Split and Durazzo. XII A Spt Cmd and RAF FBs hit Rocca and nearby gun positions, and trains and troops S of Rome. Ftrs strafe trucks and trains in Rome-La Spezia and Piombino-Leghorn areas.

Fifteenth AF: B-24's bomb Villarperosa ball-bearing works, and B-17's pound bridge and M/Ys at Bolzano. P-38's escort the B-24's all the way and accompany the B-17's almost to the tgt.

Fourteenth AF: Ftrs on armed rcn sink 3 large motor boats in Yoyang-Sinti area and damage or sink 15 sampans and a barge in Hwajung-Shasi vicinity.

Fifth AF: B-24's bomb Lakunai A/F, hit new landing ground on Duke of York I, and bomb Soerabaja. B-25's thoroughly pound Alexishafen A/F.

Thirteenth AF: 20-plus B-25's carry out strikes on Kara and Ballale I A/Fs and attack shipping between Suhane I and Tarlena.

11 November

Eighth AF: 58 HBs attack Munster, concentrating on M/Y: 111 others abort because of bad weather, which hinders assembly. 1st Bomb Div's mission to bomb Wesel is aborted over English Channel due to assembly difficulties and presence of heavy frontal cloud, and all 175 HBs return without bombing.

Ninth AF: 157 B-26's bomb military installations and T/Os in Cherbourg area, mainly at Martinvast.

Twelfth AF: US and RAF LBs and FBs, in spt of US Fifth and British Eighth Armies, hit troop and gun concentrations and comm in Rocca and Palena areas. Other NA TAF aircraft bomb town of Rocca, Bussi sul Tirino explosive works near Popoli, and docks at Civitavecchia, and strafe strongpoints at Roccaraso and Atessa. Ftrs hit motor transport in coastal area between Sangro and Pescara Rivers.

Fifteenth AF: 28 B-24's attack Annecy ball bearing plant and viaduct at Antheor.

Fourteenth AF: 6 B-24's bomb Burma Road about 375 mi W of Tungling, producing landslide and badly damaging the road. 6 P-40's S of Yoyang knock out a gun emplacement and hit a radio station, barracks, and hostels in the area. 8 more P-40's, on armed rcn in Li-Chou-Ching-Shih area, strafe pontoon bridge and troops, and sink a river steamer, a motorboat, and several small supply boats.

Fifth AF: B-24's bomb Lakunai A/F; P-39's strafe Bogadjim; and B-25's hit Madang area.

Thirteenth AF: A few B-25's and Navy F4U's strafe barges and shore installations on Matchin Bay. B-24's join Fifth AF, Navy carrier aircraft, and RAAF airplanes in attack on shipping in Rabaul harbor. This is the Thirteenth's first strike on Rabaul. Escorting ftrs claim 17 Japanese ftrs shot down while the HBs claim 5.

Seventh AF: Japanese aircraft bomb Nanumea, hitting A/F and destroying or damaging several airplanes, including 1 B-24.

12 November

Ninth AF: Ninth AF issues Tables

of Organization for IX FC, authorizing 2 air spt divs, 5 ftr wgs, 1 rcn gp, 21 ftr gps, and 65 ftr sqs. 3 combat wgs are established for IX BC: the 97th (a new LB wg), the 98th (a MB wg, formerly the 3d Bomb Wg), and the 99th (a MB wg, formerly the 44th Bomb Wg).

Twelfth AF: NATBF LBs hit guns, troops, and railway facilities near Palena, town of Atina, and road at Acquafondata. MBs hit Berat/Kucove A/F and oil refinery in Albania after failing to locate tgts near Athens. During 12/13 Nov LBs attack Arezzo M/Y and Perugia A/F. FBs of XII A Spt Cmd and DAF continue to provide close spt to US Fifth and British Eighth Armies, blasting gun positions and motor transport, and also attacking tgts (aircraft, guns, rail yards, bridge, and trains) around Bracciano Lake, Orbetello, Rieti, Sant'Elia Fiumerapido, Opuzen, Ancona, and Iesi.

Fifteenth AF: B–26's attack railroad bridges and tracks in Montalto di Castro and Orbetello areas, but heavy cloud cover prevents effective hits on the tgts. P–38's fly air-sea rescue patrol off the Semeni R mouth.

Tenth AF: 2 B–24's mine Rangoon R during 12/13 Nov.

Fourteenth AF: 10 B–25's and 24 P–40's attack Yoyang, hitting warehouse area, railroad yards, and AA positions. 5 B–25's bomb Yangchi Kang waterfront area and attack waterfront tgts at Puchi. 6 B–25's and 12 ftrs hit tgts at Yoyang. 15 P–40's and a B–25 on armed rcn hit several T/O's in Lungling area and between Yang-Chia-Kang and Sichai.

Fifth AF: B–25's and B–26's bomb

villages between Finschhafen and Saidor. B–24's attack tgts on Java and at Amboina. On this date, following a series of damaging allied strikes, Japanese remove their carrier aircraft from Rabaul, which afterwards ceases to be a serious threat to Allied forces.

Thirteenth AF: 18 B–25's bomb Tarlena; 6 others bomb Matchin Bay area; and 8 P–38's strafe Bonis A/F.

13 November

Eighth AF: 115 HBs hit port area at Bremen. 25 HBs bomb T/Os in Kiel-Flensburg area. Bad weather causes over 100 aborts. 47 P–38's escort the HBs all the way to tgt (the longest escort mission by Eighth AF ftrs to date) but are mauled badly by overwhelming number of ftrs. 7 P–38's fail to return to base.

Twelfth AF: NATBF LBs hit Palena and Atina and later bomb Civitavecchia harbor and road W of Terracina. XII A Spt Cmd FBs, along with DAF airplanes, bomb Giulianova harbor and shipping, roads leading to battle zone, and landing grounds of Aquino, Frosinone, and Marcigliana. Ftrs hit train and trucks in Pescara-Rieti area.

Fifteenth AF: Weather limits operations to air-sea rescue patrols, which are hampered by overcast.

Tenth AF: A single B–24 mines Rangoon R during 13/14 Nov.

Fifth AF: Nearly 120 B–24's and B–25's pound Alexishafen, and P–40's strafe the area. Other B–24's hit Gasmata, Kaukenau, and Timoeka. B–25's and RAAF Beaufighters claim sinking of small freighter off Tanimbar I.

Thirteenth AF: 17 B–24's pound AA positions, dispersal areas, and runway at Bonis A/F. 6 B–25's carry out low-level raid on Buka A/F. Night ftrs harass Shortland I and Kahili and Bonis A/Fs, claiming 4 grounded airplanes destroyed at the latter.

Seventh AF: Air attack for GALVANIC (assault on the Gilbert Is) begins. 18 B–24's from Funafuti bomb Tarawa. 1 HB is lost.

14 November

Twelfth AF: NATBF B–25's, escorted by P–38's, bomb Sofia M/Y. XII A Spt Cmd operations are curtailed by weather, and only battle area patrols are flown. DAF FBs hit trains on E coast of Italy near Avezzano, along Dalmatian coast SE of Metkovic, and at Sarajevo. Ftrs strafe Furbara and Tarquinia A/Fs.

Fifteenth AF: P–38's escort NATAF B–25's on raid against Sofia M/Y. The ftrs claim 5 airplanes shot down.

Fifth AF: B–25's attack supply and bivouac area W of Sio.

Thirteenth AF: P–70 night ftrs hit Shortland-Faisi area, claiming a seaplane and 2 barges destroyed.

Seventh AF: 9 B–24's from Nukufetau bomb Tarawa. 9 from Nanumea hit Mille.

15 November

Twelfth AF: XII A Spt Cmd B–25's bomb Kalamaki A/F, and its ftrs patrol battle area. Other NATAF ftrs hit road traffic S of Ancona.

Fifteenth AF: B–24's bomb Eleusis A/F; P–38's provide escort.

Fourteenth AF: 20 B–24's are dispatched against Hong Kong-Kowloon area. Bad weather prevents 15 HBs from bombing tgts; 5 bomb docks at Kowloon.

Fifth AF: Over 30 B–24's pound Alexishafen. 88 B–25's heading for Wewak and Boram with escort of 16 P–40's are intercepted by Japanese ftrs that are escorting bmrs attacking Gusap. The resulting battle causes the MBs to abort the attack. The US airplanes claim 20 of the enemy shot down. 2 P–40's are lost. P–47's claim 5 more aircraft destroyed over Wewak.

Thirteenth AF: 20 B–24's strike Buka A/F, and 18 bomb Kahili. Ftr patrols destroy or damage several barges along the coast of Bougainville and destroy 2 fuel dumps at Tonolai.

Seventh AF: 20-plus B–24's from Canton and Nanumea Is bomb Jaluit, Mille, and Makin.

16 November

AEAF: AM Sir Leigh-Mallory is named Air CinC, AEAF. Gen Butler is Deputy CG.

Eighth AF: 306 HBs attack industrial areas of Knaben and Rjukan.

Twelfth AF: B–25's bomb Sibenik and Eleusis A/Fs.

Fifteenth AF: B–17's bomb Istres-Le-Tube A/F, and B–26's hit Salon-de-Provence A/F. P–38's escort the Salon-de-Provence raid and also a NATAF B–25 attack on Eleusis A/F.

Fourteenth AF: 11 B–24's, 2 B–25's, and 4 P–40's attack docks at Kowloon. 2 B–25's damage 2 freighters near Nampang and Saint John Is, 2 more score hits on tanker off China coast S of Swatow, and 2 others bomb barracks and warehouse on Nampang I. 6 P–40's on armed rcn in Yen Bay-Dong Cuong area strafe railroad stations and barracks. 1 B–25 and 12 P–40's hit cav unit, barge, houses, and numerous sampans at Shihmen. Li-Chou area also is attacked.

Fifth AF: B–25's hit installations near Finschhafen and bomb and strafe coastal track west of Reiss Pt. P–39's, with P–40's covering, strafe barges from Saidor to Madang. P–38's battle large force of ftrs over Wewak, destroying 6. 2 P–38's are lost.

Thirteenth AF: During 15/16 Nov P–70's harass Kahili A/F. In daylight, 20 B–25's and 4 B–24's pound Buka A/F, 20-plus other B–25's fly sweeps over areas of Bougainville coastline, Buka Passage, and Sohano I. Supply dumps and barges are hit. More than 30 P–40's and P–39's also carry out sweeps over the area, hitting gun positions and other tgts at Buka Passage, several T/Os along E coast, Kieta harbor, Tonolai harbor, and Ballale I.

Seventh AF: B–24's from Nanumea and Nukufetau bomb Jaluit and Maloelap. Single aircraft hit Kwajalein, Little Makin, and Tarawa.

17 November

Twelfth AF: B–25's bomb Kalamaki A/F. Ftrs hit trucks N of Ancona at Macerata.

Fifteenth AF: B–17's hit Eleusis A/F, destroying several parked airplanes and scoring many hits on hangars, other buildings, and runways. P–38's escort the B–17's as well as NATAF B–25's attacking Kalamaki A/F.

Fourteenth AF: 8 P–40's strafe A/F and barracks at Kengtung, 4 others hit construction equipment at Dong Cuong A/F and 8 attack Pingkai and T/Os between Pingkai and Tahsai on the Salween R.

Fifth AF: B–24's bomb Soerabaja, Tjepoe, and Denpasar during 17/18 Nov, and B–25's bomb freighter off Tanimbar I. During the day, 58 B–24's are dispatched to spt attack by Australian 9th Div on Sattelberg, but because of bad weather only 3 HBs (along with 12 RAAF aircraft) get through to the tgt. P–47's strafe Japanese shipping between Saidor and Finschhafen.

Thirteenth AF: 30-plus B–25's hit Buka A/F and surrounding areas during 16/17 Nov and 2 sqs of B–24's follow with daylight strike on same tgt. 8 other B–24's bomb Buka and Bonis at various times during 16/17 Nov. During the afternoon 3 B–25's hit Kieta.

Seventh AF: More than 20 B–24's from Funafuti and Canton Is bomb Mille, Maloelap, and Tarawa.

18 November

Eighth AF: 84 B–24's hit Kjeller A/F and industrial tgts at Oslo.

Ninth AF: IX TCC's 50th Wg carries paratroops of 101st Airborne Div in a rehearsal of cross-channel operations. This is first of an extended series of trg exercises to be conducted during the several months preceding the planned invasion of W Europe.

Twelfth AF: MBs and LBs of XII A Spt Cmd and RAF attack Larissa A/F, billeting area at Rivisondoli, and road, railway and town area W of San Vito Chietino and at Lanciano. FBs hit ship in Krka R, trains at Knin M/Y and between Knin and Kosovo landing ground at Sinj, harbor and vessels at Sibenik, and defended points and gun positions along battleline in Italy.

Fifteenth AF: B–17's, with P–38 escort, pound Eleusis A/F. P–38's also escort NATAF attack on same tgt and escort supply dropping mission to Yugoslavia.

Fourteenth AF: 12 P–40's strafe troops and horses and sink a troop barge at Shihmen. 4 others, in spt of Chinese forces, strafe Tahsai ferry.

Fifth AF: Over 30 B–25's and B–26's hit enemy positions in Sattelberg area. B–24's carry out light raid on Fak Fak. P–40's bomb Iworep.

Thirteenth AF: 4 sqs of B–24's pound Buka and Kara A/Fs. 3 B–25's strafe Greenwich I.

Seventh AF: 19 B–24's from Nanumea bomb Mille. 2 others hit Tarawa.

19 November

Eighth AF: 130 HBs attack T/Os in W Germany. Malfunction of blind-bombing equipment results in no attacks on primary tgt of Gelsenkirchen.

Ninth AF: Over 100 B–26's dispatched to attack A/Fs in France abort mission when bad weather prevents rendezvous with ftr escorts.

Twelfth AF: XII A Spt Cmd A–36's and P–40's bomb bridge E of Cassino and bridge and village of Pontecorvo, and, along with DAF FBs, hit strongpoints around village of Barrea while supporting ground forces. Ftrs (mostly DAF) also strafe trucks and trains around Rieti and Metkovic.

Fifteenth AF: Weather causes recall of all aircraft dispatched.

Fourteenth AF: B–25's on shipping sweeps in S China Sea strafe 2 vessels off Hong Kong, score damaging hits on 2 vessels at Kiungshan,

damage a freighter off Tsao Tao I, and leave a gunboat and freighter sinking E of Swatow. Warehouses and wharves at Swatow also are hit.

Fifth AF: Nearly 30 B–25's and B–26's bomb positions in Sattelberg area. A–20's hit Finschhafen area. B–25's attack Kentengi Anchorage.

Thirteenth AF: 10 B–25's bomb Matchin Bay and Ballale I A/F areas.

Seventh AF: 31 B–24's from Ellice Is bases hit Tarawa and Makin.

20 November

Twelfth AF: XII A Spt Cmd and DAF ftrs carry out uneventful armed rcn. NATBF hits Porto Civitanova railway junction, Pedaso, Giulianova, and Loreto.

Fifteenth AF: Weather cancels all bmr operations. Operations are restricted to weather rcn from Decimomannu to Cape Linaro.

Fourteenth AF: 2 B–25's hit warehouses and barracks on Nampang I. Weather prevents completion of several other scheduled missions.

Fifth AF: 50 B–25's and B–26's pound Japanese positions in Sattelberg area and sink or damage at least 10 luggers in Hansa Bay. A–20's hit Lae area. 50 B–24's bomb Gasmata.

Thirteenth AF: 45 B–25's, B–34's, and P–38's attack Bonis A/F. A few other B–25's strafe coastal villages in Empress Augusta Bay region.

ZI: XX BC is officially activated with HQ at Smoky Hill AAFld.

21 November

Twelfth AF: NATBF B–25's bomb gun emplacements at Gaeta. US and RAF FBs of DAF hit strongpoints in Santa Maria Imbaro and Poggiofiorito areas. Ftrs carry out patrols and rcn along battleline along Corigliano and the Sangro R.

Fifteenth AF: B-26's bomb harbor at Civitavecchia, bridge at Fano, and M/Y at Chiusi. P-38's provide escort to the latter tgt.

Fourteenth AF: 29 P-40's strafe more than 100 sampans and small boats on Tungting Lake in Li-Chou-Changte-Ansiang area. 12 P-40's attack 5 vessels, 20 houses, and 100 men at Shihmen and between Shihmen and Li-Chou. 8 others hit troops and small river boats near Tsowshih. 12 P-40's and 4 B-25's pound town of Tzeli. 4 other B-25's on shipping sweeps over S China Sea damage a freighter and blast buildings at Taiping-hsu A/F.

Fifth AF: A-20's again hit Finschhafen area. B-24's bomb Gasmata. B-25's and B-24's hit shipping and other tgts in Aroe Is and off Manokwari.

Thirteenth AF: Gen Twining, CO MAIRSOLS, is succeeded by Gen Mitchell, USMC. A few B-25's on shipping search strafe Kieta.

Seventh AF: Following the 20 Nov amphibious landings on Tarawa and Makin Atolls, Seventh AF resumes operations against the Marshalls, in spt of the base-development phase of GALVANIC (Gilbert operations) and in preparation for invasion of the Marshalls (Operations FLINTLOCK and CATCHPOLE). B-24's from Funafuti and Nanumea bomb Nauru I.

22 November

International: Roosevelt, Churchhill and Chiang Kai-shek confer in Cairo. Talks last until 26 Nov and concern OVERLORD, possibility of expanding operations in MTO, and future operations against Japan. It is decided to make amphibious landing and offensive in Burma (CHAMPION) and to base B-29's in CBI (TWILIGHT).

Twelfth AF: Over 100 XII A Spt Cmd P-40's, B-25's, and RAF Baltimores, attack strongpoints in Lanciano-Fossacesia area, concentrating on gun positions. P-40's also hit roads and railways at Fabriano, towns of Viticuso and Vallerotonda, and as far N as Urbino. A-36's hit chemical works, harbor, and railroad yards at Civitavecchia and bomb village of San Vittore del Lazio.

Fifteenth AF: B-26's, escorted by P-38's, hit railroad center at Foligno, scoring numerous hits; others attack bridge at Ciciana.

Fourteenth AF: 12 P-40's strafe river traffic from Hofuh to Changte, and 16 attack numerous small troop boats on Tungting Lake, W of Changteh.

Fifth AF: 22 B-25's and A-20's attack villages around Sattelberg. More than 100 B-25's and B-24's bomb Gasmata and Cape Gloucester. B-24's on armed rcn score hits on freighter near Kavieng and tanker and barge in Bismarck Sea.

Thirteenth AF: P-40's in battle with 30-40 ftrs over Empress Augusta Bay claim 5 ftrs shot down. P-38's strafe barges and shore tgts at Chabai. 20-plus B-25's, along with 5 B-34's, 8 P-38's and 8 Navy F4U's, attack Buka A/F scoring hits on the airstrip and taxiways.

Seventh AF: 11 B-24's from Canton I bomb Mille. HBs claim 2 interceptors shot down.

23 November

Ninth AF: 83 B–26's bomb Berck-sur-Mer and Saint-Omer/Longuenesse A/Fs.

Twelfth AF: Weather limits operations to ftr patrols of battle area.

Fourteenth AF: 13 B–25's, 24 P–40's, and 7 P–51's pound Yoyang railroad yards and warehouse area. 8 other P–40's, on armed rcn over Hanshow area, strafe barges, boats, supplies, and cav forces.

Fifth AF: B–25's and A–20's hit villages around Finschhafen. B–24's attack convoy near Halmahera I and sink 1 vessel.

SOPAC: Gen Hubert Harmon assumes duties as Dep Cmdr for Air in SOPAC.

Thirteenth AF: Col Earl W Barnes assumes cmd of XIII FC. Chabai is attacked by 23 B–25's, 6 B–34's, and 24 Navy F4U's. 2 B–24's bomb the same tgts later in the day. 19 B–24's hit Bonis and Buka A/Fs. 4 B–25's on shipping sweep, bomb and strafe villages along Bougainville coast between Mabiri and Luluai.

Seventh AF: 6 B–24's from Nukufetau bomb Emidj and Jabor on Jaluit Atoll.

24 November

Twelfth AF: NATBF bmrs, along with DAF FBs, in close spt of British Eighth Army, hit gun positions and defended points in Fossacesia area. XII A Spt Cmd A–36's, in spt of US Fifth Army, hit roads NW of battle-line, and bomb harbor at Civitavecchia.

Fifteenth AF: B–17's, with P–38 escorts, strike Toulon submarine base and Sofia M/Y.

Fourteenth AF: 5 B–25's and 16 P–40's bomb Hanshow and strafe 15–20 small boats N of the city. 2 other B–25's attack harbor and town of Amoy. 2 direct hits are scored on a docked freighter.

Fifth AF: Col Neel E Kearby becomes CO V FC. 30-plus B–25's, B–26's, and A–20's bomb village of Kalasa. 15 A–20's and B–25's, with P–38's escorting, hit stores and supplies in Finschhafen area. More than 20 B–24's, supported by P–38's, bomb Gasmata. 18 B–25's hit shipping at Halmahera I.

Thirteenth AF: 25 B–24's bomb Buka and Chabai. 20 B–25's hit Kahili A/F, and 6 others bomb and strafe a possible radio station at Mutupina Pt. Ftr patrols strafe Gazelle and Queen Carola Harbors, sinking a barge and damaging a schooner.

Seventh AF: 20 B–24's out of Nanumea bomb Maloelap Atoll, scoring hits on landing ground and cargo vessel.

25 November

Eighth AF: Bombing by P–47's is inaugurated by VIII FC in attack on Saint-Omer A/F by 56th and 353d Ftr Gps. Two other ftr gps, the 55th (P–38's) and 352d (P–47's), carry out offensive sweeps in Lille area. The ftrs, including 2 escorting gps, fly over 330 offensive sorties. 401st Bomb Gp reaches operational status, making 22 HB gps now operational in Eighth AF.

AEAF: ACM Sir Leigh-Mallory activates his HQ. Second Tac AF, RAF, and—on 15 Dec—US Ninth AF (operationally) are included under AEAF.

Twelfth AF: LBs and MBs of XII

A Spt Cmd, along with Allied airplanes, bomb gun positions and defended points in Lanciano-Fossacesia area. MBs also hit Sarajevo, Travnik, and Ancona. US and RAF ftrs attack vehicles, gun positions, and strongpoints in Casoli-Castelfrentano-Lanciano-Fossacesia area.

Fifteenth AF: Bad weather causes recall of HBs. P–38's on supply and air-sea rescue escort duty also abort due to rain storms.

Tenth AF: In a raid on Rangoon, B–24's of the 308th Bomb Gp, borrowed from Fourteenth AF, are unable to bomb because of bad weather, but B–25's, covered by P–51's, manage to hit Mingaladon A/F, damaging the field and claiming 2 airplanes destroyed. Japanese ftrs intercept and in the ensuing battle the B–25's and P–51's claim 2 shot down. 2 P–51's are lost.

Fourteenth AF: 14 B–25's and 16 P–38's and P–51's attack A/F at Shinchiku, hitting a parking area, hangars, barracks, and other buildings. 32 enemy aircraft are claimed destroyed in the air and on the ground. 16 P–40's on armed rcn over Hanshow-Changte area sink 2 60-ft boats and 15 sampans and strafe many small supply and troop-carrying boats.

Fifth AF: P–39's strafe Bogadjim Road. Sattelberg falls to Australian 9th Div.

26 November

Eighth AF: 440 HBs attack port area of Bremen. 128 HBs assigned industrial tgts in Paris area abort mission on arrival over tgt because of complete cloud cover which totally obscures objective. 29 aircraft are lost.

Ninth AF: Almost 140 MBs attack Cambrai/Epinoy and Roye/Amy A/Fs and military constructions in town of Audinghen.

Twelfth AF: B–25's and A–20's along with RAF LBs, attack M/Y and harbor at Ancona, defended positions near Fossacesia, Lanciano, and Castelfrentano. US and RAF FBs hit these same positions and also attack troop concentrations near Palombaro and N of Casoli.

Fifteenth AF: B–17's of 2d and 99th Bomb Gps hit viaduct at Recco. 301st Bomb Gp B–17's bomb Rimini M/Y and bridge. 17th Bomb Gp B–26's bomb Cassino while B–24's of 376th Bomb Gp attack bridges in Fano, Cesano, Senigallia, and Falconara areas, scoring hits or near misses at Fano, Falconara and Senigallia.

Fourteenth AF: 5 B–25's and 16 ftrs attack Kiangling A/F. 2 other B–25's damage freighter in Honghai Bay. 12 P–40's attack numerous boats in Changte-Tehshan area. 8 other P–40's hit railroad yards at Cam Duong.

Fifth AF: Almost 40 MBs hit barge hideouts near Sio. P–40's and P–47's strafe villages and T/Os around Alexishafen, Madang, and Nubia. P–39's attack force of about 40 Japanese ftrs and bmrs in Finschhafen area, claiming 4 shot down. B–24's bomb Gasmata and score hits on cruiser near Ubili.

Thirteenth AF: Buka and Bonis A/F are hit by more than 40 B–24's, 30-plus B–25's, and more than 30 ftr aircraft. A few B–34's attack Green I, causing heavy damage in bivouac and supply area and sinking a barge. A single B–25 bombs Ballale I A/F.

27 November

Twelfth AF: During day and night Twelfth AF ftrs, LBs, and MBs and aircraft of associated RAF units of NATAF attack enemy positions, gun emplacements, roads, vehicles, railroad facilities, and T/Os in Lanciano-Fossacesia-Castelfrentano-Casoli area B–25's also bomb Porto Civitanova and Sibenik.

Fifteenth AF: B–17's, with P–38 escort, bomb M/Y and bridges at Rimini. Other B–17's hit bridges and M/Y at Grizzana and bridge approach on Reno R 25 mi SW of Bologna.

Tenth AF: B–24's, with P–38 escort, and B–25's, covered by P–51's, strike Insein. Japanese interceptors attack fiercely, shooting down 6 ftrs and 3 HBs. US airplanes claim 13 ftrs downed.

Fourteenth AF: 4 B–25's on sea sweeps attack docks and warehouses at port of Swatow and hit convoy of 9 vessels heading S toward Amoy. The MBs claim 1 destroyer sunk and a destroyer and freighter damaged by direct hits.

Fifth AF: MBs blast A/F at Boram and town and harbor at Wewak, claiming 15 airplanes and 12 barges destroyed. MBs also bomb town of Finschhafen.

Thirteenth AF: 5 B–25's, with ftr escort, bomb Queen Carola Harbor. 20-plus B–24's, with ftr spt, attack Buka A/F. 19 B–24's bomb Bonis A/F. A few B–25's and B–34's attack areas at mouth of Mobiai R and Mutupina Pt.

Seventh AF: 8 B–24's from Canton I and Nukufetau bomb Mille.

ZI: Gen Wolfe becomes CG XX BC.

28 November

International: Tehran Conference begins and lasts until 30 Nov. Roosevelt, Churchill, and Stalin discuss further action against Germany. OVERLORD and ANVIL are given priority over all other operations. Stalin agrees to commit Soviet forces against Japan after Germany's defeat.

Twelfth AF: B–25's bomb warehouses, docks, M/Ys, barracks, shipping, and other tgts in Sibenik, Zara, and Dubrovnik. DAF ftrs strafe trains between Dubrovnik and Metkovic, and Twelfth AF ftrs hit vehicles and troops in battle area. Allied FBs bomb and strafe buildings, trucks, and roads in Lanciano-Fossacesia-Casoli areas.

Fifteenth AF: B–26's are recalled over S France due to bad weather. The MBs and their ftr escort claim 5 ftrs destroyed in combat over French coast. B–25's, with ftr escort, bomb railroad viaduct at Dogna.

Tenth AF: B–24's heavily damage Botataung docks at Rangoon; the HBs claim 4 interceptors shot down. B–25's pound Sagaing.

Fourteenth AF: 8 P–40's bomb and strafe barracks area and village on W bank of the Salween near Litsaoho. 6 others strafe town area and A/F at Luang Prabang and hit radio building, barracks, and tower at Tran Ninh. 8 P–40's drop ammo to besieged Chinese troops at Changte.

Fifth AF: Nearly 50 B–24's bomb A/Fs at Wewak and Boram, and 40-plus B–25's, B–26's, and A–20's hit villages on Huon Peninsula and tracks in Finschhafen area.

Thirteenth AF: 6 B–25's bomb and strafe Mutupina Pt area. Ftrs strafe Tinputs Harbor, barges at Tonolai, and T/Os along W coast of Bougainville.

Seventh AF: 11 B–24's from Nanumea hit Nauru.

29 November

Eighth AF: 154 HBs attack port of Bremen and T/Os in the area. Unfavorable cloud conditions and malfunction of blind-bombing equipment cause more than 200 HBs to abort. 13 aircraft are lost on mission.

Ninth AF: 53 B–26's bomb Chievres A/F. 71 sent to bomb Cambrai/Epinoy A/F abort mission due to bad weather.

Twelfth AF: B–25's bomb Sarajevo and road and rail bridges at Giulianova. US, SAAF, and RAF LBs hit enemy strongpoints at San Vito Chietino and the Castelfrentano-Lanciano-Fossacesia areas. Allied FBs bomb enemy forward positions around Fossacesia and Lanciano.

Fifteenth AF: 70 B–26's bomb A/F and M/Ys at Grosseto. B–24's, with P–38 escort, bomb Furbara area. Many other MBs and HBs are prevented from bombing tgts by bad weather.

Fourteenth AF: 2 B–25's hit A/F, town area, and warehouse section at Swatow, 2 bomb power station and nearby T/Os at Amoy, and 2 attack barges in nearby coastal areas. 24 P–40's drop food and ammo to Chinese troops at Changte, strafe camp in Hsutu Lake area, damage a vessel in Tien-hsin Lake and attack numerous small craft in channels between Hsutu and Tungting Lakes and between Tsowshih and Hofuh.

Fifth AF: 35 B–25's and B–26's bomb Cape Gloucester. 6 B–24's bomb barracks at Manokwari.

Thirteenth AF: 18 B–25's, with ftr cover, attack Tinputs Harbor and T/Os in area from Numa Numa to Kieta. 21 B–24's pound Kieta. P–39's join Navy dive bmrs in strike on Mosigetta warehouse area while a ftr patrol attacks Gazelle Harbor and gun positions S of Torokina Plantation.

30 November

Eighth AF: 78 HBs hit industries at Solingen using blind-bombing equipment. 200 aircraft abort due to cloud formations which cause assembly difficulties and which require flying at altitudes not feasible for the B–24's included in the mission.

Twelfth AF: A–20's, operating in conjunction with LBs of SAAF and RAF attack ground installations and defended areas around Lanciano, Fossacesia, Orsogna, Castelfrentano, and Guardiagrele. FBs, (US, RAAF, SAAF, RAF) hit pre-arranged tgts in battle area, and by hitting T/Os on roads between Lanciano to Mozzagrogna aid in defeating counterattack against US 34th Inf Div on Monte Pantano.

Fifteenth AF: B–26's attack Monte Molino railroad bridge, Montalto di Castro, and in areas around Bastia and Torgiano. Accuracy is severely hampered by overcast. B–24's, with P–38 escort, bomb Fiume through overcast.

Fourteenth AF: 6 P–40's bomb fuel and ammo dump at Luchiangpa. 8 others strafe several boats on lake

SE of Ansiang. Supplies are dropped to Chinese troops in Changte.

Fifth AF: B–24's bomb Cape Gloucester A/F. B–25's bomb and strafe villages along coast from Borgen Bay to Riebeck Bay. B–24's hit Alexishafen. B–25's and A–20's attack Kalasa and hit trucks in Waroe area.

Thirteenth AF: 17 B–25's bomb Malai on Shortland I. Ftr aircraft (AAF and Navy) attack barges and AA guns at Tonolai, SE coast of Ballale I, NW tip of Choiseul I, Amun above Cape Moltke, Numa Numa, and Chabai. Others cover dive bmrs attacking Jakohina Mission area, gun positions at Kangu and Malabita Hill, and in Mosigetta area. A few B–34's hit Mawareka area.

Seventh AF: 10 B–24's from Canton I strike Maloelap. 20 others, sent against the same tgt from Nanumea, run into bad weather. 2 attack cargo ship and other vessels near Maloelap, the remaining 18 return to base without attacking.

1 December

Eighth AF: 281 HBs hit industrial tgts at Solingen after malfunction of Pathfinder equipment prevents attack on primary tgt at Leverkusen. Over 20 aircraft are lost on the raid.

Ninth AF: Over 175 B–26's bomb A/Fs at Chievres, Cambrai/Epinoy, Lille/Vendeville, and Cambrai/Niergnies. 28 P–51's execute a sweep over NW France, marking first Ninth AF ftr operation from UK.

Twelfth AF: B–25's bomb gun positions in Sant' Ambrogio area. FBs (including some RAF, RAAF, and SAAF aircraft) hit trucks, gun positions, and other military tgts E of

Casoli, at Lanciano, near Guardiagrele, W of Mignano, W of Minturno, and near Chieti. Several of these missions are in spt of US Fifth and British Eighth Army.

Fifteenth AF: HQ closes at Tunis and opens at Bari. Over 100 B–17's bomb Turin ball bearing works and M/Y. Escorting P–38's battle enemy ftrs without either losses or positive victories. HBs claim 2 enemy ftrs shot down. B–24's and other P–38's are recalled because of weather. B–26's, with ftr escort, attack bridges and railroad facilities at Aulla, Cecina, and Sestri Levante.

Tenth AF: B–24's bomb Insein. The HBs and escorting P–38 encounter large number of Japanese ftrs over the tgts. P–51's which failed to make rendezvous with the HBs before the attack join the formations on return trip. US losses are high: 6 B–24's and a P–51 shot down and 5 more HBs are seriously damaged. MBs hit the newly repaired bridge at Myitnge, rendering it temporarily unserviceable.

Fourteenth AF: 19 B–25's, 24 P–40's, and 10 P–51's pound Kowloon shipyards. 2 B–25's hit nearby Taikoo Docks, Hong Kong. 4 P–40's strafe truck convoy near Lashio, 16 sink about 30 boats in area around Changte, and 8 bomb Bac Ninh and vicinity.

Fifth AF: 40-plus B–24's bomb Wewak, the HBs and P–47 escorts claiming 11 enemy ftrs shot down out of interception force of about 50. 3 B–24's are lost. 16 A–20's hit Cape Gloucester area. 35 B–25's and B–26's bomb Borgen Bay area.

Thirteenth AF: 18 B–25's and 8 P–38's attack Malai. P–39's strafe

Tonolai and spt Navy dive bmrs in attack on Jaba R area near Empress Augusta Bay. Other AAF and Navy ftrs cover dive bmr strikes on Kara and Ballale I supply areas and strafe tgts at Tenekow, Chabai, and Mutupina Pt. 6 B–25's bomb Sarime Plantation.

Seventh AF: 4 B–24's, flying out of Funafuti, bomb Mille.

2 December

AEAF: CCS authorizes AEAF to attack "sky sites" in Pas de Calais area and on Cherbourg Peninsula, which RAF photography and British intelligence have virtually identified as missile-launching sites.

Twelfth AF: B–25's, A–20's, and RAF LBs spt ground forces in Monte Trocchio area, and other B–25's, A–20's, and RAF and SAAF airplanes spt ground forces near Sant' Ambrogio. More B–25's hit bridge and approaches near Chieti. Ftrs strafe trucks and trains while FBs blast gun positions along US Fifth and British Eighth Army fronts, and hit harbors and shipping along Yugoslav coast at or near Omis, Drvenicki, Trogir, Vrbnik, and Ston.

Fifteenth AF: B–24's, with ftr escort, bomb town area, railroad bridge, and M/Y at Bolzano. B–26's achieve excellent results in raid on bridge S of Orvieto and M/Y at Arezzo. B–17's blast submarine pens at Marseille.

Fourteenth AF: 18 Japanese bmrs and 30 Zeros attack Suichwan A/F. 9 P–40's intercept, shooting down 1 Japanese airplane. 2 P–40's are lost. 6 P–40's on armed rcn bomb villages between Sha Nyao and Chiao Tou Chieh. 16 others bomb Japanese positions NE of Changte.

Fifth AF: 50-plus B–25's pound Borgen Bay area. 20 B–25's and B–26's hit enemy forces in Finschhafen area. Sio area is bombed by 2 B–24's.

Thirteenth AF: 20-plus B–25's hit Malai and attack positions on Porror R and Rigu Mission at Kieta. More than 20 B–24's bomb Korovo. Ftr patrol strafes Chabai area.

3 December

Eighth AF: Note from ACM Portal to CCS states that POINTBLANK (CBO against GAF) is 3 months behind in relationship to tentative date for OVERLORD which had been set for 1 May 44. This brings more pressure on Eighth AF to destroy industrial plants of importance to aircraft production.

Twelfth AF: Twelfth AF transfers its entire II Air Serv Area Cmd with all of its subordinate units to Fifteenth AF, where it shortly becomes XV AFSC. This is a major step toward making the Fifteenth a separate, self-sufficient AF. B–25's bomb harbor and M/Y at Sibenik. FBs, along with DAF airplanes, hit tanks and trucks in Guardiagrele-Lanciano areas. Other FBs attack vessel at Sibenik and vehicles and trains N of Rome. Anzio and Nettuno are also bombed.

Fifteenth AF: B–24's, with ftr escort, hit Rome/Casale A/F. B–26's and escorting P–38's are recalled due to weather. Other P–38's escort supply mission to Yugoslavia.

Fourteenth AF: 8 P–40's attack barracks and other buildings at Wanling.

Fifth AF: More than 60 B–24's and B–25's bomb Cape Gloucester A/F. 1 B–24 sinks several barges in

Johann Albrecht Harbor while another bombs a large transport near New Hanover. 20-plus B–24's bomb Waingapoe. A–20's attack villages around Finschhafen. P–47's shoot down several airplanes over Wewak.

Thirteenth AF: 23 B–25's bomb Kieta Harbor and nearby supply and bivouac areas. 6 others hit Aitara Mission. 21 B–24's pound Bonis. Ftr aircraft (AAF and Navy) on patrol hit T/Os in areas from Numa Numa to Koromira, at Mosiga and Chabai, and W of Mutupina Pt. B–24's on armed rcn hit a variety of tgts, including Kieta, Green I, Greenwich I, and Korovo.

4 December

International: Second Cairo conference (SEXTANT) opens and lasts until 6 Dec. Roosevelt, Churchill, and Inonu attend. Churchill discusses possibility of Turkey entering the war. Plan for amphibious assault in Bay of Bengal is cancelled. A tentative timetable is set up for Pacific offensive. Unified Cmd is established in the Mediterranean effective 10 Dec.

Ninth AF: Ninth AF directive establishes Operation CROSSBOW for IX BC and provides a list of tgts to be attacked immediately. IX A Spt Cmd, constituted on 29 Nov 43, is assigned to Ninth AF, activated, and stationed at Aldermaston Court in England with Col Clarence E Crumrine as CO. 203 B–26's dispatched to attack Chievres and Lille/Vendeville A/Fs must abort mission due to bad weather.

Twelfth AF: Weather grounds Twelfth AF elements of NATAF.

Fifteenth AF: All missions are cancelled by bad weather.

Tenth AF: 5 B–24's mine Rangoon R while 12 others mine the Salween R at Moulmein during 4/5 Dec.

Fourteenth AF: 11 B–25's and 12 P–40's bomb Changte, which was taken by the Japanese earlier in the day. 11 more B–25's and 24 P–40's follow with 2 more attacks on Changte. Other P–40's drop ammo to Chinese troops on Tehshan Mt.

Fifth AF: Nearly 50 bmrs hit Cape Gloucester A/F and attack shore tgts from Rottock Bay to Rein Bay. 12 A–20's hit villages and supply dumps in Finschhafen area. 30-plus P–40's sink an oil laden lugger and 2 barges off Bogia and bomb bridge near Bogadjim.

Thirteenth AF: XIII FC completes move from the New Hebrides to Guadalcanal. 21 B–24's attack Chabai. 17 B–25's follow with strike on same tgt.

Seventh AF: 34 B–24's from Ellice and Canton Is bomb Mille. Over 20 others abort due to bad weather. 8 B–24's from Funafuti attack Nauru.

Eleventh AF: 3 bmrs return early from an armed seasearch, due to weather.

5 December

International: At Cairo Conference Roosevelt decides on Gen Eisenhower as supreme allied cmdr for OVERLORD.

Eighth AF: Around 550 HBs are dispatched to attack A/Fs at Bordeaux, Cognac, La Rochelle, and Saint-Jean-d'Angely, and industries at Paris. Cloud conditions prevent bombing of tgts except for 3 HBs that attack A/Fs at Bordeaux and Cognac. 9 aircraft are lost on the mission.

Ninth AF: 52 B–26's bomb Ligescourt, Campagne-les-Hesdin, and Saint-Josse. 200 others are forced to abandon mission because of heavy cloud cover over tgts, including V-weapon sites which the Ninth had scheduled to attack for the first time. Ninth AF P–51's (354th Ftr Gp) fly first escort mission, accompanying Eighth AF HBs in raid against tgts in areas near Amiens.

MAAF: CCS issues directive for organization of Mediterranean Allied Air Forces consolidating British and US forces of MAC and NAAF.

Twelfth AF: Weather hampers MB operations, but B–25's manage to bomb bridge at Pescara and M/Y and shipyards at Split. US FBs and ftrs (and a number of other Allied airplanes) hit gun positions S of Chieti, vessel in Poljud harbor (near Split), trains and trucks W of Aquino, bridges near Mignano and Ladispoli, town of Arezzo, A/Fs at Piombino and Aviano, and building S of Garda Lake.

Tenth AF: During 5/6 Dec B–24's mine waters in Moulmein area while 5 others lay mines in Rangoon R.

Fourteenth AF: 16 P–40's over Changte area damage several large supply sampans near Ansiang and strafe various T/Os in Tehshan and Hsutu Lake areas. More than 20 other P–40's on patrols over Changte area attack numerous boats and other tgts throughout the nearby lake region.

Fifth AF: 40 B–24's bomb Cape Gloucester. A–20's destroy small craft off New Britain. Other A–20's hit enemy forces in Finschhafen area. B–25's, B–26's, and P–40's attack tgts along Bogadjim Road.

Thirteenth AF: 23 B–25's and 20-plus Navy dive bmrs hit Monoitu, Aitara Mission, and Mosigetta area. Ftr patrols hit several areas on Bougainville and on Shortland, including Chabai, Numa Numa, Mosigetta, Monoitu, and Faisi I.

6 December

Twelfth AF: P–40 and A–36 FBs bomb bridges at Ceprano and W of Mignano. Weather cancels other operations.

Fifteenth AF: 45 B–24's bomb Eleusis A/F while 56 B–17's hit Kalamaki A/F. Other B–17's return to base with bombs because of heavy overcast. The HBs and escorting P–38's claim several enemy ftrs shot down. 1 B–24 is destroyed by flak.

Fourteenth AF: Changte is pounded throughout the day by more than 30 B–25's and numerous ftrs. Other ftrs strafe T/Os in railway yard at Hsipaw and damage train at Hopong.

Fifth AF: Nearly 100 B–24's and B–25's hit Cape Gloucester and Borgen Bay areas. P–40's strafe Cape Hoskins. A–20's and B–25's attack villages and supply dumps around Finschhafen.

Thirteenth AF: 6 B–25's bomb Monoitu Mission area, and 24 others, with ftr spt, pound Tarlena village. P–40's carry out strafing strike in Arawa Bay area near Kieta. P–38's strafe W coast of Buka. General ftr patrols strafe Chabai, Koromira, and Monoitu areas. Kieta supply area is bombed by a B–24 on armed rcn.

7 December

USSAFE: CCS accept US plan for

a strategic air cmd to coordinate operations of Fifteenth and Eighth AFs.

Twelfth AF: B–25's and A–36's bomb harbor and town of Civitavecchia. B–25's also attack Pescara, hitting railroad, road, and town area. A–36's, P–40's, and DAF ftrs hit gun position W of Orsogna, towns of Viticuso and San Vittoria, and bridge at Civitella Roveto.

Fifteenth AF: Heavy cloud cover severely restricts operations. 1 B–26 attacks bridge S of Arma di Taggia.

Fourteenth AF: Changte is hit twice by a total of 13 B–25's and several escorting ftrs. 8 P–40's strafe freight cars between Mogaung and Myitkyina.

Fifth AF: More that 90 B–24's and B–25's attack Cape Gloucester and Borgen Bay areas. A–20's bomb troop encampments and dumps in Finschhafen area. P–40's strafe boats and barges near Madang. B–24's bomb A/F and village on Haroekoe.

Thirteenth AF: 18 B–25's carry out strikes against Kahili and Kieta Harbor. Torokina I is bombed by 2 B–34's on patrol.

Seventh AF: During 6/7 Dec, 14 B–24's, staging through Tarawa, hit tgts on Maloelap and Wotje Atolls. 22 A–24's from Makin, escorted by Marine F6F's, hit Emidj. 6 B–24's from Nukufetau bomb Maloelap, and 1 other, failing to reach the primary, drops bombs on Mille. This date marks beginning of FLINTLOCK (capture and def of Kwajalein and Majuro Atolls).

8 December

USSAFE: Gen Arnold notifies Gen Spaatz that he is to cmd USSAFE (later USSTAF).

Twelfth AF: B–25's bomb bridges, industrial tgts, M/Y, and town areas of Pescara, Ancona, and Aquila. A–20's hit gun emplacements and bivouac area near Sant' Elia Fiumerapido. Other A–20's, operating with RAF and SAAF aircraft attack troop concentration and gun positions near Miglianico. FBs of AAF, RAF, RAAF, and SAAF bomb tgts in spt of ground troops near Orsogna. US A–36's and P–40's hit comm tgts (roads, railroads, bridges) at Avezzano, Frosinone, Viticuso, Gaeta, and Sant' Elia Fiumerapido.

Fifteenth AF: More than 120 B–24's and B–17's attack Tatoi and Eleusis A/Fs, railroad bridges near Orbetello Lake and town of Porto Santo Stefano. B–26's hit Spoleto viaduct, Orte M/Y, and Civitavecchia harbor. Other B–26's abort mission because of weather.

Fourteenth AF: 9 B–25's, escorted by 16 P–40's, pound Changte. 9 other B–25's bomb Hofuh and the 16 escorting P–40's bomb 2 villages to the N.

Fifth AF: B–25's attack Penfoei-Koepang area. B–25's and B–26's pound enemy supply dumps on Huon Peninsula near Finschhafen. P–39's strafe barges from Saidor to Fortification Pt.

Thirteenth AF: Ftr patrols and aircraft on armed rcn bomb and strafe several T/Os near Kieta, SE of Cape Torokina, at Baniu Plantation, and along NE coast of Bougainville.

Seventh AF: 22 B–24's from Nanumea bomb Jaluit, and 11 from Canton I bomb Mille.

Eleventh AF: 3 B–24's fly armed

rcn. During 8/9 Dec another B–24 off on a photographic mission over Kasatochi I, turns back because of mechanical trouble.

9 December

Twelfth AF: B–25's bomb railway and road bridges at Giulianova, tracks at Pescara and Teramo, and M/Y and ironworks at Terni. A–20's hit gun positions and bivouac area at Sant' Elia Fiumerapido. A–36's and P–40's attack Orsogna and coastal tgts in spt of British Eighth Army, Avezzano M/Y and villages along US Fifth Army front, troops at San Pietro Infine and Viticuso and nearby gun positions, viaduct and railway bridge E of Guidonia A/F, crossing at Furbara, and trains and trucks in Rome area. Gen Beverley takes over as new CG, XII TCC (Prov).

Fifteenth AF: P–38's carry out weather rcn over the Adriatic. B–17's of 2d and 99th Bomb Gps are recalled because of weather. All gps of 47th (B–24) and 42d (B–26) Bomb Wgs cancel operations.

Fourteenth AF: 15 B–25's bomb Wuchang and Hankow, and 3 bomb Changte. P–40's strafe sampans above Nanhsien and attack T/Os in Salween R area, including road traffic S of Hsia Chai, barracks at Tachai, and town of San Tsun.

Fifth AF: 50 B–25's bomb and strafe New Britain coast from Borgen Bay to Rein Bay. 19 B–25's and A–20's hit barges coastal installations, and roads in Fortification Pt area. 60-plus P–39's hit Bogadjim Road, barges and enemy held villages along N coast of Huon Peninsula, and enemy positions in Ramu R valley.

Seventh AF: 19 B–24's from Funafuti bomb Mille. The HBs claim 5 ftrs destroyed.

10 December

Ninth AF: 20 German aircraft attack 4 Ninth AF A/Fs in UK (Gosfield, Andrews Field, Earls Colne, and Great Dunmow), killing 8 and wounding more than 20 men.

Twelfth AF: P–40's and A–36's attack oil tanks, warehouses, railroads, and vessel at Civitavecchia, town of Acquafondata, and (with RAF, SAAF, and RAAF airplanes) hit tac tgts along British Eighth Army front, and later strafe road traffic in Canosa Sannita-Chieti area. Ftrs also bomb vessel in harbor at Split.

MAAF: MAAF is established (see 20 Dec 43).

Fifteenth AF: B–24's, with ftr escort, bomb M/Y at Sofia. B–26's hit bridge approaches W and E of Ventimiglia. P–38's fly weather rcn in Sofia and Zara areas.

Fourteenth AF: 12 B–25's and 15 P–40's attack M/Y at Hanoi. Warehouse area and railroad station suffer heavy damage. Japanese aircraft bomb Hengyang A/F. 8 P–40's intercept 1 wave of airplanes over the field, shooting down 3 of them. 2 P–40's are lost in the combat.

Fifth AF: 27 B–24's bomb tgts at Cape Gloucester and Huon Peninsula. 40 B–25's and B–26's bomb supply and bivouac areas and bridges along Bogadjim Road. P–39's strafe barges in Madang area.

Thirteenth AF: B–25's bomb Kahili supply area and A/F. P–39's bomb supply area and AA positions at Tonolai and strafe 4 barges in the harbor. B–34's hit buildings at Arigua Plantation.

11 December

Eighth AF: 523 B–17's and B–24's hit docks and industrial area of Emden. 17 aircraft are lost to enemy action.

Twelfth AF: P–40's and A–36's attack Anzio, Nettuno, Viticuso, San Vittore del Lazio, Pontecorvo, Acquafondata, railway siding at Arce, tracks and junction N of Ostia, and railway between Ostia and Lido di Roma. Weather causes abandonment of MB operations.

Fifteenth AF: All operations except weather rcn are cancelled or recalled because of bad weather.

Fourteenth AF: 14 B–25's and 10 P–40's attack Shihshow and Ansiang. 3 B–24's bomb Hankow A/F. 9 P–40's intercept about 30 airplanes over Nanchang shortly after the enemy force bombs Suichwan. The P–40's claim 10 aircraft shot down.

Fifth AF: B–25's bomb and strafe Borgen Bay area. B–25's and B–26's hit bivouacs and other installations near Fortification Pt and in Finschhafen area. B–24's bomb Makassar and Balikpapan.

Thirteenth AF: 16 B–25's, in 2 waves, attack Kahili. Several other B–25's hit Arigua Plantation. 20-plus B–24's bomb village and wharf area at Tsirogei. 8 P–39's bomb Tonolai. Several aircraft on armed rcn, operating individually or in small flights, attack T/Os scattered throughout Bougainville and Shortland area. Allied night ftrs carry out strike on Japanese bivouac along Jaba R. Others hit Buka and Bonis.

12 December

Twelfth AF: Weather curtails operations. B–25's bomb road, railroad, and landing ground at Terracina. P–40 and A–36 FBs hit trucks along roads in Chieti-Francavilla area and bomb town of Itri. Ftrs fly patrols and rcn over battle area.

Fifteenth AF: Operations are limited to weather rcn.

Tenth AF: 28 B–25's and 13 B–24's carry out saturation bombing strike against bridge at Myittha, over which large volume of Japanese goods is flowing to the N. Despite this large air effort only the approach spans suffer effective damage.

Fourteenth AF: 41 Japanese bmrs and ftrs bomb W side of Hengyang A/F, causing considerable damage. 31 P–40's and 6 P–38's intercept the enemy force, claiming 20 airplanes shot down. 2 P–40's are lost. 9 B–24's bomb Hankow A/F.

Fifth AF: P–40's dive-bomb Bogadjim Road. B–24's make light raids on Ceram and in far W part of Netherlands New Guinea.

Thirteenth AF: 6 B–25's strafe Arigua Plantation. 8 others, with ftr spt, bomb supply area at Bonis. The ftrs afterwards strafe Japanese forces between Kieta and the Aropa R. Other ftr aircraft strafe harbor at Tonolai and cover Navy dive bmr strikes against tgts in Ratsua-Porton-Chabai-Soraken areas and Kieta Harbor-Tobera Bay area. 20-plus B–24's bomb Kahili area and Poporang.

Seventh AF: 25 B–24's flying out of Ellice Is bases, bomb Emidj I.

13 December

Eighth AF: 649 B–17's and B–24's, out of 710 dispatched, bomb port areas of Bremen and Hamburg and U-boat yards at Kiel. This is first Eighth AF mission in which more than 600 HBs attack tgts. P–51's escorting the HBs reach the limit of their escort range for the first time.

Ninth AF: Nearly 200 MBs attack Schiphol A/F. IX FC P–51's, working with VIII FC P–38's, fly longest escort mission to date, escorting HBs to and from Kiel.

Twelfth AF: B–25's bomb oil depot, harbor, warehouses, and railway yard at Sibenik and Split. P–40 and A–36 FBs attack defended points in Miglionico area; quays, roads, railway yard, and gun emplacements at Terracina; and bridges at Pontecorvo and W of Isolella. Town areas and bridges at and near Atina and Acquafondata are also hit.

Fifteenth AF: Operations are restricted to weather rcn.

Tenth AF: 20 Japanese bmrs, escorted by 25 ftrs, hit Dinjan A/F before US interceptors make contact. However, little damage is done and the US ftrs catch the attackers shortly afterward. 12 Japanese bmrs and 5 ftrs are claimed knocked down.

Fourteenth AF: 12 B–25's, with ftr escort, bomb Li-Chou and Kungan. 8 B–25's pound Wuchang A/F. 16 P–40's on armed rcn strafe T/Os from Changte to Linli to Li-Chou.

Fifth AF: More than 100 B–24's and B–25's and several P–40's bomb Gasmata. A–20's hit villages along Bogadjim Road. A small flight of P–39's strafe barges along Huon Peninsula.

Thirteenth AF: 17 B–25's bomb Porton, and their ftr escorts strafe Tenekow bivouac areas during return flight. 24 B–24's bomb Bonis. 6 B–

25's carry out low-level strikes against concentrations on Numa Numa.

Seventh AF: 10 B–24's, staging through Baker I from Canton I, bomb Wotje.

14 December

Twelfth AF: MBs hit Orte, concentrating on M/Y. LBs attack road bridge SW of Pontecorvo in front of US Fifth Army lines. P–40 FBs hit bridges S of Roccasecca and E of Atina. A–36's destroy bridge at Ceprano and bomb railroad yards, town area, and highway at Sora, and docks and town area of Civitavecchia.

Fifteenth AF: More than 150 B–17's and B–24's, with ftr escorts, bomb Kalamaki, Eleusis, and Tatoi A/Fs. HBs claim 10 ftrs shot down.

Fourteenth AF: 13 B–25's, with ftr escort, bomb Shasi. 6 P–40's on armed rcn strafe Gia Lam A/F and railroad yard. 2 others strafe supply trucks S of Tengchung.

Fifth AF: In heaviest raid to date in SWPA, 228 B–24's, B–25's, and A–20's bomb Arawe in an almost continuous attack from 0645 to 1548. Gasmata is hit by B–25's and B–26's. P–39's strafe barges along Huon Peninsula. B–24's on armed rcn hit Saidor, Gasmata, and Unea.

Thirteenth AF: 18 B–24's, with ftr spt, bomb positions on Sohano I. 18 B–25's and 8 ftrs hit Manob village E of Buka Passage. Other Thirteenth AF ftrs hit gun positions, comm tgts, and other T/Os at scattered points in Bougainville-Shortland areas and cover Navy dive bmr strikes against AA positions in Chabai area.

Seventh AF: 16 B–24's, flying out of bases in Ellice Is, bomb Maloelap.

15 December

Ninth AF: Ninth AF comes under operational control of AEAF. New directive for tac bmr operations lists reduction of enemy ftr forces as basic objective. A Ninth AF planning staff, composed of officers who have had service with COSSAC, is set up in London.

Twelfth AF: B–25's bomb A/F at Mostar, and A–36 and P–40 FBs attack vessels, vehicles, and parked aircraft N and E of Peljesac Peninsula, near Mostar, and at Zemonico landing ground. B–25's and A–20's bomb roads at Pontecorvo and N of Frosinone. FBs blast gun positions along US Fifth Army front.

Fifteenth AF: B–17's, with P–38 and P–47 escorts, bomb M/Ys at Bolzano and Innsbruck. B–24's, with P–38 escort, attack Avisio viaduct. All tgts suffer considerable damage.

EAC: EAC, a combined US-British Cmd, is formed under Gen Stratemeyer, with AVM Williams as Asst Cmdr. HQ, at New Delhi, will control all operational air units in Assam and Burma which presently make up Tenth AF and RAF Bengal Air Cmd. Major components of EAC are to be Third Tac AF under AM Baldwin, Strategic AF under Gen Davidson, TCC under Gen Old, and Photo Rcn Force under Gp Capt Stewart G Wise. Strategic AF and TCC are activated on this date, the former having HQ at Belvedere Palace, Calcutta, and the latter at Comilla.

Fourteenth AF: 25 P–40's strafe parked aircraft, trucks, and several buildings at Pailochi. At least 3 enemy airplanes are destroyed. 2 B–25's on sea sweep over Gulf of Tonkin claim 1 ocean-going tug sunk. 16 P–40's on armed rcn strafe towns of Owchihow and Shihshow. 6 others attack town of Luchiangpa and villages in the area.

Fifth AF: As a preliminary to main invasion of New Britain, US forces under cmd of Gen Cunningham land on W coast of Arawe peninsula about 0700 following naval and air bombardment. B–25's pound villages in Arawe area. B–24's bomb Cape Gloucester while P–39's strafe barges at Reiss Pt. B–25's hit 2 freighters on Timor.

Thirteenth AF: 21 B–24's strike Sohano I. 6 B–25's hit installations in Numa Numa-Arigua area. 23 B–25's and 16 ftrs attack Buka, causing heavy damage in Chinatown area. P–40's destroy bridge at Runai. Numerous T/Os are attacked by AAF aircraft, operating individually and in small flights, on armed rcn over Bougainville and other N Solomons areas.

Seventh AF: 20 B–24's from Nanumea hit Maloelap. 10, staging from Canton I through Baker I, bomb Wotje. 1 B–24 is lost on Maloelap raid. 2 enemy ftrs are claimed destroyed.

16 December

Eighth AF: 535 HBs attack port area and T/Os at Bremen. Due to faulty comm, 1 combat wg mistakenly assumes mission is being abandoned and returns to base without attacking.

Ninth AF: Basic directive for IX BC trg is issued on this date. Since most of IX BC's combat units have been operational for some time earlier under VIII A Spt Cmd extensive trg will not begin until after the first of the year when inexperienced units begin to arrive.

Twelfth AF: B–25's bomb shipping at Zara and harbor and M/Y at Sibenik. A–20's attack gun positions near Mignano. P–40's and A–36's hit gun batteries and strongpoints along British Eighth Army front S and E of Chieti, gun emplacements and troop concentrations all along US Fifth Army front, especially NE and S of Cassino, and also bomb Roccasecca and docks at Civitavecchia. P–40's and P–47's hit vessel S of Zara and strafe T/Os on Peljesac Peninsula.

Fifteenth AF: B–24's attack railroad bridge and tunnel at Dogna and railroad between Dogna and Chiusaforte. Escorting P–38's strafe trains and oil tanks between Portogruaro and Latisana. B–17's, escorted by P–38's and P–47's, bomb Padua M/Y and rail junction. Rail lines, rolling stock, and buildings are damaged extensively.

Fourteenth AF: 9 B–25's and 11 P–40's hit NW part of Owchihkow. 4 B–25's on sweeps over S China Sea damage freighter S of Nampang I, bomb Tunguan docks, and shoot down 1 bmr. 15 P–40's on armed rcn strafe Pailochi A/F. 11 others strafe boats in channels N of Nanhsien. 6 P–38's strafe troop train near Changanyi and attack 25 sampans (destroying most of them) on Yangtze R just above Huangtang Lake.

Fifth AF: HBs hit Cape Gloucester. MBs hit Sio and Kelana Harbor. P–40's hit Timoeka area.

Thirteenth AF: 14 B–24's bomb Monoitu. Smaller flights of B–24's bomb Poporang I, Sohano I, and dispersal areas at Bonis A/F. 5 B–25's,

with ftr cover, hit Sankau I. B–34's attack tgts on Green I and in Mawareka, Marveiropa, and Mamaregu areas. Ftr aircraft spt Navy dive bmr strikes on Sohano I and gun positions at Bonis and afterwards strafe T/Os at several points on Bougainville.

17 December

Ninth AF: Ninth AF planning gp joins 21 Army Gp, AEAF, and RAF Second Tac AF in preparation of air section of initial joint plan (Operation NEPTUNE) for Operation OVERLORD. This begins planning which later results in massive Ninth AF plan for moving the Ninth into battle on continent of Europe.

Twelfth AF: A–20's strike arty concentration near Sant'Elia Fiumerapido. All B–25 missions are abortive. P–40's and P–51's (with SAAF escort) strafe vessel near Trpanj. A–36's and P–40 FBs bomb positions at Monte Trocchio, Cervaro, and Cardito, and M/Y, barracks, warehouses, and docks at Nettuno and Anzio.

Fifteenth AF: Operations are restricted to weather rcn.

Fourteenth AF: 6 P–40's bomb and strafe barracks near Kunlong. 6 others bomb and strafe T/Os in Hanoi.

Fifth AF: P–47's intercept 35–40 aircraft attacking Allied forces on Arawe peninsula. At least 10 airplanes are claimed shot down. Cape Gloucester and nearby shipping are attacked by B–24's and B–25's. B–25's bomb Sio area. P–39's sink 2 barges during sweep along Huon Peninsula.

Thirteenth AF: 18 B–25's strike Malai. 6 others join Navy dive bmrs in pounding Mutupina Pt area. 5 B–34's hit Poroporo and Tarekekori.

Seventh AF: 10 B–24's are dispatched from Nanumea to bomb Maloelap. 9 are recalled because of weather. 1 bombs alternate tgt of Mille.

18 December

AAF: Gen Arnold sends to ACM Portal announcement of US air officers for top cmds in Europe for 44. The list includes Gen Eaker, Allied Air Forces in MTO; Gen Cannon, Twelfth AF; Gen Twining, Fifteenth AF; Gen Spaatz, US Strategic Air Forces; Gen Doolittle, Eighth AF; and Gen Brereton, Ninth AF.

Twelfth AF: Weather limits operations. P–40 FBs attack positions in Tollo, Canosa Sannita, and Orsogna, and strafe schooner off Trogir. A–36's hit defended areas near Cassino and at Viticuso, supply dump and gun emplacement near Terracina, and positions at Monte Trocchio.

Fifteenth AF: B–26's bomb Var R bridges, destroying a highway bridge and damaging a railroad bridge. Other B–26's have less success against Antheor viaduct, although there are several near misses.

EAC: Third Tac AF is activated under AM Baldwin as a major component of EAC.

Fourteenth AF: 27 B–24's, supported by 28 P–40's, pound A/F at Namsang. Some of the P–40's strafe Laihka A/F. 2 B–25's on sea sweep claim damaging hits on a freighter and a tanker in Hainan Straits. 5 B–25's bomb SW part of Nanhsien.

Fifth AF: Over 70 B–24's, B–25's, and B–26's bomb Cape Gloucester. 20-plus B–25's bomb Borgen Bay area. Nearly 40 B–24's hit Hoskins A/F. 33 A–20's bomb and strafe dumps and bivouacs N of Finschhafen.

Thirteenth AF: 10 B–24's bomb Kahili supply area, 5 more hit Bonis supply area, and 19 others hit tgts in Chabai-Porton area. 5 B–25's carry out low-level strike on troop concentrations at Poroporo and 11 bomb Korovo. B–24's, operating individually and in small flights, on armed rcn attack Kahili, Kieta, and Poporang. Ftrs strafe T/Os at Numa Numa, Cape Pui Pui, and E coast of Buka.

Seventh AF: 14 B–24's bomb Mille. 30-plus P–39's and A–24's fly strafing and bombing raids against the same tgt.

19 December

Twelfth AF: B–25's bomb Terni M/Y and Orte M/Y and A/F. A–20's attack road, bridge, and town of Orte and hit Cassino. P–40's bomb Orsogna, Sant' Elia Fiumerapido, and dump near Arce, and hit shipping at Split, Trogir, and Solin. A–36's hit railroad and harbor area at Civitavecchia.

Fifteenth AF: About 150 B–17's attack Messerschmitt plant at Augsburg and M/Y at Innsbruck. P–38's and P–47's provide partial escort. P–47's of 325th Ftr Gp, dispatched for escort duty, miss rendezvous with HBs and instead strafe Ancona A/F, truck convoys at Porto Civitanova, train near Senigallia, and vessel at Roseto degli Abruzzi. B–26's bomb Perugia railroad installations and M/Ys at Castiglione della Valle and Foligno. 9 HBs are lost. US aircraft claim 37 ftrs shot down.

Tenth AF: 20 B–24's fly night strike against newly expanded dock area at Bangkok, causing considerable destruction.

Fourteenth AF: About 35 Japanese bmrs and ftrs attack Hengyang A/F. 26 P–40's are sent up against the attacking force and shoot down 9. 2 P–40's are lost. 12 B–25's and 8 P–40's attack Nanhsien and Ansiang.

Fifth AF: Cape Gloucester is bombed by more than 140 B–24's, B–25's, and B–26's as pre-invasion operations against New Britain increase. 37 P–40's hit Gasmata. 20 A–20's pound forces NE of Arawe. About 30 B–25's, A–20's, and P–39's hit barges, bivouac areas, and gun positions N and W of Finschhafen. 30 B–25's and B–26's pound Madang. P–47's sweep coastline of NE New Guinea.

Thirteenth AF: 24 B–25's bomb Moisuru bivouac and supply dump. 16 B–24's, escorted by 50 AAF and RNZAF ftrs, bomb town of Rabaul and Simpson Harbor. Other planes on armed rcn hit T/Os at Buka, Bonis, Ratsua, Poporang, Kara, Kahili, Koiaris, and Nissan I.

Seventh AF: 29 B–24's from Nanumea and Baker bomb barracks, hangars, and wharf areas on Mille and Maloelap Atolls. HBs claim 7 ftrs shot down. P–39's from Makin strafe Mille, destroying 3 airplanes and firing an oil dump. 2 P–39's are lost.

20 December

Eighth AF: Window—metal foil strips which, when dropped from an airplane, provide an echo which confuses radar locating equipment—is used for the first time on an Eighth AF mission, when more than 470 HBs attack port area at Bremen. Enemy opposition accounts for 27 bmrs. Nearly 80 P–51's and P–38's engage ftrs in fierce battle as twin-engine, rocket-firing German ftrs attack under protection of single engine airplanes.

Ninth AF: 35 B–26's attack V-weapon sites in N France. More than 150 others abort because of weather.

MAAF: MAAF is established, retroactive to 10 Dec 43. Commanded by ACM Tedder, MAAF is comprised of all Allied air elements (RAF, USAAF, French, and other) which are operating in MTO. These elements previously were part of MAC and NAAF, which are disbanded. USAAFNATO is established with Gen Spaatz as cmdr, to facilitate administration of AAF units of Twelfth and Fifteenth AFs.

Twelfth AF: P–40's and RAF, SAAF, and RAAF FBs blast vehicles and heavily defended areas near Chieti and Orsogna, and hit fuel dump near Manoppello. A–36's bomb Terracina and hit water towers, a train, and a railway station S of Rome.

Fifteenth AF: 30-plus B–24's bomb M/Y at Sofia, and more than 100 B–17's hit Eleusis A/F. HBs and escorting ftrs claim over 30 ftrs destroyed in combat. 9 of the escorts are lost.

Fourteenth AF: 11 B–25's and 6 P–40's from Kweilin pound Yoyang railroad yards. P–40's from Hengyang also provide spt for the MBs.

Fifth AF: Enemy bivouac is blasted by more than 90 B–24's and B–25's. A–20's hit Arawe area and P–38's in the area claim 10 enemy ftrs shot down. P–40's strafe T/O along S coast of New Britain. B–24's on armed rcn bomb merchant ship off Cape Pomas. B–26's and B–25's hit bivouacs in Finschhafen area and bomb town of Alexishafen.

Thirteenth AF: 13 B–25's, with ftr cover, bomb Korovo village and docks on Shortland I. 8 others, with ftr escort, hit Buka. Afterwards the ftrs strafe Kieta and Tenekow. Other ftrs and B–34's on armed rcn, patrol, and night snooper missions attack numerous T/Os throughout Bougainville.

Seventh AF: 16 B–24's flying out of Baker and Nanumea bomb Maloelap. 3 HBs are shot down; US gunners claim 8 ftrs destroyed.

21 December

Ninth AF: 84 B–26's bomb V-weapon sites and other tgts in France.

Twelfth AF: Gen Cannon takes cmd. B–25's bomb Terracina. P–40's hit same tgt and also bomb positions and munitions factory S of Sant' Elia Fiumerapido. A–36's bomb positions, fuel dump, and munitions factory in Cervaro area, and hit trains, seaplane base, radar station, trucks, and other tgts in Rome-Civitavecchia area.

Fifteenth AF: Operations are restricted to weather rcn and to air-sea rescue patrols N of Corfu.

Fourteenth AF: 29 B–24's pound railroad yards at Chiengmai. Warehouse area along W side of the yards suffers very heavy damage. 14 B–25's, with ftr escort, attack Hwajung.

Fifth AF: Pre-invasion air strikes continue against Cape Gloucester as more than 100 B–24's, B–25's, and A–20's pound the area. P–39's strafe tgts along Borgen and Rein Bays. P–40's and A–20's hit Hoskins A/F. P–47's claim 17 ftrs shot down in Arawe area. A–20's hit camps N of Finschhafen. B–25's bomb and cannon Madang. B–24's bomb Amahai A/F. P–40's hit Kaukenau.

Thirteenth AF: 6 B–25's attack Monoitu Mission. During 21/22 Dec snoopers bomb various bivouac areas on Bougainville.

Seventh AF: 8 B–24's from Nanumea escort 4 Navy PB4Y's on photo mission over Kwajalein Atoll. The B–24's bomb shipping and aircraft landing grounds and other facilities at Roi, Ennuebing, and Kwajalein Is. A–24's, along with Navy and Marine aircraft, hit shipping and A/Fs at Emidj I. 16 P–39's strafe fuel dumps, shipping, and AA at Mille.

22 December

AAF: Orders are issued for Gen Spaatz to take cmd of USSAFE. Gen Eaker, Eighth AF CG, is to cmd Allied AFs in MTO, after remaining in UK until mid-Jan to advise Spaatz and Gen Doolittle, the new CG, Eighth AF.

Eighth AF: 439 B–17's and B–24's bomb M/Ys at Osnabruck and Munster. Heavy cloud conditions along with malfunction of Pathfinder equipment result in a large number of HBs failing to attack tgts. 2 aircraft are lost on this mission. RAF LBs attack numerous NOBALL tgts in France in conjunction with Osnabruck-Munster raids.

Ninth AF: 210 B–26's sent to bomb special tgts in France are recalled because of bad weather.

Twelfth AF: Gen Williams reassumes cmd of XII TCC (Prov). P–

40's and Spitfires of Twelfth AF, RAF, SAAF, and RAAF hit strong points in Tollo-Miglianico-Chieti areas. P–40's blast bridge, locomotives, trucks, and railroad tracks at and near Tortoreto and Benedello. P–47's strafe T/Os in area around Zara.

Fifteenth AF: Operations are again limited to weather rcn.

Fourteenth AF: 7 B–25's, with ftr escort, bomb Hwajung. 2 others claim 3 direct hits on freighter 105 mi S of Hong Kong. 65 Japanese bmrs and ftrs attack Kunming A/F. 10 P–40's and a P–38 from Kunming and several ftrs from Yunnani engage the enemy force in a 50-min running battle, claiming 12 airplanes shot down. 2 US aircraft are destroyed on the ground. Damage to A/F is not serious. 7 P–40's intercept a force of 58 airplanes heading toward Chengkung, shooting down 3 of them and preventing attack on the A/F.

Fifth AF: 130-plus B–24's, B–25's, and A–20's continue bombardment of Cape Gloucester. Japanese air raid on Arawe causes minor damage. Nearly 40 B–25's, with P–38 escort, bomb Wewak and Boram. The P–38's, B–25's, and some P–47's on sweep claim at least 13 aircraft shot down. B–25's and P–39's bomb A/F and barges at Madang and town of Alexishafen. A–20's and B–26's pound occupied area N of Finschhafen.

Thirteenth AF: B–25's carry out strikes against Numa Numa, Kahili supply area, Buka's Chinatown area, and scattered T/Os. Ftr aircraft and B–24's attack barge concentrations and hide-outs at Sohano I, Chabai-Porton area, Anewa Bay, and Ambitle I, and several T/Os throughout Bou-

gainville. B–24's, operating individually and in pairs, attack T/Os near Bonis, near Porton, and at Sohano I.

Seventh AF: 11 A–24's from Makin dive-bomb cargo ships in Mille lagoon. Escort is provided by 32 P–39's and F6F's. The P–39's strafe the ship and AA and gasoline dumps on the island. The vessel is left burning.

23 December

Eighth AF: 3 P–47 sqs (2 sqs carrying bombs) attack Gilze/Rijen A/F.

Twelfth AF: P–40's and P–47's attempt to spt Yugoslav partisans resisting German invasion of Korcula I off Peljesac Peninsula, but bad weather prevents location of tgts.

Fifteenth AF: B–26's hit viaduct at Antheor and railroad bridge and M/Y at Imperia. Ventimiglia railroad bridge is attacked. Bridge is not hit but overpass, tunnel, tracks, and transformer station nearby are damaged.

Fourteenth AF: 29 B–24's, escorted by 7 P–51's and 23 P–40's, pound White Cloud A/F in Canton area. The HBs and ftrs claim 11 interceptors downed. 14 P–38's dive-bomb and strafe Huang Shan Kou. 2 B–25's claim 1 gunboat sunk in Formosa Straits.

Tenth AF: 19 B–24's on night raid bomb railroad terminal at Bangkok. Heavy explosions and large fires result.

Fifth AF: 61 B–24's bomb Cape Gloucester during the day. B–24's follow during 23/24 Dec with harassing attacks with small bombs, hand grenades, and beer bottles. P–39's hit barges between Borgen Bay and Rein Bay, and P–40's bomb Gasmata and strafe Cape Hoskins. 80-plus B–25's,

B–26's, and A–20's attack coastal tgts from Wewak to Hansa Bay, wide areas of Huon Peninsula, and A/Fs at Alexishafen. B–24's bomb Nabire.

Thirteenth AF: 17 B–25's attack gun positions and other tgts at Sohano I, and 6 hit positions at Malevoli in Choiseul Bay. 6 B–34's attack radar station and lighthouse on Cape Saint George. 16 P–39's on patrol bomb and strafe tgts on Shortland I. 18 B–24's bomb Taharai A/F in Rabaul area. Vunakanau also is hit. Ftr escorts claim 30 aircraft shot down over Rabaul area. This begins a CO-MAIRSOLS all-out offensive against Rabaul area that continues until the end of Mar 44.

Seventh AF: During 23/24 Dec, P–39's are airborne over Makin to intercept enemy bmrs. 2 bmrs are shot down. 1 P–39 is lost. During the day, 19 B–24's, staging through Tarawa from Nanumea, bomb Kwajalein. 9 others, staging through Baker from Canton I, hit Wotje and Maloelap. 10 A–24's, escorted by 20 P–39's, attack Mille, hitting shore installations and cargo vessel (wrecked by previous day's raid) in lagoon.

24 December

Eighth AF: 26 HB gps are now operational. 670 HBs attack 23 missile-launching sites being constructed in Pas de Calais area. This is largest number of aircraft carrying out attacks of any Eighth AF mission to date and the first of its major strikes against missile sites. No aircraft are lost.

Ninth AF: Over 60 MBs attack NOBALL tgts in Pas de Calais area. More than 30 other MBs abort due to bad weather.

Twelfth AF: Weather severely hampers operations. P–40's fail to locate tgt, a vessel at Ugljan I, but shoot down 1 airplane in the Adriatic.

Fifteenth AF: Over 100 B–26's dispatched to bomb Pisa M/Y fail to locate tgt due to overcast. 24 of the MBs bomb M/Y at Cecina.

Fourteenth AF: 18 B–24's bomb Tien Ho satellite A/F. The HBs and 18 escorting ftrs claim 20 interceptors shot down. 1 HB is lost over the tgt.

Fifth AF: Pre-invasion bombing effort against Cape Gloucester reaches its peak as nearly 190 B–24's, B–25's, and A–20's pound the area in a day-long bombardment. P–39's hit disabled destroyer offshore. Japanese forces in Arawe area are hit by A–20's. A–20's also sweep NE New Guinea coastline. B–25's bomb Atamboea.

Thirteenth AF: During 23/24 Dec, single aircraft carry out harassing strikes against Buka, Kieta, and Faisi. During the day, 24 B–25's attack seaplane anchorage at Bonis. 18 B–24's bomb Vunakanau A/F at Rabaul. 6 others hit Lakunai. Ftr cover for the strike fights fierce air action with interceptors, claiming 25 shot down. 7 Allied ftrs are lost. B–34's on armed rcn bomb barges and troops in N Bougainville and claim 2 ftrs shot down E of Cape Saint George.

Seventh AF: 18 B–24's, staging through the Gilberts from the Ellice Is, bomb Wotje.

25 December

Twelfth AF: A–36's bomb road, trucks, and town area at Pontecorvo.

P–40's, with a few SAAF Spitfires, hit motor launch in Peljesac Channel.

Fifteenth AF: B–26's pound Pisa-Porta Nuova area, scoring especially damaging hits in M/Ys. B–17's hit Bolzano M/Y. B–24's hit Pordenone M/Y and T/Os at Vicenza. B–17's of 2 gps fail to locate tgts due to bad weather, and many ftrs ticketed for escort duty fail to rendezvous with HBs in the overcast skies.

Fourteenth AF: 2 B–25's claim heavy damage to passenger ship S of Hong Kong.

Fifth AF: Cape Gloucester is subjected to almost around the clock air attacks by 180-plus B–24's, B–25's, B–26's, and A–20's. A–20's attack Japanese forces in Arawe area where Allied outposts and observation posts are being pushed back by fierce enemy assaults on beachhead.

Thirteenth AF: A few B–24's, fighting bad weather, attack Rabaul area, concentrating on Lakunai A/F. Covering ftrs claim 13 airplanes shot down. 2 P–38's are lost.

Seventh AF: 10 A–24's from Makin, supported by P–39's, attack Mille, hitting runway, ammunition storage, and an AA position.

26 December

Norwegian Sea: British Home Fleet units sink battlecruiser *Scharnhorst* off North Cape.

Twelfth AF: Weather limits operations to uneventful rcn flights.

Fifteenth AF: B–26's bomb M/Ys at Prato, Empoli, and Pistoia.

Fifth AF: US 1st Marine Div lands at Cape Gloucester at 0746. 270-plus B–25's, B–24's, and A–20's plaster the area between the Cape and Borgen Bay from 0714 to 1614.

Enemy aircraft attacking the landing force sink a destroyer and cause considerable damage to other ships, but P–38's, P–40's, and P–47's claim over 60 airplanes shot down over the invasion area.

Thirteenth AF: 7 B–25's, with 34 ftrs, attack Cape Saint George area. 25 B–25's pound bivouac and supply area at Kahili. B–34's on rcn bomb Chivaroi and Faisi.

Seventh AF: 16 B–24's, staging through Tarawa, bomb Wotje. P–39's fly rcn and strafing missions over Mille.

27 December

Twelfth AF: B–25's attack vessel near Zara. A–36's attack tgts in Italy, hitting factory and railroad at Anagni, harbor and railroad facilities at Civitavecchia, bridge at Pontecorvo, and several gun positions and vehicles.

Fifteenth AF: B–26's hit viaducts at Zoagli and Recco and attack, but fail to hit, M/Y at Poggibonsi.

Fourteenth AF: 10 P–40's strafe buildings on Pailochi A/F and sink nearby river boat. 2 locomotives N of Yoyang are also destroyed. 4 P–40's bomb Phu Tho A/F, and strafe A/F at Dong Cuong. 36 Japanese airplanes attack Suichwan A/F, destroying 1 B–25, the alert shack, and 3 fuel dumps. US interceptors claim 4 of the attackers shot down. 1 P–40 is lost.

Fifth AF: A–20's attack positions in Cape Gloucester battle zone. B–25's hit villages and tracks from Rottock Bay to Riebeck Bay and strafe barges along New Britain's S coast. B–24's bomb A/F at Hoskins. B–25's bomb Madang and hit coastal tgts along Huon Peninsula. B–24's bomb Alexishafen. P–47's strafe road near Bogia.

Thirteenth AF: 20-plus B–25's bomb seaplane anchorage at Buka, strafe AA guns SE of Ramandata, bomb Kahili supply dumps, and attack Kieta bivouac and other tgts in the area. A few B–34's hit barges at Ambitle and Anir Is. 16 P–38's join 70-plus Navy dive bmrs in strikes on Buka AA positions. About 40 Allied ftrs sweep Rabaul area, claiming 17 aircraft shot down.

28 December

Eighth AF: 20th Ftr Gp (P–38) becomes operational, making a total of 11 operational ftr gps in Eighth AF. VIII FC has flown over 17,500 sorties and destroyed more than 200 aircraft. VIII BC is charged with forming and trg special organization (Radio Counter Measure Unit) to use radio countermeasures against enemy defenses. 24 specially equipped HBs, contributed by both US and British forces, are to operate in spt of both night and day raids.

Twelfth AF: B–25's, A–20's, and A–36's, in coordination with MA CAF HBs and MBs operating against tgts in Rome area, bomb landing grounds at Ciampino, bridge at Roccasecca and road and railway to the E of town, ships and harbor at Civitavecchia, and railway sidings W of Frosinone. P–40's hit harbor at Anzio and comm in Pontecorvo and Atina areas.

Fifteenth AF: 15th Combat Mapping Sq (attached to Fifteenth AF from Mediterranean Allied Photo Rcn Wg) begins operations, carrying out rcn of area from France to Greece

and thus providing Fifteenth AF with rcn of its tgt system. Over 100 B–26's hit Guidonia and Centocelle A/Fs and railroad bridges N and S of Orvieto. A like number of B–17's and B–24's bomb Rimini M/Y and, on return flight, hit bridge over Foglia R at Pesaro and road-railway intersection S of town. 17 B–24's dispatched to hit Vicenza M/Y are attacked by about 50 ftrs before reaching tgt. 10 of the unescorted HBs are lost. Several B–24's salvo bombs over tgt area and, in the fierce battle, claim 18 ftrs shot down.

Fourteenth AF: 4 B–25's and 4 P–51's attack Yangtze R shipping at Chihchow. 1 cargo ship is claimed sunk, 2 others damaged, and an armed motor vessel set aflame. 7 P–40's bomb building on railroad siding at Yun-chi.

Thirteenth AF: 14 B–24's bomb supply areas at Bonis. 22 B–25's hit Kahili supply area. Another large ftr sweep of Rabaul area results in claims of more than 20 airplanes shot down.

Seventh AF: 15 B–24's from Funafuti and Canton Is, staging through Baker and Tarawa, hit Maloelap, Mille, and Majuro. 18 A–24's from Makin, with escort of 20 P–39's, attack Mille. This attack is followed by another against the atoll carried out by 9 B–25's from Tarawa, supported by 12 Makin-based P–39's.

29 December

Twelfth AF: P–40's hit vessel on N side of Peljesac Peninsula and railway station at Anagni. A–36's attack railway station at Ferentino, harbor and railroad yard at Civitavecchia, and truck park near Aquino.

Fifteenth AF: B–26's attack M/Y

and bridge at Certaldo, M/Ys at Poggibonsi and viaduct at Bucine, and bridge in NW part of Orvieto. B–17's blast M/Ys at Ferrara and Rimini.

Fourteenth AF: 4 P–40's on armed rcn strafe railroad station, yards, and town area at Hsipaw, hit numerous freight cars between Hsipaw and Mansam Falls, and attack railroad yards at Hopong. 3 B–25's on shipping sweep along Yangtze R claim a cargo vessel and an armed passenger ship sunk SW of Wuhu.

Fifth AF: 120-plus B–24's, B–25's, and B–26's pound positions at Cape Gloucester as US Marines take major objective, the A/F. B–25's hit Madang. B–24's bomb bivouac and comm tgts near Sio, and other B–24's fly light attack against Manokwari, hitting town and shipping.

30 December

Eighth AF: 658 HBs, escorted by P–51's and P–38's, attack oil plant at Ludwigshafen. 23 HBs are lost on mission.

Ninth AF: About 100 B–26's bomb Saint-Omer A/F and V-weapon sites on French N coast. About 100 others abort missions because of bad weather.

Twelfth AF: B–25's bomb Zara, hitting junction, railway station, repair shops, warehouse, and harbor. A–20's hit Atina. P–40's and A–36's spt ground forces, hitting tgts in Chieti-Miglianico area. Vessels are hit at Crkvice, railway sidings near Frosinone, gun positions near Arce and W of Minturno, and town areas of Sant' Elia Fiumerapido, Ferentino, and Atina are bombed.

Fifteenth AF: B–17's bomb M/Ys at Rimini and Padua. 2 HBs are lost on the Rimini mission. The HBs and escorting P–38's and P–47's claim destruction of 9 ftrs during air battles in Padua-Vicenza area, off coast E of Ravenna, and S of Aquila. B–26's hit Borgo San Lorenzo M/Y and viaduct, M/Y at Viareggio, and road junction near Roccasecca.

Tenth AF: 20 B–24's pound Monywa, hitting railway facilities and the area in general.

Fourteenth AF: 8 Japanese ftrs strafe Suichwan A/F while 12 others provide cover. 2 US airplanes are destroyed on the ground. 8 P–40's intercept the formation after the attack and shoot down 3 aircraft.

Fifth AF: A–20's hit positions in Cape Gloucester area as US Marines completely secure A/F. B–24's and B–25's bomb Alexishafen and Madang areas, Sio, and T/Os along coast of Huon Peninsula. P–39's strafe barges along Huon Peninsula. P–47's strafe Madang area and huts between Sio and Vincke Pt.

Thirteenth AF: 16 B–24's and 35 B–25's bomb Kahili and bivouac and supply areas in the vicinity. 19 B–24's, with 25 ftrs covering, attack shipping at Rabaul and also hit Tobera A/F. The escorts encounter aggressive ftr opposition and claim 12 shot down. 6 B–25's bomb Korovo area.

Seventh AF: 17 B–24's, flying from Tarawa, bomb Kwajalein. 9 B–25's from Tarawa hit town of Jabor on Jaluit Atoll. A–24's from Makin, escorted by 24 P–39's, dive-bomb gun positions on Mille. Adv HQ, Seventh AF, is moved from Funafuti to Tarawa, where it remains until completion of main campaign in Gilbert and Marshall Is.

31 December

Eighth AF: Almost 500 HBs attack tgts in France and off French coast. Tgts include a blockade runner, industries at Paris, and A/Fs at Bordeaux, Cognac, Saint-Jean-d' Angely, La Rochelle, and Landes de Bussac. 25 airplanes are lost to AA fire and ftrs. Total bomb tonnage dropped by the Eighth in Dec, 13,142 tons, for the first time exceeds that dropped by RAF BC.

Ninth AF: Around 200 B–26's bomb V-weapon sites in French coastal area.

Twelfth AF: P–40's and Spitfires of AAF, RAF, RAAF, and SAAF, strike inf and heavy arty around Tollo, Orsogna, Miglianico, Ripa, and Teatina in spt of British Eighth Army. A–36's bomb town of Formia and hit gun positions.

Fifteenth AF: 154th Tac Rcn Sq is transferred from XII Trg Cmd to Fifteenth AF for purpose of flying weather rcn, a duty presently being handled by a P–38 unit called Fifteenth AF Weather Rcn Det (and by some B–26's of 3 MB gps which are transferred to Twelfth AF after this date). Personnel and equipment of the 154th Tac Rcn Sq and the Weather Rcn Det are subsequently integrated, and the unit is redesignated the 154th Tac Rcn Sq (Weather). Operations are limited to weather rcn.

Fourteenth AF: 25 B–24's pound Lampang railroad yards, causing several big fires and many secondary explosions. 6 B–25's hit Yangtze R shipping in Anking and Lu-Kuan areas, claiming 3 cargo vessels and a troop carrier sunk. 2 others on sea sweep damage passenger vessel in Hainan Straits.

Fifth AF: A–20's hit troop concentrations in Cape Gloucester area. Nearly 50 P–40's and P–47's intercept small force of airplanes attacking Arawe beachhead area. 12 aircraft are claimed shot down. Almost 150 HBs and MBs pound Madang, Alexishafen, and Bogadjim areas.

1944

1 January

USSAFE: USSAFE is established for operational control of Eighth and Fifteenth AFs. (See 22 Feb 44.)

Eighth AF: The Operational Research Section, organized at Hq VIII BC in Oct 43, is made a special staff section, accountable directly to the CoS. It is composed mostly of civilian specialists trained in statistical analysis and other disciplines pertinent to studying operations of a strat bombing force. The section subsequently proves of great value in improving effectiveness of strat bombing.

AAFMTO: Complete reorganization of USAAF units in MTO takes place: USAAFNATO is redesignated MTO (AAFMTO); XII AFSC becomes AAFSCMTO; III Air Serv Area Cmd (Sp) becomes XII AFSC; II Air Serv Area Cmd becomes XV AFSC; XII AF Engineer Cmd (Prov) becomes AAF Engineer Cmd, MTO (Prov); and XII AF Trg Cmd is changed to XII AF Trg and Repl Cmd. XII BC is reorganized as an MB organization (3 B–25 gps and the 3 B–26 gps of 42d Bomb Wg) under Gen Knapp.

Fifteenth AF: The 3 remaining MB gps (B–26's) of Fifteenth AF are transferred to Twelfth AF, leaving the Fifteenth with 6 HB (2d, 93d, 97th, 99th, 301st, 376th) and 4 ftr gps (1st, 14th, 82d, and 325th), or 4 B–17, 2 B–24, 1 P–47, and 3 P–38 gps.

Tenth AF: 6 B–25's, along with 16 P–38's, attack bridge on Mu R between Ywataung and Monywa. Maj Robert A Erdin, piloting the lead MB, pulls up during his bomb run to avoid a tree. He releases his bombs as he noses up, and topples 2 spans of the bridge into the river. Subsequent tests prove this a good bridge-bombing maneuver. The tactic is refined and the sq (490th Sq) becomes so proficient as to gain the sobriquet "Burma Bridge Busters." Further N, 11 A–36's and 15 P–51's pound A/F at Myitkyina.

Fourteenth AF: 4 P–40's bomb and strafe T/Os in Indochina, including barracks and rafts along the Yuan R in the Cam Duong-Lao Kay area.

Fifth AF: 120-plus B–24's, B–25's, and A–20's pound Saidor area in preparation for Allied invasion. Other B–25's bomb Madang and Alexishafen. A–20's continue to hit troop concentration in Cape Gloucester area. B–25's hit positions at Borgen Bay. P–39's strafe barges along New Britain's N coast.

Thirteenth AF: 868th Bomb Sq is activated to work directly under XIII BC. The unit, equipped with SB–24's (radar equipped aircraft used for night missions), becomes known as the "Snooper Squadron." 15 B–24's, escorted by 70-plus P–38's and F6F's, bomb Lakunai A/F. Ftr and AA opposition is heavy, with 80–90 ftrs attempting interception. US airplanes claim 20 ftrs shot down. 1 B–24 is shot down and 2, severely damaged, crashland at Torokina. Allied ftrs join Navy dive bmrs in spt of ground forces in Torokina area. 6 B–25's and 2 B–24's bomb Kahili. 4 B–24's hit Manob.

Seventh AF: 16 P–39's strafe Mille harbor and attack shipping N of Mille. 2 small vessels are heavily damaged.

2 January

Twelfth AF: B–25's bomb Terni M/Y and iron works and nearby barracks. P–40's and Spitfires from AAF, RCAF, RAAF, SAAF, and RAF blast snowbound vehicles in Avezzano-Popoli area, warehouses at San Benedetto de Marsi and gun positions and defended areas around Chieti. A–36's hit Civitavecchia harbor and M/Y to the S of town, Anagni M/Y and nearby gun positions, and other T/Os. B–26's bomb bridges at Riva Santo Stefano and Ventimiglia, M/Y at Arma di Taggia, and bridge over Var R.

Fifteenth AF: P–47's fly uneventful sweep over Rome area.

Tenth AF: 27 B–25's and 16 P–39's hit fuel plant and work shops at Yenangyaung and set oilfield aflame. 13 B–24's also hit the refinery, causing large fire, and bomb a power station. 4 other B–24's bomb Akyab on W coast. About 30 A–36's and P–51's score hits on Loilaw bridge approaches and bomb towns in the vicinity.

Fourteenth AF: 8 P–40's bomb and strafe Japanese HQ and barracks at Hopang.

Fifth AF: Elements of US 32d Div make amphibious landing at Saidor following preparatory naval bombard-

ment. Bad weather prevents preparatory air strikes, but over 80 B–24's and A–20's pound positions in coordination with the landings. Harbor and A/F are captured. Other B–24's bomb Pombelaa and Amboina. B–25's and B–26's bomb Madang. P–40's strafe A/F, AA positions, barges, and supply dump at Cape Hoskins.

Thirteenth AF: 24 B–25's bomb Buka supply area. 30-plus Allied ftrs sweep Rabaul area, claiming 11 airplanes shot down. 1 Navy ftr is lost.

Seventh AF: B–24's, staging through Tarawa, bomb Maloelap. 9 B–25's hit tgts on Jaluit. P–39's strafe shipping at Mille.

3 January

Twelfth AF: Gen Morris assumes cmd of XII FC. B–25's bomb troop concentration area at Prijedor, and along with SAAF and RAF Baltimores, hit Split and Sibenik. P–40's and A–36's bomb gun positions near Cassino, Anagni railroad station, village near Vicenza, railway and trains between Ceccano and Segni, and harbor at Civitavecchia. P–40's, with SAAF and RCAF Spitfires, hit over 100 vehicles in Avezzano-Sulmona area. Other P–40's, with AAF, RAF, SAAF, and RAAF ftrs, hit tgts in Filetto-Tollo areas in spt of ground troops.

Fifteenth AF: Gen Twining becomes CG. B–17's, escorted by P–38's bomb Villarperosa ball bearing works and Lingotto M/Y and Fiat motor works in Turin area. P–47's fly top cover for the HBs as far as Italian coast, then turn and carry out uneventful sweep over Rome area.

Tenth AF: 22 A–36's and P–51's hit warehouses and dump area at

Sahmaw. 19 B–25's, along with 16 P–38's, bomb pumping station at Yenangyaung, setting oil tanks afire. 10 B–24's follow with strike on a pumping station at Yenangyaung, causing explosions and leaving tgt in flames.

Fourteenth AF: 28 B–24's attack railroad yards at Lampang. 5 FBs attack town of Pingkai.

Fifth AF: 50-plus B–24's and B–25's bomb Alexishafen area. More than 20 A–20's hit positions at Borgen Bay.

Thirteenth AF: 30-plus Allied ftrs again sweep Rabaul area, claiming 6 Zeros shot down. 6 B–24's bomb Kavieng, and several others abort due to bad weather. 6 B–25's bomb Moisuru bivouac area near Kahili, and 15 more hit supply areas near Buka Passage.

Seventh AF: 24 A–24's from Makin dive-bomb AA positions and radar and radio facilities on Mille. 20 supporting P–39's strafe runways and oil storage.

4 January

Eighth AF: Over 500 HBs attack tgts in Germany with most of them bombing port area, sub yards, and industrial area of Kiel. City of Munster is also attacked. US airplanes begin flying supplies from UK to underground resistance forces in W Europe, this operation being coded CARPETBAGGER.

Ninth AF: XIX A Spt Cmd is activated in England, and stationed at Middle Wallop. Gen Quesada assumes cmd. 253 B–26's bomb NOBALL tgts in France. Weather makes bombing difficult, and results range from unknown to good.

Twelfth AF: B–25's bomb Brodac

town area and M/Y, and town of Travnik. P–40's hit bridge and trains and fly patrols over battleline in Italy.

Fifteenth AF: Over 100 B–17's are dispatched to bomb Dupnica area in Bulgaria. 29 bomb the tgt area, but heavy cloud cover causes 77 HBs to return bombs to base. P–38's escort the HBs the total distance to and from tgts. P–47's provide escort part way.

Fifth AF: Over 100 HBs and MBs bomb Alexishafen, Madang, and Bogadjim areas and hit troops and supplies between Finschhafen and Saidor. B–25's attack arty positions in Cape Gloucester area. B–24's and B–25's hit shipping at Koepang and in nearby waters.

Thirteenth AF: B–24's bomb Sohano I, concentrating on seaplane base and supply area. B–25's pound gun positions at Tonolai and bomb Chabai. P–39's, B–34's, and night ftrs, operating individually or in small flights, hit tgts on Bougainville, including barges at Mutupina Pt and along Jaba R, and areas around Buka, Bonis, Poporang I, Papas, and Banin. 40-plus Allied ftrs attack Rabaul area and claim at least 10 airplanes shot down.

Seventh AF: 18 B–24's, staging through Tarawa, bomb Emidj.

5 January

Eighth AF: Eighth AF report concludes that US daylight strategic bombing program against Germany will be threatened unless steps are taken to reduce the enemy's ftr force, which has increased in strength in the W as a result of step-up in production, strengthening of firepower, and transfer of larger percentage of ftrs to Western Front. 426 HBs attack tgts in Germany and France. 216 of these hit Kiel while the others bomb Tours and Bordeaux A/Fs, and metals plant and M/Y at Neuss. About 25 losses are suffered in these raids.

Twelfth AF: A–36's hit gun positions N of Mignano and on S slope of Monte Porchia. Weather cancels other operations.

Tenth AF: 3 B–25's, supported by 8 P–38's, attack Mu R bridge between Monywa and Ywataung which is being rebuilt. Hits are scored on E bank near the bridge and several sheds are set afire. The escorting ftrs damage several nearby railway cars, strafe nearby town, set a barge afire, blow up 4 tin buildings, and claim a river steamer sunk.

Fifth AF: HBs and MBs bomb Alexishafen, Madang, and Bogadjim areas and attack barges from Finschhafen to Saidor. P–39's hit barges and gun positions during sweep from Sio to Bogadjim.

Thirteenth AF: B–25's bomb concentrations in Choiseul Bay area and Hahela Mission on S Buka I, while B–24's attack Tonolai, Kahili supply area, Fauro I, and Poporang building area.

6 January

USSAFE: Gen Spaatz assumes cmd and names Gen Frederick Anderson and Gen Knerr as Dep CGs for operations and administration.

Eighth AF: Gen Doolittle assumes cmd, replacing Gen Eaker who will go to Italy as CG MAAF.

Twelfth AF: B–26's bomb Pontedera hitting M/Y and Piaggio aircraft factory there, Lucca M/Y, and

railway N of Follonica. P–40 and A–36 FBs attack gun positions in Cervaro-Monte Trocchio area and near Aquino, town of Cervaro, railway at Civitavecchia, trains N and E of Rome, Velletri train station, and town of Fondi.

Fifteenth AF: Control of Fifteenth AF operations against tgts of CBO is placed under USSAFE.

Tenth AF: P–51's and A–36's carry out ground spt missions at Sumprabum and Taihpa Ga and hit cav bivouac and dumps at Kamaing. 12 P–40's attack supply dump S of Sahmaw Junction and strafe Pahok.

Fourteenth AF: 2 B–25's bomb a troop ship on the Yangtze, NE of Tungting Lake. The vessel is reported as sunk.

Fifth AF: B–24's and B–25's bomb Alexishafen and Bogadjim areas. A–20's attack tgts along road from Bogadjim to Yaula. B–25's attack T/Os on Huon Peninsula and others hit Borgen Bay area. P–39's strafe barges at Borgen and Rein Bays.

Thirteenth AF: P–38's sweep Rabaul area, claiming 9 Zeros shot down during running battle over Cape Gazelle area. B–25's and B–34's bomb and strafe tgts in Choiseul Bay area, including jetty areas and buildings at Tarekekori, tgts on Morgusaia I, and gun positions on Kondakanimboko I.

7 January

Eighth AF: 420 HBs hit I G Farben Industrie plant at Ludwigshafen. 12 aircraft are lost on mission.

Ninth AF: 35 B–36's bomb Cherbourg/Maupertus A/F. Bad weather restricts further operations.

Twelfth AF: B–25's strike Perugia A/F. A–20's hit defenses in close spt of US Fifth Army. B–26's hit M/Ys at Foligno and Arezzo and attack bridge at Roccasecca. A–36's hit gun positions, trucks, and trains in Cervaro-Aquino-Cassino area, bomb Aquino station, and hit Velletri railway yards. P–40's give close spt in Monte Maio, Monte La Chiaia, Monte Porchia, and Cedro Hill areas as Fifth Army drives toward Rapido R.

Fifteenth AF: B–17's, with P–38 escort, bomb an aircraft factory at Maribor and a torpedo factory at Fiume. The P–38's battle a superior number of enemy ftrs over Maribor area. 3 P–38's are lost and several others are missing. 4 ftrs are claimed destroyed, with 1 probably downed and 4 damaged, during the fierce half-hr fight.

Tenth AF: 7 B–25's and 15 P–38's pound Lanywa area, hitting oil plant and storage tanks, causing several fires, and strafe several AA positions. 19 A–36's and P–51's bomb supply and troop concentrations at Nanyaseik.

Fourteenth AF: 4 B–25's and 6 P–40's sink 2 large boats on the Yangtze S of Hukow and sink a large powerboat, a barge, and a small ore craft at Shihhweiyao. 11 P–38's claim between 30 and 40 sampans destroyed along the river from Hankow to Chiuchiang. 2 B–25's on sea sweep claim a 300-ft passenger vessel sunk S of Hong Kong.

Fifth AF: B–24's, B–25's, P–39's, and P–47's bomb Alexishafen-Madang area, hit Erima, Bogadjim, and tgts along Bogadjim Road, attack positions from Weber Pt to Vincke Pt, and strafe huts and barges near Saidor. B–24's bomb Cape Gloucester area. A–20's hit forces near Arawe. B–24's also hit Lorengau and Boela.

Thirteenth AF: Gen Hubert Harmon becomes CG. 8 sqs of Allied ftrs spt Navy dive bmrs in attack on Cape Saint George area. B–24's bomb Vunakanau A/F.

8 January

Twelfth AF: B–25's bomb harbor, warehouses, and railway at Metkovic. A–20's hit railway stations at Frosinone and in the Colleferro-Segni area. B–26's bomb M/Ys at Grosseto and Lucca. P–40's spt US Fifth Army in mts E and SE of Cassino, and, with A–36's, hit railway tgts S or Rome at Aquino, Frosinone, Palestrina, and Castelforte. Other P–40's hit Avezzano, and A–36's blast trains and vessels in vicinity of Tarquinia.

Fifteenth AF: The 449th and 450th Bomb Gps (B–24's) become operational, giving the Fifteenth a total of 8 HB gps. B–24's bomb Mostar A/F. B–17's hit Reggio Emilia aircraft factory. P–38's and P–47's fly escort.

Tenth AF: 20 P–51's and A–36's knock out bridge N of Hopin, destroy warehouse and railroad tracks in the area, and destroy a locomotive and damage numerous railroad cars at Tigyaingza.

Fifth AF: HBs, MBs, and a few ftrs, attack Madang area, bomb Uligan Harbor, and hit Bogadjim and Bogadjim Road. Ftrs strafe Sag Sag sawmill in Cape Gloucester area. B–25's and A–20's hit positions near Arawe. HBs bomb Kendari and other tgts on Celebes.

Thirteenth AF: B–24's bomb Kahili. B–25's hit concentrations on Siposai and Kondakanimboko Is.

Seventh AF: 15 B–24's, staging through Tarawa, bomb shipping and shore installations at several locations on Wotje, Maloelap, and Jaluit Atolls. 2 B–25's from Tarawa hit shipping and gun positions on Jaluit.

9 January

International: Churchill and De Gaulle meet at Marrakesh. They discuss cooperation of a French expeditionary force in invasion of Europe and the degree of authority of the French inside France after the invasion.

Twelfth AF: B–25's attack M/Y and docks at Ancona. P–40's hit tanks and trucks at Palena and S of Sulmona, and positions and vehicles near Cervaro. A–36's hit positions in same area.

Fifteenth AF: B–24's bomb Mostar A/F. B–17's hit aircraft factory and M/Y at Reggio Emilia. P–38's and P–47's provide escort.

Tenth AF: 21 P–51's and A–36's attack Loilaw area, severely damaging a bridge, hitting ammo storage building, and scoring direct hits on large barracks.

Fourteenth AF: 9 ftrs strafe 6 steamboats and many smaller craft on the Yangtze at Puchi. 2 B–25's on sea sweep bomb 200-ft vessel S of Swatow, reporting the ship destroyed. 8 FBs hit Sadon, and 4 bomb Atson railroad yards and Lao Kay railroad station.

Fifth AF: Ftrs and bmrs attack Alexishafen, Madang, Bogadjim, Uligan Harbor, and area E of Saidor. Cape Beechey is strafed by P–40's.

Thirteenth AF: B–25's hit Buka seaplane base and Kahili supply area. Ftrs strafe Cape Dunganon area and

along Ramusian R W of Teop. 7 sqs of Allied ftrs cover Navy dive bmr strike on Tobera. 2 sqs of B–24's pound Vunakanau A/F. 6 B–25's bomb Taharai A/F and afterwards some hit T/Os on New Ireland.

10 January

Twelfth AF: B–25's hit San Benedetto de Marsi. P–40's, with RAF, SAAF, and RAAF airplanes, hit comm, gun positions, trucks, and tanks at numerous points in and NW of battle area. Other P–40's give close spt to ground forces in Chieti area. A–36's hit trucks, tanks, trains, and other T/Os N of Rome.

Fifteenth AF: B–17's bomb Sofia, causing considerable damage in M/Ys. B–24's hit M/Y at Skoplje. P–38's and P–47's provide escort. Around 60 ftrs attack the Sofia force and fierce air battle ensues. 2 HBs are lost. The B–17's and ftr escorts claim 28 aircraft shot down.

Tenth AF: 12 A–36's and P–51's hit bivouac area at Nanyaseik. 15 P–40's attack bridge at Namti, damaging railroad tracks and the S approach to the bridge. During 9/10 Jan 7 B–24's lay mines in Menam R estuary near Bangkok and in Rangoon estuary. The HBs during the day bomb M/Y and A/F in Bangkok area and hit main jetty at Akyab. 9 B–25's mine Mokpalin ferry crossing over Sittang R.

Fourteenth AF: 8 P–31's bomb approach to Kienchang bridge and attack troop train N of Teian damaging the train and killing an estimated 100 soldiers. 3 B–25's and 8 P–40's sweep area from Anking to Chiuchiang, sinking a large motor launch, 2 100-ft barges, and a tug on the

Yangtze, and attacking a bridge at Teian and tracks S of Chiuchiang. 2 B–25's and 4 P–40's attack shipping on the Yangtze near Wusueh, sinking a launch and leaving 3 tankers burning.

Fifth AF: Over 100 HBs, MBs, LBs, and ftrs attack Madang, Alexishafen, and Bogadjim areas and coastline from Madang to Sio. P–39's strafe scattered villages and barges in New Britain. B–25's bomb Koepang.

Thirteenth AF: Gen Hubert Harmon, CG, begins HB campaign of night strikes. The 5th Bomb Gp opens the night raids sending 20 HBs on a strike against Lakunai A/F after a morning raid by 10 B–24's against nearby Vunakanau A/F. 5 B–24's hit Kahili supply area while 4 hit Chinatown area of Buka. AAF and Navy ftrs cover Navy dive bmr strike against Cape Saint George.

Seventh AF: 4 P–39's from Makin strafe Mille. 1 of the ftrs drops 2 500-lb bombs on fuel storage area. During 10/11 Jan, 16 B–24's, staging through Tarawa from Ellice Is, bomb Maloelap; 4 others, staging through Baker from Canton I, hit Mille.

11 January

Eighth AF: Over 570 B–17's and B–24's bomb industrial tgts and T/Os in Oschersleben, Halberstadt, and near Brunswick. Fierce opposition, estimated at 500 ftrs, is encountered, and 60 bmrs are lost. Among the Pathfinder aircraft are 4 B–24's, this being the first time B–24's are used in this capacity.

Twelfth AF: B–26's attack iron and steel works at Piombino during 10/11 Jan. During the day, B–25's bomb Falconara (hitting railroad junction) and railroad yards at Fabriano. P–40's and A–36's blast defenses and gun positions in Cervaro-Monte Trocchio, gun position N of Minturno, towns of Sora and Isola del Liri, road traffic in Macerata-Aquila-Popoli area, and railroad facilities at San Giorgio del Sannio.

Fifteenth AF: B–17's, with P–38 escort, bomb harbor at Piraeus. The HBs and ftrs destroy 8 attacking ftrs. 6 HBs are lost in midair collisions in heavy overcast.

Tenth AF: 36 A–36's, P–51's, and P–40's pound encampment containing about 4,900 troops and a large quantity of supplies, causing considerable damage by accurate bombing and strafing.

Fourteenth AF: Before daylight 14 Japanese bmrs hit Suichwan A/F. During the morning 3 MBs and 15 ftrs follow up with second strike. 7 P–51's and 5 P–40's intercept the second attack, claiming 3 MBs shot down. 8 B–24's bomb harbor, aluminum plant, and A/F at Takao. 1 bombs oil storage at Swatow. 4 B–24's mine harbors at Takao and Hong Kong. 1 HB is lost.

Fifth AF: B–25's, P–39's, and P–40's hit Uligan Harbor, barges and road near Bogadjim, Hansa Bay area, and town of Alexishafen.

Thirteenth AF: About 90 Allied ftrs cover 60-plus Navy dive bmrs attacking Cape Saint George area. 2 flights of P–39's strafe T/Os from Numa Numa to Koromira.

Seventh AF: 9 B–25's from Tarawa hit 5 vessels and land installations at Maloelap. A 5000-ton cargo ship and a small vessel are sunk. 4

P–39's from Makin dive-bomb and strafe runways on Mille.

12 January

Twelfth AF: Col Archibald Y Smith assumes cmd of XII AF Trg and Repl Cmd. B–25's and B–26's bomb Giulianova railway bridge and attack a dam and road bridge. A–20's hit San Donato. P–40's attack vessel in Krka R, hit enemy defensive positions at San Biagio Saracinesa, Sant' Elia Fiumerapido, Monte Trocchio, and Atina, and bomb Vallerotonda. A–36's attack Avezzano railroad yards, village near Atina, railroad facilities at Cisterna di Latina, and numerous trucks and train cars in Rome area.

Fifteenth AF: P–47's fly ftr sweep in Rome area, strafing M/Y at Teramo and buildings between Tronto and Tesino Rivers.

Tenth AF: 20-plus B–25's and P–38's hit M/Y at Letpadan, damaging warehouses, engine sheds, and other buildings. The ftrs also strafe Myohaung, setting 3 buildings afire.

Fourteenth AF: 14 B–24's bomb Bangsue M/Y at Bangkok.

Fifth AF: B–24's and B–25's attack Alexishafen area. A–20's hit Warai. B–24's attack Balikpapan, Makassar, and Dili.

Thirteenth AF: 13 B–25's of 42d Bomb Gp, on their first mission against Rabaul area, bomb Vunakanau A/F in early morning, and 16 B–24's hit Lakunai A/F during 12/13 Jan. 19 B–24's, with escort of about 50 ftrs, pound airstrip and other tgts at Tobera. 3 flights of P–39's bomb and strafe Teop, Inus Pt, Numa Numa, and Piano Mission. Other aircraft on armed rcn and sweeps hit

several T/Os throughout Bougainville area.

Seventh AF: 21 A–24's from Makin dive-bomb AA positions and storage area on Mille. 20 supporting P–39's strafe runways.

13 January

Ninth AF: 193 B–26's bomb NOBALL tgts in France. Ftr pilots report being tracked by AA rockets.

Twelfth AF: B–25's and B–26's bomb Guidonia, Centocelle, and Ciampino A/Fs. A–20's strike town of Atina. AAF, RAF, SAAF, and RAAF FBs hit shipping along Dalmatian coast at Sibenik and in Krka R. A–36's hit town and railway yards at Isola del Liri, factory at Colleferro, docks at Formia, railroad yards at Valmontone, and railway station SE of Frosinone. P–40's hit Sant' Elia Fiumerapido, San Biagio, Saracinesa, and rail and road junction near Villa Latina.

Fifteenth AF: B–17's bomb Centocelle and Guidonia A/Fs and B–24's hit Perugia A/F. P–38's provide escort, and P–47's fly top cover for the B–17 missions. The HBs destroy several ftrs in aerial combat.

Tenth AF: Gen Wolfe, CG, arrives at New Delhi with ADVON of XX BC staff. This is the first important movement of personnel for Operation MATTERHORN. 6 P–51's hit troop concentrations at Lalawng Ga and bomb Maran Ga and Shaduzup. 27 P–40's attack comm center and dumps along Kamaing-Mogaung road. 4 P–51's and a B–25 pound A/F and supply area at Myitkyina.

Fourteenth AF: 2 B–25's on sweep from Hong Kong to Hainan attack 4 large boats, several warehouses, radio station, and a car at Ft Bayard. 1 of the vessels explodes. 6 P–40's on armed rcn strafe 4 pack trains of about 15 animals each between Lungling and Tengchung.

Fifth AF: Gen Wurtsmith becomes CG V FC. 130-plus B–24's, B–25's, and P–40's attack Alexishafen. B–24's bomb Gasmata. B–24's and B–25's strike Kaukenau and Timoeka and score hit on freighter off Tanimbar Is.

Thirteenth AF: HQ moves from Espiritu Santo to Guadalcanal. During predawn hrs 11 B–25's bomb Tobera, Rapopo, Wide Bay area, and coast S of Rapopo. P–39's strafe Tinputs area.

Seventh AF: 9 B–25's from Tarawa attack harbor shipping at Wotje. 21 A–24's from Makin dive-bomb dock, barracks, and storage area on Mille. Some of 16 escorting P–39's strafe ground tgts, and 10 other P–39's carry out strafing mission over Mille.

14 January

Eighth AF: 527 B–17's and B–24's bomb 20 V-weapon sites in the Pas de Calais area.

Twelfth AF: B–25's strike Pontecorvo bridge. A–20's offer close spt to US Fifth Army forces in Monte Trocchio area. P–40's blast Loreto tank repair shops. P–40's and A–36's hit defenses in San Giuseppe, Sant' Elia Fiumerapido, and Monte Trocchio areas. A–36's also attack road and buildings E of Minturno, town of Isola del Liri, and harbor at Anzio.

Fifteenth AF: Around 200 B–24's and B–17's attack town area and A/F at Mostar. P–38's provide escort throughout the missions, and P–47's

join the B–17's at the tgt and cover the flight back to base.

Tenth AF: Bad weather limits operations to ftr patrols in Sumprabum area.

Fourteenth AF: 4 B–25's on coastal sweep from Pakhoi to Haiphong bomb group of buildings on Weichow I. 2 B–24's damage 2 vessels near Saint John I.

Fifth AF: 50-plus B–24's, B–25's, and P–40's hit Alexishafen and Erima area. B–24's bomb Cape Busching. B–25's attack T/Os along N coast of New Britain, and A–20's strike villages along S coast.

Thirteenth AF: During 13/14 Jan, 15 B–24's bomb Vunakanau and Lakunai A/Fs, Rabaul, Rapopo, and Malaguna. Just before dawn, 12 B–25's hit Au, Cape Gazelle, and Buka. P–39's join Navy SBD's in bombing Wakunai. 70-plus Allied ftrs spt strike by more than 50 Navy dive bmrs against shipping in Simpson Harbor. Ftrs claim 27 aircraft shot down.

Seventh AF: 12 B–24's, staging through Tarawa, bomb 3 islands in Kwajalein Atoll. 3 B–25's from Makin fly mission against shipping at Wotje. 2 of the MBs attack 2 small vessels, sinking 1 and damaging the other. The other B–25 bombs a runway and building on S part of Wotje.

15 January

MAAF: Gen Eaker assumes cmd of MAAF and AAFMTO, replacing ACM Tedder and Gen Spaatz, who along with AVM Coningham and numerous other American and British officers have departed for UK.

Twelfth AF: B–25's attack Foligno railway junction. B–26's bomb bridges at Orvieto, P–40's of

79th Ftr Gp and RAF 239 Wg hit San Valentino station in joint attack. A–36's and other P–40's, in spt of US Fifth Army forces, hit gun positions and strongpoints, especially at Picinisco and Atina. P–40's on armed rcn hit railroad W of Frosinone station and strafe Ceccano station and railway cars.

Fifteenth AF: B–24's bomb Prato M/Y and industrial area, and also hit roads in area and drop several bombs in town of Pistoia. B–17's concentrate on railroad yards and bridges in Florence area at Certaldo, Poggibonsi, Montalto di Castro, Arezzo, Civitavecchia, and near Porto Civitanova and Orvieto, and hit scattered T/Os. Ftrs escort all the missions.

Tenth AF: 4 P–40's and a B–25 over N Burma hit train at Pinwe.

Fourteenth AF: 2 B–25's on sea sweep along Indochina coast bomb Hongay power plant and sink gunboat in nearby cove to the SW. Coal grading building at Campha Port is also bombed. 2 B–25's on sweep off SE China coast sink wooden vessel off Swatow and damage lighthouse on Nampang I. 2 others shoot down Japanese bmr N of Chikhom.

Fifth AF: B–24's and B–25's pound Uligan Harbor. P–40's, P–47's, and B–25's hit Madang, Alexishafen, Erima, and Bogadjim area. Enemy positions along S coast of New Britain are attacked by B–25's and P–39's.

Thirteenth AF: 24 B–25's, with 60 ftrs escorting, pound East Cape. P–39's attack barges and trucks at Chabai.

Seventh AF: 9 B–25's from Tarawa flying at deck-level bomb and strafe shipping and shore in-

stallations at Maloelap. 2 vessels are hit and oil dump, hangars, other buildings, and runways are damaged. 1 B–25 crashes at sea after being hit by AA fire.

16 January

ETO: Gen Eisenhower assumes duties of Supreme Cmdr, AEF.

Twelfth AF: B–25's bomb M/Y and choke points at Terni. B–26's attack M/Y and bridge at Orte. A–20's bomb town of Atina. P–40's attack bridges in San Giorgio del Sannio area and gun emplacements near Cassino, Sant' Angelo in Theodice, and Picinisco. A–36's hit railway junction at Cecina, road and railway S of Siena, and town areas of Avezzano and Formia.

Fifteenth AF: B–24's attack Osoppo landing ground and town of Zara. The HBs claim 9 ftrs shot down. 1 B–24 is destroyed in aerial combat. B–17's bomb Messerschmitt factory at Klagenfurt and landing ground at Villaorba. Escorting ftrs claim 3 aircraft destroyed. 3 P–38's are shot down.

Fourteenth AF: 8 P–40's attack town of Pingkai and strafe T/Os in surrounding valley area.

Fifth AF: Madang, Erima, and Bogadjim areas are hit by B–25's, A–20's, and P–40's. P–39's strafe area from Sio to Bogadjim. B–25's bomb area N from Cape Croisilles. B–24's and B–25's attack positions near Arawe. B–24's carry out light raid on Amboina harbor.

Seventh AF: 25 A–24's, 16 P–39's, and 8 P–40's from Makin strike Mille. The A–24's bomb and strafe AA positions and storage areas, the P–40's bomb and strafe barracks and AA emplacements, and the P–39's strafe runways. 2 P–39's are lost. P–39's sent up on interceptor missions claim 3 airplanes destroyed over Mille and Makin.

17 January

Twelfth AF: B–25's attack M/Ys at Terni, Chiaravalle, and Montemarciano. B–26's strike Orte railway bridge and Viterbo M/Y. P–40's hit Sibenik harbor, bridge at San Giorgio del Sannio, gun positions at San Giuseppe and Formia, and docks at Anzio. A–36's bomb Anzio, Avezzano town area and road junction, and Tarquinia town and factory buildings.

Fifteenth AF: B–17's attack M/Y at Prato and M/Y and bridge at Pontassieve. B–24's bomb M/Y at Arezzo. P–38's and P–47's provide escort.

Tenth AF: A–36's and P–51's spt ground forces in Shaduzup-Ngamaw Ga area and near Taro. Others bomb supply dumps, warehouses, and rolling stock at Sahmaw. P–40's hit Myitkyina A/F.

Fifth AF: 47 B–24's and B–25's bomb Hansa Bay area. B–25's bomb Nubia. P–39's strafe Rai Coast. B–24's bomb Bandanaira.

Thirteenth AF: AAF and Navy ftrs spt Navy dive-bmr strike on shipping at Rabaul. 18 airplanes are claimed shot down. 10 Allied ftrs fail to return from mission. During 17/18 Jan, a few B–24's, in 2 flights, bomb Rabaul area, while 2 B–34's bomb Kalakapisi coast watcher station at Choiseul I.

Seventh AF: 9 B–25's from Abemama bomb and strafe Mille, hitting runway, AA positions, radio tower,

warehouse area, lagoon dredges, and possible oil dumps. 4 P–40's from Makin bomb and strafe Mille landing ground.

18 January

Twelfth AF: B–26's hit harbor, tin mills, steel works, power house, and blast furnaces at Piombino, and bomb Montalto di Castro railroad and bridge. B–25's hit town and railway viaduct at Terni, and A–20's blast gun positions in Minturno area. P–40's hit trains, wharves and vessels in Ploca and Metkovic areas. A–36's and P–40's pound troops, trucks, and gun positions in Minturno area and near Pontecorvo and Atina, hit petrol dump at Pignataro Interamna, warehouse at Fontana Liri, factory at Ceprano, rail and road junction at Avezzano, and railway at Santa Marinella.

Fifteenth AF: B–17's attack M/Ys, a bridge and an A/F in Florence area. P–38's and P–47's provide close escort.

Tenth AF: 12 P–38's hit A/F and satellite field at Meiktila. 18 B–24's and 9 B–25's bomb encampment area at Kyaukchaw. 17 A–36's and P–51's hit troops, dumps, and workshops at Sawnghka. 11 P–40's attack troops and stores at Shaduzup. 3 transport airplanes are lost to Japanese ftrs during supply dropping mission SE of Sumprabum.

Fourteenth AF: 2 B–25's bomb railroad yard and wharf at Campha Port and oil storage facilities at Mon Cay.

Fifth AF: Hansa Bay area is bombed by 40 B–24's. Other B–24's bomb Laha. 70-plus B–25's pound Madang and Bogadjim areas and positions around Shaggy Ridge. 55 P–38's and P–40's engage a like number of ftrs over Wewak, losing 3 P–38's and claiming 12 shot down.

Thirteenth AF: 34 B–25's supported by 70-plus ftrs, pound Tobera. Single B–24's on armed rcn bomb Maliai, Vunakanau, and Lakunai areas.

Seventh AF: 12 B–25's from Abemama attack barracks area, runway, and gun positions on N part of Mille. 25 A–24's and 8 P–40's from Makin pound oil storage area S of Jabor on Jaluit. The P–40's also strafe a radio station in tgt area.

19 January

Twelfth AF: B–25's bomb Rieti A/F. B–26's hit A/F at Viterbo. A–20's attack M/Y at Colleferro. P–40's bomb and strafe 2 schooners at Makarska. A–36's hit guns, trucks, and trains N of Rome and fly over 70 sorties against rail, comm and troop positions in US Fifth Army battle area as Garigliano bridgehead expands. P–40's also hit defended positions in battle area and near Scauri, Tremensuoli, and Alvito.

Fifteenth AF: B–24's and B–17's hit A/Fs at Perugia, Iesi, Centocelle, and Ciampino. P–38's fly close escort for all the missions while P–47's fly top cover over Ciampino and Centocelle and carry out sweep over Rome area.

Tenth AF: 16 B–24's bomb M/Y and Don Maung railroad station at Bangkok. 4 P–40's hit town of Wakshang. 26 A–36's and P–51's hit tgts along roads from Ngamaw Ga to Maingkwan to Mashi Daru.

Fourteenth AF: 14 P–40's and 2 B–25's attack barracks area at Mon Cay.

Fifth AF: 57 B–24's bomb Boram, 17 more bomb Amboina and Halong, and 2 others score hits on freighter near Aitape. 65 B–25's, along with RAAF airplanes, pound positions in Shaggy Ridge area. 2 P–39's bomb barges in Cape Raoult area.

Thirteenth AF: Attacks during the day are limited to isolated strikes on shipping and other T/Os by aircraft on armed rcn over Bougainville, New Ireland, and Saint George Channel. During 19/20 Jan, 11 B–24's, in 2 waves, fly strikes against Rabaul and Vunakanau tgts.

Seventh AF: 17 B–25's from Tarawa hit Mille. Flying at low altitude, the MBs score hits on gun positions, fuel dumps, and the A/F area in general. AA fire claims 2 B–25's.

20 January

USSAFE: Gen Spaatz, as CG US SAFE, formally assumes administrative responsibility for all US AAFs in UK. His HQ is located at Bushy Park, formerly Eighth AF HQ.

Twelfth AF: B–26's bomb Viterbo M/Y and attack bridge at Pontecorvo. B–25's attack railroads in Carsoli area. A–20's give close spt to US 5th Div in Minturno area. British and US P–40's follow RAF LBs in raid on Popoli station. A–36's pound rail and road crossing at Viterbo, and P–40's hit comm at Frosinone, Palestrina, and Carsoli, where a traffic block is created. A–36's and P–40's fly nearly 200 sorties in spt of US Fifth Army ground forces as 36th Div begins assault across the Rapido R in Sant' Angelo in Theodice area.

P–40's also hit tgts along British Eighth Army front.

Fifteenth AF: B–24's and B–17's bomb A/Fs at Guidonia, Centocelle, and Ciampino. P–38's provide escort, and P–47's carry out sweeps over the tgts. Other P–47's escort transport airplanes on mission to Yugoslavia.

Tenth AF: In N Burma, 40-plus A–36's and P–51's hit storage dumps along railway in Mogaung area and billets and warehouse area at Mohnyin. In S Burma, 16 P–38's and 5 B–25's knock out railroad bridge, pipeline, and railroad tracks in Nattalin area.

Fourteenth AF: 2 B–24's on sweep from Hong Kong to Swatow attack a freighter and a tanker, which are reported sinking.

Fifth AF: 37 B–25's and a B–24 bomb and strafe Hansa Bay area. Over 60 B–25's hit positions on Shaggy Ridge. P–39's strafe troops at Weber Pt. 25 A–20's hit positions between Borgen Bay and Rein Bay and hit barge hideouts and enemy held areas in Gasmata area.

Thirteenth AF: Several tgts on Bougainville are bombed by 2 sqs of B–24's. 18 B–25's, with about 70 escorting ftrs, pound A/F, fuel dump, gun positions, at Vunakanau and Rabaul.

Seventh AF: 13 B–24's, staging through Tarawa, hit Wotje Atoll during 19/20 Jan. 8 B–25's from Abemama bomb Rakaaru. Other B–25's sent from Tarawa against shipping at Ailinglapalap Atoll abort because of bad weather. 9 P–40's from Gilbert Is strafe a corvette and a schooner at Jaluit, mortally damaging both vessels. 4 other P–40's bomb Mille.

21 January

Eighth AF: 390 HBs attack 24 V-weapon sites and T/Os in France, concentrating on Pas de Calais area. Of the nearly 800 HBs dispatched, 401 are forced to abort because of clouds which prevent 12 objectives from being attacked.

Ninth AF: 119 B–25's bomb V-weapon sites in France.

Twelfth AF: B–26's hit railroad bridges N and S of Orvieto. B–25's bomb chokepoints around Rome and unsuccessfully attack Pontecorvo bridge. A–20's attack comm at Atina. P–40's hit shipping at Povlje. Other P–40's and A–36's attack strongpoints, trucks, a cmd post, HQ building, and radar station in battle area. P–40's also give close spt to US Fifth Army troops which are hard-pressed at both Garigliano and Rapido R bridgeheads. A–36's bomb Velletri, concentration at Minturno, and area S of Viterbo.

Fifteenth AF: B–17's bomb A/Fs at Istres-Le-Tube and Salon-de-Provence, railroad bridges at Porto Civitanova, and bridge and M/Y at Rimini. B–24's attack M/Ys at Pontedera and Prato. P–38's fly escort. P–47's sweep over wide areas around Rome and Florence.

Tenth AF: 11 P–40's score near misses on Loilaw bridge and strafe Budagon nearby, starting several fires. 16 A–36's and P–51's spt ground forces near Sumprabum, and 11 more bomb forces SW of Kamaing.

Fifth AF: B–25's, A–20's, and P–39's bomb Madang area, and strafe villages near Saidor and troops from Reiss Pt to Erima. B–25's and P–39's strafe barges from Cape Raoult to

Rein Bay and hit T/Os along N coast of New Britain. Single B–24's on armed rcn blast control tower at Hoskins A/F, and hit ships near Kavieng and at Lorengau. 2 B–24's bomb Waingapoe.

Thirteenth AF: 38 B–24's pound runway and revetment area at Borpop A/F. P–39's strafe Kara and Kahili. B–34's and B–24's on armed rcn bomb Kalakapisi, Nukiki, and Buka A/F.

Seventh AF: 16 B–24's staging through Tarawa during 20/21 Jan, bomb tgts on Kwajalein. 6 Tarawa-based B–25's hit Arno Atoll and 12 bomb Aur Atoll. 9 B–25's from Abemama hit gun positions, barracks, and runways on Mille. 23 A–24's and 11 P–40's from Gilbert Is base attack gun positions, ammo and oil storage, barracks, and 2 small vessels at Jaluit.

22 January

Twelfth AF: Maximum spt is given to Allied landings at Anzio, which are begun by US Fifth Army's VI Corps at 0200. FBs, LBs, and MBs direct efforts toward isolating landing area by cutting roads, bridges, and railroads and obstructing towns in the surrounding region, at Velletri, Valmontone, Colleferro, Ceprano, and Fondi, and hitting traffic and comm throughout the area. Ftrs maintain patrol over shipping and beachhead and successfully intercept several enemy FB missions directed against the landings.

Fifteenth AF: Unescorted B–17's and B–24's bomb Terni and Arezzo M/Ys, Pontedera M/Y and A/F, road and rail junction NW of Frascati, Terracina road defile, and Pontecorvo bridge and town area. P–38's strafe

tgts in Arce-Frosinone area, including several vehicles and train cars. P–47's on sweep over Rome area encounter several ftrs, and claim 5 shot down; 2 P–47's fail to return.

Tenth AF: 16 B–24's bomb encampment at Prome. 16 A–36's and P–51's and a single B–25 attack comm and supply dumps between Kumnyen and Ngamaw Ga. 12 A–36's and P–51's spt ground forces in Sumprabum area. 11 P–40's severely damage Namkwin railroad bridge.

Fourteenth AF: 11 P–40's and 5 P–51's strafe newly opened Nanchang A/F, killing about 20 troops and destroying an airplane and a truck. 12 P–38's knock out bridges at Shektan and Sheklung.

Fifth AF: B–25's strafe villages, bridges, and barges from Cape Gourdon to Cape Croisilles, and hit shipping at Papitalai, sinking small vessel and a barge and severely damaging jetty. A–20's, P–40's and RAAF aircraft hit numerous scattered T/Os on New Britain.

Thirteenth AF: 27 B–25's, with 90-plus supporting ftrs, attack Lakunai A/F, doing considerable damage to runway and revetment areas. 1 B–25 and 4 ftrs are shot down. US airplanes claim 18 Japanese downed. 6 B–25's and 30-plus B–24's pound town of Rabaul.

Seventh AF: 18 B–24's, flying from Tarawa, hit tgts on Kwajalein, Jaluit, and Mille. 10 B–25's from Abemama hit Maloelap; 9 others, flying out of Tarawa, bomb shipping and shore installations at Wotje. 3 B–25's are lost during the day's missions. 10 aircraft are claimed shot down.

23 January

Eighth AF: 23 P–47's attack Gilze-Rijen A/F.

Ninth AF: Nearly 200 B–26's bomb V-weapon sites in French coastal area.

Twelfth AF: Col William S Gravely takes cmd of XII AF Trg and Repl Cmd. B–26's bomb area S of Avezzano while B–25's hit town of Avezzano and road junction at Monte Cornacchia. A–20's bomb Vallecorsa with good results. A–36's attack Vallecorsa, road junctions at Fondi and in Priverno area, town of Ceccano, and railroad at Sezze. P–47's bomb bridge at Skradin. DAF ftrs strafe tanks and trucks on British Eighth Army front, and XII A Spt Cmd ftrs cover US Fifth Army's Anzio beachhead during the day.

Fifteenth AF: B–17's bomb road bridges at Pontecorvo and Ceprano, railroad line and bridge at Falconara Marittima, and M/Ys at Poggibonsi and Siena. P–47's escort HBs to latter 2 tgts. B–24's bomb Rieti A/F, Porto Civitanova M/Y, and T/Os, including bridge near Cagli, M/Y N of Perugia, and landing strip S of Iesi. P–47's and P–38's carry out sweeps in wide areas around Rome and Florence, reaching out to Viterbo, Rieti, Orte, and Terni.

Tenth AF: 19 B–24's, in 2 waves, attack shipping at Mergui, claiming a 350-ft vessel and 2 small boats destroyed. 6 B–25's and 16 P–38's knock out bridge at Myittha, damage bridge at Samon, and damage several trucks and railroad cars. 28 A–36's and P–51's and a single B–25 pound supply dumps at Kamaing and Mogaung, achieving excellent results. 16 P–40's hit Myitkyina A/F, railroad

cars at Pidaung, and railroad bridge at Loilaw.

Fourteenth AF: 28 P–40's and 9 B–25's from Kweilin pound Kai Tek A/F in Hong Kong-Kowloon area. 2 B–25's heavily damage 3 merchant vessels S of Wenchow.

Fifth AF: 35 B–24's, with ftr escort, bomb Wewak. 50 Japanese ftrs intercept. In the ensuing air battle US aircraft claim 12 of the ftrs shot down. 5 US ftrs are lost. P–39's strafe barges and AA positions at Uligan Harbor and on Rai Coast. A–20's hit forces and AA positions near Cape Raoult and Gasmata. B–24's hit Flores I.

Thirteenth AF: 80 AAF, Navy, and Marine ftrs spt 60-plus Navy dive bmrs in strike on Lakunai A/F and Matupi Harbor area. 3 Allied ftrs are lost. US airplanes claim more than 30 aircraft shot down. Later, 40-plus ftrs sweep Rabaul area. 20 P–39's strafe T/Os in Shortland I area. During 23/24 Jan, 7 B–25's hit Tobera and Lakunai.

Seventh AF: 21 B–25's from Tarawa and Abemama hit Taroa I. The MBs claim 3 ftrs shot down. 23 B–24's, flying out of Makin and Abemama, bomb Wotje at dusk. 1 HB bombs Mille during return flight after developing engine trouble.

24 January

Eighth AF: 857 HBs are put into the air with intentions of bombing transportation and industrial tgts at Frankfurt-Heddernheim, Frankfurt/Main, and Russelsheim. Unpredicted multi-layer clouds and haze impede assemblies, and only 452 planes are dispatched to the tgts. Cloud formations and dense contrails over English Channel make holding formation impossible, and the bmrs are recalled, with exception of a combat wg which is approaching German border. 56 planes of this wg attack power station near Eschweiler before returning to base. British and US in UK agree to place most of the available P–51's in the Eighth AF for long-range escort of HBs. Eventually the Eighth is to be equipped almost exclusively with P–51's, with the P–38's and P–47's to be transferred to the Ninth AF.

Ninth AF: More than 175 MBs attack V-weapon sites in coastal area of France.

Twelfth AF: Weather cancels all MB and LB operations. Ftrs maintain cover over Anzio beachhead (Anzio and Nettuno are captured during the day) and encounter increased air attacks. 3 ftrs are claimed destroyed in aerial combat, while 1 Allied ftr is lost. P–40 FBs hit road at Penne, while A–36's bomb Velletri and road junction E of town, and hit other comm tgts.

Fifteenth AF: B–24's bomb A/F and town area at Skoplje. B–17's hit M/Y at Vrattsa and Dolno Tserovene area, both T/Os. P–38's escort the B–24's while P–47's accompany the B–17's.

Fourteenth AF: B–25's on sea sweeps claim sinking of merchant ship W of Nampang I, 2 freighters, a cargo-passenger vessel, and a coastal cargo boat anchored in Li-Shan Bay, and a cargo-passenger vessel at Paichuan I.

Fifth AF: 40-plus B–24's bomb A/Fs at Wewak and Boram. More than 50 B–25's and P–47's hit Madang and troops in vicinity and bomb

Hansa Bay area. 38 other B–25's attack shipping and harbor installations on Manus I.

Thirteenth AF: A large concentration of AAF, Navy, Marine, and RN ZAF ftrs spt Navy and Marine TBFs dive-bombing shipping in Simpson Harbor and Keravia Bay. Several 300–500-ft vessels are damaged or sunk. US airplanes claim more than 20 ftrs shot down.

Seventh AF: 24 A–24's from Makin, supported by 12 P–39's and 7 P–40's, hit gun positions, storage areas, and barracks on Mille. In late afternoon, 8 B–25's, staging through Makin, bomb A/F on Wotje. During 24/25 Jan, 9 B–25's from Tarawa and 12 B–24's from Taroa bomb several tgts in Maloelap. 1 other B–24 bombs Mille.

25 January

Eighth AF: 62 P–47's attack Leeuwarden and Gilze-Rijen A/Fs.

Ninth AF: Nearly 150 B–26's, airborne to bomb V-weapon sites in France, are forced to abandon missions because of heavy clouds.

Twelfth AF: B–25's bomb Valmontone. B–26's hit Sezze M/Y, Sezze-Bassiano road, Amelia, and Rieti M/Y. A–20's attack Terelle. A–36's hit Civita Castellana, Itri, Velletri, and railroad rolling stock in the area. P–40's hit Velletri and Belmonte in Sabina and strafe trucks E of Fondi. P–40's and P–47's hit shipping in Dubrovnik, and nearby road and rail traffic. British and AAF ftrs of DAF hit bridge approaches at Popoli, near British Eighth Army front.

Fifteenth AF: B–17's bomb T/Os (highways and railroad bridges) at Pedaso, SE of Pedaso, at Stazione di

Monte Silvano, and on Vomano R NW of Pescara. Other B–17's return bombs to base after finding tgts obscured by bad weather.

Fourteenth AF: B–25's on sweeps of E China coast claim a patrol boat, a tanker and 2 freighters sunk S of Wenchow.

Fifth AF: 50-plus B–24's pound Hansa Bay area. 37 B–25's bomb Alexishafen and Madang. P–39's strafe barges on Rai Coast. P–40's and A–20's hit Gasmata. More than 50 B–25's bomb Lorengau and Momote.

Thirteenth AF: 19 B–24's, following 3 which drop flares, attack Lakunai A/F during late evening.

Seventh AF: 24 A–24's from Makin, supported by 12 P–39's, attack gun positions on Mille. 8 B–25's from Tarawa bomb a vessel and shore tgts at Taroa. Later, in a dusk attack, 18 B–24's flying out of Gilbert Is bomb Kwajalein, hitting runways and AA positions.

26 January

Ninth AF: 144 B–26's scheduled to bomb V-weapon sites in France are recalled because of bad weather.

Twelfth AF: A–20's attack Cisterna di Latina, toward which US Fifth Army's VI Corps is moving. A–36's and P–40's fly harassing attacks against roads and railroads, bombing at Belmonte in Sabina, Cisterna, Itri, Ceccano, Frosinone, Poggio Mirteto, and at points around these towns. A–36's destroy fuel dump and several trucks and arty caissons in Ceprano-Priverno area.

Tenth AF: 15 B–24's bomb Maungdaw. 7 B–25's and 3 ftrs hit camp at Razabil and attack T/Os between Maungdaw and Buthidaung.

Fourteenth AF: 18 P–40's from Kunming bomb and strafe A/F and barracks at Kengtung.

Fifth AF: 42 B–24's bomb Momote and Lorengau. 140-plus B–24's, A–20's, P–39's, and P–40's hit Alexishafen-Madang area. 18 B–25's bomb Bogia village. A–20's hit Cape Raoult area and P–40's strafe barges along N coast of New Britain.

Thirteenth AF: 80-plus Allied ftrs cover strike by more than 50 Navy dive bmrs on Lakunai area AA positions and revetments. 3 Allied ftrs are lost. More than 20 airplanes are claimed shot down.

Seventh AF: 9 B–25's from Makin hit several tgts in Maloelap Atoll. About 20 ftrs attack the formation. 12 P–40's, meeting the returning MBs over Aur Atoll, join battle against the ftrs, claiming more than 10 destroyed. The MBs claim 5 shot down. Several more are destroyed on ground or while taking off during the bombing raid. 9 B–25's from Tarawa hit Aineman I, Jaluit Atoll, and nearby shipping.

27 January

Twelfth AF: B–25's attack roads at Velletri, railway at Colleferro, and M/Y at Orte. B–26's bomb bridges at Ceprano and M/Y at Terni. A–20's give close spt to US Fifth Army attack near Terelle. A–26's bomb railways and buildings at Poggio Mirteto, Ceccano, and Ciampino, hit rail and road traffic S of Rome, and, with P–40's, hit town of Piedimonte. More than 70 P–40's provide close spt to Fifth Army forces in Cisterna di Latina and Atina, bombing gun positions. Allied ftrs over Anzio beachhead successfully meet increased enemy air effort, claiming 28 airplanes downed in aerial combat.

Fifteenth AF: B–17's bomb A/Fs at Salon-de-Provence and Montpellier-Frejorgues. B–24's hit Istres-Le-Tube A/F. P–38's fly escort. Other P–38's sweep Rome area, and P–47's sweep Florence area. HBs and ftr escorts claim over 20 aircraft shot down.

Fifth AF: 41 B–24's bomb Lorengau. Almost 70 B–25's, A–20's, and P–39's, along with several RAAF airplanes attack Madang and Bogia areas. B–24's hit freighter and town area at Dili and shipping at Sorong and MacCluer Gulf.

Thirteenth AF: 19 B–25's, with escort of 60-plus AAF and Navy ftrs, pound Lakunai A/F. 6 US ftrs are lost. US airplanes claim more than 20 ftrs shot down. P–39's ranging over wide areas strafe T/Os at Motupena, Gazelle Harbor, and Buka I. 2 sqs of B–24's blast concentrations at Sulphur Creek in Rabaul area.

Seventh AF: 6 B–25's from Tarawa hit Nauru, and 9 staging through Makin hit Wotje. 23 A–24's, supported by 10 P–39's, pound Mille. 7 B–24's, staging through Makin, bomb Taroa in a dusk attack.

28 January

Eighth AF: 43 B–24's bomb V-weapon site at Bonnieres, using Gee-H blind-bombing device for first time. (Gee-H is more accurate than H2X but is of use only against tgts within the 200-mi beacon range. Later, aircraft are equipped with both devices).

Twelfth AF: B–25's attack Orte M/Y. B–26's hit bridges at Orvieto and Montalto di Castro. A–20's bomb Cisterna di Latina with good results. P–40's and P–47's bomb Popoli road

junction, and A–36's hit railroad, road, and gun positions in Cassino-Vicenza-Velletri areas, Colleferro M/Y, and Atina town area. P–40's hit Terelle, Belmonte in Sabina, and Cisterna. Allied ftrs over Anzio area claim 21 airplanes shot down.

Fifteenth AF: B–17's, with ftr escorts, bomb Aviano A/F and Verona M/Y. B–24's hit M/Y at Ferrara.

Fifth AF: B–25's attack T/Os from Bogia to Cape Croisilles. A–20's attack in Cape Gloucester area. P–40's hit A/F at Hoskins. P–39's strafe barges in Rein Bay.

Thirteenth AF: AAF and Navy ftrs spt Navy dive-bmr attack on tgts in Rabaul area. 5 P–38's are lost. Allied aircraft claim about 30 airplanes shot down. At Lakunai A/F, one of the tgts, 20–30 parked airplanes are destroyed and several AA positions are destroyed or damaged. 25 B–25's, covered by 12 P–38's, pound Tobera A/F. 16 P–39's strafe Shortland I area.

Seventh AF: 9 B–25's, staging through Makin, bomb Taroa. B–24's, staging through Tarawa and Makin and taking off at varying intervals, carry out several hours of strikes against Wotje, Kwajalein, Maloelap, and Jaluit.

29 January

Eighth AF: 763 HBs led by Pathfinder aircraft hit war industries at Frankfurt/Main. 46 HBs bomb Ludwigshafen (T/O) due to deviation from planned bomb route. Ftr opposition is fierce and 29 aircraft are lost. This is first Eighth AF mission in which more than 700 aircraft attack tgts.

Ninth AF: More than 80 B–26's

bomb V-weapon sites in coastal France.

Twelfth AF: B–25's bomb San Benedetto de Marsi M/Y. B–26's hit bridges N of Rome. P–47's bomb munitions factory at Bussi sul Tirino. P–40's and A–36's, in spt of US Fifth Army forces, bomb positions in Anzio beachhead area and hit enemy forward road and rail comm. Ftrs on patrol over Anzio meet little air opposition.

Fifteenth AF: B–24's bomb Siena M/Y through overcast. B–17's bomb M/Ys at Ancona, Fabriano, Rimini, and Bologna. P–47's sweep over Rome and Florence areas.

USSR: Soviet Army clears Germans from Moscow-Leningrad rail line. Russians launch attack against German salient in Ukraine.

Tenth AF: 13 B–24's, supported by 16 P–38's, bomb gasoline plants at Yenangyaung, causing large fires. 1 HB later bombs Akyab. 6 B–25's attack bridges at Meza and Pyintha, damaging the former and blasting railroad approaches to the latter.

Fifth AF: 40-plus B–25's bomb Bogia and Nubia landing grounds. 45 A–20's hit positions in Cape Gloucester area.

Thirteenth AF: About 60 Allied ftrs cover strike by 40 Navy dive bmrs on Tobera. Lakunai A/F is pounded by 19 B–24's, escorted by P–38's and Navy ftrs. At Tobera and Lakunai, Allied airplanes claim more than 20 Japanese shot down.

Seventh AF: As US invasion force approaches the Marshalls, B–24's, attacking from bases in the Gilberts, maintain day and night attacks (both multiple-plane missions and single-plane attacks at intervals)

against Maloelap, Jaluit, Aur Atoll, Wotje, and Mille. 9 B–25's from Tarawa also carry out strike against shipping and shore installations at Wotje. 18 A–24's, supported by 12 P–40's, hit Jaluit. 12 P–39's, operating in flights of 4 aircraft, patrol and strafe Mille all day to deny use of the A/F to the enemy.

30 January

Eighth AF: 701 HBs hit city of Brunswick, using blind-bombing equipment to bomb through the overcast. 51 HBs bomb T/Os, including city of Hannover. 20 aircraft are lost on mission.

Twelfth AF: B–25's hit road junctions at Valmontone and Genzano di Roma, and bomb town of Monte Compatri. Weather cancels all B–26 operations and several B–25 missions. A–20's hit town of and road junction near Cori, and XII A Spt Cmd FBs hit Sora. US and British ftrs hit barges and fishing boats off Zara and Trojica. Ftrs on patrol over Anzio meet no air opposition.

Fifteenth AF: 451st Bomb Gp (B–24) becomes operational, making a total of 9 HB gps in Fifteenth AF. B–17's hit A/Fs and landing grounds at Villaorba, Maniago, and Lavariano. B–24's bomb Udine A/F and Fier radar station. P–38's escort B–17's on Villaorba and Maniago missions, and P–38's and some British Spitfires escort B–24's on Udine mission. P–47's carry out sweep over Villaorba area. The HBs and ftrs claim over 60 airplanes shot down and a larger number destroyed on ground.

Tenth AF: 6 B–25's attack bridges at Meza, Zawchaung, and N of Kyungon. Meza bridge is put out of commission, Kyungon bridge demolished, and Zawchaung bridge damaged. A locomotive and tender are destroyed at the latter tgt. A single B–25 attacks vehicles and other T/Os between Taihpa Ga and Tsumhpawng Ga.

Fourteenth AF: 20 P–40's fly armed rcn over E Burma. 8 of them strafe buildings at Loiwing A/F.

Fifth AF: 34 B–25's bomb Hansa Bay area and Nubia landing strip. A–20's fly barge sweep along N coast of New Britain. P–39's strafe barges and fuel dumps at Rein Bay.

Thirteenth AF: 20 P–39's attack Kunrai. 26 B–25's, with large ftr cover, bomb Lakunai A/F. 18 B–24's, supported by ftrs, hit Vunakanau A/F. 50 Allied ftrs spt Navy dive bmr strike on shipping in Rabaul area. Altogether 20-plus ftrs are claimed shot down in the attacks in New Britain area.

Seventh AF: P–40's and P–39's maintain patrols over Mille, bombing and strafing the A/F to prevent its use by the enemy against invading forces. B–24's maintain all-night strikes against Kwajalein in preparation for the invasion the following morning. Invasion of Majuro Atoll begins during 30/31 Jan.

31 January

Eighth AF: 74 B–24's bomb V-weapons site construction at Saint-Pol/Siracourt. 70 P–47 FBs, escorted by 87 P–47's and 47 P–38's, bomb Gilze-Rijen A/F; 84 ftrs are encountered and fighting is fierce; 6 P–38's are lost in battle; US aircraft account for 13 ftrs destroyed.

Twelfth AF: A–20's bomb Artena and road junction to N of town. P–

40's and A–36's, operating E of Anzio battle area, hit road junction at Sezze, town of Fondi, and junction and town area at Priverno. P–47's bomb San Benedetto de Marsi. XII A Spt Cmd flies over 250 sorties over Anzio beachhead. Air opposition is absent.

Fifteenth AF: B–17's and B–24's bomb A/F at Aviano and Udine. P–38's and P–47's provide escort. B–17's, with P–38 escort, hit Klagenfurt A/F. HBs and ftrs claim 16 airplanes shot down.

Fifth AF: A–20's attack Uligan Harbor. P–39's strafe Bogadjim, Bostrem Bay, and landing strip at Alexishafen. B–24's hit motor vessel off Ceram.

Thirteenth AF: 40-plus Allied ftrs cover strike by Navy dive bmrs on Tobera. 8 airplanes are claimed shot down. The strike is immediately followed by an attack by 17 B–24's, with ftr spt, on same tgt.

Seventh AF: As US Army and Marine troops land on Kwajalein, under overall cmd of Adm Spruance, Seventh AF hits other atolls in the Marshalls. 19 A–24's bomb Mille A/F, over which P–39's and P–40's maintain all-day cover and harassment. 9 P–40's carry out strafing mission against Jaluit. During 31 Jan/1 Feb, 8 B–24's, attacking at intervals, bomb Wotje.

Eleventh AF: 5 bmrs fly a negative sea-search mission.

1 February

Ninth AF: Col Clarence E Crumrine temporarily takes cmd of XIX A Spt Cmd, replacing Gen Quesada. The latter assumes cmd of IX A Spt Cmd, which assumes control of all the ftr and rcn units of IX FC.

Twelfth AF: B–25's bomb Albano Laziale road junction. P–40's bomb Cori, while A–36's hit Poggio Mieteto and P–47's attack station at San Valentino. Ftrs cover Anzio battle area.

Fifteenth AF: Operations are limited to ftr sweep of Orvieto-Viterbo area by P–47's and to photo and weather rcn.

Tenth AF: 6 B–24's bomb Mingaladon A/F. 1 other hits A/F at Nyaungbinwun. 32 P–51's and A–36's and a single B–25 hit main A/F at Myitkyina. Some of the aircraft then strafe Radhapur transport depot and storage area to the NW.

Fifth AF: Weather prevents 50 B–24's sent against installation in the Admiralties from reaching tgt. 2 B–24's bomb freighter NE of Vanimo, while a single B–24 on armed rcn strafes barges in Solomon Sea.

Seventh AF: B–24's from Makin hit beach defenses on Kwajalein. P–40's on armed rcn over Mille strafe beached schooner. CATCHPOLE is begun to occupy and defend Eniwetok, which is to furnish a striking base for operations against the Marianas. During the operation, Seventh AF aircraft operating from newly acquired bases in the Gilberts and Marshalls neutralize A/Fs in the Marianas and continue to pound bypassed A/Fs in the Marshalls.

2 February

Eighth AF: 96 B–24's bomb V-weapon construction sites at Saint-Pol/Siracourt and Watten.

Ninth AF: 36 B–26's attack Trieville A/F.

Twelfth AF: Gen Saville becomes CG of XII A Spt Cmd. B–25's attack Marino road junction and A–20's bomb Norma. A–36's and P–40's bomb villages, road junctions, trucks, trains, parked aircraft, supply dump, and Viterbo road during several FB missions. P–40's on patrol over battle areas attack Cisterna di Latina and Formia.

Fifteenth AF: B–24's, with Spitfire escort, bomb radar station at Durazzo.

USSR: Stalin agrees to provide 6 bases for US aircraft in USSR. Soviet Army crosses into Estonia, and in Ukraine attacks along a 60-mi front.

Fifth AF: B–24's bomb Sorong and Alexishafen. Nearly 50 A–20's pound installations in Madang area. B–25's hit New Britain coastal tgts from Cape Gauffre to Rein Bay. Other B–25's attack shipping off Tingwon Is and off SE coast of New Britain.

Seventh AF: A–24's and P–40's from Makin bomb Mille runways and gun positions and along with P–39 escort strafe NE tip of the island. B–24's from Tarawa bomb Rongelap I.

3 February

Eighth AF: 543 HBs attack Wilhelmshaven while 61 bomb Emden T/Os. Bad weather causes more than 100 HBs to abort mission.

Ninth AF: 358th Ftr Gp becomes operational. This is the first of 17 ftr gps which are to be added by 9 May 44 to the Ninth AF, which previously had only 1 ftr gp, the 354th. 52 B–26's bomb V-weapon sites on W coast of France. Weather causes over 100 other aircraft to abandon mission.

Twelfth AF: MB missions are all abortive. A–36's, hit roads and other tgts S of Rome, destroying or damaging numerous trucks and bombing towns of Sezze and Fondi as US ground forces meet strong resistance in drive toward Cassino. P–47's hit Manopello and railroad facilities at Sulmona. Ftrs patrol Anzio area.

Fifteenth AF: B–24's, finding primary tgt obscured by bad weather, bomb T/Os (railroad yards and stations) at Stimigliano and Sulmona. Other B–24's return to base without bombing. P–47's fly ftr sweep over Prato-Pontassieve area.

Tenth AF: 16 P–38's attack bridges, encampments, and buildings along Prome-Taungup road. 1 bridge is knocked out and another damaged. A tugboat is sunk at Akyab. 14 A–36's and a B–25 attack troops and camp area at Kumnyen and Lalawng Ga, and hit motor pool and repair depot at Shingban. 16 P–51's hit encampment at Sawnghka.

Fifth AF: Nearly 100 B–24's and B–25's, supported by P–38's, P–40's and P–47's, pound A/Fs in Wewak area. About 80 airplanes are destroyed on the ground and in the air. A–20's attack Alexishafen and Hansa Bay areas. P–39's and B–25's on armed rcn hit trucks at Erima, barges on New Britain coast, shipping in N Bismarck Sea, and Momote and Hyane Harbor.

Thirteenth AF: AAF P–40's and Navy ftrs cover Navy dive-bmr strike on Tobera. 15 B–24's with P–38 and Navy ftr escort bomb A/F at Lakunai. Allied aircraft claim 13 interceptors downed during the 2 strikes.

Seventh AF: P–40's from Makin bomb and strafe Mille.

4 February

USSTAF: Abbreviation for US Strategic Air Forces in Europe is changed from USSAFE to USSTAF.

Eighth AF: 433 HBs are to attack industry and railroad yards at Frankfurt/Main but due to bad weather and navigational difficulties more than 200 of them bomb T/Os, including Koblenz, Giessen, Siegen and Trier.

Ninth AF: Gen Weyland becomes CG of XIX A Spt Cmd.

Twelfth AF: Weather prevents all MB, LB, and FB missions. P–40's and Spitfires maintain patrols over Anzio area, where a strong German counter-offensive had been launched during 3/4 Feb.

Fifteenth AF: B–17's bomb Antheor viaduct and Toulon harbor. B–24's are forced by bad weather to return bombs to base. Many of the B–17's returning from Toulon raid are forced to land at various friendly fields because of unsafe flying conditions.

Tenth AF: 12 P–51's strafe runways and buildings at Indaw.

Fifth AF: B–24's and B–25's carry out small raids against Laha, Namlea, and Amboina. 170-plus B–24's, A–20's, and B–25's bomb But and Dagua A/Fs, Marienberg, and Madang-Alexishafen area. P–39's bomb and strafe Atemble and strafe T/Os in Alexishafen area.

Thirteenth AF: 25 B–25's, escorted by 40-plus ftrs, pound A/F at Tobera. 18 B–24's, covered by 30-plus P–38's and Navy ftrs, hit A/F at Vunakanau.

Seventh AF: B–24's, flying from Tarawa and Makin, bomb Wotje, Maloelap, and Mille. B–25's from Tarawa and Abemama also hit Wotje and Maloelap. P–40's based at Makin bomb and strafe Mille.

5 February

Eighth AF: 450 B–17's and B–24's attack A/Fs at Chateauroux, Avord, Tours, Chateaudun, Orleans, and Villacoublay, and aircraft works at Villacoublay. In view of previous decision to concentrate most of trg activities of Eighth AF in Comp Cmd, a decision is made to transfer HQ from Limavady, N Ireland, to Cheddington, England, to bring it closer to the combat crew trg stations over which it is to be given supervision. Most of the transfer is completed between 7 and 15 Feb.

Ninth AF: Around 180 B–26's attack 6 V-weapon sites in N France.

Twelfth AF: B–25's bomb Terni M/Y, and A–20's hit Lanuvio and Piedimonte areas. P–40's and A–36's hit road junctions at Cisterna di Latina, Vetralla, and Velletri, bomb towns of Vetralla, Ardea, and Villa Santa Lucia degli Abruzzi, and attack motor transport at several points, including areas N, NE and SE of Rome.

Tenth AF: In early morning hours, 8 B–24's bomb A/F at Heho while 6 others hit Aungban A/F. 9 B–25's follow with strikes on Heho, Sagaing, and Myittha A/Fs. During daylight hrs 14 FBs hit M/Y at Wuntho. During 5/6 Feb, 9 B–24's again hit Heho and 4 bomb Aungban.

Fourteenth AF: 8 B–24's during 5/6 Feb bomb Bangkok. 3 others hit Nakhon Nayok and unidentified A/F on Mekong R. 2 B–24's and 2 B–25's attack convoy E of Hong Kong and claim 2 freighters and 3 smaller cargo vessels sunk. 4 P–40's on armed rcn strafe big wagon and truck column

N of Hsenwi. 4 others bomb and strafe Hopang, causing large fires in the village.

Fifth AF: 70-plus B–25's and A–20's attack Hansa Bay area. 48 B–24's pound Hoskins A/F, and some also bomb Gasmata, after weather prevents attack on Kavieng. B–24's fly light raid on Kaimana. B–25's on armed rcn in W Bismarck Sea claim 1 freighter sunk; others bomb wrecked ships off New Hanover.

Thirteenth AF: 24 P–40's join 40-plus Navy ftrs in covering a strike by more than 60 Navy dive bmrs on Lakunai. This strike is followed by an attack of 13 B–24's, with 30-plus P–38 and Navy ftr escort, on same tgt.

Seventh AF: P–40's from Makin dive-bomb and strafe oil storage area, radio facilities, and small craft at Jaluit. P–39's strafe runways on Mille.

Eleventh AF: 6 B–24's and 16 P–38's join Navy aircraft to fly air cover in several relays during retirement of US light cruisers and destroyers following bombardment of installations in the Kurabu Cape-Musashi Bay areas. Shortly afterwards, the aircraft also photograph and attack installations at Paramushiru and Shimushu.

6 February

Eighth AF: 206 HBs attack A/Fs at Saint-Andre-de-L'Eure, Evreux/Fauville, Chateaudun, and Caen/Carpiquet, and rocket-launching installation at Eclimeux as T/Os. Bad weather causes more than 400 HBs to abandon mission.

Ninth AF: Around 120 B–26's bomb V-weapon sites, A/Fs, and a factory, all in France. Principal tgts bombed are at Rosieres-en-Santerre, Amiens/Glisy, Cormeilles-en-Vexin, and Grandvilliers.

Twelfth AF: B–26's bomb Orte M/Y while B–25's hit Frascati road junction. A–20's bomb Campoleone railroad station and town of Rocca-secca. P–40's bomb Cisterna di Latina, Santa Lucia (near Campoleone), Cori (and nearby road junction), and Atina. A–36's hit San Stefano al Mare, Cisterna di Latina, Frascati and Albano Laziale, and strike numerous vehicles, railroad cars and other T/Os on armed rcn missions N and S of Rome. German counteroffensive against Anzio beachhead and on Cassino front forces Allied withdrawal.

Fifteenth AF: Bad weather restricts operations to photo and weather rcn flights.

Tenth AF: 12 P–51's hit warehouses and freight cars at Wuntho and claim 4 warehouses destroyed.

Fourteenth AF: 11 P–40's on armed rcn strafe sampans and power launches between Yoyang and Puchi. 6 B–25's knock out bridges and damage 3 trains at Anxuan, Tien An, Phong Loc and Dong Hoi.

Fifth AF: B–25's and B–24's pound Bunabun Harbor, Madang, and tgts from Bogia to Cape Croisilles. Others bomb tgts in Admiralty Is (concentrating on Momote) and carry out light attacks on Talasea village and Cape Dampier gun positions in New Britain. P–39's strafe and sink barges near Nubia. A–20's hit shipping near Kairiru and Mushu Is causing considerable damage and destruction.

Thirteenth AF: B–34's and P–39's hit barges in Green I area. Lakunai A/F is hit by 32 B–25's, covered by more than 60 AAF and Navy ftrs, and shortly afterwards by 19 B–24's, escorted by nearly 50 Allied ftrs. Allied aircraft claim 16 airplanes shot down. Lakunai is practically unserviceable as result of cumulative damage.

Seventh AF: B–24's from Tarawa hit Maloelap and Wotje. A–24's and P–40's from Makin attack Mille. Tarawa-based P–39's strafe Jaluit.

7 February

Twelfth AF: B–26's bomb bridge approach S of Manziana. B–25's hit Viterbo M/Y and, in spt of US Fifth Army troops, bomb town of Cisterna di Latina as enemy counter-attack begins in Anzio area. A–20's hit Piedimonte and road junction and railway station at Campoleone. A–36's hit San Stefano al Mare and nearby railroad siding, Pontecorvo and Belmonte in Sabina, plus several T/Os and tgts in spt of ground forces in battle areas. P–40's attack observation tower at Littoria, trucks at Villa Santa Lucia degli Abruzzi, Campoleone, a railroad gun, Sezze railroad yards, Cisterna di Latina, and gun positions in battle areas. Ftrs encounter heavy aircraft activity over Anzio battle area and claim 16 shot down.

Fifteenth AF: Bad weather again limits operations to photo and weather rcn missions.

Tenth AF: A single B–25 bombs motor pool at Sumprabum.

Fourteenth AF: 16 P–40's and 4 P–51's damage railroad bridges at Kienchang and Puchi and strafe warehouses at Teian. 2 B–25's score 2 direct hits on powerplant at Thanh Hoa, strafe nearby barracks, and attack radio station at Vinh.

Fifth AF: 14 B–24's bomb Amboina and Lautem. P–39's fly strafing sweeps over New Britain. Single B–25's on rcn bomb Garua Harbor, Cape Dampier, and Kavieng.

Thirteenth AF: P–40's join Navy ftrs in covering Navy dive-bmr strike on Tobera. Several gun positions and grounded aircraft are hit and runway is bombed into unserviceable condition. 11 aircraft are claimed shot down. Vunakanau A/F is bombed by 17 B–24's, escorted by P–38's and Navy ftrs.

Seventh AF: B–25's from Tarawa and Abemama hit Wotje and Maloelap. P–40's from Makin hit storage area at Jaluit.

8 February

Eighth AF: 237 HBs attack Frankfurt/Main (using blind-bombing techniques), and 127 bomb V-weapon installations at Watten and Siracourt. 78 HBs bomb T/Os, including Wiesbaden.

Ninth AF: HQ Ninth AF extends IX BC's choice of tgts considerably, although first priority for POINT-BLANK missions (spt of CBO) and next priority for CROSSBOW tgts (V-weapon sites) is maintained. In morning raid, nearly 200 MBs attack V-weapon sites and T/Os in NW France. In afternoon raid, more than 100 B–26's bomb V-weapon sites and military installations in same general area, most of the MBs attacking Breck-sur-Mer. This is IX BC's first 2-mission day.

Twelfth AF: B–25's bomb Cisterna di Latina. B–26's hit Siena M/Y and warehouses, and railway bridge NE of Civita Castellana. A–20's bomb Piedimonte. A–36's attack gun posi-

tions near Ausonia, tracks between Rome and Orte, and town of Veroli, and fly strafing and bombing sweeps in Anzio battle area against motor transport, gun positions, road junction E of Cisterna di Latina, and town of Pontecorvo. P–40's hit Roccasecca, Castello, Caprile, Piedimonte, Aquino, and other tgts, including supply dump and gun positions. P–47's bomb Atina. DAF ftrs (US and British) destroy large number of trucks near Sora.

Fifteenth AF: 454th Bomb Gp (B–24) becomes operational, giving Fifteenth 10 operational HB gps. B–24's bomb A/Fs at Viterbo, Tarquinia, Orvieto, Piombino, and Prato. B–17's hit M/Y at Verona. P–38's and P–47's escort the Orvieto, Piombino, and Prato missions.

Tenth AF: 7 B–25's bomb bridges at Budalin and Songon, displacing a section of the former and destroying an approach to the latter. 7 others hit stronghold at Badana. 16 A–36's and P–51's and a single B–25 hit camp at Mogaung. 4 P–51's strafe railroad cars NW of Myitkyina while a lone B–25 bombs camp at Kumnyen.

Fifth AF: Nearly 50 A–20's and B–25's hit Alexishafen and Madang areas. P–39's strafe T/Os during sweeps over wide areas of NE New Guinea and New Britain. During 8/9 Feb, B–25's bomb Toeal.

Thirteenth AF: P–39's over Bougainville bomb and strafe Tiaraka huts and bivouac area.

Seventh AF: B–24's from Makin and Abemama hit Maloelap and Mille.

9 February

Ninth AF: 133 B–26's bomb V-weapon sites in coastal France, M/Ys at Tergnier, and T/Os in area. This marks the first of the IX BC raids on M/Ys.

Twelfth AF: B–25's and B–26's, in close spt to US Fifth Army forces, attack motor transport and troop concentrations in Campoleone area while A–20's blast another troop concentration to the W. P–40's hit Cisterna di Latina and gun positions. A–36's and P–40's pound concentration points of counterattack against Fifth Army beachhead in Anzio area, strike along main Fifth Army front, and attack villages of Piedimonte and Aquino and gun positions near Cassino and Ausonia.

Fifteenth AF: Weather grounds all aircraft with exception of 1 P–38 which flies weather rcn mission.

Tenth AF: B–25's, P–51's, P–38's, P–40's, and A–36's carry out 75 attack sorties against Seinnyinba, bivouac and supply areas in Mogaung-Loilaw area, bivouac and buildings at Pyindaw, camps at Kumnyen and near Maingkwan and Shingban, and storage area and bivouac on Mogaung-Kamaing road near Sawnghka. A bridge over Namtawng R near Maingkwan also is destroyed.

Fourteenth AF: 16 P–40's strafe and bomb large barracks and oil storage at Chefang and pound town areas of Homun and Mangshih. 2 B–25's demolish wireless station SW of Haiphong.

Fifth AF: Occupation of Huon Peninsula is completed as US and Australian forces meet SE of Saidor. A–20's pound village of Mindiri. B–24's bomb Amboina and Lautem.

Thirteenth AF: P–40's and Navy ftrs cover Navy dive-bmr attack on Vunakanau A/F, scoring many hits on AA positions, buildings, and runways. 24 B–24's with Navy ftr escort follow with strike on same tgt, hitting runways and revetment area. 19 B–24's, with 20 P–38's supporting, hit Tobera A/F, thoroughly saturating runway.

Seventh AF: A–24's from Makin, along with supporting P–40's, bomb and strafe oil storage and gun positions on Jaluit. During a dusk-to-dawn operation on 9/10 Feb B–24's operating at intervals from Tarawa maintain strikes against Wotje Atoll and Taroa.

10 February

Eighth AF: 138 HBs attack industrial area of Brunswick; fierce opposition accounts for loss of 29 aircraft. 28 airplanes bomb A/F at Gilze-Rijen.

Ninth AF: 114 B–26's attack V-weapon sites in coastal France, A/Fs at Poix and Beauvais/Tille, bridge at Le Crotoy, and coastal battery N of Conch R.

Twelfth AF: LB and MB missions are aborted because of bad weather. P–40's and A–36's spt unsuccessful attempt of US Fifth Army's 1st Div to stem attack in Carroceto area. P–47's fail to locate tgt (Sora) and drop bombs at T/Os.

Fifteenth AF: B–17's bomb Albano Laziale, Cisterna di Latina, and Cecina. B–24's strike Campoleone and Velletri. P–38's bomb and strafe Tivoli, Vicovaro, and Monterotondo area. P–47's fly uneventful sweeps over Cisterna di Roma and Albano. Numerous HBs are forced to abort operations because of unsafe flying conditions.

Tenth AF: 9 B–24's bomb Ban Mah arsenal at Bangkok and Don Maung A/F immediately to the N. 3 B–24's bomb Prome and Akyab, 9 B–25's pound Chiradan and Godusara, and 16 P–51's hit barracks and road at Chishidu.

Fourteenth AF: 8 P–40's bomb Wanling and vicinity while 3 others fly top cover. The tgt area, a supply, staging, and trg center, is heavily damaged. 5 B–24's during 9/10 Feb mine mouth of the Yangtze. B–25's on sea sweeps claim 2 freighters sunk near Hainan I and SW of Hong Kong. 12 P–51's and P–38's strafe boats and parked airplanes in Chiuchiang area. 12 P–40's strafe power boats and sampans along the Yangtze from Pu-chi to Yoyang.

Fifth AF: 50-plus B–24's bomb Boram A/F and harbor at Wewak. 6 B–25's and a B–24 hit Momote A/F and jetties at Manus I. P–39's strafe T/Os during sweep over wide areas of New Britain. The junction of Allied forces from Arawe and Cape Glouces-ter marks completion of campaign for W end of New Britain; occasional mis-sions will still be flown in the area, but most will be restricted to barge sweeps and patrols.

Thirteenth AF: P–40's and Navy ftrs cover Navy dive-bmr attack on Vunakanau A/F. B–25's with ftr es-cort bomb Vunakanau later in the day. Tobera is pounded by 21 B–24's supported by P–38's and Navy ftrs. The Allied airplanes claim 30-plus aircraft downed in New Britain area. P–39's hit buildings at Bonis and barges in Matchin Bay and near Green I.

Seventh AF: B–25's from Tarawa hit Wotje and Maloelap. 3 B–24's from Abemama, sent to bomb weather and radio station on Rongelap I, abort due to fuel leak in lead HB. Attempt to bomb Jaluit during return flight is unsuccessful.

11 February

Eighth AF: 180 HBs attack indus-trial tgts at Frankfurt/Main and V-weapon site at Saint-Pol/Siracourt. 130 HBs bomb Ludwigshafen and oth-er T/Os when failure of blind-bomb-ing equipment causes diversion from primary tgts. First P–51's join VIII FC.

Ninth AF: Most of 139 B–26's dis-patched to attack NOBALL tgts in N France are recalled because of bad weather. 35 manage to bomb M/Y at Amiens.

Fifteenth AF: All operations grounded by bad weather.

Twelfth AF: Bad weather cancels operations.

Tenth AF: 10 A–36's and P–51's hit supply area at Sawnghka. 12 A–36's and P–51's and a single B–25 bomb supply and bivouac area at Pyindaw. 8 P–51's hit road junction near Mogaung and nearby supply area. 8 P–51's and P–40's on armed rcn strafe large river steamer and a launch in Mandalay-Shwebo area.

Fourteenth AF: 12 P–38's knock out 1 bridge and damage another at Sheklung. 6 B–25's, escorted by 20 US and Chinese P–40's, bomb storage area at Kai Tek A/F. The P–40's claim 5 ftrs shot down. Japanese air-craft bomb and strafe Namyung, put-ting the field out of use for several days.

Fifth AF: About 50 B–24's pound

A/F at Kavieng, and 2 bomb Garove I. 7 B–24's bomb Kendari A/F and Dili. P–40's and RAAF airplanes pound forces still remaining in Saidor area. Ftr sweeps and armed rcn continue over wide areas of SWPA.

Thirteenth AF: P–40's join Navy ftrs in covering Navy dive-bmr strike on Wunapope. 22 B–25's, escorted by Navy ftrs, pound Vunakanau A/F. Tobera A/F is bombed by 15 B–24's with P–38 and Navy ftr escort.

Seventh AF: P–40's and P–39's dive-bomb and strafe hangar and A/F installations and gun positions on Mille.

12 February

Eighth AF: 85 B–24's bomb V-weapon installation at Saint-Pol/Siracourt.

Twelfth AF: B–25's attack gun positions at Campoleone and surrounding area. B–26's hit Cecina. A–36's hit airplanes and trucks on landing ground and in area near Fabrica di Roma, attack troops in the area, bomb gun positions SW of Roccasecca, and hit towns of Fondi and Lanuvio. P–40's attack Cisterna di Roma, Sezze station and road junction, Cori, and gun positions NW of Atina.

Fifteenth AF: B–17's and B–24's strike troop concentrations and highways in Cecina area and near Lake Nemi. Bad weather causes all other missions to abort.

Tenth AF: 8 P–40's hit town of Ransa and motor convoys S of Sumprabum. 40 P–51's and A–36's attack bivouacs at Walawbum, bivouac and motor pool at Padaw, storage area at road junction near Chishidu, and town of Chishidu. 30-plus P–51's and

B–25's hit camps between Tsumhpawng Ga and Walawbum, storage area and motor pool S of Kamaing, motor convoy on Myitkyina-Sumprabum road, town of Namting, and bridges at Meza and Kanni.

Fourteenth AF: 9 P–40's pound warehouse area at Wanling. 6 others bomb barracks at Vinh and strafe Dong Cuong A/F, railroad yards at Cam Duong, and sampans at Phu Tho. 5 B–25's on sea sweep in Gulf of Tonkin claim 2 trawlers sunk and hit shore T/Os SW of Haiphong. A single B–25 damages bridge at Ha Trung. 24 P–38's, P–51's, and P–40's intercept 25 ftrs near Suichwan, claiming 7 shot down. 2 US ftrs are lost.

Fifth AF: Gen Connell resumes cmd of V AFSC. About 50 A–20's blast occupied areas SE of Wewak.

Thirteenth AF: 23 B–25's, with Navy ftrs in spt, bomb Tobera A/F. 21 B–24's, escorted by P–39's and Navy ftrs, pound Vunakanau A/F. P–40's join Navy ftrs in covering Navy dive-bmr strike on Lakunai.

Seventh AF: B–25's from Tarawa and Abemama hit Wotje and Maloelap. A–24's and P–39's from Makin bomb and strafe Mille.

13 February

CCS: CCS accepts revision of CBO Plan. The tgts are reduced to a number that can be decisively attacked and tgt lists are revised to keep up with the effort of the Germans to relocate vital industrial plants. Disruption of comm lines and reduction of German air power are high priority aims included in CCS directive on this date.

Eighth AF: 377 B–17's and B–24's

bomb 17 V-weapon tgts in Pas de Calais area. 39 bomb T/Os in the area.

Ninth AF: 182 MBs attack V-weapon sites in coastal area of France. 16 others bomb secondary tgts in the area.

Twelfth AF: B–26's bomb Bucine viaduct. B–25's and A–20's spt Fifth Army forces N and E of Anzio beachhead, blasting ammo dump and troop and vehicle concentrations. P–40 and A–36 FBs give spt in same areas, hitting troop concentrations, railway tunnel, buildings, vehicles, supply dump, and gun positions.

Fifteenth AF: Operations are restricted to weather rcn.

Tenth AF: 6 P–51's and a B–25 damage road bridge and 2 warehouses in Wuntho area. 32 P–51's and A–36's hit supply area and radio installations S of Kamaing and blast bivouacs S of Walawbum. 18 P–51's hit road and railroad junction N of Sahmaw, bivouac N of Kamaing, and camp between Tsumhpawng Ga and Walawbum. During the night, 16 B–24's bomb Heho A/F.

Fourteenth AF: 23 B–24's pound railroad shops at Vinh. 4 B–25's hit convoy E of Foochow, claiming 3 freighters and a transport sunk. 4 other B–25's damage 2 vessels off SW Hainan I and bomb dock, railroad, and oil dump at Bakli. 6 P–40's bomb and strafe barracks and hangars at Phu Tho and strafe freight cars at Yen Bay and Suo Ha.

Fifth AF: 24 A–20's hit Aitape. 70-plus B–25's pound Momote A/F. 35 B–24's bomb Kavieng A/F.

Thirteenth AF: 20 B–25's bomb Tobera A/F, and 23 B–24's bomb Lakunai A/Fs. Both forces are escorted by ftrs. P–40's and Navy ftrs

escort Navy SBD's and TBF's dive-bombing runway and AA positions at Vunakanau.

Seventh AF: During 13/14 Feb, B–24's from Tarawa, operating individually at intervals, bomb Wotje, Taroa, and Mille.

14 February

SHAEF: Gen Eisenhower establishes HQ SHAEF. COSSAC comes under control of SHAEF.

Eighth AF: 46 P–47 FBs attack Gilze-Rijen A/F. (Primary tgt, Eindhoven A/F, is overcast).

Twelfth AF: Twelfth AF loses several of its operational units, the 12th Bomb and 33d and 81st Ftr Gps being transferred to India, and the 52d TC Wg and its 4 gps being sent to UK. B–25's bomb Perugia M/Y, A–20's hit Grottaferrata. A–36's attack guns in Pontecorvo area, railway yards at Civita Castellana and Frosinone, motor transport near Genzano di Roma, A/F at Furbara, and Ferentino railway station, some of the missions being in direct spt of US Fifth Army main front. P–40's bomb and strafe troop concentrations N and E of Anzio beachhead, scoring hits on tanks, motor transport, and guns near Cisterna di Roma, Cori, and Rocca di Papa. P–47's hit Colleferro and dump at Valmontone. P–40's score direct hits on vessel and fuel dump in Rogoznica area.

Fifteenth AF: B–17's attack M/Ys at Modena, Brescia, and Verona and several T/Os including A/F and Piaggio aircraft factory at Pontedera and railroad bridges and lines at Parma, Sassuolo, Rubiera, and S of Vicenza. HBs and escorting P–47's claim 20 ftrs shot down. B–24's bomb M/Ys at Mantua, Verona, Massa Lombarda, Ferrara and Arezzo, and T/Os including Pisa M/Y, Prato M/Y, A/Fs at Pisa and Pontedera, and road-rail junction near Vaiano.

Tenth AF: P–51's and A–36's carry out 70-plus sorties against a variety of tgts in Burma. Tgts include supply area at Shingban, truck convoy N of Maingkwan, supply dumps and motor transport in Kamaing area, bivouac near Mogaung, troop and vehicle concentrations between Mogaung and Kamaing, arty positions at Laawn Ga, and railroad station and warehouses at Lundaung.

Fifth AF: A–20's with P–40 spt, bomb and strafe Dagua A/F, destroying and damaging over 20 aircraft. 80-plus B–25's pound Momote A/F. More than 40 B–24's bomb A/Fs at Kavieng and Panapai.

Thirteenth AF: B–24's bomb Rabaul area in a diversionary strike while Navy TBF's lay mines in Simpson Harbor. 30 escorted B–25's pound Vunakanau A/F while 28 B–24's, also with escort, bomb Rapopo A/F. P–40's and Navy ftrs escore Navy divebmr raid on Tobera gun positions and A/F revetments. 4 B–25's also bomb Tobera. On Bougainville weather clears, permitting the first attacks, by 19 B–25's, on Kara and Kahili, in recent weeks. P–39's attack Puriata R bridges.

Seventh AF: 40-plus B–24's from 11th and 30th Bomb Gps, flying out of Makin and Tarawa, strike Ponape I in first Seventh AF raid on the Caroline Is. 2 of the HBs hit alternate tgt of Emidj I.

15 February

Eighth AF: 51 B–24's bomb V-weapon site at Saint-Pol/Siracourt. 34 P–47's bomb T/O, an A/F believed to be Coxyde or Nieuport.

Ninth AF: 194 B–26's bomb V-weapon sites, Cherbourg/Maupertus A/F, and T/Os during morning mission. 122 B–26's again bomb V-weapon construction sites in coastal area of N France during afternoon.

Twelfth AF: B–26's and B–25's bomb Monte Cassino Benedictine Abbey in spt of NZ Corps assault to establish bridgehead across the Rapido S of Cassino. Other B–26's bomb railroad at Monte Molino and M/Y at Montepescali. A/20's attack motor transport, roads, and road junction in Albano Laziale area and NW of Valmontone. P–40's bomb concentrations near Cisterna di Roma, and dumps in Valmontone and Rocca di Papa areas. A–36's hit concentrations N of Anzio beachhead, strafe trucks and barracks in Frosinone-Rieti areas, bomb Tiburtina and Trastevere M/Ys in Rome area, and hit buildings N of Velletri.

Fifteenth AF: Around 100 B–17's bomb Monte Cassino Benedictine Abbey. 60-plus B–24's attack Poggibonsi M/Y, Campoleone, and Porto d' Ascoli. Heavy cloud cover causes numerous aborts. All the missions are unescorted.

Tenth AF: P–40's, P–51's, and A–36's hit tgts in Burma, including rice mill and radio station at Waingmaw, T/Os along Hukawng-Walawbum road, motor pool and dumps in Kamaing area, troops and supplies at Padi Ga and canal bridge at Ye-u. P–40's also drop land mines on Nampaung.

Fourteenth AF: 4 B–25's on sweep

of Gulf of Tonkin coastal areas and N Indochina score direct hit on steamer at Haiphong and nearby railroad station, damage bridges near Viet Tri and patrol launch at Hanoi, and hit engine sheds at Thanh Hoa.

Fifth AF: 70-plus B–24's, A–20's, and B–25's bomb Kavieng town area, harbor, and shipping and Panapai A/F. 17 other B–24's, prevented by weather from reaching Panapai, bomb Talasea on New Britain.

Thirteenth AF: 23 B–25's, with ftr cover, bomb runway and dispersal area of Vunakanau A/F. 20 B–24's hit Borpop A/F, causing heavy damage in runway and revetment areas. In ground action, US and NZ troops land on Nissan I in Green Is, 40 mi NW of Buka; opposition is weak and organized resistance will end on 23 Feb.

Seventh AF: B–24's from Tarawa and Makin pound Ponape and Mille. 10 P–40's from Makin bomb and strafe runways and a disabled vessel at Mille.

16 February

Twelfth AF: B–25's bomb Orte M/Y and attack Campoleone area. B–26's bomb San Stefano al Mare and hit area near Perugia railroad bridge, bridge N of Orvieto, factory near Marsciano bridge, and bridge at Albinia Station. A–20's, with RAF and SAAF Baltimores and Spitfires, hit concentrations in Anzio battle area. A–36's bomb Rome/Tiburtina and Rome/Ostiense M/Ys in Rome area. P–40's attack Monte Cassino Abbey, pound tanks, trucks, and troop concentrations along US Fifth Army front, and hit towns of Fondi and Roccasec-

ca. Ftrs over Anzio encounter increased air effort in conjunction with all-out ground offensive against Allied beachhead.

Fifteenth AF: B–24's, unescorted, bomb M/Ys at Pontassieve, Siena, Poggibonsi, and Prato, bridge at Cecina, and railroad and highway near Rieti.

Tenth AF: A–36's and P–51's hit supply dumps, troop concentrations, and encampment area near Myitkyina, Kamaing, Tonkin, and Walawbum. B–25's and P–51's destroy 3 locomotives at Kyaingkwin.

Fourteenth AF: 2 B–25's knock out railroad bridge at Yen Bay and damage 2 other bridges to the S near the coast.

Fifth AF: 40-plus B–25's attack convoy off New Hanover. Over 30 B–24's bomb Panapai A/F and Kavieng, and some hit Cape Balangori and Talasea. 19 B–24's and B–25's bomb Halong. P–40's hit shipping and barges in Wewak area.

Thirteenth AF: 12 B–24's, with 30-plus P–38's and Navy F4U's, pound runway at Vunakanau A/F.

Seventh AF: B–24's from Tarawa bomb Wotje Atoll and Taroa I. P–40's from Makin fly 2 bombing-strafing strikes against Jaluit. A–24's bomb Mille.

17 February

Ninth AF: Advanced HQ, Ninth AF, is opened at Hillingdon House, Uxbridge. It is later joined in the area by advanced units of IX FC and by troop carrier units, all of which form a nucleus of advons so as to centralize tac operations in anticipation of combat on the Continent.

Twelfth AF: B–25's bomb Campoleone and Lanuvio area, B–25's hit dumps SW of Rome and N of Anzio, also hitting guns nearby. A–20's blast a dump and troop concentrations in Anzio area. P–47's bomb dumps near Valmontone. A–36's hit Carroceto, concentrations SE of Rome, and railroad underpass and a factory N of Anzio. P–40's blast enemy transport, guns, and assembly areas N of Cisterna di Latina, trucks N of Anzio and N of beachhead battleline, railroad stations at Campoleone and Carroceto, and bivouac areas, dumps, a factory, and bridge in battle area. This entire air effort (the heaviest to date in spt of troops) is aimed at helping prevent breakthrough at the beachhead, where Germans are committed to full-strength counteroffensive. A–36's bomb Monte Cassino Abbey in only air action on US Fifth Army main front.

Fifteenth AF: 455th and 456th Bomb Gps become operational giving the Fifteenth AF 12 B–24 gps. Unescorted B–17's and B–24's attack Campoleone and Grottaferrata, motor transport parks in Campoleone junction and Rocca di Papa areas, troop concentration near Frascati, stores depots in Grottaferrata area, and other tgts in adv of US Fifth Army's Anzio battle line which is under heavy counterattack by German forces.

USSR: Soviet Army completes reduction of German pockets W of Cherkassy.

Tenth AF: 38 A–36's and P–51's on armed rcn hit troops and supplies from Lonkin to Kamaing. 6 P–51's hit supply areas along roads around Lonton and Manywet; 2 others hit road junction near Maingkwan. 2 B–25's and 6 P–51's strike road bridge,

railroad station, and rail cars in Pyingaing area. 2 B–25's and 6 P–51's attack but fail to damage bridge near Ye-u.

Fourteenth AF: 4 B–25's on sweep of Gulf of Tonkin score 2 direct hits on freighter at Vinh, damage bridge approach and locomotive at Yen Xuon Station, and destroy locomotive at Yen Ly Station.

Fifth AF: 40 B–24's bomb Panapai A/F and Talasea. 16 B–25's claim 2 surface vessels and a submarine sunk off New Hanover. 16 P–47's strafe T/Os in Alexishafen area.

Thirteenth AF: 20 P–40's join 40-plus Navy ftrs in covering an attack by 70 Navy dive bmrs on shipping in Keravia Bay. 8 airplanes are claimed shot down. 2 Navy ftrs are lost. In N Solomons Allied ftrs hit Queen Carola Harbor, Kessa Plantation and bridge N of Kahili.

Seventh AF: B–24's from Tarawa and Abemama hit Ponape, Kusaie I, and Jaluit. P–40's strafe floatplanes off Emidj, as USN TF begins heavy attack on Truk.

18 February

Eighth AF: HQ issues orders to establish a photo rcn wg (8th Rcn Wg (Prov)) in Cheddington. The purpose is to make the Eighth independent in aerial rcn and to consolidate the efforts of units presently engaged in this and related activities. Col Elliott Roosevelt, Director of Rcn for Ninth AF, is named CO.

Twelfth AF: A–20's hit troop concentration near Piedimonte. XII A Spt Cmd P–40's and A–36's fly 17 missions in spt of US Fifth Army troops resisting counteroffensive, which reaches its deepest penetration into Anzio beachhead on this day. Objectives include tanks, vehicles, gun positions, troop concentrations, and railroad underpass along the Anzio-Albano Laziale axis. Ftrs over Anzio successfully intercept air strikes on beachhead. NZ troops capture Cassino Station.

Fifteenth AF: Operations are restricted to photo and weather rcn.

Tenth AF: 40-plus B–25's, A–36's and P–51's attack town of Ye-u and nearby bridge, bivouacs N of Laban, bridges in Pyingaing area and along Mu R, supply and troop concentrations at Waingmaw, radio station and supply area near Kamaing, and gun emplacements SE of Taihpa Ga. The strikes are generally successful.

Fourteenth AF: 4 B–25's on sweep of Gulf of Tonkin damage 2 large boats N of Bakli Bay, destroy ammo dump at Phu Ly, and knock out nearby railroad bridge.

Fifth AF: B–25's and RAAF Beaufighters hit Koepang. P–39's strafe T/Os at Madang and Cape Raoult.

Thirteenth AF: 34 B–25's and 18 B–24's, both forces with ftr escorts, pound Vunakanau A/F. 2 B–25's and 4 P–38's hit Tobera A/F.

Seventh AF: P–40's from Makin bomb and strafe Jaluit and Mille. US forces land at Engebi.

19 February

Twelfth AF: Col Peter S Rask becomes acting CO of XII TCC until its disbandment on 5 Mar 44. B–25's blast troop concentrations to N of Anzio beachhead. A–36's and P–40's keep troops, tanks, and motor transport in beachhead battle area under attack, flying over 200 sorties in more than 20 missions as Allied counterattack turns tide of battle. Ftrs maintain control over N part of battle area.

Fifteenth AF: Operations are again limited to rcn flights.

Tenth AF: 60-plus A–36's and P–51's and a few B–25's hit a variety of tgts in Burma. Tgts include fuel and supply dumps at Manywet and in Shaduzup area, Tonkin-Kansi road and a junction W of Manywet, Mu R bridge at Ye-u, railroad cars and tracks, locomotives, and river traffic between Monywa and Natyekan and between Alon and Segyi. Rail and road traffic in Bhamo and Hukawng Valley-Kamaing areas is also hit.

Fourteenth AF: B–24's, B–25's, and P–40's fly sea sweeps over widespread coastal areas from Formosa Straits to Indochina, claiming 3 ships sunk and others damaged. Railroad bridges, trains, and other T/Os near coastal areas are also attacked.

Fifth AF: 12 B–25's attack shipping SW of New Ireland, claiming a small freighter and a patrol boat sunk and other vessels damaged. 7 A–20's hit shipping at Kavieng. Single B–24's and B–25's carry out armed rcn over wide areas of Bismarck Sea.

Thirteenth AF: 20 P–40's and 40-plus Navy ftrs escort about 70 Navy dive bmrs in attack on Lakunai A/F. Ftr cover claims 22 airplanes shot down. 6 B–24's bomb same tgt immediately afterward. 14 B–24's, with P–38 and Navy ftr escort, hit Tobera A/F.

Seventh AF: B–24's from Tarawa and Makin pound Ponape and Kusaie I. B–25's from Tarawa hit Wotje while Makin-based P–40's bomb and strafe Mille. US forces land on Eniwetok Is.

20 February

Eighth AF: Over 1,000 HBs are dispatched to bomb German ftr aircraft production centers. Nearly 900 HBs attack assigned tgts or T/Os. This mission, the first in which the Eighth dispatches over 1,000 planes, begins "Big Week"—attacks on German aircraft plants and A/Fs.

Ninth AF: 35 B–26's bomb Haamstede A/F as a T/O, after about 100 MBs abort attacks on other A/Fs because of weather.

Twelfth AF: B–26's hit troop concentrations along roads in Vallalta area, B–25's hit dumps and assembly areas at N edge of Anzio beachhead, and A–20's bomb troop and motor transport concentration SE of Carroceto. A–26's and P–40's hit troops, trucks, and tanks NE of Carroceto, bomb town of Fondi, factory E of Carroceto, town of Piedimonte, and hit guns and T/Os along N line of beachhead. Axis attempt to achieve breakthrough is decisively defeated in center of salient created by counteroffensive and efforts end.

Fifteenth AF: B–24's blast troop concentrations in Anzio beachhead area as Axis efforts end.

Tenth AF: Bad weather limits operations to routine patrol over Sumprabum.

Fifth AF: HQ Fifth AF ADVON and HQ V BC move from Nadzab to Port Moresby. 38 B–24's bomb Alexishafen-Hansa Bay area. 18 B–24's bomb A/F at Laha and 12 others hit shipping off Kavieng.

Thirteenth AF: 35 B–25's, with ftr escort, pound Lakunai A/F. P–39's attack barge traffic, which has greatly increased off SE and NW

Bougainville, claiming 20 of the craft sunk.

Seventh AF: 9 B–25's from Tarawa bomb A/F at Wotje. P–40's from Makin strafe and bomb runways and small vessels at Mille.

21 February

Eighth AF: 764 B–17's and B–24's bomb aircraft industry at Brunswick and A/F and storage park at Diepholz. T/Os hit in W Germany because of thick overcast over primary tgts are Hannover, M/Y at Lingen, and A/Fs at Achmer, Bramsche, Hopsten, Rheine, Quakenbruck, Vorden, Ahlhorn, and Hesepe. Only 3 airplanes are lost.

Ninth AF: 18 B–26's bomb Coxyde A/F. Weather causes almost 190 aborts. The Ninth's Pathfinder Sq (provisionally activated on 13 Feb) takes part in this operation, its first venture into combat. 185 aircraft scheduled to attack other A/Fs in the Netherlands and France in afternoon are recalled because of bad weather.

Twelfth AF: B–25's bomb Orte M/Y, and B–26's hit Imperia docks. A–20's pound troop concentrations near Campoleone, along with P–40's and A–36's which also hit a fuel dump, tank and truck concentrations, and gun positions in the area. FBs also bomb and block Itri-Gaeta road.

Tenth AF: 50-plus P–51's and A–36's and a few B–25's hit cmd post at Shingban, town of Mohnyin, bridge at Loilaw, camp at Shaduzup, 2 bridges at Namkwin, and warehouses and other buildings at Kawlin and Wuntho. FBs attacking fuel dump at Pin Hmi drop bombs in wrong area. B–25's, escorted by Spitfires and Hurricanes, score effective hits on tunnel on Maungdaw-Buthidaung road.

Fifth AF: Almost 30 A–20's hit Madang and Hansa Bay area. P–39's hit Raiven Plantation. 40-plus B–24's bomb Rein Bay and Eleonora Bay areas; others attack shipping off New Hanover.

Thirteenth AF: 15 B–24's bomb Lakunai A/F; 4 others, with ftr spt, attack A/F at Rapopo. 20 P–38's join Navy ftrs in covering Navy dive bmr strikes on Lakunai gun positions. In Bougainville area 3 B–24's bomb Kara A/F while P–39's hit buildings at Tsundawan and in area S of Tabut, and bomb barges and jetty in Matchin Bay area.

Seventh AF: B–24's from Tarawa and Abemama hit Ponape, Kusaie, and Jaluit. B–25's from Abemama bomb Maloelap. P–40's from Makin hit Mille. US forces gain complete control of Eniwetok Is.

22 February

USSTAF: HQ Eighth AF is redesignated as Hq, USSTAF.

Eighth AF: HQ VIII BC is redesignated as HQ, Eighth AF. 101 HBs hit aircraft production centers at Bernburg, Halberstadt, and Aschersleben in conjunction with Fifteenth AF strike at Regensburg; 35 aircraft are lost to fierce ftr opposition. 154 HBs attack various T/Os (Wernigerode, Marburg/Lahn, Magdeburg, Bunde, Nijmegen, Arnhem, and Enschede) and fly diversionary attack against A/F at Aalborg, which cannot be bombed because of clouds; 6 aircraft are lost.

Ninth AF: 66 B–26's bomb Gilze-Rijen A/F. Bad weather causes more than 100 others to abort.

Twelfth AF: B–25's bomb Foligno M/Y and Montalto di Castro railroad bridge, and B–26's attack Albinia Station railroad bridge. A–20's hit area E of Campoleone. P–47's strike troops, gun positions, and road junction N of Carroceto, roads near Roccasecca, and town of Campoleone. A–36's hit guns NW of Carroceto and town of Formia. P–40's attack guns SE of Campoleone.

Fifteenth AF: B–17's attack Petershausen M/Y, Regensburg aircraft factory, and Zagreb. A large force of B–24's hits Regensburg aircraft plants about the same time as the B–17 attack. Other B–24's pound town of Sibenik and harbor at Zara. HBs claim 40 ftrs destroyed. 13 HBs are lost.

Tenth AF: 70-plus B–25's, P–51's, and P–40's again hit variety of tgts in Burma. Bridges are severely damaged or put out of use at Zawa, Tindeinyan, Ye-u, Namkwin, and Loilaw. Warehouses and supply dumps are hit at Segyi and at Chantha, and at Pahok road and railroad junction are blasted. Also hit are T/Os at Kawlum and along Walawbum-Kamaing road.

Fourteenth AF: P–40's on armed rcn strafe A/F at Kengtung and nearby truck convoy. At Bhamo a large rivercraft is hit and left sinking.

Fifth AF: 30-plus B–25's and P–39's attack Madang area. More than 60 B–25's and B–24's pound Iboki Plantation in spt of US Marines advancing on the area from Natamo, (and who capture Perry I).

Thirteenth AF: 20 P–40's and 40-plus Navy ftrs cover 70 Navy dive bmrs attacking Keravia Bay shipping. 40-plus B–24's, with ftr escorts, bomb Lakunai and Keravat A/Fs.

Seventh AF: 1 B–24 bombs Kusaie. 8 A–24's and 9 P–40's from Makin bomb Mille. 1 P–40 launches rockets against A/F tgts in first such attack by a Seventh AF aircraft.

23 February

Twelfth AF: P–40's hit gun position N of Campoleone and patrol Anzio area. Weather forbids other operations by Twelfth AF.

Fifteenth AF: B–24's bomb industrial complex at Steyr. Other HBs are forced to abort because of bad weather. HBs and escorting ftrs claim over 30 aircraft shot down.

Tenth AF: 14 B–24's bomb A/Fs and other tgts at Akyab and Dabaing. 3 B–25's and 12 P–51's hit radio station at Man Pang; 4 other P–51's hit warehouses at Chantha.

Fourteenth AF: 4 B–25's attack 2 ships in Gulf of Tonkin and hit railroad cars and engine shed at Van Trai Station. 4 P–40's strafe Lashio A/F.

Fifth AF: Almost 50 A–20's and B–24's blast A/F, buildings, and AA positions in Wewak area.

Thirteenth AF: 9 B–25's, with Navy ftr spt, bomb Vunakanau A/F; 10 other B–25's hit Keravat A/F. 4 B–34's on armed rcn over New Ireland strafe Cape Saint George area and bomb buildings and pier at Labur Bay. 4 B–24's attack bivouacs in upper Saua R area. 16 P–38's dive-bomb Wunapope supply area. Some attack town of Rabaul. This is first P–38 bombing raid on the Rabaul area. (P–38's, now free from constant responsibility of guarding bmrs against interceptors, will continue to dive-bomb Rabaul area through April.

During the latter part of this campaign against the famed Japanese garrison, which is to be bypassed by Allied ground forces, P–39's will add their strength due to completion of an airstrip on Nissan I in the Green Is. By 20 Apr only 120 of 1400 buildings in Rabaul will still be standing).

Seventh AF: P–40's from Makin bomb Mille. 2 small boats are destroyed by strafing. B–25's from Abemama hit Taroa. B–24's from Makin and Tarawa bomb Kusaie, Ponape, and Jaluit.

24 February

Eighth AF: 231 B–17's bomb Schweinfurt ball bearing plant (11 losses suffered) while 238 B–24's hit factory and A/F at Gotha (33 aircraft lost). 236 HBs attack secondary tgt of Rostock due to overcast at primary objectives of Poznan, Tutow, and Krzesiny. 61 HBs attack Eisenach, a T/O. RAF BC follows up with attack during 24/25 Feb of Schweinfurt.

Ninth AF: Advanced HQ IX A Spt Cmd (set up at Uxbridge on 15 Feb) assumes operational control of its gps, which hitherto had operated under orders from VIII FC. 22 B–26's bomb A/Fs at Leeuwarden, Deelen, and Gilze-Rijen on morning mission. 145 B–26's bomb NOBALL tgts between Saint-Omer and Abbeville during afternoon.

Twelfth AF: B–26's hit Fabrica di Roma landing ground. P–40's and A–36's hit gun positions, troop concentrations, trucks, and tanks in battle areas. P–47's bomb bridge at Arce.

Fifteenth AF: B–17's (in coordination with Eighth AF raids on Germany) bomb aircraft factory at

Steyr and oil refinery at Fiume. HBs and escorting ftrs claim 35 ftrs shot down. 19 US aircraft are lost.

Tenth AF: 12 B–24's pound harbor area at Moulmein, railroad sidings at Martaban, and T/Os near Mingaladon A/F and Zayat. Ftrs carry out numerous patrol and offensive sorties over Sumprabum area.

Fourteenth AF: 7 B–25's bomb warehouse and dock area at Wuhu and 3 hit railroad yards and docks at Hongay. 9 P–40's attack docks and railroad yards at Campha Port. 10 P–38's on sweep of Yangtze R from Chihchow to Pengtse claim 4 river steamers, 5 tugs, 5 motor launches, and 15 sampans destroyed.

Fifth AF: 30-plus A–20's hit Wewak area, blasting fuel dumps, trucks, A/Fs, aircraft, and supply stores. B–24's bomb Momote and Alexishafen.

Thirteenth AF: P–40's and Navy ftrs escort Navy dive bmr attack on Wunapope supply area. Some of the ftrs later strafe sub off Cape Gazelle. 20-plus B–25's, some with Navy ftr escorts, attack Tobera, Keravat, and Vunakanau A/Fs and town of Rabaul. 14 P–38's hit Wunapope and Cape Gazelle area. Cape Saint George is attacked by 24 B–24's when Vunakanau area is overcast.

Seventh AF: A–24's and P–40's from Makin bomb and strafe small vessels, radio facilities, barracks, and gun positions at Jaluit and Mille. B–25's from Tarawa pound Wotje.

Eleventh AF: 6 bmrs take off for armed rcn and shipping search over the Kurils. Only 1 gets through and jettisons bombs upon finding tgt overcast.

25 February

Eighth AF: 680 B–17's and B–24's bomb airplane factories at Regensburg, Augsburg, and Furth, and ball bearing plant at Stuttgart. This mission is flown in conjunction with Fifteenth AF attack on Regensburg and with major efforts by RAF against Schweinfurt during 24/25 Feb and Augsburg during 25/26 Feb. 31 aircraft are lost.

Ninth AF: Gen Williams becomes CG IX TCC. 191 B–26's bomb Venlo, Saint-Trond, and Cambrai/ Epinoy A/Fs in morning raid as diversion in spt of VIII BC HBs over Germany. 36 abort, mainly because of navigational error. 164 B–26's dispatched against military tgts in France during afternoon are recalled because of bad weather.

Twelfth AF: P–40's attack guns and troop concentrations E of Campoleone and in Carroceto area. A–36's bomb towns of Terracina and Sperlonga and roads in the area. P–40's also maintain patrols over Anzio.

Fifteenth AF: Continuing coordinated attacks with Eighth AF on European tgts, B–17's with ftr escorts pound Regensburg aircraft factory; enemy ftr opposition is heavy. Other B–17's hit Zara harbor and Pola. B–24's attack Fiume M/Y and port and hit Zell am See railroad and Graz A/F. Over 30 US airplanes are lost. HBs claim more than 90 ftrs shot down.

Tenth AF: 8 B–25's and 4 P–51's attack bridges at Meza, Sinthe, and Natmauk, causing light damage to the bridges and destroying 3 locomotives and several railroad cars.

Fourteenth AF: 16 P–40's attack docks, railroad yards, and warehouses at Hongay. In the harbor 1 large boat is sunk and another damaged. 2 P–40's hit a cargo vessel at Campha Port, leaving it sinking. 2 others bomb and strafe Weichow I.

Fifth AF: B–25's pound Lorengau and Alexishafen-Madang areas and Momote A/F, and A–20's bomb A/Fs at Alexishafen.

Thirteenth AF: P–39's on armed rcn bomb AA position at Monoitu, hit Aitara area, and attack barge in Cape Gazelle area. 20-plus B–25's hit Matupi and Rapopo. 21 B–24's and 17 P–38's follow shortly with another strike on Rapopo.

Seventh AF: P–40's out of Makin bomb and strafe tgts at Jaluit. B–25's from Tarawa and Abemama hit Mille and Wotje. B–24's from Abemama and Tarawa pound Ponape.

Eleventh AF: 3 B–24's from Shemya are over Matsuwa I shortly after midnight 24/25 Feb on a photo rcn and bomb run. Mission is not completed due to weather.

26 February

Twelfth AF: Weather limits operations severely, but P–47's hit shipping N and S of Velaluka.

Tenth AF: 15 B–25's and P–51's demolish warehouses, in Naba and Hopin, attack bridges at Ye-u, Bawgyo, and Tantabin, and strafe railroad cars and tracks at Tangon, Namyao, and Pyintha. The Tantabin bridge is rendered unusable while approaches of the Ye-u and Bawgyo bridges are damaged.

Fourteenth AF: 11 B–25's from Nanning attack tgts at Tourane, destroying 5 warehouses and a hangar at the A/F and a locomotive and 4 buildings at the railroad yard.

Fifth AF: B–24's bomb Wewak and Momote. B–25's, along with P–39's, hit Madang-Alexishafen area and A–20's hit Angorum.

Thirteenth AF: P–40's join Navy ftrs in covering Navy dive bmr strike on Wunapope supply and shipping facilities. 22 B–25's, with ftr spt, follow up with the day's second strike on Wunapope. Shortly afterwards, 17 P–38's strike the same tgt. 12 P–39's bomb and strafe Monoitu, Ruisei, Makapeko, and Mawareka.

Seventh AF: B–25's from Tarawa and Abemama attack Wotje and Jaluit. P–40's from Makin bomb and strafe tgts on Mille.

Eleventh AF: XI BC (Air Striking Group TG 90.1) is directed to conduct armed photo rcn missions in the Kurils, day or night, as weather permits.

27 February

Ninth AF: Gen Quesada (reappointed CG IX FC on 21 Feb) receives authority to revive IX FC (existing only on paper since creation of IX A Spt Cmd) on temporary basis as an operational HQ to function as a Combined Control Center with RAF 11 Gp at Uxbridge, where FC will prepare operations orders for Ninth AF ftr and FB gps. Quesada retains command of IX A Spt Cmd.

Twelfth AF: A–36's attack Littoria A/F, Guidonia A/F, and Ladispoli dock area. Rail cars NE of Rome are also attacked. P–40's follow up with raid against Littoria and hit trucks and other tgts in the area. Weather prevents other operations by the Twelfth.

Tenth AF: 30-plus P–51's and A–36's and 2 B–25's hit ammo dumps near the Kamaing-Walawbum road, stores and troops at Warazup, and warehouses, railroad and power facilities, bridges, and T/Os in Ye-u and Tindeinyan areas.

Fourteenth AF: 4 B–25's fly sea sweep from Vinh to Nam Dinh, bombing Nam Dinh distillery and railroad yards. No ships are sighted. 8 P–40's hit railroad bridge at Puchi, rendering it unusable.

Fifth AF: Col Jarred V Crabb becomes CG V BC. 30-plus B–24's, with P–40 spt, hit A/Fs at Boram, Wewak, and Tadji, 27 B–25's hit Hansa Bay area, and over 30 A–20's attack Alexishafen and Marakum village. More than 30 other B–25's attack Momote, Lorengau, and other tgts in the Admiralties. P–39's maintain armed rcn over New Britain.

Thirteenth AF: 16 P–39's strafe barges and other T/Os along SW coast of Bougainville throughout the day. Wunapope is attacked by 21 B–24's and 24 B–25's (both forces supported by ftr escorts) and by 14 P–38's. P–40's and Navy ftrs cover Navy dive bmr strike on Lakunai AA positions. 3 other P–38's strafe radar station at Cape Saint George.

Seventh AF: A–24's and P–40's from Makin pound Jaluit and Mille, while B–25's from Abemama hit Wotje and Mille. B–24's from Makin and Tarawa bomb Ponape.

28 February

Eighth AF: 181 B–17's and B–24's bomb 9 V-weapon sites in Pas de Calais area. Heavy clouds cause over half the HBs dispatched to return without bombing. 7 aircraft are lost, most to AA fire.

Ninth AF: 180 B–26's attack NO-BALL tgts and Rosieres-en-Santerre.

Bad weather makes bombing difficult and causes 34 other B–26's to abort.

Twelfth AF: B–25's attack Canino landing ground, but clouds prevent accurate bombing and most bombs fall W and SW of main tgt area. A–36's attack A/Fs at Littoria, Guidonia, and Marcigliana. P–47's hit motor vessels and tug off Dubrovnik and T/Os inland.

Tenth AF: 6 B–25's hit bridges and trains between Pintha and Kinu; 1 bridge is damaged and several boxcars are destroyed. 13 B–24's bomb M/Y at Mandalay and T/Os at Akyab, Monywa, and Pakokku. P–51's, A–36's and P–40's attack bridges, radio stations, supply dumps, bivouacs, troop concentrations, railroad bypasses, AA positions, and other tgts at Seton, Sinkan, Ye-u, Kawlin, Loilaw, Namkwin, Shaduzup, and Mogaung-Kamaing area.

Fourteenth AF: 6 P–40's on armed rcn strafe A/F at Myitkyina.

Fifth AF: 23 B–24's and 39 A–20's thoroughly pound Hansa Bay area. Nearly 20 other B–24's bomb Nubia and Awar A/Fs. In preparation for Allied landing, 50-plus B–25's and B–24's pound Momote, Lorengau and other tgts in Admiralty Is.

Thirteenth AF: 22 B–25's, with ftr escort, pound Rabaul; 9 mins later 12 P–38's glide-bomb Rabaul; 2 mins afterward 11 B–24's pound the same tgt. 6 other B–24's bomb Rapopo. P–40s' and Navy ftrs escort Navy dive bmrs in strike on Wunapope. P–39's attack Monoitu Mission.

Seventh AF: P–40's from Makin strafe and bomb runway and radio installation on Mille. B–25's from Tarawa pound A/F on Wotje.

Eleventh AF: 3 B–24's from Shemya search for enemy shipping. 1 HB crashes during takeoff, the others find nothing.

29 February

Eighth AF: 215 B–17's attack aircraft production plants at Brunswick. 38 B–24's bomb V-weapon site at Lottinghen.

Ninth AF: 19 B–26's bomb coastal gun position and nearby Breck-sur-Mer A/F. 216 MBs abort mission against 8 V-weapon sites in France because of total cloud cover over tgts.

Twelfth AF: B–26's bomb main and satellite A/Fs at Viterbo and several T/Os along W coast of Italy. B–25's bomb troops and gun positions W of Cisterna di Roma, while A–20's hit concentrations to the S. P–40's and A–36's strike at troop concentrations along N perimeter of beachhead. Other P–40's hit barracks and railroad yards at Littoria and tank concentration S of Cisterna. P–47's (with British aircraft) hit Giulianova railway station and shipping off Dubrovnik. Ftrs maintain patrol over Anzio beachhead.

Fifteenth AF: For fourth consecutive day, bad weather limits operations to rcn missions.

Tenth AF: 7 B–25's knock spans out of 2 bridges N of Taungtha and damage bridges S of Myingyan and between Panaing and Mahlaing. 7 B–25's and 4 P–51's bomb wireless station at Sinkan, score near misses on bridge below Kawlin, and knock out 2 bridges in Ye-u area. 40–plus P–51's, A–36's, and P–40's hit supply area S of Seton, camp and stores near Mogaung (at Pagoda Peak), and railroad station at Myitkyina.

Fourteenth AF: 23 B–24's pound warehouse area at Yoyang, causing several fires and secondary explosions. 12 B–25's bomb Yoyang railroad yards. 16 P–40's provide spt. 2 B–25's on sweep of NE China coast sink 3 sampans and damage a merchant ship at Siachwan Tao. 6 P–40's bomb and strafe ammo dumps at Kunlong. 12 P–38's and P–51's sink large motor launch NE of Anking, strafe barracks and 3 tugs in Teian area, hit barracks NW of Nanchang, and strafe railroad installations at Yangsin. 4 P–40's hit a barracks W of Nanchang. 2 B–25's sink a large rivercraft on the Yangtze near Chiuhsienchen and damage 2 more nearby.

Fifth AF: Allied amphibious forces land on Los Negros I, temporarily taking Momote A/F and then falling back to beachhead on Jamandilai Pt. Weather prevents full air spt but 7 B–24's and 8 B–25's manage to attack enemy positions and guns. Other B–24's and A–20's hit Erima, Wewak, Tadji, Awar, and Hollandia.

Thirteenth AF: 23 B–25's, with Navy ftr escort, pound Rabaul area. Later 12 P–38's hit tgts in same area. 16 AAF ftrs, along with 16 Navy ftrs, hit T/Os throughout S Bougainville and Shortland I. Numerous other ftrs, in forces of varying sizes, attack barges and scattered T/Os throughout N Solomons, Bismarck Archipelago, and waters in between.

Seventh AF: B–24's bomb Maloelap, Mille, and Wotje; B–25's hit Jaluit and Mille; P–40's attack Mille.

1 March

Eighth AF: HQ and HQ Sq, VIII AFSC is redesignated as HQ and HQ

Sq, ASC, USSTAF, after functioning as such during Jan and Feb while redesignation was being authorized. 8th Strat Air Depot Area is redesignated VIII AFSC.

Ninth AF: IX TCC establishes Pathfinder school to provide pre-invasion trg in all navigational aids.

Twelfth AF: Twelfth AF undergoes a reorganization as a result of loss of several operational units (see 14 Feb 44). XII TCC (Prov), consisting of a single wg, is disbanded and its personnel absorbed into 51st TC Wg and other units, the 51st Wg being placed under the administrative control of Twelfth AF. HQ XII BC is reduced to 1 officer and 1 enlisted man as other personnel are transferred to 57th Bomb Wg, which along with 42d Bomb Wg, is placed under the administrative control of Twelfth AF. HQ XII BC will exist as a retaining cadre until 10 Jun 44 when it is officially disbanded. P–40's attack gun positions and vehicles in US Fifth Army battle area. P–47's attack 2000-ton vessel in the Adriatic. P–40's and Spitfires of XII A Spt Cmd maintain cover over Anzio beachhead area.

Fifteenth AF: For the 5th consecutive day, bad weather forbids all operations except rcn missions.

Tenth AF: 8 P–40's score 3 hits on bridge at Namkwin. 4 others hit Myitkyina A/F dispersal area. 56 A–36's and P–51's attack stores and personnel areas at Sawnghka.

Fourteenth AF: 14 B–25's and 16 P–40's pound military zone in NE part of Nanchang.

Fifth AF: About 30 B–24's and B–25's hit Los Negros I and Lorengau. Other HBs and MBs drop supplies to Allied ground forces on Los Negros I. More than 100 B–24's, B–25's, A–20's, and ftr aircraft, along with RAAF airplanes, pound Hansa Bay, Awar Pt, A/F in Wewak area, and enemy installations and positions at Madang, Alexishafen, and Saiba.

Thirteenth AR: B–24's bomb Kahili. P–38's hit Ballale and Buka. P–39's bomb and strafe Monoitu Mission.

Seventh AF: A–24's and P–40's from Makin hit Jaluit and Mille while B–25's pound Maloelap.

Eleventh AF: XI Strat AF is activated at Shemya. It includes all units of XI BC and XI FC stationed at Near Is, and is only a tac operating agency without administrative functions.

2 March

Eighth AF: 232 HBs attack M/Y at Frankfurt/Main (using blind-bombing technique) while 133 bomb T/Os in SW Germany, including Mannheim/Ludwigshafen, Limburg, and Dernbach. 84 HBs hit A/F at Chartres. Failure of Pathfinder equipment causes many aircraft assigned to Frankfurt mission to return without bombing tgt.

Ninth AF: 353 B–26's attack NOBALL tgts, Tergnier, and Amiens/Glisy and Rosieres-en-Santerre A/Fs in morning and afternoon missions.

Twelfth AF: B–26's attack assembly area E of Carroceto and, with B–25's, bomb guns and assembly area NW of Cisterna di Roma, A–20's hit troops in beachhead battle area. P–40's and A–36's blast troops and guns throughout Anzio battle area, also hitting Cisterna and Littoria. P–47's hit motor vessel off Sibenik, leaving it burning. P–40's and A–36's fly uneventful cover over Anzio.

Fifteenth AF: 459th Bomb Gp (B–24) becomes operational, giving the Fifteenth AF 13 HB gps on combat status. Nearly 300 B–17's and B–24's, escorted by more than 150 P–38's and P–47's, spt US Fifth Army's Anzio beachhead, bombing Cisterna di Roma-La Villa area, Velletri, and troop concentrations, guns, and other military tgts in battle area at several points, including Stazione di Campoleone and Carroceto areas.

Tenth AF: 5 P–51's bomb arty positions in Maingkwan area. 20 P–40's hit fuel dump at Myitkyina, arty at Shingban, and trucks on road near Walawbum. 8 A–36's and P–51's hit encampment on Pagoda Peak near Mogaung.

Fourteenth AF: 4 B–25's sink small steamer near Mon Cay and bomb railroad shops and coal treating plant at Campho. 10 P–38's damage 2 bridges and strafe 2 barracks areas N of Nanchang. 2 P–40's bomb and strafe A/F and barracks at Kengtung.

Fifth AF: 80-plus B–24's and P–40's hit Hansa Bay area, airstrip at Nubia, and Madang-Alexishafen area. More than 60 B–25's and A–20's pound enemy forces on Los Negros I as Allied ground forces occupy Momote A/F. P–47's providing cover for the MBs claim 7 enemy ftrs shot down.

Thirteenth AF: P–40's join Navy ftrs in covering Navy dive bmr strike on shipping installations in Keravia Bay area. 12 B–25's pound Rabaul while 11 others, with Navy ftr spt, bomb Rapopo. Shortly afterwards, 20 escorted B–24's blast town area of

Rabaul. 14 P–38's follow immediately with strike on same tgt. P–39's hit Japanese-occupied Piano and Monoitu Missions.

Seventh AF: B–24's from Makin and Abemama bomb Ponape and Kusaie. B–25's bomb Maloelap.

Eleventh AF: 9 B–24's fly a futile shipping search over the Kurils. Turned back by a weather front, they either jettison or bring back their bombs.

3 March

US: Roosevelt announces that the Italian Fleet will be divided equally among US, UK, and USSR.

Eighth AF: Thick clouds cause abandonment of mission to bomb industry at Erkner, Germendorf, Annahof and Berlin. Of more than 750 HBs dispatched, 79 manage to bomb T/Os, including Wilhelmshaven and Helgoland. 11 HBs are lost on mission.

Ninth AF: 218 B–26's bomb A/Fs at Laon/Couvron, Beauvais/Tille, Rosieres-en-Santerre, Roye/Amy, and Montdidier, and military installations at Juvincourt-et-Damary and Berneval-le-Grand.

Twelfth AF: B–25's bomb Rome/Ostiense and railroad stations at San Benedetto de Marsi. Weather cancels LB and other MB operations. P–40's hit gun positions in N Anzio beachhead area while A–36's attack train and tented area between Magliano Romano and Rome. Other P–40's fly patrol over Anzio beachhead area.

Fifteenth AF: Around 200 B–17's and B–24's, with over 50 P–47's as escort, bomb M/Ys in Rome area and A/Fs and landing grounds at Viterbo, Canino, and Fabrica di Roma. More than 80 B–24's and over 100 P–38's abort because of bad weather.

Tenth AF: 22 B–25's, some supported by Spitfires and Hurricanes, bomb Ft White area; 10 B–25's and 4 P–51's pound A/Fs at Katha, Mawlu, and Shwebo. 12 B–25's and 8 P–51's hit railroad tgts and a warehouse at Kyaikthin and Kyunhla. 14 B–24's covered by 22 P–40's, hit A/Fs at Lashio, Hsenwi, and Loiwing. 70-plus P–40's, A–36's, P–51's, and B–26's hit fuel storage, supply areas, roads, and other tgts over widespread areas of Burma, including Shingban, Myitkyina, Zigyun, Mogaung, Manywet, and Washawng. 6 P–38's attack Okshitpin bridge but tgt is not damaged.

Fourteenth AF: P–40's damage coal grading building at Campha Port.

Fifth AF: More than 30 B–24's hit Hansa Bay and Alexishafen areas while 20 P–39's attack Madang and Bogadjim and 22 A–20's pound Erima. 14 A–20's and B–25's hit enemy positions on Los Negros I.

Thirteenth AF: P–40's and Navy ftrs cover Navy dive bmr strike on Rabaul and Simpson Harbor. 24 B–25's follow with attack on Rabaul, which later in the day is bombed by 20 B–24's. 5 P–38's bomb radar installations at Cape Saint George while 10 bomb Buka A/F. P–39's hit T/Os on E part of Shortland I and W part of Buka I.

Seventh AF: B–24's out of Makin bomb Ponape. B–25's from Tarawa hit Maloelap. This date marks beginning of Operation FORAGER, the capture of the S Marianas (Saipan, Tinian, and Guam) for bases for B–29 strikes against Japan. Seventh AF aircraft

maintain neutralization strikes against A/Fs in the Carolines and continue hitting Wake and the bypassed Marshalls.

Eleventh AF: 9 B–24's take off from Shemya to search for enemy shipping, but return due to heavy icing and squalls. 6 P–40's fly a search mission between Shemya and halfway to Attu.

4 March

Eighth AF: 31 B–17's bomb Kleinmachnow area SW of Berlin, becoming the first US bmrs to hit the German capital area. Around 180 HBs attack T/Os including Bonn, Dusseldorf, and Cologne. Snow flurries and clouds cause cancellation of 1 bomb div's participation in mission and more than 250 of the 510 HBs dispatched abort.

Ninth AF: 251 B–26's and 21 A–20's scheduled to bomb Malines M/Y and Bernay/Saint Martin A/F abort mission because of heavy cloud cover over tgts.

Twelfth AF: Weather cancels most Twelfth AF operations. P–40's fly a few sorties against gun emplacements in battle area, and others uneventfully patrol Anzio area.

Tenth AF: 60-plus A–36's, P–51's, and P–40's, and a single B–25 bomb dumps, roads, bivouac area, and other tgts in Seton, Sawnghka, Pinbaw, and Walawbum areas. Numerous ftrs carry out patrol and armed rcn sorties in Sumprabum area.

Fourteenth AF: 5 B–25's and 23 P–40's (16 of them Chinese) pound A/F at Kiungshan. The A/F is heavily damaged and several parked airplanes are destroyed. The MBs and ftrs claim 17 interceptors shot down.

4 P–38's and 2 Chinese B–25's claim a freighter, a tanker, and a motor launch sunk in Shihhweiyao and Wuhu areas. 6 B–25's bomb Thanh Hoa chromium mine and Campha Port docks. 2 P–40's strafe railroad yards and warehouses at Hongay and Campha Port. 5 P–40's are dispatched to bomb Cao Bang but because of bad weather attack Chinese-held Lungchow by mistake. 6 waves of Japanese airplanes bomb A/F at Suichwan, causing considerable damage.

Fifth AF: 20–plus A–20's and B–25's spt ground forces on Los Negros I. More than 30 B–24's with ftr escort, pound A/Fs in Wewak area. More than 20 other B–24's bomb Hollandia. A–20's bomb buildings and gun positions in Saidor area.

Thirteenth AF: P–40's join Navy ftrs and dive bmrs in strike on AA positions and T/Os in Rabaul area. 4 patrolling B–34's hit T/Os along both coasts on New Ireland and at Vunalama and Mandres Plantations on New Britain. 48 B–25's and 12 P–38's, along with 20–plus Navy ftrs, hit Rabaul town area in 3 closely spaced attacks. P–38's also attack T/Os on Duke of York I. 12 P–39's hit Monoitu and T/Os along SW coast of Bougainville. B–34's join Navy planes in attacks on Japanese embarkation ports around Choiseul Bay. Shortland I T/Os are hit by P–40's on patrol.

Seventh AF: P–40's from Makin bomb and strafe runways at Mille. B–25's from Tarawa bomb A/F installations and runways on Wotje.

5 March

Eighth AF: 219 B–24's are dispatched to bomb A/Fs at Mont-de-Marsan, Cazaux, and Bordeaux but bad cloud conditions force a tgt change and multiple aborts. 152 HBs bomb A/Fs (secondary and last resort tgts) at Bergerac, Cognac, and Landes de Bussac.

Ninth AF: 217 B–26's attack NO-BALL tgts in Saint-Omer-Abbeville area.

Twelfth AF: XII TCC (Prov) is disbanded at Palermo. Weather again severely hampers operations, but P–40's hit Pontecorvo and A–36's attack Formia.

EAC: During the night, Gen Wingate's Special Force of long-range penetration troops begin dropping by glider onto Japanese lines of comm in C Burma. US engineer troops drop first, followed by British 77th and 111th Brigs. Col Philip G Cochran's Air Commando unit flies them in, dropping them on a strip designated Broadway, about 50 mi NE of Indaw. Another projected drop site, Piccadilly, is unusable as the Japanese have blocked it with fallen trees. Of 67 gliders dispatched, 32 reach Broadway. 539 men, 3 mules, and 65,972 lbs of supplies are safely put down, including such items as bulldozers and lighting apparatus.

Tenth AF: B–25's, A–36's, P–51's, and P–40's fly more than 60 sorties against tgts in Burma, including arty positions, storage areas, ground troops, roads, and a bridge. The tgts are in the Zigon, Shingban, and Myitkyina areas.

Fourteenth AF: 8 B–25's bomb and strafe Chiengmai A/F, destroying 9 airplanes, the water tower, and nearby railroad station. Barracks area is also damaged.

Fifth AF: About 30 B–24's bomb enemy positions on Los Negros. In

NE New Guinea, elements of US 32d Div land at Yaula. A–20's bomb and strafe the area. P–39's pound areas around Madang and Erima. Australian ground forces break out of Ramu Valley and retreat toward Madang.

Thirteenth AF: 22 B–25's, with Navy ftr escort, bomb Simpson Harbor. 4 B–34's on patrol hit barges anchored off supply dock at nearby Raulavat Plantation. 9 B–24's follow with raid on Rabaul town area. 13 others, with Navy ftrs covering, blast revetment area and airstrip at Tobera. 11 P–38's hit Borpop A/F, and P–40's and Navy ftrs hit barges at Kabanga Bay and off Warangoi R. 16 P–39's attack AA positions at Monoitu bridge, and 3 P–38's hit Siar.

Seventh AF: The Seventh continues to hit the Marshalls and Carolines. P–40's from Makin carry out FB mission against runways and A/F installations at Mille. B–25's hit Maloelap and Mille. B–24's bomb Ponape and last resort tgts at Kusaie and Mille.

6 March

Eighth AF: 658 HBs attack Berlin area, bombing the metropolitan area and T/Os in nearby cities of Potsdam, Wittenberge, Templin, Oranienburg, and Kalkberg. Fierce ftr opposition claims 69 of the bmrs, the highest number lost by the Eighth in a single day.

Ninth AF: 260 B–26's bomb NO-BALL tgts, Hirson M/Y, and A/F at Beauvais/Tille. Heavy clouds cause over 50 B–26's and A–20's to abort missions.

Twelfth AF: P–40's pound gun positions N of Anzio beachhead (mostly NE of Ardea), and bomb Frosinone and hit guns near Littoria. A–36's fly armed rcn of roads and railroad NE of Rome, hitting several vehicles and bombing railroad cars at Capranica.

Tenth AF: 4 B–25's knock center span out of Sittang bridge and blast 2 AA positions. 14 B–25's lay mines around Kham Yai I, bomb nearby Prong I, and hit M/Y at Pegu. 18 P–51's and P–40's attack Sawnghka bridge with poor results, start fires near Lalawng Ga, and bomb dumps near Walawbum.

Fifth AF: B–25's continue to hit Japanese forces on Los Negros. B–24's bomb airstrip and other tgts in Awar-Nubia area. P–39's and RAAF airplanes hit Japanese forces around Madang. P–39's and P–38's strafe and dive-bomb Cape Hoskins-Talasea area as US Marines land about midway up the coast of Willaumez Peninsula in preparation for drive on Talasea.

Thirteenth AF: P–39's hit Monoitu Mission and huts and bridge on Miwo R. 24 B–25's, with ftr escort, pound Tobera while 24 B–24's and 12 P–38's hit Kavieng and Panapai A/F.

Seventh AF: A–24's and P–40's from Makin bomb and strafe runways at Mille. B–25's from Tarawa pound A/F at Wotje.

7 March

Ninth AF: 112 B–25's and 18 A–20's attack V-weapon sites on Channel coast of France, military installations near Criel-sur-Mer and Greny, and T/Os in the area. Bad weather causes recall of over 150 other HBs before they attack tgts.

Twelfth AF: B–25's bomb Rome/

Ostiense M/Y while B–25's hit M/Y at Littoria. A–20's strike Zagarolo railroad station. P–40's attack enemy positions in Anzio beachhead area with good results, while A–36's hit comm at Montebello, railroad station near Civitavecchia, gun emplacements near Littoria A/F, and train at Monterotondo. P–40's over Anzio beachhead encounter no air opposition.

Fifteenth AF: Around 300 B–17's and B–24's bomb Toulon submarine base, M/Ys at Poggibonsi, Prato, and Pontassieve, A/Fs at Fabrica di Roma, Viterbo, and Orvieto, and town of Castelfiorentino. P–47's and P–38's fly about 150 sorties in spt of HBs.

Tenth AF: 20-plus P–51's and A–36's on armed rcn hit T/Os from Walawbum to Shaduzup. 2 B–25's hit troop concentrations NW of Shaduzup. Another attacks road bridge and barges near Shwebo and along the Irrawaddy. Offensive rcn over several A/F in Burma results in no major action.

Fifth AF: B–24's and B–25's continue to hit tgts on Los Negros and other of the Admiralty Is and bomb Boram A/F. P–38's and RAAF airplanes attack tgts in Talasea area.

Thirteenth AF: 24 B–25's, with Navy ftr spt, hit Tobera A/F. 24 B–24's and 14 P–38's hit Panapai A/F. 19 P–40's bomb and strafe Rabaul. Ftr aircraft pound tac tgts on Bougainville, including Koromira Mission, supply area on Jaba R, and bivouac S of Maririei R near Menoavi.

Seventh AF: B–24's out of Abemama hit Kusaie and Jaluit. P–40's bomb and strafe A/F at Mille. B–25's

pound runways, AA positions, storage areas, and barracks on Taroa.

Eleventh AF: B–24's and B–25's fly negative search mission for an enemy submarine.

8 March

Eighth AF: More than 460 HBs attack ball bearing plant at Erkner with good results. 75 other HBs attack T/Os, including factory at Wildau and center of Berlin. Enemy opposition is heavy, and 36 bmrs are lost.

Ninth AF: Over 225 B–26's attack Volkel A/F once and Soesterberg A/F twice in morning and afternoon missions.

Twelfth AF: B–25's strike at Orte M/Y and Orte-Fabrica di Roma railroad. B–26's hit Rome/Tiburtina M/Y and dock area at Porto Santo Stefano. P–40 FBs hit gun positions and road junction near Rome while A–36's attack road junction near Montalto di Castro, also hitting a bridge and a train, and guns and a castle SW of Celano. P–47's hit gun emplacements. P–40's strafe vehicles near Rome/Via Appia.

Tenth AF: 23 P–51's hit A/F at Anisakan, Shwebo, and Onbauk, destroying more than 30 Japanese airplanes. Later 5 B–25's and 2 P–51's hit Shwebo, scoring hits along runway and in dispersal area and leaving several Japanese aircraft aflame. 3 B–25's hit 2 bridges at Lalawng Ga and Warazup, knocking out the latter. 16 A–36's and P–51's hit T/Os from Chanmoi to Shaduzup.

Fifth AF: B–25's carry out a number of low-level strikes as Allied ground forces capture Lombrun Plantation on Los Negros, virtually completing capture of the island. More than 70 B–24's, B–25's, and A–20's bomb Nubia and Awar airstrips; the bmrs and escorting ftrs claim 17 airplanes shot down in Wewak area. Ftrs continue to strafe coastal tgts in NE New Guinea and on New Britain.

Thirteenth AF: 23 B–24's and 23 B–25's pound Rabaul, blasting Chinatown and wharf area. 46 P–40's and P–39's pound dock area E of Rabaul. 9 P–38's, turning back from Rabaul, bomb Buka A/F.

Seventh AF: B–24's, striking from Makin, bomb Ponape and Kusaie. A–24's and P–40's, also from Makin, bomb and strafe runways and AA positions at Mille. Tarawa-based B–25's pound Wotje.

Eleventh AF: Bmrs fly negative search and patrol missions for an enemy submarine. B–24's fly cover for a convoy en route from Adak to Shemya.

9 March

Eighth AF: About 300 B–17's attack Berlin. 158 B–24's bomb other tgts, including Brunswick, Hannover, and Nienburg areas.

Twelfth AF: B–25's strike dock area of Porto Stefano, some bombs falling in Port'oErcole area. B–25's bomb bridge at Montalto di Castro. A–20's hit tank repair depot N of Tivoli. P–40's blast gun positions W of Campoleone, W of Pratica di Mare, and S of Ciampino. A–36's bomb Capranica railroad station and tgts nearby. Ftrs fly uneventful patrols over Anzio.

Tenth AF: 6 B–24's bomb Tavoy A/F and office area while 8 others hit town of Mogaung. Town area, supply dumps and road bridge at Ka-

maing are pounded by 10 B–24's, 16 P–51's, and 10 P–40's. The bridge is knocked out. 10 B–25's score numerous hits on airstrips at Indaw and Katha. P–51's, P–40's, and A–36's hit storage at Pyindaw, and spt ground forces at Walawbum and Shaduzup.

Fourteenth AF: 13 CACW B–25's and 24 Chinese P–40's pound foundry and floating docks at Shihhweiyao. 40-plus P–40's carry out several sea sweeps off Indochina coast and fly armed rcn over NE Indochina. The ftrs damage vessels off Campha Port, strafe A/F at Mon Cay, bomb A/F at Weichow I (causing heavy damage), hit barracks at Luc Nam, damage vessels at Hongay, and bomb military installations at Cao Bang.

Fifth AF: B–25's pound Lorengau and other tgts on Manus. Numerous other Fifth AF aircraft carry out armed rcn over wide reaches of SWPA, attacking a variety of tgts.

Thirteenth AF: 24 B–25's bomb dock area along N shore of Simpson Harbor at Rabaul. 19 B–24's follow with strike on Rabaul town and wharf area and also hit A/Fs in the vicinity. 40-plus P–39's and P–40's hit dock area E of Simpson Harbor. At Empress Augusta Bay, 2 sqs of B–25's hit Japanese installations on nearby hills.

Seventh AF: B–25's based on Abemama attack Taroa I. B–24's from Tarawa hit Ponape and Kusaie.

10 March

Twelfth AF: B–26's bomb Rome/ Tiburtina M/Y and unsuccessfully attack Orvieto railroad bridge, while B–25's hit Littoria M/Y. P–40's and A–36's strike at enemy positions on coast at San Felice Circeo, gun positions E of Littoria, guns and tanks at Cisterna di Roma, railroad at Montalto di Castro, train at Monte Libretti station, and railway buildings at Zagarolo. Ftrs patrol Anzio area without incident.

Tenth AF: 23 B–24's pound town areas of Mogaung and Kamaing during the afternoon, following an earlier B–25 raid on Kamaing. 40-plus P–40's, P–51's, and P–38's hit gun positions S of Walawbum, troops and storage areas W of Mogaung at Pahok, trains near Myitnge and Anisakan, A/F at Anisakan, and town area of Laban.

Fourteenth AF: 6 B–24's bomb Kowloon Docks. B–25's from Suichwan sink a motor launch and damage 2 cargo vessels and a barge in Anking area. Escorting P–38's shoot down several interceptors. P–40's and P–51's on armed rcn bomb or strafe barracks and shipping at Foochow, A/F and barracks at Nanchang, factory, barracks, and bridge near Sienning, freighters at Hongay and Campha Port, barracks at Ha Coi, and area E of Lang Son.

Fifth AF: 11 B–25's bomb Lorengau and several T/Os on Manus. B–24's and P–39's, operating singly or in pairs, attack numerous scattered T/Os throughout SWPA during armed rcn flights.

Thirteenth AF: P–40's and P–39's attack Wunapope supply area. 19 B–24's pound Rabaul area, starting several large fires. 40 B–25's hit Japanese positions in the hills near Empress Augusta Bay. P–39's attack tgts at Kepiai Plantation.

Seventh AF: A–24's and P–40's from Makin and B–25's from Tarawa attack A/Fs, AA positions, and radio installations at Mille and Wotje. B–25's, operating out of Engebi on Eniwetok Atoll (secured by invading forces on 22 Feb) in the Marshalls for the first time, bomb Kusaie I.

11 March

Eighth AF: 121 B–17's bomb Munster while 34 B–24's hit V-weapon site at Wizernes. Both attacking forces use blind-bombing techniques due to thick overcast.

Ninth AF: 61 B–26's bomb V-weapon sites in N France. 53 abort because of weather and navigational difficulties.

Twelfth AF: MBs strike at Florence, Orvieto, and Fabriano M/Ys with good results. P–40, A–36, and P–47 FBs attack supply depot, railroad station, and factory in areas NE of Monterotondo, and numerous other tgts, including gun positions in battle areas, railroad facilities, and 2 supply trains.

Fifteenth AF: About 100 B–24's, escorted by 30-plus P–38's, bomb harbor at Toulon. More than 100 B–17's, escorted by more than 50 P–47's, hit M/Y at Padua. Other B–24's bomb M/Ys at Pontassieve and Prato and hit A/F at Iesi. HBs and ftrs claim destruction of more than 30 enemy airplanes in the air.

Tenth AF: 70-plus FBs (P–40's, P–51's, and A–36's) and 2 B–25's hit fuel and ammo dumps, gun positions, roads, and general T/Os in or near Saungka, Pandaw, Walawbum, Labang Gahtawng, Shaduzup, and Mogaung.

Fourteenth AF: 10 P–40's damage 3 barges at Campha Port, hit buildings on Weichow I, and attack town area at Ha Coi.

Fifth AF: 12 B–25's pound Lorengau while 7 B–24's bomb enemy positions to the W of the town, as preliminaries for invasion of Manus increase. 80-plus B–24's, B–25's, and A–20's hit Boram A/F while more than 40 A–20's and P–39's attack tgts in Madang area. P–47's strafe Hansa Bay area. Other aircraft carry out armed rcn and sweeps over wide reaches of NE New Guinea and New Britain coastal areas.

Thirteenth AF: 40-plus B–24's and B–25's, supported by 20-plus P–38's, pound Rabaul town area. 20 P–40's bomb Wunapope. 43 P–40's bomb Mosigetta area while 4 B–24's pound Monoitu Mission.

Seventh AF: B–24's, operating out of Kwajalein for first time, carry out the Seventh's first raid from the Marshalls against Wake. P–40's and B–25's, operating from bases in the Gilberts, pound Mille and Maloelap.

12 March

Eighth AF: 52 B–24's attack V-weapon site at Saint-Pol/Siracourt, using blind-bombing technique.

Tenth AF: 50-plus P–40's, A–36's, and P–51's, along with a single B–25, pound troops and supply areas at Shedwiyang and near Kamaing, bomb town of Shaduzup, and hit storage areas near Manywet and Malakawng.

Fifth AF: 12 B–25's hit enemy positions and comm at Lorengau as landings on small offshore islands continue with beachhead being established on Hauwei I. 40-plus B–24's B–25's, and A–20's hit Wewak area.

Thirteenth AF: 22 B–25's, with Navy ftr cover, pound Rabaul area, concentrating on N rim of Simpson Harbor. 18 B–24's, with Navy ftr

cover, follow with strike against Rabaul customs wharf area. The HB strike is followed by an attack on town area of Rabaul by 64 P–40's, P–38's, and P–39's.

Seventh AF: B–24's from Tarawa bomb Mille, Wotje, Maloelap, and Nauru. B–25's hit Jaluit.

13 March

Eighth AF: 270 HBs are dispatched to bomb V-weapon installations in Pas de Calais area, but strike is cancelled because of bad weather. 7 bmrs manage to attack Paix A/F as T/O. 2 airplanes are lost to AA fire.

Ninth AF: 40 B–26's attack V-weapon site at Lottinghen/Les Grands Bois. 37 abort due to bad weather.

Twelfth AF: B–26's bomb railway bridges NW and W of Sarzana and at Viareggio, hit tracks S of the latter, and, along with SAAF LBs, bomb Fabriano M/Y. B–25's bomb Spoleto M/Y, hitting E and W chokepoints and line to Terni, and also attack Perugia M/Y with less successful results. A–36's bomb railroad station between Orte and Orvieto while P–40's hit supply dump near Velletri and gun positions along beachhead line directly S of Rome.

Tenth AF: 140-plus P–40's, A–36's, and P–51's along with 2 B–25's pound numerous T/Os in Shaduzup area, knock out a span of bridge in Shaduzup, hit town of Loilaw, pound supply and ammo dumps near Warazup and Seton, and bomb building area N of Namti.

Fourteenth AF: 8 B–24's and 4 P–40's attack A/F and seaplane anchorage at Kiungshan on Hainan I. 16

P–40's bomb bridge at Puchi, scoring direct hits on both approaches.

Fifth AF: 160-plus B–24's, B–25's, A–20's, P–47's, and P–40's thoroughly pound Wewak area; US aircraft claim 8 interceptors shot down. Other aircraft, operating singly or in flights of 2 or 3, attack several tgts in NE New Guinea-New Britain area. In the Admiralties, Hauwei I is cleared of enemy opposition and arty is brought ashore.

Thirteenth AF: 2 B–24's, with Navy ftr escort, and 22 B–25's bomb Rabaul area, hitting NW part of Rabaul and harbor and waterfront section. 27 P–39's, P–40's, and P–38's pound Wunapope supply area.

Seventh AF: B–25's from Engebi bomb Kusaie while B–24's from Tarawa hit Ponape. B–25's from Abemama and Tarawa pound Mille.

14 March

Twelfth AF: B–26's bomb Prenestina M/Y and nearby chemical plant. B–25's strike Terni and Orte M/Ys, causing considerable damage, while A–20's attack tank repair facilities unsuccessfully. P–40's attack guns in Anzio beachhead area and also hit supply dump. A–36's and P–47's hit railway stations and town of Ostia.

Tenth AF: 41 A–31's join British aircraft in hitting Japanese positions in Arakan and Chin Hills areas. 90-plus P–51's, A–36's, and P–40's, along with 3 B–25's, hit Japanese troops, bridges, dumps, and villages in Mogaung Valley.

Fourteenth AF: 20 Japanese bmrs hit A/Fs at Hengyang and Suichwan. Surprise prevents effective interception by Fourteenth AF ftrs.

Fifth AF: More than 80 B–24's, B–25's, and A–20's, supported by Allied ftrs, pound Wewak area. 17 other B–24's bomb A/F at Tadji. 8 A–20's carry out sweep over Madang area while 12 bomb airstrip at Alexishafen.

Thirteenth AF: 22 P–40's and P–39's hit Wunapope. 23 B–24's, with naval ftr cover, bomb N waterfront area of Simpson Harbor. 22 B–25's, with Navy ftr escort, bomb E section of town of Rabaul. P–39's, P–38's, P–40's, and Navy ftrs hit barges and other T/Os around coast of Bougainville and along NE New Ireland coast.

Seventh AF: B–25's from Engebi bomb Kusaie. B–25's from Tarawa hit Wotje.

15 March

Eighth AF: 330 B–17's and B–24's bomb industrial area of Brunswick. 2 P–47's each carrying 2 1,000-lb bombs, escorted by 6 P–47's, fly mission against enemy barge in Zuider Zee to test feasibility of this type of operation. The FBs score near misses.

Ninth AF: Ninth AF directive states that the Ninth is released from first priority commitment to assist Eighth AF. P–51's of the Ninth AF (committed to AEAF) will continue to escort HBs when required by the Eighth. Ninth AF Adv HQ assumes function of tgt selection and mission planning for IX BC. AEAF HQ has authority to indicate percentage of effect to be expended on each type of tgt on a long-term basis. 118 B–26's attack M/Ys at Aulnoye and Haine-Saint-Pierre and Chievres A/F. During the afternoon, 10 MBs using "Oboe" to test its accuracy, bomb Coxyde A/F with poor results. Dive-bombing missions using ftrs begin with a 7-aircraft attack on Saint-Valery-en-Caux A/F.

Twelfth AF: MBs and FBs, together with MASAF HBs and other aircraft of MATAF in greatest air effort yet made in MTO, rain bombs upon enemy concentrations in Cassino and surrounding areas as NZ Corps begins third battle of Cassino. LBs and MBs also hit a cmd post E of Ceprano and town of San Benedetto de Marsi. Ftrs on patrol and sweep over Anzio, Cassino, and Rome meet no air opposition.

Fifteenth AF: More than 300 B-24's and B-17's bomb Cassino, area S of Cassino, and areas near Venafro, in spt of US Fifth Army. Over 250 other HBs return to base without bombing because of complete cloud cover of their tgt areas. Extensive ftr cover over Cassino area is provided by P-38's, and P-47's fly 2 sweeps over Viterbo-Canino area. There is no ftr opposition.

Tenth AF: 24 A-31's join British aircraft in pounding villages and Japanese positions in Arakan area. 31 B-24's and 20-plus RAF Wellingtons and Beaufighters pound supply dumps and T/Os in Rangoon area while 8 other B-24's hit barracks near Bangkok. Numerous US and RAF MBs and FBs attack villages, Japanese positions, ammo dumps, tanks, and many other T/Os in the Chin Hills, at Chindwin, in the Mogaung Valley, and in areas around Mandalay.

Fifth AF: More than 200 B-24's, B-25's, A-20's, P-38's, P-47's, and P-40's pound Wewak township, blasting docks, warehouses, gun positions, and numerous other tgts. Ftrs claim 11 enemy airplanes shot down. 36 B-25's bomb Tingo village and Lugos

Mission area on Manus, where elements of 1st Cav Div make amphibious landing, take the mission, and head E toward Lorengau.

Thirteenth AF: Gen Hubert Harmon, CG Thirteenth AF, becomes COMAIRSOLS. 50-plus B-25's, P-40's, P-39's, and P-38's and Navy ftrs pound Wunapope supply areas. 24 B-25's, with Navy ftr escort, bomb Lakunai A/F. 22 unescorted B-24's, finding Tobera clouded over, bomb A/F at Rapopo as a secondary tgt.

Seventh AF: B-24's from Kwajalein fly first Seventh AF mission against Truk Atoll, hitting Dublon I and Eten I before dawn; alternate tgts of Oroluk Anchorage and Ponape Town are also hit. B-25's from Tarawa hit Maloelap. By this date the A-24's, P-39's, and P-40's used against Mille and Jaluit during FLINTLOCK and CATCHPOLE have returned to Oahu for rest and re-equipment.

16 March

Eighth AF: 679 B-17's and B-24's bomb aircraft factories and A/Fs at Augsburg, Friedrichshafen, Gessertshausen, and Ulm. Ftr opposition is heavy against the first force of bmrs over France and Germany. 23 US bmrs are lost on mission.

Twelfth AF: FBs, LBs, and MBs blast gun positions in Cassino-Piedimonte area as battle of Cassino rages on. FBs also hit gun positions along Anzio beachhead front.

Tenth AF: 29 A-31's hit Japanese positions in Arakan area. 6 B-25's damage bridge at Nattalin near Rangoon.

Fourteenth AF: 7 P-40's on Yangtze R sweep damage 2 launches near

Yoyang and pound barracks and storage at Sienning.

Fifth AF: 70-plus B–24's, B–25's, and A–20's hit AA positions, buildings and salvage dumps at Wewak and nearby Brandi Plantation. 19 B–25's bomb personnel and storage areas at Nubia. B–24's and Catalinas attack Japanese convoy near Hollandia. Other B–24's bomb docks and factory area at Soerabaja.

Thirteenth AF: 13 B–24's bomb Vunakanau A/F, and 12 B–25's follow with raid on Vunakanau radar installations. 9 B–25's, 12 P–39's, and 11 P–40's hit Wunapope supply areas. 10 P–38's attack Cape Tawui while 11 B–25's pound N edge of Simpson Harbor. 7 P–38's strafe barges W of Raluana Pt. At Monoitu Mission, a raid by B–24's demolishes several buildings.

Seventh AF: B–25's from Tarawa and Abemama pound Wotje, Ormed I, and Mille.

Eleventh AF: 3 B–24's take off from Shemya shortly before midnight 15/16 Mar to fly armed rcn over Matsuwa I, but turn back prematurely. Some of the bmrs jettison their bombloads over the tgt area.

17 March

Eighth AF: P–47 FBs, escorted by P–47 ftrs, attack Chartres A/F. 16 others bomb Soesterberg A/F, losing 2 aircraft to AA fire.

Ninth AF: 70 B–25's bomb M/Y at Criel-sur-Mer.

Twelfth AF: B–25's bomb Montepescali M/Y and Cecina. B–25's hit Roccasecca and Castrocielo, while A–20's hit troop concentration in Cassino area. FBs hit guns in Cassino area and attack nearby railroad

bridge and underpass with good results.

Fifteenth AF: More than 200 B–24's bomb Vienna and various T/Os. P–47's and P–38's provide escort. Over 100 B–17's abort because of bad weather.

Tenth AF: 24 B–24's and 12 P–38's attack supply dumps in Kalewa area in Chin Hills region. 18 A–31's hit villages and positions in same general area while 22 others attack troops near Thaungdut. 30-plus B–25's, P–51's, and A–36's damage Shweli and Mogaung bridges and hit positions and supply dumps in Kamaing area. 37 P–40's blast A/F at Myitkyina. Numerous other aircraft fly miscellaneous sorties over Sumprabum area. 2 B–25's cause fires among oil installations at Chauk.

Fourteenth AF: 5 B–25's bomb and strafe boatyards at Vinh and hit lumber stores and sawmills at nearby Ben Thuy.

Fifth AF: Almost 100 B–24's, B–25's, and A–20's attack Wewak area. P–38's hit Hansa Bay area while other B–25's bomb Madang-Alexishafen area. Soerabaja naval base is bombed by B–24's.

Thirteenth AF: 31 FBs and 31 B–25's pound supply areas at Wunapope and at Ralum. A few FBs hit Japanese bivouac area on Matchin Bay. 20-plus B–24's pound airstrip at Namatanai.

Seventh AF: B–24's and B–25's from Tarawa bomb, respectively, Ponape and Jaluit.

Eleventh AF: 3 B–24's fly armed rcn over Onnekotan I before dawn releasing bombs through overcast.

18 March

Eighth AF: 679 B–17's and B–24's bomb aircraft plants and A/Fs at Oberpfaffenhofen, Friedrichshafen, Lechfeld, Munich, Landsberg, and Memmingen. Enemy ftrs attack in force and AA fire is heavy. 43 US bmrs and 13 escorting ftrs are lost. Total US claims for enemy aircraft destroyed are 84.

Twelfth AF: B–25's, B–26's, and A–20's bomb Foligno M/Y, Orvieto M/Y and railroad bridge, Poggibonsi railroad bridge, Piombino dock area, Colleferro railroad tracks, and assembly area N of Anzio. P–40's, A–36's, and P–47's attack gun positions in Anzio beachhead area, factory at Carroceto, motor transport concentrations in Cassino area, fuel dump, tank repair depot, and bivouac in beachhead area, motor transport around Ladispoli, railroad bridge N of Rome, and railroad tracks and cars at other points.

Fifteenth AF: More than 350 B–17's and B–24's bomb A/Fs at Villaorba, Udine, Gorizia, Lavariano, and Maniago. 126 P–38's and P–47's carry out sweeps in Udine-Maniago area, and strafe aircraft at Udine A/F tanker S of Marano Lagoon and a hangar, 2 trains, 2 radar stations, and seaplane anchorage (destroying 6 seaplanes) at Belvedere. HBs and escorts claim 48 enemy ftrs destroyed. 9 US aircraft are downed.

Tenth AF: 12 A–31's hit Japanese positions W of Buthidaung in Arakan area. In the Chin Hills, 22 B–25's attack villages and oil storage areas near Kalewa while 16 B–24's and 41 A–31's pound same general area hitting Japanese positions and causing many fires. 20-plus P–51's and B–25's

spt ground forces near Chindwin. 14 others hit truck park and supply area near Mandalay. 20-plus FBs (P–51's, P–40's, and A–36's) bomb Kamaing area while 10 more damage several riverboats near Katha.

Fourteenth AF: 16 P–40's on Yangtze R sweep sink 1 large sailboat and strafe a transport ship at Chiuchiang. 2 P–40's damage bridge N of Haiphong and attack T/Os in the area, while 2 others sink 2 large junks at Thuong Mo. 12 P–40's on armed rcn from Nanning sink barge and damage other craft at Quang Yen, sink a transport vessel at Campha Port and damage a nearby bridge, attack a train and several buildings in Lang Son area, and damage a railroad bridge between Lang Son and Phu Lang Thuong.

Fifth AF: More than 100 B–24's B–25's, and A–20's continue to pound Wewak area, hitting AA positions and nearby Brandi Plantation. Japanese supply convoy reaches Wewak but escapes bombardment.

Thirteenth AF: 12 P–40's pound fuel stores on Keravia Bay. 13 P–38's follow with strike on ammo dump at nearby Cape Tawui. 12 P–39's later hit Keravia Bay area. Still later, 24 B–24's and 13 B–25's blast town of Rabaul and foothills nearby. 18 P–39's, along with several naval FBs, hit shipping at mouths of Jaba and Tavena Rivers.

Seventh AF: 2 B–25's from Engebi bomb and strafe Ponape. 13 B–25's from Abemama bomb Jaluit while 5 from Tawara hit the Atoll with bombs and cannon fire. 1 B–24 from Tarawa bombs Mille and photographs Mille and Majuro Atolls.

19 March

Eighth AF: 172 B–17's attack V-weapon installations at Wizernes, Watten, and Marquise. 24 P–47 FBs dive-bomb Gilze-Rijen A/F. 11 P–47's fly top cover while 39 P–51's fly uneventful supporting sweep over S Netherlands.

Ninth AF: 152 B–26's and 65 A–20's attack NOBALL tgts in Saint-Omer area during morning and afternoon missions. 16 P–47's dive-bomb A/F between Boulogne-sur-Mer and Le Touquet. The morning raids precede Eighth AF attack with HBs on V-weapon sites.

MAAF: MATAF issues directive for Operation STRANGLE, to interdict supply movements in Italy by destroying M/Ys and attacking rail lines and ports in a concentrated campaign.

Twelfth AF: B–26's attack road bridge W of Arezzo and port installations at San Stefano al Mare. B–25's hit bridge approach in S Orvieto, M/Y's at Avezzano and Orte, and bridge at Orte. Tank repair shops near Tivoli are bombed by A–20's. P–47's and P–40's strike at enemy concentrations, dumps, and guns in US Fifth Army main battle area and in area N of Anzio beachhead.

Fifteenth AF: 460th Bomb Gp (B–24) is declared operational making total of 14 HB gps operational in Fifteenth AF. 234 B–17's and B–24's, escorted by 100-plus ftrs, bomb A/F and town of Klagenfurt. Other B–24's (over 150) hit Graz factory complex M/Ys at Metkovic and Knin. Enemy ftrs provide fierce opposition and along with AA fire, shoot down 17 HBs and 1 ftr. US aircraft claim 30 enemy ftrs destroyed in combat.

Tenth AF: 20-plus B–25's and P–38's hit Wuntho. More than 20 A–31's attack villages and Japanese positions in the Chin Hills and near Chindwin. 70-plus FBs and 2 B–25's over Mogaung Valley bomb supply dumps, enemy positions, and T/Os throughout the area, concentrating attacks in and near Kamaing, Mogaung, and Sumprabum. 16 P–51's hit barracks and supply area at Meiktila A/F near Mandalay while 3 B–25's hit Indaw.

Fourteenth AF: 2 B–25's, 9 P–38's, and 3 P–51's on Yangtze R sweep damage several river vessels, hit fort at Chihchow, and bomb A/F at Nanchang.

Fifth AF: Over 100 B–24's, B–25's, A–20's, and P–47's pound Wewak area, hitting especially hard the Cape Moem and Cape Boram areas. Other B–25's and P–39's, along with RAAF airplanes, bomb Hansa Bay, Nubia, Madang, and Alexishafen area and hit tgts along Bogadjim Road. P–40's attack bivouac area and AA on Garove I. 130 B–24's, B–25's, A–20's, and P–38's virtually destroy supply convoy proceeding from Wewak toward Hollandia, sinking at least 5 vessels.

Thirteenth AF: 30-plus FBs over Rabaul area pound ammo dump and other tgts around Cape Tawui. 24 B–25's blast Wunapope area, concentrating on workers' quarters. 24 B–24's bomb airstrip at Panapai, causing considerable damage to runways.

Seventh AF: B–24's pound Wake from Kwajalein. B–25's from Abemama and Tarawa hit Maloelap, Jaluit, and Mille. 1 B–24 from Tarawa bombs Mille and photographs Mille and Majuro Atolls.

20 March

Eighth AF: 51 B–17's bomb industry and transportation tgts at Frankfurt/Main. 99 HBs attack T/Os, including Bingen, Mannheim area, and Mainz area. Bad weather and malfunction of blind-bombing equipment cause nearly 300 HBs to abandon mission.

Ninth AF: 67th Tac Rcn Gp completes series of 83 missions (begun on 23 Feb) during which photos were made of 160 mi of French coastline and 2 inshore strips, each 120 mi long; 9500 prints are produced and no aircraft are lost. Over 200 B–26's and A–20's bomb 4 NOBALL tgts and Creil M/Y. 85 P–47's dive-bomb A/Fs at Abbeville, Poix, and Conches.

Twelfth AF: 310th Bomb Gp (M) is transferred from XII FC to 57th Bomb Wg, thus consolidating all B–25 units of the Twelfth under 1 wg. B–25's strike harbor and shipping at Piombino, Poggibonsi railroad bridge, Port' Ercole, and area around Orvieto railroad bridge. B–25's hit Orvieto M/Y and underpass and road bridge nearby, Terni M/Y, and dock at San Stefano al Mare. Factory at Fontana Liri is accurately bombed by A–20's. P–40's hit troop concentrations, guns, and fuel dump in Cassino-Fontana Liri area while A–36's blast railway station at Frosinone and also drop food for troops in Cassino area. P–47's hit fuel dump at Fontana Liri.

USSR: Red Army sweeps into Bessarabia.

Tenth AF: In the Arakan area, 12 A–31's hit Japanese positions near Kaladan and Buthidaung while 6 P–

38's severely damage bridge at Lamu. 20-plus B–25's, and P–51's hit comm and transportation tgts in Katha area. 6 B–24's bomb Moulmein-Martaban area. More than 100 FBs strike Mogaung Valley buildings and supply areas, and fuel dumps at Mogaung, Myitkyina, Sumprabum, and Sahmaw.

Fourteenth AF: Photo rcn sorties are flown over C China and NE Burma.

Fifth AF: 30-plus B–24's bomb A/F at Aitape. Over 20 P–39's and A–20's hit Japanese HQ and other tgts along Bogadjim Road while B–25's and P–39's on armed rcn hit tgts at Milhanak, along Gogol R, at Yeschan, Burui A/F, and at Erima. P–40's on armed rcn hit villages and barges along Bangula Bay coast. At night B–24's bomb remnants of supply convoy off Cape Terabu.

Thirteenth AF: 20-plus FBs hit Ratawul supply area. Later 20-plus ftrs attack barges in Rabaul area while 3 B–34's blast several buildings at nearby Massava Bay. 23 B–24's bomb A/F at Vunakanau while 24 B–25's pound Lakunai. 10 P–40's and P–39's bomb Numa Numa and strafe coastal T/Os. Rcn patrol of SB–24's cover Marines moving onto Emirau I. Ftr patrol is unnecessary due to unexpected lack of opposition. After initial landing by Marines other Allied ground forces move ashore. By afternoon of 21 Mar the occupation of the island is complete. Construction of a base begins shortly.

Seventh AF: 12 B–25's from Tarawa bomb radio station and pier on Emidj. 1 other B–25 from Tarawa bombs Mille, rearms at Majuro, and again bombs Mille on return trip.

21 March

Eighth AF: 56 B–24's bomb V-weapon launching installation at Watten. 41 P–51's in a ftr sweep over S France claim 21 aircraft destroyed. About 650 B–17's and B–24's bomb Berlin area, including aircraft factories at Basdorf and Oranienburg. Of 12 brms lost, 1 B–17 is destroyed by a bomb dropped by a B–17 from a sq flying at a higher altitude.

Ninth AF: All B–26's dispatched to bomb NOBALL tgts in France are recalled because of bad weather.

Twelfth AF: B–25's make unsuccessful attempt to bomb Poggibonsi bridge. Weather cancels other B–25 missions and all A–20 operations. B–26's attack Arezzo and Bucine viaducts and Poggibonsi and Cecina railroad bridges. P–47's hit railroad bridges N of Rome while P–40's bomb tgts in Anzio area. A–36's drop food in Cassino area.

Fifteenth AF: Bad weather limits operations to photo and weather rcn missions.

Tenth AF: 30-plus A–31's hit Japanese positions near Arakan and in the Chin Hills. 25 B–25's and P–51's destroy 1 bridge and damage another near Meza, pound buildings and T/Os in Mawlu area and hit a locomotive and several trucks in Banmauk-Indaw area. 6 P–38's bomb Monywa oil dumps, causing several large fires. 80-plus FBs and 2 B–25's hit town of Manywet, storage area at Myitkyina, buildings at Kamaing and Myitkyina, and warehouses, bypass, and bridge at Hopin.

Fifth AF: 140-plus B–24's, B–25's, A–20's, P–38's, and P–40's attack numerous tgts in Wewak-Tadji-Hansa Bay-Schouten Is areas. P–39's and RAAF FBs blast Japanese positions in Madang area. P–40's and A–20's on armed rcn attack tgts on New Britain and on Garove I to the N.

Thirteenth AF: 30-plus FBs and 24 B–25's pound Lakunai A/F area. 22 B–24's bomb Vunakanau A/F. Ftrs carry out barge sweeps in Rabaul area. 14 P–39's hit Numa Numa. Small strikes are flown against Monoitu and a bridge at Meive, and FBs spt ground forces and bomb bivouac along Empress Augusta Bay.

Seventh AF: B–24's from Tarawa hit Mille, Maloelap and Ponape. Tarawa-based B–25's also pound Maloelap.

22 March

Twelfth AF: B–26's attack Poggibonsi railroad bridge and viaduct W of Arezzo. B–25's hit road bridge near Poggibonsi. P–40's bomb guns in Avezzano and Pico areas. P–40's on patrols over Anzio and Cassino claim 2 ftrs destroyed.

Fifteenth AF: Around 100 B–17's bomb M/Ys at Verona while about 100 B–24's hit M/Ys at Bologna and Rimini. P–38's and P–47's provide cover for all the missions. 2 HBs are lost to flak and another has to ditch.

CBI: Japanese move into India from Burma, penetrate to 30 mi E of Imphal.

Tenth AF: 36 A–31's hit villages of Homalin and Myothit and bomb Japanese positions near Chindwin. Over 100 ftrs and FBs over Mogaung Valley attack troops, storage, and other tgts and cause several fires throughout the area. 20-plus P–51's and B–25's carry out ground spt missions in Mawlu area near Katha. Near Rangoon 4 B–24's set fire to

Prome supply dumps while a single P–38 damages railroad bridges and several trucks at Pyinmana.

Fourteenth AF: 4 B–25's from Yangkai hit several tgts in and around Phu Dien Chau, Ha Trung, Dong Giao, and Nam Dinh. Results include 3 locomotives destroyed and another damaged, 3 125-ft steamers damaged, and a bridge roadbed weakened. 1 B–25 is lost.

Fifth AF: 130-plus B–24's, B–25's, B–20's, and P–40's attack Wewak area, hitting enemy positions, AA guns, storage areas at Wewak, Boram, and Yeschan, and hitting shipping offshore. Japanese HQ and troops are hit by 25 other aircraft in Aitape-Tadji area. P–47's hit barges at Alexishafen while P–39's hit HQ and supply dump along Bogadjim Road. A–20's hit barges near Pondo Plantation and hit Ewasse village.

Thirteenth AF: 30-plus FBs hit supply area along Laruma R. A total of 13 B–24's carry out small strikes against Buka, Monoitu, Kahili, and Kara. 23 B–25's pound Lakunai A/F, 10 B–24's bomb Tobera, and a single B–24 hits Rabaul.

Seventh AF: B–25's from Abemama and Tarawa bomb Mille and Jaluit.

23 March

Eighth AF: 767 HBs are dispatched to attack A/Fs in W Germany and aircraft factories in Brunswick area. Due to unfavorable weather conditions, only 68 HBs bomb primary tgt (A/F at Handorf). 205 bomb city of Brunswick (secondary tgt) and 432 others bomb T/Os, including Hamm M/Y, Osnabruck, Munster, Ahlen, Beckum, Neu-beckum, and Drensteinfurt. 28 aircraft are lost, mostly to ftrs.

Ninth AF: 220 B–26's on morning mission bomb Creil M/Y and A/Fs at Beaumont-le-Roger and Beauvais/Tille. In afternoon raid, 146 bomb Haine-Saint-Pierre M/Y.

Twelfth AF: B–26's bomb Florence/Campo di Marte M/Y while B–25's hit Pontassieve railway bridge and its approaches. P–40's attack guns in Cassino-Esperia area, causing many fires and explosions. A–36's bomb Cassino area with good results. Germans have been forced into narrow zone in W edge of Cassino but still hold positions commanding the town and the Abbey; NZ Corps breaks off attack.

Tenth AF: In Chin Hills region 12 A–31's hit Japanese positions, 12 B–24's and 10 P–38's bomb Kalewa, and 9 B–25's attack Kaing and Shwebo. In Katha area 12 P–51's bomb Naba Station while 12 others join 9 B–25's in attacking ammo and gas dumps at Indaw. 4 P–40's bomb stores at Kamaing while 30-plus other ftrs fly armed rcn over the Mogaung Valley in general. 12 B–24's pound Moulmein jetty and attack Moulmein-Bangkok railroad tgts, destroying 2 bridges, damaging several others, and scoring effective hits on 2 trains.

Fourteenth AF: B–25's on railroad sweep N from Vinh destroy 2 engines and several boxcars at Van Trai Station yards and attack 3 bridges between Vinh and Thanh Hoa.

Fifth AF: Nearly 100 B–24's, B–25's, A–20's, and P–47's hit numerous tgts in Aitape, Wewak, Alexishafen, and Hansa Bay areas. 29 P–40's attack Talasea and nearby bivouacs, including Gogosi. B–24's bomb Babo and during the night attack shipping in Bismarck Sea.

Thirteenth AF: 14 P–38's bomb T/Os at Komaleai Pt while 24 B–25's hit Buka area after weather prevented scheduled attacks on Rabaul. Ftrs fly sweeps over Rabaul and general New Ireland area, and 12 P–40's bomb fuel dump at Keravia Bay. 15 B–24's out of 24 dispatched plow through the bad weather and bomb Ratawul supply area.

Seventh AF: B–24's from Kwajalein bomb Wake. B–25's flying out of Eniwetok hit Ponape. Tarawa-based B–25's strike Maloelap and Jaluit, commencing a series of B–25 shuttle-missions between Tarawa or Makin and the Navy's new base at Majuro Atoll which is used as the rearming base for the return strike.

24 March

Eighth AF: 59 B–17's bomb Schweinfurt, using blind-bombing equipment. 162 other B–17's diverting from primary tgt at Schweinfurt because of clouds, bomb M/Y at Frankfurt/Main. Primary B–24 tgts, A/Fs at Metz and Nancy, are overcast, but 33 are able to bomb Nancy while 147 others bomb secondary tgt of Saint Dizier/Robinson A/F.

Twelfth AF: B–25's pound supply and bivouac areas in Piedimonte and Castrocielo and harbor installations at Leghorn. B–25's hit bridge and railroad tracks NW of Orvieto, and A–20's bomb guns in Cassino area. P–40's and A–36's in Cassino area hit guns, troop concentrations, road, and causeway. P–47's on armed rcn in Rome-Orvieto-Orte areas hit train and bridge.

Fifteenth AF: More than 100 B–24's bomb Rimini M/Ys while 32 others attack Ancona, Senigallia, and rail and road bridges over Vomano R S of Giulianova. Over 200 other B–17's and B–24's turn back before reaching tgt and before rendezvous with ftr escorts. 3 B–17's and 1 B–24 hit T/Os in Italy and Yugoslavia. 6 B–24's are lost. The HBs claim 10 enemy ftrs destroyed.

Tenth AF: Near Chindwin 50-plus A–31's attack Homalin and Tamanthi. In Mandalay area 12 B–24's and 10 P–38's bomb Pyingaing dump, 9 B–25's hit Shwebo railroad yards and a nearby factory, and 8 P–51's attack Gokteik Viaduct. 4 P–40's bomb Japanese positions near Shaduzup.

Fifth AF: P–39's and P–40's hit Alexishafen with dive bombing and strafing attack at midday. A single B–24 bombs nearby Sek I. Other B–24's on armed rcn score hit on minesweeper. Organized Japanese resistance ends on Los Negros and Bougainville, although considerable time will be required for mopping-up operations.

Thirteenth AF: 20-plus B–25's hit airstrip at Tobera. A few which lost contact with formation bomb Vunakanau instead. More than 30 P–38's, P–39's, and P–40's hit Wunapope with incendiary clusters, causing numerous fires.

Seventh AF: B–25's from Tarawa bomb Jaluit while others, flying out of Eniwetok, hit Ponape and Ant Is.

Eleventh AF: 3 B–24's fly photo mission over Onnekotan.

25 March

Ninth AF: More than 140 MBs attack Hirson M/Y.

Twelfth AF: Weather severely curtails operations. B–26's bomb Leghorn dockyard and town of Rignano sull' Arno. P–40 FBs attack gun positions in Anzio beachhead battle area. Ftrs fly cover over Anzio and Cassino areas.

Tenth AF: 50-plus A–31's attack Japanese-held villages and gun positions from Kalewa to Homalin. 8 B–24's hit Mogaung supply dumps, causing fires and much smoke. 12 P–40's bomb Kamaing area. Japanese aircraft (5 MBs and 30 ftrs) attack Allied airstrips at Chittagong, Cox's Bazaar and Anisakan. Tenth AF and RAF interceptors claim 7 airplanes shot down.

Fourteenth AF: 6 B–24's from Chengkung bomb motor pool and fuel dump at Mangshih, demolishing a sizeable portion of the tgt area.

Fifth AF: More than 100 B–24's, B–25's, and A–20's continue pounding of Wewak area, destroying supply dumps along coast from Wewak Pt to the A/F, fuel dump W of Boram, and tgts along Sauri road and in Cape Wom area. Other A–20's attack coastal area around Bunabun Harbor. P–40's attack a Japanese HQ at Cape Hoskins. B–24's bomb Babo-Urarom area. On Manus, last major battle takes place; isolated enemy positions remain to be eliminated.

Thirteenth AF: 23 B–25's pound Ratawul supply area while 34 FBs hit Keravia Bay fuel stores. 20-plus FBs hit Miwo R bridge and nearby bivouac area and bomb truck park W of Omoi R.

Seventh AF: Adv HQ in Tarawa is disbanded and the Seventh's operations in C Pacific forward area are placed under VII BC at Kwajalein. B–25's from Eniwetok pound Ponape and claim 4 ftrs shot down. B–25's from Abemama bomb Maloelap.

Eleventh AF: 2 Shemya-based B–24's bomb Kurabu Cape and N coast of Onnekotan.

26 March

Eighth AF: Nearly 500 B–17's and B–24's bomb V-weapon installations and T/Os in the Pas de Calais and Cherbourg areas.

Ninth AF: 338 B–26's and 35 A–20's attack Ijmuiden torpedo-boat pens. Nearly 140 P–47's and P–51's dive-bomb Creil M/Y and military installations in France.

Twelfth AF: Operations are at a minimum as bad weather continues. B–26's score numerous hits on Arezzo viaducts, B–25's attack Perugia railway bridge, scoring near misses, and A–20's successfully bomb troop concentrations N of Velletri. P–47's achieve direct hits on railway bridge NW of Stimigliano and near misses on railway bridge SW of Tarquinia. P–40's hit guns near Fontana Liri and N of Anzio beachhead with good results.

Fifteenth AF: 60-plus B–17's and B–24's hit port of Fiume and M/Ys at Rimini and Maniago. P–47's and P–38's provide escort. Over 150 other B–17's and B–24's abort missions because of bad weather.

Tenth AF: In Chin Hills region 40-plus A–31's pound Japanese positions in Tonzang-Kalewa area and near Kalemyo. The FBs also claim more than 20 trucks destroyed in the Kalemyo area. Near Chindwin 3 B–24's and 3 B–25's bomb troops along Imphal-Tiddim road. 70-plus FBs

and a lone B–25 attack tgts in Mogaung Valley area, including A/Fs at
Manywet   and   Myitkyina,   and
bridges, roads, railroads and T/Os at
Mogaung,   Kamaing,   and   Myitkyina. In the Katha area 8 P–51's
and 3 B–25's hit Japanese bivouac NE
of Bhamo and claim 6 warehouses destroyed at Nankan.

Fourteenth AF: 4 B–25's hit Bakli
Bay area. 2 merchant vessels are
claimed sunk, and damage is done to
tracks and loading equipment. 4 P–
40's on sweep of N coast of Gulf of
Tonkin sink ore boat and damage 4
barges.

Fifth AF: 220-plus B–24's, B–25's,
A–20's, and ftrs hit Wewak, Boram,
Cape Wom, Aitape, Hansa Bay coast,
Mushu I, and general area along N
coast of NE New Guinea, blasting
storage   areas,   barges,   shipping,
grounded airplanes, fuel dumps, and
enemy troops. Other A–20's hit Bunabun Harbor while P–39's hit Madang
area. P–39's and P–40's attack Cape
Hoskins and troops in Talasea area.
On Manus I A–20's hit buildings and
Japanese positions on S shore.

Thirteenth AF: 23 B–25's hit
Vunakanau A/F and 37 FBs attack
supply areas along Talili Bay. B–25's
continue to heckle Rabaul area during the night. In Bougainville area 3
B–24's and 20 FBs hit pillboxes and
T/Os on islands off Tekessi R mouth
and near Monoitu. FBs again spt
ground forces along Empress Augusta Bay, hitting supply dump N of
Reini R and enemy positions near
mouths   of   Tekessi   and   Maririei
Rivers. The FBs claim destruction of
a bridge over the Puriata R. 24 B–
24's on mission against Truk I fail
to reach tgt and bomb Pulusuk I in-

stead. Several of the HBs are forced
to land on Green I because of fuel
shortages.

Seventh· AF: Eniwetok-based B–
25's strike Ponape. B–25's from Tarawa hit Jaluit, rearm at Majuro, and
hit Jaluit again on return flight to
Tarawa.

27 March

Eighth AF: Almost 700 B–17's and
B–24's bomb A/Fs at Cazaux, Bor-
deaux, Pau, Biarritz, Mont-de-Marsan,
Saint-Jean-d'Angely,   La   Rochelle,
Tours, and Chartres, and an aircraft
works at Tours.

Ninth AF: 18 B–26's attack V-
weapon sites in N France. 35 others
abort due primarily to failure of
blind-bombing equipment. Onset of
bad weather makes this the last MB
mission until 8 Apr.

Twelfth AF: A–20's successfully
bomb Sesti Bagni railway station;
B–26's hit Poggibonsi railway bridge,
and tracks and train cars in the area;
and B–25's attack bridges at Marsciano, Perugia, and Grosseto railroad
bridges, scoring damaging hits at
Grosseto. P–40's hit cmd post and
supply dumps, and fly road rcn
SE of Rome with good results. A–36's
bomb Sesti Bagni railway station and
nearby trucks, while P–47's attack
bridge, junctions, and train cars on
Rome-Orvieto railroad. P–47's and
P–40's maintain cover over Cassino
and Anzio battle areas.

Tenth AF: 8 B–24's hit supply
dumps at Kamaing, while about 50
FBs and 2 B–25's hit troops in Myit-
kinya area and spt ground forces
near Kamaing. In Katha area 12 B–
25's and 16 P–38's and P–51's hit
bridge and railroad facilities near

Meza and railroad near Kawlin. 6υ A–31's pound T/Os along upper Chindwin R.

Fourteenth AF: 6 B–25's pound Viet Tri area, damaging 2 factories, a bridge, and several railroad cars. 60-plus P–40's, P–38's, and P–51's attack troops and buildings at Sienning and Kwanyinchow hit bridge, warehouse, and general area at Anyi, damage bridges at Kienchang and Puchi, and pound Nanchang A/F and surrounding areas.

Fifth AF: More than 200 B–24's, B–25's, A–20's, P–47's, P–40's, and P–39's attack storage areas, shipping, bridges, fuel dumps, enemy troop concentrations, and other tgts in areas around Wewak, Hansa Bay, Uligan Harbor, and Madang. Other aircraft carry out sweeps and armed rcn over New Britain and Bismarck Sea.

Thirteenth AF: 23 B–25's hit Wunapope with incendiaries. 34 FBs follow in rapid succession with another incendiary strike, leaving the entire vicinity in flames. 8 P–40's hit fuel dump at mouth of Tekessi R.

Seventh AF: B–25's and B–24's from Tarawa hit Maloelap, Mille, and Wotje. B–25's from Eniwetok Atoll bomb Jaluit and strafe and cannonade Ponape. A single B–24 from Tarawa bombs Jabor.

28 March

Eighth AF: 363 B–17's attack A/Fs at Dijon, Reims, Chateaudun, and Chartres. 78 B–24's dispatched to bomb port area of Ijmuiden are recalled because of thick cloud cover over North Sea.

Twelfth AF: B–25's knock out bridge approach E of Perugia and bomb railway junction and M/Y at Montepescali. B–25's bomb railway bridge S of Mignano and viaduct to the SE, and hit Certaldo railway bridge. A–20's attack tank factory N of Tivoli. P–40's strike guns in Anzio area; guns, trucks, and roads during armed rcn of Cassino-Giulianello area; and supply dumps and truck parks near Velletri and Sora. A–36's attack 2 railroad bridges and tracks at Montalto di Castro and near Orvieto. Ftrs carry out patrols over Anzio and Cassino areas.

Fifteenth AF: Almost 400 B–17's and B–24's, largest Fifteenth AF attack to date, bomb M/Ys at Verona and Mestre, and railroad and highway bridges at Cesano and Fano. P–38's and P–40's provide excellent coverage and no HBs are lost. HBs and escorts claim 12 ftrs destroyed. 5 US ftrs are lost.

Tenth AF: In the Mogaung Valley 8 B–24's bomb Kamaing storage area, while 60-plus FBs and 9 B–25's furnish ground spt in Sumprabum, Mogaung, and Kamaing areas, and bomb storage and town areas of Manywet, Mohnyin, and Kamaing. 60 A–31's over Chindwin area attack villages from Thaungdut northward, while 6 others hit Kalewa.

Fourteenth AF: 4 B–25's bomb barracks area at Vinh Yen, scoring direct hits on 4 buildings.

Fifth AF: B–24's hit Hollandia and Penfoei.

Thirteenth AF: 24 B–25's bomb Tobera A/F, causing considerable damage to landing strip. FBs hit Ratawul supply area and SW part of Rabaul. A few P–40's attack Numa Numa supply area, a single B–24 scores damaging hits on Japanese-held mission at Monoitu, and other planes hit scattered T/Os.

Seventh AF: B–25's from Abemama and Tarawa pound Jaluit, Mille, and Maloelap. A single B–24 from Kwajalein, en route to Eniwetok, bombs Rongelap. B–24's, flying night mission from Kwajalein, bomb tgts at Truk.

29 March

Eighth AF: 187 B–17's bomb industrial area of Brunswick. 40 attack T/Os, including Stedorf and Unterluss. 77 B–24's are dispatched to bomb V-weapon installation at Watten, but malfunction of Pathfinder equipment and navigational difficulties result in only 31 bombing the tgt.

Twelfth AF: B–25's attack Viterbo A/F, causing considerable damage to tgt. B–26's hit Leghorn and many small craft nearby. French B–26's attached to Twelfth AF bomb Portoferraio on Elba. P–40's attack supply dumps and bivouac area SE of Rome, tank repair shop E of Rome, and guns and supply dumps E of Velletri. P–47's cut lines at railway overpass N of Rome while A–36's bomb harbors at San Stefano al Mare and Civitavecchia and hit nearby T/Os. Spitfires, P–40's, and P–47's patrol Anzio battle area.

Fifteenth AF: About 400 B–17's and B–24's (largest Fifteenth AF total to date) bomb M/Ys at Bolzano, Turin, and Milan. P–47's and P–38's fly escort. The HBs and ftrs claim 13 aircraft destroyed. 6 US aircraft are lost.

Tenth AF: In Chindwin area 70-plus A–31's hit Japanese positions and T/Os near Tonzang, Homalin, Imphal, Ukhrul, Tamu, and Jessami.

20-plus P–51's and B–25's over Katha area hit railroad and warehouse at Indaw spt ground forces nearby. 12 P–38's join numerous RAF airplanes in strikes on A/Fs, railroads, riverboats, and a variety of tgts in Mandalay area. 12 B–24's pound Victoria Lake region near Rangoon. 80-plus FBs and a few B–25's blast tgts throughout Mogaung Valley, including Waingmaw area, Mogaung, Nanyaseik, guns NE of Kamaing, and numerous scattered fortifications, supply areas, troop concentrations, and pillboxes. 80-plus other ftrs maintain patrol of Sumprabum area.

Fourteenth AF: 12 P–40's and 3 P–51's attack railroad station area at Nanchang, causing much damage to buildings and yards. The FBs also strafe A/F and attack nearby bridge.

Fifth AF: Gen Prentiss is announced as CG V AFSC and Gen Carter as CG 54th TC Wg. B–24's bomb Hollandia. B–25's and A–20's pound Wewak area, hitting tgts at Cape Wom and Dagua and attacking shipping throughout the day. More A–20's pound Bogia-Bunabun area and P–39's hit AA position at Erima in Madang area. P–47's and P–40's on ftr sweep and armed rcn strafe coastal T/Os in NE New Guinea and New Britain.

Thirteenth AF: In Rabaul area 19 FBs hit T/Os along Miwo R and at Mawareka and Kimaku; 8 others abort because of bad weather. Ftrs sweeping vicinity of Rabaul strafe shipping in Keravia Bay and knock out gun position at Cape Tawui. 24 B–25's and 11 P–40's get through the bad weather and pound supply areas at Wunapope and Ratawul, respectively. A few P-38's hit Numa Numa while other FBs again spt ground forces at mouth of Tekessi R. B-24's of 307th Bomb Gp carry out the first daylight raid on Truk Atoll, bombing the A/F on Eten I. The mission is staged from Munda through Torokina for arming and Nissan for refueling before the strike. The unescorted HBs claim 31 interceptors destroyed, along with almost 50 airplanes on the ground. 2 B-24's are lost.

Seventh AF: B-25's from Kwajalein hit Jaluit and Rongelap. B-25's from Eniwetok strike Ponape while others from Tarawa bomb Maloelap and Jaluit.

30 March

Eighth AF: 23 P-47 FBs of 2 gps launch dive-bombing attack on Eindhoven and Soesterberg A/Fs. A third gp of P-47's strafes A/Fs at Venlo, Deelen, and Twente and other military objectives in E Netherlands and NW Germany, including M/Y at Viersen, shipping on Rhine R, flak towers, and gun emplacements. 1 ftr is lost.

Ninth AF: IX Engineer Cmd is formally activated by WD. CG is Gen Newman.

Twelfth AF: B-25's hit harbor at Leghorn and railroad bridge NW of Orte. P-40's and A-36's attack ammo dump NW of Roccasecca, trucks and supply dump NE of Tivoli and near Fumone and Gaeta, railroad bridges SE of Civita Castellana and NW of Stimigliano and Orvieto, and motor transport N of Cori and at scattered points.

Fifteenth AF: 463d Bomb Gp (B-17) becomes the fifteenth HB gp declared operational by Fifteenth AF. Nearly 350 B-24's and B-17's bomb M/Ys at Sofia and industrial complex and A/F at Imotski. Escorting ftrs and the HBs claim 13 enemy ftrs shot down. 4 HBs are lost.

Tenth AF: 17 A-31's bomb Kaing area and NW Paungbyin. 5 others hit T/Os around Thayaung. 6 P-51's hit Anisakan A/F.

Fourteenth AF: 2 B-24's fly sea sweep from Kunming, around Hainan I, and across Gulf of Tonkin to Nam Dinh. En route, a freighter is strafed. 1 HB bombs spinning mills at Nam Sinh, causing considerable damage.

Fifth AF: 60-plus B-24's, with spt from more than 90 P-38's and P-47's, hit Hollandia in first big daylight raid. A/Fs and fuel dumps are bombed. A large number of enemy aircraft are destroyed or damaged on the ground. Escorting ftrs claim about 10 interceptors shot down. B-25's, A-20's, P-47's, P-40's, and P-39's continue to blast Japanese installations and forces in areas around Wewak, Tadji, and Madang.

Thirteenth AF: 11 B-24's fly long-range strike against Moen I. The HBs score damaging hits on the A/F and claim 11 ftrs shot down. 1 B-24 is lost. The raid follows a snooper strike by 2 B-24's the previous night. In Rabaul area 10 P-38's hit SW part of the town with incendiaries while 24 B-25's pound nearby Wunapope. FBs and MBs, operating mainly in pairs, hit supply area on Mupeka R and Japanese-occupied areas at mouths of Puriata and Mamaregu Rivers. FBs continue to spt ground forces along Empress Augusta Bay perimeter hitting bivouac and truck park at

Numa Numa, fords across Hongorai R, and bridge across the Puriata.

Seventh AF: B–24's from Kawajalein and Eniwetok hit Truk before dawn. B–25's from Kwajalein and Tarawa strike Wotje, Mille, Jaluit, and Maloelap.

31 March

Twelfth AF: Weather prevents completion of most Twelfth AF operations. P–47's carry out sweep N of Rome.

Tenth AF: 24 A–31's bomb Kaing and Homalin areas. 60 A–31's hit supply dumps and villages around Mintha, Ft Keary, Thaungdut, and Ukhrul. 9 B–25's hit nearby Pinlebu area. 10 P–51's hit Japanese positions near "Broadway" airstrip. 12 P–40's bomb Warong area while others patrol around Sumprabum. Near Katha 3 B–25's and 6 P–51's hit warehouse, railroad cars, and track at Zawchaung.

Fifth AF: 60-plus B–24's, with P–38 spt, pound Hollandia for second successive day. 3 A/Fs in area are thoroughly blasted and a large number of enemy airplanes destroyed. US aircraft claim 14 interceptors shot down. Supplies, enemy troops, and coastal tgts in Tadji, Wewak, and Hansa Bay areas are hit by 120-plus A–20's and B–25's.

Thirteenth AF: 23 B–25's bomb Ratawul supply point, 11 P–40's hit Wunapope, and 26 P–39's and P–38's bomb NE part of Rabaul with incendiaries. Ftr sweeps over Rabaul and New Ireland continue. 25 FBs pound Numa Numa supply area.

Seventh AF: B–24's from Eniwetok bomb Truk in predawn mission. B–25's from Eniwetok hit Ponape

while others, flying out of Tarawa, pound Maloelap and Jaluit.

Eleventh AF: XI BC and XI FC are disbanded. Their headquarters personnel is absorbed by the 28th Bomb Gp and the 343d Ftr Gp, respectively.

1 April

Eighth AF: 438 B–17's and B–24's are dispatched to bomb chemical industry at Ludwigshafen (largest in Europe). All 192 B–17's of the lead force abandon mission over French coast due to heavy clouds. The 246 B–24's in second force became widely dispersed; 162 bomb T/Os (Pforzheim and Grafenhausen); 26 bomb Schaffhausen, Switzerland, and Strasbourg, France, mistaking them for German towns.

Twelfth AF: B–25's attack Leghorn harbor, bridges at Orvieto, and railway track S of Poggibonsi. B–26's hit Arno R railroad bridges at Signa, Riva-Trigoso, and Valdarno, while A–20's hit ammo dumps. P–40's hit tgts in vicinity of Gaeta, Formia tunnel, several fuel dumps, bridges, and guns in battle areas. P–47's bomb Poggibonsi bridge and strafe train. Ftrs patrol Anzio battle area without incident.

Tenth AF: 10 A–31's hit troop positions SW of Buthidaung. 40-plus A–31's pound Homalin-Thaungdut-Paungbyin areas. In vicinity of Mandalay 14 P–38's hit freight train and damage a factory. Near Rangoon 16 B–24's hit a railroad station and bomb Akyab while 6 B–25's damage railroad bridge near Nattalin.

Fifth AF: B–25's and A–20's hit Tadji and Hansa Bay areas. B–24's bomb Boela. B–25's attack Penfoei.

Thirteenth AF: 24 B–25's bomb supply areas at Wunapope and Ratawul. 28 P–39's and P–40's hit Toboi wharf area at Simpson Harbor. 3 P–40's follow with strike on oil and coal storage in same general area. 12 P–38's bomb mission at Monoitu. Ftrs maintain sweeps over Rabaul and New Ireland throughout the day and B–25's harass Rabaul during 1/2 Apr. 12 P–40's hit Numa Numa supply dumps.

Seventh AF: B–25's from Abemama strike Ponape; B–24's from Makin and Kwajalein hit Truk. B–25's from Tarawa bomb Maloelap and Jaluit.

2 April

Twelfth AF: MBs attack railroad bridges at Arezzo, Fano, Ficulle, Magra, N of Orvieto, and S of Poggibonsi, scoring some direct hits, hits on approaches, and several near misses. FBs hit trucks and railroad station at Fara in Sabina and E and N of Anzio, attack Formia tunnel, fly armed rcn over Atina and Arce areas, bomb factory and buildings N of Cassino, town of Pignataro Interamna, and numerous bridges, dumps, gun positions and T/Os in or around battle areas.

Fifteenth AF: 461st Bomb Gp (B–24) becomes operational, making 16 HB gps now operational in Fifteenth AF. More than 530 B–24's and B–17's (largest Fifteenth AF mission to date) attack ball bearing plant and aircraft factory at Steyr, M/Ys at Bihac and Brod, troop concentration at Bihac, and A/F at Mostar. Ftrs fly over 150 sorties in spt of the HBs. Hundreds of ftrs oppose the missions. Fierce air battles result in 19 HBs shot down and several missing. The HBs and ftr escorts claim to have destroyed over 150 ftrs in combat.

E Europe: Soviet Army enters Rumania.

Tenth AF: 12 A–31's hit troop positions E and S of Buthidaung. 60 A–31's pound positions along upper Chindwin R and hit Paungbyin and Nawngpu-awng. 12 P–40's bomb Kamaing while 6 P–51's over Katha area hit trucks near Bhamo and storage area at Indaw.

Fourteenth AF: 2 B–24's on sea sweep from Hong Kong to Formosa bomb a 215-ft ship (reported sunk) and damage a large motor launch.

Fifth AF: More than 120 bmrs and ftrs continue to hit tgts in areas around Wewak, Hansa Bay, Madang, Bogadjim, and other points along NE New Guinea coastline. MBs also hit Dili, Penfoei, and Rambutyo I.

Thirteenth AF: 31 B–24's fly strike against Dublon, causing considerable damage to warehouse and dock areas. The HBs claim 30-plus ftrs downed. 4 B–24's are lost. 40-plus FBs over Rabaul hit SE part of town, Toboi wharf area, and N section of town along Malaguna road. 7 B–25's hit Raluana Pt while 23 pound Lakunai.

XX BC: First operational B–29, piloted by Col Leonard F Harman, lands at Chakulia.

Seventh AF: B–24's from Eniwetok hit Truk during 1/2 Apr. During the day B–25's bomb Jaluit and Maloelap.

3 April

Ninth AF: Because of combat crew shortage which has caused abolition of the 50-mission limit tour of duty and resulted in fatigue and morale problems, IX BC establishes new operational leave policy. Maximum leaves for bmr crews are set at 1 week between the 25th and 30th missions and 2 weeks between the 40th and 50th missions.

Twelfth AF: MBs attack railway bridges at Orvieto, cutting approaches to bridge at N of town. Other MB attacks on bridges abort because of weather but LBs successfully bomb ammo dump. A–36's attack railway at Attigliano and bomb underpass in the area, while P–40's hit Sesti Bagni railroad station, supply dump SE of Frosinone, town of Itri, bivouac area NW of Velletri, and several trucks. P–47's successfully bomb Pignataro Interamna and nearby road junction.

Fifteenth AF: More than 450 B–17's and B–24's bomb aircraft factory and M/Y at Budapest, and M/Ys at Knin, Brod, and Drnis. 137 ftrs escort the B–17's (B–24's miss rendezvous) to Budapest. HBs and escorting ftrs claim 24 aircraft shot down.

Tenth AF: 36 A–31's bomb areas along the upper Chindwin R. In Mandalay area 4 B–25's damage Tangon bridge while 6 P–61's hit Anisakan airstrip. 20-plus FBs and 6 B–25's hit T/Os S of Mupaw Ga and W of Mogaung, troops near Bhamo, and knock out bridge near Mogaung. During 3/4 Apr 16 B–24's bomb oil and power facilities at Yenangyaung, Chauk, and Lanywa while 8 P–38's hit Meiktila A/F.

Fourteenth AF: 4 rocket-firing P–40's, with 8 other as top cover, damage 2 large river boats between Hengyang and Ichang. 4 others flying Red R sweep from Vinh Yen to Dong Cuong sink 4 small boats, damage 3 more, and strafe 50–100 persons at a loading point on the R. 3 B–24's lay mines in Haiphong area.

Fifth AF: More than 300 B–24's, B–25's, A–20's, and P–38's blast A/Fs at Hollandia. Most of the remaining Japanese airplanes there are destroyed. Of 60 intercepting ftrs, 26 are claimed shot down. Air opposition from Hollandia is very light hereafter. 50-plus P–40's, P–47's, and P–39's hit villages, comm, AA positions, and other tgts in areas around Wewak, Hansa Bay, Bogia, and Madang. B–24's hit Langgoer and B–25's bomb Babo area and Penfoei.

Thirteenth AF: 23 B–25's pound NE section of Rabaul. This strike follows larger than usual (6 B–25's) heckling raids during 2/3 Apr. 50-plus FBs blast fuel stores at Keravia Bay. On Bougainville, AF and Navy ftrs strafe Numa Numa trail area and maintain patrols.

Seventh AF: B–24's, staging through Eniwetok during 2/3 Apr, bomb Truk. B–25's from Abemama follow with daytime attack on Ponape. Other B–25's from Abemama and Tarawa hit Maloelap and Jaluit.

4 April

Twelfth AF: MB missions are aborted due to weather. LBs manage to bomb an ammo dump. FBs bomb Terracina and Formia, attack bridge and several vehicles during armed rcn of Rome-Orte area, bomb Itri and Fondi, hit numerous gun positions, a railway station, a bivouac area, and a vehicle concentration, and attack T/Os between Atina and Cassino.

Fifteenth AF: Over 300 B–24's and B–17's attack M/Y at Budapest. Ftrs fly nearly 120 sorties in spt of the mission. Between 150 and 200 enemy ftrs attack the HBs, shooting down 10. HBs and escorts claim over 50 aircraft destroyed in combat.

Tenth AF: 120-plus FBs and 4 B–25's hit rail lines, storage areas and Japanese held villages around Mogaung and Myitkyina, and spt ground forces near Kamaing and Myitkyina. 80-plus A–31's hit enemy positions E of Imphal. During 4/5 Apr, 14 B–24's bomb Moulmein railroad yards and jetties and hit Japanese HQ nearby at Nagorn Sawarn. 27 P–51's and P–38's attack Aungban and Anisakan A/Fs.

Fourteenth AF: P–38's on armed rcn strafe and destroy 2 big fuel dumps, 12 fuel trucks, and 15–20 troops in Wan Mong Kang area.

Fifth AF: 50-plus B–24's pound Wewak area. 12 P–39's hit villages, bridges, and wooded areas along coast from Cape Gourdon to Bogia.

Thirteenth AF: 12 P–40's hit barge hideout in Gazelle Harbor. 10 B–25's (rained out of Rabaul) bomb Buka A/F, 23 P–39's hit Aitara area, and 11 P–40's bomb Mamaregu barge hideout. 24 P–38's pound Mamagata, Dio Dio, and Miwo R area. Ground spt missions along Empress Augusta Bay are carried out by a variety of ftrs.

Twentieth AF: Twentieth AF is constituted and activated in Washington, DC.

Seventh AF: B–24's, flying out of the Gilberts, bomb Truk during the night. B–25's, from Abemema and Tarawa, followup during the day with raids on Ponape, Jaluit, and Maloelap.

5 April

Eighth AF: 21 B–24's bomb V-weapon installation at Saint-Pol/Siracourt. Heavy clouds and failure of blind-bombing equipment cause more than 30 other HBs to return to base without bombing. More than 450 P–47's, P–38's, and P–51's attack A/Fs and other ground tgts in Germany and W Europe.

Twelfth AF: Weather precludes all LB and MB action. P–40's hit Colleferro railway station, several fuel dumps, and gun positions in US Fifth Army battle areas. A–36's bomb Formia, and railway stations NW of Rome and in Frosinone area.

Fifteenth AF: 334 B–17's and B–24's bomb Ploesti, town area of Leskovac, and M/Y at Nish. Ftrs and AA shoot down 13 HBs.

Tenth AF: 13 B–24's bomb railroad from Moulmein to Kanchanaburi, destroying 3 bridges, damaging several others, and causing much damage to track and railroad cars. 6 A–31's over Chindwin area pound T/Os around Thaungdut.

Fourteenth AF: P–40's from Yungning pound railroad siding at Na Cham, destroying 8 boxcars and a considerable amount of track.

Fifth AF: 270-plus B–24's, B–25's, A–20's, and P–38's hit Hollandia town and dock area and villages and stores around Humboldt Bay. P–47's and P–40's blast numerous tgts in Hansa Bay-Bogia and Wewak areas. B–24's hit Kaimana and Efman I. B–25's bomb Koepang.

Thirteenth AF: 12 B–25's pound Kara. Bad weather cancels all missions against tgts in the Bismarcks.

Seventh AF: B–25's from Tarawa hit Maloelap, bomb up again at Majuro, and hit Jaluit during return trip.

6 April

Eighth AF: 12 B–24's bomb V-weapon site at Watten.

Twelfth AF: B–25's hit Perugia A/F while B–26's bomb bridge and its approaches NW of Orvieto. Weather prevents other MB operations. FBs attack railroad stations at Capronica and Maccarese, guns SE of Littoria, road bridge E of Pescasseroli, railroad bridges in Arezzo area, other rail facilities in C Italy, and small transport vessels in the Aegean.

Fifteenth AF: B–24's bomb Zagreb A/F. Numerous other B–24's and B–17's abort because of weather. Escorting ftrs and the HBs claim 17 ftrs destroyed in combat. 6 US aircraft are shot down.

Tenth AF: 6 B–25's damage railroad and rolling stock at Shwebo. 6 A–31's bomb Tamanthi area. 80-plus FBs and 2 B–25's hit troops in Namti area, spt ground forces NE of Kamaing, damage a bridge near Myitkyina, and hit troops, oil dumps, and supplies at Mogaung and Manywet.

Fourteenth AF: P–40's from Suichwan pound barrack SW of Nanchang, causing heavy damage. B–25 strike during 6/7 Apr on A/Fs near Canton is curtailed by bad weather; only 1 MB reaches tgt, dropping fragmentation bombs on revetments.

Fifth AF: P–39's, P–40's, and P–47's continue to pound coastal tgts in Wewak, Aitape, and Madang areas and at numerous other points along coast. B–25's bomb Koepang.

Thirteenth AF: 34 B–24's pound Dublon. 22 B–25's bomb Lakunai A/F and revetment area. 30-plus FBs bomb vicinity of Toboi wharf with incendiaries while more than 20 others carry out incendiary strike on Wunapope, causing severe destruction to several buildings. Ftrs maintain sweep over Rabaul and New Ireland areas.

Twentieth AF: Gen Arnold assumes cmd of Twentieth AF at Washington, DC where HQ will remain until Jul 45. CoS is Gen Hansell (currently Dep Chief of Air Staff), with Col Cecil E Combs as his dep for operations.

Seventh AF: B–24's from Kwajalein bomb Wake. B–25's from Eniwetok hit Ponape twice. B–25's from Abemama bomb Jaluit, rearm at Majuro, and hit Maloelap during return flight.

7 April

Twelfth AF: MBs attack bridges, tracks, and viaduct at Attigliano, Ficulle, Certaldo, Pontassieve, and Incisa in Valdarno, and hit Prato M/Y. LBs hit ammo dump. Ausonia, Pignataro Interamna, San Apollinare, and Terracina are bombed by P–40's along with dump and several gun positions SE of Rome. P–47's also hit bridges and trucks in this same area and attack Empoli M/Y while A–36's hit gun emplacements, train and tracks in Orvieto area and vicinity and approaches to Montalto di Castro bridge.

Fifteenth AF: Over 400 B–24's and B–17's attack M/Ys at Treviso, Mestre, Bologna, and Ferrara. Almost 100 P–38's provide escort. P–47's fly sweep over Gorizia-Udine area. HBs and ftrs claim almost 20 aircraft shot down.

Tenth AF: 9 A–31's hit Japanese positions near Buthidaung in Arakan area while 24 others over Chindwin region attack villages around Thaungdut and Tamanthi. 20-plus P–51's and

B–25's hit gun positions at Mawlu. Throughout Mogaung Valley more than 100 FBs and 2 B–25's hit numerous tgts including fuel and ammo stores near Manywet, supplies and railroad station at Myitkyina, supplies and radio station at Sahmaw, Kamaing area, bridges at Nsopzup and supply dumps W of Mogaung. 30-plus of the FBs carry out ground spt missions at Shaduzup.

Fourteenth AF: 7 P–40's strafe 3 barges and several junks at Saint John I, leaving them burning. 2 B–24's on sweep from Hong Kong to Formosa claim a large river boat and a small freighter sunk and 2 other freighters damaged. 1 HB is lost. 4 P–40's attack a large concentration of small vessels at Haiphong, sinking at least 4.

Fifth AF: B–25's, A–20's, and P–39's hit villages, barges, supply area, and coastal road in areas around Madang, Tadji, Bogia, and Uligan Harbor. Other B–25's bomb barracks at Penfoei. B–24's pound Langgoer and Wakde Is.

Thirteenth AF: 50-plus FBs pound supply areas at Ratawul. 9 B–25's hit Talili Bay, 11 bomb Vunakanau A/F, and 13 blast Tobera A/F. 6 B–25's maintain night heckling of Rabaul area. 4 P–40's bomb pillboxes near Reini R while 2 B–24's bomb Monoitu Mission.

Seventh AF: B–25's from Tarawa hit Maloelap, rearm at Majuro, and bomb Jaluit on return flight.

Eleventh AF: 8 B–24's dispatched to destroy a convoy, believed SE of Matsuwa I, turn back due to engine, navigation, and weather difficulties. A flight of F–7A's of the 2d Photo Charting Sq (1st Photo Gp, 311th Photo Wg), arrives. Its mission is mapping of Kuril Is.

8 April

Eighth AF: 3 separate forces, a total of 639 B–17's and B–24's divided into 13 combat wgs, are dispatched against A/Fs in NW Germany and aircraft factories in Brunswick area. More than 600 HBs bomb tgts, with the largest force (192 B–17's) striking at Brunswick. The other HBs bomb A/Fs including those at Oldenburg, Quakenbruck, Achmer, Rheine, Hesepe, Handorf, and Twente. 34 US bmrs are lost.

Ninth AF: 198 B–26's attack Hasselt M/Y and hit Coxyde A/F. 32 P–47's bomb area around Hasselt.

Twelfth AF: MBs attack bridge NW of Orte while A–20's successfully attack supply stores. FBs hit several bridges, motor transport, and supply dumps in C Italy, and bomb railroad tracks at Sesti Bagni and Maccarese.

USSR: Soviet forces open offensive in Crimea.

Tenth AF: 20-plus A–31's hit troop positions near Buthidaung. Nearly 50 others bomb Kohima and Homalin. Nearly 100 FBs and 2 B–25's again pound Mogaung Valley tgts, including Manywet, storage areas and railroad at Mogaung, positions at Shaduzup, and general T/Os around Kamaing. 4 B–25's damage bridge and track at Sittang.

Fourteenth AF: 11 B–24's bomb railroad yards at Hanoi. 6 B–25's damage several small ships in Yulinkan Bay. 2 others strafe A/F on Weichow I. 8 P–40's pound oil dumps at Wanling, leaving tgt area in flames. 9 B–24's bomb A/F on Samah Bay; 4 others lay mines in the bay.

Fifth AF: P–40's attack T/Os in Aitape-Wewak area. A–20's hit tgts in Hansa Bay area, firing fuel dump and destroying several warehouses and other buildings at 3 plantations, and strafing and bombing roads and bridges along the coast.

Thirteenth AF: During 7/8 Apr 6 B–25's heckle Kavieng A/F area. 50-plus FBs hit NE section of Rabaul. 24 B–25's bomb center of Lakunai A/F. 4 B–24's again pound Monoitu Mission.

Seventh AF: B–24's flying out of Kwajalein, strike Truk. Abemama-based B–25's pound Ponape. B–25's from Tarawa hit Maloelap, rearm at Mojuro, and bomb Jaluit during return flight.

9 April

Eighth AF: 399 B–17's and B–24's bomb aircraft factories and A/Fs in Germany and Poland: A/F and assembly plant at Tutow is hit by 104 B–24's; Focke-Wulf plant at Poznan by 33 B–17's; Heinkel plant at Warnemunde by 86 B–17's; aircraft plant and A/F at Rahmel by 40 HBs; A/F and assembly plant at Marienburg by 98 HBs; and A/Fs at Parchim and Rostock by 46 HBs. No ftr spt is available over the tgts because of bad weather or distance. No diversionary missions are flown. German ftrs are able to concentrate on the bmr formations, and 32 HBs are lost.

Twelfth AF: P–40 and A–36 FBs bomb railroad line between Rome and Bracciano, hitting tracks, a station, and a warehouse; attack Littoria and Terracina, repair shops NW of Valmontone, and several gun positions; and bomb scattered motor transport during armed rcn of Avezzano-Sora-Pontecorvo-Ceprano areas.

Tenth AF: 40-plus A–31's hit troop positions NW of Imphal and Thaungdut and bomb Kanglatongbi and Nawngpu-awng. The Mogaung Valley is pounded by over 100 FBs and a few B–25's; the aircraft hit town areas, bridges, storage areas, spt ground forces, and hit T/Os in general in or near Mogaung, Kamaing, Laban, Hopin, Myitkyina, and Nsopzup. 25 B–25's and P–51's hit fuel dumps at Indaw, bomb road near Manhton, and spt ground forces at Lasai. 6 B–24's bomb Mandalay railroad yards, another bombs nearby Maymyo, and 13 others mine areas near Mandalay and Magwe. Also in Mandalay area, 11 P–38's damage several locomotives, numerous railroad cars, and set a steamer afire near Ywataung.

Fourteenth AF: 2 B–25's claim a 200-ft tanker sunk off Cape Bastion and 3 ftrs shot down over Yulinkan Bay.

Fifth AF: 55 B–25's bomb Aitape area while B–24's and A–20's hit Wewak, Boram, Cape Moem, AA positions along Hansa Bay, and barges SE of Mushu I and in Wagol R. P–39's hit troops, barges, and bridges in Madang, Awar, Bogia, and Bunabun areas.

Thirteenth AF: 23 B–25's bomb Lakunai. 31 FBs hit Ralum supply areas while 22 others strike Wunapope. During 8/9 Apr 7 B–25's fly heckling missions against Rabaul.

Seventh AF: B–24's on photo rcn mission over Maloelap, Wotje, and Mille, and a single Tarawa-based B–25 bombs Taroa. B–25's, in shuttle mission from Abemama, bomb Jaluit, rearm at Majuro, and then hit Maloelap.

Eleventh AF: A weather sortie over Matsuwa is negative due to low clouds and fog.

10 April

Eighth AF: More than 650 HBs hit A/Fs at Evere, Brussels, Florennes, Diest, Maldegem, Bourges, Orleans, and Romorantin, bomb aircraft factories at Evere, Brussels, Bourges, and Orleans, and attack a V-weapon site at Marquise/Mimoyecques.

Ninth AF: 258 B–26's and 41 A–20's, including 12 aircraft dropping Window, attack coastal batteries at Le Harve/Le Grand Hameau and military installation nearby. During the afternoon 267 B–26's and A–20's bomb M/Y, A/F, coastal defenses, and NOBALL tgts at Charleroi/Montignies, Namur, Coxyde, Nieuport, and other points on N coast of W Europe. 47 P–47's dive-bomb Evreux A/F.

Twelfth AF: A–20's hit ammo dump at Gallicano nel Lazio. B–25's bomb Orvieto M/Y and 2 bridges. B–26's hit Poggibonsi and Cecina railroad bridges and tracks, and viaducts at Bucine and W of Arezzo. FBs operating over wide areas of C Italy and in battle zones hit railroad bridges, railroad cars, motor transport, barracks, and troop concentrations with good effect.

USSR: Red Army captures Odessa.

Tenth AF: 18 A–31's pound troop positions throughout Arakan area. 18 others strike troops and other tgts around Maungkan and Kangpokpi. About 100 FBs and a few B–25's pound numerous tgts, including encampment SW of Mogaung, positions near Kazu, railroad and truck park at Myitkyina, supply area S of Myit-

kyina, and bivouac area and supplies at Kamaing. Some of the FBs carry out spt of ground forces NE of Kamaing. 40-plus FBs and B–25's over Katha area hit bridge at Thityabin, troops and supplies at Shwegu, gun positions and troops S of Mawlu, and T/Os including a fuel dump. 9 B–24's bomb railroad station and jetty area at Moulmein while 4 others mine mouth of Tavoy R.

Fourteenth AF: 3 B–25's damage 2 bridges at Phu Dien Chau and destroy several buildings and some railroad track. 10 P–40's pound roads N and S of Wanling.

Fifth AF: About 60 B–24's, teaming with US destroyers offshore, bombard Hansa Bay area, concentrating on AA positions guarding A/Fs.

Thirteenth AF: 22 B–25's bomb Ratawul supply area and 40-plus FBs hit runway at Tobera, both strikes causing considerable damage. Night harassment of Rabaul area continues.

Twentieth AF: JCS informally approve MATTERHORN plan (approved in principle by Roosevelt on 10 Nov 43) for early sustained bombing of Japan by B–29's based in Calcutta area and staging through fields in area of Chengtu. The operational vehicle is to be the 58th Bomb Wg (4 bomb gps) of XX BC, soon to be assigned to the newly activated Twentieth AF, operating under Gen Arnold as executive agent for JCS.

Seventh AF: B–24's, staging through Eniwetok, bomb Truk (1 hits Ponape) while B–25's, based on Abemama, strike Ponape. B–25's, flying shuttle mission between Tarawa and Majuro, pound Maloelap and Jaluit.

Eleventh AF: 3 B–24's fly armed rcn over Matsuwa and Onnekotan Is.

11 April

Eighth AF: 830 B–17's and B–24's in 3 separate forces bomb production centers (primarily ftr aircraft factories) and T/Os in N Germany at Oschersleben, Bernburg, Halberstadt (Force I); Sorau, Cottbus, Arnimswalde, Stettin, Politz, Gulzow, Zarnglaff and Rostock (Forces II and III). Enemy opposition downs 64 HBs, one of the heaviest single-day losses of World War II.

Ninth AF: 229 B–26's and 36 A–20's, including 3 dropping Window, attack Charleroi/Montignies, military installations on coast, and Chievres A/F. Over 90 P–47's dive-bomb military installation and Gael A/F.

Twelfth AF: B–25's hit Montalto di Castro railroad bridge, while B–26's hit M/Ys at Ancona and Siena. FBs concentrate on attacks against railroad tgts NE of Rome and buildings inland from E coast. Tracks are hit hard in Arezzo-Pontassieve area as are stations at Maccarese and Cesano. Overpass, bridges, railroad cars, and dumps throughout C Italy are attacked, as is town of Gaeta.

Tenth AF: 12 A–31's attack village SW of Buthidaung. 17 P–51's and B–25's fly ground spt missions and bomb road near Maungkan. Mogaung Valley tgts are pounded by 50-plus FBs and 2 B–25's; tgts include HQ and stores at Sahmaw, HQ and ammo dump SW of Mogaung, troops at Myitkyina, and T/Os to the S, gun position S of Kamaing, and HQ at Waingmaw.

Fourteenth AF: 3 B–25's hit railroad T/Os N of Vinh and seriously damage a bridge S of Thanh Hoa.

Fifth AF: 80-plus A–20's and B–25's, supported by 30 P–47's and P–40's, blast AA positions, stores, dumps, and personnel areas at Hollandia. More than 50 B–24's bomb barges, AA guns, and other tgts along Hansa Bay which is also hit by 12 B–25's. 12 other B–25's bomb tgts on Karkar I.

Thirteenth AF: Thirteenth Air TF (Prov) is created by Gen Kenney, CG Allied AF (SWPA), from elements of Thirteenth AF and other units. About 40 FBs hit E section of Rabaul while 12 others strike Talili Bay ammo dump. 24 B–25's blast supply areas at Ratawul. On Bougainville 20-plus FBs are dispatched against coastal gun positions but fail to locate objective. 12 of the FBs bomb Aitara while 2 claim destruction of bridge near Mawareka.

Seventh AF: B–25's from the Gilberts hit Ponape, rearm at Majuro, and carry out shuttle mission against Jaluit and Maloelap.

Eleventh AF: Of 3 B–24's attempting to fly photo and bombing run over Matsuwa I installations, 2 must turn back. The third bombs the runway area.

12 April

Eighth AF: 443 B–17's and B–24's dispatched to bomb industrial tgts at Schweinfurt, Zwickau, Oschersleben, Leipzig, Schkeuditz, and Halle are forced to abandon mission because of haze and multilayer clouds. Ftr opposition is concentrated over N France and 6 HBs are lost.

Ninth AF: 231 B–26's and 20 A–20's attack railroad, shore batteries, radar installations, A/Fs, and V-weapon sites at Dunkirk, Courtrai/Wevelghem, Coxyde/Furnes, De Pannes-Bains, Saint Ghislain, Ostend, and points along coast. Over 70 P–47's dive-bomb military installations in N France.

Twelfth AF: MBs bomb rail lines approaching Monte Molino bridge and at nearby junction to Viterbo line, railroad and road bridges S of Orvieto and at Certaldo, tracks approaching bridge at Imperia, and railroad bridges over Var R and at Albenga. LBs pound Zagarolo supply dump. FBs and ftrs (some operating with British airplanes) hit comm (mainly railroad bridges), vehicles, a supply dumps at various places, including Arezzo, island of Elba, Orvieto, NE of Grosseto, NW of Bracciano, Civita Castellana, Montalto di Castro, between Piombino and Viterbo, in Castiglioncello area, NW of Montepescali, and S of Cecina.

Fifteenth AF: 483d Bomb Gp (B–17) becomes operational, increasing number of combat status HB gps in Fifteenth AF to 17. Bad weather lifts, permitting HB operations. Almost 450 B–17's and B–24's attack aircraft factories at Fischamend Markt and Wiener-Neustadt and Bad Voslau assembly plant and A/F. Over 200 P–38's and P–47's provide escort. HBs and ftrs claim over 30 aircraft shot down. 8 US airplanes are known lost and several more fail to return.

Tenth AF: 24 B–34's blast troop positions near Buthidaung. 35 A–31's hit Paungbyin and SW of Imphal. 90-plus P–40's, A–36's, P–51's, and B–25's over Mogaung Valley spt ground forces, bomb supply areas, and hit numerous T/Os in areas around Mogaung, Myitkyina, Kamaing, Taungni, and Shaduzup. 5 B–25's knock out bridge at Natmauk while 2 others damage Pyu bridge near Rangoon.

5 B–24's bomb Nagorn Sawarn while 7 hit Moulmein railroad station and jetties and bomb SE part of Prome.

Fifth AF: 180-plus B–24's, B–25's, and A–20's, supported by over 60 P–38's, bomb AA positions, A/Fs, supply areas, and shipping construction. B–24's, B–25's, A–20's, and P–39's bomb and strafe various tgts at Wewak, Madang, along Hansa Bay, and on Karkar I. Other P–39's fly barge sweep from Alexishafen up the coast as far as mouth of Sepik R. 2 B–25's bomb Penfoei.

Thirteenth AF: 5th Bomb Gp is ordered to move from Guadalcanal and New Georgia to Los Negros where it will form nucleus of Thirteenth Air TF. 23 B–25's and 11 P–39's pound W section of Rabaul, 7 other B–25's cause considerable damage in Ratawul supply area. 23 FBs blast concrete airstrip at Vunakanau. On Bougainville 12 FBs bomb and strafe Numa Numa trail and pound harbor area.

Seventh AF: B–25's, flying out of Abemama, bomb Maloelap, rearm at Majuro, and hit Jaluit on return trip.

13 April

SHAEF: Gen Eisenhower formally assumes direction of air operations out of UK at midnight (though he began informal exercise of this authority in late Mar). This assumption of authority gives Eisenhower direction over AEAF, RAF BC, and USSTAF (Fifteenth AF retains some degree of independence) along with US 1st Army Gp, 21 Army Gp, and Allied Naval Forces.

Eighth AF: 153 HBs attack industrial tgts at Schweinfurt. 230 HBs strike Augsburg, concentrating on Messerschmitt plant. 183 other bmrs hit A/Fs and other T/Os in Oberpfaffenhofen, Lechfeld, and Lauffen am Neckar. This mission is flown in conjunction with a raid on Hungary by over 500 Fifteenth AF HBs and a Ninth AF B–26 raid in S Netherlands. Although ftr opposition is dispersed, enemy aircraft and AA account for most of 38 HBs lost by Eighth AF.

Ninth AF: 121 B–26's and 37 A–20's attack M/Y, coastal batteries, A/Fs, and V-weapon sites at Namur, Chievres, Nieuport, Le Havre, and along N coast of France in general. Nearly 175 other aircraft abort missions mainly because of weather. 48 P–47's also dive-bomb V-weapon sites.

Twelfth AF: B–25's attack Terni and bridge at Marsciano while B–26's bomb Ancona M/Y and nearby railroad bridge. FBs again strike mainly at comm, town of Itri, Cesano station, factory at Fontana Liri, railroad overpass at Fara in Sabina, Anguillara, and bridges, trucks, and other tgts at points throughout C Italy.

Fifteenth AF: 535 HBs (largest HB mission to date by Fifteenth AF) bomb A/F aircraft factory, and rolling stock plant at Gyor, Vecses and Tokol A/Fs and Repulogepgyar aircraft components plant at Budapest, and M/Y at Brod. Ftrs fly over 200 sorties in spt of the HBs. Ftr opposition and AA account for 14 US HBs and 1 ftr shot down. Nearly 40 ftrs are claimed shot down and 120-plus aircraft destroyed on the ground.

Tenth AF: 24 A–31's hit gun positions and telegraph installations at Buthidaung. About 90 A–31's pound a variety of tgts at Churachandpur

Tiddim, Sagolmang, Kanglatongbi, Thayaung, Tamanthi, Minthami, and Thaungdut. 90-plus P–40's, P–51's and A–36's and a few B–25's carry out ground spt missions near Kamaing and hit assorted tgts throughout the Mogaung Valley. 12 B–25's and 11 P–51's spt ground forces at Mawlu.

Fourteenth AF: 28 ftrs attempt to intercept but fail to make contact with 13 Japanese airplanes which bomb Namyung.

Fifth AF: 80-plus B–24's and A–20's pound the A/Fs at Dagua and But on N coast of New Guinea. 33 A–20's hit Aitape. P–39's, B–25's, and B–24's fly light strikes against a variety of tgts along Hansa Bay, on Wakde, at Uligan, and several other points along the coast.

Thirteenth AF: 24 B–25's blast Talili Bay and Ratawul supply areas and town of Rabaul. 40-plus FBs strike Malaguna area NW of Rabaul. 17 FBs hit personnel and supply areas at Mosigetta, Mawareka, Meive, and Maririei. During the early morning 23 B–24's bomb Truk.

Seventh AF: B–24's out of Eniwetok strike Truk. B–25's from Abemama hit Ponape. B–25's from Tarawa bomb Jaluit, rearm at Majuro, and hit Maloelap.

Eleventh AF: 3 B–24's fly armed rcn and bombing runs over A/F at Matsuwa and installations on Onnekotan Is.

14 April

Twelfth AF: B–25's attack Viterbo A/F and Leghorn M/Y, B–26's strike at Poggibonsi, Certaldo, Cecina, and Magra, attacking mostly rail facilities and hit Arezzo bridge and viaduct and Bucine viaducts. FBs also concentrate on rail lines and bridges and hit many supply dumps, gun positions and factories, generally located NE of Rome.

Tenth AF: 20-plus A–31's hit troop positions near Buthidaung. 36 A–31's pound Paungbyin and area N of Imphal. 20 P–40's over Mogaung Valley attack camp at Manywet. 20 P–51's and 3 B–25's spt ground forces in Mawlu area.

Fifth AF: B–25's and P–39's hit barges and luggers in Vanimo Harbor and at Bogia.

Thirteenth AF: 19 B–24's on mission to the Carolines bomb Eten, Param, and Kuop Is and T/Os on Truk Atoll. 24 B–25's and 40-plus FBs blast supply area at Ratawul. 8 other FBs hit Wunapope. More than 20 FBs strike various tgts in NE part of Bougainville.

Seventh AF: A single B–24, en route from Kwajalein to Tarawa, bombs Jaluit. B–25's from Eniwetok bomb Ponape while B–25's from Abeama strike Jaluit and Maloelap, using Majuro as arming station between strikes. Japanese bmrs carry out ineffective raid on Eniwetok.

Eleventh AF: 3 B–24's fly armed photo rcn mission during early morning over Matsuwa, Onnekotan, and Paramushiru Is. Photographs taken are negative due to cloud cover.

15 April

Eighth and Ninth AFs: 530 Eighth AF and 86 Ninth AF ftrs conduct sweeps over C and W Germany. Bad weather prevents attacks on most major ground tgts. Ftrs claim 58 aircraft destroyed in air and on ground. 33 US ftrs are lost, 19 to

unknown causes (probably due mainly to bad weather) and the others to enemy action and accidents.

Twelfth AF: XII A Spt Cmd is redesignated XII TAC. MBs strike M/Y at Leghorn and a tunnel and railroad bridges in C Italy. P–47's attack rail lines, bridges, and ammo dumps NE of Rome with good results. Other P–47's and P–40's and A–36's hit numerous tgts, including rail lines, motor transport shop, vehicles, tanks, and gun positions, in C Italy and in US Fifth Army battle areas.

Fifteenth AF: Clearing weather again permits HB operations. 448 B–24's and B–17's attack Bucharest, Ploesti, and Nish M/Y. Over 150 ftrs provide escort. A special group, led by Lt Col Louis A Neveleff, flies from HQ at Bari to Medeno Polji. From there the group proceeds to Marshal Tito's HQ at Drvar, where Col Neveleff confers with Tito and spends several days laying groundwork for evacuation of downed Fifteenth AF airmen in Yugoslav hands. Also, much information is gathered regarding military organization and political trend of the partisan movement. The mission returns to Italy on 2 May. 122 men, mostly Fifteenth AF airmen, are also evacuated.

Tenth AF: 40-plus A–31's hit gun positions at Buthidaung. 12 B–24's over Andaman Is attack shipping and other tgts at Port Blair. 12 P–38's hit Heho A/F, destroying several parked airplanes.

Fourteenth AF: 3 B–25's knock out a bridge at Viet Tri and damage another.

Fifth AF: 180-plus B–24's, B–25's, and A–20's bomb landing strips, offshore islands, and entire coastal area in vicinity of Aitape. 16 P–40's strafe barges at nearby Seleo I. 20 P–39's hit villages, supply dumps, trucks, and other tgts along Hansa Bay and in Alexishafen area.

Thirteenth AF: 24 B–25's bomb ammo dump on Talili Bay; 11 P–39's follow with strike on same tgt. 3 P–38's fire Wunapope supply area; other FB strikes on same area are cancelled by weather. A few P–38's hit tgts in NE part of Bougainville.

Seventh AF: Gen Douglass becomes CG Seventh AF. B–25's, based on Tarawa, bomb Maloelap, rearm at Majuro, and hit Jaluit and Mille on return trip.

Eleventh AF: During 14/15 Apr 3 B–24's on armed rcn mission over Matsuwa and Onnekotan I hit several tgts including Matsuwa A/F. Rcn over Paramushiru fails due to overcast.

16 April

Twelfth AF: B–25's bomb approaches to Ficulle and Todi railway bridges. A–20's blast fuel supplies. P–40's, P–47's, and A–36's hit Capranica viaduct, town of Zagarolo, railway at Spigno Monferrato, M/Y at Orte-Terni, tunnel at Capranica, and tracks, vehicles, railway cars, ammo dump, bridge, and T/Os at various points in C Italy.

Fifteenth AF: 31st Ftr Gp (P–51) (transferred from Twelfth AF on 1 Apr) begins operations. It becomes the fifth operational ftr gp of Fifteenth AF. 432 HBs attack Brasov M/Y, Turnu Severin M/Y and A/F, aircraft factory and A/F at Belgrade, and M/Y at Nish. Over 90 ftrs fly escort while 50-plus others, failing to rendezvous with HBs, strafe trains on Craiova line E of Turnu–Severin.

USSR: Soviet forces capture Yalta.

Tenth AF: In Arakan area 20-plus A–31's pound troop positions S and SW of Buthidaung. More than 50 others hit Churachandpur, Homalin, Nawngpu-awng, Tiddim Road, and bridge at Manipur Road. 12 B–25's hit bridge over Mogaung R while 9 others, along with 12 P–51's, hit warehouse and railroad station at Mohnyin. 9 P–38's destroy 3 MBs at Zayatkwin near Rangoon while 2 P–51's in Mandalay area hit Anisakan A/F, destroying 2 airplanes.

Fifth AF: 170-plus B–24's, B–25's, and A–20's bomb Hollandia town and A/F and numerous other tgts in the area. P–39's hit wooded area and comm tgts along Hansa Bay and attack villages and supply dumps from Bogia to Uligan Harbor. P–38's hit Madang area. Other B–25's bomb Koepang. B–24's fly light strike against Wakde. Other aircraft, operating singly or in pairs, attack T/Os on N coast of New Guinea and SE coast of New Britain.

Thirteenth AF: 15 B–24's bomb runway at Satawan. 24 B–25's hit Ratawul supply area and alternate tgt of Raluana. At Rabaul 30-plus FBs attack area inland from Toboi wharf.

Seventh AF: B–25's, staging through Eniwetok, strike Truk. B–25's from Abemama hit Maloelap and Mille, using Majuro as a rearming base between the strikes.

17 April

Eighth AF: 14 B–24's bomb V-weapon installation at Wizernes in Pas de Calais area. No ftr opposition is offered and all US aircraft return without damage.

Twelfth AF: B–25's attack bridges N of Orte and at Monte Molino, while A–20's pound fuel dump NE of Rome. P–40, P–47, and A–36 FBs hit motor transport stores and gun positions N of Anzio, bomb Fara in Sabina station, hit tracks, trains and guns in Orte and Narni area and at other points N of Rome.

Fifteenth AF: 470 B–17's and B–24's hit Belgrade/Sava M/Y and Rogozarski A/F and aircraft factory as well as *Ikarus* aircraft factory at Belgrade, Zemun A/F, and M/Y at Sofia. More than 200 ftrs escort the missions. US aircraft claim 25 airplanes downed in combat.

Tenth AF: 36 A–31's again pound positions SW of Buthidaung. 2 B–24's bomb Akyab. 6 P–51's spt ground forces near Meza. 60-plus A–31's hit scattered villages and pound Kalewa and Yaingangpokpi. 9 P–38's destroy several airplanes at Heho A/F while 5 B–24's bomb Ywataung. 26 B–25's and 36 P–51's spt ground forces at Mawlu and bomb fuel dump at Kin. 13 other P–51's are diverted to intercept Japanese force over Imphal area and claim 3 airplanes shot down.

Fifth AF: 20-plus B–24's bomb storage areas and troop concentrations in Kai Is. P–39's attack AA positions at Bogia. Other planes, operating individually or in pairs, attack Hollandia, Uligan Harbor and vicinity, and Madang area.

Thirteenth AF: 20 B–24's bomb A/F at Satawan. 24 B–25's pound runway and revetments at Rapopo A/F. 40-plus FBs hit Matupi with incendiaries while 10 others pound runway at Keravat.

Seventh AF: B–25's, based on Tarawa, strike Maloelap and Mille, rearming at Majuro between the raids.

18 April

Eighth AF: More than 750 HBs attack aircraft industries, A/Fs and T/Os at Germendorf, Annahof, Brandenburg, Rathenow, Luneburg, Perleberg, Wittenberge, Birkenwerder, Cuxhaven, and Barnewitz, and a V-weapon site at Watten. 19 US HBs are lost.

Ninth AF: XIX A Spt Cmd is redesignated XIX TAC and becomes operational. IX A Spt Cmd is redesignated IX TAC. 277 B–26's (including 24 dropping Window) and 37 A–20's bomb gun positions and M/Ys at Dunkirk, Calais, and Charleroi/Saint Martin.

Twelfth AF: P–47 FBs cut several rail lines in Florence and Arezzo areas and strafe trains and motor transport. P–40's and P–47's hit Itri and rail bridge and fuel dumps as campaign against comm continues.

Fifteenth AF: P–38's and P–47's strafe Udine and Aiello A/Fs and T/Os in Basiliano, Sant' Andrea I, and Cervignano del Friuli areas and in Golfo di Panzano. Other ftrs fly cover for the strafing missions.

Tenth AF: 24 A–31's bomb positions SW of Buthidaung while 2 B–24's bomb Akyab. 7 B–24's bomb oil plant at Yenangyaung while 5, along with 7 P–38's, hit Ywataung. 6 B–25's score numerous hits on Mandalay-Shwebo railroad. 42 A–31's attack Ft White, Tiddim, and Tamu. 15 B–25's and 4 P–51's bomb Kamaing and hit Myitkyina-Bhamo road.

Fifth AF: The newly created (11

Apr) Thirteenth Air TF (Prov), commanded by Gen Streett and temporarily composed of elements of Thirteenth AF (which is being moved to SWPA), a few RAAF sqs, Seventh US Fleet air units, and Fifth AF units in the Admiralties and New Britain, is placed under operational control of Fifth AF/ADVON. Operating out of Momote, B–24's of Thirteenth Air TF bomb Woleai and Mariaon Is. B–24's of Fifth AF hit Manokwari and Babo. Madang area is hit by FBs.

Thirteenth AF: 14 B–24's bomb A/F at Satawan, 23 B–25's, weathered out of Vunakanau, bomb Tobera A/F. 12 others and 9 FBs which fail to reach Rapopo bomb airstrip at Keravat. Wunapope is hit by about 40 FBs, with considerable damage to the supply area.

Seventh AF: First Seventh AF attack on the Marianas takes place as B–24's escorting Navy photo airplanes on rcn mission from Eniwetok bomb Saipan. Other B–24's staging through Eniwetok hit Truk. B–25's from Tarawa bomb Ponape. B–24's from Kwajalein bomb Wake after failing to find shipping reported in the area. B–25's from Abemama bomb Jaluit and Maloelap, using Majuro as shuttle base between strikes.

Eleventh AF: 3 B–24's fly armed rcn over Matsuwa, Onnekotan, and Paramushiru Is. Cloud cover and lack of moon permit only bombing of Kashiwabara A/F and Banjo Cape area.

19 April

Eighth AF: 747 HBs in three forces bomb industrial tgts in Kassel area; A/Fs at Eschwege, Lippstadt, Werl,

Paderborn, and Gutersloh; and other tgts at Limburg, Buren, Kall, and Soest, in morning operations. During afternoon 27 B–24's bomb V-weapon site at Watten. 6 HBs are lost.

Ninth AF: After several weeks of instruction a IX AFSC trg exercise (Operation BOOMERANG) in waterproofing and landing motor vehicles gets under way. This exercise, in preparation for a cross-channel movement lasts several weeks and involves 55 units, over 650 vehicles, and more than 2,500 men. 350-plus B–26's and A–20's bomb M/Ys, city areas, and T/Os at Gunzburg, Ulm, Neu Ulm, Donauworth, and Schelklingen. Ftrs fly over 1,200 sorties against a variety of tgts in NW Europe.

Twelfth AF: Bad weather severely restricts operations. B–26's hit Cecina railroad bridge and Ancona M/Y while B–25's hit M/Y at Piombino. P–47's hit railroad tracks, M/Y, junction, and railway cars between Pontedera and Empoli and between Figline Valdarno and San Giovanni Valdarno.

Tenth AF: 50-plus A–31's hit positions and supply dumps near Buthidaung and E of Maungdaw. 40-plus A–31's hit Churachandpur, Pyingaing, Tamu, and T/Os N of Kalewa. 6 B–25's and 8 P–51's attack troops and stores NW of Banmauk. 10 P–38's hit A/F near Meiktila. 5 P–51's attack troop positions near Mawlu and bridge at Shweli.

Fourteenth AF: 3 B–25's damage a bridge at Thanh Moi and score hits on railroad and buildings S of bridge. 4 P–40's attack village of Takaw, causing several fires, and sink a ferryboat in the area.

Fifth AF: B–24's hit Urarom and Manokwari. B–25's, A–20's, and ftr aircraft strike wide variety of tgts around Hollandia, Aitape, Bogia, Uligan, Bunabun, Madang, and Cape Croisilles. B–24's of Thirteenth Air TF bomb Woleai.

Thirteenth AF: 21 B–24's bomb Satawan A/F, hitting the tgt area with about 50 tons of high explosives. 38 FBs hit Matupi supply areas while 7 bomb Rapopo airstrip. Ftrs hit Numa Numa area.

Twentieth AF: XX BC is assigned to Twentieth AF:

Seventh AF: B–24's, staging through Eniwetok, bomb Truk. B–25's from the Gilberts strike Ponape.

20 April

Eighth AF: 566 HBs attack V-weapon installations and T/Os in Pas de Calais and Cherbourg areas. 33 P–51 FBs attack A/Fs at Cambrai/Epinoy, Vitry-en-Artois, and Laon/Athies. 53 P–38's dispatched to bomb Saint-Trond A/F jettison bombs in English Channel after overcast prevents location of tgts.

Ninth AF: Almost 400 B–26's and A–20's attack gun positions at Etaples, Bazinghen, Villerville, Gravelines, and Fecamp, A/F at Poix, and V-weapon sites and T/Os in Pas de Calais area. Nearly 140 P–47's bomb M/Ys at Creil and Mantes-La-Jolie.

Twelfth AF: MBs and LBs score hits on M/Y and 3 fuel dumps at Leghorn and near misses on Cecina and Certaldo bridges and Arezzo viaduct. FBs hit railroad lines and fuel dump in Florence area; bridges, dump, rail lines, and train cars near Civitavecchia and Zagarolo, at Sezze, near Ladispoli, SW of Stimigliano and N of Monterotondo; and guns S of Albano Laziale. In battle area around Cassino FBs blast several gun positions and hit bridges, trucks, troops and other tgts at several points, including at Falconara, Recanati, San Benedetto de Marsi, and Fondi-Itri and Orte-Orvieto areas.

Fifteenth AF: More than 300 HBs attack Monfalcone shipyards, Tagliamento-Casarsa della Delizia railroad bridge, M/Ys at Fano, Vicenza, Ancona, Mestre, Treviso, and Trieste, and harbor and shipping at Venice. 180-plus other HBs dispatched against comm tgts in N Italy are forced to abort due to bad weather. About 250 ftrs provide cover for the bombing raids.

Tenth AF: 11 B–25's hit bivouac and supply area NW of Manywet. 24 A–31's pound positions at Tiddim.

Fifth AF: B–24's bomb A/Fs on Noemfoor. B–25's, A–20's, and ftrs hit a variety of tgts around Hollandia, on Cape Croisilles, in Bunabun area, and along Hansa Bay. Woleai is again bombed by B–24's of Thirteenth Air TF.

SOPAC: Gen Harris, USMC, becomes COMAIRSOLS.

Thirteenth AF: With improved weather conditions heavy bombing of tgts in the Bismarcks resumes. 22 B–25's hit Matupi supply area. 40-plus FBs blast the A/Fs at Lakunai and Keravat.

Seventh AF: B–24's from Kwajalein search area near Wake for shipping. Finding none, the HBs hit Wake and Peale Is. Tarawa-based base between strikes, bomb Maloelap B–25's, using Majuro as a shuttle and Jaluit.

Eleventh AF: A B–24 aborts a weather mission to Shasukotan I.

21 April

Eighth AF: Eighth AF offensive against German oil tgts is scheduled to start on this date, but mission is cancelled because of bad weather.

Ninth AF: 236 B–26's and 34 A–20's attack gun positions, coastal defenses and V-weapons sites at Etaples, at Berck-sur-Mer, near Doullens, and in Saint-Omer, Abbeville, and Amiens area. 4 B–26's are lost. More than 175 P–47's dive-bomb M/Ys and concentrations at Montignies-sur-Sambre, Hasselt, Namur, and Haine-Saint-Pierre.

Twelfth AF: A–20's blast ammo dump while P–47's attack train, rail lines, and motor transport behind enemy lines. Other P–47's, along with P–40's and A–36's, attack railway lines and trains between Rome and Terni, between Rome and Tivoli, and between Orte and Attigliano; hit motor transport concentration NE of Rome; and attack several bivouac areas and gun positions in battle areas.

Fifteenth AF: Over 100 B–24's bomb Bucharest M/Y and Turnu–Severin. All 17 bomb gps dispatched are recalled due to bad weather but 7 gps fail to receive recall signal. Over 150 P–38's and P–51's are dispatched as escort. 40-plus rendezvous with the B–24's and battle some 30 ftrs that attack the HB force. The other ftrs, failing to meet the HBs, engage about 40 ftrs. HBs and ftrs claim 35 aerial combat victories. 10 US aircraft are shot down.

Tenth AF: 20-plus A–31's hit villages and Japanese positions near Buthidaung. 12 B–25's and 14 P–51's pound Indaw and Mawlu, causing several fires in supply dumps and in the general tgt areas. 48 A–31's attack Tiddim Road and bridge at Manipur. 12 B–25's bomb camp and supply area at Kamaing. 8 B–24's bomb storage and fuel dumps at Lashio and bomb Namtu. 13 B–24's bomb Maymyo while 5 B–25's knock out 3 bridges in Tangon area. 4 P–51's knock out bridge at Shweli.

Fourteenth AF: 12 P–40's fly armed rcn over roads in Burma, strafing bridges, buildings, steamrollers, trucks, and troops in areas around Takaw, Bhamo, Loiwing, Kutkai, Hsenwi, and Lashio. At least 3 steamrollers and 7 trucks are destroyed.

Fifth AF: 21 B–24's bomb airstrips on Noemfoor. About 320 B–24's, B–25's, and A–20's hit numerous tgts in Tadji, Wewak, and Madang area, while a Navy carrier force hits Hollandia, Wakde, and Sawar as assault convoys approach the area.

Thirteenth AF: 307th Bomb Gp (H) is ordered to move from New Georgia and Guadalcanal to the Admiralty Is, where it will become part of Thirteenth Air TF, serving operationally under Fifth AF. In spite of heavy weather in the Bismarcks, 24 B–25's blast Matupi supply area. 11 P–39's, closed out of Rabaul, bomb Tinputs Harbor.

Seventh AF: B–24's from Kwajalein hit Wotje. B–24's from Eniwetok, staging through Kwajalein, bomb Truk. B–25's from Engebi bomb Ponape. Abemama-based B–25's, using Majuro as a shuttle base, bomb Jaluit and Maloelap.

22 April

Eighth AF: 631 B–17's and B–24's bomb M/Y at Hamm. 18 others bomb secondary tgts in Hamm while 125 attack tgts at Koblenz, Bonn, and Soest. 15 HBs are lost, mostly to AA fire. 13 escorting ftrs are lost. US HBs claim 20 airplanes destroyed and ftrs claim 34 destroyed.

Ninth AF: Over 400 B–26's and about 90 A–20's fly two missions against V-weapon sites in area of Saint-Omer and Hesdin. Nearly 275 P–47's and P–51's dive-bomb M/Ys in Belgium.

Twelfth AF: B–25's bomb bridge and tracks S of Ficulle and bridge N of the town. Other B–25's and B–26's attack San Stefano al Mare harbor, N section of Orvieto, Chiusi railroad bridge, viaducts S and W of Arezzo and Bucine, Certaldo railroad bridge, bridge approaches at Incisa in Valdarno, bridge near Siena and viaduct at Poggibonsi. A–20's hit Valmontone ammo dump and Sonnino. P–47's hit railroad, trains, and tunnels in Florence area and W of Chiusi, M/Y at Siena, vessel S of Savona, railroad lines S of Orte, and town of Gaeta. P–40's attack gun positions N of Anzio beachhead and bomb Ferentino dump area and towns of Fondi, Terracina, and Formia.

Tenth AF: More than 30 A–31's bomb Bishenpur and Kohima. 12 B–25's hit Kamaing while 5 B–25's and 6 P–51's attack ammo and other supplies at Hopin. 3 B–25's and 4 P–51's hit village NE of Bhamo while 7 P–51's attack Gokteik Viaduct.

Fourteenth AF: 6 B–24's claim 4 freighters and a gunboat sunk near Cap-Saint-Jacques. 1 other knocks out bridge SW of Vinh. P–40's on armed rcn over N Burma destroy 10 boxcars and a truck N of Lashio.

Fifth AF: More than 20 B–24's bomb airstrips on Noemfoor. 80-plus B–24's and A–20's hit Boram and But A/Fs and other tgts in Wewak area; more than 100 B–24's and B–25's pound tgts along Hansa Bay; and all through the day B–25's and FBs, in flights of 1 to more than 20 aircraft, attack areas around Hansa Bay, Wewak, Bogia, Madang, and many other points along N and E coast of New Guinea. Many of the strikes indirectly spt Allied amphibious landings on N coast to the E and W of Hollandia, toward which a pincer movement is begun.

Thirteenth AF: About 40 B–25's bomb supply areas at Ratawul and Talili Bay, pound Keravat, and hit area between Rapopo and Cape Gazelle. 40-plus FBs attack runway and gun positions at Rapopo while 9 strike Lakunai A/F. During 22/23 Apr, 17 B–24's bomb Dublon, Param, and Eten Is.

Seventh AF: During 21/22 Apr, B–24's from Kwajalein bomb Wotje. Other B–24's from Kwajalein follow with another raid on Wotje during the day. B–25's from Tarawa, using Majuro as a shuttle base for rearming, bomb Jaluit, Maloelap, and Mille.

Eleventh AF: A weather sortie is aborted soon after take off due to weather.

23 April

Eighth AF: 346 P–47's, P–38's, and P–51's fly missions against A/Fs and other tgts in N France, Belgium, and NW Germany. Results are generally good. 7 airplanes are lost, all to flak.

Ninth AF: 307 B–26's and 57 A–20's attack NOBALL tgts, gun positions, and M/Ys in Pas de Calais area and in adjacent area of Belgium.

Around 1,000 P–47's and P–51's dive-bomb numerous tgts throughout France and the Low Countries.

Twelfth AF: B–25's hit bridges and approaches at Attigliano. B–26's attack Incisa in Valdarno viaduct and bridge, Cecina M/Y, and attack, but fail to hit, Poggibonsi viaduct. P–47's, A–36's, and P–40's hit rail lines and bridges NE of Rome and along E coast in several areas including points around Orvieto, Orte, Tivoli, and Capronica.

Fifteenth AF: Weather clears and HBs can resume operations. Over 500 B–24's and B–17's attack aircraft factories and A/Fs at Wiener-Neustadt, Schwechat, and Bad Voslau. Close to 300 ftrs provide spt. Many enemy ftrs attack fiercely, downing 12 HBs and 1 ftr. The HBs and escorts claim over 40 air victories.

Tenth AF: 24 P–51's, 8 B–25's, and 51 A–31's attack Thetkegyin, Manipur bridge, Tiddim road, and Japanese positions at Indaw. 18 A–31's hit positions near Buthidaung. 12 P–38's hit Kangaung A/F near Meiktila. 21 B–24's bomb railroads and jetties at Moulmein and Martaban.

Fourteenth AF: 14 P–40's pound arty post at Sienning and cav forces at Kuan-Fou-Chiao. 2 P–40's strafe barracks S of Tengchung, and 2 P–38's hit truck convoy and barracks S of Chiengmai. 4 P–40's blast motor pool at Lashio.

Fifth AF: B–24's continue to hit airstrips on Noemfoor. The HBs claim 14 air victories. More than 90 B–24's bomb Wewak, Boram, and But A/Fs, road near Boram, and track and villages S of Dagua while 80-plus B–24's, B–25's, and A–20's pound AA positions, A/Fs, stores, and troop con-

centrations along Hansa Bay. Throughout the day A–20's, P–47's, P–38's, and P–39's pound various tgts along Hansa Bay, in Wewak area, and in vicinity of Uligan Harbor and Cape Croisilles. 20-plus B–24's of Thirteenth Air TF bomb A/F and supply areas on Woleai. In ground action Allied forces take Hollandia, Tumleo and Selo Is, and objectives around Tadji.

Thirteenth AF: Weather again curtails strikes, but several FBs hit Tobera and 20-plus B–25's blast Matupi I.

Seventh AF: B–24's based at Kwajalein hit Truk and Wotje. Makin-based B–25's hit Ponape, Jaluit, and Maloelap.

Eleventh AF: 3 B–24's fly weather and photo rcn within 100 mi of the Kuril Is and photograph Matsuwa.

24 April

Eighth AF: 716 B–17's and B–24's bomb A/Fs, aircraft production industries, and T/Os at Landsberg, Oberpfaffenhofen, Erding, Friedrichshafen, Manzell, Lowental, Gablingen, Leipheim and Neckarsulm. Although a large Fifteenth AF raid on Ploesti and Bucharest draws many ftrs, 250 German aircraft oppose this Eighth AF mission. More than 125 of these ftrs concentrate on lead force over Landsberg-Oberpfaffenhofen-Erding area and down at least 15 HBs in a 30- to 45-min battle. Total losses for the day are 39 B–17's and B–24's.

Ninth AF: 38 B–26's dispatched against tgts in France are recalled because of bad weather. 32 P–47's dive-bomb Louvain M/Y with good results.

Twelfth AF: MBs attack railroad

bridges N and S of Orvieto, at Arezzo, at Grosseto, and N and S of Incisa in Valdarno. A–20's hit dump at Valmontone. P–40's, P–47's, and A–36's hit shipping off Leghorn, Avezzano station, Orvieto and Terni M/Ys, Canino landing ground, railroad tracks at numerous points S of Orvieto, and rail lines, truck parks, and T/Os N of Rome.

Fifteenth AF: 520-plus B–17's and B–24's bomb M/Ys at Bucharest and Ploesti, hit aircraft factory at Belgrade, and attack rail line between Rimini and Ancona. Over 250 ftrs fly spt for the HBs.

Tenth AF: 36 A–31's and 8 P–38's pound positions near Buthidaung and Myohaung area. 60-plus A–31's hit troop concentration near Ft White and towns of Kohima and Ukhrul. 100-plus P–40's, P–51's, A–26's, and B–25's bomb storage areas at Kamaing, Mogaung, and Hopin, and railroads and other tgts at Myitkyina, Manywet, and Chaungwa. 25 B–25's and P–51's hit Indaw and several other B–25's bomb Pyingaing.

Fourteenth AF: B–25's damage bridges near Dara and Kengluang and strafe factory at Dhasan. P–40's on diversionary strike strafe numerous T/Os at Kengtung. B–25's on sea sweep hit 2 small steamers off Cape Bastion with cannon fire, claiming 1 vessel sunk and the other left burning.

Fifth AF: B–24's again bomb parked aircraft and other tgts on Noemfoor. 40-plus B–24's bomb A/Fs in Wewak area. More than 140 B–24's, B–25's, and A–20's hit stores, fuel dumps, and personnel areas along Hansa Bay. Throughout the day MBs and FBs hit a variety of tgts along

New Guinea coast including Karkar I, Uligan Harbor, Cape Croisilles, and Madang area. Madang falls to Allied ground forces.

Thirteenth AF: Weather continues to curtail strikes in the Bismarcks. 10 P–40's hit runway and revetments at Tobera. Ftr sweeps account for several trucks and barges in Rabaul-New Ireland area.

Twentieth AF: A B–29 piloted by Gen Saunders, CG 58th Bomb Wg, arrives at Kwanghan. Accompanying the VHB is another B–29 carrying Gen Wolfe, CG XX BC. These are the first B–29's to fly over the Hump to China.

Seventh AF: B–25's from Engebi bomb Ponape while others, based at Makin, hit Jaluit and Wotje.

Eleventh AF: A B–24 flies a photo and bomb run over Matsuwa I. Later another B–24 flies weather and bomb runs over Shasukotan, Yekaruma, Kharimkotan, and Onnekotan Is.

25 April

Eighth AF: Nearly 300 B–17's and B–24's bomb M/Ys at Mannheim and Landau, and A/Fs at Esseyles-Nancy, Metz/Frescati, and Dijon/Longvic.

Ninth AF: 240 B–26's and 69 A–20's bomb V-weapon sites in coastal area of France and gun positions at Le Treport, Varengeville-sur-Mer, Fontenay-sur-Mer/Crisbec, Ault, Fecamp, Houlgate, and Saint-Pierre-du-Mont. About 150 P–47's dive-bomb A/Fs in France and Belgium. Around 175 MBs are forced to abort missions because of bad weather.

Twelfth AF: Attacks against lines of comm N of Rome continue. A–20's hit storage areas while MBs attack

Pesaro M/Y, dumps at Manoppello, and bridges and approaches at Incisa in Valdarno, Arezzo, Asciano, Magra, Ficulle, and Orvieto. Viaducts at Incisa and Calafuria are attacked with poor results. P–40's and P–47's hit roads, gun positions, railroads, ammo dump and trucks N of Rome, near Ficulle, Orte and Orvieto. P–47's also damage destroyers off Elba.

Fifteenth AF: Around 150 B–24's bomb aircraft factory at Turin, M/Y and bridge at Parma, M/Y at Ferrara, and several T/Os. Over 300 B–24's and B–17's are forced to abort missions due to bad weather. Over 100 ftrs escort the HB missions into N Italy.

Tenth AF: 12 A–31's again hit positions at Buthidaung and bomb Paletwa. 12 A–31's bomb Kohima while 8 B–25's attack Tiddim road. 80-plus FBs and 2 B–25's hit a variety of tgts at Kamaing, Nsopzup, and Mogaung. 12 P–51's hit Japanese HQ at Katha and supply huts at Hopin. Near Mandalay 12 B–24's bomb Monywa-Alon while 21 P–38's hit A/Fs at Heho, destroying several aircraft in the air and on the ground.

Fifth AF: 12 B–25's bomb troop areas in Hollandia vicinity, attacking villages S of Tanahmerah and huts and buildings along road from Marneda to Banggerang. Other airplanes carry out similar strikes against Karkar I and along Hansa Bay.

Thirteenth AF: Just before dawn 15 B–24's hit Dublon, Moen, Fefan, Uman, and Falo Is. 23 B–25's bomb airstrip and revetments at Tobera. 12 P–39's leave stockpiles aflame at Baitsi.

Seventh AF: Kwajalein-based B–24's, during 24/25 Apr, staging through Eniwetok, strike Truk and Guam and during day hit Wotje and Maloelap. This is first Seventh AF mission against Guam. B–25's from Engebi bomb Ponape, and Makin-based B–25's hit Jaluit and Wotje.

Eleventh AF: 3 B–24's photograph and bomb installations on Matsuwa I.

26 April

Eighth AF: 292 HBs strike at industrial center of Brunswick, a secondary tgt, when heavy cloud cover prevents bombing primary tgts of industry at Fallersleben, Waggum, Paderborn, Gutersloh and Cologne. Nearly 50 other HBs bomb T/Os in Hildesheim-Hannover area. 31 P–38 FBs attack A/F near Le Mans during morning, and 24 P–51's dive-bomb Cormeilles-en-Vexin A/F in afternoon. Opposition is very light and ineffective.

Ninth AF: Ninth AF Tac Air Plan for Operation NEPTUNE is published, 10 days after receiving formal AEAF directive ordering such a plan. Around 125 MBs attack Plattling landing ground. Ftrs fly over 750 sorties against scattered tgts in NW Europe.

Twelfth AF: Bad weather greatly curtails activity. P–47's attack motor transport and railroad tracks and hit gas dump near Trasimeno Lake, landing ground at Canino, and M/Ys of Leghorn.

Tenth AF: 18 A–31's hit positions N and S of Buthidaung while 3 B–24's bomb Akyab. Near Chindwin 6 P–38's hit Tiddim road while 3 A–31's attack Japanese HQ in Kohima vicinity. 70 FBs and 3 B–25's pound numerous tgts at Mogaung, Kamaing, and several points in N part of the Mogaung Valley. In Mandalay and surrounding area, 9 B–24's bomb railroad yards and engine sheds, and 9 P–38's hit stores and hangars.

Fourteenth AF: P–40's on armed rcn from Lashio to Man Kat cause considerable damage. 2 trucks, a warehouse, a water tank, and 2 locomotives are destroyed, gun positions and a bridge are strafed, and a Japanese-occupied building is left in flames.

Fifth AF: 120-plus B–25's and A–20's pound the Wewak area, hitting A/Fs at Wewak, But, Dagua, and Boram, and supply areas, troops, and several small villages. 13 B–24's bomb Awar Pt, 20 P–39's and P–47's attack bridges and T/Os near Madang and 8 P–39's attack roads, villages, and supply dump near Bunabun Harbor. A B–25 on rcn sinks a lugger in Sepik R. Allied ground forces take Hollandia and occupy Alexishafen.

Thirteenth AF: 24 B–25's bomb runway and dispersal area at Lakunai. 35 FBs pound A/F at Tobera. 8 P–40's attack occupied areas along bays of Tabut and Wariki.

Twentieth AF: Ftrs make first interception of B–29's as the VHBs are flying over the Hump. The brief confrontation results in no losses on either side.

Seventh AF: B–24's, having landed at Los Negros after bombing Guam on 25 Apr, hit Ponape and return to Kwajalein. B–25's based on Makin hit Jaluit and Wotje.

27 April

Eighth AF: More than 450 B–17's and B–24's bomb A/Fs, M/Ys, and T/Os in France and Belgium, the principal tgts being at Chalons-sur-Marne, Blainville-sur-l'Eau, Essey-les-Nancy, Toul/Croix-de-Metz, Le Culot and Ostend/Middelkerke.

Ninth AF: About 450 B–26's and A–20's and more than 275 P–47 and P–51 dive bmrs attack gun emplacements, M/Ys, coastal batteries, A/Fs, and several military installations in France and Belgium.

Twelfth AF: Weather again severely restricts operations. P–40's attack a supply dump N of Rome, scoring 7 hits in tgt area.

Tenth AF: 24 A–31's attack positions in Buthidaung area. 12 B–25's hit Kalemyo storage area while 36 A–31's pound Kohima-Kanglatongbi area. 12 B–25's hit railroad at 4 points around Shwebo. Nearly 150 P–40's, P–51's, A–36's, and B–25's blast troops, fuel dumps, gun positions, and railroad yard at several locations in Mogaung Valley, including Myitkyina, Mogaung, Namti, Kamaing, Mohnyin, Hopin, Nanyaseik, Chaungwa, and Myothit.

Fourteenth AF: Rocket-firing P–40's attack 20 junks S of Shasi.

Fifth AF: Babo is bombed by 9 B–24's. More than 100 B–24's, B–25's, and A–20's attack Mushu and Kairiru Is and A/Fs at Wewak, Boram, Dagua, and But. 120-plus A–20's and FBs blast coastal areas of Hansa Bay and nearby villages, personnel areas NW of Bunabun, and AA positions, villages, and bridges from Bunabun to Cape Croisilles.

Thirteenth AF: 16 B–24's bomb Dublon, Eten, Moen, and Fefan Is in early morning. 24 B–25's blast Talili Bay supply area; later a few P–39's hit same tgt.

Seventh AF: B–24's, staging

through Eniwetok, bomb Truk during 26/27 Apr. B–25's from Eniwetok follow up during the day with 3 raids on Ponape. Makin-based B–25's hit Jaluit, Wotje, and Mille. 1 B–24 from Kwajalein, using Makin as a rearming base, bombs Emidj, Jabor, and Enybor.

Eleventh AF: A B–25 bombs a submarine without success.

28 April

Eighth AF: 116 B–17's bomb Avord A/F and 14 attack V-weapons site at Sottevast. 34 P–38's attack aircraft repair depot at Tours while 49 P–38's, followed by 32 P–47 dive bmrs, strike A/F at Chateaudun. Later during the day 47 B–24's bomb V-weapon site at Marquise/Mimoyecques and 11 P–47's carrying fragmentation bombs attack A/F NE of Paris.

Ninth AF: 18 B–26's bomb A/F at Cormeilles-en-Vexin as secondary tgt. Nearly 250 B–26's dispatched to bomb M/Ys are recalled because of heavy cloud over tgts.

Twelfth AF: MBs attack Piombino, railway bridges in N Orvieto, Ficulle, and W of Arezzo, and hit viaducts at Incisa in Valdarno and Piteccio. A–20's score hits on fuel dump. P–40's and P–47's hit fuel dump NW of Ferentino, warehouses S of Avezzano, several railway lines and T/Os N of Rome, Orbetello railroad yards, San Stefano al Mare harbor, rail lines at points between Rome and Avezzano, several gun emplacements, Follonica and Chiusi M/Ys, and cut railroad lines at several points NW of Rome. FBs also hit Chiusi M/Y, tracks around Castiglione della Valle, Cortona M/Y, Groseto railroad bridge, scattered motor transport, and a barge near Follonica.

Fifteenth AF: Clearing weather again permits HB operations. More than 450 B–17's and B–24's attack harbors at Piombino and San Stefano al Mare and rail and road tgts at Orbetello. P–38's, P–51's, and P–47's provide escort.

Tenth AF: 24 A–31's hit positions near Buthidaung. 36 A–31's bomb positions at Sangshak-Sansak while 12 P–38's blast Tiddim road, causing a roadblock. In Mogaung Valley 80-plus A–36's, P–40's, P–51's, and a single B–25 pound same general tgts hit on the 27th. In Mandalay area 7 B–25's knock out railroad bridge S of Myingatha and canal bridge between Ye-u and Kinu.

Fourteenth AF: 26 B–24's, escorted by 10 P–51's, damage 2 bridges over Yellow R N of Chengchow (the capture of which by Japanese troops is acknowledged by the Chinese who evacuate Hulaokuan), and pound nearby storage area. 2 P–40's on armed rcn strafe troop column NE of Tengchung. 3 B–25's on rcn damage small steamer off E coast of Hainan. 16 P–40's and 6 B–25's pound Yangsin while 18 P–40's, P–38's, and P–51's strafe Nanchang barracks.

Fifth AF: More than 160 B–24's and B–25's bomb Wakde, Biak, and Efman I A/Fs. 180-plus P–47's, P–39's, A–20's, and P–70's hit a variety of tgts along N and NE New Guinea coast including villages and supply areas in Wewak and Boram areas, barges and troops at mouth of Sepik R and at Murik Lakes, and enemy comm and hideouts from Sepik R to Cape Croisilles. 21 B–24's of Thirteenth Air TF bomb A/F on Woleai.

Thirteenth AF: 24 B–25's bomb Wunapope supply area and Rapopo A/F. 30 FBs hit runway and revetments at Vunakanau. 15 P–39's pound gun positions near Mamagata and hit nearby bivouac and supply areas.

Seventh AF: B–25's, based at Makin, strike Jaluit and Mille, using Majuro as a shuttle base between strikes. A single B–24 from Kwajalein bombs islands in Jaluit Atoll, hitting Emidj first, then rearming at Makin, and attacking Jabor and Enybor during return flight.

29 April

Eighth AF: 579 B–17's and B–24's bomb Berlin, concentrating on railway facilities in Friedrichstrasse section in center of city. 38 other HBs bomb T/Os in area, including Magdeburg. Opposition by an estimated 350 ftrs is fierce. 64 HBs claim 73 ftrs destroyed while US ftrs claim 22.

Ninth AF: 217 B–26's dispatched to bomb M/Ys in France abort mission because of heavy cloud cover over tgt area.

Twelfth AF: B–25's attack Terni viaduct and Attigliano railway bridge, while B–26's bomb bridges and bridge approaches at Pontassieve and Incisa in Valdarno. A–20's attack dump NE of Rome. P–40's and P–47's cut rail lines in many places NE of Rome, hit guns N of Anzio and dump SE of Rome, attack town of Acquapendente, hit approaches and tunnel S of Arezzo and bridge and trucks in area, bomb Sinalunga M/Y and bridge and approaches at Monte San Savino, and hit docks at San Vincenzo and boats at Follonica.

Fifteenth AF: 484th Bomb Gp (B–24) is declared operational. The Fif-

teenth AF now has 18 HB gps. Over 400 B–24's and B–17's, with ftr escorts, attack Toulon naval base, Drnis M/Y, and Rimini-Ancona railroad.

Tenth AF: 12 A–31's pound positions near Buthidaung. 21 P–38's hit A/Fs in Heho area and claim 3 aircraft downed in combat. 25 P–51's and B–25's bomb several buildings at Meza. 19 B–24's over Prome blast supply dumps in the area.

Fourteenth AF: B–25's bomb warehouse and barracks at Shayang and attack 3 motor launches at Chiuchiang, leaving them burning.

Fifth AF: More than 30 B–24's and B–25's bomb villages, AA positions, and personnel areas in Wakde Is, Maffin Bay area, and along coast of New Guinea from Takar to Verkam Pt. 40-plus A–20's hit stores at Cape Wom, and T/Os between But and Dagua. 130-plus A–20's, P–47's, and P–39's hit hideouts and movements along Sepik R and from the river's mouth to Cape Croisilles.

Thirteenth AF: More than 40 P–39's bomb and strafe tgts throughout Bougainville and Buka, including Sipaai Mission, Kieta area, Lontis, Numa Numa, Ibu, Toborei, Totavi, Aitara, and Baitsi. 24 B–25's bomb A/Fs at Kara and Buka. Allied ftr sweeps continue over N Solomons and New Ireland, where huts, barges, and other T/Os are attacked.

Seventh AF: B–24's, staging through Eniwetok from Kwajalein bomb Truk and Jaluit. B–25's from Makin also hit Jaluit and carry out 2 strikes against Ponape.

Eleventh AF: 2 B–24's abort an armed photo mission due to weather.

30 April

Eighth AF: 114 B–17's bomb Lyon/ Bron A/F, 117 B–17's bomb Clermont-Ferrand/Aulnat A/F, and 52 B–24's hit V-weapon site construction at Siracourt. In conjunction with these HB operations, 44 P–38's conduct high altitude bombing of A/F at Tours. During afternoon 22 P–38's, employing high-level bombing tactics, attack A/F at Orleans/Bricy, followed immediately by 21 P–47's that dive-bomb the tgt. Enemy opposition accounts for 1 HB and 5 ftrs.

Ninth AF: Over 300 B–26's and A–20's attack V-weapon construction works and M/Ys in France.

Twelfth AF: B–25's attack railroad bridges at Ficulle, N Orvieto and Marsciano, while B–26's hit bridges at Cortona and Incisa in Valdarno and in nearby areas. P–40's hit rail lines and storage in many locations N of Rome, hit rail lines and radar station in Orvieto area, cut railroads from Rome to Tivoli and to Civita Castellana, and hit T/Os in the area. P–47's hit numerous railroad lines, rail cars, and other tgts N of Rome.

Fifteenth AF: 464th Bomb Gp (B–24) becomes the nineteenth HB gp declared operational by Fifteenth AF. Around 500 HBs, with ftr escorts, attack M/Ys at Alessandria, Milan, and Castel Maggiore, aircraft factory at Milan, and railroad between Rimini and Ancona.

Tenth AF: In Chindwin area, 31 B–25's blast tank concentration, bridges, supply dumps, and general vicinity at Kalewa. 4 B–25's damage 2 bridges N of Yamethin.

Fourteenth AF: P–40's from Yungning knock out bridge near Dong Mo

and strafe railroad T/Os in the area.

Fifth AF: More than 80 P–39's and P–47's make almost continuous attacks throughout the day against troops and supplies along Hansa Bay. 40-plus A–20's and B–25's bomb Wewak and nearby plantation. B–24's hit Noemfoor I with light raid. B–24 rcn flights over Manokwari area and Geelvink Bay result in claims of 6 interceptors shot down. P–70's hit T/Os on W shore of Hansa Bay. 23 B–24's of Thirteenth Air TF bomb Woleai Is.

Thirteenth AF: 10 P–39's bomb Porton Plantations. 20-plus other P–39's, in 11 sweeps, attack a variety of T/Os on Buka and Bougainville, including Ivituri Mission, Kieta area, and Mamagata supply area. More than 30 P–40's and P–38's bomb Vunakanau A/F. 23 B–25's bomb Vunakambi Plantation.

Seventh AF: 41 Kwajalein-based B–24's bomb various tgts at Wake. 11 Makin-based B–25's bomb Jaluit, while 8 from Engebi bomb Ponape.

1 May

Eighth AF: More than 500 HBs are dispatched on an early morning mission to attack 23 V-weapon sites in Pas de Calais area. Bad weather causes many aborts. 129 of these HBs manage to attack V-weapon sites at Marquise/Mimoyecques, Watten, and Bois de l'Enfer and A/Fs at Paix, Montdidier, and Roye/Amy. In afternoon raid 328 B–17's and B–24's bomb M/Ys at Troyes, Reims, Sarreguemines, Metz, Liege, and Brussels.

Ninth AF: The last of the 11 bomb gps (8 medium and 3 light) of IX BC becomes operational. 450 B–26's and A–20's attack numerous M/Ys and industrial tgts in France and Belgium.

Twelfth AF: MBs attack bridges at Albinia Station, NW of Chiusi, in and near Grosseto, near Monte Molino, Calafuria, and at Pontedera. Also attacked are viaduct at Monte Catellana and M/Ys at Florence/Campo di Marte and Florence, with particularly good results at Florence. LBs hit ammo dump at Fara in Sabina. P–40's and P–47's hit rail tracks in Rome area, Priverno station, guns N of Anzio, dumps at Frascati, stations at Colleferro and Frosinone, tracks at Orbetello and Orvieto, bridge and tunnel N of Todi, road in Canino, dump and factory at Stimigliano, vessels E of Piombino, factory E of Cecina, bridge approaches at Grosseto and Arezzo, dump at Grosseto, and tunnel at Rignano sull 'Arno.

Tenth AF: 18 P–38's and A–31's hit troop positions and supply dumps. 7 P–40's over Mogaung Valley hit Kamaing and attack positions N of Nanyaseik. 30-plus B–24's bomb Maymyo, Mandalay M/Y, and oil facilities at Yenangyaung.

Fourteenth AF: 32 P–40's hit tgts over wide areas of S China, Burma and Indochina. The FBs knock out bridge at Wan Lai-Kam, pound motor pool at Wan Pa-Hsa, and strafe railroad station and A/F at Yuncheng, damage 3 bridges and hit numerous boxcars at Bac Le, Dinh Ca, and Dong Mo, and bomb carbide mines at Loc Binh. Dong Dang and Na Cham railroad yards are also strafed. 7 B–25's and 8 P–40's bomb Tangyang A/F and nearby cav post. 2 B–25's over Amoy claim a small freighter sunk. 15 enemy airplanes bomb airstrips at Ankang and Hengyang.

Fifth AF: 180-plus MBs, LBs, and ftrs pound Wewak and Hansa Bay areas throughout the day. Numerous coastline tgts are hit, including A/Fs, vehicles, comm, villages, AA positions, bivouacs, supplies, barges, and offshore islands. B–24's of Thirteenth Air TF hit Woleai and Eauriprik Is.

Thirteenth AF: 24 B–24's over Borpop area attack coastal guns. 40-plus FBs and more than 30 Navy dive bmrs pound Vunakambi Plantation. 38 P–39's, flying 18 different missions, hit a variety of tgts on SW Bougainville, including missions at Tinputs, Koromira, and Tsimba, Hongorai R crossing, Numa Numa bridge, and huts at Aravia and Kunapaupau.

Twentieth AF: By this date all 4 VHB fields in Chengtu area are open to B–29 traffic.

Seventh AF: Shore-based AF Forward Area (TF 59) is activated to control all Army, Navy, and Marine shore-based aircraft in the C Pacific forward area. The cmd is headed by Gen Hale, former CG of the Seventh. B–25's from Makin bomb Jaluit.

Eleventh AF: A single weather sortie is flown.

2 May

Eighth AF: 50 B–24's bomb V-weapon installation at Saint-Pol/Siracourt.

Ninth AF: More than 250 B–26's and A–20's bomb M/Ys at Busigny, Valenciennes, and Blanc-Misseron. Over 400 P–47's and P–51's dive-bomb A/Fs and M/Ys in France and the Low Countries.

Twelfth AF: Attacks against rail lines and bridges in N Italy continue. MBs bomb approach to bridge in N

Oriveto, bridges in S Ficulle and in Marsciano, and M/Ys in Florence/ Campo di Marte and W and NW Florence. LBs hit ammunition dump NE of Rome. P-40's and P-47's hit rail lines N of Rome, bridges SW of Rome, guns N of Anzio, road at Montefiascone, road bridge at Cecina, trucks and planes at Malignano landing ground, and several other dumps, roads, and rail lines in N Italy.

Fifteenth AF: More than 250 B-24's, most with ftr escort, attack La Spezia dock and harbor installations, M/Ys at Castel Maggiore and Parma, railroad bridges at Faenza and Orbetello, and several T/Os. Over 300 other HBs are forced to abort because of weather.

EAC: TCC, until this date a major subordinate component of EAC, is placed under Third Tac AF, another EAC component. .

Tenth AF: 24 A-31's hit villages and defensive positions near Buthidaung.

Fourteenth AF: 3 B-24's claim 2 freighters sunk in S end of Formosa Straits.

Fifth AF: 140-plus A-20's and FBs hit bridges, barges, gun positions, roads, personnel, supplies, huts, and tent areas from Wewak to Hansa Bay throughout the day. 2 B-25's bomb A/Fs at Wewak and Boram. 8 others hit Wakde I oil stores, huts, AA positions, trucks, and other T/Os. A/F on Biak I is bombed by 2 B-24's.

Thirteenth AF: 22 P-39's bomb village N of Kieta, airstrip and buildings of Koromira and Rigu Missions. 8 P-40's also hit Kieta area. Ftr sweeps over Rabaul area continue. FBs hit Vunakambi Plantation supply area with incendiaries. B-25's pound Talili area.

Seventh AF: B-24's, staging through Eniwetok from Kwajalein, bomb Truk during the night. During the day B-25's based at Makin hit Jaluit and Wotje, using Majuro as a shuttle base to rearm between strikes. B-25's from Engebi pound Ponape.

3 May

Eighth AF: 47 B-24's bomb V-weapon site at Wizernes.

Twelfth AF: B-25's and B-26's pound railway bridges at Monte Molino, Orvieto, and Taggia, bridge approaches at Ficulle and Imperia, and Ventimiglia M/Ys. A-20's attack ammo dumps. P-40's and P-47's attack rail lines, bridge, dump, guns, and building in battle area and score 4 direct hits on observation post S of Cassino; vessels and docks at Civitavecchia and Montalto di Castro, and road bridges and rail lines in the area; town of Fondi and rail lines and bridges nearby; railway bridges at Foligno, Sant'Elpidio a Mare, and Grosseto; viaduct at Terni; and numerous vehicles, dumps, railroads, vessels, and other tgts in battle areas and in N Italy.

Tenth AF: 18 A-31's again hit defensive positions near Buthidaung. 12 B-25's and 40-plus A-31's hit Kohima and Kalewa. 28 FBs pound ammo dumps and other supplies at Mohnyin and N of Nanyaseik. 9 P-38's hit A/Fs in Meiktila area. 7 P-40's attack Lakatkawng and spt ground forces in the area.

Fourteenth AF: 7 CACW B-25's bomb Mihsien town area and also hit numerous vehicles and troops NE of Mihsien, between Yochou and Hsuchang, at Chihsien and N of Yenling. The MBs also strafe town of Hsiangcheng. 4 B–25's and 8 P–40's pound storage area at Tangyang A/F. 10 CACW P–40's score 11 direct hits on bridge over the Yellow R NW of Chenghsien, and destroy 15 trucks and many troops between Loyang and Luchou. 10 other P–40's on armed rcn sink 3 sampans near Cat Ba I, knock out bridge at Bac Le, damage another at Kep, and pound Na Cham railroad yards.

Fifth AF: 72 B–24's, B–25's, and A–20's thoroughly blast Wewak and Boram A/Fs in a single raid. About 120 A–20's, B–25's, and FBs, operating throughout the day, hit Wewak and Hansa Bay areas, including tgts at Nubia, Uligan, Mushu I, Wewak, and Boram. A/Fs at Maffin Bay is bombed by B–25's.

Thirteenth AF: 8 P–39's bomb buildings at Monoitu. 17 others, in the course of 6 missions, hit T/Os, including Japanese-occupied huts and buildings at Toiemonapu, Tinputs, and Sisiruai, and bivouacs at Tarlena, Ratsua, and Mawareka. 24 B–25's bomb Kulon Plantation and a personnel concentration to the NE. Allied ftr sweeps over N Solomons and the Bismarcks continue. P–40's returning from New Britain area bomb Pororan.

Seventh AF: B–25's from Kwajalein bomb Wotje while others, based at Makin, strike both Jaluit and Wotje, using Majuro as a rearming base between raids.

4 May

Eighth AF: 851 B–17's and B–24's (13 combat wgs) take off to bomb industries at Brunswick and Berlin. Because of thick cloud conditions less than 300 HBs proceed and these are forced to abandon mission over the Low Countries. 48 B–17's manage to attack Bergen/Alkmaar A/F during withdrawal.

Ninth AF: More than 170 B–26's and 36 A–20's bomb gun emplacements and other military tgts at Etretat/Sainte-Marie-Au-Bosc, Etaples, Le Treport, Ault, Fecamp, and Ouistreham.

Twelfth AF: Main effort again is against lines of comm. MBs hit bridges, tracks, and M/Ys. P–40's, A–36's, and P–47's hit rail lines in and around Priverno, guns and radar station N of Anzio, railroad cars, rail lines, and bridge in Orte-Attigliano and Orte-Narni areas, motor transport and stores E of Frascati, M/Ys at Colleferro and Follonica, and trucks and personnel on Fondi-Pico road. Vessels at Leghorn and numerous railroad tgts at scattered points are attacked.

Tenth AF: 12 A–31's bomb Kaladan while a single B–24 bombs Akyab. 12 B–25's damage bridge at Kalemyo and bomb Tiddim, while 24 A–31's hit Kohima. 24 B–24's bomb Mandalay M/Y and barracks and general area at Maymyo. 2 P–51's knock out bypass bridge near Shweli.

Fourteenth AF: 8 P–40's hit gun positions at Pailochi. 2 B–25's strafe 12 sampans between Hong Kong and Luichow Peninsula, killing many soldiers on board.

Fifth AF: 26 B–24's of Thirteenth Air TF bomb Mokmer A/F. 60-plus B–24's, B–25's, A–20's, and P–47's pound A/Fs, road, bridges, shipping, barges, and other tgts in Wewak area. A–20's attack bridges over Awar R and T/Os in Hansa Bay area while FBs hit T/Os in Ramu R Valley and on Hansa Bay coast.

Thirteenth AF: 24 B–25's bomb Talili Bay area. 43 FBs hit Vunakanau A/F. Allied ftr sweeps over the Bismarcks continue. 38 P–39's, flying 18 missions, hit several tgts on Bougainville, including buildings at Sovele, Tinputs, Reboine Bay area, Monoitu, and in area N of Taki. T/Os in Koromira area are also attacked.

Seventh AF: 12 B–25's, based at Makin, pound Jaluit and Wotje, using Majuro as a shuttle base for rearming between the strikes. 39 B–24's from Kwajalein and Eniwetok hit Ponape.

5 May

Eighth AF: 33 B–24's bomb V-weapon installation at Sottevast.

Ninth AF: Gen Wood assumes cmd of IX AFSC.

Twelfth AF: A–20's bomb supply dump W of Albano Laziale. XII TAC A–36's, P–47's, and P–40's fly 24 missions cutting rail lines N and NE of Rome, and hitting guns N of Anzio beachhead and N of Gaeta, and a dump near Frascati. Bridges at Orvieto and W of Lake Bolsena are damaged by direct hits, a barge at San Stefano al Mare is hit, several trucks destroyed or damaged, rail lines are cut in several places near Sesti Bagni, and airplanes are hit at Canino landing ground. DAF P–47's cut tracks S of Pisa.

Fifteenth AF: 465th Bomb Gp (B–24) becomes operational, making a total of 20 HB gps operational in Fifteenth AF. 640-plus B–24's and B–17's (the largest force of HBs dispatched by Fifteenth AF to date) attack M/Y at Ploesti and troop concentrations and town area at Podgorica. Ftrs fly over 240 sorties in spt.

Tenth AF: 18 A–31's hit concentrations SE of Buthidaung. 15 P–38's hit tgts along Tiddim road while 40-plus A–31's pound gun positions, camps, villages, and supply dumps SW of Bishenpur and at Kalewa. 3 B–25's bomb Thayaung A/F area. More than 80 P–40's, P–51's, A–36's, and B–25's carry out spt of ground forces, hit gun positions and supply dumps, attack troop concentrations, and blast numerous T/Os throughout the Mogaung Valley. 11 A–31's bomb Naba and vicinity while 3 B–25's and 6 FBs hit ammo dump N of Mohnyin. 12 P–38's bomb large warehouse E of Monywa. 6 B–24's lay mines in harbor off Koh Si Chang I.

Fourteenth AF: 11 B–24's bomb docks and shipping at Haiphong. 14 P–40's damage bridges at Hsenwi and Wan Pa-Hsa and hit barracks and destroy several trucks at Kentung. 8 B–25's and 23 FBs attack warehouse area at Chiuchiang, causing large fires. 25 CACW B–25's and P–40's thoroughly pound Sinyang M/Y and storage area. 10 P–40's sweep road from Loyang to Juchou, claiming 40–50 vehicles and numerous troops destroyed.

Fifth AF: B–24's bomb Mokmer A/F while B–25's hit supply areas at Wakde I and along coast of Maffin Bay. A–20's and FBs again pound tgts around Wewak and along coast of Hansa Bay, hitting supply and personnel areas, warehouses, and occupied villages.

Thirteenth AF: 24 B–25's bomb gun positions at Buka. 34 P–39's hit various tgts on Bougainville and Buka, including buildings at Porton, Chabai, and Kohiso, pillbox at Pau I, and road near Tsundawan. Supply area at Chabai is bombed by 12 other P–39's. P–40's bomb buildings at

Kieta and at nearby Rigu Mission. Ftr patrols continue over N Solomons and the Bismarcks.

Seventh AF: During 4/5 May B-24's from Kwajalein stage through Eniwetok and bomb Truk. During the day B-25's from Eniwetok strike Ponape, and 10 from Makin hit Jaluit and Wotje, using Majuro as rearming base between the attacks.

6 May

Eighth AF: 70 B-24's bomb V-weapon site at Siracourt. Over 90 others, scheduled to attack similar installations at Sottevast and La Glacerie, fail to bomb because of total overcast at tgts.

Ninth AF: 76 B-26's and A-20's dispatched to attack coastal defenses abort mission because of weather.

Twelfth AF: A-20's pound storage area at Itri. A-36's hit rail lines in Viterbo area. P-40's hit guns, tracks, and railroad station in and around Frosinone, and rail lines, stations, roads, and town area in and near Itri, Colleferro, and Sezze. P-47's hit Certaldo M/Y and numerous railroad and highway tgts, including several bridges.

Fifteenth AF: About 300 B-17's and B-24's, escorted by P-51's and P-38's, bomb A/F, aircraft factory, and M/Y at Brasov.

Tenth AF: 24 A-31's continue pounding positions near Buthidaung. 14 B-25's bomb Indainggyi, destroy Sibong bridge, and damage road at Hpaungzeik. 40-plus A-31's bomb troop concentrations NE of Palel and hit Thaungdut area. 90-plus P-40's, A-31's, P-51's, and B-25's attack wide variety of tgts throughout Mogaung Valley. 18 FBs and 6 B-25's

spt ground forces at Mawlu while 3 B-25's and 4 P-51's hit positions at Nalong.

Fourteenth AF: 61 P-40's and 5 B-25's attack tgts throughout S China and Indochina. Numerous vehicles and troops are destroyed in Hsiangcheng, Loyang, and Luchou areas. 8 boxcars are destroyed and 70 more damaged between Thanh Moi and Bac Le and between Phu Lang Thuong and Lang Son. A barge is sunk at Campha Port and numerous sampans and small craft sunk or damaged at Cat Ba I. Main buildings at Nanchang mines are destroyed, Sienning bridge is damaged, and several railroad cars and vehicles are destroyed near Puchi. 14 B-25's and 28 FBs pound A/F and surrounding area at Hankow.

Fifth AF: B-24's bomb Penfoei and Biak I. 150-plus B-25's, A-20's, and FBs, operating almost continuously throughout the day, blast a variety of tgts from Wewak to the shores of Hansa Bay. B-24's of Thirteenth Air TF again bomb Woleai.

Thirteenth AF: 24 B-25's and 12 P-39's pound the Talili Bay area. 37 P-39's and 19 P-40's attack tgts in Porton area.

Seventh AF: B-25's from Makin and Kwajalein hit Wotje and Jaluit. B-24's, staging through Eniwetok, escort Navy airplanes on photo rcn of Guam. The B-24's bomb Guam from 20,000 ft, scoring hits on 2 A/Fs and a town area and proceed to Los Negros to prepare for return flight. The HBs claim 4 interceptors shot down.

7 May

Eighth AF: 549 B-17's bomb city

of Berlin, 167 B–24's bomb industrial center of Osnabruck, 145 B–24's strike industrial area of Munster, and around 30 other HBs bomb various T/Os in Germany in morning raids. During the afternoon 19 B–24's bomb M/Ys at Liege and 9 bomb T/Os. This is the first day in which over 900 Eighth AF HBs attack tgts and the second time in which over 1,000 are airborne on a single-day's operations. 9 bmrs are lost.

Twelfth AF: Weather remains poor and precludes MB operations. A–20's hit dump SW of Albano Laziale. FBs hit comm, especially roads, with excellent results. Roads, motor transports, trains, gun positions, bridges, tracks, M/Ys, harbor areas, and other tgts are attacked in areas around Stimigliano, Vetralla, Viterbo, Bracciano, Anzio, Manziana, Acquapendente, Civitavecchia, Terracina, Rome, and Elba I.

Fifteenth AF: 420-plus B–17's and B–24's bomb M/Ys in Bucharest. 62 P–51's escort HBs to tgt and 53 provide withdrawal escort. 84 P–38's and P–51's fly tgt cover. 38 B–17's attack bridge at Belgrade.

Tenth AF: 35 A–31's pound area around Bishenpur. 15 P–38's hit Kangaung area. 4 P–40's hit T/Os along road from N of Nanyaseik to Kamaing. 4 B–24's lay mines in Gulf of Siam off Sattahib.

Fourteenth AF: 4 B–25's hit vehicle concentrations W and NW of Hsiangcheng and bomb town of Chiahsien, and 4 P–40's destroy at least 25 trucks between the 2 towns. 8 P–40's destroy or damage 40–60 trucks, tanks, and other vehicles during road sweeps from Loyang to Yenshih and from Yehhsien to Paofeng.

8 P–40's strafe forces and equipment E of Luchou, while 4 hit railroad T/Os at Lang Son.

Fifth AF: B–24's, B–25's, and P–40's hit Urarom, Biak I, Hollandia-Wakde coast, and Sawar-Maffin Bay area. A–20's, B–25's, and FBs again attack T/Os from Wewak to area around Hansa Bay and strafe villages along Sepik R.

Thirteenth AF: 15 B–25's, hampered by bad weather, attack coastal gun on Cape Friendship and bomb W coast of Rantan I. 70-plus P–39's, P–38's, and P–40's bomb numerous tgts throughout Buka and Bougainville, including shipping and supply area at Chabai and Tsirogei, huts at Hiru Hiru, near Tonu, and at Monoitu, and bridges W of Haigi and on Miwo R.

Seventh AF: B–24's, staging through Eniwetok, bomb Truk during 6/7 May. B–25's from Engebi hit Ponape during the following day. Makin-based B–25's bomb Jaluit and Wotje.

8 May

ETO: Gen Eisenhower sets D-Day for Normandy invasion as 5 Jun. Date subsequently will be changed to 6 Jun.

Eighth AF: During the morning 378 B–17's bomb Berlin, 287 B–24's and 49 B–17's strike aircraft factories near Brunswick, and 29 HBs attack Brandenburg and scattered T/Os in the area; 36 bmrs are lost on these raids. In afternoon 52 B–17's bomb 1 V-weapon site at Sottevast, 29 B–17's bomb sites at La Glacerie, and 56 B–24's bomb M/Ys at Brussels, with 5 HBs being lost in these afternoon operations.

Ninth AF: About 450 B–26's and

A–20's bomb M/Ys, coastal defenses, bridges, A/Fs, and V-weapons sites in France and Belgium.

Twelfth AF: FBs hit roads and railroads N of Rome, supply dump N of Anzio beachhead, and station at Colleferro. Numerous trucks and railroad cars are destroyed and many troops killed. Attacks against rolling stock on Rome-Orte rail line are especially effective.

Tenth AF: 12 A–31's continue attacks on sector SE of Buthidaung. 9 B–24's and 9 B–25's bomb Moirang and a village to the N, causing considerable damage including the destruction of a road bridge. 12 P–38's hit Kangaung A/F.

Fifth AF: B–24's and P–40's operating in Geelvink Bay area attack Mokmer A/F and nearby shipping. A–20's and FBs continue to pound T/Os along NE New Guinea coast from Wewak to Hansa Bay and along Sepik R.

Thirteenth AF: FBs pound Tobera A/F and strafe T/Os in the area. 2 sqs of B–24's bomb gun positions at Sohano I and Hahilia while 30-plus P–39's and P–40's hit areas around Porton, Tsimba, Tarara, Kieta, Numa Numa, Tsirogei, and at several other points. B–25's blast coast near Banin, hit Sohano I, and bomb A/F areas at Bonis and Buka.

Seventh AF: B–25's from Engebi strike Ponape while Makin-based B–25's pound Jaluit and Wotje, using Majuro as a shuttle base between strikes. B–24's that landed at Los Negros after Guam strike on 6 May return to the Marshalls, bombing Ponape en route.

9 May

Eighth AF: A total of 797 B–17's and B–24's bomb A/Fs at Saint Dizier Robinson, Thionville, Juvincourt-et-Damary, Laon/Athies, Laon/Couvron, Lille, Nivelles, Saint-Trond, and Florennes; and M/Ys at Liege, Thionville, and Luxembourg. This is start of an offensive against A/Fs, set within a month of Normandy invasion so that the GAF will not have time to recover before D-Day.

Ninth AF: The 367th and 406th Ftr Gps become operational, bringing the ftr gp total of the Ninth AF to 18. Over 40 MBs attack M/Ys, railway batteries, coastal defense batteries, bridges, and NOBALL sites in France.

Twelfth AF: B–26's hit Incisa in Valdarno railroad bridge and viaduct while A–20's attack fuel dumps. FBs again blast roads and railroads and other tgts at various locations N of Rome, including Lake Bolsena, Civitavecchia, Colleferro, Civita Castellana, Orte, and San Giovanni Valdarno.

USSR: Soviet Army captures Sevastopol.

Tenth AF: 20-plus A–31's continue attacks on Buthidaung area, hitting troop concentrations and supply dumps. More than 100 A–31's, P–51's, and B–25's hit positions and occupied areas at Moirang, Kanglatongbi, Myothit, and SE of Palel, and severely damage bridge over Uyu R near Nawngpu-awng. Mogaung Valley tgts, including tgts in spt of ground forces near Kamaing, are pounded by more than 60 B–25's, A–36's, P–51's, and P–40's. 9 P–51's hit troops and gun positions at Mawlu and Namkwin and hit Nalong area.

3 B–24's blast barracks area at Nagorn Sawarn while 3 P–51's hit Anisakan A/F, destroying or damaging 20-plus trucks, 2 airplanes, and a locomotive. 8 B–24's lay mines in Moulmein area, 2 others make diversionary strike on Martaban, and 5 mine Mergui waterfront.

Fifth AF: More than 50 B–24's and B–25's bomb Langgoer and Faan airstrips, and Bosnik supply area and Mokmer A/F. 220-plus A–20's and FBs continue to blast numerous T/Os along NE New Guinea coastline from Wewak to Hansa Bay area. 12 B–24's of Thirteenth Air TF bomb Woleai.

Thirteenth AF: 33 FBs pound A/F at Lakunai. Ftr sweeps over New Ireland and New Britain continue. On Bougainville 30-plus P–39's and P–38's hit barges in Porton-Chabai area, huts at Kieta, and ammo dump S of Aitara Mission. 10 other P–38's and 12 B–25's bomb Bonis A/F and nearby T/Os in Buka Passage.

Seventh AF: During 8/9 May B–24's stage through Kwajalein to bomb Truk. Makin-based B–25's hit Wotje and Jaluit, using Majuro as a rearming point between attacks.

10 May

Ninth AF: About 300 MBs attack M/Ys, A/Fs, and NOBALL tgts in France and Belgium. P–47's and P–51's dive-bomb tgts in NW Europe for the sixth straight day. Bad weather causes large number of aborts.

Twelfth AF: Weather permits MB operations for first time in several days. B–25's hit bridges near San Giovanni Valdarno, Orvieto, and Monte Molino, and Terni viaduct. B–26's attack bridges W of Arezzo. FBs continue attacks on roads and railroads N of Rome. Tgts in areas of Avezzano, Civitavecchia, Furbara, Terni, Todi, Orvieto, Manciano, Perugia, Monte San Savino, and La Spezia, and near Rome are attacked.

Fifteenth AF: 485th Bomb Gp (B–24) is declared operational, giving Fifteenth AF its planned operational strength of 21 HB gps. The 52d Ftr Gp (P–51) also begins operations with the Fifteenth on this date, making a total of 6 ftr gps. Around 400 HBs attack A/F and industrial complex at Wiener-Neustadt. Over 200 ftrs provide spt. 19 HBs hit Knin railroad center. Over 300 HBs are forced to abort due to bad weather which has halted operations for the past few days. Opposition is fierce against the Wiener-Neustadt missions. 21 HBs and 1 ftr are lost. US aircraft claim 50 combat victories.

CBI: In drive to free the Burma Road, Chinese troops cross Salween R on a 100-mi front and attack Japanese positions in N Burma.

Tenth AF: 12 A–31's hit Buthidaung area. More than 70 B–25's, A–36's, P–51's, P–40's, and 10 B–24's blast numerous tgts, concentrating on barracks and storage in Myitkyina-Mogaung vicinity and also hitting gun positions and bridges at Kamaing, and railroad siding and buildings at Mohnyin. 60-plus A–31's hit Kohima and Bishenpur, and damage bridge near Kalewa. 16 P–38's destroy several aircraft in strikes on Aungban and Kangaung A/Fs.

Fourteenth AF: P–40's sink 6 large junks and damage several others in Fan Tou Bay, and destroy several trucks between Wan Pa-Hsa and Mong Ho Pung. 28 P–40's bomb Tengchung town area, strafe nearby truck convoy, damage bridges at Tingka, Bac Le and Hsenwi, hit power dam at Tasa, bomb tank and truck dispersal area at Hsiangcheng, and hit 30-plus railroad cars at Lang Giai, Dong Dang, and Na Cham.

Fifth AF: 120-plus B-24's, A-20's, and FBs, along with RAAF airplanes, maintain attacks on T/Os along NE New Guinea coast from Hansa Bay area to Wewak. 2 B-24's hit Mokmer A/F. 45 B-24's of Thirteenth Air TF bomb A/F on Eten I and warehouse area at Dublon.

Thirteenth AF: 41 FBs attack Tobera A/F. 11 B-25's hit Matupi I. Ftrs on sweep hit trucks W of Keravat. 4 B-25's bomb Muguai Mission. 61 P-39's (some back from Tobera strike) and 12 P-40's attack tgts throughout Buka-Bougainville area, including bridge over Crepers R, supply area at Mawareka, barge at Chabai, village on Schwarze Pt, pillbox at Gohi, and general area of Porton Plantations.

Seventh AF: B-24's from Kwajalein bomb Wake during 9/10 May. During the day, B-25's from Engebi bomb Ponape while Makin-based B-25's raid Jaluit and Wotje.

Eleventh AF: The Eleventh directs its components to place more emphasis on photographing and bombing of specific tgts instead of general rcn.

11 May

Eighth AF: 164 B-24's bomb M/Ys at Mulhouse, Belfort, and Epinal; 24 bomb secondary tgts of M/Ys at Chaumont; 66 attack Orleans/Bricy and other tgts of last resort. 5 bmrs are lost in these early afternoon raids.

In late afternoon 2 forces, totalling 549 B-17's, bomb M/Ys at Saarbrucken, Ehrang, Volkingen, Konz-Karthaus, Thionville, Liege, Brussels/Midi, Brussels/Schaerbeek, Bettembourg, and elsewhere in Luxembourg. 8 bmrs are lost.

Ninth AF: More than 330 MBs attack A/Fs at Beaumont-le-Roger and Cormeilles-en-Vexin and M/Ys at Aerschot and Mezieres/Charleville. Bad visibility and failure to rendezvous with ftrs cause over 100 aborts. This is start of Ninth's participation in AAF pre-invasion offensive against A/Fs.

Twelfth AF: MBs, hampered by weather, attack Portoferraio, bridges near Orvieto and Ficulle, tracks at Piombino, viaduct at Poggibonsi, and bridges at Certaldo and Signa. FBs hit Fondi, rail lines NE of Rome, A/F at Littoria, rail facilities in Perugia area, barge, harbor area, and factory in Portoferraio area, and tracks near Castiglione d'Orcia. Other FBs attack numerous positions along main front as US Fifth and British Eighth Armies begin assault through the Gustav Line and the drive toward Rome.

Tenth AF: 24 A-31's hit Japanese positions at Labawa and SE of Maungdaw. 36 A-31's hit positions at Kohima and Potsangbam. In Mogaung Valley 70-plus B-25's, A-36's, P-51's, and P-40's, attack Myitkyina and Pinbaw areas, Sahmaw, tgts NW of Kamaing, gun positions at Nsopzup, and T/Os along road from Inkangahtawng to Kamaing. 24 P-51's attack A/F at Meiktila, Anisakan, and Heho, shooting down 13 airplanes in the area. 14 B-24's pound Maymyo railroad station. 12 B-25's attack railroad in Shwebo-Sagaing area. 12 other B–25's knock out bridges at Pyu, Thawatti, Ela, and 7 mi S of Ela.

Fourteenth AF: 24 P–40's knock out main bridge N of Mangshih, bomb town area of Lungchwanchiang, damage radio station on Cat Ba I and destroy several large junks off shore, and attack power dam W of Cao Bang, buildings at Dong Dang, and boxcars and oil drums at Lang Giai. 6 B–25's and 24 P–40's (some firing rockets) pound railroad yards and depot at Sinyang, blast warehouse area 30 mi to the N, and sink a small freighter, 3 motor launches, and several sampans between Siaokan and Chienli. 2 B–25's and 4 P–40's hit troops, tanks, and trucks in Yenshih-Tengfeng-Mihsien area and in Luchou-Hsiangcheng vicinity. 6 P–40's pound supply dumps at Mienchih and 13 P–40's sink at least 5 supply boats on the Yangtze in the Hosueh area.

Fifth AF: 130-plus B–24's and B–25's bomb gun emplacements and supply areas on Wakde and Mokmer A/F and T/Os on Biak. 220-plus FBs, A–20's, B–24's, and B–25's continue to pound coastal bridges and villages, fuel dumps, vehicles, gun positions, supply areas, bivouacs, and various tgts along the shoreline from Hansa Bay to Wewak.

Thirteenth AF: 8 P–38's bomb supply-personnel area W of Tobera. 12 B–25's, 12 P–40's and 3 B–24's hit Vunakanau A/F. Ftrs on sweeps and bombing missions over the Bismarcks hit various tgts at Kabanga Plantation, Gazelle Peninsula area, N of Sae R, and at Labout. 70-plus P–39's, P–40's, and P–38's (flying total of 18 missions) attack variety

of tgts, including piers at Chabai, Ratsua, and Porton, wooded area near Pipipaia, town of Siruluna, bridge at Tokinotu, and A/F at Buka.

Seventh AF: B–24's, staging through Eniwetok, bomb Truk during 10/11 May. During day B–25's from Engebi hit Ponape while others, based at Makin, pound Jaluit.

12 May

Eighth AF: 800 B–17's and B–24's operating in 3 forces, bomb oil plants, other industrial tgts, M/Ys, A/Fs, and some unidentified T/Os at Merseburg, Lutzkendorf, Zeitz, Bohlen, Zwickau, Gera, Chemnitz, and Brux. An estimated 430 ftrs offer intense opposition. 46 HBs are lost.

Ninth AF: IX TCC carries out EAGLE, a full-scale exercise of the tactics and techniques of paradrop, glider tow, parapack in resupply, air landing of supplies, and medical evacuation as a dress rehearsal for the airborne invasion of Normandy. More than 450 MBs attack coastal defenses, A/Fs, bridges, railroads and railroad guns, and V-weapon sites in France and Belgium. Thick haze impedes visibility and causes many aborts.

Twelfth AF: A–20's blast cmd posts along main battlefront as Allied ground forces seek to break through Gustav Line. MBs hit concentration near Fondi, attack forces at Vallecorsa and Pastena, and bomb numerous positions along main front. FBs pound cmd posts, guns, bridges, road and rail traffic, and troops along assault front and in rear areas, concentrating especially on the Monte Cassino Benedictine Abbey and surrounding area.

Fifteenth AF: Around 730 B–17's and B–24's (largest HB force used by Fifteenth AF on any day to this time) attack German HQs at Massa d'Albe and Monte Soratte; town of Civitavecchia; A/Fs at Tarquinia and in surrounding area; M/Ys at Chivasso, Piombino, Marina di Carrara, Viareggio, and Ferrara; Orbetello I; Piombino harbor; docks and comm at San Stefano al Mare; harbor, M/Y, and railroad bridge at Chiavari; La Spezia M/Y and harbor; and several T/Os. 25 P–38's strafe Piacenza A/F. Other ftrs fly over 250 sorties in spt of bombing missions.

Tenth AF: 24 A–31's hit positions at Labawa and SSE of Maungdaw. 36 A–31's hit villages around Bishenpur while 4 B–25's strike at Tiddim road NNW of Tonzang. 50-plus B–25's and FBs knock out railroad bridge at Pinbaw, pound gun positions and supply area at Myitkyina and hit defensive positions near Kazu–Tiangsup. 4 B–25's damage Myothit bridge while 8 P–38's bomb Kyaukye. 21 P–51's hit A/Fs at Meiktila and Heho, claiming 8 interceptors downed. 4 B–25's knock out bridge at Daga while 2 others bomb camp at Taungbaw.

Fourteenth AF: 16 P–40's and 11 B–25's hit several tgts in S China and in Indochina. Military installations, arty positions, and tank concentrations are pounded in Yoyang area, a bridge and several trucks are damaged at Sienning, a naval vessel is attacked at Hong Kong, a radio station on Cat Ba I is bombed, and railroad yards, supply dump, and river junks are blasted in Phu Lang Thuong area.

Fifth AF: B–24's bomb Mokmer A/F and attack tgts on Ceram, Amboina and Timor. A–20's, B–25's and FBs blast villages, coastal bridges and roads, vehicles, airstrip at Boram, and other tgts throughout Wewak-Hansa Bay region.

Thirteenth AF: 12 B–25's and 20-plus P–40's and P–38's pound Tobera airstrip and nearby personnel areas; some of the B–25's returning from Tobera bomb Sohano I. 12 P–39's and about 70 Navy SBD's and TBF's sink numerous barges throughout Rabaul area, especially at Simpson Harbor and Keravia Bay. Gun positions in Matupi area are also attacked.

Seventh AF: 12 Makin-based B–25's bomb Nauru. A single B–24 from Kwajalein bombs Jaluit.

Eleventh AF: 1 B–24 reconnoiters and bombs Matsuwa I installations, concentrating on the A/F on Tagan Cape.

13 May

Eighth AF: 689 B–17's and B–24's bomb A/Fs, M/Ys, aircraft assembly plant, and T/Os at Tutow, Osnabruck, Barth, Sylt I, Stettin, and Stralsund. 12 HBs are lost.

Ninth AF: More than 300 B–26's and A–20's bomb A/Fs, coastal defenses, railway battery, and V-weapon sites in France and Belgium. P–47's carry out dive-bombing raids on various tgts.

Twelfth AF: MBs, LBs, and FBs continue to attack lines of comm but devote main effort to spt of Allied ground forces push against Gustav Line (French Expeditionary Force with US Fifth Army gains spectacular breakthrough by fierce assault). A–20's hit cmd post; B–26's damage Cortona, Certaldo, Signa, and Montepescali bridges; B–25's blast towns in rear of battleline with good results at Pastena, Pico, Vallecorsa and Itri; and FBs carry out armed rcn and scheduled attacks against comm, road and rail traffic, and gun positions along immediate battleline and in areas around Esperia, Pico, Sant' Oliva, Pignataro Interamna, Arce, Fondi, Perugia, Todi, Spoleto, Terni, Orvieto, Chiusi, Rieti, and N of Rome.

Fifteenth AF: HBs continue interdiction in spt of ground forces. 670-plus B-17's and B-24's, mostly with ftr escort, attack M/Ys at Trento, Bronzola, Fidenza, Piacenza, Faenza, Imola, Cesena, Modena, Parma, San Rufillo, Borgo San Lorenzo, Castel Maggiore and Bologna, and hit railroad bridges at Bolzano and Avisio. Ftrs sweep Bologna-Modena area.

Tenth AF: Nearly 100 P-40's and P-51's over Mogaung Valley hit gun positions, bridges, spt ground forces (near Nanyaseik), and hit numerous T/Os throughout the whole valley. 12 A-36's hit positions near Maungdaw. 19 B-25's and 46 A-31's pound several points along road and bomb troop concentrations at Bishenpur. 30-plus B-24's, B-25's, A-36's, and P-51's hit Indaw, Taungbaw, and Mohnyin. 11 B-25's bomb Monywa.

Fourteenth AF: 19 B-25's hit storage and warehouse areas at Mangshik and Lungling, bridge at Hsenwi, truck and tank concentrations SW of Loyang, and town area of Lungling. 39 P-40's hit military installations at Mengta and Tating, village N of Kaitou bridge at Tingka, and truck concentration at Yingyangchen.

Fifth AF: B-24's hit dispersal areas on Japen I, supply areas and AA guns at Bosnik, and A/Fs at Sorido, Namber, and near Moemi R. B-24's and B-25's hit A/Fs in the Wakde-Maffin-Sawar-Arare area. More than 200 FBs, A-20's, and B-25's thoroughly pound A/Fs, bridges, fuel dumps, vehicles, villages, AA guns, and supply areas in Wewak-Hansa area.

Thirteenth AF: 50-plus P-39's and P-40's attack piers at Ratsua, Porton, Chabai, and Tarlena. 30-plus other FBs hit various tgts, including supply area SE of Bonis, town of Chabai, village near Ibu, and huts and villages along Numa Numa trail. 3 B-25's hit coastal guns at Hahela Mission. 21 B-25's and more than 40 P-39's, P-40's, and P-38's pound supply areas at Talili Bay. Ftr sweeps over N New Britain and New Ireland continue. Many T/Os are strafed.

Seventh AF: B-24's, staging through Eniwetok from Kwajalein, bomb Truk during the early morning hours. Other HBs from Kwajalein bomb Maloelap and Jaluit. B-25's from Engebi hit Ponape.

Eleventh AF: 1 B-25 flies a shipping strike and strafes 2 fishing vessels.

14 May

Twelfth AF: Spt for Allied ground assault into Gustav Line continues as aircraft hit at lines of comm N and NW of Rome and blast tgts in immediate battle area. MBs claim hits on bridges, bridge approaches, and viaducts at Chiani, Marsciano, Monte Molino, Castiglione d'Orcia, San Giovanni Valdarno, Poggibonsi, Tabianello, and Arezzo. A-20's pound cmd posts in battle area. FBs hit stations, tracks, roads, town areas, bridges, gun positions, and T/Os in immediate battle area and in or near Esperia, Terni, Narni, Itri, Terracina, Perugia, Chiusi, Orvieto, San Giovanni Valdarno, Maranola, and other locations N of Rome.

Fifteenth AF: Just over 700 B–24's and B–17's attack M/Ys at Vicenza, Padua, Ferrara, Treviso, Mestre, Mantua, and Piove di Sacco, and A/Fs at Piacenza and Reggio Emilia. Ftrs fly over 170 sorties in escort. 48 P–38's strafe Aviano and Villaorba A/Fs.

Tenth AF: 24 A–31's bomb troops and gun positions at Lahaw. 12 P–38's hit Tiddim road at Tonzang, causing roadblock. 48 A–31's bomb positions at Kalewa and S of Bishenpur. 11 P–40's hit bridge and road at Kazu and railroad shed at Myitkyina. 25 B–25's and P–51's hit troop positions at Hopin. Meiktila and Heho A/Fs are hit by 20–plus P–51's and P–38's. The ftrs claim 4 airplanes downed in combat.

Fourteenth AF: 60 P–40's and P–51's hit trucks at Yoyang, river shipping, boxcars, and trucks at Pailochi and Sienning, and storage area at Shayang. 20 other P–40's bomb and strafe towns near Mamien Pass, Pingkai and areas around Mengta and Tating. 6 Japanese bmrs hit Kienow, rendering A/F temporarily unusable.

Fifth AF: B–24's bomb Bosnik supply areas and Sorido runway. In Wakde-Sawar-Maffin Bay area, villages and AA positions are pounded by B–24's and B–25's. FBs, A–20's, B–24's, and B–25's maintain strikes against A/Fs, bridges, trucks, villages, and other tgts in Wewak-Hansa Bay area.

Thirteenth AF: 23 B–25's bomb Tobera airstrip. 44 FBs pound supply and personnel areas at Vunakanau. P–39's and P–40's strafe tgts in N and E Gazelle Peninsula, and ftr patrols over Rabaul area attack several T/Os. In Buka-Bougainville area, 40–plus P–39's and P–40's bomb Hangan, Tsirogei, Tokiparo, pier at Kessa Plantation, and near Ibu.

Seventh AF: 53 B–24's from Kwajalein and 43 B–25's from Makin join Navy aircraft in pounding Jaluit.

15 May

Eighth AF: 38 B–17's attack V-weapon site at Marquise/Mimoyecques while 90 B–24's bomb similar tgt at Saint-Pol/Siracourt.

Ninth AF: 45 A–20's and B–26's bomb A/Fs at Creil and Evreux/Fauville, and Somain M/Y. Over 300 others are forced to abandon missions because of thick clouds.

Twelfth AF: MBs and LBs again hit comm lines N and NW of the front while FBs in close spt of Allied ground assault through Gustav Line blast gun positions, motor transport, ammo supplies, bridges, rolling stock, and other military tgts in the battle area. The MBs and LBs also hit harbors and vessels along coasts at Piombino, Talamone, Portoferraio, and Ancona.

Fifteenth AF: Weather cancels all operations except ftr sweep over Toulon-Marseille area.

Tenth AF: 20-plus A–31's hit gun positions W of Buthidaung and signal center to the SE. 19 B–25's pound T/Os along Tiddim road while 36 A–31's hit Moirang. 20-plus B–25's and FBs hit gun positions at Hopin and A/F at Myitkyina. 17 P–38's attack

Heho and Kangaung A/F, claiming 15 aircraft destroyed, most of them in the air. 7 B–24's bomb Myitkyina, Kalewa, and Mandalay.

Fourteenth AF: B–25's strike Kengluang bridge and hit installations near Wan Pa-Hsa. P–40's strafe troops near Pingkai, along Mamien Pass, and in the Mengta area.

Fifth AF: Wewak-Hansa Bay area is again hit by A–20's, B–24's, and FBs. B–24's and B–25's attack numerous tgts in Wakde-Sawar-Sarmi-Maffin Bay areas and on Biak I. Thirteenth Air TF B–24's from the Admiralties bomb supply and bivouac areas on Mariaon and Tagaulap Is and AA guns on Woleai and Paliau Is.

Thirteenth AF: 24 B–25's and 40-plus P–40's, P–38's, and P–39's, along with TBF's and SBD's, pound area N of Muguai, and hit Maika area between Muguai and Ebery's Lease. 40-plus ftrs on sweeps over Bougainville and Shortland Is attack AA positions, trucks, and huts at several locations including Kieta, Cape Friendship, and Chabai areas. Allied ftr sweeps continue over Rabaul area; several T/Os, including a concentration of barges in Keravia Bay, are hit.

Seventh AF: Operations are limited to photo rcn of Jaluit from Kwajalein.

16 May

International: US, UK, USSR, Belgium, Norway and the Netherlands sign agreement concerning the administration of countries as they are liberated.

Twelfth AF: MBs attack railroad bridges and a tunnel in C Italy. LBs blast guns in Roccasecca while FBs and ftrs just behind enemy lines seek out motor transport tgts, crater roads, and hit bridges, harassing the already strained comm network, while US Fifth Army troops push rapidly W and NW and British Eighth Army forces push through last defenses of Gustav Line in effort to isolate Cassino, a joint effort by British 13 Corps and Polish 2 Corps.

Tenth AF: 30-plus A–31's pound Kohima, Moirang, and S of Buthidaung. About 70 B–25's and FBs hit Myitkyina and Hopin areas. 11 B–24's hit Ywataung and Sagaing M/Ys and town of Akyab.

Fourteenth AF: 8 B–24's blast motor pool and warehouse areas at Mangshih.

Fifth AF: Fifth AF aircraft continue to pound a variety of tgts in Netherlands New Guinea and NE New Guinea. Tgts include A/Fs and supply areas on Noemfoor and Biak Is, AA guns, supplies, and occupied villages in Wakde I-Maffin-Sawar coastal area, and bridges, villages, troop concentrations, and AA positions.

Thirteenth AF: 40-plus FBs hit Vunakanau area. Ftrs on sweeps hit barges at Jacquinot Bay and Mioko Harbour, vehicles at Kurakakaul, Mandres Bay, and Vunarima, and N of Vunakanau, a small vessel in Mandres Bay, and a sawmill at Keravat. FBs hit occupied areas at Tunuru, near Kieta, near Manetai Mission, and at Tinputs.

Seventh AF: Kwajalein-based B–24's pound Wake. B–25's from Makin hit Nauru and Ponape.

17 May

Twelfth AF: Operations continue in spt of Allied ground assault.

B–26's bomb road bridges in immediate battle area with generally fair results. Roads are blocked in Frosinone. B–25's bomb landing ground at Viterbo while A–20's bomb cmd post near Valmontone and drop supplies to French troops on Monte Revole. FBs hit railroads, bridges, trucks, and gun positions behind and along battle front with good results, destroying or severely damaging 6 bridges, creating road blocks in towns of Vallecorsa and Pico, blasting gun emplacements at Cassino, and hitting numerous T/Os.

Fifteenth AF: More than 450 B–24's and B–17's bomb Piombino and San Stefano al Mare harbors and shipping in the areas, harbor area and nearby steel works in Portoferraio, causeway at Orbetello, M/Y at Ancona, and town of Bihac. P–38's strafe A/Fs at Ghedi, Villafranca di Verona, Modena, Forli, and Reggio Emilia while other ftrs fly over 130 sorties of escort duty.

Tenth AF: 20–plus A–31's hit positions S of Buthidaung and S of Labawa. An equal number pound Bishenpur-Moirang area. 18 B–25's bomb Chauk oil installations while 20 P–38's hit Kangaung A/F. B–25's and FBs fly 90 sorties against Mogaung Valley tgts, hitting T/Os at Kazu and Namti and bridge at Kamaing, and supporting ground forces in Myitkyina area.

Fourteenth AF: P–40's spt ground forces at Mamien Pass, hit Japanese positions at Tatangtzu, damage bridge and several trucks at Shweli, strafe troops at Luchiangpa, and bomb and strafe horse pack train near Tengchung. 7 B–25's and 13 P–40's pound Shayang barracks area and hit troops and vehicles NE of Shasi.

Fifth AF: Allied forces land without opposition near Arare after naval bombardment. Fifth AF B–24's and B–25's hit tgts in general vicinity at Sawar, Sarmi, and mouth of Orai R. More than 100 B–24's, with P–38 escort, pound AA positions on Bosnik, Sorido, and Mokmer, and supply areas and A/F on Noemfoor. 120–plus FBs, A–20's, B–25's, and B–24's continue to hit Wewak-Hansa Bay area.

Thirteenth AF: 25 B–25's bomb A/F at Tobera while 43 P–39's, P–40's, and P–38's, in conjunction with 40–plus Navy dive bmrs, blast Vunakanau area. Ftrs on sweeps over the Bismarcks hit Nubai R bridge and strafe tgts on Gazelle Peninsula. 39 FBs hit numerous tgts in Bougainville area, including Muguai area, bridge N of Numa Numa, barges at Banin Harbor, and area around Ratsua.

Seventh AF: B–24's from Kwajalein bomb Wake while Engebi-based B–25's hit Ponape.

18 May

Twelfth AF: MBs continue to hit rail bridges, bombing farther into the N of Italy and thus putting more pressure on the strained German comm system. LBs hit storage areas. FBs continue close spt to Allied ground forces, hitting town areas, roads, enemy positions, railroads, and numerous other tgts in battle area, including points in or around Pico, Pontecorvo, Fondi, Terracina, Ceccano, Pastena, San Giovanni Valdarno, Perugia, Terni, Spoleto, Sant'-Elpidio a Mare, Pedaso, and N of

Rome, as British Eighth Army completes reduction of Gustav Line in Liri R Valley with capture of Cassino, while US Fifth Army takes Formia.

Fifteenth AF: Almost 450 B–17's and B–24's, most with ftr escort, attack M/Ys at Belgrade and Nish and oil refineries at Ploesti. Over 300 other HBs abandon missions because of bad weather. Ftrs strafe Nish and Scutari A/Fs.

Tenth AF: 12 A–31's bomb Daletme while 36 hit tgts SW of Homalin, S of Bishenpur, and at Moirang. 140–plus FBs and 6 B–25's pound numerous tgts throughout Mogaung Valley, concentrating on bridges (at least 4 are knocked out) and spt of ground forces in areas around Myitkyina, Nanyaseik, Kamaing, Namkwin, Kazu, Lonkin, and Katkyo. 8 B–25's knock out Mu R bridge and damage Chaungu bridge approaches. 12 P–38's destroy several airplanes at Shwebo.

Fourteenth AF: 6 B–25's and 12 P–40's pound barracks and warehouse areas at Chienyangi, causing many fires. 30 P–40's spt ground forces in Salween area, hitting troops and positions at Tengchung, Tatangtzu, Mamien Pass, and Luchiangpa. 12 B–24's bomb towns of Lungling and Tengchung. 25 CACW and CAF P–40's attack trucks, armor, and troops at Chueh-shan and Loning, causing widespread destruction.

Fifth AF: More than 100 FBs, A–20's, B–25's, and B–24's pound T/Os in Wewak-Hansa Bay area throughout the day. B–24's hit T/Os on Halmahera I and bomb Bosnik. B–25's hit Larot and Saumlakki.

Thirteenth AF: 10 P–39's hit barges off Porton. 40–plus P–38's and P–39's pound supply area N of Muguai.

Seventh AF: B–25's based at Makin bomb Taroa, rearm at Majuro, and attack same tgt during return flight to base.

Eleventh AF: Over the Kurils, a B–24 on weather rcn hits a Japanese aircraft and 2 B–25's sink an auxiliary vessel. Another is sunk shortly before midnight by 2 other B–25's.

19 May

Eighth AF: 493 B–17's bomb Friedrichstrasse section of Berlin, and 49 bomb port facilities at Kiel. 273 B–24's hit industrial area at Brunswick. 8 other HBs attack T/Os and last resort tgts in Germany. Enemy resistance is heavy, and 28 HBs and 20 escort ftrs are lost. US bmrs and ftrs claim 164 aircraft destroyed.

Ninth AF: About 290 B–26's and A–20's bomb coastal defenses, port area, railway battery, and NOBALL tgts in France. More than 125 others fail to bomb because of extremely thick haze. About 300 P–47's divebomb tgts in France.

Twelfth AF: MBs hit railroad bridges in NC Italy while LBs bomb ammo dump. FBs continue spt to Allied forces advancing rapidly N and W, blasting road network in battle area, and hitting motor transport, bridges, town areas, and T/Os, in areas around San Giovanni Valdarno, Pastena, Vallecorsa, Terracina, Fondi, Pistoia and elsewhere.

Fifteenth AF: HBs hit comm tgts, ports, and oil storage in NE, C, and NW Italy. Over 500 B–17's and B–24's hit railroad bridges at Latisana, Tagliamento, Casarsa della Delizia, and Rimini, M/Ys at Forli, Faenza, and Bologna, oil storage at Porto Marghera, port and M/Y at La Spezia, harbor at Leghorn, and harbor and rail installations at Genoa. Ftrs fly over 250 sorties in spt. These operations are notable for absence of ftr opposition.

Tenth AF: A–31's again hit various tgts in Arakan area. A–31's fly over 60 sorties against villages S of Bishenpur and gun positions at Kanglatongbi. A–36's, P–40's, P–51's and a few B–25's fly 140–plus attack sorties against various tgts in the Mogaung Valley, concentrating on gun positions in Myitkyina area. 8 B–25's damage railroad tracks in Myingatha-Saye area and 16 P–38's hit A/F at Nawnghkio.

Fourteenth AF: 31 ftrs spt ground forces in Salween area at Chiangtso, Watien, and Mamien Pass. 4 P–40's knock out bridge at Shweli, 13 P–40's bomb and strafe Puchi area, and 16 P–40's and P–38's damage bridge at Tayeh and hit military installations and other buildings at Yangsin. 11 P–51's bomb village near Anking, causing large explosions and fires. 2 B–24's on sea sweep seriously damage 2 freighters S of Hong Kong. 16 CACW P–40's pound trucks, tanks, and troops in Ichang-Tangyang-Loyang area and attack river traffic at Itu on the Yangtze R.

Fifth AF: B–24's, A–20's and P–38's hit A/Fs and shipping in Manokwari-Noemfoor I area. Other B–24's pound beach defenses at Bosnik on Biak I and hit area between Bosnik and Mokmer. 270-plus A–20's, P–47's, P–38's, and B–25's continue to blast Wewak, knocking out radar and radio stations, and attack T/Os from Wewak to Hansa Bay area.

Thirteenth AF: More than 40 P–39's, P–38's, and P–40's hit Makada I. 16 B–25's bomb gun positions and supply area at Talili Bay. 20 AAF ftrs and a few Navy airplanes bomb huts and bridges at Monoitu, Porton, Toborei, Moisuru, and Tsimba.

Seventh AF: B–25's based at Engebi hit Ponape and B–25's from Makin hit Nauru.

Eleventh AF: A B–24 flies armed rcn over Shimushu and Ketoi Is.

20 May

Eighth AF: 287 B–17's and B–24's bomb A/Fs, aircraft works, and M/Ys at Orly, Villacoublay, Reims and Reims/Champagne. Large force of nearly 250 HBs scheduled to bomb at Liege and Brussels is forced to abort because of dense cloud cover over tgts.

Ninth AF: Around 450 MBs attack A/Fs, coastal defenses, and V-weapon site in France. About 250 aborts are caused mainly by bad cloud conditions and failure to rendezvous with ftrs. P–47's dive-bomb tgts in NW Europe.

Twelfth AF: Weather prevents operations by MBs and LBs. FBs continue to hit comm and gun positions in battle area. Areas in and around Vallecorsa and Terracina are hit especially hard. Ftrs maintain patrols and rcn, destroying or damaging numerous vehicles between Pisa and Pistoia.

Tenth AF: 100–plus A–36's, P–40's, and P–51's pound gun positions, attack bridges, bomb troops, and hit numerous T/Os in areas around Myitkyina, Kamaing, Nanyaseik, and Nsopzup. 16 A–31's and 2 P–38's hit tgts in Arakan area, including signal center SE of Buthidaung, gun positions SE of Maungdaw, and jetty at Akyab. 24 A–31's bomb positions at Churachandpur. About 40 B–24's and P–51's hit oil installations at Yenangyaung and Chauk, A/F at Pakokku, and town of Akyab.

Fourteenth AF: 13 B–24's attack convoy S of Hong Kong claiming 2 motor launches sunk and damaging several larger vessels. 3 HBs are lost at sea. 37 P–40's hit trucks, armored vehicles, river traffic, and troops in or near Shasi, Ichang, Tangyang, Chingmen, Loyang, and Loning. On Salween front 43 ftrs and 8 MBs spt ground forces and damage bridge N of Tengchung over Shweli R.

Fifth AF: B–24's, A–20's, and B–25's hit airstrips, revetments, supply areas, AA positions, and shipping at Manokwari, Noemfoor and Biak Is, and Mawi Bay. A–20's, B–25's, and FBs continue to pound A/Fs, coastal villages, bridges, supply dumps, trucks, and various other tgts at Wewak and from Wewak to shore of Hansa Bay.

Thirteenth AF: 22 B–25's, 44 P–39's, P–40's, and P–38's and 30-plus Navy and Marine aircraft pound AA positions, bivouacs, and supply areas from Muguai-Ebery's Lease area to Maika area. 24 other P–39's hit barges in Matchin Bay, AA guns at Sohano I, and bridges at Kieta. 3 B–24's bomb Tobera runway while 2 B–34's, with Navy ftr escort, attack barges and a launch NW of Rabaul.

Seventh AF: B–25's from Engebi bomb Ponape.

21 May

Eighth AF: 99 B–24's bomb V-weapon site at Siracourt while 25 B–17's strike similar installation at Marquise/Mimoyecques.

Ninth AF: 50 B–26's bomb A/F at Abbeville/Drucat. Over 600 P–47's and P–51's attack railroad rolling stock in France.

Twelfth AF: In NC Italy, MBs are restricted by bad weather but bomb a few bridges and roads, while LBs hit a bivouac area. FBs continue spt of ground forces, hitting troops, vehicles, roads, and railroads in or near battle areas, particularly around Sezze, Ceccano, San Giovanni Valdarno, and Pontecorvo.

Tenth AF: A few A–31's continue attacks against gun positions in Arakan area. 120-plus P–40's, P–51's, A–36's, and B–25's hit Mogaung, Myitkyina, Talawgyi-Hokat area, and Kamaing. Gun positions around Myitkyina and Mogaung are also hit. 21 A–31's hit troop concentrations at Homalin and score hits on Manipur bridge. A single B–24 bombs NW part of Mandalay.

Fifth AF: B–24's, A–20's, and P–38's attack A/Fs, town areas, barges, personnel and supply areas, and fuel dumps at Manokwari, Urarom, along Moemi R, and on Noemfoor and Biak Is. FBs, A–20's, and B–25's continue almost constant pounding of supply dumps, camps, AA positions and a variety of tgts along coast from Wewak to Hansa Bay. Thirteenth Air TF B–24's bomb Truk.

Thirteenth AF: 3 B–24's, 30-plus P–39's and P–40's, and over 40 Navy dive bmrs hit Vunakanau A/F and nearby plantation. 8 P–38's, followed shortly by Navy aircraft, bomb Lakunai A/F. More than 40 P–39's, P–38's, and P–40's fly sweeps over Bougainville. Bridges at Rigu Mission and

Shishigatero are reported demolished.

Seventh AF: 53 B–24's from Kwajalein bomb various tgts in Wotje Atoll. 41 B–25's, based on Makin, follow up with bombing, cannonading, and strafing attack on the atoll. 8 B–24's stage through Eniwetok, strike Rota, and rearm at Los Negros.

22 May

Eighth AF: Occupancy of all planned Eighth AF stations in Britain is completed with transfer of A/F at N Pickenham from RAF to the Eighth. Total stations number 77, including 66 A/Fs, occupied by 82 operational or HQ units. 269 B–17's bomb shipyards at Kiel and 23 others release bombs prematurely in Kiel area. 94 B–24's attack V-weapon site at Siracourt.

Ninth AF: Around 330 B–26's and A–20's bomb A/Fs and other tgts in Cherbourg, Calais, and Paris areas while a like number of P–47's and P–51's dive-bomb M/Ys, A/Fs and other tgts in same general areas.

Twelfth AF: 332d Ftr Gp is assigned to Fifteenth AF. This move, following a series of reassignments of ftr gps to Fifteenth AF and to India, leaves XII FC with only 1 ftr gp. MBs are inactive or abortive except for a raid on Cave. FBs maintain close spt of the ground adv, hitting at motor transport, roads, and bridges in battle areas and nearby points in C Italy, including Terracina, Ceccano, Sezze, Bastia, points between Rome and Bracciano Lake, and near Balsorano.

Fifteenth AF: As weather again clears, 550-plus B–17's and B–24's concentrate on comm and military tgts in C and NW Italy, attacking

Pescina, troop concentrations at Avezzano, port and oil depot at La Spezia, supply and ammo dumps at Marina di Carrara, port and harbor installations at Piombino, railroad and highway bridges in Pineto area, railroad from Ancona to Pescara and N of Pescara, and towns of Valmontone and Palestrina. Ftrs fly over 200 sorties in escort to HBs. There is no ftr opposition.

Fourteenth AF: 2 B–25's attack large concentration of sampans in Honghai Bay. 2 others heavily damage a 150-ft cargo vessel near Hong Kong. 22 P–51's pound town of Anking and military area NE of Nanchang. 24 P–40's hit Sienning area, bombing factory W of town, damaging bridge near town, and strafing numerous trucks in the vicinity. 23 P–40's hit road and river traffic in areas around Loyang, Loning, and Itu. 5 P–40's bomb Yangsin.

Fifth AF: B–24's and B–25's bomb Manokwari, shipping E of Cape Manggoear, and storage areas and Sorido village on Biak I. P–40's hit supply and fuel dumps, trucks, and other T/Os in area of Wakde Is. B–24's, B–25's, and FBs continue to bomb and strafe various tgts in Wewak-Hansa Bay area.

Thirteenth AF: 40-plus P–39's, P–38's, and P–40's hit T/Os in coastal area near Talili Bay. 24 B–25's pound Mioko I. 40-plus P–39's bomb Bonis supply area and blast 4 small bridges near Kieta.

Seventh AF: 8 B–25's based on Engebi bomb Ponape. Weather cancels other strikes.

Eleventh AF: 2 Attu-based B–25's on a shipping strike near Paramushiru bomb and strafe a picket boat, which is left sinking.

23 May

Eighth AF: 804 B–17's and B–24's bomb tgts at Hamburg, Saarbrucken, Metz, Epinal, Bayon, Chaumont, Etampes, Chateaudun, Caen/Carpiquet, Bourges, Avord, and Orleans/Bricy. Ftr opposition is very light; one bmr is downed by AA fire.

Ninth AF: In predawn mission 15 B–26's bomb A/F at Beaumont-le-Roger. During afternoon 58 B–26's bomb coastal batteries at Etretat/Sainte-Marie-Au-Bosc, Maisy, and Mont Fleury. Over 120 P–38's strafe and bomb rolling stock in C France.

Twelfth AF: MBs abort missions because of weather. LBs hit comm between Cisterna di Roma and Campoleone. FBs actively spt general offensive of Allied ground forces in Liri Valley and at Anzio where US and British forces break out of the beachhead. Ftrs on armed rcn join in the attacks and numerous enemy vehicles, gun positions, transport routes, and personnel are hit hard in areas in and around Terracina, Littoria, Norma, Marcigliana, Fara in Sabina, Borghetto, Arezzo, and Civita Castellena. M/Y on Empoli-Siena line is hit also.

Fifteenth AF: 300-plus B–17's and B–24's concentrate attacks on troop concentrations and comm in rear of battle area, at Avezzano, Subiaco, Valmontone, Marino, Nemi and Grottaferrata. P–38's and P–51's provide escort. Other P–38's, covered by P–47's, strafe A/F at Ferrara.

Tenth AF: 12 P–38's bomb Tiddim road and 32 A–31's bomb Kohima, Tiddim, and Kalewa. 12 B–24's bomb Indaw M/Y and Homalin. 16 P–38's attack Kangaung A/F. 23 P–40's and 4 A–36's bomb gun positions, troops, and supply dumps in Myitkyina area.

Fifth AF: B–24's hit Manokwari while B–24's, A–20's, and P–38's hit tgts at Biak I, including trucks at Borokoe, AA positions and control tower at Mokmer A/F, village of Sorido, and offshore tgts at Bransfari. P–40's hit troops on Wakde and on Biri R. P–38's spt ground forces in Aitape area. A–20's, P–39's, B–24's, and B–25's maintain bombing and strafing of Wewak-Hansa Bay area.

Thirteenth AF: 2 B–24's bomb Tobera, while 32 B–25's and 40-plus P–39's, P–38's, and P–40's attack gun positions near Rabaul, near Lakunai, and in vicinity of Tunnel Hill Road. In Bougainville area 51 P–39's and 8 P–40's attack huts, barges, bridges, and other T/Os at several locations.

Seventh AF: Makin-based B–25's strike Jaluit. B–24's returning from Los Negros, where they landed after raid on Rota on 21 May, bomb Ponape.

24 May

Eighth AF: 400 B–24's attack A/Fs at Orly, Melun, Creil, and Poix. 447 B–17's bomb Berlin while 72 attack T/Os in the area. Enemy opposition is heavy and 33 HBs are lost.

Ninth AF: More than 450 MBs attack A/Fs, coastal defenses, and V-weapon sites in France. P–38's and P–47's dive-bomb 4 landing fields in France.

Twelfth AF: MBs, LBs, and FBs fly numerous sorties in spt of rapidly advancing ground forces and in attacks against rail lines, bridges, and roads in NC Italy. MBs hit at least 5 bridges, create several road blocks and cause havoc in comm to N of battle area. LBs blast bivouac area. FBs have great success in attacks on motor transports, mainly in battle area, and in conjunction with British airplanes destroy over 300 and damage as many more.

Fifteenth AF: 620-plus B–17's and B–24's attack Avisio viaduct, Atzgersdorf aircraft components factory, town of Neunkirchen, A/Fs at Munchendorf, Graz, Wollersdorf, Bad Voslau and Zagreb, and Varazdin M/Y. Escorting ftrs fly over 250 sorties. Enemy ftr opposition is especially heavy against Bad Voslau force, downing 6 HBs.

Tenth AF: 60-plus A–31's bomb enemy positions in Palel-Chassud area, hit village near Moirang, and attack truck park beside Tiddim road. 20-plus P–40's in Myitkyina vicinity destroy 3 barracks buildings and knock out a railway bridge and a machinegun post. A single B–24 bombs Gwa in Arakan area.

Fifth AF: A–20's hit A/Fs at Namber and Kamiri. More than 200 A–20's, P–38's, P–47's P–39's, and B–25's continue to blast T/Os in Wewak-Hansa Bay area throughout the day.

Thirteenth AF: In Rabaul area 19 P–38's, P–40's, and 22 B–25's attack Hospital Point gun positions. 2 other B–25's hit town of Rabaul. Ftr patrols hit various T/Os in Rabaul area and S New Ireland. 51 P–39's, P–40's, and P–38's, and a single B–24, attack various Buka-Bougainville tgts including Buka A/F, E Bougainville coastal bridges, and Cape Lalahan radar station.

Seventh AF: B–25's from Makin pound Wotje and Jaluit, using Majuro

as a shuttle base for rearming between the strikes. B–25's based at Engebi hit Ponape.

Eleventh AF: 2 bmrs fly weather and photo rcn over Shimushu and bomb Matsuwa area.

25 May

Eighth AF: 859 B–17's and B–24's operating in 4 forces bomb M/Ys at Mulhouse, Troyes, Tonnerre, Belfort, Sarreguemines, Thionville, Metz, Blainville-sur-l'Eau, Liege, Brussels, Alost, and Charleroi; A/Fs at Esseyles-Nancy and Bretigny-sur-Orge; and coastal batteries at Fecamp and Saint-Valery–en-Caux. 2 HBs are downed by AA fire and 2 are lost to unknown causes.

Ninth AF: Over 225 MBs attack bridges near Liege and A/Fs at Lille/Nord and Monchy-Breton. About 250 P–47's dive-bomb various tgts in NW Europe.

Twelfth AF: Twelfth AF has most active day to date against enemy forces in Italy. Some MBs continue to pound bridges in NC Italy, damaging several bridges and viaducts, while others join FBs and LBs in close spt of ground troops in battle area and behind enemy lines. Motor transport N and S of Rome and N of Anzio is hit hard by the air attacks. US Fifth Army achieves a solid front with junction of VI Corps (Anzio force) and II Corps (advancing along W coast) during the morning near Borgo Grappa.

Fifteenth AF: 340-plus B–17's and B–24's attack M/Y's at Lyon, Carnoules, Amberieu-en-Buguey, and Givors, while another 250-plus HBs hit Porto Marghera oil stores, Monfalcone harbor and shipping, and Piacenza A/F and dispersal area. P–38's and P–51's fly more than 200 sorties in spt.

SE Europe: German paratroops attack Marshal Tito's HQ in Bosnia, but Tito and Maj Randolph Churchill escape to the mountains.

Tenth AF: 28 P–38's sweep over Mandalay area. 12 of them hit about 10 railroad cars near Shwebo, leaving them burning. In the Chindwin area 20 A–31's attack a bivouac and score hits on Manipur R bridge at Tonzang. B–24's hit tgts in Katha area, 6 of them bombing Indaw and 4 bombing Naba rail junction area.

Fifth AF: B–24's attack shipping at Halmahera and hit Mokmer and tgts in Wakde area. 90-plus FBs, A–20's, B–25's, and B–24's pound numerous tgts in Wewak area.

Thirteenth AF: 3 B–24's bomb Rabaul, Lakunai, and Rapopo. 8 P–38's hit Vulcan Crater barge hideout. 12 B–25's, clouded out of Vunakanau, hit Talili Bay supply area. 15 B–25's, 32 P–39's, and P–40's, and 25 Navy dive bmrs hit supply areas at Porton. 4 other P–40's hit trucks at Monoitu Mission. 16 P–39's attack several T/Os, including Cape Lalahan radar station.

Seventh AF: B–25's flying out of Engebi bomb Ponape.

Eleventh AF: 1 Shemya-based B–24 flies rcn and bombing mission in the C Kurils. Another B–24 aborts due to equipment failure.

26 May

Eighth AF: Eighth AF reaches its peak strength in number of ftr gps when 479th Ftr Gp (P–38) becomes operational. (By end of year all ftr gps except one will be converted to P–51's).

Ninth AF: Nearly 400 B–26's and A–20's attack A/Fs at Beaumont-sur-Oise and Chartres and bridges at Vernon and Poissy. 108 P–47 and P–51 FBs hit bridge at Oissel and A/Fs at Creil, Cormeilles-en-Vexin and Evreux/Fauville. P–47's and P–38's dive-bomb tgts in NW Europe.

Twelfth AF: MBs hit railway tgts in Florence area and bomb roads in battle area with good results. LBs hit Frascati. Other MBs join FBs in assault against motor transport achieving wide-spread enemy vehicle destruction, especially on the Rome-Bracciano road over which enemy is pouring reinforcements S toward battle area.

Fifteenth AF: Almost 700 B–17's and B–24's attack M/Ys at Saint-Etienne, Lyon, Nice, Chambery, and Grenoble. HBs also hit Var R bridge and troop concentrations at Bihac. Ftrs escort the HBs and strafe and dive-bomb A/F at Donji Zemunik.

Fourteenth AF: 23 P–40's sink several supply boats on Yangtze R near Shihshow, strafe troops at Shasi, hit road traffic near Loyang, and strafe pontoon bridges, supply dumps, and troops at Shanhsien. 7 P–40's bomb town of Hsing-tzu. 2 B–25's damage a small tanker N of Swatow.

Fifth AF: B–24's bomb Biak I while B–25's hit Wakde I and nearby coastal areas. Other B–25's bomb a variety of tgts in Aroe Is. 100-plus A–20's, B–25's and FBs continue to blast coastal region around Wewak. Villages and gun positions on Hansa Bay are also hit.

Thirteenth AF: 24 P–39's and P–40's hit Rabaul area while 12 B–25's bomb supply areas at Talili Bay. More than 40 P–39's and P–40's hit barges NW of Ballale I, supply areas and other tgts at Porton, and piers at Ratsua and Soraken.

Seventh AF: 45 B–25's, flying out of Makin, attack Emidj. 9 B–25's from Engebi fly successful search mission for a downed B–25 crew in the vicinity of Ponape and Pakin Is. After locating the survivors, later picked up by Navy destroyer, the MBs attack Pakin and Ponape with cannon and machinegun fire.

Eleventh AF: 2 B–24's off on an armed photo mission over Shimushu turn back due to mechanical troubles.

27 May

Eighth AF: 923 B–17's and B–24's bomb M/Ys, aircraft industries, and A/F at Ludwigshafen, Mannheim, Karlsruhe, Konz-Karthaus, Neunkirchen, Saarbrucken, Lachen/Speyerdorf, Strasbourg, and Woippy. Coastal batteries at Fecamp and Saint-Valery-en-Caux also are bombed. Opposition is heavy and 24 HBs are lost on mission.

Ninth AF: About 590 MBs attack railroad, bridges, and M/Ys in France. P–47's bomb tgts in NW Europe.

Twelfth AF: MBs concentrate efforts against lines of comm in Orvieto area. A–20's bomb storage area. FBs pound a much reduced flow of motor transport behind enemy lines and hit railroads, gun positions, bridges, and T/Os in and behind battle area, hitting tgts at Subiaco, Sora, Tivoli, Frosinone, Capena, and Orvieto, W of Bracciano Lake, between Sulmona and San Benedetto de Marsi, and at several other points.

Fifteenth AF: Almost 700 B–17's and B–24's, with P–38 and P–51 escorts, bomb M/Ys at Avignon, Montpellier-Frejorgues, Nimes, Marseilles-Blancarde, and Marseille-Saint-Charles, A/F at Salon-de-Provence, and port of Razanac.

Tenth AF: 15 B–24's bomb Pakokku and Nyaung-u.

Fourteenth AF: 24 rocket-firing P–40's hit barracks area W of Sinyang, militay installations and trucks at Nanchang, and troops, trucks, barracks, and warehouse area in Puchi vicinity.

Fifth AF: Babo A/F and Biak I are pounded by 170-plus B–24's and B–25's. After the aerial and naval bombardment, Allied amphibious forces land on Biak in the Bosnik area, secure beachhead, and gain control of trail over ridges to inland plateau to the N. About 170 A–20's, P–38's, P–40's, and B–25's blast Wewak area.

Thirteenth AF: About 200 AAF, Marine, and Navy aircraft (ftrs, dive bmrs, and B–25's) are sent against gun positions on Hospital Pt. 160-plus aircraft bomb the tgts with more than 90 tons of explosives, destroying or damaging several of the guns. Other ftrs hit T/Os in Rabaul area and a barge off SW New Ireland. 4 B–24's bomb Tobera. AAF ftrs attack beached barges in Chabai area and in Buka Passage, Aku and Nova Plantation, and bridge over Oamai R.

Seventh AF: 24 B–24's from Kwajalein and 52 B–25's from Engebi pound Ponape.

Eleventh AF: 2 bmrs fly weather and armed photo rcn and bomb Ushishiru I.

28 May

Eighth AF: Almost 900 HBs attack aircraft works, synthetic oil plants, military vehicle plants and repair depots at Ruhland, Dessau, Cologne, Merseburg, Zeitz, Konigsberg, Lutzkendorf, Magdeburg, and nearly 30 different T/Os. An estimated 450 ftrs oppose the mission with about 350 concentrating in Magdeburg area. 32 US bmrs are lost.

Ninth AF: Over 600 B–26's and A–20's bomb M/Ys, naval yards, railway bridges, and V-weapon sites in France and Belgium. 8 aircraft are lost. P–47's dive-bomb several tgts in same general area.

Twelfth AF: MBs hit bridges, viaducts, and railroad lines at several locations in C Italy, including Narni, Cortona, Terni, Ladispoli, Torrita di Siena, Magnano, Recco, Arezzo, Rapallo, Vado, Bucine, and Castiglion Fiorentino. LBs hit ammo dump while FBs continue close spt to advancing ground forces, encountering considerably less enemy motor transport behind lines because of the heavy attrition of recent days. Many roads, railroads, and bridges are hit as well as numerous other tgts along the battlefront which now stretches from W coast SW of Carroceto to the NE almost to Valmontone, then SW to just above Sezze, and from there ambles E to NE to E coast below Pescara.

Fifteenth AF: More than 100 B–24's bomb Genoa harbor and Vercelli M/Y. P–38's fly ftr sweeps against A/Fs in Kurilovec area and vehicles, comm lines, and T/Os in Knin-Bihac-Banjaluka area.

Tenth AF: 10 B–24's pound Kalemyo while 3 B–25's hit Tiddim road.

50-plus FBs and a few B–25's hit various tgts at or near Mogaung, Myitkyina, Hopin, and Sahmaw. 76 FBs and 24 B–25's bomb M/Ys at Namma and Katha, hit several tgts in Mohnyin-Hopin area, and bomb railroad between Naba and Namma.

Fourteenth AF: 14 P–40's in spt of ground forces in Salween area strafe oil storage at Hsiangta, bomb and strafe Watien area, and destroy 1 bridge and damage another on Shweli R N of Tengchung. 2 B–25's sink a patrol boat and damage another near Saint John I.

Fifth AF: In spt of ground forces on Biak I, B–24's and B–25's hit villages, supply areas, troop concentrations, and gun positions on Biak, Noemfoor, and Japen Is. A–20's, B–25's, and FBs blast troop concentrations, AA positions, and supply dumps in Wewak area. A–20's supporting ground forces in heavy fighting in Sarmi area, hit positions with minimum-level strikes. B–24's bomb Boela. Thirteenth Air TF B–24's bomb A/F on Woleai.

Thirteenth AF: 3 B–24's, followed by 23 B–25's and 12 P–38's, blast A/F at Lakunai. 33 P–39's and P–40's join 40-plus dive bmrs in strike on Tobera airstrip. 5 MBs hit Namatanai supply and personnel area. FBs hit Tsundawan supply area, huts and buildings at Gohi, Nova, and Monoitu, suspected barge hideout near Tonolai, and AA guns at Ballale I.

Seventh AF: 29 B–25's stage from Eniwetok, bomb Jaluit, and land at Makin. B–24's from Eniwetok bomb Saipan and Guam. Those bombing Guam turn S to Los Negros to rearm while the others return to Eniwetok. B–25's flying from Engebi bomb Mille.

HBs escort Navy photo planes over the Marianas.

Eleventh AF: 2 B–24's fly rcn and drop bombs on Shimushu and Matsuwa. 1 B–25 and P–38's fly guardship coverage mission, 2 other B–25's fly a negative anti-shipping sweep.

29 May

Eighth AF: 881 HBs attack synthetic oil plant at Politz, A/Fs at Hohn and Schneidemuhl, A/F and aircraft assembly plant at Tutow, and aircraft factories and assembly plants at Leipzig, Cottbus, Sorau, Krzesiny, and Poznan. 34 HBs are lost on mission.

Ninth AF: Over 450 B–26's and A–20's bomb A/F, M/Ys, railroad bridges, coastal battery, and NOBALL tgts in France and Belgium. Over 200 P–47's bomb tgts in same area.

Twelfth AF: B–25's bomb rail bridges near Bucine and at Poggibonsi and Lisciano. B–26's hit viaducts at Terni and near Stifone, railroad junction and M/Y at Terentola, Castiglion Fiorentino bridge, the Voltri shipyards, and a bridge nearby. A–20's hit troops in bivouac and bomb supply dump. FBs continue to blast motor transport between battlelines and Rome. Transports evacuate over 400 wounded from Anzio area.

Fifteenth AF: 829 B–17's and B–24's (largest number of Fifteenth AF HBs completing attacks in a single day up to this time) bomb A/Fs and aircraft factories at Wollersdorf, Wiener-Neustadt, and Atzgersdorf, and attack A/Fs, troops, and supply concentrations at Zegar, Zavalje, Prijedor, Bosanski Novi, Knin, Banjaluka, Drvar, Livno, and Basanska

Krupa. P–38's and P–51's escort the Austrian missions while P–38's accompany the HBs to Yugoslav tgts and afterwards strafe numerous T/Os. Ftr opposition over Yugoslavia is negligible but around 150 ftrs attempt interception over Austria, principally in Wiener-Neustadt area. 23 US aircraft are lost. HBs and ftrs claim over 60 ftrs shot down.

Tenth AF: 27 B–25's and 40-plus FBs pound troops and positions at Bhamo and Mohnyin, railroad at Mogaung, and warehouses at Sahmaw.

Fourteenth AF: 7 B–24's pound areas along Burma Road, 3 bomb town of Wanling, and 2 attack convoy of Hainan, claiming a 250-ft freighter sunk. 26 P–40's and P–38's attack troops at Lushan, pound barracks and demolish 7 trucks at Yuanchu, bomb and strafe general area at Nanchang, and destroy several buildings along Hsiang R N of Changsha.

Fifth AF: B–24's pound gun positions, defense areas, and troops, as first tank battle of SWPA is fought W of Parai on Biak I. Other B–24's pound A/Fs on nearby mainland at Timoeka and Babo. A–20's, B–25's, and P–47's, along with RAAF airplanes and a few HBs from the Biak strike, saturating Wewak area with continuous air strikes. In Wakde-Sarmi battle zone, B–25's and P–40's hit forces in Mount Saskin area. B–24's of Thirteenth Air TF bomb Woleai and other nearby islands in the Carolines.

SOPAC: Gen Moore, USMC, takes over as COMAIRSOLS.

Thirteenth AF: Almost 100 B–25's, P–38's, P–39's, and a variety of

Navy airplanes pound the Rabaul area, with AAF aircraft concentrating on Nordup supply area and the others concentrating on Hospital Pt AA positions. 24 P–39's and 16 P–40's blast occupied areas W of Tinputs Harbor and at Arigua Plantation.

Seventh AF: Operations are restricted to photo missions over Wotje, Mille, and Jaluit.

Eleventh AF: At dawn 2 B–25's photograph and bomb Shimushu and Matsuwa (secondary). During early afternoon 2 B–25's escorted by 4 P–38's strafe, bomb and sink a patrol boat in the Kurils. Later 4 other B–25's unsuccessfully attack 2 vessels off Shimushu.

30 May

UK: Loading of assault forces for OVERLORD begins.

Eighth AF: 911 HBs operating in 6 forces attack aircraft factories, A/Fs, and depots at Dessau, Oschersleben, Halberstadt, Rotenburg, Zwischenahn, Oldenburg, Diepholz, and Handorf; M/Ys at Brussels, Troyes, and Reims; V-weapon sites at Watten and Siracourt; and various T/Os.

Ninth AF: Over 320 MBs attack A/Fs at Denain/Prouvy and Mantes/Limay, and highway bridges at Meulan and Rouen. Nearly 400 P–47's dive-bomb tgts in NW Europe.

Twelfth AF: B–26's and B–25's destroy or damage 10 bridges, bridge approaches, and viaducts which affect supply routes to battlefronts across C Italy. LBs and FBs blast motor transports and gun positions in battle area and hit tgts in and around towns in the area, including Guidonia, Ariccia, Alatri, and Veroli. Transport airplanes evacuate wounded from Nettuno.

Fifteenth AF: Nearly 500 B–17's and B–24's attack A/F and aircraft factory at Wels, factories at Pottendorf, Neudorfl, and Neunkirchen and M/Y at Zagreb. P–38's and P–51's provide escort. Many of the ftrs strafe T/Os in areas around Zut, Brod, Susak, Bihac, Medak, and along Karlovac-Livno road.

Tenth AF: 9 B–25's attack railroad between Namma and Hopin. B–25's and FBs fly 100 sorties against railroad tgts, hitting tracks, rolling stock, stations, and bridges in vicinities of Mogaung, Myitkyina, Hopin, and Loilaw. Imphal-Tiddim road is bombed by 3 B–24's.

Fourteenth AF: 48 ftrs spt ground forces in Mamien Pass-Watien-Chiangtso area. 31 supply airplanes drop food and ammo to friendly forces in Mamien Pass area. 13 B–25's damage Wan Pa-Hsa bridge and bomb town of Lungling, destroying 6 warehouses and starting several big fires. 8 P–51's hit railroad T/Os on sweeps from Peking, Chengting, Pingting, Linfen, and Puchou. 16 P–38's and P–51's dive-bomb installations at W end of Nanchang bridge, causing much damage. 5 B–25's and 12 P–40's strafe troops, supplies, and occupied strongpoints at Loyang and at several locations along Yangtze and Yellow Rivers. Japanese air strikes on Hengyang and Liangshan A/Fs destroy 4 US airplanes, damage several others, and blow up a fuel dump.

Fifth AF: B–25's hit enemy positions as fighting on Biak I slacks temporarily. Other B–25's bomb A/F and nearby AA guns and fuel at

Timoeka. B–24's and A–20's hit Japen I. In Wakde-Sarmi battle area, B–25's bomb and strafe shoreline from NW of Sawar to Sarmi Pt. Wewak area is again blasted by 70-plus A–20's, B–24's, and B–25's, along with RAAF aircraft. Thirteenth Air TF B–24's hit Truk Atoll, Woleai, and Puluwat group.

Thirteenth AF: 23 B–25's bomb personnel areas NE of Tobera. 40-plus P–38's, P–40's, and P–39's bomb supply dump near Ratawul. 33 P–39's and 8 P–40's demolish bridges at Kirinani and over the Siaibai R. Log ramp over Miwo R is damaged and road between Puriata R and Kiaraba is hit. The FBs also attack Buka runway, Chabai barge anchorage, and Soraken supply area.

Seventh AF: B–25's from Engebi bomb Ponape, which is also hit by B–24's returning from shuttle base at Los Negros. 2 forces of B–24's from Kwajalein strike Truk and Wake.

Eleventh AF: 1 B–25 and 2 P–38's fly guardship cover.

31 May

Eighth AF: 371 HBs attack M/Ys at Schwerte, Hamm, Osnabruck, Geseke, and Roosendaal; A/Fs at Luxeuil-les-Bains, Gilze-Rijen, and Florennes; and 5 bridges in France. The mission against the bridges, using radio-controlled bombs, is unsuccessful. 6 combat wgs sent to bomb A/Fs, M/Ys, and factories in France are recalled because of bad weather. 79 P–47's using dive bombing and "Droopsnoot" (ftr equipped with bombsight) tactics attack Gutersloh A/F. 35 P–38's, unable to locate primary tgt of Lingen A/F, bomb A/F NE of Rheine, believed to be Hopsten.

Ninth AF: About 200 B–26's bomb lock and highway bridges at Bennecourt, Courcelles-sur-Seine, and Rouen.

Twelfth AF: MBs of 43d and 57th Bomb Wgs give close spt to ground forces in fierce fighting S of Rome, hitting numerous troop concentrations, roads and town areas, including points in or near Albano Laziale, Genzano di Roma, Ariccia, Frascati, Civitella Roveta, Subiaco, Cave, Nettuno, and Grottaferrata. XII TAC A–20's and FBs blast tgts in same general area, hitting troops bridges, supplies, guns, and vehicles at or near Rocca di Papa, Ariccia, Marino, Frascati, Grottaferrata, Lanuvio, Montalto di Castro, and Manciano. C–47's evacuate casualties from Anzio.

Fifteenth AF: 480-plus B–17's and B–24's bomb oil refineries and comm tgts in Ploesti area. Ftrs fly over 200 sorties in spt. 15 HBs are lost to flak and ftrs. Over 40 enemy airplanes are shot down.

Tenth AF: 12 B–25's hit Tiddim road while 36 A–31's hit supply dumps, villages, and gun positions in the Ukhrul-Moirang area. 130-plus B–25's, A–36's, P–51's, and P–40's hit troops, defensive positions, arty emplacements, boats, railroad facilities, and villages in Myitkyina-Mogaung area, buildings at Tahona, river boats at Lonkin and Kamaing, docks at Bhamo, railroad cars at Namti, and positions NW of Mohnyin. 21 other B–25's and FBs pound the Bhamo town area and A/F. 10 B–24's bomb Ye-u, demolishing several buildings.

Fourteenth AF: 51 P–51's and P–

40's pound shipping along the Yangtze, claiming direct hits on 5 small ships. 16 P–51's and P–40's bomb Kweiyi and Yoyang and installations on river to the S. 10 P–38's bomb bridge and warehouse area at Nanchang. 12 P–40's bomb Pingkiang. 4 B–25's bomb Hankow A/F, Pailochi, and motor convoy at Yoyang. 6 other B–25's knock out bridge at Kengluang. 13 B–24's pound town of Lungling, causing big fires, while 14 B–24's, supported by P–40's blast warehouse area at Lashio. 4 P–40's destroy several aircraft during strafing runs on Linfen and Hohsien A/Fs.

Fifth AF: B–25's and A–20's hit Babo area, bomb A/F near Ransiki R, cover beachhead on Biak I, and attack fishing boats on shore of Japen I. P–47's and B–25's pound villages, barges, and gun positions in Wakde-Sarmi battle area. B–24's, P–39's, and RAAF airplanes continue to hit Wewak and Hansa Bay areas.

Thirteenth AF: 12 P–38's bomb Vulcan Crater barge hideout. 22 P–39's and 12 P–40's blast supply dumps near Ratawul. 33 B–25's pound Rabaul truck concentrations, wharf area, and NE section of town. 5 B–25's bomb T/Os along NW New Ireland coast. P–39's bomb several tgts, including Soraken, Arigua, and several barges and vehicles.

Eleventh AF: During the morning 2 B–25's and 4 P–38's fly guardship cover. A bmr flies a weather mission while another reconnoiters and hits Buroton Bay.

1 June

Ninth AF: Around 100 B–26's bomb A/Fs and coastal defense batteries from Belgian border to Cherbourg Peninsula.

Twelfth AF: MBs, LBs, and FBs continue spt of ground troops, striking concentrations, bivouac areas, motor transport, railways and roads, bridges, trains and other tgts. Ftrs fly sweeps over battle areas, escort MBs, and carry out sweeps along E Italian coast.

Tenth AF: 7 B–25's pound bridges at Songon and Bongyaung and hit Imphal-Tiddim road. 20-plus others fly ammo into Imphal area. 19 P–40's hit tgts in Myitkyina area.

Fourteenth AF: 25 FBs hit Chenghsien railroad yards. 18 FBs bomb docks, gunboat, and barracks in Chiuchiang area and strafe about 300 troops at Sanyenchiao.

Fifth AF: B–24's bomb Amboina, Boeroe, and Kai Is. B–25's and A–20's attack T/Os in Kaukenau area, at Ransiki, and on Noemfoor and Biak Is. A–20's, B–25's, and P–39's hit villages, bivouac, and other T/Os in coastal area from Wakde Is to Hollandia. Bombing of Wewak-Hansa Bay coast continues.

Thirteenth AF: XIII BC moves from the New Hebrides to Los Negros. 9 B–25's bomb Matupi I and 3 hit SE part of Rabaul. 12 others pound personnel and supply area NE of Tobera. 30-plus P–38's and P–40's hit Talili Bay supply areas. 5 MBs hit barge hideout and buildings on Duke of York I. 30-plus P–39's attack Tonolai, Arigua, Arawa, and barges at Sohano I.

Seventh AF: B–25's from Eniwetok hit Ponape.

Eleventh AF: 2 B–24's from Shemya photograph and bomb installations at Buroton Bay including a suspected seaplane base and the harbor area. Of 2 B–25's and 4 P–38's taking off for guardship cover mission, 3 aircraft abort with engine trouble. 2 other B–25's fly a negative antishipping sweep.

ZI: AAF Redistribution Center is redesignated AAF Personnel Distribution Cmd.

2 June

Eighth AF: Role of bmrs from 2–5 Jun in preparation for invasion of Normandy on 6 Jun includes continuation of attacks against transportation and A/F tgts in N France and the institution of a series of blows against coastal defenses, mainly located in Pas de Calais coastal area, to deceive the enemy as to the sector to be invaded (Operation COVER). In the first mission on 2 Jun, 776 HBs attack tgts at Boulogne-sur-Mer, Wimereux, Equihen-Plage, Hardelot-Plage, Neufchatel, Dannes, Plage-Sainte-Cecile, Stella-Plage, Breck-sur-Mer, and Saint-Aubin. Opposition is confined to AA fire and is generally ineffective. The second mission of 2 Jun is carried out by 300 HBs attacking A/Fs and railroad facilities at or near Massy/Palaiseau, Conches, Beaumont-sur-Oise, Juvisy-sur-Orge, Acheres, Paris, Versailles/Matelots, Bretigny-sur-Orge, and Creil. 8 bmrs are lost to AA fire.

Ninth AF: Special conference for ground liaison officers is held by 21 Army Gp officers who present a detailed exposition of the plan for the landings in Normandy. About 350 B–26's and A–20's bomb NOBALL tgts and coastal def batteries along Channel coast. P–38's and P–47's dive-bomb tgts in the area, including V-weapon sites, fuel dump, railroad junctions and bridges.

Twelfth AF: MBs attack road and rail bridges from N of battle area just below Rome to areas N of Rome. FBs continue to blast motor transport, railways, trains, cmd posts, roads, and bridges in battle area, having particularly good success against vehicles.

Fifteenth AF: Shuttle-bombing between Italy and USSR (Operation FRANTIC) is started. Under cmd of Gen Eaker, 130 B–17's, escorted by 70 P–51's, bomb M/Y at Debreczen and land in Soviet Union— the HBs at Poltava and Mirgorod, the ftrs at Piryatin. 1 HB is lost over tgt. 27 other B–17's, forced off course en route to Oradea M/Y, also hit Debreczen. Nearly 400 other HBs attack M/Ys at Szeged, Miskolc, Szolnok, Cluj, Simeria, and Oradea. P–51's and P–38's provide escort.

Tenth AF: B–25's continue to fly ammo into Imphal area. 12 B–24's airborne against Yenangyaung fail to hit primary but unload against alternates in the area.

Fourteenth AF: 80-plus P–40's and P–51's pound troops and vehicles at Tungcheng and Chungyang and strafe concentration of about 75 sampans on Tungting Lake.

Fifth AF: B–25's bomb Kaukenau-Timoeka area while B–24's bomb positions N of Mokmer A/F. B–24's and B–25's hit bivouacs NE of Sawar A/F and near Wiske R and bomb roads along W bank of the Orai R. B–24's, P–39's, and RAAF airplanes hit Wewak area. Thirteenth Air TF B–24's bomb Dublon.

Thirteenth AF: 24 B–24's pound Nordup area. 48 P–38's, P–39's, and P–40's attack Vunakanau area. 30-

plus P–39's attack A/F at Buka and supplies in Kara-Kahili area.

Seventh AF: B–25's based at Makin strike Nauru.

Eleventh AF: 2 B–24's, finding Shimushiru overcast, bomb and photograph Matsuwa (secondary) during dawn.

3 June

Eighth AF: In Operation COVER, 338 HBs attack coastal defenses in the Pas de Calais area, bombing a total of 22 assigned tgts. In second mission of the day 215 HBs attack 16 of the tgts bombed during the first mission. No bmrs are lost on either mission.

Ninth AF: Over 250 B–26's and A–20's bomb A/Fs, highway bridges, and coastal def batteries in N France. Over 400 P–38's and P–47's dive-bomb tgts in NW Europe.

Twelfth AF: MBs pound bridges in C Italy, further damaging the enemy's comm system. FBs continue close spt of embattled ground forces immediately S of Rome and attack several bridges N of the city to hinder a possible withdrawal of enemy forces. LBs attack ammo and fuel dumps.

Fifteenth AF: Bad weather drastically curtails operations. 36 B–24's bomb waterfront area of Omis and 38 hit port area and W part of Split. Ftrs sent to strafe T/Os in tgt areas abandon mission because of low clouds over tgts.

Tenth AF: 15 B–25's pound Imphal-Tiddim road while a few P–40's hit Mogaung area. B–25 ammo lift to Imphal area continues.

Fourteenth AF: P–40's spt ground forces at Watien and Tatangtzu, de-

stroy 2 barges and damage others in Gulf on Tonkin, and strafe 40 barges carrying horses and troops in Tung-ting Lake area N of Nanhsien. B–25's, P–40's, and P–51's pound Ping-kiang area.

Fifth AF: B–25's, A–20's, and B–24's hit Timoeka A/F and nearby villages, shipping off Manokwari, Seroei Village on Japen I, and positions N of Mokmer, and strafe Mokmer, Sorido and Kamiri A/Fs. P–38's and P–47's battle ftrs over Biak I and over Babo area. P–47's and P–40's hit Sawar A/F, supplies and fuel dumps in Sarmi and Orai R areas, and hideouts and occupied areas along coast. B–24's and FBs maintain consistent pounding of numerous tgts in Wewak-Hansa Bay coastal region. B–24's of Thirteenth Air TF bomb Eten and Dublon.

Thirteenth AF: All scheduled strikes on Rabaul area are cancelled due to weather conditions. 20-plus P–39's, turned back from Rabaul area, hit Tsundawan-Porton road, vehicles in Komai area, and AA position at Kara.

Seventh AF: B–24's, staging through Eniwetok, strike Truk in pre-dawn raid. B–25's from Engebi bomb Nauru.

Eleventh AF: 2 B–25's and 2 P–38's fly guardship cover. 2 other B–25's fly a negative shipping search.

4 June

Eighth AF: In the first mission of the day the effort is to be divided between Pas de Calais (COVER) area and the Normandy assault (NEP-TUNE) area. However, D-Day is postponed 24 hrs and the NEPTUNE force is cancelled. 231 HBs attack 7 tgts in Pas de Calais area. In the second mission 283 aircraft bomb 8 coastal def positions in same area. Third mission of the day consists of attacks by 400 HBs on 10 tgts including A/Fs, railway junctions and bridges. No bmrs are lost on any of the missions.

Ninth AF: Over 300 B–26's and A–20's bomb highway bridge and coastal batteries in France. Almost 200 P–47's and P–51's dive-bomb bridges, railroad junction, rolling stock and T/Os in France.

Twelfth AF: MBs hit railroad bridges in NC Italy. FBs concentrate on motor transport on roads N of Rome over which enemy is retreating as US Fifth Army columns converge on the city amidst enthusiastic welcome by the populace. A record number of over 600 motor transport are claimed destroyed and almost as many more damaged by Twelfth AF and RAF units of MATAF.

Fifteenth AF: More than 550 B–17's and B–24's attack comm in NW Italy and on both sides of Franco-Italian frontier, hitting M/Y and repair works at Turin, M/Ys at Genoa and Novi Ligure, bridges at Gad and Orelle, and viaducts at Recco and Antheor. Ftrs fly over 200 sorties in spt of the HBs.

Tenth AF: 20-plus P–40's hit Myitkyina area while 19 others hit various points in N Burma, including Haka, Kamaing, Kamasaing, Tagwin, and Bilumyo. B–25's continue ammo lift to Imphal.

Fourteenth AF: P–40's bomb arty positions and T/Os in Watien area of Salween battle front. Others bomb railroad T/Os in NE Indochina.

Fifth AF: A–20's bomb town and harbor at Manokwari and shipping to the E in Geelvink Bay. B–24's bomb Namber and Borokoe A/Fs while ftrs battle enemy airplanes in general area. B–24's bomb area near Orai R mouth while A–20's hit Wewak and FBs pound Hansa Bay coast.

Thirteenth AF: Bad weather again prevents strikes against Rabaul area. P–39's flying a total of 55 sorties, blast truck park near Komai, strafe huts at Doure, and attack pier at Tunuru. 8 P–38's weathered out of Rabaul strike Tonolai supply area. A lone B–25 bombs Kahili.

Seventh AF: During the night B–24's, staging through Eniwetok, hit Truk. B–25's from Engebi follow with daylight raid on Ponape.

Eleventh AF: 2 B–24's fly uneventful rcn over Shimushiru. Fuel shortage and equipment failure prevent flying to Matsuwa (secondary). Later, a B–25 and 2 P–38's fly a guardship cover mission.

5 June

Eighth AF: 629 HBs attack 6 coastal def installations in Cherbourg-Caen area and 8 in Pas de Calais area, along with 3 V-weapon sites and a railroad bridge. 6 bmrs are lost. 7 P–51 FBs attack truck convoy near Lille, destroying 2 trucks.

Ninth AF: Over 100 B–26's bomb coastal def batteries in France. More than 100 P–47's dive-bomb tgts in same area.

Twelfth AF: MBs pound road bridges just N of forces retreating from Rome while FBs continue attacks against motor transport, railway lines and roads in battle areas and N of Rome, destroying many vehicles and train cars, and scoring numerous hits on bridges, tracks, and roads, as most of US Fifth Army assault forces cross the Tiber in pursuit of enemy and British Eighth Army forces E of Rome prepare to adv astride the Tiber against Terni and Rieti.

Fifteenth AF: 440-plus HBs attack M/Ys at Ferrara, Forli, Faenza, Castel Maggiore, and Bologna, bomb bridges, bridge approaches, and surrounding areas at Rimini, Fornovo di Taro, and Pioppi, and attack viaduct at Vado Ligure. P–38's and P–51's fly escort. 53 P–38's strafe Ferrara and Poggio Renatico A/Fs and 40 strafe and dive-bomb A/Fs at Bologna and Reggio Emilia.

Tenth AF: 9 B–25's bomb Bhamo and 4 hit bridge at Ledan Chaung, while others continue ammo haul into Imphal. 50 FBs pound Myitkyina area and 20-plus others hit Loilaw, Tagwin, Namti, and Mogaung.

Fourteenth AF: 12 P–40's spt ground forces at Watien and Lameng on Salween front. 18 P–24's and 12 P–40's bomb Lashio. 7 B–24's blast barracks and warehouse area at Namkham. 8 P–40's hit 15 tanks at Taying. 29 P–40's attack numerous oil barges near Yuankiang, leaving 16 of them burning.

Fifth AF: P–39's and RAAF airplanes attack Wewak area. B–24's bomb area N of Sorido A/F. During 5/6 Jun an all-night series of harassing raids by Japanese airplanes destroy several Allied aircraft on Wakde.

Thirteenth AF: 23 B–25's bomb truck park at Rabaul. 22 P–39's strike Ratawul. 11 P–38's hit barges and buildings in Vulcan Crater area.

30-plus P–39's hit vehicles in Komai-Tobago vicinity, a wooded supply area N of Buka A/F, and Cape Tanabom and Kangu Hill areas.

Twentieth AF: The Twentieth flies its first VHB combat mission. Of 98 B–29's airborne from India, 77 bomb primary tgt—the railroad shops at Bangkok. 5 VHBs are lost to non-battle causes.

Seventh AF: B–25's from Makin hit Nauru. B–24's from Eniwetok escort photo aircraft over Guam, bomb the island, and proceed to Los Negros for rearming. B–25's from Engebi strike Ponape.

6 June

Eighth AF: Eighth reaches its top strength as 493d Bomb Gp (H) becomes operational, making a total of 40 HB gps now operational. HBs fly 4 missions in spt of the invasion of Normandy. 1,361 HBs are dispatched on first mission of the day. 1,015 of the HBs attack the beach installations, 47 bomb transportation chokepoints in town of Caen, and 21 bomb alternate tgts. Overcast and inability of HBs to locate (or absence of) Pathfinder leaders causes failure of some units to attack. The second mission strikes at transportation chokepoints in towns immediately around the assault area. Total cloud cover causes most of the 528 HBs dispatched to return with their bombs but 37 bmrs manage to bomb secondary tgt of Argentan. The third mission is dispatched against the important comm center of Caen. 56 B–24's bomb through overcast skies. Transportation chokepoints in towns immediately S and E of assault area are the objectives of the fourth mission for the Eighth. 553 HBs bomb tgts including Vire, Saint-Lo, Coutances, Falaise, Lisieux, Thury-Harcourt, Pont-l'Eveque, Argentan, and Conde-sur-Noireau. In all, 1,729 HBs of Eighth AF drop 3,596 tons of bombs during D-Day, suffering only 3 losses (to ground fire and a collision). VIII FC has threefold mission of escorting HBs, attacking any movement toward assault area, and protecting Allied shipping. The ftrs fly 1,880 sorties including FB attacks against 17 bridges, 10 M/Ys, and a variety of other tgts including convoy, railroad cars, siding, rail and highway junctions, tunnel, and a dam. Very little air opposition is encountered. The ftrs claim 28 German aircraft destroyed and 14 damaged. Also destroyed are 21 locomotives and two carloads of ammunition. Numerous tgts are damaged including locomotives, trucks, tank cars, armored vehicles, goods carriers, barges, and tugboats. Tgts attacked with unreported results include warehouses, radar towers, barracks, troops, arty, staff cars, 85 trains, and a variety of other tgts. 25 VIII FC aircraft are lost.

Ninth AF: More than 800 A-20's and B-26's bomb coastal def batteries, rail and road junctions and bridges, and M/Ys in spt of the invasion forces landing in Normandy. Over 2,000 ftrs fly sweeps, escort for MBs and TCs, ground spt, and dive-bombing missions over W France. During the preceding night and during the day over 1,400 C-47's, C-53's, and gliders deliver glider troops and paratroops, including 3 full airborne divs, which are to secure beach exits to facilitate inland movement of sea-borne assault troops. A total of about 30 airplanes MBs, (ftrs and transports) are lost.

Twelfth AF: MBs, LBs, FBs, and ftrs all hit comm lines N of Rome to slow enemy retreat. Bridges, road junctions, rail lines, roads, and motor transport are continually attacked throughout the day, as British Eighth Army forces W of Tiber reach Civita Castellana and US Fifth Army forces push N and W toward Viterbo and Civitavecchia.

Fifteenth AF: Shuttlebombing (FRANTIC) continues as 104 B-17's and 42 P-51's (having flown to USSR from Italy on 2 Jun) attack A/F at Galati and return to Soviet shuttle bases. 8 enemy ftrs are shot down and 2 P-51's are lost. 570-plus other HBs, with ftr escorts, bomb oil refineries in Ploesti area, M/Ys at Brasov and Pitesti, Brasov wagon and armament works, Turnu-Severin canal, and M/Y at Belgrade.

Tenth AF: 24 B-25's attack Waingmaw, Wuntho-Hopin area, and Imphal-Tiddim road. Others maintain ammo lift into Imphal. 24 A-36's, 11 P-51's, and 45 P-40's pound Myitkyina. About 40 A-36's and P-40's hit Mogaung, Mohnyin, Lachigahtawng, Pakhren-Sakan, and Kadu areas.

Fourteenth AF: 50 P-40's attack shipping, horses, and troops in Fulinpu Kweiyi vicinity, 10 P-51's and 6 B-25's pound Tayang Chiang, and 5 B-25's bomb Pailochi A/F. 9 P-40's hit road and rail T/Os in Yellow R area. 2 others sink a junk and damage others at Kwangchow Wan.

Fifth AF: B-24's and B-25's bomb shipping near Efman and Waigeo Is. A-20's hit A/F at Babo, and A-20's and B–25's hit Namber A/F and tanks near Mokmer. P–39's, A–20's, and RAAF airplanes continue to pound Wewak-Hansa Bay area, hitting supply dumps and hideouts. B–24's hit islands in Truk Atoll.

Thirteenth AF: P–38's bomb supply dump near Nordup. P–39's and Navy aircraft hit vehicles near Hari. Other P–39's pound pier and buildings in SE Kahili.

Seventh AF: B–24's returning to Eniwetok from Los Negros (where they rearmed after bombing Guam the previous day) hit Ponape.

7 June

Eighth AF: AEAF directs air attacks against congested points to delay movement of more enemy forces into assault area. In first mission 402 HBs, including 20 Pathfinders, attack tgts at Flers, Conde-sur-Noireau, Falaise, Argentan, L'Aigle, and Lisieux. Second mission is directed at Kerlin/Bastard A/F and at bridges, railroad junctions, depots, and station at Nantes, Angers, Tours, and adjacent areas. 498 HBs attack; heavy cloud prevents almost 100 others from bombing tgts. VIII FC furnishes area spt for beachhead areas in early morning and to HB operations at midday and in late afternoon, at the same time maintaining harassment of comm and flying shipping patrol. The ftrs encounter about 150 aircraft during the day, destroying 31. Enemy ftrs account for 4 ftrs lost. FB attacks are flown against about 50 tgts, including M/Ys, sidings, trains, tunnels, bridges, convoys, A/Fs, and railroads. In almost 1,000 sorties, 25 ftrs are lost.

Ninth AF: 600-plus MBs hit bridges, junctions, trestles, coastal and field batteries, and M/Ys in France in spt of invasion. Over 1,100 ftrs spt ground troops by dive bombing and strafing, escort MBs and transports, and make sweeps throughout the battle area as Bayeux is liberated and the Bayeux-Caen road is cut. 400-plus C–47's, C–53's, and gliders resupply paratroops in the assault area.

Twelfth AF: Weather hampers MB operation but several rail and road bridges and viaducts are attacked. FBs blast retreating motor transport and troops, and hit bridges N of Rome. Numerous vehicles are destroyed immediately N of Rome and especially in Subiaco area near Rome. Many hits are scored on roads and railroads, and several railroad cars and gun emplacements are destroyed. US Fifth Army captures Civitavecchia.

Fifteenth AF: Fifteenth AF reaches its planned operational strength of 21 HB gps and 7 ftr gps as 332d Ftr Gp (P–47) begins operations. 340 B–17's and B–24's, some with ftr cover, hit Leghorn dock and harbor installations, Voltri shipyards, Savona railroad junction, and Vado Ligure M/Y, Antheor viaduct, and Var R bridge. 42 P–38's bomb Recco viaduct and 32 P–47's fly uneventful sweep over Ferrara-Bologna area.

Tenth AF: 11 B–24's bomb Wuntho and Kalemyo. 9 B–25's hit Wuntho-Shwebo railroad and bridge at Thityabin. Other B–25's continue flying ammo to Imphal. A few P–51's hit Lachigahtawng.

Fourteenth AF: 10 B–25's bomb Lashio and T/Os along Salween front.

3 B–25's and 15 FBs bomb tank concentrations at Taying, destroy several locomotives at Linfen, and pound railroad yards at Chenghsien. P–40's and B–25's strafe sampans at Ft Bayard and sink a schooner off Nampang I. 2 rocket-firing P–40's damage processing building at carbide mines at Na Duong.

Fifth AF: B–25's bomb Biak I, hitting gun positions near Bosnik, airstrip at Sorido, and Borokoe road. A–20's hit shipping in Manokwari area. B–25's blast supply areas near Orai R. FBs and A–20's continue pounding Wewak-Hansa Bay coast. Thirteenth Air TF B–24's hit various tgts on Truk Atoll (weather permits only 10 of 48-airplane force to reach tgt area).

Thirteenth AF: All scheduled strikes in Rabaul area are weathered out. P–39's and P–38's hit several T/Os on Bougainville, including occupied areas at Monoitu.

Seventh AF: B–25's from Makin bomb Ponape.

8 June

USSTAF: Gen Spaatz, CG, places oil in first priority as tgt for USSTAF as result of the destructive effect achieved by several missions against oil centers in May.

Eighth AF: Attacks are made on comm to isolate German forward elements, and A/Fs are bombed to prevent German air spt. Cloud conditions prevent over 400 HBs from executing assignments but 735 attack tgts including A/Fs at Rennes and Le Mans and bridges, M/Ys and other railroad facilities, and various T/Os at or near Tours, Nantes, Cinq Mars-la-Pile, Pontaubalt, La Vicomte-sur-Rance, Angers, Orleans, la Friliere, Etampes, and Morigny. 3 bmrs are lost. VIII FC, flying 1,405 ftr sorties on this day, sends FB attacks against nearly 75 tgts, including railroad facilities, bridges, convoys, A/Fs, barges, radio towers, troop concentration, a transformer, and a coastal gun. Ftrs and FBs destroy nearly 400 rail, ground transport, and military vehicles and claim 46 airplanes destroyed. 22 ftrs of VIII FC are lost.

Ninth AF: Around 400 MBs attack rail and road bridges and junctions, rail sidings, M/Ys, town areas, fuel storage tanks, ammunition dumps, troop concentration and strong points in the Calais area. Around 1,300 ftrs provide spt to MBs and high cover over assault area, and bomb and strafe bridges, M/Ys, gun batteries, rail facilities, vehicles, towns, and troop concentrations.

Twelfth AF: Weather again restricts activity. Many MB missions are abortive, though several bridges, railroad lines, and guns are attacked. A–20's hit town of Bolsena and tgts in surrounding areas. FBs and ftrs continue to patrol battle areas destroying motor transport, and attacking train cars, roads, rail lines, and enemy concentrations, as US Fifth Army approaches Viterbo and British Eighth Army pushes toward Orvieto.

Fifteenth AF: 52 B–17's, with P–47 escort, bomb navy yard and drydocks at Pola.

Tenth AF: B–24's mine Bangkok and Mergui areas. B–25's maintain ammo supply to Imphal. 9 B–25's pound Imphal-Tiddim road and a few A–36's and P–51's hit the enemy in Mogaung area.

Fourteenth AF: 19 P–40's bomb

docks, warehouses, and military installations at Ichang and Shasi and strafe 2 cav units at Nanying. 4 P–51's attack railroad traffic in Singtai-Chengting area.

Fifth AF: B–25's, P–38's, B–24's, and A–20's battle enemy ftrs over Manokwari and Efman-Schouten Is areas, bomb small freighter off Manokwari, and hit gun emplacements and occupied areas at Kamiri, at Namber, and near Sorido. P–40's hit supply areas and villages in vicinity of Sarmi. A–20's again hit Wewak area. B–24's from the Admiralties hit Truk.

Thirteenth AF: 24 B–25's bomb supply area at Ratawul. 32 P–39's bomb Tsirogei and supply area N of Buka. 6 P–38's hit Monoitu Mission.

Seventh AF: During 7/8 Jun, B–24's from Eniwetok bomb Truk and Ponape. B–25's from Makin follow up during day with strike against Nauru.

9 June

Eighth AF: Bad weather prevents HB operations. One ftr sq attacks shipping and another sq flies escort for photo rcn mission (not completed), losing 2 ftrs.

Twelfth AF: MBs again hit enemy comm, bombing bridges with good results. LBs hit T/Os in Acquapendente area. FBs and ftrs continue to pound motor transport retreating up Italian peninsula, and to bomb roads and railways in path of enemy retreat, as US Fifth Army reaches Viterbo, where British Eighth Army shortly makes contact with it.

Fifteenth AF: Around 500 B–24's and B–17's bomb industrial tgts and an A/F around Munich and attack oil storage at Porto Marghera. P–47's,

P–38's, and P–51's fly over 250 sorties in spt of the Munich raids. HBs and ftrs claim over 30 aircraft destroyed. 13 US airplanes are lost.

Tenth AF: 5 B–25's carry out strike on Imphal-Tiddim road while 20-plus others continue to supply ammo to Imphal area. More than 40 A–36's, P–51's, and P–40's hit Myitkyina, Mogaung, and Kadu.

Fourteenth AF: P–40's, P–51's, and B–25's fly more than 200 sorties against numerous tgts throughout the Tungting Lake area. River shipping of all description is pounded, several troop concentrations are attacked, A/Fs at Hankow and Wuchang are bombed, and towns of Ichang, Siangyin, Yuankiang, and Kiaotow are hit. 4 HB and FB sorties over S China Sea result in claims of 3 sea going vessels, a tug, and a barge sunk.

Fifth AF: B–24's bomb Peleliu A/F. A–20's bomb shipping in Manokwari harbor. B–24's, A–20's, B–25's, and P–39's, along with RAAF planes, drop about 140 tons of bombs on various tgts in Wewak area. B–24's of Thirteenth Air TF bomb Alet A/F and T/Os in Truk.

Thirteenth AF: 32 B–25's, 20 P–39's, and 5 P–38's pound supplies and gun positions in Ratawul-Talili Bay area. 5 other B–25's attack pier at New Massava Plantation and railroad to Mandres Saw Mill. P–39's hit town of Buka, supply area to the N of the A/F, and Arigua Plantation.

Seventh AF: During 8/9 Jun B–24's from Eniwetok bomb Truk.

10 June

Eighth AF: Bad weather restricts operations to NW France. 873 HBs are airborne but over 200 abort due to cloud conditions. 589 including 31 Pathfinders, attack 8 A/Fs in France and 9 coastal installations in Pas de Calais area. One B–24 is downed by AA at Evreux. VIII FC, flying over 1,600 sorties, supports HB missions and launches attacks against about 80 tgts, including railroad facilities, convoys, tank column, trucks, radar station, tunnels, gun emplacement, supply dump, and a power plant. About 225 vehicles, including train engines and cars, are destroyed, along with 16 enemy aircraft. 25 ftrs are lost.

Ninth AF: IX TAC establishes its first station on the Continent, at au Guay. 500-plus B–26's and A–20's bomb tgts in assault area in France. Tgts include military concentrations, road and rail bridges and junctions, arty batteries, M/Ys, and town areas. Aircraft of more than 15 ftr gps fly escort to bmrs and transports, and bomb numerous tgts in spt of ground assault, including rail facilities, roads, troop concentrations, arty, and town areas.

Twelfth AF: MBs attack bridges, railroads, and roads N, NE, and NW of Rome. LBs hit motor transport in town of Arcidosso. FBs and ftrs bomb and strafe motor transport and roads N of battle area, destroying numerous vehicles, especially along the roads between Rome and Vetralla. In ground action Indian 4th Div takes Pescara and Chieti, while 2d NZ Div reaches Avezzano E of Rome. XII BC is disbanded in Corsica.

Fifteenth AF: More than 550 B–17's and B–24's attack oil stores at Porto Marghera, oil refinery at Trieste, M/Ys at Mestre, Trieste, and Ancona, and A/F at Ferrara. P–51's

and P–38's fly escort, strafe T/Os between Bucharest and Danube R and S of Craiova, and dive-bomb an oil refinery at Ploesti.

Tenth AF: 23 B–24's bomb tgts at Chauk, Lonywa, and Yenangyaung while 29 others supply ammo to Imphal area. 50 A–36's, P–51's, and P–40's blast tgts at Myitkyina, Mogaung and Tapo.

Fourteenth AF: 23 P–40's and P–51's hit railroad traffic and tracks at Linfen and Loning and tank concentration at Lingpao. 6 P–40's hit bridge at Tasa. B–25's, P–40's, P–51's, and P–38's carry out 150-plus sorties against numerous tgts throughout Tungting Lake area. Numerous rivercraft are destroyed or damaged, Kukang and other villages NE of Changsha are bombed, Hankow-Wuchang A/F revetments and buildings are pounded, Changshowkai area is blasted, and several river landings and storage installations in the lake area are attacked. 3 B–24's on S China Sea sweep claim 1 small cargo ship sunk.

Fifth AF: A–20's hit A/F at Babo, destroying grounded aircraft, fuel dump, several buildings, and a gun position. A–20's, B–25's, and RAAF airplanes hit Wewak area with more than 100 tons of bombs.

Thirteenth AF: 8 P–38's skip-bomb supply tunnels at Keravia Bay while 4 others strafe nearby AA positions. AA guns S of Rapopo are attacked by 12 B–25's, 20 P–39's, and 20-plus Navy dive bmrs. Other B–25's bomb Ratawul. 31 P–39's and 20-plus Navy aircraft hit Chinatown at Buka and a supply area NE of the airstrip, a barge at Sohano I, trucks near Tsirogei, and a ford near Monoitu.

Seventh AF: B–24's, staging through Eniwetok, bomb Truk and Ponape during 9/10 Jun. B–25's from Makin hit Nauru during the day.

11 June

Eighth AF: Weather prevents operations against priority tgts in Germany so the HBs attack bridges on the Loire, bridges and A/Fs on Brest Peninsula and near Paris, and coastal defenses in Pas de Calais area. Of 1,043 HBs airborne, over 400 abort or fail to bomb due to clouds and absence or malfunction of Pathfinders. 640 HBs bomb tgts, including 10 A/Fs and landing grounds, several bridges, and various T/Os. 3 HBs are lost. VIII FC supports HBs over NW France and Ninth AF MBs attack Paris area. FBs attack over 60 tgts, including railroad yards, sidings, junctions, bridges, trains, A/Fs, convoys, an oil tanker, a power station, and warehouses. Ftrs destroy 5 aircraft. VIII FC loses 8 ftrs.

Ninth AF: 129 B–26's and A–20's bomb rail and road bridges and intersections, rail lines, oil tanks, arty, and town areas, in morning operations. Bad weather prevents afternoon operations. 10 ftr gps fly escort and strafe and bomb bridges, railroads, gun emplacements, rail and road traffic, and M/Ys in spt of Allied ground troops in France.

Twelfth AF: Weather cancels all LB and MB operations. FBs and ftrs, operating on a reduced scale, hit vehicles, roads, and bridges N of battleline which US Fifth Army's VI Corps has extended 65 mi N of Rome.

Fifteenth AF: 126 B–17's and 60 P–51's depart Russian shuttle bases for Italy to complete the first FRAN-TIC operation. On the way 121 B–17's bomb A/F at Focsani; 1 B–17 is lost. 540-plus other B–17's and B–24's attack oil installations at Constanta and Giurgiu (both raids having ftr escorts) oil refinery and M/Y at Smederovo. The HBs and ftrs claim total of 50 airplanes destroyed during the day's missions.

Tenth AF: 30 B–25's continue flying ammo to Imphal area. 55 A–36's, P–51's, and P–40's attack tgts at Myitkyina, Mogaung, Indawgyi Lake, and Padaung.

Fourteenth AF: In China's Tungting Lake area 80-plus P–40's, P–51's, and P–38's pound towns of Lanchi and Anking, hit cav compound at Kintsing, attack Japanese HQ, positions, and river traffic N of Changsha, destroy or damage several boats, barges, and sampans at Changsha, and strafe numerous T/Os throughout the entire region. In Yellow R area, 27 B–25's and P–40's pound barracks, fortifications, tank concentration, several armored vehicles, and cav forces at Iching and Lingpao. 3 B–25's on sea sweep in S China Sea claim 1 600-ft freighter sunk.

Fifth AF: B–24's bomb Sorido A/F and surrounding areas as US carrier forces attack Saipan, Tinian and Guam. B–25's, A–20's, and P–47's continue to saturate Wewak-Hansa Bay coastline with bombs. Other B–24's bomb Dublon and Peleliu A/F.

Thirteenth AF: 130-plus B–25's, P–38's P–39's, and Navy dive bmrs pound AA positions S and SW of Rapopo. P–39's fly 44 sorties against occupied areas at Komai, Kakaura, and Quaga, AA guns at Kangu Hill, and plantations at Arigua and Tsirogei.

Seventh AF: B–24's from Eniwetok hit Truk during 11/12 Jun. B–25's follow with raid against Ponape during the morning.

12 June

Eighth AF: With bad weather over top priority tgts in Germany, HB efforts are directed against A/Fs and landing grounds in NE France and rail and road bridges on the Brest Peninsula. 1,278 HBs, including 25 Pathfinders, drop 3,295 tons of bombs on 22 of the primary tgts and on secondary and T/Os. 8 HBs are lost, mostly to ground fire. VIII FC furnishes spt for HB missions and Ninth AF MBs, and attacks enemy communications and troop movements. Ftrs damage M/Ys at Juvisy-sur-Orge and Melun and several freight trains, and destroy 108 locomotives, train cars, trucks, tanks, and other vehicles. One gp of P–47's is attacked by 50 German ftrs in a fierce battle, 8 P–47's and 5 Me 109's being shot down. During the day VIII FC flies 1,002 sorties and claims 26 aircraft destroyed. Losses total 17.

Ninth AF: 509 B–26's and A–20's bomb M/Ys, road and rail junctions, bridges, arty, town areas, troop concentrations, and various T/Os in France. Aircraft of more than 15 ftr gps fly close and area spt for bmrs and bomb and strafe rail lines, gun batteries, bridges, fortifications, radar installation, tanks, ammo dumps, town areas and strongpoints in battle area of France.

Twelfth AF: MBs hit bridges, viaducts, and rail lines at Collazone, Perugia, Foligno, Massa Lombarda, Pietrasanta, Cattolica, Pesaro, Arezzo, and Bucine. LBs hit Arcidosso and motor transport in the area. FBs are restricted by bad weather but attack several bridges and roads in line of enemy retreat which at its farthest point is N and W of Viterbo.

Tenth AF: More than 30 B–25's continue to supply troops at Imphal with ammo. 16 P–40's hit Mogaung and T/Os in N Burma.

Fourteenth AF: 50 P–40's, P–51's, and B–25's hit troop concentrations in Yellow R area at Lingpao and S of Loyang. In Tungting Lake area about 100 P–40's and P–51's attack numerous supply boats and other river and lake traffic, and hit dock areas and warehouses at Lanchi, Yuankiang, and at scattered points. Also hit are villages and troops in Changsha and Kuanchuang areas.

Fifth AF: Fierce ground fighting continues on Biak I while Japanese airplanes attack Allied ground forces and shipping offshore; P–47's battle attacking aircraft, shooting down several. P–47's and A–20's hit troop concentrations, comm, and various other tgts in Wewak and Hansa Bay areas. B–24's bomb Peleliu A/F and Dublon I.

Thirteenth AF: 6 B–24's bomb runways at Tobera and Rapopo. 22 P–39's and 10 P–38's join 20-plus Navy airplanes in attacks on supply dumps near Ralum. 20 B–25's pound Malapau village. 44 P–39's hit Baku A/F, Tsirogei plantation, barges and pier S of Kleine I, and occupied area W of Komai.

Seventh AF: Eniwetok-based B–24's hit Truk during 11/12 Jun and again during the day.

13 June

Eighth AF: Bad weather cancels large-scale bombing of high priority tgts in Germany. Overcast bombing against tac tgts in NW France is undertaken. On first mission of the day cloud cover is less than anticipated and visual runs are made by 128 B-17's against A/Fs at Dreux, Saint-Andre-de-L'Eure, and Evreux. On second mission 208 HBs, including 15 Pathfinders, attack A/Fs at Beauvais/Nivillers and Beaumont-sur-Oise, and bridges and scattered tgts between Brittany and the assault area. Bridges bombed are at Porcaro, Montfort-sur-Meu, Ploermel, La Vicomte-sur-Rance, Saint-Vincent-sur-Oust, and Vannes. AA fire downs 2 B-24's. VIII FC furnishes spt for the HB missions and conducts FB and strafing attacks against bridges, trains, trucks, and other vehicles. The ftrs, flying a total of 782 sorties, claim 6 airplanes, bomb 5 bridges, and destroy 3 locomotives, 23 trucks, and 4 other vehicles. Losses of VIII FC total 4.

Ninth AF: 397 B-26's and A-20's bomb rail and road junctions, M/Ys, and fuel dumps in assault areas in France. Aircraft of 9 ftr gps escort bmrs and attack bridges, M/Ys, troop areas, rail and road traffic, gun emplacements, ammo dumps, and other tgts.

UK: The first V-1 lands in S England. More land during 13/14 Jun, and throughout the rest of the month.

Twelfth AF: MBs bomb shipping at Leghorn with excellent results and score numerous hits on bridges, viaducts, rail lines, and roads in NC Italy. FBs continue to disrupt retreat over entire area N of battle zone as British Eighth Army's 13 Corps pushes toward Orvieto and 10 Corps reaches Terni.

Fifteenth AF: 560-plus B-17's and B-24's, most with ftr escorts, attack A/F at Oberpfaffenhofen, aircraft component plants at Munich-Allach, M/Ys at Innsbruck, Munich, and Porto Marghera, and several T/Os in Germany, Austria, and Italy. HBs and ftrs claim over 30 aircraft shot down. 10 US airplanes are lost and several others are missing.

Tenth AF: A few P-51's hit Mogaung while 39 B-25's fly ammo to Imphal area.

Fourteenth AF: 18 B-25's and 56 FBs pound M/Y at Wuchang. About 70 other B-25's and FBs attack a variety of other tgts in the Tungting Lake region, including many river vessels, A/F at Pailochi, troop positions NE of Changsha, warehouse and factory area at Shasi, and numerous general T/Os. 12 FBs hit Japanese HQ and barracks at Loyang. 4 B-24's over S China Sea claim 1 cargo vessel sunk. 4 P-40's pound Japanese positions at Watien and Kaitou.

Fifth AF: More than 100 A-20's and a few B-25's and P-39's attack miscellaneous tgts in Wewak area. P-39's hit area around Hollandia and P-47's bomb bridge over Orai R and fuel dumps near Sarmi. A-20's blast enemy positions N of Borokoe. B-24's bomb airstrip at Liang. B-24's from Admiralty Is bomb Woleai, Dublon, and Satawan.

Thirteenth AF: 9 P-38's and 23 P-39's hit Ralum and AA positions to the S. 24 B-25's bomb Tobera AA guns and A/F; 15 others, in 2 waves, bomb Praed Pt. 6 B-24's also bomb Tobera. 31 P-39's and 12 Navy aircraft attack supply dumps at Buka and Tapsadawato, bomb approach to

Abia R bridge, and hit garden area at Tabago.

Seventh AF: Attack during 12/13 Jun by B–24's from Eniwetok against Truk and Ponape is followed by daylight attack by Makin-based B–25's against Nauru and Ponape.

Eleventh AF: During 12/13 June 6 B–24's dispatched to fly an offensive sweep and provide air cover for a naval TF abort missions due to weather.

14 June

Eighth AF: Bad weather again covers all strategic tgts in Germany except one in the extreme NW. Major effort is against tac objectives, mainly in France. 1,314 HBs attack tgts, including oil refinery at Emmerich, an A/F and a bridge in Germany, 16 A/Fs in France and 1 in Belgium, 14 bridges, CROSSBOW supply sites, and scattered T/Os in France. HB losses total 14. VIII FC ftrs escort the HBs and engage in heavy aerial combat as ftrs intercept the HB forces. VIII FC loses 4 aircraft while destroying 4 of the enemy. P–47's bomb and strafe 3 A/Fs, 2 M/Ys, an ammo dump, and several other T/Os.

Ninth AF: Over 500 B–26's and A–20's attack rail comm SW of Paris and highway comm centers S of beachhead area. Junctions, bridges, M/Ys, gun emplacements, and various defensive strongpoints are included. Over 15 ftr gps fly escort and attack numerous ground tgts, including rail lines running from SW of Paris to Rennes area, and highway traffic in Cherbourg Peninsula and S of beachhead area to the Loire R.

Twelfth AF: MBs bomb several bridges and viaducts in NC Italy, with especially good results on viaduct and railway bridge N of Arezzo. Ships in Leghorn harbor also are hit. LBs pound ammo supplies. FBs continue to attack roads and bridges in and just N of battle area (only small number of vehicles are seen) as US Fifth Army forces take Magliano and Orvieto falls to elements of British Eighth Army.

Fifteenth AF: More than 550 B–17's and B–24's attack oil refineries and other tgts in Hungary and Yugoslavia, including Budapest, Petfurdo, Komarom, Osijek, and Sisak. P–38's, P–47's, and P–51's escort HBs and P–38's strafe and dive-bomb A/F at Kecskemet.

Tenth AF: 21 B–25's continue ammo supply to Imphal vicinity. A few P–40's hit Mogaung area.

Fourteenth AF: 43 P–40's attack river shipping, troops, and villages in Tungting Lake area, at or near Lanchi, Changsha, Chulianchiao, and Linyang.

Fifth AF: A–20's, B–25's, and P–39's hit Wewak area. B–24's bomb Kamiri A/F. A–20's hit A/F at Babo, Orai R bridge, and fuel dumps, and other tgts near the river's mouth. Halong seaplane base is hit by B–24's.

Thirteenth AF: 80-plus B–25's, P–38's, P–39's, and Navy aircraft hit supply areas and underground storages along N shore of Gazelle Peninsula from Vulcan Crater to Wunapope. Ralum, Keravia Bay, and Wunapope stores are the hardest hit. P–39's fly 27 sorties along E shoreline of Bougainville from Bonis to Kieta, hitting Monoitu, Bonis, and pier at Kieta Mission.

Eleventh AF: 4 B–24's fly extensive photo rcn over the C and N

Kurils. They are attacked by some 20 ftrs of which 3 are damaged.

15 June

Eighth AF: 1,225 HBs operating in 8 forces bomb Misburg oil refinery in Germany and numerous tac tgts in France, including 9 A/Fs, an aircraft plant, a CROSSBOW supply site, 11 bridges, a M/Y, and various scattered tgts. Losses total 4 HBs. VIII FC escorts the HBs, flies shipping patrol, and carries out FB attack on bridges at Etaples. Ftr attacks destroy a locomotive and 5 trucks, along with 5 aircraft. A total of 762 ftr sorties are flown. No losses are suffered.

Ninth AF: Over 550 B–26's and A–20's direct main attacks against fuel and ammo dumps, rail and highway comm, and armd div HQ S of bridgehead on Douve R. Over 1,400 ftrs fly armed rcn in Valognes-Cherbourg area, W part of Cherbourg Peninsula, and along comm lines S to Loire. Ftrs also attack shipping between the Channel Is and Cherbourg Peninsula.

Twelfth AF: MBs blast rail and road bridges in La Spezia sector and in area S of Florence. LBs again hit ammo supplies. FBs and ftrs hit bridges and roads N of battlelines (again only scattered motor transport tgts are available for strafing). US Fifth Army patrols move into Grosseto and British Eighth Army pushes beyond Todi toward Perugia.

Fifteenth AF: Weather cancels bombing operations. P–51's and P–38's strafe La Jasse, Orange/Plan de Dieu, Orange/Caritat, Avignon/Chateau-Blanc, and Avignon/Pujaut A/Fs.

Tenth AF: 30 B–25's fly ammo to Imphal area. 27 A–36's, P–51's, and P–40's pound Mogaung and Myitkyina.

Fourteenth AF: 24 P–40's hit Japanese cav forces at Chuchou and several supply boats on Siang-Chiang R. 10 P–40's destroy or damage several tanks, trucks, and train cars between Loyang and Shanhsien. 24 B–24's bomb warehouse area at Canton, causing heavy damage.

FEAF: FEAF is formed with jurisdiction over Fifth and Thirteenth AFs. Gen Kenney becomes CG FEAF, with HQ in Brisbane. FEAF HBs, MBs, LBs, and ftrs attack barges in Manokwari area, village in Wakde area. Also bombed are A/Fs on Timor and Truk. Thirteenth AF airplanes still in Solomon-Bismarck area hit Tobera A/F and forces on Bougainville. Amphibious forces of US Marines land on Saipan.

SOPAC: COMAIRSOLS is dissolved, to be replaced by a new cmd, Air Comd, Northern Solomons (COMAIRNORSOLS).

Thirteenth AF: HQ Thirteenth AF moves from Guadalcanal to Los Negros, from which the HBs have been operating since Apr as Thirteenth Air TF. Gen Streett becomes CG Thirteenth AF, which becomes part of FEAF. The MBs and ftrs, together with other COMAIRSOLS airplanes, continue to maintain the neutralization of Rabaul and the pounding of the Bougainville-Buka area through Jul and into Aug.

Twentieth AF: B–29's bomb Japan. With the exception of Eleventh AF's raids on the Kurils, this is first air attack against Japan since Doolittle's raid. 47 B–29's, operating out of Chengtu, bomb primary tgt of Imperial Iron and Steel Works at Yawata. The Twentieth's first combat loss during a bombing mission results when ftrs destroy a B–29 down with engine trouble at Neihsiang A/F in China.

Eleventh AF: 2 B–24's fly armed photo rcn over Shimushiru I.

16 June

Eighth AF: 313 HBs, including 22 Pathfinders, attack 4 A/Fs and 4 CROSSBOW supply sites in France, losing a B–17 to ground fire. P–38's of VIII FC cease flying shipping patrol as of this date. 18 escort HB missions and attack a concentration of stalled trains between Angouleme and Poitiers, dropping external fuel tanks on them and firing the tanks by strafing. The same tactics are used on trains in M/Y at Saint-Pierre-d'Excideuil. Heavy damage is inflicted on both tgts, including heavy troop casualties. At Saint-Pol-sur-Ternoise a large number of railroad cars are burned by oil and phosphorous bombs and strafing attacks. Other M/Ys, a power station, railroad station, trains, barges, tanks, trucks, gun emplacements, AA tower, and an armored vehicle are attacked. A total of about 400 railroad cars are attacked and about half of them set on fire. In general the ftr attacks are highly effective.

Ninth AF: Bad weather prevents bmr operations. More than 500 ftrs strafe and bomb rail lines, bridges, and highway traffic in Cherbourg Peninsula.

Twelfth AF: B–26's and B–25's hit rail and road bridges, viaduct, and other comm tgts at Casalecchio di

Reno/Villa Vergano, Lissone, Viareggio, Pisa, Vernio, Grizzana, and Pietrasanta. A–20's continue to hit ammo supplies. FBs continue interdiction by hitting bridges, trucks, rail lines, and other tgts closer to the front, which now reaches across Italy from W coast near Grosseto to E coast in vicinity of Macerata.

Fifteenth AF: Almost 600 HBs attack oil tgts at Vienna and Bratislava. Between 200 and 250 ftrs attack the formations and 15 US aircraft are shot down. HBs and escorting ftrs claim 70 airplanes destroyed.

Tenth AF: 28 A–36's, P–51's, and P–40's hit Myitkyina and T/Os in N Burma.

FEAF: Bmrs and ftrs hit widespread tgts in SWPA and in SOPAC. Personnel areas and barges along coast in Wewak and Hansa Bay areas are hit throughout the day. A/Fs and shipping at Efman and Samate Is and at Babo and Sorong are attacked. Dublon and Yap are bombed. HBs hit Vunakanau A/F at Rabaul. HBs, MBs, LBs and ftrs attack a large variety of T/Os on Gazelle Peninsula from Tobera A/F to Rabaul.

SOPAC: Gen Mitchell, USMC, becomes head of COMAIRNORSOLS.

Seventh AF: B–25's, based at Makin, hit Ponape.

17 June

Eighth AF: During first mission, 231 HBs, including 16 Pathfinders, attack 8 A/Fs in N France. Clouds and malfunction of blind-bombing equipment cause nearly 100 aborts. 2 HBs are lost. Favorable break in weather over N France permits a second mission. 273 B–24's bomb 3 A/Fs and 2 landing strips, along with some T/Os, in same general area hit by the earlier mission. 1 B–24 is lost to AA fire. VIII FC ftrs escort both HB missions and during first mission P–38's bomb 2 bridges N of Paris, damaging 1 of them severely. After escorting second mission, a P–51 gp bombs 2 M/Ys with good results. Other ftrs bomb a bridge and a M/Y as T/Os. 15 locomotives, train cars, trucks, and other vehicles are destroyed, along with 5 airplanes. VIII FC loses 8 ftrs while flying 1,027 sorties during the day.

Ninth AF: Operational control of air-ground coordination of FB missions moves from HQ Ninth AF and 21 Army Gp Combined Control Center (in UK) to Adv HQ IX TAC (in Normandy) operating in close proximity to US First Army. 265 MBs attack fuel dumps, a bridge and a railway line S of battle area in France. Over 1,300 ftrs fly escort and top cover, and strafe and bomb troop concentrations, military vehicles, bridges, gun emplacements, tanks, and other tac tgts.

Twelfth AF: Except for a B–26 attack on 1 bridge and an A–20 raid on an ammo dump, weather prevents completion of LB and MB missions. FBs are also restricted but manage to hit several gun positions, comm tgts, boats, small ships, barges, and T/Os in battle area and at various other locations including Capo d'Enfola and other points on Elba (where French forces land and begin clearing island), and Rio Marina.

Fifteenth AF: Operatons are limited to rcn missions.

Tenth AF: 8 A–36's attack forces at Mogaung. 25 B–25's fly ammo to Imphal area.

Fourteenth AF: B–25's and FBs attack large troop concentrations at Shanglishih and Fenglinpu, bomb town of Lanchi and nearby villages, attack 4 villages in Chuchou area, hit troop barges at Changsha, damage several supply boats at Yiyang, and bomb military installations at Ichang.

FEAF: MBs, LBs, and ftrs hit shipping in Sorong harbor and airstrips in Babo area. In Wewak area, A–20's, B–25's, and ftrs continue to pound barges and villages. HBs again bomb Truk, hitting tgts on Eten and Dublon. HBs hit Lakunai A/F while A–20's, B–25's, and ftrs attack numerous tgts between Rapopo and Tobera.

Seventh AF: B–24's, flying from Kwajalein, bomb Ponape. B–25's from Makin hit Nauru.

Eleventh AF: 12 B–25's fly 3 air cover missions for Naval TF on withdrawal, following the shelling of Kurabu Cape installations.

18 June

Eighth AF: 1,239 HBs operating in 4 forces attack oil industries at Oslebshausen, Hamburg, and Misburg, dock area and city of Hamburg, A/Fs at Stade and Hassum, and various tgts at Brunsbuttelkoog, Bremerhaven, Nordenham, and Helgoland, and V–weapon site at Watten. A total of 566 ftrs fly uneventful escort to the HB missions, all returning safely to base. 11 HBs are lost, 10 to AA fire and the other to unknown causes.

Ninth AF: About 130 A–20's and B–26's bomb fuel dumps at Foret d'Andaine and Conches and M/Ys at Rennes and Meudon during the morning, and NOBALL tgts in the afternoon. Ftrs, in addition to escort duty, continue strafing and bombing rail lines, troop concentrations, and highway traffic in Cherbourg Peninsula.

Twelfth AF: Bad weather grounds MBs and LBs. FBs and ftrs are restricted to patrols, mainly over Piombino area and island of Elba, during which several gun positions, boats, and barges are hit.

Tenth AF: 16 A–36's, P–51's, and P–40's hit Myitkyina and Mogaung.

Fourteenth AF: B–25's and P–40's bomb Yoyang and hit shipping and posts in Siang-Chiang R delta area. P–40's and P–51's attack about 100 supply boats in lower Tungting Lake area, strafe cav forces between Siangyin and Changsha, and hit village just E of Changsha.

FEAF: A–20's, B–25's, and ftrs, along with RAAF airplanes, continue to pound supplies and occupied areas along coast in Wewak area. B–24's hit tgts in Truk. A variety of ftr and bmr aircraft unload 18 tons of bombs on numerous tgts around Rabaul. Ftrs continue sweeps against T/Os along coastal areas of Bougainville.

Seventh AF: B–25's from Makin pound Nauru. B–24's stage through Eniwetok to bomb Truk.

19 June

Eighth AF: During the morning 259 B–17's bomb A/Fs at Cazaux, Bordeaux/Merignac and Landes de Bussac, and landing strip at Corme-Ecluse. Bad weather causes nearly 200 aborts among the HBs and prevents nearly 200 ftrs from effecting rendezvous and providing escort for the bmrs. 217 P–38's and P–51's manage to complete escort missions. On another morning mission, 201 HBs bomb 17 V–weapon sites in Pas de Calais area. None of the HBs or the 95 escorting P–38's are lost. In the afternoon, 270 HBs bomb 18 V–weapon sites, including most of those bombed in the morning mission. A P–38 gp, after completing escort duty, dive-bombs and strafes transportation tgts in NE France, destroying a locomotive and 3 barges. Losses during the day amount to 7 HBs and 16 ftrs.

Ninth AF: A/F at Cardonville, the first US field in France, becomes operational. Around 200 ftrs carry out uneventful armed rcn and patrols in the morning, and dive-bomb 6 NOBALL tgts in the afternoon.

Twelfth AF: Weather again grounds LBs and MBs. FBs of 87th Ftr Wg spt French forces which complete occupation of island of Elba during afternoon. FBs of the 87th and other units of XII TAC hit railroads, gun emplacements, factory, and shipping in and N of battle area at scattered points in countryside and in and near towns of Pontedera, Leghorn, Sestri Levante, and Viareggio.

Tenth AF: 30 B–25's complete ammo run to Imphal. 33 A–36's, P–51's, and P–40's strike Myitkyina, Mogaung, and Pinbaw.

Fourteenth AF: About 150 FBs and 8 B–25's again pound a variety of tgts throughout Tungting Lake area. Tgts include much shipping from Siangyin to Chuchou, and at various points along Siang-Chiang R, villages and compounds between Yiyang and Changsha, and boats and river area at Anking. 18 P–40's damage 2 bridges and destroy about 20 fuel trucks at Yuncheng. On Salween front 15 P–40's hit trucks and military installations. 4 B–25's bomb Kengluang bridge.

FEAF: Over 100 A–20's and FBs maintain strikes along coast around Wewak, hitting supply and bivouac areas, roads, personnel, and a coastal gun position. A–20's hit A/Fs at Manokwari, Noemfoor I, and Moemi. B–25's hit forces in Cape Orford region. HBs bomb Dublon and Eten.

Seventh AF: B–24's, staging through Eniwetok, strike Truk. B–24's from Kwajalein and B–25's out of Makin pound Ponape.

Eleventh AF: 2 B–24's fly armed photo rcn over Paramushiru and bomb Suribachi area with unobserved results.

20 June

Eighth AF: In the morning 1,257 B–17's and B–24's attack 14 strategic tgts in N Germany, including oil refineries, synthetic oil plants, a tank ordnance depot, and a military vehicle manufacturing plant. The HBs are escorted by 760 ftrs of which nearly half strafe 6 A/Fs and several other ground tgts, with claims of 13 aircraft and 10 locomotives destroyed. Also during the morning 130 B–24's bomb 10 V–weapon sites in Pas de Calais area; 42 P–47's provide spt, destroying 3 aircraft. During the afternoon 216 HBs attack 10 V–weapon sites in same area and T/Os which are mainly A/Fs in France and Belgium. 108 P–47's and P–51's provide uneventful escort. Total losses for the day are 50 HBs and 7 ftrs. HBs and ftrs claim 76 aircraft destroyed.

Ninth AF: About 370 B–26's and A–20's bomb 9 V–weapon sites in France and a coastal def battery at Houlgate. Over 1,000 ftrs operating over frontline areas, Cherbourg Peninsula, and S to Dreux, bomb and strafe rail lines, M/Ys, bridges, troop concentrations and other tgts.

Twelfth AF: Weather continues to hamper operations but 60-plus MBs manage to attack rail tgts between Genoa and La Spezia. FBs destroy several road bridges in battle area and to the N, and damage several other road and rail bridges as Allies' rapid adv slows down due to enemy's ability to strengthen his position and form a delaying line across Italy to S of Gothic Line (Pisa-Rimini) where he is prepared to make a stand. FBs also damage a 20,000-ton aircraft carrier in Genoa harbor.

EAC: AC Mellersh assumes cmd of Strategic Air Force, EAC.

Tenth AF: 5 B–24's fly fuel to Kamaing while 13 B–25's supply ammo to Imphal. 2 B–25's hit bridge at Banchaung. 8 A–36's and 3 P–40's attack tgts at Myitkyina.

Fourteenth AF: In Yangtze R-Tungting Lake area about 120 B–25's and FBs again attack a wide variety of tgts, pound river shipping at numerous points, hit villages and supply lines in Pinkiang area, and bomb towns of Changsha, Pingsiang and Ikiawan. In Salween R area 24 B–25's pound Lungling and 16 P–40's hit troops and positions at Tengchung and Chenanso. In Yellow R area 8 P–40's pound railroad yards and strafe about 75 trucks, destroying more than 20 of them. 3 B–24's over S China Sea attack shipping, claiming a 5,000-ton commercial ship sunk.

FEAF: A–20's, P–39's, and RAAF aircraft, pound areas along coast in general area of Wewak. B–24's bomb Kamiri A/F and attack Woleai and Dublon. B–25's, P–38's, and other Allied airplanes (including some of RNZAF) blast AA positions S and SW of Rapopo.

Seventh AF: B–25's from Makin strike Ponape. Kwajalein based B–24's bomb Truk.

21 June

Eighth AF: The Eighth begins shuttle bombing missions (FRANTIC) between UK and bases in USSR. P–47's (2 gps) escort the HBs from just off German coast to Stendal where a P–51 gp continues escort to, and spt over, the tgt (synthetic oil plant at Ruhland). 123 B–17's bomb primary tgt, 21 bomb Elsterwerda, and a lone B–17 bombs Riesa due to a bomb rack malfunction. After the attack, the supporting P–51 gp is relieved 50 mi SE of Poznan by 65 other P–51's which are to accompany the HBs to USSR. 50 mi SE of Brest Litovsk 20 to 30 ftrs attack the force. In the resulting battle 1 US and 6 German ftrs are destroyed. A single B–17 is lost (to unknown causes) on the flight. 144 HBs land in USSR, 73 at Poltava, and the rest at Mirgorod. The 64 remaining P–51's land at Piryatin. The shuttle run is made in conjunction with a large-scale effort against tgts in Berlin area. 935 HBs attack city areas, motor industries, and T/Os in and near Berlin, Genshagen, Basdorf, Rangsdorf, Trebbin, Belzig, Potsdam, Stendal, and surrounding areas. 19 HBs are lost. Ftrs fly 902 sorties in spt of this mission, claiming 18 ftrs destroyed, with a loss of 6. In late afternoon 31 B–24's bomb CROSSBOW supply sites at Oisemont/Neuville and Saint-Martin-L'Hortier and 39 bomb rocket site at Siracourt. AA fire shoots down 1 B–24. 3 ftr gps fly 101 sorties, meeting no enemy aircraft, but 1 gp strafes railroad and canal tgts. During 21/22 Jun the 73 B–17's which earlier landed at Poltava are attacked for 2 hrs by an estimated 75 German bmrs led by airplanes dropping flares. 47 HBs are destroyed and most of the remainder severely damaged. Heavy damage is also suffered by stores of fuel and ammo.

Ninth AF: Over 250 B–26's and A–20's bomb 13 V–weapon sites in Pas de Calais area. Over 700 ftrs escort Eighth AF HBs over Germany, bomb bridges S and W of Paris, and strafe rail and road traffic and comm centers N and W of Paris.

Twelfth AF: MBs have excellent results against rail bridges in N and NC Italy, also hitting viaducts, road bridges, and other comm tgts, and bombing ships at Leghorn harbor. LBs again hit ammo supply while FBs concentrate on rail and road bridges over large area including locations in vicinity of Gothic Line and at points to the N.

Tenth AF: 34 B–25's maintain ammo run to Imphal. 61 A–36's, P–51's, and P–40's pound Myitkyina and Mogaung.

Fourteenth AF: 11 FBs hit river shipping, barracks, and cav forces at Siangtan and Hengshan.

FEAF: P–39's and RAAF airplanes hit dumps and bivouacs at Suain and attack other tgts in Wewak area. A–20's attack various T/Os in Paniai Lakes area while B–25's hit villages on coast of Netherlands New

Guinea E of Maffin Bay. B–24's bomb Kamiri A/F and other tgts on Noemfoor and attack shipping in Palau Is and at Dublon.

Seventh AF: B–24's based on Kwajalein, bomb Truk.

22 June

Eighth AF: In morning mission 216 HBs attack 12 CROSSBOW installations in Pas de Calais area. Some of the 212 spt ftrs strafe coastal defenses. During the afternoon 718 HBs attack 22 tgts in France and Belgium, including M/Ys transformer stations, A/Fs, bridges, fuel storage facilities, railroad facilities, CROSSBOW supply site, and numerous T/Os. Ftrs escort the mission and 3 P–47 gps strafe and bomb transportation tgts, destroying an ammo train, 6 other freight cars, and a truck. 8 HBs are lost, mostly to ground fire. Because of attack on B–17's at Poltava on shuttle mission, the B–17's at Mirgorod and P–51's at Piryatin are moved farther E into USSR. They are to be returned to Mirgorod and Piryatin to be dispatched to bases in Italy as soon as weather permits. The move is fortunate as German bmrs strike both Piryatin and Mirgorod during 22/23 Jun.

Ninth AF: Around 600 B–26's and A–20's and over 1,200 ftrs fly missions during the day. The main effort consists of an attack on tip of Cherbourg Peninsula in spt of US VII Corps assault on port of Cherbourg. Beginning 1 hr before ground attack and continuing until attack begins ftrs and FBs pound whole area S of city from low level. As ground assault begins, B–26's and A–20's strike

series of strongpoints selected by US First Army, forming a 55-min aerial barrage moving N in adv of ground forces. Later in the day MBs attack M/Ys, fuel dumps and a German HQ. FBs fly armed rcn over various railroads and bomb rail facilities, trains, road traffic, and gun emplacements in France. 25 FBs are lost during the day's operations.

Twelfth AF: MBs attack railway bridges and viaducts in NC Italy, at Marzabotto, Boccheto, and Gricigliana, A–20's again hit ammo supplies. FBs pound road and rail bridges, mainly in Pisa area, and cut rail lines between Bologna and Pistoia.

Fifteenth AF: Following 5 consecutive days of bad weather more than 600 HBs bomb tgts in N Italy, hitting motor transport works at Turin and Chivasso, M/Ys at Parma, Modena, Fornovo di Taro, Bologna, Castel Maggiore, and Ferrara, oil storage at Fornovo di Taro, harbor at Pola, A/F at Poggio Renatico, and highway and railroad bridges at Nervesa della Battaglia and Rimini. Ftrs fly more than 250 sorties in spt of the missions.

Tenth AF: 6 B–24's fly fuel to Kamaing while 40 B–25's supply Imphal with ammo. 40 A–36's, P–51's, and P–40's hit Mogaung and Myitkyina while 10 others hit tgts at Hopin, Namma, and Sahmaw.

Fourteenth AF: 18 P–40's destroy 20-plus trucks between Hsuchang and Lohochai. 4 P–40's damage a troop steamer in Tungting Lake. 13 B–24's bomb Bakli harbor, damaging dock facilities and claiming 1 freighter sunk.

FEAF: B–25's, A–20's, and P–47's

hit shipping at Efman I and A/Fs and T/Os on Noemfoor, attack Manokwari, and hit villages in the Sarmi area. Attacks by A–20's and ftrs, along with RAAF airplanes, on wide coastal area around Wewak continue. B–24's bomb Yap, Sorol, and Woleai. B–25's join the Allied aircraft in pounding Nordup and Ralum.

Seventh AF: B–24's, staging through Eniwetok from Kwajalein, hit Truk; 1 bombs Ponape. First ftrs of Seventh AF arrive in Marianas; 22 aircraft of 19th Ftr Sq, taking off from aircraft carrier, land on Saipan.

23 June

Eighth AF: At midday 211 HBs attack 12 CROSSBOW installations, damaging at least 6 of them. Ftr spt is furnished by 4 P–51 gps (161 aircraft) all of which afterward strafe transportation tgts in Paris area, destroying 3 locomotives, 100 pieces of rolling stock, and 14 motor vehicles. An exploding ammo train causes a low-flying P–51 to crash, the only airplane lost on the mission. During the late afternoon 196 HBs attack A/Fs at Juvincourt-et-Damary. Laon/Athies, and Coulommiers, and a railroad bridge at Nanteuil-sur-Marne. Over 100 HBs abort because of heavy clouds over tgts. 226 P–47's and P–51's provide spt. Afterwards part of a P–47 gp bombs and strafes a M/Y while the remainder of the gp bombs and strafes a train carrying trucks and armored cars, destroying the locomotive, 3 trucks, and an armored car, and damaging 20 freight cars. Total losses are 7 HBs, mostly to AA fire.

Ninth AF: Bad weather prevents MB and LB missions during morning. In the afternoon over 175 B–26's and A–20's bomb 7 V–weapon sites in France. Around 630 ftrs provide escort and also bomb and strafe rail and road traffic and comm centers. 200 C–47's and C–53's fly supplies to the Continent.

Twelfth AF: Weather cancels MB operations. A–20's continue to attack ammo supplies. FB operations are restricted but P–47's hit rail comm at 4 different points in battle area as fierce struggle for Chiusi takes place.

Fifteenth AF: More than 400 B–17's and B–24's attack oil storage at Giurgiu, 2 oil refineries at Ploesti, and M/Y at Nish. More than 100 US aircraft are shot down. HBs and escorting ftrs claim more than 30 aircraft destroyed.

Tenth AF: 12 B–24's fly gasoline to Kamaing while 29 B–25's make ammo run to Imphal. About 80 A–36's, P–51's, and P–40's attack Mogaung, Myitkyina, Taungni, and bridge at Namkwi.

Fourteenth AF: 20 B–24's bomb docks at Hankow. In Tungting Lake area 70-plus B–25's and FBs attack wide variety of river shipping at several locations, bomb runway at Hengyang, strafe cav troops in the area, and hit towns and villages of Chuchou, Ikiawan, Chuting, Chwanchishih, and Siangtan. 30 B–25's and FBs hit various T/Os along Yellow R.

FEAF: Wewak area is again pounded throughout the day by A–20's, P–39's, P–47's, and RAAF airplanes. A few A–20's and A–26's on barge search bomb offshore islands near Manokwari. This marks SWPA debut of the A–26. P–47's on sweeps strafe areas E of Maffin. B–24's hit A/F at Yap and Woleai. HBs on armed rcn bomb Dublon, Koror, and Peleliu. B–24's bomb Tobera A/F. B–25's along with other Allied airplanes, hit AA positions S and SW of Rapopo.

Seventh AF: Eniwetok-based B–24's strike Truk. B–25's from Engebi pound Ponape. During the evening, B–24's from Kwajalein also attack Ponape.

Eleventh AF: 2 B–25's fly a negative shipping sweep.

24 June

Eighth AF: During the morning 317 B–17's bomb dock area, aircraft factory, steelworks, and coke oven plant at Bremen, and shipyard, railroad station and warehouses at Warnemunde. 6 ftr gps provide escort: 1 gp strafes A/F and rail transport in the Munster and Hamm areas. A second force of 334 B–24's attack tgts in France, including railway bridges at Saumur and Tours/La Riche, A/Fs and landing strip at Toussus-Le-Noble, Orleans/Bricy, Chateaudun, and Foret-de-Bourse, and T/Os at Conches, Dreux, and Pont-Audemer. 288 ftrs fly escort, part of which afterwards strafe road and rail transport, destroying 4 locomotives and a rail tank car, along with 4 enemy ftrs in aerial combat. 4 HBs and 1 ftr are lost, all to AA fire. 145 HBs airborne to attack 12 CROSSBOW sites in Pas de Calais area are prevented by overcast from bombing the sites, but 12 fly S and release bombs near the industrial area of Rouen losing 1 B–17 to AA fire. During the afternoon 163 HBs attack 5 electrical stations, 7 V-weapon sites, Saint-Pol-sur-Mer M/Ys, and a

missile platform. 118 sorties are flown by supporting ftrs which, after HBs withdraw, attack ground tgts destroying 1 airplane a locomotive, and a truck.

Ninth AF: 430-plus B–26's and A–20's attack tgts in France, including 4 gun positions, 3 V-weapon sites, 3 fuel dumps, 2 M/Ys, and a railroad bridge. Over 200 transports fly supplies to the Continent. 11 ftr gps provide escort, attack fuel dumps, rail tgts and bridges W of Paris and S of the Loire, and fly armed rcn S of Cherbourg Peninsula and SW of Paris.

Twelfth AF: Weather cancels MB operations. FB activity is restricted but P–47's attack several bridges, railway lines, guns, and other tgts in Lucca area and other points along and N of battleline.

Fifteenth AF: 335 B–17's and B–24's bomb railroad repair depot at Craiova, railroad bridge at Piatra, and oil refinery at Ploesti. 33 P–51's sweep Ploesti-Bucharest area while other P–51's, P–38's, and P–47's fly 220-plus sorties in spt of HBs. HBs and ftrs claim over 20 aircraft shot down. 10 US airplanes are downed and several others are missing.

Tenth AF: 11 B–24's fly gasoline to Kamaing while 35 B–25's supply Imphal with ammo. 60-plus A–36's, P–51's, P–40's, and P–38's attack Myitkyina, Mogaung, Mawlaik-Kin area, Pinbaw, and Hopin.

Fourteenth AF: 60-plus P–40's and P–38's bomb towns of Siangsiang and Yuankiang, attack cav forces in Hengyang area, and damage a pontoon bridge between Tungcheng and Pingkiang. 4 B–25's and a few P–40's knock out bridge N of Chenghsien.

FEAF: Fifth AF and RAAF airplanes continue to blast stores, personnel areas, roads, and bridges in general area of Wewak. B–25's, A–26's, and A–20's hit enemy positions in caves E of Mokmer A/F, attack shipping in Babo area (on MacCluer Gulf), and bomb Kamiri and Kornasoren A/Fs. HBs, MBs, and ftrs, along with other Allied airplanes, hit Tobera A/F, AA guns at Wunapope, and buildings at Nordup.

Seventh AF: P–47's, based on Saipan, strafe remnants of enemy forces on the island and also hit forces left on Tinian.

Eleventh AF: 3 B–24's at dawn bomb area N of A/F at Kurabu Cape. Later 2 B–25's fly a negative shipping search.

25 June

Eighth AF: During the morning 236 B–17's bomb Toulouse/Francazal and Toulouse/Blagnac A/F's and oil dumps at Montbartier. 10 B–17's bomb scattered T/Os. 107 B–24's bomb Avord and Bourges A/Fs. 176 B–17's drop supplies to French interior forces. A total of 8 HBs are lost. VIII FC flies 639 sorties in supporting operations. In addition 5 ftr gps carry out strafing activities, claiming numerous ground tgts including 6 airplanes on a landing ground and the A/F at Bourges. 19 enemy ftrs are claimed destroyed in aerial combat. During midday 153 B–24's bomb 17 power and transformer stations in effort to disrupt flow of electric power to V-weapon stations. 64 B–24's, hampered by cloud over primary aiming points, bomb miscellaneous last resort tgts, including A/Fs at Peronne and Nuncq.

Ftr spt is provided by 3 gps. All airplanes return safely. In night mission 300 B–17's and B–24's bomb 7 railway bridges and 2 A/Fs in Paris area. 69 HBs attack alternate tgts, including A/Fs of Orly, Romilly-sur-Seine, and Etampes/Mondesir. Ftrs fly 346 sorties in escort and tgt area spt. A P–38 gp strafes ground tgts in Angers, Le Mans-Laval area, and a P–47 gp bombs and strafes an alternate landing ground near Evreux/Fauville A/F. HB losses total 7. Ftrs claim 6 airplanes destroyed against no losses. In USSR, Eighth AF HBs and ftrs are flown, at daybreak, from dispersal bases to Poltava and Mirgorod and loaded and fueled with intentions of bombing oil refinery at Drohobycz and proceeding to base in Italy. Bad weather cancels the mission until the following day. The aircraft return to dispersal bases for the night as precaution against air attacks.

Ninth AF: 400-plus B–26's and A–20's hit fuel dumps at Foret d'Andaine, Foret d'Ecouves, and Senonches, and rail bridges at Cherisy, Chartres, Oiseme and Epernon. 14 ftr gps send airplanes on escort, and on armed rcn and dive bombing missions over Chartres, Dreux, Argentan, Tours, and Orleans areas. Transports fly supply and evacuation missions to France.

Twelfth AF: Bad weather again prevents operations by MBs. LBs hit enemy ammo supply. FBs bomb towns of San Quirico di Moriano and Castelfiorentino and several rail lines and bridges in battle area near Gothic Line. Piombino falls to US Fifth Army during the day, and the enemy withdraws from Chiusi during 25/26 Jun after several days of resisting British Eighth Army forces attacking the town.

Fifteenth AF: 650-plus B–17's and B–24's attack M/Y and oil installations at Sete and Balaruc-le-Vieux, telephone exchange at Le Pontet, railroad bridges at Tarascon and Arles, M/Ys and bridges at Avignon, and harbor facilities along S coast of France. Ftrs fly almost 200 sorties in spt. 1 ftr gp strafes tgts along Fiume-Senje road and at other points on Istrian peninsula.

Tenth AF: More than 50 B–25's make ammo run to Imphal. 60-plus A–36's, P–51's, and P–40's pound Myitkyina and Mogaung. 2 B–25's bomb Mohnyin-Mawhun railroad.

Fourteenth AF: 31 B–25's, P–40's, and P–51's hit towns of Siangtan and Ichang, attack sampans at Wukou, destroy about 50 trucks and strafe concentrations of troops and horses in Tangyang-Pingkiang and Siangtan-Yungfengshih areas, and pound river dock and sampans at Siangsiang. 7 CACW B–25's bomb Shayang storage area. 23 B–25's and P–40's bomb storage area and damage bridge at Chenghsien.

FEAF: Wewak area continues under attack of Fifth AF and RAAF aircraft. Personnel areas at But, Dagua, and Suain and barges at Mushu and Kairiru Is are hit. P–40's and B–24's strike Kamiri A/F while A–20's, P–47's, and B–25's hit villages along Tor R and P–47's hit tanks along Wiske R. B–24's pound Yap and Sorol. MBs and ftrs, along with other Allied airplanes, hit AA positions near Wunapope and blast plantations along Wide Bay.

Seventh AF: P–47's based on Saipan carry out rcn and strafing mis-

sions over Saipan and Tinian. B–24's based on Kwajalein hit Truk and Wotje.

Eleventh AF: Two B–24's bomb the A/F at Kurabu Cape.

26 June

Eighth AF: 72 B–17's leave Poltava and Mirgorod, rendezvous with 55 P–51's from Piryatin, bomb oil refinery and M/Y at Drohobycz (1 returns to USSR because of mechanical trouble), and then proceed to Foggia. Fifteenth AF P–51's meet formation an hr after the attack and escort the B–17's to Italy. It is planned to return the HBs to bases in UK on 27 Jun but bad weather delays this move until 5 Jul.

Ninth AF: Weather cancels all Ninth AF operations save a few ftr sorties which result in claims against a few military vehicles and 3 airplanes as US ground forces capture Cherbourg. 3 US ftrs are lost.

Twelfth AF: Bad weather grounds MBs. FBs, operating on reduced schedule, hit railroad tgts and other tgts in battle area S of Gothic Line.

Fifteenth AF: 677 B–17's and B–24's attack tgts in Vienna area, hitting aircraft factory at Schwechat, M/Y at Vienna/Floridsdorf, and refineries at Korneuburg, Vienna/Floridsdorf, Moosbierbaum, Schwechat, Winterhafen, and Lobau. Ftrs fly over 260 sorties in spt. An estimated 150 to 175 enemy ftrs attack formations. Nearly 30 US aircraft (mostly HBs) are lost. US claims total more than 60 enemy ftrs.

Tenth AF: 30-plus B–25's fly ammo to Imphal. More than 80 A–36's, P–51's, and P–40's pound Myitkyina. 7

other FBs hit Waingmaw, Loilaw, and Pyindaw.

Fourteenth AF: 14 B–24's blast Hankow, causing heavy damage and fires. 180-plus MBs and FBs attack river shipping and several villages in Tungting Lake area. Towns of Yuankiang, Sinshih, Siangtan, Liling, and Hengshan are bombed, as is warehouse area at Yuhsien. Numerous troop and truck concentrations and other T/Os throughout the entire region are attacked. In Salween area 14 B–25's and 36 P–40's knock out bridge at Tingka, damage another near Mangshih, bomb military installations at Tengchung, strafe Japanese positions at Lungling, and hit T/Os between Lungling and Tengchung. Japanese bomb Lingling A/F, damaging runway and destroying a P–51.

FEAF: Wewak area is hit throughout the day by Fifth AF B–24's and P–39's, along with US Navy and RAAF airplanes. P–38's, P–47's, A–20's, A–26's, B–24's, and B–25's attack A/Fs, shipping, villages, town areas, roads, and numerous other tgts at Efman, Noemfoor, Japen, and Biak Is, at Manokwari and Ransiki, and near Sarmi. B–24's bomb tgts on Yap and Sorol Is; others on armed rcn bomb airstrips at Woleai and Peleliu. AAF and other Allied aircraft hit A/Fs, AA positions, and other tgts in Rabaul and Cape Orford areas.

Seventh AF: Saipan-based P–47's continue to hit enemy forces remaining on Saipan and on Tinian while P–61's carry out night patrols over Saipan. B–25's from Makin pound Ponape and Nauru.

Eleventh AF: 12 B–25's fly 3 4-plane air cover missions for Naval TF on withdrawal following shelling of Kurabu Cape installations.

27 June

Eighth AF: 40 B–24's bomb CROSSBOW supply site at Saint-Leu-d'Esserent while 51 others bomb M/Ys and A/F at nearby Creil. 5 B–24's are downed by AA fire. 101 B–17's bomb CROSSBOW supply sites at Saint-Martin-l'Hortier, Biennais, Beauvoir-Riviere, and Domleger, and a canal lock at Espierres, losing 1 plane to AA fire. 183 P–51's spt the HBs, losing 2 ftrs to enemy aircraft and destroying 6 ftrs. After completing escort, the P–51's bomb and strafe T/Os, including M/Ys, bridges, railroads, transportation and A/F installations, and dispersal areas.

Ninth AF: Bad weather precludes bmr operations. Over 700 ftrs take part in various operations. Most of them fly high cover over assault areas and bomb and strafe rail and road traffic and comm centers in France.

Twelfth AF: Continued bad weather cancels MB operations. LBs again hit ammo supplies. FBs hit roads, bridges, rail lines, and other tgts in and near battleline.

Fifteenth AF: Around 300 B–17's and B–24's bomb M/Ys at Budapest and Brod. 75 to 90 enemy ftrs attack the formations. 3 HBs are lost. HBs and escorting ftrs claim over 30 planes shot down. 90 P–51's sweep Budapest area, claiming 7 ftrs destroyed.

Tenth AF: 8 B–24's fly gasoline to Kamaing while 52 B–25's continue ammo run to Imphal.

Fourteenth AF: In Tungting Lake area 160 MBs and FBs hit troop concentrations, supplies, and river and road traffic between Changsha and Hengyang, bomb arty concentrations at Sinsiang, attack waterfront and docks at Hengshan, pound villages near Chuchou, and attack numerous T/Os throughout the lake region. 4 B-25's over Formosa Strait claim 2 cargo vessels sunk and others damaged.

FEAF: Fifth AF and RAAF LBs and FBs continue to attack Wewak area, hitting troop concentrations, villages, ammo dumps, and warehouses. B-24's, B-25's, A-20's, A-26's, P-40's and P-47's hit A/Fs, gun positions, and various other tgts in or near Babo, Manokwari, Biak I, Noemfoor I, Ransiki, Waren, and Moemi. B-24's bomb Yap and Sorol; others on photo rcn flight bomb Woleai and Ifalik Is. Thirteenth AF ftrs and bmrs join other Allied airplanes from the N Solomons in bombing AA positions at Ralum and other tgts in Rabaul area.

Seventh AF: P-47's continue strafing and rocket attacks on Tinian, Saipan, and Rota while P-61's carry out defensive night patrols. B-24's, staging through Eniwetok, pound Truk. During the night a single B-24 bombs Ponape.

28 June

Eighth AF: 672 B-17's and B-24's bomb A/Fs at Laon/Couvron, Laon/Athies, and Juvincourt-et-Damary; rail bridges at Fismes and Anizy-le-Chateau; fuel storage dump at Dugny; M/Ys at Saarbrucken; and T/Os, including A/Fs at Denain/Prouvy, Le Bourget, and Florennes, and railroad chokepoint near Tergnier. Nearly 300 HBs abort because of heavy cloud and dense contrails

at operational level. 566 ftrs spt the HBs, destroying 2 ftrs in aerial combat and suffering no losses. HB losses total 2. About one-third of the escorting ftrs afterward bomb and strafe transport tgts, claiming 3 locomotives and an armored vehicle destroyed.

Ninth AF: 220-plus ftrs, based on Continent, attack railroad facilities, bridges, fuel and ammo dumps, arty, troop concentrations, vehicles, and other tgts. Bad weather cancels bmr and ftr operations from UK.

Twelfth AF: Bad weather cancels all LB and MB operations. FBs carry out rail-cutting missions N of battleline in NC Italy.

Fifteenth AF: 229 B-24's bomb M/Y and 2 oil refineries at Bucharest; 138 others hit Karlovo A/F. 40 ftrs carry out sweep over Bucharest area while other ftrs fly more than 230 sorties in escort of HBs. 20-plus enemy ftrs are claimed shot down, mostly by the ftrs during sweep over Bucharest.

Tenth AF: 8 B-24's fly fuel to Kamaing. Ammo delivery to Imphal is continued by 47 B-25's. 14 other B-25's pound Naba-Mawlin railroad.

Fourteenth AF: In Yangtze R-Tungting Lake area B-25's and FBs fly more than 160 sorties attacking river shipping at several locations, bombing towns of Hengshan, Liling, and Pingkiang, and bombing Japanese HQ and gun sites in Siangsiang area. Also in Hengyang area the MBs and FBs hit rear supply bases and cav and inf concentrations.

FEAF: Attacks on Wewak area continue. Japanese HQ and comm in Suain-Karowop Plantation area and coastal road from Babiang to Nyaparake are hit. A/F and fuel dumps on Noemfoor I, Japanese positions and occupied areas and buildings on Biak and Efman Is, village near Babo, and Tor R and Maffin Bay areas are attacked. B–24's bomb A/F and town on Yap and comm on Sorol and Woleai. AA guns E of Tobera area are attacked.

Seventh AF: P–47's and P–61's carry out daylight raids and defensive night patrols over Saipan, Tinian, and Rota.

29 June

Eighth AF: 82 B–17's bomb synthetic oil plant at Bohlen, 61 strike aircraft components factory at Wittenberg, 31 bomb aero engine works at Leipzig/Taucha, 39 hit ftr assembly plant at Leipzig/Heiterblick, and 42 bomb T/Os at Wittenberg, Quakenbruck, and Limbach-Oberfrohna. 390 B–24's bomb aircraft assembly plant at Bernburg, ftr assembly factory at Oschersleben, aero engine works at Magdeburg-Neustadt, aircraft components factory at Aschersleben, airpark at Stendal, and T/Os including A/Fs at Burg and Gardelegen and M/Y at Oebisfelde-Kaltendorf. 51 B–24's bomb motor transport plant at Fallersleben and personnel camp S of Mittelland Canal. Clouds cause assembly problems and over 400 HBs abort without reaching enemy territory. Total HBs losses for the day number 15. 14 gps from VIII FC and 1 from Ninth AF escort the HBs. Flights from 9 of these gps afterwards strafe parked aircraft, trains, barges, a factory, road vehicles, and soldiers. 3 ftrs are lost. 33 enemy airplanes are claimed destroyed.

Ninth AF: Almost 200 B–26's and A–20's bomb gun batteries on Cap de

la Hague, bridges and rail lines in Rennes-Saint-Hilaire-du-Harcourt-Vitre areas, and rail bridge at Oissel. Ftrs fly armed rcn and attack enemy airplanes, road and rail traffic, gun positions, bridges and other tgts in wide areas throughout NW France.

Twelfth AF: FBs, MBs, and LBs attack ammo dumps, viaducts, bridges, railroad cars, landing grounds, roads, motor transport, and other tgts along battleline in NC Italy and at various points to the N.

Tenth AF: 16 B–24's continue fuel lift to Kamaing. 45 B–25's haul ammo to Imphal. 23 other B–25's bomb Tamu. 19 A–36's, P–51's, and P–38's hit Myitkyina and Myitnge bridge. A B–25 bombs tgts in Mohnyin-Naba area.

Fourteenth AF: In Tungting Lake area 60-plus MBs and FBs hit shipping, gun positions, troop concentrations, and general T/Os at several locations, including Lingyang, Liling, Hengyang, Yuhsien, Hengshan, Siangsiang, Chaling, and Yiyang. 3 B–24's bomb Takao docks. P–40's damage bridge and attack rail traffic at Phu Lang Thuong.

FEAF: Japanese concentrations at Aitape and a variety of T/Os including barges, villages and bivouacs in Wewak area are hit by A–20's, B–25's, and FBs. B–24's, B–25's, A–20's, and FBs attack A/Fs and AA guns at Babo, Manokwari, Waren, and Moemi, barges at Noemfoor, and villages E of Maffin Bay. AA positions S of Ralum are bombed.

Seventh AF: P–47's carry out bombing and strafing missions over Saipan, Tinian, and Rota. B–24's, staging through Eniwetok, pound Truk while B–25's based at Makin hit Ponape.

Eleventh AF: 2 B–25's fly a negative shipping sweep.

30 June

Eighth AF: 136 HBs attack A/Fs at Montdidier, Evreux/Fauville, Conches, Le Culot, and Coxyde/Furnes. P–51's furnish escort and afterwards strafe M/Ys, A/Fs, barges, barracks, a train, a factory, and a warehouse with good results. No enemy aircraft are encountered and no airplanes are lost.

Ninth AF: 125-plus B–26's and A–20's, using blind-bombing methods in bad weather, bomb fuel dumps and road junctions at Conde-sur-Vire, Foret de Conches, Conde-sur-Noireau, and Thury-Harcourt. Around 250 others are forced to abort due to weather. 600-plus ftrs escort bmrs, fly cover over the beach, and bomb M/Ys at Chartres and Verneuil-sur-Avres, bridges E of Paris, and Evreux-Bueil, and Breux-sur-Avre-Trappes rail lines. The ftrs fly armed rcn in Seine-Loire gap and along the Loire, and Continent-based ftrs of IX TAC attack comm tgts in adv of US and British positions.

Twelfth AF: Weather again restricts MB operations but B–25's attack Pietrasanta railway bridge and Marradi viaduct and tunnel. FBs hit rail lines, bridges, railroad cars, guns, motor transport, and other tgts along battleline and area to the N in Pistoia area.

Fifteenth AF: Bad weather causes over 450 HBs and more than 150 ftrs to abort missions. 188 HBs, escorted by 138 ftrs, hit A/F at Zagreb and T/Os in Hungary and Yugoslavia, including M/Ys at Kaposvar, Osztopan and Split, highway bridge at Brac I, A/F at Banjaluka, and city of Buda-

pest. 130-plus ftrs provide escort.

Tenth AF: 47 B–25's continue Imphal ammo run while 17 B–25's haul gasoline to Kamaing. 18 B–25's bomb Tamu and 6 hit Wainggyo. 11 P–38's attack Myitnge bridge.

Fourteenth AF: MBs and FBs again pound numerous tgts in Tungting Lake area, concentrating on river shipping, town areas, troop concentrations, and road traffic. Towns bombed include Pingkiang, Hengshan, Liling, Yuhsien, Siangyin, and Chuchou. Also hit is A/F at Hengyang and bridges at Leiyang and Liling. 15 P–40's over NE Indochina damage bridge approaches at Phu Lang Thuong and blast 3 trains.

FEAF: Barges, troop concentrations, and other T/Os near Nyaparake and Suain are attacked. Kamiri and Namber A/Fs, supply areas, and defensive positions on Noemfoor I are hit. Tobera and Erventa I are also bombed.

Seventh AF: P–47's on Saipan continue to pound entry forces remaining on Saipan, Tinian, and Rota.

1 July

Eighth AF: 325 HBs are dispatched to bomb 14 V-weapon sites in N France but are recalled because of clouds. Recall messages by mistake are not sent to 3 sqs; 2 of these abort on decision of sq leaders; the other continues on mission and 9 of its planes bomb a V-weapon site at Mont Louis Ferme. P–51's, relieved of escort duty by recall of HBs, claim 5 aircraft destroyed in aerial engagements.

Ninth AF: IX ADC is activated in UK by Ninth AF to provide air defense behind the advancing Allied ground forces in N Europe. CG is Gen Richardson. Weather prevents operations by IX BC. 47 ftrs escort TCs and fly sweeps in Vire area where about 20 ftrs bomb tac tgts.

Twelfth AF: LBs and MBs hit fuel dumps, rail bridges, viaducts, and docks in NC Italy. FBs concentrate on road and rail bridges behind battle area, destroy several ftrs in combat over Reggio Emilia A/F, and hit guns S of Carsoli.

Tenth AF: 8 P–40's fly ground spt missions in Myitkyina area. 2 B–25's bomb rail tgts at Mohnyin and Naba.

Fourteenth AF: B–25's and FBs again pound tgts throughout Tungting Lake region. River shipping is attacked on large scale at numerous locations and 250–300 trucks are strafed between Tungcheng and Pingkiang. Hengyang A/F is bombed as are towns of Pingkiang, Hengshan, Liling, and Yuhsien. Pontoon bridge and Japanese positions at Leiyang are also hit. B–24's lay mines in river at Canton during the night.

FEAF: B–24's bomb A/F at Namlea and hit shipping throughout the Amboina-Ceram-Boeroe area. Other B–24's, B–25's, A–20's and FBs hit A/F, AA guns, bivouacs, supplies, and Japanese defenses on Noemfoor I in preparation for Allied landings on 2 Jul. A/F at Manokwari is also bombed. Bmrs and ftrs continue to pound Wewak coastal area; many of the strikes are in conjunction with Navy PT boats. A few B–24's on armed rcn bomb tgts on Yap and Peleliu.

Seventh AF: P–47's fly bombing and strafing missions over Saipan, Tinian, and Rota. B–24's, staging through Eniwetok, hit Truk during 1/2 Jul and follow up with another raid during the day. Makin-based B–25's bomb Ponape.

Eleventh AF: At dawn 4 B–24's radar-bomb southern Shimushu and Kurabu Cape A/F through overcast.

2 July

Eighth AF: 280 HBs attack 13 V-weapon sites in Pas de Calais area. 41 P–51's, temporarily in Italy while en route from USSR to UK during shuttle mission, join Fifteenth AF ftrs in escorting Fifteenth AF HBs against tgts in Budapest area, claiming 9 aircraft destroyed and suffering 4 losses.

Ninth AF: All IX BC missions cancelled due to bad weather. Ftrs of 7 gps of IX TAC fly interception missions in Caen area and cover over beach area, attack rail lines along the Loire, and hit a HQ and supply dumps and strongpoints near La Haye-du-Puits.

Twelfth AF: MBs and LBs continue to pound enemy comm lines N of battle area (mainly along and N of Pisa-Florence line) and hit several fuel dumps with good results. FBs are active against motor transport and bridges immediately N of battleline.

Fifteenth AF: 620-plus B–17's and B–24's attack 2 M/Ys, an A/F, and 2 oil refineries at Budapest, industrial area at Gyor, railroad bridge at Szolnok, and M/Ys at Brod and Vinkovci. Ftrs sweep over Budapest area. HBs and ftrs claim 50-plus ftrs shot down. 14 US aircraft are shot down and as many more are missing.

Tenth AF: 7 P–40's continue spt of ground forces in Myitkyina area. 2 B–25's hit railroad tracks at Pinwe and Katha.

Fourteenth AF: 11 B–25's and 42 FBs again attack river shipping, compounds, and troop concentrations in Tungting Lake region. Also town of Hengshan is bombed. B–25's and P–51's pound A/F and town area at Lupao.

FEAF: B–24's, B–25's, and A–20's, and FBs, along with naval guns, bombard Kamiri area of Noemfoor I, after which Allied amphibious forces land with little opposition and secure beachhead. Other B–25's attack barges near Manokwari.

Seventh AF: P–47's on Saipan bomb and strafe forces on Saipan, Tinian, and Rota.

3 July

Eighth AF: 55 B–17's in Italy on USSR shuttle mission join Fifteenth AF HBs in bombing M/Ys at Arad. 38 P–51's of VIII FC, also on shuttle run, fly escort on the mission.

Ninth AF: Nearly 275 ftrs strafe and bomb strongpoints, gun positions, fuel dump, comm lines, bridges, and patrol beach in vicinity of Lessay and Periers, S of US First Army's adv.

Twelfth AF: B–26's and A–20's pound enemy fuel dumps while B–25's hit bridges tunnels, and viaducts at Pietrasanta, Canneto sull'Oglio and Saviano, and fuel storage tanks in Pontelagoscuro area. FBs blast motor transport and bridges in battle area as US Fifth Army begins drive on Leghorn. Vehicle park, ammo dump, and a barge are also hit.

Fifteenth AF: More than 600 B–24's and B–17's attack oil storage, oil refinery, and locomotive works at Bucharest, oil storage at Giurgiu, railroad tgts at Turnu–Severin, bridge at Piatra, M/Ys at Arad and

Timisoara, bridge at Szeged, and oil storage at Belgrade. Ftrs fly over 250 sorties in spt of missions.

Tenth AF: 20-plus FBs spt ground forces in Myitkyina area, which also is covered by 10-plane combat patrol.

Fourteenth AF: In Tungting Lake area 4 B–24's bomb Yoyang railroad yards. B–25's and P–40's pound river shipping, bridges, gun sites, compounds, and villages at several locations, including Leiyang, Ssutang, Yungfengshih, and Tsungyang. B–25's drop ammo to Chinese ground forces at Hengyang. P–40's damage bridge at Phu Lang Thuong and hit nearby T/Os.

FEAF: P–38's and B–25's hit personnel and supply areas S of Kamiri and spt invading ground forces as they push E along N coast of Noemfoor I. Efman I, Manokwari, and Biak I are attacked by B–24's, A–20's, and ftrs. Wewak coastal area continues under sustained air attack as Allied airplanes pound tgts including forces at Brandi Plantation and supplies and a bridge near But. HBs hit airstrips, AA positions, and T/Os in Yap group, at Woleai, and at Peleliu. Larat and Saumlakki are also bombed.

Seventh AF: P–47's continue to hit troops remaining on Saipan, Tinian, and Rota. B–24's, staging through Eniwetok, bomb Truk.

4 July

Eighth AF: 256 HBs attack 7 A/Fs N and W of Paris, plus several T/Os. Bad weather and mechanical failures cause over 350 others to abort. VIII FC flies 594 sorties during HB ecort and strafing assignments against transportation tgts.

Ninth AF: Although bad weather curtails bmr operations, 95 B–26's and A–20's bomb rail bridge at Oissel and strongly defended positions N of Anneville-sur-Mer, using Pathfinder technique. More than 900 ftrs strafe and bomb numerous tgts in France including troop concentrations, gun positions, rail lines, M/Ys, tunnel, radio station, bridges, highways, and a cmd post. Ftrs also fly escort and cover beach and assault areas.

Twelfth AF: Weather cancels LB and MB operations. FB operations are greatly reduced but attacks are made on bridges, rail lines, roads, and guns in and N of battle area as US Fifth Army elements clear parts of Rosignano, overrun Mount Vitalba and area to its E, and push into Casole d'Elsa.

Fifteenth AF: 250-plus B–17's and B–24's bomb bridge and railroad repair works at Pitesti and oil refinery at Brasov. 350-plus ftrs escort HBs and carry out sweeps in tgt area. Claims of enemy ftrs destroyed total 17. 1 ftr gp strafes 2 landing grounds and a troop train in Yugoslavia on return trip to base.

Tenth AF: 30-plus P–40's continue spt of ground forces near Myitkyina. 20-plus P–47's and P–51's fly offensive sweep over Lashio area, patrol Mogaung area, and bomb T/Os at Taungni, Nampadaung, and Mogaung. 4 B–25's hit bridges and railroad tracks in Hopin and Naba areas.

Fourteenth AF: 38 MBs and 74 FBs pound tgts throughout Tungting Lake-Yangtze R region and in Yellow R and Canton areas. River shipping is hit hard, particularly along Siang-Chiang R. Troop concentrations, road traffic, and general T/Os are hit at many locations. Towns bombed include Shasi, Lukou, Yungfengshih, Liling, Siangtan, anl Yuhsien. A/F at Hengyang is bombed and supplies are dropped to Chinese troops in the area. A/Fs and warehouses in Canton area are bombed and T/Os at Linfen, Wenhsi, and Puchou in Yellow R region are strafed.

FEAF: A–20's continue spt of Allied ground forces pushing E and SE from Kamiri A/F area of Noemfoor I and taking Kamiri village and Kornasoren A/F. P–47's strafe T/Os at nearby Biak I while B–24's bomb A/F at Efman I. Other aircraft bomb and strafe troops E of Maffin Bay. Personnel areas at But and Dagua and barges at Wewak Pt are also attacked. B–24's hit shipping and A/Fs in Amboina-Ceram area. B–24's bomb Yap and hit airstrips on Woleai, Sorol, and Peleliu.

Seventh AF: P–47's on Saipan continue FB operations against forces on Saipan, Tinian, Aguijan and Rota Is. B–24's, staging through Eniwetok, pound Truk.

5 July

Eighth AF: 233 HBs attack 3 A/Fs in the Netherlands and 2 in Belgium, a factory near Mol, and 3 V-weapon supply sites in France. 184 ftrs fly sorties in spt of the HBs. 70 B–17's on shuttle mission (UK-USSR-Italy UK) attack M/Y at Beziers (with Fifteenth AF B–24's) while on last leg from Italy to UK. 42 VIII FC P–51's return to UK with the B–17's. (Of the 11 P–51's remaining in Italy, 10 return to UK the following day and the last several days later.)

Ninth AF: About 180 MBs and LBs bomb bridges at Caen and also rail sidings, tracks, and rolling stock.

In the afternoon 4 NOBALL HQ are hit. 600-plus ftrs escort IX BC, carry out armed rcn of comm and enemy movements, attack rail lines, rolling stock, M/Ys, bridges, supply dumps, and cover beach area.

Twelfth AF: B-25's bomb Villafranca di Verona M/Y, Aulla railroad bridge, and Ostiglia fuel dumps while A-20's blast supply dump and rail lines. FBs hit tracks, bridges, roads, and other tgts in battle area as US Fifth Army continues fierce fighting around Rosignano.

Fifteenth AF: Almost 500 B-17's and B-24's bomb Montpellier and Beziers M/Ys and Toulon submarine pens and harbor installations. Close to 200 ftr sorties are flown in spt of the missions.

Tenth AF: 20-plus P-40's and A-36's continue spt in Myitkyina sector while 12 other airplanes fly armed rcn in same area. 20-plus other P-40's, P-51's, and A-36's hit T/Os in areas around Hopin, Namma, and Naungtalaw. The town area of Naungtalaw also is pounded by 11 B-25's.

Fourteenth AF: 136 FBs and 64 MBs attack tgts throughout Tungting Lake area. Tgts include river shipping, warehouses, troops, arty, trucks, and other T/Os at Liling, Lukou, Pingkiang, Yungfengshih, Siangyin, and Chuting. Hengyang A/F is bombed, and supplies are dropped to Chinese forces in the vicinity. In Salween area 40 transports drop supplies to Chinese forces on battleline, and 4 FBs pound town and vicinity of Tengchung. 22 B-24's bomb supply and ammo depot at Canton. 6 MBs attack A/Fs in the area. 5 B-24's lay mines in Shanghai harbor.

FEAF: In area around Wewak A-20's and FBs hit dumps at Dagua and attack barges during 4/5 Jul. B-24's bomb airstrips and AA guns at Yap and Woleai; Sorol and Paliau I are also hit. Light strikes are flown in spt of troops on Noemfoor I and against barges, A/Fs, and troop concentrations at Efman and Biak Is and at Moemi, Manokwari, and in Wakde area.

Seventh AF: P-47's fly FB operations over Saipan, Rota, and Tinian.

6 July

Eighth AF: 231 B-24's bomb dock area at Kiel during morning while 687 HBs bomb 18 V-weapon sites, 7 A/Fs, a M/Y and a highway intersection. 3 HBs and 2 ftrs are lost. In the late afternoon 220 HBs strike 6 V-weapon sites and supply installations, 3 railroad bridges, a highway bridge, and an A/F in N France. 471 ftrs escort the HBs. Afterwards a sq of P-47's dive-bombs 3 A/Fs in Conches area. No aircraft are lost on afternoon mission.

Ninth AF: During the morning around 500 B-26's and A-20's bomb bridges and rail lines at 8 locations in France. In afternoon 5 tgts are attacked, including bridges, fuel dumps, railroad tracks, and V-weapon location. Over 15 ftr gps escort bmrs, fly armed rcn of rail lines, roads, and M/Ys, damaging or destroying tracks, trains, tunnel, building, and supply dump. Ftrs also cover beach and bomb and strafe troop concentrations and gun positions.

Twelfth AF: A-20's hit ammo ship at La Spezia during 5/6 Jul and continue attacks on fuel supplies during the day. MBs again hit comm, concentrating on bridges N of battleline, and attack enemy warehouses and HQ. FBs hit rail lines (with especially good results betwen Viareggio and Massa Lombarda) and damage several bridges just N of battle area as US Fifth Army continues clearing Rosignano and takes Castellina Marittima and Mount Vaso.

Fifteenth AF: 530-plus B–17's and B–24's attack Verona M/Y, Bergamo steel works, Avisio viaduct, Tagliamento-Casarsa della Delizia railroad bridge, Aviano oil and gasoline storage, Porto Marghera oil storage, and Trieste oil refinery. P–51's and P–38's provide escort.

Tenth AF: 12 P–40's attack bridge near Myitkyina while 40-plus others spt ground forces in the area. Several other P–40's attack Maingna, barracks at Sahmaw, train at Taungni, and troops at Sakangyi. 6 B–25's bomb Maingna and 2 hit Mohnyin.

Fourteenth AF: B–25's, P–40's, and P–51's continue to pound river shipping, bridges, troop concentrations, road traffic, and general T/Os throughout wide area around Tungting Lake and along the Yangtze. Hit particularly hard are town area and supply depot at Sinshih. B–25's near Burma border cause considerable damage at Tengchung and drop supplies to Chinese ground forces on Salween front, and during 6/7 Jul bomb Tien Ho A/F at Canton.

FEAF: B–25's, A–20's, and FBs continue to pound Wewak area, concentrating on troops S of Matapau. B–25's and FBs sweep N coast of Vogelkop Peninsula and offshore islands, hitting T/Os. Other FBs hit Manokwari area and buildings at Ransiki, Moari, and Oransbari. A/Fs, gun positions, comm tgts, and supply

dumps in area around Babo are hit by B–24's, A–26's, A–20's, and P–38's. B–24's bomb town and warehouse area of Yap and a few hit A/F at Woleai.

Twentieth AF: Gen Saunders becomes CG XX BC.

Seventh AF: P–47's bomb and strafe forces on Saipan, Rota, and Tinian. B–24's, staging through Eniwetok, pound Truk during 5/6 Jul and follow with another raid during the day. B–25's, based at Makin, hit Nauru.

7 July

Eighth AF: Over 1,000 HBs attack 3 synthetic oil plants, 8 aircraft assembly plants and engine works, 2 A/Fs and an equipment depot, 2 M/Ys a railway station, railway repair shops, and city of Hameln, all in Germany. 37 HBs are lost during the day's operations, 649 ftrs escort HBs. 42 P–38's and 124 P–47's make strafing attacks, destroying parked aircraft, locomotives, and rolling stock. Ftrs claim 77 aircraft destroyed in aerial combat and 4 on ground. 6 ftrs are lost.

Ninth AF: 100-plus A–20's and B–26's bomb rail bridge near Tours, and T/Os in Lisieux and Beuzeville areas. Over 500 ftrs fly escort and area cover, carry out armed rcn of comm and troop activity, and bomb railroads, rolling stock, M/Ys, ammo dumps, and bridges in frontline areas and wide areas of W France.

Twelfth AF: During 6/7 Jul A–20's bomb La Spezia harbor and motor transport in the area, and resume attack on fuel supplies during the day. B–26's and B–25's score direct hits on railway bridges at Reggio

Emilia, and over the Fratta R and possible hits on Santa Maria di Mugnano bridge and 2 other bridges in the area; they also hit Collecchio fuel dump, causing many fires and explosions. FBs attack Ferrara A/F, town of Empoli, and rail lines, bridges, fuel and ammo dumps, motor transport, and numerous other tgts in battle area as US Fifth Army forces complete clearing of Rosignano.

Fifteenth AF: 560-plus B–24's and B–17's bomb 2 synthetic oil plants at Blechhammer, synthetic oil and coking plant at Odertal, and Zagreb A/F and M/Y. HBs and ftr escorts claim more than 50 aircraft shot down during fierce battle with 275–300 ftrs mainly in Vienna-Budapest area. 18 US aircraft are listed as destroyed and a larger number missing.

Tenth AF: 20 FBs hit T/Os at Okkyin and Namkwin and strafe trucks near Myitkyina. 4 B–25's attack bridges and railroad tracks at Hopin and Naba.

Fourteenth AF: In Tungting Lake area B–25's and FBs hit Yoyang, Siangtan, Liling, and Yungfengshih, strafe cav forces N of Yuhsien, hit river shipping, troops, and pontoon bridge at Siangsiang, attack compounds in Leiyang area, and bomb storage at Shihshow. 10 mi E of Ichang on the Yangtze P–40's thoroughly blast Japanese post. B–25's and P–51's bomb Tien Ho and White Cloud A/Fs and pound town of Tsingyun.

FEAF: B–24's and A–20's bomb Moemi and Nabire A/Fs; supply dumps along Wiske R are also attacked. A few FBs and RAAF aircraft attack barges, gun positions, and troops along coast in Wewak area. B–

24's bomb Yap, Sorol I radio station, and runway on Woleai.

Twentieth AF: 14 B–29's, operating out of Chengtu during 7/8 Jul, bomb Sasebo, Omura, and Tobata (most of the planes hitting Sasebo area). 3 others attack secondary and last resort tgts at Laoyao and in Hankow area.

Seventh AF: P–61's carry out interceptor missions over Guam, Saipan, and Rota during 6/7 Jul.

8 July

Eighth AF: 467 HBs, operating in 4 forces, bomb 13 railroad facilities (bridges, junctions, sidings, lines, viaducts, and embankments), 3 M/Ys, a highway junction, 5 A/Fs, and 10 V-weapon installations, all in France. Nearly 450 others are forced to abort, mainly because of very heavy cloud conditions. 9 HBs are lost. 14 ftr gps spt day's operations. 596 ftrs complete sorties, claiming 20 aircraft, 15 locomotives, and several railroad cars and road vehicles destroyed by strafing and bombing. 1 ftr is lost.

Ninth AF: About 280 MBs and LBs bomb V-weapon HQ at Chateau-de-Ribeaucourt, numerous strongpoints in Caen battle area, rail bridges at Mantes-La-Jolie, Saumur, Nogent-le-Roi, and Caen and (late in evening) fuel dumps in Rennes and bridge at Nantes. Ftrs escort the bmrs and fly armed rcn throughout wide areas of France, concentrating on frontline area. Tgts hit include M/Ys, bridges, ammo and supply dumps, troop concentrations and tanks.

Twelfth AF: During 7/8 Jul A–20's bomb areas in or near Empoli, Agliana, and Lucca, and hit fuel dumps the following day. MBs pound M/Ys at Novi

Ligure, Piacenza, Mantua, and **Ferrara** and tracks near Parma. FBs again blast railroads, roads, and bridges N of battleline, which is advancing N from above Cecina toward Leghorn.

Fifteenth AF: 520-plus HBs attack tgts in Vienna area, bombing refineries at Vosendorf and Korneuburg, A/F at Zwolfaxing, Markersdorf, and Munchendorf, and M/Y and oil storage at Vienna/Floridsdorf, and A/F at Veszprem. Ftrs fly well over 200 sorties in spt of HB missions which are opposed by more than 100 ftrs. 14 US aircraft are lost. HBs and ftrs claim more than 50 ftrs shot down.

Tenth AF: 30-plus A–36's and P–40's hit bridge at Myitkyina and spt ground forces in the area. 12 B–25's also pound Myitkyina.

Fourteenth AF: MBs and FBs fly nearly 100 sorties against tgts in Tungting Lake area. River shipping is hit hard throughout the whole lake area. Trucks, bridges, warehouses, supply dumps, troop concentrations, Japanese posts, and T/Os are attacked at Sinshih, Sinyang, Leiyang, Liling, Chuchou, Puchi, Siangsiang, and Yuhsien. 18 B–24's bomb military area near Canton, and 37 P–40's attack Japanese-held villages and river shipping NW of Canton. In Indochina 10 P–40's hit shipping all along coast while 5 B–25's knock out 2 bridges at Cam Lo. 20 Japanese airplanes bomb Suichwan A/F, rendering it temporarily unusable. Enemy airplanes also damage Kanchou A/F.

FEAF: MBs and FBs hit fuel dumps, barges, villages, and various other tgts at Babo, Fak Fak, Sagan, Kokas, at mouth of Maroe R, along Cape Kariensore, and W of Namber.

B–25's, A–20's, FBs and a few HBs attack Woleai, hitting barges, gun positions, and comm tgts.

Seventh AF: P–47's fly FB operations against troops on Saipan, Pagan, and Tinian. During 7/8 Jul B–24's stage through Eniwetok and bomb Truk. More B–24's follow with another raid during the day.

9 July

Eighth AF: During morning mission 140 B–17's bomb 2 railroad bridges, a railroad viaduct, a road bridge, and an A/F in France. 1 HB and 2 supporting ftrs are lost. Later, 24 B–17's and 35 B–24's bomb 3 CROSSBOW installations and 2 A/Fs in France; bad weather causes over 100 other HBs to abort. 168 ftrs escort the HBs. 1 P–47 gp afterwards joins RAF Spitfires in aerial battle against 15 Me 109's. The P–47's claim 5 ftrs destroyed against no losses; Spitfires down 6 Germans.

Ninth AF: Of more than 250 MBs and LBs dispatched, about 60 bomb tgts in France; bad weather prevents others from bombing. Tgts hit are rail bridge, crossing, overpass and highway bridge at Ablis, Orleans, Vendome, and Montfort-sur-Risle. Ftrs escort IX BC, provide area cover over battle area, and bomb and strafe gun positions, vehicles, rail cars, bridges, and tanks.

Twelfth AF: Weather greatly curtails operations. FBs attack rail lines between Empoli and Montelupo Fiorentino with good results. Other tgts include roads, bridges and gun positions.

Fifteenth AF: In the Fifteenth's first Pathfinder-led mission, 222 B–17's and B–24's bomb Xenia and Concordia Vega oil refineries at Ploesti. P–38's and P–51's fly escort. Other P–51's sweep Ploesti area during the attacks. HBs and ftrs claim destruction of 14 of the 40–50 opposing ftrs. 6 US aircraft are shot down.

Tenth AF: 60-plus A–36's, P–51's, P–47's, and P–40's spt ground forces and hit bridge in Myitkyina area, strafe gun positions at Shwebo and tgts along the Irrawaddy in Katha area, and attack T/Os in areas around Loilaw, Hopin, Mohnyin, Maingna, Anisakan, and Onbauk. 19 B–25's hit storage sheds at Waingmaw and railroads and bridges at Mohnyin, Naba, and Hopin.

Fourteenth AF: 40 P–40's and 8 B–25's hit town area, trucks, and supply sampans at Shayang and damage tunnel entrances and highway bridge at Sinyang. 5 B–25's bomb power plant and building area at Tinh Soc.

FEAF: A–20's and FBs pound shipping, A/Fs, troops, and other tgts at Babo, Manokwari, Efman, Biak and various points along coastline of Geelvink Bay. B–25's and FBs sink a 3,000-ton vessel and several barges around Halmahera I. Dumps at Marubian, Kairiru, and Niap and bridge at But are bombed by B–25's, A–20's, and FBs. B–24's bomb Namlea A/F and attack Yap and Woleai.

Seventh AF: P–47's hit remnants of Japanese forces on Saipan and Tinian, as organized resistance on Saipan ends. Saipan will become a base from which B–29's will bomb Japan. Makin-based B–25's bomb Jaluit.

10 July

Ninth AF: Ftrs bomb and strafe gun positions, bridges, rail overpass,

inf concentrations, and highway junctions, and cover battle area.

Twelfth AF: MBs successfully hit M/Ys, railroad bridges, and viaducts in NC Italy. Weather restricts FBs and ftrs but several tgts are hit, including A/F at Modena and scattered gun positions, rail lines, and roads.

Tenth AF: 24 P–40's and P–51's spt ground forces at Myitkyina. 20-plus A–36's P–51's, P–47's, and P–40's hit Mogaung, buildings and boxcars at Mohnyin, trucks at Sahmaw, factory at Loiwing, and Punga pagoda. Railroad supply area at Mohnyin is bombed by 6 B–25's.

Fourteenth AF: 70 P–40's and 6 B–25's hit river shipping between Siangtan and Siangsiang, between Changsha and Chuchou, and N of Hengyang; strafe and bomb posts and trucks in Pingkiang, Tungcheng, and Tsungyang areas and in Changsha-Kweilin area; and bomb A/Fs at Hankow and Wuchang.

FEAF: B–24's attack Laha, Namlea, and T/Os in Boeroe-Ceram-Amboina area. A–20's, FBs, and a B–25 hit troops, villages, and barges in Wewak area. B–24's bomb A/Fs and town areas at Yap, Gagil-Tomil I and Sorol. Operations also include small-scale strikes in Wakde area and snooper and armed rcn missions over the Carolines.

Seventh AF: P–47's hit troops and gun positions on Tinian. B–24's, staging through Eniwetok, pound Truk during 9/10 Jul and again during the day.

11 July

International: Roosevelt announces that US will recognize French Committee of National Liberation as *de* *facto* administrative authority in France.

Eighth AF: 969 HBs attack Munich while 38 others bomb Augsburg and M/Ys at Eppingen. Ftrs fly 762 sorties in spt. Overcast hinders strafing attacks but ftrs manage to destroy a parked airplane and a locomotive, and hit Worms M/Y. 20 HBs and 4 ftrs fail to return to base.

Ninth AF: A–20's and B–26's strike fuel dumps at Foret d'Andaine, Chateau-de-Tertu, Flers, and Foret d' Ecouves; NOBALL sites at Chateau d'Helicourt and Chateau d'Ansenne; and a rail bridge at Bourth. Ftrs escort IX BC, patrol battle area, and attack trains, gun positions, ammo dumps, and other tgts in areas around Lessay, Periers, Saint-Lo, Lonrai, Tours and Folligny.

Twelfth AF: Weather again hampers operations. MBs attack M/Y at Alessandria, hit approach to railroad bridge at Chiavari, and score near misses on other bridges. FBs hit A/F at Rimini and attack fuel dumps, rail lines, gun positions, bridges, and T/Os N of battleline as US Fifth Army engages in hard fighting in Pastina and Laiatico area.

Fifteenth AF: Bad weather curtails HB effort. The only tgt attacked is Toulon harbor, where 87 B–24's hit jetties, oil stores, nearby telegraph cable factory, barracks, repair shops, adjoining M/Y, and submarines in drydock.

Tenth AF: 70-plus FBs pound barracks at Myitkyina, bridges at Namkwin and Mohnyin, A/F at Lashio, and T/Os at several other locations, including Nanyinbya, Indaw, Katha, Bhamo, and Anisakan-Shwebo area. 11 B–25's hit bridges at Hsenwi.

Fourteenth AF: 28 B–24's bomb storage base at Sinshih. 24 P–40's hit river traffic at Hengyang and E of Siangsiang. 22 other P–40's attack town of Hengyang, hitting Japanese-occupied buildings and a bridge. 33 more P–40's attack villages, road traffic, and T/Os at Leiyang and from Chuchou to Hengyang to Yungfengshih. 3 B–25's bomb Liling and Yuhsien. 14 P–51's bomb town of Pakmoi Hu and hit gun positions at Lupao. 8 B–25's pound railroad yards at Sinyang. 12 B–25's and 14 FBs bomb Mangshih on Burma Road and spt Chinese ground forces between Tengchung and Lungling.

FEAF: B–24's pound A/F at Babo while A–20's hit supply dumps at Kokas. B–25's bomb A/Fs at Manokwari, Waren, and Moemi during the night. A–20's, MBs, and FBs spt ground forces in Sarmi-Sawar area and bomb A/Fs, shipping, and various occupied areas and installations on Halmahera, in Schouten Is, on Boeroe, and the Palau group, and at Woleai.

Seventh AF: P–47's pound forces on Tinian and Pagan.

12 July

Eighth AF: 131 B–24's, with escort by 144 RAF Spitfires, are dispatched against 10 V-weapon sites in Rouen area but abort because of thick blanket of low cloud over tgt area. 1,117 HBs bomb M/Ys, aero engine plant, and A/F at Munich. 754 ftrs spt the HBs. 24 HBs are lost, 13 to AA fire and the rest to accidents and unknown causes.

Ninth AF: Over 300 MBs and LBs fly morning and afternoon missions against fuel dumps at Foret d'Andaine and Foret d'Ecouves, military concentrations at Foret de Cinglais, rail bridges at Merey, Cinq Mars-la-Pile, Saumur, Nantes, and Nogent-le-Roi, and other rail and road tgts. Ftrs furnish escort, cover battle area, and fly armed rcn over wide areas, attacking rail lines S and W of Rambouillet, bridges and fuel dump in Nantes vicinity, trains and military transport at Vitry-le-Francois, and grounded airplanes S of Chateaubriant, bridges at Craon, Le Mans, Pontorson, Mayenne, S of Rennes, N of Angers, and Tours, rail traffic S of Fougeres, and inf and arty positions near Periers.

Twelfth AF: A–20's bomb scattered motor transport in Florence-Leghorn area during 11/12 Jul. MBs begin air offensive (MALLORY MAJOR) against road and rail bridges over the Po R during the day. A–20's continue attacking ammo supplies. FBs hit barges and small boats on Arno R and attack roads, ammo dumps, gun positions, tracks, vehicles, and a number of other tgts in that general area N of battleline.

Fifteenth AF: More than 420 B–24's attack tgts in SE France, scoring numerous hits on Nimes and Miramas M/Ys and cutting rail lines at Theoule-sur-Mer bridge and Var R bridge in Provence. Around 50 enemy ftrs oppose the missions. HBs and escorting ftrs claim 14 shot down. 7 US aircraft are lost.

Tenth AF: 44 P–40's spt ground forces in Myitkyina area. 28 P–51's and P–47's hit bridge and other tgts in Hopin, bomb Maingna pagoda, and hit Alanbo and Tagwin areas. 13 B–25's bomb bridges at Mongyin and hit T/Os in Myitkyina area.

Fourteenth AF: 60-plus P–40's hit towns of Liling and Yuhsien, river shipping at Hengyang, troop concentrations at Leiyang and near Yuhsien, A/F at Siangtan, and fuel dumps NW of Changsha. 34 P–51's bomb Tsingyun and pound Japanese concentrations at Lienchiangkou. 11 P–40's bomb railroad yards at Yuncheng and hit radio station N of Tungkuan with rocket fire. 12 B–25's bomb Tengchung and 15 P–40's bomb and strafe storage areas, villages, troop areas, and general T/Os in Lungling and Mangshih areas.

FEAF: B–24's hit Manokwari A/F; weather curtails further operations in Geelvink Bay area. A–20's, MBs, and FBs again hit troop concentrations and barges in Wewak area. Smaller strikes by B–24's and B–25's are flown against A/F at Laha, Dili, and on Koer I. B–24's pounds Yap.

Seventh AF: During 11/12 Jul B–24's stage through Eniwetok to bomb Truk. During the day B–24's hit Truk again. P–47's on Saipan continue to hit Tinian.

13 July

Eighth AF: 888 HBs, flying in 3 forces, bomb Saarbrucken M/Ys and aircraft engine plant at Munich. 548 ftrs execute escort assignments. In addition 1 flight of P–47's strafes a M/Y N of Karlsruhe, destroying 4 locomotives. 10 HBs are lost, along with 5 ftrs. 12 enemy aircraft are claimed destroyed.

Ninth AF: Bad weather prevents bmr operations and restricts ftrs. Ftrs fly armed rcn in Sens-Montargis area, hitting rail and highway traffic, warehouses, barracks, and armored cars and tanks. Rail lines and bridges are hit in Saint-Florentin-Dreux-Evreux-Chartres-Mamers-Gassicourt areas. IX TAC ftrs furnish area cover, bomb troop concentrations, vehicles, and gun positions in Lessay-Coutances area, and attack rail traffic W of Angers, landing field W of Alencon, M/Y at Vendome, and bridge at Tours.

Twelfth AF: MBs again bomb bridges in the Po Valley. A–20's hit ammo plant. FBs attack tgts, mainly railroads, in areas N of Arno R in adv of the battlefront.

Fifteenth AF: 581 B–17's and B–24's attack tgts in NE Italy, hitting M/Ys at Verona, Mestre, Brescia, and Mantua, Pinzano al Tagliamento railroad bridge, and oil storage at Porto Marghera and Trieste. P–38's and P–51's fly escort. Other P–51's carry out sweep over Po Valley.

Tenth AF: 44 P–40's and P–51's spt ground forces in Myitkyina area. 40 more A–36's, P–51's, and P–47's hit bridges at Nyaunggon, Mohnyin, Myothit, Mawlu, and Henu, and attack Hopin, Lashio, and Indawgyi Lake areas.

Fourteenth AF: 16 B–25's bomb Pailochi A/F, causing large fires and considerable damage. 45 P–40's attack trucks, compounds, river shipping, and troop concentrations between Hengyang and Siangtan, pound town of Liling and Siangtan A/F, and strafe shipping from Changsha S along Siang Chiang R. 8 B–25's bomb Chenghsien railroad yards and storage area. 12 B–25's bomb Tengchung and Mangshih.

FEAF: B–24's again bomb Yap and Sorol. B–24's, B–25's, and A–20's bomb gun positions and A/F at Babo and in Manokwari area and hit supply depot at Kokas. FBs spt Allied ground forces in Aitape area while A–20's and FBs pound occupied areas and gun positions in Wewak area and on Mushu I. B–24's also hit Amahai A/F.

Seventh AF: P–47's continue to hit Tinian. Kwajalein-based B–24's bomb Truk. B–25's from Makin pound Nauru.

14 July

Eighth AF: With conversion of 55th Ftr Gp from P–38's to P–51's, the Eighth acquires majority of P–51 gps to provide longer-range high-altitude escort for the HBs. Conversion to P–51's will continue until by the end of the year every gp except 1 will be equipped with them. In morning mission 319 B–17's drop supplies to French interior forces in S France. 4 P–51 gps fly 499 sorties in spt. No bmrs or ftrs are lost. HBs claim 9 enemy ftrs destroyed and the ftrs claim 4. During the evening 93 B–24's bomb A/Fs at Peronne and Montdidier. Nearly 40 other HBs do not bomb because of failure of blind-bombing equipment. Ftrs fly 83 uneventful sorties in spt. No aircraft are lost.

Ninth AF: Weather again curtails operations. 62 B–26's and A–20's, using Oboe, bomb railway embankment at Bourth and rail bridge at Merey. Ftrs provide escort and fly armd rcn over widespread areas of W France, attacking bridges, trains, rail lines, and military transport tgts. 85 enemy ftrs give battle near Brezolles and Alencon. 6 ftrs are claimed by US ftrs, against 5 missing from IX FC. IX TAC strafes and bombs defended positions ahead of US First Army.

Ftrs cut rail lines in L'Aigle-Alencon area, bomb troop concentrations near Periers, and M/Ys at Chateaudun and Aube-sur-Rile.

Twelfth AF: MBs concentrate on Po R Valley bridges. 600 ft (2 center spans) of Taglio di Po road bridge and 1 span of Piacenza rail bridge are destroyed, and damaging hits are scored on Corbola road and railroad bridges. FBs again hit gun positions and lines of comm in and N of battle areas while LBs attack supplies.

Fifteenth AF: 430-plus HBs attack 4 oil refineries at Budapest and Petfurdo and M/Y at Mantua. P-51's and P-38's provide escort. P-51's fly uneventful sweep of Budapest area. P-38's strafe trains N of La Spezia and dive-bomb Ghedi A/F.

Tenth AF: 49 P-40's pound enemy forces in Myitkyina vicinity. 38 P-51's and P-47's hit bridges at Mohnyin, Kadu, Henu, and Mawlu, bomb supplies at Nyaungbintha, spt ground forces near Myitkyina, bomb rice mill at Mohnyin, and hit several buildings at Hopin.

Fourteenth AF: FBs and MBs hit ftr strip N of Changsha, arty positions at Leiyang, town of Sungpai, and road and river traffic from Hengyang to Yuhsien and from Sienning to Tungshan; also attacked are various T/Os around towns of Hengyang, Changsha, and Chaling. During the night FBs blast Pailochi A/F, destroying more than 20 enemy airplanes. B-25's bomb roads in Tengchung area. B-25's and P-40's pound railroad yards at Siangsiang.

FEAF: B-24's continue to blast Yap. Oil reservoirs and wells at Boela are bombed and strafed by A-20's. B-24's and B-25's attack barge facilities and gun positions at Lautem. On Vogelkop Peninsula night ftrs hit A/Fs while B-25's bomb barge terminal at Kokas. A-20's hit Japanese forces at Sauri and bomb A/F at But. FBs spt ground forces in Aitape area along Driniumor R and Koronal Creek and blast troop concentrations near Afua.

Seventh AF: P-47's again hit Tinian.

15 July

Ninth AF: Weather cancels most operations but 4 B-26's (92 others abort) hit L'Aigle rail bridge during afternoon. 3 FBs fly uneventful sweep. Ftrs of IX TAC fly area cover and bomb inf, arty, M/Y, railroad, and a bridge in Saint-Lo, Argentan, and Falaise areas.

Twelfth AF: MB campaign against Po R Valley bridges (MALLORY MAJOR) reaches successful conclusion (though interdiction program against the bridges is subsequently continued on expanded scale) as most of the rail and road bridges in tgt area are destroyed or severely damaged by previous attacks and raids which struck bridges at Bozzolo, Desenzano de Garda, Cremona, Borgoforte, Ostiglia, Polesella, Sermide, Ferrara, Aulla, Filattiera, Ficarolo, and Chiavari and M/Y at Villafranca di Verona. FBs attack road bridges N of battleline and hit gun positions, roads, motor transport, and other tgts, while supporting ground forces slowly advancing N along a line extending E from the coast below Leghorn.

Fifteenth AF: More than 600 B-17's and B-24's bomb 4 oil refineries in Ploesti area and Teleajenul pumping station. P–51's and P–38's fly over 300 escort sorties.

Tenth AF: 38 P–40's continue spt of ground forces in Myitkyina area. 60-plus P–47's and P–51's attack bridges at Manla, Henu, and Mawlu, sweep Lashio, Katha, and Talawgyi areas, and hit motor pool at Kadu and T/Os around Sangin and Mohnyin. 20 B–25's attack Myitkyina area and hit bridges and supply area at Mawhun.

Fourteenth AF: More than 100 B–25's, P–40's, and P–51's blast towns of Sinshih, Chuchou, Siangtan, Siangsiang, Sungpai, and Chaling, concentrating on military and railroad installations and river shipping. Villages, troop concentrations, and river craft are attacked N and W of Hengyang and from Chaling to Yuhsien. In Salween area 26 P–40's spt Chinese forces and 12 B–25's bomb Mangshih and Lungling. 12 B–25's and P–40's bomb railroad yards at Hsuchang, causing considerable damage.

FEAF: B–24's blast Yap, scoring numerous hits in Yap town area and on radio station and barracks area. B–24's, penetrating heavy weather front, bomb A/F at Efman while B–25's hit enemy forces along Korrido Anchorage, and A–20's blast gun emplacements on island off Manokwari. B–25's, A–20's, and FBs again pound troop concentrations over wide area around Wewak.

Seventh AF: P–47's bomb and strafe Tinian. B–24's, staging through Eniwetok, hit Truk.

16 July

Eighth AF: 577 B–17's bomb Munich and surrounding area. Tgts include M/Ys, aircraft engine plants, Munich/Riem A/F, and city of Augsburg. 409 bomb Saarbrucken M/Ys and adjacent areas. Ftrs fly 684 supporting sorties and also strafe Bruges A/F and rail transportation. 11 HBs and 3 ftrs are lost.

Ninth AF: Gen Williams, CG IX TCC, arrives in Italy from UK, and activates Prov TC Div which will take part in invasion of S France. About 375 B–26's and A–20's, during morning and evening operations, bomb strongpoints in Saint-Lo area, bridges in frontline area, and bridges and fuel dump SE of Rennes. Ftrs escort the bmrs and fly armed rcn over frontlines in Chateaudun-Orleans-Tours areas.

Twelfth AF: MBs hit bridges in Po Valley at Peschiera del Garda, Mantua, Torre Beretti, Piacenza, Casale Monferrato, and Bressana Bottarone. FBs hit railroads and bridge just N of battleline as US Fifth Army forces take territory SE of Leghorn and push to within sight of Arno R Valley. British Eighth Army elements take Arezzo and thrust through to the Arno R.

Fifteenth AF: Around 380 HBs attack oil and aircraft tgts in Vienna area, bombing Munchendorf A/F, Winterhafen oil depot, Vienna M/Y, and Wiener Neudorf engine factory. P–51's and P–38's fly more than 150 sorties in escort while 132 other P–51's sweep Vienna area. More than 100 ftrs oppose the raids. 10 US airplanes are lost and several others are missing. US claims of ftrs shot down total over 30.

Tenth AF: 27 P–40's continue to hit forces in Myitkyina area. 20-plus P–51's and P–47's attack railroad bridges at Namkwin, Manla, and Hopin, and hit general T/Os in Hopin area. 12 B–25's bomb town of Maingna and bridges at Mohnyin.

Fourteenth AF: 23 B–24's pound Changsha, causing heavy damage. 40 P–51's and P–40's hit river shipping at Changsha, attack T/Os S of Hengyang, and bomb building area at Ikiawan.

FEAF: B–24's continue bombing Yap. Other B–24's pound AA positions at Manokwari. FBs bomb supply dumps N of Moemi and attack shipping in Kokas-Babo area. Bmrs and ftrs again hit troop and supply concentrations in Wewak sector. B–24's hit Atamboea A/F. TC missions to forward bases, especially Biak, increase.

Seventh AF: P–47's continue to pound Tinian.

17 July

Eighth AF: In the morning 592 HBs operating in 3 forces attack 12 railroad bridges, 3 rail junctions, a railway chokepoint, a V-weapon supply site, a M/Y, an A/F, and an oil storage dump in France. 463 ftrs complete sorties in spt of bmrs; elements of 4 gps afterwards strafe ground tgts, claiming 23 locomotives, 18 trucks, and 55 train cars destroyed. During the evening 126 HBs attack 12 V-weapon sites in NW France. 5 P–51 gps provide escort.

Ninth AF: With operations limited by weather, 69 MBs hit fuel dumps at Rennes while 37 LBs strike fuel dumps at Bruz and M/Y at Dol-de-Bretagne. Ftrs escort transports, fly area cover, attack fuel dumps and landing field at Angers, dive-bomb defenses at Coutances in spt of US First Army, attack Nevers M/Y, and

hit troop concentrations in spt of First Army assault in Saint-Lo area.

Twelfth AF: MBs concentrate on Po Valley bridges, hitting road and rail bridges and viaducts at or near Alessandria, Ostiglia, Bogliasco, Borgoforte, Moline, Imperia, Asti, Mollere, and Casale Monferrato. FBs continue to hit tgts N of battle area, concentrating on bridges and rail lines, while US Fifth Army elements take Luciana, and reach Arno R Valley, but make little progress toward Leghorn. British Eighth Army forces pursue enemy toward Florence.

Fifteenth AF: 162 B–24's attack M/Y and railroad bridges at Avignon and railroad bridges at Arles and Tarascon. P–51's and P–38's provide escort.

Tenth AF: 60-plus P–40's, P–47's, and P–51's continue to hit forces in Myitkyina area, pound Tagwin, and bomb M/Y at Mohnyin.

Fourteenth AF: 22 B–24's bomb Changsha. 7 B–25's and 21 P–40's pound railroad yards at Kaifeng. 6 B–25's and 12 P–40's hit Tengchung.

FEAF: Operations against the Carolines are restricted to snooper missions against Yap and Woleai. B–24's bomb gun positions around Manokwari and A/F at Moemi. B–25's sink large lugger in Kaiboes Bay. A–20's, B–25's, and P–39's hit troop concentrations and supplies between Aitape and Wewak at Abau, Parakaviu, Nyaparake, and E of Tadji and bomb Boram A/F and Cape Moem. Fuiloro is bombed by B–25's.

Seventh AF: P–47's bomb and strafe Tinian. 48 B–25's from Makin stage through Engebi to bomb Ponape. 47 of the MBs (1 aborts) attack

A/F facilities, AA positions, and other tgts throughout the atoll.

18 July

Eighth AF: 437 HBs attack tgts in Germany, including Hemmingstedt oil refinery, Kiel port area, Peenemunde experimental establishment, scientific HQ at Zinnowitz, T/Os of Cuxhaven, and M/Ys at Stralsund. 454 ftrs fly supporting sorties. 3 HBs and 3 ftrs are lost. 571 B–24's (in conjunction with Ninth AF and RAF BC) bomb enemy equipment and troop concentrations in spt of assault by British Second Army in Caen area. 90 RAF Spitfires fly uneventful spt for the HBs.

Ninth AF: 400-plus B–26's and A–20's hit various military tgts in spt of ground forces in Caen area, and later in day bomb rail and highway bridges beyond the frontlines. Large number of ftrs fly escort, dive-bomb gun positions at Rouen and Mantes-la-Jolie, hit military tgts in Chartres area (using rockets), attack gun positions, bridges, and other tgts in Benney-Alencon-Saint-Lo area, and fly armed rcn and ftr sweeps over wide areas of N and W France.

Twelfth AF: A–20's bomb road junction S of Campi and Sarzana and attack La Spezia area during 17/18 Jul. During the day bad weather cancels MB missions. FBs, operating on reduced scale, hit several bridges, roads, rail lines, and other comm tgts and guns N of and in battle area as US Fifth Army forces reach Leghorn.

Fifteenth AF: 200 B–24's and B–17's attack Memmingen A/F Dornier aircraft works at Manzell, and Casarsa della Delizia railroad bridge. Between 250 and 300 ftrs oppose the formations attacking tgts in Germany, beginning interception at N Adriatic coast, continuing to the tgts and back as far as Brenner Pass. 20 US aircraft are lost. HB's and escorting ftrs claim 66 ftrs shot down.

Tenth AF: 25 P–40's hit Myitkyina area. 8 P–47's attack Theinin, and 16 P–51's spt ground forces at Pyindaw. 9 B–25's bomb Myitkyina and Naungtalaw.

Fourteenth AF: In Hengyang-Tungting Lake region 30-plus P–40's strafe shipping between Chaling and Hengyang, bomb town of Hengyang, and hit the A/F and several AA positions in the area. 16 P–51's and P–40's hit river shipping from Lienchiangkou to Samshui to Sainam. 13 P–40's hit fuel dump on railroad near Kangtsun-i.

FEAF: B–24's strike Yap, bombing town and Blelatsch peninsula; several of the HBs bomb Sorol I. Bad weather prevents strikes on Vogelkop Peninsula. FBs continue to hit barges, supply routes, and troop concentrations in coastal area from Aitape to Wewak.

Seventh AF: P–47's pound Tinian and Pagan. 5 B–24's, flying out of Kwajalein, hit Wotje. 25 B–24's, staging through Eniwetok, attack Truk.

19 July

Eighth AF: More than 1,100 HBs, operating in 5 forces, attack tgts in Germany, including 2 plants producing hydrogen peroxide (an ingredient in V-weapon fuels), a chemical plant, 2 aircraft factories, 4 ball bearing plants, 6 M/Ys, 4 A/Fs, and a river dam. Attacks in the Munich area are followed, within 90 mins, by Fifteenth AF attacks. 731 ftrs, operating in 19 separate units, spt the HBs; 8 of these units afterwards strafe ground tgts, including parked aircraft, locomotives and rolling stock, and road vehicles. 15 HBs and 7 ftrs are lost. The HBs claim destruction of 6 aircraft, and the ftrs claim 17 destroyed in aerial combat and 39 on the ground.

Ninth AF: In the afternoon 262 B-26's and A-20's bomb bridges on the Loire and Seine and a fuel dump at Bruz. Ftrs provide escort and, though limited by bad weather, hit rail lines and scattered enemy installations and movements in Amiens-Tours-Chartres area and along Ghent-Brussels railroad.

Twelfth AF: Weather again restricts MB operations, but in late afternoon B-26's hit bridges at Piacenza and Ostiglia. B-25's bomb bridge at Sassuolo. FBs are limited to a few railroad tgts as US Fifth Army takes Leghorn and moves N.

Fifteenth AF: More than 400 B-17's and B-24's bomb an ordnance depot, an aircraft factory, a motor works, and an A/F in the Munich area. P-51's and P-38's fly more than 300 sorties in spt. Enemy ftr opposition is weak but flak is heavy and accurate. 16 US airplanes are shot down and several are missing.

Tenth AF: 30-plus P-40's and P-51's hit Myitkyina area and spt ground forces near Kamaing. Myitkyina is also bombed by 9 B-25's.

Fourteenth AF: 80-plus P-40's hit shipping in Tungting Lake area, attack T/Os, supply areas, and troop concentrations around Hengyang, bomb radio station, storage facilities, and shipping at Changsha, hit A/F at Siangtan, and sink about 15 sampans between Changsha and Siangtan. 31

P-40's and P-51's bomb and strafe Samshui town and dock area and hit several troop compounds in Lienchiangkou vicinity. 4 P-40's over NE Indochina coast claim 25 junks sunk.

FEAF: B-24's, striking in 2 waves, attack A/F on Yap. Several of the B-24's become separated from the formations and bomb Ngulu and Sorol Is. Weather again cancels strikes on Vogelkop Peninsula area. FB's hit stores, gun positions, and T/Os along Dandriwad R and spt Allied ground forces in Sarmi-Sawar sector.

Seventh AF: P-47's continue to bomb and strafe Tinian.

20 July

Eighth AF: Over 1,200 HBs strike numerous objectives in C Germany, in Erfurt-Leipzig area and near Mainz. Tgts include 4 aircraft and aircraft engine factories, a ball bearing plant, a motor vehicle works, 5 A/Fs, 2 synthetic oil plants, an optical instruments works, an armament factory, 5 M/Ys, and the cities of Koblenz, Bad Nauheim, and Bad Salzungen. 727 ftrs spt the Eighth's HBs and afterwards several units strafe ground tgts. 19 HBs and 8 ftrs are lost. HBs claim 6 aircraft destroyed while the ftrs claim 11 destroyed in the air and 11 on the ground.

Ninth AF: Weather forbids morning operations. In afternoon 62 MBs and LBs strike Senonches fuel dump and Chaulnes M/Y. Ftrs escort bmrs and transports and fly armed rcn against rail lines, bridges, and gun positions S of frontlines.

Twelfth AF: XII AF Trg and Repl Cmd is disbanded in Algeria. MBs continue to pound Po Valley bridges in or near Ostiglia, Parma, Mantua, Ferrara, and Alessandria. FBs again hit tgts N of battle area, concentrating on rail lines and destroying or damaging large number of railroad cars as US Fifth Army forces push to point SE of Pisa.

Fifteenth AF: Around 450 B–17's and B–24's bomb A/F at Memmingen, and A/F, Zeppelin works, and aircraft factory at Friedrichshafen. P–38's and P–51's provide escort and, with HBs, claim 19 airplanes shot down.

Tenth AF: A few P–40's attack tgts in Myitkyina area.

Fourteenth AF: In Tungting Lake area 11 B–24's bomb E half of Changsha, causing heavy destruction. 140-plus P–40's and P–51's attack river shipping and road traffic at several locations throughout the region, pound supply villages S of Changsha and Sinshih, bomb motor pool at Tsungyang, hit warehouse area at Siangtan, and attack troop compounds and gun positions N of Hengyang and at Leiyang and Chaling.

FEAF: B–24's bomb W part of Yap town. Other B–24's hit A/F and AA guns at Manokwari and AA at Moemi. B–25's hit shipping off Sorong, in Kaiboes Bay, and off Misool I, and bomb Kasim I. A–20's spt Allied ground forces in Sarmi sector. B–24's bomb Namlea A/F and shipping in Kayeli Bay. B–25's hit shipping at Dili. A–20's and a B–25 bomb supply dumps at Cape Moem, Wom, and Sauri while FBs hit T/Os along Yakamul coastal road and troops on Kairiru I.

Seventh AF: P–47's pound Tinian. B–25's from Engebi bomb Ponape.

21 July

Eighth AF: 960 HBs, attacking in 4 forces, bomb tgts in Germany, among them 4 aircraft plants, 2 ball bearing plants, and numerous T/Os in Duren area, Stuttgart area, and 11 other towns and cities, including Munich and Saarbrucken. 711 ftrs, operating as 33 tac units, execute escort assignments and later ftrs from 7 units strafe ground tgts, destroying a small number of parked aircraft and rail and road transport tgts. 31 HBs and 10 ftrs are lost. HBs claim 9 airplanes destroyed, and ftrs claim 6 destroyed in the air and 3 on the ground.

Ninth AF: Weather prevents all combat operations except for 1 ftr gp which is dispatched on armed rcn but is recalled before reaching the Continent. Less than 15 rcn and evacuation sorties are flown.

Twelfth AF: Weather cancels MB operations. LBs hit supply dump while FBs attack rail and road bridges in Po Valley and hit rail lines N of battleline which is pushing into the Arno R Valley SE of Pisa.

Fifteenth AF: 362 B–17's and B–24's bomb Brux synthetic oil refinery and M/Y at Mestre. More than 100 other HBs are forced to abort due to bad weather. P–38's and P–51's provide escort.

Tenth AF: 6 B–25's bomb railroad at Mohnyin and 1 hits town of Naba.

Fourteenth AF: 41 P–40's hit town area, A/F, trucks, river shipping, and troops at Changsha; trucks, horses, and junks at Sinshih; and troop concentrations, arty sites, and pillboxes at Hengyang.

FEAF: B–24's again pound Yap I, concentrating on the A/F. Ftrs, many dropping phosphorus bombs on the HB formation, attack fiercely but ineffectively; the B–24's claim 7 ftrs shot down. Other B–24's bomb AA positions and A/F at Manokwari. A–20's hit barracks at Nabire. P–39's hit caves and barge hideouts on N coast of Biak I and spt ground forces along Verkam R. B–25's hit shipping at several points around the long coastline of Vogelkop Peninsula. B–25's and A–20's pound But, and P–39's bomb bridge nearby. P–47's follow with attack on But and also hit Wewak jetties and Kairiru I.

Seventh AF: P–47's attack enemy forces on Tinian. 28 B–24's, staging through Eniwetok, pound Truk. US Marines and Army troops land on Guam.

22 July

Ninth AF: 1 gp of LBs and 2 gps of MBs attack rail bridge at Bourth and fuel dumps at Foret de Conches and Flers. 4 gps of FBs fly armed rcn and rail cutting missions during late evening. 1 gp escorts IX BC. Ftrs of IX TAC escort over 100 C–47's on supply-evacuation run to the Continent, and provide cover over battle area.

Twelfth AF: Weather again curtails operations. During night and day operations A–20's carry out armed rcn of Lucca, Florence, Genoa, and Milan areas, bombing scattered motor transport, and attack munitions factory. B–25's bomb bridges at Ronco Scrivia and Cogoli. FBs hit roads, railroads, bridges, gun positions, trains, and vehicles in and N of battle area, and strafe airplanes at Bergamo A/F.

Fifteenth AF: 76 P–38's and 58 P–51's begin second Fifteenth AF shuttle missions, attacking A/Fs at Zilistea and Buzau (claiming destruction of 56 enemy airplanes) and landing at FRANTIC bases in the USSR. 458 B–17's and B–24's (with ftr escorts) bomb oil refinery at Ploesti and other HBs hit alternate tgts of Verciorova M/Y, Orsova railroad bridge, and Kragujevac M/Y.

Tenth AF: 14 P–40's attack forces in Myitkyina area. 7 B–25's bomb railroad at Mohnyin while 2 hit storage sheds at Maingna.

Fourteenth AF: 120-plus P–40's and P–51's attack town area, A/F, railroad yards, and shipping at Hengyang, bomb towns of Chaling, Yuhsien, and Chuchou, hit river shipping, troops, trucks, and T/Os in areas around Changsha, Kiaotow, Siangtan, and Sinshih, and hit troop compounds and shipping at Yuhsien. 25 B–24's bomb Changsha, causing heavy damage. 31 P–40's and P–51's blast Tsingyun and strafe about 40 junks to the S of town. 4 P–40's sink several large junks off NE Indochina coast.

FEAF: B–24's again attack A/F on Yap. B–24's, B–25's, A–20's, and an assortment of FBs direct their main attacks against several shipping terminals in the Vogelkop Peninsula area, sink sub chaser off Morotai, bomb Saumlakki, and hit But A/F and personnel areas, barge hideouts, supply and ammo dumps, bridges and roads at, and to the W of, Wewak.

Seventh AF: P–47's from Saipan, using fire-bombs for the first time, hit Tinian and Pagan. Makin-based B–25's pound Ponape.

Eleventh AF: 2 B–25's flying negative shipping search encounter bmr which evades contact.

23 July

Eighth AF: 243 HBs attack A/Fs

at Juvincourt-et-Damary, Laon/Couvron, Laon/Athies, and Creil, while a single B-24 bombs T/O. 1 HB is lost. Ftrs fly 187 sorties in spt of the HBs. No enemy aircraft are encountered.

Ninth AF: 330-plus A-20's and B-26's bomb rail bridges along Argentan-Paris and Lisieux-Bernay-Evreux railroads, and hit fuel dumps at Foret de Conches. Ftrs escort bmrs, attack rail lines, enemy installations, and movements in Argentan-Alencon-Chartres-Evreux areas, and bomb bridges, strongpoints, and a supply dump in spt of US First Army.

Twelfth AF: A-20's bomb and strafe motor transport in Po Valley during 22/23 Jul. B-25's and B-26's hit bridges and bridge approaches in the Valley, at or near Antoniassi, Acqui, Molare, Ferrara, Ostiglia, Borgoforte, and Cervo. FBs, operating in small numbers, hit comm lines between battle area (along Pisa-Florence line) and Po Valley.

Fifteenth AF: 42 B-24's bomb Berat oil refinery. 15 P-51's provide tgt cover for the HBs and afterwards strafe roads and T/Os in Yugoslavia near Albanian border.

Tenth AF: 100-plus FBs hit enemy positions in Myitkyina area, spt ground forces at Szigahtawng, bomb Kamaing and Mogaung areas, blast troops and supplies at Kalang, Kyungon, and Tinzai, and hit T/Os at Pegu, Namma, Sahmaw, Taungni, and Hopin. 9 B-25's hit Myitkyina and Naungtalaw areas while 8 bomb Namting.

Fourteenth AF: 62 P-40's attack warehouses, trucks, and troops in Changsha-Sinshih-Fulinpu area, bomb A/F and river craft at Siangtan, hit enemy-held areas of Hengyang, and

strafe and bomb troop compounds and villages N of it. 6 B-25's and 21 P-40's hit warehouses and railroad yards in Yellow R area. 10 P-40's hit Japanese positions on Salween front in spt of Chinese forces.

FEAF: B-24's again bomb Yap I, hitting town area and A/F. A/Fs and shipping terminals over widespread areas of Vogelkop Peninsula and nearby islands are pounded by B-24's, B-25's, A-20's, and FBs. But A/F is again the main tgt in NE New Guinea. Comm, supplies, barges, and troop concentrations from Wewak to Yakamul are also bombed and strafed throughout the day.

Seventh AF: Saipan-based P-47's hit Tinian. B-25's begin arriving on Saipan. B-25's from Makin attack Nauru. B-24's staging through Eniwetok, bomb Truk while others, flying out of Kwajalein, hit Wotje.

24 July

Eighth AF: Eighth AF HBs are scheduled to participate in US First Army offensive (Operation COBRA) to penetrate German defenses W of Saint-Lo and secure Coutances. Bad weather causes the ground forces to delay attack until next day, and cloud conditions cause 1,102 HB aborts. In all, 352 HBs attack primary tgt area near Saint-Lo, and 132 bomb other points, including road intersections and railway lines. 405 ftrs of 10 gps fly spt sorties. Later 3 of the P-47 gps strafe ground tgts. 3 ftrs and 3 bmrs are lost.

Ninth AF: 11 gps of bmrs scheduled to participate in Operation COBRA have missions cancelled due to weather. 5 gps of MBs hit rail bridges and 5 gps of MBs and LBs strike 3 fuel and ammo dumps. Ftrs fly escort to IX BC, fly area cover, bomb installations in Laval-Nantes-Le Mans-Chartres areas, and hit bridges and supply dumps in spt of US First Army.

Twelfth AF: MBs attack bridges at Chivasso, Peschiera del Garda, Imperia, and Ronco Scrivia, and viaduct at Ovada. A–20's hit ammo supplies while FBs attack rail lines in Po Valley, destroying and damaging numerous railway cars, as US Fifth Army begins regrouping along the Arno.

Fifteenth AF: More than 200 B–17's and B–24's attack tank repair and ball bearing works in Turin, the harbor at Genoa, A/Fs at Valence/La Tresorerie and Les Chanoines, and troop concentrations at Sjenica, Prijepolje, Pljevlja, and Andrijevica. Ftrs provide escort and strafe Prizren area.

Tenth AF: 14 P–51's hit Kamaing and Mogaung areas while 28 P–40's hit Myitkyina. 8 B–25's bomb Mohnyin and Naungtalaw.

Fourteenth AF: 13 B–25's and 20 P–40's bomb railroad facilities at Sienning. 22 P–40's pound Pailochi A/F, destroying about 30 airplanes and causing heavy destruction in general. 9 B–25's and 20 P–40's hit town of Puchi, causing several fires. 46 P–40's hit river and road traffic, enemy concentrations, and T/Os at Changsha, Sinshih, Fulinpu, Hengshan, Liling, Leiyang, and Hengyang. In Canton area 7 P–51's dive-bomb White Cloud A/F and town of Tsingyun. 3 P–40's on armed rcn bomb Ben Thuy railroad yards and strafe junks and barges in coastal areas.

FEAF: Operations in the Caroline Is are restricted to snooper strikes by HBs. Bad weather cancels scheduled strikes in Vogelkop Peninsula area. B–24's bomb AA positions at Saumlakki. 18 A–20's and a B–25 bomb But A/F, P–47's hit supply areas at Sauri, and P–39's bomb and strafe bridges and supply dumps in Suain area.

Seventh AF: P–47's hit Tinian, on which US Marines land, and Rota. B–25's from Engebi bomb Ponape.

Eleventh AF: 2 B–25's fly a negative shipping search.

25 July

Eighth AF: HBs spt US First Army assault (Operation COBRA) with saturation bombing in VII Corps area in Marigny-Saint-Gilles region, just W of Saint-Lo. 1,495 HBs attack primary tgt and 13 bomb alternate tgt. Due to personnel error, bombs from 35 HBs fall within US lines. 102 US troops, including Gen McNair, are killed and 380 wounded. 485 ftrs execute escort assignments, including protection of Ninth AF MBs. Afterward 4 of the 10 gps strafe ground tgts, and 2 gps sweep inland and engage German ftrs. 5 HBs and 3 ftrs are lost to AA fire. Ftrs claim 12 aircraft destroyed in the air and 2 on the ground. Late in the afternoon 106 HBs dispatched to bomb tgt in Brussels area are recalled because of heavy cloud formations.

Ninth AF: During the morning 11 gps of MBs and LBs attack tac tgts in vicinity of Saint-Lo in spt of US First Army. In afternoon 4 gps bomb bridges on the Seine and Loire. 42 MBs of IX BC, repeating errors of previous day, short-bomb behind US lines. Casualties again are concentrated in 30th Inf Div. Ftrs strafe and bomb military tgts in Saint-Lo area in spt of COBRA, fly area patrol and sweeps S of battle area, and carry out armed rcn against installations in Laval-Ghent-Amiens areas.

Twelfth AF: A-20's hit storage dump and rail lines while MBs pound bridges in NW Italy at Borgo San Dalmazzo, Fossano, Albenga, Casale Monferrato, Cervo, Legnano, Rovigo, and Chivasso. FBs continue to attack comm in Po Valley, hitting numerous tgts and completely destroying railroad bridge at Crema.

Fifteenth AF: 420 B-17's and B-24's bomb Hermann Goring tank works in Linz while other HBs hit Villach M/Y and T/Os in Austria and Yugoslavia. Ftrs provide escort and carry out sweeps. 175-200 enemy ftrs oppose the attacks. 21 US aircraft are lost. HBs and ftrs claim over 60 ftrs shot down. Operating from Russian FRANTIC bases, 34 P-51's and 33 P-38's attack A/F at Mielec and return to Russia.

Tenth AF: 24 P-40's and P-51's hit tgts around Myitkyina, Kamaing, and Mogaung.

Fourteenth AF: 24 B-24's bomb Yoyang, blasting storage area and railroad yards. 51 P-40's and P-51's attack road and river traffic, troop compounds and cav units at Chaling, Siangsiang, Changsha, Siangyin, and Sinshih and NW of Hengyang. 27 P-40's escorting the B-24's over Yoyang claim 6 interceptors shot down. 11 FBs spt Chinese ground forces in Salween area.

FEAF: B-24's bomb A/F and other tgts on Woleai. Bad weather again cancels strikes in Vogelkop Peninsula, but TCs complete 48 missions to Biak I despite the weather. Comm and

troop concentration along coast in general area of Wewak are attacked throughout the day.

Seventh AF: P-47's continue to hit Tinian and Pagan. B-24's, based at Kwajalein, bomb Truk.

26 July

Ninth AF: Weather forces recall of several gps of MBs and LBs, assigned to spt US First Army, but about 160 aircraft manage to bomb fuel dump at Senonches with good results. Ftrs escort bmrs, fly cover over assault area, carry out close spt for ground troops in Saint-Lo area, and fly armed rcn in Poix, Amiens, Chartres, Laval, and Angers areas.

Twelfth AF: During 25/26 Jul A-20's bomb roads and motor transport in Vado Ligure area and hit fuel supplies during following day. B-25's and B-26's hit bridges in N Italy at Ronco Scrivia, Vado, Asti, Ostiglia, Carasco, Verona, and Poggio Renatico. FBs attack road and rail bridges in N Italy at several points, strafe and bomb many gun positions, destroy or damage over 20 airplanes at Valence A/F, and hit numerous T/Os.

Fifteenth AF: Ftrs on second shuttle mission leave Russian FRANTIC bases, strafe enemy aircraft in Bucharest-Ploesti area, and return to bases in Italy. 330-plus B-17's and B-24's attack Wiener Neudorf aircraft factory, A/F at Markersdorf, Thalerhof, Zwolfaxing, and Bad Voslau, and T/Os in Vienna area. Also hit are Szombathely A/F and oil storage at Berat. Ftrs fly escort and carry out patrols and sweeps in Brod-Zagreb and Ploesti-Bucharest areas. HBs and ftrs claim over 70 airplanes shot down.

Tenth AF: 42 P-40's pound Myitkyina area while 16 P–51's hit Mogaung and Kamaing sectors. About 20 other FBs hit T/Os at Hopin, Bhamo, Myothit, Wuntho, and N part of Mandalay. 9 B–25's bomb storage sheds at Mohnyin.

Fourteenth AF: 27 B–25's and 3 P–40's blast town of Tengchung, breaching SE wall in several places. 32 P–40's and P–38's attack T/Os throughout Tengchung, Lungling, and Mangshih areas. 97 P–40's attack troops, horses, trucks, fortified points river shipping, and other T/Os at numerous locations in or near Siangtan, Changsha, Hengshan, Fulinpu, Leiyang, Pingkiang, Hengyang, Chaling, and Nanyo, A/F at Hengyang is also bombed.

FEAF: B–24's again hit supply areas, comm, and other tgts on Woleai. Other B–24's bomb A/Fs at Babo and Ransiki. A–20's and B–25's, along with RAAF FBs, hit troop concentrations, small shipping, mortar positions, shore guns, and other T/Os along Hollandia-Aitape-Wewak coastline. B–25's bomb Langgoer.

Seventh AF: P–47's and B–25's from Saipan pound Tinian. B–25's from Engebi attack Ponape.

27 July

Eighth AF: 67 B–24's bomb coastal battery at Gravelines, GAF signals equipment at Brussels, and oil installations and industrial plants at Ghent. 79 HBs return to base without bombing due to low-lying haze which obscures coastal tgts. 3 ftr gps perform escort duty and strafe ground tgts, destroying aircraft, 2 vehicles, 2 locomotives, and some rolling stock. Only single ftr is lost.

Ninth AF: Bad weather causes recall of MBs and LBs sent to bomb Loire and Seine bridges. Ftrs attack rail lines enemy installations and movements NW and SW of Paris, and bomb gun positions and other military tgts in the Coutances-Saint-Lo area in spt of US ground forces which break through W of Saint-Lo.

Twelfth AF: A–20's fly night patrols on 26/27 Jul over Po Valley, bombing lights and vehicles at Piacenza, Modena, and Verona. Both MBs and FBs concentrate on bridges in Po Valley and NW Italy throughout the day. Numerous hits are scored on bridges and other tgts, including parked airplanes, guns, and railroads.

Fifteenth AF: 366 B–17's and B–24's bomb armament works at Budapest. 24 other B–24's attack Pecs M/Y. P–38's and P–51's escort the Budapest mission.

Tenth AF: 40-plus FBs hit Taungni, Myitkyina, Kamaing-Mogaung area, and bridge at Sahmaw.

Fourteenth AF: 17 P–40's hit river and lake shipping S of Yogang and in Siangtan area, strafe truck columns S of Changsha, and bomb and strafe troops, horses, and compounds in Nanyo area.

FEAF: B–24's hit A/F on Woleai and supply areas on Mariaon and Tagaulap Is. Other B–24's bomb A/Fs at Lolobata and Miti while B–25's hit Galela A/F. B–24's and B–25's bomb shipping and air facilities at Ransiki, Moemi, and Babo, hit freighter in Kaiboes Bay, and bomb AA positions at Kokas, while A–20's blast fuel dumps at Nabire. P–39's strafe concentrations and small vessels along W coast of Geelvink Bay. A–20's, B–25's, and FBs hit troop concentrations, supply dumps, gun positions, barges, and a variety of other tgts along coast from Aitape to Wewak to Cape Moem. B–24's bomb Laha, Namlea, Cape Chater, and Dili.

Seventh AF: P–47's and B–25's from Saipan hit Tinian. B–24's from the Marshalls bomb Truk. B–25's based at Makin, hit Jaluit.

28 July

Eighth AF: 653 B–17's bomb synthetic oil plant at Merseburg while 57 others bomb Wiesbaden M/Ys and aircraft engine factory at Taucha. 437 ftrs fly supporting sorties and strafe ground tgts, destroying 8 locomotives and 7 trucks. 7 B–17's and 2 P–51's are lost. Bmr and ftr claims of aircraft destroyed total 7. 111 B–24's dispatched to bomb tgts in Brussels are recalled, along with escorting ftr gp, because of complete cloud cover over the tgt. 180 B–24's dispatched against tgts in France fail to bomb tgts because of heavy cloud. Ftrs fly 237 sorties in spt, and also strafe trains, destroying 2 locomotives and some rolling stock. No aircraft are lost.

Ninth AF: Gen Schramm assumes cmd of IX ADC. IX BC operates in spt of US First Army, bombing rail bridges, supply dumps and ammo dumps in Foret de Conches, Dreux, and Le Mans areas. Ftrs escort bmrs, fly armed rcn in Le Mans, Laval, and Dreux areas and furnish cover over assault areas and armed columns.

Twelfth AF: LBs bomb scattered lights and vehicles in Po Valley during 27/28 Jul. During day LBs, MBs, and FBs hit tgts in Po Valley, concentrating on bridges. Some FBs attack motor transport in Rhone Valley.

Fifteenth AF: 345 B–17's and B–24's attack 2 oil refineries at Ploesti and M/Y at Florina. P–51's and P–38's provide spt for the Ploesti raid.

Tenth AF: More than 100 FBs hit Myitkyina, Kamaing, Mogaung, and Taungni areas. 16 others attack T/Os at Bhamo, Indaw, Mohnyin, and hit bridge at Sihet. 8 B–25's pound troop area at Sihet.

Fourteenth AF: 18 B–25's, with ftr spt, pound Yoyang railroad yards. Other B–25's in gps of 1 to 3 hit Yellow R bridge and White Cloud, Tien Ho, and Hankow A/Fs. 18 P–40's hit Pailochi A/F, destroying several airplanes. 30-plus P–40's and P–51's on armed rcn hit troop concentrations, river and road traffic and other T/Os at Leiyang, Chaling, Chinlanshih, and in Tungting Lake area.

FEAF: Tgts in Woleai I are bombed by 4 sqs of B–24's; A/F and supply area are well covered. B–24's and A–20's pound A/Fs at Manokwari and Babo, bivouac areas at Kasoeri, and shipping in Kaimana Bay. P–39's hit Windissi and other Geelvink Bay villages. A–20's and FBs blast stores, troop concentrations, comm tgts, barges, and T/Os in Wewak, Cape Moem, and But areas. Laha and Cape Chater are hit by B–24's while B–25's bomb supply dumps at Maumere.

Seventh AF: B–25's and P–47's based on Saipan bomb and strafe Tinian.

29 July

Eighth AF: 568 B–17's bomb synthetic oil plant at Merseburg and 32 bomb T/Os in 2 nearby towns. Ftrs of 9 gps fly 477 sorties in spt of HBs; 2 gps later strafe ground tgts. A second force of 444 B–17's bombs oil refinery near Bremen. 2 P–51 gps fly escort. A third force of 74 B–24's escorted by 2 ftr gps attacks A/Fs at Laon/Couvrron and Juvincourt-et-Damary. Overall, 14 HBs and 7 ftrs are lost. Claims of airplanes destroyed amount to 26 by the HBs and 20 by the ftrs (including a jet aircraft near Bremen.)

Ninth AF: Bad weather cancels all IX BC missions. Ftrs fly armed rcn in Rouen, Amiens, Beaumont-en-Beine, Tours, Vendome, and Le Mans areas, furnish assault area cover, carry out armed rcn of enemy installations and movement in battle area, and provide cover in spt of US First Army.

Twelfth AF: Weather cancels MB operations. FBs, operating on reduced scale, hit buildings at Diano Marina and bridges, rail lines, A/Fs, and vehicles in N Italy.

Fifteenth AF: Weather cancels all bombing operations. 14 P–38's, taking off from Russian bases, sweep Kecskemet area.

Tenth AF: About 100 FBs bomb Myitkyina, Kamaing, and Mogaung areas and strafe Indaw. More than 20 others attack tgts at Myothit, Chyahkan, Mainghka, Nawna and Nansawlaw, and hit bridge at Panghkam. Troop area at Naungtalaw is bombed by 9 B–25's.

Fourteenth AF: 26 B–24's bomb Samah Bay storage area. 27 B–25's hit Yulin harbor, Hankow A/F, Kaifeng railroad yards, and town of Tengchung. 80-plus P–40's and P–51's on armed rcn hit bridges, troops, supplies, and river, road, and rail traffic throughout vast area including towns of Liling, Sinsiang, Hengshan, Changsha, Siangtan, Chaling, Liuyang, and Chuchou.

FEAF: B–24's bomb supply areas on Woleai I; nearby islands of Mariaon and Tagaulap are also hit. Other B–24's bomb A/Fs at Boela, Namlea, and Cape Chater, and pound Moemi, Sagan, Otawiri, and Urarom. MBs hit oil tgts at Karaka, shipping off Sorong and Cape Fatagar, and a supply village W of Babo. P–39's bomb Windissi and strafe troop concentrations along W shore of Geelvink Bay for third consecutive day. In NE New Guinea bmrs and ftrs continue pounding the N coast, hitting troops, bridges and stores at Wewak and along Harech Creek, and T/Os in Yakamul area.

Twentieth AF: Over 70 B–29's out of Chengtu bomb Showa Steel Works at Anshan and harbor at Taku. The first VHB to be shot down on a combat mission falls to 5 ftrs near Chenghsien (which the B–29 bombs after engine trouble causes abort from primary mission). Another B–29 bombs Chinwangtao before making forced landing at friendly field near Ankang.

Seventh AF: P–47's continue to hit Tinian. B–24's hit Truk and B–25's attack Ponape.

Eleventh AF: 3 B–24's fly bombing and rcn runs over Shimushu and Paramushiru sites including Kurabu Cape installations.

30 July

Eighth AF: HQ issues order regularizing under VIII AF Comp Cmd certain special and prov units carrying out special tac activities. This is result of suggestion made on 2 Mar by Gen Doolittle, CG Eighth AF, that units engaged in CARPETBAGGER, H2X (blind-bombing), night leaflet, and weather missions be put under centralized control.

Ninth AF: 450-plus A–20's and B–26's bomb defenses in Chaumont area in spt of US First Army. Ftrs fly escort, cover assault area and armd columns, and carry out armd rcn in Orleans-Paris area. IX TCC flies supply and evacuation missions to Continent, using over 200 transport airplanes.

Twelfth AF: During 29/30 Jul LBs bomb Savona and surrounding areas. Overcast in W Po Valley causes some MB aborts but several bridges at Ovada, Bistagno, Cherasco, and Ferrara are successfully attacked. FBs attack road and rail bridges in N Italy, hit shipping between Savona and Ventimiglia, silence 8 flak guns at Ferrara bridge, and hit several transportation T/Os.

Fifteenth AF: 300-plus B–17's and B–24's bomb Duna A/F and aircraft factory at Budapest, and M/Ys at Brod. P–38's and P–51's escort the missions.

Tenth AF: 30-plus FBs attack Myitkyina and Kamaing-Mogaung area and hit bridge at Sihet. Japanese cmdr at Myitkyina orders withdrawal and commits suicide.

Fourteenth AF: 11 B–24's pound town of Wuchang. 70-plus P–40's and P–51's attack bridge and town area at Liling, railroad yards at Hsuchang, and troop concentrations, storage, and road, river and rail traffic in areas around Yungfengshih, Puchou, Hengyang, Chuchou, Chaling, Tungting Lake, and Liuyang. More than 20 P–40's and P–38's hit shipping and road traffic around Hanoi, Lang Son, Dong Dang, Mon Cay, and Campha Port.

FEAF: Supply area on Woleai I

is again bombed by B–24's. Other B–24's and P–38's attack A/F and oil installations at Boela while more P–38's attack shipping off E Ceram, off Amboina, and near Talaga. B–25's hit A/Fs at Penfoei and Koepang. B–24's hit Morotai I. P–39's spt Allied ground forces on Biak I and continue to patrol W Geelvink Bay, hitting barges in Bentoni Bay and troops at Idorra. Allied forces (TF TYPHOON) land on N coast of Vogelkop Peninsula near Mar. The landings, made without preparatory bombardment to achieve surprise, meet no opposition. Bmrs and ftrs continue to pound troop concentrations, barges, ships, fuel dumps, comm and other tgts between Wewak and Aitape.

Seventh AF: B–25's and P–47's from Saipan again hit Tinian. B–25's from Makin bomb Jaluit.

31 July

Eighth AF: 651 B–17's supported by 5 P–51 gps bomb M/Ys at Munich and aero engine plants at Munich-Allach, A/F at Schleissheim, and scattered T/Os. 8 P–51 gps give withdrawal spt. 447 B–24's, escorted beyond Dutch coast by 3 ftr gps, bomb chemical works and city at Ludwigshafen, and SW part of city of Mannheim. 85 B–24's escorted by a P–47 gp bomb A/Fs at Laon/Athies and Creil. 667 ftrs complete missions in spt of HBs and in weather scouting duties. 10 B–17's are lost at Munich and 6 B–24's at Ludwigshafen. Ftrs suffer 3 losses.

Ninth AF: Around 500 A–20's and B–26's attack bridges on the Seine, Loire, Mayenne, and Ruisseau la Forge Rivers and a fuel dump at

Foret de la Guerche. Ftrs fly armd rcn of activities in Dieppe-Rouen areas, escort bmrs, provide armd column cover, dive-bomb military tgts in spt of US First Army and fly a few night intruder missions over enemy territory.

Twelfth AF: Weather grounds MBs. FBs hit several bridges in W Po Valley while ftrs strafe A/Fs with good results. The FBs also destroy around 50 railroad cars and damage numerous others.

Fifteenth AF: 360-plus B–17's and B–24's, with ftr escort, bomb 2 oil refineries at Bucharest, 1 each at Ploesti and Doicesti, and oil storage at Targoviste.

Tenth AF: 20 FBs hit Myitkyina, 11 attack Kamaing-Mogaung area, 12 bomb bridge at Mohnyin, 14 spt ground forces near Myitkyina, and 11 others hit T/Os at Sahmaw, Bilumyo, and Pinhe. 9 B–25's pound Hopin troop area. Japanese are in retreat down Tiddim road.

Fourteenth AF: 12 B–24's bomb Wuchang railroad yards. B–25's, operating individually or in pairs, bomb Hengshan, Siangtan, and Hankow and attack Tien Ho, White Cloud, Hengyang, and Wuchang A/Fs. 60-plus P–40's and P–51's attack troop compounds, town areas and road and river traffic at several locations in or near Changsha, Hengyang, Kaishowkiao, Liling, Luchi, and Liuchow.

FEAF: B–24's again strike Woleai. A/Fs at Lolobata and Galela also are hit by B–24's. P–39's continue to hit villages on W coast of Geelvink Bay. In NE New Guinea FBs continue pounding Japanese concentrations and T/Os on N coast, particularly between Wewak and Yakamul.

A–20's spt Australian ground forces in Hansa Bay area, hitting troop positions W of Sepik R and troop concentrations at Singarin and Kopa.

Seventh AF: B–25's and P–47's based on Saipan bomb and strafe Tinian. B–25's from Makin pound Nauru. B–24's from the Marshalls bomb Truk.

1 August

Eighth AF: 191 B–17's drop supplies to French interior forces; 3 P–51 gps furnish escort. 75 B–17's bomb A/F at Tours; escort is flown by 1 P–51 gp. 387 B–17's escorted by 1 P–51 gp attack 5 A/Fs and a railway bridge in area S and SW of Paris. A fourth force of B–17's (320) is dispatched to bomb tgts in Paris environs. Bad weather causes over 100 aborts but 219 planes bomb 4 A/Fs, 5 bridges, railway facilities and a rail and highway junction, mostly T/Os. 3 ftr gps provide spt. The fifth force of 100 B–24's, sent against 8 V-weapon sites in NW France, runs afoul of bad weather which causes multiple aborts. 34 of the planes manage to bomb 3 sites. Another force of 156 B–24's is dispatched against 7 V-weapon sites in same area plus oil storage depot at Rouen. Bad weather prevents attacks on the sites but 85 HBs bomb the oil depot and railroad junction nearby. 4 ftr gps strafe rail and ground vehicles during course of day's actions. 5 bmrs and 3 ftrs are lost during the day.

Ninth AF: XIX TAC becomes operational in conjunction with the US Third Army on the Continent. The Ninth's ftr and FB gps (Ninth AF refers to them collectively as FB gps) are divided between IX and XIX TACs.

About 250 MBs and LBs bomb rail bridges at Mezieres-sur-Seine, Maintenon, Les Ponts-de-Ce, Chartres, Cinq Mars-la-Pile, Bouchmaine, Nogent-sur-Loir, and Bourth. XIX TAC ftrs carry out armd rcn and rail bombing missions in Alencon, Dreux, Chartres, Nogent-sur-Loir, Le Mans, Sable-sur-Sarthe, Laval and Sille-le-Philippe areas, while IX TAC ftrs fly armd column and assault area cover, and armed rcn in battle areas.

Twelfth AF: MBs hit bridges in Po Valley, N of Genoa, at Canneto sull'Oglio, Balossa, Vigone, Ronco Scrivia, and Ovada, and M/Y at Imperia. FBs concentrate on A/F in Po Valley (at Villanova d'Albenga, Airasca, and Venaria Reale) hit small landing grounds throughout the area, and attack several comm tgts including roads, rail lines, bridges, and railroad cars.

Fifteenth AF: Bad weather limits operations to rcn missions.

Tenth AF: 8 B–25's bomb several points along railway from Naba to Hopin. FBs attack Shwegu, hit bridges in Mohnyin area, and spt ground forces in Myitkyina and Taungni sectors.

Fourteenth AF: 8 B–25's bomb Wuchang A/F. 2 others hit town of Siangyin. More than 90 P–40's and P–51's on armed rcn hit trucks, troops, supplies, and river shipping in and around Hengyang, Leiyang, Sinshih, Hengshan, Liling, Changsha, and Siangyin. AF and railroad yards at Hengyang are also bombed.

FEAF: B–24's bomb Utagal. Weather cancels scheduled strikes against Vogelkop Peninsula area, but a few MBs hit shipping in islands to the W, sinking luggers off Kaboe and Salawat Is and strafing troops on shores of MacCluer Gulf. The weather also restricts operations against Wewak area; a few P–39's strafe coastal trails. B–24's bomb Namlea A/F.

AAFPOA: Army Air Forces Pacific Ocean Areas is activated at Hickam Field with Gen Millard Harmon as CG. Harmon is to be responsible to Gen Robert C Richardson, Jr, CG, USAFPOA, for logistics and administration, and to Adm Nimitz, CINCPOA, for operations of AAF air units except those of Twentieth AF. Harmon also is Dep Cmdr of Twentieth AF and is responsible directly to Gen Arnold in all matters affecting the Twentieth in POA.

Seventh AF: Seventh AF comes under control of AAFPOA. Makin-based B–25's hit Ponape. Organized resistance ends on Tinian. P–47's and P–61's on Saipan will continue steady daylight and night combat patrols and strikes almost around the clock to the fall of Guam on 10 Aug. Most of the P–47 flying is devoted to neutralizing A/Fs on Pagan and Rota and to direct spt of Marine and Army forces fighting on Saipan, Guam, and Tinian.

2 August

Eighth AF: 2d and 3d Bomb Divs fly 2 late afternoon operations against tgts in France. 289 B–17's and B–24's attack 12 tgts including oil dumps and depots, supply depots, railway bridges, junctions, canal lock, A/Fs, and M/Ys. 3 P–51 gps provide escort, 2 of them later strafing rail and highway traffic NE of Paris. In the second mission, over 390 HBs attack 15 V-weapon sites, 5 bridges, an A/F, and a rail junction and bridge.

5 P–51 gps provide escort and 3 of these gps later strafe rail transportation tgts. Overall losses for the day's operations total 6 HBs and 6 ftrs, most to AA fire. No enemy aircraft are encountered.

Ninth AF: IX BC halts bombing of bridges, fuel dumps, and similar tgts in Brittany except on request of 12th Army Gp, as US Third Army wants use of bridges access to all fuel they may find in their adv across France. Around 300 A–20's and B–26's attack bridges at Mezieres-sur-Seine, Mainvillers, Cinq Mars-la-Pile, Nantes, and Lisle, and ammo dumps at Caudebec-les-Elbeuf and Le Lude. Ftrs fly armed rcn in wide areas surrounding Paris and SW as far as Laval, escort IX BC, and provide cover for armd columns and close spt for ground forces.

Twelfth AF: MBs strike at bridges near border between Italy and France, doing some damage at Gilette, Taggia, Alessandria, and at 2 points along the Var R. FBs pound bridges and A/Fs in NW Italy and S France and attack T/Os in the area.

Fifteenth AF: 330-plus B–17's and B–24's attack Genoa harbor and hit tgts in S France, including Le Pouzin oil storage, Portes-les-Valences torpedo factory and M/Y, Le Pontet oil storage, and Avignon railroad bridges. P–38's and P–51's provide escort.

Tenth AF: P–51's, P–47's, and A–36's spt ground forces in Taungni area. P–51's and P–47's on patrols and armed rcn hit various T/Os around Katha, Mainghka, Meza, Helon, Mohnyin, Bilumyo, and Namma. P–40's attack gun positions and strongpoints at Myitkyina.

Fourteenth AF: 11 B–25's and 32 P–40's and P–38's bomb and strafe town of Tengchung. 9 P–40's and P–38's damage bridge at Tingka. Yangtze R shipping and supplies are attacked at Shihlipu by 8 P–40's.

FEAF: B–24's bomb A/F at Yap I. A–20's bomb Nabire A/F while in Wewak area bmrs and ftrs hit bridge and A/F at Boram and bridges, comm lines, troop concentrations, and other tgts along coastline, especially between But and Cape Karawop. MBs and HBs carry out wide sweeps over the Moluccas and Lesser Sunda Is, hitting A/Fs at Maumere, Amahai, and Liang, and shipping off Ceram and Amboina. HBs hit Cape Chater and Lautem while MBs bomb camp near Poeloeti. FBs hit Mapia I and coastal vessels and shore tgts at Talaud.

3 August

Eighth AF: In early afternoon nearly 400 B–17's and B–24's bomb M/Ys in France and 1 in Germany, an oil refinery in Germany, and an A/F, road and rail junctions, bridges, and a few individual tgts in France. 3 of the 6 P–51 gps providing escort later strafe transportation tgts and A/Fs. 12 aircraft are claimed destroyed. 6 HBs and 6 P–51's are lost. Later in the afternoon 515 bmrs attack 20 V-weapon sites in France. 2 A/Fs and a railroad bridge and a junction in France, 2 oil refineries and a storage depot in Belgium, 4 oil facilities in France, a road and rail bridge in the Netherlands, and M/Ys in Belgium. 6 ftr gps provide uneventful escort. One HB is lost.

Ninth AF: 180-plus A–20's and B–26's bomb rail bridges, overpasses, and junctions at Mantes-la-Jolie, Chartres, La Chenaie and Merey, fuel dump at Maintenon, and alternate rail tgts in N France. Ftrs escort IX BC bmrs and a few C–47's, provide cover for ground forces, and fly armed rcn over wide areas of N and W France.

Twelfth AF: MBs achieve fair results in attacks on bridges at Gilette, Levens, Lesegno, Albenga, and Asti, and at 2 locations along Var R. FBs have successful day against comm tgts (mainly road and railroad bridges) and A/Fs in N Italy. At least 15 bridges are damaged or demolished and several parked aircraft are destroyed.

Fifteenth AF: More than 600 B–17's and B–24's hit industry in Friedrichshafen area, including chemical works, fabric works, and 2 aircraft factories, and bomb comm tgts in Brenner Pass area, attacking Avisio viaduct and bridges at Ora and San Michele all'Adige. Ftrs fly about 300 sorties in spt. HBs and ftrs claim 18 enemy aircraft shot down. 11 US airplanes are destroyed.

Tenth AF: B–25's bomb Wanling, knock out bridge at Panghkam, and attack bridges along the railroad from Naba to Myitkyina. P–51's and P–47's spt ground forces N of Taungni and near Sahmaw, hit towns of Shwegu and Mosit, attack factory area at Mohnyin, and pound boats, troop concentrations, and gun positions at Myitkyina and Maingna.

Fourteenth AF: 23 B–24's bomb town of Yoyang. 6 B–25's hit Mangshih. Nearly 150 P–40's, P–51's, and P–38's on armed rcn attack T/Os, including A/Fs, troops, town areas, supply areas, and rail, road, and river

traffic at numerous locations, including areas of Tengchung, Tingka, Mangshih, Loyang, Changsha, Hengyang, Tangyang, Chingmen, Chaling, Siangyin, Nanchang, Siangtan, Hengshan, Chuchou, Ikiawan, and Leiyang.

FEAF: B–24's bomb Yap and islands in Woleai group. Bad weather cancels scheduled strikes over Vogelkop Peninsula area, However, MBs hit troop concentrations at Bira and other points on MacCluer Gulf, bomb Urarom, and spt Allied ground forces on Biak by hitting troops in Korim Bay area. An ammo dump and oil derrick at Boela are also destroyed. Supply dumps, comm tgts, and bridges are hit as FBs and A–20's continue to blast areas around But, Dagua, and Wewak.

Seventh AF: VII Air Serv Area Cmd is activated. B–24's from the Marshalls pound Truk.

4 August

Eighth AF: In late morning and midafternoon raids, over 1,250 HBs attack 4 oil refineries, 4 aircraft factories, 4 A/Fs, Peenemunde experimental establishment, and torpedo plants in Germany, 2 coastal batteries in Pas de Calais area, and 2 V-weapon sites, 2 A/Fs, a M/Y, a railroad crossing, and a bridge in NW France. All of the Eighth's 15 ftr gps spt the operations, flying 782 sorties. HBs claim 3 airplanes destroyed and ftrs claim 39 destroyed in air and 15 on ground. Strafing claims include numerous items of rolling stock. 14 HBs and 15 ftrs are lost during the day.

Ninth AF: 62 A–20's and B–26's bomb rail bridges at Oissel, Epernon, and Saint-Remy-sur-Avre and an ammo dump and bivouac area in Foret de Sille. Ftrs furnish cover over battle area and for an armd column, fly sweeps, dive-bomb enemy positions and also fuel dumps at Angers, attack ammo dump at Tours, and fly armed rcn in Quimper-Nantes, Amines, and Saint-Quentin areas.

Twelfth AF: Weather severely hampers the day's operations. MBs attacking bridges at Levens, Ventimiglia, Fontan, and along Var R achieve poor results. FBs in same general area hit bridges, tracks, guns, junction, and A/F, and strike at Nice harbor.

Fifteenth AF: In an attempt to comply with the first direct Soviet request for AAF air strikes, 70-plus P–38's and P–51's leave Italy, attack A/F and town of Focsani and land at FRANTIC bases in USSR.

Tenth AF: B–25's bomb town of Sahmaw in spt of advancing Allied ground forces. P–51's also spt ground forces in the Sahmaw-Taungni area. FBs hit various tgts, including town areas, gun positions, troops, and comm lines in or near Shwegu Pinbaw, Kazu, Bhamo, Myitkyina, Bilumyo, Mawhe, Mainghka, and Onsansaing.

Fourteenth AF: 20 B–25's bomb town of Mangshih and A/Fs at Lashio and Hsenwi. 32 P–40's hit town area and T/Os at Tengchung. 70 P–40's attack troops, supplies, river shipping, and trucks at several points in Tungting Lake-Yangtze R region. 4 P–38's knock out 2 bridges at Mongyu.

FEAF: B–24's bomb supply area on Utagal I and A/F at Yap. Other B–24's bomb oil installations at Boela and attack Faan. B–25's and A–20's

hit oilfields at Klamono and at Kasim I and bomb Nabire A/F. P–39's strafe Pegun I. A–20's and FBs in spt of Allied forces pound enemy concentrations, supplies, and barges E of Driniumor R, at Abau, S of Torricelli Range, at Boram, and just W of Wewak.

Seventh AF: Saipan-based B–25's fly 2 strikes against Guam. B–25's staging from the Marshalls, hit Ponape.

Eleventh AF: 4 P–38's accompanied by 1 B–25 fly top cover for naval force near Massacre Bay. 4 MBs fly an uneventful shipping sweep.

5 August

Eighth AF: In the morning 1,062 HBs strike Magdeburg-Brunswick-Hannover region, bombing oil, aircraft, and engine works and A/F. 14 ftr gps provide spt, 657 airplanes completing sorties. The HBs and ftrs encounter about 100 ftrs and claim 30 destroyed. The ftrs of 6 gps fly strafing missions against highway and rail traffic and several A/Fs. 14 HBs and 6 ftrs are lost. During afternoon 38 B–17's, escorted by P–51 gp bomb 6 V-weapon sites and an A/F in France. No losses are suffered.

Ninth AF: In order that operations controlled by Ninth AF be developed in close association with HQ 12th Army Gp, the Ninth's HQ at Uxbridge and Grandcamp-les-Bains are closed and a single HQ opened the following day (6 Aug) at Saint-Sauveur-Lendelin near both Adv HQ 12th Army Gp and Adv HQ AEAF. 50th and 53rd TC Wgs of IX TCC are attached to MAAF for purpose of forming, with 51st TC Wg, a Prov TC Air Div to handle the airborne phase of the invasion of S France. 300-plus A–20's and B–26's bomb Saint-Malo harbor and Foret de Sille fuel dump during 4/5 Aug, and during the day, rail bridges at 6 cities in N and W France, and M/Y at Compiegne. Ftrs furnish cover for ground forces and fly armed rcn over wide areas of N France.

Twelfth AF: Weather again restricts operations. A–20's on armed rcn in Po Valley during 4/5 Aug attack lights and vehicles. FBs fly a few unsuccessful missions against bridges.

Tenth AF: 14 B–25's bomb town area of Taungni and stores area at Bilumyo. 50 P–51's also pound Taungni area. 21 P–47's attack T/Os throughout widespread area around Bhamo.

Fourteenth AF: 15 B–25's bomb town of Wanling. 3 hit Lashio A/F. 36 P–40's again pound Tengchung. In Tungting Lake area 50-plus P–40's attack comm tgts, troops, and numerous trucks.

FEAF: B–24's bomb personnel and supply areas on Yap. Other B–24's bomb oil facilities at Boela while B–25's hit villages and small boats near Seleman Bay and afterwards bomb Besar I. B–24's attack seaplane anchorage at Kokas while P–39's strafe barges in W Geelvink Bay area. Despite bad weather, P–39's manage to hit Luain gun positions and ammo dump. A few B–24's bomb Sasa A/F.

Seventh AF: B–25's from Saipan fly 2 strikes against Guam.

Eleventh AF: A weather mission is followed by a shipping sweep flown by 2 MBs which is aborted early due to weather.

6 August

Eighth AF: The Eighth strikes 5 aircraft and engine factories, torpedo plant, 7 oil refineries, and an A/F in Berlin and Hamburg-Kiel areas, and 2 V-weapon sites in Pas de Calais area. 953 HBs attack their tgts. 25 fail to return. The 554 ftrs in spt lose 6 of their number. Total claims of enemy airplanes destroyed amount to 34. The bombing is very effective and 10 major tgts are severely damaged during one of the best days the Eighth experiences. In conjunction with the operations against the Berlin and Hamburg-Kiel areas, the Eighth begins its second shuttle-bombing mission to the USSR. 78 B–17's are dispatched, but 3 return to UK due to mechanical troubles. The HB formation is met by a P–51 gp 60 mi E of Jutland. 75 B–17's bomb aircraft factory at Rahmel, near Gdynia, with good results. Another P–51 gp picks up the formation as it withdraws toward USSR. No aircraft are lost and the HBs land at Poltava and Mirgorod while the P–51's land at Piryatin.

Ninth AF: MBs and LBs hit bridges, fuel and ammo dumps, and a locomotive depot at Beauvais, Beaumont-sur-Sarthe, Courtalain, Foret de Perseigne, and Blois. Ftrs escort IX BC and furnish cover to ground troops in Vire, Rennes, and Redon areas.

Twelfth AF: MBs strike bridges in SE France in Rhone Valley and areas to the E, in or near Tarascon and Arles, and along Var R. FBs enjoy successful day against tgts in NW Italy and SE France, including bridges, railroad lines, motor transport, trains, roads, A/Fs, and town areas, plus shipping at Imperia, Genoa, and La Spezia.

Fifteenth AF: 60 ftrs take off from Soviet FRANTIC bases, attack Craiova M/Y and other railroad tgts in Bucharest-Ploesti area, and land at Italian bases. Close to 700 B–17's and B–24's, operating against tgts in SE France, attack oil storage at Le Pouzin, Le Pontet, and Lyon, railroad bridges at Le Pouzin, Avignon, Tarascon, Rambert, and Givors, M/Ys at Portes-les-Valences and Miramas, and submarine pens at Toulon. 43 P–38's dive-bomb A/Fs at Orange/Plan de Dieu, and Valence. P–38's and P–51's fly about 200 sorties in spt of bombing missions.

Tenth AF: 6 B–25's bomb town area of Mohnyin while 2 others destroy bridge at Hsenwi. 21 P–51's hit 4 railroad bridges in the Naba-Pinbaw area, destroying 2 of them. P–51's and P–47's hit numerous T/Os at Mohnyin, Hopin, Bhamo, Myothit, Katha, Indaw, and other points in N Burma. A few P–40's strafe T/Os in Myitkyina area.

Fourteenth AF: 28 P–40's again pound Tengchung. 47 P–40's and P–51's hit trucks, troop compounds, and gun positions in Hengyang area. 19 P–40's attack sampans and trucks around Changsha. 20 others hit supplies, trucks, barracks, and T/Os at Chefang and Mangshih, between Changsha and Hengyang, and between Siangyin and Siangtan.

FEAF: Yap supply area is bombed by B–24's. Heavy frontal weather activity over Vogelkop Peninsula and the Moluccas cancels strikes in that area. On the mainland of New Guinea, MBs and ftrs, though restricted by weather, spt ground operations near

Sarmi, hit gun positions at Dagua, and strafe fuel dumps and T/Os at Cape Djeruen.

Seventh AF: B–25's from Saipan strike Guam twice. B–25's flying out of the Marshalls hit Ponape, and others from the Gilberts hit Nauru. B–24's from Kwajalein bomb Wotje.

7 August

Eighth AF: Shuttle mission continues from USSR. In accordance with Soviet request, tgt is oil refinery in Poland. 57 B–17's and 37 P–51's are dispatched. 55 HBs (2 return to base early) bomb refinery at Trzebinia. P–51's engage 6 to 8 enemy ftrs over tgt and claim destruction of 3 of them. The airplanes return to FRANTIC bases in USSR. In UK 902 HBs, supported by 10 ftr gps, are dispatched to bomb oil dumps and bridges in France. Cloud conditions cause multiple aborts, but 483 HBs bomb 11 oil dumps, 5 bridges, 3 A/Fs, and an M/Y. 3 HBs are lost. 8 gps of FBs attack M/Ys and rail transportation N and E of Paris.

Ninth AF: To maintain close association with ground forces, IX TAC and XIX TAC constitute mobile units to accompany Adv HQ of US First and Third Armies, respectively, as they adv rapidly to the E. Gen Brereton relinquishes cmd of Ninth AF to become CG First Allied Airborne Army. 380-plus A–20's and B–26's bomb bridges at Nogent-sur-Seine and Neuvy-sur-Loire. Ftrs escort IX BC, furnish defensive cover in Vire, Laval, and Rennes areas, and spt ground forces in assault area.

Twelfth AF: A–20's bomb shipping at Monaco, Genoa, Finale Ligure, and Alassio during 6/7 Aug. During day,

B–25's and B–26's bomb bridges at Les Censies, Ventimiglia, La Voulte-sur-Rhone, Livron, Avignon, and Pont-Saint-Esprit. FBs hit rail and road bridges, M/Ys at Alessandria and Albenga, shipping at Imperia and Nice, and A/Fs in NW Italy and S France.

Fifteenth AF: 353 B–17's and B–24's bomb 2 synthetic oil refineries at Blechhammer; over 300 ftrs provide spt. 76 B–24's hit Alibunar A/F and Novi Sad oil facilities. HBs and ftrs claim nearly 30 aircraft shot down.

Tenth AF: B–25's destroy 2 bridges, damage 2 others, and hit T/Os in areas around Naba and Mawhun. FBs attack Mohnyin, Myothit, and Pinbaw, hit motor pool at Namana, damage 2 bridges S of Bhamo, and attack T/Os during sweeps of Onbauk A/F and town of Bhamo. FBs also spt ground forces in Taungni area.

Fourteenth AF: 37 P–40's hit Hengyang and trucks, troops, and gun positions in the surrounding area. 21 P–40's bomb Changsha, 4 hit rivercraft at Siangsiang, 4 bomb wall at Tengchung, and 6 attack Hsiaoshuipu.

FEAF: B–24's bomb power plant, AA positions, and barracks area on Yap, phosphate plant on Fais I, and A/Fs at Galela and Lolobata, where 35–50 aircraft are destroyed or damaged.

Seventh AF: Saipan-based B–25's hit Guam twice during the day.

8 August

Eighth AF: Shuttle mission continues as B–17's with P–51 escort, leave bases in USSR. While 36 hit Buzau A/F others hit A/F at Zilistea.

No ftrs are encountered during mission. 359 B–24's from UK bomb 10 V-weapon sites and 4 A/Fs in NE France. 6 P–51 gps provide escort. 2 gps bomb and 3 gps strafe rail facilities and rail and motor transportation with good results. 497 B–17's bomb troop concentrations and strongpoints and T/Os S of Caen. 2 P–51 gps give spt, 1 later strafing traffic in Rouen area. 10 HBs and 4 P–51's are lost, mostly to AA fire. 4 gps of FBs (163 planes) strafe and bomb M/Ys, a bridge, and T/Os N and W of Dijon and in Paris-Amiens-Saint-Quentin area. Eighth AF during the day and RAF during 7/8 Aug drop over 5,200 tons of bombs, mainly in spt of Canadian First Army (accompanied by a Polish armd div) offensive toward Falaise.

Ninth AF: Gen Vandenberg assumes cmd of Ninth AF. 406 B–26's and A–20's bomb rail enbankment and bridges at 8 locations in N and W France, attack radar installations between Argentan and Alencon, and give tac spt to ground forces near Saint-Malo. Ftrs escort IX BC, give defensive air cover, and fly armed rcn E of Paris and in battle area.

Twelfth AF: MBs attack tgts in Po and Rhone Valleys, hitting bridges and railroad tracks in or near Alessandria, Avignon, and Pont-Saint-Esprit, and along Var R. A–20's hit storage dump and nearby town of Savigliano. FBs hit barge in San Stefano al Mare harbor and pontoon and railroad bridges nearby, and attack Mantua causeway and nearby bridges, scoring many hits and destroying several vehicles.

Fifteenth AF: Bad weather limits operations to rcn missions.

Tenth AF: B-25's are weathered out of their primary tgt, the town of Shwekyina. The MBs hit alternates, destroying Meza bridge and damaging 3 others, and bombing railroad tracks at several points between Naba and Meza. Weather severely curtails FB missions.

Fourteenth AF: 6 B-25's and 7 P-40's bomb storage area in Hengshan and destroy several trucks in the area. 29 P-40's hit gun positions and T/Os in Hengyang vicinity. 14 P-51's and P-40's hit bridge, trucks, and river craft at Siangtan while 8 blast trucks, barges, and compound between Siangtan and Hengyang. 12 P-40's attack river shipping from Sinti to Hankow. 15 P-40's bomb storage areas and radio stations at Amoy and Swatow.

FEAF: B-24's bomb Yap and Gagil-Tomil Is, concentrating on airstrips, A/Fs at Galela, Lolobata, and Babo, and towns of Urarom and Manokwari. A-20's bomb radio station near Hollandia and hit troop concentrations in Musu area. FBs bomb bridges and buildings at Boram, troops at But, and guns at Dagua.

Seventh AF: Saipan-based B-25's bomb Guam where effective resistance ends. B-25's from the Marshalls hit Ponape while B-24's bomb Truk.

9 August

Eighth AF: More than 500 HBs attack aircraft engine plant at Sindelfingen and several T/Os, including M/Ys at Saarbrucken, Luxembourg, and Saint-Vith. 18 HBs are lost, mostly to AA fire. 15 ftr gps fly 570 sorties in spt, claiming 33 aircraft destroyed in air and 30 on ground, plus numerous ground tgts in strafing attacks.

15 FB gps bomb and strafe rail tgts, including 12 M/Ys, in France. 325th Photographic Wg (Rcn) is activated to replace 8th Rcn Wg (Prov).

Ninth AF: Close to 400 MBs and LBs attack ammo dump in Foret de Blois, shipping at Brest, and other tgts, including rail bridges at 10 locations in N and W France. Ftrs escort IX BC, cover ground forces, and fly armed rcn in wide areas of N France (around Paris, as far S as Orleans, and as far NE as Reims and Chalons-sur-Marne).

Twelfth AF: MB efforts are restricted by bad weather. However, during 8/9 Aug A-20's hit tgts along coastal road from Nice to Genoa, and during the day B-25's hit railroad at Ventimiglia and B-26's attain excellent results on Bergamo/Orio al Serio AF. FBs sink motor vessel in Imperia harbor and attack railroad facilities in NW Italy.

Fifteenth AF: Around 400 B-24's and B-17's, with ftr escorts, bomb 2 A/Fs and an oil refinery at Budapest, rolling stock plant and aircraft assembly plant at Gyor, and M/Y and oil refinery at Brod.

Tenth AF: 24 FBs spt ground forces in Taungni-Sahmaw area. Several others unsuccessfully attack bridge N of Hopin and bomb town of Tagwin.

Fourteenth AF: 6 B-25's bomb compound and vehicle shed on NE edge of Hengyang. 36 P-40's and P-51's attack trucks, gun positions, and buildings at several points in Hengyang-Siangtan area. 21 P-51's and P-40's knock out pontoon bridge and hit junks and sampans at Changsha, and attack rivercraft at points along the C Yangtze.

FEAF: B–24's blast AA positions in 3 different areas of Yap I. Other B–24's bomb A/Fs at Boela and at Liang. A–20's hit shipping facilities at Asap I and bomb Nabire A/F. Ftrs strafe villages S of Manokwari. B–25's bomb forces on N coast of Waigeo I. A–20's and FBs hit troops at Dagua and near Haur and bomb stores at Cape Moem and machine-guns at Cape Wom.

10 August

Eighth AF: 45 P–51's in Italy during FRANTIC mission are dispatched with Fifteenth AF aircraft to escort on a troop carrier evacuation mission. Over 150 B–24's from UK bomb 2 bridges and 3 fuel dumps SE of Paris, plus T/O near Brienon-sur-Armancon. 5 ftr gps and a sq afford escort, claiming 8 airplanes destroyed in combat. Rail and transportation facilities are strafed in Paris, Troyes, Dreux, Chartres and Evreux areas. 11 gps of FBs, in 2 operations, bomb large number of rail and highway transportation tgts, including 15 M/Ys S and E of Paris, and along French-Belgian border.

Ninth AF: Almost 200 MBs and LBs bomb rail bridges and embankments in wide areas around Paris. Ftrs escort bmrs, spt ground forces, give defensive cover, and fly armed rcn in battle areas and around Amiens, Paris, Cambrai, Meaux, Dijon, and Troyes.

Twelfth AF: MB and LB missions are cancelled by bad weather. FBs, operating on reduced scale, hit gun positions along S coast of France in preparation for Allied invasion of S France (Operation DRAGOON).

Fifteenth AF: More than 450 HBs, with ftr escort, hit 6 oil refineries in Ploesti area.

Tenth AF: 9 B–25's bomb town of Shwekyina. A few P–51's spt ground forces by hitting railroad station at Mingon.

Fourteenth AF: 9 P–40's strafe Taiyuan A/F claiming more than 20 aircraft destroyed. 16 P–40's destroy 4 trucks and damage about 50 others at Siangtan and in Changsha area. 2 P–40's strafe numerous junks along S China coast.

FEAF: B–24's attack Yap, concentrating on AA positions, A/Fs and town of Yap. Others hit A/Fs at Galela, Lolobata and Namlea. B–25's bomb Langgoer A/F. FBs attack Sorong, Manokwari, and villages along W coast of Geelvink Bay. FBs continue to pound forces between Aitape and Wewak. Large-scale TC missions are flown to forward bases, especially in Schouten Is.

Twentieth AF: 2 missions are flown during 10/11 Aug. In one, 24 B–29's, out of Chengtu, bomb urban area of Nagasaki and 3 others hit T/Os. The B–29's claim 1 ftr shot down, the first such claim (except probables) by the B–29's. In other missions, the first staged through China Bay, 31 B–29's bomb oil refineries at Palembang, 8 mine the Moesi R nearby, and 3 hit T/Os and a secondary tgt. The first attack, from Ceylon to Sumatra, is the longest single-stage combat flight (about 3,900 mi) by B–29's during the war.

Seventh AF: B–24's, flying their first mission from Saipan, pound Iwo Jima, beginning the AAF's neutralization campaign of that island. Saipan-based P–47's hit Tinian and Pagan Is. All organized resistance on

Guam ends. B-24's from Kwajalein hit Wotje.

Eleventh AF: 4 B-25's on a shipping sweep spot 2 patrol boats 75 mi ESE of Shimushu I. One is sunk, the other is damaged.

11 August

Eighth AF: More than 850 HBs attack 13 M/Ys, fuel dumps, A/Fs, and T/Os, in NE France and Paris area, and 23 arsenal areas, barracks, concrete emplacements and heavy arty posts in and around Brest, escorted by 8 ftr gps and a sq. 5 gps later strafe ground tgts.

Ninth AF: LBs and MBs from 97th, 98th, and 99th Combat Bomb Wgs attack bridges at Montrichard, Oissel, Fismes, and Creil/Saint-Maximin, gun defenses at Ile de Cezembre and Saint-Malo, and ammo dump at Foret de Roumare. Ftrs cover assault area, escort IX BC, and fly armed rcn in battle area and extensively over N France.

Twelfth AF: B-25's, B-26's, and P-47's strike gun positions along French and Italian coasts W of Genoa as DRAGOON assault force begins movement from Naples area toward tgts in S France.

Tenth AF: 5 B-25's bomb encampment area and underground shelters at Kadu. 4 others abort because of bad weather. 6 P-40's attack Japanese-occupied temple at Shwekyina and Japanese HQ at Bhamo.

Fourteenth AF: 23 B-24's bomb Changsha, 16 B-25's pound Hengyang over 40 P-51's and P-40's bomb bridges, villages, warehouses, trucks, troops, and other T/Os in Hengyang area. 26 P-40's attack T/Os at or near Chuting, Puchou, and Yungfengshih.

FEAF: A-20's hit shipping off Urarom and in Wandammen Bay and barges and a radar station along coast of Geelvink Bay. A-20's pound Japanese HQ and bivouac areas S of Sawar, A-20's and B-25's bomb forces at Haur village while P-39's hit Kairiru I barge terminal, coastal guns at several points, and troops, supplies, and buildings from But to Rocky Pt.

Seventh AF: Makin based B-25's hit Ponape.

12 August

Eighth AF: Shuttle-bombing mission UK-USSR-Italy-UK is completed. Of 72 B-17's taking off from Fifteenth AF bases in Italy, 3 have various problems. The others bomb Toulouse/Francazal A/F and then proceed to UK. 62 P-51's (part of the shuttle-mission force) and 43 from UK provide escort. No aircraft are lost. 70 HBs and 58 P-51's land in UK. 5 HBs and 6 P-51's, either left in Italy or returning there during mission, subsequently return to UK. Over 500 other HBs attack 7 A/Fs and M/Ys in the Paris area. 6 ftr gps provide escort, 1 escorts Ninth AF MBs. 2 of the gps afterwards strafe transportation tgts. In 2 operations nearly 900 FBs attack transportation tgts in NE France, a large number of which are bombed with good results by over 700, at a loss of 13 ftrs.

Ninth AF: IX BC LBs and MBs attack Oissel rail bridge, Corbeil-Essonnes refueling siding, and numerous points along highways in Argentan area with aim of bottling up enemy troops. Ftrs fly ground forces cover and armed rcn over wide areas of W and N France, also escort IX BC.

Twelfth AF: MBs, LBs, and FBs attack tgts, mainly gun positions, in battle area N of Arno R and in S France.

Fifteenth AF: Almost 550 ftr-escorted HBs bomb gun positions in Savona, Genoa, Marseille, and Sete areas. 100-plus P–51's strafe radar installations and other coast-watching facilities along French S coast. These and Twelfth AF strikes are preparatory to DRAGOON.

Tenth AF: About 20 FBs hit Shwekyina, damage bridge near Manla, bomb railroad yards at Pinwe, strafe river boat near Bhamo, and attack troops in Myothit area. 24 FBs spt ground forces in Taungni-Pinbaw area.

Fourteenth AF: 7 B–25's bomb railroad yards at Hengyang. 19 P–51's and P–40's hit T/Os in this area. 39 P–40's attack various T/Os at Chiuchiang, Yungfengshih, Loyang, Siangtan, and Tengchung.

FEAF: FEAF long-range rcn is greatly increased thanks to strategic position of newly acquired Schouten Is bases. B–24's pound A/F at Babo while B–25's and P–39's hit Nabire A/F. Other P–39's attack defenses at Mansinam I and shore concentrations along W Geelvink Bay. P–47's spt ground operations in area of Sansapor Pt by bombing Dore. A–20's and P–47's hit forces and T/Os in Sarmi area and along Metimedan R. A–20's and P–39's attack troops at Haur, coastal tgts in cooperation with PT boats, and fuel dumps at Boram.

Seventh AF: Saipan-based B–24's hit shipping, seaplane base, and A/F at Chichi Jima, B–25's pound Pagan I while P–47's hit Rota. B–24's from the Marshalls bomb Truk while Gilberts-based B–25's pound Nauru.

Eleventh AF: 4 B–24's and 2 F–7A's over Paramushiru and Shimushu hit tgts which include shipping in Higashi Banjo Strait and buildings and runway on Suribachi. Enemy ftrs give battle. The B–24's score 3 kills and 13 probables and damaged. 6 more MBs fly an uneventful shipping sweep and take photos over Shimushiru I.

13 August

Eighth AF: Over 1,200 HBs escorted by 6 ftr gps attack railroad bridge, 3 coastal batteries, and several highways along with T/Os along the Seine from Le Havre to Paris during a battle area spt mission. 13 HBs are lost. Over 800 FBs attack M/Ys, bridges, tunnels, moving traffic and other transportation facilities in wide area NE of the Seine. 13 FBs are lost.

Ninth AF: Around 575 B–26's and A–20's bomb fuel storage at Les Buissons, points along highways around Lisieux and SE to Rugles with aim of containing enemy in Falaise pocket, railroad tgts at Peronne, Doullens, and Corbeil-Essonnes. Ftrs escort IX BC, cover ground forces, and fly armed rcn in Alencon, Le Mans, Domfront, and Chartres areas. About 125 transports fly ferry and evacuation missions. During 13/14 Aug, 28 B–26's bomb Foret de Halouze ammo dump and bivouac area.

Twelfth AF: MBs blast coastal def guns in Marseille area while LBs during 12/13 Aug attack tgts along Monaco-Toulon road, and FBs hit guns and barracks in the area. Ftrs strafe A/Fs at Les Chanoines, Montreal,

Avignon, La Jasse, Istres-Le-Tube, Valence, and Bergamo. A–20's attack explosive stores in battle area in Arno R Valley.

Fifteenth AF: Almost 500 B–24's and B–17's attack gun positions around Genoa, Toulon, and Sete, and strike at bridges at Pont-Saint-Esprit, Avignon, Orange, and Crest. 31 P–38's dive-bomb Montelimar A/F. Other ftrs fly 180-plus sorties in spt of HB missions. 28 HBs hit military installations at Pec.

Tenth AF: 20 FBs hit troops and supplies at Mankwi, Myothit, and Tali. 7 others knock out bridge at Kyauktalon and damage another near Namkwin. 26 FBs attack village of Pinwe and hit T/Os near Mawlu and Pinbaw. 9 B–25's strike bomb storage area at Pinwe considerably damaging the village.

Fourteenth AF: 30-plus B–25's bomb Tungling, Sinsiang, and Hengyang, Pailochi A/F, shipping at Takao harbor and nearby coastal areas. 3 cargo vessels are claimed sunk. 51 P–40's and P–51's attack trucks, bridges, railroad yards, troops, and other T/Os in Hengyang area. 18 P–40's and P–38's pound Tengchung. 50-plus other P–40's, P–51's, and P–38's attack troops, bridges, railroad tracks, shipping, trucks, and other T/Os at several locations including Lienhwa, Siangsiang, Sinshih, Puchou, Tungyangtun, Hengshan, Weichow I, Luichow Peninsula, Tingka, Mangshih, Nanchang, Puchi, and along Yunglo R.

FEAF: Bad weather in SWPA curtails operations. B–24's bomb bivouacs and supply dumps at Manokwari. Bmrs hit Cape Wom storage area while P–39's cooperate with PT boats to hit Dagua personnel areas and Suain coastal positions. P–47's and P–39's hit Cape Wom, troops at Ulban, Matapau, and Suain, and spt ground forces at Sarmi. TC aircraft complete nearly 90 missions to Owi I and other forward bases.

Eleventh AF: Of 3 B–24's departing Shemya during 12/13 Aug, 1 aborts while the other 2 bomb Kashiwabara staging area. Later 6 B–25's fly a shipping sweep E of the N Kurils during which ftr is downed.

14 August

Eighth AF: Over 1,100 HBs attack 9 A/Fs, 2 aero engine factories, 1 oil plant, 2 bridges, 2 rail junctions and other secondary and T/Os in SW Germany, E France, and Bordeaux region. Ftrs fly 388 sorties in spt and destroy 10 aircraft, 19 locomotives, and numerous other ground tgts. 6 FB gps attack tgts within 130-mi radius of Paris, 136 FBs bombing various transportation tgts.

Ninth AF: IX BC MBs and LBs hit several highway and rail bridges, junctions and sidings mostly beyond battlelines in France to delay and complicate German retreat. Ftrs escort bmrs, fly armed rcn over Falaise, Broglie, and Chartres areas, and spt ground forces, especially 7 armed and inf divs, over wide areas of N and W France. A XIX TAC sq uniquely effects surrender of a number of German ground troops, Germans on roads being strafed by sq NE of Carrouges wave white flags, whereupon planes buzz the road and shepherd enemy troops into a column which then proceeds to US lines to surrender.

Twelfth AF: MBs hit coastal def

guns while FBs pound various gun positions, tracks, enemy HQ, and T/Os in the Toulon-Nice area. Ftrs strafe radar installations and T/Os along the French S coast as DRAGOON forces approach. During 13/14 Aug A–20's hit T/Os in W Po Valley and fuel dump N of Italy battle area.

Fifteenth AF: 540 B–24's and B–17's bomb gun positions in Toulon and Genoa areas as DRAGOON convoy heads for French Mediterranean coast. 145 P–38's and P–51's strafe radar installations at several coastal points.

Tenth AF: B–25's bomb Mohnyin and Indaw. 18 P–51's pound tgts in Myothit area. 46 other FBs hit various N Burma tgts including Naba junction, active area near Pinbaw, building and T/Os at Thaikwagon, cmd post at Hopin, motor pool at Nansiaung Forest, ammo and other supplies in Mohnyin area, and bridges S of Bhamo one of which is slightly damaged.

Fourteenth AF: 24 B–25's blast Lungling while 16 P–40's hit fortified pass and T/Os to the S. 12 B–25's bomb railroad yards at Siangtan. 31 P–40's and P–51's hit railroad yards, river shipping, and general T/Os at Hengyang. 13 P–40's attack Tengchung. 13 others hit trucks, troops, and rivercraft at Pailochi and Siying and 4 bomb bridge at Hsenwi.

FEAF: B–25's and B–24's attack Ternate I, AA positions, oil dumps, barracks, supply areas, and other tgts throughout the Halmaheras. B–24's pound A/F at Babo while A–20's and FBs, along with RAAF airplanes, blasting bivouac, and troops at Terabu, Kaiten, and Wewak Pt.

Seventh AF: The Seventh is reorganized as a "mobile tac airforce," retaining only units that will function in the combat area. VII BC includes 11th, 30th, 41st, anl 494th Bomb Gps; VII FC includes 15th and 318th Ftr Gps and 8th Night Ftr Sq; and the recently activated VII Air Serv Area Cmd is composed of 4 serv gps. Saipan-based B–24's bomb Iwo Jima and B–25's hit Pagan. P–47's hit Rota. From the Marshalls, B–25's hit Ponape and B–24's bomb Wotje.

15 August

Eighth AF: More than 850 HBs attack 11 NW German, Dutch, and Belgian A/Fs in conjunction with 1,000 RAF HBs and Mosquitos raiding 9 A/Fs in the Netherlands and Belgium, all supported by 607 VIII FC sorties. 17 Eighth AF HBs and 6 ftrs are lost. HBs claim 13 aircraft destroyed while ftrs claim 14 in air and 8 on ground, along with 29 locomotives and a large number of other ground tgts. 33 P–47's dive-bomb and skip-bomb repair shop and locomotives in M/Y at Braine-le-Comte.

Ninth AF: 50th and 53d TC Wgs, on loan to MAAF, participate in invasion of S France as part of Prov TC Air Div. 330-plus A–20's and B–26's bomb Marseille-en-Beauvaisis and Foret de Chantilly ammo and fuel dumps, rail bridges at Auvers-sur-Oise and L'Isle-Adam, Serqueux M/Y, and coastal defense at Saint-Malo. Ftrs fly cover for 5 inf and armd divs, escort IX BC, and fly extensive armed rcn over N and W France.

Twelfth AF: During 14/15 Aug A–20's bomb Le Vallon, Istres, and Orange/Plan de Dieu A/Fs and other

Rhone Valley tgts while US Seventh Army carries out preliminary operations to isolate DRAGOON invasion beaches. US Special Serv Force invades Levant and Port-Cros Is and secures left flank of assault area. French commandos land E of Cap Negre and clear coastal defenses, French Naval Assault Gp lands SW of Cannes and secures right flank. 1st Airborne TF drops in rear of assault beaches and blocks off invasion area from the interior. Main force, US VI Corps, lands 3 divs abreast between Nice and Toulon at 0800. A–20's bomb barracks in invasion area while B–25's, B–26's, P–38's, and P–47's, supporting invasion, pound beaches, enemy concentrations, and gun positions in coastal areas and later in the day move attacks inland to interdict enemy comm lines successfully hitting numerous bridges. Ftrs maintain constant patrol over convoys and invasion area.

Fifteenth AF: In Fifteenth AF's first HB mass night raid, 252 B–17's and B–24's after predawn takeoff pound beaches in Cannes-Toulon area in immediate adv of Operation DRAGOON. 28 other ftr-escorted B–17's bomb highway bridges over Rhone R. B–17's sent against coastal gun positions abort mission owing to poor visibility. 166 P–51's escort MATAF C–47's carrying airborne invasion troops.

EAC: AM Coryton assumes cmd of Third Tac AF, a major component of EAC. Tac AF functions remain under Coryton until it is dissolved on 4 Dec 44.

Tenth AF: More than 70 P–51's, P–47's, P–40's, and A–36's hit numerous N Burma tgts including general T/

Os in Bhamo area, monastery at Pegu, troops E of Mawhun, Loiwing and Lashio A/F and rail tgts between Naba and Hopin. Close spt strikes are flown for ground forces in Pinbaw and Naba areas. Supply dumps at Mainghka are bombed and 2 villages N of Kazu are hit and burned out.

Fourteenth AF: 12 B–25's bomb Kutkai, demolishing 2 large buildings and leaving 14 burning. 35 P–40's attack Tingka, Hsenwi, Lungling, and Tengchung. Nearly 100 P–40's and P–51's attack troops, horses, trucks, river shipping, arty pieces, warehouses, and general T/Os in or near Sungpai, Sinshih, Hengyang, Chaling, Leiyang, Sinyang, Siangtan, Hukow, and Changsha. 4 P–40's hit coastal shipping at Hongay and Nam Dinh.

FEAF: B–24's bomb Lolobata A/F and B–25's attack shipping in Ternate area, setting a 1,200-ton vessel afire and damaging several luggers and barges. P–39's dive-bomb AA positions at Wewak Pt. FEAF aircraft on armed rcn hit T/Os in Ceram area and Tanimbar Is.

Thirteenth AF: XIII FC moves from Guadalcanal to Sansapor Pt.

16 August

Eighth AF: Over 950 HBs attack 11 oil refineries, aircraft plants and several T/Os in C Germany. 16 ftr gps fly over 600 spt sorties. 24 HBs are lost. Ftrs claim 32 air victories.

Ninth AF: The 4 gps of 98th Combat Bomb Wg move during 16–30 Aug from UK to the Continent. About 130 MBs and LBs hit Foret de Roumare ammo dump and rail bridges at Pont-Audemer, Thibouville, Brionne,

Nassandres, and Le Bourg. Ftrs escort IX BC, give air cover to armd div and inf forces, and fly patrol and armed rcn over N and W France.

Twelfth AF: In spt of DRAGOON forces, ftrs and FBs continue to blast enemy defenses and comm on the beaches and in the invasion area of S France. A–20's hit lights and vehicles during 15/16 Aug from N of beachhead to Rhone R and during the day raid ammo stores. MBs pound Rhone R bridges and gun positions throughout the general area.

Fifteenth AF: 89 B–24's, with ftr escort, bomb chemical works at Friedrichshafen. 108 B–17's, supporting DRAGOON, attack railroad bridges at Saint-Vallier, Saint-Pierre-d'Albigny, Grenoble, and Isere-Valence. 42 P–51's escort MATAF C–47's on supply dropping mission to DRAGOON beachheads.

Tenth AF: As last Japanese resistance in India ceases, 16 B–25's bomb Indaw. 20 P–51's hit A/Fs at Lashio, Nawnghkio, Shwebo, Anisakan, and Onbauk. 37 P–40's and P–51's hit strong points, pillboxes, and machine-gun positions in Pinbaw area. 19 P–47's and P–51's attack T/Os at Katha, bridge S of Bhamo, town of Tagwin, railroad T/Os between Naba and Hopin, enemy-held monastery, and ammo dump at Pegu.

Fourteenth AF: 18 B–25's bomb Wanling area and warehouses while 12 hit Chaling area and warehouses at Siangtan. 90 P–40's and P–51's hit bridges, fortified positions, troops, trucks, rivercraft, supplies, gun positions, and other T/Os in Hsenwi and Lungling areas and in widespread area around Tungting Lake and C Yangtze R.

FEAF: B–24's and B–25's bomb Miti and Lolobata A/Fs, warehouses and shipping facilities at Ternate I, shipping in Wasile and Weda Bays, installations on Ajoe and Japanese positions at Tanimbar Is. Off Alor I B–25's sink small vessel. A–20's spt ground forces in Maffin Bay area while P–39's hit troops and positions from Manokwari to Windissi and bomb A/F at Ransiki, Moemi, and Waren.

Seventh AF: B–24's from Saipan hit Chichi Jima and Pagan. Marshall-based B–24's bomb Truk.

17 August

Eighth AF: 10 B–24's dispatched against Les Foulons rail bridge abort because of cloud cover over tgt. 20 ftr gps strafe and bomb between Brussels and Paris, 11 M/Ys, 2 A/Fs and numerous T/Os and destroy many locomotives, train cars, and road vehicles along with bridges, towers, warehouses and barges.

Ninth AF: 400-plus A–20's and B–26's bomb road bridges at Montfort-sur-Risle, Pont-Audemer, Nassandres, Beaumont-le-Roger, Le Bourg, Brionne, and Beaumontel, and rail bridge at La Ferriere-sur-Risle. Ftrs fly ground force cover over Saint-Malo and Dreux and armed rcn in NW France. IX TAC ftrs attack and severely damage Gestapo HQ near Chateauroux.

Twelfth AF: Despite bad weather, MBs attack railroad bridges leading to beachhead area of S French coast and hit coastal guns SW of Toulon. LBs hit motor transport during night and drop ammo to invasion forces.

FBs and ftrs on armed rcn and patrol score excellent results against motor transport and rail cars and destroy several airplanes on A/Fs in S France.

Fifteenth AF: 53 B–17's, with ftr cover, bomb Nish A/F. 250 B–24's, escorted by P–51's, bomb 3 oil refineries and T/Os in Ploesti area.

Tenth AF: 47 FBs spt ground forces in Pinbaw area. 9 B–25's bomb Katha. 12 FBs pound town areas of Nanyinbya and Bilumyo. 12 other FBs attack arty positions and storage areas in Momauk area. India is cleared of all Japanese forces.

Fourteenth AF: 25 B–24's blast Yoyang. 18 B–25's bomb railroad yards and storage area at Chiuchiang and 4 hit road and A/F in Hengyang area and storage buildings at Nanyo. 100-plus P–40's, P–51's, and P–38's on offensive rcn attack town areas, bridges, hangars, supply dumps, railroad tgts, and road and river traffic in E Burma, around Hsenwi, Tungling, and Tengchung, and throughout Tungting Lake-C Yangtze R area, particularly in Hengyang area. 8 P–40's attack shipping in Haiphong area and between Dong Trieu and Ha Duong.

FEAF: B–24's pound A/Fs on Amboina, Ceram and Boeroe Is. B–25's strafe installations at Dili, on Moloe, and in NW Kai Is. MBs sink transport vessel off Halmahera I. A–20's bomb Klamono oil fields while FBs hit gun positions, storage areas, and other tgts at Ransiki and Manokwari and troop concentrations along N shore of MacCluer Gulf. On Biak P–40's, supporting ground forces landing at Wardo, pound shore positions and troops inland as enemy remnants on Biak break up into small groups.

P–39's strafe troops from Cape Wom to Dandriwad R and near But, and hit gun positions at Marubian.

Seventh AF: B–24's from Saipan bomb Iwo Jima. Makin-based B–25's hit Ponape.

18 August

Eighth AF: More than 700 HBs attack 15 assigned tgts including bridges, A/Fs, fuel dumps, an aero engine plant, and several T/Os, in France and Belgium supported by 8 ftr gps (1 other gp escorts MBs of Ninth AF). 3 of the escorting gps later strafe 3 A/Fs in France, destroying 48 parked airplanes. 12 FB gps successfully attack A/Fs and transportation facilities in the Seine-Brussels area encountering about 100 ftrs. 15 FBs are lost. 10 ftrs are claimed destroyed.

Ninth AF: Nearly 100 B–26's and A–20's strike fuel dump, ammo dump, rail and road overpass, rail embankment, and junction beyond battleline to disorganize retreating German forces. Over 1,000 ftrs fly cover over ground forces in Argentan-Paris area, along Seine R, and armed rcn over N and W France.

Twelfth AF: MBs blast coastal guns in Toulon area and shipping in Toulon harbor. FBs closely spt beachhead troops, hit rolling stock and rail lines, and generally disrupt comm as US VI Corps overruns primary defenses in coastal area of SE France. Ftrs maintain beachhead patrols and area cover for bmrs.

Fifteenth AF: 370 ftr-escorted B–17's and B–24's bomb 5 oil refineries around Ploesti. 89 B–24's, with ftr cover, bomb Alibunar A/F.

Tenth AF: 16 P–47's and P–51's

knock out road bridge, attack town areas, and hit general T/Os in Bhamo area. 4 P-47's knock out both approaches to bridge in Hsenwi. Troop concentration in Moda is pounded by 15 P-47's and P-51's and an A-36. 39 P-47's, P-40's and P-51's closely spt ground forces in various Pinbaw area sectors. 8 P-47's sweep Lashio A/F, strafing several T/Os.

Fourteenth AF: 12 B-25's bomb storage areas at Mangshih. 6 pound storage area at Changsha. 60-plus P-40's, P-51's, and P-38's on armed rcn attack troops, town areas, bridges, and other T/Os in E Burma, Lashio, Tengchung, Lungling, and Mangshih areas, and in Tungting Lake-C Yangtze R area at points including Yoyang, Chaling, Yuhsien, Hengshan, Chuchou, and Hsuchang.

FEAF: FBs and A-20's pound troops and storage area at Suain and hit def lines near Sarmi. Armed rcn missions continue over wide stretches of SWPA including Amboina-Ceram, Palau Is, and Halmahera I. Several T/Os are attacked.

Seventh AF: P-47's from Saipan bomb and strafe Pagan I.

19 August

Ninth AF: 50th and 53d TC Wgs, on loan to MAAF to participate in invasion of S France, are ordered to return to UK. No IX BC operations. Ftrs cover ground forces in battle areas and fly armed rcn along Seine R and surrounding areas and in wide areas around Paris, Orleans, and Tours.

Twelfth AF: A-20's hit M/Ys while B-25's and B-26's bomb road and rail bridges throughout SE France. FBs and ftrs continue to pound enemy comm N and W of beachhead and guns in the immediate battle area as US Seventh Army's TF Butler crosses Durance R and moves N to Sisteron and Digne.

Fifteenth AF: Bombing Ploesti area for fourth consecutive day, 65 B-17's supported by 125 P-51's blast 2 oil refineries.

Tenth AF: 4 P-47's spt ground forces SW of Thaikwagon. 4 others strafe trucks carrying troops between Bhamo and Myothit.

Fourteenth AF: 25 B-24's bomb Puchi, severely damaging warehouse area. 11 B-25's hit Sienning. 3 hit railroad tracks and runway N of Hengyang. More than 70 P-40's and P-51's on armed rcn attack river shipping, troops, trucks, and other T/Os at or near Pengtse, Hengyang, Chaling, Yoyang, Siangtan, and Changsha.

FEAF: Weather restricts operations. P-40's bomb port of Napido. P-39's bomb and strafe coastal positions along W shore of Geelvink Bay. A-20's operating in force in spt of ground troops pound tgts in Sawar-Sarmi sector. P-39's spt ground forces in Wewak area.

Seventh AF: Saipan-based P-47's bomb installations on Anatahan and drop fire-bombs on Tinian to aid ground forces in mopping-up operations.

Eleventh AF: A weather sortie and a 4-plane shipping sweep are flown with negative results.

20 August

Ninth AF: 61 B-26's bomb troop and equipment concentration waiting at Foret de la Lande to be ferried across the Seine. Ftrs fly armed rcn along Seine, spt ground troops in battle area, and fly escort mission to over 100 troop carriers on supply and evacuation run.

Twelfth AF: During 19/20 Aug A–20's attack lights and motor transport from battleline NW to the Rhone. B–26's, joined by FBs and ftrs, hit coastal def guns in Toulon area, while B–25's bomb Rhone Valley bridges and A/Fs achieving especially good results at A/F near Valence.

Fifteenth AF: 460-plus B–24's and B–17's, some ftr-escorted, bomb A/F and M/Y at Szolnok, and oil refineries at Dubova, Czechowice and Auschwitz.

Tenth AF: 24 P–47's and P–51's fly close spt strikes for ground forces immediately S of Thaikwagon. 4 P–51's hit T/Os at Myintha and Aledaw.

Fourteenth AF: 4 B–25's and 7 P–40's damage buildings and a pontoon bridge and strafe about 30 sampans in the Hengyang area. 13 P–40's hit buildings, trucks, and river shipping in Hengshan area. 60-plus P–40's and P–51's attack numerous trucks, rivercraft, and general T/Os at Tingka, Anjen, Yangtien, S of Yoyang, between Hankow and Chinchiang, and between Sinshih and Changsha.

FEAF: B–24's bomb town and A/F of Namlea. B–25's bomb Langgoer A/F. B–24's pound personnel areas and warehouses at Tobelo. P–39's hit Windissi and enemy shipping off Manokawri while P–40's pound gun positions, buildings and stores at Manokwari. Other P–40's spt ground forces by hitting troop concentrations at Napido. A–20's and FBs hit personnel center near Marubian, supplies at Wom, and numerous tgts during coastal sweeps in Wewak general area.

Twentieth AF: 61 Chengtu-based B–29's bomb Imperial Iron and Steel Works at Yawata during the day, followed by 10 more during 20/21 Aug, 5 hitting tgts other than the primary. 14 B–29's are lost, including 1 to AA and 4 to enemy airplanes (1 by air-to-air bombing and 1 by ramming). B–29 gunners claim 17 air victories.

Seventh AF: Saipan-based B–24's hit Yap for the first time. A B–24 bombs Alamagan while P–47's pound Pagan. Marshalls-based B–24's bomb Truk.

Eleventh AF: 4 B–25's fly a negative shipping sweep.

21 August

International: A series of conferences begins at Dumbarton Oaks. Delegates from US, UK, USSR, and China discuss postwar issues.

Ninth AF: Bad weather grounds all bmrs and ftrs. Less than 20 transports fly supply and evacuation missions.

Twelfth AF: MBs hit roads and bridges in Po Valley while A–20's during 20/21 Aug strike motor transport in the W part of the Valley and bomb Alessandria barracks during the day. FBs and ftrs again blast enemy comm lines and gun positions in S France, M/Y and rail lines at Alessandria and Casale Monferrato, and motor transport and train cars in NW Italy and SE France.

Fifteenth AF: 117 B–24's, escorted by P–51's, bomb Nish A/F. 102 B–24's, with P–51 escort, hit Hajduboszormeny A/F which 46 other P–51's sweep, some making low-level strafings on parked aircraft.

Tenth AF: 6 B–25's knock out and

damage 3 river bridges at Mu area and at Hsipaw, 36 P–51's spt ground forces near Pinlon, Ingyingon, and Nansankyin. 8 P–51's bomb storage area at Chyahkan.

Fourteenth AF: 8 B–25's bomb Anjen and T/Os in surrounding area. 7 others attack Hengyang A/F, town of Nanyo, and several buildings and other T/Os near Yangtien. 90-plus FBs hit town areas, river and road traffic, and other T/Os at Pengtse, Kinhwa, Tengchung, Anjen, Hengyang, and Yangtsishih; S of Sintsaing, N of Tungting Lake, between Hankow and Sinti, and in Changsha area.

FEAF: B–24's blast supply dumps and AA guns on Wasile Bay coast. B–25's hit Kaoe A/F and town. B–25's hit villages and supply areas on Karakelong I. FBs blast warehouses and other tgts in Manokwari area. A–20's and FBs hit supply dumps in Sawar-Sarmi sector and attack troops along coast, particularly from Babiang to Luain.

Seventh AF: B–24's from Saipan hit Yap, P–47's bomb Pagan, and Makin-based B–25's hit Nauru.

22 August

Ninth AF: IX BC operations are cancelled because of weather. Ftrs fly sweeps, provide air cover for 2 inf and 1 armd div, strafe numerous military and transportation tgts, and fly armed rcn from Evreux to Troyes.

Twelfth AF: Weather restricts operation in SE France. B–26's attack tgts in Po Valley where they destroy 1 bridge and severely damage another. A–20's hit motor transport SW of Alessandria and in Nice area during 21/22 Aug and hit industrial buildings in S France during the day. Ftrs hit motor transport W of the Rhone and in scattered parts of SE France.

Fifteenth AF: Around 530 B–17's and B–24's supported by P–51's and P–38's bomb oil refineries at Korneuburg, Odertal, and Blechhammer (2), and oil storage at Lobau.

Tenth AF: P–51's and P–47's fly 53 sorties against Tengchung in spt of attacking Chinese forces. 28 P–47's attack buildings, supply dumps, troops, and gun positions near Ingyingon, Nansankyin, and Pinlon. 8 P–47's strafe T/Os between Tingka and Bhamo. 2 rocket-firing P–51's seriously damage several buildings at Aledaw. 9 B–25's bomb Hopin.

Fourteenth AF: 11 P–40's and P–38's hit bridges and road tgts around Tingka, Mangshih, Loiwing, and Pangpying. 6 others attack landing strip and river traffic at an island near Foochow.

FEAF: FBs continue to blast supply and personnel tgts in Manokwari and surrounding areas. FBs again hit N coastal New Guinea areas, including shipping facilities at Wewak, barge terminal on Mushu I, and trains and troop positions at various coastal points.

Seventh AF: Saipan-based B–24's bomb A/Fs on Yap and Pagan. P–47's also pound Pagan A/F and AA emplacements. Kwajalein-based B–24's hit Mille.

23 August

Eighth AF: 150-plus FBs bomb and strafe rail transportation from Saint-Omer to Reims. Over 80 bomb Hamm M/Ys and 9 others, and strafe miscellaneous ground and river tgts.

Ninth AF: IX BC sends 4 B–26's to

drop leaflets on Lisieux-Bernay area. Ftrs fly ground forces cover, sweeps, armed rcn over battle areas and along Seine R, and attack arty positions. Over 150 transports fly supply and evacuation missions and several hundred rcn aircraft fly tac, visual, photographic, and arty adjustment rcn missions.

Twelfth AF: MBs attack road and rail bridges N of Arno R and roads leading N from Florence, and also hit bridges in Rhone Valley. Widespread haze in parts of France and Italy prevents accurate bombing. FBs continue to attack comm, gun positions, and road movements in Provence battle areas.

Fifteenth AF: 472 B–24's and B–17's supported by P–51's and P–38's bomb S industrial area of Vienna, Wiener-Neudorf aircraft engine factory, Vosendorf oil refinery, and Markersdorf A/F, and attack tgts at Ferrara, missing river bridge but hitting synthetic rubber factory.

Tenth AF: 32 P–47's spt British advances down railroad in Pinbaw area hitting gun positions, troops, and HQ buildings, immediately N or Pinbaw, and along Nansonti Creek. 6 P–47's pound Onsansaing, 8 P–51's bomb encampment near Kadu, and 4 hit Lungling and Mangshih. 5 others attack guns, fuel dump, and other T/Os along Burma Road from Wanling to Lungling while 7 more hit buildings and vehicles during sweeps of the general Mangshih-Chefang area. 12 P–51's hit T/Os SW of Lungling and 2 P–40's strafe trucks at Chefang.

Fourteenth AF: 7 B–25's and 21 FBs attack villages, compounds, other T/Os near Hengyang, Ling-

yang, and Anjen. More than 40 FBs hit villages, shipping, troops, supplies, and other T/Os around Ichang, Yangtien, Siangtan, and Yiyang, and S of Sungpai and Siangyin.

FEAF: B–24's pound Galela area and Langgoer A/F and Saumlakki. FBs hit A/F at Nabire, Moemi, and Urarom, village of Moari, and town of Manokwari. B–25's, A–20's, and FBs continue to attack barge hideouts, troops, villages, and general T/Os around Wewak.

Seventh AF: B–24's from Saipan bomb Yap and Iwo Jima while P–47's hit Pagan and Aguijan. Gilbert-based B–25's attack Ponape.

24 August

Eighth AF: Almost 400 HBs attack armament factory and 17 oil installations, aircraft assembly plants and aero engine works and over 20 T/Os in Germany, losing 27 HBs, but claiming 10 enemy airplanes destroyed. VIII FC flies over 600 sorties in spt of mission, claiming 10 combat victories. 4 gps strafe A/Fs near Brandenburg and Nordhausen, an M/Y near Brunswick, and the Neuenhaus-Nordhorn area. Ground tgts destroyed include 14 airplanes, 7 locomotives, trucks, and boats.

Ninth AF: Weather cancels IX BC mission against 4 fuel dumps N of the Seine. Ftrs give air cover to ground forces, mainly for 3 armd and 2 inf divs, bomb Seine bridges, and fly armed rcn along Seine and around Troyes, Orleans, and Tours. About 275 transports fly supply and evacuation missions.

Twelfth AF: A–20's during 23/24 Aug hit motor transport and T/O in Rhone Valley and at Genoa, Milan, and Turin. MBs bomb bridges at Montpellier, Avignon, Lunel, Solignano Nuovo, and Castel del Rio, and score direct hits on gun positions in Marseille area. Ftrs bomb and strafe gun positions, vehicles, roads and bridges throughout SE France.

Fifteenth AF: 530–plus B–17's and B–24's bomb 3 oil refineries at Kolin and Pardubice, Vinkovci M/Y, Szeged, and Ferrara railroad bridge and several T/Os. Around 70–80 fts attack the Czechoslovakian missions. US HBs and escorting ftrs claim nearly 40 air victories.

Tenth AF: 9 B–25's bomb Kangon. 3 P–47 flights spt British troops NE of Pinbaw, hitting forces and gun emplacements near Namyin Te and Nansankyin. 4 P–47's bomb Nankan. 4 P–51's strafe vehicles along Shweli R and bomb storage area S of Hopin.

Fourteenth AF: Town areas, river and road traffic, railroad tgts, and other T/Os in or near Hengyang, Chuchou, Siangtan, and Yangtien are attacked by 8 B–25's and 25 P–40's. 19 other P–40's hit similar T/Os at Yungcheng, Anjen, along C Yangtze R, and S of Mangshih.

FEAF: Shipping in Lembeh Strait is attacked by B–25's, while B–24's bomb Lolobata A/F.

Twentieth AF: Advanced air echelon of Gen O'Donnell's 73d Bomb Wg HQ flies into the Marianas, the first Twentieth AF contingent to arrive. Ground echelon arrives by water on 16 Sep.

Seventh AF: Saipan-based P–47's pound Aguijan and Pagan. Marshall-based B–24's bomb Truk while B–25's hit Nauru.

25 August

Eighth AF: Over 1,100 HBs attack 4 aircraft plants, 3 A/Fs, 2 experimental stations and 15 T/Os in Germany. 19 HBs are lost. 15 ftr gps fly over 600 supporting sorties downing 11 enemy aircraft. 4 gps later strafe ground tgts including numerous parked airplanes of which 30 are claimed destroyed. In a follow-up operation 92 HBs attack 5 liquid oxygen plants in Belgium and N France. 5 ftr gps fly escort.

Ninth AF: About 240 A–20's and B–26's attack various enemy strongholds in and around Brest supporting ground forces' attempt to capture Brest harbor. Ftrs provide air cover for 5 divs, fly armed rcn along Seine R, and sweeps in wide areas around Paris which is liberated. Ftrs of IX TAC raid, and set afire with napalm tanks, the reported HQ of FM Model (CinC West) and Verzy.

Twelfth AF: A–20's hit T/Os during 24/25 Aug, and during the day fly armed rcn over Po and Rhone Valleys, and hit ammo stores in S France. B–25's and B–26's attack Rhone R bridges at Avignon, Culoz, Saint-Alban-du-Rhone, Pont d'Ain, and Loyes, and hit gun positions around Marseille. FBs on armed rcn in SE France battle area and along battleline N of Arno R attack gun positions, roads, and bridges.

Fifteenth AF: More than 300 B–17's and B–24's supported by P–38's and P–51's bomb aircraft factories at Brno and Kurim and A/Fs at Brno and Prostejov.

Tenth AF: 9 B–25's bomb Kondangyi. 4 P–47's knock out bridge S of Bhamo and hit several T/Os in the area. 2 P–51's bomb probable factory at Hopin. 6 flights of P–51's attack buildings and T/Os at Pinlon and Kyagyigon. 32 other P–51's spt ground forces at Ingyingon and along Hsai-hkao and Namsang R.

Fourteenth AF: 3 B–24's bomb Kowloon docks. 3 B–25's and 12 P–40's hit buildings, troop compounds, and general T/Os in Yangtien area. 4 B–25's and 21 P–40's attack similar tgts in and around Anjen. 2 B–25's bomb ftr strip at Leiyang and 2 others hit town of Nanyo. 40 P–51's and P–40's attack wide variety of T/Os throughout Hengyang, Siangyin, Siangtan, and Siangsiang areas, Chenghsien, Lishui, Samshui, Chiangmen, Luichow Peninsula, and Red R delta.

FEAF: B–24's strike Koror and Malakal I. B–24's pound Lolobata. B–25's on shipping sweep over Lembeh Strait claim a merchant ship sunk and hit several small vessels. In Lesser Sunda Is a few B–25's on shipping sweep attack several small vessels. A–20's and FBs hit Babo A/F, Sagan, and Otawiri. P–39's strafe troops near But.

Seventh AF: B–24's from Saipan hit A/F on Iwo Jima while P–47's blast AA positions and troops on Pagan. A B–24 bombs Yap. Gilbertsbased B–25's bomb Ponape.

Eleventh AF: 1 B–24 flies rcn over Shasukotan, Onnekotan, and Harumukotan Is but drops no bombs due to accurate AA fire.

26 August

Eighth AF: HBs are dispatched in 4 operations against tgts in France and Germany. In first operation 95 B–24's bomb synethetic oil plant at Ludwigshafen, M/Ys at Ehrang and

Konz-Karthaus, and other tgts at Alzey and Meisenheim. 2 ftr gps fly spt, with 1 gp later strafing Speyer A/F. In second operation 171 B–17's escorted by 1 P–51 gp bomb 8 gun positions at Brest while clouds prevent over 150 other HBs from bombing. In the third operation over 400 B–17's and B–24's bomb 2 synthetic oil plants, 2 oil refineries, a fuel depot, 2 A/Fs, and T/Os in NW Germany. 7 ftr gps escort, with 1 gp later conducting strafing attacks. In last operation an attack by 30 B–17's against 3 liquid oxygen plants in Belgium is aborted because of thick haze. 1 P–51 gp gives uneventful spt.

Ninth AF: IX TCC is relieved of its assignment to the Ninth AF upon transfer of the cmd and its serv organizations from IX AFSC to First Allied Airborne Army commanded by Gen Brereton. IX BC strikes fuel dumps at Saint-Gobain, Fournival/Bois-de-Mont, and Compiegne/Clairoix, and troop and equipment concentrations at Rouen. Ftrs fly escort to BC, ground forces and assault area cover, and armed rcn in Rouen, Dijon, Chatillon-sur-Seine and S Loire areas.

Twelfth AF: During 25/26 Aug FBs on armed rcn over W Po Valley and over Nice area bomb vehicles and other T/Os, and during day bomb ammo dumps in SE France and in NC Italy. MBs hit guns in Marseille area but several missions into Rhone Valley are aborted due to bad weather. FBs and ftrs fly armed rcn over N Italy and SE France, attacking rail lines, roads, guns, vehicles, and other T/Os.

Fifteenth AF: 470–plus HBs escorted by P–38's and P–51's attack viaducts and bridges at Venzone, Avisio, and Latisana, and hit train ferry and terminal at Giurgiu, A/F at Otopeni, barracks and troops in Baneasa area and viaduct at Borovnica.

Fourteenth AF: 3 B–24's bomb storage area at Amoy. 3 B–25's bomb barracks area near Wenchow harbor and damage bridge near Sincheng. 31 FBs attack railroad tgts, troops, sampans, and other T/Os in or near Yangtien, Yungfengshih, Siangsiang, Anjen, Laiyuan, Kinhwa, and Pengtse.

FEAF: B–24's bomb Koror and Peleliu A/Fs. Other B–24's bomb Haroekoe and Liang A/Fs. A–20's in close ground spt hit troop concentrations in the Sarmi sector. FBs hit T/Os in Wewak and Suain areas. P–39's maintain patrols over W shore of Geelvink Bay.

Seventh AF: Saipan-based B–24's bomb Iwo Jima A/F. P–47's blast AA guns and trooops on Pagan and Aguijan. A B–24 on armed rcn bombs Woleai and Yap.

Eleventh AF: 3 B–24's hit Kashiwabara staging area during early morning, starting several fires. Later 6 B–25's strafe and bomb E coast of N Kurils, sinking a patrol boat. 1 out of 4 interceptors and one of the B–25's are hit. 7 more B–24's bomb tgts on Kashiwabara and on Otomari Cape, including docks, piers, boats, and a fuel dump. 6 P–38's unsuccessfully attempt to intercept 4 unidentified aircraft W of Attu.

27 August

Eighth AF: Over 1,200 HBs fly against Berlin area tgts but abort mission due to high clouds. Over 150 of the HBs attack T/Os in German coastal area and Danish peninsula, including 4 A/Fs, 2 M/Ys, 2 islands, 3 cities, and scattered tgts. 11 P–51 gps provide escort and strafe ground tgts in Germany, destroying several including 24 locomotives. 5 B–17's and 10 P–51's are lost. 8 FB gps strafe and bomb rail transportation in E France and the Saar, claiming, among other tgts, over 100 locomotives and over 200 train cars destroyed.

Ninth AF: IX BC attacks troop concentrations in Rouen area, Rouen bridge, Boulogne-sur-Mer/Boursin navigational beam station, and Bucyles-Pierrepont and Foret de Samoussy fuel dumps. Ftrs cover ground forces and fly sweeps and armed rcn in Senlis area and S of Loire R claiming 16 aircraft (11 in the air) destroyed, and losing 6.

Twelfth AF: MBs hit gun emplacements in Marseille area and bomb bridges at Berceto. FBs continue armed rcn in Po Valley and over roads leading N from battle line N of the Arno R. LBs bomb T/Os in Po Valley during 26/27 Aug, fly armed rcn and during the day hit ammo stores in NC Italy.

Fifteenth AF: 530-plus ftr-supported HBs attack 2 oil refineries in Blechhammer, railroad bridge at Ferrara, and viaducts at Avisio, Venzone, and Borovnica.

Tenth AF: 23 P–47's spt ground forces in Pinbaw area, hitting Kondangyi and troops and strongpoints near Pinbaw.

Fourteenth AF: 7 B–25's bomb Hengyang, Tien Ho, White Cloud, and Pailochi A/Fs. 9 others hit road and river traffic in Yoyang, Hankow, Changsha, and Hengyang areas. 120-plus P–40's and P–51's hit T/Os in the above areas plus Yangtien, Chachiang, Anjen, Leiyang, Sintsiang, Siangsiang, and Siangtan, damaging or destroying numerous trucks, many rivercraft and hittig several troop concentrations.

FEAF: FBs hit Miti and A/Fs at Babo, Ransiki, Sagan, and Manokwari. FBs hit bivouacs near Boram, troops between Abau and Boikin, and a fuel dump and barges at Kairiru I.

Seventh AF: A Saipan-based B-24 bombs Iwo Jima while another, after photo rcn of Woleai, bombs Yap. P-47's bomb AA positions on Pagan and strafe buildings on Alamagan.

Eleventh AF: 5 B-24's bomb and photograph Kashiwabara in 2 raids. 4 B-25's on a shipping sweep E of the N Kurils bomb and strafe picket boats damaging 1 and leaving another sinking.

28 August

Eighth AF: Weather prevents HB operations. 8 P-51 gps fly strafing sweeps against rail and road traffic in areas in or around Brussels, Antwerp, Namur, Mezieres, Metz, Strasbourg, Trier, and Bad Kreuznach. Claims include 8 aircraft and nearly 150 locomotive destroyed. 16 P-51's are lost. FBs fly 2 strafing and bombing operations. The first is flown by 6 gps against rail and road traffic in and around Strasbourg, Saarbrucken, Sarrebourg, Metz, and Trier. In the second, 5 gps attack rail and road traffic in NW France, Belgium, and the Netherlands including bombing 13 M/Ys.

Ninth AF: B-26's and A-20's of IX BC bomb fuel dumps at Doullens, Barisis-aux-Bois, ammo dump at

Querrieu, ammo and fuel dump at Compiegne/Foret de Laigue, and alcohol distillery and fuel storage depot at Hamm. Ftrs escort BC and about 400 transports on supply and evacuation runs, attack A/Fs at Bourges and Peronne, spt ground forces, and fly armed rcn from Amiens to E of Dijon.

Twelfth AF: B-25's bomb railroad bridges in Lyon area. B-26's destroy several airplanes at Villafranca di Verona A/F and bridge at Parma. A-20's hit motor transport and other T/Os during 27/28 Aug, fly armed rcn over Po Valley and blast cmd post SE of Genoa. FBs hit vehicles in Rhone Valley, bomb and strafe roads and bridges in battle area N of Arno R and hit shipping in Imperia and Savona harbors.

Fifteenth AF: 560-plus HBs escorted by P-38's and P-51's strike Moosbierbaum oil refinery and adjacent chemical works, oil refinery at Szony, railroad bridges and viaducts at Szolnok, Zambana, Avisio, and Ora, and M/Ys at Miskolc.

Tenth AF: 4 P-47's bomb tank pool at Momauk, while 5 others hit Myintha. 2 P-47's spt ground forces in Pinbaw area.

Fourteenth AF: 8 B-25's bomb Tien Ho, White Cloud, Hankow, and Pailochi A/Fs. 8 more attack river and road traffic from Chiuchiang to Hankow and from Hengyang to Puchi. 32 P-40's pound T/Os at Hengyang and Pailochi. 23 P-40's attack Taying storage buildings and 10 P-40's and P-51's hit Anjen and nearby T/Os.

FEAF: B-24's hit Koror, A/F on Peleliu, and seaplane base on Arakabesan. FBs hit Kokas, vessels off Point

Karakra, barracks at Nabire, storage facilities at Moemi and Manokwari and Boram fuel dumps. A–20's and FBs attack small vessels along E coast of Ceram.

Twentieth AF: Gen Hansell assumes cmd of XXI BC. Gen Norstad succeeds Hansell as CoS of Twentieth AF.

Seventh AF: Saipan-based B–24's pound Iwo Jima by day and night. P–47's hit Pagan and Maug Is. A B–24 on armed rcn bombs Yap. Gilberts-based B–25's strike Ponape; Marshalls-based B–24's hit Truk.

29 August

Eighth AF: 5 FB gps attack rail transportation in N France, Belgium, and W Germany. 2 A/Fs, 3 M/Ys, rail lines at several points, and a large number of rail and road vehicles are attacked.

Ninth AF: Bad weather allows only minimum bmr and ftr operations. B–26's attack 1 fuel dump while a few ftrs fly sweeps over NW France. Over 100 transports complete supply and evacuation missions.

Twelfth AF: MBs hit 4 bridges and a viaduct in NE Italy while LBs hit fuel station. FBs hit roads and bridges in N Italy and spt ground forces in Arno R Valley. P–47's of 87th Wg fly MB escort and armed rcn, claiming 100 vehicles destroyed. XII TAC ftrs attack tgts in Rhone Valley.

Fifteenth AF: 550 HBs strike comm tgts in Po Valley and in the Hungarian Plain, oil refineries and comm tgts in the Silesian Plain, including Bohumin area, steel works and M/Y, Moravska-Ostrava M/Y, oil refineries and industrial area including tank works, Szolnok and Sze-

ged M/Ys, and railway bridges at Szeged, Borovnica, Salzano, and Ferrara. P–38's bomb Latisana bridge.

Tenth AF: 8 B–25's attack tgts in Katha and hit 2 bridges just N of the town area. 8 P–51's attack Bilumyo. 5 P–47's destroy road bridge at Mainghka and 5 others hit buildings in Bhamo.

Fourteenth AF: 24 B–24's escorted by 45 ftrs, blast railroad yards at Yoyang. 15 B–25's bomb Pailochi, White Cloud, Tien Ho, and Hankow A/Fs. 10 others hit trucks and other T/Os from Hengyang to Yoyang, from Hankow to Chinchiang, and near Anjen. 18 P–40's hit storage area and T/Os around Tangyang. 17 attack trucks and buildings from Siangtan to Changsha. 14 P–40's claim 8 ftrs downed over Shayang. 22 others attack trucks, supplies, and troops at Wuhu, Ichang, S of Isuho, SW of Lungling, and N of Hengshan.

FEAF: B–24's bomb Koror, Malakal, seaplane base on Arakabesan, and supply area N of Ngesebus A/F. B–24's bomb barracks at Amboina and P–38's hit seaplane base at Halong.

Twentieth AF: Gen LeMay becomes CG XX BC.

Seventh AF: Saipan-based B–24's bomb Iwo Jima and Pagan during the evening. P–47's strafe AA positions on Pagan while a B–24 on armed rcn bombs Yap. Gilberts-based B–25's bomb Nauru.

30 August

Eighth AF: About 200 HBs supported by 16 P–51's bomb 8 V-weapon sites in Pas de Calais area. Later in the day over 600 B–17's supported by 7 P–51 gps bomb U-boat base and shipyards at Kiel, and aircraft plant and other industry in the Bremen area.

Ninth AF: About 75 A-20's and B-26's bomb fuel dump near Arques-la-Bataille, Rouxmesnil-Bouteilles, and gun positions around Ile de Cezembre. Weather grounds ftrs.

Twelfth AF: Weather grounds MBs. LBs hit T/Os during 29/30 Aug and fuel storage while FBs pound roads and railroads in Po Valley and, on armed rcn over Rhone Valley, attack rail lines and motor and horse-drawn vehicles, as US Seventh Army elements continue up Rhone Valley toward Lyon.

Fifteenth AF: Over 100 B-24's and B-17's bomb railroad bridges at Cuprija, Novi Sad, and Vranjevo. Nearly 100 P-51's strafe Kecskemet and Oradea A/Fs.

Tenth AF: Several P-47's bomb and strafe town of Man Sai.

Fourteenth AF: B-25's attack Hengyang, Pailochi, and Hankow A/Fs, roads in Nanyo and Changsha areas, and boats between Changsha and Hengyang, and Kichun and Wuh-sueh. In Kweiyi and Sintsiang areas 33 P-40's claim 58 trucks destroyed, 175 damaged, and at least 100 Japanese killed. 10 P-51's hit scattered T/O's in same areas. 21 P-40's hit barracks, trucks, and a bridge in Siangsiang and Siangtan region. 34 P-40's and P-51's attack a variety of tgts, including railroad traffic and facilities, occupied areas, and trucks, at Yangtien, between Hengshan and Nanyo, NE of Ichang, SW Hengshan, and near Hengyang.

FEAF: Koror and Malakal are pounded by B-24's. B-24's hit Wasile Bay storage and personnel areas while B-25's make low-level attack on Kaoe town. P-38's bomb oil tanks, barracks, and AA positions at Boela. P-47's hit Urarom runway and Man-okwari storage area, P-38's bomb A/Fs at Babo and Ransiki, and P-39's hit T/Os along W coast of Geelvink Bay.

Seventh AF: A B-24 on armed rcn from Saipan bombs Yap. P-47's strafe positions and storage areas on Pagan. Kwajalein-based B-24's hit Mille.

31 August

Ninth AF: 99 B-26's and A-20's bomb ammo dump at Foret d'Arques and gun positions at Ile de Cezembre. Ftrs fly armed rcn in Amiens, Saint-Quentin, Albert, and Arras areas, ground forces cover for 3 armd divs, battleship cover, and also dive-bomb Ile de Cezembre.

Twelfth AF: MBs attack railroad bridges in Po Valley, cutting the bridge at Mira. A-20's attack T/Os in Po Valley during 30/31 Aug and along with FBs hit comm N of Arno R. Other FBs attack comm tgts in France as US Seventh Army pushes toward Lyon.

Fifteenth AF: 45 P-51's strafe A/F at Reghin, while 97 others strafe A/Fs at Oradea and Kecskemet. Ftrs claim a record number of over 150 aircraft destroyed on the ground. Starting Operation REUNION, 36 B-17's evacuate US airmen interned in Rumania from Bucharest (which falls to the Soviet Army today) to Bari.

Tenth AF: 6 B-25's bomb T/Os at Katha and 3 hit bridges at Baw-gyo and Hsenwi.

Fourteenth AF: 12 B-24's bomb Takao harbor, damaging dock area and claiming 2 tankers sunk. 14 B–25's attack Tien Ho, White Cloud, Kai Tek, and Hengyang A/Fs. 8 B–25's attack numerous trucks S of Sintsiang and near Sinshih, hit roads S of Nanyo and damage a freighter near Sinshih. 60-plus FBs attack trucks, barracks, supplies, rivercraft, bridges and troops in or near Sinshih, Changsha, Yangtien, Hengyang, Nanyo, Siangtan, Teian, and Shihhweiyao.

Seventh AF: Saipan-based P–47's strafe gun positions at A/F on Pagan. Yap and Pagan are bombed by single B–24's.

1 September

Eighth AF: 950-plus HBs sent against tgts in E France and Germany are recalled because of bad weather. 1 HB bombs railroad at Hasloch. 11 ftr gps offer spt, 1 gp strafing a locomotive. A P–47 gp on sweep strafes transportation tgts in Brussels-Antwerp area. 7 P–47 gps bomb and strafe rail lines in N and E France and A/F W of Nancy claiming 5 combat victories and 5 destroyed on the ground.

Ninth AF: IX TCC comes under administrative control of USSTAF and under operational control of First Allied Airborne Army, to increase efficiency, especially for planning, trg, and preparation of airborne operations. SHAEF now can deal directly with all elements of an airborne force through a single unified cmd instead of through various army gps and AFs (*i.e.* 12 and 21 Army Gps, Ninth AF, and RAF components). MBs attack fortifications in Brest area which arty fire had been unable to reduce. Escorting ftrs fly sweeps and armed rcn in N and E France, and fly cover for 6 divs in Brussels, Amiens, Saint-Quentin, Cambrai, Reims, and Verdun areas.

Twelfth AF: During 31 Aug/1 Sep A–20's hit gun positions and T/Os in W Po Valley. Weather grounds B–26's during day but B–25's score excellent results against road and railroad bridges N and NE of Venice. FB and ftrs bomb and strafe roads, troop concentrations, supply dumps, and German HQ in battle area N of Florence, and fly armed rcn from Ventimiglia along coast to La Spezia.

Fifteenth AF: 480-plus HBs attack Boara Pisani, railroad bridges at Tesica/Moravac, Mitrovica, and Kraljevo, railroad bridges at Szolnok, and Mezotur, M/Ys at Szajol, Debreczen, Berettyoujfalu, and Novi Sad, and A/F at Nish. 51 P–51's successfully strafe Debreczen A/F. 16 B–17's evacuate interned US airmen from Rumania. Ftrs spt bombing and evacuation missions.

Tenth AF: A few P–47's attack Bhamo and strafe river boats in the area.

Fourteenth AF: 4 B–24's claim a small freighter sunk in Formosa Strait. 12 B–25's bomb Kai Tek A/F and a supply depot S of Canton. B–25's hit road S of Nanyo, runway at Hengyang, and T/Os near Anjen. 61 P–40's and P–51's attack bridges, roads, shipping, A/Fs troops, and other T/Os at or near Yangtien, Nanyo, Hengyang, Anjen, Changning, and Chiuchiang.

FEAF: 50-plus B–24's bomb Sasa, Matina, and Likanan A/Fs. Others, failing to reach Mindanao, hit Beo. FBs hit Boela and A/F at Amahai. A–20's, P–40's and B–25's bomb runways at Babo and Urarom.

Seventh AF: Saipan-based P–47's carry out rocket and strafing strike against Pagan. A lone B–24 on armed rcn bombs Yap. Marshalls-based B–24's bomb Truk.

Eleventh AF: A B–24 bombs Kashiwabara during 31 Aug/1 Sep. A B–25 bombs a shack on SW coast of Paramushiru and sinks a nearby ship. 5 other B–25's on this mission turn back due to overcast.

2 September

Eighth AF: A P–47 gp strafes gun positions and road and rail traffic in Bruges-Ghent-Courtrai-Roulers area.

Ninth AF: IX TAC, moving with US First Army, transfers HQ to Versailles. On 11 Sep HQ follows the ground forces to Jamioulx. Weather grounds bmrs. Ftrs fly armed rcn and area spt to ground forces in Belgium and NW, NE, and E France.

Twelfth AF: B–25's bomb 3 bridges in Po Valley, following raid during 1/2 Sep by A–20's which hit pontoon bridge and T/Os in the Valley. FBs blast roads, bridges and gun emplacements in Po Valley, docks at Savona, and shipping off shore. France-based FBs, hampered by poor weather, hit barracks and rail lines in Lyon area.

Fifteenth AF: XV FC (Prov) is activated and given control of the 305th Ftr Wg (Prov) and 306th Ftr Wg (Prov)—shortly to be organized—and their 7 ftr gps. 380-plus HBs hit Kraljevo railroad bridge and M/Y, railroad bridge at Mitrovica, road bridge at Supovac, and 3 M/Ys at Nish. 27 P–38's dive-bomb Cuprija road bridge while 57 P–38's and 112 P–51's strafe roads and railways in Nish and Belgrade areas. Other P–51's escort Nish and Supovac bombing missions.

Tenth AF: 8 B–25's hit tgts along Burma Road S of Wanling, including the road itself and bridges at Kawnghka and Namhpakka. Another B–25 hits alternate tgt, an area in Indaw. 24 B–24's haul fuel to Kunming.

Fourteenth AF: 2 B–25's bomb runway at Hengyang A/F. 30 P–40's attack gun positions, troop concentrations, and sampans in Hengyang and Changning areas. 20 P–40's hit similar tgts S of Changsha, W of Pengtse, and in Siangtan area. 12 P–51's damage bridge at Yangtien.

FEAF: B–24's operating in strength bomb warehouses at Lasang, shipyards and personnel areas at Bunawan, and A/F at Likanan. B–25's hit warehouses and shipyards along Lembeh Strait, while other B–25's hit position near Pitoe A/F on S Morotai I. B–24's bomb Koror. FBs hit Sorong area and forces at Cape Pus and Boikin.

Seventh AF: 2 Saipan-based B–24's hit Yap and Pagan. P–47's hit AA positions on Pagan with rocket and strafing attacks. Marshalls-based B–25's bomb Ponape and Nauru.

3 September

Eighth AF: Over 300 B–17's bomb Ludwigshafen/Opau synthetic oil plant. 5 escorting P–51 gps claim 7 combat victories. Nearly 400 B–17's bomb 16 gun batteries and def installations in Brest area, escorted by P–51 gp, which claims 7 aircraft destroyed. 3 P–47 gps strafe transportation tgts in Tilburg, Namur and Cologne areas. Bad weather cancels FB mission against strongpoints in

Brest area. Over 50 B–24's fly supplies to Orleans/Bricy A/F.

Ninth AF: MBs and LBs supporting ground troops pound strongpoints and bridges in Brest area. Ftrs fly armed rcn, ground spt, and sweeps in N and E France, Belgium, and W Germany.

Twelfth AF: MBs pound railroad and road bridges in W Po Valley while FBs blast motor transport and rolling stock in Turin area. On 2/3 Sep A–20's on armed rcn of N Italy, start fires in Genoa harbor. FBs blast German vehicles retreating up Rhone Valley. Capture of Lyon is completed by French elements of US Seventh Army.

Fifteenth AF: Over 300 HBs hit key escape routes of retreating German forces in the Balkans, and bomb rail comm and supply lines S from Budapest, 3 bridges in Belgrade area, bridges at Szajol and Szeged, and badly damage ferry docks at Smederovo. 3 B–17's evacuate interned airmen from Bucharest. 40 P–38's divebomb Smederovo ferry and strafe Kovin and Baviniste A/Fs and a landing ground, destroying many parked aircraft, motor transport, vehicles, and fuel tanks. 75 P–51's strafe roads, railroads, vehicles, bivouac areas, railroad repair shops, and miscellaneous tgts in Skoplje-Nish-Krusevac-Belgrade areas.

Tenth AF: 4 B–25's attack and slightly damage Tahpalai bridge NE of Hsipaw. 1 B–25 knocks out center span of a railroad bridge in the area and another causes considerable damage at Indaw.

Fourteenth AF: 12 B–24's pound M/Ys at Nanking. 7 B–25's destroy at least 45 trucks and damage about 100 others during armed rcn from Hengyang to Tungting Lake and Yoyang. 2 others bomb Hengyang A/F. More than 100 P–40's, P–51's, and P–38's attack troops, railroad tgts, bridges, and other T/Os in areas around Changning, Hengyang, Sungpai, Chuki, Yangtien, Hengshan, and near Haiphong and in Red R Valley.

FEAF: B–24's pound Langoan A/F and Lembeh Strait warehouses and shipping. B–25's hit village of Tobelo. FBs hit Babo, Waren and Nabire A/Fs, Manokwari storage and personnel areas, strafe areas along MacCluer Gulf, and fly coastal sweeps in Wewak area, strafing troops, supplies, and occupied areas. FBs hit oil tanks and radio station at Boela.

Thirteenth AF: XIII BC moves from Los Negros to Wakde.

Seventh AF: Saipan-based B–24's bomb Iwo Jima. P–47's hit Pagan and Maug Is with rockets. A lone B–24 on armed rcn bombs Yap.

4 September

Ninth AF: Weather prevents bmr activity. Ftrs fly armed rcn over Belgium, E France, Luxembourg, and E and C Germany, and defensive night patrols over W and NW France. British complete liberation of Brussels and clear most resistance from Antwerp.

Twelfth AF: B–25's and B–26's hit several road and railroad bridges and tunnel in Po Valley while FBs strike pontoon bridges, roads, bridges, and motor transport in preparation for Allied ground assault on Gothic Line. During 3/4 Sep A–20's on armed rcn of Po Valley bomb vehicles in Turin-Milan areas. Ftrs fly armed rcn and offensive patrols in Po and Rhone Valleys.

Fifteenth AF: 305th Ftr Wg (Prov) is organized and given control of the 3 P–38 gps of 306th Ftr Wg. Almost 400 HBs, with ftr escort, attack submarines in Genoa harbor and hit comm in N Italy including Avisio viaduct, M/Ys at Trento, Bronzola, and Ora, and railroad bridges at Ora, Casarsa della Delizia, and Latisana.

Tenth AF: 24 B–24's haul 32,000 gals of fuel to Kunming. Though heavy rains curtail combat operations, 9 P–47's attack Bhamo and Myothit.

Fourteenth AF: 12 B–25's blast sampan, barge, and motor launch concentrations in Kweiyang area. 6 B–25's, with P–51 spt, pound Paishui and Lingling areas, considerably damaging town of Lingling and killing an estimated 60 soldiers and 10 horses. 100-plus P–40's and P–51's on armed rcn kill large numbers of troops and horses, pound river and road traffic, and a variety of other T/Os in the E Burma-SW China region around Changning and Lungling and throughout areas mainly to the S of Tungting Lake-Yangtze R section of inland SE China, mainly around Hengyang, Lingling, Leiyang, Yangtien, and Kiyang.

FEAF: Bad weather cancels most large-scale operations. A–20's and B–25's hit Urarom A/F and FBs attack Moemi and hit Napido. During 4/5 Sep B–24's bomb Kendari A/F.

Seventh AF: 5 B–24's, on armed rcn, snooper mission, and trg flight, bomb Iwo Jima, Marcus, Yap, and Pagan Is. P–47's hit Pagan with rockets and strafing attacks. B–24's from Kwajalein strike Wotje.

Eleventh AF: 6 B–25's fly anti-shipping sweep close to Paramushiru and draw shore-based AA fire. 8 ftrs intercept but there are no losses on either side.

5 September

Eighth AF: Over 650 HBs attack Stuttgart aero engine plant, Ludwigshafen synthetic oil plant, Karlsruhe M/Y, and various T/Os. 9 ftr gps fly spt and several gps strafe A/Fs. Ftrs claim 19 aerial combat victories. Nearly 150 B–17's supported by a P–51 gp bomb 5 gun emplacements in Brest area. 5 ftr gps in sweeps over Frankfurt/Main, Stuttgart and Rotterdam areas strafe A/Fs and rail, road, and river traffic and claim 9 air victories and 62 aircraft destroyed on ground. In Germany 2 FB gps bomb 3 A/Fs and strafe 2, claiming destruction of 66 parked aircraft. Nearly 90 B–24's fly supplies to France.

Ninth AF: 300-plus MBs and LBs bomb strongpoints in Brest area and coastal battery at Pointe du Grand Gouin. Ftrs hit gun positions and other military tgts in Brest area and fly cover for 6 armd and inf divs.

Twelfth AF: MBs again strike with excellent results road and rail bridges in Po Valley while FBs blast rail lines and rolling stock S of the river. A–20's hit Milan and Genoa areas during 4/5 Sep and attack ammo stores during the day. Ftrs fly sweeps through Rhone Valley and spt limited ground force adv in preparation for major assault on Gothic Line.

Fifteenth AF: 430-plus HBs, with ftr escort, attack comm tgts in Hungary and N Italy to impede withdrawal from the lower Balkans and to disrupt railroad comm in Italian N. Tgts hit are 2 railroad bridges at Budapest and 1 each at Szolnok and Szob and a railroad bridge at Ferrara. HBs dispatched to Yugoslavia cannot bomb tgt because of total cloud cover.

Tenth AF: 8 B–25's pound tgts at Indaw. 21 B–24's fly fuel to Kunming. Numerous other cargo and TC sorties are flown to various CBI terminals.

Fourteenth AF: 25 B–25's pounding Kiyang and Hengyang cause considerable damage in both towns and at the Hengyang A/F. 6 others attack trucks and other T/Os at Siangtan ferry crossing, near Hengyang and Kiyang, in Lingling and Yoyang areas, and at Samshui. 2 more B–25's bomb Kowloon shipyards. 26 P–40's blast concentrations of river junks, troops and horses in Kiyang-Wangyang area. Other FBs, operating individually or in flights of 2–10 aircraft, hit a variety of T/Os throughout Hengyang, Kiyang, Yungfengshih, and Lishui area.

FEAF: B–24's hit Peleliu A/F, a few bombing Saipan. Small-scale B–24 strikes hit Kendari A/F while FBs attack Galela and nearby villages, Soepiori Peninsula villages and Waren and Moemi A/Fs. Almost 60 B–24's blast Langoan A/F while a sizeable B–25 force bombs Djailolo A/F, several villages, and Kaoe AA positions.

Seventh AF: 20 Saipan-based B–24's bomb Iwo Jima. 2 others on armed rcn hit Marcus and Yap. P–47's make strafing and rocket attacks on AA positions on Pagan. Gilberts-based B–25's attack Nauru and Ponape.

6 September

Eighth AF: About 200 ftrs strafe rail and highway traffic in Rotterdam, Aachen and Koblenz areas losing 4 aircraft to flak. 70 B–24's fly supplies to battle area.

Ninth AF: MBs and LBs hit Brest area strongpoints, coastal battery at Pointe du Grand Gouin, defenses at Saint-Pierre-Quilbignon, and Brest area bridge. Ftrs hit Brest area gun positions and ammo dump and fly cover for several armd and inf divs.

Twelfth AF: During 5/6 Sep A–20's attack T/Os in Savona and Milan areas. During the day weather grounds XII TAC aircraft except for a few ftrs based in France which fly armed rcn over Belfort, Dijon, and Colmar areas, destroying or damaging numerous motor transport and railroad cars and several locomotives, field guns, trailers, and a tank.

Fifteenth AF: 542 HBs attack comm tgts in Rumania, Yugoslavia and Hungary and troop and tank concentrations in S Yugoslavia. Tgts include 2 M/Ys at Oradea, and 2 nearby bridges over Sebes Koros R, M/Y at Novi Sad, bridge at Belgrade, tanks and troops at Leskovac, and M/Y at Nyiregyhaza. 2 HBs, with ftr escort, evacuate interned airmen from Bucharest.

Tenth AF: 6 B–25's hit Indaw while 3 bomb Katha. 24 B–24's fly about 34,000 gals of fuel to Kunming. Large-scale daily TC and cargo operations to a variety of CBI terminals continue.

Fourteenth AF: 20 B–25's pound Yiyang, Lingkuantien railroad yards,

trucks N of Lingling, troops and occupied areas around Kiyang and Paishui, and Hengyang A/F. 45 P–40's
and P–51's on armed rcn attack
troops, shipping, and comm tgts in
Yiyang area, bomb warehouses at
Hukow, destroy fuel barge at Pengtse,
hit railroad yards, trucks, troops, and
sampans at Kweiyang and Lingkuantien, and attack general T/Os at
Yangtien.

FEAF: B–24's pound Santa Ana
port. B–25's bomb Buayan A/F in
the first MB raid in Phil Is since
early 1942. Several B–24's, turning
back from the Santa Ana strike,
bomb Rainis. B–25's hit Galela and
S coast of Morotai while FBs hit
Kaoe A/F and bomb Djailolo runway. A–20's, B–25's, and FBs hit A/
Fs at Manokwari, Moemi, Ransiki,
and Waren, and stores and personnel
area at Nabire. P–40's attack S Soepiori I and Napido. Other P–39's
strafe barges and huts at Suain.

Seventh AF: Saipan-based B–24's
strike Iwo Jima while P–47's make
strafing and rocket runs on AA positions on Pagan. B–24's on armed rcn
bomb Marcus. Eniwetok-based B–24's
bomb Truk.

7 September

Ninth AF: Bad weather grounds
bmrs. Ftrs provide air cover for US
8th and 29th Inf Divs.

Twelfth AF: Weather cancels all
flying except for weather rcn by a
few P–47's.

Tenth AF: 22 B–24's fly fuel to
Kunming. Many other TC and cargo
sorties are flown to numerous CBI
terminals.

Fourteenth AF: 24 B–25's attack
town areas, river shipping and

trucks in and around Kiyang, Lingling, and Yoyang. 11 B–25's bomb
Tien Ho and White Cloud A/Fs and
2 bomb Siangtan ferry. 5 B–24's hit
4 freighters SW of Hong Kong. Nearly 100 P–40's and P–51's on armed
rcn over vast areas of SE China attack numerous T/Os including troops,
railroad tgts, river shipping, warehouses, and bridges. 4 P–38's hit T/
Os in Hanoi-lower Red R area.

FEAF: B–24's pound Menado area
and B–25's hit Wasile Bay villages.
Other B–24's strike Galela in force
while P–38's dive-bomb Djailolo A/F.
A–20's bomb Boela A/F and B–25's
sink lugger in Bara Bay. A–20's hit
Mongosah A/F while FBs hit Manokwari airstrip and villages in Schouten
Is and strafe and bomb Wewak A/F
and surrounding areas.

Seventh AF: Saipan-based P–47's
make strafing and rocket attacks on
Pagan and Aguijan. B–24's on snooper and armed rcn missions hit Iwo
Jima and Marcus.

Eleventh AF: 6 B–25's on a shipping sweep attack a small fishing
fleet between Paramushiru and Onnekotan.

8 September

ETO: The first V–2 fired in combat explodes in Paris suburb; the
second strikes a London suburb a few
hrs later.

Eighth AF: About 950 HBs escorted by 7 P–51 gps attack an oil
refinery, M/Y, tank and armored vehicle factory, and ordnance plant in
the Rhineland, plus 11 T/Os. 22
HBs are lost. 2 P–51 gps strafe tgts
in   Heidelberg-Darmstadt-Wurzburg
and Frankfurt/Main-Koblenz   areas,
while 5 FB gps strafe and bomb rail

transportation E of the Rhine. Over 100 B–24's fly "trucking mission," carrying supplies to battle area.

Ninth AF: Weather prevents bmr missions. Ftrs fly cover for troops in Brest area and for US 2d, 5th, 8th, and 29th Inf Divs, and XX Corps area, escort troop movements and fly defensive patrols. Several hundred transports fly supply and evacuation missions.

Twelfth AF: A–20's fly supply missions to A/F near Lyon. Bad weather grounds MBs. P–47's FBs on armed rcn in Po Valley area attack 2 pontoon bridges and several barges, cut a road, and hit several vehicles and other T/Os. Ftrs strafe Belfort area, hitting 10 trains with good results, and blast a horse-drawn vehicle convoy near Strasbourg.

Fifteenth AF: 354 B–17's and B–24's escorted by P–38's hit railroad bridges at Brod and Belgrade and M/Ys at Sarajevo and Nish. 77 P–51's strafe A/Fs at Ecka, Petrovgrad, Ilandza, and Alibunar. Other P–51's escort RAF Beaufighters to Trieste and MATAF C–47's on evacuation missions to Bucharest and back to Italy.

Tenth AF: 9 B–25's bomb Katha. 23 B–24's haul fuel to Kunming. Large-scale TC operations to many CBI terminals continue.

Fourteenth AF: 18 B–24's attack 5 railroad bridges at Giap Nat, Dui Giang, Hue, Trach, Duc Tho, and Quang Tri, knocking out Quang Tri bridge. 3 others claim a destroyer sunk S of Hong Kong. 5 B–25's destroy bridge near Kiyang, bomb Hengyang and Lingling, and damage bridge near Hengyang. 100-plus P–40's and P–51's on armed rcn hit

large variety of T/Os including troops, river shipping, bridges, airstrips, supplies, trucks, and railroad tgts over vast SE China areas at Lingling, Kiyang, Tunganhsien, Hengyang, Lingkuantien, and Leiyang.

FEAF: B–24's pound Langoan A/F. B–25's hit Galela and Tobelo while B–24's bomb Lolobata and P–47's attack Kaoe A/F and AA positions, Djailolo A/F and barges at Point Lelo. B–24's bomb A/Fs at Langgoer, Faan, Letfoean, and Toeal. P–38's hit Boela while B–25's hit small shipping at Ceram. FBs and A–20's hit airstrips and T/Os at Efman, Samate, Babo, Urarom, Manokwari, Moemi, and Ranski. P–39's strafe Wewak coastal area.

Twentieth AF: 90 Chengtu-based B–29's bomb Showa Steel Works at Anshan, 3 others bomb other tgts in Anshan, 5 hit Sinsiang railroad yards, and 3 others hit various T/Os. Gen LeMay (CG, XX BC) accompanies the mission. During 8/9 Sep Japanese bmrs attack HQ, storage areas, and parked airplanes at Hsinching (near Chengtu) damaging a B–29, a C–46, and wounding 2 soldiers.

Seventh AF: Saipan-based B–24's bomb Iwo Jima and Pagan and hit shipping at Chichi Jima. B–25's from the Gilberts hit Ponape and B–24's from Kwajalein bomb Wotje.

9 September

Eighth AF: 350-plus B–17's bomb M/Ys at Mannheim and Mainz, armament plant at Dusseldorf and 10 T/Os. 8 B–17's are lost, mostly to AA fire. 8 P–51 gps and a sq give escort, 1 gp later strafing rail traffic S of Wurzburg. 1 P–47 gp sweeps Lingen-

Munster-Haltern area to spot flak positions and troop concentrations, and strafe an A/F. 5 FB gps bomb and strafe shipping between German mainland and Schouwen, Overflakee, and Walcheren Is, installations on the islands, and rail and road traffic NW and NE of Frankfurt/Main. 9 FBs are lost. Ftrs claim 13 aircraft destroyed. Training functions are removed from VIII AF Comp Cmd control and distributed within the combat gps in anticipation that combat gps will have to train their own replacements upon deployment from ETO to other theaters.

Ninth AF: Bmrs fly leaflet mission to coastal France and Belgium. Ftrs fly escort, furnish ground force cover for US VIII Corps in the Brest area, 2d, 5th, and 8th Inf Divs of US Third Army's XX Corps area W of Metz, and fly armed rcn in areas around Aachen, Cologne, Koblenz, Bonn, Saarbrucken, and Nancy. Ftrs also hit bridges at Custines and Pompey. Over 700 transports fly missions.

Twelfth AF: B–26's achieve excellent results against rail bridges in the E Po Valley while B–25's bomb troop concentrations and supply points S of Bologna. FBs and ftrs attack railways and roads in Po Valley and from Genoa to Turin. Motor transport and rolling stock are bombed and strafed in N Italy and E France, with particular success in Belfort-Mulhouse-Freiburg areas.

Tenth AF: 9 B–25's bomb Japanese HQ and other buildings at Manwing. 17 B–24's run fuel to Kunming. Numerous other transport sorties are flown to several points in CBI.

Fourteenth AF: 24 B–25's hit river traffic and troop compounds in areas around Kiyang, Lingling, and Lingkwantien, bomb towns of Lingling and Samshui, and knock out W end of bridge at Lingling. About 50 P–40's and P–51's hit numerous T/Os throughout inland SE China including rivercraft and troop areas around Lingling, Lupao, Tsingyun, Kiyang, Leiyang, and Yungfengshih, and a railroad bridge at Tunganhsien. 5 B–24's over S China Sea claim 4 freighters sunk or heavily damaged.

FEAF: B–24's bomb Mapanget A/F. More than 100 FBs and A–20's pound A/Fs at Liang, Haroekoe, Boela, and Namlea. FBs hit Moemi, Manokwari, and Ransiki airstrips while B–25's hit Babo A/F. B–24's hit Galela A/F.

Seventh AF: A B–24 on snooper mission from Saipan bombs Iwo Jima during 9/10 Sep. B–25's based in the Gilberts bomb Nauru.

Eleventh AF: 6 B–25's hunt shipping off Paramushiru. 4 return to Attu with bombs, finding no tgts. One hits mast of a vessel and ditches in water. The other lands on one engine in Petropavlovsk. 3 B–24's make an uneventful raid during 9/10 Sep on Kashiwabara. Later 2 photo planes escorting 2 bmrs over Kurils on a mapping project are attacked by ftrs which inflict no damage.

10 September

Eighth AF: Over 1,000 HBs attack aircraft, tank, motor transport and engine plants, A/Fs, and jet-propulsion units plant in SC Germany, along with Ulm and Heilbronn M/Ys and several other secondary and T/Os. 12 gps of escorting ftrs claim 6 aircraft destroyed in air and 73 on ground. 12 HBs and 12 ftrs are lost. 3 P–47 gps strafe A/Fs and ground and rail traffic in sweep over Cologne, Frankfurt/Main, and Kassel areas, claiming destruction of 40 parked planes. 8 P–47's are lost, mostly to flak.

Ninth AF: Adv HQ, Ninth AF, assigns rail lines approaching the Rhine from the W, N of Karlsruhe, to be attacked by IX and XIX TAC in first of series of orders setting up rail interdiction programs to cut lines W and E of the Rhine in Sep and early Oct. Changes and additions to tgts appear on 12 and 14 Sep when a list of all lines to be cut is published. About 340 MBs and LBs hit strongpoints and ammo stores in Foret de Haye, Custines rail bridge, and road bridge over Mosel R. Escorting ftrs provide general air cover in Metz-Nancy area, and spt US Third Army ground forces in stemming counterattack there. 800-plus transports complete supply and evacuation missions. Southern invading forces and those of the Normandy invasion meet. City of Luxembourg is liberated.

Twelfth AF: MBs continue campaign against railroad bridges in Po Valley and execute 4 attacks against supply and ammo dumps. FBs of 87th Wg hit dumps and comm as ground assault on Gothic Line commences during early morning. France-based XII TAC ftrs and FBs blast comm in Belfort and Dijon areas, cutting railroads and hitting several trains.

Fifteenth AF: 344 B–17's and B–24's bomb 5 ordnance depots and SE industrial area in Vienna and 2 oil refineries in the area. 88 B–24's escorted by P–38's and P–51's bomb

Trieste port. 45 B–24's, with P–51's escorting, fly supply mission to Lyon.

Tenth AF: TC and cargo hauls continue on large scale to numerous points in CBI. 24 B–24's haul fuel to Kunming.

Fourteenth AF: 45 B–25's bomb towns of Kutkai, Ssutang, Samshui, Tunganhsien, Lingling, and Tunghsiangchiao, and hit fuel dump near Lingling. About 140 P–40's and P–51's on armed rcn over E Burma, SW China, and inland SE China attack a huge number of T/Os including troops, aircraft, river shipping, trucks, runways, bridges, and supply areas.

FEAF: B–24's pound A/Fs at Langoan and Mapanget and hit Tomohon and waterfront area of Menado. Lolobata and Hate Tabako A/Fs are bombed and areas along Wasile Bay strafed. MBs, A–20's, and P–38's hit A/Fs and oil storage at Namlea, Amahai, and Boela while B–24's hit Laha A/F. A–20's and ftrs hit A/Fs at Samate, Sagan, Nabire, Urarom, Manokwari, Moemi, and Ransiki.

Seventh AF: B–24's from Saipan hit Iwo Jima and strike shipping near Iwo Jima. Eniwetok-based B–24's bomb Truk.

Eleventh AF: 6 B–25's fly shipping sweep off Suribachi.

11 September

International: Second Quebec conference opens. Roosevelt and Churchill discuss Pacific war plans and completion of European war.

Eighth AF: The Eighth begins another FRANTIC shuttle-bombing mission, as 75 B–17's with 64 P–51's attack armament plant at Chemnitz, and land at USSR bases. 1 P–51 is lost. FRANTIC mission lasts until 17 Sep and takes the planes from UK to USSR to Italy to UK. Over 850 other HBs, escorted by 14 ftr gps, bomb 6 synthetic oil plants, an ordnance depot, an engine works, a M/Y, a tire plant, and numerous other scattered T/Os, along with several German cities. An estimated 525 ftrs attack the formations or are engaged by Eighth AF planes. 52 HBs and 32 ftrs are lost. HBs claim destruction of 17 ftrs while the US ftrs claim 116 in the air and 42 on the ground.

Ninth AF: 358 MBs and LBs, in spt of US Third Army, hit gun positions and strongpoints in Metz area. Ftrs escort bmrs, fly armed rcn over Lissendorf and Duren areas, and spt Third Army ground forces in Metz area. Armored rcn elements of this Army cross into Germany, the first Allied unit to do so. Ftrs also spt ground forces in Brest area.

Twelfth AF: B–26's hit defensive positions as US Fifth Army elements push through N Italian mountain passes toward Gothic Line defenses. B–25's bomb railroad bridges at Vigevano and Canneto sull'Oglio and supply areas. FBs and ftrs attack roads, railroads, guns, supply areas, bridges, and other tgts at Vernio, and in Alessandria, Turin, Piacenza, and Milan areas.

Fifteenth AF: Bad weather limits operations to supply mission by 54 B–24's to France.

Tenth AF: 12 P–47's hit roads, towns, and general T/Os in Tengchung, Lungling, and Bhamo areas. 23 B–24's fly fuel to Kunming. Numerous other transport flights throughout CBI continue.

Fourteenth AF: 18 B–24's blast storage area at Manling. 30 B–25's bomb Tunganhsien and Kiaotow and hit T/Os in Lingling area. 12 P–40's blast trucks along Burma Road and around Lungling. 59 P–40's and P–51's hit river shipping, railroad tgts, troop concentrations, supply dumps, and other T/Os in Canton-Tungting, Lake area.

FEAF: B–24's hit A/Fs at Galela and Miti. B–25's bomb Kairatoe A/F and village and Boela A/F while P–38's hit A/Fs at Namlea and Amahai and oil tanks at Boela. A–20's and B–25's hit Kaoe A/F and scattered T/Os. A–20's strike Otawiri, Sagan, Nabire, and Urarom A/Fs while FBs hit A/Fs and AA guns at Manokwari and Ransiki.

Seventh AF: Saipan-based B–24's bomb Iwo Jima and hit shipping off Chici Jima. P–47's pound Pagan with strafing attacks and rockets.

Eleventh AF: 4 B–25's on a shipping search sink a small craft off Shimushu. 2 other B–25's fly search mission for B–25 (which force-landed in USSR on 9 Sep but is still reported as missing).

12 September

Eighth AF: Over 800 HBs escorted by 15 ftr gps attack 4 synthetic oil plants, 2 oil refineries, an oil depot, an aero engine works, and numerous T/Os including several C and NW German cities. 400 to 450 aircraft are encountered by the HBs and ftrs. HBs lose 45 of their number and claim destruction of 27 ftrs. 13 P–51's are lost. US ftrs claim 63 air victories plus 26 on the ground.

Ninth AF: MBs and LBs hit Westwall fortifications, Sankt Wendel station where an armd div and important technicians are to entrain, and fortifications around Nancy. Ftrs continue ground spt in French-German border area. 400-plus transports complete supply and evacuation missions.

Twelfth AF: Gen Chidlaw assumes cmd of XII FC. B–26's blast defended positions in C battle sector of Gothic Line. B–25's pound Po R railroad bridges and attack guns and strongpoints in battle zone as enemy falls back to prepared Gothic Line defenses and rapid Allied adv halts. FBs strike at guns, troop concentrations, strongpoints, and flak positions in Genoa and Milan areas. France-based FBs cut tracks in Belfort, Basel, and Freiburg areas.

Fifteenth AF: Nearly 330 B–17's and B–24's supported by P–38's and P–51's bomb Lechfeld A/F, Munich/Allach engine works, and Wasserburg jet aircraft factory. 50-plus B–24's fly supply mission to S France.

Tenth AF: 4 B–25's pound buildings in Katha area. 25 B–24's haul fuel to Kunming. 8 P–47's sweep river from Bhamo to Katha, 3 strafe official buildings at Bhamo, and 16 hit T/Os on Burma Road from Lungling to Wanling to Namhkam and blast gun positions N of Loiwing A/F.

Fourteenth AF: 10 B–25's and 6 P–40's pound Lungling. 14 B–25's hit town area and destroy 2 bridges and damage another at Sungpai. 22 others bomb Kaochishih, Tunghsiangchiao, and area E of Kiyang. 27 P–51's and P–40's on armed rcn over Hunan and other areas of inland SE China attack road and river traffic and general T/Os around Lingling, Hengyang, Kiyang, Yangtien, and Patpo. 15 P–40's hit coastal and river shipping in S China and in Indochina on S China Sea, in Chikhom Bay, and along the Red R.

FEAF: B–24's pound 3 A/Fs in Menado area. B–24's and B–25's bomb Kaoe and Galela, A/Fs, and radar facilities on Morotai I. B–24's hit Lautem. P–38's dive-bomb Namlea runways while P–47's hit Boela. A–20's, B–25's, and FBs hit A/Fs, AA guns, and other tgts at Babo, Mongosah, Manokwari, Sagan, Moemi, and Samate.

Seventh AF: P–47's from Saipan hit AA positions on Pagan with rocket and bombing attack. A lone B–24 on armed rcn bombs building area on Marcus. B–25's from the Gilberts bomb Nauru.

Eleventh AF: 6 bmrs fly a negative shipping sweep over Shimushu. 3 more attack Suribachi A/F and offshore shipping tgts. 1 B–24 flies negative rcn.

13 September

Eighth AF: 70-plus B–17's, escorted by a P–51 gp, continuing UK-USSR-Italy-UK shuttle-bombing mission, take off from USSR bases, bomb steel and armament works at Diosgyor and proceed to Fifteenth AF bases in Italy. 750-plus HBs from UK bomb 3 synthetic oil plants, 2 aero engine factories, 3 M/Ys, an A/F, motor works, ordnance depot, fuel depot, and several cities and isolated T/Os in C and SW Germany. 11 ftr gps escorting later strafe A/Fs and miscellaneous ground tgts. 28 HBs and 9 P–51's are lost. P–51's claim 33 aircraft destroyed in the air and 20 on the ground. A P–51 gp sweeping S of Munich strafes aircraft dispersal area, A/F and a M/Y.

Ninth AF: XIX TAC HQ accompanies US Third Army HQ to Chalons-sur-Marne. B–26's fly leaflet mission to coastal N France and Belgium. Ftrs spt ground forces in Brest and Nancy-Metz areas (air-ground coordination being especially effective between XIX TAC and French 2d Armd Div in defeating enemy move on Vittel), and fly armed rcn over Cologne, Aachen, Koblenz, Linz/Rhine, and Wahn areas. XIX TAC inaugurates rail cutting campaign. Transports fly numerous supply and evacuation missions.

Twelfth AF: B–25's destroy bridge at Peschiera del Garda, cutting the Milan-Verona line. B–25's and B–26's bomb guns and defensive positions N of Florence. FBs attack railroads, rolling stock, and bridges in N Italy, although heavy overcast hampers operations in NW.

Fifteenth AF: 350-plus ftr-escorted B–17's and B–24's bomb Auschwitz oil and rubber works and Odertal and Blechhammer oil refineries, hit Cracow-Auschwitz area and bomb M/Y at Vrutky. Over 100 other HBs attack Avisio viaduct, Mezzocorona and Ora railroad bridges.

Tenth AF: 8 P–47's hit tgts at Mawhun and some of the FBs afterwards strafe T/Os on the Irrawaddy R from Katha to Shwegu. 8 others sweep the river between Bhamo and Katha. 12 more hit tgts along road in Kutkai area. Large-scale transport operations in CBI continue.

Fourteenth AF: B–24's claim 3 cargo vessels sunk off Pescadores Is.

FEAF: B–24's and B–25's hit 4 A/Fs and bomb villages on Morotai

I. B–25's hit Langgoer A/F while A–20's and FBs hit 2 A/Fs in Efman I. A–20's, B–25's, and FBs hit Babo AA positions and A/Fs at Manokwari and Ransiki.

Thirteenth AF: Thirteenth AF moves from Los Negros to Hollandia.

Seventh AF: Saipan-based P–47's hit buildings on Pagan with rockets and machinegun fire. B–24's on armed rcn, snooper, and training missions bomb Iwo Jima, Marcus, and Pagan.

14 September

Ninth AF: XXIX TAC (Prov) is activated at Vermand, in anticipation of operating with US Ninth Army, shortly to join 12th Army Gp. Gen Nugent is CG. About 140 B–26's and A–20's bomb gun emplacements and strongpoints in Brest area. Ftrs fly armed rcn in various battle areas. Transports continue large-scale supply and evacuation missions.

Twelfth AF: MBs attack def positions in E and C parts of Gothic Line as enemy fiercely resists, especially at Il Giogo Pass and on Monte Altuzzo. FBs continue strikes against comm and movement in Po Valley despite bad weather which limits France-based ftrs to a few sweeps in S France.

Tenth AF: 4 B–25's drop fragmentation-boobytrap bombs on Bhamo. Large-scale transport operations continue to various points in CBI.

Fourteenth AF: 6 B–25's bomb Tunganhsien. 91 P–40's and P–51's attack inland shipping, troop compounds, supplies, and numerous buildings around Lungling area, throughout vast expanse of inland SE China, mainly in Hunan, and other areas S of Tungting Lake.

FEAF: B–25's pound Mapanget airstrip on Menado area. B–24's hit 4 A/Fs on Halmahera. A–20's and B–25's bomb Babo A/F while FBs make scattered small raids on AA positions, A/Fs, and T/Os on Vogelkop Peninsula.

Seventh AF: B–24's from Saipan bomb Iwo Jima. P–47's make strafing and rocket attacks on warehouses and shelters on Pagan. B–24's on armed rcn bomb Marcus. B–24's from Eniwetok bomb Truk while Gilberts-based B–25's hit Ponape.

Eleventh AF: During 13/14 Sep 3 B–24's strike Kurabu Cape shipping and A/F.

15 September

Eighth AF: The 3 ftr wgs and 15 ftr gps of VIII FC are transferred to the 3 bomb divs.

Ninth AF: Ninth AF main HQ moves from Sunninghill Park to Chantilly. Bad weather prevents bmr operations. IX TAC supports US First Army troops and flies armed rcn around Cologne and from Trier to Rhine R area. XIX TAC supports US Third Army and flies armed rcn in Nancy-Strasbourg area.

Twelfth AF: 87th Ftr Wg, 47th Bomb Gp, 57th Ftr Gp, 86th Ftr Gp, and several other units are transferred from XII TAC to XII FC. XII TAC passes under operational control of Ninth AF. All MB missions are cancelled or aborted due to weather. FBs, though restricted by weather, carry out armed rcn against enemy comm and defensive positions in Milan-Genoa-Modena-Pistoia areas, as Allied forces (joined on this date by elements of Brazilian Expeditionary Force) attempt to penetrate enemy strongholds in the N Apennines.

Fifteenth AF: 276 B–17's and B–24's bomb Tatoi, Eleusis, and Kalamaki A/Fs and Salamis submarine base. P–38's and P–51's fly escort, tgt cover, and sweep tgt areas. The attacks are aimed at hampering withdrawal of enemy forces from the area. 53 B–24's fly supply mission to S France. 24 B–24's begin evacuating aircrews formerly imprisoned in Bulgaria from Cairo to Bari.

EAC: Combat Cargo TF is formed as a cmd of EAC. Gen Evans is CG. HQ is temporarily located at Hastings AB and later moved to Comilla. The cmd is responsible to air deliver supplies to British Fourteenth Army and other organizations as required, a task it fulfills until its disbandment on 1 Jun 45.

Tenth AF: 8 P–47's bomb Kutkai, 16 sweep river from Bhamo to Katha and bomb Naba, Katha, and Mohnyin. Several other P–47's sweep Burma Road from Lungling to Muse to Bhamo and strafe boat on river at Myothit. 12 P–51's hit Mawhun while 8 B–25's hit fuel storage and T/Os in Chefang area. 13 B–24's fly fuel to Liuchow.

Fourteenth AF: 19 B–24's bomb military storage area at Hengyang. 20 B–25's hit Chuanhsien and 5 pound ferry crossing and bus station at Lingling. More than 90 P–40's and P–51's on armed rcn attack river shipping, numerous buildings, troops, and general T/Os from NE of Ichang to Liuchow Peninsula concentrating on Kiyang and Changsha areas.

FEAF: B–24's, A–20's, and P–47's bomb Kaoe, Lolobata, and Hate Tabako. P–39's bomb Manokwari A/F and town area.

W Pacific: US forces land on Morotai and Peleliu.

Seventh AF: P–47's from Saipan hit AA positions on Pagan with machinegun and rocket fire. A lone B–24 on a snooper mission bombs Iwo Jima. All other B–24 missions abort.

16 September

Eighth AF: 7 ftr gps, 4 carrying bombs, strafe Hannover-Bremen-Osnabruck areas and bomb Ahlhorn A/F and Mannheim-Kaiserslautern area.

Ninth AF: HQ Ninth AF begins reorganization of IX BC as 9th Bomb Div, implementing the redesignation of 30 Aug. 150-plus MBs and LBs attack Bath dike and Arnemuiden road and rail embankment. Ftrs escort bmrs, fly sweeps, and armed rcn over Rastatt and Haguenau, and spt US Third Army's XII and XV Corps in repelling counterattacks in NE France.

Twelfth AF: MBs attack fuel and supply dumps and defensive positions in Bologna and Rimini areas while FBs and ftrs bomb and strafe rail and road tgts N of battle areas in the N Apennine Mts as US Fifth Army forces struggle to break through strong enemy defenses in hills N of Prato, along main Monte Altuzzo ridge, on Monte Veruca, Monte Monticelli, and other mountain positions.

Fifteenth AF: Bad weather cancels bombing operations. 2 P–38's fly weather rcn and 54 B–24's fly supplies to S France.

Tenth AF: 19 B–24's haul fuel to Liuchow. In spite of bad weather, 4 P–47's sweep Lungling-Wanling-Loiwing road and 5 damage bridge approach at Manyut.

Fourteenth AF: 20 B–24's bomb Hengyang. 12 B–25's bomb Kutkai. 28 B–25's hit tgts in China, including Yuangshaho ferry, Pakmushih, Chuanhsien, and Lengshuitang. 130-plus P–40's and P–51's on armed rcn hit T/Os in Mangshih and Lungling area and from N of Tangyang and along the Yangtze R southward including areas around Changsha, Kiyang, Samshui, Chuanhsien, Lingling, and Kwongning.

FEAF: B–24's bomb Kendari air depot and Ambesia A/F while B–25's attack large warehouse at Gorontalo. B–25's and B–24's pound Namlea, Liang, Haroekoe, Kairatoe, Laha, and Kamarian. FBs hit Manokwari, Sagan, Moemi, and Waren airstrips.

Seventh AF: 17 Saipan-based B–24's bomb Iwo Jima. 3 others on trg and armed rcn missions bomb Pagan and Marcus. P–47's pound enemy positions on Pagan. B–24's in the Marshalls bomb Emidj.

Eleventh AF: 3 B–24's bomb Kataoka naval base. 4 B–25's abort a shipping sweep due to weather and mechanical difficulties.

17 September

Eighth AF: UK-USSR-Italy-UK shuttle mission is completed as 72 B–17's and 59 P–51's fly without bombs from Italy to UK. 2 B–17's and a P–51 abort and a P–51 crash-lands SW of Paris. 70 B–17's and 57 P–51's land safely in UK. Over 800 B–17's escorted by 3 ftr gps bomb 117 flak batteries and installations and an A/F, all in the Netherlands. 16 ftr gps escort airplanes of First Allied Airborne Army making parachute and glider drop of 20,000 troops into the Netherlands to secure axis of adv toward Zuider Zee for British Second Army, as part of MARKET-GARDEN, 17–30 Sep. Troops dropped are I Airborne Corps, consisting of British 1st Airborne Div (with Polish Para Brigade) and US 82d and 101st Airborne Divs. The ftr gps also bomb and strafe flak positions and other ground tgts, encountering intense flak and about 30 ftrs. 16 US ftrs are lost. Claims include 8 airplanes and 107 flak positions destroyed.

Ninth AF: No combat bmr missions are flown. Weather permits 1 leaflet mission. XIX TAC supports US VIII Corps in Brest area and flies armed rcn over Trier and Saarbrucken areas. IX TAC flies armed rcn in the Dusseldorf, Duren, Cologne, and Linz/Rhine areas, supports US 2d and 5th Armd Divs and 4th Inf Div in the Netherlands, and participates in MARKET-GARDEN.

Twelfth AF: B–25's hit troop concentrations in British Eighth Army battle area in vicinity of Rimini. B–25's pound rail bridges in W Po Valley, while FBs operating in the Valley attack rails, roads, rolling stock, road bridges, motor transport and other tgts. In the mountains S of the Valley US Fifth Army forces break through Gothic Line at Il Giogo Pass, take Monte Altuzzo and Pra-

tone, finish clearing Monte Veruca, and gain crest of Monte Monticelli. US Seventh Army's French 2d Corps makes contact with US Third Army's French 2d Armd Div near Bains-les-Bains.

Fifteenth AF: 440-plus HBs, with ftr escort, attack 2 oil refineries and 4 M/Ys in Budapest area in an attempt to hit Germany's principal remaining oil supply and to aid Soviet and other friendly forces on S Russian front by pounding the focal rail traffic point in that area. Some of the escorting ftrs strafe T/Os in the general tgt area. Bad weather hampers all but 8 of 54 B–24's flying supplies to S France. 25 HBs return from Cairo to Italy with Allied airmen formerly imprisoned in Bulgaria. 2 B–17's, escorted by 41 P–51's, evacuate wounded airmen from Czechoslovakia to Italy.

Tenth AF: 8 P–47's bomb Katha, 8 hit Momauk and Wanling, and 8 others attack Bhamo. 6 B–25's hit Mangshih while 3 others bomb Indaw. 16 B–24's haul fuel to Liuchow. TC aircraft fly over 200 sorties delivering personnel and supplies to various points in CBI.

Fourteenth AF: 29 B–24's bomb Changsha. 27 B–25's hit Hwangshapu, Kiyang, and Nanyo. 130-plus P–51's and P–40's on armed rcn attack town areas, strongpoints, shipping, railway tgts, gun positions, trucks, and other T/Os from NE of Ichang southward through Hunan province and beyond. Areas hit include Changsha, Kiyang, Lingling, Chuanhsien, Siangtan, Hengshan, Kweiyang, and Lingkuantien, plus scattered T/Os elsewhere.

FEAF: B–25's bomb Buayoan A/F.

B-24's, B-25's, and P-38's hit Langoan A/F. B-25's and P-39's, fighting bad weather, attack a variety of tgts, including A/Fs and villages in Amboina-Ceram area. P-47's and P-40's pound Samate A/F.

Seventh AF: A B-24 on a snooper mission from Saipan bombs Iwo Jima. Armed rcn over Marcus is unsuccessful due to bad weather. Gilberts-based B-25's pound Nauru.

Eleventh AF: 2 B-24's weather-abort a mission to Suribachi. 4 B-25's fly an unsuccessful shipping sweep.

18 September

Eighth AF: 12 ftr gps escort airplanes of First Allied Airborne Army as second troop echelon is dropped in the Netherlands to participate in heavy fighting in Arnhem area. Ftrs bomb and strafe flak positions and other ground tgts and encounter heavy flak and over 100 enemy ftrs which claim 7 US ftrs. US claims include 29 ftrs and 33 flak positions destroyed. Almost 250 B-24's, supported by nearly 200 ftrs, drop supplies to First Allied Airborne Army in the Netherlands. Intense flak downs 16 B-24's and 21 ftrs. 2 of the ftr gps strafe rail and highway traffic and over 50 ftrs bomb flak positions. In last Eighth AF shuttle-bombing mission, 18-22 Sep, UK-USSR-Italy-UK, 110 B-17's and 150 P-51's (64 P-51's to continue to USSR) drop supplies to Polish forces at Warsaw. 3 B-17's abort and 2 are lost. After completing supply drop, 105 B-17's and the 64 P-51's proceed to USSR.

Ninth AF: First 9th Bomb Div HQ on European continent opens at Chartres. Weather cancels all bmr activity. Less than 100 ftrs spt US VII Corps in W Germany and fly cover in area of Brest where organized resistance comes to an end.

Twelfth AF: B-25's continue to hit troop concentrations and gun positions in spt of British Eighth Army forces which opens assault on defenses in Rimini area. Despite bad weather B-26's and P-47's maintain attacks on bridges, rail lines, and transportation in Po Valley.

Fifteenth AF: 463 B-17's and B-24's, some with ftr escort, hit Subotica and Szeged M/Ys and railroad bridges at Novi Sad, Belgrade, Szob, and Budapest (2). Ftrs maintain cover over Budapest area.

Tenth AF: 9 P-47's pound Japanese positions in Myothit area. 8 B-25's hit supply dumps and installations at Chefang. 18 B-24's fly fuel to Liuchow. 200-plus other sorties by TC aircraft deliver men and supplies to several points in CBI.

Fourteenth AF: 30 B-25's attack town areas and fuel dumps at Lingling, Taohsien, and Chuanhsien and damage the approaches to Lingling ferry crossing. 4 B-24's over Formosa Strait claim 1 freighter sunk. About 115 P-40's and P-51's on armed rcn attack troops, trucks, tanks, shipping, town areas, and other T/Os throughout Hunan province S of Tungting Lake to Luichow Peninsula and Chikhom Bay.

FEAF: B-24's blast several tgts in Davao area, including oil storage at Sasa. B-25's hit Langoan A/F and lake area. Others hit Samate A/F. Bad weather forces B-24's over Ceram-Amboina area to individually attack tgts which include 4 A/Fs.

FBs hit A/F and town of Manokwari and AA guns at Moemi.

Seventh AF: 2 B–24's on armed rcn from Saipan bomb Marcus. 28 Eniwetok-based B–24's bomb Truk. Gilberts-based B–25's pound Ponape.

19 September

Eighth AF: Nearly 800 B–17's are dispatched against tgts in NW Germany. Weather prevents about half from bombing primary tgts but most manage to bomb secondaries or T/Os. Over 650 B–17's bomb 10 M/Ys and several bridges, railroads, factories, barges, storage areas, city areas and numerous scattered T/Os in NW Germany. 6 ftr gps furnish spt. 4 P–51 gps supporting First Allied Airborne Army in the Netherlands engage well over 100 ftrs, downing 23. 9 P–51's are lost. As UK-USSR-Italy-UK shuttle mission continues, over 90 B–17's and their ftr gp take off from USSR, bomb M/Y at Szolnok, and fly to Fifteenth AF bases in Italy.

Ninth AF: Bmrs hit M/Ys in Duren area to prevent reinforcements from reaching Aachen area by rail. IX TAC supports US V Corps in repelling counterattack at Wallendorf bridgehead, supports Operation MARKET-GARDEN and flies armed rcn in W Germany. XIX TAC escorts LBs and MBs, flies cover both for MARKET-GARDEN and in Brest and Nancy areas, and armed rcn over Metz area.

Twelfth AF: Bad weather grounds MBs. FBs hit guns and defensive positions along Gothic Line and attack roads and bridges in Bologna area.

Fifteenth AF: 96 B–24's attack railroad bridges at Kraljevo and Mitrovica. 70 P–38's provide tgt area cover.

Tenth AF: 18 B–24's fly fuel to Liuchow and Chengkuing. TC transports fly over 100 sorties carrying men and supplies to several CBI locations.

Fourteenth AF: 28 B–25's bomb Lingling, Lengshuitang, Chuanhsien, Sinning, and Shanhsien. 150-plus P–40's and P–51's pound numerous T/Os during armed rcn flights from Tungting Lake-C Yangtze R area to the S China Sea. The FBs particularly concentrate on road transport in Changsha area and supply dumps, buildings, and trucks near Sintsiang.

FEAF: Striking all principal tgts in NE Celebes, B–24's, B–25's, and P–38's hit Amoerang port area, Menado fuel tanks and shipping personnel areas and AA guns at Mapanget and Sidate, bivouac, supply areas, and lookout towers along Lembeh Strait, Langoan A/F, and Kakas rest camp.

Seventh AF: 29 Saipan-based B–24's blast shipping at Chichi Jima. 24 P–47's bomb and strafe AA positions and storage areas on Pagan. 3 B–24's on snooper and armed rcn missions bomb Iwo Jima and Marcus.

Eleventh AF: 2 B–25's fly shipping sweep over Tomari Cape. 4 B–24's off to strike Kurabu Cape turn back due to weather and mechanical failures.

20 September

Eighth AF: Over 600 ftrs spt First Allied Airborne Army in Arnhem and Nijmegen areas, strafing and bombing ground tgts. Intense light flak claims 5 ftrs. Air attacks aid ground troops in taking valuable bridges in the area and in adv toward Arnhem.

Ninth AF: The Ninth's adv HQ

follows US 12th Army Gp to Verdun. About 40 MBs hit Trier M/Y and defensive positions at Herbach to complicate rail transportation and aid in Allied ground attack on Aachen. Ftrs fly air cover for US V and VII Corps in W Germany near Dutch boundary and US XV and XX Corps in Nancy area, and fly armed rcn over Bonn, Mannheim, Hamburg, Koblenz, and Ruhr Valley areas.

Twelfth AF: 27th and 79th Ftr Gps are added to XII FC which on this days begins operations in spt of US Fifth Army. Weather again grounds MBs and severely restricts ftrs which fly uneventful rcn missions.

Fifteenth AF: 500 B–17's and B–24's escorted by P–38's and P–51's attack 3 railroad bridges at Budapest, 2 M/Ys at Hatvan and 1 at Gyor and bomb Malacky A/F and Bratislava oil district.

Tenth AF: P–47's hit Kadu rail siding, Nyaungbintha, Indaw, and troops at Hkaungtung. 3 B–25's weathered out of Bhamo area hit alternates at Indaw. TC aircraft continue large-scale operations to several points in CBI.

Fourteenth AF: 27 B–25's bomb Lingling, Chuanhsien, and Kiyang and hit T/Os throughout Chuanhsien area. More than 100 P–51's and P–40's on armed rcn over wide areas of SE China attack troops, horses, trucks, shipping, and other T/Os, particularly concentrating on areas around Chuanhsien, Lingling, Kiyang, Changsha, and Yiyang.

FEAF: Despite poor weather over Celebes, Menado area is again attacked. B–24's hit Mapanget and Sidate A/Fs and supply dumps and other T/Os. B–24's hit Djailolo and A–20's and P–47's during 19/20 Sep strike Kaoe A/Fs. B–24's, B–25's, and FBs, striking during 19/20 Sep and during day, pound A/Fs at Amahai, Namlea, Liang and Laha, town of Lautem, and several T/Os. FBs hit AA guns and T/Os at Moemi and Ransiki A/Fs and hit supply dump further E along Orai R. During 20/21 Sep a few B–24's again hit Menado and Sidate areas.

Seventh AF: P–47's from Saipan bomb and strafe gun positions on Pagan. A lone B–24 on armed rcn bombs Marcus. B–24's in the Marshalls hit Jaluit while Makin-based B–25's pound Nauru.

21 September

Eighth AF: Nearly 450 HBs escorted by 3 P–51 gps attack synthetic oil plant at Ludwigshafen/Opau, M/Ys at Koblenz and Mainz, and T/Os in Rhineland. 3 ftr gps spt First Allied Airborne Army airplanes dropping supplies and paratroops of Polish 1st Brig near Driel. Bad weather forces recall of 1 gp near Dutch coast. Other gps encounter about 50 ftrs, claiming 20 destroyed against 4 aerial combat losses. Over 80 B–24's carry gasoline to France.

Ninth AF: 79 MBs and LBs bomb M/Ys at Gerolstein, Pronsfeld, and Ehrang. Ftrs escort bmrs, fly armed rcn over Bonn, Koblenz, Karlsruhe, Cologne, and Strasbourg area, and spt US First and Third Armies in W Germany and E France. IX TAC is exceptionally effective in aiding V Corps withdrawal from Wallendorf bridgehead. During the evening IX ADC ftrs patrol Luxembourg-Chaumont area.

Twelfth AF: Bad weather and unserviceable landing grounds cancel all operations.

Fifteenth AF: 345 HBs attack M/Ys at Debreczen, Bekescsaba, and Brod, railroad and highway bridges at Baja, in Kiskore area, and at Tiszafured, plus Novi Sad railroad bridge. 42 P–38's dive-bomb Osijek M/Y. Other ftrs escort HBs. 2 C–47's (1 from Balkan AF), with 8 P–51's escorting, evacuate Fifteenth AF personnel from Yugoslavia to Italy.

Tenth AF: 7 B–25's hit Man Mawn. 1 other bombs Indaw. 21 B–24's haul fuel to Liuchow. 170-plus other transport sorties are flown to various terminal points in CBI.

Fourteenth AF: 27 B–25's pound Kiyang, Yungming, Lingling and areas to the N, and area W of Chuanhsien. 100-plus P–40's and P–51's attack buildings, river shipping, troops, horses, and supplies at numerous points especially around Sinshih, Kiyang, Wuchou, and Isuho.

FEAF: B–24's attack Laha and Kairatoe A/F and shipping in Piroe Bay. P–38's and B–25's hit Menado, Tomohon, Kakas rest camp, small craft near Belang I, Kairatoe, and Namlea A/F, and barge off Kaoe Pt. FBs hit Windissi and Ransiki T/Os and strafe T/Os near Orai R. During 21/22 Sep FBs hit Geelvink Bay-Bentoni Bay area.

Seventh AF: 5 B–24's on armed rcn and trg missions from Saipan bomb Marcus and Pagan. B–25's, based in the Gilberts, strike Ponape.

22 September

Eighth AF: Over 600 HBs from UK escorted by 6 P–51 gps bomb 3 armd vehicle and motor transport factories at Kassel along with 6 T/Os at Wetzlar. Over 100 B–24's fly gasoline to France. Last Eighth AF UK-USSR-Italy-UK shuttle mission ends as 84 B–17's escorted by 51 P–51's return directly to UK bases from Italy. Remaining aircraft return on 8 Oct.

Ninth AF: XIX TAC HQ accompanies US Third Army HQ from Chalons-sur-Marne to Etain. No bmr missions are flown. Ftrs attack railroads, supply and ordnance depots, and strongpoints, and fly sweeps and armed rcn over Cologne, Dusseldorf, Aachen, Koblenz, Trier, Bonn, Mannheim, and Strasbourg areas.

Twelfth AF: Operating N of Italian battle area, MBs bomb road and rail bridges, while FBs continue hitting roads, railroads, and transportation, and spt ground forces as US Fifth Army elements prepare to pursue enemy withdrawing from N of Pistoia and to drive N to Raticosa Pass and NE to Imola. British Eighth Army forces battle enemy along Marecchia R.

Fifteenth AF: 366 B–24's and B–17's escorted by 270 ftrs bomb NE industrial area of Munich and Munich/Riem A/F. 76 B–24's bomb Larissa M/Y. 68 B–24's fly supply mission to S France.

Tenth AF: 13 B–24's fly fuel to Liuchow. TCs fly more than 170 other sorties to various points in the CBI.

Fourteenth AF: 24 B–24's pound Hankow. 12 B–25's and 7 P–51's hit Hengyang road junction and ferry. 7 B–25's bomb Kianghwa while 6 P–51's damage nearby bridge. 5 B–25's hit Yungming. 44 P–40's and P–51's blast T/Os along roads in Changsha, Siangtan, and Sintsiang areas. 50-plus other P–40's and P–51's hit various T/Os around Chuanhsien, Paoching, Lingling, Hankow, and Kiyang.

FEAF: B–24's again pound Sidate and Mapanget. B–24's and B–25's bomb Amahai and Liang villages and Haroekoe A/F. A–20's pound Urarom A/F while FBs hit Idorra, Windissi, Moemi, and Kaimana.

Seventh AF: 15 Sapan-based B–24's strike shipping at Chichi Jima. 24 P–47's strafe Pagan and bomb Anatahan I. 3 B–24's on snooper mission and armed rcn flight bomb Iwo Jima and Marcus. 15 B–25's, flying out of Makin, bomb Nauru.

23 September

Eighth AF: 14 ftr gps bomb and strafe flak positions and other ground tgts in 2 landing zones in Nijmegen area, immediately preceding the arrival of the remainder of US 82d and 101st Airborne Divs and Polish 1st Brig, and engage over 150 ftrs. US ftrs claim 27 destroyed. Over 150 B–24's fly gasoline to France.

Ninth AF: MBs and LBs sent against tgts in W Germany are recalled due to weather. Ftrs spt US First Army in W Germany, US Third Army in Chateau-Salins area, escort bmrs (recalled), and fly armed rcn over wide areas of W Germany.

Twelfth AF: Although several missions are aborted because of bad weather, MBs attack several railroad bridges in Po R Valley. FBs hit guns and rail and road tgts in battle area as US Fifth Army pushes on through Gothic Line defenses.

Fifteenth AF: 147 B–17's, escorted by 290 P–38's and P–51's bomb Brux synthetic oil refinery and Wels M/Y. 229 B–24's attack comm tgts in Italy, including viaduct at Venzone and road and railroad bridges at Casarsa della Delizia, Pinzano al Tagliamento, Ponte di Piave, Latisana, San Dona di Piave, and Susegana.

Tenth AF: 19 P–47's attack bridges along a line Wanling-Bhamo-Myitkyina destroying 1 bridge. 6 B–25's hit bridges S of Meza, destroying 1 and extensively damaging several others. 19 B–24's fly fuel to Liuchow while 2 deliver fuel to Kunming.

Fourteenth AF: 15 B–24's pound Burma Road in Chefang area. 36 B–25's hit Chuanhsien and T/Os in surrounding areas. 6 B–25's bomb Kuanyang, 5 hit Yungming, 6 damage Dara bridge, 12 bomb Lungling, and 2 knock out bridge near Jinyang. 2 B–24's bomb docks at Amoy. Again more than 90 P–40's and P–51's hit numerous T/Os throughout SE China concentrating on Japanese troops in Chuanhsien area and various tgts around Jungyun, Yuankiang, Yungming, Lingling, and Hsuchang.

FEAF: During night and day raids B–24's and B–25's concentrate on Sidate and Mapanget A/Fs. P–47's pound Kaoe A/F. P–47's and P–40's bomb AA guns at Manokwari, Moemi, and Ransiki A/Fs.

Thirteenth AF: Thirteenth AF moves from Hollandia to Noemfoor I.

Seventh AF: 15 B–24's from Saipan bomb Chichi Jima, Haha Jima, and Ani Jima. 2 B–24's on armed rcn bomb Marcus while 1 on trg mission hits Pagan. On 23/24 Sep a B–24 from Kwajalein bombs Wake.

24 September

Eighth AF: Nearly 50 B–24's transport fuel to France.

Ninth AF: No bmr operations are flown. XIX TAC supports 7th Armd Div of US Third Army in E France and flies armed rcn over E France and W Germany. IX ADC flies night patrols from Paris to Aachen.

Twelfth AF: Weather cancels MB and LB operations. FBs spt ground forces, bombing and stafing strongpoints, troop concentrations, and frontline comm tgts as US Fifth Army pushes through N Apennines.

Fifteenth AF: 362 B-24's, with ftr escort, bomb Eleusis, Kalamaki, and Tatoi A/Fs, M/Y at Salonika, and harbor at Skaramanga. P-51's escort B-24's transporting personnel from Bari to Marcianise.

Tenth AF: P-47's fly 20 attack sorties against tgts in Mawhun area, including Pinlon. Other P-47's fly 13 sorties against tgts in Bhamo area, demolishing bridge at Manyut and hitting enemy positions at Chayuhkwang. 11 B-24's haul fuel to Liuchow. 240-plus other transport sorties are flown to various points in the CBI.

Fourteenth AF: 26 B-25's bomb Mangshih, Taohsien, and Kuanyang, attack White Cloud A/F, and knock out Dara bridge. 3 others hit T/Os near Changtuikuan and along Lingling-Siangtan road. 70-plus P-51's and P-40's on armed rcn over SW and SE China pound numerous T/Os, especially town areas and river shipping at Takhing and Sinshih.

FEAF: B-24's and B-25's bomb Amahai, Namlea, and Haroekoe A/Fs and Boela. HBs hit Lautem. FBs attack Babo, Urarom, and Manokwari A/Fs while B-25's bomb Sorong.

Seventh AF: 18 B-24's from Saipan hit shipping and harbor facilities in the Bonins, mostly at Chichi Jima. 2 others on armed rcn mission bomb Marcus. 16 ftrs strafe AA positions on Rota. 26 B-24's from Kwajalein bomb Truk while 11 B-25's, based in the Gilberts, hit Ponape.

Eleventh AF: 8 B-24's striking Kurabu Cape A/F are challenged by 12 ftrs. 1 of 2 damaged B-24's forcelands in USSR. One ftr is downed. 4 B-25's fly negative shipping search.

25 September

Eighth AF: About 100 HBs escorted by 14 ftr gps attack 3 M/Ys and a synthetic oil plant at Ludwigshafen and Koblenz, industrial area of Frankfurt/Main and several T/Os. About 175 B-24's haul fuel to France.

Ninth AF: No bmr missions are flown. IX TAC flies cover for US First Army units in W Germany, dive-bombs rail lines, and flies armed rcn over Trier-Koblenz-Aachen area. IX ADC flies night patrols from Paris E to Luxembourg and the German border.

Twelfth AF: MBs and LBs cancel operations due to bad weather. FBs hit barracks areas, railroads, roads, and transportation in or near Bologna, Bozzolo, Parma, Castelfranco Veneto, and Canneto sull'Oglio, and in immediate battle areas as US Fifth Army meets strong opposition, especially in vicinity of Monte Bastione, and near Torre Poggioli, Monte Gamberaldi, and Monte Castelnuovo.

Fifteenth AF: 51 B-24's, with P-51's and P-38's providing tgt cover and close escort, bomb Piraeus, Skaramanga, and Salamis harbors.

Tenth AF: 13 P-47's attack towns of Haungton, Myintha, and Mawlu. B-24's again haul fuel to China, 15 landing at Kunming, 3 at Liuchow, and 1 at Yungning. Tenth AF flies 220-plus other transport sorties to various CBI terminals.

Fourteenth AF: 12 B–25's blast barracks area at Mangshih. 12 bomb Kweiyang, and 6 hit town area and railroad yards at Hengyang. 11 B–24's pound Nanking. About 120 P–51's and P–40's on armed rcn over vast expanses of China S of the Yangtze R attack large variety of T/Os at numerous locations including troops, buildings, and comm tgts in Paoching area and between Siangtan and Fulinpu.

FEAF: B–24's hit Kendari A/F and B–25's bomb Langoan A/F. A–20's fire storage areas and hit personnel areas on W shore of Kaoe Bay. Namlea A/F is again bombed by B–24's. P–38's pound Kairatoe and Boela A/Fs. B–25's and A–20's hit Sagan and Urarom A/Fs while P–40's attack Kaimana.

Seventh AF: Saipan-based B–24's strike Iwo Jima and Marcus. During 25/26 Sep Kwajalein-based B–24's stage through Eniwetok on strike at shipping at Truk. Failing to locate primary tgts the HBs bomb Tol, Eten, Param, and Moen while others hit Wake during 25/26 Sep.

Eleventh AF: 2 B–25's fly negative shipping sweep.

26 September

Eighth AF: 400 B–17's bomb 2 M/Ys, 2 aircraft plants, a steel works, and 2 A/Fs at Osnabruck, Hamm, Bremen, Rheine, and Hesepe, plus 3 T/Os in NW Germany. 9 P–51 gps fly escort. 8 ftr gps, including 2 attached from Ninth AF, spt First Allied Airborne Army, claiming 32

ftrs destroyed in combat. Over 160 B–24's fly fuel to France.

Ninth AF: No bmr missions are flown. IX TAC supports US First Army in Bonn area and cuts rail lines W of Rhine. XIX TAC hits fortifications near Metz.

Twelfth AF: During 25/26 Sep A–20's bomb T/Os in Po Valley. Throughout the day B–25's and B–26's pound rail and road bridges in E and NW parts of the Valley while FBs and ftrs of XII FC attack road nets, rails, motor transport, and supply points at many locations in the valley.

Tenth AF: 2 P–47 flights hit tgts in Bhamo-Myothit area, including Sinkin, Momauk, and Nanhlaing. 3 other flights hit tgts in Pinwe-Mawlu area, including town of Nyaungbintha. 20-plus P–47's in 2 flights hit Tingka, fuel storage at Chefang, and repair shops at Wanting. 9 B–25's blast troop concentrations and stores in Hinlong. 19 B–24's haul fuel to Liuchow, Yangtong, and Yungning.

Fourteenth AF: 12 B–25's bomb Lungfukwan and Mangshih while several P–40's hit T/Os in same areas. 6 B–25's and 4 P–38's attack and slightly damage Dara bridge and destroy road machinery nearby. About 50 P–40's and P–51's continue armed rcn over vast inland areas of S China, attacking troops, buildings, and other T/Os.

FEAF: B–25's bomb Maumere Bay. B–25's and B–24's bomb Liang and Kendari A/Fs. P–40's hit Kokas.

Twentieth AF: 83 B–29's, staging from Chengtu, bomb Anshan most of them striking Showa Steel Works with poor results. 15 others bomb Dairen, Sinsiang, and various T/Os.

During 26/27 Sep, Japanese aircraft bomb Chengtu area, damaging 5 B–29's. This attack along with the one on 8 Sep set pattern for Japanese raids which usually follow B–29 missions and continue until 19 Dec but are of light nature and annoying rather than seriously damaging.

Seventh AF: 2 B–24's from Saipan on armed rcn bomb Marcus. During 26/27 Sep another B–24 snooper hits Iwo Jima. B–25's from the Gilberts bomb Nauru. B–24's from the Marshalls hit Wake during 26/27 Sep.

Eleventh AF: A B–24 flies weather rcn. Later 4 B–24's radar-bomb Suribachi A/F.

27 September

Eighth AF: Nearly 1,100 HBs bomb 2 M/Ys, 2 synthetic oil plants, 2 motor works, and a tank and armored vehicle plant, at Cologne, Ludwigshafen, Mainz, and Kassel, and T/Os in W Germany. 15 escorting ftr gps claim 31 aircraft destroyed. Over 160 B–24's carry gasoline to France.

Ninth AF: Nearly 300 MBs and LBs abort due to weather. 8 manage to bomb tgt at Foret de Parroy. Ftrs fly armed rcn, cover US First and Third Army forces in W Germany and E France and later fly night patrols in Belgium, Luxembourg, and W German areas.

Twelfth AF: During 26/27 Sep A–20's bomb motor transport in Po Valley. During the day bad weather cancels MB operations and restricts XII FC. Yet FBs effectively spt US Fifth Army, especially on Monte Oggioli, blasting defensive positions, troop concentrations, roads, and

motor transport, and cutting rail lines between Parma and Piacenza.

Tenth AF: 13 P–47's bomb area near Katha. 30 P–47's in 5 flights hit ammo stores and town area of Myothit, and attack Sinkin, Bhamo, and Ma-ubin. 7 other P–47's damage approaches to railroad bridge at Nansiaung, 7 more hit bivouac area at Pinwe, and 7 B–25's pound Hsenwi. 10 B–24's fly fuel to Liuchow and Yungning. TCs fly 200-plus sorties to various points in CBI.

Fourteenth AF: 40-plus P–40's and P–51's on armed rcn attack comm tgts, river shipping, buildings, and troops in Kiyang, Lungfukwan, Sungpai, Chuanhsien, Lingling, Paishui, and Paoching areas.

FEAF: B–24's bomb Menado personnel and supply areas. B–25's attack oil tanks at Boela and hit Old Namba A/F. P–40's hit Ransiki, Kokas, and Waren A/F and shipping in Vogelkop Peninsula area.

Seventh AF: Saipan-based P–47's bomb and strafe Pagan. 2 B–24's on armed rcn hit Marcus. 14 Marshalls-based B–24's strike Truk.

28 September

Eighth AF: Nearly 1,000 HBs attack 2 synthetic oil plants, a motor plant, and city area—all in or near Magdeburg, Kassel, and Merseburg plus T/Os in C Germany including Eschwege A/F. 15 supporting ftr gps claim 26 aircraft destroyed. Over 30 HBs fail to return. Nearly 200 B–24's carry fuel to France.

Ninth AF: 9th Bomb Div hits defended area of Foret de Parroy. Ftrs escort bmrs, attack railroads W of the Rhine, fly sweeps and armed rcn in Arnhem (from which British airborne troops have relinquished their hold because of strong German opposition), Koblenz, Strasbourg, Karlsruhe, and Mannheim areas, and spt US First and Third Armies in E France and W Germany. Night patrols continue over Belgium, Luxembourg, and Germany.

Twelfth AF: Weather grounds LBs and MBs. FBs, operating on reduced scale bomb Bologna and hit roads and rail lines at 4 locations.

Fifteenth AF: Bad weather cancels bombing operations, limiting missions to weather rcn.

Tenth AF: 4 P–47's bomb and strafe Mawhun and Nansiaung. 21 B–24's fly fuel to Liuchow, Yungning, and Kunming.

Fourteenth AF: 26 B–24's pound town of Samshui. 31 B–25's attack towns of Taochuan and Shangchiehshou, Tien Ho and White Cloud A/Fs, and river and road traffic around Lingling, Siangtan, and Chuchou. More than 100 P–40's, P–51's, and P–38's on armed rcn attack numerous T/Os including bridges, town areas, troops, and road, rail, and river traffic throughout inland SE China and, on a smaller scale, in SW China and in Indochina.

FEAF: B–25's on shipping sweep attack small vessels off Kairatoe. A–20's bomb Langoan A/F. P–38's hit barge and town area at Pajahi. P–47's pound Manokwari A/F.

Seventh AF: B–24's from Saipan bomb naval installations at Chichi Jima. P–47's bomb defenses on Pagan.

29 September

Ninth AF: 400-plus MBs and LBs hit M/Ys and rail sidings at Prum,

Euskirchen, and Bingen, dragon's teeth antitank defenses near Webenheim, and M/Ys, rail sidings, warehouses and barracks at Julich and Bitburg. Over 1,500 ftrs escort bmrs, hit railroads, fly sweeps and armed rcn over wide areas of the Netherlands, Luxembourg, Belgium, E France, and in W Germany as far E as Frankfurt/Main.

Twelfth AF: LBs and MBs are again grounded by weather. FBs, hampered by weather, fly 52 sorties in afternoon, cutting rail lines leading S from Milan.

Tenth AF: 11 B–25's attack and damage the main bridge, knock out the bypass bridge and silence adjoining AA positions on Burma Road near Uamhkai. 18 B–24's haul fuel to Yungning, Liuchow, and Kunming.

Fourteenth AF: 11 B–25's bomb Mangshih, 24 bomb Tien Ho and White Cloud A/Fs, and 15 hit T/Os around Chuanhsien, Taochuan and Taohsien. About 100 P–51's, P–40's, and P–38's again attack various T/Os throughout vast expanses of China S of the Yangtze R, hitting road, rail, and river tgts, troops, and town areas.

FEAF: Kendari A/F is bombed by B–24's. B–25's hit both Namlea A/Fs while B–24's blast Liang and Haroekoe A/F. A–20's and RAAF airplanes, continue to pound Urarom A/F; other A–20's bomb Faan A/F.

Seventh AF: 3 B–24's from Saipan bomb Marcus. 2 others hit Iwo Jima and Pagan. P–47's bomb and strafe gun positions on Pagan. B–24's from Eniwetok pound Truk.

Eleventh AF: 2 B–24's bomb Katooka naval base and Kokutan Cape.

30 September

Eighth AF: More than 750 HBs attack 3 M/Ys and an A/F at Bielefeld, Hamm, Handorf, and Munster, Munster city area and several other tgts in the area is bombed by over 200 HBs. 13 ftr gps escort and 2 more fly spt sweeps. Over 100 B-24's haul gasoline to battle areas on the Continent.

Ninth AF: 14 B-26's bomb Arnhem road bridge. Results poor. Ftrs fly sweeps over Belgium, E France, and W Germany and attack rail tgts.

Twelfth AF: B-25's bomb road and railroad bridges in Po Valley at Piacenza, Voghera, Sesto Calende, Lonate Pozzolo, Galliate, Cittadella, Borgoforte, and Tortona. B-26's hit fuel dumps at Cremona, and bridges at Padua, Turbigo, and San Nazzaro. XII FC ftrs hit motor transport, rail lines, roads, bridges, and rolling stock in Po Valley.

Tenth AF: 50-plus P-47's hit various tgts in Myothit and Bhamo areas, attack T/Os at Khalayang, sweep Anisakan and Nawnghkio A/F areas, bomb Nansiaung railroad bridge, and hit T/Os on or near Burma Road between Mangshih and Lashio. 11 B-25's knock out a span of the main bridge and damage 2 bypass bridges at Hsenwi. 18 B-24's haul fuel to Liuchow, Yungning, and Kunming.

Fourteenth AF: 29 B-24's and 12 B-25's bomb Tien Ho and White Cloud A/Fs and Wuchou. 6 B-25's hit T/Os S of Lungfukwan. Nearly 100 P-40's and P-51's on armed rcn over wide areas of China S of the Yangtze R again hit numerous T/Os, concentrating on river shipping.

FEAF: B-24's strike oil installations at Balikpapan. Ambesia A/F is pounded by B-24's while B-25's hit Mapanget, Langoan, and Sidate, and P-38's hit shipping in Wasile Bay. Other B-25's attack shipping in the Halmahera waters. P-38's hit Amahai, Kairatoe, and Haroekoe A/Fs and Halong seaplane base. A-20's and FBs hit Babo, Urarom, and Fak Fak. A-20's and B-25's bomb Faan.

Seventh AF: Saipan-based P-47's blast A/F area on Pagan. Later in the day a B-24 hits same tgt. During 30 Sep/1 Oct a Kwajalein-based B-24 bombs Wake.

1 October

Ninth AF: XXIX TAC (Prov) locates adv HQ at Arlon. Weather prevents bmr operations. A few ftrs fly armed rcn over E France and wide areas of W Germany and patrol battle areas. Night patrols are flown over E France and Luxembourg.

Twelfth AF: B-25's and B-26's attack bridges, fuel dumps, factory, and barracks in C and W Po Valley, including 3 attacks on Piacenza while XII FC's LBs hit fuel dump and bivouacs and FBs blast guns and comm in mountainous battle areas between Florence and Bologna.

Fifteenth AF: 5th Photo Gp, Rcn, with component units, is assigned to Fifteenth AF, completing the full establishment of 21 HB gps, 7 ftr gps, and 1 rcn gp, as authorized in WD directive of 23 Oct 43. Weather permits only photo and weather rcn missions.

Tenth AF: 34 P-47's bomb Thetkegyin while 20 others hit railroad tgts throughout N Burma railroad corridor and troop concentrations at Ponlon. 4 P-47's bomb Shwegugale while 6 others hit Lungling and sweep Burma Road in the area.

Fourteenth AF: 18 B–25's bomb Tien Ho and White Cloud A/Fs, town of Wuchou, and T/Os in Samshui and Canton areas. 100-plus P–40's and P–51's on armed rcn throughout China areas S of the Yangtze hit variety of T/Os, concentrating on comm tgts and troops in Mangshih and Hsinganhsien areas.

FEAF: B–24's bomb Langoan while B–25's hit Lembeh I, Menado, and Bolaang-oeki port. B–24's bomb Taka while P–38's hit Amahai, Kairatoe, and shipping off Amboina. B–25's and P–38's on shipping sweeps off Halmahera I destroy several barges and luggers. A–20's and P–38's attack Urarom A/F and Fak Fak supply dumps, while P–40's hit Doom I and T/Os in Windissi, Idorra, and MacCluer Gulf. P–47's and A–20's hit Doeroa, Langgoer, and Faan A/Fs.

Seventh AF: B–24's from Saipan strike A/F on Iwo Jima. B–25's from Makin bomb Nauru while B–24's, staging through Eniwetok, hit Truk.

2 October

Eighth AF: Over 1,100 HBs, escorted by 17 gps of ftrs, attack 4 assigned tgts at Bettenhausen ordnance depot, Henschel plant and other Kassel areas, Cologne motor works, Hamm M/Y, and several T/Os in these areas. 15 HBs and 11 ftrs fail to return.

Ninth AF: IX TAC moved advanced HQ to Verviers, maintaining close association with US First Army. HQ XXIX TAC (Prov) goes into operation along with US Ninth Army. This new TAC is formed from elements of IX and XIX TAC. 9th

Bomb Div strikes industrial area of Ubach and defended positions at Herbach. Ftrs fly armed rcn (and later night patrol) over Belgium, E France, and W Germany and spt US First, Third, and Seventh Armies in E France and W Germany.

Twelfth AF: Weather grounds MBs and restricts ftrs to rcn and patrols. During 1/2 Oct LBs bomb T/Os in Po Valley.

Fifteenth AF: Unfavorable weather again cancels bombing missions and limits operations to weather rcn.

Tenth AF: 49 P–47's pound several towns and bridges in Bhamo area and destroy buildings in Shwekyina, Kaungsin, Maingka, Kyungyi, Singan, and Kabani. 20-plus P–47's hit N Burma railroad tgts and troops at Man He and Manla. 7 P–47's bomb Kutkai while 8 sweep Lungling-Loiwing area, destroying a warehouse at Selan. 8 B–25's slightly damage road bridges N of Lashio. 4 others bomb and damage Namhkai road bridges and their vicinity. TC airplanes fly 260-plus sorties, delivering men and supplies to various points in CBI.

Fourteenth AF: 11 B–25's attack town of Pingnam while 16 bomb Tien Ho and White Cloud A/Fs and town of Samshui. 70-plus P–40's and P–51's on armed rcn over S China attack various T/Os, chiefly river traffic and troop areas around Chuanhsien, Taochuan, Takhing, Wuchou, Dosing, and Wenchow peninsula, and attack shipping in Campha Port-Hongay area.

FEAF: B–25's pound Laha A/F while B–24's hit Haroekoe. P–38's cover Laha raid, attack shipping in Seri and Amboina Bays and hit

Amahai and Kairatoe A/Fs. Off Halmahera I B–25's fly barge sweep, bomb Laboehan, and attack coastal villages on Weda and Boeli Bays. P–40's attack vessels off Tamoelol village and Misool I and bomb Otawiri and Ransiki A/Fs.

Seventh AF: Saipan-based B–24's hit Marcus and shipping W of Chichi Jima.

Eleventh AF: Photo rcn missions, by 4 B–25's to Paramushiru and by 2 B–24's to Onnekotan, abort due to weather.

3 October

Eighth AF: Almost 1,000 HBs attack 3 A/Fs W of Nurnberg, city of Nurnberg, synthetic oil works at Wesseling, and a motor works and A/F in Karlsruhe area (all assigned tgts), and hit several other tgts in Nurnberg-Cologne-Karlsruhe areas. 16 ftr gps give escort.

Ninth AF: 220-plus MBs and LBs sent to bomb tgts at Duren, Aldenhoven, and Arnhem are recalled because of weather. Ftrs fly armed rcn over W Germany, hit railroads W of Rhine, and spt US Third Army in Metz area. IX ADC continues night patrols.

Twelfth AF: MBs continue to pound road and rail bridges and fuel dumps in Po Valley. LBs, FBs, and ftrs of XII FC hit fuel dumps, rail lines, and transportation in the Valley and spt US Fifth Army forces in battle areas in the N Apennines S and SW of Bologna and N of the Arno R Valley.

Fifteenth AF: For the eighth consecutive day bad weather prevents bombing operations.

Tenth AF: TCs fly 240-plus sorties,

delivering men and supplies to various points in CBI.

Fourteenth AF: 23 B–25's attack Pingnam, trucks and rivercraft in Wuchou, Samshui, and Canton areas, and bomb Tien Ho and White Cloud A/Fs. 100 P–51's and P–40's continue armed rcn over wide expanses of China S of the Yangtze, attacking rivercraft, road traffic, troops, town areas, and other T/Os. Hsinganhsien, Pingnam, and Chuanhsien areas are covered exceptionally well.

FEAF: For second time B–24's bomb oil refineries in Balikpapan area, MBs hit shipping and bomb Sanana. MBs smash Kaoe runway and bomb Galela. MBs and HBs over Ceram-Amboina hit barge and coastal T/Os and pound Taka A/F, while FBs attack Halong seaplane base and Namlea and Haroekoe A/Fs. On Vogelkop Peninsula FBs again hit Fak Fak and Otawiri.

Seventh AF: B–24's from Saipan hit shipping in the Bonins while P–47's pound gun positions, buildings, and wharf on Pagan. B–24's on special rcn missions bomb A/F at Iwo Jima.

Eleventh AF: 2 B–24's flying offshore rcn over Onnekotan, Harumukotan, and Shasukotan also strafe several small vessels.

4 October

Ninth AF: Bmrs drop leaflets in Metz, Saint-Die, and Saarburg areas. Ftrs spt US First and Third Armies in W Germany and E France, escort MBs, and fly armed rcn in forward areas, attacking rail and military tgts.

Twelfth AF: Weather restricts MBs to attacks on 2 bridges at Bistagno and Villafranca d'Asti. FBs closely spt ground forces fighting in Loiano-Quinzanod'Oglio-Sassoleone areas, and hit comm N of battle areas.

Fifteenth AF: 327 B–17's and B–24's, with ftr escort, bomb Munich W M/Y. Around 400 other HBs attack rail line in Trento-Mezzaselva area (covering over 50 mi of the Brenner route), Aviano A/F, Avisio viaduct, and railroad and road bridges at Pinzano al Tagliamento, Pordenone, Latisana, Casarsa della Delizia, Mezzocorona, Ora, and San Dona di Piave. 39 P–51's strafe Tatoi, Kalamaki, and Eleusis A/Fs. Other P–51's escort MATAF C–47's and fly rcn.

Tenth AF: 8 P–47's damage approaches to bridge between Myitkyina and Bhamo. 16 P–47's hit town of Palwesho. 4 others hit small towns S of Bhamo, including Man The and Hantet.

Fourteenth AF: 5 B–25's hit Hsinantien and areas N of Chefang. 80-plus P–40's and P–51's continue to attack T/Os during armed rcn over areas of China S of the Yangtze. More than 20 FBs hit buildings, troops, and river shipping in Paoching area.

FEAF: B–25's bomb Sidate and and Bolaang-oeki. P–40's and B–25's attack Galela and Kaoe A/Fs. B–25's and A–20's on shipping sweep bomb town and port area of Amboina, hit wharf at Halong, and attack shipping and shore T/Os at various points.

Seventh AF: B–24's from Saipan attack shipping W of Iwo Jima and bomb A/Fs, radio station, buildings, and area tgts on Marcus, Pagan, and Iwo Jima. P–47's hit gun positions,

beach defenses, buildings, and wharf area on Pagan. B–24's from the Marshalls bomb A/F at Moen.

Eleventh AF: A B–24 weatheraborts a photo run off Matsuwa. 4 B–25's bomb a freighter and a barge off Shimushu. 15–17 ftrs intercept and the B–25's score one victory.

5 October

International: Sec of the Treasury Morgenthau and Lord Keynes begin series of talks on the course of Lend-Lease between V-E and V-J Days.

Eighth AF: GO 507 implements decision of 15 Sep to assign staff officers of HQ VIII FC to HQ Eighth AF to represent units in administrative functions, thus eliminating administrative and operational control from HQ VIII FC and placing it under Eighth AF HQ. This is necessitated by the transfer of ftr gps to bomb divs. Over 900 HBs, escorted by 15 ftr gps, strike 4 primary tgts (a M/Y and 4 A/Fs) in NW Germany and several secondary tgts and T/Os (M/Y, A/F, city areas) in the same area, especially around Dusseldorf and Cologne.

Ninth AF: 330-plus MBs and LBs dispatched against tgts in Arnhem, Aldenhoven, and Duren are recalled. Ftrs hit pillboxes along Westwall, spt ground forces of XV Corps in France, fly armed rcn in Prum, Bonn, Koblenz, Trier and Landau areas, hit tgts along Rhine-Marne Canal, and during 5/6 Oct fly patrol in Belgium, E France, and W Germany.

Twelfth AF: During 4/5 Oct A–20's bomb T/Os in battle area in mountains S of Bologna and N of Arno R Valley. During the day weather grounds MB wgs and XII FC.

Fifteenth AF: Bad weather causes recall of HBs.

Tenth AF: 11 P–47's hit Mawlu and attack locomotives and T/Os in Naba area. 8 B–25's attack bridges at Namhkai, damaging the main bridge. TCs fly over 250 sorties to various locations in CBI.

Fourteenth AF: 12 B–25's and 22 FBs attack Samshui, Koyiu and Takhing. 8 hit T/Os in Canton-Wuchou area, and 3 bomb storage area at Mangshih. 50-plus P–40's and P–51's over wide areas of S China attack rivercraft, road traffic, bridges, town areas, and troops.

FEAF: B–24's bomb A/Fs in Kendari area. B–25's and P–38's hit Kairatoe A/F, town of Amboina and numerous coastal and shipping T/Os in Amboina-Ceram area. A–20's, B–25's, and FBs attack Urarom, Simora Pt area, Doom I, Babo, Efman and Samate A/Fs and disposal areas. A–20's blast Japanese bivouacs and supply areas near Sarmi.

Seventh AF: Saipan-based P–47's hit Pagan with rockets and bombs. A B–24 bombs gun positions on the islands. B–25's from the Gilberts bomb runways and gun positions on Nauru while B–24's from the Marshalls bomb an A/F at Moen and during 5/6 Oct strike Wake.

Eleventh AF: At dawn 2 B–24's bomb Kashiwabara and Kurabu Cape.

6 October

Eighth AF: Nearly 1,200 HBs attack 11 primaries, including oil plants, aircraft factories, ordnance facilities, and AF trg school, in N Germany, and 19 T/Os including A/Fs at Stralsund and Stade. 16 ftr gps in escort claim 19 air victories.

Ninth AF: 300-plus MBs and LBs hit M/Ys, barracks, and ammo dump at Hengelo and Duren and bridges at Arnhem and Aldenhoven. Ftrs fly armed rcn in Dusseldorf, Aachen, Trier, Dieuze, and Koblenz areas, sweeps and patrols in forward areas, attack railroads in Dorsel area, and spt US First, Third, and Seventh Armies' forces in E France and W Germany.

Twelfth AF: Weather cancels all operations of MB wgs and XII FC.

Fifteenth AF: Weather cancels bombing operations. 35 P–38's strafe A/Fs at Sedhes, Megalo Mikra, Megara, Eleusis, and Tatoi A/Fs, and 55 P–51's strafe Kalamaki A/F.

Tenth AF: 20-plus P–47's bomb troop concentrations in Mawlu and Bilumyo and damage approach to bridge at Seywa. 8 B–25's attack bridges at Hsenwi, damaging main bridge but causing little harm to bypass bridges. Transport operations continue on large scale in CBI.

Fourteenth AF: 12 B–25's bomb Wuchou and attack boats and other T/Os in Canton area. 50-plus P–40's and P–51's on armed rcn over areas of China S of the Yangtze R attack rivercraft, bridges, town areas, troop concentrations and T/Os along N Indochina coast.

FEAF: P–38's hit Kaoe A/F and shipping near Djailolo. P–47's bomb Kaimana. In Ceram-Amboina-Boeroe area B–25's and P–38's attack Namlea, Waai, Amahai, and several small craft.

Twentieth AF: The first P–61 night ftrs arrive in Chengtu on eve of third air raid. (In 10 attacks from 6 Sep to 19 Dec, only 43 aircraft participate).

Seventh AF: B–24's from Saipan hit Iwo Jima in harassment attacks during 6/7 Oct. A B–24 from Kwajalein bombs heavy gun battery on Emidj. During 6/7 Oct, 3 B–24's bomb Wake.

7 October

Eighth AF: Over 1,300 HBs, in 4 forces, bomb 5 synthetic oil plants, an armament, a tank, and an aero engine works in C and NE Germany, plus 16 identified and 19 other unidentified tgts in the area. 19 escorting ftr gps claim 22 air victories including 4 jets. Air opposition and ground fire is heavy. 52 HBs and 15 ftrs are lost.

Ninth AF: HQ cancels previous instructions against bombing bridges and opens to attack all bridges on US front, except those over the Rhine R. 300-plus MBs and LBs strike bridges at Arnhem, Bullay, and Dillingen, supply depot at Euskirchen, and M/Y and warehouse at Hengelo and Trier. Ftrs fly bmr escort, sweeps and armed rcn in forward areas, hitting railroads, barges, and troop concentrations, and spt ground forces in E France and W Germany.

Twelfth AF: Weather again grounds MBs. FBs hit guns and troop concentrations in battle area, which extends over wide front S of Bologna in region of Monte Stanco, Monte Cauala, Monte Castellaro, and Monte Ceci, and comm to the N.

Fifteenth AF: 350-plus B–17's and B–24's bomb Lobau and Schwechat oil refineries and Winterhafen oil depot in Vienna area. Nearly 30 others hit T/Os in Hungary includ-

ing M/Ys at Szombathely and Zalaegerszeg. 330-plus HBs, escorted by P–38's and P–51's, attack M/Ys at Nove Zamky and Komarom and A/F at Gyor. 6 B–17's escorted by 54 P–51's, evacuate US airmen from Czechoslovakia to Italy.

Tenth AF: 5 P–47's bomb supplies and troops at Man Hpa. Large-scale transport operations continue to deliver men and supplies to various points in CBI.

Fourteenth AF: 53 P–51's and P–40's on armed rcn attack troop concentrations, bridges, river and rail traffic, town areas, and supply dumps around Tunghsiangchiao, Pingnam, Hsinganhsien, Chuanhsien, Lingling, Wuchou, Houmachen, Chiuchiang, and Paoching.

FEAF: B–24's over Mindanao bomb Zamboanga while a P–38 cover force hits seaplanes, shipping, and other T/Os in the area. B–25's bomb Langoan, Tompaso, and Tondegesang. P–38's attack Kaoe I, and hit Boela oil tanks. B–25's bomb storage area on W Amboina. P–38's and B–25's strike Doom I and Babo A/F.

Seventh AF: B–24's from Saipan, on armed rcn, attack Marcus and nearby shipping.

8 October

Ninth AF: Revision and elaboration (from 28 Sep–8 Oct) of Ninth AF interdiction program against railroads connected with Rhine R results in issue of a new interdiction program. It includes rail lines further to the E and requires attacks by all 4 TACs of the Ninth AF, plus aid from British Second Tac AF. More than 300 MBs and LBs hit strongpoints and bridges over wide areas of E

France and W Germany. Ftrs spt ground forces of US VII, XV, XIX, and XX Corps in E France and W Germany, escort 9th Bomb Div, and attack A/Fs, railroads, and numerous military tgts in forward areas.

Twelfth AF: Bad weather forces MBs to cancel missions. XII FC ftrs are airborne to spt ground forces over battle area and abort all missions.

Fifteenth AF: Bad weather limits operations to rcn and sea-search missions.

Tenth AF: 20-plus P–47's hit T/Os in Mawhun and Manyut areas, knock out bridge at Seywa, and bomb railroad tracks in N Burma. 5 B–25's damage 1 bridge and score hits on the other bridge approaches at Namhkai and knock out 2 bridges at Wuntho and Kawlin.

Fourteenth AF: 12 P–40's and P–51's hit locomotives, trucks, and river traffic at Yuncheng and NE of Pengtse.

FEAF: P–47's bomb Amahai and Boela. P–38's hit Dodinga Bay barge hideouts, supplies and T/Os along Wasile and Kaoe Bays. B–25's, A–20's, and FBs hit Sorong, Doom I, runways and T/Os at Efman and Samate, and gun positions, bivouacs, and supplies at Simora Pt.

Seventh AF: 3 Saipan-based B–24's hit Pagan and Marcus. 24 P–47's hit buildings, beach defenses, and gun positions on Pagan. During the day and 8/9 Oct B–24's from the Marshalls bomb Wake.

Eleventh AF: Photo missions to Paramushiru, Matsuwa, Onnekotan and Shasukotan turn back due to weather.

9 October

International: Churchill and Eden, with Harriman, US presidential representative, as observer, arrive in Moscow. Polish PM arrives later. Talks with Soviets deal with spheres of influence, the Balkans, and Poland's position.

Eighth AF: Over 1,000 HBs strike 2 M/Ys and an engine plant at Mainz, and hit Koblenz, Gustavsburg, Schweinfurt, and 2 T/Os in W Germany. 19 ftr gps, including 2 from Ninth AF, provide spt.

Ninth AF: HQ gives the TACs an initial attack list of 10 bridges on US front. Other lists follow. 30 9th Bomb Div aircraft attack rail bridge at Euskirchen. Ftrs provide escort and fly uneventful armed rcn. Dive bmrs sent against A/Fs in Germany are recalled because of bad weather.

Twelfth AF: Weather again grounds MBs. FBs, and ftrs hit roads, rail crossing, transport and other tgts in Bologna and Sabbioso areas.

Fifteenth AF: Bad weather restricts operations to weather rcn missions.

Tenth AF: 50-plus P–47's knock out bridge at Manyut and thoroughly pound town area, bomb enemy positions at Nyaunggon, Pinhe, and near Mawhun, damage bridge near Mawlu, and hit a variety of tgts in Katha area. 9 B–25's attack road bridges SW of Lashio, knocking out Na-lang and Nampawng bridges. The MBs hit several T/Os in the area. Transport aircraft continue steady supply of various points in CBI.

Fourteenth AF: 2 B–25's bomb area N of Mangshih. 3 B–24's hit shipping along lower Yangtze R. 29 P–51's and P–40's on armed rcn attack river traffic, troops, bridges, and other T/Os in areas around Tanchuk, Tengyun, Anking, and Amoy. Airstrip at Tanchuk is temporarily put out of commission.

FEAF: B–25's, A–20's, and FBs attack Boela, Namlea, Kairatoe, and Liang, concentrating on oil tanks and A/Fs. B–25's and FBs hit Lolobata and Hate Tabako A/Fs and nearby barges, supplies, and other T/Os. A–20's and FBs strike Faan and Langgoer A/Fs. P–40's hit Manokwari and B–25's bomb Samate.

Seventh AF: 18 B–24's from Saipan pound Iwo Jima. 25 B–25's from the Marshalls bomb Truk.

10 October

Ninth AF: Weather cancels daytime bmr and ftr operations. IX ADC during 10/11 Oct flies patrol over Belgium and W Germany.

Twelfth AF: MBs are again grounded due to weather. FBs, though also hampered by weather, manage to closely spt ground forces, particularly at Monte delle Formiche where US 85th Inf Div elements are stopped short of the crest, and attack comm N of battle area in the N Apennines.

Fifteenth AF: Almost 170 B–17's and B–24's attack 4 M/Ys at Treviso and Mestre and bridges at Susegana and San Dona di Piave plus rail lines in surrounding areas. About 90 ftrs provide spt in Udine-Treviso area. 350-plus other HBs are forced to abort because of weather.

Tenth AF: 28 P–47's spt ground forces near Pinhe, bomb towns of Tawbon and Man Naung, and hit T/Os in and near Momauk. Transport operations to various points in CBI

continue at the rate of 250-plus sorties.

Fourteenth AF: 12 B–25's bomb and considerably damage Kunlong ferry. 38 P–40's and P–51's on armed rcn attack bridge and other T/Os near Mangshih, hit troop areas around Tanchuk and Wuchou, river traffic near Dosing, and locomotives and barges along N Indochina coast.

FEAF: B–24's strike oil refineries and an A/F in Balikpapan area. The HBs and escorting P–47's and P–38's claim over 30 Japanese ftrs downed. P–38's and B–25's bomb Djailolo, Kaoe, and Hate Tabako A/F and Wasile town area. P–47's hit Liang A/F. A–20's hit Sarmi area. A–20's and B–25's bomb Urarom A/F.

Seventh AF: 14 B–24's from Saipan bomb A/F at Iwo Jima and shipping off the E shore. 24 P–47's pound buildings and storage caves on Pagan. Later a B–24 bombs the radio station N of Pagan A/F. 12 B–25's from Makin bomb runways and adjacent AA positions on Nauru.

Eleventh AF: 4 B–24's abort a strike at Kashiwabara due to weather.

11 October

Eighth AF: 130 B–17's bomb Wesseling synthetic oil plant and Koblenz M/Y. 3 P–47 gps give spt.

Ninth AF: 99 MBs and LBs sent to bomb Camp-de-Bitche military camp are recalled when Pathfinder equipment malfunctions and weather prevents visual bombing. Ftrs escort bmrs, fly armed rcn, cut rail lines in Aachen-Rhine area, and spt US VII and XIX Corps in Aachen area, and US XII, XV, and XX Corps in Metz-Saarlautern area.

Twelfth AF: Despite bad weather MBs attack bridges and supply dumps in Po Valley. FBs and ftrs closely spt ground forces in Apennine Mountains between Florence and Bologna where fierce fighting rages on Monte delle Formiche, Livergnano escarpment, Monte delle Tombe, Gesso ridge, and Monte Battaglia. Also hit are comm behind battle area and as far W and N as Genoa, Turin, and Savona.

Fifteenth AF: About 180 B–17's and B–24's, with ftr escort, bomb Vienna S ordnance depot, Graz motor works, S and SW areas of Vienna, towns of Hirtenberg and Enzesfeld, M/Y at Zeltweg, Dravograd railroad bridge on Yugoslav-Hungarian boundary, railroad and highway bridges at Cesara, and Trieste harbor. Over 250 HBs fail to complete missions because of bad weather. 18 P–51's strafe tgts in Bratislava and Budapest areas, including supply dumps, and trains and destroy 17 airplanes at Esztergom landing ground. 37 other P–51's strafe Prostejov A/F and T/Os in surrounding area, destroying nearly 30 aircraft and trucks, locomotives, and railroad cars.

Tenth AF: 15 P–47's hit guns and enemy positions near Pinhe while 9 attack town of Manwein and hit T/Os in the area. 8 others hit towns of Nayakaung and Nansiaung. 8 B–25's attack bridges at Man Pwe, Tahpalai, and Namyao damaging only Man Pwe bridge. 23 P–47's hit troops and stores near Tawbon and at Hkawan, knock out Kawnghka bridge and damage Wanling bridge. Transport flights continue to points throughout CBI.

Fourteenth AF: 2 B–25's knock out bridge S of Mangshih. 3 P–40's attack sampans from Tanchuk to Tengyun while 8 hit general T/Os N of Mangshih.

FEAF: B–24's bomb Koeandang and Langoan area. P–38's pound Miti A/F. A–20's and FBs attack Liang, Kairatoe, Laha, Haroekoe, and Namlea A/F. Langgoer A/F is bombed by P–47's. P–47's hit Babo A/F while A–20's attack Sarmi troop concentrations. At night B–24's bomb Sasa Matina and Buayoan A/F.

Seventh AF: Saipan-based P–47's hit buildings on Pagan with rockets and bombs. A Kwajalein-based B–24 bombs Wake during the night.

Eleventh AF: 4 B–25's over Shimushiru and Paramushiru blow up 3 buildings and damage 2 others at Cape Namikawa.

12 October

Eighth AF: Over 500 HBs attack M/Y at Osnabruck, aircraft industries at Bremen, and T/Os including Diepholz A/F. 11 ftr gps escort HBs, claiming 18 ftrs downed.

Ninth AF: Ninth AF is delegated administrative (in addition to operational) control over XII TAC hitherto assumed by USSTAF. Advanced HQ XIX TAC arrives at Nancy, following the adv of US Third Army. Almost 250 MBs and LBs bomb Camp-de-Bitche military camp, rail bridges at Grevenbroich and Ahrweiler, city areas of Langerwehe, Aldenhoven, and Venraij, and various T/Os. Escorting ftrs fly also armed rcn and rail cutting in Dusseldorf, Aachen, and Belfort areas, and spt VIII, XII, XV, and XX Corps in E France and W Germany.

Twelfth AF: MBs, supporting US Fifth Army, attack comm, supply dumps, and bivouac and barracks areas S of Bologna. FBs and XII FC ftrs, mainly in spt of US Fifth Army, blast supply dumps, gun positions, troop concentrations, and comm in the high country S of Bologna (while DAF gives similar spt to British Eighth Army in Rimini area).

Fifteenth AF: Around 700 HBs, with ftr spt, pound ammo and fuel dumps and depots, bivouac area, barracks, vehicle repair shop, munitions factory and T/Os in Bologna area (Operation PANCAKE) supporting US Fifth Army offensive in that sector. 160 P–51's strafe mainline railroad and Danube R traffic in Vienna-Gyor-Budapest areas and strafe Seregelyes A/F, disrupting traffic and destroying many enemy airplanes.

Tenth AF: 18 P–47's bomb railroad tgts in the Naba-Mawlu rail corridor damaging a bridge approach, and strike troops and stores near Nayakaung. 12 other P–47's hit various tgts at Pintha and Nyaunggon. 4 B–25's knock out a bridge just N of Lashio. 3 others knock out bridge at Kawlin and damage tracks near Man Pwe bridge.

Fourteenth AF: 3 B–25's and 12 P–40's hit Chefang storage area and bridge and general T/Os in Mangshih area. 40-plus P–40's and P–51's on armed rcn covering wide areas of S China and extending into W Burma attack troop concentrations, river traffic, storage areas, and buildings in areas around Taochuan, Kweiping, Hsinganhsien, Yuncheng, Tanchuk, and Hsenwi.

FEAF: B–24's bomb Ambesia, Langoan, Mapanget, and Sidate A/Fs.

B–25's, A–20's, and P–47's again pound A/Fs at Liang, Laha, Namlea, Kairatoe and Haroekoe, and town of Boela. P–38's hit numerous T/Os on Halmahera I. FBs hit Manokwari and Urarom and A–20's bomb pillboxes in Sarmi area.

Twentieth AF: First B–29 *(Joltin' Josie, the Pacific Pioneer)* arrives at Saipan, piloted by Gen Hansell, CG XXI BC, for whom temporary HQ are set up on Saipan. Also the regular air echelon of 73d Bomb Wg arrives at Saipan on this date, followed during Oct and first week in Nov by 4 bomb gps and 4 air serv gps. (313th Bomb Wg will be established in the theater in Dec 44, 314th in Jan 45, 58th in Mar, and 315th in Apr. In Mar 45 VII FC will be established at Iwo Jima from where some of its units escort B–29 missions).

Seventh AF: B–24's from Saipan bomb harbor and shipping at Chichi Jima, shipping S of Haha Jima, AA positions on Marcus, and A/F area on Pagan. P–47's hit Pagan A/F area with bombs and rockets. B–24's from Kwajalein bomb Wake during 12/13 Oct.

Eleventh AF 3 B–24's hit A/F and shipping tgts in the Matsuwa-Onnekotan area.

13 October

Ninth AF: 9th Bomb Div hits bridges at Saarlouis, Roermond, Venlo, Euskirchen, and Mayen, plus several T/Os. Escorting ftrs also fly armed rcn over areas of Metz and extensively over W Germany, attacking railroads and other tgts, and spt US First, Third, and Seventh Armies.

Twelfth AF: Weather cancels all

MB operations except for attacks on 4 tgts (bridges and supply dumps) in the battle area S of Bologna. FBs spt US Fifth Army operations more successfully in the area, hitting gun emplacements, troop concentrations, supply dumps, bridges, and vehicles.

Fifteenth AF: More than 650 ftr-escorted HBs bomb oil refineries at Blechhammer and Vienna/Floridsdorf, motor works, locomotive shops, and M/Y at Vienna, Graz, Banhida, Szekesfehervar, Papa, Hranice and Mezirici. Some of the escorting ftrs strafe railroads, roads, and A/F in areas of Balaton and Neusiedler Lakes, Vienna, and Prostejov. Other ftrs strafe roads, railroads, and Danube R traffic in Vienna-Gyor-Budapest areas.

Tenth AF: 38 P–47's strike Okkyin, Yebyangale, and Theinlon, and hit troops in Myothit area. 8 P–47's spt ground forces in Mohnyin area, 12 attack and considerably damage Wanling bridge and 4 hit T/Os in the area. Transports fly over 280 sorties hauling troops and supplies to CBI terminals.

Fourteenth AF: 138 P–40's and P–51's on numerous armed rcn missions throughout S China and into W Burma attack troop areas, rivercraft, town areas, bridges, trucks, and other T/Os. 71 of the FBs hit tgts in Kweiping area while the others attack tgts around Chuanhsien, Litou, Shepchung, Tengyun, Lungfukwan, Kingshan, Mangshih, and Chefang.

FEAF: B–25's bomb Menado and surrounding area. P–38's hit AA positions, enemy concentrations, and other tgts in NE Celebes and Halmaheras. A–20's and FBs attack Boela

oil installations and A/Fs at Amahai, Kairatoe, and Namlea.

Seventh AF: B–24's from Saipan bomb Yap. From the Marshalls B–24's pound Truk. Gilberts-based B–25's bomb Nauru.

Eleventh AF: 4 B–25's bomb Kurabu A/F and bomb and strafe buildings on Tomari Cape, scoring hits on canneries, warehouses, and barracks. Later, 4 B–24's photograph and bomb tgts at Kashiwabara.

14 October

Eighth AF: About 1,100 HBs bomb 7 M/Ys at Saarbrucken, Kaiserslautern, and Cologne, city of Euskirchen, and T/Os in the Cologne area. 15 ftr gps give escort.

Ninth AF: Bad weather grounds 9th Bomb Div. Ftrs escort leaflet mission, fly sweeps and rail cutting operations, armed rcn over E France and W Germany, and spt US Third Army.

Twelfth AF: Bad weather cancels all MB operations. Over 100 ftrs and FBs pound troop concentrations, gun positions, supplies, bridges, roads, and rail lines S of Bologna where hard fighting is taking place in Monterumici, Livergnano, and Gesso ridge areas.

Fifteenth AF: 317 B–17's and B–24's hampered by bad weather, bomb oil refineries at Blechhammer and Odertal, and several T/Os including M/Ys at Bratislava, Nove Zamky, Komarom, Komarom and Nove Zamky railroad bridges, Borzavar industrial area, and Ugod military garrison. Escorting ftrs strafe A/Fs, rail and road traffic and other T/Os in tgt areas. 52 B–24's bomb railroad bridge and M/Y at Maribor. 54 P–51's on strafing mission in Balaton Lake area attack A/Fs at Szekesfehervar and Seregelyes. 55 P–38's escort MATAF C–47's carrying airborne forces to Megara A/F.

Tenth AF: Transport aircraft fly more than 200 sorties, delivering men and supplies to various points in CBI.

Fourteenth AF: 32 P–51's and P–40's on armed rcn attack troops, town areas, and river traffic around Samshui, Mangshih, Kweiping, Hsinganhsien, Konghow and Tajungchiang.

FEAF: B–24's again bomb oil refineries and associated industries in Balikpapan area. Others bomb Pombelaa mine. A–20's, B–25's, and FBs again hit Laha and Haroekoe A/Fs.

Twentieth AF: 103 Chengtu-based B–29's bomb aircraft plant at Okayama. 12 more hit last-resort tgts and T/Os. This is first Twentieth AF mission during which over 100 VHBs attack tgts and the first of a series of missions against Formosa in conjunction with US invasion of Leyte.

Seventh AF: 3 B–24's on armed rcn from Saipan bomb Marcus. P–47's on sweep over Pagan bomb and strafe storage caves. 1 B–24 from the Marshalls bombs Wake during 14/15 Oct.

Eleventh AF: 4 B–25's bomb and strafe buildings at Otomae Bay.

15 October

Eighth AF: More than 1,000 HBs attack 9 M/Ys and gas unit plant in and around general area of Cologne, along with several other tgts including oil facilities at Reisholz and Monheim. 3 ftr gps give general area spt while 12 gps provide close escort. 2 P–47 gps attack comm in Hannover and Munster-Kassel areas.

Ninth AF: Weather prevents bmr operations. Ftrs fly rail cutting missions and spt elements of US First, Third, Seventh, and Ninth Armies in E France and W Germany.

Twelfth AF: B–25's bomb bridges in W Po Valley. B–26's hit bridges in the E part of the Valley, and have excellent success bombing a railway fill at Ossenigo, trapping over 300 railway cars N of the tgt. Ftrs and FBs concentrate efforts toward spt of ground forces along wide front in the mountains S of Bologna.

Fifteenth AF: Bad weather limits operations to weather rcn missions.

Tenth AF: About 40 P–47's attack positions in Mohnyin area and at Man Naung, supply concentrations at Kyungyi, railroad tgts in Mawhun area, ammo stores at Manwing, and buildings near Muse. 12 B–25's hit town of Onbauk, storage facilities at Indaw, and vicinity of Thabeikkyin. Transport operations in CBI continue on large scale.

Fourteenth AF: 28 B–24's, 33 P–51's, and 18 P–40's pound White Cloud A/F and shipping in Hong Kong area. 2 B–24's bomb Amoy. 6 FBs hit T/Os near Mangshih and Tajungchiang.

FEAF: A–20's again pound A/Fs and oil storage on Ceram. P–38's carry out shipping sweep over Flores area and on Halmahera bomb Pitoe and Kaoe areas. P–38's bomb Amahai A/F while bmrs on armed rcn hit nearby T/Os. P–47's attack Sagan A/F.

Seventh AF: 27 B–24's from Saipan strike fuel storage, AA positions, and installations at A/F on Iwo Jima. 1 other HB bombs A/F at Pagan. 2

B–24's from the Marshalls bomb Wake on 15/16 Oct.

Eleventh AF: 4 B–25's on armed rcn over Paramushiru turn back when flight drifts off course. 1 B–24 strafes a freighter off Shimushiru.

16 October

Ninth AF: Ninth AF adv HQ follows HQ 12th AG to Luxembourg. All operations cancelled due to weather.

Twelfth AF: MB operations are cancelled by bad weather. LBs and FBs hit troop concentrations, bridges, gun positions, road, rail lines, and vehicles in battle area, particularly in Monte Belmonte vicinity.

Fifteenth AF: Nearly 600 HBs, with ftr escort, hit tank factory, tank assembly plant, and aero engine works at Steyr, benzol plant and ordnance depot at Linz, plus alternate tgts and T/Os in Austria, including Graz-Neudorf aircraft engine factory, Trieben, Linz, Graz, Villach, Salzburg, Klagenfurt, Spittal an der Drau and Zeltweg M/Ys, town of Sankt Veit an der Glan, Brux synethetic oil refinery, and armament works in Plzen. Over 20 P–51's and P–38's fly photo and weather rcn missions and sea patrol. 29 P–38's escort MATAF C–47's (transporting airborne troops) to Greece and back to Italy.

Tenth AF: 11 P–47's attack 2 railroad bridges in Naba-Mawlu area, damaging approaches to both tgts. 5 other P–47's hit Japanese forces in NW part of Madangyang. 12 B–25's, supported by escort of 8 P–47's, pound A/F at Shwebo. Transports fly over 300 sorties in CBI.

Fourteenth AF: 28 B–24's, 8 B–25's, 26 P–51's, and 21 P–40's blast shipping and Kowloon Dock area. 15 cargo vessels are damaged or sunk. 3 other P–51's hit Wuchou area. 36 P–40's, P–51's, and P–38's hit village and town areas, bridges, and troop concentrations in Kweiping, Tanchuk, Hsinganhsien, Tingka, and Chefang areas.

FEAF: P–38's hit harbor, shipping, A/F and trucks at Cagayan. B–24's blast Makassar area. B–24's, B–25's, and FBs again pound the Boeroe-Ceram A/Fs and towns of Boela and Amboina and hit shipping in Binnen Bay. FBs hit Timoeka and Mongosah and Sagan A/Fs. Langgoer A/F is pounded by A–20's.

Twentieth AF: Over 40 B–29's, out of Chengtu, bomb Okayama aircraft plant and Heito A/F. 20-plus other B–29's bomb alternate or chance tgts at Takao, Swatow, Toshien, and Sintien harbors, Hengyang, and several A/Fs, including Taichu.

Seventh AF: 15 P–47's and 1 B–24 from Saipan hit Pagan. From the Marshalls 14 B–24's hit Truk.

Eleventh AF: 7 B–24's fly cover sorties for naval TF.

17 October

Eighth AF: More than 1,200 HBs attack 5 M/Ys and 2 T/Os at Cologne. 15 ftr gps give spt.

Ninth AF: All Rhine rail and road bridges are cleared for attack. 2 days later Adv HQ prescribes bridges as having priority on tgt list second only to rail lines. 35 MBs hit rail bridge at Euskirchen. Ftrs escort MBs, fly armed rcn in Strasbourg-Colmar-Mulhouse area, attack railroads in Allendorf an der Lahn-Gemunden area, and M/Y at Dielkirchen.

Twelfth AF: Weather cancels all MB operations and limits FBs to limited sorties in the battle area S of Bologna, hitting roads, rail lines and bridges. A–20's during 16/17 Oct on armed rcn over Po Valley bomb T/Os and cause explosions on N edge of Ravenna.

Fifteenth AF: 330-plus HBs attack Blechhammer S oil refinery and industrial area of Vienna, plus alternate tgts and T/Os including M/Ys at Banhida, Nagykanizsa, Szombathely, Strass, Graz, and Maribor, railroad bridge at Maribor, rail line at Furstenfeld, and T/Os scattered throughout the Balkans. P–51's escort a C–47 picking up personnel at Valjevo A/F, a B–17 carrying a photo crew to Rumania (to photograph Ploesti), and several C–47's transporting personnel to Araxos A/F.

Tenth AF: 15 P–47's bomb supply area near Naba, hit Japanese HQ and supply area near Mawhun, and blast supply base and permanent camp at Myazedi. 8 B–25's bomb Nawnghkio A/F and 3 attack bridges near Kawlin and Thityabin. Approach to the latter bridge is damaged. Transports fly almost 300 sorties to various points in CBI.

Fourteenth AF: 15 B–25's, 12 P–40's, and 10 P–51's pound supply depot at Tien Ho A/F. 2 B–24's bomb supply depot at Victoria Harbor. 44 P–51's and P–40's on armed rcn attack rivercraft, troop concentrations, villages, and other T/Os around Kweiping, Tengyun, Mangshih, Tajungchiang, Wuchou, and Dosing. Runway at Tanchuk A/F suffers considerable damage.

FEAF: FBs and B–25's hit A/Fs, shipping and scattered T/Os in the Halmahera area. In Ceram-Amboina-Boeroe area A–20's, B–25's, and FBs continue to pound A/Fs and oil facilities. In the principal strike of the day almost 60 B–24's hit oil installations, barracks, and shore tgts on Ilang and N Davao Bay areas.

Thirteenth AF: XIII BC moves from Wakde to Morotai.

Twentieth AF: 10 B–29's, flying out of Chengtu, bomb Einansho air depot. 14 others bomb alternate tgts.

Seventh AF: 11 B–24's from Saipan hit shipping off Haha Jima and town of Okimura. Later, during 17/18 Oct, 1 B–24 bombs A/F on Iwo Jima. B–25's from the Gilberts hit Nauru.

Eleventh AF: 7 B–24's fly cover sorties for naval TF.

18 October

Eighth AF: Over 450 HBs hit aircraft plants at Kassel, motor plant and M/Y at Cologne, and chemical works at Leverkusen, along with nearby T/Os. 12 ftr gps provide escort and 2 gps later strafe rail traffic between Cologne and Kassel.

Ninth AF: Weather prevents operations of all cmds (including 9th Bomb Div) except IX TAC ftrs which fly sweeps, rail cutting missions, and night patrols, and provide air cover for US 1st Inf Div in Aachen area.

Twelfth AF: Most MB missions are aborted because of weather, but B–26's effectively hit Castel San Pietro dell'Emilia warehouses and railroad bridge at Padua. Ftrs and FBs, operating on restricted schedule due to weather, offer effective close spt to ground forces in mountains S of Bologna and hit comm tgts in Bologna and Modena areas. On 17/18

Oct LBs on armed rcn bomb lights and vehicles E of Bologna.

Fifteenth AF: 38 P–38's dive-bomb Vinkovci. 41 P–51's escort C–47's to Greece.

Tenth AF: 13 P–47's attack Mingaladon A/F, 21 spt ground forces in Mohnyin area, 8 knock out 2 bridges at Wanting, and 6 hit troops near Hwemun. 6 B–25's damage approaches to 2 road bridges at Wuntho. 6 other B–25's damage approaches to 2 bridges at Namhkai and Meza. Transports again fly nearly 300 sorties to several locations in CBI.

Fourteenth AF: 100-plus P–40's and P–51's fly armed rcn over vast areas of China S of the Yangtze R, attack town areas, troops, rivercraft, gun positions, supply facilities, A/Fs, and other T/Os around Kweiping, Shangkaishow, Tajungchiang, Konghow, Wuchou, Shepchung, Hsinganhsien, Tengyun, Liutu, Tanchuk, and Takhing. Railroad tgts at Lang Son are also attacked.

FEAF: Bad weather curtails major strike on Balikpapan. Of 120-plus HBs and ftrs, only 8 B–24's and 8 P–38's reach the tgt. P–38's hit barges, small shipping, and vehicles on W coast of Mindanao. B–24's attack Sagan and Babo A/Fs. M/Bs and FBs again hit Namlea, Amboina, Liang, and nearby tgts, attack T/Os at Djailolo and in Wasile Bay area, and pound Urarom, Manokwari, Babo, Sagan, Otawiri, and other Vogelkop area tgts.

Seventh AF: B–24's out of Saipan bomb Haha Jima while P–47's bomb and strafe Pagan.

Eleventh AF: 4 B–25's bomb Kurabu Cape A/F and Suribachi. 8–12

interceptors attack the B–25's, which claim 2 victories.

19 October

Eighth AF: More than 900 HBs attack Gustavsburg diesel engine and armored vehicle plant, Mainz M/Y, arty tractor plant at Mannheim, and several nearby towns and T/Os. 15 ftr gps fly escort.

Ninth AF: Weather prevents bmr operations. Ftrs attack tank concentration E of Luneville, strafe tgts NW of Kaiserslautern, fly rcn in W Germany, and provide cover for US Third and Seventh Army forces in E France.

Twelfth AF: XII AF redesignates XII FC as XXII TAC following a reorganization period during which the XXII TAC was temporarily referred to as "X" TAC and "X-Ray" TAC, to distinguish it from XII FC HQ around which it was formed. B–26's attack Mantua causeway, railway fill at Ossenigo, and bridges at Calcinato and Peschiera del Garda. Ftr attack NW of Mantua accounts for 2 MBs lost and 1 missing. At least 2 of the attacking ftrs are destroyed. B–25's attack bridges in Milan area at Lonate Pozzolo, Cameri, and Magenta. FBs of XXII TAC hit tgts in spt of ground forces, concentrating on Monte Grande area, and attack rail lines and bridges N of battle zone. On 18/19 Oct LBs hit T/Os during armed rcn in Genoa and Bologna areas.

Fifteenth AF: Bad weather restricts operations to rcn missions.

Tenth AF: 10 P–47's blast approaches to 2 bridges in Mawlu area and 15 spt ground forces in Mohnyin area, hitting village of Nyaunggaing and damaging nearby bridge and pounding railroad station at Kadu.

Fourteenth AF: More than 100 P–51's and P–40's on armed rcn over S China hit numerous T/Os from Tungting Lake area to Luichow Peninsula. The FBs concentrate on rivercraft, troop compounds, and building areas.

FEAF: B–24's hit Parepare. FBs hit Amboina and Boela A/F and shipping from Zamboanga S in Sulu-Mindanao area, pound Cebu A/F, hit nearby shipping, and strafe Miti, Djailolo, and Hate Tabako. A–20's and FBs blast A/Fs at Urarom, Sagan, and Babo.

Seventh AF: B–24's on armed rcn from Saipan bomb bridge, pier, and town area at Yap.

Eleventh AF: A B–24 bombs Kurabu Cape.

20 October

Ninth AF: 9th Bomb Div hits Geertruidenberg/Parenboom and Moerdijke rail bridges. Attacks on other tgts are aborted because of bad weather. Ftrs fly armed rcn over E France and widespread areas of W Germany, attack railroads and various military tgts, and spt US Third and Seventh Armies' elements in E France.

Twelfth AF: Weather clears, permitting for the first time in several days a maximum effort by MBs which attack 12 bridges and railroad fills in Po Valley. FBs of XXII TAC, operating on full scale, blast gun positions, troop concentrations, supply dumps, and comm tgts in close spt of US Fifth Army's drive on Bologna from the S. The FBs concentrate on ap-

proaches to Monte Grande area to prevent counterattacks.

Fifteenth AF: 480-plus HBs attack oil refinery at Brux, oil storage at Regensburg, A/F at Bad Aibling, M/Ys at Rosenheim and Innsbruck, motor transport, armament plants, and ordnance works at Milan, plus scattered T/Os. P–38's and P–51's escort Brux and Regensburg missions.

Tenth AF: 9 P–47's hit encampments and stores near Naba. 5 others knock out road bridge near Wanling and hit supply dump in the area, while 4 more attack troops and supplies in Nansiaung area. Transports fly over 200 sorties in the CBI.

Fourteenth AF: 18 B–25's bomb docks and storage area at Samshui and town of Kweiping. 28 P–51's and P–40's join attack on Samshui area. 77 P–40's and P–51's on armed rcn pound road, river, and rail traffic, town and village areas and other T/Os around Kweiping, Menghsu, Shawan, Kaotienhsu, Pingnam, Hsenwi, Wuchou, Dosing, Tanchuk, and coastal areas of Indochina including Hongay.

FEAF: B–24's bomb Davao. B–25's hit Amboina town.

Seventh AF: 6 Saipan-based P–47's bomb and strafe Pagan. Later in the day 4 B–24's hit the island. During 20/21 Oct a B–24 on a snooper mission bombs Iwo Jima.

21 October

Ninth AF: Bad weather grounds bmrs. Ftrs fly armed rcn and attack railroads in W Germany and spt elements of US Third and Seventh Armies in E France and W Germany.

Twelfth AF: B–26's, in the day's only MB mission, attack Nervesa della Battaglia railroad bridge and causeway. Ftrs and FBs operate in close spt of US Fifth Army forces S of Bologna and FBs also hit comm in N Italy as far N as Verona and as far W as Turin. During 20/21 Oct LBs bomb T/Os during intruder missions N of battle area.

Fifteenth AF: 104 B–24's with ftr escort attack M/Ys at Gyor and Szombathely. Almost 100 P–38's and P–51's strafe Szombathely and Seregelyes A/Fs and rail lines between Sajoszentpeter to Ipolyszog.

Tenth AF: 15 P–47's damage at least 3 bridges throughout the railroad corridor in N Burma. 15 other P–47's spt ground forces in Mohnyin area, hitting gun positions and defensive works at Ywathit. 12 others attack positions and occupied areas around Bhamo and Muse, 6 knock out Paungni R bridge, and 4 attack town of Mawhun. About 270 sorties are flown by Tenth AF transports in CBI.

Fourteenth AF: 3 B–25's and 130–plus P–40's and P–51's attack shipping, gun positions, troop areas, bridges, town areas, road traffic, and other T/Os around Yuma, Takhing, Dosing, Konghow, Shawan, Kuanyang, Kweiping, Tungpingchi, Tingka, Muse, Wan Lai-Kam, Shekpo, Menghsu, and Amoy.

FEAF: B–24's bomb Cagayan and Parepare. B–25's and FBs hit Misamis and blast truck convoy near Kibawe. Other FBs hit Kaoe Bay supply areas. FBs hit Boela A/F and Amboina town area. Mongosah and Sagan A/Fs are also bombed.

Seventh AF: 28 B–24's from Saipan bomb Iwo Jima. 2 B–24's, in first US air strike from Guam, hit Yap.

22 October

Eighth AF: 492d Bomb Gp (CARPETBAGGER gp under control of VIII FC) is transferred to 1st Bomb Div to operate as night bombing gp, one sq remaining on CARPETBAGGER duty. This reduction of supply-dropping forces results from recapture of major portions of France. The remaining sq will supply underground forces in Scandinavia, the Low Countries, and Germany until V–E Day. More than 1,000 HBs attack 2 military vehicle plants at Brunswick and Hannover, 2 M/Ys at Hamm and Munster, and 11 T/Os. 15 ftr gps fly spt.

Ninth AF: Adv HQ XXIX TAC (Prov) moves from Arlon to Maastricht to maintain close association with Ninth Army. Weather forbids bmr operations. Ftr sweeps and armed rcn spt US Third and Seventh Army elements in E France and W Germany.

Twelfth AF: Bad weather grounds all MBs and LBs. Ftrs and FBs, flying less than 20 sorties, hit rail lines and trains in N Italy.

Fifteenth AF: Bad weather limits operations to rcn flights.

Tenth AF: 40-plus P-47's hit a variety of tgts including bridges at Panghkam, and at 2 other points along N Burma rail corridor, towns of Manna and Kyaungle, bivouac in Indaw area, and various T/Os.

Fourteenth AF: 2 B–25's knock out 2 railroad bridges at Pingnam while 8 P–51's pound town area. 54 P–40's and P–51's on armed rcn attack town areas and general T/Os at Nampang, Wanling, Kuanyang, Shekpo, Pingnam, Kweiping, and near Menghsu.

FEAF: B–25's and P–38's attack

shipping in Sulu Archipelago and Jolo and Zamboanga harbors while B–24's hit Opon and Lahug A/Fs. B–25's hit Ternate and B–24's pound Matina A/F, Cagayan, and Likanan. B–25's hit Piroe Bay supply dumps and gun positions and FBs hit Kairatoe and Amahai A/Fs and T/Os in Binnen Bay. A–20's blast pillboxes and occupied areas in Metimedan-Sawar Rivers sector.

Seventh AF: Guam-based B–24's hit Yap with harassment raids during the day, operating singly or in groups of 2 or 3. Makin-based B–25's bomb Nauru.

23 October

Ninth AF: Weather prevents all cmds, including 9th Bomb Div, from flight operations.

Twelfth AF: Bad weather grounds MBs. Ftrs and FBs although cancelling many operations, cause much damage to transportation, destroying or damaging numerous locomotives, railroad cars, and motor transport, and damaging vessels in Savona, Turin, Padua, and Genoa areas.

Fifteenth AF: Around 500 B–24's and B–17's bomb Skoda armament works at Plzen, Rosenheim M/Y, Plauen industrial area, Munich airplane engine plant, Augsburg diesel engine factory, and Regensburg oil storage depot, and comm tgts in N Italy including M/Y at Bressanone, bridges at or near Casarsa della Delizia, Pordenone, Santo Stino di Livenza, and Maniago, and rail line running N to Brenner area. Ftrs escort missions to Germany and Czechoslovakia.

Tenth AF: 20 P–47's hit Japanese concentrations at Nanhlaing and

Kyungyi. 16 spt ground forces at Mawlu and Henu and in nearby areas. Bivouac area S of Indaw is pounded by 4 FBs while 7 knock out bypass bridge at Panghkam. 3 B–25's blast train cars and sidings at Kyaukme, 3 hit nearby motor pool, 2 hit motor pool at Namhsim, and 1 blasts rail line at Nawngpeng. Transports fly 270-plus sorties in CBI.

Fourteenth AF: 3 B–25's knock out bridge at Lohochai while 7 P–40's hit trucks and locomotives nearby. 6 B–25's and 11 P–51's pound town area of Menghsu. 50-plus P–40's and P–51's hit small towns and other T/Os in Menghsu area. 40-plus others attack shipping, bridges, and general T/Os around Anfu, Kweiping, Shepchung, Kuanyang, Ssuwangshu, Mangshih, Chefang, Panghkam, Wanling, Takhing, Tanchuk, Dosing, Wuchou, and Tengyun.

FEAF: B–24's and P–38's maintain shipping sweeps in Makassar area. B–25's, A–20's, and FBs hit Boela oil storage, Amboina town, 2 A/Fs, and other tgts in Amboina-Ceram-Boeroe area. FBs hit Sagan while A–20's spt ground forces further E in Sawar R-Orai R area. Vehicles and small vessels in Mindanao area are attacked by FBs while B–25's attack small shipping in Sulu Archipelago. FBs over Halmahera I hit scattered bivouacs.

Seventh AF: 8 B–24's from Guam bomb Yap. 2 from Saipan hit Pagan and, during 23/24 Oct, 1 bombs Iwo Jima.

Eleventh AF: 3 B–24's hit Kashiwabara tgts. 3 more B–24's bomb Otomari and fly a photo mission over Onnekotan. 5 B–25's bomb Asahi Bay area.

24 October

Eighth AF: By this date, all Path-finder aircraft of 482d Bomb Gp (engaged in H2X and other radar trg at RAF Alconbury) have been dispersed to HB gps within the bomb divs, which set up their own H2X trg. Over 400 FBs are dispatched to attack aircraft and ground tgts in Hannover-Kassel area. 73 bomb flak positions at Elburg, factory near Nienburg, and miscellaneous ground tgts. Bad weather causes other FBs to jettison bombs in Channel and Zuider Zee. The FBs strafe transportation and other ground tgts with good results.

Ninth AF: Bad weather cancels all operations except ftr patrols by IX and XXIX TAC over W Germany. The ftrs attack rail tgts.

Twelfth AF: Weather grounds MBs. Over 300 XXII TAC ftrs and FBs attack tgts in spt of US Fifth Army S of Bologna and hit comm and shipping in Turin-Genoa and E Po Valley areas, destroying 14 locomotives and over 100 railroad cars. During 23/24 Oct LBs attack T/Os in Po Valley.

Fifteenth AF: Weather cancels all offensive operations.

Tenth AF: From 24 Oct through 27 Oct FBs and MBs steadily spt Allied troops on the N Burma front, pounding road and rail comm, troop concentrations and supply dumps, and sweeping A/Fs. The strikes include close spt of British troops advancing on the right flank of the front known as the "Rail Corridor," and of Chinese forces pushing down the left flank along the Myitkyina-Bhamo road. CBI is split into 2 theaters—India-Burma and China.

Fourteenth AF: About 80 P–40's, P–51's, and P–38's on armed rcn over SE China, SW China, and E Burma hit runways, storage facilities, town areas, troops, horses, gun positions, and other T/Os around Amoy, Lohochai, Tanchuk, Sinthe, Menghsu, Pingnam, Mangshih, Chefang, and Lashio.

FEAF: B–24's bomb Buayoan A/F while B–25's on armed rcn hit small shipping and troops. B–24's, B–25's, and FBs hit Sandakan area. P–38's bomb Amboina reservoir areas. A–20's and FBs again pound Babo, Moemi, Sagan, Manokwari, Otawiri, and other Vogelkop Peninsula area tgts.

Seventh AF: Guam-based B–24's bomb Yap while Saipan-based P–47's hit Pagan.

Eleventh AF: 3 B–24's bomb Kashiwabara and Kurabu Cape. 4 B–25's weather-abort a photo mission to Paramushiru. 2 others on a shipping sweep off Kurabu hit a freighter, which is observed listing and smoking, and strafe 2 subchasers.

25 October

Eighth AF: Nearly 1,200 HBs in 5 forces attack 3 oil refineries, Neumunster A/F and aircraft repair works, synthetic oil tgts at Gelsenkirchen and Scholven/Buer, and several other tgts including M/Ys at Munster and Hamm. 11 ftr gps provide spt.

Ninth AF: First Tac AF (Prov) is established, but not yet organized, therefore Ninth AF continues to administer, supply, and control all XII TAC and assigned units until mid-Nov when First Tac AF assumes full control. 9th Bomb Div's missions are cancelled because of bad weather. Ftrs fly sweeps, hit rail and military tgts in Saarbrucken area, and spt US XIX Corps in W Germany.

Twelfth AF: Weather again grounds MBs. FBs blast guns, vehicles, and comm in battle area S of Bologna while ftrs destroy over 20 locomotives in Piacenza area.

Fifteenth AF: Weather again limits operations. 3 B–17's bomb Klagenfurt aircraft factory and Sankt Veit and der Glan M/Y. 5 P–38's complete 3 weather rcn missions.

Fourteenth AF: 6 B–25's and 4 P–38's damage railroad tracks at Dara bridge. 7 P–38's and P–51's hit Mongyu bridges and destroy Kawnghka bridge. 4 others strafe Nawnghkio A/F. 20-plus P–51's and P–40's on armed rcn attack T/Os at Tengyun, Kweiping, and Ssuanghsu, and about 50 strike tgts throughout Menghsu area.

FEAF: 50-plus B–24's, supported by P–38's and P–47's, attack naval forces in Mindanao Sea, firing small vessels and claiming a light cruiser damaged. B–24's bomb Ambesia A/F and attack shipping in Makassar-Kendari area. FBs hit barges and villages in areas of Dodinga and Wasile Bays. B–25's, A–20's, and FBs hit Piroe, Boela, Halong, Amboina, Saparoea, Haroekoe, and N Ceram coastal tgts. A–20's pound supply and fuel dumps in Sarmi area.

Twentieth AF: 59 B–29's, flying out of Chengtu, bomb aircraft plant at Omura. Several other VHBs hit alternate tgts and T/Os.

Seventh AF: 29 Saipan-based B–24's bomb Iwo Jima during the morning. Later during the day 4 B–24's from Saipan and Guam, on armed

rcn missions, bomb Yap. 8 P–47's from Saipan bomb Pagan.

26 October

Eighth AF: Over 1,100 HBs attack synthetic oil plant at Bottrop, ordnance and storage depot at Bielefeld, aircraft repair works and M/Y at Munster, military vehicle plant near Hannover, aqueduct and Mittelland Canal at Minden, and other tgts including city of Hannover. 14 ftr gps provide escort.

Ninth AF: No bmr operations as bad weather prevails. Ftrs sweep areas of E France and W Germany from Metz to Cologne, attacking rail and road traffic, rail bridges, and M/Ys.

Twelfth AF: Weather suspends all Twelfth AF operations.

Fifteenth AF: Weather curtails operations. 7 B–17's bomb M/Y at Innsbruck.

Fourteenth AF: B–24's and B–25's attack shipping off E Luichow Peninsula. B–25's also hit river shipping from Dosing to Takhing and Yellow R bridge. Ftrs attack town of Menghsu, hit T/Os around Menghsu and Kweiping, and make armed rcn attack on Hongay. B–25's and ftrs bomb railroad yards at Hsuchang.

FEAF: B–24's attack naval force of 2 battleships, 5 carriers, and 5 destroyers W of Panay I. P–38's hit vehicles in Davao area and B–25's bomb Iligan. Hits are claimed on a battleship and 2 carriers. P–40's attack T/Os in Dodinga-Kaoe Bay area, Djailolo, supply area S of Galela, and guns S of Doro. A–20's and B–25's bomb Urarom.

Seventh AF: 8 Saipan-based P–47's bomb and strafe Pagan. 15 B–

25's based in the Gilberts, bomb A/F area on Nauru.

Eleventh AF: Of 6 B–24's which abort a naval TF cover mission after failing to find the ships, 2 bomb installations on Onnekotan I.

27 October

Ninth AF: Gen Robert C Richardson reassumes cmd of IX ADC. Adverse weather prevents all operations except patrols by XIX TAC and supply dropping missions (to VI Corps near Saint-Die) by XII TAC.

Twelfth AF: Weather curtails operations. FBs on armed rcn in Genoa-Novi Ligure-Turin area hit comm and transportation tgts.

Fifteenth AF: Bad weather limits operations to 5 weather rcn flights.

Fourteenth AF: Ftrs bomb and strafe town of Mengmao and nearby hill positions, river traffic, troops, and horses from Tanchuk to Tengyun, bridges NE of Hsinganhsien, town of Kaotienhsu, troops in Kweilin area, rail traffic W of Puchi, and A/Fs at Siangtan and Changsha.

FEAF: 40-plus FBs, operating in 3 waves, hit shipping off Cebu and W of Mactan I. B–24's attack Malili and Palopo.

Seventh AF: 2 B–24's on armed rcn from Saipan bomb Yap. During 27/28 Oct a B–24 on snooper mission hits Iwo Jima.

Eleventh AF: 7 B–24's weather-abort an attempt to fly cover for naval TF.

28 October

Eigth AF: 350-plus B–17's escorted by 4 ftr gps bomb M/Ys at Hamm and Munster.

Ninth AF: HQ 9th Bomb Div transfers to Reims. 45 9th Bomb Div aircraft bomb rail bridges at Sinzig, Kempenich, and Ahrweiler, and A/F at Euskirchen. Ftrs escort bmrs, fly sweeps and armed rcn over W Germany, attack 6 bridges and 1 tunnel, and spt US XIX Corps in Belgium near German border.

Twelfth AF: Bad weather again grounds MBs, and restricts XXII TAC. FBs and ftrs, flying 65 sorties, attack vehicles and trains in Turin-Milan-Genoa area.

Fifteenth AF: Bad weather again limits operations. 10 B–17's bomb Klagenfurt aircraft factory. 6 P–38's fly rcn missions, during early part of the night. 8 B–17's bomb Munich W M/Y. 1 bombs Erlsbach.

Tenth AF: 80-plus FBs pound numerous tgts including town areas, troops, railroad facilities, and a variety of T/Os at Mannaun, Manoi, Sinkan, Winwa, Man Mao, Myazedi, Pinwe, Naba, Yebawgyi, and Kangon.

Fourteenth AF: Ftrs strafe villages, troops, and horses in Menghsu-Konghow area, pound bridges around Kaotienhsu, and hit Yangtong A/F and shipping at Hongay and Wuchou.

FEAF: B–24's, fighting bad weather, bomb A/F at Puerto Princesa. During 28/29 Oct, B–24's bomb Wilhelmina Docks area. B–25's and P–38's blast town of Amboina.

Twentieth AF: Marianas-based XXI BC flies its first combat mission when 14 B–29's attack sub pens on Dublon I. 4 others (1 carrying Gen Hansell, CG XXI BC) abort. About a third of the bombs fall in general tgt area.

Seventh AF: B–24's from Saipan bomb Haha Jima while others, from

Guam, hit Yap. Saipan-based P–47's bomb Pagan.

Eleventh AF: 8 B–25's fly cover for naval TF.

29 October

Ninth AF: About 170 MBs and LBs bomb rail bridges at Mayen, Konz-Karthaus, Ellern, Moerdijke, and Euskirchen. Ftrs fly escort to bmrs, sweeps, defensive patrols, armed rcn over wide areas of E France, the Netherlands, and Germany, bomb rail tgts and bridges, and fly cover for US XIX Corps in Belgium.

Twelfth AF: Weather again restricts operations. XXII TAC FBs fly 15 sorties against railroad tgts in Po Valley.

Fifteenth AF: 35 B–24's of over 155 HBs dispatched with ftr escort, bomb Munich W M/Y. The remainder and 670 other HBs, dispatched against tgts in S Germany, abort mission due to bad weather. 30 P–38's, after escort duty, strafe comm lines from Wels to Kienberg, destroying 17 locomotives and several other road and rail transportation tgts.

Tenth AF: 80-plus FBs again attack a wide variety of tgts including troop concentrations, bridges, supply dumps, and numerous T/Os at Kawlin, Wingnang, Hsenwi, Bhamo, Shwegu, Kyungon, Tugyaung, Yebyangale, Henu, and Kayin.

Fourteenth AF: Ftrs in spt of Chinese ground forces blast hill positions in Lungling and Mangshih areas. Others damage bridge at Sinshih, bomb Kweiyi and Paoching, hit railroad tgts between Siaokan and Sinyang, and strafe A/Fs at Chingmen, Tangyang, and Ichang.

FEAF: FBs and B–25's, operating in small forces, are active against A/Fs, AA positions, and T/Os on Halmahera I. FBs also hit Ransiki while FBs, A–20's, and B–25's bomb Urarom and Soeli and strafe T/Os throughout Urarom-Kaimana area.

Thirteenth AF: Thirteenth AF moves from Noemfoor I to Morotai I.

Seventh AF: 19 B–24's from Saipan bomb Chichi Jima. 2 from Guam strike Yap.

Eleventh AF: 4 B–25's on rcn hit Tomari Cape buildings and a freighter which is left listing.

30 October

Eighth AF: Over 600 HBs supported by 15 ftr gps attack oil refineries near Hamburg and 11 other tgts including M/Ys at Hamm and Munster. Clouds cause abort of around 600 other HBs.

Ninth AF: 9th Bomb Div bmrs are recalled from mission (mainly against bridges) because of bad weather. Ftrs fly patrols and armed rcn over NE France and in W Germany around Aachen and Rhine R. XIX TAC escorts 9th Bomb Div and HBs of Eighth AF.

Twelfth AF: Weather again grounds MBs and limits XXII TAC FBs and ftrs to 51 sorties against scattered tgts in Po Valley.

Fifteenth AF: During 30/31 Oct 3 B–24's bomb Klagenfurt M/Y, P–38's fly rcn missions, while bad weather cancels all other operations.

Tenth AF: 10 B–25's knock out bridges at Namhkai, Wuntho, Thegyaung, and Nankan and damage others at Okkyin and Zawchaung. 50-plus P–47's knock out Hpao Nam R bridge and strafe T/Os at several locations;

hit several bridges throughout N Burma rail corridor, damaging or knocking out each tgt; spt ground forces at Naba Station and Pinwe; and hit troop concentrations at Mansi and Man yut.

Fourteenth AF: 13 B–24's lay mines in Victoria Harbor. P–40's bomb installations around Phu Lang Thuong and hit junks at sea.

FEAF: B–24's pound Bacolod A/F, while B–25's and FBs hit San Roque A/F and barges at Zamboanga. P–38's hit Sandakan A/F. B–24's bomb Makassar wharf area while P–40's, over NE peninsula, hit various T/Os. P–38's hit Piroe. Urarom A/F is again bombed by A–20's and B–25's.

Twentieth AF: 8 B–29's from the Marianas bomb sub pens on Dublon I, 9 others bomb 2 mi beyond tgt.

Seventh AF: 8 B–24's on armed rcn missions from Guam bomb Yap. 1 B–24 from Saipan, during 30/31 Oct snooper mission, bombs Iwo Jima. Saipan-based P–47's hit Pagan. B–25's from Makin strike Nauru.

Eleventh AF: 3 B–24's fly armed rcn over Matsuwa and Onnekotan.

31 October

Ninth AF: Weather forbids bmr operations and limits ftrs. XII and XIX TACs fly patrols, sweeps, and armed rcn over E France and W Germany. XII TAC also supports US Seventh Army elements in Metz area.

Twelfth AF: B–26's hit bridge and causeway at Nervesa della Battaglia and bridges at Montebello and Piazzola sul Brenta. FBs attack guns and positions in battle area S of Bologna in the Apennines, and comm

and shipping tgts in Po Valley and on Po R.

Fifteenth AF: P–38's fly photo and weather rcn. 174 B–24's, dispatched against tgt in Yugoslavia, are forced to return because of weather.

Tenth AF: 60-plus P–47's attack occupied areas and supply areas at Namun, Bhamo, and Nakang, and railroad bridges, locomotive shelters, and rolling stock along the Kyaikthin-Naba line. 2 B–25's attack T/Os from Katha to Bhamo along the Irrawaddy R.

Fourteenth AF: 6 P–51's hit shipping T/Os at Swatow and Amoy. About 70 ftrs spt Chinese ground forces by pounding positions in Lungling area. 4 B–25's and 12 P–40's bomb railroad bridge at Pengpu.

FEAF: P–47's and A–20's bomb Kairatoe A/F and Saharoe village. B–25's and P–40's hit Loloda and Soasioe. P–38's and A–20's, concentrating on A/Fs, attack Samate, Efman, Sagan, and Doom I.

Seventh AF: During 31 Oct/1 Nov a B–24 on snooper mission from Saipan bombs Iwo Jima.

Eleventh AF: 4 B–25's score direct hits on a cannery at Tomari Cape and leave nearby buildings burning. 1 of 2 B–25's hit by AA heads for and safely lands in USSR.

1 November

Eighth AF: Over 300 HBs attack 2 synthetic oil plants near Gelsenkirchen, a bridge at Rudesheim, and M/Ys at Koblenz and Hamm. 9 ftr gps fly escort.

Ninth AF: Weather prevents bmr operations. Ftrs fly patrols, sweeps, armed rcn over Belgium, E France, and large areas of W Germany and attack bridges, railroads, and various other tgts.

Twelfth AF: Operations are again curtailed by bad weather. However, ftrs and FBs successfully attack bridges, rail lines, roads, vehicles, and trains in C Po Valley and hit scattered tgts elsewhere in N Italy.

Fifteenth AF: 320-plus B-17's and B-24's, with ftr escorts, bomb diesel works, ordnance works, and M/Y at Vienna. Also hit are M/Ys at Graz, tank factory at Kapfenberg, T/Os including M/Ys at Gussing, Ljubljana, and Cakovec, and scattered comm tgts in S Germany, Hungary, Austria, and Yugoslavia. Several ftrs strafe road and rail transport tgts and troops in Gyor-Parndorf and Neusiedler Lake areas.

Tenth AF: 70-plus FBs knock out bridge at Panghkam, slightly damage bridges in the Wingkang and Kawnghka area, hit railroad T/Os between Indaw and Naba, attack Japanese positions near Bhamo, Si-in, Hantet, and Shwegu, and bomb towns of Loiwing and Lagaw. 9 B-25's damage bridge approaches at Hsenwi, Namhkai, and Kawnghka.

Fourteenth AF: About 70 ftrs again spt Chinese ground forces in Lungling area. 13 ftrs strafe river, road, and rail traffic from Kunghsien to Loyang.

FEAF: B-24's bomb A/Fs at Cebu City, and Alicante and supply dumps at Del Monte. FBs hit Bacolod, Alicante, and Carolina A/Fs. A-20's and B-25's hit Babo A/F. P-38's and B-25's pound Namlea A/Fs. P-47's attack shipping and shore tgts during sweep over Sulu Archipelago.

Seventh AF: 8 B-24's from Guam attack shipping NE of Iwo Jima. 12 B-24's escorting Navy photo airplanes over Iwo Jima, Haha Jima, and Chichi Jima, bomb A/Fs, a warehouse, and shipping. P-47's from Saipan strafe Pagan. During 1/2 Nov a B-24 on snooper mission from Saipan bombs Iwo Jima.

Eleventh AF: A B-24 on an armed weather mission bombs Otomari Cape.

2 November

Eighth AF: Eighth AF is ordered to increase size of 406th Bomb Sq (Night Leaflet), as liberation of Europe and conquest of Germany accelerate. About 1,100 HBs in 5 separate forces attack synthetic oil plant at Merseburg/Leuna, Castrop-Rauxel, Sterkrade, and Bielefeld/Schildesche railroad and M/Y, along with several T/Os. Opposition is heavy with an estimated 500 ftrs attacking, mainly against the Merseburg/Leuna force claiming 40 HBs. The 17 escorting ftr gps lose 28 planes. Total of over 160 ftrs are claimed destroyed.

Ninth AF: 147 bmrs of 9th Bomb Div attack rail bridges at Mayen, Euskirchen, Bullay, Konz-Karthaus, and Trier. Ftrs fly escort to 9th Bomb Div and Eighth AF, attack bridges, fly armed rcn and night patrol, and provide spt for ground forces in frontline areas.

Twelfth AF: Clouds over Po Valley prevent MB operations. XXII TAC aircraft are also grounded due to unserviceable fields and bad weather over Italian battle areas.

Fifteenth AF: Bad weather curtails operations. 5 B-17's bomb Moosbierbaum oil refinery, while 2 others hit an A/F N of the city and bomb Klagenfurt. 6 P–38's fly weather rcn missions. All other operations are cancelled.

Tenth AF: Tenth AF moves from New Delhi to Myitkyina. 80-plus P–47's hit variety of tgts. The FBs bomb bridge at Ho-hko, spt ground forces at Myothit, bomb supply dumps at Namdaungmawn personnel and supply areas at Naungletgyi and Mawtaung, knock out bridge at Meza, hit nearby railroad cars, attack A/Fs at Nawnghkio and Sinlanzu and strike boats and boxcars S of Katha. 8 B–25's knock out 2 bridges at Tangon and Tantabin. A single B–25 bombs Indaw. Transports fly 268 sorties to forward areas.

Fourteenth AF: 100-plus P–40's, P–51's, and P–38's on armed rcn over SW and SE China and N Indochina attack T/Os in Lungling and Mangshih area, knock out bridge at Dara and hit Nantingshun and Pinglo towns. The FBs also damage 4 factories at Kweilin, hit tanks and troop concentrations N of town, attack T/Os near Pinglo, Tahsu and E of Yungfu, and A/F, barracks, town area, and trains at Gia Lam.

FEAF: B–24's over Ormoc Bay attack Japanese convoy, claiming 1 transport sunk and another damaged. P–38's hit smaller shipping in Ormoc Bay, strafe vehicles from Ormoc to Valencia, and bomb San Enrique. B–25's pound Matina, Libby, Davao and Likanan A/Fs. During 2/3 Nov B–24's bomb Makassar, concentrating on wharf area.

Twentieth AF: 17 Marianas-based B–29's bomb sub pens on Dublon I.

Seventh AF: 11 Saipan-based B–

24's bomb Chichi Jima. 3 from Guam, on armed rcn, hit Marcus.

Eleventh AF: 4 B–24's bomb Suribachi and Onnekotan. 4 B–25's on a photo and offensive sweep bomb tgts at Torishima Is and Hayakegawa setting fire to 15 buildings, including a cannery.

3 November

Ninth AF: 140-plus MBs and LBs hit rail overpass at Kaiserslautern, and rail bridges at Neuwied-Irlich, Bad Munster am Stein, Morscheid and Konz-Karthaus. Ftrs fly armed rcn, ground forces cover, attack railroads, bridge, and observation posts in W Germany, and escort 9th Bomb Div.

Twelfth AF: Heavy clouds over most of N Italy begin to disperse. MBs are still grounded but FBs manage to fly 8 sorties against gun positions in mountains S of Bologna.

Fifteenth AF: 46 B–17's and B–24's (in an operation adapted to bad weather and flying without escort) bomb Vienna S ordnance depot, Moosbierbaum oil refinery, Munich W M/Y, Klagenfurt aircraft factory, towns of Innsbruck and Graz, and rail line SE of Graz. The HBs attack individually, depending on cloud cover for protection. Over 30 other HBs abort due to clearing weather.

Tenth AF: 12 B–25's, supported by 18 P–47's, hit Nawnghkio A/F. A single MB attacks T/Os between Myitkyina and Lashio. 90-plus FBs attack bridges, enemy forces, town areas and numerous T/Os at Kawngmu, Namhai, Tonlon, Ho-hko, Hinlong, Namhsum, Hkusan, Hkawngwa, Wingkang, Namhkam, and S of Mansi. Tenth AF transports fly 240-plus sorties to forward areas.

Fourteenth AF: 69 P–40's, P–51's, and P–38's on armed rcn over E Burma, SW and SE China, and N Indochina hit T/Os in Lungling area, damage railroad bridge S of Lashio, hit town of Mangshih and destroy nearby warehouse. The FBs hit town areas and docks at Takhing and Tengyun, attack troops in Mosun area, destroy 2 Japanese ftrs near Amoy, hit trains at Hongay, and bomb areas on Hainan I.

FEAF: B–25's bomb Alicante A/F. P–40's hit highway and oil dump N of Ormoc. A–20's and B–25's bomb Babo A/F. During 3/4 Nov harassing strikes are flown at A/Fs in C Phil Is, on NE peninsula of Celebes, and on Halmahera.

Twentieth AF: 49 B–29's, operating from rear bases in Calcutta area, bomb Malagon railroad yards. Almost as many others hit alternate tgts.

Seventh AF: 14 B–24's from Guam pound shipping at Chichi Jima and Haha Jima. 34 P–47's from Saipan bomb and strafe Pagan. B–24's from Saipan continue armed rcn and snooper missions over Marcus and Iwo Jima.

4 November

Eighth AF: More than 1,000 HBs operating in 6 forces attack synthetic oil plants, oil refineries, and benzol plant at Bottrop, Gelsenkirchen, Hamburg, Hamburg/Harburg, Misburg, and Neunkirchen, and several T/Os. 17 ftr gps, including a Ninth AF gp, provide spt.

Ninth AF: 218 MBs and LBs hit Trier ordnance depot, Baumholder depot, and Eschweiler gun positions. Ftrs escort the 9th Bomb Div, attack railroads, bridges, and other tgts, and

spt US XIX Corps in Aachen area.

Twelfth AF: Over 200 B–25's and B–26's of 42d Bomb Wg hit railway and road bridges in Brenner Pass. More than 130 B–25's of 57th Bomb Wg strike comm in W Po Valley, cutting at least 4 bridges. Ftrs and FBs of XXII TAC concentrate on comm tgts and trains in Po Valley and defenses in battle area S of Bologna. Some XXII TAC aircraft hit guns on N Italian coast, some hit rocket launching site and comm N of battle area, and 4 P–47's bomb Milan hotel where Hitler is rumored to be staying.

Fifteenth AF: 715 HBs with ftr escorts pound oil storage at Regensburg, M/Ys at Munich and Augsburg, main M/Y and a benzol plant at Linz, a troop concentration at Podgorica, as well as attacking several alternate tgts and scattered T/Os including M/Ys at Wels and Kufstein, Erding, A/F, railroad tgts in and near Rosenheim, and towns of Strass and Muhldorf.

Tenth AF: 17 P–47's pound Shwebo A/F while 6 others bomb stores of guns and ammo at Mong Yaw.

Fourteenth AF: 34 P–40's, P–51's, and P–38's attack road traffic and other T/Os in Mangshih and Lungling areas. 4 P–38's bomb pass near Menghsu, blocking the highway.

FEAF: B–24's again pound Alicante A/F.

Seventh AF: 18 Saipan-based B–24's bomb Iwo Jima A/Fs. 2 others, on shipping rcn, bomb Haha Jima. 2 B–24's on armed rcn from Guam bomb Marcus. 16 P–47's bomb landing strip on Pagan.

Eleventh AF: 6 B–24's strike A/F,

buildings, and offshore shipping at Suribachi and Kurabu.

ZI: First report is received of Japanese balloon SW of San Pedro; USN recovers some apparatus, envelope, and rigging.

5 November

Eighth AF: More than 1,200 HBs attack M/Ys at Frankfurt/Main, Ludwigshafen, Karlsruhe, Hanau, and Kaiserslautern, and synthetic oil plant at Ludwigshafen, rail facilities at Landau, and 8 T/Os. 15 ftr gps give spt. 37 HBs and ftrs are lost.

Ninth AF: 160 MBs and LBs strike ammo, ordnance, and supply depots at Hamburg. Ftrs escort bmrs, fly armed rcn, attack railroads and bridges, and cover ground forces of V and XIX Corps. IX TAC aids US 28th Inf Div in withstanding counterattack near Kommerscheidt.

Twelfth AF: MBs, flying over 300 sorties, bomb bridges in Brenner Pass and in the NE Po Valley to interdict the Germans' 2 main supply routes from the N. Ftrs and FBs hit defenses and forces in battle areas in the N Apennines S of Bologna and attack comm tgts to the N as well as in battle zone.

Fifteenth AF: 500 B–24's and B–17's bomb Vienna/Floridsdorf oil refinery in largest operation against a single tgt during World War II. 10 other HBs bomb about 20 scattered T/Os and 1 alternate tgt (Kapfenberg tank works). 139 P–38's and 198 P–51's provide escort. 16 of the ftrs strafe T/Os in tgt area. 42 other B–24's, with ftr escort, bomb troop concentrations at Mitrovica and Podgorica.

Tenth AF: About 70 P–47's attack Lashio A/F, hit gun positions on Kyundaw I, bomb Kanbalu M/Y, hit T/Os along Naba-Wuntho railroad and on Burma Road and bomb town of Namhpakka and Lasai area. 28 other P–47's maintain patrols S of Myitkyina. Transports fly 300-plus sorties carrying men, equipment and supplies to various forward areas.

Fourteenth AF: 49 P–40's, P–38's, and P–51's attack storage facilities and other T/Os around Mangshih, Chefang, Wanling, and Kweihsien.

FEAF: B–24's and P–40's attack A/Fs and barges in the C Phil Is. B–24's also hit town of Bima and Waingapoe Bay shipping at Soembawa. B–25's and FBs strike A/Fs, troop concentrations, and comm tgts throughout the Halmahera area and NE peninsula of Celebes. FBs and A–20's hit Amahai and T/Os on S coast of Ceram. Almost 50 A–20's, supporting ground forces, blast installations in Sarmi area.

Twentieth AF: 24 Marianas-based B–29's bomb 2 Iwo Jima A/Fs, starting tac operations against the island in preparation for its invasion. 53 Calcutta-based B–29's bomb Singapore naval base putting the King George VI Graving Dock (one of the world's best drydocks) out of operation for 3 months, and blast other tgts at the base. 7 other B–29's bomb secondary tgt and Pangkalanbrandan refinery while 4 more hit other tgt.

Seventh AF: B–24's from Guam hit shipping in the Bonins and, during armed rcn mission, bomb Marcus.

Eleventh AF: 4 B–25's abort an offensive sweep off Suribachi due to intense shore fire. 4 more B–25's fly armed rcn over Shimushu and deck-level bomb Torishima Is tgts. Of

4 ftrs intercepting the B–25's, 1 is downed. 4 B–24's bomb Onnekotan and Matsuwa. 3 more B–24's bomb Kataoka naval base, starting fires. 7 ftrs intercept and the HBs down 1.

6 November

Eighth AF: Over 1,000 HBs in 6 forces attack 6 oil and chemical installations, a canal aqueduct and aircraft repair plant, along with 3 M/Ys, an A/F, and several T/Os in N and NW Germany. 16 ftr gps afford close escort and later strafe ground tgts in NW Germany and the Netherlands.

Ninth AF: Weather grounds 9th Bomb Div. Ftrs, during armed rcn, attack railroads and bridges. IX TAC also supports ground forces in Schmidt area.

Twelfth AF: MBs strike electric transformers and converters, railway bridges and railway fills on the rail line through Brenner Pass. FBs and ftrs again hit troops and gun positions in the battlelines S of Bologna and comm tgts N of the battle area.

Fifteenth AF: 580-plus ftr-escorted HBs bomb Moosbierbaum oil refinery and Vienna S ordnance depot, alternate tgts of Kapfenberg steel works, Deutsch Wagram, Graz and Maribor M/Ys, and railroad power sub station at Bolzano.

AAF, India-Burma Theater: AAF, India-Burma Sector, China-Burma-India Theater is redesignated AAF, India-Burma Theater.

Tenth AF: 70-plus P–47's, sweep A/Fs at Anisakan, Onbauk, Shwebo, Kin, and Kawlin; destroy and damage bridges at Hinlong and Wingkang; bomb town of Mawtaung and M/Y at Kanbalu; hit boxcars at Wuntho and Meza, boats along the Ir-

rawaddy from Katha to Twinnge, and attack several scattered T/Os. 28 P–47's fly combat patrols S of Myitkyina. 8 B–25's bomb military area at Namun and supply dump at Mansi. Large-scale transport operations continue.

Fourteenth AF: 16 P–40's pound Mangshih and Lungling areas. 15 others hit buildings and other T/Os at Wanling and around Chefang and Kweihsien.

FEAF: B–24's strike Lahug and Fabrica A/Fs, while FBs pound Palompon, bridge N of Valencia, and barges in Ormoc Bay. B–24's bomb Malili.

Seventh AF: B–24's from Saipan bomb shipping at Okimura and Higashi-minato and hit island of Ani Jima. During 6/7 Nov a snooper mission is flown over Iwo Jima A/Fs. Dispersal areas and runways are bombed. Beginning on this date and continuing through 24 Dec 44, B–24's on Saipan fly 24 missions to lay 170 mines in several anchorages throughout the Bonin Is.

Eleventh AF: 4 B–25's bomb Torishima Is, score a hit on a large building, sink two nearby barges, and probably hit other shipping tgts. About 20 ftrs intercept, downing 1 B–25. The MBs claim 3 victories.

7 November

Ninth AF: No bmr operations because of unfavorable weather. Ftrs fly patrols and armed rcn, attacking railroads, guns positions and other tgts. IX TAC supports US V Corps as fierce counterattacks force US 28th Inf Div to retreat from village of Kommerscheidt. V Corps decides to withdraw Kall R bridgehead.

Twelfth AF: AG officially orders *de facto* action of 19 Oct redesignating XII FC to XXII TAC. MBs of 42d Bomb Wg aid DAF in supporting British Eighth Army's attack on Forli. 57th Bomb Wg continues interdiction campaign against railway supply lines in NE Italy. FBs closely spt US Fifth Army forces astride Idice R in mountains S of Bologna and bomb comm N of the Apennines, scoring many hits on bridges between Piacenza and Bologna.

Fifteenth AF: More than 550 HBs attack Maribor, Alipasin Most, and Brunico M/Ys, Vienna/Floridsdorf oil refinery, Brenner Pass railroad route, railroad bridges at Pinzano al Tagliamento, Casarsa della Delizia, Mezzocorona, Ora, and Albes, and troop concentrations at Novi Pazar, Sjenica, Prijepolje, and Mitrovica. Ftrs escort all operations except the attacks on troop concentrations. 124 P–38's strafe troop concentrations at Podgorica and roads and railroads near Raska, between Visegrad-Prijepolje-Sjenica and from Sjenica to Novi Pazar.

Tenth AF: 80-plus P–47's hit gun positions, supply areas, and troops at Bhamo, Pintin, and in vicinity of Myazedi, bomb A/Fs at Kawlin, Shwebo, and Onbauk, hit fuel dump near Panghkam road junction, attack railroad T/Os between Indaw and Shwebo, and T/Os along the Irrawaddy between Bhamo and Katha. 28 other P–47's maintain overlapping patrols over area S of Myitkyina. Transports fly 260-plus sorties to forward areas.

Fourteenth AF: 6 B–25's bomb railroad yards at Yuncheng. 2 B–25's

and 21 P–51's, P–40's, and P–38's hit T/Os around Mangshih, Chefang, Wanling, and Lungling.

FEAF: B–24's and FBs hit Fabrica, Alicante, Bacolod, and Opon A/Fs, shipping at various C Phil locations, and comm and supply tgts at Tambuco, Ormoc, Palompon, Valencia, and other areas. P–38's and B–25's hit Del Monte A/F and T/Os in Macajalar Bay, Mindanao, and Mandai A/F. B–25's hit Tanamon, Mapanget, and Langoan. B–25's and FBs hit Galela, Miti, and Kaoe A/Fs. In sweeps over Boeroe and Ceram small groups of B–25's and P–38's hit runways and small shipping. B–24's bomb Raba Estate.

Seventh AF: B–24's from Guam strike Iwo Jima and, during armed rcn flight, bomb AA positions on Marcus. P–47's strafe A/F on Pagan during the early morning and follow up with rocket and strafing runs later in the morning.

8 November

Eighth AF: Transfer of trg functions from VIII AF Comp Cmd to combat gps is completed. VIII AF Comp Cmd ceases to function as personnel are attached to Air Disarmament Cmd (Prov) by USSTAF. A/F at Denain/Prouvy is assigned to Eighth AF. This is first step in establishing an VIII AFSC Serv Center on the European continent so that Eighth AF can service and administer its own aircraft and personnel in the area. Over 250 HBs attack synthetic oil plants at Merseburg/Leuna and M/Y at Rheine, along with 5 T/Os. Bad weather causes recall of over 350 other HBs. 18 ftr gps provide escort and later strafe ground tgts with good results. 23 ftrs are lost.

Ninth AF: Weather cancels operations against military depots and troop concentrations in Germany, and fortified positions in France. Mission against rail bridges in Germany is recalled due to weather. Ftrs fly escort, attack railroads, bridges, factories, supply dumps, and cmd posts. IX and XIX TACs spt US 28th Inf Div in Schmidt area (V Corps begins withdrawing Kall R bridgehead) and Third Army elements start assault on enemy fortifications in Metz area.

Twelfth AF: MBs strike rail line in Brenner Pass and other lines running into Italy from NE and bomb bridges in C and W Po Valley, damaging several and destroying the bridge at Mantua. Ftrs and FBs hit comm in Bologna area, but concentrate most of their operations against bridges and rail lines in Parma area in effort to disrupt battle area supply lines.

Fifteenth AF: 34 B–24's bomb troop concentrations at Mitrovica, Prijepolje, and Sjenica. Heavy cloud over tgts forces over 70 others to abort.

Tenth AF: 80-plus P–47's spt ground forces in Mawlu area, bomb personnel, supplies, and comm facilities at Tunhong, Chaungdauk, and Kutkai, gun positions at Hsipaw, Man Hpa town area, Kawlin A/F and T/Os along Kawlin-Pinwe railroad. 8 B–25's knock out Bawgyo railroad bridge. 270-plus transports fly sorties to forward areas.

Fourteenth AF: In S China and N Indochina 2 B–25's hit railroad tracks at Lohochai and 2 others hit tracks at Duc Tho. 4 P–51's blast road machinery near Muse. 15 B–25's, 13 P–40's and P–51's pound storage buildings, villages, and other T/Os throughout Mangshih area.

FEAF: B–24's again hit Alicante A/F. B–25's bomb Langoan A/F while P–38's on sweeps over Kendari area hit parked airplanes, shipping, nickel mine, and other T/Os. B–25's attack Kaoe and Hate Tabako A/F while others hit T/Os on Ceram.

Twentieth AF: 17 XXI BC B–29's are airborne against Iwo Jima A/F. 6 manage to bomb through a hole in cloud cover. Others fail to bomb tgt. Enemy aircraft drop phosphorous bombs on formations, damaging 1 B–29. 1 VHB ditches, the first aircraft lost by XXI BC on a combat mission.

Seventh AF: B–24's from Saipan hit shipping at Chichi Jima and Haha Jima. A single HB on a snooper mission bombs Iwo Jima during 8/9 Nov. P–47's attempt ftr sweep over Pagan but must abort because of bad weather.

Eleventh AF: An 8-aircraft shipping sweep is cancelled due to weather.

9 November

Eighth AF: Over 1,100 HBs (in conjunction with Ninth AF aircraft) hit TAC tgts in Metz and Thionville area as US Third Army forces launch full-scale attack on Metz. Other tgts include Saarbrucken M/Ys, bombed by over 300 of the HBs. 11 ftr gps give escort and 6 gps of FBs bomb and strafe tgts between Frankfurt/Main and Mannheim. Over 40 HBs and ftrs are lost.

Ninth AF: 74 planes of 9th Bomb Div attack road junctions, barracks, ordnance arsenals, arty camps, military storage depot, and other tgts in Dieuze, Landau, Sankt Wendel, and Faulquemont areas. IX TAC flies sweeps over W Germany and attacks M/Y at Duren, while XXIX TAC escort attacks Rahling and an A/F and supports US Third Army elements (2 inf and 2 armd divs) as all-out assault on Metz is pushed.

Twelfth AF: Bad weather hampers MBs operations in Po Valley as 7 of 9 missions abort. In the 2 others, bridges in the Valley are hit. Ftrs and FBs fly less than 100 sorties, but successfully strike road and railroad bridges in Bologna-Modena areas.

Fifteenth AF: Bad weather limits operations to 4 weather rcn missions.

Tenth AF: 70-plus aircraft bomb concentrations and supply areas at Kutkai, Shwebo, Mawtawng, and Kunhailong, bomb A/F at Kawlin, knock out bridge at Ho-hko, and spt ground forces and hit T/Os near Chyauhkawng, Namakyaing, Sepein, Tonlon, and at other points in the same general area. 6 B–25's bomb rail yards at Kanbalu. Transports continue large-scale operations, flying nearly 300 sorties to forward areas.

Fourteenth AF: 8 B–25's bomb Mangshih while 10 P–38's hit T/Os in Mangshih-Chefang area. 6 B–25's bomb Kaifeng while 6 others hit sampans, storage areas, and other T/Os in Yiyang area. 160 P–40's, P–38's, and P–51's on armed rcn over wide expanses of S China and N Indochina attack trucks, gun positions, river and coastal shipping, and other T/Os at or near Pingnam, Kweihsien, Changsha, Yoyang, Siangtan, Lushan, Kioshan, Paoching, Hengyang, Liangshan, Liuchow, Suikai, Gia Lam,

Kien An, and Weichow I.

FEAF: FBs attack convoy off W coast of Leyte and hit barges and shipping near Ormoc. B–24's bomb Carolina A/F. B–25's attack several A/Fs and villages in the NE peninsula of Celebes and Halmahera. A–20's strike Piroe.

Seventh AF: B–24's from Guam, fly shipping rcn over the Bonins attacking vessels and AA positions at Haha Jima, shipping and town at Okimura, and returning, strafe Iwo Jima. P–47's from Saipan strafe storage caves on Pagan. During 9/10 Nov a lone B–24 from Guam, on snooper mission, bombs Iwo Jima.

Eleventh AF: An 8-plane armed rcn sweep and a 4-plane bombing mission are cancelled due to weather.

10 November

Eighth AF: More than 600 HBs attack A/Fs, M/Y and chemical plant at or near Hanau, Wiesbaden, and Cologne; and 4 T/Os. 14 ftr gps give escort to HBs and 2 FB gps bomb and strafe transportation-comm tgts in NC Germany.

Ninth AF: 150-plus bmrs dispatched against ordnance arsenal and camp area are recalled due to weather. 7 others drop leaflets. XXIX TAC attacks railroads while XIX TAC escorts bmrs and supports 80th and 5th Inf Divs in US Third Army assault in Metz area.

Twelfth AF: HQ and HQ Sq, XII TAC; HQ and HQ Sq, 64th Ftr Wg; 324th Ftr Gp; 415th Night Ftr sq; 11th Tac Rcn Sq; and several signal, ftr control, and serv units are relieved from duty with Twelfth AF and assigned to ETOUSA and First TAC AF (Prov). MBs continue interdiction

campaign against railways in NE
Italy, principally the Brenner Pass,
Brenta R and Po R bridges, rail ferry
at Ostiglia, and several dumps. FBs
hit rail tgts and guns at several points
in Po Valley.

Fifteenth AF: Continued bad
weather limits operations to rcn missions and rcn escorts by P–38's.

Tenth AF: 60-plus P–47's again
attack a variety of tgts including
Japanese concentrations at Bhamo,
Indaw, Hkapra, and Nawngtao, town
of Naba Station bridges at Meza and
in Kawlin area, and T/Os along the
Irrawaddy and along the railroad corridor in N Burma and spt ground forces S of Bhamo. Transports fly more
than 250 sorties to forward areas.

Fourteenth AF: 11 B–25's pound
storage buildings and town area of
Wanling. 130-plus P–40's, P–38's,
and P–51's on armed rcn over S China
attack river, road and rail traffic, storage, A/F and villages at or near
Tingka, Chefang, Kweilin, Yoyang,
Nanyo, Changsha, Paoching, Kweihsien, Yungfu, Wuchou, Siangtan,
Tanchuk, Mosun, Kweiping, Yuncheng, Chenghsien, Hankow, and
Chikhom.

FEAF: FBs again hit Ormoc Bay
shipping while B–25's join Navy aircraft in shipping strikes throughout
same area. At least 3 destroyers are
claimed sunk. B–24's in the area bomb
town of Ormoc. B–25's and A–20's
over Ceram bomb Haroekoe A/F,
Piroe, and T/Os on S coast.

Seventh AF: 27 Saipan-based B–
24's pound Iwo Jima. 6 from Angaur
I bomb Koror.

11 November

Eighth AF: 400-plus HBs attack

Oberlahnstein, Koblenz, and Rheine
M/Ys, Scholven/Buer oil plant, and
Bottrop synthetic oil plant, along with
other tgts. 11 ftr gps provide escort.

Ninth AF: 190 MBs and LBs hit
strongpoints at Putzlohn and rail
bridges at Sinzig, Euskirchen, Ahrweiler, and Mayen. IX TAC hits railroads and other tgts, escorts 9th
Bomb Div, and supports US 28th Inf
Div in Schmidt area. XXIX TAC hits
tgts in W Germany. XIX TAC flies
armed rcn and supports US XII and
XX Corps in Thionville-Metz area.

Twelfth AF: MBs strike at railroad
bridges in NC and NE Italy, damaging bridge at Piazzola sul Brenta and
knocking out 2 spans of bridge at
Latisana. FBs continue spt of ground
forces S of Bologna, attack vehicles,
trains, and comm in Genoa-Alessan-
dria area, bomb Villafranca di
Verona A/F and set most of the area
aflame. During 10/11 Nov A–20's
bomb Ghedi A/F and T/Os in Po
Valley.

Fifteenth AF: 220-plus HBs attack
M/Ys in Rosenheim, Salzburg, Villach, Linz, and Lienz, railroad at Zell
am See, highway bridge at Sillian,
Wurzen Pass, railroad bridges at Pinzano al Tagliamento, Latisana, and
Casarsa della Delizia, and Aviano
A/F. Ftrs escort all missions except
the bridge attacks. Bad weather
grounds 100-plus other HBs, and another 320-plus are recalled before
reaching tgt areas.

Tenth AF: Nearly 90 P–47's hit
troop concentrations at Chaungdauk,
Nawngtao, Mankang, and in Indaw
vicinity; damage and knock out
bridges at Meza and S of Kawlin, score
near misses on bridges in Hsenwi-
Namhkai area; blast radio installa-

tion near Manoi, bomb Kawlin A/F, hit rail traffic between Shwebo and Padu, and attack T/Os along the Irrawaddy from Tigyaing to Twinnge. Transports fly 237 sorties to forward areas.

Fourteenth AF: 18 B–25's hit Phuc Yen, Wan Lai-Kam, and damage bridge on Mekong R. 10 B–25's bomb Kweilin A/F while 4 hit Wanling. 5 B–25's and 6 P–40's attack Chingmen A/F. 70-plus P–40's, P–51's and P–38's over S China and N Indochina on armed rcn hit T/Os at several locations, concentrating on Lampang, Changsha, Lingling, and Hengyang areas.

FEAF: B–24's hit Dumaguete A/F while FBs hit shipping in Palompon area and T/Os at Valencia. Over Halmahera FBs and B–25's hit shipping and Namlea A/F. P–38's hit Kendari A/F and B–24's bomb Ninring R area.

Twentieth AF: The last of the 6 preliminary trg missions of XXI BC is directed at Truk atoll. 8 B–29's bomb Dublon I sub pens.

Seventh AF: Escorted by newly arrived P–38's (some of which also escort B–29 raid on Truk) 29 Guambased B–24's pound Iwo Jima A/Fs. 16 Saipan-based P–47's hit Pagan beach defenses and storage caves.

12 November

Eighth AF: Operational tour of duty for ftr pilots is set at 270 hrs.

Ninth AF: Weather prevents operations by 9th Bomb Div. Ftr operations are limited but IX and XIX TAC's fly patrols and armed rcn in W Germany and along French-German border.

Twelfth AF: Bad weather grounds

MBs. FBs spt ground forces in the N Apennines and hit railway tgts in Po Valley, cut rail lines in 18 places and destroy or seriously damage 8 bridges. During 11/12 Nov LBs hit motor transport, Bergamo A/F, and Po R crossing at San Benedetto Po.

Fifteenth AF: 107 ftr-escorted B–24's strike at bridges at Ora, Albes, and Mezzocorona, viaduct at Avisio, plus alternate tgt of Casarsa della Delizia railroad bridges and T/Os in NE Italy including Latisana railroad bridge and an A/F to the N.

Tenth AF: 16 P–47's spt ground forces in Pinwe area and near Indaw. 24 attack supplies and comm tgts in Kawlin area while 9 bomb Japanese concentrations at Indaw and Man Hkong. Town of Pegon is attacked by 11 P–47's and 20-plus others and 9 B–25's hit T/Os during the sweeps of the Irrawaddy from Singu to Katha anl along rail lines at several points in N Burma. 250-plus transport sorties are flown to forward bases and frontline areas.

Fourteenth AF: 8 B–25's knock out a railway bridge and damage 2 others near Thanh Hoa. 4 B–25's bomb town of Man Pwe while 4 attack Wanling. 38 P–51's and P–40's hit Hengyang A/F and attack river, rail, and road traffic, arty pieces, pillboxes, and storage around Hengyang, Lingling, and Kweilin. 13 P–40's hit Changsha area. 40 P–51's and P–38's hit various T/Os at several other locations scattered throughout S China and N Indochina.

FEAF: B–24's bomb Alicante A/F while FBs hit Linao barges of W coast of Leyte, and shipping in Ormoc Bay. B–25's bomb Daliao and Matina A/F. B–24's and FBs over NE Celebes and Halmahera I attack shipping and Djailolo A/F. 50-plus B–25's blast Mapia and Asia Is.

Twentieth AF: 29 Chengtu-based B–29's bomb Omura. Over 20 others bomb last resort tgt of Nanking (due to bad weather over Omura), and 20-plus more hit various alternate tgts and T/Os.

Seventh AF: 29 Saipan-based B–24's with P–38 escort bomb A/F on Iwo Jima. 11 P–47's strafe runway and storage area on Pagan. During the night a B–24 on snooper mission bombs Iwo Jima. B–24's from Angaur bomb Koror.

Eleventh AF: 2 B–24's fly armed rcn over Onnekotan and Matsuwa.

13 November

Ninth AF: Weather prevents all operations except for night patrol and weather rcn by IX TAC.

Twelfth AF: During 12/13 Nov A–20's bomb ammo dumps, pontoon bridge, and T/Os in Po Valley. Thick overcast covering N Italy the following morning vastly curtails MBs which attack only a railway bridge at Padua. FBs continue to hit comm N of battle area and also oil pipeline across the Po R at Ostiglia.

Fifteenth AF: During 12/13 Nov 14 MBs hit Blechhammer oil refinery. 5 others hit alternate tgts and T/Os at scattered locations including Gleiwitz, Karvina, Ruzomberok, and Vac. Day operations are limited to rcn missions.

Tenth AF: 100-plus FBs pound numerous tgts in N Burma. Close spt strikes are made on Pinwe area, bridges at Namhkai, Meza, and Thegyaung, on troop concentrations and on supplies at Loi-Lum and Namhpakka. Ferry crossing at Shweli

is hit by 12-hr delay bombs, Nawnghkio landing ground is strafed, and numerous T/Os along the Irrawaddy and rail lines in N Burma are hit. Transports fly over 300 sorties to forward areas.

Fourteenth AF: 4 B–25's bomb Man Pwe while 4 others blast 3 warehouses at Wanling. 60-plus P–40's, P–51's, and P–38's on armed rcn over S China and as far W and SW as Burma and Thailand hit numerous T/Os including shipping, troops, and railroad tgts.

FEAF: B–24's pound Fabrica A/F while FBs hit shipping and other T/Os. A few FBs hit Legaspi A/F. B–25's, with P–38 cover, hit San Roque A/F and town of Zamboanga. Over Halmahera I and in Ceram area FBs and A–20's bomb A/Fs and various T/Os. Pegun I is blasted by 2 waves of 70 A–20's.

Seventh AF: 6 B–24's from Guam, escorting Navy photo aircraft over Iwo Jima and the Bonins, attack shipping at Futamiko. 1 B–24 from Saipan, carrying out unsuccessful shipping search, bombs Iwo Jima. 7 B–24's from Angaur hit oil storage on Malakal I and attack bridge between Malakal and Koror.

14 November

Ninth AF: Weather prevents all operations except a few ftr patrols and rcn flights.

Twelfth AF: Bad weather restricts operations to FB attacks by 17 P–47's on rail lines and road N of battleline.

Fifteenth AF: Bad weather limits operations to rcn missions.

Tenth AF: 12 B–25's bomb supply area near Lashio. 56 FBs hit supply areas, enemy concentrations, town areas, and general T/Os at Kutkai, Sandaya, Palaung, Kawlin, Tingka, and in Shwebo-Kyaukmyaung area. 12 spt ground forces in Pinwe area, 4 bomb Sindaw R bridges and 30-plus others maintain patrols S of Myitkyina. 300-plus transport sorties are flown to forward areas.

Fourteenth AF: In E Burma and in China-Burma boundary areas 8 B–25's bomb Wanling and Hsenwi. 15 P–38's and P–40's on armed rcn hit T/Os around Wanling and Mangshih.

FEAF: B–25's pound Pegun I in preparation for allied amphibious landings early the following morning. B–24's, with P–38 and P–47 cover, bomb Bacolod A/F while FBs hit trucks and buildings in Valencia area and near Linao and hit shipping S of Ormoc. B–25's and FBs pound Lahug and Opon A/F. B–24's strike Langoan A/F.

Seventh AF: 22 Saipan and Guam-based B–24's bomb Woleai hitting an A/F and adjacent installations and firing an oil dump. 4 Saipan-based P–47's hit Pagan A/F. During 14/15 Nov a B–24 from Saipan on snooper mission attacks shipping SW of the Bonins.

15 November

Ninth AF: XII TAC, along with 71st Ftr Wg, 50th, 358th, and 371st Ftr Gps, 86th Air Depot Gp, and 83d and 312th Serv Gps, is assigned to the First Tac AF (Prov). When hostilities cease the First Tac AF will be disbanded and all of its units will revert to Ninth AF. Weather prevents bmr operations and limits ftrs. XIX TAC flies armed rcn in Merzig-Trier-Saarbrucken area and supports XX Corps in same area.

Twelfth AF: Twelfth AF loses HQ & HQ Sq, 63d Ftr Wg; HQ and HQ Sq, 42d Bomb Wg; 17th and 320th Bomb Gps, and 310th Serv Gp to ETOUSA. Bad weather cancels all operations except for rcn by 4 P–47's and attack by 2 on railroad bridge and rolling stock in Po Valley.

Fifteenth AF: 80 B–17's and B–24's attack benzol plant at Linz, M/Y at Innsbruck, and troop concentration at Novi Pazar (all primary tgts), and make single bmr attacks on Wolfsburg, Salzburg, Hieflau, Kapfenberg steel works, Schwaz, Ybbs, and A/Fs near Linz, Passau, and Traunstein. Ftrs escort the Novi Pazar raid.

Tenth AF: 12 B–25's attack A/F at Kawlin. 42 P–47's hit supplies, troop and vehicle concentrations, and T/Os at Mansak, Gyogon, Banmauk, Namtao, and Wuntho. 20 spt ground forces in Pinwe area while 16 attack bypass bridges at Kawnghka and Namhkai, knocking out the latter. 8 P–47's bomb Kyaikthin rail sidings and junction, 8 strafe Anisakan A/F, and 12 hit T/Os during N Burma road sweeps. 280 transport sorties are flown.

Fourteenth AF: 19 B–25's and 16 P–51's and P–40's over SW China, W Burma, and N Indochina hit railroad tgts, villages, town areas, and general T/Os at or near Wanling, Mangshih, Tingka, Quang Yen, Nam Dinh, Thanh Hoa, and Man Pwe.

FEAF: B–25's and FBs spt allied amphibious landings in Mapia Is. B–24's, with P–38 spt, bomb La Carlota A/F while B–25's hit Lahug. B–25's and FBs attack T/Os on Cebu and shipping off W coast of Leyte. On Mindanao B–24's hit 3 A/Fs while P–38's hit shipping and other T/Os. In NE Celebes B–24's bomb

Tanamon while other B–24's, B–25's, and FBs hit scattered T/Os in Celebes anl Halmahera I.

Seventh AF: Guam-based B–24's on shipping strike to the Bonins, attack vessels at Haha Jima and near Chichi Jima. 1 Saipan-based B–24, during 15/16 Nov snooper mission, bombs Iwo Jima after failing to find shipping tgts in the Bonins.

Eleventh AF: 8 B–25's weather-abort armed photo rcn over Paramushiru.

16 November

Eighth AF: About 1,200 HBs, along with Ninth AF and RAF airplanes, attack tac tgts E of Aachen in spt of US First and Ninth Armies' offensive. 9 ftr gps fly escort and 2 gps later strafe transportation tgts in Giessen, Marburg, and Berleburg areas.

Ninth AF: 80 9th Bomb Div bmrs hit defended areas and strongpoints at Echtz, Luchem, and Eschweiler. IX TAC FBs dive-bomb gun positions and other tgts in Stolberg and Hurtgen areas and XIX TAC supports US XX Corps in Merzig, Trier, Saarbrucken area. XXIX TAC attacks tgts in 12 W German towns. US First and Ninth Armies begin eastward thrust (Operation QUEEN) into areas hit by IX and XXIX TACs.

Twelfth AF: MBs fly over 250 sorties against rail lines in Brenner Pass and other parts of NE Italy destroying the railroad bridge at Sacile. FBs in spt of British Eighth Army adv to NW of Forli hit guns, ammo supplies, and other military tgts, attack pipeline crossings of the Po at Ostiglia and Ferrara, and pontoon stores near Ficarola, as well

as hitting comm tgts N of battle area.

Fifteenth AF: More than 550 HBs attack Munich W M/Y and troop concentrations at Visegrad as well as alternate tgt of Innsbruck M/Y and scattered T/Os. Over 250 P–51's and P–38's spt the attack on Munich. 26 other P–38's strafe transport tgts on roads between Sarajevo and Novi Pazar.

Tenth AF: 30 P–47's hit troop concentrations and supply areas at Naungmo, Nawngmoloi, and Lashio. 11 spt ground forces in Pinwe area, 4 attack bridges at Meza and over Sindaw R. 4 bomb Meza railroad station, 16 sweep railroad from Sagaing to Kanbalu, and 16 strafe Nawnghkio and Hsumhsai A/Fs. Transports fly 270-plus sorties to forward bases and frontline areas.

Fourteenth AF: 23 B–24's bomb Changsha. 8 B–25's hit Lohochai and bomb Wanling area. 16 B–25's hit Nghia Trang, Duc Tho, Nha Trang, and Do Len. 70-plus P–40's and P–51's over SE and SW China on armed rcn attack road, river, and rail traffic, town areas, and other T/Os at several scattered locations.

FEAF: In C Phil Is and in Mindanao area B–25's, B–24's, and FBs hit A/Fs, harbors, shipping, and T/Os. In Kendari area and on NE peninsula of Celebes, and on Halmahera, HBs, MBs, and FBs pound A/Fs, villages and shipping. MBs also spt ground forces in Mapia Is and bomb Namlea A/F.

Thirteenth AF: Col Willard R Wolfinbarger becomes CO of XIII FC.

Seventh AF: 12 Saipan-based B–24's bomb shipping at Chichi Jima while 2 others attack barges at Haha Jima. 12 P–47's and 3 P–38's hit A/F on Pagan in the first combat strike by P–38's in the Marianas. During a 16/17 Nov snooper mission in the Bonins a B–24 attacks shipping.

17 November

Ninth AF: 30 bmrs of 9th Bomb Div hit Haguenau. Weather prevents 100-plus bmrs from attacking tgts. Ftrs escort bmrs, fly patrol and armed rcn over wide area of W Germany, and spt US 104th and 4th Inf Divs and 2d Armd Div, E of Aachen and near Hurtgen.

Twelfth AF: For the first time in several months the Twelfth's MBs attack tgts in Yugoslavia, hitting bridges along the Brod-Zagreb-Maribor railroad. MBs also hit rail bridges and viaducts in NE Italy, concentrating on Brenner Pass where ground haze and smoke screen at Avisio viaduct hamper the attacks. FBs of XXII TAC cut rail lines, hit larger concentrations of railroad cars, and blast several ammo and fuel dumps N of the battleline below Bologna. FBs closely supporting ground forces also hit guns and other military tgts in battle area.

Fifteenth AF: 630-plus HBs attack Blechhammer S and Vienna/Floridsdorf oil refineries, industrial area in and near Vienna, M/Ys at Maribor, Gyor, Graz, Salzburg, Villach, and town of Sankt Johann in Tirol, plus several scattered T/Os. Ftrs escort HBs and fly rcn and rcn escort missions.

Tenth AF: 33 P–47's hit troop and vehicle concentrations and supply areas at Manlu, Loi Lum, Nawng Moloi, and Kyaukme. 10 P–47's spt ground forces in N Burma railroad corridor near Meza. 16 others sweep rail line from Hsipaw to Sedaw hitting rolling stock, gun positions and other T/Os while 3 bomb Meza railroad station. 16 others strafe A/Fs at Nawnghkio, Anisakan, and Onbauk. 9 B–25's bomb bridges at Lashio, knocking out a bypass bridge and damaging others. Several machinegun positions are silenced in the bridge area. Transports continue to operate on large scale, flying 266 sorties to forward areas.

Fourteenth AF: 3 B–24's bomb Kowloon Docks. 15 B–25's, in flights of 2 or 3 MBs each, attack gun positions, storage areas, and village and town areas N of Chuchou, S of Hpalen, W of Nanyo, and at Chefang and Nanyo. Also a bridge at Tingka is knocked out. 100-plus P–40's and P–51's hit T/Os throughout SE and SW China, concentrating on Mangshih and Changsha areas.

FEAF: B–24's bomb Legaspi A/F. In Mindanao area B–24's bomb Sasa and Likanan A/Fs. Other B–24's and B–25's fly heckling missions over C Phil Is, Mindanao, and NE Celebes. B–25's continue to spt ground forces on Mapia Is.

Seventh AF: 15 B–24's, flying shipping strike out of Saipan, attack vessels SW of Muko Jima and attack harbor and town of Okimura.

Eleventh AF: 4 B–24's bomb Suribachi A/F. 2 ftrs intercept and damage 1 B–24 which force-lands on Kamchatka.

18 November

Eighth AF: 8 ftr gps strafe oil storage depots in Hanau and Ulm areas, A/Fs at Leipheim and Lechfeld, and miscellaneous ground tgts. About 70 ftrs are encountered. US ftrs claim 26 air victories and 69 destroyed on the ground. 8 US ftrs are lost.

Ninth AF: 340-plus bmrs of 9th Bomb Div strike barracks areas, rail bridges, rail facilities, strongpoints, and defended positions at 13 locations in Germany. Ftrs escort Bomb Div, fly sweeps and armed rcn over W Germany, and spt ground forces E of Aachen and in Sarreguemines area.

Twelfth AF: MBs bomb bridges at Pizzighettone, Romano di Lombardia, Castelnuovo di Garfagnana, Migazzone, Casarsa della Delizia, Casale Monferrato, and at Zidani Most and also pound Brod-Ljubljana railway, the principal German escape route in the Balkans. FBs continue successful attacks on rail lines, dumps, guns, and pipelines in the N Apennines and the Po Valley, XXII TAC claiming over 100 train cars, 8 locomotives, and nearly 75 vehicles destroyed.

Fifteenth AF: 680-plus HBs bomb Vienna/Floridsdorf and Korneuburg oil refineries, A/Fs at Aviano, Villafranca di Verona, Udine, and Vicenza, and troop concentrations at Visegrad. 126 P–38's escort Austria missions while 12 others bomb the troop concentrations at Visegrad. 186 P–51's provide cover for raids on the Italian A/Fs and sweep tgt areas. Over 50 other ftrs fly rcn and rcn escort.

Tenth AF: 27 FBs spt ground forces S of Pinwe and in Bhamo area. 16 attack troops and supply area at Panglong and Ngapwegyi while 7 hit ferry area at Meza, 20 hit T/Os along Kanbalu-Wuntho railroad and at Maymyo and Wetwin. 9 B–25's pound Man Pwe rail yards, destroying warehouses and other buildings anl causing much general damage. Transports continue large-scale operations to forward areas.

Fourteenth AF: 10 B–25's blast stores at Hengshan and hit populated areas from Ishan to Liuchow. 130-plus P–51's, P–40's, and P–38's pound T/Os scattered over vast areas of S China. Troops, shipping, supplies, trucks, and railroad tgts are hit particularly hard N of Lingling, from Liuchow to Ishan, from Hengshan to Hengyang, from Kweilin to Liuchou, from Siangtan to Paoching, and at Chuanhsien, Hwaiyuanchen, Chingmen, Chuchiang, and Shihkiachwang.

FEAF: In Mindanao-NE Celebes areas B–24's, B–25's and A–20's again hit A/Fs and T/Os. FBs, A–20's, and B–25's over several locations in Phil Is pound shipping, supply and personnel areas, harbors, barges, airstrips, and comm tgts. B–24's, with P–38's and P–47's supporting, launch major strike against oil installations at Tarakan. Other B–24's and B–25's hit shipping off Tarakan and in Brunei Bay. In the Makassar-Kendari area B–24's bomb Polewali shipyards. B–24's pound A/Fs in Ceram-Amboina area while P–38's strafe shipping. B–25's continue to spt ground forces in Mapia Is.

Seventh AF: B–24's from Saipan and Guam hit shipping at Chichi Jima and Haha Jima. P–38's and B–24's from Saipan escort photo planes over Iwo Jima.

Eleventh AF: 4 B–24's strike Suribachi shore batteries, including one on Takikawa Cape. A shipping sweep by 6 B–25's is cancelled due to weather.

19 November

Ninth AF: 450-plus A–20's, A–26's, and B–26's bomb storage depots, bridge, junction, ordnance depots, and defended positions in or near 10 German towns and cities. Ftrs escort 9th Bomb Div, carry out patrols, and fly armed rcn hitting rail facilities and other tgts over W German areas including Euskirchen, Trier, Saarbrucken, Julich, and Cologne. IX, XIX, and XXIX TACs spt US VII, XII, XIX, and XX Corps areas E of Aachen and near Hurtgen, between Metz and Saarlautern and near Sarreguemines.

Twelfth AF: Fog and low clouds force cancellation of missions against W Po Valley tgts and limit FBs to a midday attack on rail lines, guns, troop concentrations, motor transport, and other military tgts in and near battle area S of Bologna. During 18/19 Nov A–20's on armed rcn bomb Ghedi A/F and tgts in Bologna, Ferrara, Mantua, Cremona, and Parma areas.

Fifteenth AF: More than 500 B–24's and B–17's bomb Schwechat and Vosendorf oil refineries, Winterhafen oil depot and Lobau oil plant, Wiener-Neudorf aircraft factory, Linz benzol plant, Horsching A/F, Gyor, and Maribor M/Ys, plus several scattered T/Os. 19 P–38's dive-bomb troop concentrations at Prijepolje and Novi Pazar, while 126 P–51's strafe roads and railroads between Esztergom and Veszprem and Vienna, and also attack Veszprem and Tapolcza A/Fs. Other ftrs cover HB and rcn missions.

Tenth AF: 15 P–47's spt ground forces attacking Bhamo and fighting in the Pinwe area. 36 P–47's pound enemy concentrations at Man Mao, Sekang, and Manlu. Transports fly 290 sorties to forward areas.

Fourteenth AF: 3 B–24's bomb Samah Bay docks. 10 B–25's damage 2 buildings N of Chefang and score hits on bridges at Tingka and Wan Lai-Kam. 8 P–40's and P–38's hit T/Os S of Tingka and Chefang. 19 P–40's blast troops and river, rail, and road traffic in Hankow area. 27 P–40's, P–51's, and P–38's hit numerous T/Os in Mangshih area.

FEAF: B–24's bomb Alicante and Palompon while P–47's hit Valencia and Ormoc areas. On Mindanao B–24's hit Libby A/F. Others bomb A/Fs at Sasa, Sidate, Mapanget, and Borebore. B–25's and A–20's hit A/Fs and shipping in Ceram-Amboina-Boeroe. B–25's and A–20's hit Asia Is tgts.

Seventh AF: 5 B–24's from Guam, on armed rcn over Iwo Jima and the Bonins, bomb A/Fs on Iwo Jima while 15 hit shipping at Chichi Jima and Haha Jima. 1 B–24 from Angaur in the Palaus bombs Legaspi A/F.

20 November

Eighth AF: Almost 200 B–17's sent against Eudenbach A/F must abort because of bad weather. Over 150 others bomb Scholven/Buer synthetic oil plant and Munster M/Y, with 7 ftr gps in spt. 6 other gps strafe W German ground tgts.

Ninth AF: Bad weather prevents 9th Bomb Div operations. Ftrs fly sweeps and night patrols over broad areas of W Germany and strafe and bomb numerous railroads, trains, buildings and various military tgts.

Twelfth AF: During 19/20 Nov 44 A–20's attack Po R crossings, A/Fs and lights in the Po Valley. During the day bad weather prevents MBs from successfully attacking tgts. FBs able to operate during the late morning destroy 2 factories E of Modena, and supply dumps near Parma, and cause large explosions in dump near San Felice del Benaco.

Fifteenth AF: 192 B–24's and B–17's bomb Blechhammer S oil refinery and town of Prerov (a T/O). 284 others encounter bad weather and attack several alternate tgts and T/Os in Czechoslovakia including town of Zlin and M/Ys at Brno, Hodonin, and Breclav and other T/Os in C and SE Europe. 92 B–24's attack Sarajevo M/Y, and railroad bridges at Doboj, Zenica, and Fojnica. 11 P–38's dive-bomb M/Y at Brod, while 43 others strafe comm between Esztergom, Veszprem, and Vienna. Other ftrs fly HB escort, rcn, and rcn escort.

Tenth AF: 7 B–25's knock out Hsipaw road bridge. 4 others fail to damage Bawgyo bridge. 12 P–47's spt ground forces in Pinwe sector. 20-plus others hit defenses at Mong Nge, horse transport unit at Selan, bomb storage areas at Kyungon and Kyakataing, Japanese HQ and troop concentration at Man Mao, and several scattered T/Os. Transports maintain continuous flights to forward bases and frontline areas.

Fourteenth AF: 8 B–25's hit barracks area at Lashio. 60-plus P–38's, P–40's, and P–51's on armed rcn over parts of SE and SW China and Indochina attack shipping–especially severely in the Chiuchiang area–and barracks, radio stations, villages, and other T/Os.

FEAF: B–25's bomb Haroekoe and Laha A/Fs. P–38's hit T/Os over Sidate and in Makassar areas.

Seventh AF: Bad weather cancels all bombing missions.

Eleventh AF: 3 B–24's fly an air cover mission for the Navy.

21 November

Eighth AF: Over 1,100 HBs attack synthetic oil plant at Merseburg/Leuna, 2 oil refineries at Hamburg, and several other tgts including 4 towns, 4 M/Ys, an A/F, flak position, and about 30 T/Os. 16 ftr gps escort, later strafe ground tgts, and combat large number of ftrs over Merseburg area. US ftrs claim over 70 destroyed. 34 US ftrs and HBs are lost.

Ninth AF: 9th Bomb Div hits rail bridges and defended areas at several points including Bergstein, Echtz, Sinzig, Neuwied, and Derichsweiler. Ftrs escort B–26's and also Eighth AF B–17's (to Merseburg), fly area cover, sweeps, and dive-bombing missions in W Germany, and spt US 1st, 8th, and 104th Inf Divs in Hurtgen area and XII and XX Corps between Merzig and Sarreguemines.

Twelfth AF: B–25's blast defenses and troop concentrations in Faenza area as British Eighth Army's 5 Corps opens general offensive N towards that town. FBs hit tgts in US Fifth Army battle area S of Bolonga, in Po Valley, and in NE Italy. Particularly good results are achieved against supply dumps and rail line in Brenner Pass is cut in 3 places.

Fifteenth AF: 25 B–24's bomb troop concentrations, railroad, and highways at Novi Pazar and Cacak. 155 P–38's dive-bomb comm lines in S Yugoslavia, destroying several vehicles, blasting roads at Vucitrn, Rogatica, Tvrdosevo, and Duga Poljana, hitting bridges at Vrbasici, and

Kukavica and causing landslide at Pavlica. 87 P–51's strafe comm over wide areas of S Yugoslovia. Other ftrs fly rcn missions.

Tenth AF: 28 P–47's spt ground forces in Pinwe and Bhamo areas. 37 others hit supply areas, troop concentrations and strongholds at Langwa, Pinmalut, Hlebwe, Mutawng, and Nawnghkem. 15 P–47's hit T/Os while sweeping Kyaukme-Namyao road. 10 B–25's knock out bridges at Hsipaw and Bawgyo. Transports fly 280-plus sorties to forward areas.

Fourteenth AF: 42 P–51's and P–38's on armed rcn attack fuel supplies and town area at Ishan and road and rail traffic and other T/Os in Chiuchiang area, N of Wanling, S of Foochow, and at Hsuchang, Sincheng, and Sheklung.

FEAF: B–24's bomb Matina and Lumbia A/Fs. FBs hit troop barges and supply dumps in Ormoc Bay and numerous T/Os throughout the C Phil Is. B–25's hit Langoan and Mapanget A/Fs while B–24's in Kendari area bomb A/F at Ambesia.

Twentieth AF: 61 B–29's from Chengtu bomb aircraft plant at Omura. 13 B–29's bomb Shanghai, and several others hit alternates and T/Os. The VHBs claim 27 ftrs downed, the highest Twentieth AF claim to date.

Seventh AF: Seventh AF serv gps are reassigned from VII Air Serv Area Cmd to VII BC and VII FC, with one serv gp to spt each tac gp in the field. B–24's from Guam bomb shipping and naval shore installations at Chichi Jima and Haha Jima. During 21/22 Nov a lone B–24 on snooper mission bombs Iwo Jima.

Eleventh AF: Adv HQ is estab-lished on Shemya with Gen Harry A Johnson as Dep Cmdr. 5 B–24's fly air coverage for naval units. Another fleet coverage mission by 10 B–25's is cancelled due to weather. Before clearance can be obtained from Russians through diplomatic channels, a B–24 air-drops provisions to marooned crew of B–24 which force-landed on Kamchatka on 17 Nov 44.

22 November

Eighth AF: 2d and 4th Combat Bomb Wgs of 3d Bomb Div are combined to form the Administrative Bomb Wg (Prov). This type of unit is expected to be highly suitable for conditions in Pacific theater where bomb div HQ might be located far from its wg HQ. Under this new plan, the administrative wg can absorb many functions of the div HQ. This experiment will be judged acceptable during Feb 45.

Ninth AF: Bmr operations are cancelled due to bad weather. Ftr operations are limited. 16 aircraft from IX and XIX TAC patrol over V and VII Corps area (SE of Aachen), Bonn-Cologne area, and fly rcn around Saarbrucken, Homburg/Saar, Neukirchen, Kaiserslautern, and Sarrebourg.

Twelfth AF: B–25's again pound defenses in Faenza area as British Eighth Army forces push into that area from the SE. FBs and ftrs fly nearly 350 sorties against rail lines in Po Valley and very successfully hit guns, vehicles, troops and other tgts in US Fifth Army battle area S of Bologna, and supply dumps and pipelines N of the battle area.

Fifteenth AF: 205 HBs hit E and W M/Ys at Munich. 214 others fail to reach primaries because of impenetrable weather and attack alternates and T/Os including M/Ys at Regensburg, Salzburg, Lienz, and Villach and several T/Os at scattered points. Ftrs provide escort to Munich. 88 B–24's attack bridge at Ferrara and rail line at Carbola, while 39 P–38's bomb Osoppo motor transport depot.

Tenth AF: 15 P–47's spt ground forces at Bhamo while 37 others fly close spt in Pinwe area. Supply and personnel areas at Nawngchio, Kutkai, Ingon, Selong, Man Mao, and in vicinity of Kanbalu are pounded by more than 40 P–47's. 12 others attack A/F at Kawlin. Transports fly 188 sorties to forward areas.

Fourteenth AF: 22 B–24's bomb Hankow. 11 B–25's pound Ishan and Liuchenghsien areas while 8 hit storage facilities at Wanling and Kutkai. 95 P–51's, P–40's, and P–38's on armed rcn over wide expanses of S China attack town areas, supplies, and road and rail traffic, hitting Chefang area especially hard.

FEAF: B–24's, B–25's, and FBs pound Bacolod A/F, Ipil, and Ormoc area bridges, barges, and T/Os. B–24's bomb Sasa A/F. FBs hit T/Os in Makassar area, B–24's bomb nickel mine and T/Os in Kendari area and hit A/Fs in NE Celebes. Other B–24's hit small shipping during sweep over Brunei Bay.

Seventh AF: 22 B–24's from Saipan escorted by 22 P–38's (the first long-range P–38 escort of Seventh AF bmrs), bomb A/Fs on Moen and Param. P–47's from Saipan pound A/F on Pagan.

Eleventh AF: 4 B–25's abort an air coverage mission due to weather.

23 November

Eighth AF: Over 140 B–17's escorted by 2 ftr gps bomb benzol manufacturing plant near Gelsenkirchen and M/Y at Duisburg.

Ninth AF: Unfavorable weather cancels all flights.

Twelfth AF: Bad weather restricts operations. MBs over Faenza area abort due to overcast, P–47's hampered by low clouds over the Apennines, fly only 16 sorties, against rail lines S of Bologna, but succeed in cutting the lines in 6 places.

Fifteenth AF: 81 B–24's attack road and railroad bridges at or near Zenica Brod, and Doboj. 30 P–38's bomb Doboj M/Y, 13 hit Doboj road and rail bridge, and 4 attack, but miss, bridge at Maglaj. 13 B–24's and B–17's drop supplies at points in Yugoslavia.

Tenth AF: More than 50 P–47's spt ground forces in Pinwe and Bhamo areas. 16 sweep and strafe A/Fs and many T/Os from Anisakan to Nawnghkio. 3 hit ammo dump at Man Naung. 21 P–47's sweep roads in Ye-U area and strafe rail installations at Kanbalu. 10 B–25's knock out Tantabin main bridge and Tangon and Thegyaung bypass bridges, and blast approaches to Tangon main bridge and Tantabin bypass bridge. 282 transport sorties are flown to forward bases and frontline areas.

Fourteenth AF: 12 B–25's bomb storage area near Lashio and 8 hit Kutkai and Wanling. 2 B–24's bomb Kowloon Docks. More than 120 P–40's, P–51's and P–38's hit T/Os throughout SW and SE China. 32 of the FBs spt ground forces in Chefang area.

FEAF: B–24's bomb Matina A/F.

Seventh AF: 17 B–24's from Guam hit shipping at Chichi Jima and Haha Jima and bomb town of Okimura.

24 November

Ninth AF: Weather cancels all operations except for 3 XIX TAC ftrs which fly night intruder mission in Saarbrucken, Zweibrucken, and Homburg/Saar areas.

Twelfth AF: B–25's, in spt of British Eighth Army, bomb defenses in Faenza area. Bad weather restricts FBs to 2 missions which damage a road bridge and cut rail line S of Modena.

Fifteenth AF: P–38's and P–51's fly photo and weather rcn missions.

Tenth AF: 32 P–47's fly close spt strikes in Pinwe and Bhamo sectors. 50 P–47's attack troops and supply areas at Panma, Hpa-Hpen, Nawng-Sang, Kawlin, Wahkyet, Kawng ai, and in Pintha area, 8 damage bridges at Meza, Namhkai, and Hsenwi while 10 others hit Lashio A/F. 6 B–25's pound storage and ferry area at Meza and 4 damage approaches to Namhkai and Hsenwi road bridges. 323 transport sorties are flown to forward areas.

Fourteenth AF: 21 B–24's bomb warehouse area and docks at Hankow. 3 others hit Haiphong area. 22 B–25's bomb storage area near Lashio, T/Os in Hankow area, and towns of Wanling, Siangtan, Wuchang, and Wan Lai-Kam. 120-plus P–40's, P–38's and P–51's on armed rcn attack many T/Os in E Burma and SW and SE China, concentrating on river and rail traffic and supplies at Chefang, Hengshan, and Sinshih-Changsha area.

FEAF: B–24's bomb AA positions and T/Os at Camp Downes and Panalisan Pt and US ftrs attack and destroy several airplanes over Carigara Bay and Leyte area. B–24's hit AA positions and other tgts at Matina A/F.

Twentieth AF: XXI BC flies its first mission against Japan. Objective is Tokyo. The 111 B–29's are led by 73d Bomb Wg CG, Gen O'Donnell piloting *Dauntless Dotty*, copiloted by Maj Robert K Morgan, erstwhile pilot of the famed B–17, *Memphis Belle*. 35 VHBs bomb primary tgt, Musashino aircraft plant; 50 bomb secondary tgt, urban area and docks; 17 abort en route; the remainder are unable to bomb due to mechanical difficulties. 1 B–29 crashes off Honshu when a ftr rams the bmr, shearing off the elevator and right horizontal stabilizer, becoming the first XXI BC VHB lost to Japanese action. 1 other ditches after running out of fuel. B–29 gunners claim 7 aircraft downed.

Seventh AF: 2 B–24's from Saipan on shipping rcn attack vessels at Haha Jima and Chichi Jima. 3 B–24's from Guam on armed rcn bomb Marcus. 14 Saipan-based P–47's strafe landing ground on Pagan.

25 November

Eighth AF: More than 900 HBs attack Merseburg/Leuna synthetic oil plant, Bingen M/Y and several T/Os. All bombing utilizes Pathfinder technique due to very heavy clouds. Escorting ftrs fly over 800 sorties. Over 65 HBs fail to return from mission but many land safely in Allied-occupied territory. 36th Bomb Sq starts daily operations as a screening force for bomb divisions. It is assigned task of protecting the Eighth's primary VHF and ftr-to-bmr comm from interception during assembly. Increase of flak batteries around German military and industrial installations soon compels the 36th to increase radar countermeasures on each mission. The sq remains on this assignment until end of war in Europe

Ninth AF: 9th Bomb Div hits Landau ordnance arsenal, road junctions, and ammo dump at Neustadt and Kaiserslautern. Ftrs escort 9th Bomb Div and Eighth AF, fly armed rcn over Germany, and spt ground forces E of Aachen and between Merzig and Sarreguemines.

Twelfth AF: Bad weather again hampers operations. 3 ftr gps fly only 53 sorties against railway tgts and T/Os N of US Fifth Army battle area, cutting lines at 14 places and destroying several vehicles.

Fifteenth AF: During 24/25 Nov over 40 B–17's and B–24's bomb Linz benzol plant, Klagenfurt, Innsbruck, and Munich W M/Ys, and 2 unidentified T/Os. During the day P–38's fly photo and weather rcn missions.

Tenth AF: 24 FBs spt ground forces in Bhamo area. 24 bomb an A/F at Kawlin while 8 more strafe Tabingaung A/F and town area. 12 attack Meza railroad station and boxcars in nearby bridge area, storage and personnel areas in Lashio area and at Nawngyang, Ashang, and Man Mao. 8 P–47's strafe T/Os along Wuntho-Shwebo rail line. Transports fly 325 sorties to forward bases and frontline areas.

Fourteenth AF: 12 B–25's hit warehouses, village and town areas at Lashio and Wanling. 6 attack rail tgts, trucks, and buildings at Phu Lang Thuong. 75 P–40's, P–51's, and P–38's on armed rcn attack river, road, and rail traffic, troops, buildings, and other T/Os at several Thailand, Burma, S China, and N Indochina locations, including areas around Lampang, Paoching, Ankang, Ishan, Hochih, Bhre, Namsang, Mongyu, and Phu Lang Thuong.

FEAF: FBs range over wide areas of Masbate, Cebu, Leyte, and surrounding waters, attacking shipping, A/Fs, bivouacs, and a variety of tgts. B–25's and FBs hit A/Fs on Ceram and Boeroe and B–24's on armed rcn over N Borneo hit shipping and other T/Os. During 25/26 Nov B–25's hit A/Fs in NE Celebes and Halmahera.

Seventh AF: 7 Guam-based B–24's, escorting photo aircraft over Bonin and Kazan Is, bomb Chichi Jima, Muko Jima, and Haha Jima.

Eleventh AF: A B–24 aborts an armed photo mission over Matsuwa due to weather and instead radar-bombs Kurabu A/F. B–25's cancel a shipping sweep due to weather.

26 November

Eighth AF: 1,000-plus B–17's and B–24's bomb rail viaducts at Altenbeken and Bielefeld, Misburg oil refinery, M/Ys at Hamm, Osnabruck, Hannover, Gutersloh, Bielefeld, and Herford, and 7 T/Os. 15 ftr gps fly escort. About 550 ftrs are encountered. HB losses total over 35 (25 to ftrs). US ftrs claim over 100 air victories.

Ninth AF: 173 MBs and LBs bomb supply, storage, stores, and ordnance depots at Gaulsheim, Bergzabern, Giessen, Reichenbach, and Homburg/Saar. Ftrs fly sweeps and armed rcn over W Germany, search for lost A–20, escort 9th Bomb Div, and spt US 29th Inf Div at Bourheim and XX and XII Corps in area of the Maginot Line and German-French border.

Twelfth AF: Slight improvement in weather permits FBs to increase operations. P–47's closely spt ground forces in US Fifth Army battle area in the Apennines S of Bologna and cut rail lines in over 30 places N of the immediate battle zone.

Fifteenth AF: 39 P–38's fly offensive sweep over Seregelyes A/F and strafe nearby road and rail traffic. Other ftrs fly rcn and escort.

Tenth AF: 16 P–47's continue close spt strikes. About 60 FBs hit concentrations, supply and ammo dumps, and rail tgts at Panghkai, Kunmong, Mabein, Lashio, Panku, and around Meza. 7 others on railroad sweep hit T/Os between Maymyo and Man Pyen. Transports fly more than 300 sorties to forward areas.

Fourteenth AF: 19 B–25's and 20 P–51's blast railway cars, station, and track, hit several trucks, and hit town areas at Hochih and Phu Lang Thuong 6 B–25's damage bridge at Kengluang. 90-plus P–40's, P–51's, and P–38's hit river, rail, and road traffic and other T/Os over wide S China areas, 40 of them concentrating on tgts between Kweiyi and Changsha and around Liuchow.

FEAF: 40-plus B–24's, some with ftr spt, bomb La Carlota and Talisay A/Fs. FBs hit A/F and various T/Os throughout the area. B–25's pound A/Fs in Amboina-Ceram area and B–24's bomb A/F near Davao. Others bmrs and ftrs fly light strikes and armed rcn missions against a variety of tgts in N Celebes, N Borneo, S Luzon, Mindanao, and Halmahera.

Seventh AF: P–47's from Saipan strafe A/F on Pagan. During the night a B–24 on snooper mission from Guam bombs Iwo Jima. B–24's from Angaur bomb Arakabesan.

Eleventh AF: Shipping sweep by 4 B–25's is called off due to weather.

27 November

Eighth AF: More than 450 HBs attack Bingen and Offenburg M/Ys and 5 T/Os, 5 ftr gps fly escort. 10 gps of ftrs (2 of FBs) sent against oil tgts in NC Germany fail to locate primaries. Several FBs bomb and strafe rail tgts and A/F in Stendal area. 8 gps are jumped by about 750 ftrs (largest sighting to date) in Magdeburg-Munster-Hannover areas when the Germans mistake them for HB formations. US ftrs claim 98 destroyed against 11 losses. After combat 4 ftr gps resume strafing of ground tgts.

Ninth AF: Weather forbids bmr missions. Ftrs patrol over W Germany, dive-bomb bridge at Rurdorf, and spt US 104th, 8th, and 1st Inf Divs near Hurtgen and in Weisweiler-Franz area, and XIX Corps (mainly 2d Armd Div) at Merzenhausen.

Twelfth AF: Weather grounds all missions except 5 weather rcn sorties.

Fifteenth AF: P–51's and P–38's fly rcn and rcn escort missions. Bad weather cancels other operations.

Tenth AF: 12 P–47's fly close spt strikes in Pinwe area. 21 FBs destroy bridges at Inailong and Thegyaung and damage bridges at Ho-hko and Kawnghka. 60-plus FBs attack personnel and supply areas at Kutkai, Kyungon, Kodaungbo, Mongmit, Datwin, Man Namsawk, Old Lashio, and Ugingyi. Transports fly 280-plus sorties, carrying men and supplies to forward bases and frontline areas.

Fourteenth AF: 17 B–24's bomb

Gia Lam. 17 B–25's blast Hochih area, 6 bomb Phu Lang Thuong, and 8 pound warehouses at Lashio. 56 P–40's, P–51's, and P–38's on armed rcn over E Burma, N Indochina, and vast areas of S China attack town areas, railroad tgts, bridges and other T/Os around Lampang, Phu Binh, Pachai, Ishan, Wanling, Chefang, Hsenwi, and Kawnghka.

FEAF: B–24's bomb Malogo, Bacolod and Daliao A/Fs. B–25's blast Namlea, Liang, and Laha A/Fs. A variety of FEAF aircraft attack A/Fs, shipping, and T/Os on Celebes, N Borneo, and in the Halmahera and the Ceram areas.

Twentieth AF: Operating from Calcutta area, 55 B–29's bomb Bangsue railroad yards at Bangkok. 3 others hit individual tgts. 81 Marianas-based B–29's fly against Tokyo. None of the VHBs bomb the primary tgts (Musashino and Nakajima plants) but 59 hit secondary (urban area and docks). 7 bomb Hamamatsu, a T/O. While the mission is in progress 11 enemy airplanes attack Isley Field on Saipan, destroying or damaging several B–29's. AA and intercepting ftrs down 10 aircraft.

Seventh AF: 24 B–24's from Saipan, escorted by 12 P–38's, hit Iwo Jima. 29 more B–24's, from Guam, fly a second strike against the island. 25 B–24's from Angaur bomb Del Monte A/F.

28 November

Ninth AF: 9th Bomb Div hits defended villages of Birgel and Merken, rail bridge at Sinzig, and Billiger Forest ammo dump. Ftrs fly escort, night intruder missions, and armed rcn in Kall-Trier area, and

spt US 1st, 8th, and 104th Inf Divs as they take Langerwehe, Jungersdorf, Hurtgen, and bridge at Inden.

Twelfth AF: B–25's hit railroad bridges at Magenta, Torre Beretti, and Casale Monferrato, and an abandoned ship at La Spezia harbor. Ftrs and FBs spt ground forces in battle area in Apennines S of Bologna, hit comm tgts N of battle zone, and cut railroad lines in more than 40 places in Brenner Pass and NC Po areas.

Fifteenth AF: Bad weather limits operations to rcn flights.

Tenth AF: 39 P–47's spt ground forces in Pinwe and Bhamo areas. Supply and personnel concentrations and T/Os at Nwegyo, Kutkai, Meza area, Mankang, Manai, Nawnglok, Nawnglong, Loimawk, Man Myeng, Mong Wi and Kungmong are attacked by about 80 FBs. 16 hit T/Os along Maymyo-Bawgyo rail line. Transports fly 317 sorties to forward areas.

Fourteenth AF: 17 B–24's, escorted by 12 P–51's, bomb Gia Lam. 6 B–25's hit railroad bridge at Phu Lang Thuong. 3 blast 6 warehouses at Hsenwi, 3 bomb Wan Lai-Kam, 1 hits Kutkai, and 4 attack buildings in Wanling and Chefang areas. 60-plus P–40's, P–51's, and P–38's on armed rcn over wide areas of E Burma and S China hit troops, bridges, horses, and other T/Os at many locations.

FEAF: B–24's bomb Daliao and Matina A/Fs. Small attacks by HBs, MBs, and FBs are launched against A/Fs, shipping, and T/Os over wide areas of SWPA, including C Phil Is, Halmahera, and Timor area.

Seventh AF: 21 Saipan-based B–24's bomb Iwo Jima A/F. 3 others, flying armed rcn mission, bomb Marcus. During 28/29 Nov 1 B–24 on snooper mission hits Iwo Jima. 3 B–24's from Angaur bomb Araka-besan radio station.

Eleventh AF: 1 B–24 photos and bombs Matsuwa shore area.

29 November

Eighth AF: Over 1,000 HBs hit viaducts at Altenbeken and Biele-feld, Misburg oil refinery, Hamm M/Y, and several T/Os. 16 ftr gps escort HBs and 5 gps later strafe transportation tgts.

Ninth AF: 301 MBs and LBs hit defended areas, barracks, and military depots at Wittlich, Mariaweiler, Pier, Elsdorf, Limburg, Rastatt, and Landau. Ftrs escort 9th Bomb Div and Eighth AF, fly armed rcn over W Germany, and spt 104th Inf Div in holding action against counterattacks at Inden and Lammersdorf, 8th Inf Div at Hurtgen, and 7 Armd Div in XIII Corps drive toward the Roer.

Twelfth AF: During 28/29 Nov A–20's fly armed rcn over Po Valley, dropping incendiaries at several points including bridges at Piacenza and Castel Maggiore and A/Fs at Ghedi and Villafranca di Verona. During the day weather grounds MBs. However ftrs and FBs can operate, and blast enemy comm on Brenner line and in NC Po Valley, cutting rail lines in numerous places and destroying a large number of vehicles and railroad cars.

Fifteenth AF: Weather limits operations to photo and weather rcn missions.

Tenth AF: 50–plus FBs fly close spt strikes in battle areas around Bhamo and Pinwe. Bridges at Tonbo,

Pauktaw, Man Loi, Meza, Bon Chaung, and at 2 unnamed points in N Burma are pounded by 60–plus FBs. 8 others bomb supplies, personnel and ammo stores at Tigyaing. 323 transport sorties are flown to forward areas.

Fourteenth AF: 6 B–25's bomb Ninh Binh, 8 hit Lashio, and 3 attack Hsenwi. 20 P–40's, P–38's, and P–51's hit T/Os in Chefang area. 23 P–38's and P–51's attack bridges, horses, shipping, and rail traffic around Hochih, Nanning, Hsenwi, Quang Yen, Kawnghka, and Namhkai.

FEAF: B–24's bomb Matina A/F while A–20's and P–47's hit A/F at Pangsagan. B–24's, with ftr cover, pound Puerto Princesa and Kendari A/F. HBs, MBs, and FBs fly several light raids against Halmahera A/Fs and against shipping and other T/Os in Phil Is, Ceram area, N Celebes, and N Borneo.

Twentieth AF: 24 Marianas-based B–29's strike Tokyo dock and industrial area during 29/30 Nov. 2 VHBs bomb last resort tgts of Yokohama and Numazu.

Seventh AF: 18 B–24's from Guam bomb Iwo Jima. 4 P–47's from Saipan strafe Pagan.

Eleventh AF: 3 B–24's bomb Kashiwabara. B–25's call off a shipping sweep due to weather.

30 November

Eighth AF: Around 1,200 HBs strike 4 synthetic oil plants at Bohlen, Zeitz, Merseburg/Leuna, and Lutzkendorf, and M/Ys at Neunkirchen and Homburg/Saar. 16 Eighth AF and 3 Ninth AF ftr gps providing escort encounter sporadic ftr opposition. Intense accurate flak downs at least 29 HBs of a total loss of around 40.

Ninth AF: 288 MBs and LBs attack defended villages of Vettweiss, Stockheim, Erp, and Pirmasens, armd vehicle repair center at Gemund, a rail tunnel, a military camp at Malsbenden, and M/Y at Zweibrucken. Ftrs escort 9th Bomb Div, give area spt to Eighth AF HBs at Leipzig, fly sweeps, dive bombing missions, and rcn over W Germany, and spt elements of US VII Corps in Hurtgen area (especially 104th Div at Lammersdorf and Inden).

Twelfth AF: B–25's bomb bridges at Romano di Lombardia and Crema. Ftrs and FBs attack comm in Po Valley, cutting rail lines and destroying a large number of railroad cars and motor transport. Tgts also include bridges, guns, and buildings.

Fifteenth AF: On 29/30 Nov 18 B–17's bomb Linz benzol plant. 3 others hit M/Ys at Villach, Klagenfurt, and Gmunden. B–24's hit M/Ys at Munich and Innsbruck. During day P–38's and P–51's fly rcn over Yugoslavia, Italy, and Germany.

Tenth AF: 9 B–25's knock out and damage bridges at Bawgyo, Namhkai, and Hsenwi. 16 P–47's spt ground forces at Bhamo. Town of Pinwe is found to be free of enemy forces. About 70 FBs attack troops and supply areas at several locations including Molo, Naungmo, Namun, Hkumpen, Myadaung, Kutkai, Kanbalu, Kyauk, and Natpe. 13 others attack bridges at Meza and in Bawdwin area. 8 strafe T/Os along Kyaukme-Panglong road. 321 transport sorties are flown to forward areas.

Fourteenth AF: 12 B–25's and 8 P–51's damage 2 railroad bridges

and several buildings at Phu Lang Thuong and Phu Ly. 11 bomb 5 warehouses and several other buildings at Lashio, and Wanling. 9 FBs hit shipping, rail tgts, and troops at various points in Thailand. 23 FBs attack T/Os in Chefang area.

FEAF: B–24's in major strikes of the day hit Malimpoeng and Parepare, Legaspi A/F, Matina A/F, and 4 A/Fs on Halmahera. B–25's strike Dumaguete A/F. FBs, HBs, and MBs fly armed rcn, harassing strikes, and light raids over various areas of NEI and Phil Is.

Seventh AF: 23 B–24's from Saipan bomb A/F on Iwo Jima. 8 Guam-based B–24's, escorting photo airplanes over the Kazan and Bonin Is, bomb Haha Jima. 37 from Angaur hit Legaspi A/F. During 29/30 Nov 2 B–24's from Guam and Saipan, bomb Iwo Jima A/F during snooper missions.

Eleventh AF: A weather sortie is the only mission.

1 December

Ninth AF: 134 MBs and LBs strike defended areas at Fraulautern, Ensdorf, and Saarlautern. Ftrs fly sweeps, armed rcn, and bombing missions over W Germany and spt US VII Corps elements at Inden and Hurtgen Forest and 8th Inf Div of V Corps at Tiefenbach Creek and Brandenberger Forest.

Twelfth AF: B–25's attack 4 railroad bridges in W Po Valley, damaging the bridges at Voghera and Torre Beretti. XXII TAC hits motor transport and train cars at several points in N Italy and hit rail lines over widespread area N of the Apennines, including Brenner Pass where lines are cut at 3 points.

Tenth AF: 30–plus P–47's continue spt of ground forces in Bhamo area. Town areas, troops, warehouses, and supply dumps at Myitson, Mingon, Alezeik, Lenaung, and Old Lashio are pounded by 30-plus P–47's. 17 more hit bridges in N Burma and 8 strafe Hsenwi landing ground. 290 transport sorties are flown to forward areas.

Fourteenth AF: 6 B–24's attack T/Os in S China Sea. 8 B–25's destroy 3 storage buildings and damage 6 others at Wanling. 9 FBs pound troop positions in the area and destroy or damage several trucks. Several other FBs hit trucks, locomotives, and villages in Chefang area, between Lashio and Hsenwi, from Linfen to Taiyuan, and at Kunlong.

FEAF: Major FEAF strikes include B–24 raids on Bacolod and Fabrica A/Fs and B–25 attack, with P–47 spt, on Lahug A/F. B–25's attack Cagayan A/F. B–25's and FBs also hit several A/Fs and numerous T/Os on Halmahera during a series of raids. Other FEAF aircraft maintain armed rcn and sweeps over wide area of NEI and Phil Is.

Seventh AF: 26 Guam-based B–24's pound A/F on Iwo Jima. During 1/2 Dec a B–24 bombs Iwo Jima during a snooper mission.

2 December

Eighth AF: Around 275 HBs attack M/Ys at Bingen, Oberlahnstein, and Koblenz-Lutzel, along with a railroad and 4 T/Os. Over 150 HBs abort because of heavy clouds. 8 ftr gps fly spt, encounter over 100 ftrs and claim 17 destroyed. Ftrs

down 8 B–24's at Bingen. 3 ftr gps fly sweeps over Cologne-Kassel-Mannheim-Frankfurt/Main area, meet about 50 ftrs and claim 15 destroyed.

Ninth AF: 210 A–20's, A–26's, and B–26's bomb areas of Saarlautern, Ensdorf, and Fraulautern. Ftrs escort 9th Bomb Div, fly armed rcn over W Germany (tgts hit include M/Y and bridges), and spt US 1st Inf Div at Luchem, 104th Inf Div at Inden, and 8th Inf Div in Brandenberger Forest-Tiefenbach Creek area.

Twelfth AF: MBs hit several bridges in N and NE Italy, scoring effective hits on 2 bridges across the Piave and Brenta Rivers and 4 on the Brenner line. Ftrs and FBs attack comm in Po Valley and spt US Fifth Army forces in battle area S of Bologna. On 1/2 Dec A–20's hit Ghedi A/F and T/Os in NC Po Valley and trains on Brenner line.

Fifteenth AF: Around 500 HBs attack Blechhammer N and S, Odertal and Vienna/Floridsdorf oil refineries, and Strasshof and Celldomolk M/Y and Medvedov highway bridge, plus scattered T/Os in C and E Europe. Ftrs fly escort and carry out rcn missions.

Tenth AF: 40 FBs fly close spt strikes in Bhamo battle sector. Supply areas, ammo dumps, personnel and tank concentrations, and strongholds at Mayathein, Kwingyi, Nanthe, Hsai-hkao, Hsenwi, Man Hkam, Wuntho, Tedaw, and Old Lashio are hit by 60-plus FBs. 16 others hit rolling stock on rail line between Hsipaw and Lashio and strafe supply train in Pangkyawng. 10 B–25's pound several N Burma bridges, knocking out road bridges at Tonglau and Nam Nung and 2 railroad bridges at Tangon. Transports fly 286 sorties to forward areas.

Fourteenth AF: 4 B–25's damage several buildings at Hsenwi. 39 P–51's, P–40's, and P–38's on armed rcn attack troops, horses, trucks, railroad yards, shipping, storage facilities, and road machinery between Yungfengshih and Paoching, from Wanling to Lashio, in Chiuchiang area, N of Wanling and Nan-Tan, and at Kichang and Lashio.

FEAF: B–24's hit Dumaguete, Matina, and Cagayan A/Fs. B–24's and B–25's attack Borebore A/F and Kendari. FBs in C Phil and Mindanao spt ground forces and hit supplies, comm, and a variety of T/Os. MBs bomb Namlea A/F and attack shipping off Ceram.

Seventh AF: 23 B–24's from Guam hit Iwo Jima. During 2/3 Dec 3 B–24's on snooper missions from Saipan and Guam bomb A/F on Iwo Jima.

3 December

Ninth AF: Weather cancels bmr operations. Ftrs fly defensive patrols and armed rcn, hitting rails and bridges and dive-bomb tgts in W Germany including M/Y at Grevenbroich. 104th Inf Div is supported as it extends Inde R bridgehead beyond Lucherberg, US 1st Inf Div as it seizes Luchem, US 8th Inf Div in Brandenberger Forest-Tiefenbach Creek area, and units of US XII Corps at Sarre-Union as it checks a counterattack.

Twelfth AF: Weather hampers operations. Many missions are aborted. MBs score effective hits only on bridge E of Mantua. 57th and 350th Ftr Gps fly 60 sorties against tgts in US Fifth Army battle area S of Bologna and against comm in N Italy. During 2/3 Dec LBs bomb lights throughout Po Valley.

Fifteenth AF: 85 B–24's and B–17's bomb Vienna SE freight depot, Linz industrial area, M/Ys at Innsbruck, Villach, and Klagenfurt, and various T/Os. P–38's and P–51's escort HBs and fly rcn and rcn escort. 14 B–17's and B–24's drop supplies in Yugoslavia.

Tenth AF: 32 P–47's continue close spt of ground forces attacking Bhamo. 18 others damage road bridges at Hay-ti and Tonbo and 6 attack several railroad bridges in N Burma. 4 drop delay-fuse bombs on Myitson ferry landing. 30-plus FBs hit troop and equipment concentrations, fuel and other supplies, arty, ammo dumps, and general town areas in or near Hopaw, Loipao, Man Kat, Namhpai, and Indaw. 9 strafe T/Os along Shwebo-Wuntho rail line. 4 B–25's during 3/4 Dec destroy train on Tangon railroad bridge and attack several other T/Os. 323 transport sorties are flown to forward bases and frontline areas.

Fourteenth AF: 5 B–24's place delayed action bombs near Pengpu bridge. 4 B–25's and 10 P–51's bomb Sintsiang storage area. 67 FBs on armed rcn blast trucks, railroad tgts, warehouses, shipping and other T/Os at Wanling, Loyang, Yuncheng, Hei-Shih Kuan, Wuhu, and particularly in areas around Shihhweiyao and from Hengyang to Siangtan and Lingling.

FEAF: Major B–24 strikes include raids against Malimpoeng and Mandai. B–25's pound 4 A/Fs on Halmahera while A–20's attack Point

Noejew. FBs hit storage area at Palompon and A/Fs near Masbate.

Twentieth AF: Almost 70 XXI BC B–29's based in the Marianas bomb Musashino aircraft plant and docks and urban areas at Tokyo. 6 VHBs are lost.

Seventh AF: 17 Guam-based B–24's pound Iwo Jima. 7 others, escorting photo airplanes over Bonin and Kazan Is, bomb Haha Jima and Iwo Jima. B–24's on snooper missions from the Marianas during 3/4 Dec continue to bomb Iwo Jima.

4 December

Eighth AF: Over 1,100 HBs bomb M/Ys at Kassel, Soest, Bebra, Giessen, and Mainz and as secondary tgts Friedberg and Koblenz M/Ys, along with city of Fulda, and several unidentified T/Os. 15 ftr gps fly spt. Most of the 70 ftrs and HBs failing to return to UK land safely on the Continent.

Ninth AF: Weather prevents bmr operations. Ftrs fly armed rcn and spt US 1st, 8th, and 104th Inf Divs at Luchem, Bergstein, and E of Inde R; and XII and XX Corps in drive toward the Saar R and around Saarlautern.

Twelfth AF: B–25's hit defenses in Bagnacavallo and Faenza areas and ammo dump at Tortona. XXII TAC aircraft hit tgts in US Fifth Army battle area S of Bologna in the Apennines and comm to the N of the battle zone. During 3/4 Dec LBs again bomb T/Os in Po Valley.

Fifteenth AF: 26 P–38's bomb railroad bridge at Zenica. 14 B–17's and B–24's drop supplies in N Italy. P–38's and P–51's fly rcn and escort missions. Bad weather prevents HB bombing.

Tenth AF: 28 P–47's attack and damage bridges at Kawnghka, Namyao, Nampawng, Namhkai, and Hsenwi and demolish main bridge at Ho-kho. 8 P–47's spt ground forces in Bhamo area. 60-plus FBs hit enemy-held positions, troop concentrations, supply areas, warehouses, and general T/Os at Man Mau, Nwegyo, Hkayanzatkon, Mogok, Pangpong, Namahokgyi, Kyusa, Man Maw, Mongnaw, and Man Htam. Transports fly 308 sorties to forward areas.

Fourteenth AF: 24 B–25's, supported by 12 P–40's, hit bridges, buildings, and river, road, and rail traffic at several points in China, Indochina, and Burma including Lashio, Kutkai, Namhkai, Saiping, Hsiangcheng, Lingling, Kweilin area, between Minkiang and Sinantien, and between Sinyang and Saiping. 90-plus FBs on armed rcn pound numerous T/Os from Hsenwi to Nanning, Lang Son, and Namhkai and across S China from Burma border to Amoy.

Seventh AF: 3 B–24's from Guam hit Marcus while 3 from Saipan bomb Pagan. Snooper missions continue as 2 Marianas-based B–24's bomb Iwo Jima during 4/5 Dec.

Eleventh AF: A weather aircraft aborts shortly after takeoff.

5 December

Eighth AF: More than 500 HBs attack munitions and tank works at Berlin, Munster M/Y, and 10 T/Os. 15 escorting ftr gps encounter an estimated 275–300 ftrs and claim 90 destroyed.

Ninth AF: 172 A–20's, A–26's, and B–26's attack M/Y, road junction, fuel storage dump, defended positions, and rail bridge at 8 W German locations. Ftrs escort 9th Bomb Div, fly numerous armed rcn missions, and provide cover for US 1st, 8th, and 104th Inf Divs in Luchem, Bergstein, and Lucherberg areas.

Twelfth AF: Bad weather severely restricts operations. MB missions are cancelled except for a weather rcn flight. Ftrs and FBs hit a few rail lines and other comm tgts in E Po Valley but devote major effort to closely spt US Fifth Army in battle area S of Bologna.

Fifteenth AF: Bad weather again cancels HB operations. P-38's, escorted by P-51's, fly photo and weather rcn missions.

Tenth AF: 31 FBs spt ground forces in Bhamo area. 25 FBs hit Hay-ti, Meza, and 3 other road bridges. 20-plus FBs attack town areas, troop concentrations and storage facilities in or near Kawng-wai, Kunmong, Settawagon, and Thit-poklwin. 8 attack T/Os along Shwebo-Wuntho rail line. Transports complete 285 sorties carrying troops to forward bases and dropping supplies to frontline forces. 10 B-25's bomb comm center, supplies, and personnel concentration at Mogok. On this date Tenth AF airplanes begin Operation GRUBWORM, flying Chinese 14th and 22d Divs from Burma to China in preparation for Yunnan campaign to counter a probable Japanese drive toward Kunming.

Fourteenth AF: 7 B-24's on sweeps over Gulf of Tonkin, S China Sea, and Formosa Strait bomb Ft Bayard and Kowloon Docks and damage a freighter. 6 B-25's pound T/Os from Liuchow to Liuchenghsien. 61 P-40's, P-51's, and P-38's on armed rcn hit river, road, and rail traffic and other T/Os at scattered points mainly in S China.

FEAF: B-24's strike Hate Tabako, Galela, and Djailolo A/Fs. B-25's and A-20's lightly raid Miti and Kaoe A/Fs. B-25's hit Langoan while B-24's flying in pairs hit T/Os nearby and in N Borneo. FBs over C Phil area hit Japanese positions, barges, and comm tgts.

Seventh AF: P-47's from Saipan strafe runway on Pagan.

Eleventh AF: 6 B-24's off for a strike on Kakumabetsu abort due to weather. B-25's cancel a shipping sweep.

6 December

Eighth AF: Over 650 HBs, supported by ftrs flying over 750 sorties, bomb synthetic oil plant at Merseburg/Leuna, Minden aqueduct, Bielefeld M/Y, and several other tgts.

Ninth AF: 154 A-20's and B-26's bomb defended areas of Munstereifel, Erkelenz, Nideggen, and Daun. Ftrs escort bmrs, fly armed rcn and night patrol, attack bridges, gun positions, and other tgts, and provide air cover for US V, VII, and XII Corps in areas of Bergstein, Lucherberg, and Sarreguemines and along Saar R.

Twelfth AF: Heavy cloud cover, increasing in density throughout the day, severely restricts operations. MBs are grounded except for 1 rcn sortie. XXII TAC ftrs and FBs fly less than 100 sorties, attacking comm in Brescia, Verona, and Mantua areas.

Fifteenth AF: 270-plus HBs attack M/Ys at Graz, Szombathely, Sopron, Nagycenk, Hegyeshalom, Maribor, Bratislava, and Devinska Nova Ves, and town of Zalaegerszeg, plus scattered T/Os. P–51's and P–38's escort HBs, cover RAF supply missions to Yugoslavia, and strafe Vienna.

Tenth AF: 9 P–47's damage bridge at Namhkai and knock out bridge at Mongmit. 10 B–25's knock out main bridge at Bawgyo and damage bypass. 15 P–47's spt ground forces in Bhamo area, 4 bomb Hsenwi A/F, and 8 strafe Bawgyo AA positions. 12 P–47's hit troops, arty, and supplies at Banmauk, W side of Indawgyi Lake, and Namhkam. Transports fly 300 sorties to forward areas.

Fourteenth AF: 8 P–51's attack road traffic in Hsenwi area and from there to Wanling.

FEAF: B–24's pound Bacolod A/F. P–38's over Bacolod and others covering convoy off S Leyte claim several airplanes downed. B–25's, with P–47 spt, hit Cagayan, Jacgol, and Del Monte A/Fs. B–24's hit A/Fs at Kendari and Borebore. FBs and B–25's attack Halmahera I A/Fs while A–20's and B–25's bomb Namlea area.

Eleventh AF: 4 B–24's bomb Suribachi A/F, scoring hits on the runway, and blast batteries. On return flight, 1 is hit by AA fire. 1 B–25 flies a negative shipping search. A B–24 weather airplane force-lands in USSR.

7 December

Ninth AF: All missions except a few ftr patrols are cancelled because of bad weather.

Twelfth AF: Weather grounds MBs. Ftrs and FBs, despite weather, attack railroads, roads, bridges, rolling stock, and other tgts over widespread areas of N Italy, from La Spezia to N of Po Valley. Bad weather obscures most primaries but alternate tgts are fairly successfully hit.

Fifteenth AF: 31 B–17's and B–24's make predawn raids on Salzburg, Klagenfurt, Villach, and Lienz M/Ys, comm tgts in Wolfsberg, Spittal an der Drau, Mittersill, Sankt Veit in Defereggen, and Trieste. P–38's, and P–51's fly rcn and rcn escort missions.

Tenth AF: 9 B–25's knock out E span of road bridge at Tonbo. 21 P–47's spt ground forces in Bhamo area. 63 blast concentrations of enemy troops and supplies at Male while 4 others hit supplies at Myauk-le. 14 P–47's knock out bridge at Mansam and damage 3 bridges at Mongmit and Namyao. 17 others hit Nawnghkio and bomb supply areas at Na-kawnkongnyaung. Transport fly 267 sorties to forward areas.

Fourteenth AF: 8 B–25's hit storage area at Lashio. 4 B–25's and 8 P–40's attack and considerably damage Sankiao. 4 B–25's, operating individually, attack truck convoys and other T/Os in Hengyang area and in Siang-Chiang Valley. 2 B–24's claim 1 cargo vessel sunk in S China Sea while 15 P–51's hit shipping at Hong Kong, claiming a destroyer and freighter sunk. 65 P–51's, P–40's, and P–38's on armed rcn over wide areas of China attack storage areas, troops, bridges, railroad tgts, and gun positions around Paoching, Anking, Hengyang, Tuhshan, Nan Tan, Kengtung, and Luchai and between Kweilin and Liuchow.

FEAF: B–24's pound Malogo A/F, town of Masbate, and Legaspi A/F. B–25's hit Miti, Kaoe, Galela, and Lolobata A/Fs. Other FEAF aircraft fly armed rcn and harassing missions over Mindanao, N Borneo, and Makassar areas, attacking various T/Os.

Twentieth AF: 80 B–29's, operating from Chengtu, bomb Manchuria Airplane Manufacturing Company and adjacent arsenal at Mukden. 10 other B–29's bomb a rail yard short of the primary, and several other bmrs strike alternates. The VHBs claim 20 ftrs downed.

Seventh AF: Immediately following an enemy bombing raid on Saipan, 4 P–47's fly rcn over Pagan searching for aircraft but observe none.

Eleventh AF: 9 bmrs fly 2 negative shipping searches.

8 December

Eighth AF: As part of move to create self-sustaining, mobile air divs, all sub-depots are relieved from assignment to VIII AFSC and assigned to the 3 bomb divs with VIII AFSC retaining technical supervision.

Ninth AF: 29 A–26's hit Sinzig rail bridge. Ftrs escort RAF, bomb gun positions, bridges, and city areas, fly armed rcn, and spt US V and VII Corps W of Schmidt and Duren, and XX Corps and XII Corps in Sarreguemines and Dillingen areas.

Twelfth AF: Weather again greatly curtails operations. 4 P–47's on weather rcn of W Po Valley attack trains, claiming destruction of 4 locomotives and damage of almost 100 train cars. On 7/8 Dec 3 A–20's bomb T/Os in Po Valley.

Fifteenth AF: Again hitting comm tgts in predawn attack 24 B–17's and B–24's bomb Moosbierbaum oil refinery and Graz, Klagenfurt,

and Villach M/Ys. Later in the day P–38's fly photo and weather rcn missions. P–51's escort the photo rcn flights over Vienna area, W Hungary, and N Yugoslavia.

Tenth AF: 30-plus P–47's spt ground forces in Bhamo area. 28 hit supply areas at Kyingyi, Loi-Lun, and Hke-hkun. 12 bomb troop concentrations at Namti and 4 hit village on Nawnghkem. 16 FBs attack Shwebo motor pool and radio station while 6 others hit Namun ferry landing. 7 aircraft knock out a bypass bridge at Namhkai and 8 FBs hit railroad T/Os between Sedaw and Nawnghkio. Large-scale transport operations continue.

Fourteenth AF: 4 B–25's hit Nan Tan area, killing many horses. 14 P–51's hit A/F and other tgts at Nanking, claiming 24 airplanes, a freighter, and 2 locomotives destroyed. 15 P–40's blast railroad tgts and buildings from Nan Tan area to Liuchow. 25 P–51's hit Hochih and troops, warehouses, trucks and ammo dump in the area. 20-plus other FBs on armed rcn hit various T/Os around Lipo, Shihhweiyao, Tuhshan, Santon, Paoching, Hengyang, Taiyuan, and Linfen areas.

FEAF: 60-plus B–25's and FBs (along with RAAF airplanes) hit A/F and various other tgts on Halmahera. 60-plus B–24's bomb Mandurriao, Lahug and La Carlota A/Fs while FBs hit San Isidro area. FEAF aircraft fly armed rcn and light raids over N Borneo, N Celebes, Flores, and Wewak area.

Twentieth AF: 60-plus B–29's from the Marianas join P–38's, B–24's and Navy cruisers in strike against A/Fs on Iwo Jima from which Japanese strikes against US A/Fs in the Marianas are being launched. (Japanese aircraft strike the A/Fs on 2, 7, and 27 Nov, 7 and 25 (the largest attack—25 aircraft) Dec, and from 25 Dec 44 to 2 Jan 45 in very minor degrees. Altogether about 80 aircraft attack, and nearly 40 are downed. 11 B–29's are destroyed and 43 damaged).

Seventh AF: 89 B–24's from Guam and Saipan join B–29's and naval vessels in bombarding Iwo Jima A/Fs. 28 P–38's escort the B–29's. The strikes are aimed at reducing the raids against US bases in the Marianas.

9 December

Eighth AF: Nearly 400 B–17's bomb 2 A/Fs and a M/Y in Stuttgart area, along with 5 T/Os. 7 ftr gps fly escort and strafe transportation tgts.

Ninth AF: 254 A–20's, A–26's, and B–26's bomb defended villages, storage depots, barracks area, and M/Y in W Germany. Ftrs escort 9th Bomb Div, sweep Landau and Saarbrucken areas, attack Zulpich and bridge at Euskirchen, and spt XII and XX Corps in Sarreguemines and Saar R area and around Dillingen.

Twelfth AF: Bad weather grounds MBs. Ftrs and FBs attack comm in C and NE Po Valley.

Fifteenth AF: 170 HBs attack Linz industrial area and Villach M/Y, Regensburg oil refinery, and several Plzen armament works. P–51's and P–38's escort the HBs and fly rcn missions.

Tenth AF: 12 P–47's knock out a bridge at Mongmit, damage another and blast approach to Namyao bridge. Villages and building areas, supply dumps, and T/Os are attacked at Man Mao, Etgyi, Namhsim, Tawma and other points in N Burma. Transports continue flying men and supplies to forward areas, completing nearly 300 sorties.

Fourteenth AF: 12 B–25's bomb Lipo, Tuhshan, and Hochih. A B–25 attacks truck convoy in Siang-Chiang Valley while a B–24 claims 1 cargo ship sunk in S China Sea. 19 P–40's and P–51's hit river, road, and rail shipping and other T/Os from Kweiyi to Siangtan. 65 P–51's and P–40's hit similar T/Os around Kweilin, Liuchow, Lingling, Hengyang, Tuhshan, and Chuchou. 50 more FBs hit T/Os at several other locations scattered throughout S China.

FEAF: B–24's bomb Lingkas tank farm, Dondang R bridge and Sanga Sanga oil installations, and 3 A/Fs in Amboina-Ceram area. P–38's hit Old Namlea A/F. B–25's attack Wasile Bay area.

Seventh AF: 2 B–24's from Saipan during 9/10 Dec fly harassment strikes against Iwo Jima.

10 December

Eighth AF: Over 450 HBs strike M/Ys at Bingen and Koblenz-Lutzel and several T/Os supported by 10 ftr gps. 2 other gps sweep E of tgt area.

Ninth AF: About 130 B–26's bomb defended positions at Birkesdorf, and Huchem-Stammeln. Ftrs escort 9th Bomb Div, strafe and dive-bomb numerous tgts in W Germany, and spt US 8th, 9th, 83d, and 104th Inf Divs and 3d and 5th Armd Divs in areas around Bergstein, Duren, and along W bank of the Roer.

Twelfth AF: MBs bomb bridges,

fills, and tunnel in Brenner Pass area, hit Fidenza bridge and barracks at Bologna, and spt British Eighth Army in Faenza area, bombing defensive positions. XXII TAC tgts are again predominantly comm N of US Fifth Army battle zone.

Fifteenth AF: 550-plus B–17's and B–24's dispatched to bomb oil tgts in Germany are recalled because of overcast weather. 6 B–17's manage to bomb Klagenfurt M/Y as a T/O.

Tenth AF: 20 P–47's fly close spt strikes in Bhamo area. 8 others blast approaches to Hay-ti road bridge. 50-plus P–47's hit warehouses and other storage areas, troop concentrations, and positions at Daungbin, Myebalin, Kyaunghkam, Pongon, Thinbaung, Kawnghkang, Pangteng, and Hsipaw. 12 B–25's hit storage areas at Meza, Namun, and Kungmong. Transports fly 178 sorties to forward areas.

Fourteenth AF: 25 B–24's bomb city of Hankow. 3 others bomb Samah Bay docks. 8 B–25's bomb Kutkai and hit T/Os in Liuchow area. 118 P–40's, P–51's, and P–38's on armed rcn over wide areas of China attack numerous T/Os, concentrating on rail, river, and road traffic, especially in the Hochih, Changsha, and Yuncheng areas.

FEAF: In principal strikes of the day B–24's hit Pamoesian tank farm and nearby alternates of Lingkas tank farm, Labuan docks, and Lutong refinery, while B–25's pound Sidate A/F. In smaller raids P–38's hit port Misamis. B–25's bomb A/Fs on Boeroe and Amboina, and FBs pound storage facilities and T/Os in C Phil Is.

Seventh AF: 3 B–24's from Saipan and 1 from Guam fly harass-

ment strikes against Iwo Jima during 10/11 Dec.

11 December

Eighth AF: Over 1,400 HBs attack M/Ys at Frankfurt/Main, Hanau, and Giessen, and road and rail bridges at Mannheim and Maximiliansau, along with several T/Os. 15 ftr gps fly escort and 1 gp later strafes tgts in Kassel-Minden area.

Ninth AF: Over 200 bmrs dispatched to bomb defended villages and storage areas in Germany are recalled because of weather. 1 bmr manages to bomb stores depot at Reichenbach. Ftrs escort RAF, dive-bomb tgts in German cities, and spt US 3d Armd Div in Echtz-Geich area, 104th Inf Div at Merken, 9th Inf Div at Merode and Derichsweiler, and 83d Inf Div at Strass.

Twelfth AF: MBs hit Motta di Livenza bridge. Ftrs and FBs hit occupied areas, houses, guns, and defensive positions S of Bologna and attack railroad tgts in C Po Valley. During 10/11 Dec LBs attack vehicles, lights, railway lines, roads, river ferries, and pontoon bridges in Po Valley.

Fifteenth AF: 435 HBs, with ftr escorts, attack Moosbierbaum oil refinery, and in Vienna/Matzleinsdorf railroad station, S ordnance depot, and SE goods depot. Alternate tgts include Kapfenberg tank works, town of Tulln, Parndorf A/F, Graz M/Y, and various T/Os.

Tenth AF: 12 B–25's hit stores area at Hpaklon. 16 P–47's spt ground forces in Bhamo area. 21 P–47's knock out and damage bridges at Mongmit, Man Aitau, Ho-hko, and Pa-mao. 7 FBs severely damage Hsipaw ferry.

Supply and personnel concentrations and town areas are hit at Lawa, Myitson, Pemnegon, Nam Pan, Hsenwi, and Nawngpeng. 270 transport sorties are flown to forward areas.

Fourteenth AF: 6 B–24's and 6 B–25's, supported by 8 P–51's, pound Hai Duong area. 12 B–25's bomb Kutkai. 16 FBs attack Tien Ho A/F, Kengtung barracks, Lashio, and Wan Lai-Kam.

FEAF: In major air activity B–24's bomb Mandurriao A/F. B–25's, with P–47 spt, hit Padada A/F and Fifth AF ftrs join Marine aircraft in attacks on 13-ship convoy off NW Leyte. B–25's, A–20's, and FBs hit Goeroea. Other FEAF planes make small raids on oil and shipping tgts around N Borneo.

Seventh AF: Col Lawrence J Carr becomes CO of VII BC. 28 B–24's from Guam pound A/F and ammunition storage area on Iwo Jima. Night harassment of Iwo Jima continues as individual B–24's from Guam and Saipan fly 3 snooper strikes against the island during 11/12 Dec.

Eleventh AF: 4 MBs fly negative enemy shipping search.

12 December

Eighth AF: Nearly 1,200 HBs hit M/Ys at Darmstadt, Hanau, and Aschaffenburg, and synthetic oil plant at Merseburg/Leuna (all primary tgts); and other tgts including Friedberg M/Y, Gelnhausen, Nordhausen, Dieburg, and several T/Os. 15 ftr gps fly escort, 4 of them later strafing ground tgts.

Ninth AF: 90 B–26's and A–20's strike defended villages of Gemund, Harperscheid, Hellenthal, Schoneseiffen, Wollseiffen, and Schleiden, and towns of Dorsel, Mayen, and Wiesbaden. Ftrs fly armed rcn and strafing and bombing missions in W Germany and spt US 83d Inf Div in Strass-Gey area, cover VII Corps in Duren area, and spt XII and XX Corps in Habkirchen and Bliesbruck areas (35th Inf Div assault across Blies R) and Saarlautern-Dillingen.

Twelfth AF: Bad weather cancels all except 11 weather rcn sorties.

Fifteenth AF: 75 B–17's and B–24's bomb Blechhammer S oil refinery, Moravska-Ostrava, and several T/Os. Around 40 P–51's and P–38's fly rcn and rcn escort.

Tenth AF: 11 B–25's bomb several storage areas N of Lashio. 20-plus P–47's knock out bridges at Namyao, Inailong, and Kunlong, and damage others at Ho-hko, Hinlong, and Kunlong. 40-plus FBs hit Japanese HQ, trucks, town areas, troop concentrations, and supplies at Sedo, Pale, Chaunggyi, Tada-u, Hsenwi, Shwebo, and Thabyetha. 263 transport sorties are flown to forward areas.

Fourteenth AF: 6 B–25's bomb Kutkai, damaging 3 warehouses and 2 other buildings. 50-plus P–40's, P–51's, and P–38's on armed rcn attack many T/Os including town areas, road and rail traffic, and supplies at or near Wan Pa-Hsa, Chiengmai, Sinantien, Paoching, Hengyang, Changsha, Kweilin, Nan-Tan, Hochih, and Szeenhsien. Several FBs drop napalm on Yangtong A/F.

FEAF: B–24's, with ftr cover, bomb Bacolod A/F while B–25's hit San Roque A/F. B–24's pound Kendari A/F. In Amboina-Ceram-Boeroe area B–25's hit 3 A/Fs and attack barges. A–20's hit A/F on Efman I.

Twentieth AF: Serv gps of 313th Bomb Wg arrive on Tinian.

Seventh AF: 24 Saipan-based B-24's pound Iwo Jima. Individual B-24's from Saipan and Guam fly 5 snooper strikes against Iwo during 12/13 Dec.

Eleventh AF: The weather aircraft aborts mission due to weather.

13 December

Eighth AF: Over 200 B-17's dispatched against tgts in Germany are recalled when weather grounds ftr escort.

Ninth AF: 250 A-20's, A-26's, and B-26's hit supply dump at Schleiden, plus defended positions in several villages and M/Y at Euskirchen. Ftrs escort 9th Bomb Div, fly night bombing missions, attack tgts in Cologne area, and spt XX Corps in Dillingen-Saarlautern bridgehead area, and XII Corps in Habkirchen-Bliesbruck area along Blies R.

Twelfth AF: Weather again hampers operations. The only B-25 bombing mission of the day aborts. Ftrs and FBs attack mainly occupied areas and buildings in battle area S of Bologna, comm throughout C Po Valley, and coastal def and AA guns S of La Spezia.

Fifteenth AF: Weather restricts operations to rcn and escort missions.

Tenth AF: 12 B-25's bomb storage and personnel area at Mongmit. 7 P-47's damage approach to Hay-ti road bridge while 4 spt US inf forces near Tonkwa. Supply areas, personnel, Japanese-held buildings, vehicles, and general T/Os are hit by 60-plus FBs at several places including Hosi, Longkin, Kyauktaing, Tigyaing, Kantha, Man-pwe, and Konnyaung.

260-plus transport sorties carry men and supplies to forward areas.

Fourteenth AF: 6 B-25's severely damage warehouse area at Hsenwi. 2 bomb town of Wuming. 24 P-51's and P-38's hit town of Bac Ninh and rail yards at Phu Lang Thuong, and damage bridge at Chiengmai.

FEAF: B-24's bomb Carolina and Talisay A/Fs. B-25's bomb San Roque, Haroekoe, Amahai, Old Namlea, and Liang A/Fs. B-25's, P-38's, and P-47's on small raids hit shore positions at Galela Bay, while covering attempted rescue of downed pilot by PT boat, and bomb Goeroea supply area. Other B-25's and B-24's on rcn hit T/Os in Sulu Archipelago.

Twentieth AF: 70-plus B-29's from the Marianas bomb and considerably damage Mitsubishi aircraft engine plant at Nagoya as bombing accuracy is improved.

Seventh AF: With most of its personnel aboard the *Sea Flasher* and its equipment aboard the *Cape Catoche*, Seventh AF HQ arrives at Tanapag. Remainder of HQ arrives by air, 14–19 Dec. 15 Guam-based B-24's bomb Iwo Jima. 3 from Saipan, on armed rcn mission, bomb Marcus I. During 13/14 Dec 6 B-24's make individual harassment raids against Iwo Jima from Saipan and Guam.

Eleventh AF: 4 MBs weather-abort a shipping search.

14 December

Ninth AF: Bad weather grounds bmrs. Ftrs fly armed rcn, hit rail tgts and bridges, and spt US 2d and 99th Inf Divs in Monschau Forest, 8th Inf Div in Bergstein area, 78th Inf Div in Simmerath-Kesternich area, and XII and XX Corps around Habkirchen and Saarlautern.

Twelfth AF: MBs score effective hits on railroad bridges at Parma and Chivasso. Ftrs and FBs attack rail lines N of the immediate battle area and in Po Valley and hit guns and occupied areas on US Fifth Army front S of Bologna.

Fifteenth AF: Bad weather cancels all operations except 1 P-38 rcn mission.

Tenth AF: 12 B-25's again bomb supply and personnel area at Mongmit. Bodegon railroad bridge is severely damaged by 4 P-47's. 48 P-47's hit troop concentrations, supplies, and areas of active enemy movement at Panghkam, Hohai, Dobin, Kyaukpyintha, Ho-naw, Kunlong, and Nawngkyaung. 4 others spt ground forces near Tonkwa. Large-scale transport operations to forward areas continue. Japanese garrison at Bhamo prepares to withdraw.

Fourteenth AF: 6 B-25's bomb Loi Mwe while 10 P-38's and P-51's hit Kentung.

FEAF: B-24's pound A/Fs on Negros. B-25's hit Zettle Field in Sulu Archipelago and Namlea. Other planes carry out sweeps, armed rcn, and light raids against various tgts in C Phil Is, Luzon, Mindanao and Palawan Is, Halmahera, N Borneo, and Sulu Archipelago.

Twentieth AF: 33 B-29's, flying out of Calcutta area, bomb railroad bridge at Bangkok. 14 others hit T/Os and alternate tgts.

Seventh AF: 24 Saipan-based B-24's pound Iwo Jima. During 14/15 Dec 6 B-24's from Guam and Saipan fly individual snooper strikes against Iwo Jima.

15 December

Eighth AF: Around 650 HBs strike Hannover M/Y, Kassel tank factories and M/Y, and 9 T/Os. 11 ftr gps fly escort.

Ninth AF: 300-plus A-20's, A-26's, and B-26's hit defended positions, camp area, and oil storage at Heimbach, Wollseifen, Harperscheid, Schonau, Ruthen, and Dorsel. Ftrs escort 9th bomb Div, hit supply and ammo dumps and other tgts during bombing attacks and armed rcn, and spt US 2d and 99th Inf Divs in area of Westwall fortifications, 78th Div at Kesternich, and 8th Inf and 5th Armd Div N of Kesternich. Ftrs spt XX and XII Corps in Dillingen-Saarlautern area and at Habkirchen and heights along Blies R.

Twelfth AF: B-25's, attack ammo dumps at Cremona, Bologna, and Pavia, fuel dump at Castellar Guidobono, and severely damage railway bridges S of Asti and at Voghera. Ftrs and FBs again hit tgts in US Fifth Army battle area S of Bologna and comm in C Po Valley and make numerous rail cuts throughout the area (especially on the vital Brenner Line) destroying many vehicles and train cars. Several bridges are hit, 3 being left impassable.

Fifteenth AF: 330-plus HBs attack main M/Ys, main station, and freight yard at Linz, M/Ys at Amstetten, Salzburg, Innsbruck, and Rosenheim (all primary tgts) and T/Os including Klagenfurt and Waldhausen M/Y and town of Sankt Johann in Tirol. Schwaz M/Y is also hit (due to malfunction of instruments). 250-plus P-38's and P-51's provide escort.

Tenth AF: 10 B-25's destroy Hsipaw railroad bridge and a bypass bridge at Namhkai and damage other bridges at Namhkai. 4 P–47's severely damage 2 bridges at Ho-hko. 7 P–47's fly close spt strikes along Namh-Kam-Bhamo road. Japanese garrison at Bhamo escapes through Chinese lines early in the morning and later Chinese troops occupy the town. 13 P–47's hit Lashio A/F. Town areas, troop concentrations, and supply areas are attacked at Panglong, Nanponpon, Panghkam, Kinu, Man Hpai, and Namhkam. Steady air movement of men and supplies to forward bases and frontline areas continues.

Fourteenth AF: 6 B–25's blast storage building at Kunlong. 5 P–51's hit and damage a bridge and a building S of Huizan. 4 P–38's knock out bridge at Hawng Luk.

FEAF: In major strikes of the day, FBs hit fuel dump at San Fernando; B–24's and B–25's bomb Sasa and San Roque A/Fs; B–24's bomb Puerto Princesa; and B–25's hit A/Fs on Ceram and Amboina. Miscellaneous armed rcn and light raids by ftrs and bmrs are flown against A/Fs on Boeroe I and on Halmahera; shipping and other T/Os are attacked at several points throughout NEI.

Seventh AF: 13 B–24's from Guam bomb Iwo Jima. During 15/16 Dec a B–24 on snooper raid from Guam hits the island.

ZI: Continental AF is activated to coordinate the work of the 4 domestic AFs and I TC Cmd but will not assume jurisdiction until 8 May 45.

16 December

Eighth AF: Over 100 B–17's supported by 3 ftr gps bomb Stuttgart M/Y, city of Bietigheim, and a T/O.

Ninth AF: Bad weather cancels 9th Bomb Div combat operations. Ftrs escort RAF, fly night patrol and intercept missions, and spt US First Army elements in Ardennes as German FM von Rundstedt begins all-out counteroffensive, and XII and XX Corps at Saarlautern bridgehead and in Saint-Avold-Saarbrucken area where news of Ardennes counteroffensive cancels XII Corps plans for assault on Westwall.

Twelfth AF: Bad weather grounds MBs. XXII TAC FBs hit occupied buildings and guns in battle zone S of Bologna, continue attacks on Brenner rail line effecting 16 rail cuts, hit and set aflame 3 vessels in La Spezia drydock, and blast several railroad bridges N of battle area.

Fifteenth AF: Almost 600 B–24's and B–17's bomb synthetic oil plant at Brux and armament works at Plzen, benzol plant at Linz, and M/Ys at Innsbruck and Villach, plus several scattered T/Os. P–38's and P–51's escort operations to Czechoslovakia. Other P–38's fly rcn missions while P–51's fly rcn escort.

Tenth AF: 4 P–47's spt US ground forces near Tonkwa. Locomotives, storage areas, buildings, personnel, and areas of Japanese activity are attacked at Se-eng, Nanponpon, Kangon, Winghsa, Inywa, Molo, and Mabein. Large-scale air supply to forward areas continues.

FEAF: Major operations of FEAF include B–24 strikes on Padada and Puerto Princesa A/Fs. B–25's, A–20's, and FBs attack A/Fs and T/Os including shipping in Ceram area and in C Phil Is. T/Os are also attacked in N Borneo and in Vogelkop Peninsula area.

Seventh AF: Daytime activities are

limited to rcn flights by B–24's over the Bonin and Kazan Is and by P–47's over Pagan. During 16/17 Dec 3 B–24's from Guam and Saipan fly individual snooper strikes against Iwo Jima.

17 December

Ninth AF: Weather prevents bmr operations. Over 1,000 ftrs fly armed rcn, defensive patrols, and attacks on bridges and gun positions. IX and XIX TACs also spt ground forces (8th, 28th, 78th, 99th, and 106th Inf Divs, 5th Armd Div, V, VII, VIII, XII, and XX Corps) against counteroffensive in the Ardennes and in battle to hold Saarlautern bridgehead.

Twelfth AF: Bad weather again cancels MB operations. XXII TAC hits comm in Po Valley and attacks Trento M/Y on rail line running N to Brenner Pass.

Fifteenth AF: 550-plus HBs bomb oil refineries at Blechhammer N and S, Odertal and Moravska-Ostrava, M/Ys at Gross Strehlitz, Villach, Saak, Salzburg, and Wels. P–38's and P–51's escort HBs, fly rcn, strafe railroad running from Rosenheim into Austria, and escort photo rcn operations. Enemy ftrs appear in force for first time since Aug HBs and ftrs claim 55 air victories.

Tenth AF: 8 P–47's spt ground forces in Namhkam sector. 8 more P–47's hit rail T/Os between Kyaikthin to Kinu, then E to the Irrawaddy and up the river to Tigyaing. 4 hit rivercraft at Tagaung. 50-plus FBs attack storage areas, vehicles, bivouacs, personnel areas, and general T/Os at Pang-hsao, Kyaukme, Manai, Kutkai, Ma-ugon, Hpa-ye, and Man Namman. 12 more strafe T/Os during

Kyaukme-Nampyao railroad sweep. 290 transport sorties are flown.

Fourteenth AF: 9 B–24's pound Camranh Bay area. 5 B–25's bomb road at Wan Pa-Hsa while 12 FBs hit nearby railroad bridge, damaging it severely.

FEAF: B–24's pound Bacolod A/F while B–25's hit Silay A/F. P–40's join Marine FBs in attacking Cananga area and P–38's destroy several aircraft during sweeps over Negros. B–25's bomb Likanan while B–24's with P–47 spt, hit Jolo A/F. FBs hit positions at Valencia. B–24's and FBs attack Jesselton and Laha A/Fs.

Seventh AF: 24 B–24's from Saipan and 26 from Guam pound Iwo Jima. 3 from Saipan, on armed rcn, bomb Woleai Atoll and Eauriprik. During 17/18 Dec B–24's from Saipan and Guam fly 3 single-plane harassment strikes against Iwo Jima.

18 December

Eighth AF: Over 350 HBs hit M/Ys at Cologne-Kalk, Kaiserslautern, and Mainz, areas of Koblenz, Lutzel, and Bonn, and several T/Os. Bad weather causes over 500 aborts. 7 ftr gps fly escort.

Ninth AF: 160-plus A–26's, A–20's, and B–26's hit defended positions at Harperscheid, Hellenthal, Blumenthal, Dreiborn, and Herhahn. Ftrs fly sweeps and armed rcn over W Germany (claiming over 40 enemy airplanes downed plus hitting numerous ground tgts) and spt US 2d, 4th, 28th, and 106th Inf Divs W of Butgenbach, W of Trier, SE of Clervaux, and SE of Saint-Vith, and XII Corps at Niedergailbach. IX TAC hits Panzer units spearheading Bulge.

Twelfth AF: Weather again curtails operations. XXII TAC ftrs and FBs hit comm in E Po Valley, scoring particular success against lines in N part of the Valley in Padua region, and spt US Fifth Army operations in battle area S of Bologna.

Fifteenth AF: 560-plus HBs hit oil refineries at Blechhamer (2), Odertal, Vienna/Floridsdorf, Moravska-Ostrava, and Auschwitz; M/Ys at Graz, Studenzen, and Sopron; Bruck an der Mur industrial area, and various scattered T/Os. Ftrs fly escort and rcn missions.

Tenth AF: 12 B–25's knock out two railroad bridges at Wetlet and damage another at Saye. 17 P–47's destroy bypass bridges at Hinlong and Wingkang. 11 P–47's hit A/F at Nawnghkio while 12 others sweep A/Fs at Anisakan, Hsumhsai, and Nawnghkio. 9 FBs provide close spt to ground forces in Namhkam. 17 P–47's attack personnel and supply areas at Man Ton and Hseing-hkai. 292 transports fly men and supplies to forward bases and battle areas.

Fourteenth AF: 33 B–24's bomb barracks and administrative buildings at Hankow. 23 B–25's hit Wuchang. 7 B–25's bomb barracks and damage a bridge at Siaokan A/F while 6 others pound storage buildings at Kunlong. 149 P–40's and P–51's spt the Hankow, Siaokan, and Wuchang raids and claim 42 aircraft downed and destroyed on the ground. 20 P–51's and P–38's follow the B–25 strike on Kunlong with napalm attacks, causing considerable damage. 28 other P–40's and P–51's attack various T/Os around Hochih, Nanning, Mengmao, Wanling, Sang Song, and Phu Lang Thuong.

FEAF: FBs destroy bridge on Palompon-Cananga road on Leyte and pound Calatagan A/F. B–25's hit San Roque A/F. FBs attack Tanao harbor and A/F and T/Os in Tarakan area, strafe seaplane facilities at Sanga Sanga, and bomb Haroekoe A/F.

Twentieth AF: 63 B–29's flying out of the Marianas hit Mitsubishi aircraft plant at Nagoya. 10 others bomb last resort tgts and T/Os. 84 B–29's, flying out of Chengtu area, drop incendiaries on docks at Hankow in the first mass firebomb attack by B–29's. The strike is made in conjunction with 200 aircraft of Fourteenth AF. 5 other VHBs hit alternates.

Seventh AF: 6 Guam-based B–24's flying armed photo rcn over Moen, Param, and Eten bomb Dublon. After photographing A/Fs on the 3 islands, the HBs return by way of Woleai, Puluwat, and Namonuito and photograph all 3 atolls. During 18/19 Dec, 4 B–24's from Guam and Saipan fly snooper strikes against Iwo Jima.

19 December

Eighth AF: Over 300 HBs attack Ehrang and Koblenz M/Ys and 8 W German rail and road junctions, rail and road chokepoints, and railhead tgts. Only 1 ftr gp flies escort as weather grounds others.

Ninth AF: All administrative sections and extra operational equipment of XXIX TAC are moved from Maastricht to Saint-Trond to avert transportation problems should XXIX TAC be subsequently forced into a hasty withdrawal. Weather grounds bmrs. Ftrs fly armed rcn in W Germany, escort RAF Lancasters, fly patrols from Belgium to the Rhine, spt US 1st, 2d, 99th, and 106th Inf Divs, and 7th Armd Div (N and E of Malmedy and SE and SW of Saint-Vith), and fly cover for US Twelfth Army troops and XII Corps near Verdun and Saint-Avold.

Twelfth AF: Weather grounds MBs. XXII TAC ftrs and FBs, unable to reach primary tgts further N, hit comm N of battle area but concentrate mainly on gun positions in La Spezia area.

Fifteenth AF: More than 400 B-24's and B-17's attack Blechhammer N and S and Moravska-Ostrava oil refineries, Rosenheim rail sidings and M/Y and Strasshof, Villach, Klagenfurt, Graz, Innsbruck, and Sopron M/Ys, town of Sternberk, and several scattered T/Os. P-38's and P-51's fly rcn missions and escort HBs.

Tenth AF: 12 B-25's hit road junctions at Mongmit and S of Kyaukme, Kyaukme railroad station, and Hsenwi bridge. 7 P-47's severely damage Tonbo road bridge, and 11 others hit T/Os during Onmaka-Hsoplong rail sweep. 42 P-47's pound supply and personnel areas and troops at Myadaung, Tantabin, and Twinnge, village of Nyaugbintha, and truck park near Humon. 300-plus transport sorties are flown to forward areas.

Fourteenth AF: 16 B-25's, escorted by 24 P-40's, attack Pengpu. 4 P-38's bomb Wanling-Mongyu road causing traffic block. 4 P-51's claim 2 freighters sunk off Hong Kong. 2 P-40's destroy 3 locomotives and a truck at Sinyang.

FEAF: Ftr-supported B-25's bomb Fabrica A/F. Ftrs on sweep over Ponay, Negros, and Leyte hit Fabrica, Bacolod, Silay, Dumaguete and Alicante A/Fs, and town of Palompon. B-24's bomb Legaspi A/F while P-38's hit Batangas A/F. B-25's, A-20's, and P-38's pound Kairatoe area. Other FEAF aircraft on armed rcn, sweeps, and small strikes hit T/Os at many locations throughout NEI and Phil Is.

Twentieth AF: 17 B-29's, from Chengtu area, hit aircraft plant at Omura, 13 others hit secondary tgt of Shanghai, and another 2 strike other alternates.

Seventh AF: HQ Seventh AF is officially opened at Tanapag. 27 B-24's from Saipan and 25 from Guam strike Iwo Jima. 3 on armed rcn from Guam bomb Marcus. 14 P-38's from Saipan, with 3 B-29's as navigational escort, strafe A/Fs on Iwo Jima. 4 B-25's from Guam and Saipan carry out 3 snooper strikes against Iwo Jima during 19/20 Dec.

ZI: 4 ftrs of Fourth AF, directed by Los Angeles Control Gp to search for Japanese balloon reported over Santa Monica, are unable to locate the tgt.

20 December

Ninth AF: Bad weather prevents all combat operations, except night intruder mission by 2 ftrs.

Twelfth AF: Continued bad weather limits operations. MBs are grounded and overcast prevents ftrs and FBs to reach many tgts in C and E Po Valley. However, the Brenner line is cut S of Trento and trains are successfully attacked near Padua and Treviso. Armed rcn in W Po Valley accounts for several locomotives, vehicles, and other T/Os, and railroads, bridges, and T/Os are hit in the La Spezia and Genoa areas. During 19/20 Dec LBs attack lights at 5 locations in E Po Valley.

Fifteenth AF: For fifth consecutive day, HBs hit Axis oil production. 454 HBs hit Regensburg oil refinery, M/Ys at Linz, Salzburg, and Villach, and armament works at Plzen. Over 300 P–38's and P–51's provide escort. 40-plus others fly rcn and rcn-escort missions.

Tenth AF: 9 B–25's destroy 3 road bridges at Mongmit, bypass bridges at Tangon and Tantabin, and 3 bridges in N Burma. 3 other MBs blast ferry area at Thabeikkyin. 12 P–47's knock out Hay-ti road bridge and damage Pa-mao bridge. 12 other FBs sweep the Irrawaddy from Sheinmaga to Twinnge, strafing several T/Os. 13 P–47's spt ground forces in Namhkam sector. Troops, supply areas, and buildings are pounded at Hseing-hkai, Tigyaing, Na-kawnkongnyaung, and Man Hkunhawng. Transport operations to front areas total 284 sorties.

Fourteenth AF: 118 P-51's and P–40's on armed rcn over S China and E Burma attack road, rail, and river traffic and other T/Os, mainly in or near Wanling, Mongyu, Monhkong, Lashio, Hochih, Chinchenchiang Hong Kong, Sinyang, Lohochai, Leiyang, Kweilin, Sintsiang, Siangtan, Paoching, Liuchenghsien, Hengshan, and Hengyang.

FEAF: 150-plus B–24's, B–25's, and FBs pound 10 A/Fs throughout C Phil Is and 3 on Mindanao. In NEI B–24's hit Malang A/F and B–25's hit Haroekoe. Numerous other single FEAF flights and small forces attack a large variety of T/Os throughout NEI and the Phil Is.

Seventh AF: 23 B–24's, based on Saipan, pound Iwo Jima. During 20/21 Dec 6 B–24's from Guam and Saipan hit Iwo Jima with 5 snooper strikes.

Eleventh AF: A B–24 flies armed rcn over the Kurils. Another B–24 strikes Onnekotan installations, while 2 more flying armed photo mission over Kashiwabara and Kataoka also strafe buildings on Onnekotan and bomb Nemo Bay. 4 B–25's abort a fighter-decoy mission due to weather.

21 December

Ninth AF: IX and XXIX TACs are transferred from Ninth AF to British Second Tac AF control to operate against the N line of the Bulge. XIX TAC flies armed weather and intruder rcn in Saarbrucken-Trier area. Weather grounds all operations.

Twelfth AF: During 20/21 Dec A–20's attack highways, secondary roads, and T/Os in N and C Po Valley. During the day, bad weather grounds MBs and reduces ftr and FB operations of XXII TAC. However, XXII TAC aircraft are effective against railroad tgts in Treviso area and damage Ghedi A/F. Trains, vehicles, guns, and buildings are attacked in or near Mantua, Milan, Turin, La Spezia, Padua, and Mestre.

Fifteenth AF: 84 B–24's bomb main M/Y and railroad sidings at Rosenheim. 40 P–51's provide escort. Over 40 P–38's fly photo rcn and rcn escort missions.

Tenth AF: 12 B–25's bomb supply and personnel area at Magyidon. 13 P–47's damage bridges at Hay-ti, Mong Long, and Pa-Mao. Rail T/Os from Hsumhsai to Hsipaw are attacked by 12 P–47's. More than 20 FBs hit troop concentrations at several points including Man Ka-lao and general area E of Shweli R. 12 P–47's bomb and strafe Lashio area. 290-plus transport sorties are flown to forward bases and frontline areas.

Fourteenth AF: 145 P–40's and P–51's fly armed rcn over wide expanses of S China, E Burma and N Indochina. The ftrs attack chiefly troops and river, road, and rail traffic and a variety of T/Os at numerous locations. 9 B–25's bomb Kunlong and Minkiang.

FEAF: B–24's, B–25's, and FBs pound 10 A/Fs mostly on Negros and elsewhere in C Phils. Leyte-based FBs fly over 100 attack sorties. Likanan A/F is also hit by HBs. B–25's pound Goeroea, Anggai, and Lolobata.

Twentieth AF: 19 B–29's from Chengtu attack Mukden. The primary objective (Manchuria Airplane Manufacturing Company) suffers little damage and nearby arsenal and rail yards are slightly damaged. 8 other VHBs bomb alternates and T/Os.

Seventh AF: 23 Guam-based B–24's hit Iwo Jima. During 21/22 Dec, 4 B–24's from the Marianas fly 3 harassment strikes against Iwo Jima.

22 December

Ninth AF: 3 ftr gps of IX TAC are transferred to XIX TAC to concentrate air power for cooperation with US Third Army to which main effort against the Bulge has been assigned. The gps return to control of IX TAC on 25 Dec. Ftrs fly a few strafing, weather rcn, intruder patrol, and alert missions. Bad weather cancels all other missions.

Twelfth AF: During 21/22 Dec A–20's hit scattered tgts in Po Valley. Clearing weather during the day enables MBs to hit bridges at Torre Beretti, Pontetidone, and at Chiari. FBs concentrate on railway tgts, destroying 5 bridges in N Italy and making numerous cuts in rail lines, several on the important Brenner line. Motor transport and guns N of battle area are also successfully attacked.

Fifteenth AF: Bad weather restricts operations to rcn, supply dropping, and escort missions over Germany, Austria, Czechoslovakia, Hungary, and Yugoslavia.

Tenth AF: 12 B–25's bomb supply area at Magyidon. 8 P–47's knock out Namhkai bypass bridge and damage 2 bridges at Kinu. 16 hit T/Os along Irrawaddy R from Tagaung to Thabeikkyin and along road E and N to Mongmit. 12 P–47's bomb and strafe personnel area at Onbauk and bridge at Na-lang. More than 300 transport sorties are flown to forward areas.

Fourteenth AF: 4 B–25's damage bridge at Song Hoa. 2 B–25's bomb Yungning. 80-plus P–51's and P–40's on armed rcn over wide reaches of S China, E Burma, and N Indochina hit numerous T/Os. A/Fs at Heho and Tien Ho are strafed and several airplanes are destroyed in battles over Canton and Kai Tek A/Fs. Rail facilities, river and road traffic, and other T/Os are hit at several locations including Chinchengchiang, Wanling, Gia Lam, and Pingsiang-Yungning area.

FEAF: B–24's, with P–47 spt, bomb Clark Field while P–40's bomb and strafe Lipa A/F. B–24's bomb Carolina A/F while B–25's, with P–47 cover, hit Fabrica A/F. On Mindanao B–24's bomb storage and personnel areas while B–25's hit waterfront at Zamboanga. FEAF aircraft fly numerous shipping searches, armed rcn, and sweeps over Mindanao and throughout NEI. Numerous FBs pound Wasile R and Goeroea areas and Hate Tabako A/F. US and RAAF B-24's, B-25's, and FBs bomb Lolobata and Hate Tabako A/Fs and Goeroea area.

Twentieth AF: 48 B-29's from XXI BC hit Mitsubishi aircraft industrial complex. Total cloud cover prevents accuracy, and damage is light. B-29's claim 9 ftrs downed.

Seventh AF: During 22/23 Dec 2 Guam and Saipan-based B-24's make harassing strikes on Iwo Jima.

23 December

Eighth AF: Almost 400 HBs attack M/Ys at Ehrang, Kaiserslautern, and Homburg/Saar, comm centers at Junkerath, Ahrweiler, and Dahlem, rail junction at Homburg/Saar, and several T/Os. 7 P-51 gps fly escort and encounter an estimated 75-100 ftrs, claiming 23 shot down. 3 ftr gps on sweeps encounter about 350 ftrs and claim 46 destroyed.

Ninth AF: Around 500 B-26's and A-20's attack rail bridges, comm tgts, villages, rail junction and T/Os in Germany losing 31 bmrs. Ftrs fly bmr escort, armed rcn, and patrols (claiming over 100 aircraft downed and 3 A/Fs bombed), and spt ground forces between Werbomont and Butgenbach along N battleline of Bulge and US III, VIII, and XII Corps forces along S battleline of the Bulge.

Twelfth AF: On 22/23 Dec A-20's on intruder patrols hit Po R crossings and T/Os. Bad weather during day grounds MBs. FBs operate in W Po Valley, mainly against railway comm. A/F near Milan is attacked, and several enemy airplanes destroyed.

Fifteenth AF: Bad weather again limits operations to rcn, supply dropping, and escort missions over C and E Europe.

Tenth AF: 15 P-47's knock out and damage bridges at Mong Long, Pa-mao, and Man Pwe. 12 B-25's destroy bridges at Tonbo, Saye, Ketka, and Nampawng, and damage several others. 40-plus FBs attack storage areas, bivouacs, and enemy-held points at Namhkam, Nyaunggyin, Hseinghkai, Mongyin, and Kutkai. Transport sorties to forward bases and front-line areas total 353.

Fourteenth AF: 8 B-25's pound points along Burma Road. 13 B-25's hit town areas, trains, and other T/Os at Vinh, from Dap Cau to Lungchow, and from Lang Son to Yungning. In China 3 B-25's and 5 P-40's damage about 50 railroad cars in area S of Yellow R. 16 P-51's over Wuchang and Hankow damage 2 ferry ramps and blast 3 oil dumps. 12 P-51's and P-38's damage 2 hangars at Heho A/F, 12 P-51's pound railroad shops at Chenghsien, and bomb Houmachen with napalm.

FEAF: B-24's bomb Fabrica and Silay A/Fs. P-38's and P-47's provide cover. B-24's bomb Grace Park A/F and B-25's pound San Roque A/F and Davao and Zamboanga areas. B-25's and FBs blast Lolobata, Hate Tabako, and Goeroea area. Again numerous FEAF aircraft fly various small strikes, armed rcn, and sweeps over Phil Is and NEI. FBs are especially active against tgts in C Phil Is and Halmahera.

Seventh AF: 12 B-24's from Saipan and 14 from Guam hit Iwo Jima. 3 others from Guam, flying armed rcn mission, bomb Woleai. During the night 2 B-24's from Guam and Saipan fly harassing strikes against Iwo Jima.

Eleventh AF: The weather mission finds squall conditions and is aborted.

24 December

Eighth AF: Almost 1,900 (of over 2,000 dispatched) HBs attack 11 A/Fs, 14 comm centers, and numerous other tgts including 2 M/Ys, 5 cities, and over 50 T/Os—all in battle areas. 13 ftr gps meet over 200 enemy ftrs and claim 70 destroyed.

Ninth AF: 276 MBs and LBs hit rail bridges and comm centers in W Germany. Ftrs escort 9th Bomb Div, fly armed rcn, and spt US III, VIII, and XII Corps along S battleline of the Bulge, stretching from Echternach to area NW of Neufchateau, as 4th Armd Div reaches enemy's ring around Bastogne.

Twelfth AF: Weather again holds operations to a minimum. However, P–47's carry out very successful raid on Thiene A/F, causing considerable damage and destroying several enemy airplanes. Other missions find little activity and result in destruction of only a few trucks and trains.

Fifteenth AF: Unfavorable weather curtails all but photo and weather rcn missions.

Tenth AF: 38 P–47's hit troop concentrations and supply areas at Pangkai, Man-namman, Man Om, Mong Nge, and Kyanhnyat. 6 spt ground forces in Si-U sector while 12 hit T/Os along Sinlum-Nawghkio rail line. 8 P–47's strafe A/F at Lashio. 287 transport sorties are flown to forward areas.

Fourteenth AF: 6 B–25's blast Kunlong ferry area. 3 B–24's claim 1 tanker sunk in S China Sea. 100- plus P–40's, P–51's, and P–38's on armed rcn attack T/Os throughout S China, especially river, road, and rail traffic, troops, and buildings around Hengyang, Lingling, Siangtan, and Changsha. Also Hong Kong area shipping is pounded (1 tanker claimed sunk and other ships damaged) and 30-plus enemy airplanes claimed destroyed at Tsinan A/F.

FEAF: B–24's bomb Clark Field, Puerto Princesa, and Kudat A/Fs. B–25's and FBs blast Goeroea area, bomb Silay A/F and hit San Roque barracks, Zamboanga waterfront, and Davao Bay shipping. Again FEAF aircraft on miscellaneous small operations attack many tgts throughout NEI and Phil Is.

Twentieth AF: 23 XXI BC B–29's attack 2 A/Fs on Iwo Jima.

Seventh AF: 12 B–24's from Saipan and 38 from Guam strike Iwo Jima. 17 Saipan-based P–38's make low-level strafing attack on Iwo Jima. 23 other B–24's, based on Saipan, bomb Chichi Jima. 2 B–24's on harassment strikes from the Marianas hit Iwo Jima during 24/25 Dec.

25 December

Eighth AF: Over 350 HBs hit 18 tgts (mostly rail bridges and comm centers) in the tac area W of the Rhine. 9 escorting ftr gps encounter over 300 ftrs and claim more than 40 kills.

Ninth AF: Nearly 650 MBs and LBs hit rail and road bridges, comm centers and T/Os in W Germany and breakthrough area. Ftrs, including an Eighth AF gp loaned to Ninth, escort 9th Bomb Div, fly patrols and armed rcn, and spt US III, VIII, and XII Corps along S battleline of enemy salient from Echternach to NW of Neufchateau.

Twelfth AF: Clearing weather in Po Valley permits FBs to successfully cut numerous rail lines running N to Brenner Pass, and lines in E Po Valley, destroying or damaging several locomotives.

Fifteenth AF: 253 HBs hit Brux synthetic oil plant and main M/Y at Wels. 145 others bomb M/Ys at Plattling, Villach, Hall, Graz, Innsbruck (2), and Rosswein and Innsbruck AA position and rail siding. Over 30 ftrs escort Brux-Wels-Rosswein-Plattling raids. Other P-38's and P-51's fly rcn escort and cover MATAF B-25's on Yugoslav supply run.

Tenth AF: 4 P-47's bomb and strafe troop concentrations and supplies at Mabein. 8 others sweep Burma Road stretches and strafe Lashio A/F. Transports fly 259 sorties delivering men and supplies to forward bases and frontline areas.

Fourteenth AF: 6 B-25's and 8 FBs knock out bridge at Wan Pa-Hsa. 22 P-51's pound railroad ferry, damage tanker at Nanking, and hit nearby A/F, claiming 13 airplanes destroyed. 30-plus other P-51's, P-40's, and P-38's on armed rcn hit various T/Os around Yungning, Kunming, Kiungshan, Paoching, Wanling, Man Pong, and Mong Long.

FEAF: B-24's, with ftr spt, bomb Mabalacat, Sasa, Sandakan and Jesselton A/Fs. B-25's, along with RAAF FBs, hit Galela area. Other B-25's and FBs pound Mindanao and Halmahera I tgts again during several smaller raids throughout the day.

Seventh AF: 12 B-24's from Saipan bomb Iwo Jima. B-24's from Guam and Saipan continue night strikes against Iwo Jima during 25/ 26 Dec.

26 December

Eighth AF: Over 100 HBs attack 3 M/Ys and 2 bridges at Andernach, Neuwied, Sinzig, and Niederlahnstein, and 3 other tgts in W German battle area. 5 ftr gps fly escort and 2 others fly sweeps in Bonn area.

Ninth AF: 9th Bomb Div attacks road junctions, rail bridges, rail head, comm and casual tgts in breakthrough area as enemy's westward drive ends short of the Maas R. Ftrs fly escort, armed rcn, sweeps, and spt US III and VIII Corps S of Bastogne, as US 4th Armd Div breaks ring around the city.

Twelfth AF: Good weather permits operations in force for first time in several days. During 25/26 Dec A-20's bomb area between battleline and Bologna, attack lights, motor transport, and railroads in Po Valley, and hit Vicenza A/F. During the day MBs concentrate on Brenner Pass and hit Padua, San Ambrogio di Valpolicella, Ponte di Piave, Dolce, Pordenone railroad bridge, and 2 dumps in Bologna area. FBs bomb railways, especially Brenner line, bridges in Po Valley, and NE Italy, spt US Fifth Army forces S of Bologna and in Serchio R Valley where Germans begin series of counterattacks, and hit shipping at La Spezia and Genoa.

Fifteenth AF: Around 380 B-24's and B-17's bomb Odertal, Blechhammer S, and Auschwitz oil refineries, railroad bridge at Ora and viaduct at Avisio, plus scattered T/Os. 26 P-38's bomb railroad bridge at

Latisana. P–38's and P–51's escort the HB missions.

Tenth AF: 8 B–25's knock out and damage bridges at Taunggon, Padan, and Kyaukhlebein. 34 P–47's hit troop concentrations at Panghai, Mongyu, Na-hsang, Man Om, and Hpa-lin. 8 others hit stores area and distributing point at Hsenwi, 11 attack supplies at Pangpao, and 2 bomb rafts, boats, and landing points at Myitson ferry. 4 B–25's fly offensive night rcn against comm lines. 275 transport sorties are flown to forward areas.

Fourteenth AF: 6 B–25's bomb Wan Lai-Kam. 5 B–25's hit T/Os in Formosa Strait, in Siang-Chiang Valley, and at Ikiawan and Changsha. 12 P–51's attack Tsinan A/F. 46 P–51's, P–38's, and P–40's hit railroad tgts, shipping, storage and other T/Os at or near Kinkiang, Anking, Ka-chun, Lampang, Monglong Valley, and Man Pong.

FEAF: B–24's pound Clark Field. B–25's hit Matina A/F, shipping in Davao R, and bomb nearby Samal I. B–24's hit Libby A/F. B–25's, B–24's, and FBs hit Galela, Lolobata, and Hate Tabako. Miscellaneous attacks by other FEAF airplanes are flown against tgts in N Borneo, NE Celebes, and Halmahera.

Seventh AF: 13 Guam-based B–24's hit Iwo Jima. 3 from Saipan fly armed rcn and bomb Marcus. 2 HBs from the Marianas strike Iwo Jima during 26/27 Dec.

27 December

Eighth AF: Nearly 600 HBs attack tgts in battle area of W Germany, including 8 M/Ys, 4 rail bridges, 2 rail junctions, cities of Hildesheim and Eckfeld, and 13 T/Os. 4 ftr gps fly spt. 5 other gps on sweeps engage about 200 ftrs in combat, claiming about 30 kills.

Ninth AF: 9th Bomb Div attacks rail bridges, comm centers, and T/Os in Germany and Belgium. Ftrs escort bmrs, fly patrols and armed rcn, and spt US 3d Armd and 82d Airborne Divs in Manhay and Trois-Ponts area, and III, VIII, and XII Corps in Saint-Hubert-Bastogne-Martelange area.

Twelfth AF: On 26/27 Dec A–20's bomb pontoon bridges at Ficarolo, road bridges at Ostiglia and Castel Maggiore, San Benedetto Po crossing, Turin A/F, and several Po Valley roads. MBs blast 3 Brenner area routes leading into Austria and Yugoslavia, and bomb 2 supply dumps in Bologna area. FBs devote main effort to spt US Fifth Army in Serchio Valley area where counterattacks are being successfully halted. Other FBs hit comm in Po Valley and escort MBs and C–47's dropping supplies to Italian partisans.

Fifteenth AF: 520-plus HBs bomb Vosendorf oil refinery, Linz ordnance depot, M/Ys at Wiener-Neustadt, Villach, Klagenfurt, Bruck an der Mur, Graz, and Maribor, Feldbach railroad junction, Brenner rail line, Venzone viaduct, and Vipiteno and Bressanone railroad bridges. 44 P–38's bomb bridges at Latisana and Casarsa della Delizia. 29 P–51's strafe railroad tgts between Vienna and Linz. Other ftrs fly over 250 escort sorties.

Tenth AF: 8 B–25's attack bridges at Kin and Kyaukhlebein, damaging the former. 28 P–47's hit troop and supply areas at Se-hai, Man Hkam, Mong Yok, and Mong Nge. 285 transport sorties are flown to forward areas. 4 B–25's continue offensive rcn against comm lines during 27/28 Dec.

Fourteenth AF: 6 B–25's bomb area W of Kengtung. 2 B–25's and 8 P–40's hit Ishan area. 29 P–40's and P–51's attack area S of Puchi. 17 P–51's over White Cloud, Whampoa, and Tien Ho A/Fs claim 10 airplanes destroyed. 2 P–51's are lost. 40-plus P–40's and P–51's hit T/Os at or near Kweiyi, Vinh Yen, Lungan, Mong Long, Mong Khong, and Namtao.

FEAF: B–24's bomb San Jose-Talisay and Matina A/Fs. Small miscellaneous strikes are carried out over Borneo, Celebes, and Lesser Sunda Is.

Twentieth AF: B–29's and crews of 313th Bomb Wg (VH), commanded by Col John H Davies, begin to arrive on Tinian, joining the 73d Bomb Wg as the XXI BC's second operational wg. 39 B–29's from the Marianas bomb Tokyo's Nakajima and Musashino aircraft plants. 13 attack alternates and T/Os. Enemy ftrs are active, flying over 250 individual attacks on the VHBs. B–29's claim 21 downed. 3 VHBs are lost, 1 to ftrs and 2 to mechanical difficulties.

Seventh AF: 13 Saipan-based B–24's hit Iwo Jima while 21 more bomb Chichi Jima. 35 from Guam also pound Iwo Jima while P–38's strafe the island on which 2 B–24's also make snooper strikes during 27/28 Dec.

28 December

Eighth AF: More than 1,100 HBs attack 9 M/Ys, 4 bridges, and several cities and T/Os in W German tac area.

11 gps of P–51's fly spt. 4 other ftr gps sweep Bonn-Koblenz area.

Ninth AF: Weather prevents all combat operations except night-ftr missions.

Twelfth AF: MBs attack troop concentration at Aulla, dump at Mirabello Monferrato, 3 rail lines from Austria and Yugoslavia into NE Italy by hitting bridges at Chiusaforte and Bodrez, and viaduct at Borovnica. XXII TAC planes spt US Fifth Army in Serchio Valley, where counterattacks are repulsed, hit roads and bridges, and destroy a number of vehicles, many at a motor transport depot near Aulla which the ftrs bomb and strafe. During 27/28 Dec LBs bomb lights and motor transport at almost 50 places throughout Po Valley and Brenner area.

Fifteenth AF: 480-plus HBs attack Regensburg oil storage and freight yard in Germany, M/Ys at Zwettl, Amstetten, Kallwang, Hieflau, and Salzburg, oil refineries at Kralupy nad Vltava, Kolin, and Pardubice, oil storage and sidings at Roudnice nad Labem, Nymburk railroad bridge at Kammern, Brenner rail line, and Bressanone and Venzone railroad bridges. P–38's and P–51's fly over 350 sorties in spt of HBs.

Tenth AF: 23 P–47's knock out bridge at Nampawng and damage others at Man Pwe and Hsenwi. 8 B–25's destroy bridges at Kin and Kyaukhlebein, hit an already unserviceable bridge at Padon, damage a bypass road at Lashio and bomb troop concentrations, supplies, and arty at Mong Hseng, Mong Tat, and Kathe. 297 transport sorties are flown to forward areas. 4 B–25's continue offensive rcn over comm lines during 28/29 Dec.

Fourteenth AF: 2 B–25's and 16 FBs hit town areas, railroad tgts, and gun positions in Hengyang-Leiyang area. 20 P–51's and P–38's attack Gia Lam A/F, pounding barracks area, hangars, shops, and railroad facilities. 40-plus other P–51's, P–40's, and P–38's on armed rcn over S China and over Indochina hit T/Os at several locations including areas around Anking, Kinkiang, Wanling, Mongyu, Namtao, Yungning, Hanoi, Lang Son, Man Pong, Siangtan, and Yuncheng.

FEAF: B–25's pound Laha, Kairatoe, and Haroekoe A/Fs while FBs hit Namlea A/F. In Soembawa-Flores I area, B–24's attack Japanese shipping. FEAF ftrs and bmrs on numerous small raids hit tgts on Palawan, Mindanao, Borneo, Celebes, Halmahera, Timor and Tanimbar Is, Lingayen Gulf, and W of Mindoro I.

Seventh AF: 13 B–24's, flying out of Saipan, bomb A/F on Iwo Jima which is hit again during 28/29 Dec when HBs from Guam and Saipan fly 2 single-plane strikes.

29 December

Eighth AF: 750-plus HBs strike 5 M/Ys, 4 bridges, 6 comm centers, dock area, 5 city areas, and several T/Os in W Germany. 10 P–51 gps fly close escort and 2 gps later strafe rail transportation. 3 other gps fly area spt.

Ninth AF: Weather causes recall of over 100 bmrs except for 7 which bomb Saint-Vith comm center and Keuchingen road bridge. XIX TAC flies armed rcn over Belgium and Germany and supports US III, VIII, and XII Corps in Neufchateau-Bastogne-Arlon areas.

Twelfth AF: During 28/29 Dec LBs pound motor transports, ferry crossings, road bridges, rail line, and T/Os throughout NW and NC Po Valley. MBs during the day blast the Rovereto bridge and Lavis viaduct, attack several bridges in NE Italy destroying center span of bridge at Pordenone, and severely damage bridge at Motta di Livenza. FBs concentrate on comm tgts in extreme W end of battle area, with excellent results on bridges in Massa Lombarda area and destroy numerous vehicles and several locomotives.

Fifteenth AF: Almost 450 HBs attack M/Ys at Innsbruck, Passau, Rosenheim, Landshut, Salzburg, and Verona (2), Brenner rail line, Castelfranco Veneto and Udine locomotive repair depots, and Bressanone railroad bridge. 14 P–38's bomb road bridge S of Rosenheim. Around 300 other P–38's and P–51's fly escort and rcn missions.

Tenth AF: 9 B–25's bomb troops and supplies at Panma. 15 P–47's hit supply area at Twinnge and troop concentration at Wetwun. 4 B–25's continue armed night rcn over comm facilities. Transports fly 289 sorties to forward bases and frontline areas.

Fourteenth AF: 4 B–25's attack T/Os from Dong Hoa to Lang Son. 37 P–51's and P–40's on armed rcn attack Gia Lam A/F and hit various T/Os E of Man Pong, E of Tsingsinghsien, N of Mongyu, and at Shanhsien and Hei-Shih Kuan.

FEAF: B–24's bomb Sasa A/F while B–25's and FBs hit Namlea. FBs hit NE Celebes A/Fs while B–24's bomb Limboeng. FEAF aircraft fly small strikes against a wide range of tgts in N Borneo, C Phil Is, S Luzon, and on Timor.

Seventh AF: 26 B–24's, based on Guam, pound Iwo Jima which is bombed again for a 6-hr period during 29/30 Dec by 9 HBs, flying at varying intervals.

Eleventh AF: 3 B–25's on a ftr-decoy mission abort due to weather. 2 of them are missing on return flight. A B–24 bombs Kataoka.

30 December

Eighth AF: Over 1,200 HBs hit 8 M/Ys, 6 bridges, rail junction and city area, and 13 T/Os in W Germany. 11 ftr gps fly escort, 2 others fly area sweeps.

Ninth AF: Weather forces recall and cancellation of 9th Bomb Div and IX TAC missions. XXIX TAC flies armed rcn over battle area and around Wallersheim and XIX TAC covers large areas of France, Belgium, and Germany hitting numerous ground tgts and supports US III, VIII, and XII Corps in Saint-Hubert, Bastogne and Diekirch areas.

Twelfth AF: MBs concentrate major effort on rail line running N to Brenner Pass, hitting fill at Dolce and bridges at Calliano, Ala, and Santa Margherita d'Adige, and ammo dump at Bologna. FBs blast road bridges, spt US Fifth Army SE of La Spezia, and hit bridges in Mantua and Modena areas. During 29/30 Dec LBs hit T/Os at numerous N Italian locations, including Ghedi A/F, and train S of Mantua.

Tenth AF: 12 P–47's knock out and damage bridges at Man Pwe, Ho-hko (2), and Inailong. 17 B–25's blast troop and supply area at Kyat-

pyin. 28 P–47's and P–38's hit troops, supplies, and areas of enemy activity at Myethin, Manna, Nanponpon, Lawa, Sabenago, Hmattawmu, and Hosi. Transports complete 338 sorties to forward areas. 4 B–25's continue single-plane offensive rcn over comm lines during 30/31 Dec.

Fourteenth AF: 4 B–24's damage a bridge W of Kengtung while 2 others NE of Thanh Moi damage a bridge, railroad tracks, and more than 40 boxcars. 40-plus P–51's and P–40's on armed rcn attack T/Os at several points including areas around Mong Nawng, Man Pong, Mong Long, Ka-chun, Shanhsien, Ichang, and Shayang.

FEAF: In the principal action of the day, FBs pound A/Fs in C Phil, N Borneo, and N and SW Celebes while B–25's hit barge anchorage and supplies at Haroekoe. Smaller strikes by B–25's, B–24's, and FBs are flown against shipping, oil tgts, A/Fs, and T/Os throughout Phil Is and NEI.

Seventh AF: 14 Saipan-based B–24's bomb Iwo Jima which is hit again over an almost 7-hr period, 30/31 Dec, by 9 HBs singly operating from Guam.

31 December

Eighth AF: 1,200-plus HBs hit 5 oil refineries, an aircraft plant, U-boat yards, 2 A/Fs, T/Os in N Germany, 6 bridges, 3 comm centers, 3 M/Ys, a detraining point, a city area, several T/Os in W Germany and Helgoland I. 14 escorting ftr gps engage about 150 ftrs, mostly in Hamburg area, and claim about 60 kills. HBs lose 14 to the ftrs, and claim 26 ftrs destroyed.

Ninth AF: Weather grounds bmrs.

Ftrs fly sweeps and armed rcn, attacking numerous ground tgts. XIX TAC supports US III, VIII, and XX Corps around Bastogne and between Mosel and Saar Rivers in Merzig area.

Twelfth AF: During 30/31 Dec A-20's again fly intruder missions, bombing a variety of tgts, including motor transport, bridges, and railroads in Po Valley. During the day MBs hit bridge at Bodrez, railroads at Piazzola Sul Brenta and near Padua, and a dump. XXII TAC FBs destroy 5 and damage 2 railway bridges in Po Valley, cut rail lines at numerous places, destroy several locomotives, and destroy or damage 200-plus railway cars.

Tenth AF: 28 P-47's strafe Laihka, Namsang, Aungban, Kunlon, and Heho A/Fs. 5 P-47's damage bridge at Namhkai. A total of 65 P-47's and P-38's hit Japanese Div HQ at Ongyaw and troop concentrations and supply areas at Mongmit, Nawngka, Kawngtawng, Pangnim, Mong Tat, Kutkai, and Man Namman. A few B-25's fly night harassment missions against A/Fs. About 300 transport sorties are flown to forward areas throughout the day.

Fourteenth AF: 4 B-24's claim 1 freighter sunk and another damaged off Hainan I. 4 B-25's damage 2 bridges and destroy or damage 5 buildings at Mong Ping. 35 P-40's and P-51's attack troops, horses, town areas, and railroad tgts at or near Hankow, Saiping, Siangtan, Hengyang, Lingling, and Kweilin. 29 other ftrs on armed rcn hit T/Os at several points in N Indochina, E Burma, and S China.

FEAF: B-24's and B-25's bomb A/Fs in C Phil, on Luzon and Mindanao. Other B-24's bomb Ambesia A/F, hit Dili, and pound A/Fs and supply areas throughout Halmahera I. FBs are active against A/Fs, shipping, AA guns, and various T/Os on Halmahera and in N Celebes.

Twentieth AF: Gen Hansell and his XXI BC Forward Echelon HQ staff close Saipan HQ and move to Guam where ground echelon arrived in early Dec.

Seventh AF: From Guam 19 B-24's hit Iwo Jima A/Fs during the day. 10 more HBs hit the island with individual harassment raids over a 6-hr period during 31 Dec/1 Jan.

1945

1 January

Eighth AF: The 3 Bomb Divs of the Eighth are redesignated Air Divs. Over 700 HBs attack 3 oil tgts, 5 Rhine R bridges, and rail junctions, 3 M/Ys, various other tgts in 10 cities, and several T/Os—all in Germany. 14 escorting ftr gps battle over 120 ftrs in Frankfurt/Main and Hannover areas, claiming 17 kills, including a jet ftr.

Ninth AF: GAF launches attack of 700–800 airplanes against Ninth AF and Allied A/Fs, mainly in Brussels and Eindhoven areas, and to a lesser degree in Metz area. 127 operational Allied aircraft are destroyed. Allied ftrs claim 160 air victories while AA claims 300. 190 A-20's, A-26's, and B-26's hit rail bridges, comm centers, road junction, a cmd post, and HQ, all in Belgium and Germany. Ftrs escort 9th Bomb Div and Eighth AF bmrs, fly patrols, sweeps, and armed rcn (claiming 39 air victories and numerous ground tgts destroyed) and spt US III, VII, and XII Corps between Saint-Hubert and the Mosel R.

Twelfth AF: MBs attack bridges at Palazzuolo sull'Oglio, Parma, and Calcinato (latter 2 tgts are missed) and ammo dump at Parma. FBs spt ground forces S of Bologna, hit comm and numerous T/Os to the N and completely destroy a fuel dump at Parma. LBs on intruder missions during 31 Dec/1 Jan achieve excellent

results on motor park near Molinella and hit M/Y near Milan.

Fifteenth AF: Unfavorable weather permits only P-38 rcn flights.

Tenth AF: 71 P-47's and P-38's attack villages, general supply areas, fuel dumps, tanks and other vehicles, and troop concentrations at several locations including Man Hio, Bahe, Mongmit, Hatka, Namhpakha, Loihseng, Mong Yaw and in Hsenwi area. 4 others hit T/Os along the Irrawaddy from Tanaung to Kyungyi. 4 B-25's harass comm lines during 1/2 Jan. Large-scale air transport operations continue.

Fourteenth AF: 3 B-24's bomb Ft Bayard. 40 P-51's and P-40's pound railroad tgts, warehouses, industrial works, and gun positions from Yoyang to Puchi. 8 P-51's hit Suchow A/F, claiming 25 airplanes destroyed. 47 other P-40's and P-51's on armed rcn hit troops, horses, town areas, and rail and road traffic at several locations. Especially at Liuchenghsien and between Siaokan and Hsuchang.

FEAF: B-25's and FBs make low-level attacks on Negros I A/Fs. B-24's, with P-38 cover, bomb Clark Field. Others pound Sasa area and along with B-25's hit Djailolo, Wasile Bay bivouac areas, and Miti ammo dump. B-25's bomb A/Fs on Ceram and barracks at Laoag. FBs are active against tgts in Manila area and also hit Silay. A/Fs, shipyards, and other tgts in Borneo, Celebes and Lesser Sunda Is also sustain light raids, by FEAF ftrs and bmrs, which also fly armed rcn.

Seventh AF: 19 B–24's from Saipan bomb Iwo Jima. 9 more, during 1/2 Jan snooper missions, hit the island at varying intervals.

Eleventh AF: 5 B–24's fly coverage for a naval force upon aborting bomb mission to the Kurils.

2 January

Eighth AF: HQ VIII AFSC (Adv) is established in Brussels, along with a "Far Shore" staff division. Through this HQ, the CG AFSC can administer his cmd and closely communicate with other cmds operating on the Continent. This arrangement functions until 29 Apr when it is relieved by 5th Strategic Air Depot at Merville. About 950 HBs attack 5 M/Ys, 6 bridges, 5 comm centers, a rail junction, 2 tank concentrations, and several T/Os in battle area of W Germany. 10 ftr gps escort HBs while 2 others spt MBs of Ninth AF. 3 gps fly sweeps in which 1 gp strafes transportation tgts near Frankfurt/Main and Giessen.

Ninth AF: 135 A–20's, A–26's, and B–26's hit rail bridges and comm centers in Belgium and Germany. Ftrs escort 9th Bomb Div, fly patrols, sweeps, and armed rcn and spt US III and VIII Corps in Bastogne area and XII Corps S of Clerf R and W of the Sauer R.

Twelfth AF: FBs concentrate effort in W Po Valley and Brenner area, claiming large number of rail lines cut and many vehicles and trains destroyed and damaged. Milan M/Y

is hit hard and good coverage is achieved on spt tgts in US Fifth Army battle area. LBs during 1/2 Jan continue intruder missions over Po Valley.

Fifteenth AF: Again bad weather restricts operations to rcn flights.

Tenth AF: Troop concentrations and supplies are attacked at Mabein, Panghka, Mansut, Letpangon, Loimun, Panghkai, Namhsan, Thabeikkyin, and in Lashio area by 66 P–47's and 13 P–38's. 546 transport sorties are flown to forward bases and frontline areas.

Fourteenth AF: 6 B–25's bomb Kentung. 30-plus P–40's and P–51's on armed rcn attack T/Os, mainly railroad traffic, at or near Lohochai, Pengpu, Man Pong, Wanling, Wan Pa-Hsa, and Sinyang.

FEAF: P–38's and A–20's hit shipping in San Fernando harbor. B–24's pound Clark Field and B–25's hit Batangas. A/Fs in C Phil area are bombed by B–25's, A–20's, and FBs while B–24's strike Likanan, Menado, and Wasile Bay area. Other FEAF aircraft make armed rcn and harassing strikes on T/Os throughout C Phil area and NEI.

Twentieth AF: 44 B–29's, operating from Calcutta area, attack railroad bridge at Bangkok. 2 others hit alternate and T/O.

Seventh AF: 12 Guam-based B–24's hit Haha Jima while 14 others pound Iwo Jima. During 2/3 Jan 10 HBs, flying snooper strikes out of Guam, hit Iwo Jima over a 7-hr period.

3 January

Eighth AF: Almost 1,100 HBs, escorted by 11 ftr gps, bomb tgts in W

Germany, including 11 M/Ys, 3 comm centers, 2 rail junctions, a railhead, 2 city areas, and T/Os. 2 ftr gps fly area sweeps in spt.

Ninth AF: All combat operations are cancelled because of weather.

Twelfth AF: MBs score direct hits on 2 railroad bridges at Lavis and fly good coverage of Chiusaforte, Canale d'Isonzo, and Padua railroad bridges. FBs hit large number of comm tgts (mainly railroad tgts) in Po Valley which is also subjected to intruder missions during 2/3 Jan, when pontoon bridges, vehicles, and Ghedi A/F are hit.

Fifteenth AF: Bad weather curtails operations for fifth successive day. P–38's fly photo and weather rcn missions.

Tenth AF: 10 B–25's, supported by 12 P–47's, attack A/F at Aungban. Troop concentrations and supply and ammo dumps are pounded at several locations, including Man Kun, Loi Hkam, Ngawnga, Chakau, Mulaw, and Man Pwe. 575 transport flights are completed to forward areas.

Fourteenth AF: 10 P–51's hit A/F at Tsinan, claiming 13 airplanes destroyed. 6 P–51's claim several river steamers sunk in Hankow-Chiuchiang area while 6 others damage bridges at Chinchengchiang. 20-plus other P–40's, P–51's, and P–47's on armed rcn attack various T/Os in Wuchang-Hankow and Shwangliu areas, at Namtao, S and SW of Man Pong, and W of Wanling.

FEAF: B–24's pound Clark Field and Mabalacat areas. B–25's hit 5 A/Fs in C Phil Is while B–24's bomb 2 on Mindanao. B–24's attack Djailolo supply area, while B–25's bomb Namlea A/F. Numerous other FEAF

aircraft on armed rcn, harassing raids, and light strikes attack a vast variety of tgts throughout NEI and Phil Is.

Twentieth AF: 57 Marianas-based B–29's bomb docks and urban areas of Nagoya. 21 others bomb alternates and T/Os. Japanese ftrs fly 300-plus attacks on the B–29's. 5 VHBs are lost. B–29 gunners claim 14 kills.

Seventh AF: 22 B–24's from Saipan bomb Iwo Jima. 3 from Guam, on armed rcn, hit Marcus. During a 6-hr period on 3/4 Jan, 10 HBs from Guam hit Iwo Jima.

Eleventh AF: B–25's fly coverage for a naval force over the Kurils.

4 January

Eighth AF: Transfer of HQ, VIII FC from Bushey Hall to Charleroi begins. HQ is to provide administrative and operational spt for ftr gps operating with Ninth AF on tac spt missions.

Ninth AF: All combat operations, except a defensive patrol by 4 ftrs, are cancelled because of bad weather.

Twelfth AF: MBs hit bridges at Lavis and Calliano. Ftrs and FBs interdict Po Valley comm and hit ammo dump at San Felice del Benaco. During 3/4 Jan LBs successfully hit stores dump and bridge near Mestre, and destroy or damage over 50 vehicles.

Fifteenth AF: 370-plus B–24's and B–17's bomb M/Ys at Verona (2), Bronzolo (2), Vicenza, Padua (2), Trento, and Bolzano, and station sidings at Trento. 54 P–38's attempt high-level bombing of Cismon del Grappa but fail to hit tgt. 9 B–24's drop supplies in Yugoslavia. P–38's and P–51's fly rcn and escort opera- tions. Over 200 ftrs accompany HBs.

Tenth AF: 13 B–25's, escorted by 12 P–47's, bomb Namsang A/F. 12 P– 47's hit bypass road bridges at Inai- long and Bawgyo, damaging ap- proaches to the latter. Troops and supply areas are hit at Man Kat, Hsenwi, Yi-ku, Se-hai, and near Nawnghkio by 36 P–47's and P–38's. 6 P–47's bomb cable and pontoons along N riverbank at Na-lang. 6 hit enemy activity near Twinnge and 5 attack truck dispersal area and ware- houses at Mogok. Transports fly 597 sorties to front areas and forward bases.

Fourteenth AF: 4 B–24's bomb Ft Bayard and Samah Bay areas. 6 B– 25's damage a bridge and a warehouse, and destroy 2 other buildings at Ken- tung. 21 P–40's on armed rcn pound T/Os in Wanling area. 8 P–51's knock out bridge at Huizan and damage an- other, and 20 other ftrs hit T/Os around Lohochai, Sinyang and Han- kow.

FEAF: B–24's pound Puerto Princesa. B–25's hit railroad and highways in San Pedro area. B–25's and P–38's hit Tanamon and Sidate. Other B–24's and B–25's, flying small- scale strikes, hit A/Fs in S Luzon, on Mindanao, in NE Celebes, and in C Phil Is, and bomb shipyards in N Borneo.

Seventh AF: 13 Guam-based B– 24's pound Iwo Jima. During 4/5 Jan, 10 more hit the island with individ- ual harassment strikes.

5 January

Eighth AF: Over 850 HBs, sup- ported by 11 ftr gps, bomb 9 M/Ys, 8 comm centers, 3 rail tgts, 5 city areas, and 15 T/Os in battle areas and C Germany. 1 ftr gp flies un- eventful sweep while another bombs and strafes Siegen M/Y.

Ninth AF: 9th Bomb Div attacks rail bridges at Ahrweiler, Simmern, and Bullay and comm centers at Gouvy, Houffalize, Massen, and near Durler. Ftrs escort 9th Bomb Div and VIII BC, fly armed rcn, attack A/Fs, comm center, traffic concentra- tion, and other tgts, and spt US III and VIII Corps W and E of Bas- togne and 2d and 3d Armd Divs near Manhay.

Twelfth AF: During 4/5 Jan A– 20's on S Po Valley intruder mission bomb Modena area. Bad weather can- cels all other operations.

Fifteenth AF: 1 B–24 bombs Zag- reb railroad sidings. 69 others abort due to total cloud cover over tgt. 38 P–51's fly cover over tgt area. 33 P– 38's bomb N railroad bridge at Doboj. Other operations are limited to rcn, supply drops, and escort.

Tenth AF: 16 B–25's flying A/F sweep inflict considerable damage on Laihka, Aungban, Kunlon, and Mong Long A/Fs. In Namhkam sector, 2 P–47's join ground forces in blasting arty positions at Wingkang and Kun- long. 9 P–47's damage bypass bridges at Mongmit. 70-plus FBs attack stor- age areas, tanks and trucks, and troop concentrations at Mong Yaw, Hsenwi, Hpa-Pen, Man Ton, Tunghka, Man Peng, and Longhsu. Transports fly 550-plus sorties to forward bases and frontline areas. Operation GRUB- WORM, one of the major transport achievements of the war, is completed on this date 1 month from its start. Chinese 14th and 22d Divs, Chinese Sixth Army HQ, a heavy mortar co, a signal co, and 2 portable surgical hospitals have been airlifted. The move required 1,328 transport sorties. ATC provided 597 sorties; the air commando sqs, 488; and Tenth AF, 243. The lift included more than 25,000 Chinese soldiers, 396 US soldiers, 1,596 animals, 42 jeeps, 48 howitzers, 48 heavy mortars, and 48 antitank guns. The troops and supplies have been landed at Chanyi, Kunming, Luliang, and Yunnani. Only 3 planes were lost during the operation.

Fourteenth AF: 4 B–25's pound 13 storage buildings at Kengtung. 5 B–25's knock out bridge at Dara. 3 B–25's bomb Wan Pa-Hsa and Hawng Luk while 1 B–24 bombs Cap-Saint-Jacques area. 29 P–40's and P–51's hit A/Fs at Hankow and Wuchang, claiming 50 airplanes destroyed in the air and on the ground. 23 P–51's and P–38's hit A/F and other tgts in Samah Bay area, claiming 11 airplanes destroyed. 30 P–40's and P–38's attack various T/Os, Sinsiang, Kengtung, and Wan Pa-Hsa, and in Wanling area. 4 P–40's pound fortified hill positions in Salween area.

FEAF: In major strikes of the day B–25's hit shore installations along Lingayan Gulf, and bomb Menado. B–24's attack Miri A/F. Numerous smaller strikes are flown throughout Phil Is and NEI. A–20's and FBs attack A/Fs in Luzon, C Phil area and Mindanao, FBs and B–24's hit Pombelaa, Tondano area, and T/Os in NE Celebes. Other FEAF aircraft fly scattered strikes at various tgts in Borneo, Lesser Sunda, and Tanimbar Is.

Seventh AF: 22 B–24's from Saipan, in morning and afternoon raids, pound Iwo Jima. 7 P–38's, with 3 B–24's as navigational escort, fly strafing mission against Iwo Jima. Other B–24's act as airborne spotters for naval bombardment of Chichi Jima and Haha Jima.

Eleventh AF: 4 B–24's fly an air coverage mission for a naval TF on its approach to Suribachi.

6 January

Eighth AF: More than 750 HBs attack 6 M/Ys, 4 bridges, a comm center, a city area, and 14 T/Os in battle zone of W Germany. 7 ftr gps fly escort and 1 gp strafes A/F and transportation tgts. 1 gp of FBs bombs Siegen M/Y.

Ninth AF: 26 bmrs of 9th Bomb Div strike Prum. Bad weather prevents all ftr operations.

Twelfth AF: Bad weather over N Italy grounds MBs. XXII TAC ftrs and FBs hit rail lines and bridges in Genoa-La Spezia coastline area, and bomb vessels in harbors at Genoa and Imperia.

Fifteenth AF: Bad weather precludes all operations except a single rcn mission by 2 P–38's.

Tenth AF: Bad weather cancels all combat missions. Transports manage 310 sorties, landing men and supplies at advanced bases and dropping supplies to frontline troops.

Fourteenth AF: 40 P–40's, P–51's, and P–47's pound Hankow-Wuchang area. 9 airplanes are claimed destroyed. 4 B–24's bomb Cap-Saint-Jacques area.

FEAF: In the day's major operations, B–24's bomb Clark Field while B–25's, A–20's, and FBs blast bridges and T/Os at Calumpit and Plaridel and in nearby S Luzon areas. B–24's bomb Nichols Field and Nielson A/F.

A–20's, with P–38 cover, bomb Carolina A/F. B–25's and FBs hit Mapanget A/F. FEAF flies numerous smaller strikes against various points throughout NEI and Phil Is.

Twentieth AF: 28 Chengtu-based B–29's bomb aircraft factory at Omura. 13 bomb secondary tgt at Nanking while 6 attack T/Os.

Seventh AF: 15 B–24's, based at Guam, bomb Iwo Jima A/Fs. During 6/7 Jan, 9 B–24's on individual snooper strikes continue to pound the A/Fs.

Eleventh AF: 2 B–24's bomb Suribachi Bay A/F, also hitting buildings and pier areas. 10 B–25's fly single air coverage sorties for naval TF.

7 January

Eighth AF: Over 1,000 HBs, escorted by 11 ftr gps, bomb 7 M/Ys, 6 comm centers, 3 bridges, railroad lines, along with several city areas and T/Os in Germany. 2 ftr gps sweep Cologne and Osnabruck areas.

Ninth AF: XXIX TAC ftrs escort VIII BC HBs. All other cmds and 9th Bomb Div cancel operations as weather is bad.

Twelfth AF: Weather grounds MBs and LBs. XXII TAC ftrs and FBs make 6 cuts on Brenner rail line, damage W end of rail bridge at Cittadella, and hit M/Y S of Trento. Most of XXII TAC's effort is concentrated against land and water comm in La Spezia-Genoa area, including attacks on shipping at Savona and San Remo harbors.

Fifteenth AF: Unfavorable weather again curtails operations. 3 P–38's complete photo and weather rcn missions.

Tenth AF: Bad weather cancels all combat missions. Transports complete 383 sorties to forward areas.

Fourteenth AF: 5 B–24's bomb Ft Bayard and attack shipping in Samah Bay, claiming 1 vessel sunk.

FEAF: In major strikes of the day, large numbers of B–25's and A–20's, supported by P–38's, hit network of airstrips from Clark Field to Angeles A/F. B–24's bomb Nielson and Grace Park A/Fs and Nichols Field, and B–25's and FBs pound bridges in the Plaridel and Calumpit areas. B–24's raid Padada and Daliao A/Fs. B–25's and FBs hit Lembeh Strait and Langoan areas. Other FEAF aircraft on small-scale armed rcn missions strike T/Os throughout Phil Is.

Seventh AF: 11 B–24's, flying out of Saipan, bomb A/F on Iwo Jima. During 7/8 Jan, 10 more HBs again pound A/Fs, striking in single-bmr snooper missions over a 7-hr period.

8 January

Eighth AF: Nearly 600 HBs, given area spt by 6 ftr gps, bomb 4 M/Ys, 12 comm centers, a rail-over-road bridge, and 5 T/Os in Germany.

Ninth AF: Weather prevents operations.

Twelfth AF: XXII TAC A–20's fly 33 effective sorties in Po Valley during 7/8 Jan. Bad weather sharply reduces daytime operations. Of 3 MB missions dispatched, only 1 reaches tgt (Chivasso railway bridge) where only 6 MBs bomb through overcast. Less than 20 XXII TAC ftrs hit scattered tgts in Po Valley.

Fifteenth AF: More than 300 B–17's and B–24's bomb Linz main station yard and N main M/Y plus M/Ys at Graz, Villach, Klagenfurt, and Salzburg, escorted by 200-plus P-38's and P-51's. Over 30 other P-38's fly rcn and rcn escort.

Tenth AF: 21 B-25's hit troops and supply areas at Nampeng and Mong Long. 74 P-47's and P-38's attack troop concentrations and supply areas at Tunhunghkam, Mongyu, Hpa-hpun, and Man Om. 12 P-47's knock out bypass bridge at Namhkai. Transports complete 470-plus sorties to forward bases and frontline areas.

Fourteenth AF: 8 P-51's hit T/Os E of Muse and E of Wanling.

FEAF: In the main strikes during the day, P-51's and P-40's strafe A/Fs in the Lingayen Gulf area. A-20's pound railroad yards at Cabanatuan, motor convoys between Cabanatuan and Bongalion and between Bongabon and Mojon, Rosales and San Quintin rail installations, bridges at Cuyapo, Paniqui, and near Santa Rosa. P-47's hit rail yards and truck convoy in San Jose area. B-24's and A-20's attack Nichols Field and Nielson, Lipa, and Calingatan A/Fs. B-25's with P-47 cover, bomb Fabrica A/F, while B-24's bomb Likanan A/F and oil storage at Matina. P-38's attack Manggar and Sepinggang A/Fs. Numerous small-scale attacks over the Phil Is and NEI continue.

Seventh AF: 26 Guam-based B-24's bomb A/Fs on Iwo Jima, which, during 8/9 Jan, 10 more B-24's subject to individual snooper strikes over a 6-hr period.

9 January

Ninth AF: 15 B-26's bomb Rinnthal rail bridge with aim of isolating 3 enemy armd divs in Landau area. XXIX TAC ftrs escort the MBs. Weather prevents other operations.

Twelfth AF: MBs attack bridges at Palazzuolo sull'Oglio, Pontetidone, Romano di Lombardia, and assembly area at Crespellano. Ftrs and FBs in excellent day against comm in W and C Po Valley and other points in N Italy make numerous rail cuts, destroy or damage many vehicles and trains and effectively hit ammo and fuel dumps, guns, and strongpoints along US Fifth Army front in the N Apennines.

Fifteenth AF: Bad weather permits only rcn missions.

EAC: Col Minton W Kaye assumes cmd of Photo Rcn Force, a component of EAC.

Tenth AF: 8 P-47's hit div HQ at Ho-na while 4 others spt ground forces in Si-U sector. 90-plus FBs hit supply areas, tanks, AA positions, and troop concentrations at Man Kat, Tonghsim, Kong-lin, Bawdwin, Mong Tat, and in Hsenwi vicinity. 488 transport sorties are flown to forward areas.

Fourteenth AF: 6 B-25's hit railroad tgts, road bridge, and building area NE of Thanh Moi. 25 P-40's, P-38's, and P-51's hit T/Os S, SW, and NE of Wanling. 8 P-51's bomb railroad repair shops at Sinsiang while 3 P-40's hit road W of Muse, causing traffic block.

FEAF: Amphibious forces of US Sixth Army begin landing on shores of Lingayen Gulf at 0930. In N Luzon, B-24's bomb Mabalacat while B-25's, A-20's, and FBs destroy several bridges and numerous vehicles and trains throughout Luzon, and bomb several A/Fs. B-24's also hit Nielson A/F and Nichols Field. FEAF airplanes make small-scale attacks on barges, A/Fs, and T/Os on Mindanao, Halmahera, Ceram area, N Borneo, and on Timor.

Twentieth AF: 39 B–29's from Chengtu bomb harbor at Kirun. This raid is first of several such operations against Formosa in conjunction with the US invasion of Luzon. 6 B–29's bomb last resort tgts along China coast. 72 Marianas-based B–29's are dispatched against Musashino aircraft plant near Tokyo. High winds break up formations so that only 18 V HBs can bomb the primary tgt. A large number hits alternates and T/Os

Seventh AF: 24 B–24's, based on Saipan, hit A/F on Iwo Jima which is struck again by 8 HBs on individual snooper missions during 9/10 Jan.

Eleventh AF: For the first time the Eleventh radar-bombs with H2X equipment as 4 B–24's hit Suribachi Bay A/F.

10 January

Eighth AF: Over 912 HBs attack 10 bridges, 6 M/Ys, 5 A/Fs, and numerous T/Os. 3 ftr gps fly close escort and 3 other gps give area spt. 1 gp of P–51's bombs M/Ys in Neustadt area. Heavy AA fire accounts for almost 20 HBs.

Ninth AF: Over 30 B–26's sent against comm center and road bridge abort due to weather. XIX TAC escorts MBs, flies patrols, attacks bridges and other tgts and supports US III, VIII, XII, and XX Corps in Saint-Hubert-Bastogne-Wiltz area, in Diekirch and Echternach area and points to the SE.

Twelfth AF: Weather restricts operations but FBs effectively attack comm and supply dumps in C and N Po Valley. The strikes are concentrated in the N and around

Piacenza, and score nearly 50 rail cuts, along with destruction of 80 motor transports and several trains. Fuel and ammo dumps in Milan area are bombed and a 400-ft naval vessel at Venice is destroyed.

Fifteenth AF: Weather restricts operations to photo and weather rcn missions.

Tenth AF: 75 FBs pound troop concentrations, supplies, tanks, arty, and buildings at Kawnglang, Nampachi, Man Namman, Pangkai, Mong Yai, Namhsan, Namyao, Se-ping, Panghai, and in Hosi area. 17 P–47's knock out a bridge, damage another at Bawgyo and 2 others at Ho-kho. 8 P–47's spt ground forces in Si-U battle sector. 8 others hit supplies and ferry crossing at Tamawngtawn. 472 transport sorties are flown to forward bases and front-line areas.

Fourteenth AF: 2 B–24's bomb Cap-Saint-Jacques area. 50-plus P–51's, P–40's, and P–38's pound various T/Os throughout Wanling area. 6 P–40's hit T/Os in Muse area.

FEAF: B–24's bomb Grace Park A/F and warehouse area, A–20's and FBs pound trucks, trains, railroad yards, railroads, and highways over wide areas of N and S Luzon, and bomb Vigan and Laoag A/Fs. About 60 P–40's bomb and strafe Galela area. B–25's and P–38's hit Kendari A/F. Other B–25's, A–20's, and FBs, operating in smaller forces, hit numerous shipping and comm tgts, A/Fs, and other tgts throughout the Phil Is.

Thirteenth AF: XIII FC moves from New Guinea to Leyte.

Seventh AF: 30 Guam-based B–24's operating in 2 separate formations, bomb A/Fs on Iwo Jima. 2 other HBs, on armed rcn, hit A/F at Woleai. Iwo Jima A/Fs are hit again on 10/11 Jan by B–24's flying snooper missions from Guam.

Eleventh AF: 3 B–24's on an armed photo mission bomb and photograph Kurabu A/F scoring hits on the runway.

11 January

Ninth AF: About 120 A–20's, A–26's, and B–26's attack comm centers and rail bridges in Belgium and Germany. Ftrs escort bmrs, hit Mayen ammo dump, and patrol areas around Malmedy and NE of Trier.

Twelfth AF: During 10/11 Jan LBs attack T/Os in W Po Valley. Clearing weather during the day enables increase of ftr and FB attacks in Po Valley and in US Fifth Army battle area in the N Apennines. Many ammo and fuel dumps, rail lines, trains, and vehicles are pounded, and an alcohol refinery at Piacenza is severely damaged.

Fifteenth AF: Bad weather limits operations. P–38's fly rcn and rcn escort missions.

Tenth AF: 12 P–47's spt ground forces in Si-U and Namhkam sectors. 3 others strafe trucks between Namkham and Selan. Troop concentrations, vehicles, arty pieces, supply areas, and general enemy movement are pounded by 80-plus FBs. 12 B–25's bomb storage buildings in Lashio area. 509 transport sorties are flown to forward areas.

Fourteenth AF: 5 B–25's damage bridge at Wan Mai-Lo. 12 FBs hit T/Os NE of Wanling, 7 drop napalm on T/Os NE of Muse, and 11 attack T/Os SE of Wanting and in E end of Wanting R valley.

FEAF: Large numbers of B–24's, B–25's, A–20's, and FBs concentrate on comm tgts throughout N Luzon and attack A/Fs, comm, and town areas in S Luzon, C Phil, and on Mindanao. B–25's and P–38's attack Kendari A/F.

Twentieth AF: 25 B–29's out of Calcutta bomb 2 large drydocks at Singapore. Around 15 others bomb Penang I, Mergui, and various T/Os.

Seventh AF: 23 B–24's from Saipan pound A/Fs on Iwo Jima. Bombing of Iwo Jima is continued during 11/12 Jan by 3 HBs flying individual snooper strikes from the Marianas.

Eleventh AF: 3 B–24's on an armed rcn to Suribachi bomb NW of Taro Lake. 5 B–25's hit Kotani Shima.

12 January

Ninth AF: All combat operations are cancelled because of weather.

Twelfth AF: 319th Bomb Gp and a serv gp, relieved of assignment to the Twelfth AF, return to US. These are the first Twelfth AF gps to return directly to ZI from the theater of operations. Weather severely curtails operations, but ftrs and FBs of XXII TAC score successfully against comm tgts in W and C Po Valley, claiming over 50 rail cuts and destruction or damage of 100-plus vehicles.

Fifteenth AF: For fourth consecutive day, all bombing operations are cancelled by bad weather. P–38's fly photo and weather rcn and escort missions.

Tenth AF: 16 FBs spt ground forces in battle sectors at Si-U and at Lawa on the Irrawaddy. More than 70 FBs hit troops, supplies, vehicles, and general enemy movement at Namsa-lap, Longmao, Hsaihkao, Mangpu, Pangnim, and near Lashio, Hsipaw, and Hsenwi. Transports fly 544 sorties, landing men and supplies at forward bases and dropping supplies to troops in battle sectors.

Fourteenth AF: 6 B–25's again damage bridge at Wan Mai-Lo. 35 FBs pound T/Os around Wanting and Muse.

FEAF: B–24's bomb San Jose del Monte area and bivouac areas in N Luzon. Other B–24's hit Legaspi, Batangas and Matina A/Fs while B–25's bomb Fabrica warehouses.

Seventh AF: 28 Guam-based B–24's bomb A/Fs at Iwo Jima. 3 HBs, on armed rcn from Saipan, bomb Marcus. Iwo Jima is hit by snooper strikes during 12/13 Jan by 4 B–24's from the Marianas.

13 January

Eighth AF: 900-plus HBs bomb 7 Rhine bridges, 3 M/Ys, a rail junction, and T/Os in battle zone. 7 ftr gps fly close escort while 5 gps fly area spt. 1 P–51 gp bombs M/Y.

Ninth AF: 95 9th Bomb Div bmrs strike road and rail bridges at Dasburg, Steinebruck, and Simmern to disrupt enemy movements. Ftrs escort 9th Bomb Div, Eighth AF, and RAF bmrs, fly armed rcn and patrols, and bomb and strafe numerous ground tgts. IX TAC supports US VII Corps near Houffalize, XIX TAC supports US III, VIII, XII, and XX Corps elements in Saint-Hubert-Bastogne-Wiltz areas and points E and S near Clerf and Mosel Rivers.

Twelfth AF: Bad weather pro-

hibits all but weather rcn and a scramble mission, all uneventful.

Fifteenth AF: For fifth successive day no bombing operations are flown. Weather permits only rcn and escort missions.

Tenth AF: 10 FBs hit Aungban A/F while 4 others spt ground forces along the Irrawaddy at Molo. 20-plus FBs hit horses and vehicles at Hsaihkao, buildings at Man Ping, and troops at Mankang and Man Sang. Transports fly 556 sorties to forward areas.

Fourteenth AF: 6 B–25's blast 6 storage buildings at Kengtung. 3 others damage bridge at Hawng Luk. 31 P–51's, P–38's, and P–40's hit T/Os in Wanting area. 16 P–51's hit T/Os around Shanhsien, Chiatsochen, and Chaling.

FEAF: B–24's over Luzon hit Tarlac barracks and storage area, Batangas A/F, and troop concentrations at San Juan, Del Monte, Muzon, and San Vicente. P–47's fly sweep from Laguna de Bay to Tarlac, destroying parked airplanes and vehicles. A–20's hit town of Batangas and nearby railroads and highways, and bomb Lucena and Calingatan A/Fs. Also the N Luzon area is hit throughout the day by small raids.

Seventh AF: 14 Saipan-based B–24's hit Iwo Jima A/F. 2 HBs from Guam and Saipan, again raid the A/Fs on 13/14 Jan.

14 January

Eighth AF: Over 650 HBs attack 4 oil tgts, 2 steel mills and benzol plant W of Berlin, plus M/Y, Wangerooge I, and T/Os. 150-plus other HBs bomb 3 bridges in Cologne area. 15 escorting ftr gps battle about 250 ftrs, claiming about 100 kills. 4 gps on ftr sweeps engage over 150 ftrs, claiming over 40 destroyed.

Ninth AF: 280-plus MBs and LBs strike bridges and comm centers in base area of Ardennes salient and in other areas of W Germany. Ftrs escort 9th Bomb Div and Eighth AF HBs, fly armed rcn and patrols, attack numerous ground tgts, and spt US First Army in Vielsalm area and US Third Army around Diekirch.

Twelfth AF: Weather again cancels all combat missions.

Fifteenth AF: For sixth consecutive day bad weather permits only rcn missions.

Tenth AF: 12 B–25's hit troops, stores area, and knock out 3 bridges near Nampawng and Hay-ti. 26 FBs spt ground forces at Si-U and at Mabein. 60-plus FBs pound supply areas, troop concentrations, and general T/Os at or near Hsenwi, Se-u, Kongnyaung, Kutkai, Mongmit, Man-ai, and Kawnghka. Transports fly 487 sorties to forward areas.

Fourteenth AF: 27 B–24's, supported by 45 P–51's and P–40's, pound Hankow. 8 enemy airplanes are claimed destroyed. 7 B–25's hit tgts at and W of Kengtung. 42 P–47's, P–40's, and P–51's attack A/Fs at Wuchang and Hankow. 17 Japanese airplanes are claimed destroyed. 21 P–40's and P–51's hit T/Os in Wanting area. 5 P–51's blast trucks and buildings at Shanhsien. 8 others attack shipping on the Yangtze near Anking.

FEAF: B–25's pound Aparri A/F while supporting P–51's destroy several parked aircraft. A–20's bomb Clark Field destroying numerous parked airplanes, while B–24's hit troop concentrations at Cabanatuan. B–24's, B–25's, A–20's, and FBs over wide areas of Luzon hit tanks, trucks, and other vehicles near Norzagaray, Masbate, Tartaro, Bulac, Banglos, and San Felipe; bomb bridge N of Bocaue; hit A/Fs at Tuguegarao, Malabang, Batangas, and Silay; bomb Cotabato supply area; and attack numerous other tgts. B–25's bomb Goeroea area.

Twentieth AF: 54 B–29's, out of Chengtu, bomb air installations at Kagi while 1 VHB bombs Heito. 22 others hit alternates and T/Os at several points, among them Taichu A/F and Hengyang. 40 B–29's from the Marianas bomb Mitsubishi aircraft plant at Nagoya. Over 20 others hit alternates and T/Os.

Seventh AF: 22 B–24's from Saipan and 21 from Guam bomb A/Fs on Moen. 9 P–38's escort the Saipan-based HBs. 12 B–24's from Guam pound A/F on Iwo Jima. 2 B–24's from the Marianas fly snooper strikes against Iwo Jima A/Fs during 14/15 Jan.

15 January

Eighth AF: 600-plus HBs, escorted by ftrs from 10 gps, bomb 4 M/Ys at Ingolstadt, Freiburg, Reutlingen, and Augsburg, and several other tgts in SW Germany. 3 ftr gps fly sweeps and strafe ground tgts while 3 gps of FBs bomb M/Ys, roads and rail tgts.

Ninth AF: 16 9th Bomb Div bmrs hit Simmern bridge to help thwart movement in Trier area. XIX TAC escorts MBs, flies armed rcn and patrols, and supports US III and VIII Corps in Houffalize-Bastogne-Wiltz areas.

Twelfth AF: Operations resume as weather clears. MBs concentrate on Brenner rail line, flying nearly 150 sorties against bridges at San Michele all'Adige, Rovereto, Ala, Lavis, Santa Margherita d'Adige, and Motta di Livenza. XXII TAC attacks comm in Po Valley and further N, destroying or damaging several bridges and a very large number of railway cars (most of them at Como M/Y). During 14/15 Jan LBs hit tgts in Po Valley, including Po crossings at Borgoforte, Piacenza, and San Benedetto Po.

Fifteenth AF: 400-plus B–24's and B–17's escorted by 270-plus P–38's and P–51's, bomb M/Ys and other railroad comm in NE and SE Vienna and M/Y at Treviso.

Tenth AF: 12 B–24's bomb troop concentration and supply area at Mong Ngaw. 6 FBs damage bridge at Namhkai. 11 spt ground forces along the Irrawaddy, bombing Mabein, hitting cable crossing at Myitson, and attacking ferry landing on Nampaw R, a tributary. Troops, supplies, tanks and T/Os are attacked at several points in N Burma including Mong Tat, Mong Yok and Mong Pa. Transports fly 527 sorties to forward areas. Gens Wedeymeyer, Stratemeyer, and Sultan confer at Myitkyina and agree that an AAF HQ to cmd US Tenth and Fourteenth AFs should be set up in China.

Fourteenth AF: 18 B–25's, supported by 20 P–51's and P–40's, attack Hankow. Others hit Wan Pa-Hsa town area and damage nearby bridge, attack shipping near Amoy, and hit T/Os in Siang-Chiang and Hsiang Valleys and from Hong Kong to Foochow. 130-plus P–40's and P–51's on armed rcn attack numerous T/Os throughout S China from Burma border to SE coast.

FEAF: B–24's, B–25's, A–20's, and FBs attack objectives on Luzon, in C Phil, and on Palawan, hitting highways, railroads, A/Fs and numerous T/Os including tanks, trucks, and other vehicles. B–24's also bomb Jesselton A/Fs.

Seventh AF: 12 B–24's from Saipan hit A/Fs on Iwo Jima. 2 HBs, operating singly from Guam and Saipan, strike Iwo Jima A/Fs during 15/16 Jan.

16 January

Eighth AF: Over 550 HBs, supported by 13 ftr gps, bomb 2 synthetic oil plants, 2 aircraft engine plants, 2 M/Ys, a tank factory and several T/Os in C Germany. Due to heavy fog a large percentage of the HBs are diverted to various landing fields in UK and on Continent.

Ninth AF: 311 A–20's, A–26's, and B–26's hit road and rail bridges, comm centers, motor transport repair center, and other tgts in Germany. Ftrs escort 9th Bomb Div and Eighth AF HBs, fly armed rcn and defensive patrols, and spt US First Army elements along battleline NE of Houffalize, and III Corps along battleline SE of Houffalize.

Twelfth AF: During 15/16 Jan A–20's exploit a break in the bad weather and blast motor transport around Genoa and NE of Milan. During the day bad weather returns, grounding MBs and limiting FBs to 16 completed sorties against comm in Po Valley and NE Italy.

Fifteenth AF: Bad weather restricts operations to rcn and rcn escort missions by 30 P–38's.

Tenth AF: 12 B–25's attack troop concentration and supply dump at Namtoi. 15 P–47's spt ground forces near Yenya-u and S of Shadaw. 22 bomb A/Fs at Anisakan and Nawnghkio. Troop concentration, supplies, town areas, vehicles, and other tgts are attacked by 40-plus FBs. Transports fly 550 sorties to forward areas.

Fourteenth AF: 4 B–25's and 8 P–40's destroy train N of Hankow. 8 B–25's pound Wanting. 180-plus P–51's, P–40's, and P–38's on armed rcn over vast expanses of China S of the Yangtze and from Burma border to S China Sea attack numerous T/Os. Wanting, Muse, and Changsha areas are hit especially hard.

FEAF: In the day's principal strikes B–24's, A–20's, and FBs pound Japanese concentrations, trains, trucks, and T/Os on Luzon. Other B–24's hit A/Fs in N Borneo and Halmahera I. B–25's, A–20's, and FBs on small raids, armed rcn, and harassing strikes hit Negros A/Fs and A/Fs, comm tgts, trains, trucks, and other T/Os throughout Luzon.

Twentieth AF: 313th Bomb Wg (VH) flies shakedown mission. 32 of 44 B–29's bomb A/F on Pagan I.

Seventh AF: 10 B–24's from Guam bomb A/F on Iwo Jima. 12 P–38's from Saipan assigned to high cover for the HB strike fail to make contact with the formation due to bad weather. 3 of the ftrs strafe beached vessels. 3 B–24's fly snooper strikes against Iwo Jima A/Fs during 16/17 Jan.

17 January

Eighth AF: 650-plus HBs, supported by 8 ftr gps in close escort and 3 more in area sweeps, bomb 3 oil refineries, 2 viaducts, a M/Y, a U-boat yard, an A/F, and T/Os in NW Germany. The ftrs strafe rail tgt.

Ninth AF: Weather cancels all bmr operations and limits ftrs. XIX TAC flies night patrol while IX TAC flies leaflet mission and patrols XIX Corps area around Hurtgen Forest.

Twelfth AF: MBs, taking advantage of improved weather conditions, attack 6 rail tgts on Brenner rail line, blocking line at Calliano, cutting tracks at Ora, and destroying a section of bridge at Sacile. In NE Italy ftrs and FBs concentrate large effort on rail lines and bridges, destroying 4 and damaging another, cutting tracks at numerous points, and blasting vehicles and trains.

Fifteenth AF: Continued bad weather cancels all operations.

Tenth AF: 4 B–25's demolish 2 bypass bridges at Ho-hko. 8 pound village of Mansam. 20 P–47's spt ground forces along the Irrawaddy, hitting tgts at Konkha, Onbaing, and Wabyudaung. Troop concentrations and supplies are bombed by 75 FBs at Nawngchio, No-na, Man Hpa-yaw, Man Namket, Nanhu, Panghai, Mong Nge, and Ho-Pok. Transports fly 489 sorties to forward bases and frontline areas.

Fourteenth AF: 12 B–25's bomb town area, river shipping, and trucks at Ishan. 3 B–25's and 8 P–40's pound sampans and storage areas W of Hengshan while 2 B–25's hit oil dump and other T/Os in Hsiang Valley and another blasts troop compound at Chaling. 4 B–25's damage bridge at Phu Lang Thuong. 180-plus P–40's, P–51's, and P–38's hit large number of T/Os from Burma border to Shanghai, concentrating on Wanling area and A/Fs in Shanghai,

Wuchou, and Wuchang areas.

FEAF: In principal strikes of the day B–24's bomb railroad yards at Legaspi while B–25's hit roads and railways E of Manila, destroying many railroad cars and troop-laden trucks. Other B–24's pound Daliao area on Mindanao and Talisay A/F. B–25's, A–20's, and FBs continue to fly small strikes and armed rcn against bridges, shipping, port areas, A/Fs, trucks, and other T/Os throughout Luzon and at C Phil Is.

Twentieth AF: Nearly 80 B–29's, out of Chengtu, bomb A/F at Shinchiku. 8 other VHBs hit alternates and T/Os in SE China.

Seventh AF: 14 B–24's from Saipan pound A/Fs on Iwo Jima. 3 from Guam, on armed rcn flight, bomb Marcus. 2 B–24's, from Guam and Saipan, fly individual harassment strikes against Iwo Jima during 17/18 Jan.

18 January

Eighth AF: Over 100 B–17's supported by 3 ftr gps bomb Kaiserslautern M/Y. Most of the HBs are diverted, after bombing, to bases on Continent because of heavy clouds.

Ninth AF: IX TAC returns to operational control of Ninth AF (from Second Tac AF) as US First Army returns from 21st Army Gp to 12th Army Gp. IX TAC HQ (Rear) returns to Verviers from Charleroi. Weather prevents all Ninth AF operations except for alert flights by 11 ftrs of IX and XXIX TACs.

Twelfth AF: During 17/18 Jan A–20's attack Po R crossings, lights and movement throughout Po Valley. During the day MBs pound tgts on the Brenner line, including temporary

bridge between San Michele all'Adige and Ora, and overhanging cliff over railroad at San Ambrogio di Valpolicella. Ftrs and FBs blast comm lines in NE Italy and fuel and supply dumps in Piacenza area, destroying numerous railroad tracks, trains, and vehicles, and causing explosions or fires in most of the dumps.

Fifteenth AF: Weather prevents bombing operations. P–38's and P–51's fly photo rcn and escort missions.

Tenth AF: 23 P–47's and P–38's hit Anisakan and Hsumhsai A/Fs. 12 B–25's bomb A/F at Nawnghkio. 20-plus P–47's spt ground forces at Si-U and near Yenya-u and Mahlainggon. Troops, supplies, and general T/Os are attacked at Antawsai, Mong Nak, Namhpakka, Mong Yok, Loi-pyek, Kyawnghkam, Pangnok, and in Namtu vicinity. 529 transport sorties are flown to forward areas.

Fourteenth AF: 29 B–24's bomb Hong Kong. 7 B–25's bomb Ishan and Chinchengchiang, 4 B–25's and 12 P–40's hit shipping in Puchi area, 4 B–25's bomb town of Wanting, and 2 hit troop compounds at Chaling. 11 B–25's and 12 FBs attack Phu Lang Thuong. 25 P–40's pound shipping and railroad tgts at Hong Kong. About 140 P–51's, P–40's, and P–38's on armed rcn over S China from Burma boundary to Hong Kong attack a huge variety of T/Os.

FEAF: B–25's blast Cotabato area. B–24's bomb tgts in Miti area, B–25's hit troop concentrations at Bamban, A–20's hit warehouses and highway traffic N of Bataan, and P–38's strafe parked airplanes at Tuguegarao and vehicles at Enrile, Calarian, and Butigui. A variety of FEAF aircraft fly small-scale raids and armed rcn missions against road and rail tgts, bridges, A/Fs, and numerous T/Os throughout the Phil Is.

Seventh AF: 19 Saipan-based B–24's bomb tgts on Chichi Jima and Haha Jima, damaging naval base and town of Okimura. 10 B–24's from Guam pound A/F on Iwo Jima. 3 B–24's during 18/19 Jan continue snooper strikes against Iwo Jima A/Fs.

Eleventh AF: 3 B–24's fly unsuccessful rcn to Kurabu A/F. One of the B–24's force-lands in USSR on return trip.

19 January

Ninth AF: Bad weather cancels bmr operations. Ftrs fly patrols and armed rcn. XIX TAC also supports elements of US III and VIII Corps NE of Houffalize and around Clervaux, and 5th Inf Div around Bettendorf.

Twelfth AF: During 18/19 Jan A–20's bomb motor transport movements, lights, roads, and railroads throughout Po Valley. Weather cancels MB operations and prevents FBs from completing XXII TAC's only mission airborne during the day.

Fifteenth AF: Over 400 HBs attack N and S M/Ys, a railroad bridge, and a highway bridge at Brod. Because of overcast, only 1 of 112 HBs sent against Zagreb M/Y bombs tgt while others abort. 46 P–38's bomb S railroad bridge at Doboj and 59 P–51's sweep from Zagreb to Gyor. Other P–38's fly rcn missions and rcn escort and cover MATAF B–25's on supply run.

Tenth AF: 9 B–25's bomb troops and stores at Na-mon and near Hsenwi. 28 FBs spt ground forces in Si-U and Namhkam battle sectors and

along the Irrawaddy near Yenya-u, Kyaukpyu, and Myitson. 4 others bomb causeway in lake at Mogok. Troops, supplies, and arty are hit by 80-plus FBs at Tonghsim, Konghsa, Mankang, Mong Pa, Pangkawlong, Saihkao, Man Hio, Man Mao, and other locations in N Burma. Transports complete 500-plus sorties to forward areas.

Fourteenth AF: 4 B–25's bomb Mongyu and vicinity, 5 bomb Ishan, 8 hit shipping and rail tgts at Song Cau, and 4 hit shipping, railroad tgts, and bridge at Do Len. About 115 P–51's, P–40's, and P–38's on armed rcn over S China and N Indochina attack a great variety of T/Os covering especially Wanting area.

FEAF: In principal missions of the day, B–24's and B–25's bomb La Carlota and Bacolod A/Fs. A–20's attack shipping at Salomague and Callaguip. B–25's, A–20's, and FBs attack throughout Luzon, hitting A/Fs, vehicles, storage areas, highways, and a variety of other tgts.

Twentieth AF: 62 XXI BC B–29's hit Kawasaki aircraft plant at Akashi. 9 others bomb alternates and T/Os.

Seventh AF: 7 B–24's from Saipan bomb harbor installations at Chichi Jima. 9 from Guam hit A/Fs on Iwo Jima. 7 B–24's escort photo planes over the Bonin and Kazan Is and 1 bombs Iwo Jima. During the night 3 B–24's on individual snooper strikes from the Marianas bomb Iwo Jima.

Eleventh AF: 1 B–24 flies radar-ferret mission over Shimushu and Onnekotan. 2 other B–24's hit Matsuwa and Onnekotan.

20 January

International: Provisional National Government of Hungary signs armistice in Moscow with US, USSR, and Great Britain.

Eighth AF: Approximately 675 HBs attack 3 M/Ys, a synthetic oil plant, and 2 T/Os in W Germany. 9 ftr gps fly close escort, 2 others fly area patrols in Duren and Frankfurt/Main areas, strafing ground tgts.

Ninth AF: Bmr operations cancelled due to weather. Ftrs fly armed rcn, alerts, and night patrol. IX TAC also supports 7th Armd Div on Dutch-German boundary.

Twelfth AF: MBs destroy 1 and damage another bridge near San Michele all'Adige, and score good coverage on Trento M/Y. XXII TAC FBs very successfully blast comm and fuel and ammo dumps in Po Valley.

Fifteenth AF: The tac organization of Fifteenth AF becomes fully developed when a supply-dropping gp, 15th Special Gp (Prov), organized on 18 Jan, is given control of the 859th (B–24) and 885th (B–17) Bomb Sqs which drop supplies in France, Italy, and Yugoslavia. (In Mar the 15th Gp will be redesignated the 2641st Special Gp (Prov) and with its units attached to Twelfth AF for operational control, the Fifteenth retaining administrative control). 345 B–17's and B–24's attack N and S main M/Ys and station sidings at Linz, M/Ys at Salzburg and Rosenheim, and oil storage at Regensburg. Ftrs escort HBs and fly rcn and rcn escort missions.

Tenth AF: 16 FBs spt ground forces along the Irrawaddy near Mabein, Shadaw, and Myitson. 8 others hit ammo dump at Namhkai and

supply dump at Kutkai. Also hit are troop concentrations, supply areas and T/Os at Kyaunghkam, Panghung, Kawnglom, Namhsan, Loi-kang, and in Hsenwi area. 482 transport sorties are flown to advanced bases and battle sectors.

Fourteenth AF: 4 B–25's hit bridge and railroad cars near Hanoi. 3 B–25's attack T/Os W of Hengshan, 2 hit troop compound and other tgts at Chaling and Anjen, and 1 damages a small freighter in E China Sea. 32 P–51's pound A/Fs in Shanghai area, claiming 22 airplanes destroyed. More than 200 P–40's, P–51's, and P–38's on armed rcn over vast S China and N Indochina areas attack bridges, town areas, rail, road and river traffic, and other T/Os at numerous points.

FEAF: B–24's pound Fabrica A/F and bomb underground storage area at Bamban. A–20's and B–25's hit railroads and trains near Bicol R and between Calauag and Legaspi. Other A–20's and FBs hit Aparri-Laoag and Tubang A/Fs, hit arty positions W of Bong Bong and destroy railroad bridge at Aloneros.

Twentieth AF: Gen LeMay takes cmd of XXI BC. Gen Ramey officially becomes CG XX BC.

Seventh AF: 12 Guam-based B–24's bomb A/Fs on Iwo Jima. 5 from Saipan hit town of Okimura. During 20/21 Jan, 10 HBs from Guam fly separate snooper strikes against Iwo Jima A/Fs.

Eleventh AF: 4 B–24's bomb Kataoka area.

21 January

Eighth AF: About 750 HBs hit M/Y and tank factory at Aschaffenburg, military vehicle plant, bridge, comm center and M/Y at Mannheim, M/Ys at Heilbronn and Pforzheim, comm center at Arnbach, town of Reutlingen, and 3 T/Os. 9 ftr gps fly close spt and strafe 4 A/Fs plus numerous miscellaneous ground tgts. 1 P-51 gp flies area sweep in spt of HBs and another supports Ninth AF MBs.

Ninth AF: IX TAC HQ (main) returns to Verviers from Liege. 166 A-26's, A-20's, and B-26's hit rail junction and bridge at Euskirchen and M/Y and defended positions at Mayen. Ftrs fly armed rcn, escort bmrs, bomb bridges, and spt US 7th Armd Div.

Twelfth AF: Weather restricts operations during 21/22 Jan to armd rcn by 5 A-20's. The LBs bomb comm tgts in Po Valley. During day B-25's hit bridges at Rovereto and Lavis, destroy bridge at Pontetidone, and blast railroad fill at San Michele all' Adige, and supply dump at Cremona. Ftrs and FBs concentrate on comm in same area as MBs, destroying 1 bridge, inflicting 36 rail cuts, hitting fuel and ammo dumps, and destroying and damaging many vehicles and much railroad rolling stock, mostly in Milan area.

Fifteenth AF: 170 B-17's bomb Lobau and Schwechat oil refineries at Vienna. 131 P-51's and P-38's provide spt. 43 P-38's bomb oil refinery at Fiume. Other ftrs escort rcn missions and accompany supply-dropping operations to Yugoslavia.

Tenth AF: 10 B-25's bomb Heho A/F. 12 P-38's bomb bridge area at Nampawng. 26 P-47's spt ground forces near Twinnge, Mahlainggon, and Konkha along the Irrawaddy, and in the Si-U sector. 50-plus P-38's

and P-47's hit troop concentrations, supplies, and T/Os at Me-han, Mogok, Hsenwi, Na-makhkaw, Kutkai, Kunhkan, and Man On. Nearly 500 transports sorties are flown to forward areas.

Fourteenth AF: 30 B-24's pound Hong Kong area. 12 P-51's hit Nanking A/F (claiming 11 enemy airplanes destroyed) and T/Os along the Yangtze to Hankow. 30 P-51's and P-40's on armed rcn hit T/Os at several locations. 12 of the FBs concentrate on Wanting area.

FEAF: B-24's bomb Marikina A/F and hit barracks and coastal def guns at Calabasan. B-25's, A-20's, and FBs fly sweeps, small strikes, and armed rcn attacks on A/Fs, road networks, bridges, gun positions, numerous vehicles, and other T/Os throughout C and S Luzon.

Twentieth AF: 30 B-29's, flying out of the Marianas, bomb Moen A/F.

Seventh AF: 12 Guam-based B-24's bomb A/Fs on Iwo Jima. During 21/22 Jan, 8 more, flying separate snooper strikes from Saipan, pound the A/Fs.

22 January

Eighth AF: Nearly 200 B-17's, supported by 85 ftr sorties, bomb Sterkrade-Holten synthetic oil plant, Rheine M/Y, Dinslaken, Osnabruck, and T/Os. 2 P-51 gps fly area sweeps (1 in escort to Ninth AF MBs).

Ninth AF: 304 B-26's, A-26's, and A-20's bomb M/Y, railhead, and road and rail bridges in Germany with aim of obstructing troop movement. Ftrs escort 9th Bomb Div, fly armed rcn and sweeps and A/F cover, and spt US 7 Armd Div near Montfort, III, VIII, and XII Corps from S of Saint-

Vith along battlefront to NW of Echternach, and 4th, 5th, 94th, and 95th Inf Divs from Echternach S to just W of Saarlautern.

Twelfth AF: B–25's score damaging hits at Rovereto, San Michele all' Adige and on Dogna bridge, and attack Chiari and Crema bridges with fair results. FBs range over practically all of N Italy destroying and damaging large number of vehicles and railway cars and several locomotives, also hitting fuel and ammo dumps around Mantua.

Fifteenth AF: Bad weather limits operations to 1 P–38 weather rcn flight.

Tenth AF: 46 P–47's spt ground forces near Si-U, Namhkam, and along the Irrawaddy near Twinnge, Bahe, Nam Mit R, Myitson, and Banwe. 12 others hit T/Os along roads near Kutkai, Hsenwi, Lashio, and Namtu. Troop concentrations, fuel and ammo dumps, vehicles, and general supplies are pounded at Kin, Padan, Man Lom, Namtu, Hkamtung, Kabaing, Nammaw-hpek, Panglaw, and Na-hsang. Transports fly 449 sorties to advanced bases and frontline areas.

Fourteenth AF: 16 P–40's and P–51's on armed rcn attack various tgts in Wanting area and in SW China. 10 P–51's bomb buildings at Kunlong ferry. 14 P–51's and P–40's hit Sintsiang railroad yards and destroy several locomotives and trucks E of Tsinan and Suchow.

FEAF: B–24's, escorted by P–38's, bomb Heito A/F in first major Fifth AF strike on Formosa. Other B–24's bomb barracks in the Cabaruan Hills and gun positions across Manila Bay and hit Fabrica A/F. In smaller miscellaneous strikes, FEAF ftrs and bmrs over C and S Luzon hit enemy positions, small shipping, and highways at several points, and damage bridge over Magata R.

Seventh AF: 20 B–24's from Guam blast A/Fs at Iwo Jima, while 8 more B–24's flying individual strikes from Guam pound the A/Fs again during 22/23 Jan.

23 January

Eighth AF: 150-plus B–17's, escorted by 2 P–51 gps, bomb M/Y and bridge at Neuss. A P–51 Continent-based gp flies uneventful sweep over Neuss area.

Ninth AF: A small B–26 force hits troop concentrations, road bridge, and military transport tgts at Blankenheim, Dasburg, and Arzfeld. Ftrs fly armed rcn, alert flights, and patrols, and spt US III, VIII, and XII Corps and 4th, 94th, and 95th Inf Divs from S of Saint-Vith, S and E along the battleline to just W of Saarlautern.

Twelfth AF: During 22/23 Jan A–20's bomb lights, roads, and river crossings at over 50 locations in Po Valley, hit several T/Os, and attack Borgoforte and San Benedetto Po and A/Fs at Villafranca di Verona and Ghedi. Weather cancels MB operations during the day. FBs operate mainly against comm, principally railroad tgts, in Po Valley but also hit ammo dumps, shipping, guns, vehicles, and other tgts in N Italy scattered from Genoa to NE Italy.

Fifteenth AF: Continued bad weather cancels all operations.

Tenth AF: 12 B–25's bomb A/Fs at Aungban and Hsumhsai. 34 P–47's spt ground forces near Namhkam and along the Irrawaddy in the Twin-nge and Bahe areas. 55 P–47's and P–38's hit troop concentrations, stor-age areas and vehicles at Kawngwang, Sati, Kyaukme, Wengnan, Hko-lawng, Lothke, and Panglaw. Transports fly 542 sorties, carrying men and supplies to advanced bases and drop supplies to troops in frontline areas.

Fourteenth AF: 40 P–51's and P–40's on armed rcn attack T/Os (main-ly river, road, and rail traffic) at sev-eral locations in both S China and in N China plain, including Wanting-Suchow and Yuankiang areas, lower Tungting Lake region, points between Kiaotow and Kweiyi, and points as far N as Peking.

FEAF: On 22/23 Jan B–24's again hit Formosa in force, bombing alumi-num factory at Takao. In the day's principal missions, B–24's bomb Baguio and, along with A–20's, hit Corregidor I. Other A–20's attack Aparri A/F while FBs hit bridge at Digdig, luggers S of Alcala, guns on Grande I, bridge over Magata R, and base at Camp John Hay. B–24s hit Silay A/F.

Twentieth AF: 28 B–29's of XXI BC bomb Mitsubishi engine plant at Nagoya. 27 hit secondary tgt, the urban area of the city. 9 bomb other alternates and T/Os. An estimated 600-plus ftrs offer heavy and agres-sive opposition but down only 1 VHB. US gunners claim 32 ftrs downed.

Seventh AF: 12 B–24's from Sai-pan bomb Iwo Jima A/Fs. 3 from Guam fly armed rcn over Woleai, 2 of them bombing the main runway on the island. During 23/24 Jan, 10 B–24's from Saipan strike Iwo Jima singly at about 45-min intervals.

Eleventh AF: 1 B–24 flies rcn

sortie along Onnekotan-Matsuwa E coasts. 4 B–24's strike Kakumabetsu cannery and tgts on Paramushiru. 8–10 ftrs intercept and the B–24's claim 2 victories. 1 B–24 is lost.

24 January

Eighth AF: 2 P–51 gps fly sweeps over Wahn A/F-Dorweiler area and Karlsruhe-Koblenz area, claiming 3 ftrs downed.

Ninth AF: 25 9th Bomb Div bmrs hit comm centers at Schleiden, Stadt-kyll, and Pronsfeld. Ftrs fly armed rcn, sweeps, A/F cover, and bomb 1 bridge. XIX TAC supports US III, VIII, XII, and XX Corps elements along battlefront at several points from SW of Saint-Vith to Saarlau-tern area.

Twelfth AF: Cloud conditions and ground fog at bases nearby halt oper-tions. 1 MB flies weather rcn over Venice area and P–47's fly weather rcn over Bologna-Parma area. 2 of the P–47's destroy a truck and damage a train near Parma.

Fifteenth AF: Unfavorable weather limits operations to 1 complete weather rcn mission.

Tenth AF: 12 B–25's bomb Hsum-hsai A/F. 17 P–47's spt ground forces at Padin near Namhkam, and along the Irrawaddy in Bahe area. 6 P–47's knock out Inailong bypass bridge. Troop concentrations and supply areas are attacked at Nawngang, Pangsan, Mansak, Konsan, Yaun-ggwin, Mangkung, Nawngngun, Mong Long, Mogok, Namhsan, and in Mongmit area. Transports again fly over 500 sorties to forward areas.

Fourteenth AF: 12 P–51's on armed rcn attack railroad tgts N of Siangsiang, between Loyang and Kaifeng, and near Tungchen. 21 locomotives are claimed destroyed.

FEAF: B–24's pound Corregidor, Cavite, Canacao peninsula seaplane base, and Grande I. FEAF ftrs and bmrs on sweeps, armed rcn, and light raids attack a variety of tgts all over Luzon including small shipping, A/Fs, def positions, storage and town areas, roads, and vehicles. During 24/25 Jan, B–24's on snooper mission again hit Takao A/F.

Twentieth AF: 20 B–29's of 313th Bomb Wg hit 2 A/Fs on Iwo Jima.

Seventh AF: 33 B–24's, from Guam and Saipan, pound Iwo Jima during 4 raids. 6 others act as airborne spotters for naval bombardment of Iwo. During 5 hrs of 24/25 Jan, 10 HBs maintain harassment strikes against the island's A/Fs.

Eleventh AF: 4 B–25's on a low-level attack on Torishima abort due to mechanical trouble. 4 more B–25's bomb buildings on Torishima. AA fire damages 2 B–25's. 6 ftrs take off after radar reports an unidentified tgt SE of Attu. They spot a balloon which they shoot down with tracers.

25 January

US: Gen Stilwell is assigned cmdr of Army Ground Forces.

Eighth AF: 2 ftr gps sweep over wide areas of SW Germany, claiming 2 ftrs downed NE of Mannheim and E of Kirrlach.

Ninth AF: 170 MBs and LBs hit comm centers and railroad bridges, overpasses, and lines in W Germany with aim of harassing and obstructing troop movement. Ftrs of the 3 TACs fly armed rcn, alerts and night patrols, escort bmrs, and attack numerous ground tgts. XIX TAC supports US 5th Inf Div in Echternach area.

Twelfth AF: During 24/25 Jan A–20's make several intruder attacks on roads, motor transport, bridges, and trains. Bad weather during the day greatly curtails flying. The only MB mission dispatched achieves poor results on Cremona ammo dump. FBs and ftrs of XXII TAC hit comm and dump areas, mainly in Milan area, with good general success.

Fifteenth AF: Weather curtails operations. P–38's fly photo and weather rcn. P–51's escort the photo rcn missions.

Tenth AF: 24 P–47's spt ground forces in Namhkam area, near Molo, and near Myitson. 12 B–25's pound A/F at Heho. 80-plus FBs attack troops, supplies, and T/Os at Hsenwi, Loi-weng, Ho hpong, Loi Nan, Tingyet, Mong Tat, Ho-mong, Mong Long, Pangkwai, and in Kutkai area. Transports fly 581 sorties to forward areas.

Fourteenth AF: 21 P–51's hit rail tgts and A/Fs in Peking area, claiming 4 locomotives and 40 aircraft destroyed. 16 P–40's and P–51's attack railroad tgts around Kaifeng, Shihkiachwang, Pengpu, and Chingmen. 42 locomotives are claimed destroyed.

FEAF: B–24's, operating in force, again pound Corregidor I. B–24's, B–25's, A–20's, and FBs on sweeps, armed rcn, and small-scale strikes hit vehicles, enemy positions, A/Fs, ammo and supply dumps, barges, comm, and T/Os in general, over wide areas of Luzon, Palawan, and in C Phil Is. During 25/26 Jan B–24's fly harassing raid on Takao.

Seventh AF: 14 Saipan-based B–24's bomb Iwo Jima in the afternoon. During 25/26 Jan, 10 more, flying individual harassment strikes at intervals, pound the island.

26 January

Eighth AF: 1 P–51 gp, based on Continent, flies uneventful ftr sweeps over Heilbronn, Aschaffenburg, Giessen, and Trier areas.

Ninth AF: 27 B–26's bomb Euskirchen rail bridge to interdict rail traffic SW from Euskirchen, much of which comes from Cologne and Bonn. The 3 TACs fly armed rcn, alert flights, and patrols. XIX TAC supports US Third Army elements from S of Saint-Vith to W of Saarlautern.

Twelfth AF: During 25/26 Jan A–20's fly armed rcn of Po Valley, bombing Po R crossings, Ghedi A/F, and general movement throughout the area. Both 57th Bomb Wg and XXII TAC cancel all operations for the day because of bad weather.

Fifteenth AF: Weather prevents bombing operations. P–38's fly rcn and rcn-escort missions and escort RAF supply drop over Yugoslavia.

Tenth AF: 8 FBs spt ground forces in Namhkam area. 140-plus FBs hit trops, supplies, guns, railroad tgts, and T/Os at Tangtong, Panghai, Man Pwe, Kyaunghkam, Mong Pa, Nalang, Hsenwi, Molo, Mong Tat, Humon, Tonghkan, Pangnim, Konghsa, Namtu, Namhsan, and in Nampok area. Transports fly more than 500 sorties to advanced bases and frontline areas.

Fourteenth AF: 15 P–51's and P–40's hit Chenghsien A/F and locomotives, tracks, and motor transport at Nanking and Sinsiang.

FEAF: B–24's hit coastal guns on Corregidor and in Balete Pass.

B–25's bomb Cabcaben A/F area and coastal guns on Carabao I and A–20's attack Grande I coastal defenses. B–25's bomb Likanan and Sasa. P–38's strafe same tgts and also hit Padada. A–20's and FBs, along with a few B–24's, continue armed rcn and miscellaneous attacks against A/Fs, comm, vehicles, coastal guns, town areas, and other tgts throughout Luzon and in C Phils.

Twentieth AF: During 25/26 Jan, 70-plus B–29's of XX BC mine the 6 approaches to Singapore harbor and at Saigon, Camranh Bay, Pakchan R, Penang harbor, Koh Si Chang Channel, and Phan Rang Bay.

Seventh AF: 17 Guam-based B–24's bomb Iwo Jima A/Fs. During 26/27 Jan the A/Fs are hit by 9 B–24's on individual harassment missions.

27 January

Ninth AF: Weather grounds 9th Bomb Div and XIX TAC. IX and XXIX TACs fly armed rcn over battle area and parts of W Germany, along with alert flights and leaflet mission.

Twelfth AF: Bad weather during morning causes all MBs to abort except for an attack on bridge at Bressana Bottarone. XXII TAC ftrs and FBs continue interdiction of comm with good results against motor transport, trains, rail lines, bridges, and storage dumps. P–47's of 57th Ftr Gp destroy oil plant near Fornovo di Taro.

Fifteenth AF: For sixth consecutive day bad weather restricts operations to rcn and escort missions.

Tenth AF: 30-plus FBs spt ground forces at Man Sak, Molo Ywama, area

S of Molo, and area S of Banwe. 8 others knock out bypass bridge at Bawgyo. About 100 FBs hit troop concentrations, supplies, and T/Os at or near Man Kyan, Kuinkuiloi, Hohkun, Pongalau, Hsenwi, Kutkai, Hsatong, Ping hoi, Ho-mong, Padon, and Kyaung-hen. Transports fly 527 sorties to advanced bases and over forward areas, landing men and landing and dropping supplies.

Fourteenth AF: 22 P–40's and P–51's attack locomotives, trucks, and shipping at Sinsiang, Kihsien, and Nanking, from Taiyuan to Puchou, and E of Yiyang.

FEAF: B–24's pound Canacao seaplane base, Cavite, and Grande I while B–25's hit Cabcaben and A/F at Calingatan. Other FEAF aircraft continue small-scale strikes against numerous other A/Fs, town areas, gun emplacements, harbors, and comm and transportation tgts throughout Luzon.

Twentieth AF: By this date the complete forward dets of the 4 B–29 gps in the Chengtu area have evacuated their bases and moved to more permanent bases in India. This move complies with JCS directive formulated on 15 Dec 44 and received on 18 Dec. The long-existing understanding that XX BC might be moved from CBI when more convenient bases are available is thus put into its initial stage when XX BC's CG, Gen LeMay, and JCS agree that on logistical grounds XX BC's operating scheme is basically unsound, a situation made more apparent when in Nov the Japanese had overrun Luchou and Yungning and threatened Kunming. This development necessitated air tonnage flown over the Hump being diverted to Chinese ground forces and Fourteenth AF, resulting in curtailed supplies to XX BC and providing the catalyst for beginning movement of the cmd from China. 22 XX BC B–29's based in India hit navy yard and arsenal at Saigon. 1 bombs bridge at Bangkok. Results are poor. 76 B–29's of 73d Bomb Wg are airborne from the Marianas against Musashiho and Nakajima aircraft plants near Tokyo. Clouds and high winds over tgt area prevent bombing of the primary. 56 VHBs bomb secondary tgt of Tokyo urban area and 6 others attack alternates and T/Os. Ftr opposition is the heaviest to date and 5 B–29's are downed. 4 others ditch or crashland. B–29 gunners claim 60 ftr kills, the highest VHB claim to date.

Seventh AF: 19 B–24's, based at Saipan, bomb Iwo Jima. 10 HBs from Saipan and Guam follow up with individual harassment raids against the island during 27/28 Jan. 1 B–24 from Angaur bombs Arakabesan.

28 January

Eighth AF: Nearly 900 HBs attack 2 benzol plants, 3 M/Ys, 3 bridges, 4 city areas, and T/Os in W Germany. 5 P–51 gps fly escort. 1 gp escorts MBs of Ninth AF.

Ninth AF: 95 9th Bomb Div bmrs hit comm center at Mayen, rail bridges and overpass at Eller, Sinzig, Remagen, and Kaiserslautern, T/Os in W Germany, and fly cover for US First Army forces on frontline in Monschau-Butgenbach area.

Twelfth AF: Weather again hampers operations. B–25's have good results on railroad bridges at Lavis and San Michele all'Adige. XXII

TAC aircraft operate effectively against comm and transport tgts throughout N Italy including at Milan, Pavia, Cremona, Nervesa della Battaglia, Treviso, Genoa, Padua, and Lake Maggiore areas.

Fifteenth AF: Continued bad weather (seventh successive day) restricts operations to 3 weather rcn flights.

Tenth AF: 40 FBs spt ground forces SE of Banwe, E of Molo, S of Molo Ywama, and near Namhkam. 80 FBs hit troop concentrations, supply areas, and enemy movement and active areas at or near Namsangsok, Namlan, Pangmakmo, Wengnan, Kutkai, and Mu-lwat. Again well over 500 sorties are flown to forward areas by transports. First convoy from Ledo crosses Chinese border heading for Kunming.

Fourteenth AF: 23 P-40's and P-51's attack railway and river traffic at Wuhu, Sinyang, and Linfen, in Sinsiang-Hantan area, between Loyang and Sinyang, and along Pinghan railroad.

FEAF: B-24's, B-25's, A-20's and FBs concentrate attacks on Luzon, heaviest tonnage (from B-24's) falling on Corregidor. Cavite and tgts between Manila and Subic Bay, including Laoag A/F, are also hit. A-20's concentrate on tgts in Aparri-Gattaran area while FBs and A-20's hit A/Fs in Cagayan Valley and troops, trucks, and roads in San Felipe and Talavera areas.

Seventh AF: 10 B-24's from Guam and 10 from Saipan bomb A/Fs on Iwo Jima. 10 more follow during 28/29 Jan with single-bmr harassment raids on the A/Fs. 2 B-24's from Angaur bomb Arakabesan.

29 January

Eighth AF: 1000-plus HBs bomb 7 M/Ys, 2 rail centers, 2 viaducts, a city area, military vehicle and aircraft factories, and T/Os in W Germany. 14 ftr gps fly spt and strafe ground tgts.

Ninth AF: 364 A-20's, B-26's, and A-26's bomb rail bridges, supply and comm centers, and defended areas in W Germany. Ftrs escort the bmrs, fly armed rcn and patrols and spt US Third Army units at points along frontlines from S of Saint-Vith to bridgehead area around Saarlautern.

Twelfth AF: Gen Barcus becomes CG XII TAC. Due to high winds and generally bad weather, MBs successfully bomb only 2 tgts, the railway bridges at Calliano and Rovereto, and attack with less success bridges at Motta di Livenza, Lavis, Mantua, and Chiusaforte, and railway station at Lavis. XXII TAC ftrs and FBs operate primarily against comm throughout Po Valley. Results are generally good and bridge at Nervesa della Battaglia is cut. Bridges or their approaches at Cittadella, Santa Margherita d'Adige and Cismon del Grappa are damaged along with a variety of tgts. During 28/29 Jan intruder LBs hit rail facilities, pontoon bridge, lights, and motor transport at nearly 50 locations in Po Valley.

Fifteenth AF: Weather prevents bombing operations for eighth consecutive day. P-38's fly photo and weather rcn missions.

Tenth AF: 13 B-25's knock out road bridges at Loi-leng and Tonglau and hit several nearby T/Os. 26 P–47's hit troop positions in Namhkai area. 11 P–38's and 16 P–47's attack A/Fs at Aungban and Heho. 8 P–47's spt ground forces near Banwe. 70 P–47's and P–38's pound troop concentrations and supplies at Panglong, Tangyan, Wengnan, Homang, Mong Long, Namtu, Mongyin, Mong Yang, and Namhsam. Large-scale transport operations continue.

Fourteenth AF: Pailochi A/F, river and road shipping, troops, gun positions, buildings, and other T/Os are attacked at Kweiyi, Hankow, Sinyang and Chihkiang, between Hengshan and Siangtan, between Wuhu and Anking, N of Hengyang, and E and S of Yutze.

FEAF: Heavy B–24 daylight raids concentrate on Heito A/F area and Corregidor while B–25's bomb nearby Cabcaben. FBs and A–20's hit T/Os from Aparri to Echague. Further S ftrs hit gun positions in the Batangas and Verde Is areas. A–20's spt ground forces inland from Lingayen by hitting Carranglen road net. Others hit Talavera and Carabao I.

Twentieth AF: About 30 Marianas-based B–29's strike at 2 A/Fs on Iwo Jima.

Seventh AF: 19 Guam-based B–24's bomb Iwo Jima A/Fs. 2 from Saipan, on armed rcn flight, bomb Marcus. 1 B–24 from Angaur bombs Arakabesan. During 29/30 Jan, 5 HBs from Saipan continue harassment raids on Iwo Jima A/Fs.

30 January

International: Preliminary part of Malta-Yalta conferences begin at Malta.

Ninth AF: Weather cancels bmr operations. Ftrs fly nightfighter and intruder rcn missions. Ftr cover for US 5th Armd Div W of Gemund is recalled during the day.

Twelfth AF: Good weather in Po Valley permits full-scale operations against comm lines. During 29/30 Jan intruding A–20's pound scattered movement (much of it near Milan), several Po R crossings including at Borgoforte, Piacenza, and San Benedetto Po, harbor at La Spezia, and fuel dumps and other tgts at many locations. B–25's effectively strike Brenner rail line during the day, especially Lavis and Trento M/Ys and bridges at Lavis and Calliano. XXII TAC ftrs and FBs strike railroads and bridges in NE Italy cutting many lines and damaging several bridges, and hit fuel dumps and factories around Parma.

Fifteenth AF: For ninth successive day weather prevents bombing operations. During 29/30 Jan, 13 B–24's drop supplies in N Italy. During the day P–38's fly rcn and rcn-escort and carry out supply missions and strafing attacks in Austria.

Tenth AF: 65 FBs spt ground forces in Banwe, Yenya-u, Hsenwi, Molo, and Mongmit areas. 5 others knock out bridge E of Mong Long. 100-plus FBs attack troops, supplies, arty, and comm tgts at several locations including Kutkai, Bawgyo, Ham ngai, Namhsan, Naleng, Pangsari, Hsenwi, and Wengnan. Transports again fly over 500 sorties to forward areas.

Fourteenth AF: 27 B–24's bomb Hankow. 32 P–40's and P–51's spt the HBs. 8 P–51's hit T/Os in areas around Loyang, Yuncheng, and Sinantien.

FEAF: Bad weather cancels most of scheduled strikes over Luzon. However, B-24's bomb Cavite while FBs flying spt for ground forces hit arty and troop concentrations NE of Labayug and others attack ammo dumps N of San Isidro.

Seventh AF: 17 B-24's from Saipan bomb Iwo Jima A/F. 3 others bomb A/F on Woleai. 5 B-24's from Angaur strike Koror and Arakabesan. During 30/31 Jan, 10 HBs from Saipan fly single-bmr snooper raids against Iwo Jima A/Fs.

31 January

International: Conference at Malta begins. Churchill, Eden, Stettinius, and the CCS discuss Western Front strategy, Anglo-US forces of occupation in Germany, and shipping problems.

Eighth AF: 400-plus HBs and 4 gps of escorting ftrs are recalled from mission against tgts in Germany because of expected bad weather at UK bases and heavy clouds.

Ninth AF: All operations cancelled due to weather.

Twelfth AF: MBs attack railroad bridges at Chiusaforte, Voghera, Lavis, Rovereto, and San Michele all' Adige, and M/Y at Rovereto, with only fair results. Ftrs and FBs hit bridges, rail lines, trains, vehicles, and other tgts over widespread areas of N Italy. During 30/31 Jan LBs hit several railroad tgts during intruder missions in Po Valley.

Fifteenth AF: 670-plus B-24's and B-17's bomb Moosbierbaum oil refinery, M/Ys at Graz and Maribor, and scattered T/Os. P-38's and P-51's fly

over 300 escorting sorties for the HBs. Other P-38's fly rcn and rcn escort and drop supplies into Austria. During 30/31 Jan B-24's drop supplies in N Italy.

Tenth AF: 12 B-25's hit troops and stores at Namlan. 50-plus P-47's attack troops and supplies at several locations including Na-mawtawng, Tawkut, Mong Long, Hsipaw, Hsenwi, and Namhpakka. Transports complete 535 sorties to forward bases and frontline areas.

Fourteenth AF: P-51's strafe T/Os along Pinghan railroad.

Thirteenth AF: Gen Barnes again assumes cmd of XIII FC.

Seventh AF: 20 B-24's from Guam bomb A/Fs and AA defenses on Iwo Jima. During 31 Jan/1 Feb, 9 more HBs, flying single-bmr harassment strikes, hit the island.

1 February

Eighth AF: 600-plus HBs hit 3 M/Ys at Mannheim, Ludwigshafen, and Krefeld, and 3 bridges at Wesel and Mannheim, along with towns of Pforzheim and Barth and T/Os in the area. 6 ftr gps fly close and freelance spt.

Ninth AF: 146 B-26's, A-26's, and A-20's bomb rail bridges and defended areas on Rhine and Mosel Rivers and in W Germany near battlefront. IX and XIX TACs escort MBs and LBs, fly armed rcn, and attack Euskirchen M/Y and town of Arloff.

Twelfth AF: Bad weather curtails operations. LBs and MBs are grounded and ftrs and FBs fly only 14 sorties, 12 against comm tgts N of battle area and 2 weather rcn sorties.

Fifteenth AF: Over 300 B–17's and B–24's attack Moosbierbaum oil refinery and M/Ys at Graz, Furstenfeld, and Klagenfurt. 1 HB bombs Pula. P–38's and P–51's fly 270-plus sorties escorting HBs. Other P–38's carry out rcn and rcn escort missions.

Tenth AF: 28 FBs spt ground forces around Hosi and Molo. 12 B–25's knock out Mong Pawn bridge. 8 P–47's damage approach to Pa-mao bridge. 8 others hit Hsumhsai A/F. 90-plus FBs hit troops, supplies, vehicles, ferry crossing, and various T/Os at several locations including Nauchye, Hsenwi, Man Pwe, Pongkalau, Nawng Mawn, Na-lang, Kunhkan, and Panghtu-lin. 550 transport sorties are flown to forward areas.

Fourteenth AF: 6 B–24's attack shipping off Indochina coast, claiming 1 cargo vessel sunk and a patrol boat damaged. 4 P–40's attack div HQ SW of Yungning.

FEAF: B–24's pound Canacao peninsula and Cavite areas. Tgts include shipyard, seaplane base, comm, and supply. B–25's hit Puerto Princesa. B–24's bomb Okayama A/F during 31 Jan/1 Feb and hit Okayama and Heito A/F and Toko seaplane base during the following day.

Twentieth AF: 67 B–29's bomb the Admiralty IX Floating Drydock (and vessel berthed in it) at Singapore navy yard. 21 other B–29's bomb West Wall area of the naval base. 21 others hit alternate tgts at Martaban and George Town.

Seventh AF: 21 Saipan-based B–24's hit Iwo Jima in the afternoon, and 10 more, flying individual snooper raids, hit the island during 1/2 Feb. 20 B–24's from Angaur bomb Corregidor.

2 February

Eighth AF: 1 ftr gp flies uneventful sweep in Koblenz-Wetzlar-Siegen-Siegburg area.

Ninth AF: 350-plus B–26's, A–26's, and A–20's bomb road and rail bridges to block E-W movement E of the Rhine and defended localities E of battlefront in W Germany. Ftrs hit bridges and fly escort, armed rcn and patrols, and spt US Third Army elements along the Our-Sauer Rivers.

Twelfth AF: MBs, taking advantage of improving weather conditions in NE Italy, hit bridges at Lavis, Chiusaforte, Calliano, Mantua, Rovereto, Calcinato, and Dogna. Bad weather at bases restricts XXII TAC aircraft to 5 weather rcn sorties.

Fifteenth AF: Bad weather cancels bombing operations. 1 B–17 and 1 B–24 drop supplies in N Italy. 33 P–51's, with 14 others flying top cover, strafe Kurilovec A/F. 11 other P–51's escort RAF supply dropping mission over Yugoslavia. 11 P–38's fly photo and weather rcn. Photo rcn is covered by 24 other P–38's.

Tenth AF: 11 B–25's pound troops and supplies at Loilem. 60-plus FBs spt ground forces in Molo, Hosi, and Mabein areas. Troops, supplies, town areas, and vehicles are attacked at Panma, Kan-loi, Pansak, Man Ho Pang, Pongkalau, Hsenwi, Namtu, Panghai, Kong kang, and Ondon. Transports complete 485 sorties to forward bases and over frontline areas.

Fourteenth AF: 4 P–40's attack regimental HQ and a storage area at Lungchow.

FEAF: B–24's continue to pound Corregidor and Cavite. In the Cagayan Valley B–25's attack pillboxes, gun positions, and river barges. A–20's hit Baler Bay area. B–24's hit Okayama A/F during dawn raid.

Thirteenth AF: Col Carl A Brandt becomes CO XIII BC.

Seventh AF: 20 Guam-based B–24's pound Iwo Jima storage area. During 2/3 Feb, 10 more, flying individual harassment raids, bomb the island's A/Fs. 4 P–47's, on rcn flight, strafe buildings on Pagan. 22 B–24's from Angaur bomb Corregidor.

3 February

Eighth AF: Over 1,200 B–17's and B–24's bomb M/Y in Berlin and a synthetic oil plant and transportation tgts at Magdeburg. Around 900 ftrs spt the HBs.

Ninth AF: 9th Bomb Div attacks Berg-Gladbach storage and repair depot, Dahlem comm center, rail bridges at Ahrweiler and Sinzig, and M/Y at Junkerath. Ftrs escort 9th Bomb Div, fly patrols, and carry out armed rcn over W Germany.

Twelfth AF: Weather restricts combat operations to an attack by 4 P–47's on Sonico M/Y.

Fifteenth AF: Weather again cancels bombing operations. P–38's fly photo and weather rcn. P–51's escort photo rcn while other P–38's escort MATAF B–25's on transport run to Yugoslavia.

Tenth AF: 12 B–25's attack troops and supplies at Loilem. 27 FBs close by spt ground forces in Molo, Hosi, and Myitson areas. 80-plus FBs hit troop concentrations, supplies, town areas, tanks, and other tgts at Kyaung-hen, Mongkyet, Hsipaw, Hsenwi, Nasang, Konghsa, and Hkaihsi. Transports complete 531 sorties, landing men and supplies at

advanced bases and dropping supplies to forward troops.

FEAF: B–24's again pound Corregidor and Canacao peninsula. Other B–24's hit Aparri and Tuguegarao. In Batangas area A–20's continue ground spt missions. B–24's bomb Cebu City and surrounding tgts. B–25's and P–38's hit Matina, Daliao, and Padada A/Fs.

Seventh AF: 9 Saipan-based B–24's hit Chichi Jima. 10 others hit Iwo Jima while 9, flying single-bmr harassment strikes, pound Iwo Jima during 3/4 Feb. 15 P–38's, part of a force escorting photo airplanes, strafe the island in 2-wave attack.

4 February

International: US-British-Soviet conference opens at Yalta. Stalin, Churchill, Roosevelt, their CoS, Molotov, Eden, Stettinius, and Hopkins attend. Discussed are USSR's entry into war against Japan, policy toward Germany, Polish problem, Security Council voting formula, policy toward liberated Europe, and the calling of a United Nations conference.

Ninth AF: 9th Bomb Div attacks repair depot at Mechernich, Arloff road and rail junction, and flies a leaflet mission. IX and XIX TACs patrol battle area.

Twelfth AF: MBs bomb railroad bridges at Ala, San Michele all' Adige, Lavis, Dogna, and Bodrez, and attack Ala M/Y. XXII TAC ftrs and FBs escort MBs and, in widespread areas of N Italy, destroy 2 bridges, damage 8 others, and blast rolling stock.

Fifteenth AF: Bad weather cancels bombing operations for third successive day. 24 B–24's and 1

B–17 drop supplies and leaflets in N Yugoslavia. 8 P–38's carry out photo and weather rcn missions.

Tenth AF: 54 P–38's and P–47's destroy or damage bridges at Inailong, Bawgyo, Ho-hko, Hay-ti, Mong Long, and Pa-mao. 26 P–47's spt ground forces in Myitson and Hosi areas. Troops, supplies, and vehicles are attacked at Nam Yem, Na-makhkaw, Mansam, Kong kang, Nawngsong, Mong Yai, Nalang, and Pangmit. Again transports complete more than 500 sorties to advanced bases and over forward areas, where supplies are dropped to troops.

Fourteenth AF: 10 P–40's bomb A/F and Japanese HQ at Yungning and railroad yards at Sinyang. 2 of the P–40's over Sinyang are lost to ground fire.

FEAF: B–24's continue to hit Corregidor and Cavite. In spt of ground forces B–25's bomb and strafe coast tgts from San Felipe to Maloma, hit tgts around Iba, and drop napalm on San Jose del Monte. A–20's bomb Lipa and Calingatan A/Fs.

Twentieth AF: For the first time XXI BC sends VHBs from 2 wgs (73d and 313th) against Japanese Home Islands. 69 B–29's bomb urban area of Kobe. 30 others, including 15 hitting Natsusaka, bomb last resort tgts and T/Os. About 200 attacking ftrs down 1 B–29 and damage 35 others. 1 other crashes upon landing at Saipan. B–29's claim 4 ftrs downed, 20 probably destroyed, and 39 damaged.

Seventh AF: 9 B–24's from Guam bomb AA defenses on Iwo Jima while 10 hit town of Okimura. 2 B–24's from Saipan, on armed rcn flight, bomb Marcus. 23 B–24's from Angaur bomb Caballo I. During 4/5 Feb, 8 Guam-based B–24's, operating singly, pound A/Fs on Iwo Jima.

5 February

Ninth AF: Weather cancels all operations except IX TAC ftr patrols over US First Army area around Butgenbach.

Twelfth AF: B–25's score excellently against San Ambrogio di Valpolicella landslide (overhanging cliff collapses on railroad by bombing) and bridges at San Michele all' Adige and Calliano. During 4/5 Feb XXII TAC A–20's intruder missions hit lights, motor transport, and roads in Po Valley and areas S of Bologna. Ftrs and FBs fly over 270 sorties against comm tgts in N Italy. Incendiary bombing of a truck park damages numerous vehicles.

Fifteenth AF: 730–plus HBs bomb oil storage at Regensburg, main station and 2 M/Ys at Salzburg, M/Ys at Rosenheim and Villach, and Straubing railroad installations. 6 HBs bomb Comeglians road bridge. P–38's and P–51's escort HBs, fly rcn and rcn spt missions, and accompany 25 B–24's on supply mission to Yugoslavia.

Tenth AF: 35 P–47's spt ground forces in Myitson, Hosi, and Molo areas. 8 P–38's bomb Mong Long. 60 P–38's and P–47's hit troops and supplies at Kan-loi, Namyang, Man-Peng, Pangmakhe leng, Kwangteng, Mong Pa, and Mansam. Transports fly 554 sorties to forward areas.

Fourteenth AF: 14 P–51's and P–40's attack locomotives and trucks at Pinghan railroad yards, Hsiangcheng, and Lohochai. At least 9 locomotives and an undetermined number of trucks are destroyed.

FEAF: 60 B–24's deliver heaviest attack yet on Corregidor. Spt for ground forces continues in various Luzon battle zones. B–25's on shipping sweep of E coast claim 9 barges and luggers sunk and several more damaged. B–24's bomb Manggar and Sepinggang A/Fs.

Seventh AF: 21 B–24's from Saipan bomb AA positions, def installations, and bivouac on N end of Iwo Jima. During 5/6 Feb Iwo Jima A/Fs are pounded by 10 Saipan-based B–24's flying individual snooper strikes.

Eleventh AF: 5 B–24's bomb Kataoka through solid overcast. A shipping sweep by B–25's is cancelled due to weather.

6 February

Eighth AF: 1,300-plus HBs attack M/Ys at Chemnitz and Magdeburg, and over 20 T/Os, including Gotha M/Y. 15 P–51 gps fly spt and 2 of the gps strafe ground tgts.

Ninth AF: 261 MBs and LBs attack Rheinbach ammo dump, Sotenich comm center, Vlatten defended village, Berg-Gladbach motor transport center, and several casual tgts. Ftrs fly armed rcn, alert flights and patrols, dive-bomb Horrem bridge, cut rails, and escort 9th Bomb Div.

Twelfth AF: B–25's attack railroad tgts on the line running N to Brenner Pass, damaging bridges at Rovereto and Ala. M/Ys at Rovereto and San Ambrogio di Valpolicella and bridge at Crema are less successfully hit. FBs cut railroad bridges at Nervesa della Battaglia and San Michele all'Adige. The P–47's claim 3 ftrs destroyed in combat N of

Verona and attack numerous T/Os throughout tgt areas. During 5/6 Feb A–20's attack lights, roads, and motor transport in C Po Valley.

Fifteenth AF: Bad weather permits only supply and rcn missions. 5 P–38's complete weather and photo rcn while 12 B–24's and 1 B–17 drop supplies in Yugoslavia.

Tenth AF: 86 P–47's and P–38's and 25 B–25's pound troop concentrations, supplies, and AA positions in Lashio area. 4 P–38's damage approach to Mong Tong bridge. Transports complete 514 sorties, carrying men and supplies to forward areas.

Fourteenth AF: 20 P–51's pound and considerably damage Peking A/F, claiming 7 airplanes destroyed. Other FBs on armed rcn hit several T/Os (mainly rail and river traffic) around Tsingpu, Wuhu, Suchow, Hsiangcheng, Ichang, Chingmen, and Yungning. FBs sink numerous river craft on Mekong R from Wan Mai-Lo to Nguen.

FEAF: B–24's bomb Corregidor gun positions. B–25's and P–38's hit Echague and camp on Rosario-Baguio road. A–20's attack gun positions and defenses at Nichols Field in spt of ground forces and bomb Caballo I. A–20's attack Fabrica A/F. B–24's and B–25's fly coastal sweeps hitting various tgts at Divilacan Bay, Hondagua, and Bicol Peninsula. B–24's, with P–38 spt hit Manggar and Sepinggang A/Fs.

Seventh AF: 9 Guam-based B–24's hit AA defenses and radar and radio installations on Iwo Jima. 10 more bomb Ototo Jima island and town of Omura. 1 B–24 from Angaur bombs Koror, 2 hit Bulan A/Fs and 19 bomb Corregidor. 8 B–24's from Guam fly individual strikes against Iwo Jima A/Fs during 6/7 Feb.

7 February

Eighth AF: High, heavy clouds necessitate recall of about 300 B–17's and 3 ftr gps from mission to attack tgts in W Germany.

Ninth AF: 16 B–26's strike rail siding at Lipp. Weather cancels other operations.

Twelfth AF: During 6/7 Feb A–20's bomb lights and movement over extensive areas of N Italy. During day B–25 blasts cut bridges at Bodrez and Lavis, viaduct at Lavis, and block rail lines at San Michele all'Adige and Mantua. XXII TAC P–47's destroy 4 railroad bridges and damage another severely in NE and C Po Valley and Brenner Pass, and blast dumps and sugar refineries in the Mantua, Brescia, and Reggio Emilia areas.

Fifteenth AF: 680 B–17's and B–24's bomb oil refineries at Moosbierbaum, Lobau, Schwechat, Vienna/Floridsdorf, Korneuburg and Kagran in Vienna area, oil storage at Pula, shipyard and harbor of Trieste, town of Bratislava, A/F at Zwolfaxing, and several scattered T/Os. 274 P–38's and P–51's provide escort. 8 B–24's drop supplies in Yugoslavia. 18 P–51's strafe Zeltweg A/F and surrounding area while 10 P–38's sweep Zagreb-Karlovac-Sisak area. Other P–38's fly rcn and escort operations.

Tenth AF: 11 B–25's attack tanks and troops at Man Namman. 50 P–47's spt forces preparing to cross Shweli R in Myitson area. 40-plus P–47's and P–40's attack troops and supply areas at Nawngkalio, Man Li, Hsunkwe, Nawnghkio, Loi Hkam, Panghsapye, Na-lang, Wingnang, and Pang Eng Hkye. 464 transport sorties are flown to advanced bases and frontline areas.

Fourteenth AF: 11 P–51's knock out bridge at Hengshan. 34 P–40's hit river, road, and rail traffic from Kweiyi to Hengshan, from Chiuchiang to Wuhu, from Wan Mai-Lo to Luang Prabang, from Siaokan southward, in area S of Tsinan, and N of Tehsien. 2 FBs hit warehouse area at Kweihsien.

FEAF: B–24's, with P–38 spt hit T/Os at Heito A/F and other points (after weather prevents bombing of Takao). A–20's, supporting ground operations, attack hills W of Clark Field. B–25's, with P–51 cover, fly several sweeps over Formosa, claiming a sub sunk, a tanker set afire, a large motor launch sunk, other shipping damaged, and several vehicles and an airplane destroyed. B–24's hit Bago and Mandaue. Other B–24's bomb Tawau and—in another mission—Miri A/F, Tutong oil refinery pump station and power house.

Twentieth AF: 44 B–29's bomb primary tgt of Saigon (11 drop prematurely and 33 hit residential section), 19 hit T/O of Pnom Penh, and 2 bomb last resort tgt, a M/Y at Martaban. In a more successful mission, almost 60 B–29's bomb and effect the collapse of most of middle span of Rama VI bridge at Bangkok (3d strike at this tgt) and destroy NE approach. 1 VHB bombs Martaben M/Y.

Seventh AF: 6 B–24's from Saipan bomb town of Okimura. 8 B–24's hit AA positions and radio and radar installations on Iwo Jima, while 2 others bomb Woleai A/F. From Angaur 20 B–24's bomb Silay and Tali-

say A/Fs and 1 bombs Opon A/F on
Mactan I. 9 B–24's, during 7/8 Feb
snooper raids from Saipan, bomb Iwo
Jima A/Fs.

Eleventh AF: 6 B–24's off to Kataoka abort mission when all aircraft accidentally drop bombs prior
to bombing run. 4 B–25's weather
abort.

8 February

Eighth AF: Over 400 HBs dispatched to attack tgts in W Germany
are recalled before leaving UK coast
due to clouds over bases, routes, and
tgts. 2 Continent-based P–51 gps
strafe rail tgts and parked aircraft.

Ninth AF: 320-plus B–26's, A–20's,
and A–26's strike road junction, M/
Y, 3 defended areas, and 10 casual
tgts in Germany. Ftrs fly armed rcn,
bomb numerous ground tgts, and
spt US XII Corps which has, on 7
Feb, crossed Our and Sauer Rivers
between Vianden and Echternach and
established bridgeheads.

Twelfth AF: During 7/8 Feb on
intruder missions A–20's bomb various tgts at 58 points in Po Valley
and Brenner Pass area. MBs during
day attack bridges at Calliano,
Chiusaforte, Dogna and Piacenza.
Ftrs and FBs closely spt US Fifth
Army forces in Serchio Valley—
where counterattacks oppose Allied
offensive—and destroy Nervesa della
Battaglia railroad bridge and oil
dump N of Mestre.

Fifteenth AF: Over 500 B–24's and
B–17's bomb SE Vienna comm tgts
and M/Y at Graz, plus several T/Os.
270-plus P–38's and P–51's escort. 12
B–24's drop supplies in Yugoslavia. 11
P–51's sweep Zagreb area. Other P–
51's and P–38's fly rcn and rcn escort.

Tenth AF: 72 P–47's spt ground
forces in Myitson area. 37 P–47's
and P–38's hit troops, supply areas,
ammo dumps, and T/Os at Namsaw,
Hsun-kwe, Loi-Kong, Nawng-un,
Hsipaw, Panghai, and Kongnio, and
bomb village near Pangkawn. Transports fly 581 sorties carrying men
and supplies to forward bases and
dropping supplies to frontline areas.

Fourteenth AF: 10 P–51's knock
out bridge at Shihtangchung and
blast bridge approach at Changsha.
9 other ftrs knock out another bridge
N of Changsha. 4 ftrs hit railroad
T/Os from Linfen to Yutze to Shihkiachwang and bomb Tsinan A/F.

FEAF: B–24's bomb town of Mariveles. B–25's sink or damage several small vessels along Luzon's E
coast and hit Legaspi A/F. B–24's
bomb Manggar and Sepinggang A/F.

Twentieth AF: 30 B–29's from the
Marianas bomb Moen I A/F number 1.

Seventh AF: 20 B–24's from Guam
bomb radar and radio installations
and AA defenses on Iwo Jima in the
afternoon. During 8/9 Feb, 10 fly
single-plane snooper strikes against
the island's A/Fs.

Eleventh AF: 4 B–25's abort mission to Masugawa R when unable to
identify the tgt.

9 February

International: Malta-Yalta conferences end. Conferees agree to plan
for invasion of Japan following defeat of Germany, anticipated for
about 1 Jul 45. Until then pace of the
Pacific war will be slowed. USSR will
acquire parts of Manchuria in return
for participating in war against
Japan.

Eighth AF: 1,200 HBs operating

in 6 forces attack Rothensee and Lutzkendorf synthetic oil plants, Bielefeld/Schildesche rail viaduct, Arnsberg viaduct, and numerous secondary tgts and T/Os. 15 ftr gps provide escort, with 6 gps later strafing rail and road transportation, hangars, and an ammunition dump.

Ninth AF: 347 A–20's, A–26's, and B–26's bomb comm centers at Viersen and Kempen, M/Ys at Rheydt, Grevenbroich, and Viersen, and rail bridges at Neuwied-Irlich and Sinzig. Ftrs fly armed rcn over E and W of the Rhine, attack rail bridges, and spt US XII Corps bridgeheads across the Our and Sauer Rivers.

Twelfth AF: During 8/9 Feb A–20's and A–26's on intruder missions attack comm tgts throughout C and NE Po Valley. Weather restricts daytime operations to weather rcn and supply dropping missions.

Fifteenth AF: During 8/9 Feb 1 B–17 and 10 B–24's drop supplies in N Italy. During the day 49 HBs hit Moosbierbaum oil refinery. 5 others bomb M/Ys at Graz and Bruck an der Mur. 11 B–24's drop supplies in C Yugoslavia, while P–38's and P–51's fly rcn missions and rcn and supply escort.

Tenth AF: 10 B–25's damage bridge at Tonglau and destroy 1 bridge and damage another at Ke-hsi Mansam. 2 others pound trucks, gun positions, and buildings during road sweep from Hsipaw to Loilem to Lashio. 9 P–47's knock out bridge at Bawgyo and damage another at Inailong. 22 P–47's spt ground forces in Myitson area. Troops, supplies, and comm are attacked at Tangtong, Man Mau, Se-u, Mansam, Panghai, Nalang, and Man hpat by 40-plus FBs.

479 transport sorties are flown to forward areas.

Fourteenth AF: 8 ftrs hit rail bridges in Kiyang and Lukou areas, damaging 1 bridge. Several trucks are strafed and destroyed. 3 ftrs on railroad sweep destroy several locomotives between Peking and Sinsiang. Several other ftrs bomb railroad yards at Kaifeng and A/F at Sinsiang. CACW ftrs make surprise strike at Tsingtao A/F, claim about 100 airplanes destroyed and damaged, and also destroy several nearby locomotives.

FEAF: B–24's fly morning and afternoon raids against Corregidor gun positions. A–20's also hit the island fortress. Mariveles and S part of Bataan Peninsula are pounded by B–24's and A–20's throughout the morning and afternoon. B–25's and P–51's hit shipping near Legaspi and in San Miguel Bay and destroy buildings at San Fernando. In spt of ground forces, A–24's and P–40's over Balete Pass area attack bridges and roads.

Twentieth AF: 29 XXI BC B–29's hit Moen I for second consecutive day, bombing A/F number 2.

Seventh AF: 22 B–24's from Guam and Saipan bomb A/Fs, def and radar-radio installations and AA positions on Iwo Jima. During 9/10 Feb, 11 more B–24's from Saipan make separate strikes against A/Fs and AA defenses.

10 February

Eighth AF: 150 B–17's bomb Dulmen oil depot, Ijmuiden sub pens, and town of Lingen. 3 ftr gps escort HBs. 2 gps of FBs sent against transportation tgts abort because of bad weather.

Ninth AF: 320-plus bmrs of 9th Bomb Div attack comm centers at Kempen, Horrem, and Euskirchen, vehicle center and depot at Munstereifel and at Berg-Gladbach, and several casual tgts including rail bridge at Bullay. Ftrs escort bmrs, fly patrols and armed rcn, bomb bridges, attack railroad cars and other tgts, and spt US VIII and XII Corps in Prum area on Prum R and in bridgehead area E of Sauer R NW of Echternach.

Twelfth AF: During 9/10 Feb A-20's and A-26's hit railroads, lights, and movement in Po Valley and Brenner area and bomb docks at La Spezia. Weather cancels all but 2 MB missions. However, the B-25's cut bridges at Palazzuolo sull' Oglio and Romano di Lombardia. FBs concentrate on railroads in NE Italy, and destroy numerous vehicles in truck park in Mantua area.

Fifteenth AF: Bad weather prevents bombing. 12 B-24's drop supplies in Yugoslavia while P-38's fly rcn and escort missions.

Tenth AF: 5 B-25's destroy Laihka bridge. 4 others hit Namsang bridge, with poor results. 9 P-47's knock out approaches to Pa-mao bridge while 8 others destroy half of bridge at Inailong. 15 P-47's spt ground forces in Mongmit area, concentrating on Japanese positions S of Myitson. 76 FBs attack troops and supply areas at Panglong, Namsangsok, Namtu, Kutkai, Mong Yaw, Mongmit, Ho-mong, Man Pwe, Namsam, and Loiya. Again transports fly more than 500 sorties to forward areas.

FEAF: B-24's again blast Japanese gun positions while P-51's and P-38's, supporting ground forces hit comm tgts in Bayambang-Santa Fe area, while B-25's in the area blast villages where vehicles are hidden. B-24's, A-20's, and FBs completely saturate the S part of Bataan Peninsula with bombs during morning and afternoon attacks, thoroughly pummelling defenses and forces. P-47's on ftr sweep over Formosa claim 10 air victories.

Fifth AF: Gen Frederick H Smith Jr becomes CG V FC.

Twentieth AF: 84 B-29's, from the Marianas, hit Nakajima aircraft plant at Ota. 12 B-29's are lost. 21 aircraft are downed.

Seventh AF: 10 Guam-based B-24's bomb Okimura. 6 P-38's escort photo mission and fly ftr sweep over Iwo Jima. 17 B-24's from Guam, with P-38 escort, pound Iwo Jima in late afternoon, and 9 more make single-bmr harassment strikes on the island during 10/11 Feb.

11 February

International: US, Britain, and USSR issue Yalta declaration.

Eighth AF: Over 120 B-17's bomb Dulmen oil depot and a T/O (road junction). A P-51 gp provides close escort. 4 P-51 gps strafe rail and road transportation in E Netherlands and NW Germany, while 1 other gp bombs and strafes a truck park in Germany.

Ninth AF: 97 B-26's and A-20's bomb Bingen and Modrath M/Ys. Ftrs fly armed rcn and patrols, attack special tgts and T/Os, and attack in cooperation with US XII Corps across Sauer R NW of Echternach.

Twelfth AF: LBs on night intruder

missions attack enemy movement and lights at various points in N Italy, hit bridges in Po Valley, and attack frontline positions in N Apennines. in NE and C Po Valley and stores Weather grounds MBs but ftrs and FBs blast railroad bridges and lines and supply dumps in C and W Po areas.

Fifteenth AF: Bad weather limits operations to B–24 supply mission to Yugoslavia during 10/11 Feb and to P–38 rcn missions.

Tenth AF: 11 B–25's bomb troops and supplies at Loilem. 22 P–47's spt ground forces in Mongmit area, hitting buildings at Nabu and Japanese positions S of Myitson. 100-plus FBs pound troop concentrations, supplies, ammo dumps, gun positions, and T/Os at several locations including Pangsang, Taung-gaing, Panghsapye, Nam Pok, Byaungbyan, Manai, Kutkai, Mongmit, Namun, and Pangmahe-leng. Transports complete 503 sorties to forward bases and over frontline areas (dropping supplies).

Fourteenth AF: 17 B–25's hit railroad yards at Sinyang and Lohochai and locomotive foundry at Hsuchang. 23 P–47's pound Hankow A/F. 8 ftrs hit Anyang A/F and Pinghan railroad T/Os. B–24's claim 2 cargo vessels sunk in S China Sea.

FEAF: B–24's attack Corregidor almost continuously throughout the day. FBs spt ground forces blasting numerous tgts from Cauringan to Taytay and at Wawa, Montalban, Antipolo, and Marikina. P–47's blast train NE of Heito. B–24's fly light strike against Bago.

Twentieth AF: 56 B–29's bomb storage dumps around Rangoon. Mis-

sion is flown in conjunction with B–24's of EAC's Strategic AF which hit tgt. 9 B–29's from the Marianas carry out rcn mission for Navy. 1 other returns early. Tgt area covers 135–00E to 148–00E to 30–00N.

Seventh AF: 21 B–24's from Saipan, operating in 2 separate forces, bomb A/Fs and defenses on Iwo Jima. 3 others, on armed rcn, bomb Marcus. 25 B–24's based on Angaur bomb Corregidor. During 11/12 Feb, 10 B–24's from Saipan fly individual harassment strikes against Iwo Jima.

Eleventh AF: Of 7 B–24's off on an air cover mission for a naval TF, only 3 reach the tgt.

12 February

Ninth AF: All combat operations cancelled because of bad weather.

Twelfth AF: LBs, during 11/12 Feb, bomb comm tgts in Po Valley and NE Italy, including Brenner Pass area. Bad weather during day restricts MB operations to bombing the bridge at Ala and a sugar refinery at Legnago. Only 1 ftr gp, the 57th, can operate, hitting bridges, rail lines, and guns in Po Valley.

Fifteenth AF: Continued bad weather restricts operations to rcn and rcn escort by P–38's and P–51's.

Tenth AF: 23 P–47's spt ground forces hitting NE of Nabu and bombing mortar positions S of Myitson. 4 others spt forces at Loiya. 3 P–47's severely damage bridge at Pa-mao. 60-plus P–47's and P–38's pound supply areas, troops, tanks, and trucks at various locations including Hukawt, Kongtap, Namtu, Namta-gun, Mongmit, Loingu, and Tonsing. 520

transport sorties are flown to forward areas throughout the day.

Fourteenth AF: 6 P–51's destroy 6 locomotives between Suchow and Pengpu and strafe Nanking and Suchow A/Fs. Other ftrs claim at least 10 more locomotives destroyed in areas S of Yellow R. P–40's bomb troops in Hsiancheng area and hit trains on Pinghan railroad.

FEAF: B–24's continue to pound Corregidor. A–20's sweeping S Bataan Peninsula, sink about 30 barges loaded with troops, ammo, and supplies. Throughout the day MBs and ftrs directly spt ground forces on Bataan Peninsula and from Lingayen Gulf area to Nichols Field.

Twentieth AF: 8 B–29's complete rcn mission for Navy covering from 135–00E to 148–00E and to 30–00N. 21 other B–29's from the Marianas bomb heavy AA on Iwo Jima in preparation for amphibious invasion of the island on 19 Feb.

Seventh AF: 9 Guam-based B–24's pound Chichi Jima naval installations while 19 bomb A/Fs and defenses on Iwo Jima. During 12/13 Feb, 8 B–24's from Guam fly single-bmr harassment strikes against both Iwo and Chichi Jima.

Eleventh AF: B–25's cancel cover mission for a naval force because of weather.

13 February

Ninth AF: 320-plus B–26's, A–26's, and A–20's, attack rail bridges at Sinzig, Neuwied-Irlich, and Euskirchen, military transport depots at Schwelm and Iserlohn, defended points at Wittlich, and T/Os. Ftrs escort MBs and LBs, bomb Neuss and Zieverich bridges and other tgts, fly

armed rcn, and spt Third Army elements from Prum to Saarlautern along the Our, Sauer, and Saar R bridgehead areas.

Twelfth AF: During 12/13 Feb LBs attack enemy movement in C and NC Po Valley. MBs hit bridges at Calcinato, Dogna, and Chiusaforte and bridge approach at Lavis. FBs fly nearly 350 sorties against enemy comm in N Italy including M/Ys at Verona, Parma, and Vicenza.

Fifteenth AF: In the Vienna area 640-plus HBs with ftr spt hit S ordnance depot, S and SE goods yards and depot, C repair shops, and Matzleinsdorf M/Y, and M/Ys at Graz, Sarvar, Zagreb (2) and Maribor (2), Pula harbor, Maribor locomotive depot and rolling stock repair shops, and several T/Os. P–38's and P–51's carry out rcn and rcn escort missions.

Tenth AF: Troops concentrations, supply areas, and T/Os are pounded by 70 FBs at several locations including Kongpaw, Namtu, Kyaohpak, Laihka, Kon-wet, Mong Pa, Hkom-nio, and Naung-lang. 19 FBs spt ground forces in Mongmit-Myitson area. 16 FBs knock out approach to main bridge and damage bypass bridge at Hay-ti. 477 air supply sorties are flown by transports throughout the day.

Fourteenth AF: Ftrs sweep railroad from Sinyang to Hsuchang, bomb approach to Hsuchang bridge, and strafe Sinyang and Ichang A/Fs. B–25's bomb Hsuchang foundry.

FEAF: B–24's continue to pound Corregidor as large segment of HBs attack main coastal guns and score direct hits on several batteries. B–24's bomb Mariveles while A–20's and P–47's bomb and strafe T/Os throughout S part of Bataan Peninsula. MBs and ftrs attack small shipping during sweeps of E and N coasts of Luzon. B–25's, with ftr spt, hit Kagi A/F.

Seventh AF: 25 B–24's from Saipan fly two strikes against Iwo Jima, while 10 others hit Haha Jima. During 13/14 Feb, 5 B–24's, flying individual harassment strikes, bomb Iwo Jima at intervals over an 8-hr period.

14 February

Eighth AF: Nearly 1,300 HBs attack M/Ys at Dresden, Chemnitz, Magdeburg, and Hof, road bridge at Wesel, Dulmen oil depot 2 A/Fs, 10 town aras, and numerous T/Os. 16 ftr gps escort HBs or fly area sweeps, strafe ground tgts, and battle over 75 ftrs, claiming 20 destroyed.

Ninth AF: 600-plus A–20's, A–26's, and B–26's attack rail bridges, M/Y, comm centers, ammo dump, prime mover depot, and several T/Os in Germany in morning and afternoon missions aimed primarily at obstructing enemy movement and supply. Ftrs fly armed rcn over wide areas of Germany, escort 9th Bomb Div, attack river traffic, bridges, and other tgts, and spt US Third Army elements E of Our and Sauer Rivers.

Twelfth AF: During 13/14 Feb A–20's bomb bridge approach at Castelnuovo di Garfagnana and hit T/Os in Po Valley. During the day MBs bomb bridges or bridge approaches at San Michele all'Adige, Tarvisio, Bressanone, and hit guns near Ponte Gardena. Ftrs and FBs, operating in poor weather, attack mainly comm tgts in Po Valley.

Fifteenth AF: More than 500 B–24's and B–17's bomb Moosbierbaum,

Lobau, Vienna/Floridsdorf, and Schwechat oil refineries in Vienna area, M/Ys at Graz, Gleisdorf, Klagenfurt, Villach, Celje, Maribor, and Zagreb, and several scattered T/Os. P–38's also bomb Moosbierbaum refinery and Maribor M/Y. Other P–38's and P–51's escort HBs, fly photo and weather rcn, and escort rcn missions.

Tenth AF: 12 B–25's attack vehicles along roads from Lashio to Takaw to Hopong. 7 P–47's strafe Laihka A/F. Bad weather cancels other scheduled offensive missions. Transports continue to operate despite the weather, completing 520 sorties to forward areas.

Fourteenth AF: P–47's bomb Kaifeng A/F and P–51's hit Shihkiachwang A/F, destroying several parked airplanes. The P–51's afterwards blast 7 locomotives between Puchou and Sinsiang. Other ftrs destroy 7 more locomotives between Sinyang and Hsuchang, bomb railroad yards at Lohochai, and destroy fuel dump at Hsiangcheng.

FEAF: B–24's continue to bomb Corregidor, concentrating on dock area and gun positions. Other B–24's bomb Mariveles and B–25's bomb A/F at Tuguegarao. MBs and ftrs provide excellent spt for ground forces, blasting guns and troops W of Clark Field, N of Marikina A/F, and N of Montalban. A–20's pound general area of S Bataan. B–25's bomb barges at Zamboanga and P–38's bomb Matina A/F. Ftrs on armed rcn strafe A/Fs on Negros and Cebu. A few MBs bomb Kagi A/F and nearby T/Os.

Twentieth AF: B–29's from the Marianas again carry out rcn mission for the Navy, covering area northward from base line at 28–02N 145–55E to 28–44N 148–00E.

Seventh AF: 17 Guam-based B–24's pound defenses and radar and radio installations on Iwo Jima at midday. During 14/15 Feb 5 more HBs, flying individual snooper missions bomb Iwo Jima A/F and AA positions while 4 in separate strikes hit Susaki A/F.

Eleventh AF: 3 B–24's bomb and photograph Suribachi A/F (secondary).

15 February

Eighth AF: Over 1,000 HBs attack Magdeburg synthetic oil plant, M/Ys at Dresden, Cottbus, and Rheine, and several T/Os. 9 ftr gps fly escort and strafe transportation tgts.

Ninth AF: Around 90 B–26's bomb Sinzig and Mayen rail bridges and 4 T/Os in the area. Ftrs patrol points along battlefront, attack railroads and other special tgts, fly armed rcn and spt US VII, VIII, XII, and XX Corps along Roer and Prum Rivers and in Saar R bridgehead area.

Twelfth AF: MBs bomb Spilimbergo ammo dumps through overcast, but are forced by the bad weather to cancel all other operations. FBs, limited by weather, concentrate on railway tgts in NE and W Po Valley.

Fifteenth AF: Over 650 B–24's and B–17's bomb 5 station freight yards, SE goods depot, Korneuburg oil refinery, and Vienna/Floridsdorf, Matzleinsdorf, and Penzing M/Ys—all in Vienna area, plus M/Ys at Klagenfurt-Wiener-Neustadt and Graz, Graz ordnance depot, shipyards in Fiume and scattered T/Os are also

hit. Ftrs escort HBs and fly rcn and rcn escort missions.

Tenth AF: 12 B–25's hit buildings, troops, and other T/Os during sweep from Lashio to Loilem and along road E and W from Loilem. 20 P–47's fly close spt strikes in Mongmit-Myitson area. Bridge at Hay-ti is knocked out by 6 P–47's. 56 P–47's attack troops, town areas, and supplies at Paukmyaing, Nam-hpuktok, Namtoi, and Namhu-tau. 8 P–47's hit Li-lu ferry area. Large-scale transport operations continue. 511 sorties are flown to forward areas.

Fourteenth AF: 15 FBs attack railroad tgts at Saiping, in Hankow area, N of Sinantien, between Hsuchang and Loyang, and along the Yangtze from Wuhu to Hankow.

FEAF: B–25's attack bridges in S part of Formosa. HBs again blast Corregidor with A–20's and FBs bombing and strafing its few remaining gun positions. FBs hit Caballo I and FBs, B–25's, and A–20's hit Bataan Peninsula all day. Also hit are troops and gun positions in Ft William McKinley area and A/Fs at Tuguegarao and Echague.

Twentieth AF: 33 Marianas-based B–29's bomb Mitsubishi aircraft engine works at Nagoya. Almost 70 others hit last resort tgt and T/Os, 54 of them bombing Hamamatsu.

Seventh AF: 24 B–24's from Saipan, in two separate strikes, bomb Iwo Jima A/Fs and AA defenses. 12 others hit A/F at Chichi Jima. 4 B–24's from Guam, escorting photo airplanes over Truk, bomb A/Fs at Param and Moen Is. 5 B–24's fly night harassment raids against Iwo and Chichi Jima.

16 February

Eighth AF: Nearly 1,000 HBs attack benzol plants at Dortmund and Gelsenkirchen, oil refineries at Dortmund and Salzbergen, MYs at Osnabruck, Hamm, and Rheine, Wesel rail bridge, and several secondaries and T/Os. 4 ftr gps provide spt.

Ninth AF: 300-plus B–26's and A–20's bomb Mayen rail bridge, Rees comm center, Solingen turbo-jet component works, Unna ordnance depot, and a T/O. Ftrs escort the bmrs, fly patrols, sweeps, and armed rcn, attack bridge, railroads, and other special tgts. XIX TAC also supports US VIII, XII, and XX Corps W of Prum R, E of Sauer R, and in Saarlautern area.

Twelfth AF: Bad weather grounds MBs. FBs cut rail lines at S end of Garda Lake, and bomb ammo and fuel dump E of Nervesa della Battaglia and ammo dump E of Villafranca in Lunigiana.

Fifteenth AF: 630-plus B–24's and B–17's bomb A/Fs at Regensburg, Landsberg, and Neubiberg, M/Ys at Rosenheim, Hall, Innsbruck, Bolzano, and Vipiteno, plus scattered T/Os in Austria and N Italy. P–38's and P–51's escort HBs, fly rcn missions, and escort rcn and supply operations.

Tenth AF: 12 B–25's bomb troops, storage areas, and vehicles during offensive rcn along roads S of Lashio and from Hsenwi to Loilem. 31 P–47's spt ground forces in Myitson area. About 160 FBs attack town areas, troop concentrations, arty positions, transportation tgts, and general T/Os at Namtu, Wengkau, Hsipaw, Namhsawng-hawng, Hunhla, Mong Yai, Sinkin, Panghung, Hatka,

Na-kyeh, and Panglong and similar tgts at Kyawngsu, Kunsanlek, Namloi, Man-kyawng, Tonsing, Sam-Lau, and Mong Li. Transports fly 632 sorties delivering men and supplies to forward bases and dropping supplies to frontline troops.

Fourteenth AF: 33 FBs attack A/Fs in Nanking area, railroad yards at Hsuchang and Tungpu, and hit rail and river traffic from Wuhu to Hankow, in Sinsiang area, in Luang Prabang area, and from Muong Soui to the Mekong R.

FEAF: Ftrs attack vehicles and trains in S part of Formosa. 120-plus A–20's and B–24's pound Corregidor during early daylight hours. Amphibious and airborne landings follow and the paratroops soon link up with the beachhead. A–20's and FBs also bomb nearby Caballo I. B–25's spt ground forces in Mariveles area, hit facilities at Baguio and Santa Fe, and bomb Camalaniugan A/F. P–38's hit Likanan and Matina A/F. B–24's pound Kendari A/F.

Seventh AF: 2 Guam-based B–24's on armed rcn flight bomb Marcus. 42 sent against Iwo Jima are recalled due to total cloud cover over the tgt. During 16/17 Feb, 4 Guam-based B–24's, striking separately, hit Susaki A/F.

17 February

Eighth AF: Over 300 B–17's bomb Frankfurt/Main M/Ys and several T/Os including Giessen M/Y, Aschaffenburg, and Hanau. Nearly 600 other HBs abort from synthetic oil tgts in Germany because of bad cloud conditions. 3 P–51 gps provide escort and strafe ground tgts.

Ninth AF: 31 B–26's strike Mayen

rail bridge and T/O at Reinfeld. Ftrs of IX and XIX TAC fly patrols, sweeps, and armed rcn. XXIX TAC cancels operations due to bad weather.

Twelfth AF: MBs bomb bridges at Chiusaforte, Bressanone, Crema, and Dogna. Ftrs and FBs hit comm tgts in Po Valley and damage bridges at Nervesa della Battaglia, Cittadella, Calliano, Ala, and Pordenone. Also bombed are guns and dumps from S of La Spezia E to battle area below Bologna.

Fifteenth AF: About 500 HBs attack main M/Y, station, and benzol plant at Linz, steel works at Judenburg, tank works at Steyr and Sankt Valentin, M/Ys at Graz, Wels, Bruck an der Mur, and Villach, plus shipyards and harbors at Fiume, Trieste, and Pula. P–38's and P–51's escort HBs, rcn missions, and supply drops, strafe rail lines in Vienna-Linz area and aircraft at Ardning and Grafenstein, and fly weather and photo rcn.

Tenth AF: 14 P–47's spt ground forces in Mongmit-Myitson area. 140-plus FBs strike at troop concentrations, supply points, transport, animal concentrations, tanks, and arms and ammo stores are pounded in N Burma including at Hko-lawng, Hai-pu, Na-kyeh, Man Sang, Samlan, Hkumman-mao, Mong Lang, Na-leng, Honwo, and Loi-pyek. 10 B–25's bomb troops and supplies at Hai-hseng. 603 transport sorties are flown.

Fourteenth AF: 30 B–25's bomb Linfen and Yuncheng. A single B–25 hits railroad T/Os from Hengyang to Lingling. 27 P–40's and P–51's attack animal transport, barracks, railroad tgts, and town area at Puchi. 16 P–47's hit Hankow-Wuchang area. 37 other FBs attack railroad yards and T/Os and road and river traffic near Tsinan, Changsha, and Kweiyi, and at Sinyang, Linfen, and Lung Hai.

FEAF: B–24's, with ftr spt attack A/F, railroad yard, and aluminum plant at Takao. A–20's spt ground forces in Mariveles area and hit caves and dugouts in hills W of Ft Stotsenburg. A–20's, B–25's, and FBs attack Tuguegarao and coastal town of San Fernando. B–24's pound Miri A/F.

Twentieth AF: 9 B–29's from Saipan bomb Dublon I sub pens.

Seventh AF: 42 B–24's from Saipan blast def installations and bivouac area. 3 others, on armed rcn flight, bomb Marcus. 3 B–24's from Guam, escorting photo plane over Truk Atoll bomb Param, Uman, and Eten in the atoll. 5 B–24's from Saipan fly individual snooper strikes during 17/18 Feb against Chichi Jima.

Eleventh AF: 4 B–25's provide air coverage for naval TF en route to Paramushiru.

18 February

Ninth AF: 60-plus B–26's bomb Dottesfeld rail bridge, T/O at Daun, and 5 other T/Os in Germany as 9th Bomb Div starts campaign to isolate the Ruhr. XIX TAC escorts B–26's and flies weather rcn and armed rcn. IX and XXIX TACs are grounded because of weather.

Twelfth AF: During 17/18 Feb A–20's bomb tgts in Po Valley, including towns of Nogara, Castelfranco Veneto, Modena, Cremona, Bovolone, and Isola della Scala, bridges at Cittadella and Villafranca in Lunigiana, and A/Fs at Ghedi and Villafranca in Lunigiana. All B–25 missions abort due to weather except attack on Ala rail bridge. Ftrs and FBs fly less than 100 sorties, hitting ammo dumps and railroad bridges and lines, mainly in Po Valley.

Fifteenth AF: During 17/18 Feb 24 B–24's drop supplies in N Italy. During the day 160 B–17's bomb benzol plant, main M/Y and station at Linz. 20 P–38's provide escort. Almost 290 B–24's, with ftr escorts, are recalled because of weather from missions dispatched against tgts in Austria. Weather also causes recall of 52 P–51's on strafing mission. A few P–38's complete rcn missions but most are recalled as weather worsens.

Tenth AF: 12 B–25's demolish bridges at Namsang and Ke-hsi Mansam. 30-plus FBs spt ground forces in Mongmit-Myitson-Nabu area. More than 100 FBs pound troop concentrations, supplies, vehicles, and other tgts immediately in adv of the southward moving battleline in Burma. Transports fly 602 sorties to forward areas.

Fourteenth AF: 25 FBs attack Sinyang railroad yards and A/F and T/Os along Pinghan railroad, at Chiuchiang, in Nanking area, E of Lohochai, and SE of Hsuchang. 4 B–24's over S China Sea claim damage on 2 vessels.

FEAF: B–24's bomb Takao, Okayama, and Toshien A/Fs. P–38's provide spt. B–25's and ftrs pound comm tgts and T/Os throughout Formosa. MBs and ftrs continue to fly numerous missions in spt of ground forces on Luzon. B–24's bomb Labuan A/F.

Twentieth AF: 35 Marianas-based B–29's bomb 2 A/Fs on Moen I.

Seventh AF: 36 Guam-based B–24's dispatched against Iwo Jima are recalled because of complete cloud cover over the tgt. 3 others on armed rcn bomb Marcus. During 18/19 Feb, 9 B–24's from Guam individually strike Chichi Jima.

Eleventh AF: 7 B–24's fly cover sorties for naval force during its approach to Kurabu Cape.

19 February

Eighth AF: Nearly 1,100 HBs attack primary tgts: 3 benzol plants at Bochum and Gelsenkirchen, oil refinery at Dortmund, tank plant near Siegen, M/Ys at Siegen, Rheine, Munster, and Osnabruck, and Wesel rail bridge, plus Haselunne and Haltern. 8 ftr gps fly escort and strafe rail traffic. 4 other ftr gps effectively strafe rail and road transportation in Hannover, Brunswick, and Magdeburg areas.

Ninth AF: 9th Bomb Div B–26's, A–26's, and A–20's, strike Mechernich prime mover depot, rail bridges at Pracht, Niederscheld, and Neuwied-Irlich, Wiesbaden ordnance depot, and 4 T/Os. Ftrs escort 9th Bomb Div, attack railroads and bridges, fly armed rcn and alerts, and cooperate with VIII, XII, and XX Corps E of Our R, between Westwall and Prum R, and in the Saar-Mosel triangle.

Twelfth AF: Gen Morris takes cmd of XII AFSC (until 1 Jan 44 designated the III Air Serv Area Cmd). Bad weather grounds MBs. FBs, some bombing by radar-control because of heavy clouds, attack-comm and dumps in W Po Valley and NE Italy, and claim several rail line cuts in Brenner area.

Fifteenth AF: During 18/19 Feb, 11 B–24's drop supplies in N Italy. During the day almost 500 B–24's and

B–17's, escorted by about 220 P–51's and P–38's, bomb 2 M/Ys and S station area in Vienna, M/Ys at Klagenfurt, Graz, Bruck an der Mur, and Maribor, shipyards in Fiume, and Pula harbor and military installations. 51 P–51's strafe rail and river traffic and A/Fs between Linz and Vienna and in Graz area. Other P–51's and P–38's fly escort and rcn missions.

Tenth AF: 24 B–25's and 31 P–47's fly close spt strikes in Mongmit-Myitson area. 70-plus FBs hit troop concentrations, supplies, and villages behind the battleline in C Burma. Heavy transport operations continue.

Fourteenth AF: 14 P–51's and P–40's blast rail and river traffic at Chiuchiang, Hsuchang, Lung Hai, and Tsinpu.

FEAF: B–24's bomb Koshun, Heito, and Takao A/Fs. MBs and ftrs on sweeps over the island attack a large number of T/Os including trains parked airplanes, buildings, and coastal vessels. In C Phil, USMC Corsairs under tac cmd of Thirteenth AF fly napalm strikes against A/Fs and other tgts. Ftrs, B–25's, and A–20's continue to spt ground forces at San Augustin, Carranglen, Balete Pass, and Bataan Peninsula and bomb Japanese-held sectors on Corregidor. B–24's bomb Miri A/F.

Thirteenth AF: Gen Wurtsmith becomes CG Thirteenth AF.

Twentieth AF: Around 50 B–29's bomb Central Railroad Repair Shops at Kuala Lumpur, some bombing from only 1,000 ft. 4 other VHBs hit alternates of Alor Star A/F, and M/Y at Martaban. 150 B–29's are airborne against Musashino aircraft plant hoping to draw air reinforcements away from Iwo Jima which US Marines invade. Thick clouds completely cover the primary so 119 B–29's bomb port and urban area of Tokyo. 12 others hit last resort tgts and T/Os. 6 B–29's are lost. US gunners claim 39 ftrs downed.

Seventh AF: 44 B–24's from Saipan are sent against Iwo Jima. 14 pound def positions and bivouac and storage areas little more than an hr before elements of US 4th and 5th Marine Divs make amphibious landing on SE coast at 0900. The other 30 HBs abort because of cloud cover, mechanical trouble, or arrival over tgt too late to make a bomb run. 26 B–24's from Angaur bomb Likanan A/F. During 19/20 Feb, 8 Saipan-based B–24's fly individual heckler strikes over Chichi Jima.

Eleventh AF: 6 B–24's fly photo rcn over Shimushu and bomb Kurabu Cape A/F. 6 ftrs intercept; the B–24's claim 4 damaged. 4 B–25's weather-abort a mission to hit tgts along the Hayakegawa R.

20 February

Eighth AF: 850-plus HBs bomb main station and M/Y at Nurnberg, plus 14 T/Os. Thick cloud en route to tgt forces about 400 other HBs to abort. Ftrs fly 438 effective spt sorties. About half of the escort strafes ground tgts. 4 other gps strafe rail and road tgts in Nurnberg and Straubing areas.

Ninth AF: IX Engineer Cmd is relieved of its assignment to Ninth AF and assigned to USSTAF. (After V-E the cmd will revert to control of the Ninth.) Weather grounds 9th Bomb Div. Ftrs fly armed rcn E and W of Rhine R, attack bridge and defended area, and spt US VIII, XII, and XX Corps in Lichtenborn area, W of Prum R, and in Saar-Mosel triangle.

Twelfth AF: Twelfth AF loses more units to ETOUSA as 2 ftr gps (27th and 86th) and an air serv gp are transferred to First Tac AF (Prov). A–20's on night intruder missions during 19/20 Feb bomb T/Os at over 30 points in C Po Valley, several rail diversions, and M/Ys at Villafranca in Lunigiana, Roncanova, Bovolone, Cerea, Legnago, Cittadella, Casa di David, Isola della Scala, Castelfranco Veneto, and Nogara. FBs devote main effort to spt US Fifth Army offensive in Monte Torraccia area. MBs bomb bridges at Montebello, Chiusaforte, Salzano, and Calcinato.

Fifteenth AF: 520-plus B–17's, with ftr escort, and B–24's bomb Lobau and Schwechat oil refineries and Vienna/Floridsdorf M/Y, steel works at Kapfenberg, harbor at Pula, and shipyards at Trieste and Fiume.

Tenth AF: 44 P–47's fly close spt strikes in Mongmit battle sector. 8 spt ground forces in Namhsan area. 13 P–38's severely damage bridge at Mong Long. Nearly 100 P–47's and P–38's pound troop concentrations, supply and ammo dumps, and general T/Os behind enemy lines. Large-scale transport operations continue.

Fourteenth AF: 34 P–51's pound locomotives, railroad cars, and other T/Os at Tsingtao and Puchi. About 30 other FBs on armed rcn hit T/Os (mainly rail and river traffic) at scattered locations including Changsha, Lohochai, Tsingtao, Chukiatsi,

N of Lingling, and between Siangsiang and Siangtan.

FEAF: B–24's bomb runways and warehouse at Jesselton A/F. Buildings at Puerto Princesa and underground installation on Corregidor are pounded. B–25's and ftrs over Formosa thoroughly blast town of Choshu, and also hit railroad yards, vehicles, railway rolling stock, and buildings.

Seventh AF: 2 Guam-based B–24's on armed rcn flight bomb Marcus. During 20/21 Feb 7 B–24's flying individual raids, bomb town of Okimura and A/F on Chichi Jima.

21 February

Eighth AF: 1,200-plus HBs attack tank plant, main railroad station, M/Ys and locomotive shops at Nurnberg, and 13 T/Os in the area. 12 ftr gps fly escort and 10 of them later strafe ground tgts. 2 other gps escort Ninth AF MBs while another gp strafes tgts in Meiningen, Coburg, and Nurnberg areas.

Ninth AF: 9th Bomb Div hits rail overpass and bridges, oil storage depot, M/Ys, comm centers, and 13 T/Os in Germany. Over 1,100 ftr sorties are completed as IX, XIX, and XXIX TACs escort 9th Bomb Div, attack railroads, A/F, and other selected tgts, fly armed rcn over wide areas of Germany including US First Army area between Duren and Losheim, and spt VIII, XII, and XX Corps along Prum R, the West wall, and in Saar-Mosel triangle.

Twelfth AF: Night ftrs and A–20's on intruder missions during 20/21 Feb continue to attack comm and supplies in Po Valley. MBs, during the day, bomb bridges at Dogna,

Crema, and Romano di Lombardia. FBs devote their main effort to close spt of ground forces along W and C US Fifth Army front, and also hit comm to the N of the battleline and in the Po Valley.

Fifteenth AF: During 20/21 Feb, 1 B–17 and 13 B–24's drop supplies in N Italy. During the day over 500 B–17's and B–24's with ftr escorts bomb Vienna railroad tgts (C yards, S station, and Matzleinsdorf M/Y), M/Ys at Bruck an der Mur, Wiener-Neustadt, Zeltweg, and Sopron, and shipyards at Trieste and Fiume.

Tenth AF: 16 P–47's provide close spt for ground forces in Namhsan area. 15 spt ground forces in Mongmit sector. 100-plus FBs strike supply and troop concentrations and make offensive sweeps of roads along battleline areas. Transports continue to land men and supplies at forward bases and drop supplies to frontline troops.

Fourteenth AF: 21 B–25's, supported by 12 P–51's, pound Taiyuan. 2 B–25's and 12 P–40's hit Yoyang. About 100 FBs on armed rcn attack troops, trucks, horses, railroad tgts, river shipping, and other T/Os at many locations throughout S and E China.

FEAF: B–24's bomb Japanese positions in hills W of Ft Stotsenburg. P–47's pound Corregidor and strafe Bagae-Pilar road and P–40's spt ground forces at Marikina, San Mateo, and on Corregidor. Basco is hit by B–25's, A–20's, and P–38's. B–24's bomb Kudat and Sandakan A/Fs while A–20's attack Jesselton A/F and town.

Seventh AF: 24 P–47's from Saipan hit Pagan with napalm. P–38's from Guam escort photo airplanes over Truk and strafe aircraft on Moen and wharf on Falas I. 3 Guam-based B–24's on armed rcn flight bomb A/F on Marcus. During 21/22 Feb, 6 HBs fly individual snooper raids from Guam against Chichi Jima.

22 February

Eighth AF: 1,359 HBs attack rail facilities and comm tgts (in conjunction with RAF and Ninth AF which attack similar objectives) including over 20 M/Ys and a total of about 40 tgts altogether, in N and C Germany. Ftr participation, including escort, strafing sweeps, and weather scouting, amounts to 822 effective sorties. (Fifteenth AF simultaneously hits tgts further S).

Ninth AF: Ninth AF joins other USAAFs in ETO and MTO, along with RAF, in Operation CLARION with objective of paralyzing the already decimated German railway system. 450-plus A–20's, A–26's, and B–26's of the 9th Bomb Div bomb SW German tgts including 46 rail bridges, 12 M/Ys, 11 stations, plus junctions, roundhouses, viaduct, crossing, workshop. CLARION marks first low-level operations by MBs since May 43. Over 1,000 ftrs of IX, XIX, and XXIX TACs escort the MBs and LBs, attack several assigned ground tgts, fly armed rcn, and cooperate with US VIII, XII, and XX Corps along Prum R and in Saar-Mosel Triangle.

Twelfth AF: A–20's during 21/22 Feb attack ammo dump, railroad bridges and lines, and road lights in Po Valley. B–25's bomb railroad bridges and M/Ys at Lavis, Bressanone, and Ala, cutting the bridge at Lavis and the through tracks at Ala M/Y. Ftrs and FBs continue to spt US Fifth Army forces S and SW of Bologna and hit comm tgts, dumps, vehicles, and guns in and N of battle area in Apennines and in Po Valley, and bomb A/Fs at Ghedi and Bergamo.

Fifteenth AF: The Fifteenth's participation in Operation CLARION includes over 350 HBs bombing 50-plus separate comm tgts in Germany, Austria, and Italy, including some 25 M/Ys and numerous railroad lines and bridges. Ftrs fly over 300 escort and strafing sorties.

Tenth AF: 29 P-47's spt ground forces in Namhsam area. 11 closely spt forces in Mongmit sector. About 100 FBs attack troop concentrations, gun positions, supply points, trucks, and animal transport in battle areas and behind enemy lines. Transports complete over 600 sorties to forward areas throughout the day.

Fourteenth AF: 19 FBs hit villages, tanks, and trucks from Hsiangcheng to Hsuchang, attack railroad traffic around Sinsiang and Linfen, hit river craft, trucks, and troops in Chiuchiang area, and claim 1 freighter sunk on the Yangtze between Hankow and Nanking. A single B-25 attacks convoys in Siang-Chiang Valley near Hengyang.

FEAF: 100 B-24's hit troop concentrations NW of Ft Stotsenburg. P-47's pound Corregidor. A-20's hit concentrations at Pugo, SW of Baguio, B-24's bomb supply areas N and W of Baguio while P-51's hit Angin and Marikina. B-24's bomb Tarakan and Labuan A/Fs.

Seventh AF: 3 B-24's on armed rcn from Guam bomb A/F on Marcus. During 22/23 Feb, 6 HBs fly individual harassment strikes against Susaki A/F and town of Okimura.

23 February

Eighth AF: As a follow-up to the previous day's attacks on transportation facilities, 1,193 HBs strike 10 M/Ys and numerous T/Os, mostly rail comm, in C Germany. Ftrs fly over 600 effective escort and strafing sorties.

Ninth AF: 9th Bomb Div hits comm centers E of Roer R as US Ninth Army crosses the river and begins assault (Operation GRENADE) toward the Rhine. Ftrs fly armed rcn, patrols, and alerts and spt US 104th and 8th Inf Divs near Duren, XIII and XIX Corps' attack across the Roer at Linnich and Rurdorf, and VIII, XII, and XX Corps at Prum R, E of Our R, and E of Saar R.

Twelfth AF: A-20's on intruder missions during 22/23 Feb hit M/Ys and A/Fs throughout N Italy. MBs concentrate on N end of Brenner Pass, damaging bridges at Campo San Pietro and railroad fill at San Felice del Benaco and hitting bridges at Dogna. FBs pound A/Fs, and enemy movement in C and N Po Valley, and damage 5 bridges and cut rail lines at numerous points.

Fifteenth AF: About 380 HBs hit M/Ys at Villach, Worgl, Knittelfeld, Klagenfurt and Udine, plus Kitzbuhel railroad junction. 140-plus P-38's and P-51's provide escort. Some of the ftrs strafe areas NW of Linz and N of Munich. 35 other P-38's dive-bomb Worgl M/Y and afterwards 30 of them strafe rail line Rosenheim-Innsbruck-Landeck. Other P-38's and P-51's fly rcn and escort missions.

Tenth AF: 20-plus P-47's spt ground forces in Mongmit sector and near Lashio, hitting Japanese concentration. 12 B-25's and 120-plus FBs continue pounding troop concentrations, supply areas, road traffic, and ammo dumps in frontline areas and behind enemy lines. Large transport effort completes 655 sorties.

Fourteenth AF: 29 B-24's and 22 ftrs scheduled to attack Shihkiachwang abort because of bad weather. 8 P-51's hit railroad T/Os near Siaokan and attack river traffic from Nanking to Hankow. 5 B-24's sweep Gulf of Tonkin and S China Sea, damaging 1 vessel. 4 P-40's attack T/Os in Kaifeng area.

FEAF: Strikes supporting ground forces continue throughout battle zones on Luzon. P-47's hit Jesselton A/F while B-24's bomb Sandakan, Lahat Datu, and Miri A/Fs. B-25's on shipping sweeps bomb vessels in Phan Rang harbor and hit small convoy SW of Camranh Bay.

Seventh AF: 26 B-24's from Angaur bomb San Roque A/F. 2 P-47's from Saipan on armed rcn strafe Pagan. On 23/24 Feb, 7 B-24's from Guam fly snooper raids against A/F on Chichi Jima and town of Okimura on Haha Jima. Marines raise US flag on summit of Mount Suribachi on Iwo Jima.

ZI: A P-38 from Santa Rosa AAFld shoots down Japanese balloon over Calistoga.

24 February

Eighth AF: 1,050 HBs attack 4 oil refineries, 3 M/Ys, shipyards, 2 rail bridges, an industrial area, and a city area—all in Germany. 12 P-51 gps spt the HBs, 8 of them strafing numerous ground tgts.

Ninth AF: Nearly 500 MBs and LBs hit 5 comm centers, 2 M/Ys, 3 rail bridges, 6 town areas, and a T/O as part of interdiction operations against troops during Rhineland campaign. Ftrs spt 8th and 104th Inf Divs in Duren area, XIII and XIX Corps at Roer R bridgehead area, and VIII, XII, and XX Corps E of and along Prum R and in Saarlautern area.

Twelfth AF: During 23/24 Feb A-20's bomb M/Ys, including those at Castelfranco Veneto, Rovereto, Villafranca di Verona, and Legnago, and A/Fs at Villafranca di Verona, Ghedi, and Bergamo. MBs bomb rail lines, bridges, bridge approaches, and fills at Bozzolo, Santa Margherita d'Adige, San Michele all'Adige, Pizzighetone, and Lavis, and severely damage Sesto Calende industrial complex. FBs hit comm, mainly A/Fs, railroad bridges, lines, and M/Ys at several points including Villafranca, Calliano, N of Nervesa della Battaglia, N of Santa Margherita d'Adige, Bergamo, Pavullo nel Frigano, Isola della Scala, and Motta di Livenza. Ftrs and FBs spt US Fifth Army forces, hitting gun positions in adv of battlefront, at Montese and E of Modena, and blast tgts in battle area as 10th Mountain Div reaches summit of Monte Torraccia.

Fifteenth AF: More than 500 HBs (with ftr escorts) attack Udine, Padua, Verona, and Ferrara M/Ys and Ferrara railroad bridge, M/Ys at Graz and Klagenfurt, and several

T/Os. During previous night 20 HBs continue supply drops in N Italy.

Tenth AF: 8 P–47's in close spt of ground forces near Lashio pound vehicle and troop concentration. 12 B–25's and about 125 FBs strike against tgts immediately behind lines, hitting troops, supply areas, occupied towns and villages, vehicles, and general T/Os. Transports complete 600 sorties carrying men and supplies to forward areas.

Fourteenth AF: 5 B 24's on individual sweeps over S China Sea and Gulf of Tonkin claim 4 vessels sunk.

FEAF: On Luzon, strikes in spt of ground forces continue, especially W of Ft Stotsenburg. FBs attack forces holding out on Corregidor. B–24's bomb Sepinggang and Manggar A/Fs. B–25's sweep off China coast, bombing naval base at Ryukyu-Sho.

Twentieth AF: In an all-incendiary attack 105 B–29's hit Empire Dock area at Singapore, burning out about 40 per cent of the warehouse area. This is the last 100-aircraft strike of XX BC.

Seventh AF: 28 B–24's from Angaur bomb Ising. 3 B–24's on armed rcn from Guam bomb Marcus A/F. During 24/25 Feb, 5 B–24's out of Guam fly individual snooper strikes against Chichi Jima A/F and town of Okimura.

Eleventh AF: 4 B–25's on shipping sweep attack Hayakegawa. Returning, the B–25's sight and photograph a Japanese bomb-carrying balloon.

25 February

Eighth AF: 1,141 HBs attack 2 tank factories, 4 M/Ys, 2 A/Fs, an oil depot, and 3 T/Os (city areas) in SC Germany. 11 ftr gps on close escort and area patrols cover the HBs.

Ninth AF: 9th Bomb Div strikes 4 rail bridges, 4 comm centers, M/Y and 9 T/Os as part of interdiction campaign against Germany. Ftrs escort 9th Bomb Div, attack assigned ground tgts, fly armed rcn, and spt 8th and 104th Inf Divs in Duren area, XIII and XIX Corps E of the Roer, and VIII, XII, and XX Corps along the Prum and Saar Rivers.

Twelfth AF: A–20's (24/25 Feb) attack M/Ys at Villafranca di Verona, Cittadella, Castelfranco Veneto, Trento, and Turin, and A/Fs at Villafranca di Verona and Bergamo. MBs cut or damage bridges at Vipiteno, Dogna, Ala, and Campo San Pietro, and railroad fill at San Felice del Benaco. XXII TAC ftrs and FBs are restricted by ground haze in Po Valley but attack rail lines, M/Ys, rolling stock, motor transport, and dumps.

Fifteenth AF: Over 600 B–17's and B–24's bomb M/Ys in Amstetten, Linz (2) Villach (2), and Salzburg, plus Linz benzol plant and ordnance depot and several T/Os. Ftrs escort and some afterwards strafe T/Os in Austria, SE Germany, and W Czechoslovakia. 37 P 51's strafe railroad tgts in Rosenheim-Muhldorf-Landshut-Augsburg areas. Routine rcn and supply missions continue.

Tenth AF: In joint operations with British and Chinese army forces, 16 P–47's spt British 36th Inf Div in Mongmit sector while 31 P–47's spt Chinese 38th and 50th Divs near Lashio and Namtu, respectively. Low B–25 strike knocks out suspension bridge at Namsang. 9 B–25's and 85 FBs blast troop concentrations, supply areas, road traffic, and general T/Os behind enemy lines. 600-plus transport sorties are completed to forward areas.

Fourteenth AF: 6 B–25's, supported by 5 P–40's, hit sampans and buildings in Puchi area. 3 B–25's and 19 P–40's pound Isuho ferry and attack river and road traffic from Siangtan to Hengyang. A single B–25 bombs truck convoys S of Hengyang. 4 B–24's over Gulf of Tonkin and S China Sea claim damaging hits on 2 vessels. 44 P–51's and P–40's hit bridges, river shipping, troop areas, and motor transport at Kweiyi, Paoching, and Siangtan, from Lingling to Hengyang and Leiyang, from Anjen to Chaling, N of Liuchow, and W of Ishan.

FEAF: B–24's bomb Takao. P–51's hit T/Os along E Formosa coast. B–24's attack troop concentrations on E side of Ipo R and pound Japanese positions between Ipo and Osboy. B–24's bomb Tawau and Labuan A/Fs.

Twentieth AF: Gen Millard F Harmon, CG AAFPOA and Dep Cmdr of Twentieth AF, is lost near Kwajalein when his aircraft disappears en route to Washington DC. (On 2 Mar Gen Hale, AAFPOA dep cmdr for operations, assumes Harmon's positions). 172 B–29's bomb urban area of Tokyo. Around 30 others hit alternates and T/Os. This is XXI BC's largest mission to date and its first 3-wg strike against Japan as the 73rd and 313th Bomb Wgs are joined by the 314th.

Seventh AF: 9 Guam-based B–24's hit blockhouses, and mortar and rocket-launching positions on NW part of Iwo Jima. 8 B–24's, flying separate harassment strikes, pound A/Fs on Chichi Jima during 25/26 Feb.

26 February

Eighth AF: 1,102 HBs hit 3 railroad stations in Berlin, plus T/Os including Eberswalde. 15 ftr gps provide escort.

Ninth AF: 235 A–20's, A–26's, and B–26's attack comm center at Wickrath, rail and road junctions at Zieverich and Gladbach, a supply and ammo depot (casual tgt), towns of Kapellen, Viersen, and Munstereifel, and T/Os. Weather limits ftr operations to armed rcn flights in Aschaffenburg-Wurzburg area by XIX TAC.

Twelfth AF: A–20's, during 25/26 Feb, considerably damage M/Ys at Castelfranco Veneto and Bazzano. MBs bomb railroad bridges at Legnago, Ala, Pontetidone, and San Michele all'Adige. Ftrs and FBs hit bridges, M/Ys, rail lines, and transport tgts at numerous points including Nervesa della Battaglia, Ora, Bologna, Trento, Vicenza, Castelnuovo di Garfagnana, and Avisio, and bomb A/Fs at Ghedi and Bergamo. XXII TAC aircraft also spt US Fifth Army forces in battle area S of Bologna.

Fifteenth AF: During 25/26 Feb supply drops to N Italy continue. During the day 32 P–38's dive-bomb and strafe Graz-Bruck an der Mur-Wiener-Neustadt rail lines. 12 others fly top cover. Other P–38's and P–51's fly rcn and escort missions. 102 B–24's, with ftr escort, dispatched against tac tgts in Yugoslavia, are recalled when clouds completely cover objectives.

Tenth AF: 12 P–47's spt troops of British 36th Div in Mongmit area.

8 spt MARS TF (US 533d Brig) in Lashio sector while 16 others fly close spt for Chinese 50th Div troops near Namhsam. 8 B-25's on low-level strikes knock out bypass bridges at Mong Pawn and Loi-leng. 80-plus FBs and 4 B-25's continue to attack troops, supplies, road traffic, and other tgts immediately behind lines. Again 600-plus transport sorties are flown.

Fourteenth AF: 20 B-25's, some with ftr escort, bomb Ishan, Luchai, Siangtan, and hit bridges at Chuchou and Loshan. 9 B-25's attack bridges, railroad tracks, and heavy port equipment at Ha Trung, along the Chu R, and at Hongay and Haiphong. 70-plus FBs on armed rcn over S and E China and N Indochina attack numerous T/Os including A/Fs, town areas, and river, rail, and road traffic.

FEAF: B-24's over Formosa hit Takao A/F while ftrs on sweep strafe railroad tgts. B-24's bomb troop concentrations in Ipo Dam area and spt ground forces NE of Manila. A-20's and FBs spt ground forces in Echague A/F area, at Ternate, Trinidad, and Antipolo, and hit troops W of Ft Stotsenburg. A-20's, P-38's, and P-47's hit Puerto Princesa. B-24's hit Manggar and Sepinggang A/Fs. B-25's bomb Zettle A/F.

Seventh AF: 9 B-24's sent from Guam against positions on Iwo Jima are recalled due to cloud cover. 8 HBs hit Chichi Jima during 26/27 Feb, flying individual harrassment strikes.

27 February

Eighth AF: 1,012 HBs, in 3 forces, bomb Leipzig rail traffic center, Halle M/Y and T/Os including Bitterfeld M/Y. 14 P-51 gps fly close escort while a P-47 gp patrols Halle-Leipzig area. 11 gps later strafe road and rail tgts.

Ninth AF: 118 MBs and LBs attack Ahrweiler rail bridge, comm centers at Glessen, Munstereifel, and Monheim, and a T/O. Ftrs fly leaflet missions, attack Frankfurt/Main oil storage tanks, fly alerts, and strafe from W of Duisburg to Worringen. XXIX TAC also flies spt for XIII and XIX Corps SW and S of Monchen-Gladbach.

Twelfth AF: A-20's on 26/27 Feb bomb enemy movement at 14 different places in Po Valley, M/Ys at Villafranca di Verona and Isola della Scala, town of Bazzano, and A/Fs at Villafranca di Verona and Ghedi. XXII TAC FBs concentrate on railroad cutting in Brenner area and NE Italy, claiming 36 cuts, and attack rolling stock in Villach area. MBs destroy railroad diversion bridge at San Michele all'Adige and cut approaches on Ala and Lavis bridges and effectively blast Spilimbergo and Pagnocco dumps.

Fifteenth AF: 540-plus B-24's and B-17's, with ftr escort, bomb M/Ys at Augsburg, Salzburg, Lienz, and Jenbach, plus several T/Os. Escorting ftrs strafe T/Os during return flight. Routine rcn and supply missions continue.

Tenth AF: 18 P-47's closely spt ground forces in Mongmit area. 4 others knock out small bypass bridge at Hay-ti. About 100 FBs attack troop concentrations, supplies, gun positions, elephant transport, and road traffic along battlefronts and behind enemy lines. Transport operations continue on large-scale as 589 sorties are completed.

Fourteenth AF: 12 B–25's knock out 4 bridges and damage 2 others in N Indochina. 12 others bomb Ishan and Hwaiyuanchen. 4 B–24's over Gulf of Tonkin and S China Sea attack shipping, claiming 2 vessels sunk. 19 FBs hit barracks SW of Ishan, 15 attack Kiungshan A/F, 12 hit T/Os in Yoyang area, 23 hit T/Os around Kiyang, and 30 others hit scattered T/Os at other points in S and E China.

FEAF: B–24's, A–20's, and P–38's strike Puerto Princesa in preparation for the following morning's allied amphibious landings. On Luzon ground spt continues on large-scale. P–51's bomb Baguio. On Mindanao P–38's and USMC aircraft hit A/Fs. B–24's bomb Tarakan and Jesselton A/Fs. Takao is hit by B–24's. Ftrs sweep W coast of Formosa. Sweeping China coast, B–25's hit fleet of junks and sampans near Hong Kong destroying and damaging more than 25.

Twentieth AF: Personnel of 58th Bomb Wg (VH) begin shipping out of Calcutta for Tinian and Guam, implementing redeployment orders of 6 Feb WD directive. Final shipment arrives in the Marianas on 6 Jun, completing transfer of the wg from India without loss of a single life or aircraft. During 27/28 Feb, 10 B–29's mine Johore Strait. 1 other mines Penang harbor.

Seventh AF: 9 Guam-based B–24's blast pillboxes, arty emplacements, blockhouse, and mortar positions on N part of Iwo Jima. 22 B–24's from Angaur bomb Daliao and Libby A/Fs. During 27/28 Feb, 9 HBs, flying snooper strikes out of Guam, bomb

A/Fs, radio stations, and town of Omura.

28 February

Eighth AF: 1,054 HBs, using blind-bombing techniques, strike 6 M/Ys, 2 rail viaducts, a tank plant, a castings plant, and a few T/Os in WC Germany. 9 ftr gps give close escort, airplanes from 5 gps later strafing ground tgts. 5 other P–51 gps conduct successful strafing attacks on numerous tgts while a P–47 gp bombs M/Ys and factory buildings.

Ninth AF: 340-plus A–20's, B–26's and A–26's bomb rail bridges at Mayen, Niederscheld, and Colbe, Unna ordnance depot, Kamp road junction, Siegen and Sankt Wendel M/Ys, town of Rheinburg, and T/Os. Ftrs escort 9th Bomb Div, fly sweeps, patrols and armed rcn, attack special tgts, and spt US 3d Armd Div at Paffendorf bridgehead, US Ninth Army elements near Monchen-Gladbach and Neuss (2d Armd Div reaches point within 6 mi of the Rhine), and VIII, XII, and XX Corps between the Prum and Kyll Rivers and near Trier.

Twelfth AF: On 27/28 Feb A–20's attack a few M/Ys, bridges, rail lines, and general movement but because of bad weather are recalled by midnight. XII TAC FBs continue to pound comm and other tgts, including Ghedi and Vicenza A/Fs, ammo dumps near Codroipo and W of Villafranca di Verona, and shell loading plant SW of Piacenza. MBs bomb bridges at Ala, Santa Margherita d'Adige, San Michele all'Adige, Ponte di Piave, and Pordenone, and railway embankment at Salorno.

Fifteenth AF: About 680 B–17's

and B-24's bomb M/Ys at Lienz, Ora, Bolzano, Vipiteno, Vicenza, Fortezza, Bressanone, Brunico, Brescia, and Conegliano, and bridges at Albes and Verona-Parona di Valpolicella. 109 P-51's provide escort. 75 P-38's dive-bomb Sankt Veit an der Glan M/Y and strafe rail lines in Sankt Veit-Klagenfurt-Villach-Ljubljana areas. Other P-38's and P-51's (about 25) strafe rail traffic around Bruck an der Mur, Innsbruck, Klagenfurt, Worgl, and Passau, and attack Bjelovar A/F, destroying enemy-held B-24 and P-38. Rcn and supply flights are maintained.

Tenth AF: 28 P-47's spt forces of British 36th Div in Mongmit area. 75 FBs continue pounding troop concentrations, supply dumps, and road traffic behind enemy lines. 552 transport sorties are flown, landing men and supplies at forward bases and dropping supplies to frontline troops.

Fourteenth AF: 2 B-25's attack T/Os in Hsiang R Valley while 2 P-51's hit T/Os NE of Hengyang. A single B-24 damages a cargo vessel in S China Sea.

FEAF: B-24's strike A/Fs at Sandakan and Labuan. B-24's bomb Caldera Pt and B-25's hit San Roque A/F. B-25's fly napalm raid against Sanga Sanga A/F.

Seventh AF: 8 Guam-based B-24's pound Susaki A/F. 23 B-24's from Angaur bomb Sasa A/F. During 28 Feb/1 Mar 6 HBs from Guam, flying separate harassment strikes, bomb Susaki A/F again.

1 March

Eighth AF: 1,153 B-17's and B-24's bomb 8 M/Ys in SW Germany, plus 2 T/Os. 9 P-51 gps provide close escort, 7 gps afterward strafe transportation facilities and A/Fs.

Ninth AF: 340-plus MBs and LBs attack ordnance depot at Giessen, comm centers at Pulheim, Rheinbach, Rommerskirchen, and Stommeln, rail bridge at Pracht, a road bridge, and 8 T/Os. Ftrs escort MBs and LBs, fly alerts, scheduled patrols, and armed rcn, hit assigned ground tgts and spt US 3d Armd Div at Erft R bridgehead near Paffendorf, 9th Armd Div between Neffelbach and Rotbach (creeks), XVI and XIII Corps in Venlo area and along Niers R, XIX Corps in Monchen-Gladbach area, VIII Corps astride the Prum R, XII Corps between Prum and Nims Rivers and along the Kyll R, and XX Corps in Trier area.

Twelfth AF: A-20's fly intruder missions during 28 Feb/1 Mar against tgts at Lecco and in Parma area, starting large fires and causing several explosions during strike on Casarsa della Delizia temporary railroad bridge, and hit bridges at Nervesa della Battaglia and Sacile. Weather cancels all daytime operations except for rcn and supply runs.

Fifteenth AF: 630-plus B-24's and B-17's bomb Moosbierbaum oil refinery and alternate tgts and T/Os including M/Ys at Sankt Polten, Amstetten, Villach, Klagenfurt, Knittelfeld, Feldbach, Jesenice, and Maribor, plus several scattered T/Os. Over 220 ftrs provide escort. 22 P-38's bomb Moosbierbaum refinery and Tulln M/Y (afterward 12 of them strafe Wiener-Neustadt-Gloggnitz rail lines). 47 other P-38's strafe rail traffic around Graz and W of Vienna.

USAFIME: USAFIME takes over NW Africa from MTOUSA and is redesignated AMET (Africa-Middle East Theater).

Tenth AF: 27 P–47's spt ground forces in Mogok area. 16 fly close spt strikes near Lashio. 14 P–47's damage approaches of bypass bridge at Na-lang, but leave the bridge serviceable. About 100 FBs attack troops, supply areas, comm tgts, a ferry landing, and general T/Os along battlefronts and immediately behind German lines. Large-scale transport operations continue.

Fourteenth AF: 6 B–25's and 5 P–51's pound S side of Ishan while 17 other P–51's hit E and W sections of the city. 9 P–51's attack T/Os of Chinchengchiang while 4 others hit troops and road traffic between Chinchengchiang and Hwaiyang.

FEAF: B–24's over Formosa and the Ryukyu Is bomb Takao aluminium plant, Tainan A/F and nearby satellite field. Ftrs hit buildings at Keishu and storage tanks, railroad yards, and T/Os throughout the Ryukyus. Troops on Corregidor and W of Ft Stotsenburg are hit with napalm. Other B–24's bomb Tarakan, Labuan, and Manggar A/Fs. B–25's hit Zettle Field.

Thirteenth AF: Thirteenth AF moves from Morotai to Leyte. XIII FC moves from Leyte to Palawan.

Seventh AF: VII FC is removed from control of Seventh AF and transferred to AAFPOA. 7 B–24's from Guam bomb Susaki A/F. 1 other hits Haha Jima. During 1/2 Mar, 5 HBs make separate harassment strikes on Susaki A/F and town of Omura.

2 March

Eighth AF: 1,159 HBs bomb synthetic oil plants at Bohlen, Ruh-land, and Magdeburg, 2 oil refineries at Rositz and Schonebeck, M/Ys at Chemnitz, Dresden, and Magdeburg, and T/Os in Germany and Czechoslovakia. 15 ftr gps fly 675 effective supporting sorties. Also part of 3 of these gps strafe A/Fs.

Ninth AF: 9th Bomb Div hits 5 bridges, 2 comm centers, 3 ordnance and motor transport depots, several city areas, and 6 T/Os. Objectives are to hinder movement of enemy troops trying to help German army caught in front of US Third Army, to obstruct movement in general, and to damage enemy repair and refitting capabilities. Over 1,700 ftrs escort 9th Bomb Div, hit special tgts, fly armed rcn and patrols, and spt US 3d Armd Div at expanding bridgehead on the Erft R, XVI and XIX Corps in Sevelen, Monchen-Gladbach, and Neuss area, and VIII, XII, and XX Corps E of Prum R, astride the Kyll R, and in Trier-Saarburg area.

Twelfth AF: Weather again grounds MBs, FBs and ftrs hit comm, ammo and stores dumps, 2 sugar refineries, guns, vehicles, and buildings S of Bologna and in Po Valley, and A/F at Aviano and Lonate Pozzolo.

Fifteenth AF: 470 B–24's and B–17's, with ftrs flying escort, bomb M/Ys at Linz, Sankt Polten, Amstetten, Graz, Knittelfeld, and Brescia. 31 P–51's on strafing mission attack rail and river comm from Linz to Regensburg, while 18 others fly top cover. P–38's fly rcn missions. B–24's drop supplies during 1/2 Mar in N Italy and C Yugoslavia.

Tenth AF: 20-plus P–47's fly close spt strikes in Mogok area. 2 B–25's damage ferry slips at Li-lu while

10 others hit bridges at Tonglau, Na-lang, Mong Pawn, and Namsang. 90-plus FBs attack gun positions, troops, supply areas, and highway T/Os in general battle areas and behind enemy lines. Transports complete 564 sorties to forward areas.

Fourteenth AF: 3 B–24's on sweeps over Gulf of Tonkin and S China Sea claim 2 vessels sunk and 3 damaged.

FEAF: B–24's, B–25's, A–20's, and FBs hit Matsuyama, Toyohara, Kagi, and Kato A/Fs. Other B–24's pound Sepinggang and Manggar A/Fs and waterfront area of Sandakan.

Twentieth AF: Around 50 B–29's bomb shop and warehouse area at naval base in Singapore. 5 others hit alternates on Bukum I, at Arang Hill, and at Khao Huakhang.

Seventh AF: 7 Guam-based B–24's make daylight raid on Chichi Jima A/F and 5 more bomb same A/F and town of Omura during 2/3 Mar.

3 March

Eighth AF: 1,048 HBs operating in 6 forces bomb 10 primary tgts (6 oil refineries, an oil plant equipment works, motor transport factory, tank plant, and a rail bridge) in NC and E Germany along with several secondaries, last resort tgts, and T/Os including M/Ys, casting plant, tank plant, and industrial and city areas. 657 effective ftr sorties are flown in spt. Ftrs also strafe ground tgts.

Ninth AF: 9th Bomb Div hits Wiesbaden, Giessen, Bergisch Born, and Nahbollenbach ordnance and storage depots, rail bridges at Remagen and Simmern, comm center at Heimersheim, motor transport concentration at Schwelm, Rheinbach ammo dump, Kirn M/Y and town, and several T/Os. Ftrs fly bmr escort, hit special tgts, fly patrols and armed rcn, and spt US 9th Inf Div, 3d Armd Div, and VII Corps astride Erft R W of Euskirchen and area near Roggendorf W of the Rhine R, XIII, XVI, and XIX Corps E of Sevelen, NE of Krefeld, and W of the Rhine in Dusseldorf area, and VIII, XII, and XX Corps in the area between the Prum and Kyll R and along the Mosel in Trier area.

Twelfth AF: Overcast skies and turbulent winds hamper MB missions against comm in Brenner area, allowing only limited success against tgts. Crema and Fidenza bridges in Po Valley are damaged. XXII TAC FBs, destroy a sugar refinery at Verona and achieve good results against comm and dumps in C Po Valley and Brenner area. Other ftrs and FBs spt US Fifth Army S of Bologna. A–20's during 2/3 Mar hit roads, ammo supplies, and vehicles at several points in Po Valley, particularly in Bologna-Modena regions, and bomb Legnano M/Y.

Fifteenth AF: Rapidly deteriorating weather cancels bombing operations. P–51's strafe rail traffic between Leibnitz and SW of Spittal an der Drau and attack A/F S of Graz. P–38's fly rcn and rcn escort. 1 B–24, of 6 dispatched, drops supplies in N Yugoslavia.

Tenth AF: 24 P–38's and P–47's spt forces of Chinese 50th Div near Mansam. 16 spt British 36th Div in Mogok area. 10 P–47's knock out Na-lang bridge while 2 B–25's drop delay-action bombs in good pattern around Loi-leng bridge. 10 B–25's join 80-plus FBs in attack on troops, supplies, tanks, trucks, gun positions, and transport elephants behind enemy lines. 29 of the FBs concentrate on Kankang area. 643 air supply sorties are completed.

Fourteenth AF: 4 B–24's over Gulf of Tonkin and S China Sea attack shipping T/Os, claiming 1 vessel sunk and 3 damaged. 3 B–25's hit Kep, damaging several locomotives and boxcars and hit a bridge. 12 P–51's over Indochina hit T/Os between Vinh and Nam Dinh (2 direct hits are scored on bridge at Minh Koi) while 2 others blast HQ building in Hanoi.

FEAF: B–24's pound Tainan area and Kiirun while ftrs sweeping over Formosa hit numerous T/Os. FBs bomb Koshun A/F. B–25's bomb San Roque A/F. B–24's and B–25's attack Zettle Field. Echague, Ternate, and Caballo I areas are bombed by A–20's. B–25's, aborting strike against Formosa, bomb airstrip at Basco.

Seventh AF: 10 B–24's from Guam pound Susaki A/F in afternoon strike, and 4 more, flying individual strikes, hit same tgt during 3/4 Mar.

4 March

Eighth AF: Over 1,000 HBs are dispatched to bomb tgts in SW Germany. Bad weather causes over 300 aborts. 656 HBs bomb M/Ys at Ulm, Ingolstadt, Offenburg, military vehicle plants and ordnance depot at Ulm, jet aircraft plant at Schwabmunchen, and 6 city areas. 13 ftr gps fly 467 uneventful supporting sorties.

Ninth AF: About 180 B–26's, A–20's, and A–26's strike M/Ys and rail junction at Recklinghausen, Lenkerbeck, and Herne, comm centers at Bruhl, Sechtem, and Rheinbach, and several other tgts including

rail bridge and towns. Weather limits ftr operations. A few ftrs fly armed rcn E of the Rhine and others fly cover for XX Corps.

Twelfth AF: Good flying weather permits full-scale effort by Twelfth AF. MBs hit 7 railroad bridges on Brenner line and in NE Italy. Salorno railroad fill receives a particularly good concentration of bombs. XXII TAC P–47's concentrate on comm tgts in Po Valley, knocking out a span of the Cittadella railway bridge. Brazilian P–47's blast ammo dump at Villafranca di Verona. A–20's during 3/4 Mar bomb bridge and bridge approaches at Casarsa della Delizia, Ostiglia, and Nervesa della Battaglia, radar station at Vignola, and lights, motor transport, roads, and other T/Os at over 30 places in the C Po Valley.

Fifteenth AF: 630-plus B–24's and B–17's, with ftr escort, bomb M/Ys at Sopron (2), Szombathely, Knittelfeld, Zeltweg, Graz, Sankt Veit an der Glan, Wiener-Neustadt, Zagreb (2) and Ljubljana, and several scattered T/Os. Other B–24's, with P–51 escort, drop supplies in Yugoslavia. P–38's and P–51's fly rcn and rcn escort operations.

Tenth AF: 100 FBs attack troop concentrations, villages, roads, tanks, trucks, animal transport, and supplies along and immediately behind the battlelines running from SW to NE across C Burma. Meiktila is largely occupied by forces of Indian 17th Div.

Fourteenth AF: 4 B–24's on sea sweep damage a destroyer escort in S China Sea.

FEAF: B–24's bomb Sasa and Likanan A/Fs and town of Zamboanga and pound gun positions, ammo storage, and T/Os at Antipolo and Wawa, supply dumps and town area at Bamban, T/Os in Cagayan Valley, fortifications on Caballo I, and A/Fs at Aparri and Tuguegarao.

Twentieth AF: Gen Giles becomes Dep Cmdr of Twentieth AF and CG of AAFPOA. A B–29 makes an emergency landing on Iwo Jima. This begins a series of over 2,400 such emergency landings on the island during World War II. 192 Marinanas-based B–29's are airborne against Musashino (Musashi) but heavy clouds prevent bombing the primary. 159 of the VHBs bomb secondary tgt, the urban areas of Tokyo, and almost 20 others hit alternate tgts. This aborted try at Musashino marks end of XXI BC's effort to knock out Japanese aircraft industry by high-altitude, daylight precision bombing. (The indirect effect of causing Japanese industrialists to lose confidence in their supposed immunity from air attacks exceeds the effect of actual bomb damage to the aircraft industry). During 4/5 Mar, 11 B–29's, staging from Luliang, mine the confluence of the Hwangpoo and Yangtze Rivers and the Tai-hsing Narrows. 1 VHB drops mines at Tungting Lake.

Seventh AF: 10 B–24's from Guam bomb Susaki A/F. During 4/5 Mar, 3 HBs make separate harassment raids on the A/F.

5 March

Eighth AF: Almost 400 HBs attack M/Y at Chemnitz, oil refinery at Hamburg/Harburg, and T/Os including 2 railway storage sidings and 3 town areas. 587 supporting sorties

are flown by ftrs. A gp of P–51 FBs bomb M/Ys, a tunnel, a rail line, and a road. 2 other gps escort MBs of Ninth AF.

Ninth AF: 565 MBs and LBs attack 6 M/Ys, comm center, ordnance depot, a city area and T/Os with aim of obstructing reinforcements and supplies to German forces being pushed back across the Rhine R. Ftrs escort 9th Bomb Div, drop leaflets in Cologne-Bonn area, and fly armed rcn over Ruhr and Hamm-Duisburg area.

Twelfth AF: A–20's hit lines of comm in N Po Valley during 4/5 Mar. Results are generally good. Bad daytime weather grounds MBs. XXII TAC FBs and ftrs operate on greatly reduced scale, mostly in C Po Valley, hitting bridges at Casarsa della Delizia, Nervesa della Battaglia, Ostiglia, and Ostellato, and attacking town of Vignola.

Fifteenth AF: Bad weather limits operations to supply, escort, and rcn missions.

Tenth AF: 50-plus P–47's spt forces of British 36th Div in Mogok sector and forces of Chinese 50th Div in Mansam area. 46 P–47's and 12 B–25's hit troop concentrations in battle areas and attack supply areas, road traffic, and general T/Os behind enemy lines. 664 air supply sorties are flown to forward areas.

Fourteenth AF: 30 B–25's knock out bridges at Phu Xuyen, Thinh Duc, Phu Ly, Ninh Binh, and Phu Lang Thuong and damage bridge at Kep. 2 B–25's, escorted by 8 P–47's, knock out bridge at Changtuikuan while 4 bomb Chikhom. 40-plus P–51's and P–40's on armed rcn hit road, rail, and river traffic, town areas, and other T/Os in Indochina, C Yangtze R area, and elsewhere in S and E China.

FEAF: B–25's hit San Roque A/F. B–24's with ftr spt hit troops in Antipolo area while FBs dive-bomb San Pablo, hit Ft Drum, attack troops W of Ft Stotsenburg, and spt guerrilla forces NE of Lingayen Gulf. Tgts on Formosa and in the Ryukyus are hit by ftrs on sweeps and B–24's on armed rcn. The ftr sweeps are especially effective against railroad tgts. B–25's hit Zettle Field.

Seventh AF: Susaki A/F is pounded by 11 B–24's from Guam. During 5/6 Mar, 5 more hit the A/F in individual snooper strikes. 22 B–24's from Angaur bomb Matina A/F.

6 March

Ninth AF: 260-plus A–26's, and B–26's hit Recklinghausen, Siegburg, and Opladen M/Ys, Siegburg storage depot, and town of Bochum as a T/O. Weather grounds IX and XIX TAC. XXIX TAC flies alerts and covers US XVI Corps as it completes drive to the Rhine in Rheinburg area.

Twelfth AF: MBs pound comm in Brenner Pass and hit bridges at Pordenone, Ossenigo, Enego, Ora, Pizzighetone, and San Ambrogio di Valpolicella. Ftrs and FBs concentrate on close spt of US Fifth Army S and SW of Bologna. During 5/6 Mar a few A–20's bomb T/Os in Po Valley.

Fifteenth AF: Bad weather restricts all operations except rcn and a supply mission, with escort, to Yugoslavia.

Tenth AF: 31 P–47's spt British 36th Div forces in Mogok area. 12 B–25's join 60-plus FBs in striking troop concentrations, road traffic, supply and fuel dumps, and other tgts in vicinity of the battlefront and in areas close behind enemy lines. Transport operations continue on a large scale with 663 sorties completed to forward areas throughout the day.

Fourteenth AF: 4 B–25's bomb Chikhom. About 50 FBs hit storage, troops, railroad tgts, and river and road traffic around Hankow, along Pinghan railroad, Kaifeng, Suchow, Hsuchang, Changsha, Yoyang, Liuyang, and Hengyang, and on railroads from Liuliho to Chengtung and from Tungpu to Tatung.

FEAF: HBs pound San Roque and Zamboanga areas. Other HBs, MBs, and FBs hit Antipolo area, bomb Balete Pass, and spt guerrillas near San Fernando, Ft Drum, and Caballo I. B–25's and P–38's attack Hainan I and considerably damage Samah A/F. Ftrs sweeping over Formosa hit Koshun area.

Seventh AF: 11 Guam-based B–24's again pound Susaki A/F. 5 more hit the A/F during 6/7 Mar in separate strikes. 28 P–51's and 12 P–61's land on Iwo Jima.

Eleventh AF: Mission to the Kurils is cancelled due to inclement weather.

7 March

Eighth AF: 873 HBs attack benzol plant and oil refinery at Dortmund, benzol plants at Datteln and Castrop/Rauxel, rail viaduct at Bielefeld, and M/Ys at Soest, Paderborn, Siegen, Giessen, and city of Fulda. 7 ftr gps provide close area spt.

Ninth AF: Weather cancels combat operations except for XXIX TACs spt of US XVI Corps along the Rhine in Wesel area.

Twelfth AF: B–25's continue interdiction of enemy comm, damaging railroad bridge at Longarone and railroad fills at Peri and Ossenigo. XXII TAC concentrates on comm in NE Po Valley and fuel and ammo dumps in C part of the Valley with generally good results. During 6/7 Mar LBs hit Ostiglia crossing and bridges at Nervesa della Battaglia and Casarsa della Delizia, and bomb T/Os in Brenner area.

Fifteenth AF: Continued bad weather limits operations to a supply drop in Yugoslavia and routine rcn and escort missions. All bombing operations are cancelled and 42 P–51's sent on strafing mission against railroad comm in Austria are recalled.

Tenth AF: 30 P–47's spt troops of British 36th Div in Mogok area. 18 others spt elements of Chinese 50th Div near Mansam. Elements of Chinese 38th Div occupy Lashio. 12 B–25's and 35 FBs attack road tgts, troops, vehicles, and a variety of T/Os immediately behind enemy lines. Transports fly 630 sorties supplying forward areas with men and equipment.

Fourteenth AF: 4 B–25's and 9 P–40's blast railroad tgts N of Kiaotow. Single B–25's hit truck convoys in Hsiang R Valley, waterfront at Changsha, and bridge and other T/Os on Pinghan railroad. 130-plus FBs attack numerous tgts throughout S and E China, concentrating on railroad, road, and river tgts in the areas around Nanking, Yoyang, Sintsiang, and Changsha.

FEAF: B–24's hit Balete Pass area while A–20's and FBs hit troop concentrations and gun positions near Antipolo and near San Fernando, NW of Ft Stotsenburg, and in Bayombong-Solano area and T/Os in Lake Taal area, towns of Santa Fe, Lal-lo and Vigan, and on Caballo I. Numerous ground spt missions are flown throughout Luzon.

Seventh AF: 11 Guam-based B–24's hit Susaki A/F and town of Okimura and Haha Jima. 5 more hit Susaki during 7/8 Mar in individual harassment strikes.

Eleventh AF: 8 B–25's, dispatched to strike a reported convoy, abort due to weather. So do 8 B–24's after departing on a shipping sweep and a strike on Kataoka.

8 March

Eighth AF: 1,201 HBs bomb 6 benzol plants, 7 M/Ys, aircraft plant, rail center, synthetic oil plant, and a city area in WC Germany. 287 sorties by 6 P–51 gps provide spt.

Ninth AF: Operational HQ of XXIX TAC moves from Maastricht to Monchen-Gladbach. 328 MBs and LBs hit 7 comm centers, 2 M/Ys, road overpass, and military transport depot in furtherance of interdiction program. Weather prevents ftr operations except for small alert mission by XXIX TAC.

Twelfth AF: MBs are hampered by heavy clouds but hit Novara M/Y, Longarone and Mori rail fills, and Rovereto bridge. Ftrs and FBs pound comm and supplies, destroy road bridge SW of Bologna, severely damage ammo plant and surrounding complex NW of Milan, and hit several other tgts, including bridge near Montebello which Brazilian P–47's operating with XXII TAC cut in half. A–20's, operating during 7/8 Mar, attack river crossings at

Borgoforte, Cremona, Ostiglia, San Benetto Po, Viadana, and Ora, and numerous vehicles, lights, and general movement in C Po Valley and along Brenner line.

Fifteenth AF: Over 550 HBs hit Hegyeshalom, Komarom, and Verona M/Ys, Maribor locomotive depot, and Kapfenberg steel works. P–51's and P–38's fly escort and rcn missions.

Tenth AF: 20 P–47's spt British 36th Div. 40 FBs hit troop concentrations and supply areas along battlefront and behind enemy lines. 39 others sweep roads S of the bomb line, attacking gun positions and other T/Os. Transports fly 554 sorties to advanced bases and over frontline areas.

Fourteenth AF: 34 B–24's, supported by 21 P–51's, pound Shihkiachwang. 3 B–24's claim transport sunk in S China Sea. 16 B–25's and 6 P–40's attack railroad tracks, boxcars, gun positions, sampans, and locomotives, knock out 2 bridges and damage another, and destroy and damage several locomotives at or near Hengshan, Yehhsien, Lohochai, and Chungmow. 140-plus FBs fly armed rcn over wide areas of S and E China, attacking numerous T/Os, mainly river, road, and railroad tgts, storage areas, gun positions, and troops, concentrating around Changsha, Changanyi, and bridge at Puchi.

FEAF: B–24's pound Zamboanga area. B–24's hit road tgts at Balete Pass while A–20's spt guerrilla forces in San Fernando area. FBs hit fuel dumps, gun positions, and other tgts near Angat and Ipo dam and numerous T/Os in Antipolo area, personnel and storage areas near Baguio, and several tgts in Cagayan Valley (including town of Caggay, Dummun R area, and barges at Naguilian).

Seventh AF: 14 B–24's from Guam bomb Susaki A/F through heavy cloud layers. 5 more HBs hit Susaki again during 5 individual harassment strikes during 8/9 Mar.

9 March

Eighth AF: 1,007 B–17's and B–24's bomb 6 M/Ys, a large tank factory, and a castings plant at Frankfurt/Main, Kassel, Munster, Osnabruck, and Rheine. 5 ftr gps fly close escort and 3 fly area patrol.

Ninth AF: 600-plus MBs and LBs hit 6 M/Ys, storage and vehicle depots, ammo-filling plants, and 12 T/Os as part of interdiction campaign in Germany. Ftrs fly armed rcn, hit special tgts, cover Remagen bridgehead and spt US 9th Inf and 9th Armd Divs committed there, spt 4th Armd Div at Mosel bridge at Treis, XX Corps along Mosel and Saar Rivers, and XVI Corps along the Rhine R near Wesel.

Twelfth AF: B–25's hit bridges at San Ambrogio di Valpolicella, San Michele all'Adige, Bozzolo, Santa Margherita d'Adige, Ora, and Montebello, M/Y at Ora, and bridge approach at Ala. Ftrs and FBs attack bridges, railroads, vehicles, trains, supply dumps, parked airplanes, buildings, and other tgts over wide areas of N Italy, including Milan, Cittadella, Ala, Santa Margherita d'Adige, La Spezia, Ghedi, Lecco, and battle area in N Apennines. A–20's, on intruder missions during 8/9 Mar bomb river crossings in Po Valley at several locations, among them Ostiglia, San Benedetto Po, and Borgoforte.

Fifteenth AF: 372 B–17's and B–

24's, with ftr escorts, bomb M/Ys at Graz (2), Klagenfurt, Sankt Stefan, Sankt Paul, and Ljubljana. River bridges at Sankt Paul are also bombed. 27 P–38's bomb Knittelfeld M/Y and 13 others strafe Graz-Maribor railroad lines. Routine supply, rcn, and escort missions continue.

Tenth AF: 16 P–47's spt elements of Chinese 50th Div near Mansam. 80-plus FBs operating over and behind enemy lines attack trucks, horses and carts, troops, and arty pieces. 568 air supply sorties are flown to forward areas.

Fourteenth AF: 32 B–24's, escorted by 5 P–51's, bomb railroad yards at Sinsiang. 15 B–25's and 2 P–40's knock out 2 bridges at Hwaiyuanchen and E of Jungtse, and hit railroad tgts and other T/Os at Yehhsien, at Chowkiakow, at Hsuchang, and E of Junan. 50-plus FBs on armed rcn attack railroad tgts, river and road traffic, bridges, gun positions, and troops at several locations, particularly around Kweiyi, Hengyang, Nanking, and Sinyang.

FEAF: B–24's bomb Zamboanga. B–25's, in cooperation with PT boats, attack tgts on Basilan I. B–24's hit Ipo area, B–25's and FBs spt ground forces E of Manila Bay, hit Japanese-occupied areas at Mahiga, Lipa Bay, and Ternate, and bomb and strafe T/Os on Caballo I. B–25's, A–20's, and FBs hit bridges at Bayombong, town of Makati, Cabugao, and Cauayan, San Fernando and Solvec Cove areas on NW coast, town of Cauayan, and Aparri A/F. B–24's pound dock area at Takao.

Seventh AF: 13 Guam-based B–24's fly daylight strike on Susaki A/F while 5 more, on single-bmr

raids, hit the A/F during 9/10 Mar. 24 Angaur-based B–24's pound town of Zamboanga.

Eleventh AF: 3 B–24's fly a negative shipping search.

10 March

Eighth AF: 1,321 HBs strike 6 M/Ys, 2 rail viaducts, 4 railway centers, and a town area—all in W Germany. 10 ftr gps fly 484 supporting sorties. 2 other gps spt Ninth AF MBs.

Ninth AF: 383 LBs and MBs strike 5 M/Ys, comm center, 2 city areas, miscellaneous tgts in Koblenz-Braubach area, and a T/O. Ftrs escort MBs and LBs, attack ground tgts, fly patrols, armed rcn, and provide cover and ground spt over Remagen bridge area where US 9th Inf Div expands bridgehead against fierce opposition, spt 4th Armd Div in Koblenz area and XX Corps in Saarburg area, and cooperate with XVI Corps near Wesel.

Twelfth AF: LBs bomb bridges and other comm tgts in E Po Valley during 9/10 Mar. B–25's bomb bridges at Ora, Bozzolo, and San Michele all'Adige, and railroad fill at Ceraino railroad station. Ftrs and FBs hit comm and T/Os at various locations in E Po Valley, including several bridges, and numerous ammo dumps and vehicles.

Fifteenth AF: 191 HBs hit Verona-Parona di Valpolicella railroad bridge. 1 other bombs Voghera M/Y. Supply missions to Yugoslavia and rcn operations continue.

Tenth AF: 13 P–47's spt forces of British 36th Div in Mogok area. 46 P–47's and P–38's sweep roads S of bomb line. 49 others hit supply areas behind enemy lines, attack a bivouac near Nam-yang, and bomb a truck park N of Mong Yai. 537 air supply sorties are flown to forward areas.

Fourteenth AF: 32 B–24's blast railroad yards at Tsanghsien and Tehsien. 10 B–24's and 4 P–40's attack Siangtan and nearby T/Os. 60-plus FBs hit river, road, and railroad tgts, gun positions, warehouses, airstrips, and troops around Sinyang, Yiyang, Changsha, Kiyang, Yoyang Hengyang, Hankow, and Wuchang.

FEAF: B–24's and B–25's over Zamboanga Peninsula area bomb town of Zamboanga, Calarian A/F, Pangasahan, Port Holland, Kulibato Point, and Sibago I. B–24's bomb Ipo area and Aparri A/F. B–25's and A–20's spt guerrillas near San Fernando and bomb Cabugao. FBs hit Caballo I, bomb town of Minanga, hit enemy concentrations at Burgos, near Ft Stotsenburg, in Batangas province, and at other locations on Luzon, and attack Teresa. B–24's bomb Kudat and Jesselton A/Fs.

Twentieth AF: 24 B–29's bomb M/Y at Kuala Lumpur. (1 of the VHBs drops over half of its bombs at Alor Star A/F). 3 others attack Khao Huakhang, and freighter in channel leading to Port Swettenham. During the predawn hours 279 B–29's, of 325 airborne, blast Tokyo urban area with incendiaries, destroying more than 267,000 buildings—about one-fourth in the city—and killing more than 83,000 people. This death total is the highest of any single day's action during the war, (exceeding the deaths caused by the first atomic bomb on Hiroshima). 20 other B–29's bomb alternates and

T/Os. 14 VHBs are lost. The participating B–29's are from the XXI BC's Bomb Wgs, the 73d, 313th, and 314th, based on Guam, Tinian, and Saipan. The raids are flown at levels ranging from 4,900 to 9,200 ft.

Seventh AF: 10 B–24's from Guam hit Susaki A/F which 9 HBs again hit during 10/11 Mar on separate snooper strikes. 23 B–24's from Angaur bomb Calarian A/F.

Eleventh AF: 5 B–24's radar-bomb tgts on Kataoka, Suribachi, and Kakumabetsu with unobserved results. 1 ftr is sighted but no attack is made. 2 other B–24's on this mission abort due to weather and mechanical trouble. B–25 missions to Hayakegawa and Paramushiru are also cancelled due to weather.

11 March

Eighth AF: U-boat yards at Kiel and Bremen and shipyard and refinery area at Hamburg are bombed by 1,212 HBs. Close escort is provided by 14 P–51 gps while 1 P–47 gp flies area spt in Kiel area.

Ninth AF: 696 A–20's, A–26's, and B–26's, hit 4 A/Fs, 3 comm centers, 2 ammo filling plants, and several city areas and other casual tgts. Attacks are to obstruct air operations and supply and troop movements in general. Ftrs fly patrols and armed rcn, escort 9th Bomb Div, spt US 9th Inf Div push at Remagen bridgehead and fly cover over the area, and spt XX Corps E of Trier and Saarburg.

Twelfth AF: B–25's of 57th Bomb Wg score damaging hits on bridge and fills at San Michele all'Adige, Volargne, and Ossenigo, and, attacking tgt in Austria for first time, bomb bridge at Drauburg. Ftrs and FBs of XXII TAC hit rail lines and dumps in C Po Valley and in Brenner area. During 10/11 Mar LBs hit several Po R crossings, Ghedi and Pavia A/Fs, road junctions, and other tgts in Po Valley.

Fifteenth AF: Bad weather limits operations to rcn and supply missions.

Tenth AF: 14 B–25's pound stores, troops, vehicles, and ammo dumps at Konghsa, Kwai-Kong, Man Kat, and Mong Yai. 4 P–38's knock out bridge at Mong Tong. 8 P–47's hit troop concentration at Kyaukme. 30-plus P–47's hit T/Os during road sweeps behind enemy lines. Transports fly 547 sorties to forward areas.

Fourteenth AF: 4 B–25's knock out 1 bridge and hit numerous box-cars at Kep and near Don Met. 5 B–24's over S China Sea and Gulf of Tonkin claim 1 freighter sunk and another damaged. 10 P–40's and P–51's blast locomotives on Tsinpu railroad and demolish 3 villages E of Lohochai.

FEAF: B–24's bomb Zamboanga area, Mercedes village, and San Roque A/F. B–25's hit Mercedes, spt ground forces near Zamboanga, and in conjunction with PT boats, hit Isabela, Barlak, Taluksangay, and HQ N of Zamboanga. B–24's hit Aparri area and spt ground forces at Wawa. A–20's and FBs fly ground spt missions and attack supply dumps and numerous T/Os throughout Luzon. FBs hit Takao and B–24's bomb Mako.

Twentieth AF: Attacking at altitudes ranging from 5,100 to 8,500 ft, 285 B–29's bomb Nagoya urban area with incendiaries during 11/12 Mar.

Seventh AF: 11 B–24's from Guam again hit Susaki A/F, while 8 more during 11/12 Mar, pound the A/F individually. Iwo Jima-based P–51's also bomb Susaki and strafe Okimura and Kitamura.

12 March

Eighth AF: 1,309 HBs strike Swinemunde area and 7 M/Ys at Friedberg, Wetzlar, Marburg/Lahn, Siegen, Frankfurt/Main, Betzdorf, and Dillenburg. 523 P–51 sorties are flown in spt of HBs.

Ninth AF: 9th Bomb Div MBs and LBs attack 8 M/Ys, ammo-filling plant, city areas and T/Os. Attacks on M/Ys are aimed at blocking troop movements by rail into Ruhr and Remagen areas. Ftrs escort 9th Bomb Div, bomb special tgts, fly armed rcn, cover Remagen area, and spt US 9th Inf Div in Kalenborn and Hargarten areas and XX Corps in Saarburg bridgehead area.

Twelfth AF: B–25's hit 7 railroad bridges, cutting two, and fills— severely damaging one and a train— in Brenner area and in NE Italy as far E as Yugoslav border area. FBs blast comm in N Italy, making 36 rail cuts, 19 of them on the Brenner line. P–47's also bomb and severely damage a munitions factory NW of Zagreb. During 11/12 Mar LBs on intruder missions hit Po crossings, sugar refinery, vehicles, and trains.

Fifteenth AF: 790 B–24's and B–17's bomb Vienna/Floridsdorf oil refinery and alternate tgts of Graz, Zeltweg, and Wiener-Neustadt M/Ys. 98 P–38's bomb Knittelfeld railroad bridge (2 others hit nearby T/Os) and strafe comm in Wiener-Neustadt-Graz-Klagenfurt areas. 12 P–38's sweep Zagreb area. Bad weather forces 60 P–51's sent against Austrian comm to abort. Supply mission to Yugoslavia and rcn operations are successful.

Tenth AF: 13 B–25's and 35 P–47's hit troop concentrations, supplies, vehicles, and AA guns along battlefront and behind enemy lines. 66 P–47's hit transportation tgts and a bridge during several road sweeps in C Burma. 12 others damage bypass bridge at Hay-ti. Transports complete 677 sorties delivering men and supplies to advanced bases and dropping supplies to frontline forces.

Fourteenth AF: 4 B–25's knock out Song Rang bridge. 6 P–51's hit road comm at Hwayuan and bomb a building at Ha Coi.

FEAF: B–24's hit Mercedes and Malabang. Other B–24's bomb Japanese troops near Ipo. B–25's hit supply area at Bangued and troops at Pattao. A–20's and FBs fly ground forces spt missions throughout Luzon. FBs also bomb Calallo I. On Formosa B–24's, with P–38 spt bomb Takao Tainan. P–51's also hit Tainan and bomb Jitsugetsu power plants.

Twentieth AF: 44 B–29's hit oil storage facilities on Bukum I, Samboe, and Sebarok Is. 1 other VHB bombs Arang Hill. Results are poor.

Seventh AF: 16 P–51's bomb and strafe Okimura. 13 B–24's fly daylight strike against Susaki A/F. During 12/13 Mar, 8 HBs hit Susaki and Okimura. 24 B–24's from Angaur hit Sarangani Bay storage area.

Eleventh AF: 5 B–24's bomb Kurabu A/F area. 8 B–25's weather-abort a mission to Hayakegawa.

13 March

Eighth AF: 16 continent-based

P–51's fly uneventful aircraft sweep in Remagen-Koblenz area.

Ninth AF: 450-plus A–26's, A–20's, and B–26's, bomb 3 M/Ys, 2 A/Fs, rail sidings, and several T/Os in continuing interdiction campaign in Germany. Ftrs fly escort, patrols, and armed rcn, attack assigned tgts, cover US First Army area in general along the Rhine R from Dusseldorf to Linz/Rhine, spt US 9th Inf Div around Hargarten, cover Remagen bridgehead, and spt XX Corps as it opens offensive SE from Saarburg bridgehead.

Twelfth AF: B–25's bomb railroad bridges and fills at Perca, Vo Sinistro, Pizzighetone, Salorno, and Sacile. Ftrs and FBs attack bridges, flak positions, ammo and supply dump, rail lines, various other tgts, and fly close spt to US Fifth Army force as XXII TAC operates over wide areas of N Italy from the N Apennines through the Po Valley, and into NE Italy. On 12/13 Mar LBs hit railroads, Po R crossings, dumps, and movement, mainly in Po Valley.

Fifteenth AF: 569 B–24's and B–17's bomb Regensburg M/Y. 3 other HBs bomb Landshut M/Y and T/Os. Over 280 P–38's and P–51's provide escort and several strafe rail traffic in Germany and Austria during return flight. 41 P–51's on strafing mission attack rail traffic in Munich-Landshut-Regensburg and Ingolstadt areas and between Vienna and Wiener-Neustadt. Photo rcn is particularly extensive, with 18 P–38's covering areas of Germany, Austria, Czechoslovakia, Yugoslavia, Hungary, and N Italy. 41 ftrs escort photo missions.

Tenth AF: 16 P–47's spt forces of

Chinese 50th Div, hitting Japanese positions along Namtu R in Namhsan area. 26 P–38's hit road tgts S of bomb line in C Burma. 12 B–25's attack troop concentrations, supplies, and gun positions behind enemy lines. 4 P–47's hit wooded area in British 36th Div battle sector. Other FBs make ineffective bridge strikes. Transports complete more than 500 sorties to forward areas.

Fourteenth AF: 7 B–24's over Gulf of Tonkin and S China Sea claim a cargo vessel and a large junk destroyed. 13 P–40's, P–38's, and P–51's destroy a storehouse and damage a compound at Chingchengchiang and knock out a bridge and hit machinegun positions and other T/Os at Lang Son.

FEAF: B–24's hit tgts in Sarangani Bay area and effectively hit town of Lagao. MBs spt ground operations in Zamboanga area. B–25's, A–20's, and ftrs spt ground forces hitting forces and positions in Cagayan Valley. B–25's hit sampans off Hainan I while P–51's sweep Samah A/F. B–24's hit installations in WC Formosa. B–24's bomb Mako.

Twentieth AF: In the third of the Twentieth AF's great fire raids, 274 B–29's begin bombing Osaka shortly after midnight, 13/14 Mar. The heart of the city, an area of 8.1 sq mi, is wiped out during 3 hrs of bombing from altitudes of 5,000 to 9,600 ft.

Seventh AF: 6 B–24's from Guam hit Woleai while 10 bomb Susaki A/F. During 13/14 Mar 8 more, flying individual strikes, pound Susaki. 24 B–24's from Angaur bomb storage area on Sarangani Bay.

14 March

Eighth AF: 1,188 HBs hit 3 tank and armored vehicle plants, 2 oil refineries, 2 M/Ys (all in the Hannover area), M/Ys at Gutersloh, Holzwickede, Giessen, Osnabruck, and Hameln, 2 rail bridges and a M/Y near Herford, road bridge near Minden, and jet castings plant at Hildesheim. 13 ftr gps fly 610 effective supporting sorties. 3 other gps spt Ninth AF MBs.

Ninth AF: 350-plus MBs and LBs hit 3 A/Fs, 4 rail bridges, a junction, 5 towns, and 3 T/Os as interdiction operations continue. Ftrs escort 9th Bomb Div, attack railroads and other special tgts, fly patrols, sweeps, and armed rcn, cover Remagen area, and spt US XII Corps as it begins drive from the Mosel R to the Rhine R, and XX Corps operations W of Trier and Saarburg.

Twelfth AF: B–25's damage bridges at Casarsa della Delizia, Cittadella, Vipiteno, and Campo. Ftrs and FBs attack comm, ammo and supply dumps, motor transport, trains, buildings, and other tgts, escort MBs, and spt ground forces, operating over much of N Italy from the Apennine battle area N and NE. LBs hit river crossings and T/Os in Po Valley during 13/14 Mar.

Fifteenth AF: 634 HBs, with ftr escorts, hit Szony and Almasfuzito oil refineries and M/Ys at Komarom, Nove Zamky, Zagreb, Wiener-Neustadt, Graz, and Knittelfeld. 90 P–38's dive-bomb bridges at Ptuj, 42 of them afterwards strafing rail traffic in Yugoslavia and Austria. 21 P–51's also strafe rail traffic in Austria. B–17's and B–24's drop supplies in N Italy and in Yugoslavia.

P–38's continue rcn missions, including larger than usual number of photo rcn flights (most of them heavily escorted) over Italy, Germany, Austria, and Yugoslavia.

Tenth AF: 20 P–37's fly close spt for elements of Chinese 50th Div in Mansam area. 3 B–25's knock out bridge at Laihka while 11 others bomb troop and vehicle concentration nearby. 39 P–47's hit troop concentrations, supplies and vehicles at Laihka and Namlan while 29 others sweep roads S of bomb line. 614 air supply sorties are flown to forward areas.

Fourteenth AF: 3 B–24's claim 1 cargo vessel sunk in S China Sea. 1 B–25 and 4 FBs damage 12 track sections near Tungyangchen. 4 P–51's hit railroad T/Os near Chihsien. 19 P–51's and P–38's blast barracks area at Vinh Yen.

FEAF: B–24's bomb Konel area while B–25's and B–24's hit village and AA positions near Zamboanga and dock area at Isabela. A–20's and numerous FBs (including some Marine aircraft) hit installations and defensive positions throughout Luzon. A–20's over Palawan hit Pandanan I. B–24's bomb Mako naval base. B–25's on armed rcn and shipping sweep along China coast bomb secondary tgts when no ships are sighted.

Seventh AF: 11 B–24's from Guam bomb Susaki A/F while 23 from Angaur hit Sarangani Bay supply area. 5 Iwo-based P–51's strafe and fire-bomb positions on N tip of Mindanao. 16 more strafe and dive-bomb Susaki A/F, town of Omura, and several gun positions on Chichi Jima.

During 14/15 Mar, 5 more B–24's flying individually hit Susaki.

Eleventh AF: Of 12 B–25's taking off to cover naval TF on its way to Matsuwa, 6 abort due to weather and failure to locate the TF. The others fly coverage sorties throughout the day.

15 March

Eighth AF: 1,282 HBs bomb primary tgts of Army HQ at Zossen and M/Y at Oranienburg, along with T/Os including M/Ys at Stendal and Birkenwerder, rail sidings at Gardelegen, rail center at Wittenberge, road bridge at Gusen, and town of Havelberg. 14 ftr gps in close escort and 1 in area patrol fly 732 effective spt sorties.

Ninth AF: 9th Bomb Div A–20's, A–26's, and B–26's attack comm centers at Neunkirchen and Pirmasens, M/Ys at Turkismuhle and Erbach, 3 flak positions, and several other tgts, as well as dropping leaflets on Koblenz. Ftrs hit Overberge M/Y and other tgts, escort 9th Bomb Div, fly sweeps and armed rcn, and spt US XII Corps crossing Mosel in offensive toward the Rhine, and XX Corps E of Trier and Saarbrucken.

Twelfth AF: B–25's attack railroad bridges and fills at Salzano, Canale d'Isonzo, Rovereto, Palazzolo sull'Oglio, Romano di Lombardia, and Mori. Ftrs and FBs of XXII TAC concentrate on comm lines in NE Italy, particularly the Brenner rail line, and also blast several supply and ammo dumps. LBs continue intruder missions during 14/15 Mar hitting Po R crossings and fills in San Ambrogio di Valpolicella area.

Fifteenth AF: 109 B–17's bomb

Ruhland oil refinery (marking the Fifteenth's deepest penetration into Germany). 103 others bomb alternate tgt of Kolin refinery. 470-plus other HBs attack tgts in Austria, including Moosbierbaum, Schwechat, and Vienna/Floridsdorf oil refineries, M/Ys at Wiener-Neustadt, Sankt Polten, Graz, Bruck an der Mur, Klagenfurt, and Murzzuschlag, and bridge at Klagenfurt. Supply missions to N Italy and Yugoslavia continue, along with extensive photo and weather rcn. Ftrs fly over 300 sorties in escort of HBs and supply and rcn flights.

Tenth AF: 30 P–47's spt elements of Chinese 50th Div in Namhsan area. 32 P–38's sweep roads S of bomb line. Transports fly 625 sorties to forward areas.

Fourteenth AF: 4 B–24's claim 1 vessel sunk in S China Sea. 4 B–25's hit area E of Pingsiang. 4 P–51's hit locomotives between Sinsiang and Shihkiachwang and 4 attack motor transport in Paotou area.

FEAF: In spt of US ground forces on Luzon B–24's, A–20's, and P–38's hit HQ area at Baguio. P–47's hit Minuli bridge and enemy concentrations in Balete Pass and W of Ft Stotsenburg. A–20's and P–47's hit gun positions and occupied areas around Batangas. B–24's and B–25's hit personnel N of Sarangani Bay and troops and gun positions in Zamboanga area. B–24's bomb Lahug. P–47's dive-bomb Takao power installations.

Seventh AF: 8 Guam-based B–24's bomb Susaki A/F. 3 more, on snooper strikes, hit Susaki during 15/16 Mar.

Eleventh AF: 1 B–24 flies air coverage for naval TF. 7 others weather-abort.

16 March
Ninth AF: 280-plus MBs and LBs hit Landau barracks area and comm center, Niederscheld town area and rail bridge, 6 other town areas, a M/Y, rail junction, crossroads, and also drop leaflets. Ftrs escort 9th Bomb Div, fly patrols, sweeps, armed rcn, and cover VIII, XII, and XX Corps in assault across the Mosel from W of Koblenz and N of Boppard, at one point, as far E as Bad Kreuznach, and as far S as Merzig.

Twelfth AF: B–25's of 57th Bomb Wg, flying their farthest N penetration to date, bomb Brixlegg railroad bridge. The MBs also hit Spilimbergo power plant, with excellent results, and lightly damage 3 bridges on Brenner line, 1 in C Po Valley, and 1 in NE Italy. XXII TAC FBs continue to attack comm in Po Valley and NE Italy, while LBs bomb bridges and T/Os on night intruder missions along Po R and in N Po Valley.

Fifteenth AF: 720-plus B–24's and B–17's bomb Korneuburg, Vienna/Floridsdorf, Schwechat, and Moosbierbaum oil refineries and M/Ys at Sankt Veit an der Glan, Amstetten, Graz, Varazdin and Pragersko. 52 P–51's strafe rail lines in Vienna, Linz, Passau, and Regensburg areas and A/F at Mettenheim. B–17's and B–24's continue supply drops to N Italy and Yugoslavia while P–38's fly extensive weather and photo rcn missions. Ftrs fly more than 300 sorties in escort of HBs, supply runs, and rcn operations.

Tenth AF: 23 P–47's spt forces of Chinese 50th Div in Hsipaw area.

4 P–38's, supporting British 36th Div, bomb arty positions NE of Mogok. 12 B–25's blast fuel dump and troop concentration at Panghai. 40 P–38's sweep roads S of bomb line. Transport operations continue on steady basis.

Fourteenth AF: 32 B–24's, escorted by 10 P–51's, pound N railroad yards at Shihkiachwang. 1 B–25 and 2 P–51's attack railroad between Sinsiang and Shihkiachwang.

FEAF: A–20's and B–24's continue pounding Japanese installations at Baguio. P–51's strike Patapat, hitting vehicles and supplies. Ftrs on patrol hit Caballo I. Batangas area is again pounded by FBs and A–20's. B–24's hit Talisay and Carolina A/Fs and bomb tgts pinpointed by guerrillas on Cebu. B–25's bomb San Roque A/F and attack Tarakan and Jesselton A/Fs. B–24's also hit town of Taihoku, A/Fs at Heito, and Okayama naval airbase.

Twentieth AF: 307 XXI BC B–29's, of 331 airborne, fire-raid Kobe in the heaviest attack to date, bombing from 5,000 to 9,500 ft during the predawn hours of 16/17 Mar. About one-fifth of the city's area is burned.

Seventh AF: 13 Guam-based B–24's bomb Susaki A/F. 16 Iwo-based P–51's dive-bomb and strafe radio and radar installations, gun positions, and storage area on Chichi Jima. During 16/17 Mar Susaki is hit again, by 5 B–24's flying individual harassment strikes. Iwo Jima is declared secure although fierce resistance continues on some parts of the island.

Eleventh AF: Because of a navigational error, 2 B–24's on a photo mission to Matsuwa reach 130 mi S of the island, the deepest penetration of the Japanese Home Islands to date. The B–24's turn N, photograph Matsuwa and bomb Shimushiru with unobserved results.

17 March

Eighth AF: 1,260 HBs hit 2 synthetic oil plants, 2 power stations, an instruments works, an industrial complex around a tank factory, 2 M/Ys, and 5 city areas in W and NC Germany. 13 P–51 gps, plus an extra P–51 section, provide spt.

Ninth AF: 650-plus A–20's, A–26's, and B–26's bomb 5 M/Ys, 2 comm centers, an ordnance depot, 3 city areas, and several T/Os. Attacks are to impede enemy movement of troops, equipment, and supplies in face of advancing Allied forces. Ftrs fly escort, patrols, and armed rcn, cover Remagen bridgehead, spt US III Corps NE of Remagen, cooperate with XII Corps which has penetrated several mi E of Bad Kreuznach at one point, and operate with XX Corps which at one point reaches as far E as Birkenfeld.

Twelfth AF: A–20's and B–26's during 16/17 Mar bomb Po R crossings, other bridges, lights, and movements in Po Valley. B–25's bomb railroad bridges and fills at Cittadella, San Michele all' Adige, Aldeno, Bozzolo, Canneto sull' Oglio, Pontetidone, Pizzighettone, and Pontevico. Ftrs and FBs are greatly restricted by bad weather but score effectively against dumps, bridges, railroads, M/Ys, trains, and buildings mainly in Po Valley.

Fifteenth AF: Bad weather grounds HBs. 98 P–38's dive-bomb Ptuj and

Zagreb railroad bridges, Klinca Sela M/Y, and Sisak M/Y and bridge. B-24's, with ftr escort, drop supplies in Yugoslavia and P-38's and P-51's fly rcn and rcn escort. During 17/18 Mar B-24's drop supplies in N Italy.

Tenth AF: 16 P-47's spt British 36th Div around Mogok. 12 B-25's bomb troops and supplies near Namlan. 33 P-47's hit road tgts behind enemy lines, concentrating on Hay-ti and Mong Yai sectors. 40-plus other FBs attack troops, supplies, tanks, and trucks behind the battleline including Ta-mun, Namsaw, Pansupe, Tal-ti, and Kankang areas. Transports continue to fly troops and supplies to frontline areas.

Fourteenth AF: 1 B-25 and 12 P-51's damage 21 locomotives and a river launch in Peking area, around Tsinan, and between Taiyuan and Tatung.

FEAF: Formosa A/Fs are pounded by B-24's operating in force. On Luzon nearly 500 sorties are flown in spt of ground forces by B-25's, A-20's, and ftrs. B-24's hit Panay beaches preparatory to allied landings on 18th and bomb troops in combat areas on Mindanao. Bacolod A/F is also bombed.

Twentieth AF: 70 B-29's hit storage dump at Rangoon. 2 others bomb T/Os—Sagyi A/F and warehouses at Bassein.

Seventh AF: 11 Guam-based B-24's hit Chichi Jima. During 17/18 Mar, 5 more hit Susaki A/F.

Eleventh AF: 2 B-24's fly bombing and photo missions over Matsuwa, concentrating on the A/F, and on returning photograph Shasukotan, Harumukotan, and Onnekotan.

18 March

Eighth AF: 1,251 HBs attack 2 rail centers and 2 tank and armament plants in Berlin area, along with several T/Os including 2 M/Ys, 3 town areas, and an industrial area near Berlin (secondary tgt). 14 P-51 gps fly 645 effective supporting sorties.

· Ninth AF: 660-plus MBs and LBs hit M/Ys at Wetzlar, Worms, Kreuztal, and Bad Durkheim, comm center at Bad Durkheim, and 4 town areas with aim of hampering enemy movement. Ftrs escort 9th Bomb Div, attack assigned tgts, fly patrols, and armed rcn, and cooperate with US III Corps of Remagen, with XII Corps as it begins assault toward Mainz-Worms sector of the Rhine, and with XX Corps as it moves rapidly eastward through Sankt Wendel area toward Kaiserslautern.

Twelfth AF: During 17/18 Mar A-20's and A-26's continue intruder missions in Po Valley, concentrating on Po R crossings. B-25's bomb railroad bridges at Bozzolo, and Palazzuolo sull' Oglio, railroad fill at Salorno, and causeway at Mantua. Ftrs and FBs hit dumps and spt ground forces S of Bologna, and attack comm tgts over wide areas of Po Valley. The most devastating raid of the day is flown against Novara M/Y where 14 locomotives are destroyed.

Fifteenth AF: Bad weather limits operations to rcn and supply missions, a FB attack by P-38's on Varazdin railroad bridge, after which many of the P-38's strafe railroad comm in Zagreb, Varazdin, Maribor, and Villach areas, and a strafing mission against rail comm and A/Fs in Graz, Wiener-Neustadt, Maribor, and Szombathely areas.

Tenth AF: 12 P–47's spt Chinese ground forces near Hsipaw. 8 others spt British 36th Div troops by dropping napalm NE of Mogok. 11 B–25's and 20 FBs hit troop concentrations and supplies immediately behind the battlefront. Roads S of bomb line are swept by 16 P–38's. Transports continue steady operations.

Fourteenth AF: 6 B–24's sweep Gulf of Tonkin and S China Sea, claiming 1 freighter damaged. 2 P–51's over N Indochina strafe trucks, troops, and horsecarts.

FEAF: In S Luzon HBs, A–20's, and ftrs spt ground forces by hitting Ipo area and various tgts in Batangas Province. B–24's again bomb Bacolod, hit several tgts on Cebu, and bomb Sepinggang and Jesselton A/Fs. A/F at Tainan, seaplane base at Takao, and emergency field at Koshun are also hit.

Twentieth AF: During 18/19 Mar, 290 XXI BC B–29's continue fire raids on Japanese cities, bombing Nagoya from 4,500 to 9,000 ft with incendiaries for the second time this month. This mission ends the Mar fire raids.

Seventh AF: 16 P–51's from Iwo Jima dive-bomb radar and radio installations and barges at Chichi Jima. 14 B–24's from Guam pound Susaki A/F. 1 other hits Haha Jima. During 18/19 Mar 5 more HBs individually strike Susaki.

Eleventh AF: A weather sortie is flown.

19 March

Eighth AF: 1,223 HBs attack M/Ys at Fulda and Plauen, industrial areas around military vehicle and optical works at Jena and Zwickau, A/Fs and jet aircraft plants at Neuburg an der Donau, Baumenheim, and Leipheim, and industrial and city areas at Plauen and Saalfeld. P–51's fly 606 effective sorties in spt of HBs. Over 100 ftrs, including 36 jets in formation (largest number yet seen as a unit) are encountered. US ftrs claim 42 ftrs destroyed (including 3 jets).

Ninth AF: 9th Bomb Div strikes 2 M/Ys, 5 rail bridges, comm center and several casual tgts as part of interdiction program to impede enemy movement. Ftrs escort 9th Bomb Div, fly patrols and armed rcn, spt US III Corps W of Remagen, cooperates with XII Corps' 4th Armd Div E of Kaiserslautern as it drives toward the Rhine. FBs of XIX TAC, on special mission, bomb HQ of CinC West (FM von Rundstedt) at Ziegenberg.

Twelfth AF: XXII TAC LBs strike heavily against general movement in Po Valley during 18/19 Mar, and are followed during day by ftr and FB attacks on comm in C Po Valley and NE Italy where numerous rail cuts are made, 3 bridges damaged, and several supply dumps hit. MBs damage bridge at Muhldorf, bridges and fills at Perca, and at 7 other locations on the N Italian approaches to Brenner Pass.

Fifteenth AF: 800-plus HBs, with ftr escorts, hit M/Ys at Landshut, Passau, Sankt Veit an der Glan, Lambach, Muhldorf, Plattling, Garching an der Alz, Klagenfurt, and Altenmarkt an der Alz. 54 P–51's strafe railroads in the HB tgt areas. 36 P–38's bomb Varazdin M/Y. B–24's drop supplies in Yugoslavia while P–38's and P–51's fly rcn and escort.

Tenth AF: 24 P–38's spt forces of Chinese 50th Div near Hsipaw. 12 P–38's sweep roads S of bomb line while 27 P–47's operating over and behind enemy lines hit troop concentrations and supplies at Namlan, Namio, and Nam-maw-long and Japanese-held monastery at Nam-maw-long. Transports fly 502 sorties to forward areas.

Fourteenth AF: 5 B–24's on sweep over S China Sea and Gulf of Tonkin claim a large freighter sunk. 4 P–38's strafe trucks from Son La to Hoa Binh.

FEAF: B–24's and FBs again hit installations in N Luzon. B–24's hit variety of tgts on Cebu including town of Minglanilla.

Seventh AF: 16 P–51's from Iwo Jima bomb and strafe Susaki A/F, radio installation, and storage area on Chichi Jima. 12 Guam-based B–24's follow up with another attack on the A/F and radio installations later in the day. During 19/20 Mar Susaki is hit again by 5 B–24's flying separate snooper strikes.

Eleventh AF: 5 B–24's bomb and photograph Kashiwabara naval base. 8 B–25's bomb canneries along the Masugawa and Asahigawa Rivers.

20 March

Eighth AF: 407 B–17's and B–24's bomb shipyard and dock area at Hamburg and oil refinery at Hemmingstedt. Ftrs of 8 gps complete 298 effective sorties in spt.

Ninth AF: 360-plus A–20's, A–26's, and B–26's bomb Geisecke M/Y, Sythen ammo-filling plant, town of Gronau (including a rail bridge), and several casual tgts in or near 9 other towns. Ftrs escort MBs and LBs, fly

patrols and armed rcn, spt US III and VII Corps just E of the Rhine R between Bad Honningen and the Sieg R, and XII and XX Corps as they push to the Rhine R at Worms and at a point N of Mannheim.

Twelfth AF: XXII TAC LBs during 19/20 Mar continue intruder missions into Po Valley while ftrs and FBs pound comm tgts in the Valley during the day and severely damage fuel dumps near Mantua. MBs hit 4 bridges on Brenner line and 2 others in NE Italy and hit other bridge approaches nearby.

Fifteenth AF: 760-plus HBs, with ftr escort, hit Korneuburg and Kagran oil refineries, M/Ys at Wels, Sankt Polten, Amstetten, Wiener-Neustadt, and Klagenfurt, and tank works at Steyr. Routine supply, rcn, and escort missions continue.

Tenth AF: 20 P–47's sweep roads S of bomb line in C Burma. 16 others hit supply dumps behind Japanese lines. Transports continue to supply forward areas.

Fourteenth AF: 4 P–38's claim 11 trucks destroyed and 9 damaged between Son La and Hoa Binh.

FEAF: B–24's, A–20's, and FBs fly numerous ground spt missions and hit tgts at Balete Pass, Bayombong, Tuguegarao, Antamok, San Fernando, Bontoc and along roads. B–24's pound supply and personnel area E of Cebu City and N of Mambaling, defensive positions NW of Talisay and AA guns to the N, and also bomb Talisay. Other B–24's bomb town of Tainan. B–25's on shipping sweep sink 3 small vessels near Qui Nhon.

Seventh AF: 12 Guam-based B–24's bomb Susaki A/F. During 20/21

Mar, 4 other HBs fly single strikes against the A/F.

21 March

Eighth AF: Preparatory air operations for forthcoming (23 Mar) crossing of lower Rhine R by allied ground forces begin. 1,254 HBs (in conjunction with aircraft of RAF and Ninth AF attacking other tgts) bomb 10 A/Fs in NW Germany, tank factory at Plauen and M/Y at Reichenbach during morning raid. During afternoon 90 B-24's bomb Mulheim an der Ruhr A/F. Ftrs fly nearly 750 effective sorties in spt of the 2 operations.

Ninth AF: 580-plus A-20's, A-26's, and B-26's strike 6 comm centers and a M/Y E of the Rhine R (along with several casual tgts) in interdiction campaign to obstruct enemy movement. Ftrs fly patrols and armed rcn, attack railroads and bridges, spt US VII Corps as its units reach Sieg R near Siegburg, cooperate with XII Corps as more of its elements reach the Rhine at various points between Boppard and Worms, and spt XX Corps as additional units reach the Rhine between Worms and Mannheim.

Twelfth AF: LBs continue to attack comm in Po Valley especially Po R crossings during 20/21 Mar. During the day FBs concentrate on railroad tgts (lines, trains, bridges, and viaducts) and dumps in Po Valley and areas N of battleline in N Apennines. MBs bomb railroad fill at Salorno, bridges at Casarsa della Delizia and Pizzighettone, M/Ys at Vipiteno and Brennero, and bridge approaches at Campo.

Fifteenth AF: 660-plus B-24's and B-17's, with ftr escorts, bomb Neuburg an der Donau A/F, M/Ys at Villach (2), Klagenfurt, Graz, Bruck and der Mur, and Pragersko, 3 oil refineries and a goods depot at Vienna, and 4 scattered T/Os. Supply and rcn missions with escort are flown.

Tenth AF: 30 P-47's spt Chinese ground forces in Hsipaw area. 34 P-38's sweep roads S of bomb line. 13 B-25's and 18 P-47's attack troop concentrations and vehicles at several points behind Japanese lines. 526 air supply sorties are flown to forward areas. In ground action in the area of the British Fourteenth Army's 33 Corps, organized resistance ceases in Mandalay. Allied forces completely take over that city.

Fourteenth AF: 4 P-51's damage several locomotives and boxcars at Vinh A/F and along railroad to the N. 6 B-24's claim 1 vessel damaged in S China Sea.

FEAF: On Luzon B-25's, A-20's, and ftrs continue large-scale spt missions, hitting a variety of tgts including Japanese defenses at Lipa and Tarlac and town of Naga and Camiling. In C Phils B-24's hit tgts near Cebu City while A-20's pound other towns on Cebu. B-24's bomb Samah A/F. B-25's on shipping sweep attack and set afire a freighter SE of Nanao I.

Seventh AF: 16 P-51's from Iwo Jima strafe and bomb barracks and radio and radar installations on Chichi Jima. 13 B-24's, based on Guam, hit Susaki A/F, which is hit again during 21/22 Mar by 5 more, flying separate strikes.

ZI: A P-63 from Walla Walla A/F intercepts Japanese balloon near Redmond, and, after chase that includes

2 refueling stops, shoots it down near Reno.

22 March

Eighth AF: Air attacks in preparation for lower Rhine R crossing by Allied ground forces continue. 1,284 HBs hit 4 A/Fs and 3 M/Ys E of Frankfurt/Main, 10 military encampments in the Ruhr, and 2 city areas nearby. 9 P–51 gps fly spt and strafe aircraft at several A/Fs.

Ninth AF: Nearly 800 A–20's, A–26's, and B–26's bomb 9 comm centers and a M/Y E of the Rhine R (plus 7 towns, flak positions, and a T/O) as part of interdiction program to impede movement of supplies and troops. Ftrs escort 9th Bomb Div, attack railroads and other assigned tgts, fly patrols and armed rcn, spt US 1st and 9th Inf Divs SE of Honnef and along the Wied R, cooperate with XII Corp as it begins crossing Rhine in Mainz-Oppenheim areas and with XX Corps which begins attack on Ludwigshafen.

Twelfth AF: A–20's and A–26's during 21/22 Mar, continue intruder raids concentrating on Po R crossings in the E Po Valley. During the day P–47's blast rail lines, trains and other comm tgts, especially in E Po Valley and areas to the N. B–25's destroy bridge at Brixlegg, severely damage Steinach bridge, and hit bridge approaches at Muhlberg and town of Matrei am Brenner. Weather prevents successful attacks on 2 tgts in N Italy.

Fifteenth AF: 680-plus HBs (with ftr escort) hit Ruhland and Kralupy nad Vltava oil refineries (some HBs on Ruhland raid bomb Lauta aluminum works to the N), a railroad comm and ordnance depot, a M/Y, and 2 oil refineries at Vienna, M/Ys at Graz, Wels, Zeltweg, Klagenfurt, and Neratovice, and scattered T/Os. Rcn and rcn escort missions are also flown.

Tenth AF: 16 FBs spt Chinese ground forces near Hsipaw. 12 B–25's and 41 FBs hit numerous tgts along and immediately behind enemy lines. Troops, supplies, and comm are attacked and 2 bridges are knocked out. 547 air supply sorties are flown to forward areas.

Fourteenth AF: 24 FBs and a single B–25 attack railroad traffic and railroad yards in and around Shihkiachwang, at Chukiatsi, and from Sinsiang to Chenghsien.

FEAF: B–24's and A–20's (along with Marine aircraft) hit Cebu City, defenses at several locations on Cebu I, and tgts on Inampulugan I nearby. On Luzon B–24's, B–25's, A–20's, and ftrs continue to hit numerous objectives, chiefly Balete Pass, Tangadon, San Fernando, and Batangas areas. Other B–24's hit Tainan and Okayama A/Fs, destroying several hangars, planes, and gun positions.

Twentieth AF: 76 B–29's, operating in 2 waves, blast storage dumps at Rangoon.

Seventh AF: 16 Iwo-based P–51's bomb and strafe weather station, fuel storage, and radar installations on Chichi Jima. Later in the day 13 B–24's from Guam bomb Susaki A/F. 20 B–24's from Angaur bomb Cebu I. During 22/23 Mar, 4 B–24's from Guam make individual raids on Susaki A/F.

23 March

Eighth AF: Allied ground assault

across lower Rhine begins. 1,240 HBs attack 10 assigned M/Ys E of the Rhine (primary tgts) and 4 other M/Ys as secondary tgts and T/Os, along with a power station, aluminum works, and benzol plant. 14 P-51 gps give close and area spt, flying 355 effective sorties.

Ninth AF: Around 800 MBs and LBs strike 7 comm centers, a factory, and T/Os (including several flak positions). Attacks on comm centers are aimed at obstructing movement of reinforcements to the front. Ftrs escort 9th Bomb Div, fly patrols and armed rcn, attack assigned ground tgts, spt US III and VII Corps SE of Honnef and E of Wied R and XII and XX Corps astride and on W bank of the Rhine R between Mainz and Worms.

Twelfth AF: LBs attack loading points and crossings along Po R during 22/23 Mar. P-47's concentrate on comm and general movement in lower Brenner area during the day. The FBs also blast several dumps in C Po Valley. B-25's hit bridges, railroad fills, and bridge approaches in Brenner area at Matrei am Brenner, Pordenone, Salorno, San Michele all' Adige, Vo Sinistro, Longarone, and Perca.

Fifteenth AF: 658 HBs (with ftr escort) hit oil refineries at Ruhland, and at Vienna, M/Ys at Budejovice, Gmund, Sankt Polten and Sankt Valentin, and tank works at Sankt Valentin, plus scattered T/Os. Over 40 P-38's and P-51's fly rcn.

Tenth AF: 15 P-47's spt Chinese ground forces, bomb troop, positions at Nampongpang and Nakang. 16 P-47's hit T/Os along roads from Mong Nawng to Wan Sing to Kun-long. 11 P-47's hit quarters at Monglawng while 3 others attack supply dumps at Laihka. 9 B-25's bomb comm routes, creating 2 road blocks behind enemy lines. In large-scale air supply operations, 536 sorties are flown.

Fourteenth AF: 28 B-24's bomb Tsinan railroad shops and Yellow R bridge. 5 B-25's bomb town areas, storage facilities, and T/Os at Sinsiang and Wuyang and chiefly in the Hsiangcheng area. 50-plus FBs attack troops, horses, and river, road, and railroad tgts in N Indochina and S and E China.

FEAF: B-24's, B-25's, A-20's, and ftrs hit the Visayan Is, bombing Cebu City, hitting defenses on Cebu and other islands, and bomb Antamok mines, Balete Pass, and Tangadon areas, along with several other tgts. B-24's also hit tgts on Mindanao. FBs attack Takao.

Seventh AF: 15 P-51's from Iwo Jima bomb and strafe various tgts on Chichi Jima, Haha Jima, and Ani Jima. During 23/24 Mar 5 Guam-based B-24's, flying single-bmr strikes, pound Susaki A/F.

Eleventh AF: An 8-bmr strike is called off due to weather.

24 March

Eighth AF: In conjunction with allied ground forces assault across the lower Rhine R the Eighth flies bombing, supply, and armed rcn missions. During morning 1,033 HBs strike 14 A/Fs in W Germany. 85 ftr sorties are flown in spt. At midday 235 B-24's drop supplies to allied forces in assault area E of the Rhine. During the afternoon 443 HBs, supported by 113 effective ftr sorties, bomb 5

A/Fs, a M/Y, and a railroad in NW Germany. The ftrs claim 27 kills in aerial combat. All during the day, ftrs fly 1,065 effective sorties in armed rcn patrols attacking numerous ground tgts and claiming 30 ftrs downed.

Ninth AF: Almost 700 A-20's, A-26's, and B-26's blast comm centers, rail bridges, flak positions, and numerous other tgts in cooperation with combined land-airborne assault across the Rhine R (PLUNDER-VARSITY) by the British Second and US Ninth Armies and the US XVIII Corps of the First Allied Airborne Army. Over 2,000 transports and gliders of IX TCC drop and land British 6th Airborne and US 17th Airborne Divs (plus arty, vehicles, ammo, and other supplies) E of the Rhine N and NW of Wesel as British Second and US Ninth Armies cross river to the NW and SE. Ftrs attack with bmrs before the drop and carpet the landing zones with fragmentation bombs, immobilizing numerous flak batteries. Ftrs escort bmrs and transports, cover assaulting 30th and 79th Inf Divs, attack troop concentrations, flak positions, supply and ammo dumps, A/Fs, defended villages, and road and rail traffic, and patrol the perimeter of the battle sector. Ftrs also spt US First Army elements across the Rhine E of Remagen between Koblenz and the Sieg R as they prepare for breakout assault, and US Third Army's XII Corps as it strengthens its Rhine bridgehead E of Oppenheim and commits its armor to push through toward the Main R.

Twelfth AF: Gen Cannon takes cmd of AAFMTO, and shortly afterwards also takes over MAAF. A-20's and A-26's during 23/24 Mar pound M/Ys, river crossings and other bridges, and a variety of other tgts in Po Valley and NE Italy where ftrs and FBs during the day destroy or damage numerous rail lines and train cars. B-25's bomb bridges or bridge approaches at Piacenza, Chiari, Perca, Casarsa della Delizia, Palazzolo sull'Oglio, Muhlberg, and Steinach.

Fifteenth AF: 660 B-24's and B-17's bomb tank works at Berlin and A/Fs at Munich and Neuburg an der Donau, plus Budejovice M/Y, and alternate tgts and T/Os including A/Fs at Plattling, Erding, and Udine. P-38's and P-51's escort the missions against German tgts and fly rcn.

Tenth AF: 31 FBs and 9 B-25's operating over battlefront and behind enemy lines in C Burma pound troop concentrations, supply areas, truck park, and general T/Os. 9 other FBs attack T/Os along roads S of bomb line. 504 air supply sorties are flown, landing men and supplies at advanced bases and dropping supplies to frontline forces.

Fourteenth AF: 34 B-24's, with escort of 9 ftrs, pound Chenghsien locomotive park and Yellow R bridge. 30-plus B-25's and over 100 FBs, operating in forces of 1-8 airplanes, attack tanks, trucks, locomotives, troop concentrations, storage areas, airstrips, bridges, gun positions, and general T/Os throughout S and E China.

FEAF: B-24's and A-20's pound Cebu City and defenses and installations on Cebu I. B-24's, B-25's, A-20's, and P-38's attack Balete Pass, Legaspi, Batangas area, and scattered tgts throughout Luzon. B–24's hit harbor at Takao and power plant and alcohol factory E of Okayama.

Twentieth AF: 23 B–29's, from the Marianas, attack Mitsubishi aircraft engine plant at Nagoya during 24/25 Mar. 5 VHBs are lost.

Seventh AF: 9 B–24's from Guam bomb torpedo storage area on Marcus. 24 Angaur-based B–24's bomb defensive positions and town of Naga. 16 Iwo-based P–51's hit air, naval, and radar installations and T/Os on Chichi Jima. During 24/25 Mar, 5 Guam-based B–24's hit A/F and town of Omura.

25 March

Eighth AF: Nearly 250 B–24's bomb oil storage depots near Brunswick, Hamburg, and Lauenburg. 5 ftr gps provide escort. Over 700 B–17's are recalled because of bad weather. 1 gp of P–51's bomb ammo dump.

Ninth AF: 9th Bomb Div hits 4 comm centers, 3 M/Ys, and T/Os, including flak positions. Ftrs fly escort, armed rcn, and missions against several ground tgts. Ftrs spt US 79th Inf Div as it pushes 2 mi to the E of the Rhine (SE of Wesel), III and VII Corps as they begin breakout assault toward Altenkirchen and in Epgert and Willroth areas, and XII Corps as it establishes bridgeheads on the Main in Hanau and Aschaffenburg areas.

Twelfth AF: During 24/25 Mar A–20's and A–26's continue intruder missions, attacking Po R crossings and railroad and motor transport tgts. P–47's, during the day, raid railroad bridges and lines, hitting tgts at Lavis, Casarsa della Delizia, San Michele all'Adige, Pavia, Santa Mar-

gherita d'Adige, and other points in Po Valley and NE Italy, and bomb fuel dumps N of battle area. 6 MB missions against bridges and fills in Italy and Austria are ineffective because of bad weather.

Fifteenth AF: Over 650 HBs strike 2 A/Fs and a tank works at Prague (patterns of bombs also hit 2 other nearby A/Fs) and an A/F at Cheb. Alternate tgts bombed include Wels and Udine A/F. P–38's and P–47's escort HBs, and sweep and strafe Nurnberg-Eibelstadt-Wurzburg-Regensburg areas, and fly rcn operations.

Tenth AF: 26 P–47's spt forces of Chinese 50th Div in Hsipaw area. 44 FBs and 14 B–25's attack troops and supplies and hit T/Os along roads behind battleline in C Burma. 557 transport sorties are flown to forward areas.

Fourteenth AF: 20-plus B–25's and 150-plus ftrs, operating individually and in flights of up to 8 aircraft, continue attacks on numerous tgts including river, road, and rail traffic, A/Fs, troop concentrations, storage areas, horses, and gun positions throughout S and E China.

FEAF: Cebu City is thoroughly pounded by nearly 70 B–24's. Other B–24's hit Legaspi, and B–25's and FBs fly numerous ground spt missions throughout Luzon, especially between Montalban and Laguna de Bay. B–25's attack Pandanan I.

Seventh AF: 16 Iwo-based P–51's bomb and strafe Susaki A/F, and naval and radar installations on Chichi Jima. 16 more follow with attacks on radar station and personnel concentration on the island. 23 B–24's from Angaur bomb defenses on Cebu

I. During 25/26 Mar, 5 B–24's from Guam hit Susaki A/F. Marines complete reduction of final resistance pocket on Iwo Jima.

26 March

Eighth AF: Over 300 B–17's bomb Zeitz synthetic oil plant, Plauen tank factory, and cities of Meiningen, Wurzburg, Oelsnitz, and Markt Erlbach. 12 P–51 gps fly close and area spt.

Ninth AF: Around 300 MBs and LBs hit M/Ys at Wurzburg, Gemunden, and Flieden, town of Ruckers, and 2 T/Os. Ftrs escort 9th Bomb Div, fly armed rcn, hit special tgts and spt various ground forces along the front. Ftr spt is accorded US 2d, 3d, 7th, and 9th Armd Divs in Hachenburg, Montabaur, and Limburg areas, XII Corps along the Main R from Frankfurt/Main to Aschaffenburg, and Ninth Army elements in bridgehead area around Gahlen.

Twelfth AF: Weather grounds MBs and hampers operations in general. During 26/27 Mar 3 LBs hit bridges at Cittadella and Verona. FBs, operating on reduced scale, hit comm tgts in W Po Valley, cutting a road bridge and several railroads, and attacking several T/Os.

Fifteenth AF: Over 500 B–17's and B–24's, escorted by P–51's and P–38's attack M/Ys at Wiener-Neustadt, Strasshof, Bruck an der Leitha, Neunkirchen, Bratislava and Szombathely. 46 P–38's dive-bomb bridge at Ybbs while 26 P–51's, covered by 13 others, strafe rail traffic in Wiener-Neustadt-Vienna-Budejovice areas. Other P–38's and P–51's fly rcn operations.

Tenth AF: 28 P–47's and 10 B–25's operating over and behind C Burma battlelines attack arty positions, troop concentrations, road comm, and supply areas. 522 air supply sorties are being completed throughout the day.

Fourteenth AF: 15 B–25's and 80-plus FBs, operating individually or in small flights, continue to disrupt mobility and supply lines throughout S and E China, hitting numerous T/Os chiefly trucks, tanks, supply areas, horses, troops, arty pieces. Several of the FBs also damage considerably Puchou A/F.

FEAF: B–24's, B–25's, A–20's, and FBs bomb Legaspi and tgts in the area including fuel dump at Camalig. FBs hit numerous tgts in N Luzon at Solvec Cove, Baguio, Mankayan, Sante Fe, and other areas. In SW Luzon A–20's and FBs spt US ground forces, hitting Ternate, and towns in Tayabas and Batangas Provinces. B–24's and A–20's in C Phil hit Cebu City and E coast tgts. B–24's hit Takao.

Seventh AF: 21 P–51's from Iwo Jima bomb and strafe Susaki A/F while 16 bomb and strafe weather and radar stations on Chichi Jima and town of Kitamura. 9 Guam-based B–24's pound Marcus. During 26/27 Mar 3 HBs from Guam on individual snooper strikes hit Chichi Jima. Enemy makes final attack on Iwo Jima in early morning attempt to infiltrate bivouac area. Capture and occupation phase of Iwo ends at 0800 when Gen Chaney becomes Island Cmdr.

Eleventh AF: 2 missions, each by 4 B–25's, attempt to bomb canneries on the Masugawa and the Hayakegawa rivers. Ftrs drive off Masugawa mission. Other mision cannot find tgt due to weather. 4 B–24's bomb Kataoka naval base.

27 March

Eighth AF: 3 ftr gps escort RAF bmrs attacking Paderborn.

Ninth AF: Weather cancels 9th Bomb Div operations. IX TAC ftrs patrol US First Army front. XIX TAC hits M/Ys, patrols Third Army front, flies area cover from Koblenz to Aschaffenburg to Worms, and supports VIII and XII Corps along Rhine R in Wiesbaden area and Main R in Frankfurt/Main-Aschaffenburg area.

Twelfth AF: Weather cancels all combat operations.

Fifteenth AF: Bad weather limits operations to 3 P–38 rcn flights.

Tenth AF: 80-plus FBs over battle areas and behind enemy lines in C Burma pound troops and supplies at several locations including Mong Kung, Man Namkat, Nam-yang, Tonglau, Ho-na, Hkai-wun, Longwai, Monglawng, Laihka, and Namlan areas. Transports are exceptionally active, flying 635 sorties to forward areas.

Fourteenth AF: 25 B–25's hit towns, rail, road, and river traffic, and T/Os around Kweilin, Liuchow, Hengyang, Hochih, Nanyang, Kaifeng, Anlu, Ishan, Kiyang, and Siang Chiang Valley. 44 FBs hit trucks, trains, sampans, power facilities, and other tgts around Hongay, Nanyo, Son Tay, Na Cham, Cao Bang, Lang Son, Moc Chau, Muong Hang, and Bac Quang. 28 FBs knock out bridge NE of Liuchow, hit town of Szeenhsien, and attack ammo dumps and road and river traffic around Hochih,

Ishan, Liuchow, Pingnam, Liangfeng, and Kweilin.

FEAF: B–24's, B–25's, A–20's, and FBs bomb Legaspi, Balete area, Ipo-Siniloan sector, Batangas area, and several other locations throughout Luzon. Ftrs spt US amphibious landings on Caballo I. In C Phil area B–24's bomb Negros A/Fs while B–25's and P–38's hit Cebu City area. Other B–25's bomb Kinsui, and B–24's lightly attack Sandakan.

Twentieth AF: 150-plus Marianas-based B–29's flying the first of many raids in spt of impending Okinawa invasion, hit Tachiarai and Oita A/Fs and Omura aircraft factory. 97 B–29's mine Shimonoseki Strait during 27/ 28 Mar. This is first of many mining operations by B–29's in Japanese waters.

Seventh AF: 16 P–51's from Iwo Jima bomb ammo stores and town of Kitamura. During 27/28 Mar 5 B–24's, flying individual strikes from Guam, hit Susaki A/F.

28 March

Eighth AF: Nearly 900 HBs attack tank factory and armament plant in Berlin, tank plant, M/Y, and city area at Hannover, and numerous other tgts including Stendal and Minden. 8 P–51's gps fly spt.

Ninth AF: 215 MBs and LBs hit Neuenheerse and Erbach oil storage depots and 11 T/Os. Ftrs escort 9th Bomb Div, fly armed rcn and area cover over wide expanse of German territory, and spt US XII Corps in breakout attacks across the Main R in Dornigheim area and 2d and 8th Armd Divs in Dorsten area.

Twelfth AF: Bad weather grounds MBs and LBs. Ftrs and FBs are limited to weather rcn and some armed rcn in Milan area where they harass comm.

Fifteenth AF: Unfavorable weather restricts operations to rcn flights by 5 P–38's.

Tenth AF: 30-plus FBs operating over and behind battlelines in C Burma attack troop concentrations, supply areas, elephant transport, and general T/Os at or near Wan Hong, Ho-na, Kyu-sawk, Nawnghkio, and Na-ti. 642 air supply sorties are flown to advanced bases and over front-lines, where supplies are dropped, throughout the day.

Fourteenth AF: 6 B–24's bomb Haiphong and Hanoi docks and Bakli Bay barracks. 9 B–25's and 8 P–40's hit rivercraft and other tgts from Yanglowtung to Sienning. 9 other B–25's hit junks, storage, and T/Os in Lushan area and 7 bomb Ching-men. 14 B–25's, operating in gps of 1 to 4 aircraft, hit rivercraft and scattered T/Os at several other points in S and E China. 120-plus FBs over Indochina and S and E China continue to pound numerous T/Os, mainly river, road, and rail traffic and troop concentrations. River craft and A/Fs in areas around Kai Tek, Canton, Hankow, and Wu-chang are severely hit.

FEAF: B–24's and FBs hit Balete Pass tracts and ridges, installations at Santa Fe, and ground spt tgts N of Laguna de Bay and in Cavite and Batangas Provinces. B–25's and A–20's attack troop concentrations at Baguio and Ilagan. FEAF bmrs hit Cebu City area and pound A/Fs on Negros. B–24's bomb Likanan A/F. Other B–24's hit Takao

and Tainan while B–25's hit shore tgts along Indochina coast.

Twentieth AF: During 28/29 Mar, 10 B–29's mine mouth of the Hwang-poo R and S channel of the Yangtze R at Shanghai. About 50 other VHBs fly missions mining waters at Saigon, Camranh Bay, and in Singapore area.

Seventh AF: 15 P–51's from Iwo Jima hit Chichi Jima A/Fs and de-fenses. 10 Guam-based B–24's bomb Truk and, flying separate snooper strikes, 5 hit Susaki A/F during 28/29 Mar.

29 March

Ninth AF: All combat operations cancelled because of weather except for 2 ftrs of IX TAC which patrol US Third Army front.

Twelfth AF: Clear weather during 28/29 Mar permits LBs to hit rail loading points, trains, vehicles, roads, and bridges at many places in Po Valley as well as river crossings at Borgoforte, Lodi, San Benedetto Po, Ostiglia, and Casalmaggiore, factory at Brescia, and motor transport move-ment in Milan-Piacenza area. Bad morning weather cancels MB opera-tions except for a pamphlet mission over Bologna. When weather clears about noon, XXII TAC FBs hit dumps at La Spezia and other points near battle area, Lavis viaduct, railroad bridges or approaches at Ora, Santa Margherita d' Adige, Nervesa della Battaglia, Rovereto, Ala, and other locations, and many vehicles and train cars and other T/Os throughout Po Valley and NE Italy.

Fifteenth AF: Continued bad weather limits operations to rcn and rcn escort missions by 23 P–38's.

Tenth AF: Bad weather curtails operations in C Burma. 6 B–25's hit troop concentrations and 8 others attack unsuccessfully 2 bridges immediately behind enemy lines. Transports complete 560 sorties to forward areas.

Fourteenth AF: 18 B–25's, escorted by 12 P–40's, bomb railroad yards at Yoyang. 11 B–24's attack shipping in S China Sea, at Bakli Bay, at Samah Bay, and at Haiphong, heavily damaging a destroyer and a merchant vessel. 4 B–25's claim 6 small steamers sunk and several vessels damaged in Liuchow area while 2 others hit town area and railroad tgts in Dong Giao area. Single B–25's hit T/Os at or near Loyang, Loning, Neihsiang, Yiyang, and Hsuchang. 90-plus FBs over S and E China and over Indochina attack troops, supplies, transport, and comm tgts at several places, concentrating strikes around Hengyang, Chuchou, Isuho, Nanking, and Namyung, and among many tgts hit A/Fs at Amoy and Kai Tek.

FEAF: B–24's and B–25's attack Toshien, Byoritsu, and Eiko. B–24's bomb Camalaniugan, B–24's and P–51's hit Legaspi and surrounding area, and A–20's and numerous ftrs hit various tgts in SW Luzon. Cebu is bombed by B–25's in spt of ground forces while A–20's spt troops landing on Negros. B–24's bomb Oelin A/F.

Twentieth AF: 24 B–29's fly last mission under XX BC, attacking oil storage facilities on Bukum I during 29/30 Mar. 2 other VHBs bomb individual tgts on Malay Peninsula.

Seventh AF: 31 Iwo-based P–41's

bomb and strafe Haha Jima. 9 B–24's from Guam bomb Dublon.

Eleventh AF: 6 B–24's bomb Kataoka naval base. 8 B–25's weather-abort a mission to Tomari Cape. 1 B–24 flies radar-ferret mission along Paramushiru coast.

30 March

Eighth AF: 1,250-plus HBs attack U-boat yards and port areas at Hamburg, Bremen, and Wilhelmshaven, and oil storage and city area at Hamburg and Bremen. 16 ftr gps provide close and area spt.

Ninth AF: 337 MBs and LBs attack Bad Oeynhausen tank factory, Munden ordnance depot, Ebenhausen oil depot, 2 town areas and 6 T/Os, and drop leaflets. Ftrs escort 9th Bomb Div, fly patrols and armed rcn, and spt ground forces. Ftr spt is provided for US 3d and 7th Armd Divs near Paderborn and at Edersee dam on Eder R, XII Corps N of Frankfurt/Main, XX Corps in Hersfeld and Hanau areas, and XVI Corps in Marl-Polsum area.

Twelfth AF: During 29/30 Mar LBs continue to pound Po R crossings, loading points, and other comm in Po Valley. During the day XXII TAC ftrs and FBs fly some 400 sorties against fuel and ammo dumps, stores, bridges, rail lines, M/Ys, buildings, motor vehicles, trains, and a variety of tgts over wide areas of N Italy. Weather forces MBs to attack mainly alternate tgts. The B–25's bomb railroad bridges (or bridge approaches) at San Ambrogio di Valpolicella, Rovereto, Chiari, Palazzolo sull'Oglio, Legnago, Ora, and Romano di Lombardia.

Fifteenth AF: 60-plus B–17's and

B–24's bomb Vienna N stations and goods depot, Graz and Klagenfurt M/Ys, Kapfenberg tank works, and several minor T/Os. 28 P–38's and P–51's sweep Zagreb-Graz area. Others fly rcn.

Tenth AF: In C Burma battle area 41 P–38's and P–47's hit enemy troops and supplies at Loiwing, Pawngleng, and Nawnghkio. 7 B–25's hit personnel, supply area, and trucks behind enemy lines in and near Laihka and at Kongleng. 7 other B–25's attack road bridges, knocking out bridge at Loi Putau. Transports complete 612 sorties to forward areas.

Fourteenth AF: 4 B–25's, supported by 24 P–40's, knock out bridge at Chungmow. 10 B–25's bomb Hsuchang, 9 bomb Changanyi, and 9 pound Yanglowtung railroad yards. 15 P–40's fly escort. 5 B–24's bomb Samah Bay area. 2 B–25's bomb Hankow A/F, 2 bomb Neihsiang, and single B–25's attack tgts around Fang-cheng, Nanyang, and Anlu. 100-plus FBs over S and E China hit troops, railroad tgts, trucks, tanks, supplies, and rivercraft especially around Hankow, Wuchang, Kanchou, and Hangchow. A/F area at Kanchou and A/F and railroad yards at Hangchow are hit particularly hard.

FEAF: B–24's bomb Balete Pass and Solvec Cove areas. P–38's hit arty positions in Santa Fe area. B–24's and A–20's hit Legaspi Port and nearby Little Batsan. A–20's and FBs continue ground spt missions in Laguna de Bay area and W of Ft Stotsenburg. B–24's and A–20's spt ground forces on Cebu. B–24's, B–

25's, and P–38's hit Bongao I, Sanga Sanga, and Kuching area.

Twentieth AF: 12 B–29's attack Mitsubishi aircraft engine plant at Nagoya shortly past midnight during 30/31 Mar while 80-plus B–29's mine Shimonoseki Strait.

Seventh AF: 10 Guam-based B–24's bomb A/F on Marcus. During the night 5 others individually strike Chichi Jima A/F.

Eleventh AF: 8 B–25's cancel shipping strike because of weather.

31 March

Eighth AF: Nearly 1,300 HBs bomb Zeitz synthetic oil refinery, Halle M/Y, oil depot near Erfurt, cities of Gotha and Brandenburg, and 11 T/Os. 15 ftr gps provide spt.

Ninth AF: 550-plus MBs and LBs hit storage depots at Ebrach, Wurzburg, and Marienburg, M/Y at Wurzburg, town area of Rothenburg ob der Tauber, and a T/O. Ftrs escort 9th Bomb Div, hit special tgts, fly armed rcn, and spt US 3d and 9th Armd Divs near Paderborn, XII Corps as it charges toward Eisenach, XX Corps along Fulda and Eder Rivers, and XVI and XIX Corps S of Haltern and NW of Lippstadt.

Twelfth AF: MBs bomb several tgts (mostly alternates) in Po Valley and Brenner area despite bad weather. B–25's hit bridges or bridge approaches at San Michele all'Adige, Steinach, Crema, Canneto sull'Oglio, Legnago, and Manerbio, and rail embankment at Salorno. XXII TAC A–20's and other aircraft hit Po R crossings during 30/31 Mar at Casalmaggiore, Ostiglia, Borgoforte, and San Benedetto Po, rail facilities at Piacenza and Cittadella, plus nearby ammo dumps and other tgts. FBs continue to pound comm and dumps at Lavis, Casarsa della Delizia, San Ambrogio di Valpolicella, Legnago, and several other points in Po Valley and NE Italy.

Fifteenth AF: 540 B–24's and B–17's bomb Linz main railroad station and sidings, M/Ys at Villach and Treviso, and 3 minor T/Os. P–51's and P–38's provide escort. 37 other ftrs on sweeps and strafings attack railroad tgts in Munich-Linz-Regensburg area and 43 hit similar tgts in Prague area. Still other P–38's and P–51's fly extensively rcn and rcn escort.

Tenth AF: 12 B–25's hit troop dispersal areas behind enemy lines in C Burma and hit 1 road bridge. 8 P–38's attack supply dump at Namsang A/F.

Fourteenth AF: 30 B–24's, with escort of 9 P–51's, blast railroad yards at Shihkiachwang. 12 B–25's bomb railroad yards at Sinyang while 4 hit Yanglowtung yards. 6 B–25's damage bridge and hit gun position at Sienning while 6 more knock out bridge near Ninh Binh and hit storage area at Samah Bay. 26 P–51's attack Ningpo A/F, destroying or damaging several airplanes. 6 of the P–51's are lost. About 125 other FBs and several B–25's (operating individually) attack numerous tgts in Indochina and S and E China including bridges, troops, supplies, and rail, road, and river traffic.

FEAF: A–20's attack army camp at Saiatan while P–51's sweep from Babuyan Channel to SW Formosa. Ftrs attack tgts in Cagayan Valley and N of Laguna de Bay, blasting bridges and gun positions over wide stretches of Luzon. B–25's, A–20's, and FBs hit Cebu tgts, several of the strikes being flown in spt of ground forces. B–24's again bomb Bongao I and hit Oelin. Ftrs harass N Borneo A/Fs. B–24's bomb harbors and shipping at Kiirun, Formosa and Yulin.

Twentieth AF: 137 B–29's strike Tachiarai machine works and Omura A/F. This is diversionary strike preceding invasion of Okinawa which begins at 0830 on 1 Apr.

Seventh AF: 15 P–51's from Iwo Jima bomb and strafe vessels, air installations, and T/Os on Chichi Jima. 16 more follow with attacks on vessels and harbor area. During the night 5 B–24's from Guam, flying individual harassment strikes, hit Susaki A/F.

1 April

Ninth AF: No bmr operations due to weather. Ftrs fly patrols, armed rcn, and spt US 3d and 9th Armd Divs in Paderborn-Lippstadt and Warburg areas, XX Corps astride and E of the Fulda R, anl XII Corps which reaches the Werra R W of Meiningen.

Twelfth AF: A–20's and A–26's on intruder missions during 31 Mar/1 Apr over Po Valley continue to attack road and railroad bridges, motor transport, loading points, and other tgts. Principal strikes are made at Po R bridges. Ftrs and FBs during the day strike rail bridges, dumps, rail lines, M/Ys, trains, vehicles, gun positions, several buildings (including ammo plant and truck factory), and a variety of T/Os in Po Valley and NE Italy. MBs hit railroad bridges at Calcinato, Crema, Mantua, Monselice, Colle Isarco, San Ambrogio di Valpolicella, and Perca.

Fifteenth AF: Almost 400 B–24's and B–17's bomb Maribor railroad bridge, M/Ys at Sankt Polten, Selzthal, Zeltweg, Graz, and Villach, railroad bridge at Krieglach, and gun positions on Adriatic coast near Venice. 82 P–38's bomb Ybbs railroad bridge while 52 P–51's strafe rail traffic in Prague-Plzen area. Other P–38's and P–51's fly rcn and rcn escort.

Tenth AF: 10 B–25's attack roads and bridges behind enemy lines in C Burma. 478 transport flights are made throughout the day. British 36th Div forces begin to push down railroad from Mandalay to Rangoon.

Fourteenth AF: 7 B–24's bomb Ft Bayard storage area. 6 B–25's and 6 P–51's attack river shipping and warehouses in Sienning-Puchi area. 4 B–25's attack railroad tgts at Ninh Binh and Minh Koi. 5 B–25's hit warehouses and other buildings at Hsuchang while 3 damage bridge at Changtuikuan. Single B–25's bomb T/Os around Sanshihlitun, Sichuan, Loning, and Suicheng. 23 P–51's pound A/Fs in Shanghai area. 70-plus other FBs attack river, road, and rail traffic, storage areas, troops, and general T/Os throughout wide areas of occupied S and E China.

FEAF: B–24's attack Giran A/F while B–25's and P–47's sweep wide areas. On Luzon B–24's, A–20's, and FBs hit Legaspi area (where US amphibious landing is taking place), tgts N of Balete Pass, Batangas area, and spt troops over parts of S and NW Luzon. In C Phil B–25's and A–20's spt ground forces near Cebu City and on Negros. B–24's hit Oelin A/F.

2 April

Eighth AF: Over 700 HBs dispatched against 6 A/Fs in Denmark, along with 12 ftr gps, abandon mission because of bad weather in tgt area.

Ninth AF: Weather prevents operations by 9th Bomb Div and XXIX TAC. IX and XIX TACs fly patrols and armed rcn over wide expanses of Germany claiming 17 airplanes downed and IX TAC supports US 9th Armd Div at Diemel R bridgehead near Warburg.

Twelfth AF: Gen Chidlaw takes cmd of Twelfth AF (in Italy) and will shortly take over MATAF also. A–20's and A–26's continue intruder missions during 1/2 Apr concentrating on Po R crossings and other Po Valley comm tgts. B–25's bomb railroad bridges at Fornovo di Taro, Drauburg, San Michele all' Adige, Matrei am Brenner, Steinach, and Colle Isarco, and railroad fill at Vo Sinistro. Ftrs and FBs again hit comm in Po Valley but divert sizeable effort to attacks on methane plants in C Po area. The P–47's are attacked by about 40 ftrs during the day, 13 are claimed destroyed.

Fifteenth AF: Almost 600 B–24's and B–17's, with ftr escorts, bomb comm tgts in Austria including M/Ys at Graz, Sankt Polten, and Krems, and railroad bridge on Sulm R. 38 P–38's dive-bomb railroad bridge at Wildon. 71 P–38's and 55 P–51's strafe Vienna-Munich and Wiener-Neustadt-Maribor rail traffic. Others carry out photo and weather rcn and rcn escort flights.

Tenth AF: Bad weather cancels all offensive missions. Air supply missions continue with 469 sorties being flown to forward areas.

Fourteenth AF: 28 B–25's knock out bridge SE of That Khe, bomb town area of Vinh, damage bridge approaches at Kep, hit shipping and other T/Os along coast of Gulf of Tonkin, and blast town area of Luc Nam. 25 B–25's attack trucks, tanks, rivercraft, and T/Os at Sichuan, Neihsiang, Sinyang, Mingkiang, Siangtan, Kweiping, Nanning, and Hengshan. 4 B–24's bomb Kowloon Docks and hit shipping at Bakli Bay and Samah Bay. 32 P–51's pound A/Fs in Shanghai area. 140-plus other FBs attack numerous tgts scattered throughout S and E China, including troops, trucks, horses, river shipping, bridges, gun positions, A/Fs, rail traffic, and town areas.

FEAF: B–24's bomb harbor at Hong Kong. B–25's and FBs attack Bamban bridges, Balete Pass-Baguio area and Penablanca. Troops at Cebu City and on Negros are bombed by B–25's and FBs. B–24's bomb Sarangani Bay area. Other B–24's hit Sandakan shipyards and Tawau A/F. Bongao I is hit by HBs.

Twentieth AF: During the first 4 hrs after midnight (1/2 Apr), 6 B–29's mine harbor at Kure while more than 100 bomb Nakajima aircraft factory at Tokyo. 9 B–29's mine waters off Hiroshima during 2/3 Apr.

Seventh AF: 12 Guam-based B–24's bomb Marcus.

Eleventh AF: A B–24 on weather rcn returns early due to mechanical trouble. Another B–24 investigates radar jamming on Kresta Point.

3 April

Eighth AF: Over 700 HBs attack U-boat yards at Kiel (2 HBs bomb Flensburg A/F as a T/O). 12 ftr gps fly close and area spt.

Ninth AF: Operational HQ of XXIX TAC moves to Haltern. About 230 MBs and LBs attack Holzminden and Hameln M/Ys, town of Gottingen, 2 T/Os, and fly leaflet mission. Ftrs fly escort, fly patrols and armed rcn, spt US 9th Armd Div in Warburg area, XX Corps E of Werra R toward Muhlhausen and in Kassel area, XII Corps in Gotha and Suhl areas, and 2d and 8th Armd Divs in Teutoburger Forest and Neuhaus.

Twelfth AF: During 2/3 Apr LBs bomb M/Y at Mantua, several Po R crossings and other comm tgts in Po Valley. Weather hampers operations during the day. MBs cancel most missions, but manage to bomb Po Valley bridges at Camposanto, Usigliano, and Modena. XXII TAC (including Brazilian and SAAF units) blast comm, fuel dumps, methane plants, trains motor transport at numerous points in N Italy (mainly Po Valley), including Parma, Modena, Fidenza, Lodi, Bergamo, Reggio Emilia, and Piacenza.

Fifteenth AF: 95 P–38's divebomb Tainach-Stein railroad bridge. Other P–38's and P–51's fly rcn and escort missions. Bad weather prevents HB operations.

Tenth AF: Bad weather again causes cancellation of most scheduled strikes. A few FBs hit Japanese-held wooded area near Kenglong. Transports complete 383 sorties to forward areas.

Fourteenth AF: 17 B–25's bomb Pinglo, Ninh Binh railroad yards, knock out bridge at Thinh Duc, and damage bridges at Gian Khau and Mon Cay. 60-plus FBs knock out bridges at Hsitu and between Chuting and Hengyang, destroy pontoon bridges in Kanchou area, hit Yangtong A/F, pound Hai Duong railroad yards, and hit river traffic and other T/Os at several locations including Hongay, Cao Bang, Tayu, Hankow, Kanchou, Yoyang, and Ishan-Hwaiyuanchen areas.

FEAF: Hong Kong docks are again bombed by B–24's. Other B–24's and B–25's hit A/F, butanol plant, and railroad yards at Kagi while A–20's sweep other rail tgts. On Luzon FBs and A–20's hit Balete Pass-Baguio-Naguilian area N Cagayan Valley supply tgts, Laguna de Bay area, and Infanta, also, Miri A/F, troops in Cebu City area, and tgts on Tarakan I are bombed. MBs attack N Hainan I.

Twentieth AF: During 3/4 Apr, 9 B–29's mine waters off Hiroshima. Twice during early morning, 48 B–29's hit aircraft plant at Shizuoka, 68 attack Koizumi aircraft factory and urban areas in Tokyo, and 100-plus strike aircraft plant at Tachikawa and urban area of Kawasaki.

4 April

JCS: JCS designates Gen Mac-Arthur CINCUSAFPAC and Adm Nimitz CINCPOA.

Eighth AF: 939 HBs, supported by 826 effective ftr sorties, bomb 5 A/Fs and 2 landing grounds in N Germany, submarine yards at Hamburg and Kiel, and munitions plant near Ulzen.

Ninth AF: XXIX TAC returns to operational control of Ninth AF (from Second Tac AF) as US Ninth Army reverts to control of 12th Army Gp (from 21st Army Gp). The British ground and air HQ have operationally controlled XXIX TAC and Ninth Army since shortly after the Ardennes breakthrough and the Battle of the Bulge. 330-plus MBs and LBs hit Ebrach oil depot, Crailsheim M/Y and barracks area, Grossaspach supply depot, town of Ellswangen, Backnang rail and road junction, and 2 T/Os. Ftrs escort 9th Bomb Div, fly patrols, sweeps, and armed rcn, attack special tgts, and spt US 104th Inf Div at Scherfede and Hardehausen, 9th Armd Div in Warburg area, XX Corps in Muhlhausen-Kassel areas, 2d and 5th Armd Divs in Hameln and Minden areas on the Weser R, and 8th Armd Div as it assaults Ruhr pocket in Lippstadt area.

Twelfth AF: B–25's continue to blast comm along Brenner rail line, ranging from railroad bridge at Drauburg to Camposanto railroad bridge. The MBs also inflict considerable damage on Merano methanol plant. P–47's concentrate on enemy movement, rail lines, and ammo and fuel dumps throughout Po Valley.

Fifteenth AF: Again bad weather prevents HB operations and limits effort to rcn and escort missions and to strafing attacks by 94 P–51's on rail traffic in Munich, Regensburg, Plzen, Linz, and Gmunden areas.

Tenth AF: Combat operations are restricted to attacks on a troop concentration and rice and fuel supplies behind enemy lines in C Burma. Transports operate on steady basis throughout the day.

Fourteenth AF: 2 B–25's sink a junk in Gulf of Tonkin. 6 P–38's strafe trucks around Dien Bien Phu, Moc Chau, and Son La.

FEAF: B-24's bomb Toyohara A/F, Mako harbor, and Tokichito I. A-20's hit Shinchiku factories and rail yards. B-24's bomb harbor at Hong Kong. P-38's and P-51's pound various tgts in C Luzon while A-20's and P-38's hit Calauag area. A-20's pound NW Negros and B-24's bomb tgts in C Mindanao.

Seventh AF: 24 B-24's from Angaur hit building at Bunawan.

5 April

International: USSR notifies Japan that it wishes to abrogate 5-year Russo-Japanese neutrality pact signed in 1941.

Eighth AF: Over 1,000 HBs attack 5 M/Ys, 4 ordnance depots, an armament works, an A/F, an aircraft parts factory, and 2 town areas in SC Germany. 12 ftr gps spt the HBs.

Ninth AF: Weather prevents operations by 9th Bomb Div. Ftrs fly patrols, sweeps, and armed rcn, and spt US 7th Armd Div's attack on Ruhr pocket SW of Brilon, XX Corps' drive E in Muhlhausen area, XII Corps' adv in Meiningen area, 2d Armd Div bridgehead astride the Weser R S of Hameln, 8th Armd Div (preparing for assault on Soest), and 5th Armd Div near Minden.

Twelfth AF: B-25's bomb 5 bridges in N Italy and Austria, at Steinach, Matrei am Brenner, Modena, Salorno, and San Michele all'Adige, and blast gun positions at La Spezia. These attacks follow night raids by A-20's and A-26's on bridges at Lavis, Ala, San Michele all'Adige, San Ambrogio di Valpolicella, Piazzola sul Brenta, Cittadella, and Montebello,

and other tgts. Ftrs and FBs devote their largest effort to close spt of ground forces, blasting occupied areas and gun positions in Massa Lombarda area, and also attack comm and dumps in Po Valley.

Fifteenth AF: 457 B-24's and B-17's attack railroad bridge at Dravograd, M/Ys and locomotive depots at Brescia, Alessandria, and Turin, and A/F at Udine. 96 P-38's dive-bomb Radovljica railroad bridge, 27 P-51's with 13 flying top cover, strafe rail comm in Munich, Regensburg, Passau, and Linz areas. 20-plus P-38's fly rcn missions. Around 300 ftr sorties are flown to escort transport, rcn, and HB missions (including RAF raid on Monfalcone shipyards).

Tenth AF: Bad weather cancels scheduled strikes. Transports continue large-scale operations to forward areas.

Fourteenth AF: 27 FBs on armed rcn attack troops, horses, and river, road, and rail traffic at Shanhsien, Shihkiachwang, and Son La, and in Tehsien and Loyang-Pinglo area.

FEAF: B-24's bomb Kowloon Docks and nearby A/F, while other B-24's bomb Kiirun harbor. 180-plus sorties in spt of ground forces are flown in Luzon. A-20's and patrolling P-61's spt troops on Cebu and Negros. P-38's hit Tarakan I and Tawau.

Seventh AF: 18 B-24's from Guam hit tgts on Eten anl Dublon Is. 22 from Angaur pound bivouac area at Bunawan.

6 April

Eighth AF: 641 HBs bomb M/Y at Halle, rail traffic center at Leipzig, M/Y and industrial complex at Gera, and city area of Eisleben. 15

ftr gps fly around 600 effective sorties in spt of the HBs.

Ninth AF: 99 MBs and LBs hit M/Ys at Gottingen and Northeim and city area of Herzberg, and drop leaflets over 3 city areas. Ftrs fly escort, alerts, sweeps, and armed rcn, and spt US VIII Corps in Eisenach area, and XX Corps E of the Werra near Muhlhausen.

Twelfth AF: Gen Darcy takes cmd of XXII TAC. A–20's and A–26's on night intruder missions, 5/6 Apr, bomb several bridges in Po R Valley, scoring good results on 8 of the tgts, also hitting assembly area along the Po R. XXII TAC ftrs and FBs hit lines of comm, mainly in Po Valley, and spt US Fifth Army forces attacking toward Massa Lombarda. B–25's cancel missions against tgts on Brenner line due to weather, but hit 6 bridges in C Po Valley and gun positions at La Spezia.

Fifteenth AF: 387 HBs, with ftr escort, bomb M/Y flak positions and ordnance depot at Verona and M/Y and small arms plant at Brescia. 179 other HBs sent against tgts in N Italy are recalled. 81 P–38's dispatched to bomb bridge in Austria abort due to weather. 14 manage to attack bridges near Austro-Italian border. 6 P–51's (of 54 airborne) strafe railroad tgts in Straubing-Plattling area. Others fly rcn missions.

Tenth AF: With improving weather conditions combat strikes in C Burma battle area increase. 70-plus FBs attack troop concentrations, arty positions, tanks, trucks, fuel dumps, and general T/Os along and immediately behind enemy lines. Tgts are located in several areas including Paklu, Nawnghkio, Loilem, Takaw, Mong Hko, Kongleng, Nawng-Hsan Pu, and Indaw. Air supply sorties continue on steady basis throughout the day.

Fourteenth AF: 3 B–24's hit T/Os in Bakli Bay area. 4 P–38's knock out bridge in Dien Bien Phu area. 8 P–51's blast railroad T/Os, troops, horses, and boat landings in Chenghsien area and along Lung Hai railroad and Yellow R.

FEAF: B–25's bomb town of Hokko. Ground spt sorties continue in areas around Balete Pass, W of Ft Stotsenburg, N, NE, and S of Laguna de Bay, and around Legaspi. Ftrs also hit Carabao I and Infanta. B–24's bomb town N of Cebu City while ftrs spt ground units on Cebu. A–20's spt ground forces on Negros. B–25's pound Bunawan. B–24's bomb Jolo I defenses and ammo and supply dumps. At Manila AFPAC is established under Gen MacArthur. 400 *Kamikaze* planes make all-out effort against Okinawa shipping and beachheads. 2 destroyers, 2 ammo ships, a mine sweeper and an LST is sunk. Other vessels are damaged. Nearly 300 Japanese planes are expended.

Seventh AF: 11 B–24's from Guam pound positions and A/F on Marcus. 23 from Angaur bomb barracks and wharf at Bunawan.

Eleventh AF: 8 B–24's attack and photograph Kurabu, especially the A/F, while 8 B–25's hit radar installations in an all-out attack on Hayakegawa, Kotani Shima, and Minami Cape, dropping napalm-filled incendiaries for the first time. Buildings and shipping in N part of Hayakegawa are hit especially hard. Another B–25 flies weather rcn.

7 April

Eighth AF: Over 1,200 HBs hit 6 A/Fs, 5 M/Ys, 2 explosives plants, 2 oil storage depots, and an ordnance depot in C and N Germany. 15 ftr gps, providing spt, meet well over 100 conventional ftrs and 50-plus jets. The German ftrs attack fiercely and in the ensuing air battle down 15 HBs. US ftrs claim over 60 ftrs destroyed including a few jets against negligible losses. HBs claim 40 of the ftrs destroyed.

Ninth AF: 268 MBs and LBs strike M/Ys at Northeim and Gottingen, plus 2 town areas. Ftrs fly escort, patrols, and armed rcn, and spt US 7th Armd Div at Schmallenberg, 3d and 9th Armd Divs along the Weser R E of Warburg, VIII, XII, and XX Corps in Muhlhausen, Eisenach, and Meiningen areas (including strong air spt against counterattack on XII and XX Corps at Struth), 2d Armd Div along Sarstedt-Hildesheim road, and XVI Corps between Lippe and Ruhr Rivers in Essen area.

Twelfth AF: During 6/7 Apr A-20's and A-26's bomb bridges at Lavis, Ala, Rovereto, and San Ambrogio di Valpolicella, and several Po R crossings. During the day weather grounds MBs. XXII TAC ftrs and FBs, operating on limited scale, hit Montechino oilfield, ammo dumps and comm tgts N of battle area, and gun positions in Monte Belvedere-Strettoia area in which US Fifth Army forces push N.

Fifteenth AF: 128 B-17's and B-24's attack Mezzocorona railroad bridge and nearby road bridge, Verona-Parona di Valpolicella railroad bridge, and M/Ys at Innsbruck, Sankt Veit an der Glan, and Klagenfurt. Over 500 HBs return to base without bombing because of multilayer clouds. 82 P-38's bomb Tainach-Stein railroad bridge. 74 others sent against bridge in S Austria abort due to weather.

Tenth AF: 95 FBs operating over and behind Japanese lines in C Burma pound troop concentrations, trucks, and supply areas, and sweep roads S of bomb line.

Fourteenth AF: 14 B-25's hit town areas and T/Os at Sichuan, Hsihhsiassuchi, Neihsiang, Shaoyang, and Nanchang. 4 B-24's bomb harbors and dock areas at Bakli and Samah Bays and at Haiphong. 8 P-38's hit T/Os around Dien Bien Phu and along Nam Hon area. 24 P-51's attack river, road and rail traffic in Yellow R area, S of Anyi, at Yuncheng, and at Tengfeng.

FEAF: Bad weather hampers strikes N of the Phils. B-24's and P-38's over Formosa hit various T/Os. Ftrs fly 130-plus sorties in spt of ground forces at Solvec Cove, Villa Verde Trail, Ipo and Marikina Rivers, and NE Laguna de Bay. B-24's again bomb Bunawan. Other B-24's and P-38's hit Jolo I. B-24's bomb Bima A/F.

Twentieth AF: 101 B-29's bomb Nakajima aircraft engine plant at Tokyo while 150-plus hit Mitsubishi aircraft plant at Nagoya. Nearly 30 others hit last resort tgts. 91 P-51's of VII FC escort the VHBs to Japan for the first time and claim 21 kills.

Seventh AF: 24 B-24's from Angaur bomb barracks area at Bunawan.

Eleventh AF: A B-24 flies a radar-ferret mission along the coasts of Paramushiru and Harumukotan.

8 April

Eighth AF: More than 1,150 HBs strike 3 A/Fs, 4 M/Ys, an oil storage depot, 2 ordnance depots, a railroad yard workshop, and an aircraft parts and repair factory, in areas N and NW of Leipzig, SE of and near Nurnberg, and SW of Chemnitz. 14 ftr gps fly escort.

Ninth AF: HQ IX TAC moves from Bruhl to Marburg/Lahn. Around 620 A–20's, A–26's, and B–26's bomb Munchenbernsdorf oil storage depot, Sonderhausen comm center, Nienhagen oil refinery, Celle M/Y, and 8 city areas. Ftrs escort 9th Bomb Div, attack A/F, fly patrols and armed rcn, and operate in conjunction with US VIII, XII, and XX Corps in Thuringer Forest and Erfurt areas.

Twelfth AF: During 7/8 Apr LBs hit cmd posts and dumps. MBs, despite bad weather bomb railroad bridges at Salorno, San Michele all' Adige, Vo Sinistro, and Bondeno, railroad fill and canal at Salorno, and gun positions at La Spezia. XXII TAC FBs concentrate efforts on Brenner area comm (cutting lines in 31 places and damaging 4 bridges), oil fields in C Po Valley, and points further N.

Fifteenth AF: More than 500 B–24's and B–17's, with ftr escorts, attack comm in N Italy, concentrating on transportation system feeding into Brenner Pass. Bridges, viaducts, and M/Ys are hit at or near Bressanone, Campodazzo, Vipiteno, Fortezza, Campo di Trens, Mezzocorona, Avisio, Brescia, Gorizia, Pordenone, and Ponte Gardena. (power dam at Ponte Gardena is also hit). 168 P–38's bomb Rattenberg and Garmisch railroad bridges and strafe rail traffic in Munich-Salzburg-Linz areas.

Tenth AF: 50-plus P–38's and P–47's operating in C Burma battle areas attack troops, supplies, gun positions, and trucks at several points along and behind enemy lines, and sweep roads S of bomb line. Transports maintain operations throughout the day.

Fourteenth AF: 31 P–51's knock out bridge S of Shaoyang, destroy section of track at Sincheng, and hit numerous road and rail T/Os in Yellow R areas and points to the S, from Shanhsien to Loning, at Hungtung, and S of Hei-Shih Kuan. 4 B–24's attack shipping T/Os in S China Sea and in Bakli and Yulin Bays and bomb Kowloon Docks.

FEAF: For second consecutive day bad weather prevents attacks on primary tgts N of the Phil Is. MBs and HBs hit secondary tgts including Chomosui A/F and Tainan town and railroad yards, towns of Takao, Toko, and Kaiko, and other scattered objectives. A–20's and FBs over Luzon spt ground forces particularly in areas E of Manila. B–24's join A–20's and FBs in spt of ground forces on Cebu and Negros. Other HBs bomb N Davao Bay area and Jolo I.

Twentieth AF: 48 B–29's strike 2 A/Fs at Kanoya and 1 at Kokubu.

Seventh AF: 25 B–24's from Angaur bomb Bunawan area. During 8/9 Apr, 6 night ftrs from Iwo Jima, operating singly at 2-hr intervals, bomb Chichi Jima, Haha Jima, Ani Jima, and Ototo Jima.

9 April

Eighth AF: 10 jet A/Fs, a M/Y and rail center, an ammunition plant, and an oil storage facility in SC Germany are bombed by around 1,200 HBs. 15 ftr gps give close and area spt.

Ninth AF: Over 700 MBs and LBs strike M/Ys at Jena and Saalfeld, oil tgts at Bad Berka and Dedenhausen, ordnance depots at Naumburg and Amberg-Kummersbruck, and several T/Os. Ftrs escort 9th Bomb Div, attack several A/Fs and a fuel storage facility, fly area patrols and armed rcn, and spt III Corps along Lenne R, 3d Armd Div E of the Weser R toward Nordhausen, VIII Corps in Arnstadt area and XII and XX Corps in Thuringer Forest and around Erfurt.

Twelfth AF: A-20's and A-26's on intruder missions during 8/9 Apr bomb bridges, vehicles, and T/Os in Po R Valley and NE Italy. During the day B-25's and XXII TAC FBs (in conjunction with DAF FBs and MASAF HBs) blast gun positions, troop concentrations, enemy HQ, and strongpoints in Lugo-Imola area in spt of British Eighth Army offensive. Other XXII TAC FBs hit comm in N Italy (including Brenner line) and methane plant and ammo and fuel dumps in WC Po Valley.

Fifteenth AF: 825 B-24's and B-17's in close coordination with the British Eighth Army, pound gun positions and other forward military tgts SE of Bologna, in the area immediately W and SW of Lugo. 88 P-51's provide tgt cover. 150-plus P-38's bomb and strafe railroad bridges at Rattenberg, Seefeld, Telfs, Rosenheim, and to the S near Austro-German border, and also hit rail lines in Munich-Rosenheim area. Over 90 P-51's escort supply (to N Italy) and transport missions and spt MATAF aircraft attacking positions in Imola area. Other airplanes continue rcn operations.

Tenth AF: More than 70 P-38's and P-47's attack troops, supplies, gun positions, and general T/Os along and behind C Burma battleline around Mong Pawn, Wan Htum, Pang po, Kyawkku, Mong Hko, Hanhwe-Mu, Laihka, and other points. Transports complete 415 sorties to forward areas.

Fourteenth AF: 9 B-24's bomb docks at Canton and Kowloon and attack T/Os at Bakli Bay. 8 B-25's bomb Sinyang railroad yards and nearby T/Os. 13 other B-25's knock out bridge N of Hsuchang and hit various tgts around Laohokow, Sichuan, Sinyang, Likuanchiao, Lichen, and along the Han R. 19 P-51's hit T/Os in or near Neihsiang, Laohokow, and Sichuan. 2 P-38's blast trucks in Dien Bien Phu area.

FEAF: A-20's and FBs spt ground forces on Luzon in Balete Pass, Baguio, and Solvec Cove areas and at several points in SW Luzon, and attack Japanese forces in Legaspi area. B-24's and FBs spt ground forces in C Cebu and on Negros. Several B-24's on armed rcn missions hit China and Indochina coastal tgts.

Twentieth AF: 16 B-29's mine Shimonoseki Strait.

Seventh AF: 16 P-51's from Iwo Jima bomb and strafe military installations at Chichi Jima during the early morning. 17 Guam-based B-24's pound Marcus A/F and def installations. 22 from Angaur hit troop concentration at Kabacan.

10 April

Eighth AF: 1,224 HBs hit 8 A/Fs 2 M/Ys, a factory A/F and repair hangars, an ordnance depot, and HQ buildings—all in N Germany. 15 ftr gps provide close and area spt and strafe numerous A/Fs, claiming 335 parked airplanes destroyed. About 60 jets and a few conventional ftrs are encountered. US ftrs claim over 20 aerial victories. Enemy ftrs and AA account for 16 HBs.

Ninth AF: 423 A–20's, A–26's, and B–26's strike oil storage and ordnance depots, rail bridge and viaduct (all primary tgts) and several other tgts including a M/Y and an industrial area. Ftrs escort 9th Bomb Div, fly patrols, rail cutting operations, and armed rcn, and spt US 13th Armd Div crossing the Sieg R near Siegburg, 3d Armd Div approaching Nordhausen, 9th Armd Div in Hain area, XII Corps near Coburg, XX Corps W of Weimar and the Saale R, 2d and 5th Armd Divs crossing Oker R in Ahnsen and Schladen areas, and XVI Corps along the Ruhr R in Essen area.

Twelfth AF: During 9/10 Apr LBs hit guns and other close spt tgts along British Eighth Army front (which stretches from W of Imola to Comacchio Lagoon and the coast) and also hit several Po R crossings and attack Brenner line bridges at Lavis, Rovereto, and San Michele all'Adige. During the day B–25's and XXII TAC FBs continue pounding spt tgts along the battlefront. FBs also attack bridges on the Brenner line and comm and other tgts in Po Valley.

Fifteenth AF: 648 B–24's and B–17's, in spt of British Eighth Army forces, blast arty positions, machinegun nests, and inf defenses along the Santerno R. This effort represents the largest number of Fifteenth AF HBs attacking tgts in a single day as of this date. 88 P–51's fly tgt cover. 152 P–38's dive-bomb bridges, a tunnel and a M/Y at Seefeld and Worgl.

Tenth AF: About 30 FBs attack troop concentrations at Tonglau, at points along Zawgyi, and at other locations in C Burma battle area. 455 transport sorties are flown to forward areas.

Fourteenth AF: 23 B–24's pound Yungcheng storage areas. 50-plus B–25's and 180-plus FBs (operating in small flights) attack numerous tgts throughout S and E China. Tgts hit are mainly troops, horses, town areas, storage areas, and river, road, and rail traffic.

FEAF: HBs bomb town of Koshun. A–20's and FBs again spt ground forces in SW Luzon and in Balete Pass, Baguio, and Solvec Cove areas, and pound Legaspi area. B–24's and FBs spt ground forces in C Cebu. B–24's bomb Liang and Bingkalapa A/Fs.

Seventh AF: During 10/11 Apr, 6 Iwo Jima-based night ftrs, flying individual strikes bomb and strafe Chichi, Muko, Ani, and Haha Jima.

Eleventh AF: In coordinated operations with Navy aircraft, 7 B–24's napalm-bomb Kataoka naval base. 4 B–25's attempt to hit radar installations on Minami Cape, the primary air warning station in the Kurils, but fail to release bombs due to approach error. 3 other B–25's deck-level bomb Masugawa R cannery. A B–24 investigates ice floes along Kurils.

11 April

Eighth AF: Over 1,250 HBs attack 6 M/Ys, 2 A/Fs, 2 ordnance depots, 2 oil storage depots, and an ammunition factory in S Germany. 15 ftr gps provide close and area spt.

Ninth AF: 689 MBs and LBs strike M/Ys at Bernburg, Oschersleben, Zwickau, and Kothen, Naumburg ordnance depot, Bamberg motor transport plant, and several other tgts. Ftrs escort 9th Bomb Div, fly patrols, sweeps, leaflet mission, and armed rcn (claiming 43 aircraft shot down), and spt US 3d and 9th Armd Divs in Nordhausen and Ringleben-Sachsenburg-Rothenberga areas, 2d Armd Div as it reaches Elbe R S of Magdeburg in a record drive of 57 mi, XVI Corps along the Ruhr R at Witten, XX Corps as it crosses the Saale R at Weimar and overruns Buchenwald concentration camp and Allied prisoner camp nearby, XII Corps in Coburg-Rottenbach area, and VIII Corps as it approaches the Saale R S of Weimar.

Twelfth AF: During 10/11 Apr LBs bomb bridges at Lavis, Ala, Rovereto, San Michele all'Adige, and San Ambrogio di Valpolicella, and hit vehicles, Po R crossings and T/Os in Po Valley. MBs continue to spt British Eighth Army forces between Imola and Comacchio Lagoon, bomb guns SE of La Spezia in front of US Fifth Army adv, and bomb 4 bridges on the Brenner line. XXII TAC FBs also fly spt on Eighth Army front, and hit comm (including Brenner line) and fuel and ammo dumps in N Italy.

Fifteenth AF: 544 B–24's and B–17's hit comm in N Italy, concentrating on transportation system feeding into Brenner area, in effort to hamper enemy's supply and escape routes. The HBs bomb bridges at Padua, Vipiteno, Campodazzo, Ponte Gardena, and Campo di Trens, M/Ys at Bronzolo and Ora, vehicle repair shop at Osoppo, and fuel depot at Goito. 40 P–38's dive-bomb Rosenheim railroad bridge. 40 other P–38's and 29 P–51's strafe rail traffic in Munich, Regensburg, Plzen, Linz, and Salzburg areas. Over 250 ftrs escort HB missions, rcn and supply missions, and operations against N Italian tgts by MATAF aircraft.

Tenth AF: 54 FBs hit troop and supply concentrations near Mong Kung and Mong Nim, attack trucks and T/Os in other areas behind battleline, and sweep several roads S of bomb line. Transports fly 424 sorties carrying men and supplies to forward areas.

Fourteenth AF: 7 B–25's bomb Hsihhsiassuchi, 5 pound Pinglo barracks and storage area, and a few others hit Yanglowtung railroad yards and T/Os E of Paoching. 150-plus FBs attack troops, river, road and rail traffic, and a variety of T/Os scattered throughout S and E China and N Indochina.

FEAF: B–24's bomb Cotabato. Japanese defenses NW of Guadalupe are pounded by HBs. A–20's hit bivouac E of Negritos. On Luzon B–24's, B–25's, A–20's, and FBs bomb numerous tgts including Fuga I, Cagayan Valley areas, Santa Fe, bridges and other comm in Iligan, Naguilian, Manga, and Tuguegarao, and troops and supply concentration N of Imugan. Troop spt strikes are flown in Solvec Cove area and E of Manila. Baguio and troop concentration in Batangas area and on Bicol peninsula are bombed. At Iriga, defenses are hit with napalm. B–24's bomb Okayama while B–25's hit several tgts including Ts'eng Wen sugar refinery, Seiko, Sunbon-sha, and Shasekiryo. P–38's attack gun positions at Tarakan.

Seventh AF: 24 B–24's from Angaur hit Cotabato supply and personnel areas. 18 Guam-based B–24's pound positions on Eten I.

Eleventh AF: P–38's together with Navy aircraft pick up bomb-filled paper balloons over Attu and E of Adak. One balloon over Attu is shot down.

12 April

US: President Roosevelt dies.

Eighth AF: 2 ftr gps escort MBs of Ninth AF in attack on ordnance depot.

Ninth AF: 167 MBs and LBs attack Hof rail bridge, Kempten ordnance depot, and Goppingen M/Y, plus a town area and a casual T/O. Over 275 planes abort because of weather. Ftrs escort 9th Bomb Div, attack town of Kothen, fly armed rcn and sweeps over wide areas of Germany and spt ground forces. Ftrs also spt US III, XVI, and XVIII Corps as they continue to reduce the Ruhr pocket, 9th Armd Div on Saale R near Werben and Bad Lauchstadt, XX Corps from Saale R N and S of Jena E across the Weisse Elster R, VIII Corps along the Saale further S of Jena, XII Corp SE of

Coburg on Hasslach R, 2d Armd Div across the Elbe R near Randau S of Magdeburg, 5th Armd Div on W bank of the Elbe R at Wittenberge, and XVI Corps as it continues fighting in Duisburg and Dortmund areas.

Twelfth AF: LBs, during 11/12 Apr, hit Po R crossings, MBs, restricted by low clouds, bomb approaches to Maribor bridge, hit tgts along Brenner rail line, and spt British Eighth Army in Argenta area. FBs attack NE Italian railroad lines, including fuel dumps and comm tgts in Po Valley.

Fifteenth AF: 400-plus HBs hit comm in N Italy and S Austria, attacking railroad bridges at Padua, Ponte di Piave, Nervesa della Bataglia, and Sankt Veit an der Glan, ammo dump at Malcontenta, and supply dump at Peschiera del Garda. 124 P–51's provide escort. 123 P–38's bomb railroad bridges at Unzmarkt and Arnoldstein. 128 B–24's, with P–51 escort, sent against N Italian comm abort due to bad weather. 38 P–51's escort MATAF B–25's on raids in N Yugoslavia.

Tenth AF: 75 FBs continue to pound tgts in C Burma battle area. Troop concentrations, gun positions, supplies, vehicles, and general T/Os are attacked along battlefront, behind enemy lines, and along roads S of bomb line. 369 air supply sorties are flown throughout the day.

Fourteenth AF: 12 B–24's supported by 14 P–51's, bomb Wuchang railroad yards and A/F. 7 B–25's bomb Hsuchang railroad yards, 3 hit Loning, 2 attack Likuanchiao, 2 bomb Tenghsien, and single B–25's attack storage areas at Pingyao and Huaiching. 100-plus FBs attack troops, horses, bridges, river shipping, trucks, and railroad tgts at several locations in Indochina and at points scattered over S and E China.

FEAF: P–38's and A–20's spt ground troops on Cebu and Negros. B–24's bomb Sapakan, Kabacan, and Davao Bay areas. P–38's hit Cotabato and also Kabacan. Other B–24's, B–25's, A–20's, and FBs pound tgts throughout Cagayan Valley, blast defenses at Balete Pass and in Baguio area, and hit troops, comm tgts, and defenses at numerous points in SW and SE Luzon. B–24's attack Tainan and bomb Okayama A/F.

Twentieth AF: 94 B–29's strike Nakajima aircraft factory at Tokyo while 11 hit secondary tgt of Shizuoka engine plant. VHB gunners claim 16 ftrs downed. 130-plus other B–29's bomb 2 chemical plants at Koriyama. 32 more VHBs hit various T/Os. During 12/13 Apr, 5 B–29's mine Shimonoseki Strait. Ftrs from VII FC escorting the daylight operations over Tokyo area claim 15 aircraft downed.

Seventh AF: 24 B–24's, based on Angaur hit personnel area at Kabacan. During 12/13 Apr, 6 Iwo-based ftrs, operating singly at intervals, bomb and strafe tgts at Kita, Chichi, Haha, and Ani Jima.

Eleventh AF: P–38's shoot down paper bomb-balloons over Attu.

13 April

Eighth AF: Over 200 B–17's bomb Neumunster M/Y. 8 ftr gps spt HBs and strafe numerous A/Fs, claiming 284 parked airplanes destroyed.

Ninth AF: A special mission is flown by IX TAC FBs against HQ of FM Model's Army Gp B at Haus Waldesruh in the Ruhr pocket.

The air attack is followed by an arty barrage. As a result the HQ is moved to Haan. IX TAC pilots sight Soviet ftrs in the air for the first time. Weather grounds 9th Bomb Div. Ftrs fly patrols and armed rcn, and spt US XVIII Corps in Huckeswagen and Hagen areas, III Corps between Ruhr and Honne Rivers, 3d Armd Div on Saale R in Alsleben, Nelben and Friedeburg area, XX Corps astride and between the Weisse Elster and Zwickauer Mulde Rivers N of Gera, XVI Corps NW of Hagen, 2d Armd Div in Elbenau-Grunwalde area, and 5th Armd Div along the Elbe in Tangermunde area.

Twelfth AF: B–25's are restricted by weather to 1 mission, an attack on road bridge at Mollinella. FBs continue to hit comm and dumps in Po Valley and guns in La Spezia area. LBs during 12/13 Apr attack Po R crossings at San Benedetto Po, Ostiglia, Piacenza, and Casalmaggiore, bridges at San Ambrogio di Valpolicella, and motor transport and T/Os in Milan area.

Fifteenth AF: Bad weather limits operations to rcn and escort missions.

Tenth AF: 30-plus P–47's and P–38's attack troops and supplies in Hamn gai, Loi-hseng, and Wan Yin areas and sweep roads S of bomb line in C Burma. Air transport operations to front areas total 450 sorties.

Fourteenth AF: 11 B–25's bomb railroad yards and warehouse area at Kaifeng, 6 knock out bridge at Ningming, and 6 hit fort at Bac Ninh. 7 B–25's hit shipping in S China Sea and Bakli Bay and town areas of Tenghsien and Liuchow. 4 others, along with 5 P–51's, knock out bridge and hit town area and shipping at Puchi. 24 P-38's and P-51's knock out 3 bridges, damage another, and hit several T/Os in N Indochina. About 140 FBs fly armed rcn and strikes throughout S and E China, hitting rail, road, and river traffic, town areas, troops, and general T/Os.

FEAF: B-24's hit Hong Kong waterfront (Taikoo Docks) and storage areas in Canton. Other B-24's hit A/Fs at Tainan and Okayama while B-25's attack railroads. Numerous sweeps are flown over Cagayan Valley and ground spt missions are continued on Luzon, Cebu, and Negros. B-24's bomb Davao area. B-25's hit various tgts on Mindanao and in Sulu Archipelago.

Twentieth AF: During 13/14 Apr almost 330 B-29's bomb Tokyo arsenal area.

Seventh AF: 18 Guam-based B-24's pound enemy positions on Marcus. 23 from Angaur bomb personnel and storage areas at Kabacan. 2 Saipan-based P-61 night ftrs bomb and strafe Pagan I.

Eleventh AF: At Attu 27 P-38's and P-40's scramble following radar reports of unidentified plots. Later, they shoot down 9 of 11 Japanese paper bomb-balloons sighted over the W Aleutians.

14 April

Eighth AF: 1,161 HBs hit 22 defensive installations, consisting of AA and arty positions and strongpoints covering the Gironde estuary. Other Allied AFs and French naval units attack similar tgts. The air attacks precede a ground assault by French det of 6th Army Gp on the defense pockets which deny Allies use of port facilities in Bordeaux area.

Ninth AF: Operational HQ of XXIX TAC moves to Gutersloh. 18 B-26's fly leaflet mission in Ruhr area. Ftrs fly patrols, sweeps, and armed rcn, and spt US 3d Armd Div SW of Elbe/Mulde R junction near Dessau, 9th Armd Div in Borna and Lobstadt area, XX Corps elements which continue to arrive at Zwickauer Mulde R, VIII Corps along the Weisse Elster R S of Gera, XII Corps elements in Bayreuth area, 2d and 5th Armd Divs along the Elbe in Barby-Magdeburg and Tangermunde areas.

Twelfth AF: During 13/14 Apr LBs continue to hit comm in Po Valley. Bad weather over N part of Brenner line prevents MB attacks but the B-25's hit alternates on S part of line at Salorno, San Ambrogio di Valpolicella, and Chiusaforte, bomb guns SE of La Spezia in spt of US Fifth Army, and hit 5 defensive positions along British Eighth Army front in Argenta area. FBs concentrate on supporting Fifth Army forces SW of Bologna.

Fifteenth AF: 318 HBs hit ammo factories at Avigliana, Spilimbergo, Malcontenta, and Palmanova, motor transport depot at Osoppo and Klagenfurt M/Y as a T/O. 158 ftrs provide escort. 29 P-38's bomb and strafe railroad tgts in Munich-Linz-Regensburg areas. 54 P-51's fly escort for MATAF B-25's bombing tgts in N Italy.

Tenth AF: 41 P-47's and P-38's attack troops, supplies, and fuel dumps at Tawnghkam Nawng-hkam, Mong Kung, Loi-makhkawn, and Nawngkaw. 8 P-38's damage bridges at Kong pau and Kyawngpeng. 446

transport flights are flown to forward areas.

Fourteenth AF: 24 B–24's, supported by 12 P–51's, bomb Loyang and knock out bridge over Yellow R. 30-plus B–25's and more than 130 FBs attack bridges (knocking out at least 6), river, road, and rail traffic, troops, storage areas, town areas, and general T/Os over vast expanse of S and E China.

FEAF: B–25's sweep Canton-Hong Kong waterways, hitting shipping and other tgts. B–24's bomb four A/Fs on Formosa. In the Phil Is B–24's, B–25's, A–20's, and FBs fly numerous strikes in spt of ground forces and against A/Fs, gun positions, defenses, and troop concentrations throughout Luzon, Cebu, Negros, and Mindanao.

Seventh AF: 24 Angaur-based B–24's pound supply and personnel areas at Tigatto.

15 April

Eighth AF: The sole operational employment of napalm bomb by Eighth AF is carried out against German ground installations (pillboxes, gunpits, tank trenches, and heavy gun emplacements) in defensive pocket at Royan by nearly 850 HBs. Results are negligible and HQ recommends its discontinuance against this type of tgt. A total of 16 defensive installations on Gironde estuary are bombed by 1,280 HBs supporting assault by French ground troops under 6th Army Gp. 2 ftr gps escort Ninth AF MBs attacking Ulm M/Y.

Ninth AF: 258 B–26's and A–26's bomb M/Ys at Gunzburg and Ulm (primary tgts) and several other tgts

including 3 M/Ys. Ftrs escort 9th Bomb Div, fly patrols and armed rcn, and spt US 3d Armd Div near Dessau and across Mulde R near Torten, 9th Armd Div along Mulde R NW of Borna, VIII Corps along Weisse Elster R between Gera and Plauen, XX Corps astride the Mulde R NE of Chemnitz (where 6th Armd Div awaits Red Army forces), and 2d Armd Div on Elbe R near Magdeburg.

Twelfth AF: During 14/15 Apr LBs concentrate on comm tgts in Po Valley, particularly the Po crossings. During the day MBs and FBs concentrate on direct spt of US Fifth and British Eighth Army drives, hitting troop concentrations, guns, strongpoints, and a variety of tgts in areas S of Bologna, around Medicina and Sasso Marconi, and at other points in battle areas.

Fifteenth AF: 830 B–17's and B–24's, in spt of US Fifth Army, blast gun positions, supply dumps, troop concentrations, maintenance installations, and German HQ along highways leading from Bologna. 145 P–38's furnish escort. Another force of 312 B–17's and B–24's bomb rail diversion bridges at Nervesa della Battaglia, Ponte di Piave, and Casarsa della Delizia, and ammo factory and stores at Ghedi. 191 P–51's provide escort. 36 P–38's and 36 P–51's strafe rail comm in area bounded by Munich, Salzburg, Linz, Plzen, and Regensburg. 12 of the P–38's skipbomb rail tgts in Salzburg-Linz area, including Vocklabruck M/Y. 8 P–38's furnish top cover for the strafing missions. 128 P–51's provide uneventful escort for MATAF bmrs on 3 missions to N Italy. Other P–38's and P–51's carry out rcn and rcn escort operations. Today's effort is the largest of World War II by Fifteenth AF (most ftrs and brms dispatched and attacking, and largest bomb tonnage dropped) during a 24-hr period. 1,142 HBs bomb tgts.

Tenth AF: 62 P–38's and P–47's attack troop concentrations and supply areas at Loi-Mwe, Lawksawk, Thongdan, and near Laihka. 312 transport sorties are flown to forward areas.

Fourteenth AF: 3 B–25's knock out Pa Ching pontoon bridge, 7 pound storage depot at Fang-cheng, 4 bomb Tunganhsien, and 3 hit Paoching. 1 B–24 bombs Canton docks. Almost 200 FBs ranging over all of S China and up into the N China plain hit numerous tgts including bridges, river shipping, town areas, trucks, railroad traffic, gun positions, storage areas, and general T/Os. Paoching, Hengyang, Yungfengshih, and Hsihhsiassuchi areas are especially hard hit.

FEAF: On Formosa B–24's bomb Toyohara, Shinchiku, and Shinshoshi A/Fs. B–25's hit Shoka rail yards. B–24's and FBs bomb island fortifications in Manila Bay, FBs hit bivouacs and other tgts in N Luzon and spt ground forces E of Manila and on Carabao I. FBs and B–24's fly spt missions for ground forces on Negros and Cebu. B–24's bomb Davao area and B–25's join Marine aircraft in hitting highways and vehicles.

Twentieth AF: During 15/16 Apr, 194 B–29's strike Kawasaki urban area while 109 hit urban area of Tokyo.

Eleventh AF: A B–24 flies weather rcn.

16 April

Eighth AF: During morning 486 B–17's bomb tank ditch def line at Pointe de Grave on S side of Gironde estuary in spt of ground assault in that area. In the afternoon 715 HBs bomb M/Ys at Plattling, Regensburg, and Landshut, and rail bridges and siding at Regensburg and Straubing. 15 ftr gps provide uneventful close and area spt and then strafe over 40 landing grounds and installations in Czechoslovakia and Germany, claiming a record 747 parked ftrs destroyed. 34 ftrs are downed mostly by automatic AA weapons.

Ninth AF: About 450 MBs and LBs bomb Zerbst comm center, Gunzenhausen M/Y, Kempten ordnance depot, and Wittenberg M/Y and gun positions. IX TAC's ftrs claim 25 air victories during the day as they escort 9th Bomb Div, fly patrols, area cover, and armed rcn, attack A/Fs and other tgts, and spt US 3rd Armd Div SW of Dessau, 9th Armd Div in Bennewitz-Colditz area along the Mulde R, XX Corps which remains at Zwickauer Mulde R bridgehead NE of Chemnitz, VIII Corps crossing Weisse Elster R between Gera and Plauen, 2d Armd Div on the Elbe R near Magdeburg, XIX Corps E of Barby, and V Corps near Leipzig. The 354th Ftr Gp (the pioneer P–51 gp of the Ninth AF) claims its 900th air victory.

Twelfth AF: During 15/16 Apr LBs hit Po R crossings, towns of Vignola, Zocca, and Sassuolo, and several T/Os in Po Valley. During the day MBs bomb bridges on Reno R near Bologna, blast troop reserve areas SE of Portomaggiore on British Eighth Army front, and attack troop concentrations S of Portomaggiore. Ftrs and FBs concentrate most of their effort on close spt tgts in US Fifth Army battle area S and SW of Bologna.

Fifteenth AF: 98 B–24's bomb positions SW of Bologna. 102 P–51's fly escort. Almost 700 B–24's and B–17's abort due to bad weather. 36 P–51's sweep areas S of Munich, Plzen, and Linz. 4 strafe A/F E of Munich. Other P–51's and P–38's fly escort and rcn missions.

Tenth AF: 22 FBs pound troop concentrations in Ke-hsi Mansam vicinity. 19 others attack road bridges behind enemy lines, claiming 1 bridge destroyed. Air transport operations to forward areas continue on steady basis.

Fourteenth AF: 18 B–24's pound storage area at Linfen. 3 bomb T/Os in Bakli Bay and Canton areas. 10 B–25's bomb Yungfengshih, Kweilin, and Shanhsien, knocking out 1 bridge and hitting buildings, river shipping, and rail traffic. About 120 FBs over S and E China hit river, road, and rail traffic, town areas, troops, and general T/Os at many scattered locations.

FEAF: B–25's hit Taien A/F, while B–24's and P–51's bomb Giran and Matsuyama A/Fs and nearby areas. FBs hit N Luzon bivouacs and other tgts and spt strikes and sweeps are flown over Cebu, Negros, and Mindanao with B–25's hitting highways on Mindanao, B–24's hit defenses at Carabao I. P–38's pound Lingkas Tank Farm and other tgts at Tarakan. During 15/16 Apr B–24's bomb Taihoku.

Seventh AF: 18 Guam-based B–24's pound Marcus. 2 P–61's from Saipan bomb and strafe Pagan.

VII FC: In first VLR ftr operations from Iwo Jima, VII FC P–51's with B–29 navigational escort from Twentieth AF, strafe and bomb tgts at Kanoya. B–25's continue to furnish navigational escort in all subsequent VII FC strikes (through 14 Aug) on Japan from Iwo Jima.

Eleventh AF: B–25's abort mission to bomb Hayakegawa because of weather front. 6 B–24's radar-bomb Kataoka naval base. Another B–24 flies a radar-ferret sortie.

17 April

Eighth AF: More than 950 HBs attack 8 railway centers, junctions, stations and M/Ys and 1 oil depot in E Germany and W Czechoslovakia. 15 ftr gps fly spt, encountering about 50 ftrs, mostly jets, and claiming 13 destroyed (including 4 jets) in aerial combat. The ftrs strafe numerous A/Fs and claim over 250 parked aircraft destroyed.

Ninth AF: 9th Bomb Div attacks defended city of Magdeburg (including numerous gun positions in the area), M/Y and ordnance depot at Aalen, M/Y and ordnance depot at Tubingen, and ordnance depot at Ravensburg. Ftrs fly escort to 9th Bomb Div, fly patrols, area cover, and armed rcn, hit A/Fs at Marianske Lazne and Michalovy Hory, and spt US 3d Armd Div mopping up S of the Elbe R and W of the Mulde R near Dessau, 9th Armd Div along the Mulde R E of Leipzig, VIII Corps in Greiz-Zwickau area, XX Corps SW of Chemnitz, 5th Armd Div at Knesebeck Forest, S of Wittingen, and 2d armd Div opening assault on Magdeburg.

Twelfth AF: LBs during 16/17 Apr hit Po R crossings and several towns W and SW of Bologna. During the day B–25's of 57th Bomb Wg successfully attack 4 Reno R bridges near Bologna and close spt tgts on British Eighth Army front to the SW, and extensively damage 4 bridges in N Italy and Austria on Brenner rail line. XXII TAC ftrs and FBs concentrate on close spt of US Fifth Army S and W of Bologna.

Fifteenth AF: 751 B–24's and B–17's, in spt of US Fifth Army, hit troop concentrations, supply dumps, gun positions, and HQ immediately S and SW of Bologna. 143 P–51's provide escort. 147 P–38's dive-bomb railroad bridges at Seefeld and Mariahof. 14 P–51's, with 10 flying top cover, strafe T/Os in Munich, Plzen, and Linz areas. 61 P–51's escort MATAF supply missions to N Italy and bombing raids on bridges in W Austria. Other P–38's and P–51's fly rcn and rcn escort.

Tenth AF: 18 FBs hit troops and supplies near Mong Kung and Wan Hpun. 12 others attack vehicles and other T/Os along roads S of bomb line. 489 transport sorties are completed to forward areas throughout the day.

Fourteenth AF: 4 B–25's and 4 P–51's blast river shipping S of Yiyang. 6 B–25's bomb area around Kwangsi University at Liang-feng. 2 B–24's bomb Bakli Bay dock area. 70-plus P–51's and P–40's hit troops, town areas, road traffic, river shipping, and general T/Os at several locations in S and E China including

Changsha, Sinning, Sinhwa, Yiyang, Tungting Lake, Paoching, Yungfengshih, Shanhsien, Lingling, Pingsiang, Tsinkong, and Hochih.

FEAF: B–24's bomb Taichu, Shinshoshi, Toyohara, and Okayama A/Fs. B–25's hit A/F at Taito. Numerous sweeps and sorties are flown in spt of ground forces over Luzon, Cebu, Negros, Mindanao and Sulu Archipelago. B–24's over Mindanao bomb Cotabato and Kabacan.

Twentieth AF: Almost 120 B–29's bomb A/Fs at Tachiarai, Kokubu, Izumi, Nittagahara, and Kanoya (2). Beginning on this date and continuing through 11 May, XXI BC devotes about 75 per cent of its combat effort to spt of Okinawa campaign. During this period the B–29's fly more than 2,100 sorties against 17 A/Fs on Kyushu and Shikoku Is which are dispatching air attacks (including *Kamikaze* raids) against US Navy and Marine forces.

Seventh AF: 18 P–51's flying two strikes from Iwo Jima, attack vessels in Futamiko.

18 April

Eighth AF: More than 750 HBs attack 7 M/Ys, a rail bridge and junction, and 2 transformer stations in W Czechoslovakia and SE Bavaria. 13 ftr gps fly escort. 2 other gps escort Ninth AF MBs over Germany.

Ninth AF: About 590 B–26's, A–26's, and A–20's attack oil storage at Neuburg an der Donau, M/Ys at Juterbog and Nordlingen, and rail junctions at Falkenburg and Juterbog. Ftrs escort 9th Bomb Div, fly patrols, sweeps, and armed rcn, attack assigned tgts, and spt ground forces including US V Corps assaulting Leipzig, VII Corps in Dessau-Halle areas,

5th Armd Div near Steimke, and 2d Armd Div at Magdeburg and other XIX Corps elements astride the Elbe R S of Barby. Organized German resistance in the Ruhr pocket ceases.

Twelfth AF: During 17/18 Apr LBs pound comm in S Po Valley and towns of Vignola, Bazzano, and Sassuolo in US Fifth Army battle area. MBs hit 2 railroad fills and a bridge on the S Brenner line and troop concentrations on Fifth and British Eighth Army fronts, SW of Bologna and in Dugnano Paderno area. FBs of XXII TAC also concentrate on spt tgts in Fifth Army battle area.

Fifteenth AF: 473 B–24's and B–17's, with escort of 89 P–51's, spt Fifth Army offensive in Bologna area, blasting defensive positions and comm in areas around the city. 78 P–38's dive-bomb railroad bridge at Malborghetta Valbruna, while 87 others dive-bomb 2 railroad bridges at and SE of Kolbnitz. P–51's sweep Augsburg, Plzen, and Linz areas, escort rcn missions flown by P–38's, and escort MATAF B–25's and C–47's on bombing and supply operations.

Tenth AF: 21 P–38's attack troop concentration, tanks, arty positions, and bivouac area near Man Li and Kongsam. 5 P–61's hit supply area W of Laihka. Transports land or drop 806 tons of supplies at forward bases and frontline areas.

Fourteenth AF: 3 B–25's hit trucks and other T/Os E of Siangtan. 52 P–51's and P–40's attack river shipping, town areas, rail and road traffic, tanks, and bridges at several S and E China locations including Sinhwa, Hengyang, Changsha, Luchai, Paoching, Kweiyang, Yenkou, Sinning, and Siangtan.

FEAF: On Formosa B–25's bomb Karenko A/F, B–24's hit Tainan, Giran, Toyohara, Hobi, and Soton A/Fs, and P–38's on sweeps hit rail and road transportation. FBs and A–20's hit Balete Pass area and spt ground forces on Luzon, Negros, and Cebu. B–24's bomb Piso Point. B–25's and P–38's hit Tarakan and Sandakan.

Twentieth AF: B–29's hit Japanese A/Fs, as 100-plus VHBs strike A/Fs at Tachiarai, Izumi, Kokubu, Nittagahara, and Kanoya (2), the same tgts attacked on the 17th.

Seventh AF: During 18/19 Apr 3 Iwo Jima-based P–61's flying individual strikes, bomb and strafe Futamiko and radio station on Chichi Jima.

19 April

Eighth AF: Over 550 HBs hit 3 M/Ys, rail bridge, rail junction and other railroad facilities in SE Germany and NW Czechoslovakia. 11 ftr gps give close and area spt, encountering over 30 ftrs and claiming 12 destroyed, including several jets.

Ninth AF: 9th Bomb Div hits M/Ys at Ulm, Neu Ulm, and Gunzburg (primary tgts), city of Donauworth and T/O at Schelklingen. Weather prevents over 70 of the 450-plus dispatched aircraft from bombing tgts. Ftrs fly escort to 9th Bomb Div, carry out patrols and armed rcn, bomb radio station, and cooperate with US VII Corps in Halle-Dessau area, XII Corps attacking SE from S of Bayreuth, XX Corps in Bamberg-Nurnberg area, preparing to drive toward Austria, and XIX Corps along the Elbe R in Magdeburg area.

Twelfth AF: During 18/19 Apr LBs bomb roads, vehicles, and lights in Bologna, Turin, Milan, and Mantua areas, and continuing to pound Po R crossings, hit 8 bridges. MBs bomb bridges in Brenner Pass and spt ground forces at several points including Budrio, Vignola, and San Martino in Soverzano areas. FBs hit dumps, comm, and close spt tgts in US Fifth Army battle areas S and W of Bologna.

Fifteenth AF: 619 HBs attack rail comm in S Germany, Austria, and N Italy, bombing Rattenberg railroad bridge and M/Ys at Lienz, Klagenfurt, Bischofshofen, Linz and Rosenheim, Avisio viaduct, Vipiteno railroad bridge, AA batteries near Grisolera and Santo Stino di Livenza, and several minor T/Os. 78 P–38's dive-bomb M/Y at Weilheim. Other P–38's and P–51's fly rcn and rcn escort, and escort MATAF B–25's and C–47's.

Tenth AF: 14 P–38's hit supplies near Paklu, fuel dump at Hainang, and bridges near Kunna. 1 bridge is knocked out. 6 other P–38's attack T/Os along roads behind enemy lines. Air supply operations continue as 800 tons of supplies are landed or dropped in forward areas.

Fourteenth AF: 12 B–24's bomb railway repair shops at Taiyuan. 3 others attack Bakli Bay T/Os, 8 B–25's attack bridges and rail and road traffic N and NE of Anyang and NE of Taiku, damaging or destroying several locomotives and numerous boxcars. 100-plus P–40's, P–51's, and P–47's attack town areas, troops, river, road, and rail traffic, and general T/Os all over S and E China and hit a few T/Os in N Indochina.

FEAF: B–24's over Formosa bomb Tainan A/F and Shinchiku town. Numerous missions are flown in spt of ground forces on Luzon, Cebu, and Negros. Other B–24's bomb personnel areas at Kabacan, Cagayan, and along Davao R. Tarakan on Borneo is hit by light B–25 strike while B–24's returning from Indochina coastal sweep bomb Sandakan. B–25's, with P–51 cover, hit Haimi.

Seventh AF: 8 P–51's from Iwo Jima bomb and strafe Futamiko. 25 B–24's, based in the Palaus bomb nearby Arakabesan and Koror. 17 B–24's from Guam hit Dublon, Fefan, and Eten. During 19/20 Apr, 6 P–61's from Iwo Jima, operating singly and at intervals, bomb and strafe Chichi, Haha, and Muko Jima.

VII FC: Ftrs from Iwo Jima carry out 106 effective strike sorties against Atsugi-Yokosuka area. 24 airplanes are claimed destroyed in the air and 14 on the ground.

Eleventh AF: 8 B–25's off to bomb Kuril tgts abort due to weather.

20 April

Eighth AF: Around 800 HBs attack 8 M/Ys, 3 rail junctions, a rail bridge, other rail facilities, and an A/F, located in 7 cities in an arc from NNW to SSW of Berlin, 3 towns in E and SE Bavaria, and a town in Czechoslovakia. 15 ftr gps give close and area spt, and claim 7 ftrs downed.

Ninth AF: 564 MBs and LBs strike oil storage at Deggendorf and Annaburg, M/Ys at Memmingen and Wittenberg, ordnance depots at Nordlingen and Straubing, and other tgts including flak positions. Ftrs escort 9th Bomb Div, fly patrols, sweeps, and armed rcn, attack special tgts, and cooperate with US ground forces including VII Corps W of Dessau, VIII

Corps between Plauen and Chemnitz, XII Corps in Grafenwohr area, XX Corps attacking toward the Danube and Regensburg, and XIX Corps in Magdeburg-Barby area.

Twelfth AF: LBs on night intruder missions during 19/20 Apr continue to pound Po R crossings and vehicle movement throughout the Valley. MBs considerably damage 4 of 6 railroad bridges and fills attached on Brenner line, and also hit HQ in battle area and 2 Reno R bridges N of Bologna. FBs again spt US Fifth Army elements S and W of Bologna as they begin to emerge from the Apennines onto the Po plain.

Fifteenth AF: HBs again pound railway systems and road bridges in effort to hinder supply or withdrawal of enemy forces in N Italy. Over 700 B-24's and B-17's hit railroad bridges at Campodazzo, Ponte Gardena, and Campo di Trens, viaduct at Avisio, M/Ys at Vipiteno, Fortezza, and Brennero, and road bridges at Lusia, la Carrare, and Boara Pisani, and Mariahof viaduct and Innsbruck M/Y. 115 P-38's dive-bomb railroad line Innsbruck - Rattenberg - Rosenheim, hitting M/Ys at Hall, Schwaz, Jenbach, Kundl, Worgl and Kiefersfelden, 4 rail bridges, and several box cars, and cut rail lines at 42 places between Innsbruck and Rosenheim. Other P-38's and P-51's escort HBs, MATAF supply runs to N Italy, Hungary, and Yugoslavia, and MATAF B-25 raids in N Italy, and fly rcn.

Tenth AF: 32 P-38's knock out 3 bridges and damage 5 others in C Burma behind enemy lines. 12 P-47's hit troop concentration and ration dump at Tonglau, 18 attack troop concentration around monastery at Kengkawmanhaung, and 12 attack troops along stream near Wan Nahpeit. 497 transport sorties land or drop 784 tons of supplies in forward areas.

Fourteenth AF: 7 B-25's hit town of Neihsiang and attack railroad T/Os from Saiping to Lohochai and from Linying to Hsuchang. 9 B-25's bomb Loyang and Luchou. 100-plus P-51's, P-40's, and P-47's concentrate attacks against town areas throughout S and E China, also hitting troops, gun positions, river traffic, and other T/Os.

FEAF: B-24's bomb Tainan A/F while P-51's attack Koshun A/F. Large-scale FEAF spt of ground forces on Luzon, Cebu, and Negros continues. B-24's bomb Sepinggang and Labuan A/Fs and P-38's and B-25's hit Tarakan I.

Seventh AF: 11 P-51's from Iwo Jima bomb Haha Jima.

21 April

Eighth AF: 300-plus HBs attack Munich M/Y, town of Ingolstadt, and Landsberg A/F. Around 200 other HBs abort because of bad weather. 7 ftr gps fly close spt while 1 gp sweeps Munich area.

Ninth AF: Gen Stearley takes over as CG, IX FC, and also takes cmd of IX TAC. 121 bmrs of 9th Bomb Div hit Attnang-Puchheim M/Y. Ftrs fly escort, patrols, armed rcn and cooperate with US VIII Corps as elements of 6th Cav Gp cross Czechoslovakian border to reach Hranice and, Trojmezi, XII Corps in Grafenwohr-Weiden area, and XX Corps E of Nurnberg.

Twelfth AF: During 20/21 Apr LBs bomb Po R crossings, with good results. Weather curtails daytime operations but MBs score hits on Matrei am Brenner bridge on Brenner rail line and in late afternoon hit Po R crossings. XXII TAC ftrs and FBs, grounded most of the day, fly close spt to US Fifth Army which drives into Bologna (a longstanding objective) and begins to push rapidly across the plain toward the Po R.

Fifteenth AF: 240 B–17's and B–24's, with P–51 escort, bomb M/Ys at Rosenheim, Attnang-Puchheim, Spittal an der Drau, and Vocklabruck. Over 400 B–24's and their ftr escorts, sent to attack comm in N Italy, abort due to bad weather. 138 P–38's bomb railroad lines and facilities in Munich-Rosenheim-Rattenberg areas. Other P–38's fly rcn while P–51's escort rcn flights, MATAF MB operations to Austria, and US and RAF supply and transport missions to Yugoslavia.

Tenth AF: Bad weather over C Burma causes cancelling or aborting of all combat missions. However, transports complete 464 sorties, landing or dropping 682 tons of supplies to forward areas.

Fourteenth AF: 5 B–25's bomb Loyang. A single B–24 hits Bakli Bay T/Os. 30 P–51's and P–47's attack railroad and road tgts, barracks area, buildings, and bridges at or near Paoching, Chihsien, Taiku, Hsihhsiassuchi, Shaho, Linfen, Luan, Yutze, and Shanhsien.

FEAF: FEAF continues large-scale spt of ground forces on Luzon, Cebu, Negros and on Jolo Is. B–24's bomb Miri, Kudat, Manggar, and Sepinggang A/Fs and P–38's hit Tarakan and Sandakan, Miri A/F, oil storage near Lutong, and, with B–24's, attack T/Os along SW Celebes coast.

Twentieth AF: XXI BC continues to hit A/Fs in Japan. 217 B–29's blast A/Fs at Oita, Kanoya (2), Usa, Kokubu, Kushira, Tachiarai, Izumi, and Nittagahara. Other B–29's hit T/Os including city of Kagoshima.

Seventh AF: 18 Guam-based B–24's bomb Marcus.

22 April

Ninth AF: XXIX TAC moves operational HQ to Brunswick. Weather prevents combat operations by 9th Bomb Div and IX TAC. XIX TAC flies armed rcn over E Germany and W Czechoslovakia, flies area cover over Wurzburg-Bayreuth areas, patrols Third Army front (Bayreuth-Nurnberg areas), and XII Corps in German-Czech border area near Weiden.

Twelfth AF: Entire night and day effort is concentrated against German forces retreating N across the Po R in face of allied forces which send adv elements racing to S bank. MBs fly 16 missions against ferries and pontoon bridge sites on the Po between Casalmaggiore and Polesella. XXII TAC LBs, FBs, and ftrs maintain night and day attacks on Po crossings and enemy movement. The cmd claims over 900 motor and horse-drawn vehicles destroyed.

Fifteenth AF: Bad weather cancels all HB operations. 258 P–51's and P–38's fly armed rcn over NE Italy, bombing M/Ys, bridges, railroads, highways, and several buildings and strafing an A/F, rail and road traffic, and numerous other T/Os. Other P–38's fly rcn while P–51's escort rcn and supply missions.

Tenth AF: Bad weather again cancels scheduled air strikes. 464

transport sorties fly 664 tons of supplies to forward areas.

Fourteenth AF: 2 B–24's bomb T/Os at Bakli Bay and Canton. 5 B–25's bomb Hsuchang and hit area to the NW. 19 P–51's and P–47's attack trains, trucks, troops, horses, and town areas at or near Linfen, Luan, Sincheng, Fentingtukou, Taiku, Chenghsien, Sinsiang, and Kaifeng.

FEAF: Numerous missions in spt of ground forces on Luzon, Cebu, and Negros continue. B–24's bomb Manggar and Jesselton A/Fs, B–29's hit Tarakan, and P–38's hit Kuching. B–24's hit shipping and harbor installations at Saigon.

Twentieth AF: Strikes against A/Fs continue. 80-plus B–29's bomb A/Fs at Izumi, Kushira, Miyazaki, Tomitaka, and Kanoya.

VII FC: 99 effective sorties are flown during ftr attack from Iwo Jima against Akenogahara and Suzuko A/Fs. The ftrs claim 10 aircraft downed and 15 destroyed on the ground.

23 April

Ninth AF: Weather cancels combat operations by 9th Bomb Div. Ftrs patrol Magdeburg area and US Third Army front (E of Bayreuth-Nurnberg area), fly armed rcn over E Germany and W Czechoslovakia, and operate in conjunction with XII Corps as it presses forward N of Regensburg between Danube R and Czech Border. Soviet Army forces enter Berlin.

Twelfth AF: During 22/23 Apr LBs and night ftrs hit Po crossings, M/Y, A/Fs, vehicles, trains, and T/Os in general in N and W Po Valley. During the day MBs pound Po cross-

ings, road bridges over Brenta R, and hit Brenner rail line at 4 points. The ftrs and FBs on armed rcn in N and W Po Valley attack motor transport, road bridges, and numerous tgts in spt of US Fifth Army, elements of which cross the Po R.

Fifteenth AF: 719 B–24's and B–17's attack bridges over Brenta and Adige Rivers (at Bonavigo, Zevio, Albaredo d'Adige, Legnano (2), Badia, Padua (3), and Cavarzere) and hit supply dump at Peschiera del Garda. 165 P–38's and P–51's on armed rcn of NE Italy bomb and strafe rail and road bridges, highways, trains and vehicles, and other T/Os. Other P–38's fly rcn. Other P–51's escort rcn flights and MATAF B–25 missions against tgts in N Italy.

Tenth AF: 7 P–61's attack with napalm, rockets, and cannon several tgts during sweeps from Laihka to Loilem to Hopong to Wan Yin. Laihka A/Fs, bridge S of Wan Yin, trucks, and other tgts are successfully pounded. 40-plus FBs attack troop concentrations along and behind lines at several points including Loilem, Nawng Leng, Mong Pawn, and Naungtaw. Bridge at Namhkok is temporarily out due to bomb damage to approaches. 570 transport sorties are flown to forward areas throughout the day.

Fourteenth AF: 5 B–25's blast Hsuchang railroad yards, completely demolishing a locomotive repair shop. 2 B–24's attack T/Os in S China Sea. 39 P–47's and P–51's attack troops, horses, trains, and rivercraft at or near Taiku, Shanhsien, Nanyang, Hsihhsiassuchi, Loning, Sinyang, Chenghsien, Sichuan, Lushan, and along

Pinghan railroad, and render a rail-road tunnel near Sinyang unusable.

FEAF: B–25's hit Shinei railroad yards. P–51's hit Karenko A/F and P–38's attack various T/Os. FBs continue to spt ground forces in N and S parts of Luzon pounding numerous arty positions, supply areas, and general T/Os. B–24's bomb military depot at Shanghai and shipping in Yulin harbor on Hainan I. B–29's also hit Hainan and Woody Is. B–24's bomb naval base at Saigon. Other B–24's bomb A/Fs at Sepinggang and Jesselton. P–38's drop napalm on Tarakan I tgts. Other B–24's fly shipping sweep over Makassar Strait and damage several small vessels.

Seventh AF: First element of Seventh AF, a det of 28th Photo Rcn Sq, arrives on Okinawa. 13 B–24's from Guam pound positions at Marcus.

24 April

Ninth AF: 9th Bomb Div hits A/F at Landau an der Isar and oil depot at Schrobenhausen. Ftrs fly A/F cover, escort 9th Bomb Div, fly armed rcn, and operate in conjunction with XII Corps as it continues SE between the Danube and the Czech border, and with XX Corps as it reaches the Danube SW and E of Regensburg.

Twelfth AF: During 23/24 Apr LBs bomb A/Fs at Villafranca di Verona, Ghedi, and Bergamo, M/Ys at Trento, Piacenza, and Fidenza, and vehicles and other T/Os throughout Po Valley and elsewhere in N Italy. MBs hit 6 Po R crossings and (as ground forces reach and cross the Po at several points, relieving necessity for many attacks along the river) then carry out 6 attacks between Ver-

ona and Trento on Brenner rail line. Ftrs and FBs blast vehicles on Po Valley roads N of the river and up to Brenner rail line, and also hit roads and vehicles betweeen La Spezia and Parma.

Fifteenth AF: About 700 B–24's and B–17's attack railroad bridges at Malborghetto Valbruna, Kolbnitz, Drauburg, Fermata di Brondolo, Casarsa della Delizia, Arnoldstein, and Latisana, road bridges at Spilimbergo, Bassano del Grappa, and Friola, motor transport depot at Osoppo, M/Ys at San Ambrogio di Valpolicella and Rovereto, and supply dump at Peschiera del Garda. 79 P–38's and 90 P–51's fly armed rcn over wide areas of N Italy, many strafing tac tgts N of the advancing US Fifth and British Eighth Armies. The P–38's carry out several dive-bombing missions, claiming 1 bridge destroyed and 5 damaged. Other P–51's and P–38's fly 186 sorties in escort of HBs, rcn missions, and MATAF operations. 22 P–38's complete rcn flights.

Tenth AF: About 40 P–47's and P–38's attack troop concentrations, storage areas, vehicles, and T/Os in Mong Nawng vicinity, W of Mong Kung-Laihka road, S of Loilem, and at Wan Hsan. Transports land or drop 747 tons of supplies at adv bases and in frontline areas.

Fourteenth AF: 2 B–24's bomb Hongay railroad yards and attack T/Os in S China Sea. 2 others damage a vessel at Bakli Bay. 4 B–25's hit railroad T/Os from Siaokan to Sinyang while 2 damage bridge at Kuanshuishih. 50-plus P–51's, P–61's, and P–40's attack rivercraft, railroad tgts, trucks, bridges, troops, horses, and other T/Os at numerous S and E

China locations as pressure by allied air and ground forces mounts against enemy movement and supply routes.

FEAF: A–20's and FBs continue to strike in spt of ground forces on Luzon. A–20's hit sugar refineries at Mizukami and Shinei while B–24's bomb Tainan and Hokko. Other B–24's bomb Tabanio and Miri.

Twentieth AF: 101 B–29's strike Hitahi aircraft plant at Tachikawa. 21 others hit alternates and T/Os, 5 VHBs are lost. The B–29's claim 16 ftrs destroyed.

25 April

International: Delegates from 50 nations begin Conference on International Organization in San Francisco for purpose of organizing the United Nations.

Eighth AF: Around 275 B–17's escorted by 4 P–51 gps bomb Plzen-Skoda armament works and A/F in Czechoslovakia. This is the Eighth's final HB mission against an industrial tgt. A comparable number of B–24's bombs transformer station near Traunstein, M/Ys at Hallein and Bad Reichenhall, and M/Y at Salzburg. 4 ftr gps fly spt.

Ninth AF: 296 MBs and LBs strike Erding A/F and Freilassing ordnance depot. Ftrs fly A/F cover and escort missions, and operate in conjunction with US XII Corps as it pushes along N bank of Danube SE of Passau and spt XX Corps on the Danube at Regensburg and surrounding areas. US and Soviet forces establish contact near Torgau.

Twelfth AF: All combat operations are aimed at plugging retreat routes and disrupting transport in N Po Valley and points to the N. MBs hit Adige R crossing at Cavar-

zere and M/Y at Gorizia, and attack 5 bridges and fills on Brenner line in Austria and N Italy, damaging 2 of the tgts. Ftrs and FBs harass retreating forces in N Po Valley. During 24/25 Apr LBs and night ftrs attack crossings of Adige and Po Rivers and the Canale Bianco, and strike A/Fs at Villafranca di Verona, Udine, and Bergamo, and M/Ys at Brescia and Verona.

Fifteenth AF: 467 B–17's and B–24's bomb main M/Y station, and sidings, N and S main M/Ys and freight yard at Linz, the major Austrian traffic center along railline running N to Prague, plus Wels M/Y (an alternate) and several T/Os. 119 P–38's and P–51's fly armed rcn over N Italy, a few strafing road traffic. The P–38's dive-bomb road and rail bridges and raillines. P–38's and P–51's fly almost 300 sorties in escort of HBs, P–38 rcn flights, and MATAF B–26 raids.

Tenth AF: 16 P–38's attack truck parks, fuel dumps, and supply areas at Hopong and Hotang. 20 other P–38's hit troops at Wan Kinglong and at other points in C Burma battle area. Transports complete 445 sorties to forward areas, landing or dropping 624 tons of supplies.

Fourteenth AF: 2 B–24's bomb railroad yards at Hongay. 4 B–25's and 4 P–47's damage bridge and knock out AA position N of Anyang. More than 50 P–47's and P–51's hit river, road, and rail tgts, troops, horses, and buildings in areas around Loning, Hsihhsiassuchi, Linfen, Kuanshuishih, Saiping, Yungcheng, Sichchuan, and Tsingsinghsien.

FEAF: B–24's bomb harbor at Saigon, Balete Pass bridges, and Boeloedowang and Basco A/Fs. B–25's, A–20's, and ftrs concentrate on Cagayan Valley bridges and spt ground forces around Balete Pass, Baguio, and Solvec Cove. Other FEAF spt missions continue in S Luzon from Ipo Dam to New Bosoboso, E of Santa Maria, NE of Siniloan, Anuling, Monte Banahao, near Legaspi, and S of Camalig, and in Monte Mandalagan-Monte Silay area.

Twentieth AF: Gen Joseph Smith assumes cmd of XX BC.

26 April

Ninth AF: HQ IX TAC moves from Marburg/Lahn to Weimar. 125 9th Bomb Div bmrs hit Plattling A/F. Ftrs escort 9th Bomb Div, fly A/F cover, carry out armed rcn in Germany and Czechoslovakia, drop leaflets, and cooperate with US XII Corps as its forces cross into Austria SE of Passau, and XX Corps as it begins full-scale assault across the Danube at Regensburg. Ftrs claim 19 combat victories.

Twelfth AF: During 25/26 Apr XXII TAC aircraft hit M/Ys, A/Fs, motor transport, and other comm tgts, mainly in N Po Valley. MBs complete 1 of 4 missions dispatched (cloud obscures 3 tgts), hitting Chioggia bridge and knocking out a span. XXII TAC ftrs and FBs attack enemy movement throughout afternoon, destroying over 150 motor transport.

Fifteenth AF: 107 B–24's bomb motor transport depot at Tarvisio, and M/Ys at Sachsenburg, Lienz, Spittal an der Drau, and Klagenfurt (all T/Os). 117 B–17's and 196 B–24's, also dispatched against tgts in N Italy, abort due to bad weather. 155 ftrs provide escort. 75 P–38's and 102 P–51's fly armed rcn over N Italy. Of these, 12 P–38's and 48 P–51's strafe T/Os. All of the P–38's dive-bomb raillines and road bridges. 16 other P–38's dive-bomb NW part of Alesso. Rcn and rcn escort and supply escort missions by P–38's and P–51's continue as usual.

Tenth AF: 30 P–38's and P–47's attack troop concentrations E of Wan Sing, at Naungtaw, and in Loilem vicinity. Transports land or drop 553 tons of supplies at forward bases and frontline areas.

Fourteenth AF: 2 B–24's bomb docks at Hongay. 10 B–25's and 4 P–47's knock out bridges near Wuchang and N of Taiku and damage bridge near Kaifeng. 80-plus FBs blast troops, horses, road and rail transport, tanks, gun positions, and T/Os at numerous places in S and E China as the campaign against the occupying Japanese intensifies.

FEAF: B–24's bomb Shanghai. B–25's hit Heito sugar refinery and nearby T/Os. P–38's on sweep also hit several T/Os. B–25's, A–20's, and FBs continue to fly numerous sorties in spt of ground forces in N and S Luzon. B–24's join USMC aircraft in pounding Cebu tgts. Other B–24's hit Miri A/F. B–25's and ftrs hit tgts on Tarakan I.

Twentieth AF: 195 B–29's (some escorted by ftrs of VII FC) bomb A/Fs at Usa, Oita, Saeki, Tomitaka, Imabari, Nittagahara, Miyazaki, Kanoya, Kokubu, and Miyakonojo. Other VHBs hit T/Os.

Seventh AF: 13 B–24's from Guam bomb Eten I.

27 April

Eighth AF: By this date the flow

of P-51, B-17, and B-24 replacement aircraft has stopped and authorization of 68 planes per bomb gp and 96 per ftr gp is reduced to original 48 and 75, respectively.

Ninth AF: Weather grounds 9th Bomb Div. Ftrs fly sweeps, A/F cover, and armed rcn, and attack A/Fs. Other ftrs fly air cover for US XII Corps as 11th Armd Div reaches Czech border N of Bischofsreuth and other elements move further into Austria toward Linz, and spt XX Corps as it receives surrender of Regensburg and expands its Danube bridgehead.

Twelfth AF: Bad weather throughout N Italy holds operations to a minimum. XXII TAC ftrs and FBs operate during latter part of afternoon, closely supporting ground forces in battle area N of Po R, hitting guns, vehicles, railroads, train cars, and Bergamo A/F as US 1st Armd Div spearheads the drive to the NW.

Fifteenth AF: Bad weather cancels HB operations and hampers ftr missions. 8 P-51's and 2 P-38's complete weather rcn missions. Other ftrs sent on rcn escort and armed rcn flights abort.

Tenth AF: 37 P-38's and P-47's hit troop concentrations in Wan Pong and Nawng Leng areas. 12 other FBs sweep roads S of the bomb line. Transports complete 408 sorties throughout the day, landing or dropping 618 tons of supplies at forward bases and frontline areas.

Fourteenth AF: 5 B-25's and 70-plus FBs attack bridges, positions, villages and town areas, gun emplacements, and river, road, and rail traffic at many points in S and E China chiefly around Fantung.

FEAF: B-25's attack Japanese installations at Cabatuan, La-lo, and Garit Norte. A-20's hit towns throughout the area. In S Luzon FBs and A-20's hit tgts E of Manila, in Legaspi area, and at other scattered points. B-24's hit Jesselton A/F and B-25's bomb Tarakan I. During 26/ 27 Apr B-29's bomb Tansui seaplane base. B-24's bomb Mandai A/F. HBs hit Soerabaja.

Twentieth AF: More than 100 B-29's strike A/Fs at Izumi, Miyazaki, Kokubu, Miyakonojo, Kanoya, and Kushira.

Seventh AF: 11 Guam-based B-24's bomb Woleai.

Eleventh AF: 6 B-24's drop fragmentation bombs on Kataoka naval base. 1 B-24 hits Minami Cape, and another flies a radar-ferret mission.

28 April

Ninth AF: Weather prevents all Ninth AF combat operations.

Twelfth AF: Weather severely curtails operations. XXII TAC ftrs and FBs, flying just over 100 sorties, hit enemy movement in battle area at several points from S of Piacenza to NW of Milan. MBs are grounded. Partisans apprehend Mussolini who dies before a firing squad on Lake Como.

Fifteenth AF: Continued bad weather cancels HB operations and limits ftrs to escort and weather rcn missions.

Tenth AF: 8 P-38's attack cav rgt and supplies in Namhok area. 6 others hit bivouac area near Pawngleng. 22 P-47's are detailed to strike

at troops, arty positions, trucks, elephants, and carts along and behind
enemy lines in C Burma. Despite bad
weather most of the FBs complete
missions. Transports make 441 flights
to forward areas, landing or dropping 610 tons of supplies.

Fourteenth AF: 10 B–25's bomb
Paoching A/F and Shaho railroad
yards, knock out bridge near Kaifeng, and damage bridge W of Showyang. About 80 FBs attack troops,
A/Fs, storage facilities, railroad tgts,
rivercraft, trucks, and enemy positions in S and E China, again concentrating on Fantung area. A B–24
claims a freighter sunk in S China
Sea.

FEAF: B–25's hit tgts in Itogon
area of N Luzon. A–20's attack Itogon mines and start fires among huts
at Fabrica. FBs attack Balete Pass,
Cagayan Valley, Tuguegarao, Trinidad, and Cervantes. In S Luzon A–
20's and FBs spt ground forces at
various points including Batangas
sector and hit tgts around Norzagaray, Ipo Dam, Montalban, New Bosoboso, and along San Andres trail.
B–24's bomb Toshien and several
secondary tgts. Other B–24's hit
Kuching while B–25's and P–38's hit
Tarakan I and T/Os along Sarawak
coast. B–24's over Celebes bomb
Masamba, Malimpoeng, and Mandai
A/Fs. B–25's sink about 20,000 tons
of merchant shipping in Saigon
harbor.

Twentieth AF: Around 120 B–
29's hit A/Fs at Kushira, Kanoya,
Miyakonojo, Kokubu, Miyazaki, and
Izumi. The VHBs claim a total of 14
downed ftrs.

Seventh AF: 12 B–24's from Guam
hit Param I during early morning

hours. 12 more attack Param during
the afternoon. 20 P–47's from Saipan
sweep Truk, strafing small vessels
and A/Fs at Param and Moen.

29 April

Ninth AF: Weather cancels operations by 9th Bomb Div. Ftrs fly patrols and A/F cover, hit special
tgts, fly armed rcn over E Germany
and W Czechoslovakia, and cooperate with XII Corps moving SE between the Danube and the Czech
border N of Linz, and with XX Corps
as some of its units establish bridgeheads and begin crossing the Isar R
in Plattling-Landau an der Isar-Landshut-Passau areas.

Twelfth AF: Weather again restricts operations. MBs are grounded.
Ftrs and FBs attack retreating forces
and comm throughout NE Italy including Thiene A/F and claim over
350 motor transport destroyed. Enemy forces in Italy, cmd by Gen von
Vietinghoff surrender unconditionally
at Caserta, effective 2 May.

Fifteenth AF: Bad weather again
prevents HB operations. 8 P–51's and
P–38's complete weather and photo
rcn missions. 39 P–51's fly armed rcn
over NE Italy. 5 of the ftrs bomb
and 4 strafe various T/Os, claiming
4 motor transports destroyed and a
rcn car and 2 parked aircraft damaged.

Tenth AF: 5 P–47's attack Laihka A/F. 6 others strafe troops and
horses at Tadamo. Transports fly 427
sorties to forward areas, landing or
dropping 537 tons of supplies.

Fourteenth AF: 3 B–25's and 4
P–47's blast tgts at Taiyuan railroad
yards. About 50 FBs, operating in
forces of 1–4 aircraft, blast numer

ous T/Os in S and E China, hitting especially the Fantung area.

FEAF: In spt of ground forces FBs hit troop concentrations, supply areas, pillboxes, gun positions, vehicles, and other tgts mainly in the Balete Pass, Baguio, and Echague areas. A–20's hit New Bosoboso area, where ftrs also spt ground forces concentrating in Ipo Dam area. B–24's pound Kuching A/F while B–25's bomb Tarakan I. Other B–24's hit Langoan, Mandai, and Mapanget A/Fs. P–38's sweep Indochina and strafe Thu Dau Mot A/F.

Twentieth AF: 111 B–29's strike Miyazaki, Miyakonojo, Kokubu, Kanoya (2), and Kushira A/Fs. The B–29's claim nearly 30 aircraft shot down.

Seventh AF: 20 Saipan-based P–47's sweep Truk, strafing A/Fs, defenses, and gun positions on Moen and Param and hit Param and Falas with rockets. 24 Guam-based B–24's subsequently attack the same A/Fs. 20 B–24's, operating in 2 forces, pound air installations on Marcus.

Eleventh AF: 12 B–25's attempting to bomb tgts in the Kurils abort due to weather front. 6 B–24's radar-bomb Kataoka naval base.

30 April

International: Hitler commits suicide in the bunker of his chancellery.

Ninth AF: Weather cancels 9th Bomb Div and XXIX TAC operations. IX TAC flies A/F cover, sweeps, and armed rcn. XIX TAC flies patrols and armed rcn, and cooperates with XII Corps moving SE between the Danube and the Czech border N of Linz and with XX Corps crossing the

Isar R at several points in Landau an der Isar-Landshut area.

Twelfth AF: During 29/30 Apr A–20's and A–26's hit motor transport near Lake Como and roads in Trento, San Michele all'Adige, and Bolzano areas. Bad weather grounds MBs. FBs fly armed rcn over N Italy, blasting guns, vehicles, and other T/Os.

Fifteenth AF: For fourth consecutive day bad weather cancels HB operations. P–38's fly rcn, escorted by P–51's. Other P–51's and P–38's escort supply-dropping missions to N Italy and Yugoslavia.

Tenth AF: Bad weather cancels scheduled combat strikes. Air supply operations to forward areas continue on a steady basis.

Fourteenth AF: 6 B–25's and 9 P–47's hit railroad yards at Taiyuan. 50-plus P–47's, P–51's, and P–40's attack troops, defensive positions, bridges, rail tgts, and scattered T/Os in S and E China, concentrating around Laohokow, Hsihhsiassuchi, and Loning.

FEAF: B–24's hit Toshien fuel storage and bomb Tainan, Takao, and Okayama A/Fs while B–25's hit Taito. Escorting P–38's attack numerous T/Os. P–51's bomb Okayama A/F. Numerous missions are flown over Luzon and Negros by B–25's, A–20's, and FBs in spt of ground forces. B–24's attack Davao area. P–38's hit Tarakan and B–24's bomb Manggar A/F. Other B–24's bomb Malimpoeng A/F.

Twentieth AF: 120-plus B–29's hit A/Fs at Tachikawa, Kanoya (2), Kokubu, Oita, Tomitaka, and Saeki, and city of Hamamatsu. 20-plus other B–29's hit alternates and T/Os. The

VHBs claim 10 aircraft downed. Ftrs sent from VII FC to provide VLR escort fail to rendezvous.

Seventh AF: In a thorough strafing and rocket strike on several islands of Truk Atoll, 20 P–47's from Saipan attack seaplane base, several small vessels, A/F, barracks, radio station, and numerous other tgts. 24 B–24's from Guam pound the A/Fs on Moen and Param. 22 B–24's, operating in 2 waves about 3 hrs apart, bomb air installations on Marcus.

1 May

Eighth AF: Almost 400 B–17's drop food supplies in The Hague and Rotterdam areas.

Ninth AF: 9 A–26's bomb ammo plant at Stod. IX TAC escorts LBs, flies A/F cover, and patrols Leipzig-Schwarzenberg area. XIX TAC flies patrols and armed rcn over E Germany, W Czechoslovakia, and Austria, dive-bombs Berchtesgaden, and operates with US XII Corps which is advancing SE between the Danube and the Czech border and N into Czechoslovakia N of Passau, and with XX Corps whose adv elements speed toward the Inn R at Wasserburg.

Twelfth AF: During 30 Apr/1 May A–20's and A–26's bomb T/Os in N Italy. Bad weather during the day cancels MB operations. FBs destroy numerous motor and horse-drawn vehicles in NE Italy. US Fifth Army forces approach Brenner Pass on Austro-Italian border, while British Eighth Army elements make contact with Yugoslav troops of Marshal Tito near Monfalcone.

Fifteenth AF: Despite bad weather 27 B–17's bomb main station M/Y at Salzburg. This is the final Fifteenth AF bombing mission of World War II. P–38's and P–51's fly rcn and rcn escort missions.

Fourteenth AF: During May the Japanese decide to give up their Greater E Asia Corridor and withdraw from S China. Fourteenth AF further concentrates its attacks on rail and road movements and river shipping and thus plays a major role in critically reducing the enemy's mobility and supply lines. 2 B–25's and 16 P–51's knock out bridges near Taiku and Kiehsiu and hit AA positions and locomotives near the bridges, blast gun emplacements in Loning area, and hit several locomotives, near Shihkiachwang. Gen Wedemeyer selects Gen Stratemeyer to cmd AAF China Theater, with both Tenth and Fourteenth AFs under his cmd.

FEAF: B–25's hit Heito sugar refinery and town of Kagi. FEAF continues to spt ground forces on Luzon and Negros. B–24's spt Australian landings on Tarakan I and bomb Tawau. B–25's attack Jesselton, Tarakan, Sandakan, and Kudat, concentrating on A/Fs.

Seventh AF: 16 Guam-based B–24's bomb A/F on Marcus while 10 hit air installations on Param. During the night 9 more, flying individual snooper strikes, hit A/Fs on Param and Moen.

Eleventh AF: 1 B–24 flies weather rcn over the Kurils.

2 May

Eighth AF: Almost 400 B–17's drop food supplies in populated areas in the Netherlands, mostly at Schiphol and Alkmaar A/Fs, Vogelenzang, Hilversum, and Utrecht.

Ninth AF: Weather cancels 9th Bomb Div operations. Ftrs fly A/F cover, defensive-freelance patrols, sweep over Dessau area, and patrol Straubing-Ingolstadt area and US Third Army front in Austria and Czechoslovakia. Soviet forces are in complete cmd of Berlin.

Twelfth AF: Bad weather continues. MBs are grounded while XXII TAC flies uneventful armed rcn in NE Italy.

Fifteenth AF: Bad weather limits operations to 1 weather rcn mission.

Fourteenth AF: 5 B-24's mine areas of Yangtze R. 20-plus B-25's and about 130 FBs attack comm tgts and supply lines and hit a large variety of T/Os throughout S and E China as the air campaign accelerates with aim of disrupting imminent withdrawal of Japanese and abandonment of their Greater E Asia Corridor.

FEAF: B-24's and P-51's pound troops near Ipo Dam while B-25's, A-20's, and ftrs hit Cagayan Valley tgts. FEAF strikes in spt of ground forces continue on Luzon and on Cebu I. B-25's continue spt for Australian troops on Tarakan I and, in conjunction with Navy airplanes, bomb Kudat A/F.

Seventh AF: 12 Iwo-based P-51's strike radio station on Chichi Jima. 12 B-24's from Guam pound Param A/F while 21, flying in 2 forces, hit A/Fs and gun positions on Marcus. During 2/3 May 9 more HBs make individual harassment bombings on Param, Moen, and Tol I.

3 May

Eighth AF: 390-plus B-17's drop food supplies at Schiphol and Alk-

maar A/Fs, and near Vogelenzang, Hilversum, and Utrecht.

Ninth AF: 132 A-26's (on final 9th Bomb Div raid) bomb Stod ammo plant. IX TAC escorts 9th Bomb Div and C-47's and flies A/F cover. XIX TAC patrols US Third Army front, flies armed rcn over Germany, Austria, and Czechoslovakia in frontline areas and around Kiel and Lubeck, and escorts 9th Bomb Div. XXIX TAC escorts C-47's, flies sweeps, and hits shipping in Kiel-Lubeck area.

Twelfth AF: To assure that the enemy implements surrender terms and to observe road activity, ftrs fly rcn missions over N Italy and SW Austria. MBs drop leaflets in several areas where enemy troops might be unaware of the surrender.

Fifteenth AF: Bad weather again restricts operations to rcn and rcn escort missions by 20 P-38's and escort of MATAF B-25 leaflet dropping mission in N Italy.

Tenth AF: With the fall of Rangoon on this date (Indian 26th Div elements occupy the city), the war against the Japanese in Burma is successfully concluded. Pockets of resistance remain W of the Irrawaddy and between that river and the Mandalay-Pegu railway. However, during May AAF operations are reduced drastically due to lack of suitable air tgts and because of the onset of bad weather preceding the monsoon. Tenth AF is withdrawn from combat and moved back to India (see 15 May 45). 1 sq of P-38's remains in Burma to patrol the roads leading into China.

Fourteenth AF: 9 B-25's and 6 FBs attack truck convoys in Hsiang

Valley and near Paoching, Changsha, and Hengyang, and pound railroad T/Os and bridges in Taiku, Singtai, and Linfen areas. 90-plus FBs attack troops, town areas, ammo dumps, river shipping and other T/Os over wide areas of S and E China.

FEAF: Saigon is bombed by B-24's, which greatly damage a boat-yard and oil storage areas. On Luzon B-24's and P-51's pound Ipo area while A-20's and ftrs spt ground forces. B-25's continue spt of ground forces on Tarakan and, with B-24's, carry out small raids against numer-out tgts on Borneo and Celebes. Manggar A/F is heavily hit by B-24's. P-38's and Navy airplanes hit warehouses in Brunei Bay area.

Twentieth AF: 68 B-29's bomb A/Fs at Tachiarai, Miyazaki, Miya-konojo, Kanoya (2), and Kokubu. 88 other B-29's mine Shimonoseki Strait and Inland Sea. 10 ftrs are claimed destroyed by B-29's on the Tachiarai mission.

Seventh AF: 10 Guam-based B-24's bomb A/Fs and T/Os on several islands of Truk Atoll. During 3/4 May 8 more separately strike Param, Eten, Moen, and Truk A/Fs.

4 May

Ninth AF: No bmr operations. IX TAC flies patrols and armed rcn, XIX TAC flies patrols and armed rcn and operates in concert with XII Corps assault on Linz, and with XX Corps which crosses the Inn R and pushes E and SE. XXIX TAC sweeps Dessau and Wittenberg areas and attacks shipping in Kiel and Flensburg areas. German forces in the Netherlands, NW Germany and Denmark surrender.

Twelfth AF: XXII TAC continues flying visual rcn during night and day in N Italy. US 85th Inf Div reaches Austrian border near San Candido and pushes on to Brenner Pass at Vipiteno without opposition.

Fifteenth AF: No offensive operations. Activity is limited to rcn missions (with escort), escort of MATAF leaflet drops in N Italy, and escort of C-47's on supply dropping missions to Yugoslavia.

Fourteenth AF: 12 B-25's and 180-plus FBs, mostly operating in flights of 2 to 4 aircraft, attack town areas, storage, troops, horses, trucks, river shipping, A/Fs, and many other T/Os scattered over vast expanse of S and E China.

FEAF: B-25's bomb Tuguegarao area while other B-25's, A-20's, and FBs, in spite of bad weather, spt ground forces in N and S Luzon and on Negros. P-38's pound Itu Aba I. B-24's heavily damage oil installations at Saigon. B-25's and P-38's spt ground forces on Tarakan I and B-24's hit Sandakan and Kota Baru and bomb Mandai and Masamba A/Fs.

Twentieth AF: 47 B-29's attack A/Fs at Oita, Omura, Saeki, and Matsuyama.

Seventh AF: 22 B-24's from Angaur bomb AA positions on Koror. 11 from Guam hit A/F on Marcus.

Eleventh AF: Gen Isaiah Davies replaces Gen Johnson as CG Eleventh AF on an interim basis.

5 May

Eighth AF: About 400 B-17's drop food at Schiphol and Alkmaar A/Fs, Vogelenzang, Hilversum, and

Utrecht, in the third food mission to these locations.

Ninth AF: No Ninth AF operations except tac and photo rcn in forward areas.

Twelfth AF: XXII TAC ftrs continue rcn flights over N Italy, SW Austria, and as far N as Munich. Ftrs destroy numerous aircraft at A/F SE of Munich.

Fifteenth AF: 14 P–51's escort MATAF C–47's on supply-dropping missions over Yugoslavia.

Fourteenth AF: 3 B–25's knock out bridge at Singtai and hit railroad traffic in Sinsiang area. 5 B–25's hit railroad cars and other T/Os at Kaifeng, Hsihhsiassuchi, and in Tungkuan and Luan areas. 76 FBs, operating in flights of 2–4 aircraft, attack variety of T/Os throughout S and E China.

FEAF: In first FEAF strike on Amoy area, B–24's bomb A/F and oil storage plant. B–24's bomb Shinchiku A/F while B–25's and FBs hit Taito sugar refinery, Shoka railroad yards, and Giran and Matsuyama A/Fs. A–20's and FBs continue to hit Cagayan Valley tgts and spt ground forces at various Luzon locations. B–25's and P–38's spt Australian forces on Tarakan I. On Borneo P–38's hit Miri waterfront on W coast and Keningau A/F in the N. B–24's bomb Kuching waterfront on W coast.

Twentieth AF: 45 B–29's bomb A/Fs at Oita, Tachiarai, Kanoya, and Chiran; 148 (including B–29's of 58th Bomb Wg flying their first attack of Japan from Tinian) hit navy aircraft factory and arsenal at Kure, and 86 drop mines in Tokyo Bay, Ise Bay, and at points in the Inland Sea. The B–29's claim 11 ftrs downed.

Seventh AF: 12 Angaur-based B–24's bomb Koror.

Eleventh AF: 1 B–24 flies weather mission over the Kurils.

6 May

Eighth AF: Around 380 B–17's drop food supplies at Schiphol and Alkmaar A/Fs, Vogelenzang, Hilversum, and Utrecht.

Ninth AF: No operations by 9th Bomb Div and IX and XIX TACs. XXIX TAC flies demonstration mission in Klotze area.

Twelfth AF: Gen Israel takes cmd of XXII TAC. Ftrs fly rcn over French and Italian Alps.

Fifteenth AF: 9 P–38's escort Balkan AF supply-dropping missions to Yugoslavia.

Fourteenth AF: 3 B–25's and 4 P–51's knock out bridge at Hsihhsiassuchi. 111 FBs, operating in flights of 2 to 4 aircraft, attack numerous T/Os throughout S and E China.

FEAF: B–24's bomb Matsuyama A/F and secondary nearby tgts and later bomb Toshien, Toko, and Kiirun. B–25's pound town of Mato. A–20's and FBs fly numerous attack sorties in spt of ground forces in N and S Luzon. FBs fly spt missions over Panay I. B–24's bomb Kudat and Keningau A/Fs. P–38's hit Ranau and Labuan airstrips while B–25's spt Australian troops at Tarakan I. B–24's bomb Limboeng A/F. B–25's over Indochina bomb Dong Hoi warehouses.

Seventh AF: 18 P–47's from Saipan sweep Truk Atoll, strafing A/F on Moen, seaplane base at Dublon, and shipping off Param, off Moen, and between Dublon and Fefan.

7 May

International: German High Command surrenders unconditionally all land, sea, and air forces at Reims effective 9 May.

Eighth AF: 220-plus B–17's drop food near Schiphol A/F, Vogelenzang, Hilversum, and Utrecht.

Ninth AF: XIX TAC flies sweeps over E Germany and W Czechoslovakia and carries out demonstration flights over PW camps.

Twelfth AF: P–47's fly rcn over Austrian Alps.

Fifteenth AF: 13 P–51's escort 3 Balkan AF supply dropping missions to Yugoslavia.

Fourteenth AF: 3 B–25's and 4 P–47's knock out bridge N of Singtai. 3 B–24's attack Yellow R T/Os, damaging at least 1 bridge. 131 FBs again hit various T/Os throughout S and E China, concentrating on railroad tgts.

FEAF: B–25's, A–20's, and FBs hit tgts in Cagayan Valley and spt ground action in Cervantes area, Balete Pass and N of Laguna de Bay. P–38's hit Bintula, Kudat, and Ranau while B–25's, and P–38's hit gun positions and HQ on Tarakan I. B–24's bomb Bingkalapa A/F and harbor at Soerabaja. B–25's hit railroad tgts between Cap Batangan and Cap Varella.

Twentieth AF: 41 B–29's bomb A/Fs at Usa, Oita, Ibusuki, and Kanoya. 34 aircraft are claimed destroyed by B–29's during Usa and Oita missions.

Seventh AF: 16 Saipan-based P–47's strafe radio station, A/F installations, and gun positions on Moen and Falas. 11 Guam-based B–24's pound runways on Marcus.

8 May

Ninth AF: IX and XIX TACs patrol Leipzig, Chemnitz, Adorf and Linz areas, and fly sweeps and demonstration missions.

Twelfth AF: Transports carry out evacuation and supply missions in S Europe.

Fifteenth AF: All Fifteenth AF aircraft stand down on V-E Day. Fifteenth AF offensive operations end. Subsequent operations involve transport, supply, trg, and movement flights.

Fourteenth AF: 13 B–25's knock out bridge at Do Cam and damage others at Do Len, over the Song Chu R, and N of Kaifeng. A single B–24 damages bridges at Huto. 20 P–51's pound rail and road traffic along Indochina coast while 12 P–51's and P–38's hit T/Os in several cities. About 100 FBs over wide areas of S and E China continue to hit numerous T/Os, concentrating on shipping and dock area at Taku.

FEAF: P–38's hit Jesselton, Sengkawang, and Kudat A/Fs while B–25's bomb Kuching and Labuan A/F areas. B–24's, B–25's, and FBs continue to pound Cagayan Valley. B–24's hit Davao while P–38's hit Labugan A/F area. Other B–24's bomb Mandai A/F. B–25's bomb railway installations between Phan Rang and Binh Dinh.

Twentieth AF: 40 B–29's hit A/Fs at Kanoya, Miyakonojo, Oita, and Matsuyama.

Seventh AF: 12 Guam-based B–24's bomb A/F on Marcus. 12 others from Guam pound runway on Param I.

VII FC: P–51's from Iwo Jima fly 94 effective sorties in strike against Kisarazu A/F.

9 May

Eighth AF: 453d Bomb Gp, first bomb gp to be redeployed after cessation of hostilities, begins departure from Old Buckenham to US. It is only bomb gp departing by ship.

Ninth AF: XIX TAC patrols Linz-Klatovy areas and carries out further demonstration flights.

Twelfth AF: With combat operations in S Europe at an end, transport aircraft continue supply and evacuation missions.

Fourteenth AF: 14 B–24's, 14 B–25's, and 26 P–51's blast Paoching and various nearby T/Os. Some of the FBs also attack T/Os W of Hengyang. 4 P–51's pound boxcars, locomotives, and other railroad tgts from Tourane to Hue.

FEAF: B–24's bomb 2 A/Fs in Canton area. A–20's and ftrs fly offensive sweeps over Cagayan Valley and spt ground forces in the Cervantes Baguio-Balete Pass area and the Ipo-New Bosoboso-Infanta area. B–24's bomb area around Dalirig and Maluko preparatory to allied landings in Macajalar Bay area on 10 May. P–38's over Borneo hit Brooketon, Sarawak and Tarakan I.

Seventh AF: 14 P–47's from Saipan sweep Truk. 29 B–24's from Guam, operating in 3 forces over a 6-hr period, bomb A/Fs, barracks, and T/Os on Param and Moen Is.

Eleventh AF: Radar discloses considerable shipping between Para-

mushiru and Shimushu. Thus, 12 B–24's take off and radar-bomb through overcast. Another B–24 flies a radar-ferreting sortie over Paramushiru and Shimushu.

10 May

Eighth AF: Effective this date, Gen Doolittle, CG, is relieved of duty in ETO and assigned to HQ AAF, Washington. He is relieved by Gen Kepner.

Ninth AF: 9th Bomb Div is redesignated 9th Air Div. No operations for TACs and 9th Air Div.

Fourteenth AF: 19 B–25's and 4 P–47's attack bridges at Fengstun and Pinyang, on the Song Chu R, and N of Singtai (Pinyang tgt is destroyed), hit Yungfengshih and Chingshuping, and bomb A/F at Paoching. 100–120 FBs pounding T/Os over S and E China, disrupt enemy movement and supply lines.

FEAF: B–24's bomb A/F in Canton area. A–20's and FBs hit Cagayan Valley tgts and spt ground action in battle zones throughout Luzon. B–24's hit Impasugong, Kalasungay, and Malaybalay and B–25's in spt of ground forces attack Kibawe and Tagolaan. B–24's bomb Makassar ship basins, shore tgts at Balikpapan on Borneo, and Limboeng A/F on Celebes. B–25's, with ftr escort, hit Kari and comm T/Os on Formosa.

Twentieth AF: 42 B–29's hit A/Fs at Matsuyama, Usa, Miyazaki, and Kanoya. 302 others bomb Tokuyama naval fuel station and coal yards, Otake oil refinery, and Amami-O-Shima naval oil storage facilities. B–29's claim 10 aircraft destroyed.

Seventh AF: 11 Guam-based B–24's bomb A/F on Marcus in the morning. During afternoon 19 B–24's flying in 2 forces, hit A/Fs on Param and Moen.

Eleventh AF: The Eleventh and Fleet Air Wing Four execute the heaviest and most successful joint mission to date. 12 B–24's bomb shipping tgts at Kataoka naval base, and fly photo rcn over E and W Paramushiru on return trip. Next, 16 Attu-based B–25's take off. 1 aborts while the others hit shipping between Kashiwabara and Kataoka. Heavy AA fire claims 1 B–25. A B–24 and a B–25 forceland in the USSR.

11 May

Fourteenth AF: 6 B–25's and 4 P–47's knock out Chungmow bridge and damage bridge at Sincheng. 2 B–25's bomb truck convoys in Paoching, Hengyang, and Changsha areas. 60-plus FBs hit troops, arty positions, comm tgts, and general T/Os in S and E China, concentrating on Yangchi and Fantung areas.

FEAF: B–24's bomb Toshien A/F and towns of Koshun, Kato, Takao, Toko, and Shajo. B–25's pound Kagi. B–25's, A–20's, and FBs continue to spt ground action near Paranum and in Ipo Dam sector. B–24's bomb A/F at Keningau and B–25's bomb Brunei Bay area. B–24's hit Mandai and Boeloedowang A/Fs.

Twentieth AF: About 50 B–29's attack A/Fs at Oita, Saeki, Nittagahara, Miyazaki, and Miyakonojo. 92 others bomb Kawanishi aircraft plant at Kobe. B–29's claim 9 ftrs downed on Kobe mission. Missions against Japanese A/Fs terminate air campaign, begun on 17 Apr, during which Twentieth AF has devoted major effort toward hitting sources

of *Kamikaze* raids against US Navy and Marine forces in the Battle of Okinawa.

Seventh AF: 14 P–51's from Iwo Jima strafe and bomb radio station at Chichi Jima. 10 Guam-based B–24's hit A/F on Param, while 13 pound Marcus I runways.

12 May

Ninth AF: XIX TAC flies demonstration missions.

Twelfth AF: Large-scale redeployment of Twelfth AF units officially begins (although first large movement to ZI has earlier taken place on 12 Jan 45, followed by redeployment of various units to all the theaters). On 12 May the Twelfth has 198 units assigned and 8 attached. By the end of May, 17 assigned units will be redeployed from the theater, 43 assigned serv units disbanded (and personnel used to form 21 new serv units), 9 assigned units transferred to other HQ in the theater, and 1 attached unit released —leaving 150 assigned and 7 attached units intact.

Fourteenth AF: 17 B–25's and 8 P–51's bomb barracks and storage area at Loyang and hit railroad tgts around Sinsiang and Sinyang, from Hankow to Sinyang, from Chenghsien to Szeshui, from Kioshan to Lohochai, and between Hengshan and Yoyang and knock out bridge N of Hengyang. 150-plus FBs again hit scattered tgts in S and E China, concentrating on road, rail, and river traffic and supply lines.

FEAF: A–20's and FBs spt ground forces on Luzon and Negros. B–24's pound several railroad and road bridges at Binh Dinh, Phu My, Bong

Son, Lai Ha, Tuy Hoa, and Phu Hiep and attack railroad yard at An Trach and other railroad tgts. B-24's, B-25's, and P-38's hit tgts in Brunei Bay area including Labuan, Brooketon, and Jesselton A/Fs and troops on Tarakan I. B-24's bomb Makassar shipyards and Limboeng A/F.

Seventh AF: 9 Guam-based B-24's bomb A/F on Marcus while 12 more hit A/F on Param.

13 May

Fourteenth AF: 5 B-24's lay mines in Yangtze R. 10 B-25's and 5 ftrs knock out bridges at Hankow and Hengyang but fail to hit bridge N of Siaokan. 130-plus FBs over areas of S and E China attack troops, bridges, rail traffic, town areas, and other T/Os and generally disrupt Japanese movement and comm.

FEAF: B-24's again pound bridges along Indochina coast. Bmrs and ftrs pound Cagayan Valley tgts and continue spt of ground forces on Luzon. B-24's hit troop concentrations and caves in Bugnay area. Other B-24's bomb Oelin and Tabanio A/Fs while B-25's and P-38's bomb Sandakan and spt ground forces on Tarakan I.

Twentieth AF: During 13/14 May 12 B-29's drop mines in Shimonoseki Strait.

Seventh AF: 10 B-24's from Guam bomb underground hangar on Moen. 9 other HBs strike A/F on Marcus.

14 May

Fourteenth AF: B-24's mine the Yangtze R. 15 B-25's and 6 FBs hit river shipping near Hengshan and pound bridges and other railroad

tgts around Chushihtien, Sinyang, Kioshan, Kuanshuishih, Hengyang, Chuchou, Changsha, Yoyang, Sintien, Hsuchang, Saiping, and Hengshan. 120-plus FBs over S and E China hit numerous T/Os at several locations concentrating on Liping and Tungkow areas.

FEAF: B-24's bomb Hozan (largest military and air supply center on Formosa). A-20's and FBs spt ground forces on Luzon and Negros. B-24's attack Jesselton and Sepinggang A/Fs. B-25s hit Jesselton, Kudat, and Bintula A/Fs and spt ground forces on Tarakan I. B-24's lightly raid Makassar harbor, Sidate A/F, and Parepare warehouses and bomb Bima A/F on Soembawa.

Twentieth AF: 472 B-29's blast urban area of N Nagoya. 11 VHBs are lost. About 20 enemy ftrs are downed. This is the XXI BC's first 4-wg raid as VHBs of the 58th Bomb Wg join bmrs from the 73d, 313th, and 314th Wgs in a single mission.

15 May

Tenth AF: Tenth AF moves from Myitkyina to Piardoba.

Fourteenth AF: A single B-24, supported by 2 P-51's, seriously damages 3 bridges near Singtai and Linmingkuan. 20 B-25's, some with ftr escort, bomb bridges, barracks, troops, horses, road and railroad tgts, and general T/Os around Sinyang, Yoyang, Changsha, Hsuchang, Chenghsien, Sichuan, Pinyang, Tsinkong, Luchou, Kweiping, Tanchuk, Laohokow, Siangyang, Nanying, Paoching, and Hengyang. 150 FBs over S and E China attack a variety of tgts chiefly road, rail, and river traffic, troops, and bridges, at many scattered locations. Liping and Tungkow areas are again well covered.

FEAF: B–24's bomb Shinchiku. Other B–24's and B–25's hit Miri and Kudat A/Fs and spt ground forces on Tarakan I. P–38's pound troop concentrations and gun positions on Mount Mandalagan.

Eleventh AF: 13 B–24's bomb Kashiwabara-Kataoka area, claiming one ship destroyed, and a direct hit on another, and investigate radar activities. Low fog limits observation of other results. AA fire damages 2 B–24's, 1 of which forcelands in USSR.

16 May

Fourteenth AF: B–24's continue to lay mines in Yangtze R. 33 B–25's and 16 P–47's and P–51's attack railroad tgts, barracks, HQ, bridges, town areas, river shipping, and T/Os at or near Kaifeng, Sinyang, Chungsiang, Chienyangi, Ichang, Chingmen, Yanglowtung, Kiyang, Loyang, Szeshui, Hsihhsiassuchi, Shanhsien, Neihsiang, Liuchou, Kweiping, Nanyo, Shihlipu, Hojung, Mingkiang, and Kioshan. 100-plus FBs attack river, road, and rail traffic, troops, gun positions, and generally harass Japanese movement and supply lines in S and E China hitting especially T/Os in Yangchi.

FEAF: Nearly 100 P–38's pound tgts in Ipo Dam area with napalm. B–24's hit Manggar, Tondano, and Balikpapan while B–25's and P–38's hit Miri, Brooketon, Bintula, Ft Brook, and a flak ship near Labuan I. P–38's also spt ground forces on Tara-

kan I. B–24's bomb Taichu and B–25's hit alcohol plants and railroad yards.

Twentieth AF: 25 B–29's mine Shimonoseki Strait and Maizuru and Miyazu harbors.

Seventh AF: 13 Guam-based B–24's bomb A/F on Marcus. 11 others sent against Marcus abort because of bad weather.

17 May

Fourteenth AF: 16 B–25's and about 100 ftrs continue to disrupt comm and supply lines and hinder enemy withdrawal from numerous locations of S and E China, pounding town areas, troop concentrations, storage areas, river, road, and rail traffic and general T/Os.

FEAF: During sweeps over Formosa, B–25's and P–51's cause widespread damage hitting railroad yards, bridges, and alcohol plants. B–24's bomb A/Fs at Nanseiho and Matsuyama. Ftrs fly 130-plus sorties against Ipo Dam area. B–24's bomb Sepinggang, Manggar, and Sidate A/Fs.

Twentieth AF: Between 0300 and 0600, 457 B–29's pound urban area of S Nagoya. 11 others hit T/Os.

Seventh AF: Ftrs from Iwo Jima fly 41 effective strike sorties against Atsugi. Pilots claim 10 parked aircraft destroyed. During 17/18 May 2 P–47's of 318th Gp, presently arriving on Ie Shima (between 13–19 May), fly heckling mission over Kyushu—the first such Seventh AF mission against Japan.

18 May

Eighth AF: Troop Movement Section is organized at HQ Eighth AF under Director of Operations. It is to be the control unit over all redeployment activities.

Fourteenth AF: 9 B–25's blast Siangtan supply areas. 8 B–25's, supported by 7 P–51's, hit railroad tgts and other T/Os around Sinyang, Kiaotow, Sintsiang, and Chenghsien. About 75 FBs and rcn airplanes continue harassment of enemy movement and supply lines throughout S and E China, escort of C–47 transports, and surveillance of enemy forces.

FEAF: B–24's bomb Taichu and Tainan A/Fs. B–25's and FBs sweep Formosa hitting numerous tgts. B–25's, A–20's, and FBs spt ground forces in N Luzon and pound concentrations in S Luzon. FBs also spt ground forces on Negros. B–24's and B–25's hit Ft Brook and Sarawak while B–24's and P–38's attack defenses on Tarakan I.

Twentieth AF: Adv air echelon of 509th Comp Gp arrives at North Field on Tinian. The 509th is scheduled to deliver atomic bomb attacks on Japan. Its CO is Col Paul W Tibbets Jr, a pilot with a distinguished record in the 97th Bomb Gp (H) in Europe and N Africa. During 18/19 May, 30 B–29's mine Shimonoseki Strait and Tsuruga Harbor.

Seventh AF: 8 P–47's from Ie Shima make bombing, strafing, and rocket attacks on radar and ground installations on Kume Jima in Amami Gunto. Other P–47's fly heckler strikes against Kyushu during 18/19 May.

Eleventh AF: 8 B–24's bomb naval, harbor, and A/F tgts in Kataoka. Another B–24 searches for enemy radar along the Kuril Is.

19 May

Fourteenth AF: 4 B–25's blast Kaifeng warehouse area, destroying at least 5 warehouses, while another hits nearby railroad tracks. Another B–25 bombs town of Shanhsien. About 90 FBs attack river, road, and rail shipping, troops, supplies and general T/Os, continuing the disruption of troop movement and withdrawal in S and E China.

FEAF: B–24's pound Kiirun harbor. B–25's sweep W Formosa coast, hitting several tgts including Toyohara, Nisui, and along the Ts'eng-Wen R, hitting railroad yard, storage facilities, and damaging alcohol plant on the Ts'eng Wen. Ftrs sweep Giran, Tainan, and Heito areas. B–25's, A–20's, and FBs spt ground forces throughout Luzon, concentrating in Ipo Dam area. P–38's spt ground action on Cebu. B–24's bomb Oelin A/F and, along with P–38's, attack tgts on Tarakan I.

Twentieth AF: 272 B–29's bomb city of Hamamatsu.

Eleventh AF: 8 B–25's try to bomb Minami Cape radar installation and cannery on the Naka R. Only one gets near tgts and bombs and strafes the area, while intense AA fire and enemy ftrs drive off the rest and down 1 B–25. Another is missing and a third reaches Petropavlovsk.

20 May

Fourteenth AF: 55 P–51's and P–40's pound truck concentrations, fuel dumps, gun positions, supply areas, troops, bridges, rail, road, and river traffic, and various T/Os around Liping, Yangchi, Siangtan, Yoyang, Yungfengshih, Paoching, Taohwaping, Hengyang, Tungkow, and Changsha.

FEAF: Despite bad weather B–25's over Formosa bomb various comm tgts and alcohol plant at Meiji. B–25's, A–20's, and FBs pound Cagayan Valley tgts. B–24's bomb Piso Pt, and FBs spt ground action in Bukidnon area. P–38's hit Sandakan, Keningau, and Tarakan I. B–25's hit shipping at Balikpapan harbor and nearby barracks area and sawmill.

Twentieth AF: During 20/21 May, 30 B–29's mine Shimonoseki Strait, Maizuru harbor, and He-Saki anchorage.

Seventh AF: 16 Saipan-based P–47's strafe A/Fs on Moen and Eten and seaplane base and barges off Dublon. 10 Guam-based B–24's hit air operations building on Marcus. 9 P–47's from Ie Shima hit hangar and 2 boats at Fukue-Shima. 32 others hit A/Fs, railroads, buildings, and radar facilities on Kyushu.

21 May

Fourteenth AF: 8 B–25's bomb bridge approach N of Hankow, 1 damages railroad track between Changsha and Kweiyi, and 2 score near misses on bridge at Kuanhsuishih. 3 B–25's and 6 P–51's damage bridge at Chihsien and hit railroad T/Os in Anyang area. 50-plus FBs on armed rcn continue attacks against river, road, and rail traffic, positions, troops, bridges, and numerous other tgts in S and E China.

FEAF: B–25's blast numerous tgts in Cagayan Valley while A–20's and P–51's spt ground forces in NW Luzon sectors. P–38's napalm-bomb Ipo Dam and Marikina R sectors and hit positions throughout Negros I.

B–24's hit Brunei, Melak airstrip, Samarinda shipyards, and troop concentrations on Tarakan I. P–38's strafe railroad rolling stock in Saigon area.

Seventh AF: P–47's fly heckler strikes against Kyushu during 21/22 May.

22 May

Fourteenth AF: 15 B–25's and 7 FBs knock out rail bridge at Hei-Shih Kuan, damage bridge approach at Hwayuan, and hit a variety of tgts S of Kuo-lueh-chen. 10 P–51's drop napalm on trucks, barracks, storage, trains, and town areas at Sinyang, and Shanyangchen. 45 other FBs and photo rcn airplanes attack railroad tgts, bridges, troops, and other tgts at several S and E China points and survey enemy movements.

FEAF: B–24's bomb Toshien and Okayama while B–25's hit oil plant W of Kagi and several T/Os. B–25's, A–20's, and FBs attack Santa Fe, Fula, and Casambalangan areas in the N part of Luzon and spt ground forces in Ipo Dam and Marikina areas in the S. HBs, MBs, and FBs attack Jesselton, Kudat, Bintula, and Tarakan I.

Twentieth AF: During 22/23 May, 30 B–29's mine Shimonoseki Strait and approaches.

23 May

Ninth AF: Gen Weyland assumes cmd of Ninth AF. Gen Sanders becomes CG XIX TAC. XIX TAC flies navigational patrol to Gmunden, Liezen, Radstadt, and Innsbruck.

Fourteenth AF: 14 B–25's and 6 P–51's attack bridge and gun positions N and S of Hwayuan, knock out bridge and hit boxcars at Chungmow, damage bridge N of Lohochai, damage bridge and nearby gun positions at Kuanshuishih, and pound truck convoys around Paoching, Hengyang, and Changsha. 30-plus FBs hit various T/Os around Liping, Yoyang, Changsha, Hengyang, Luntangpu, Chingmen, Shasi, and Ichang.

FEAF: A–20's and B–25's hit Cagayan Valley and Balete Pass tgts. P–51's spt ground forces in Baguio area and P–38's hit Ipo-Antipolo areas. Tawau, Bintula, Samarinda, and Miri are hit by HBs, Ft Brook and Weston by MBs, and Tarakan I by FBs.

Twentieth AF: During 23/24 May, 520 out of 562 B–29's sent against Tokyo bomb an urban-industrial area S of the Imperial Palace along W side of the harbor. 5 others hit T/Os. 17 B–29's are lost. This is the largest number of B–29's participating in a single mission during World War II.

Seventh AF: 32 P–47's from Saipan strafe Moen A/Fs and boats off Tol, buildings on Tarik, and seaplane base, buildings, and small boats at Dublon.

Eleventh AF: 7 B–24's radar-bomb Kataoka naval base area while another flies a radar-ferret mission in the same area.

24 May

Ninth AF: Gen Sanders becomes CG 9th Air Div.

Fourteenth AF: 5 B–25's knock out railroad bridge N of Anyang. 30-plus FBs attack railroad tgts, truck convoys, bridges, and other T/Os around Anyang, Sichuan, Kuolueh-chen, Kuantaokou, Luntangpu, Houpo, Laohokow, Sinsiang, Nan-

yang, Kiehsiu, Linfen, Taiyuan, Puchou, and Yutze.

FEAF: B–24's pound Cagayan Valley tgts including Aparri. B–25's, A–20's, and P–51's hit numerous tgts throughout the Valley and in NW and S Luzon, including Vira, Callang, Santa Cruz, Baguio, Balete Pass, Ipo, and Antipolo areas. FBs also spt ground forces on Negros. B–24's, B–25's, and P–38's attack Ft Brook, Bintula, Tawau, Beaufort, Jesselton, along the Lawas R, and Malinau.

Twentieth AF: During 24/25 May, 25 B–29's lay mines in Shimonoseki Strait and at Niigata, Nanao, and Fushiki.

Seventh AF: 26 Guam-based B–24's pound A/F and surrounding area on Marcus. P–47's fly heckler strikes against Kyushu during 24/25 May.

VII FC: 120 Iwo Jima-based ftrs dispatched against Matsudo and Tokorozawa abort because of weather.

25 May

JCS: JCS approve directive for Operation OLYMPIC, the invasion of the Japanese Home Islands, scheduled for 1 Nov 45.

Fourteenth AF: 5 B–25's and 2 P–51's knock out a bridge N of Kioshan, damage another N of Changtuikuan, and pound railroad tgts around Sinyang, Saiping, Sinantien, Hsuchang, and Chenghsien. 16 FBs on armed rcn hit various T/Os in Anyang, Hantan, Chenghsien, Kaifeng, Linfen, Shihkiachwang, Sinsiang, Miyanghsien, Nanyang, Tenghsien, Loning, Sichuan, and Hsuchang areas.

FEAF: B–25's, A–20's, and FBs fly numerous strikes and ground spt missions. FBs also spt ground forces on Cebu I. B–24's bomb Oelin, Ft Brook, and Tarakan I while B–25's and P–38's hit Kudat. P–38's also spt ground action on Tarakan.

Twentieth AF: During 25/26 May, 464 B–29's pound urban area of Tokyo immediately S of the Imperial Palace just N of that bombed on 23/24 May, including financial, commercial, and governmental districts as well as factories and homes. 26 B–29's are lost on this mission, the highest single-day loss of VHBs in World War II. US gunners claim 19 ftrs destroyed.

VII FC: By concurrence of CINCPOA, VII FC, with its subordinate units, is assigned to operational and administrative control of Twentieth AF. Iwo Jima-based ftrs fly 73 effective strike sorties against Matsudo and Tokorozawa.

Eleventh AF: 2 B–24's fly a radar-ferret mission over Matsuwa and bomb Tagan Cape area. Another B–24 flies armed weather rcn.

26 May

Twelfth AF: Gen Myers assumes cmd of Twelfth AF.

Fifteenth AF: Gen Mollison assumes cmd of Fifteenth AF.

Fourteenth AF: 12 B–25's and 6 P–51's damage 2 bridges N of Hankow. 4 B–25's hit railroad tgts around Lohochai and between Kinkiang and Kioshan. 3 B–25's attack truck convoys in Siangtan and Paoching areas and along Paoching-Hengyang-Changsha highway. 80-plus FBs over several areas in S and E China continue to harass Japanese movements, attacking troops and positions and hitting rail and road traffic. Japanese complete withdrawal from Yung-ning, severing land connection with Indochina. Chinese retake Nanning.

FEAF: B–25's and P–38's sweep W part of Formosa causing extensive damage to a variety of comm and industrial tgts. A–20's and FBs pound numerous Luzon tgts, particularly in Balete Pass area. B–24's bomb Tuguegarao and Echague. FBs also spt ground forces on Cebu. B–24's, B–25's, and FBs hit Tarakan I, Beaufort, Weston, Tenom, Trusan Haji, Sandakan, and Jesselton.

Twentieth AF: During 26/27 May, 29 B–29's mine waters in Shimonoseki Strait and at Fushiki, Fukuoka, and Karatsu.

Seventh AF: 16 P–47's from Saipan strafe A/Fs on Moen, seaplane base on Dublon, and several T/Os. 10 Guam-based B–24's bomb A/F on Marcus.

27 May

Fourteenth AF: 15 B–25's bomb textile mill at Chenghsien, attack trains, railroad track and bridge in Lohochai area, and bomb railroad yards at Sinyang. 80-plus FBs attack town areas, trucks, railroad tgts, bridges, and general T/Os at scattered S and E China locations.

FEAF: B–24's pound railroad yards and rolling stock at Muong Man and Phan Rang. B–25's and FBs attack tgts at Koshun, Shinei, Tairin, Ensui, Kohyo, and Kobi and attack numerous T/Os at many other Formosan locations. B–24's, A–20's, and FBs hit Cagayan Valley tgts while other FBs spt ground forces in Balete Pass, Baguio, and Ipo Dam sectors. HBs, MBs, and FBs attack Tawau, Kudat, Langkon, and Sandakan, and hit tgts on Tarakan I.

Twentieth AF: During 27/28 May 9 B–29's drop mines in Shimonoseki Strait and in Moji area.

Seventh AF: 16 Saipan-based P–47's sweep Truk, strafing A/F, aircraft, and radio tower and facilities at Moen, buildings at Dublon seaplane base and on Udot I, and small craft off Dublon and Fanamu.

28 May

Fourteenth AF: 19 B–25's, along with 8 FBs, hit railroad, road, and river traffic around Vinh, Quang Tri, Dap Cau, and Song Chu, knock out bridge at Hwayuan, and demolish tunnel opening near Wuchang. 16 P–51's cause heavy damage and casualties blasting a bridge and military installations near Wuchang. 27 P–51's hit bridges, troops, storage, trucks, trains, rivercraft, and other tgts in Yoyang area. 65 other FBs attack T/Os at several locations throughout S and E China. 15 photo rcn airplanes continue to maintain good coverage of enemy movements.

FEAF: B–24's again bomb railroad yards E of Saigon at Phan Rang and Muong Man. B–25's and FBs attack industrial T/Os at Shoka, Taichu, Ujitsu, Byoritsu, and other Formosan locations. B–24's, B–25's, A–20's, and FBs attack Pateng, Ipo Dam area, Tuguegarao and Ugac airstrips, Anuling, Baguio area, guns and defenses in Balete Pass area, and spt ground forces at several points. B–24's, B–25's, and ftrs hit gun positions and other tgts at Balikpapan. P–38's dive-bomb Keningau and Jesselton A/Fs.

VII FC: Ftrs from Iwo Jima hit Kasumigaura and its A/F. 6 planes are claimed destroyed and 40-plus damaged. P–47's fly heckler strikes against Kyushu during 28/29 May. Japanese wage their last strong air effort on Okinawa hitting a number of ships and sinking destroyer USS *Drexler*.

29 May

Fourteenth AF: A single B–24 damages railroad bridge over Huto R. 4 B–25's and 4 P–51's knock out bridge S of Kuanshuishih. 2 B–25's over Indochina attack locomotives near Vinh. About 30 FBs attack comm and transportation tgts around Yoyang, Thanh Hoa, Vinh, Quang Tri, Vinh Yen, and Chenghsien.

FEAF: More than 100 B–24's bomb Kiirun and several other towns on Formosa. B–25's, and FBs hit Tainan alcohol plant and T/Os in Tokyo area. B–24's, B–25's, and A–20's hit a variety of tgts in N while other FBs hit C part of Luzon including Cagayan Valley, Baguio, Balete, and Ipo areas. HBs hit A/Fs at Oelin, Tabanio, and Ft Brook.

Twentieth AF: Ground echelon of 509th Comp Gp begins to arrive on Tinian. 454 B–29's, escorted by 101 P–51's from the VII FC for first time on a fire-bomb raid, bomb Yokohama with incendiaries and destroy the main business district (a third of the city's area) along the waterfront. Burned out area of Yokohama now amounts to almost 9 sq mi. About 150 ftrs attack the formations. 7 B–29's and 3 P–51's are lost. The P–51's claim 26 ftrs shot down while the VHBs claim 6.

Eleventh AF: 4 B–25's weather-abort a shipping sweep along the E coasts of Paramushiru and Shimushu.

30 May

Fourteenth AF: 7 B–25's pound railroad yards at Sinsiang and knock out bridge at Sincheng. 28 FBs attack bridges, enemy positions, trucks, railroad tgts, barracks, and general T/Os around Anyang, Liuchow, Chingmen, Chungmow, Linfen, Huluehchen, Kweilin, Hsinganhsien, Leiyang, and Yenkoupu.

FEAF: On Formosa 100-plus B–24's pound Takao while ftrs sweep coastal areas. B–25's concentrate on Shinei area. A–20's hit Cagayan Valley tgts. HBs and ftrs hit several tgts in Borneo, concentrating on Tawau personnel and supply area and airstrip at Ranau.

Seventh AF: 10 Guam-based B–24's hit Marcus A/F. 14 P–47's strafe barges at Truk Atoll. 28 P–47's from Ie Shima hit shipping and lighthouse at Amami-O-Shima and Okino Erabu.

31 May

AAF: USAAF units, including Tenth AF and US components of EAC, are withdrawn from SEAC and returned to operational control of AAF. EAC is inactivated, along with the Strategic AF and Combat Cargo TF.

Fourteenth AF: 5 B–25's and 4 P–47's hit railroad tracks and cars in Chenghsien and Kaifeng areas, knock out bridge at Sinyang, damage bridge at Lohochai, and strafe AA positions at both bridges. 30-plus FBs damage 4 bridges, hit several railroad tgts and rivercraft, attack trucks and troops, and strafe numerous T/Os around Shihkiachwang, Changsha, Yoyang, Yenkoupu, Taohwaping, Changanyi, Chiuchiang, Liuchow, Tsingkong, and Paoching.

FEAF: B–24's, B–25's, and FBs attack Formosan tgts, with 90-plus HBs concentrating on Takao. Other planes hit Koshun, Giran warehouses and comm tgts, and blast transportation and comm tgts over wide areas of Formosa. B–25's, A–20's, and FBs hit tgts in Cagayan Valley, in Balete Pass, and in Baguio and Ipo areas. FBs also hit Negros I. B–25's and FBs hit troop concentrations on Tarakan I and occupied building area at Belait. FBs also blast A/Fs at Kudat, Jesselton, Keningau, and Labuan.

Seventh AF: 8 P–47's from Ie Shima strafe buildings, barracks, and seaplane ramps at Amami-O-Shima.

1 June

Eighth AF: The Operational Analysis Section ceases to function as a unit after a successful career of statistical research which assisted materially in improving the effectiveness of US strategic bombing.

Fourteenth AF: 6 B–25's bomb Sinsiang railroad yards while 4 B–25's and 4 P–47's damage bridge N of Linmingkuan. 18 P–51's hit river shipping, warehouses and other tgts in Yoyang area. 20 other FBs knock out bridge near Szeshui, pound river shipping near Yoyang, and attack various tgts in Huluehchen area.

FEAF: B–24's pound Takao while ftr aircraft sweep Formosa coastline. B–25's, A–20's, and FBs continue to hit tgts in Cagayan Valley, at Pingkian, Kayapa, Gattaran, Cumao, Bone, and in Ipo area. Many of the missions are ground spt strikes. B–24's and P–38's hit Tarakan I troop concentrations while B–24's, B–25's, and P–38's hit Kota Belud, Victoria,

Jesselton, Langkon, and Labuan I.

Twentieth AF: 458 B–29's attack city of Osaka. 148 P–51's of VII FC, en route to escort rendezvous with the VHBs, encounter a severe weather front. Flying behind in excessive turbulence, many of the ftrs collide. 27 are lost. 27 others manage to find the B–29's and escort them over the tgt. 10 B–29's are lost. The B–29's claim 16 ftrs destroyed.

Seventh AF: In the Ryukyus 12 P–47's from Ie Shima fly strafing and rocket attacks against Kikaiga, Tokuno, and Amami Gunto.

Eleventh AF: A 4-plane shipping strike is called off due to weather.

ZI: AAF Center is established with jurisdiction over AAF School of Applied Tactics (formerly AAF Tac Center), Proving Ground Cmd, and AAF Board.

2 June

Fourteenth AF: 2 B–25's blast fuel and ammo dumps NE of Nanyang. 20 FBs attack A/F at Tsinan, railroad yards and T/Os at Anyang and warehouse area at Paoching, knock out bridge S of Singtai, and hit trucks, tanks, and armd vehicles in Liuchow area.

FEAF: B–25's, A–20's, and FBs continue to hit Cagayan Valley in force, spt ground forces in Balete Pass and Ipo sectors, and attack areas E of Manila and N of Baguio. FBs hit areas near Mount Mandalagan on Negros and dug-in positions NW of Bogo. B–24's hit Pontianak A/F and Tarakan and Labuan Is while B–25's and ftrs attack Kudat, Sandakan, and Miri. B–24's bomb Hozan and hit warehouses and dock facilities at Kiirun.

Seventh AF: 11 Guam-based B–24's attack A/F area on Moen. P–47's fly heckler strikes against Kyushu during 2/3 Jun.

3 June

Fourteenth AF: 5 B–25's and 25 P–51's blast warehouse area and river traffic at Liuchow. 2 B–25's bomb Sinyang-Lohochai railroad. A single B–24, escorted by 2 P–51's, damages bridge N of Shihkiachwang. 4 P–51's damage bridge E of Kiehsiu and strafe train and lumber carts N of Linfen. Bad weather curtails other scheduled FB missions.

FEAF: HBs and ftrs hit resistance areas on Negros. HBs attack Kota Waringin and Muara I, while HBs bomb Batavia. P–51's hit coastal cargo vessels over SE China coast.

Seventh AF: P–47's on heckler patrol strafe T/Os an Amami-O-Shima.

Eleventh AF: 1 B–24 flying a radar-ferret mission to Kataoka is followed by 8 others, radar-bombing and photographing scattered tgts in the naval base area. 7 B–25's take off for Kurils, 4 are turned back by weather. The others low-level bomb Masugawa R Cannery.

4 June

Fourteenth AF: 12 B–25's heavily damage railroad yards and warehouses at Sinsiang. 10 B–25's and 4 P–51's in repeat attack on the yards cause numerous fires. 2 B–25's and 3 P–51's hit road and railroad T/Os from Sinyang to Hsuchang. 17 ftrs bomb or strafe bridges, railroad traffic, and other T/Os around Chihsien, Linfen, Shihkiachwang, and Liuchow.

FEAF: FBs attack T/Os in Cagayan Valley and A–20's and FBs supporting ground forces strike defensive positions in Balete Pass, Aritao, Mount Imugan, Carulay, and Bambang. B–24's bomb Taihoku. B–24's bomb Balikpapan and Manggar and spt ground forces on Tarakan I. B–25's hit Manggar, Djembajan, and Kudat.

Seventh AF: 8 P–51's from Iwo Jima bomb radio station on Chichi Jima and strafe town of Okimura during return flight. 13 Guam-based B–24's hit A/F and boat basin on Marcus. P–47's fly heckler strikes against Kyushu during 4/5 Jun.

Eleventh AF: 8 B–25's abort a shipping strike at Kurabu Cape due to weather. 11 B–24's, however, get through and radar-bomb Kataoka naval base.

5 June

Fourteenth AF: 32 B–25's and 8 P–51's bomb city of Nanyang, hit railroad yards at Anyang, damage bridge approach at Chuanhsien, and bomb ferries at Ninh Binh and Dap Cau. 40-plus ftrs bomb and strafe rail, river, and road traffic and general T/Os throughout S and E China.

FEAF: B–25's, A–20's, and FBs hit Cagayan Valley tgts while other FBs spt ground actions in Cervantes, Balete Pass, and Ipo battle zones and hit forces E of Manila. B–24's bomb Melak, Asa, and Kuching A/Fs and Tarakan and Labuan Is, while B–25's and ftrs concentrate on Tuaran, Mensalung, and Kudat. HBs pound Taito.

Twentieth AF: 473 B–29's pound city of Kobe with incendiaries. 11 VHBs are lost. US gunners claim 86 ftrs downed. The attack burns off over 4 sq mi and damage over half of the city.

Seventh AF: P–47's from Ie Shima patrol over Amami Gunto. Lighthouse is strafed.

6 June

Ninth AF: HQ Ninth AF moves from Chantilly to Bad Kissingen.

Fourteenth AF: 11 B–25's and 9 P–51's bomb railroad yards N of Siaokan and damage bridges, strafe gun positions, and attack general T/Os around Saiping and Hwayuan. 30-plus ftrs bomb or strafe bridges near Chihsien and Fengstun and hit troops, railroad tgts, and T/Os around Linfen, Laohokow, Changsha, Peking, Kweilin, Dap Cau, and Thanh Hoa.

FEAF: A–20's and FBs blast bridges in Cagayan Valley. Other FBs pound Balete Pass area. B–24's, B–25's, and FBs hit Labuan supply areas, spt troops on Tarakan, and bomb Kota Waringin and Pontianak A/Fs, areas along Belait R, around Brunei, and strike Miri, Jesselton, Kudat, and Beaufort. Bad weather cancels all missions against Formosan tgts.

Seventh AF: 12 Guam-based B–24's hit oil storage buildings on Eten. 36 Ie Shima-based P–47's, sweeping S part of Kyushu, hit numerous T/Os with rockets and machinegun fire, and claim 9 aircraft downed. In the Ryukyus, Ie Shima-based P–47's patrol over Amami Gunto, strafing lighthouse and buildings.

7 June

Twelfth AF: Maj Gustav M Minton Jr, takes cmd of XXII TAC, which ceases to function. Maj Minton continues in the cmd until transfer to AAFSCMTO on 12 Aug.

Fourteenth AF: 7 B–25's and 4 P–47's damage bridge near Anyang, bomb buildings N of Changsha and airstrip at Paoching, and hit T/Os during road and river sweep from Siangtan to Yoyang. 45 ftrs bomb or strafe numerous tgts including troops, river traffic, town areas, and supplies in S and E China and knock out bridges at Singtai and Chihsien.

FEAF: A–20's and FBs hit personnel and def positions near Infanta, at Mount Mapatad, in Marikina area, and in other areas in Ipo sector. In the N FBs pound numerous Cagayan Valley tgts and spt ground forces N of Baguio and E of Manila. B–24's pound Brooketon and Muara. MBs and FBs hit Kudat, Ft Brook, Belait, Jesselton, and Keningau.

Twentieth AF: 409 B–29's, escorted by VII FC P–51's, drop incendiary and high explosive bombs on Osaka, hitting E–C section of the city which contains industrial and transportation tgts and the Osaka Army Arsenal (largest in Japan). Despite being forced to bomb by radar because of heavy undercast, the B–29's burn out over 2 sq mi of the city, destroying over 55,000 buildings. 26 other B–29's mine Shimonoseki Strait and waters around Fukuoka and Karatsu.

Seventh AF: 24 B–24's from Angaur bomb boat repair basin on Aurapushekaru I. 20 P–47's from Ie Shima hit T/Os (radio station, warehouses, freighter, and motor launches) on Kyushu, and claim 5 aircraft downed.

8 June

Ninth AF: XXIX TAC (having been activated as a prov cmd on 14 Sep 44) is activated by Ninth AF.

Fourteenth AF: 15 P–51's and P–40's attack bridges near Hankow, N of Sinsiang, and SE of Tayung, knocking out the latter. 17 other ftrs bomb and strafe rivercraft, warehouses, trucks, A/F, town areas, and general T/Os around Hwangkang, Ichang, Hengyang, Laohokow, and Tehsien.

FEAF: Bad weather cancels Formosa strikes and limits operations on Luzon to FB strikes against Cagayan Valley tgts. Labuan I A/F is bombed by B–24's, while other B–24's and B–25's and P–38's attack gun positions at Balikpapan.

VII FC: Iwo Jima-based ftrs dispatched against Kagamigahara A/F and Meiji abort due to bad weather.

9 June

Fourteenth AF: 3 B–25's and 60-plus P–47's, P–51's, and P–40's damage 4 bridges, hit river shipping, pound town areas and villages, and attack various T/Os around Hwayuan, Changte, Suchow, Sinyang, Hankow, Laohokow, Nanyang, Tatung, Tashihkiao, Pinyang, Luchai, Kiehsiu, Linfen, Tsinan, and Shihkiachwang.

FEAF: Labuan I is bombed by B–24's. Other HBs drop napalm on Brooketon. FBs hit Cagayan Valley tgts and spt ground forces in Cervantes areas as ground forces penetrate last defensive position on Mindanao. Bad weather cancels operations N of the Phil Is.

Twentieth AF: 110 B–29's attack aircraft factories at Nagoya, Akashi, and Narao. 26 others mine Shimono-seki Strait during 8/9 Jun.

Seventh AF: 20 P–47's from Ie Shima strafe various T/Os on Kyushu.

VII FC: 57 ftrs from Iwo Jima pound Kagamigahara A/F and surrounding area. 20-plus parked airplanes are claimed destroyed or damaged.

Eleventh AF: In coordination with Navy surface and air forces attacking in the Kurils, 6 B–24's and 8 B–25's fly extensive armed weather rcn and anti-shipping sweeps over Kurabu and Otomari Capes, Ichino-watashi, and Asahigawa. The B–24's score no results, half of them jettisoning their bombs. The B–25's then fly a diversionary bombing mission over Araido where they are attacked by 8 ftrs. To evade them, the B–25's fly over Kamchatka where Soviet AA fire shoots down one, killing its crew. Another damaged B–25 crashlands in Petropavlovsk. This is the first time Soviet AA hits a US aircraft.

10 June

Fourteenth AF: 14 P–51's damage bridge near Singtai and attack barracks, rivercraft, fuel dumps, trucks and other T/Os around Taohsien, Lingling, Liuchow, and Kaifeng.

FEAF: FBs again pound Cagayan Valley area and spt ground forces E of Manila. HBs bomb Labuan I and Brooketon in coordination with landings of Australian 9th Div on shore of Brunei Bay and on islands of Labuan and Muara.

Twentieth AF: 280 B–29's, some escorted by P–51's of VII FC, bomb aircraft plants at Tomioka, Chiba,

and Ogikubo, seaplane base at Kasumi-gaura, Tachikawa Army Air Arsenal, and engineering works at Hitachi. The ftrs claim 26 ftrs downed.

Seventh AF: 39 Ie Shima-based P–47's sweeping Kyushu, strafe numerous ground T/Os, and claim 17 aircraft shot down.

Eleventh AF: 2 B–24's fly with Navy aircraft on shipping attack and hit a small cargo vessel.

11 June

Fourteenth AF: 4 B–25's, with ftr escort, bomb railroad yards at Kuan-shuishih. 29 ftrs attack bridges, rail and road traffic, rivercraft, and T/Os in general around Fenglochen, Liu-chow, Samshui, Luchai, Lipu, Lei-yang, and Kweilin.

FEAF: B–25's, A–20's and FBs hit Cagayan Valley tgts and pound forces E of Manila in Ipo-Infanta areas and various tgts N of Baguio. Ground spt strikes are flown in Mari-kina R sector. B–24's spt ground forces on Tarakan I and bomb Kota Baru, Laoet I, and Tawau. P–38's hit Beaufort while B–25's spt ground forces in Brunei Bay sector.

Twentieth AF: Combat crews of 509th Comp Gp begin to arrive at North Field, Tinian, with their B–29's. 26 B–29's mine Shimonoseki Strait and Tsuruga Bay.

VII FC: Iwo Jima-based ftrs hit Tokorozawa. Pilots attacking the A/F claim 18 parked airplanes destroyed and over 30 damaged.

Eleventh AF: 8 B–24's on shipping sweep over the Kurils do not find tgts because of overcast and instead radarbomb installations on Kurabu Cape and in Kataoka areas.

12 June

Fourteenth AF: 2 B–25's knock out bridge S of Yutze while 4 escorting P–47's hit nearby AA positions and afterwards pound railroad tgts at Linfen. 9 P–51's and 2 P–61's damage bridge N of Hengyang, hit storage area at Yunganshih, and attack railroad tgts, troops, horses, AA positions, and road traffic in Neikiuhsien and Hengyang.

FEAF: B–24's inflict heavy destruction on navy yard and dock area at Hong Kong and railroad yards at Saigon. 2 B–32's bomb airstrip on Batan I. Numerous FBs and B–25's hit Cagayan Valley tgts while other FBs spt ground forces N of Baguio and Balete Pass and E of Manila, and yet others concentrate on Tarakan I, Brunei Bay area, and coastal routes in N Borneo.

Seventh AF: 12 Guam-based B–24's pound A/F on Marcus.

Eleventh AF: 4 B–25's strafe shipping off Paramushiru, near Arahata Cape, damaging 4 freighters and 2 barges. One of the B–25's is shot down.

13 June

Fourteenth AF: 11 B–25's and 7 P–51's considerably damage Kaifeng railroad yards and strafe comm center S of Puchou. 8 P–51's damage 2 bridges at Fenglochen and Shihkiachwang and hit railroad T/Os around Fenglochen and Suchow.

FEAF: Bad weather hinders B–24's over Formosa. A few hit Toshien, the primary tgt. Others hit alternates including Toko, Koshun, Kontei, Garan-bi Point, Taito, Mako naval base and other Formosan tgts. 2 B–32's bomb Koshun A/F. A–20's and FBs attack Cervantes area, Marikina area, tgts in Cagayan Valley, and islands N of Luzon. B–24's bomb Balikpapan-Sepinggang area. B–25's and FBs spt ground forces in Brunei Bay area and, sweeping N Borneo from Kudat to Miri, hit numerous T/Os.

Twentieth AF: 29 B–29's drop mines in Shimonoseki Strait and in waters at Niigata, during 13/14 Jun.

Seventh AF: 13 B–24's from Guam bomb A/F on Moen. Over 40 P–47's from Ie Shima strafe and fire rockets at vessels, buildings, radio station, barracks, and A/Fs at Amakusa Jima, Amami-O-Shima, and Tokuno.

14 June

JCS: Gens MacArthur and Arnold and Adm Nimitz are directed to prepare for immediate occupation of Japan in the event the enemy suddenly collapses or surrenders.

Fourteenth AF: 42 P–51's attack bridges, shipping, AA positions, railroad tgts, trucks, and comm around Hengyang, Hankow, Yoyang, Lingling, Anyang, Szeshui, Hohsien, Shihkiachwang, Neikiuhsien and Puchou.

FEAF: B–25's, A–20's, and FBs pound areas around Cagayan Valley, Cervantes and N of Baguio and E of Manila. B–24's bomb warehouses at Parepare and personnel area at Sidate. B–24's bomb Balikpapan AA positions.

15 June

Fourteenth AF: 3 B–25's and 47 P–51's and P–47's knock out bridge W of Shihkiachwang, damage and attack others, and hit trucks, barracks, rivercraft, storage facilities, gun positions, railroad tgts, and T/Os.

Tgts are in Pinghan RR, Kukong, Lingling, Chenhsien, Kuotaichiao, Pakonghow, Kweilin, Anyang, Shihkiachwang, Loyang, Liuchow, and Paoching areas.

FEAF: B-24's bomb Taichu A/F. B-25's hit town of Rokko and A/F at Okaseki. On Luzon numerous B-25's, A-20's, and FBs pound various objectives, concentrating on Cagayan Valley, Cervantes area, and Antipolo-Ipo sector. B-24's blast gun positions at Balikpapan and B-25's and P-38's hit areas between Brunei and Kudat.

Twentieth AF: 44 B-29's fly incendiary mission against Osaka-Amagasaki urban area, ending a month of concentrated fire raids against large Japanese cities. 30 other B-29's mine Shimonoseki Strait and waters around Fukuoka, Karatsu, and Fushiki. VII FC escort for Osaka raid aborts due to bad weather.

16 June

Fourteenth AF: 2 B-25's hit supply movements on Paoching-Hengyang road. 41 P-51's attack bridges, shipping, road transport, power facilities, and railroad traffic, knocking out bridges near Siangtan, Changsha, and Suchow. Rail, road and river traffic is attacked near Yoyang, Hengyang, Kuanyang, Shou-yang, Peking, and Linfen. Power plant at Uong Bi is heavily damaged.

FEAF: B-25's, A-20's, and FBs hit personnel and supply tgts in Cagayan Valley and E of Manila, and spt ground forces in Cervantes sector. B-24's bomb Balikpapan gun emplacements, Tawau, and Samarinda, while B-25's hit Brunei Bay area and FBs attack Miri, Jesselton, Ken-

ingau A/Fs and N Borneo T/Os. 90-plus B-24's pound Kiirun harbor and town of Takao. 3 B-32's bomb Taito.

Seventh AF: P-61's arrive on Ie Shima and take over night heckler missions against Kyushu from the P-47's. Other P-61's fly night intruder missions over Amami Gunto, bombing various T/Os. 38 P-47's from Ie Shima dive-bomb boats, AA positions, runways, and buildings on Kikai I.

Eleventh AF: 4 B-24's bomb and strafe shipping off Suribachi Bay and a radar site on Minami Cape. One of the B-24's crashes into the water. 4 B-25's on a shipping strike score near misses on a freighter in Asahi Bay and bomb tgts along the Torishima Chain. Mechanical failures force 2 of the B-25's to fly to Petropavlovsk.

17 June

AAF: Gen Arnold requests of Gen Wedemeyer that Gen Stratemeyer replace Gen Chennault as head of AFs in China.

Fourteenth AF: 2 B-25's bomb road and rail supply movements in Paoching and Hengyang areas. 2 B-25's and 4 P-47's severely damage bridge at Linmingkuan. 54 P-51's, P-47's, and P-61's hit road transport, railroad, river traffic, gun positions, bridges, and T/Os around Kukong, Hankow, Lingkuantien, Changsha, Yoyang, Loyunghsien, Luchai, Hwangshapu, Kiyang, Kweilin, Kaifeng, and Shihkiachwang. 4 P-47's blast comm center at Puchou.

FEAF: B-25's, A-20's, and FBs pound Cagayan Valley tgts and numerous other objectives throughout N Luzon. Many of the strikes spt US Sixth Army forces. B-24's pound Balikpapan area oil tgts and gun positions. B–25's and P–38's hit Limbang town and sweep from Beaufort to Jesselton, hitting Beaufort buildings, several comm tgts at various points, and personnel areas at Labuan I. B–24's bomb industrial and railroad tgts at Kiirun. P–38's pound railroad bridge and trucks at Soton.

Twentieth AF: 450-plus B–29's bomb urban areas of Kagoshima, Omuta, Hamamatsu, and Yokkaichi, with incendiaries, while 25 others mine Shimonoseki Strait and waters around Kobe—all during 17/18 Jun.

Seventh AF: 33 P–47's from Ie Shima bomb and strafe shipping, A/F, villages, bridge and radar and radio facilities on Amami Gunto and Tokuno. During 17/18 Jun 2 P–61's from Ie Shima fly unsuccessful (due to weather) intruder strike over Amami Gunto and Kyushu. This begins a campaign of night and day intruder missions over Kyushu I and the Ryukyu Is by the night ftrs (12 more are flown during Jun).

Eleventh AF: 4 B–25's bomb shipping near Kataoka. One ship is observed exploding, another burns after a strafing run. 4 other B–25's fly a shipping sweep from Shimushu to Kurabu Cape. A number of vessels are sighted but cannot be attacked because of land-based AA.

18 June

Fourteenth AF: 70-plus P–51's, P–61's, and P–47's continue to disrupt Japanese withdrawal from S and E China, attacking bridges, villages and town areas, barracks, troop concentrations, motor transport, shipping and rail traffic, and T/Os throughout wide areas.

FEAF: Supporting US Sixth Army forces on Luzon, B–25's, A–20's, and FBs continue to attack tgts in Cagayan Valley, Balete Pass area, Cervantes area, and other locations. B–24's blast troop concentrations in Balikpapan and S of Miri, Manggar A/F and Sepinggang defenses. B–25's spt ground forces on Labuan I. B–24's destroy a block of buildings and several warehouses and small vessels in Kiirun harbor area. P–51's hit Taien and Toyohara A/Fs and T/Os while P–38's start numerous fires in town of Kari.

Eleventh AF: 6 B–24's join Navy aircraft in attacking Kataoka and Tomari Cape. Cloud cover prevents observation of effects. 1 B–24 flies radar-ferret mission over the Kurils.

19 June

Fourteenth AF: 5 B–25's and 4 P–47's knock out bridge on Pinghan railroad while 4 P–51's knock out another NE of Kihsien on Tungpu railroad. 70-plus other P–51's damage several bridges, hit rail, road and river traffic, supplies, troops, and general T/Os throughout S and E China.

FEAF: A–20's and FBs continue to pound Luzon, chiefly around Cagayan Valley, SE of Aparri, and around Cervantes. Heavy strikes in C Cagayan area are in spt of guerilla offensive. B–24's bomb fortifications and AA guns at Balikpapan while B–25's hit N Borneo tgts including Keningau A/F and tgts N and NW of Kudat. Other B–24's bomb docks, warehouses, and railroad yards at Kiirun. B–25's pound Shoka railroad yards and P–51's attack AA positions between Rokko and Toyohara. 2

bridges in Shoka area are destroyed or badly damaged.

Twentieth AF: About 480 B–29's fly incendiary bombing raids on Toyohashi, Fukuoka, and Shizuoka during 19/20 Jun, while 28 others mine Shimonoseki Strait and waters at Niigata, Miyazu, and Maizuru.

Seventh AF: 22 Guam-based B–24's bomb A/F on Marcus. 47 Ie Shima-based P–47's bomb A/F on Tokuno while 16 others patrol uneventfully over Amami-O-Shima.

VII FC: Ftrs dispatched from Iwo Jima against Kagamigahara A/F and Meiji abort because of bad weather.

Eleventh AF: In a coordinated shipping search, a B–24 flies theater's longest mission, a 2,700-mi round-trip lasting 15 1/2 hrs and flying as far as Uruppu I. Turning N the B–24 bombs a small convoy 25 mi SW of Shimushu Bay, sinks vessel, heavily damages another, and sets 2 more afire. Another B–24 bombs and photographs Matsuwa I. 4 B–25's break off a shipping sweep due to presence of ftrs.

20 June

Fourteenth AF: 8 B–25's and 6 P–51's knock out 2 bridges near Quang Tri and My Chanh and blast surrounding AA positions. 8 FBs sink at least 3 river steamers in canal at Haiphong. 37 P–51's hit rail, road, and river traffic, bridges, and general T/Os around Liuchow, Kweilin, Juchai, Hankow, Siangtan, Changsha, Hengshan, Sintsiang, Kweiyi, Kueiyangshih, and Ft Bayard. Bridge at Hankow is destroyed and several others damaged.

FEAF: A–20's and FBs blast resistance on Luzon and directly spt

guerilla offensive in C Cayagan Valley. HBs again pound AA positions in Balikpapan area. B–24's bomb Shinchiku A/F.

Seventh AF: From Ie Shima 14 P–47's bomb and strafe vessels, buildings, lighthouse, and village on Amami Gunto A/F on Tokuno I. 38 others bomb A/F at Omura and hit Tokuno I on return trip.

21 June

Eighth AF: Gen Larson relieves Gen Kepner as CG, Eighth AF.

Fourteenth AF: 16 B–25's bomb enemy fort at Bac Ninh, hit railroad yards and trains at Thanh Hoa, Phu Dien, Yen Li Station, Ha Trung, and Ninh Binh, damage tunnel at La Son, bomb barge concentration at Ha Dong, and attack a train near Duc Tho bridge. 40-plus P–51's and P–38's hit road, rail, and river transport, coastal shipping, troops, supply lines, and T/Os in Indochina and S and E China.

FEAF: FBs attack positions and supply areas in the Cagayan Valley, other locations in N Luzon and in the Marikina and Infanta areas in C Luzon. B–24's pound Balikpapan town area, Manggar A/F, Sepinggang defenses, and Oelin A/F. B–25's bomb town on Keningau while P–38's blast the nearby A/F. The FBs attack Kudat and caves near Jesselton. P–38's hit tgts at Mato and Kagi and T/Os along W coast.

Twentieth AF: 25 B–29's mine the sea approaches around Fushiki, Senzaki, Nanao, and Yuya Bay during 21/22 Jun.

Seventh AF: 24 B–24's from Guam bomb fuel oil storage and power plant buildings on Eten I.

22 June

Fourteenth AF: 23 B–25's and 4 P–47's pound trucks, trains, and gun positions in Hanoi area, bomb railroad yards and barracks area at Sinsiang, hit rail and road tgts, buildings, and radar station in Showyang area, knock out bridge S of Saiping, and damage bridge N of Hsuchang. 40-plus ftrs hit rail, road, and river traffic, arty emplacements, line positions, and other tgts in Indochina and S and E China.

FEAF: FBs supporting ground action continue to hit concentrations and positions in Cagayan Valley. B–24's pound Balikpapan area gun and def positions while B–25's hit nearby warehouses and numerous other buildings. P–38's dive-bomb and score direct hits on pillboxes. B–24's hit Toshien oil facilities and P–38's attack Mato. 2 B–32's blast gun positions and barracks at Heito. US ground forces complete capture of Okinawa.

Twentieth AF: About 130 B–29's bomb aircraft plants at Himeji, Kagamigahara, Akashi, and Tamashima. 162 others pound naval arsenal at Kure.

Seventh AF: Over 40 P–47's from Ie Shima fly combat patrols over Amami Gunto, claiming 11 aircraft downed.

Eleventh AF: Gen Brooks becomes CG, Eleventh AF.

23 June

Fourteenth AF: 4 B–25's knock out E approach to Phu Lang Thuong bridge. 12 P–51's strafe A/Fs in Canton area. 4 P–38's bomb locomotives and barracks area at Les Pins and Lang Son. 17 other ftrs strafe railroad tgts and river traffic around Wuchou, Siaokan, Peking, Hanoi, and Vinh.

FEAF: 150-plus B–24's, B–25's, and FBs continue heavy strikes against Balikpapan area concentrating on gun emplacements and def positions. A–20's and FBs pound troop concentrations and occupied areas in Cagayan Valley. FBs attack pockets of resistance at Infanta and Antipolo areas. B–24's bomb butanol plant at Kobi.

Twentieth AF: During 23/24 Jun, 26 B–29's mine harbors of Fukuoka, Karatsu, Sakai, and Niigata.

Seventh AF: Gen White becomes CG, Seventh AF. 38 P–47's from Ie Shima bomb A/Fs at Hakata and Itazuke and, during return flight, attack 2 boats off Amami Gunto. 40 other P–47's bomb Saitozaki A/F.

VII FC: Ftrs from Iwo Jima fly 99 effective sorties against A/Fs on Kagamigahara and Hyakuri. 19 aircraft are claimed downed and 21 destroyed on the ground.

Eleventh AF: 2 B–24's on shipping sweep between Matsuwa and Paramushiru sink 1 freighter, damage 2 more, and hit a whale boat. 1 ftr is claimed destroyed. 6 more B–24's bomb Kataoka.

24 June

Fourteenth AF: 13 B–25's and 12 FBs knock out bridges at Lohochai and S of Chenghsien and hit surrounding AA positions, attack animal-drawn transport at Hsiangcheng, attack railroad T/Os in Shihkiachwang area, and hit railroad yards at Siaokan. 40-plus FBs continue harassing enemy withdrawals in S and E China where numerous comm tgts, gun positions, bridges, and rail, road, and river traffic are attacked.

FEAF: Fifth AF A–20's and FBs spt US Sixth Army and Filipino troops in Kiangan sector and N and NE of Tuguegarao, blast numerous tgts throughout Cagayan Valley, Cervantes area concentrations, and Infanta-Antipolo resistance pockets. B–24's bomb Balikpapan town and coastal guns. FBs pound coastal guns while B–25's bomb warehouses and nearby Manggar A/F.

Seventh AF: At dawn 1 B–24 from Guam bombs buildings on Marcus. During the afternoon 18 more bomb the A/F. 36 P–47's from Ie Shima attack boats and village in Sakishima Archipelago, wharf at Kuro I, Ishigaki I, and buildings, villages, T/Os and several points in the Ryukyus.

Eleventh AF: 2 B–24's on shipping sweep instead radar-bomb Kurabu Cape, because of overcast and turbulence. Another planned shipping strike by 6 B–25's is also cancelled due to weather.

25 June

Fourteenth AF: 18 B–25's and 14 P–51's and P–47's knock out bridges N of Shihkiachwang and N of Saiping, bomb power plant, barracks, and warehouse at Sinsiang, bomb Nanyo-Hengyang road, and hit railroad yard at Siaokan. 80-plus FBs attack bridges, gun positions, river, road, and rail traffic, and generally harass Japanese movements throughout S and E China, particularly around Hengyang, Yoyang, Liuchow, Changsha, Lipu, and Luchai.

FEAF: Oil facilities, shore defenses and nearby Manggar A/F on Balikpapan area are well covered by HBs, MBs, and FBs. B–24's bomb Mandai A/F. On Luzon MBs and FBs hit tgts (mostly troop concentrations and resistance pockets) in Cagayan Valley, in Cervantes area, and in Infanta sector.

Twentieth AF: During 25/26 Jun 26 B–29's plant mines in Shimonoseki Strait and at Maizuru and off Obama I.

Seventh AF: At dawn 3 B–24's from Guam attack heavy AA positions on W coast of Marcus.

26 June

Fourteenth AF: 21 P–51's bomb or strafe road, river, and rail traffic, motor pools, gun positions, and buildings around Yoyang, Hengyang, Chenghsien, Linfen, and Tsinan, and knock out bridge SW of Yutze.

FEAF: FBs hit tgts in Infanta area and troop concentrations in Cagayan Valley and Kiangan area. Ground spt strikes are flown in Cervantes area and E of Manila. Strikes against Balikpapan area continue by B–24's and B–25's hitting oil tgts and nearby A/F at Manggar. B–24's bomb Trombol airstrip. Other B–24's bomb A/F at Limboeng. P–61's during 25/26 Jun set fires at Ensuiko sugar refinery while B–24's hit sugar refinery at Tanshi during the day.

Twentieth AF: 450-plus B–29's, escorted by VII FC P–51's, attack aircraft plants at Kagamigahara, Nagoya, and Akashi, light metals industries and arsenals at Osaka and Nagoya, oil refinery at Yokkaichi (bombed by 315th Bomb Wg on its first raid on Japan from Guam), other factories at Nagoya, and several alternate tgts and T/Os, including city of Tsu. B–29's claim more than 20 ftrs downed.

Seventh AF: 1 Guam-based B–24 attacks heavy AA positions on W side of Marcus at dawn.

27 June

FEAF: During 26/27 Jun HBs over Soerabaja Strait area bomb Tandjoeng-perak A/F. For the fifteenth consecutive day, B–24's pound Balikpapan destroying oil facilities and shore defenses. B–25's hit warehouses, other buildings, and general waterfront area. Other B–24's bomb Mandai and Limboeng A/Fs. FBs hit Kiangan area, troop concentration NW of Bolog, Pagong area, and Bontoc-Sabangan area, provide ground spt near Montalban, and hit tgts in Infanta sector.

Twentieth AF: During 27/28 Jun, 29 B–29's mine harbors of Hagi, Kobe, and Niigata.

Seventh AF: In early morning raid from Guam, 3 B–24's bomb underground storage area and fortifications on Marcus. At midday 18 B–24's pound A/F on Moen. 20 P–47's from Ie Shima hit shipping and village at Kikai I. AA from vessels downs 2 P–47's. 1 vessel is left aflame. 12 other P–47's hit shipping off Kakeroma I, while 20 more attack vessels and T/Os throughout Sakishima Archipelago. During 27/28 Jun, 5 P–61's fly intruder attacks, hitting vessels off Amami Gunto and Wan A/F.

VII FC: Ftr strikes, from Iwo Jima, against Kasumigaura, Imba, and Tsukuba are aborted because of weather.

28 June

Fourteenth AF: 7 B–25's and 4 P–51's bomb town of Changsha, troop concentration and supply area, and blast truck convoys and ammo trains in Yoyang area. 28 P–51's hit comm center S of Puchou, knock out bridges near Kiehsiu and Neikiuhsien, bomb gun emplacements and defensive positions SE of Hsihsiakou, and attack railroad traffic and damage a road bridge in Suchow and Yoyang areas.

FEAF: B–24's pound installations in Manggar area while B–24's, B–25's, and P–38's hit defenses near Balikpapan. The P–38's also skip-bomb oil storage. Other HBs hit runways at Tabanio and Oelin. B–24's bomb A/Fs at Limboeng and Langoan. FBs hit troop concentrations in Kiangan area while supporting ground forces and attack Japanese concentrations and positions between Ipo and Infanta. B–24's strike Keishu butanol plant.

Twentieth AF: During 28/29 Jun, 487 B–29's carry out fire-bomb attacks on Okayama, Sasebo, Moji, and Nobeoka.

Seventh AF: 3 B–24's from Guam bomb fuel storage on Marcus. 39 P–47's from Ie Shima attack shipping at Koniya with rocket and bombing and hit Tokuno I with rockets and machinegun fire. 26 more hit T/Os in Sakishima Archipelago including vessels, docks, A/F, floatplane, and village.

29 June

Fourteenth AF: 15 B–25's and 4 P–47's knock out bridge at Chungmow and damage another. 18 P–51's attack troop concentrations, gun emplacements, villages, bridges, and T/Os around Hsihsiakou, Yutze, Anyang, Puchou, and Szeshui and knock out bridge at Szeshui.

FEAF: Continuing offensive against Balikpapan, B–24's, B–25's, and FBs bomb def positions and oil installations. Other B–24's bomb Ft Brook and Oelin A/Fs. FBs spt ground forces in Kiangan area and in Cervantes sector. Other B–24's bomb oil refinery at Shinchiku.

Twentieth AF: During 29/30 Jun, 32 B–29's bomb Nippon Oil Company at Kudamatsu while 25 others mine W Shimonoseki Strait and waters around Maizuru and Sakata.

Seventh AF: 34 P–47's from Ie Shima hit A/Fs at Kanoya and Kushira on Kyushu with rockets and machinegun fire, and attack shipping while returning, claiming 7 small vessels sunk.

30 June

Twelfth AF: Organization charts show a further net loss during Jun. 16 units have been transferred to other HQ within the theater, 1 sent directly to the Pacific, another redeployed to US, 3 disbanded, 9 prov units discontinued, and 5 attached units relieved (plus a Brazilian unit attached for operations being released). Only 2 units are added to the Twelfth.

AAF, China Theater: HQ AAF, China Theater is established by a GO from HQ, US Forces, China Theater. Gen Stratemeyer is appointed CG. Subordinate elements are Tenth and Fourteenth AFs, China ASC, and a photo gp.

Fourteenth AF: 2 B–25's attack bridge at Lohochai, causing little

damage. 4 FBs pound hill positions and hit arty emplacement SW of Hsihsiakou. 3 others bomb and strafe enemy-held temple and a troop area at Likuanchiao.

FEAF: FBs spt ground forces in Cervantes sector, N of Baguio and pound gun positions and other tgts in Kiangan area as Luzon campaign officially ends at midnight. B–24's again pound Balikpapan. B–25's pound tgts in NE Borneo and cause considerable damage at Tawau and Tandjoengredeb.

Twentieth AF: 509th Comp Gp, scheduled to deliver first atomic bomb attack on Japan, begins combat flight training from Tinian. For most crews, this involves 5 or 6 practice missions such as a navigation trg flight to Iwo Jima, bombing Rota during the return flight; 2 or more short bombing missions against Rota or Guguan I; and 1 long bombing mission against Truk; and 1 against Marcus—all run in flights of from 2 to 9 VHBs.

Seventh AF: 2 Guam-based B–24's attack boat basin on Marcus.

1 July

Fourteenth AF: A few B–25's bomb bridge and ferry terminal at Chungmow and near Kaifeng. 4 escorting P–47's strafe Kaifeng A/F and locomotives in the area. 4 other P–47's bomb railroad yards at Yuhsiang. 4 P–51's knock out bridge E of Kiehsiu. On this date Chinese forces capture Liuchow.

FEAF: B–24's pound defenses at Balikpapan as Australian forces make amphibious landings. B–24's, B–25's, and P–38's hit A/Fs at Oelin, Tabanio, and Trombol, and bomb

Tawau area. B–24's hit Limboeng and Mandai airstrips. FBs hit troops and gun positions in Kayan-Tadian area.

Twentieth AF: 530-plus B–29's carry out incendiary attacks on Ube, Kure, Shimonoseki, and Kumamoto. During 1/2 Jul, 24 other B–29's mine Shimonoseki Strait and waters at Nanao and Fushiki.

Seventh AF: 2 B–24's from Guam bomb building concentration on Marcus. 33 B–25's, operating in two flights from Okinawa, bomb Chiran A/F on Kyushu. 2 others hit Yaku I.

VII FC: 84 Iwo Jima-based ftrs hit tgts at Kasumigaura, Itami, Hamamatsu, and Nagano.

ZI: HQ, Weather Wg is redesignated HQ, AAF Weather Serv.

2 July

Fourteenth AF: 28 P–51's hit rail, river, and road traffic, bridge, and buildings around Hengyang, Hankow, and Yoyang, attack bivouac area and HQ E of Changsha, bomb troop concentration and buildings at Yangan. The FBs pound HQ, buildings, fortified compound, barracks, general T/Os around Tartin, and **troop concentration** near Sichuan.

FEAF: B–24's bomb defenses in Balikpapan area and P–38's spt Australian forces as they complete capture of Balikpapan and its oil installations. B–25's hit Bintula personnel area. FBs hit resistance pockets near Kiangan and supply areas in the Cervantes sector. B–24's pound Toyohara A/F.

Twentieth AF: During 2/3 Jul, 39 B–29's bomb oil refinery at Minoshima.

Seventh AF: 3 B–24's from Guam attack radar installation on Marcus.

3 July

Fourteenth AF: 3 B–25's knock out bridge near Suicheng while 2 P–47 escorts hit nearby AA positions. 70-plus P–51's and P–47's continue to disrupt Japanese withdrawal, attacking transport, supply, and comm tgts, troops, bridges and Japanese-held points. The tgts are near Hengyang, Paoching, Kueiyangshih, Changsha, Kweilin, Lingling, Kukong, Hankow, Siangtan, Isuho, Chiuchiang, Fahsien, Tanchuk, Lohochai, and Luichow Peninsula. The FBs also hit shipping, cement plant, A/F, and barracks area near Haiphong.

FEAF: Fifth AF ftrs fly their first mission over Japan, P–51's destroying floatplanes in Fukuoka harbor area. FBs hit resistance areas in Mankayan and Kiangan sectors. B–24's bomb runways at Mandai and Limboeng A/Fs. B–24's pound Batu Kawa airstrip SE of Kuching and def positions near Balikpapan in spt of Australian drive inland.

Twentieth AF: Air echelon of XX BC, including Gen Joseph Smith, CG, sails for Okinawa. The rest of the cmd sails in 2 lots, on 12 Jul and 4 Aug, leaving only a few small dets in India-Burma. (58th Bomb Wg earlier sailed to the Marianas. *See* 27 Feb). 560-plus B–29's drop incendiaries on Kochi, Himeji, Takamatsu, and Tokushima, during 3/4 Jul. 26 others mine Shimonoseki Strait and waters at Funakawa and Maizuru during the predawn hrs of the 4th.

Seventh AF: 2 B–24's from Guam attack water storage buildings on Marcus. 36 B–25's from Okinawa, attacking in two flights, hit Chiran A/F.

4 July

AAF, China Theater: A group of officers arrives at Chungking to organize HQ, AAF China Theater.

Fourteenth AF: 30 P–51's and P–38's over Indochina and S and E China attack docks and shipping at Haiphong, Red R shipping between Hanoi and Hung Yen, small craft between Mon Cay and Pakhoi, between Hongay and Pai-lung Wei Cape, and between Pai-lung Wei Cape and Umpo. The FBs also hit road traffic on Luichow Peninsula and sampans E of Tanchuk.

FEAF: P–51's fly massive sweep along W coast of Kyushu. FBs spt ground forces in Cagayan Valley. Others attack Batan I. B–24's again pound defenses near Balikpapan. B–25's bomb Sibuti. Other B–24's pound Donggala seaplane base and runways at Boeloedowang and Limboeng A/Fs.

Seventh AF: 3 B–24's from Guam attack AA installations on SW corner of Marcus.

VII FC: Iwo Jima-based ftrs fly 161 effective strike sorties against Yokosuka naval base, Imba, Tsukuba, and Kasumigaura.

Eleventh AF: 8 B–24's radar-bomb Kataoka naval base.

5 July

Ninth AF: Col Roger J Browne takes cmd of XIX TAC.

Fourteenth AF: 8 B–25's sink several sampans and junks at Haiphong and damage several larger vessels. 2 B–25's and 2 P–47's knock out bridge S of Chumatien. 37 P–51's over Indochina and S and E China blast shipping in Hongay and Haiphong area, pound docks and small vessels at Chikhom, knock out bridge at Chumatien, blast barracks area at Anyang, and hit river and rail traffic around Tanchuk and Chenghsien.

FEAF: B–24's bomb Toshien, Takao, Toyohara and nearby Kamioka supply area, and Taihoku A/F. FBs fly nearly 100 sorties in spt of ground forces in Kiangan area. B–24's bomb Manggar and Riko. Australian troops cross Balikpapan Bay and land on W shore. P–51's sweeping Kyushu strafe T/Os and down several aircraft.

Seventh AF: 46 B–24's and 24 B–25's all from Okinawa bomb Omura A/F and 2 towns in the Omura-Nagasaki area.

VII FC: 100-plus ftrs, based on Iwo Jima, strike Ibaraki, Yatabe, Yawatasaki Cape, and Maruta.

6 July

AAF, China Theater: Gen Stratemeyer officially assumes cmd as CG AAF China Theater. He arrives in China several days later.

Fourteenth AF: 98 P–51's and P–38's over Indochina and S and E China continue to disrupt Japanese retreat and hit transport and supply tgts. Rail, road, and river traffic, coastal shipping, bridges, troops, Japanese-held areas, and general T/Os are blasted at many locations chiefly around Kweilin, Kukong, Yangso, Haiphong, and Hanoi. On this date Gen Chennault, CG Fourteenth AF, requests permission to retire, which is soon granted.

FEAF: FBs continue to spt ground forces N of Kiangan and bomb town of Mankayan. B–24's bomb Heito, Ryutan, and Taien A/Fs and A–26's pound Taito railroad yards. B–24's over Borneo bomb Bandjermasin warehouses, Tandjoengredeb buildings, Samarinda shipyards, and Balikpapan and Manggar areas. P–51's hit transportation tgts in Kagoshima Bay area.

Twentieth AF: Taking off during late evening hours of 6 Jul, 517 B–29's drop incendiaries on Chiba, Akashi, Shimizu, and Kofu between 0700–0800 on 7 Jul. 59 others bomb Maruzen Oil Refinery at Osaka during the same hr.

VII FC: Ftrs from Iwo Jima hit tgts (mainly A/Fs) in Japan, including Kumagaya, Yamagata, and Chiba.

7 July

Fourteenth AF: 80-plus P–51's and P–38's over Indochina and S and E China continue to disrupt Japanese withdrawal, pounding numerous comm and transport tgts and general T/Os particularly in the Yangso, Kweilin, and Fenstun areas.

FEAF: B–25's and FBs strike at remnants of Japanese army in the Laguna de Bay and Marikina areas. FBs also hit areas of resistance near Kiangan, Penablanca, and Mankayan. B–24's, B–25's, and P–38's spt Australian ground forces in area near Balikpapan. B–24's bomb Matsuyama and Taihoku A/Fs in force.

VII FC: 100-plus ftrs dispatched from Iwo Jima to hit tgts in Japan abort because of bad weather.

8 July

Fourteenth AF: 6 B–25's and 4 P–47's severely damage bridge N of Sinsiang and hit nearby trains. 60-plus P–38's, P–47's, and P–51's pound river shipping, rail traffic, supplies, and troops at Haiphong, Do Son, Tourane and at numerous locations in S and E China.

FEAF: P–38's and P–51's supporting ground operations hit supply and personnel areas near Kiangan and Penablanca. B–24's bomb Shinchiku A/F, B–25's start fires at Getsubi alcohol plant and on Koto I, and P–38's attack oil production area at Gyuni Kuki. B–24's and B–25's, supporting Australian forces, hit Balikpapan area def positions, Samarinda shipyards, various tgts along Samarinda road, and warehouses at Tandjung. B–24's (including some of RAAF) bomb Donggala warehouses.

VII FC: 100-plus ftrs from Iwo Jima pound A/Fs and other tgts at Hyakuri, Chofu, Tokorozawa, and Yachimata. 5 aircraft are claimed downed and at least 25 destroyed on the ground. 8 US ftrs are lost.

9 July

Fourteenth AF: 5 B–25's knock out 2 bridges in Sinantien area. 14 P–51's and P–38's knock out bridges near Hengyang and Sinshih, damage bridge near Chihsien, and attack shipping and railroad T/Os around Hankow, Lukou, Sinshih, and Dong Hoi.

FEAF: P–38's and P–51's fly ground spt in Iguig area of Cagayan R Valley and hit Sabangan. Nearly 50 P–51's are weathered out of Kyushu sweep. B–24's bomb Okaseki, Toyohara, and Takao A/Fs. A–26's attack Karenko. B–24's and P–38's supporting Australian forces, hit Japanese forces in areas near Balikpapan, Manggar, and Sepinggang. (Australian and Dutch forces complete encirclement of Balikpapan Bay).

Other HBs hit Samarinda shipyards. B–25's in spt of operations in Brunei Bay area bomb Japanese-occupied area E of Beaufort.

Twentieth AF: During 9/10 Jul, 475 B–29's attack Sendai, Sakai, Gifu, and Wakayama with incendiaries. 61 bomb oil refinery at Yokkaichi, and 31 mine Shimonoseki Strait and waters at Niigata and Nanao.

Seventh AF: 43 B–24's from Okinawa bomb Omura A/F (1 other bombs A/F on Kikai I. 50-plus Okinawa-based B–25's hit Tokuno A/F on Tokuno I.

VII FC: 100-plus Iwo Jima-based ftrs hit tac tgts at Itami, Hamamatsu, Aichi, and Washinomiya, claiming 12 air victories and 5 parked airplanes destroyed.

10 July

Fourteenth AF: 14 B–25's bomb town of Dong Anh, railroad shops at Phu Lang Thuong, and truck convoys moving through Siang Chiang Valley. 22 P–51's and P–38's bomb warehouses at Wuchang, hit railroad T/Os near Yoyang, strafe 3 railroad stations N of Chuanhsien, bomb buildings N of Kanchou, knock out bridge approach S of Chuting, damage bridge near Hengyang, and hit T/Os at Weichow I, Laohokow, and Tourane.

FEAF: P–38's and P–51's spt ground action in N Cagayan Valley and hit enemy pockets E of Manila. B–24's bomb Tainan A/F, destroying several planes, and bomb warehouses at Takao. Bad weather again prevents ftr sweep over Kyushu. B–24's hit town of Muarakaman and A/F at Tabanio while P–38's strafe numerous T/Os in SE Borneo. B–24's bomb Donggala warehouse area.

Seventh AF: During 10/11 Jul 1 B–24 from Okinawa bombs Karasehara A/F. 43 other Okinawa-based B–24's bomb Wan and Sateku A/Fs on Kikaiga I. 50-plus B–25's bomb Wan A/F on Kikaiga I and Saha-Saki on Naka-No I, both in the Ryukyus, and Kurume.

VII FC: Ftrs, based on Iwo Jima, fly over 100 effective strike sorties against Hashin, Nishinomiya, Sano, and Tokushima, mostly hitting A/Fs.

Eleventh AF: 4 B–24's fly a search down the W coasts of Paramushiru and Shimushu and then radar-bomb Minami Cape. 1 B–24 flies a radar-ferret mission over N Kurils.

11 July

Fourteenth AF: 25 P–51's and P–40's attack bridges, troops, gun positions, rail traffic, rivercraft, coastal shipping, and various scattered tgts at or near Nanchang, Kweiyi, Puchi, Tanchuk, and Luichow Peninsula.

FEAF: P–51's sweep Kyushu. B–24's bomb Shinchiku A/F. B–25's and FBs pound troop concentrations and defenses in Cagayan Valley. B–24's pound troop concentrations on Negros I. B–25's and P–38's pound highway tgts in Balikpapan area.

Twentieth AF: During 11/12 Jul, 25 B–29's mine Shimonoseki Strait and waters at Miyazu, Maizuru, Obama I and, in the first B–29 operation to Korea, at Pusan and Najin.

Seventh AF: During 11/12 Jul, 2 B–24's from Okinawa attack Byu and Miyazaki A/Fs.

Eleventh AF: 5 B–24's radar-bomb Kataoka. 4 B–25's fly shipping sweep and bomb Otomae Bay fishery, scoring hits among the buildings.

12 July

Twelfth AF: XII AFSC is disbanded at Siena.

Fourteenth AF: 3 B-25's blast supply convoys moving through Siang Chiang Valley. 43 P-51's and P-38's attack bridges, rivercraft, barracks road traffic, and coastal shipping around Changsha, Hsinching, Hamrong, Tonkin area, Cao Bang, Luichow Peninsula, and Nanchang. 2 bridges are knocked out and others damaged, A/Fs are strafed at Vinh and Kiungshan.

FEAF: P-51's sweep Kyushu. B-24's bomb Canton. Other B-24's bomb Toshien while A-26's hit numerous tgts at Tamazato. P-51's hit tgts along W Formosan coast. FBs hit pillboxes E of Iguig, attack concentrations in Bontoc-Kiangan area, and spt ground forces E of Manila. (Town of Kiangan falls to 6th Inf Div, but resistance in area continues). B-24's over Negros I in spt of ground forces bomb concentration NE of Mount Mandalagan. B-24's destroy Tandjung barrack area. B-24's hit Donggala warehouses.

Twentieth AF: During 12/13 Jul 453 B-29's drop incendiaries on Utsonomiya, Ichinomiya, Tsuruga, and Uwajima. 53 others bomb petroleum center at Kawasaki.

Seventh AF: HQ Seventh AF on Okinawa is declared open by GO on this date. 47 B-24's from Okinawa, failing to bomb primary (Tsuiki) because of clouds attack A/F on Kikaiga I at Amami Gunto. 2 Okinawa-based B-24's bomb Byu and Miyazaki A/Fs during the night. 50-plus B-25's bomb Kanoya A/F and town of Aburatsu on Kyushu and Tokuno A/F on Tokuno I. Chiran A/F is

pounded by 70 B-25's and A-26's. (This is first strike against Japan by Seventh AF A-26's.) 2 more A-26's hit Ibusuki seaplane station.

Eleventh AF: 4 B-25's on shipping sweep bomb and strafe a freighter. 1 B-25 is lost.

13 July

Fourteenth AF: 14 B-25's and 12 P-51's attack bridges, railroad yards, AA guns, and T/Os at Anyang, Puchi, and Do Cam. 33 P-51's and P-38's attack river shipping, buildings, road traffic, rail tgts, and general T/Os around Trung Khanh Phu, Tonkin Delta area, Cao Bang, Wangypan, Luichow Peninsula, Thanh Hoa, Pinglo, Changsha, and Wuchou.

FEAF: B-24's bomb storage areas of Canton. B-24's bomb boatyards and buildings at Suo while A-26's hit Karenko railroad yards. B-24's bomb concentrations NE of Mount Mandalagan. MBs and FBs hit Kiangan area, attack Japanese pockets E of Iguig and N of Tuguegarao, pound pillboxes, ammo dumps, and vehicles in Cervantes sector, and blast hostile areas near Siniloan, NE of Laguna de Bay. P-38's attack gun entrenchments in Miri area. P-38's on sweep over SW Celebes hit vehicles and comm tgts.

Twentieth AF: During 13/14 Jul, 30 B-29's mine Shimonoseki Strait and waters at Fukuoka, ports at Seishin, Masan, and Reisui.

14 July

Fourteenth AF: 25 P-51's and P-38's bomb or strafe ammo and supply dumps, river, road, and rail traffic, and coastal shipping around Laohokow, Hung Yen, Bac Ninh, Tinpak,

Hongay, Mon Cay, Vinh, Koyiu, and Yutze.

FEAF: On this date Seventh AF officially joins Fifth and Thirteenth AFs as part of FEAF. A–26's hit Taiharo refinery and warehouse area. P–51's over W coast blast railroad tgts. P–47's sweep N China coast and attack coastal cargo vessels NW of Tinghai. FBs spt ground forces in Mankayan and Kiangan areas and hit enemy positions in Ipo-Infanta sector. B–24's spt ground forces on Negros I, bombing area NE of Mount Mandalagan. Other B–24's bomb airstrips at Boeloedowang, Limboeng, Mapanget, and Tanamon and Japanese HQ at Sindjai.

Seventh AF: The Seventh is assigned from AAFPOA and overall operational control by the Navy to FEAF. Seventh AF units in the Ryukyus, operating under Tac AF, Ryukyus (Tenth Army Tac AF) since Apr when first element of the HQ Seventh AF arrived, are now under operational control of HQ Seventh AF which opens in Okinawa on this date. Move from Saipan takes place between 18 Jun and 28 Jul.

VII FC: Ftrs from Iwo Jima sent on strike against Meiji and Kagamigahara abort because of weather.

15 July

Fourteenth AF: 3 B–25's blast truck convoys moving through Siang Chiang Valley. 39 P–51's and P–47's attack rivercraft, troops, coastal shipping, bridges, railroad yards, gun positions, trains, and other tgts around Luichow Peninsula, Anyang, Yutze, Sinsiang, Fentingtukou, Paoching, Tanchuk, Kweiyi, Pac Muong, and Haiphong.

FEAF: B–24's bomb arms plant at Canton. On Formosa P–51's sweep W coast, blasting a warehouse and other buildings S of Takao and T/Os on Hoko I. P–38's and P–51's spt ground forces in N Cayagan Valley, in Kiangan sector, and in Cervantes area. B–25's and P–51's bomb def positions in Infanta sector. 58 B–24's hit A/Fs at Tomitaka and Usa. 25 pound Kikai I, Miranoura on Yaku I, and A/F at Tamega I.

Twentieth AF: During 15/16 Jul, 26 B–29's mine waters at Naoetsu, Niigata, Najin, Pusan, and Wonsan. 59 other B–29's bomb Nippon Oil Company at Kudamatsu.

VII FC: Iwo Jima-based ftrs fly over 100 effective sorties against A/Fs and other tac tgts at Meiji, Kagamigahara, Kowa, Akenogahara, Nagoya, and Suzuko.

16 July

International: Conference opens at Potsdam to draw up terms for Japanese surrender and to discuss military and political problems connected with the ending of hostilities.

US: The first atomic bomb is successfully exploded at Los Alamos.

Eighth AF: HQ Eighth AF issues its last movement order in ETO. After much reorganization and redeployment of units, HQ relieves VIII FC from assignment to Eighth AF and directs HQ and HQ Sq to move from Charleroi back to UK (the unit moves to High Wycombe the following day, 17 Jul) where VIII FC is to assume control over all Eighth AF units remaining in UK. HQ Eighth AF is transferred without personnel, equipment, or combat elements to Okinawa, where Eighth and Twentieth AFs are to comprise USASTAF under cmd of Gen Spaatz. By this date over 90,000 persons (more than 50 per cent of the Eighth's strength on 30 Apr 45) have been redeployed to US, N Africa, and various parts of ETO.

AAF, India-Burma Theater: Gen Hanley assumes cmd of AAF, India-Burma Theater.

Fourteenth AF: 5 B-25's pound enemy truck convoys moving supplies through Siang-Chiang Valley and S of Kweilin. 60-plus P-51's, P-38's, and P-47's continue to hit river, road, and rail traffic, bridges, troops, supplies, and other tgts at many points in Indochina and S and E China.

FEAF: B-24's bomb warehouses at Watampone. P-51's and B-25's spt ground forces in Kiangan-Baguio sector and area E of Manila. P-51's on sweep of Formosa attack comm tgts, hitting railroad station and locomotive shed at Byoritsu and scoring direct hit on bridge SW of Koryu. B-24's, A-26's, B-25's, P-51's and P-47's from Okinawa and Ie Shima pound Kyushu. P-51's hit several E coast tgts, concentrating in Kagoshima Bay area. 27 A-26's, 1 B-24, and 39 P-47's hit A/F and bridge at Miyazaki; 33 B-24's bomb bridges at Nobeoka; 36 B-25's, a B-24 and an A-26 pound Sadohara bridge; 6 B-24's bomb harbor and town of Aburatsu; and 5 P-47's hit Yanagawa.

Twentieth AF: HQ is officially moved to Harmon Field, Guam. XX BC is inactivated, effective 18 Jul, and HQ and HQ Sq, XXI BC is redesignated HQ Sq, Twentieth AF. Thus the BCs are brought to an end as actual establishments. Their wgs pass to direct control of HQ, Twentieth AF of which Gen LeMay takes

cmd on this date. During 16/17 Jul, 466 B-29's drop incendiary bombs on Numazu, Oita, Kuwana, and Hiratsuka.

VII FC: Ftrs based on Iwo Jima fly over 100 effective sorties against tgts (mainly A/Fs) at Kameyama, Kiyosu, Komaki, Okazaki, Suzuko, and Akenogahara. 22 air victories are claimed.

Eleventh AF: 2 B-24's fly a negative shipping search mission to Shimushiru I. 4 B-25's on enemy shipping sweep deck-level bomb and strafe enemy freighter. 3 of the bmrs then bomb and strafe Torishima Is (secondary).

17 July

Fourteenth AF: A single B-25 attacks 3 truck convoys in Siang-Chiang Valley and bombs area along river at Hengyang. 70-plus P-51's and P-47's continue to disrupt enemy movement in Indochina and S and E China, attacking bridges, railroad yards, rail, road, and river traffic, A/Fs, gun positions, and many other tgts at various locations, especially around Suichwan, Linfen, and Sinsiang.

FEAF: Nearly 150 B-24's, B-25's, and A-26's pound Chiang Wan A/F. P-47's attack shipping and warehouses in Taishan I area while others hit Tinghai A/F. P-51's over Kyushu and N Ryukyu Is attack shipping, severely damaging a 10,000-ton cargo vessel in harbor on Amami-O-Shima. P-47's dive-bomb railroad tunnels NW and SW of Kagoshima. B-24's bomb Limboeng barracks and strafe schooner off SW Celebes. B-25's attack Jesselton A/F and Itu Aba I.

Twentieth AF: During 17/18 Jul,

27 B–29's mine Shimonoseki Strait and waters in Nanao-Fushiki area, at Henashi Cape, Iwase and at Seishin. Also, units of British Pacific Fleet join US Third Fleet units in bombardment of Japan.

Eleventh AF: Unsuccessful shipping sweeps are flown by 2 B–24's over Shimushiru and by 4 B–25's between Kurabu and Paramushiru.

18 July

Fourteenth AF: 4 B–25's blast Dong Anh railroad yards. 36 P–51's and P–38's hit river traffic, rail tgts, coastal shipping, enemy positions, trucks, and other tgts around Viet Tri and other areas of Indochina and near Yoyang, Suichwan, Lingling, Chikhom, Kukong, and Dosing.

FEAF: About 150 B–24's, B–25's, and A–26's, covered by 54 P–47's, hit Shanghai area, A/Fs at Chiang Wan, Wusung, and Lunghua, Shanghai docks, shipping on Whangpoo R, and airstrips on Chusan I. Other P–47's attack various T/Os on Kyushu and P–51's attack comm lines, bridges, shipping, towns, and other tgts throughout Kyushu and the Ryukyus. P–38's hit comm and transportation tgts throughout N part of Formosa while B–24's pound A/F at Matsuyama. B–24's bomb Boetoeng and Watampone, B–25's hit Jesselton, and P–38's attack Langkon. P–38's hit Japanese concentration along Kibawe trail.

USASTAF: USASTAF is established at Guam under Gen Spaatz.

Eleventh AF: 2 routine search and weather sorties are flown.

19 July

Fourteenth AF: 20 B–25's, 16 P–

51's, and 4 P–47's blast railroad yards at Shihkiachwang. 7 other B–25's and 2 P–51's hit bridges S of Yoyang and bomb truck convoys in Siang-Chiang Valley, particularly around Siangtan area. 37 FBs disrupt enemy movement over wide areas of Indochina and S and E China, attacking numerous T/Os.

FEAF: P–38's hit suicide boat hideout at Sandakan while B–25's bomb Jesselton A/F. P–38's spt ground forces, hitting positions along Kibawe trail. B–25's hit Itu Aba. 90-plus P–51's pound numerous tgts on sweeps over Nagoya area and hit A/Fs, factories, power facilities, and gun positions at locations including Kagamigahara, Nishinomiya, and Osaka.

Twentieth AF: On 19/20 Jul, 27 B–29's lay mines in Oyama, Niigata, Miyazu, Maizuru, Tsuruga, Nezugaseki, Obama I, and Kobe-Osaka areas and at Wonsan. 470 VHBs (also operating during the night) drop incendiaries on Fukui, Hitachi, Chosi, and Okazaki while 83 others bomb oil facilities at Amagasaki.

VII FC: Iwo Jima-based ftrs strike A/Fs, factories, railroads, power lines and other tac tgts at Kagamigahara, Nagoya, Meiji, Izumi, Nishinomiya, and Tambaichi.

20 July

Fourteenth AF: 10 B–25's and 6 P–51's hit truck convoys around Hengyang and Wuchang, storage on island near Changsha, locomotive shops at Phu Thuong, and power plant and railroad tgts in Vinh area. 50-plus P–51's, P–38's, and P–61's disrupt enemy movement and general withdrawal in Indochina and S and

E China, attacking river, road, and rail traffic, coastal shipping, supplies, and other tgts.

FEAF: P-38's attack town of Langkon while B-24's pound Togian I. P-38's hit T/Os in SW Celebes. B-25's hit Itu Aba and W of Palawan for second consecutive day. A-20's and FBs spt ground action in Kiangan area and in lower Cagayan Valley. B-25's and FBs hit Japanese positions in Marikina and Infanta areas. B-24's bomb area S of Fabrica.

Twentieth AF: The 509th Comp Gp begins series of 12 precision attacks over Japan for purpose of familiarizing crews with tgt area and tactics contemplated for scheduled atomic bomb missions. The strikes (on 20, 24, 26, and 29 Jul) are mostly against (or near) cities previously bombed, in the general area of cities chosen for possible atomic attack, and involve from 2 to 6 aircraft in order to accustom the Japanese to sight of small formations of B-29's flying at high altitudes.

VII FC: Ftrs based on Iwo Jima fly nearly 100 effective sorties against tgts, mainly A/Fs, at Kamezaki, Meiji, Okazaki, Nagoya, Kagamigahara, Hamamatsu, and Komaki.

Eleventh AF: 8 B-24's fly the heaviest and most successful mission of the month, bombing hangars and revetments at Matsuwa A/F.

21 July

Fourteenth AF: 11 B-25's and 2 P-51's attack truck convoys in Siang-Chiang Valley, bomb HQ near Wuchang, and hit bridge, trains, warehouses, and AA positions in Sienning area. 40-plus P-51's, P-38's, and P-61's again attack numerous tgts and

disrupt enemy movement in Indochina and S and E China, hitting comm tgts, supplies, transport, and other T/Os.

FEAF: B-25's and A-26's bomb shipping at Naze-Ko. P-38's hit Kiangan area. Bad weather restricts activity in NEI, Phil Is, Japan, and other tgt areas mainly to light raids and snooper missions.

22 July

Fourteenth AF: 16 B-25's and 8 FBs blast truck convoys moving supplies through Siang-Chiang Valley, bomb railroad yards at Siaokan, and knock out 2 bridges S of Sincheng and Lohochai. 50-plus P-51's, P-47's, and P-38's continue campaign to disrupt enemy movement and withdrawal in Indochina and S and E China, pounding numerous rail, road, and river tgts, supply dumps, and coastal shipping.

FEAF: 22 B-24's from Okinawa hit Chiang Wan and 1 hits Tinghai A/F. 37 B-25's bomb oil plant at Shanghai and destroyer in Whangpoo R. P-47's from Ie Shima join the MB attack on Shanghai area, hitting destroyer, gunboat, and freighter in the Whangpoo R, and factories and railroad shops. 34 P-51's from Okinawa also hit Whangpoo shipping. 37 A-26's hit A/F at Tachang. B-24's on night shipping search and weather mission bomb A/Fs at Tinghai on Chusan I, Pusan, and Yonago. B-25's, P-51's, and P-38's, hampered by bad weather, fly 30-plus ground spt sorties in Gubano, Cervantes, and Mankayan areas.

Twentieth AF: During 22/23 July, 23 B-29's, staging through Iwo Jima, mine Shimonoseki Strait and Korea coast at Najin—which is the longest B–29 combat mission of the war—and in Pusan-Masan area. 72 others bomb coal liquefaction company at Ube. (See 10 Aug 44 and 14 Aug 45 for longest single-stage missions).

VII FC: 100-plus Iwo Jima-based ftrs hit A/Fs, rail installations, and other tac tgts at Itami, Hanshin, Sano, Tokushima, Takamatsu, and Minato.

23 July

Fourteenth AF: 8 B–25's and 4 P–51's bomb railroad yards at Sinyang and hit warehouse at Ichang. 100-plus P–51's, P–38's, and P–40's attack numerous tgts, including rail, road, and river traffic, A/Fs, coastal shipping, bridges, storage facilities, and railroad yards, at many locations over S and E China, especially in the Paoching area and, to a smaller degree, over Indochina.

FEAF: B–25's pound Jesselton while B–24's over other areas of NEI bomb Amboina and Tolonoeoe Is. Ftr aircraft spt ground forces in Kiangan area. B–25's bomb Itu Aba I. B–24's hit Miho and Saeki. Single HBs on armed rcn hit several tgts including Tinghai A/F, Kure harbor, and Tanega I.

Eleventh AF: 2 B–24's radar-bomb Kurabu Cape A/F.

24 July

Fourteenth AF: 8 B–25's and 6 P–51's pound truck convoys in Hengyang area, hit river shipping near Pakonghow, and damage bridge and storage area and knock out AA positions at Puchi. 80-plus P–51's, P–38's, and P–47's over Indochina and S and E China continue to disrupt Japanese

withdrawal, pounding dozens of T/Os at numerous locations. 15 P–51's blast Changsha area, destroying an estimated 28 warehouses and 8 fuel storage buildings.

FEAF: 100-plus Fifth AF B–24's fly their first strike from Okinawa, bombing Chiang Wan A/F N of Shanghai. Seventh AF B–25's from Okinawa hit Wusung and Lunghua A/Fs in the Shanghai area while A–26's and B–25's attack Tachang and Tinghai A/Fs. FBs hit shipping and T/Os throughout the general area attacked by the bmrs. Thirteenth AF B–25's pound Jesselton A/F. B–24's hit Oelin and Tabanio A/Fs. Other B–25's hit Itu Aba I. Fifth AF FBs spt ground forces in the Infanta and Leyban areas.

Twentieth AF: 570 plus B–29's bomb aircraft plants at Handa, Nagoya, and Takarazuka, arsenal and metals industry at Osaka, and urban areas of Tsu and Kawana, plus several T/Os.

VII FC: 91 P–51's, operating out of Iwo Jima, hit A/Fs and other tac tgts at Hamamatsu, Suruga Bay, and other points in Nagoya area.

25 July

Fourteenth AF: 10 B–25's and 3 P–38's knock out bridges at Tho Linh and Quang Tri and damage a barge and a river steamer in Wuchou area. 30 P–51's and P–38's attack river, road, and rail traffic, railroad yards, and other tgts in the areas of Duc Tho, Bac Ninh, Vinh, Hanoi, Kukong, Samshui, Wuchou, and West R.

FEAF: B–24's bomb Pontianak and Kuching A/Fs while MBs and ftrs attack dispersal area in Jesselton A/F area. B–24's pound enemy troops on Negros I. B–25's bomb Itu Aba I. B–24's bomb Kikai I and town of Tsuiki.

Twentieth AF: During 25/26 Jul, 75 B–29's bomb oil refinery and petroleum center at Kawasaki while 29 others mine waters at Nanao, Fushiki, Obama I, Tsuruga, Seishin, and Pusan.

26 July

International: Potsdam ultimatum is issued. Japan is told to surrender unconditionally or face "utter destruction."

Fourteenth AF: 8 B–25's and 4 P–51's bomb railroad yards at Lohochai and hit storage area and animal transport in Pinking area. 100-plus P–51's, P–38's, and P–61's pound enemy movement and withdrawal in Indochina and S and E China, hitting supplies, troops, river, road, and rail traffic, coastal shipping, railroad yards, bridges, town areas and other tgts at numerous locations.

FEAF: B–24's hit Tabanio, Trombol, Sengkawang, and Oelin A/Fs. FBs and B–25's over Luzon (where Thirteenth AF now provides ground spt) aid ground forces in Mankayan area and near Tuguegarao. B–24's plaster Japanese positions on ground spt strikes over Negros. B–25's bomb Itu Aba I. Other B–25's on shipping search attack convoy at Tsutsu Bay sinking 3 small cargo vessels, a freighter, and a few small craft. B–24's on snooper strikes attack several tgts, including various tgts in the Ryukyus, A/Fs at Tinghai and at Nakazu, and docks at Pusan.

Twentieth AF: During 26/27 Jul, 350 B–29's drop incendiary bombs on Matsuyama, Tokuyama, and Omuta.

Eleventh AF: 7 B–24's successfully hit Kataoka naval base with incendiaries, leaving smoke columns 5,000 ft high in their wake. No airborne opposition. AA fire is moderate and inaccurate. Another B–24 flies a radar-ferret mission over the N Kurils.

27 July

Fourteenth AF: 13 B–25's, some with P–51 spt, hit supply movement in Siang-Chiang Valley, bomb railroad yards at Siaokan and Sinyang, and hit coastal shipping in Do Son area. 50-plus P–51's and P–38's concentrate on attacking river shipping at numerous points of Indochina and S and E China also hitting road and rail traffic, coastal vessels, storage areas, and bridges.

FEAF: 60-plus Fifth and Seventh AF B–24's pound M/Y at Kagoshima. 50 escorting P–51's attack numerous nearby T/Os. 150-plus P–47's over Kyushu hit comm and industrial tgts, including tunnel S of Kurino, bridges at Okasa, Hitosuse-gawa, and Matsu-base, and factories and power plant at Yatsushiro. B–24's of Thirteenth AF hit airstrip N of Pontianak.

Twentieth AF: During 27/28 Jul, 24 B–29's drop mines in Shimonoseki Strait, at Fukuoka, Niigata, Maizuru, Senzaki, and in Fukawa Bay.

28 July

Fourteenth AF: 7 B–25's and 4 P–51's attack supply movement through Siang-Chiang Valley, hit a freighter and 2 smaller vessels off Shuitang, and pound troops near Kian. About 90 P–51's, P–47's, and P–61's disrupt Japanese movement throughout S and E China and in Indochina. The FBs concentrate on river transport.

FEAF: 137 Ie Shima-based P–47's rocket and strafe A/Fs, oil stores, railroad yards, warehouses, industry, gun positions, and other tgts on Kyushu at or near Kanoya, Metatsubara, Tachiarai, Kurume, Saga, and Junicho. 21 more P–47's attack shipping at Yatsushiro. A–26's and B–25's pound A/Fs at Kanoya. P–51's and B–25's, sweepig over Inland Sea, destroy 2 small cargo vessels and a patrol boat. 70-plus B–24's bomb shipping at Kure, claiming direct hits on a battleship and aircraft carrier. B–25's and P–38's in spt of ground forces hit enemy positions in Mankayan-Kiangan area and in Marikina area. Other P–38's hit troop concentrations on Jolo I. B–24's spt ground forces on Negros I.

Twentieth AF: During 28/29 Jul, 471 B–29's drop incendiary bombs on Tsu, Aomori, Ichinomiya, Ujiyamada, Ogaki, and Uwajima, while 76 others bomb oil refinery at Shimotsu.

VII FC: 140-plus P–51's, based on Iwo Jima, hit 9 objectives (A/Fs and military tgts) in wide area around Tokyo and attack a destroyer escort along Chiba Peninsula, leaving it burning.

29 July

Fourteenth AF: 4 B–25's and 2 P–51's hit shipping off Luichow Peninsula near Cape Kami, barracks at Chingmen, and cannon-strafe trucks at Kuanshuishih and oil storage at Yingtak. About 100 P–51's, P–38's, and P–61's attack a variety of tgts over a vast area from Haiphong to Peking, continuing the steady campaign against enemy movement and withdrawal.

FEAF: P–47's from Ie Shima and B–24's, B–25's, and A–26's from Okinawa pound tgts in the Japanese Home Islands. 70-plus B–24's pound shipping at Kure. 41 B–24's hit factory and storage area NW of Aburatsu, shipping and engine works in Nagasaki and vicinity, and towns of Nobeoka and Oita. B–25's hit Kagoshima, Kibana, bridge, barracks and other buildings at Miyazaki, warehouses, lighthouse, and navigation light at Tozaki-hana, and bomb Tokuno I. A–26's pound naval base and engine works at Nagasaki. Numerous P–47's hit harbor at Kure, shipping and seaplane station at Ibusuki, railroad station, docks, and town area of Makurazaki, Chiran and Izumi A/Fs, and shipping at Kagoshima Bay. P–51's hit numerous T/Os on S coast of Korea and on S part of Kyushu, where shipping, railroads, and Omura and Sashiki factories are also attacked. B–24's hit Sidate A/F and warehouses at Watampone. Other B–24's over Negros bomb resistance pocket S of Fabrica. B–25's and P–38's hit Japanese positions near San Mariano and W of Kiangan, troop concentrations in Marikina watershed, and ridge emplacements in Bantayan area. Several buildings are destroyed at Pasco Point.

Twentieth AF: During 29/30 Jul, 24 B–29's mine Shimonoseki Strait and waters at Fukuoka, Karatsu, and Najin.

30 July

Japan: Japanese reject Potsdam ultimatum. Nevertheless Gen Marshall directs Gens MacArthur and

Wedemeyer and Adm Nimitz to proceed with plans for a surrender.

Fourteenth AF: 2 B–25's bomb supply convoys moving through Siang-Chiang Valley. 40-plus P–51's, P–38's, and P–61's hit various tgts in S and E China, and in Indochina, chiefly river transport, but also troop concentrations, railroad traffic, and many T/Os. Tgt areas include Nanyang, Suchow, Hankow, Sinyang, Anking, Anyang, Lohochai, Kukong, Takhing, Koyiu, Samshui, Pingsiang, Kian, Yungcheng, Yingtak, and Wuchou.

FEAF: 60-plus B–25's and A–26's bomb Omura A/F. 4 of the planes hit A/F at Izumi. P–47's spt the strike and also hit numerous nearby T/Os. B–25's, failing to find tgts on shipping sweep over Korean waters, bomb shipping, a railroad, and a warehouse in Sendai area. Covering P–51's also hit nearby T/Os. 80-plus P–47's bomb Sendai, leaving much of the town in flames. P–51's on photo rcn of S Kyushu destroy trains and small craft. Nearly 80 P–47's attack Miyazaki, Karasehara, and Tomitaka areas, firing warehouses and damaging barracks, hangars, towers, and other buildings, and blast buildings and construction on and near Shibushi A/F. B–24's bomb Kota Waringin A/F. B–25's and P–38's spt ground forces E of Ilagan, near Kiangan, and E of Manila in Infanta sector.

VII FC: Iwo Jima-based ftrs attack A/Fs, railroads, and other tac tgts throughout the Kobe-Osaka area.

Eleventh AF: 8 B–24's on way to the Kurils are soon recalled because of weather disturbances.

31 July

Twelfth AF: Organizational charts show great decrease in Jul in size of Twelfth AF due to redeployment, transfer, disbandment, and discontinuance of 50 units. Only 5 new units are added to the Twelfth. This leaves 77 assigned and 3 attached units compared to 122 assigned and 2 attached the previous month. The Twelfth practically ceases to be a flying AF as only 2 MB gps, a night ftr sq, and a rcn gp remain as flying units. The planes from these units are shortly transferred to AAFSC, MTO.

Fourteenth AF: 3 B–25's continue to bomb supply convoys moving through Siang-Chiang Valley. 52 P–51's and P–61's over S and E China attack rivercraft, trucks, railroad traffic, coastal shipping, ammo dumps, and other tgts at several locations including areas around Yanglowtung, Changsha, Siangyin, Hengyang, Hankow, Paoching, Nanyang, Nanking, Kulo, Hoihow, and Yoyang.

FEAF: 80-plus B–24's pound Kagoshima railroad yards and several other tgts in the general area including Sasebo naval base, Yaki-shima, and Nagasaki. A–26's and B–25's bomb Kanoya and Miyazaki A/Fs and nearby tgts, Sasebo naval base, Marushima, warehouses at Nagasaki, and a factory and power plant on Koyagi I. P–51's attack flak positions at Moji, blast shipping at Iki I and off NW and W coast of Kyushu, hit island WSW of Sasebo, bomb railroad tgts and warehouses in Izumi area, and in general attack railroad and road net and other comm tgts throughout Kyushu. P–61's continue harassing missions during the night. P–51's over the Ryukyus bomb airstrips in Miyako I, and bomb town in Koniya area. B–25's and P–38's spt ground action on Luzon, hitting forces in Cagayan Valley and in Cervantes and Infanta sectors. B–24's pound area S of Fabrica.

1 August

Tenth AF: Gen Hegenberger becomes CG Tenth AF. Tenth AF moves from Piardoba to Kunming. (HQ at Kunming was officially opened on 23 Jul). The scheduled role of the Tenth AF in China is almost identical with its completed Burma mission: to act as the tac AF giving direct spt and providing air supply to Chinese ground forces operating S of 27th parallel N.

Fourteenth AF: Bad weather severely curtails operations. P–61's effectively sweep rivers in Wuchou, Canton, and Tsingyun areas, sinking several large junks and sampans.

FEAF: B–24's bomb shipyards at Pontianak. Other HBs hit barracks and AA guns along Makassar Strait. P–38's strafe locomotives in Soerabaja area. Other P–38's spt ground forces ENE and SE of Mankayan and, along with USMC aircraft, pound enemy positions and concentrations in Upian area. B–24's bomb Tourane M/Y while escorting P–51's strafe boxcars at Quang Nam. Other B–24's strike Takao military stores. About 50 B–24's bomb tgts in Nagasaki dock and harbor area. B–25's and FBs in Nagasaki area hit docks, railroad yards, and shipping. Other B–24's bomb Koniya A/F and hit Kakeroma I. 80-plus P–47's hit railroad bridges and other railroad tgts at Sendai. Also P–47's fly their first combat mission from Iwo Jima, joining VII FC P–51's in sweep over S Honshu. Rolling stock and A/Fs are attacked in Okazaki, Itami, and Nagoya areas.

Twentieth AF: 627 B–29's, on night of 1/2 Aug, carry out fire-bomb raids on Japanese cities of Hachioji, Toyama, Nagaoka, and Mito; 120 others bomb Kawasaki petroleum facilities; and 37 drop mines in Shimonoseki Strait, in Nakaumi Lagoon, at Hamada, Sakai, Yonago, Najin, and Seishin. The total of 784 B–29's (of 836 dispatched) bombing tgts is the largest Twentieth AF single-day effort of World War II.

VII FC: 30-plus Iwo Jima-based P–51's hit A/Fs and other tgts in Osaka-Nagoya area. Bad weather prevents numerous other ftrs from reaching tgts.

2 August

Fourteenth AF: 10 B–25's, escorted by 2 P–47's, knock out bridge at Sinyang and severely damage bridge at Lohochai. 7 B–25's bomb town of Sinning, and hit several truck convoys between Siangtan and Changsha and in Siang-Chiang Valley. 31 P–51's also bomb town of Sinning. 40-plus P–47's and P–51's knock out at least 3 bridges and damage others and attack shipping, fuel dumps, gun positions, trucks, railroad yards and general T/Os around Sichuang, Shangkao, Yoyang, Hankow, Mingkiang, Sincheng, Yutze, Houmachen, Yuncheng, Anyang, and Kaoyi.

FEAF: Bad weather cancels all FEAF missions from Okinawa. Thirteenth AF P–38's spt ground forces on N Luzon, hitting pockets of resistance W of Kiangan and blasting enemy occupied caves on ridge NW of Bontoc.

Twentieth AF: Gen Twining becomes CG Twentieth AF. Gen LeMay is assigned to USASTAF as CoS.

Eleventh AF: 6 B–24's radar-bomb Kokutan Cape and visually bomb Kataoka.

3 August

Fifteenth AF: Gen Lee takes cmd of Fifteenth AF.

Fourteenth AF: 16 B–25's pound various railroad tgts in E China. 50-plus FBs attack bridges, railroad yards, storage areas, enemy troops, river and rail traffic, and various other tgts as the campaign to disrupt Japanese retreat from S and E China continues in spite of considerable bad weather.

FEAF: P–38's and B–25's spt ground forces on N Luzon, hitting buildings in Apunan area and Japanese positions at various locations including ridges SW of Kiangan and W of Banaue. B–24's bomb airstrips at Tanamon and Sidate and bomb seaplane base at Kangean I.

VII FC: Ftrs from Iwo Jima fly nearly 100 effective sorties throughout Tokyo area, hitting A/Fs, rail installations, and trains.

4 August

Ninth AF: Gen Kepner takes cmd of Ninth AF.

Fourteenth AF: Bad weather hampers operations. However, 4 B–25's damage Sincheng railroad bridge, 4 B–25's and 2 P–51's bomb Pailochi A/F and hit trucks in the area, and 7 P–51's damage 12 locomotives between Taiyuan and Tsinan, destroy or damage several trucks near Shihkiachwang, and bomb bridge near Chihsien.

FEAF: B–25's over Kyushu hit industrial area near Takanabe, bombing warehouses, factories, railroad bridge, and M/Y. B–25's and P–38's spt ground forces on Luzon, hitting Japanese forces near Santa Ines, in Butitio area, and near Mount Obudan. B–24's spt ground action S of Fabrica. B–24's bomb Miti A/F. P–38's on sweep over Singapore claim 2 Japanese planes downed.

5 August

Fourteenth AF: 20 P–51's knock out bridge NW of Anyang and damage another NE of Kiehsiu, attack railroad tgts during sweeps from Taiyuan to Suchow and Tehsien to Pengpu, and strafe rivercraft between Ichang and Lokchang.

FEAF: 330-plus B–24's, B–25's, A–26's, P–47's, and P–51's pound Tarumizu town, industrial area on Kyushu and many T/Os on Kyushu and in the Ryukyus. P–38's spt ground forces on Luzon, hitting Japanese concentrations ENE of Naguilian, near Mount Data, and at other points. B–24's pound Japanese positions S of Fabrica. Other B–24's bomb supply and personnel areas and AA positions in Makassar area. B–24's also bomb Miti.

Twentieth AF: During 5/6 Aug, 470-plus B–29's fly incendiary raids against cities of Saga, Mae Bashi, Imabari, and Nishinomiya-Mikage, 106 bomb coal liquefaction company at Ube, and 27 mine waters of Sakai, Yonago, Nakaumi Lagoon, Miyazu, Maizuru, Tsuruga, Obama, Najin and Geijitsu area.

VII FC: VII FC is officially assigned to Twentieth AF. 100-plus P–51's strike A/Fs and military installations in large area around

Tokyo, scoring especially effective hits at Katori A/F.

6 August

Fourteenth AF: 10 P–51's and P–47's damage 10 locomotives between Tehsien and Suchow and 5 around Anyang, Kaifeng, and Loyang, and lightly damage bridges N of Chihsien and S of Houmachen.

FEAF: Okinawa-based aircraft pound tgts on Kyushu. 150-plus P–47's and A–26's fight bad weather to hit the primary, Miyakonojo. 170-plus B–24's, B–25's, and P–47's hit Kagoshima as secondary tgt. 60-plus B–25's and P–51's attack shipping and ground T/Os in Tsushima Strait area and in N Ryukyus. P–51's operating in area between Kyushu and Korea bomb A/F and strafe numerous T/Os on Saishu I. P–47's bomb Anjo on Tanega I. Other aircraft, operating individually or in pairs, hit various T/Os on S Korea coast, in Inland Sea, S Honshu, W Shikoku I, throughout the N Ryukyus, and in Shanghai area. B–24's pound resistance pockets on Negros I.

Twentieth AF: The world's first atomic attack takes place. At 0245 Col Paul W Tibbets pilots the B–29 *Enola Gay* off the runway at North Field, Tinian. At 2-min intervals, 2 observation B–29's follow Maj Charles W Sweeney's *Great Artiste* and Capt George W Marquardt's No 91. At 0915 (0815 Japan time) the atomic bomb is released over Hiroshima from 31,600 ft. It explodes 50 secs later. More than 80 per cent of the city's buildings are destroyed and over 71,000 people (Japanese figures; US figures say from 70,000 to 80,000) are killed. The

Enola Gay lands on Tinian at 1458, followed within the hr by the 2 observation planes.

VII FC: Almost 100 ftrs from Iwo Jima attack A/Fs and military installations at 6 locations throughout general area around Tokyo.

7 August

Fourteenth AF: Fourteenth AF moves from Kunming to Paishiyi.

FEAF: P–47's cover Twentieth AF B–29 strike against Kyushu tgts. B–24's and A–26's over Kyushu pound Tsuiki A/F. Other B–24's start fires at Omura. B–25's hit bridges and other tgts at Matsubase and Kawajiri and bomb convoy off Pusan. Other B–25's hit Chiran and Izumi A/Fs. FBs attack and considerably damage comm and transportation facilities throughout Kyushu. B–24's bomb Takao A/F. B–25's and P–38's spt ground forces near Ambuclao, Kiangan, Batangan, Aparri, Mankayan, Bontoc, and Tabayoc and Palugloko Mountains. In NEI B–24's bomb area E of Bandjermasin, and P–51's hit harbor at Soerabaja.

Twentieth AF: 124 B–29's, escorted by VII FC ftrs, bomb naval arsenal at Toyokawa. During 7/8 Aug, 29 others drop mines in Shimonoseki Strait, at Miyazu, Maizuru, Tsuruga, Obama and at Najin. FEAF P–47's provide cover.

VII FC: After escorting B–29's on bombing mission, P–51's attack railroad tgts and shipping in and near Magarimatsu, Chofu, Atsugi, and Sagami.

Eleventh AF: 5 B–24's bomb Kataoka A/F. AA fire damages 2 B–24's.

8 August

International: USSR declares war on Japan.

Fourteenth AF: 10 P–51's hit buildings, trucks, rivercraft, and other T/Os in Paoching, Hengyang, and Chuanhsien areas.

FEAF: Okinawa-based B–24's, B–25's, A–26's, P–51's, and P–47's carry out numerous strikes against tgts on Kyushu. Tgts include Usa and Tsuiki A/Fs, comm and transport tgts all over Kyushu, shipping between Kyushu and Korea, and T/Os in the Ryukyus, on China coast, and on Formosa. P–47's escorting B–29's claim 10 Japanese planes downed. B–24's bomb Shinchiku A/F. B–24's on shipping search hit Lolobata A/F. B–24's spt ground forces in Lenatin R Valley and SSE of Mankayan. P–38's spt ground action SSE of Mankayan, in Kiangan area, and NW of Bagabag.

Twentieth AF: Shortly before noon, 221 B–29's drop incendiaries on Yawata. Late in the afternoon about 60 VHBs bomb aircraft plant and arsenal complex at Tokyo, while during 8/9 Aug 91 others hit Fukuyama with incendiaries.

VII FC: 100-plus ftrs from Iwo Jima hit A/Fs, factory buildings, barracks, and rail installations in Osaka area.

9 August

International: Soviet troops pour into Manchuria.

Tenth AF: Tenth AF moves from Kunming to Liuchow. When the war ends, the deployment of Tenth AF units to China is still in progress. So, for the Tenth, war ends amidst a major reorganization.

Fourteenth AF: 5 B–25's, with P–51 escort, damage Puchi railroad bridge, and hit rail traffic N of Sinsiang. The P–51's strafe AA positions and T/Os near the bridge. 4 other B–25's operating individually, attack truck convoys and T/Os S of Changsha, S and N of Yoyang, and in Siang-Chiang Valley, and hits S end of town of Siangtan.

FEAF: B–25's over Kyushu bomb A/Fs at Kanoya, town of Noma, shipping in Beppu Bay, bridges, factories, and oil storage at Tsurusaki, and shipping, coastal villages, and comm tgts in Tsushima Strait area. A–26's and A–20's hit Kanoya A/F and industrial areas of Kushikino, Minato, and Shimahira. B–24's over W Honshu bomb A/F at Iwakuni. Over 200 P–47's and P–51's hit numerous tgts on Shikoku, Kyushu, and in the Ryukyus including A/Fs, barracks, harbor installations, bridges, shipping, vehicles, and various factories and storage facilities. B–24's bomb military stores at Matsuyama. B–25's and P–38's spt ground forces in areas N of Baguio, SSE of Mankayan, S of Kabayan, SE of Cervantes, near Kiangan, and NW of Infanta. B–24's over Amboina-Ceram bomb Laha barracks.

Twentieth AF: Second and last atomic bomb of World War II is dropped on Japan. Maj Charles W Sweeney pilots a B–29, *Bock's Car,* off runway at North Field, Tinian, at 0230. He is followed by 2 observation B–29's—the *Great Artiste* piloted by Capt Frederick C Bock (who has exchanged planes with Sweeney for the mission) and another VHB piloted by Maj James I Hopkins (who loses contact with the other 2 B–29's). The primary tgt, Kokura, is obscured by bad weather. The attack is made against the secondary tgt, Nagasaki. The bomb, dropped from 28,900 ft at 1158 (1058 Nagasaki time), explodes about a min after release. Japanese reports claim nearly 24,000 killed. US figures estimate about 35,000. The attacking B–29's refuel on Okinawa, and return to Tinian by 2339. During 9/10 Aug, 95 B–29's bomb Nippon Oil Refinery at Amagasaki.

10 August

Fourteenth AF: Gen Stone assumes cmd of Fourteenth AF, replacing Gen Chennault. 5 B–25's and 4 P–51's bomb bivouac S of Siangyin, hit convoys S of Siangtan and in Siang-Chiang Valley, pound storage area and AA positions at Nanchang, and hit truck concentration N of Hengshan. More than 50 P–47's and P–51's attack rivercraft, railroad tgts, troops, trucks, and bridges at several points in S and E China.

FEAF: 80 B–24's, 118 MBs, and 220-plus P–47's and P–38's pound Kumamoto area. 20-plus B–24's bomb Oita area. 39 P–51's provide cover over both tgts. Nearly 40 B–25's attack destroyers, cargo ships, and small vessels during shipping sweep between Kyushu and Korea. P–47's bomb Sasebo Harbor. P–51's hit various T/Os on Honshu and Kyushu and B–25's bomb T/Os in the N Ryukyus. B–24's bomb Shinchiku. P–38's hit troop concentrations near Mount Pulog and ENE of Dupax.

Twentieth AF: 70 B–29's bomb arsenal complex at Tokyo. VII FC provides escort. During 10/11 Aug, 31 VHBs mine Shimonoseki Strait,

Nakaumi Lagoon, and waters at Sakai, Yonago and Wonsan.

11 August

Fourteenth AF: 9 P–51's attack troops, trains, and rivercraft around Chenhsien, Tehsien, and Hengyang.

FEAF: Okinawa-based B–24's, B–25's, A–26's, A–20's, and ftrs flying about 530 sorties cause extensive destruction of shipping and shore installations in the Inland Sea, in Tsushima area, and of comm, transportation, and other tgts throughout Kyushu. Phil Is-based B–24's bomb Heito A/F and Laha barracks. P–38's hit buildings near Dibuluan and field-guns near Kiangan.

12 August

International: Soviet troops move into Korea.

Ninth AF: Col Reginald F Vance becomes cmdr of 9th Air Div.

FEAF: B–24's from Okinawa bomb Matsuyama A/F. B–25's and A–26's hit Chiran and Kanoya A/Fs while other A–26's and A–20's and P–47's hit towns of Kushikino, Akune, and Miyazaki. More B–25's and FBs hit shipping and comm tgts in Kyushu, N Ryukyus, and between Japan and Korea. The aircraft claim several small merchant ships sunk and damaged, and numerous bridges, railroads, factories, and other T/Os hit. B–24's from the Phil Is pound Kagi A/F and Takao M/Y. P–38's spt ground forces in or near Kabayan, Kiangan, and Uldugan.

Eleventh AF: 4 B–24's make a combined visual and radar bomb run over Kataoka. 3 more bomb Suribachi A/F, hitting runways and buildings. 1 B–24 flies a radar-ferret mission.

13 August

FEAF: B–24's and B–25's from Okinawa pound shipping in waters off Korea and Kyushu and in Inland Sea claiming several vessels sunk and damaged. P–47's over Keijo encounter 20 aircraft and claim at least 16 shot down. B–25's attack Japanese forces near Palacian. P–38's hit shipping in Singapore area.

Eleventh AF: Eleventh AF dispatches its last combat mission when 6 B–24's radar-bomb Kashiwabara staging area, leaving huge columns of smoke.

14 August

FEAF: B–25's, P–47's, and P–51's attack shipping in Korea and Kyushu waters, claiming several vessels destroyed and damaged. P–47's over Osaka-Nagoya area claim several Japanese aircraft shot down.

Twentieth AF: 302 B–29's bomb naval arsenal at Hikari and Osaka Army Arsenal while 108 bomb railroad yards at Marifu. VII FC planes escort VHBs over Osaka area. During 14/15 Aug, 160-plus B–29's attack Kumagaya and Isezaki with incendiaries while 132 (in the longest nonstop unstaged B–29 bombing mission from the Marianas—3,650 mi) bomb Nippon Oil Company at Tsuchizakiminato. 39 others mine waters at Nanao, Shimonoseki, Miyazu, and Hamada. These are the final B–29 combat missions against Japan. Before the last B–29's return, President Truman announces the unconditional surrender of Japan. Immediately thereafter, 11th Airborne Div leaves Phil Is by air for Okinawa, where it goes on standby as the initial occupation force for Japan.

VII FC: After escorting B–29 strike over Osaka area, 160-plus ftrs (from VII FC on Iwo Jima) fly last ftr strike against Japanese Home Islands, hitting A/Fs and other military installations in Nagoya general area.

15 August

International: Gen MacArthur is notified that he is Supreme Cmdr for Allied powers. All offensive action against Japan ends.

Twelfth AF: All units are transferred or redeployed with exception of 6719th WAC HQ Pltn (an assigned unit) and Det, 1054th MP Co, Avn.

21 August

Eleventh AF: 2 B–24's are prevented by cloud cover from taking photos of Soviet occupation of Kurils. 4 others abort a photo mission to Paramushiru and Shimushu due to weather.

23 August

Eleventh AF: 4 B–24's fly photo mission over Paramushiru and Shimushu.

24 August

Eleventh AF: B–24's try to photo Soviet occupation of the Kurils but are impeded by clouds.

27 August

Thirteenth AF: XIII BC moves from Morotai to Clark Field.

Twentieth AF: B–29's begin supplying prisoners-of-war and internee camps in Japan, China, and Korea with medical supplies, food, and clothing. The first supply drop (to Weihsien Camp near Peking) is followed by a concentrated effort of 900 sorties in a period of less than a month. 4,470 tons of supplies are dropped to about 63,500 prisoners in 154 camps.

28 August

Twelfth AF: With discontinuance of 6719th WAC HQ Pltn, the Det, 1054th MP Co, Avn, remains the only unit still attached to Twelfth AF.

Japan: Occupation of Japan officially begins as adv party arrives in Home Islands.

30 August

Japan: Occupation in force begins when 11th Airborne Div is flown to Atsugi A/F and Marines land at Yokosuka naval base.

31 August

Twelfth AF: Twelfth AF is inactivated in Italy.

Fifteenth AF: Col Elmer J Rogers Jr assumes cmd of Fifteenth AF until its inactivation on 15 Sep 45.

2 September

International: Hostilities with Japan end officially with the signing of the instrument of surrender aboard the USS *Missouri* in Tokyo Bay.

3 September

Eleventh AF: A C–54 on its way from Atsugi to Washington DC refuels at Adak. The aircraft carries motion pictures of the Japanese surrender aboard the *Missouri*.

4 September

Eleventh AF: 2 B–24's fly high-altitude photo rcn of Paramushiru and Shimushu, encountering Soviet ftrs.

6 September

Eleventh AF: A radiogram from COMNORPAC officially cancels all further missions.

15 September

Fifteenth AF: Fifteenth AF is inactivated in Italy.

GLOSSARY OF TERMS AND ABBREVIATIONS

AA——antiaircraft
AAB——Army Air Base
AAF——Army Air Force(s)
AACS——Army Airways Communications System
AAFIB——Army Air Force in Britain
AAFld——Army Air Field
AAFMTO——Army Air Forces, Mediterranean Theater of Operations
AAFPOA——Army Air Forces, Pacific Ocean Areas
AAFSCMTO——Army Air Forces Service Command, Mediterranean Theater of Operations
AAFWS——Army Air Forces Weather Service
AB——air base
ABDA——American-British-Dutch-Australian Forces
ABDACOM——American-British-Dutch-Australian Forces Command
AC——Air Commodore
ACM——Air Chief Marshal
ADC——Air Defense Command
Adm——Admiral
Adv——Advance
ADVON——Advanced Echelon
AEAF——Allied Expeditionary Air Force
AEF——Allied Expeditionary Force
A/F——airfield—used collectively to mean both the landing field and the fixed facilities
AFBC——Air Force Base Command
AF Comp Cmd——Air Force Composite Command
AFPAC——US Army Forces, Pacific
AFSC——Air Force Services Command
AG——Adjutant General
Air Div——Air Division
AM——Air Marshal
AMET——Africa-Middle East Theater
ammo——ammunitions
armd——armored, armoured
arty——artillery
ASC——Air Service Command
A Spt Cmd——Air Support Command

Asst——Assistant
ATC——Air Transport Command
AVG——American Volunteer Group
AVM——Air Vice Marshal
Avn——Aviation
AWPD——Air War Plans Division
BC——Bomber Command
Bd——Board
BLADE Force——British armored unit in TORCH operations
bmr——bomber
Bn——Battalion
bomb——bombardment
Bomb Div——Bombardment Division
Bomb Gp——Bombardment Group
Bomb Sq——Bombardment Squadron
Brig——Brigade
C——central
CACW——Chinese-American Composite Wing
CAF——Chinese Air Force
C/AS——Chief of Air Staff (RAF)
CATF——China Air Task Force
cav——cavalry
CBI——China-Burma-India
CBO——Combined Bomber Offensive (Plan)
CCRC——Combat Crew Replacement Center
CCS——Combined Chiefs of Staff (US-British)
CG——Commanding General
CinC——Commander-in-Chief
CINCPAC——Commander-in-Chief, Pacific
CINCPOA——Commander-in-Chief, Pacific Ocean Areas
CINCUSAFPAC——Commander-in-Chief, United States Army Forces, Pacific
cmd——command
Cmdr——Commander
CO——Commanding Officer
Co——company
COMAIRNORSOLS——Commander Air North Solomons
COMAIRSOLS——Commander Air Solomons

691

COMAIRSOPAC——Commander Aircraft South Pacific Forces

COMGENSOPAC——Commanding General of US Army Forces in the South Pacific

comm——communications

COMNORPAC——Commander North Pacific

Comp——Composite

Comp Cmd——Composite Command

COMSOPAC——Commander-in-Chief, South Pacific

CONUS——Continental United States

CoS——Chief(s) of Staff (US)

COS——Chiefs of Staff (British)

COSSAC——Chief of Staff, Supreme Allied Commander

DAF——Desert Air Force

DATF——Desert Air Task Force

def——defense

dep——deputy

det——detachment

Div——Division

DS——Detached Service

DSC——Distinguished Service Cross

E——East, eastern

EAC——Eastern Air Command

EAME Theater——European-African-Middle East Theater

ETO——European Theater of Operations

ETOUSA——European Theater of Operations, United States Army

FB——fighter-bomber

FC——Fighter Command

FEAF——Far East Air Force

FM——Field Marshal

Ft——Fort

ftr——fighter

Ftr Gp——fighter group

GAF——German Air Force

GASC——Ground Air Support Command

Gds——Guards

Gee——Device used for blind-bombing, though primarily a navigational apparatus. It depended on beams transmitted from ground stations and had short operational range

GHQ——General Headquarters

GO——General Order

Gp——Group

HB——heavy bomber

HE——high explosive

HQ——headquarters

I——Island(s)

IATF——India Air Task Force

IC——Interceptor Command

IG——Inspector General

inf——infantry

JCS——Joint Chiefs of Staff

LB——light bomber

MAAF——Mediterranean Allied Air Forces

MAC——Mediterranean Air Command

MASAF——Mediterranean Allied Strategic Air Force

MATAF——Mediterranean Allied Tactical Air Force

MB——medium bomber

ME——Middle East

MP——Military Police

MTO——Mediterranean Theater of Operations

MTOUSA——Mediterranean Theater of Operations, United States Army

Mts——Mountains

M/Y——marshalling yard

N——North, northern

NAAF——Northwest African Air Forces

NAASC——Northwest African Air Service Command

NACAF——Northwest African Coastal Air Force

NAS——Naval Air Station

NASAF——Northwest African Strategic Air Force

NATAF——Northwest African Tactical Air Force

NATBF——Northwest African Tactical Bomber Force

NATC——Northwest African Training Command

NATOUSA——North African Theater of Operations, United States Army

NEI——Netherlands East Indies

NORPACFOR——North Pacific Forces

NZ——New Zealand

Oboe——Blind-bombing device of a rather short range because of dependence on beams transmitted by ground stations. Oboe was one of most accurate of blind-bombing devices

Pathfinder——Aircraft equipped with devices allowing blind-bombing under cloudy or overcast conditions or in darkness

Phil Is——Philippine Islands

Photo——Photographic

Pltn——Platoon
PM——Prime Minister
POA—Pacific Ocean Areas
Prov——Provisional
Pt——point
PT——patrol vessel, motor torpedo boat
Pur——Pursuit
R——River
RAAF——Royal Australian Air Force
RAD——Rear Admiral
RAF——Royal Air Force
RCAF——Royal Canadian Air Force
rcn——reconnaissance
repl——replacement
Rgt——Regiment
RN——Royal Navy
RNZAF——Royal New Zealand Air Force
S——South, southern
SAAF——South African Air Force
SBD——Navy (Douglas) Scout Bomber
SEAC——Southeast Asia Command
serv——service
SHAEF——Supreme Headquarters Allied Expeditionary Force
Slot, the——300 mi long open-water passage from the Shortland Is to Florida and Savo Is
SOPAC——South Pacific
SOS——Service of Supply
Sp——Special
SPOBS——Special Observer Group, US Army
spt——support
strat——strategic
Sq——Squadron
SWPA——Southwest Pacific Area
TAC——Tactical Air Command
TBF——Navy (Grumman) Torpedo Bomber
tac——tactical
TC——troop carrier
TCC——Troop Carrier Command
TF——Task Force
TG——Task Group
tgt——target
T/O——target of opportunity
trg——training
Trg and Repl Cmd——Training and Replacement Command
UK——United Kingdom

US——United States
USA——United States Army
USAAF——United States Army Air Force(s)
USAAFNATO——United States Army Air Forces, North African Theater of Operations
USAAFUK——United States Army Air Forces in United Kingdom
USAFBI——United States Army Forces in British Isles
USAFIA——United States Army Forces in Australia
USAFIME——United States Army Forces in the Middle East
USAFISPA——United States Army Forces in South Pacific Area
USAFPOA——United States Army Forces, Pacific Ocean Areas
USAMEAF——United States Army, Middle East Air Forces
USFIA——United States Forces in Australia
USMC——United States Marine Corps
USN——United States Navy
USS——United States ship
USSAFE (later USSTAF)——United States Strategic Air Forces in Europe
USSR——Union of Soviet Socialist Republics
USSTAF (formerly USSAFE)——United States Strategic Air Forces in Europe
USASTAF——United States Army Strategic Air Forces in the Pacific
VAD——Vice Admiral
V-E Day——Victory in Europe
VHB——very heavy bomber
VHF——very high frequency
V-J Day——Victory in Japan
VLR——very long range
W——West, western
WAC——Women's Army Corps
WD——War Department
WDAF——Western Desert Air Force
Wg——Wing
WPB——War Production Board
WTF——Western Task Force (in TORCH)
ZI——Zone of Interior (continental US)

GLOSSARY OF CODE NAMES

ANVIL——Plan for invasion of S France.

ARCADIA——Washington conference, 20 Dec 41–14 Jan 42, on proposed Anglo-American offensive against Germany. Participants include the President, the Prime Minister, and their military staffs.

ARGUMENT——Coordinated attacks by Eighth and Fifteenth AFs on German aircraft production, with an assist by RAF. The plan is drafted 2 Nov 43 and presented on 29 Nov 43 by Combined Operational Planning Committee and thereafter repeatedly modified. Operations are conducted 20–25 Feb 44.

AVALANCHE——Invasion of Italy at Salerno, 9 Sep 43.

BAYTOWN——British invasion of Italy near Reggio di Calabria, Sep 43.

BOLERO——Buildup of US armed forces in United Kingdom for attack on Europe.

BOOMERANG——Pre-Normandy invasion exercise in water-proofing and landing motor vehicles.

CARPETBAGGER——Air operation from United Kingdom to drop supplies to patriot forces in occupied W Europe.

CATCHPOLE——Operations against Eniwetok and Ujelang Atolls, Marshall Is, early 1944.

CHAMPION——Plan made in late 1943 for offensive in Burma.

CLARION——Large-scale air strike by all available air power of AAF and RAF against transportation and comm tgts in Germany (22–23 Feb 45).

COBRA——US First Army operation to penetrate German defenses W of Saint-Lo and secure Coutances.

COVER——Series of aerial blows preceding the Normandy invasion, chiefly in the Pas de Calais coastal area of France, to deceive the enemy as to the sector to be invaded.

CROSSBOW——RAF code name for operations against German missile launching sites (code name also used by USAAF).

DRAGOON——Invasion of S France, Aug 44.

EAGLE——Pre-Normandy invasion exercise of paradrops, glider tows, and related tactics and techniques.

EUREKA—Tehran Conference, Nov 43.

FLAX——Attacks on Axis transports between Tunisia and Europe.

FLINTLOCK——Operations against Kwajalein and Majuro Atolls in the Marshall Is, early 1944.

FORAGER——Capture and def of the southern Marianas (Saipan, Tinian, and Guam) during spring and summer of 1944.

FRANTIC——Shuttle-bombing of Axis-controlled Europe from bases in UK, Italy, and USSR.

GALVANIC——Assault on the Gilbert Is, late 1943.

GYMNAST——Early Allied plan for seizure of Casablanca and invasion of NW Africa.

HALPRO——Bombing det for China–Burma–India Theater.

JUNIOR——Twelfth Air Force.

LANDGRAB——Invasion of Attu.

MALLORY MAJOR——Offensive against Po R bridges, Jul 44.

MARKET–GARDEN——Operation to secure bridgehead over Rhine R, Sep 44.

MATTERHORN——Plan approved in Apr 44 for bombing of Japan by B–29's based in Calcutta area and staging through adv fields in Chengtu area.

NEPTUNE——Actual operations within OVERLORD. Used for security reasons on OVERLORD planning documents bearing place names and date.

NOBALL——Codename for tgts consisting of German missile-launching sites. *See also* V–weapons and rocket sites.

OCTAGON——US–British conference at Quebec, Sep 44.

OVERLORD——Overall plan for invasion of W Europe in 1944.

PANCAKE——MATAF and MASAF operation to destroy enemy supplies and equipment in the Bologna area, annihilation of enemy forces on the Bologna approaches, and the isolation of the battle area, Dec 44.

PLUNDER——Allied land assault across the Rhine, 24 Mar 45.

POINTBLANK——The Combined Bomber Offensive of US and British AFs against German AF and aircraft industry.

QUEEN——12th Army Group operation between Wurm and Roer Rivers.

REUNION——Evacuation of US airmen interned in Rumania, from Bucharest.

ROUNDUP——Plans for invasion of Western Europe, Spring 1943.

SEXTANT——International Cairo Conference, Nov–Dec 43.

SLAPSTICK——British airborne landing on heel of Italy, 9 Sep 43.

STARKEY——Combined air attack on Pas de Calais area, Aug–Sep 43. Rehearsal of invasion of France.

STRANGLE——Air operation to interdict movement of enemy supplies in Italy.

SUPERCHARGE——British 30 Corps breakout, Egypt, 1942. Revised plan of assault on Mareth Line, Mar 43.

SUPERGYMNAST——Projected plan to combine US and British plans for seizure of Dakar, Casablanca, and Tunisia.

TIDALWAVE——Bombing of Ploesti, Aug 43.

TORCH——Plan for Allied landings in North and Northwest Africa, Nov 42.

TRIDENT——US–British Conference in Washington, May 43.

TWILIGHT——Plan to base B–29's in CBI.

VARSITY——Airborne drop E of the Rhine near Wesel, 24 Mar 45.

INDEX
GLOSSARIES OF ABBREVIATIONS USED IN INDEX

Countries and Localities. Abbreviations are also provided for frequently used sub-divisions and provinces of several countries to facilitate identification of little-known place names.

Ad	Admiralty Islands	HK	Hong Kong
Al	Alaska	Hu	Hungary
Ala	Alabama	IJ	Iwo Jima
Alb	Albania	In	India
Alg	Algeria	Ind	Indochina
Au	Austria	Int	International
Aus	Australia	It	Italy
Be	Belgium	Ja	Java
Bi	Bismarck Archipelago	Jap	Japan
Bo	Borneo	Kas	Kansas
Bon	Bonin Islands	Ko	Korea
Br	Britain	Ku	Kurile Islands
Bu	Burma	Li	Libya
Bul	Bulgaria	Lu	Luxembourg
Ca	Caroline Islands	Ma	Mariana Islands
Cal	California	Mal	Malayan States
Can	Canada	Mar	Marshall Islands
Ce	Ceram	Mas	Massachusetts
Cel	Celebes	Me	Maine
Cey	Ceylon	ME	Middle East
Ch	China	Mi	Michigan
Cz	Czechoslovakia	Mo	Moluccas
DC	Dist of Columbia	Mon	Monaco
De	Denmark	Mor	Morocco
D'E	D'Entrecasteaux Islands	NAf	North Africa
Eg	Egypt	NCa	New Caledonia
El	Ellice Islands	Ne	Netherlands
Fi	Fiji Islands	Nev	Nevada
Fla	Florida	New G	New Georgia
Fo	Formosa	NG	New Guinea
Fr	France	NH	New Hebrides
FWA	French West Africa	NI	Northern Ireland
Gi	Gilbert Islands	No	Norway
Gr	Greece	No Sea	North Sea
Gu	Guam	O	Ohio
Gua	Guadalcanal	Oc	Oceania
Ha	Hainan Island	Or	Oregon
HI	Hawaiian Islands		

697

Countries and Localities (Continued)

Pa	Palau Islands	So	Solomon Islands (*incl* protectorates)
Pak	Pakistan		
Pal	Palestine	Su	Sunda Islands
Pe	Pescadores Islands	Sum	Sumatra
Ph	Phoenix Islands	Sw	Switzerland
PI	Philippine Islands	Th	Thailand
Po	Poland	Ti	Timor
Ru	Rumania	Tu	Tunisia
RI	Ryukyu Islands	US	United States
Sa	Sardinia	USS	USSR
Sar	Sarawak	VI	Volcano Islands
Si	Sicily	Wa	Washington (state)
Sin	Singapore	Yu	Yugoslavia

Geographic Features.

Arch	Archipelago	I	Island and Islet
At	Atoll	Mt	Mountain
C	Cape	Pens	Peninsula
Ch	Channel	Pt	Point
Cr	Creek	Plt	Plantation

Ranks and Titles.

AC	Air Commodore	FM	Field Marshal
ACM	Air Chief Marshal	GEN	General
ADM	Admiral	GENofA	General of the Army
AG	Adjutant General	Gp CAPT	Group Captain
AM	Air Marshal	LTC	Lieutenant Colonel
AVM	Air Vice Marshal	LTG	Lieutenant General
BG	Brigadier General	MAJ	Major
BRIG	Brigadier	MAR	Marshal
CAPT	Captain	MARof-RAF	Marshal of the RAF
COL	Colonel		
COL-GEN	Colonel-General	MG	Major General
		RAD	Rear Admiral
1LT	First Lieutenant	2LT	Second Lieutenant
FADM	Fleet Admiral	VAD	Vice Admiral

Units and Components. *See* main glossary for explanation of proper abbreviation.

AE	AEAF	H	HAF
AF Al Def Cmd	Air Force Alaska Defense Command	MA	MAAF
		MAS	MASAF
Al Def Cmd	Alaska Defense Command	NA	NAAF
		USAME	USAMEAF
FE	FEAF	USAST	USASTAF

Alphabetical Listing

Note: Entries in the Chronology are indexed by date (numerically by day-month-year) and by numbered or named Air Force or major AAF component. Thus, 1–1–4/12 denotes 1 Jan 1944, Twelfth AF; 18–7–5/FE refers to 18 Jul 1945, Far East Air Forces. Abbreviations of named Air Forces are included in the Index Glossary.

Aachen, Ge, 6–9–4/8, 9–9–4/9, 13–9–4/9, 19–9–4/9, 20–9–4/9, 22–9–4/9, 24–9–4/9, 25–9–4/9, 6–10–4/9, 11–10–4/9, 12–10–4/9, 18–10–4/9, 30–10–4/9, 4–11–4/9, 16–11–4/8, 17–11–4/9, 18–11–4/9, 19–11–4/9, 22–11–4/9, 25–11–4/9

Aalborg, De, 22–2–4/8

Aalen, Ge, 17–4–5/9

Abaiang, Gi, 20–2–3/7

Abau, NG, 17–7–4/FE, 4–8–4/FE, 27–8–4/FE

Abbasanta, It, 14–5–3/NA

Abbeville, Fr, 13–3–3/8, 16–7–3/8, 31–7–3/8, 15–8–3/8, 20–8–3/8, 24–2–4/9, 5–3–4/9, 20–3–4/9, 21–4–4/9

Abbeville/Drucat, Fr, 12–7–2/8, 19–8–2/8, 6–9–2/8, 8–11–2/8, 6–12–2/8, 10–7–3/8, 16–8–3/8, 9–9–3/8, 21–5–4/9

Abel's Field, NG, [09–37S 148–49E], 9–11–2/5

Abemama, Gi, 26–1–3/7, 26–5–3/7, 28–5–3/7, 24–6–3/7, 18–9–3/7 19–9–3/7, 17–1–4/7, 18–1–4/7, 20–1–4/7, 21–1–4/7, 22–1–4/7, 23–1–4/7, 4–2–4/7, 7–2–4/7, 8–2–4/7, 10–2–4/7, 12–2–4/7, 17–2–4/7, 21–2–4/7,

Abemama, (Continued)

23–2–4/7, 25–2–4/7, 26–2–4/7, 27–2–4/7, 2–3–4/7, 7–3–4/7, 9–3–4/7, 13–3–4/7, 16–3–4/7, 18–3–4/7, 19–3–4/7, 22–3–4/7, 25–3–4/7, 28–3–4/7, 1–4–4/7, 3–4–4/7, 4–4–4/7, 6–4–4/7, 8–4–4/7, 9–4–4/7, 10–4–4/7, 12–4–4/7, 13–4–4/7, 14–4–4/7, 16–4–4/7, 18–4–4/7, 21–4–4/7

Abia R, So, 13–6–4/13

Ablis, Fr, 9–7–4/9

Abuari, NG, 27–10–2/5, 29–10–2/5

Aburatsu, Jap, 12–7–5/7, 16–7–5/FE, 29–7–5/FE

Acerno, It, 17–9–3/12, 22–9–3/12

Acheres, Fr, [48–58N 02–04E?], 2–6–4/8

Achmer, Ge, 21–2–4/8, 8–4–4/8

Acquafondata, It, 12–11–3/12, 10–12–3/12, 11–12–3/12, 13–12–3/12

Acquapendente, It, 21–10–3/12, 29–4–4/12, 7–5–4/12, 9–6–4/12

Acqui, It, 23–7–4/12

Adak I, Al, 28–6–2/11, 28–7–2/11, 14–8–2/11, 16–8–2/11, 25–8–2/11, 30–8–2/11, 1–9–2/11, 9–9–2/11, 10–9–2/11, 12–9–2/11, 13–9–2/11, 16–9–2/11, 21–9–2/11, 1–10–2/11, 2–10–2/11, 3–10–2/11, 4–11–2/11, 12–

Arakan, Bu, 1–2–3/10, 14–3–4/10, 15–3–4/10, 16–3–4/10, 18–3–4/10, 20–3–4/10, 21–3–4/10, 7–4–4/10, 10–4–4/10, 16–4–4/10, 19–5–4/10, 20–5–4/10, 21–5–4/10, 24–5–4/10

Aranci, It, 30–5–3/NA

Arang Hill, Mal, 2–3–5/20, 12–3–5/20

Arare, NG, 13–5–4/5, 17–5–4/5

Aravia, So, 1–5–4/13

Arawa, So, 1–6–4/13

Arawa Bay, So, 6–12–3/13

Arawe, Bi, 5–11–2/5, 22–11–2/5, 22–12–2/5, 23–12–2/5, 24–12–2/5, 4–2–3/5, 19–3–3/5, 10–4–3/5, 26–4–3/5, 18–5–3/5, 20–7–3/5, 14–12–3/5, 15–12–3/5, 17–12–3/5, 19–12–3/5, 20–12–3/5, 21–12–3/5, 22–12–3/5, 24–12–3/5, 25–12–3/5, 31–12–3/5, 7–1–4/5, 8–1–4/5, 16–1–4/5, 10–2–4/5

Araxos, Gr, 6–10–3/12, 3–11–3/12, 3–11–3/15, 17–10–4/15

Arbatax, It, 23–4–3/NA, 24–5–3/NA

ARCADIA Conference, 22–12–1/Int, 14–1–2/Int

Arce, It, 3–10–3/12, 20–10–3/12, 11–12–3/12, 19–12–3/12, 30–12–3/12, 22–1–4/12, 22–1–4/15, 24–2–4/12, 2–4–4/12, 13–5–4/12

Arcidosso, It, 10–6–4/12, 12–6–4/12

Arco dei Fileni, *see* Marble Arch

Ardea, It, 5–2–4/12, 6–3–4/12

Ardennes, Be, (*see also* Bulge), 16–12–4/9, 17–12–4/9, 14–1–5/9, 4–4–5/9

Ardning, Au, 17–2–5/15

Arehe, NG, [?], 20–9–2/5

Arezzo, It, 12–11–3/12, 2–12–3/15, 5–12–3/12, 7–1–4/12, 15–1–4/15, 17–

Arezzo, (Continued)
1–4/15, 22–1–4/15, 14–2–4/15, 19–3–4/12, 21–3–4/12, 22–3–4/12, 26–3–4/12, 2–4–4/12, 6–4–4/12, 10–4–4/12, 11–4–4/12, 12–4–4/12, 14–4–4/12, 18–4–4/12, 20–4–4/12, 22–4–4/12, 24–4–4/12, 25–4–4/12, 28–4–4/12, 29–4–4/12, 1–5–4/12, 10–5–4/12, 14–5–4/12, 23–5–4/12, 28–5–4/12, 12–6–4/12, 14–6–4/12, 16–7–4/12

Argatala, In, 25–1–3/10

Argenta, It, 12–4–5/12, 14–4–5/12

Argentan, Fr, 6–6–4/8, 7–6–4/8, 25–6–4/9, 15–7–4/9, 23–7–4/9, 8–8–4/9, 12–8–4/9, 18–8–4/9

Argonne, USS, 10–7–2/7

Argos, It, 4–10–3/12, 9–10–3/12, 14–10–3/12

ARGUMENT, (*see* "Big Week")

Ariana, Tu, 6–5–3/NA

Ariano, It, 10–9–3/12, 11–9–3/12, 12–9–3/12

Ariccia, It, 30–5–4/12, 31–5–4/12

Arigua, So, 15–12–3/13, 31–5–4/13, 1–6–4/13, 11–6–4/13

Arigua Plt, So, 10–12–3/13, 11–12–3/13, 12–12–3/13, 29–5–4/13, 9–6–4/13

Aritao, PI, 4–6–5/FE

Arles, Fr, 25–6–4/15, 17–7–4/15, 6–8–4/12

Arloff, Ge, 1–2–5/9, 4–2–5/9

Arlon, Be, 1–10–4/9, 22–10–4/9, 29–12–4/9

Arma di Taggia, It, 7–12–3/15, 2–1–4/12

Armies (numbered)
First Allied Airborne Army, 7–8–

Loimawk, Bu, [22–30N 97–20E], 28–11–4/10

Loi-mun, Bu, [18–51N 97–29E], 2–1–5/10

Loi Mwe, Bu, 14–12–4/14, 15–4–5/10

Loi Nan, Bu, 25–1–5/10

Loingu, Bu, 12–2–5/10

Loipao, Bu, 3–12–4/10

Loi Putau, Bu, 30–3–5/10

Loi-pyek, Bu, [23–10N 97–50E], 18–1–5/10, 17–2–5/10

Loire R, Fr, 11–6–4/8, 14–6–4/9, 15–6–4/9, 24–6–4/9, 30–6–4/9, 2–7–4/9, 19–7–4/9, 25–7–4/9, 27–7–4/9, 31–7–4/9, 26–8–4/9, 27–8–4/9

Loi-weng, Bu, [21–48N 97–46E?], 25–1–5/10

Loi wing, Bu, [23–13N 97–28E], 2–1–3/10, 9–1–3/10, 12–4–3/14, 30–1–4/14, 3–3–4/10, 21–4–4/14, 10–7–4/10, 15–8–4/10, 22–8–4/14, 12–9–4/10, 16–9–4/10, 2–10–4/10, 1–11–4/10, 30–3–5/10

Loiya, Bu, [23–17N 96–56E], 10–2–5/10, 12–2–5/10

Lokanu, NG, 29–12–2/5, 18–7–3/5

Lokchang, Ch, 5–8–5/14

Lolobata, Mo, 27–7–4/FE, 31–7–4/FE, 7–8–4/FE, 8–8–4/FE, 10–8–4/FE, 15–8–4/FE, 16–8–4/FE, 24–8–4/FE, 25–8–4/FE, 8–9–4/FE, 10–9–4/FE, 15–9–4/FE, 9–10–4/FE, 7–12–4/FE, 21–12–4/FE, 22–12–4/FE, 23–12–4/FE, 26–12–4/FE, 8–8–5/FE

Lolobau I, Bi, 2–2–3/5, 3–5–3/5

Loloda, Mo, 31–10–4/FE

Lombrum Plt, Ad, 8–3–4/5

Lonate Pozzolo, It, 30–9–4/12, 19–10–4/12, 2–3–5/12

London, Br, 8–4–2/Int, 12–4–2/AAF, 26–5–2/Int, 29–5–2/Int, 18–6–2/8, 25–6–2/8, 18–7–2/Int, 15–12–3/9, 8–9–4/Eto

Longarone, It, 7–3–5/12, 8–3–5/12, 23–3–5/12

Long distance (*incl* long range) flying escort, 3–9–2/11, 15–6–3/8, 24–1–4/8

Longeau, Fr, 20–8–2/8, 13–3–3/8

Longfellow, Newton, COL/BG, 27–7–2/8, 2–12–2/8, 1–7–3/8

Longhsu, Bu, 5–1–5/10

Long Kesh, NI, 12–9–2/8, 13–11–2/8

Longkin, Bu, 13–12–4/10

Longmao, Bu, 12–1–5/10

Longstop Ridge, *see* Djebel el Ahmera

Longuenesse A/F, *see* Saint-Omer/Longuenesse

Longwai, Bu, [22–20N 97–35E], 27–3–5/10

Loning, Ch, 18–5–4/14, 20–5–4/14, 22–5–4/14, 10–6–4/14, 29–3–5/14, 1–4–5/14, 8–4–5/14, 12–4–5/14, 23–4–5/14, 25–4–5/14, 30–4–5/14, 1–5–5/14, 25–5–5/14

Lonkin, Bu, 12–2–3/10, 13–2–3/10, 17–2–4/10, 18–5–4/10, 31–5–4/10

Lonlan, Bu, 9–11–4/10

Lonrai, Fr, 11–7–4/9

Lontis, So, 29–4–4/13

Lonton, Bu, [25–06N 96–17E], 17–2–4/10

Lonywa, Bu, 10–6–4/10

Lorengau, Ad, 18–10–2/5, 13–11–2/5, 18–12–2/5, 23–12–2/5, 4–2–3/5, 22–2–3/5, 19–3–3/5, 22–3–3/5, 23–3–3/5, 7–4–3/5, 9–4–3/5, 18–5–3/5, 7–1–4/5, 21–1–4/5, 25–1–4/5, 26–

Marneda, NG, [02–37S 140–21E], 25–4–4/5

Maroe R, NG, 8–7–4/FE

Marquana Bay, So, 21–8–3/13

Marquardt, George W, CAPT, 6–8–5/20

Marquise, Fr, 19–3–4/8

Marquise/Mimoyecques, Fr, (*see also* Mimoyecques), 10–4–4/8, 28–4–4/8, 1–5–4/8, 15–5–4/8, 21–5–4/8

Marradi, It, 30–6–4/12

Marrakesh, Mor, 9–1–4/Int

Marsala, Si, 11–4–3/NA, 6–5–3/NA, 11–5–3/NA, 12–5–3/NA, 29–5–3/NA, 15–6–3/NA, 3–7–3/NA, 5–7–3/NA, 7–7–3/NA, 12–7–3/NA, 14–7–3/NA

Marsciano, It, 16–2–4/12, 27–3–4/12, 13–4–4/12, 30–4–4/12, 2–5–4/12, 14–5–4/12

Marseille, Fr, 15–5–3/NA, 2–12–3/15, 15–5–4/15, 12–8–4/15, 13–8–4/12, 24–8–4/12, 25–8–4/12, 26–8–4/12, 27–8–4/12

Marseille-en-Beauvaisis, Fr, 15–8–4/9

Marseille-St Charles, Fr, 27–5–4/15

Marseilles-Blancarde, Fr, 27–5–4/15

Marshall, George C, GEN/GEN of A, 9–3–2/AAF, 7–4–2/US, 8–4–2/Int, 12–4–2/AAF, 14–4–2/Int, 20–6–2/8, 18–7–2/Int, 5–9–2/8, 5–12–2/SOPAC, 30–7–5/Jap

Marshall Is, 17–6–3/7, 6–11–3/7, 21–11–3/7, 22–12–3/7, 30–12–3/7, 29–1–4/7, 31–1–4/7, 1–2–4/7, 3–3–4/7, 5–3–4/7, 10–3–4/7, 11–3–4/7, 8–5–4/7, 27–7–4/7, 31–7–4/7, 3–8–4/7, 4–8–4/7, 6–8–4/7, 8–8–4/7, 12–8–4/7, 14–8–4/7, 16–8–4/7, 20–8–4/7,

Marshall Is, (*Continued*) 24–8–4/7, 28–8–4/7, 1–9–4/7, 2–9–4/7, 16–9–4/7, 20–9–4/7, 26–9–4/7, 27–9–4/7, 4–10–4/7, 5–10–4/7, 8–10–4/7, 9–10–4/7, 13–10–4/7, 14–10–4/7, 15–10–4/7, 16–10–4/7

Marsicano, It, 23–10–3/12, 27–3–4/12, 13–4–4/12

Martaban, Bu, 24–2–4/10, 20–3–4/10, 23–4–4/10, 9–5–4/10, 1–2–5/20, 7–2–5/20, 19–2–5/20

Martelange, Be, 27–12–4/9

Martin, Frederick, L, MG, 18–12–1/H

Martinvast, Fr, 11–11–3/9

Martuba, Li, 15–11–2/9

Marubian, NG, 9–7–4/FE, 17–8–4/FE, 20–8–4/FE

Marushima, Jap, 31–7–5/FE

Maruta, Jap, [37–44N 139–08E?], 5–7–5/VIIFC

Maruzen Oil Refinery, Jap, 6–7–5/20

Marveiropa, So, 16–12–3/13

Maryut, Eg, 31–8–2/USAME

Marzabotto, It, 22–6–4/12

Masamba, Cel, [02–34S 120–19E], 28–4–5/FE, 4–5–5/FE

Masan, Ko, 13–7–5/20, 22–7–5/20

Masaweng R, NG, 3–8–3/5

Masbate, PI, 25–11–4/FE, 3–12–4/FE, 7–12–4/FE, 14–1–5/FE

Mashi Daru, Bu, 19–1–4/10

Mason, Charles P, RAD, 16–2–3/SOPAC

Massacre Bay, Al, 13–10–3/11, 4–8–4/11

Massa d'Albe, It, 12–5–4/15

Massa Lombarda, It, 14–2–4/15, 12–

⋆U.S. G.P.O. 1991– 282-282:40042